OXFORD MEDICAL PUBLICATIONS

Oxford Textbook of Psychiatry

Oxford Textbook of Psychiatry

MICHAEL GELDER
Professor of Psychiatry, University of Oxford

DENNIS GATH
Clinical Reader in Psychiatry, University of Oxford

RICHARD MAYOU
Clinical Reader in Psychiatry, University of Oxford

SECOND EDITION

Oxford   New York   Melbourne
OXFORD UNIVERSITY PRESS

Oxford University Press, Walton Street, Oxford OX2 6DP

Oxford New York Toronto
Delhi Bombay Calcutta Madras Karachi
Kuala Lumpur Singapore Hong Kong Tokyo
Nairobi Dar es Salaam Cape Town
Melbourne Auckland Madrid
and associated companies in
Berlin Ibadan

Oxford is a trade mark of Oxford University Press

First published 1983. Reprinted with corrections 1984, 1985, 1986, 1988
Second edition 1989
Reprinted 1990, 1991 (with corrections), 1993

British Library Cataloguing in Publication Data
Gelder, Michael G. (Michael Graham)
Oxford textbook of psychiatry.—2nd ed.
1. Medicine. Psychiatry
I. Title II. Gath, Dennis III. Mayou,
Richard
616.89
ISBN 0–19–261629–3 pbk

Library of Congress Cataloging-in-Publication Data
Gelder, Michael G.
Oxford textbook of psychiatry / Michael Gelder, Dennis Gath,
Richard Mayou.—2nd ed.
(Oxford medical publications)
Bibliography. Includes Index.
1. Psychiatry. I. Gath, Dennis. II. Mayou, Richard.
III. Title. IV. Series.
[DNLM: 1. Mental Disorders. 2. Psychiatry. WM 100 G315o]
RC454.G42   1989   616.89—dc19   88-38712
ISBN 0–19–261629–3 (pbk.)

Printed in Great Britain by
Butler & Tanner Ltd
Frome and London

Preface to the second edition

In this edition the main aims and general approach are the same as in the first edition, but the text has been extensively revised. This revision has been undertaken with three aims: to incorporate the latest systems of classification, namely the draft ICD10, and DSMIIIR, in the sections dealing with clinical syndromes; to introduce advances in knowledge and practice; and to correct errors.

In preparing this second edition we have been greatly helped by:

Dr D. H. Clark   Dr I. B. Glass
Dr P. J. Cowen   Dr A. Hope
Dr K. E. Hawton   Mr H. C. Jones
Dr D. Jones   Professor D. Shaffer
Professor P. McGuffin   Professor Sir David Weatherall
Dr G. Stores

We acknowledge with gratitude the permission of the World Health Organization to quote material from the 1988 Draft of Chapter V of ICD10, Categories F00–F99, Mental, Behavioural and Developmental Disorders; Clinical Descriptions and Diagnostic Guidelines, World Health Organization, Division of Mental Health, Geneva, 1988 (MNH/MEP/87.1, Rev.2). The copyright of ICD and the trial drafts are held by WHO. The authors wish to make it clear that the trial drafts are provisional and subject to alteration in the final version.

Oxford   M.G.
1988   D.G.
                                                                          R.M.

Preface to the first edition

This book is written primarily as an introductory textbook for trainee psychiatrists, and also as an advanced textbook for clinical medical students. We hope that the book will also be useful, for purposes of revision and reference, to psychiatrists who have completed their training and to general practitioners and other clinicians.

The subject matter of this book is the practice of clinical psychiatry. Recent years have seen the increasing development of sub-specialties such as child and adolescent psychiatry, forensic psychiatry, and the psychiatry of mental retardation. This book is mainly concerned with general psychiatry, but it also contains chapters on the sub-specialties. Throughout the whole book, our purpose has been to provide an introduction to each subject, rather than a fully documented account. It is assumed that the trainee psychiatrist will go on to consult more comprehensive works such as the *Handbook of psychiatry* (Shepherd 1983), the *Comprehensive textbook of psychiatry* (Kaplan *et al.* 1980), and specialized textbooks dealing with the sub-specialties. In some chapters references are made to basic sciences such as psychology, genetics, biochemistry, and pharmacology. Discussion of these subjects is based on the assumption that the reader already has a working knowledge of them from previous study.

The chapters dealing with psychiatric treatment fall into two groups. First, there are three chapters wholly devoted to treatment and concerned only with general issues. In this group, Chapter 17 deals mainly with drug treatment and electroconvulsive therapy; Chapter 18 deals with psychological treatments; and Chapter 19 discusses the organization of services for the rehabilitation and care of patients with chronic psychiatric disorders. Second, there are the various chapters on individual syndromes, which include sections on the treatments specific to those syndromes. In these chapters, treatment is usually discussed in two parts. The first part examines the evidence that a particular treatment is effective for a particular syndrome; the second part discusses (under the heading of management) practical issues in treatment, such as ways of using various treatments singly or in combination at different stages of a patient's illness. The separation of chapters on general issues from those on specific issues means that the reader has to consult more than one chapter for complete information on the treatment of any disorder. None the less this arrangement is preferred because a single treatment may be used for several syndromes. For example, antipsychotic drugs are used to treat mania and schizophrenia, and supportive psychotherapy is part of the treatment of many disorders.

In this book there is no separate chapter on the history of psychiatry. Instead certain chapters on specific topics include brief accounts of their history. For example, the chapter on psychiatric services contains a short historical review of the care of the mentally ill; and the chapter on abnormal personality includes some information about the development of ideas about the subject. This arrangement reflects the authors' view that, at least in an introductory text, historical points are more useful when related to an account of modern ideas. The historical references in this book can be supplemented by reading a history of psychiatry such as that by Ackerknecht (1968) or Bynum (1983).

The use of references in this book also needs to be explained. As this is an introductory postgraduate text, we have not provided references for every statement that could be supported by evidence. Instead we have generally followed two principles: to give references for statements that may be controversial; and to give more references for issues judged to be of topical interest. In an introductory text it also seemed appropriate to give references mostly to the Anglo–American literature. For all these reasons the coverage of the literature may seem uneven; but—as explained above—the book is written in the expectation that the trainee psychiatrist will progress to other works for more detailed literature surveys. Suggestions for further reading are given at the end of each chapter.

Oxford   M.G.
May 1983   D.G.
                                                                                    R.M.

Acknowledgements*

In writing this book we have been greatly helped by advice and comments generously given by colleagues. We wish to thank:

Dr S. Abel, Dr J. Bancroft, Mr J. Beatson, Miss V. L. Bellairs, Dr S. Bloch, Dr L. Braddocks, Dr S. Crown, Professor J. E. Cooper, Dr J. Corbett, Dr P. Cowan, Dr N. Eastman, Professor Griffith Edwards, Dr G. Forrest, Dr K. W. M. Fulford, Professor D. P. B. Goldberg, Dr G. Goodwin, Professor D. G. Grahame-Smith, Professor J. C. Gunn, Dr J. Hamilton, Dr K. E. Hawton, Dr A. Hope, Dr T. Horder, Professor R. E. Kendell, Professor I. Kolvin, Professor M. H. Lader, Dr J. P. Leff, Dr R. Levy, Dr P. F. Liddle, Professor W. A. Lishman, Professor H. G. Morgan, Dr J. McWhinnie, Dr D. J. Nutt, Dr W. Ll. Parry-Jones, Professor E. S. Paykel, Dr J. S. Pippard, Miss S. Rowland-Jones, Dr G. Stores, Dr C. A. Storr, Dr T. G. Tennent, Dr C. P. Warlow, Dr G. K. Wilcock, and Dr H. H. O. Wolff.

We are also grateful to many other colleagues who have given advice and to our secretaries. We are particularly indebted to Mrs Susan Offen who has given invaluable help at all stages of the preparation of the typescript and the checking of references.

* This Acknowledgements section is reprinted from the first edition of this book.

Contents

1 Signs and symptoms of mental disorder

Psychiatry can be practised only if the psychiatrist develops two distinct capacities. One is the capacity to collect clinical data objectively and accurately by history taking and examination of mental state, and to organize the data in a systematic and balanced way. The other is the capacity for intuitive understanding of each patient as an individual. When the psychiatrist exercises the first capacity, he draws on his clinical skills and knowledge of clinical phenomena; when he exercises the second capacity, he draws on his general understanding of human nature to gain insights into the feelings and behaviour of each individual patient, and into ways in which life experiences have affected that person's development.

Both capacities can be developed by accumulating experience of talking to patients, and by learning from the guidance and example of more experienced psychiatrists. From a textbook, however, it is inevitable that the reader can learn more about clinical skills than about intuitive understanding. In this book several chapters are concerned with aspects of clinical skills. This emphasis on clinical skills in no way implies that intuitive understanding is regarded as unimportant but simply that it cannot be learnt from reading a textbook.

The psychiatrist can acquire skill in examining patients only if he has a sound knowledge of how each symptom and sign is defined. Without such knowledge, he is liable to misclassify phenomena and make inaccurate diagnoses. For this reason, questions of definition are considered in this first chapter before history taking and the examination of the mental state are described in the second.

Once the psychiatrist has elicited a patient's symptoms and signs, he needs to decide how far these phenomena resemble or differ from those of other psychiatric patients. In other words, he must determine whether the clinical features form a syndrome, which is a group of symptoms and signs that identifies patients with common features. When he decides on the syndrome the psychiatrist combines observations of the patient's present state with information about the history of the disorder. The purpose of identifying a syndrome is to be able to plan treatment and predict the likely outcome by reference to accumulated knowledge about the causes, treatment, and outcome of the same syndrome in other patients. The principles involved are discussed in Chapter 4, which is concerned with classification, and also in the chapters dealing with the different syndromes.

Since the present chapter consists mainly of definitions and descriptions of symptoms and signs, it may be less easy to read than those which follow. It is suggested that the reader should approach the chapter in two stages. The first reading can be applied to the introductory sections and to a general understanding of the more frequent abnormal phenomena. The second can focus on details of definition and the less common symptoms and signs.

Before individual phenomena are described, it is important to consider some general issues concerning the methods of studying symptoms and signs and the terms used to describe them.

Psychopathology

The study of abnormal states of mind is known as **psychopathology**, a term that denotes three distinct approaches.

The first approach, **phenomenological psychopathology** (or **phenomenology**), is concerned with the objective description of abnormal states of mind in a way that avoids, as far as possible, preconceived theories. It aims to elucidate the basic data of psychiatry by defining the essential qualities of morbid mental experiences and by understanding what the patient is experiencing. It is entirely concerned with conscious experiences and observable behaviour. According to Jaspers (1963), phenomenology is 'the preliminary work of representing, defining and classifying psychic phenomena as an independent activity'.

The second approach, **psychodynamic psychopathology**, originates in psychoanalytical investigations. Like phenomenological psychopathology, it starts with the patient's description of his mental experiences and the doctor's observations of his behaviour. However, unlike phenomenological psychopathology it goes beyond description and seeks to explain the causes of abnormal mental events, particularly by postulating unconscious mental processes. These differences can be illustrated by the two approaches to persecutory delusions. Phenomenology describes them in detail and examines how they differ from normal beliefs and from other forms of abnormal thinking such as obsessions. On the other hand, the psychodynamic approach seeks to explain the occurrence of persecutory delusions, in terms of unconscious mechanisms such as repression and projection. In other words, it views them as evidence in the conscious mind of more important disorders in the unconscious.

In the third approach, often called **experimental psychopathology**, relationships between abnormal phenomena are examined by inducing a change in one of the phenomena and observing associated changes in the others. Hypotheses are formulated to explain the observed changes, and then tested in further experiments. The general aim is to explain the abnormal phenomena of mental disorders in terms of psychological processes that have been shown to account for normal experiences in healthy people. (An example is given on p. 25 where mood disorders are discussed.)

It should be noted that the term experimental psychopathology is also used to cover a wider range of experimental work that might throw light on psychiatric disorder. This usage includes studies of animals as well as of humans; for example, studies of animal learning and behavioural responses to frustration or punishment.

This chapter is concerned mainly with phenomenological psychopathology, although reference will also be made to relevant ideas from dynamic or experimental psychopathology.

The most important exponent of phenomenological psychopathology was the German psychiatrist philosopher, Karl Jaspers. His classical work, *Allgemeine Psychopathologie [General psychopathology]*, first appeared in 1913, and was a landmark in the development of clinical psychiatry. It provides the most complete account of the subject and contains much of interest, particularly in its early chapters. The seventh (1959) edition is available in an English translation by Hoenig and Hamilton (Jaspers 1963). Alternatively, useful outlines of the principles of phenomenology have been given by Hamilton (1985) and by Scharfetter (1980).

The significance of individual symptoms

It is often mistaken to conclude that a person is mentally ill on the evidence of an individual symptom. Even hallucinations, which are generally regarded as hallmarks of mental illness, are sometimes experienced by healthy people, for example when falling asleep. Symptoms are often recognized as indicating mental illness because of their intensity and persistence. None the less, even when intense and persistent, a single symptom does not necessarily indicate illness. It is the characteristic grouping of symptoms into a syndrome that is important.

Primary and secondary symptoms

The terms primary and secondary are used in describing symptoms, but with more than one meaning. The first is temporal; primary meaning antecedent and secondary meaning subsequent. The second is causal; primary meaning a direct expression of the pathological process and secondary meaning a reaction to the primary symptoms. The two meanings are often related—the symptoms appearing first in time being direct expressions of the pathological process.

It is preferable to use the terms primary and secondary in the temporal sense because it is factual. However, many patients cannot give a clear account of the chronological development of their symptoms. In these cases a distinction between primary and secondary symptoms in the temporal sense cannot be made with certainty. If this happens it is only possible to conjecture whether one symptom could be a reaction to another; for example, whether the fixed idea of being followed by persecutors could be a reaction to hearing voices.

The form and content of symptoms

When psychiatric symptoms are described, it is usual to distinguish between form and content, a distinction that can be best explained with an example. If a patient says that, when he is entirely alone, he hears voices calling him a homosexual, then the form of his experience is an auditory hallucination (i.e. a sensory perception in the absence of an external stimulus) while the content is the statement that he is homosexual. A second person might hear voices saying he is about to be killed: the form is still an auditory hallucination but the content is different. A third might experience repeated intrusive thoughts that he is homosexual but realize that these are untrue. He has an experience with the same content as the first (concerning homosexuality) but the form is different—in this case an obsessional thought.

Description of symptoms and signs

Introduction

In the following sections, symptoms and signs are described in a different order from the one adopted when the mental state is examined. The order is changed because it is useful to begin with the most distinctive phenomena—hallucinations and delusions. This change should be borne in mind when reading Chapter 2 in which the description of the mental state examination begins with behaviour and talk rather than hallucinations and delusions.

The definitions in this section generally conform with those in the Present State Examination (PSE) a widely used standardized rating system developed by Wing *et al.* (1974) and adopted by the World Health Organization for an international study of major mental disorders. The PSE definitions were developed in several stages. The original items were chosen to represent the clinical practice of a group of psychiatrists working in western Europe. The first definitions were modified progressively through several editions. The seventh edition was used in a large Anglo–American diagnostic project; the eighth included modifications arising from a study of schizophrenia carried out in countries in Europe, Asia, and the Americas; while the ninth, published in 1974, incorporates further refinements suggested by analysis of the previous studies. The PSE therefore provides useful common ground between psychiatrists working in different countries and contains definitions that can be applied reliably.

Before we consider individual symptoms it is appropriate to remind the reader that it is important not only to study individual mental phenomena but also to consider the whole person. The doctor must try to understand how the patient fulfils social roles such as worker, spouse, parent, friend, or sibling. He should consider what effect the disorders of function have had upon the remaining healthy parts of the person. Above all he should try to understand what it is like for this person to be ill, e.g. to care for small children while profoundly depressed or to live with the symptoms and disabilities of schizophrenia. The doctor will gain such understanding only if he is prepared to spend time listening to patients and their families and to interest himself in every aspect of their lives.

Disorders of perception

Perception and imagery

Perception is the process of becoming aware of what is presented through the sense organs. **Imagery** is an experience within the mind, usually without the sense of reality that is part of perception. **Eidetic imagery** is a visual image which is so intense and detailed that it has a 'photographic' quality. Unlike perception, imagery can be called up and terminated by voluntary effort. It is usually obliterated by seeing or hearing. Occasionally, imagery is so vivid that it persists when the person looks at a poorly structured background such as plain wallpaper. This condition is called **pareidolia**, a state in which real and unreal percepts exist side by side, the latter being recognized as unreal. Pareidolia can occur in acute organic disorders caused by fever, and in a few people it can be induced deliberately.

Alterations in perception

Perceptions can alter in intensity and quality. They can seem more intense than usual, e.g. when two people experience the same auditory stimulus, such as the noise of a door shutting, the more anxious person may perceive it as louder. In mania, perceptions often seem very intense. Conversely, in depression colours may seem less intense. Changes in the quality of sensations occur in schizophrenia, sensations sometimes appearing distorted or unpleasant. For example, a patient may complain that food tastes bitter or that a flower smells like burning flesh.

Illusions

Illusions are misperceptions of external stimuli. They are most likely to occur when the general level of sensory stimulation is reduced. Thus at dusk a common illusion is to misperceive the outline of a bush as that of a man. Illusions are also more likely to occur when the level of consciousness is reduced, for example in an acute organic syndrome. Thus a delirious patient may mistake inanimate objects for people when the level of illumination is normal, though he is more likely to do so if the room is badly lit. Illusions occur more often when attention is not focused on the sensory modality, or when there is a strong affective state ('affect illusions'), e.g. in a dark lane a frightened person is more likely to misperceive the outline of a bush as that of an attacker. (The so-called **illusion of doubles** or **Capgras syndrome** is not an illusion but a form of delusional misinterpretation. It is considered under paranoid syndromes in Chapter 11.)

Hallucinations

A hallucination is a percept experienced in the absence of an external stimulus to the sense organs, and with a similar quality to a true percept. A hallucination is experienced as originating in the outside world (or within one's own body) like a percept, and not within the mind like imagery.

Hallucinations are not restricted to the mentally ill. A few normal people experience them, especially when tired. Hallucinations also occur in healthy people during the transition between sleep and waking; they are called **hypnagogic** if experienced while falling asleep and **hypnopompic** if experienced during awakening.

Pseudohallucinations

This term has been applied to abnormal phenomena that do not meet the above criteria for hallucinations and are of less certain diagnostic significance. Unfortunately the word has two meanings which are often confused. The first, originating in the work of Kadinsky, was adopted by Jaspers (1913) in his book *General psychopathology*. In this sense, pseudohallucinations are especially vivid mental images; that is, they lack the quality of representing external reality and seem to be within the mind rather than in external space. However, unlike ordinary imagery, they cannot be changed substantially by an effort of will. The term is still used with this meaning (see, for example, Scharfetter 1980).

The second meaning of pseudohallucination is the experience of perceiving something as in the external world, while recognizing that there is no external correlate to the experience. This is the sense in which the term is used by Hare (1973) and Taylor (1979).

Both definitions are difficult to apply because they depend on the patient's ability to give precise answers to difficult questions about the nature of his experience. Judgements based on the patient's recognition of the reality of his experience are, not surprisingly, difficult to make reliably because the patient is often uncertain himself. Although the percepts must be experienced as either in the external world or within the mind, patients often find this distinction difficult to make.

Taylor (1981) has suggested that the two kinds of pseudohallucination should be distinguished by separate names: 'imaged' pseudohallucinations that are experienced within the mind and 'perceived' pseudohallucinations that are experienced as located in external space but recognized as unreal. In everyday clinical work it seems better to abandon the term pseudohallucinations altogether, and simply to maintain the term hallucination as defined at the beginning of this section. If the clinical phenomena do not meet this definition, they should be described in detail rather than labelled with a technical term that provides no additional information useful for diagnosis. Readers requiring a more detailed account of these problems of definition are referred to Hare (1973), Taylor (1981), and Jaspers (1963, pp. 68–74). Further information about the phenomena themselves will be found in Sedman (1966).

Types of hallucination

Hallucinations can be described in terms of their complexity and their sensory modality (see Table 1.1). The term **elementary hallucination** is used for experiences such as bangs, whistles, and flashes of light; **complex hallucination** is used for experiences such as hearing voices or music, or seeing faces and scenes.

Hallucinations may be auditory, visual, gustatory, olfactory, tactile, or of deep sensation. **Auditory hallucinations** may be experienced as noises, music, or voices. Hallucinatory 'voices' are sometimes called **phonemes**, but this usage is at variance with the dictionary definition of the term as a specific sound in a specific language. Voices may be heard clearly or indistinctly; they may seem to speak words, phrases, or sentences; and they may seem to address the patient, or talk to one another referring to the patient as 'he' or 'she' (**third person hallucinations**). Sometimes voices seem to anticipate what the patient thinks a few moments later, or speak his own thoughts as he thinks them, or repeat them immediately after he has thought them. In the absence of concise English technical terms, the

Table 1.1. Description of hallucinations

---

1. According to complexity
     elementary
     complex

2. According to sensory modality
     auditory
     visual
     olfactory and gustatory
     somatic (tactile and deep)

3. According to special features
     (a) auditory: second person
                       third person
                       Gedankenlautwerden
                       écho de la pensée
     (b) visual: extracampine
4. Autoscopic hallucinations

---

last two experiences are sometimes called **Gedankenlautwerden** and *écho de la pensée* respectively.

Visual hallucinations may also be elementary or complex. They may appear normal or abnormal in size; if the latter, they are more often smaller than the corresponding real percept. Visual hallucinations of dwarf figures are sometimes called lilliputian. **Extracampine visual hallucinations** are experienced as located outside the field of vision, that is, behind the head. **Olfactory and gustatory hallucinations** are frequently experienced together, often as unpleasant smells or tastes.

Tactile hallucinations, sometimes called **haptic hallucinations**, may be experienced as sensations of being touched, pricked, or strangled. They may also be felt as movements just below the skin which the patient may attribute to insects, worms, or other small creatures burrowing through the tissues. **Hallucinations of deep sensation** may occur as feelings of the viscera being pulled upon or distended, or of sexual stimulation or electric shocks.

An **autoscopic hallucination** is the experience of seeing one's own body projected into external space, usually in front of oneself, for short periods. This experience may convince the person that he has a double (*doppelgänger*), a theme occurring in several novels, including Dostoevsky's *The Double*. In clinical practice this is a rare phenomenon, mainly encountered in a small minority of patients with temporal lobe epilepsy or other organic brain disorders (see Lukianowicz 1958 and Lhermitte 1951 for detailed accounts).

Occasionally, a stimulus in one sensory modality results in a hallucination in another, e.g. the sound of music may provoke visual hallucinations. This experience, sometimes called **reflex hallucinations**, may occur after taking drugs such as LSD, or, rarely, in schizophrenia.

As already mentioned, **hypnagogic** and **hypnopompic hallucinations** occur at the point of falling asleep and of waking respectively. When they occur in healthy people, they are brief and elementary—for example hearing a bell ring or a name called. Usually the person wakes suddenly and recognizes the nature of the experience. In narcolepsy, hallucinations are common but may last longer and be more elaborate.

Diagnostic associations

Hallucinations may occur in severe affective disorders, schizophrenia, organic disorders and dissociative states, and at times among healthy people. Therefore the finding of hallucinations does not itself help much in diagnosis. However, certain kinds of hallucination do have important implications for diagnosis.

Both the form and content of **auditory hallucinations** can help in diagnosis. Of the various types—noises, music, and voices—the only ones of diagnostic significance are voices heard as speaking clearly to or about the patient. As explained already, voices which appear to be talking to each other, referring to the patient in the third person (e.g. 'he is a homosexual') are called **third person hallucinations**. They are associated particularly with schizophrenia. Such voices may be experienced as commenting on the patient's intentions (e.g. 'he wants to make love to her') or actions (e.g. 'she is washing her face'). Of all types of hallucination, commentary voices are most suggestive of schizophrenia.

Second person hallucinations appear to address the patient (e.g. 'you are going to die') or give commands (e.g. 'hit him'). In themselves they do not point to a particular diagnosis, but their content and especially the patient's reaction may do so. For example, voices with derogatory content suggest severe depressive disorder, especially when the patient accepts them as justified (e.g. 'you are wicked'). In schizophrenia the patient more often resents such comments.

Voices which anticipate, echo, or repeat the patient's thoughts also suggest schizophrenia.

Visual hallucinations may occur in hysteria, severe affective disorders, and schizophrenia, but they should always raise the possibility of an organic disorder. The content of visual hallucinations is of little significance in diagnosis.

Hallucinations of taste and smell are infrequent. When they do occur they often have an unusual quality which patients have difficulty in describing. They may occur in schizophrenia or severe depressive disorders, but they should also suggest temporal lobe epilepsy or irritation of the olfactory bulb or pathways by a tumour.

Tactile and somatic hallucinations are not generally of diagnostic significance although a few special kinds are weakly associated with particular disorders. Thus, hallucinatory sensations of sexual intercourse suggest schizophrenia, especially if interpreted in an unusual way (e.g. as resulting from intercourse with a series of persecutors). The sensation of insects moving under the skin occurs in people who abuse cocaine and occasionally among schizophrenics.

Perception and meaning

A percept has a meaning for the person who experiences it. In some psychiatric disorders an abnormal meaning may be associated with a normal percept. When this happens we speak of **delusional perception**. In some neurological disorders percepts lose their meaning. This is called **agnosia**. These abnormalities are considered further on pp. 17 and 30 respectively.

Disorders of thinking

Disorders of thinking are usually recognized from speech and writing. They can also be inferred from inability to perform tasks; thus one psychological test of thought disorder requires the person to sort objects into categories.

The term disorder of thinking can be used in a wide sense to denote four separate groups of phenomena (Table 1.2). The first group comprises particular kinds of abnormal thinking—delusions and obsessional thoughts. The second group, disorders of the stream of thought, is concerned with abnormalities of the amount and the speed of the thought experienced. The third group, known as disorders of the form of thought, is concerned with abnormalities of the ways in which thoughts are linked together. The fourth group, abnormal beliefs about the possession of

Table 1.2. Disorders of thinking

1. Particular kinds of abnormal thoughts
   Delusions
   Obsessions

2. Disorders of the stream of thought (speed and pressure)

3. Formal thought disorder (linking of thoughts together)

4. Abnormal beliefs about the possession of thoughts

thoughts, comprises unusual disturbances of the normal awareness that one's thoughts are one's own.

The second and third groups are considered here, whilst the first and last will be discussed later in the chapter.

Disorders of the stream of thought

In disorders of the stream of thought both the amount and the speed of thoughts are changed. At one extreme there is **pressure of thought**, when ideas arise in unusual variety and abundance and pass through the mind rapidly. At the other extreme there is poverty of thought, when the patient has only a few thoughts, which lack variety and richness, and seem to move through the mind slowly. The experience of pressure occurs in mania; that of poverty in depressive disorders. Either may be experienced in schizophrenia.

The stream of thought can also be interrupted suddenly, a phenomenon which the patient experiences as his mind going blank, and which an observer notices as a sudden interruption in the flow of conversation. Minor degrees of this experience are common, particularly in people who are tired or anxious. By contrast, **thought blocking**, a particularly abrupt and complete interruption, strongly suggests schizophrenia. Because thought blocking has this importance in diagnosis, it is essential that it should be identified only when there is no doubt about its presence. Inexperienced interviewers often wrongly identify a sudden interruption of conversation as thought blocking. There are several other reasons why the flow of speech may stop abruptly: the patient may be distracted by another thought or an extraneous sound, or he may be experiencing one of the momentary gaps in the stream of thought that are normal in people who are anxious or tired. Thought blocking should only be identified when interruptions in speech are sudden, striking, and repeated, and when the patient describes the experience as an abrupt and complete emptying of his mind. The diagnostic association with schizophrenia is strengthened if the patient also interprets the experience in an unusual way, e.g. as having had his thoughts taken away by a machine operated by a persecutor.

Disorders of the form of thought

Disorders of the form of thought can be divided into three subgroups, flight of ideas, perseveration, and loosening of associations. Each is related to a particular form of mental disorder, so that it is important to distinguish them, but in none of the three is the relationship strong enough to be regarded as diagnostic.

In **flight of ideas** the patient's thoughts and conversation move quickly from one topic to another so that one train of thought is not completed before another appears. These rapidly changing topics are understandable because the links between them are normal, a point that differentiates them from loosening of associations (see below). In practice, the distinction is often difficult to make, especially when the patient is speaking rapidly. For this reason it may be helpful to tape record a sample of speech and listen to it several times. The characteristics of flight of ideas are: preservation of the ordinary logical sequence of ideas, using two words with a similar sound (clang associations) or the same word with a second meaning (punning), rhyming, and responding to distracting cues in the immediate surroundings. Flight of ideas is characteristic of mania.

Perseveration is the persistent and inappropriate repetition of the same thoughts. The disorder is detected by examining the person's words or actions. Thus, in response to a series of simple questions, the person may give the correct answer to the first but continue to give the same answer inappropriately to subsequent questions. Perseveration occurs in dementia but is not confined to this condition.

Loosening of associations denotes a loss of the normal structure of thinking. To the interviewer this appears as muddled and illogical conversation that cannot be clarified by further enquiry. Several features of this muddled thinking have been described (see below), but in the end it is usually the general lack of clarity in the patient's conversation that makes the most striking impression. This muddled thinking differs from that of people who are anxious or of low intelligence. Anxious people give a more coherent account when they have been put at ease, while those with subnormal intelligence can express ideas more clearly if the interviewer simplifies his questions. When there is loosening of associations, the interviewer has the experience that the more he tries to clarify the patient's thoughts the less he understands them. Loosening of associations occurs most often in schizophrenia.

Loosening of associations can take several forms. **Knight's move** or **derailment** refers to a transition from one topic to another, either between sentences or in mid-sentence, with no logical relationship between the two topics and no evidence of the forms of association described under flight of ideas. When this abnormality is extreme it disrupts not only the connections between sentences and phrases but also the finer grammatical structure of speech. It is then called **word salad**. The term **verbigeration** refers to a kind of stereotypy in which sounds, words, or phrases are repeated in a senseless way.

One effect of loosened associations on the patient's conversation is sometimes called **talking past the point** (also known by the German term **vorbeireden**). In this condition the patient seems always about to get near to the matter in hand but never quite reaches it.

Several attempts have been made to devise psychological tests to detect loosening of associations, but the results have not been particularly useful to the clinician. Attempts to use the tests to diagnose schizophrenia have failed.

In addition to these disorders of links between ideas, thoughts may become illogical through **widening of concepts**, i.e. the grouping together of things that are not normally regarded as closely connected with one another.

Neologisms

Although not a disorder of the form of thought, neologism is conveniently described here. In this abnormality of speech the patient uses words or phrases, invented by himself, often to describe his morbid experiences. Neologisms must be distinguished from incorrect pronunciation, the wrong use of words by people with limited education, dialect words, obscure technical terms, and the 'private words' which some families invent to amuse themselves. The interviewer should always record examples of the patient's words and ask what he means by them.

Theories of thought disorder

Many theories have been proposed but none is convincing (see Payne 1973 for a review). Each theory attempts to explain a particular aspect of the thought disorder found in schizophrenia. Thus Goldstein (1944) built his theory round the apparent difficulty in forming abstract concepts ('concreteness'), while Cameron (1938) developed Bleuler's original observation that there is a 'loosening of associations', i.e. that the boundaries between concepts are less clear then in normal people. Payne and Friedlander (1962) developed the theory that concepts are too wide (over-inclusive) and devised ways of testing for over-inclusiveness with problems requiring the sorting and classification of objects. Bannister (1962) used Kelly's personal construct theory as the basis of a similar scheme, in which schizophrenics were supposed to have constructs that are not as consistent as those of other people and not as well structured. Bannister and Fransella (1966) devised an ingenious test in which these aspects of personal constructs are assessed by asking subjects to rate photographs of unknown people for a number of attributes such as kindness, honesty, and selfishness. Although the test provides a method of measuring one aspect of thought disorder, the theory has not succeeded in explaining how the abnormality arises.

Delusions

A delusion is a belief that is firmly held on inadequate grounds, is not affected by rational argument or evidence to the contrary, and is not a conventional belief such that the person might be expected to hold given his educational and cultural background. This definition is intended to separate delusions, which are indicators of mental disorder, from other kinds of strongly held belief found among healthy people. A delusion is usually a false belief, but not invariably so.

The hallmark of the delusion is that it is firmly held on inadequate grounds, that is, the belief is not arrived at through normal processes of logical thinking. It is held with such conviction that it cannot be altered by evidence to the contrary. For example, a patient who holds the delusion that there are persecutors in the adjoining house will not be convinced by evidence that the house is empty; instead he will retain his belief by suggesting, for example, that the persecutors left the house before it was searched. It should be noted that non-delusional ideas of normal people can sometimes be equally impervious to reasoned argument, for example, certain shared beliefs of people with a common religious or ethnic background. Thus a person who has been brought up to believe in spiritualism is unlikely to change his convictions when presented with contrary evidence that convinces a non-believer.

Although delusions are usually false beliefs, in exceptional circumstances they can be true or subsequently become true. A well recognized example is pathological jealousy (p. 334). A man may develop a jealous delusion about his wife, in the absence of any reasonable evidence of infidelity. Even if the wife is actually being unfaithful at the time, the belief is still delusional if there is no rational ground for holding it. The point to stress is that it is not falsity that determines whether the belief is delusional, but the nature of the mental processes that led up to the belief. Conversely, it is a well-known pitfall of clinical practice to assume that a belief is false because it is odd, instead of checking the facts or finding out how the belief was arrived at. For example, improbable stories of persecution by neighbours, or of attempts at poisoning by a spouse, may turn out to be arrived at through normal processes of logical thinking, and, in fact, to be correct.

The definition of a delusion emphasizes that the belief must be firmly held. However, the belief may not be so firmly held before or after the delusion has been fully formed. Although some delusions arrive in the patient's mind fully formed and with total conviction, other delusions develop more gradually. Similarly, during recovery from his disorder, a patient may pass through a stage of increasing doubt about his belief before finally rejecting it as false. The term *partial delusion* is sometimes used to denote these phenomena (as in the Present State Examination, see p. 4). It is safest to use the term partial delusion only when it is known to have been preceded by a full delusion, or (with hindsight) to have later developed into a full delusion. Partial delusions are sometimes found during the early stages of schizophrenia. When partial delusions are met, they cannot be given much weight in themselves, but a careful search should be made for other phenomena of mental illness.

Although a patient may be wholly convinced that a delusional belief is true, this conviction does not necessarily influence all his feelings and actions. This separation of belief from feeling and action is known as *double orientation*. It occurs most often in chronic schizophrenics. Such a patient may, for example, believe that he is a member of a Royal Family while living contentedly in a hostel for discharged psychiatric patients.

Delusions must be distinguished from *overvalued ideas*, which were first described by Wernicke (1900). An overvalued idea is an isolated, preoccupying belief, neither delusional nor obsessional in nature, which comes to dominate a person's life for many years and may affect his actions. The preoccupying belief may be understandable when the person's background is known. For example, a person whose mother and sister suffered from cancer one after the other may become preoccupied with the conviction that cancer is contagious. Although the distinction between delusions and overvalued ideas is not always easy to make, this difficulty seldom leads to practical problems because diagnosis of mental illness depends on more than the presence or absence of a single symptom. (For further information about overvalued ideas the reader is referred to McKenna 1984.)

Delusions are of many kinds, which will now be described. In the following section, the reader may find it helpful to refer to Table 1.3.

Primary, secondary, and shared delusions

A **primary** or **autochthonous** delusion is one that appears suddenly and with full conviction but without any mental events leading up to it. For example, a schizophrenic patient may be suddenly and completely convinced that he is changing sex, without ever having thought of it before and without any preceding ideas or events which could have led in any understandable way to this conclusion. The belief arrives in the mind suddenly, fully formed, and in a totally convincing form. Presumably it is a direct expression of the pathological process causing the mental illness— a primary symptom. Not all primary delusional experiences start with an idea; a **delusional mood** (see p. 17) or a **delusional perception** (see p. 17) can also arrive suddenly and without any antecedents to account for them. Of course, patients do not find it easy to remember the exact sequence of such unusual and often distressing mental events and for this reason it is difficult to be certain what is primary. Inexperienced interviewers usually diagnose primary delusional experiences too readily because they do not probe carefully enough into their antecedents. Primary delusions are given considerable weight in the diagnosis of schizophrenia, and it is important not to record them unless they are present for certain.

Secondary delusions can be understood as derived from some preceding morbid experience. The latter may be of several kinds, such as: a hallucination, e.g. someone who hears voices may come to believe that he is being followed; a mood, e.g. a person who is profoundly depressed may

Table 1.3. Descriptions of delusions

---

1. According to fixity
     complete
     partial

2. According to onset
     primary
     secondary

3. Other delusional experiences
     delusional mood
     delusional perception
     delusional memory

4. According to theme
     persecutory (paranoid)
     delusions of reference
     grandiose (expansive)
     delusions of guilt and worthlessness
     nihilistic
     hypochondriacal
     religious
     jealous
     sexual or amorous
     delusions of control
     delusions concerning possession of thought
     delusions of thought broadcasting

5. According to other features
     shared delusions

---

believe that people think he is worthless; or an existing delusion, e.g. a person with the delusion that he has lost all his money may come to believe he will be put in prison for failing to pay debts. Some secondary delusions seem to have an integrative function, making the original experiences more comprehensible to the patient, as in the first example above. Others seem to do the opposite, increasing the sense of persecution or failure, as in the third example.

The accumulation of secondary delusions may result in a complicated **delusional system** in which each belief can be understood as following from the one before. When a complicated set of interrelated beliefs of this kind has developed the delusions are sometimes said to be **systematized**.

Shared delusions: as a rule, other people recognize delusions as false and argue with the patient in an attempt to correct them. Occasionally, a person who lives with a deluded patient comes to share his delusional beliefs. This condition is known as shared delusions or **folie à deux**. Although the second person's delusional conviction is as strong as the partner's while the couple remain together, it often recedes quickly when they are separated. The condition is described more fully on p. 340.

Delusional moods, perceptions, and memories

As a rule, when a patient first experiences a delusion he also has an emotional response and interprets his environment in a new way. For example, a person who believes that a group of people intend to kill him is likely to feel afraid. At the same time he may interpret the sight of a car in his driving mirror as evidence that he is being followed. In most cases, the delusion comes first and the other components follow.

Occasionally the order is reversed: the first experience is change of mood, often a feeling of anxiety with the foreboding that some sinister event is about to take place, and the delusion follows. In German this change of mood is called **Wahnstimmung**, a term usually translated as **delusional mood**. The latter is an unsatisfactory term because there is really a mood from which a delusion arises. At other times, the first change may be attaching a new significance to a familiar percept without any reason. For example, a new arrangement of objects on a colleague's desk may be interpreted as a sign that the patient has been chosen to do God's work. This is called **delusional perception**: this term is also unsatisfactory since it is not the patient's perceptions that are abnormal, but the false meaning that has been attached to a normal percept. Although both terms are less than satisfactory, there is no generally agreed alternative and they have to be used if the experience is to be labelled. However, it is usually better simply to describe what the patient has experienced and to record the order in which changes have occurred in beliefs, affect, and the interpretation of sense data.

In a related disorder a patient sees a familiar person and believes him to have been replaced by an impostor who is the exact double of the original. This symptom is sometimes called by the French term **l'illusion de sosies** (illusion of doubles), but it is of course a delusion, not an illusion. The symptom may be so persistent that a syndrome, the **Capgras syndrome**, has been described in which it is the central feature (see p. 339). The opposite false interpretation of experience occurs when a patient recognizes a number of people as having different appearances, but believes they are a single persecutor in disguise. This abnormality is called the **Fregoli delusion**. It is described further on p. 339.

Finally, some delusions concern past rather than present events, and are known as **delusional memories**. For example, if a patient believes that there is a plot to poison him he may attribute new significance to the memory of an occasion when he vomited after eating a meal, long before his delusional system began. This experience has to be distinguished from the accurate recall of a delusional idea formed at the time. The term is unsatisfactory because it is not the memory that is delusional, but the interpretation that has been applied to it.

Delusional themes

For the purposes of clinical work, delusions are grouped according to their main themes. This grouping is useful because there is some correspondence between themes and the major forms of mental illness. However it is important to remember that there are many exceptions to the broad associations mentioned below.

Persecutory delusions are often called **paranoid**, a term which strictly speaking has a wider meaning. The term paranoid was used in ancient Greek writings in the modern sense of 'out of his mind', and Hippocrates used it to describe febrile delirium. Many later writers applied the term to grandiose, erotic, jealous, and religious, as well as persecutory, delusions. For this reason, it is preferable not to use the term paranoid to describe a persecutory delusion. However, the term paranoid applied in its wide sense to symptoms, syndromes and personality types retains its usefulness (see Chapter 10).

Persecutory delusions are most commonly concerned with persons or organizations that are thought to be trying to inflict harm on the patient, damage his reputation, make him insane, or poison him. Such delusions are common but of little help in diagnosis, for they can occur in organic states, schizophrenia, and severe affective disorders. However, the patient's attitude to the delusion may point to the diagnosis: in a severe depressive disorder he characteristically accepts the supposed activities of the persecutors as justified by his own guilt and wickedness, but in schizophrenia he resents them, often angrily. In assessing such ideas, it is essential to remember that apparently improbable accounts of persecution are sometimes true and that it is normal in certain cultures to believe in witchcraft and to ascribe misfortune to the malign activities of other people.

Delusions of reference are concerned with the idea that objects, events, or people have a personal significance for the patient: for example, an article read in a newspaper or a remark heard on television is believed to be directed specifically to himself. Alternatively a radio play about homosexuals is thought to have been broadcast in order to tell the patient that everyone knows he is a homosexual. Delusions of reference may also relate to actions or gestures made by other people which are thought to convey something about the patient; for example, people touching their hair may be thought to signify that the patient is turning into a woman. Although most delusions of reference have persecutory associations they may also relate to grandiose or reassuring themes.

Grandiose or expansive delusions are beliefs of exaggerated self-importance. The patient may think himself wealthy, endowed with unusual
abilities, or a special person. Such ideas occur in mania and in
schizophrenia.

Delusions of guilt and worthlessness are found most often in depressive
illness, and are therefore sometimes called depressive delusions. Typical
themes are that a minor infringement of the law in the past will be
discovered and bring shame upon the patient, or that his sinfulness will
lead to divine retribution on his family.

Nihilistic delusions are strictly speaking beliefs about the non-existence
of some person or thing, but their meaning is extended to include
pessimistic ideas that the patient's career is finished, that he is about to
die, that he has no money, or that the world is doomed. Nihilistic delusions
are associated with extreme degress of depressed mood. Comparable ideas
concerning failures of bodily function (e.g. that the bowels are blocked
with putrefying matter) often accompany nihilistic delusions. The resulting
clinical picture is called **Cotard's syndrome** after the French psychiatrist
who described it (Cotard 1882). The condition is considered further in
Chapter 10.

Hypochondriacal delusions are concerned with illness. The patient may
believe wrongly, and in the face of all medical evidence to the contrary,
that he is ill. Such delusions are more common in the elderly, reflecting
the increasing concern with health among mentally normal people at this
time of life. Other delusions may be concerned with cancer or venereal
disease, or with the appearance of parts of the body, especially the nose.
Patients with delusions of the last kind sometimes request plastic surgery
(see p. 418).

Religious delusions: delusions with a religious content were much more
frequent in the nineteenth century than they are today (Klaf and Hamilton
1961), presumably reflecting the greater part that religion played in the
life of ordinary people in the past. When unusual and firmly held religious
beliefs are encountered among members of minority religions, it is
advisable to speak to another member of the group before deciding
whether the ideas (e.g. apparently extreme ideas about divine punishment
for minor sins) are abnormal or not.

Delusions of jealousy are more common among men. Not all jealous
ideas are delusions; less intense jealous preoccupations are common, and
some obsessional thoughts are concerned with doubts about the spouse's
fidelity. However, when the beliefs are delusional they have particular
importance because they may lead to dangerously aggressive behaviour
towards the person thought to be unfaithful. Special care is needed if the
patient follows the spouse to spy on her, examines her clothes for marks
of semen, or searches her handbag for letters. A person with delusional
jealousy will not be satisfied if he fails to find evidence supporting his

beliefs; his search will continue. These important problems are discussed further in Chapter 10.

Sexual or amorous delusions: both sexual and amorous delusions are rare but when they occur, they are more frequent among women. Delusions concerning sexual intercourse are often secondary to somatic hallucinations felt in the genitalia. A woman with amorous delusions believes that she is loved by a man who is usually inaccessible, of higher social status, and someone to whom she has never even spoken. Erotic delusions are the most prominent feature of **De Clérambault's syndrome** which is discussed in Chapter 10.

Delusions of control: the patient who has a delusion of control believes that his actions, impulses, or thoughts are controlled by an outside agency. Because the symptom strongly suggests schizophrenia, it is important not to record it unless definitely present. A common error is to diagnose it when not present. Sometimes the symptom is confused with the experience of hearing hallucinatory voices giving commands that the patient obeys voluntarily. At other times it is misdiagnosed because the patient has mistaken the question for one about religious beliefs concerning the divine control of human actions. The patient with a delusion of control firmly believes that individual movements or actions have been brought about by an outside agency; for example that his arms are moved into the position of crucifixion not because he willed them to do so, but because an outside force brought it about.

Delusions concerning the possession of thoughts: healthy people take for granted that their thoughts are their own. They also assume that thoughts are private experiences that can be known to other people only if spoken aloud, or revealed by facial expression, gesture, or action. Patients with delusions about the possession of thoughts may lose these convictions in several ways. Those with delusions about **thought insertion** believe that some of their thoughts are not their own but have been implanted by an outside agency. This experience differs from that of the obsessional patient who may be distressed by unpleasant thoughts but never doubts that they originate within his own mind. As Lewis (1957) said, obsessional thoughts are 'home made but disowned'. The patient with a delusion of thought insertion will not accept that the thoughts have originated in his own mind. Patients with **delusions of thought withdrawal** believe that thoughts have been taken out of their mind. This delusion usually accompanies thought blocking, so that the patient experiences a break in the flow of thoughts through his mind and believes that the 'missing' thoughts have been taken away by some outside agency, often his supposed persecutors.

In **delusions of thought broadcasting** the patient believes that his unspoken thoughts are known to other people, through radio, telepathy, or in some other way. Some patients also believe that their thoughts can be heard by other people (a belief which also accompanies the experience of hearing one's own thoughts spoken, *Gedankenlautwerden*).

All three of these symptoms occur much more commonly in schizophrenia than in any other disorder.

The causes of delusions

So little is known about the processes by which normal beliefs are formed and tested against evidence, that it is not surprising that we are ignorant about the cause of delusions. This lack of knowledge has not, however, prevented the development of several theories, mainly concerned with persecutory delusions.

One of the best known theories was developed by Freud. The central ideas were expressed in a paper originally published in 1911 (Freud 1958): 'the study of a number of cases of delusions of persecution has led me as well as other investigators to the view that the relation between the patient and his persecutor can be reduced to a simple formula. It appears that the person to whom the delusion ascribes so much power and influence is either identical with someone who played an equally important part in the patient's emotional life before illness, or an easily recognizable substitute for him. The intensity of the emotion is projected in the shape of external power, while its quality is changed into the opposite. The person who is now hated and feared for being a persecutor was at one time loved and honoured. The main purpose of the persecution asserted by the patient's delusion is to justify the change in his emotional attitude'. Freud further summarized his view as follows: delusions of persecution are the result of the sequence. 'I do not *love* him—I *hate* him, because he persecutes me'; erotomania of the sequence 'I do not love *him*—I love *her*, because *she loves me*'; and delusions of jealousy of the sequence 'It is not *I* who loved the man—*she* loves him' (Freud 1958, pp.63–4, emphases in the original). This hypothesis suggests therefore that patients who experience persecutory delusions have repressed homosexual impulses. So far, attempts to test this idea have not produced convincing evidence in its favour (see Arthur 1964). Nevertheless, the general idea that persecutory delusions involve the defence mechanism of projection has been accepted by some writers.

Several existential analyses of delusions have been made. These describe in detail the experience of the deluded patient and make the important point that the delusion affects the whole being—it is not just an isolated symptom. Conrad (1958), using the approach of Gestalt psychology, described the delusional experience as having four stages starting from a delusional mood which he called trema (fear and trembling), leading via the delusional idea which he called apophenia (the appearance of the phenomenon), to the person's efforts to make sense of the experience by revising his whole view of the world. These efforts break down in the last stage (apocalypse) when thought disorder and behavioural symptoms appear. While a sequence of this kind can be observed in a few patients it is certainly not invariable.

Learning theorists have tried to explain delusions as a form of avoidance of highly unpleasant emotions. Thus Dollard and Miller (1950) suggested that a delusion is a learned explanation for events which avoids feelings of guilt or shame. This idea is as unsupported by evidence as all the other theories of delusion formation. Readers who wish to find out more about the subject should consult Arthur (1964).

Obsessional and compulsive symptoms

These symptoms are more common than delusions but generally of less serious significance. Obsessional and compulsive symptoms are best described separately although they often occur together.

Obsessions are recurrent, persistent thoughts, impulses, or images that enter the mind despite the person's efforts to exclude them. The characteristic feature is the subjective sense of a struggle—the patient resisting the obsession which nevertheless intrudes into his awareness. Obsessions are recognized by the person as his own and not implanted from elsewhere. They are often regarded by him as untrue or senseless—an important point of distinction from delusions. They are generally about matters which the patient finds distressing or otherwise unpleasant.

The presence of resistance is important because, together with the lack of conviction about the truth of the idea, it distinguishes obsessions from delusions. However, when obsessions have been present for a long time, the amount of resistance often becomes less. This seldom causes diagnostic difficulties because by the time it happens, the nature of the symptom has usually been established.

Obsessions can occur in several forms (Table 1.4). Obsessional **thoughts** are repeated and intrusive words or phrases, which are usually upsetting to the patient; e.g. repeated obscenities or blasphemous phrases coming

Table 1.4. Obsessional and compulsive symptoms

1. Obsessions: thoughts
    ruminations
    doubts
    impulses
    obsessional phobias

2. Compulsions (rituals)

3. Obsessional slowness

into the awareness of a religious person. Obsessional **ruminations** are repeated worrying themes of a more complex kind; e.g. about the ending of the world. Obsessional **doubts** are repeated themes expressing uncertainty about previous actions, e.g. whether or not the person turned off an electrical appliance that might cause a fire. Whatever the nature of the doubt, the person realizes that the action has, in fact, been completed safely. Obsessional **impulses** are repeated urges to carry out actions, usually actions that are aggressive, dangerous, or socially embarrassing. Examples are the urge to pick up a knife and stab another person; to jump in front of a train; to shout obscenities in church. Whatever the urge, the person has no wish to carry it out, resists it strongly, and does not act on it.

Obsessional phobias are obsessional thoughts with a fearful content; e.g. 'I may have cancer'; or obsessional impulses that lead to anxiety and avoidance; e.g. the impulse to strike another person with a knife with the consequent avoidance of knives. The term is confusing (see below under phobias).

Although the themes of obsessions are various, most can be grouped into one or other of six categories: dirt and contamination, aggression, orderliness, illness, sex and religion. Thoughts about **dirt** and **contamination** are usually associated with the idea of harming others through the spread of disease. **Aggressive** thoughts may be about striking another person or shouting angry or obscene remarks in public. Thoughts about **orderliness** may be about the way objects are to be arranged or work is to be organized. Thoughts about **illness** are usually of a fearful kind; e.g. a dread of cancer or venereal disease. This fearfulness has resulted in the name **illness phobia**, but this term should be avoided because the phenomena are not examples of anxiety arising in specific situations (which is the hallmark of a phobia, see below). Obsessional ideas about **sex** usually concern practices which the patient would find shameful, such as anal intercourse. Obsessions about **religion** often take the form of doubts about the fundamentals of belief (e.g. 'does God exist?') or repeated doubts whether sins have been adequately confessed (**scruples**).

Compulsions are repetitive and seemingly purposeful behaviours, performed in a stereotyped way (hence the alternative name of **compulsive rituals**). They are accompanied by a subjective sense that they must be carried out and by an urge to resist. Like obsessions, compulsions are recognized as senseless. A compulsion is usually associated with an obsession as if it has the function of reducing the distress caused by the latter. For example, a handwashing compulsion often follows obsessional thoughts that the hands are contaminated with faecal matter. Occasionally, however, the only associated obsession is an urge to carry out the compulsive act.

Compulsive acts are of many kinds, but three are particularly common.

Checking rituals are often concerned with safety; e.g. checking over and over again that a gas tap has been turned off. **Cleaning** rituals often take the form of repeated handwashing but may also involve household cleaning. **Counting** rituals may be spoken aloud or rehearsed silently. They often involve counting in a special way, e.g. in threes, and are frequently associated with doubting thoughts such that the count must be repeated to make sure it was carried out adequately in the first place. In **dressing** rituals the person has to lay out his clothes in a particular way, or put them on in a special order. Again, the ritual is often accompanied by doubting thoughts that lead to seemingly endless repetition. In severe cases patients may take several hours to put on their clothes in the morning.

Obsessional slowness is usually the result of compulsive rituals or repeated doubts but it can occur occasionally without them (primary obsessional slowness).

The differential diagnosis of obsessional thoughts is from the ordinary preoccupations of healthy people, from the repeated concerns of anxious and depressed patients, from the recurring ideas and urges encountered in sexual deviations or drug dependency, and from delusions. Ordinary preoccupations do not have the same insistent quality and can be resisted by an effort of will. Many anxious or depressed patients experience intrusive thoughts (for example, the anxious person may think that he is about to faint, or the depressed person that he has nothing to live for), but they do not find these ideas unreasonable and they do not resist them. Similarly, sexual deviants and drug-dependent people often experience insistent ideas and images concerned with their sexual practices or habits of drug taking, but these ideas are usually welcomed rather than resisted. Delusions are likewise not resisted, and are firmly held to be true.

Theories about the **aetiology** of obsessions are discussed in Chapter 7, where obsessional neuroses are considered.

Disorders of emotion

The glossary of DSM III recommends that the term affect should be used for short-term states and mood for sustained ones. However, in everyday clinical practice, the words are often used interchangeably. In mental disorder, affect may be abnormal in three ways: its nature may be altered; it may fluctuate more or less than usual; and it may be inconsistent either with the patient's thoughts and actions or with events that are going on at the time.

Changes in the nature of emotion can be towards anxiety, depression, elation, or anger. Changes in any of these emotions may be associated with an obvious cause in the person's life, or arise without reason. Emotional disorders usually include several components other than the mood change itself. Thus feelings of anxiety are usually accompanied by autonomic over-activity and increased muscle tension, and feelings of depression by gloomy preoccupations and psychomotor slowness. These other features are part of the syndromes of anxiety and depressive disorders and as such are described in later chapters.

Abnormal fluctuation of mood may take the extreme form of total loss of emotion and inability to feel pleasure. The latter is sometimes called **apathy** (i.e. without feeling), a sense of the word that contrasts with the everyday usage of indolence or lack of initiative. When the normal variation of emotion is reduced rather than lost, affect is described as **blunted** or **flattened**. When emotions change in an excessively rapid and abrupt way, affect is said to be **labile**. When mood changes are very marked, the term **emotional incontinence** is sometimes used.

Normally, emotional expression seems appropriate to a person's circumstances (e.g. looking sad after a loss) and congruent with his thoughts and actions (when a person looks sad he is likely to be thinking gloomy thoughts). In psychiatric disorders, there may be **incongruity** of affect. For example a patient may laugh when describing the death of his mother. Such incongruity must be distinguished from laughter indicating that someone is ill at ease when talking about a distressing topic. It should be noted that failure to show emotion in distressing circumstances, although equally incongruous in the everyday sense, is called flattening of affect, not incongruity.

Disorders of emotion are found in all kinds of psychiatric disorder. They are the central feature of the affective disorders (depression and elation) and of anxiety disorders. They are also common in other neuroses, organic disorders, and schizophrenia.

Experimental psychopathology of mood

So far the most fruitful applications of experimental psychopathology have been to anxiety and depressive disorders. In anxiety disorders, research has focused on ways in which thinking about symptoms can increase and prolong anxiety. Thus anxious patients frequently think that physical symptoms such as palpitations signify an impending heart attack, that feelings of dizziness are a precursor of losing consciousness, or that increasing mental tension will lead to loss of control (Beck *et al.* 1974*a*; Hibbert 1984*a*). Changing these cognitions through cognitive therapy (see p. 736) appears to improve the outcome of anxiety neuroses.

Experimental studies of the psychopathology of depression have been mainly concerned with the relationship between mood and memory. Depressive mood change, whether in normal states of sadness or in depressive disorders, is associated with greater accessibility of unhappy as compared with happy memories (Teasdale and Fogarty 1979; Clark and

Teasdale 1982). Since thinking about unhappy events leads to depressive mood (an everyday observation that has been confirmed experimentally by Teasdale and Bancroft 1977) a circular process may ensue, leading to progressive deterioration of mood. [See Teasdale (1983) for a further account of these ideas.]

Phobias

A phobia is a persistent irrational fear of and wish to avoid a specific object, activity, or situation. The fear is irrational in the sense that it is out of proportion to the real danger and is recognized as such by the person experiencing it. The person finds it difficult to control his fear and often tries to avoid the feared objects and situations if possible. The object that provokes the fear may be a living creature such as a dog, snake, or spider, or a natural phenomenon such as darkness or thunder. Fear-provoking situations include high places, crowds, and open spaces. Phobic patients feel anxious not only in the presence of the objects or situations but also when thinking about them (**anticipatory anxiety**).

Isolated phobic symptoms are common among normal people and have been described since the earliest medical writings (see Lewis 1976 or Errera 1962 for a historical account). The variety of feared objects and situations is great. In the past, Greek names were given to each one (Pitres and Régis 1902 labelled some seventy in this way), but there is nothing to be gained by this practice.

As pointed out earlier, obsessional thoughts leading to anxiety and avoidance are often called **obsessional phobias**; e.g. a recurrent thought about doing harm with knives is sometimes called a phobia of knives because the person is anxious in the presence of these objects and avoids them. Similarly, obsessional thoughts about illness are sometimes called illness phobias (e.g. 'I may have cancer'). Strictly speaking neither of these symptoms is a phobia. Nor is dysmorphophobia, which is a disorder of bodily awareness (see p. 417).

Depersonalization and derealization

Depersonalization is a change of self-awareness such that the person feels unreal. Those who have this condition find it difficult to describe, often speaking of being detached from their own experience and unable to feel emotion. A similar change in relation to the environment is called **derealization**. In this condition, objects appear unreal and people appear as lifeless, two-dimensional 'cardboard' figures. Despite the complaint of inability to feel emotion, both depersonalization and derealization are described as highly unpleasant experiences.

These central features are often accompanied by other morbid experiences. There is some disagreement whether these experiences are part of depersonalization and derealization or separate symptoms. These accompanying features include changes in the experience of time; changes in the body image such as a feeling that a limb has altered in size or shape; and occasionally a feeling of being outside one's own body and observing one's own actions, often from above. These features do not occur in every case (Ackner 1954*a*).

Because patients find it difficult to describe the feelings of depersonalization and derealization, they often resort to metaphor. Unless careful enquiry is made, this can lead to confusion between descriptions of depersonalization and of delusional ideas. For example, a patient's description of depersonalization may be 'as if part of my brain had stopped working', or of derealization 'as if the people I meet are lifeless creatures'—statements which must be explored carefully to distinguish them from delusional beliefs that the brain is no longer working or that people have really changed. At times, this distinction may be very difficult to make.

Depersonalization and derealization are experienced quite commonly as transient phenomena by healthy adults and children, especially when tired. The experience usually begins abruptly and in normal people seldom lasts more than a few minutes (Sedman 1970). The symptoms have been reported after sleep deprivation (Bliss *et al.* 1959), after sensory deprivation (Reed and Sedman 1964), and as an effect of hallucinogenic drugs (Guttman and Maclay 1936). The symptoms also occur in many psychiatric disorders when they may be persistent, sometimes lasting for years. They are particularly associated with generalized and phobic anxiety disorders, depressive disorders, and schizophrenia. Depersonalization has also been described in epilepsy, especially the kind arising in the temporal lobe. Some psychiatrists, notably Shorvon *et al.* (1946), have described a separate depersonalization syndrome (see p. 214). Because depersonalization and derealization occur in so many disorders, they do not help in diagnosis.

There are several **aetiological theories** about depersonalization. Mayer-Gross (1935) proposed that it is a 'preformed functional response of the brain' in the sense that an epileptic fit is a preformed response. Others have suggested that depersonalization is a response to alterations in consciousness (which is consistent with its appearance during fatigue and sleep deprivation in normal people).

A third suggestion is that depersonalization occurs when anxiety becomes excessive. Thus Lader and Wing (1966) described one anxious patient who developed depersonalization during an experiment in which skin conductance and heart rate were being measured. An accompanying fall in these measures suggested that depersonalization might have been an expression of some mechanism that reduced anxiety. However, depersonalization can occur when consciousness is normal and anxiety is absent so that, at best, these ideas can explain only a proportion of cases. Moreover, in states with undoubted changes in consciousness (acute organic psychosyndromes) depersonalization is found in only a minority of patients. The same argument can be applied to states of anxiety. Other writers have suggested that depersonalization is the expression of a disorder of perceptual mechanisms, and some psychoanalytic authors regard it as a defence against emotion. These various theories, none of which is satisfactory, have been reviewed by Sedman (1970).

Motor symptoms and signs

Abnormalities of social behaviour, facial expression, and posture occur frequently in mental illness of all kinds. They are discussed in Chapter 3 where the examination of the patient is considered. There are also a number of specific motor symptoms. With the exception of tics these symptoms are mainly observed among schizophrenic patients. They are described briefly here for reference, and their clinical associations are discussed in Chapter 9.

Tics are irregular repeated movements involving a group of muscles, e.g. sideways movement of the head or the raising of one shoulder. **Mannerisms** are repeated movements that appear to have some functional significance, e.g. saluting. **Stereotypies** are repeated movements that are regular (unlike tics) and without obvious significance (unlike mannerisms): for example, rocking to and fro. **Posturing** is the adoption of unusual bodily postures continuously for a long time. The posture may appear to have a symbolic meaning, e.g. standing with both arms outstretched as if being crucified; or may have no apparent significance, e.g. standing on one leg. Patients are said to show **negativism** when they do the opposite of what is asked and actively resist efforts to persuade them to comply. **Echopraxia** is the imitation of the interviewer's movement automatically even when asked not to do so. Patients are said to exhibit **ambitendence** when they alternate between opposite movements, e.g. putting out the arm to shake hands, then withdrawing it, extending it again, and so on. **Waxy flexibility** is detected when a patient's limbs can be placed in a position in which they then remain for long periods whilst at the same time muscle tone is uniformly increased.

Disorders of the body image

The body image or body schema is a person's subjective representation against which the integrity of his body is judged and the movement and positioning of its parts assessed. To the earlier neurologists the body schema was a postural model (see Head 1920). Schilder (1935), in his book *The image and appearance of the human body*, argued that this postural model is only the lowest level of organization of the body schema, and that there are also higher psychological levels founded on emotion, personality, and social interaction.

It is certainly true that, in clinical practice, abnormalities of body image are encountered that affect far more than the appreciation of posture and movement. These abnormalities arise in neurological as well as psychiatric disorders, and in many cases organic and psychological factors appear to be acting together. Unfortunately, in neither neurological nor psychiatric disorders are the causes of body image disturbances understood completely. In the account that follows, we follow broadly the scheme proposed by Lishman (1987) and we recommend the relevant sections (pp. 59–66) of his book and the review of Lukianowicz (1967) to the reader who requires more detailed information about these disorders.

Phantom limb is a continuing awareness of a part of the body that has been lost. As such it is perhaps the most convincing evidence for the concept of a body schema. It occurs usually after limb amputation but has been reported after removal of breasts, genitalia, or eyes (Lishman 1987, p. 91). Phantom limbs may be experienced as painful. The phantom limb is usually present immediately after amputation and normally fades gradually, although a minority persist for years (see textbooks of neurology or the review by Frederiks 1969 for further information).

Unilateral unawareness and neglect is the most frequent neurologically determined disorder of body image. It usually affects the left limbs, and arises most often from lesions of the supramarginal and angular gyri of the right parietal lobe, often following a stroke. When the disorder is marked, the patient may neglect to wash one side of his body or to shave one side of his face, or may put on only one shoe. In its mildest form, it can be detected only by special testing using double stimulation (e.g. if both wrists are touched with cotton wool but the patient reports a touch from only one side, even though the sensation on the other side is present when tested on its own). Further information is given by Critchley (1953) whose book gives detailed information about syndromes arising from lesions in the parietal lobes.

Hemisomatognosis: this disorder, which is also known as hemidepersonalization, is much less frequent than unilateral unawareness. The patient reports the feeling that one of his limbs is missing, usually on the left. The disorder can occur on its own, or together with hemiparesis. There is often a coincident unilateral spatial agnosia. The nature of the patient's awareness is variable; some patients know that the limb is present though it feels to be absent, whilst others believe wholly or partly that the limb is really absent.

Anosognosia is a lack of awareness of disease, and it too is more often manifest on the left side of the body. Most often it occurs briefly in the early days after acute hemiplegia but occasionally it persists. The patient does not complain of the disability on the paralysed side and denies it when pointed out to him. There may also be denial of dysphasia, blindness (**Anton's syndrome**), or amnesia (most marked in Korsakov's syndrome). **Pain asymbolia** is a disorder in which the patient perceives a normally painful stimulus but does not recognize it as painful. Although these disorders are clearly associated with cerebral lesions, it has been suggested that there is a psychogenic element whereby the awareness of unpleasant things is repressed (see, for example, Weinstein and Kahn 1955). Although it is hardly possible that structural damage could act in the absence of psychological reactions, it seems unlikely that the latter can be the sole cause of a condition that is so much more frequent on the left side of the body.

Autotopagnosia is the inability to recognize, name, or point on command to parts of the body. The disorder may also apply to parts of the body of another person, but not to inanimate objects. It is a rare condition which arises from diffuse lesions, usually affecting both sides of the brain. Nearly all the cases can be explained by accompanying apraxia, dysphasia, or disorder of spatial perception (see Lishman 1987, p. 63).

Distorted awareness of size and shape includes feelings that a limb is enlarging, becoming smaller, or otherwise being distorted. Unlike the phenomena described so far, these experiences are not related closely to lesions of specific areas of the brain. They may occur in healthy people especially when falling asleep, or in the waking state, when very tired. They are sometimes reported in the course of migraine, in acute brain syndromes, as part of the aura of epilepsy, or after taking LSD. Changes of shape and size of body parts are also described by some schizophrenic patients. The person is nearly always aware that the experience is unreal, except in some cases of schizophrenia.

Reduplication phenomenon is the experience that part or all of the body has doubled. Thus the person may feel he has two left arms, or two heads, or that the whole body has been duplicated. These phenomena have been reported rarely in the course of migraine and temporal lobe epilepsy as well as in schizophrenia. In an extreme form the person has the experience of being aware of a copy of his whole body, a phenomenon already described under the heading of autoscopic hallucinations.

Coenestopathic states are localized distortions of body awareness, for example the nose feels as if it is made of cotton wool.

Disorders of memory

Failure of memory is called **amnesia**. Several kinds of memory failure are met in psychiatric disorders, and it might be expected that these would correspond broadly to the processes of memory thought to exist in healthy people. Although psychologists do not agree completely about the structure of normal memory, the following general scheme is widely accepted. Human memory behaves as if organized in three kinds of 'stores'. **Sensory stores** have a limited capacity to receive information from the sense organs and to retain it for a brief period (about 0.5 s), presumably so that processing can be undertaken. The second store—**primary memory** or **short-term memory**—also has a limited capacity, but information is held for rather longer than in the sensory store, being lost in about 15–20 s. Information can be retained for longer by repeated rehearsal (as in repeating an unfamiliar phone number until it has been dialled fully). There may be two short-term stores, one for verbal and the other for visual information, located respectively in the left and right hemispheres.

The third kind of store is secondary memory or **long-term memory** which receives information that has been selected for more permanent storage. Unlike short-term memory, this kind of store has a large capacity and holds information for a long time. Information in this store is 'processed' and stored according to certain characteristics such as the meaning or sound of words. Information also seems to be stored partly according to the emotional state of the person at the time when the event occurred, and to be more easily recalled when the person is in the same state; thus memories of events occurring during an unhappy mood are recalled more readily in an unhappy than in a happy state. Two useful distinctions can be made about the working of long-term memory. The first is between memory for events (**episodic memory**) and memory for language and knowledge (**semantic memory**). The second is between the **recognition** of material presented to the person, and **recall** without a cue: the latter is the more difficult.

Memory is affected in several kinds of psychiatric disorder. Thus in depressive disorders there is differential recall of unhappy memories (p. 25). Organic brain disorder generally affects all aspects of secondary memory, but some organic conditions give rise to an interesting partial effect known as the amnestic syndrome (p. 354) in which the person is unable to remember events occurring a few minutes before (impaired episodic memory), but can converse normally (intact semantic memory).

After a period of unconsciousness there is poor memory for the interval between the ending of complete unconsciousness and the restoration of full consciousness (**anterograde amnesia**). Some causes of unconsciousness (e.g. head injury and ECT) also lead to inability to recall events before the onset of unconsciousness (**retrograde amnesia**).

In some neurological and psychiatric disorders, patients have a peculiar disturbance of recall, either failing to recognize events that have been encountered before (*jamais vu*), or reporting the recognition of events that are in fact novel (*déjà vu*). Some patients with extreme difficulty in remembering may report as memories, events that have not taken place at the time in question (or may never have involved the person at all)—a disorder known as **confabulation**.

For a review of psychological studies of memory see Baddeley (1976).

Disorders of consciousness

Consciousness is awareness of the self and the environment. The level of consciousness can vary between the extremes of alertness and coma. The quality of consciousness can also vary: sleep differs from unconsciousness, and stupor differs from both (see below).

Many terms have been used for states of impaired consciousness. **Coma** is the most extreme form. The patient shows no external evidence of mental activity and little motor activity other than breathing. He does not respond even to strong stimuli. Coma can be graded by the extent of the remaining reflex responses, and by the type of EEG activity. **Sopor** is an infrequently used term for a state in which the person can be aroused only by strong stimulation. **Clouding of consciousness** refers to a state in which the patient is drowsy and reacts incompletely to stimuli. Attention, concentration, and memory are impaired and orientation is disturbed. Thinking seems slow and muddled, and events may be interpreted inaccurately.

Stupor refers to a condition in which the patient is immobile, mute, and unresponsive but appears to be fully conscious, usually because the eyes are open and follow external objects. If the eyes are closed, the patient resists attempts to open them. Reflexes are normal and resting posture is maintained, though it may be awkward. (Note that in neurology the term implies impaired consciousness.)

Confusion means inability to think clearly. It occurs characteristically in organic states, but in some functional disorders as well. In acute organic disorder confusion occurs together with partial impairment of consciousness, illusions, hallucinations, delusions, and a mood change of anxiety or apprehension. The resulting syndrome has been called a confusional state, but this term is not well defined and it is preferable to avoid it (see p. 348). Three variations of this syndrome may be mentioned. The first is an **oneiroid** (dream-like) state in which the patient, although not asleep, describes experiences of vivid imagery akin to that of a dream. When such a state is prolonged it is sometimes called a **twilight state** (see p. 348). **Torpor** is a state in which the patient appears drowsy, readily falls asleep, and shows evidence of slow thinking and narrowed range of perception.

Disorders of attention and concentration

Attention is the ability to focus on the matter in hand. Concentration is the ability to maintain that focus. These abilities may be impaired in a wide variety of psychiatric disorders including depressive disorders, mania, anxiety disorders, schizophrenia, and organic disorders. Therefore the finding of abnormalities of attention and concentration does not assist in diagnosis. Nevertheless these abnormalities are important in management: for example, they affect the patient's ability to give or receive information, and poor concentration can interfere with a patient's ability to work or pass his leisure time, for example in reading or watching television.

Insight

Insight may be defined as awareness of one's own mental condition. It is difficult to achieve, since it involves some knowledge of what constitutes a healthy mind, and yet doctors cannot agree among themselves about the meaning of terms such as mental health and mental illness. Moreover, insight is not simply present or absent, but rather a matter of degree. For this reason it is better to consider four separate questions. First, is the patient aware of phenomena that other people have observed (e.g. that he appears to be unusually active and elated)? Second, if so, does he recognize that these phenomena are abnormal (or does he, for example, maintain that his unusual activity and cheerfulness are merely normal high spirits)? Third, if he recognizes the phenomena as abnormal, does he consider that they are caused by mental illness, as opposed to, for example, a physical illness or the results of poison administered to him by his enemies? Fourth, if he accepts that he is ill, does he think he needs treatment?

The answers to these questions are much more informative—and much more likely to be reliable—than those of the single question: is insight present or not? Newcomers to psychiatry often ask this question because they have read that loss of insight distinguishes psychoses from neuroses. While it is generally true that neurotic patients retain insight and psychotic patients lose it, this is not invariable; nor is this in practice a reliable way of distinguishing between the two. Also the concepts of neurosis and psychosis are themselves unsatisfactory (see p. 79). On the other hand, the four questions listed above can help the clinician decide whether the patient is likely to co-operate with treatment.

The mechanisms of defence

So far, we have been concerned with aspects of descriptive psychopathology; or in other words with abnormal mental experiences which the patient can describe and with changes in behaviour which other people can observe. We now turn to an aspect of dynamic psychopathology that deserves special attention at this stage. It is concerned neither with mental events that the patient can describe, nor with his behaviour. Instead it is a set of processes that may help to *explain* certain kinds of experience or behaviour. These processes are called mechanisms of defence. They originated in the work of Sigmund Freud and have been elaborated by his daughter Anna Freud (1936). In the following account, the more important defence mechanisms are defined and brief examples given of the kinds of mental events and behaviour that they may explain. It is important to understand, at the start, that defence mechanisms are automatic and unconscious: they imply the patient is not acting deliberately nor is he aware of his real motives at the time, though he may become aware of such motives later either through introspection or because they have been pointed out to him by another person.

Defence mechanisms have been used to account for what Freud called the psychopathology of everyday life and to explain the aetiology of mental disorders. The illustrations of mechanisms of defence that appear in the following paragraphs are all concerned with everyday thoughts and actions. This is because these kinds of explanation are useful in understanding many aspects of the day-to-day behaviour of patients whether they have psychiatric or medical conditions. In subsequent chapters consideration is given to theories that have attempted to explain neurotic symptoms and personality disorders in terms of the same mechanisms.

Repression is the exclusion from awareness of impulses, emotions, and memories that would cause distress if allowed to enter consciousness. For example, a memory of an event in which a person was humiliated may be kept out of his awareness. **Denial**, a closely related concept, is inferred when a person behaves as though unaware of something which he may reasonably be expected to know. For example, a patient who has been told that he has cancer, may subsequently speak and act as though not aware of it.

Projection refers to the unconscious attribution to another person of thoughts or feelings that are one's own, thereby rendering the original feelings more acceptable. For example, someone who dislikes a colleague may impute feelings of anger and dislike to him. In this way, his own feelings of dislike may appear justified and become less distressing.

Regression refers to the unconscious adoption of a pattern of behaviour appropriate to an earlier stage of development. It is commonly seen among physically ill people who adopt a child-like dependency on nurses and doctors. During the acute stage of illness this dependency is often an adaptive response enabling the patient to accept the requirements of intensive medical and nursing care; however, if it persists, it can impede rehabilitation.

Reaction formation refers to the unconscious adoption of behaviour opposite to that which would reflect true feelings and intentions. For example, excessively prudish attitudes to the mention of sexual intercourse in conversation, books, or the media may occur in someone who has strong sexual drives that he cannot consciously accept.

Displacement refers to the unconscious process of transferring emotion from a situation or object with which it is properly associated, to another which will give rise to less distress. Thus after the recent death of his wife a man may blame the family doctor for failing to give her adequate treatment, instead of blaming himself for putting his own work before her needs in the last months of her life.

Rationalization refers to the unconscious provision of a false but acceptable explanation for behaviour which has other, less acceptable origins. For example, a husband who neglects his wife and goes to entertainments without her may give himself the false explanation that she is shy and would not enjoy them.

Sublimation is a related concept which refers to the unconscious diversion of unacceptable impulses into acceptable outlets; for example, turning angry feelings into vigorous sporting activities, or turning the wish to dominate other people into organizing charitable activities.

Identification refers to the unconscious process of taking on some of the activities or characteristics of another person, often to reduce the pain of separation or loss. For example a widow may take on the same work in local government that her husband used to undertake, or she may try to think about things in the way that he would have done.

Further reading

Jaspers, K. (1963). *General psychopathology*, trans. from the 7th German edition by J. Hoenig and M. W. Hamilton, Chapter I; Phenomenology. Manchester University Press, Manchester.

Scharfetter, C. (1980). *General psychopathology: an introduction* Trans. from the German by H. Marshall. Cambridge University Press, Cambridge.

Schneider, K. (1949). The concept of delusion. Reprinted and translated in Hirsch, S. R. and Shepherd, M. (eds.) (1974). *Themes and variations in European psychiatry*. John Wright, Bristol.

Shepherd, M. and Zangwill, O. L. (eds.)(1983). *Handbook of psychiatry*, Vol. 1. Cambridge University Press. (See especially: Introduction; The sciences and general psychopathology by M. Shepherd; and The historical background pp. 9–56).

Sims, A. (1988). *Symptoms in the mind; an introduction to descriptive psychopathology*. Baillière Tindall, London.
Wing, J. K., Cooper, J. E., and Sartorius, N. (1974). *The measurement and classification of psychiatric symptoms* (see Glossary of definitions, pp. 141–88). Cambridge University Press, Cambridge.

2 Interviewing, clinical examination, and record keeping

In psychiatry, as in medicine generally, correct diagnosis depends on careful history-taking and thorough clinical examination. However, psychiatry differs from the rest of medicine in that the interview is used not only to obtain the history but also as a way of eliciting clinical signs. This chapter begins, therefore, with an account of the technique of interviewing. Whilst this account draws attention to important points of technique, it should be remembered that interviewing is a practical skill that the trainee can acquire only through carrying out interviews under supervision and watching experienced interviewers at work.

The following section outlines an approach to interviewing that is widely used and effective in practice. There are of course other effective ways of conducting an interview. Whatever the approach, it is important that the interviewer should have definite aims and a clear plan for attaining them.

The diagnostic interview

Before the interview begins there are certain preliminary requirements. The interview should be carried out in a room that is reasonably sound-proof and free from interruptions. The patient should not be seated directly opposite the interviewer, nor should his chair be so much lower that he has to look upwards. In this way he will feel at ease rather than under constant scrutiny. For a diagnostic interview the interviewer should sit at a writing table in order to take notes (a psychotherapeutic interview may require less formal arrangements with patient and therapist both in armchairs). He should not attempt to memorize the interview and write notes afterwards, as this is time-consuming and likely to be inaccurate. The least obtrusive way of taking notes is to place the patient at the side of the desk, and on the left side of a right-handed interviewer. This creates a suitably informal atmosphere and allows the interviewer to attend to the patient whilst writing.

The first encounter with the patient is important. The interviewer should welcome him by name, and give his own name. If the patient is accompanied by a companion it is good practice for the interviewer to welcome this person as well and to explain how long he may expect to wait before being interviewed himself. If the patient is seen at the request of a general practitioner, the interviewer should indicate that the latter has written to him, but should not reveal the contents of the letter in detail.

The interviewer should explain how he proposes to proceed: e.g. 'First, I should like to hear about your present problems. Only when I am sure that I have understood these shall I ask you how they began'. The interviewer then asks an open question such as 'Tell me about the problems' or 'Tell me what you have noticed wrong', and the patient is encouraged to talk freely for several minutes. During this time the interviewer makes two separate kinds of observations—how the patient is talking, and what he has to say. The first helps the doctor decide *how* to interview the patient, whilst the second tells him *what* to ask about.

Whilst deciding how to interview the patient, the interviewer observes whether he seems co-operative, reasonably at ease, and able to express his ideas coherently. The most frequent difficulty is that the patient is over-anxious. The interviewer should consider whether such anxiety is part of the presenting disorder or merely fear on coming to a psychiatrist. If the latter, the interviewer should take time to discuss the patient's apprehension before proceeding with the interview. Usually reassurance and a calm, unhurried approach will put the patient more at ease.

Sometimes the patient seems unco-operative and resentful when he begins to talk. This may be because the interview is taking place against his wishes: for example, his spouse may have persuaded him to attend, or the psychiatrist may be interviewing him after admission to a general hospital for treatment of drug overdosage. Faced with this kind of resentment the interviewer should talk over the circumstances of the referral and try to persuade the patient that the interview is intended to be in his own interests. Patients may appear resentful for other reasons. Some patients act in a hostile way when anxious, and some depressed or schizophrenic patients seem unco-operative, because they do not regard themselves as ill. At times it becomes apparent that a patient cannot respond adequately to the interview because of impaired consciousness. When this seems likely, orientation, concentration, and memory should be tested, and if impaired consciousness is confirmed, an informant should be seen before returning to the patient.

Provided there are no immediate problems of this kind, the interviewer should consider whether there are likely to be difficulties in guiding the interview effectively. Some patients, such as successful business men, attempt to dominate the interview, especially if the interviewer is younger than themselves. Others adopt an unduly friendly attitude that threatens to convert the interview into a social conversation. In either case, the interviewer should explain why he needs to guide the patient to relevant issues.

As mentioned above, the interviewer, whilst listening to the patient's opening remarks, also begins to think what questions he should ask. These should begin with further enquiries about the *nature* of the patient's presenting symptoms. It is a common mistake to start asking about the timing of such symptoms before their nature is clearly established. For example, patients sometimes say they are depressed, but further enquiry shows that they are experiencing anxiety rather than low spirits. If there is any doubt, the patient should be asked to give examples of his experiences. The interviewer should clearly understand the nature of the symptoms before asking about their timing and the factors that make them better or worse.

When all the presenting complaints have been explored in this way, direct questions are used to ask about other relevant symptoms. For example, a person who complains of feeling depressed should be asked about ideas concerning the future, sleep pattern, appetite, etc. The subsidiary questions required for each presenting symptom will be apparent from reading the chapters in this book on psychiatric syndromes.

Next, the mode of onset of the complaint is asked about and its course noted, including any exacerbations or periods of partial remission. Considerable persistence may be needed to date the onset accurately, and if necessary it should be related to events the patient can remember accurately (e.g. was it before or after your birthday; had it already started before Christmas?).

Controlling the interview

As the interview continues, the doctor's task is to keep the patient to relevant topics by bringing him back to the point if he strays from it. In doing this the interviewer should use a minimum of leading or closed questions (a leading question suggests the answer; a closed question allows only the answers yes or no, thus preventing the person from volunteering information). Thus instead of the closed question 'are you happily married?' the interviewer might ask 'how do you and your wife get on with one another?'. When there is no alternative to a closed question, the answer should be followed by a request for an example.

Taciturn patients can often be encouraged to speak more freely if the interviewer shows non-verbal expressions of concern (e.g. leaning forward a little in the chair with an expression of interest). It is less easy to curb the flow of an over-talkative patient. Sometimes this can be done only by waiting for a natural break in the flow of speech to explain that, because time is limited, the interviewer proposes to interrupt the patient when appropriate to help him focus on the issues that are important for planning treatment. Provided such advice is given tactfully, most garrulous patients are relieved to be given it.

Although it is essential to ask direct questions about specific items of information, it is equally important to give the patient an opportunity to talk spontaneously, as unexpected material may be revealed in this way. Spontaneous talk can be encouraged by prompting rather than by questioning, e.g. by repeating in an enquiring tone the patient's reply to previous questions or by using non-verbal prompts. Also, before ending the interview, it is useful to ask a general question such as 'Is there anything else you wish to tell me?'.

History taking

Whenever possible, the history from the patient should be supplemented by information from a close relative or another person who knows him well. This is much more important in psychiatry than in the rest of medicine, because psychiatric patients are not always aware of the extent of their symptoms. For example, a manic patient may not realize how much embarrassment he has caused by his extravagant social behaviour, or a demented patient may not fully understand the extent to which his work is impaired. Alternatively patients may know what their problems are, but not wish to reveal them; for example, alcoholics often conceal the extent of their drinking. Also, when personality is being assessed, patients and relatives often give quite different accounts of characteristics such as irritability, obsessional traits, and jealousy.

The history should always be recorded systematically and in the same order to ensure that important themes are not forgotten by the interviewer, and to make it easier for colleagues to refer to the notes. However, it is not always possible to gather information in the same order with every patient. Some flexibility must be allowed if the patient is not to feel unduly restricted by the interviewer.

In this section, a standard scheme of history taking is given in the form of a list of topics to be covered. This will serve as a check-list for the beginner, and a reminder for the more experienced interviewer, of the topics that make up a complete history. However, it is neither necessary nor possible to ask every question of every patient. Common sense must be used in judging how far each topic needs to be explored with a particular patient. The trainee must learn by experience how to adjust his questioning to problems that emerge as the interview proceeds. This is done by keeping in mind the decision about diagnosis and treatment that will have to be made at the end of the interview.

The scheme given below is followed by notes explaining how to record the different items, and why they are important. After this the assessment of personality is discussed in more detail.

A scheme of history taking is given below. For ease of reference, this scheme is presented simply as a list of headings and items. However, it is essential that the trainee should understand how to record the different items, and why they are important; these topics are outlined in the subsequent notes on history taking. It is recommended that the scheme and subsequent notes be studied together.

The scheme of history taking

Informant

Name, relation to patient, intimacy, and length of acquaintance. Interviewer's impression of informant's reliability.

Source of referral and reasons for referral

Present illness

Symptoms with duration and mode of onset of each. Description of the time relations between symptoms and physical disorders and psychological or social problems. Effects on work, social functioning, and relationships. Associated disturbance in sleep, appetite, and sexual drive. Any treatment given by other doctors.

Family history

Father: age now or at death. (If dead give cause of death.) Health, occupation, personality, quality of relationship with patient. **Mother**: the same items. **Siblings**: names, ages, marital status, occupation, personality, psychiatric illness, and quality of relationship with patient. **Social position of family**—atmosphere in the home.

Family history of mental illness—psychiatric disorder, personality disorder, epilepsy, alcoholism. Other neurological or relevant medical disorders (e.g. Huntington's chorea).

Personal history

Early development: abnormalities during pregnancy and at birth. Difficulties in habit training and delay in achieving milestones (walking, talking, sphincter control, etc.). Separation from parents and reaction to it. **Health during childhood**: serious illness, especially any affecting the central nervous system, including febrile seizures. **'Nervous problems' in childhood**: fears, temper tantrums, shyness, stammering, blushing, food-fads, sleep-walking, prolonged bed wetting, frequent nightmares (though the significance of these behaviours is doubtful, see p. 165). **School**: age of starting and finishing each school. Types of school. Academic record.

Sporting and other achievements. Relationships with teachers and pupils. **Higher education**: comparable enquiries. **Occupations**: chronological list of jobs, with reasons for changes. Present financial circumstances, satisfaction in work. **Service or war experience**: promotion and awards. Disciplinary problems. Service overseas.

   Menstrual history: age of menarche, attitude to periods, regularity and amount, dysmenorrhoea, premenstrual tension, age of menopause and any symptoms at the time, date of last menstrual period. **Marital history**: age of patient at marriage. How long spouse known before marriage and length of engagement. Previous relationships and engagements. Present age, occupation, health, and personality of spouse. Quality of the marital relationship.
Sexual history: attitude to sex. Heterosexual and homosexual experience. Current sexual practices, contraception.
Children: names, sex, and age of children. Date of any abortions or stillbirths. Temperament, emotional development, mental and physical health of children.

Present social situation

Housing, composition of household, financial problems.

Previous medical history

Illness, operations, and accidents.

Previous psychiatric illness

Nature and duration of illness. Date, duration, and nature of any treatment. Name of hospital and of doctors. Outcome.

Personality before present illness

Relationships: friendships, few or many; superficial or close; with own or opposite sex. Relations with workmates and superiors. **Use of leisure**: hobbies and interests; membership of societies and clubs. **Predominant mood**: anxious, worrying, cheerful, despondent, optimistic, pessimistic, self-depreciating, over-confident. Stable or fluctuating. Controlled or demonstrative. **Character**: sensitive, reserved, timid, shy; suspicious, jealous, resentful; quarrelsome, irritable, impulsive; selfish, self-centred; self-conscious, lacking in confidence; dependent; strict, fussy, rigid; meticulous, punctual, excessively tidy. **Attitudes and standards**: moral and religious. Attitude towards health and the body. **Habits**: food, alcohol, tobacco, drugs.

Notes on history taking

The scheme just outlined lists the items to be considered when a full history is taken, but gives no indication why these items are important, or what sort of difficulties may arise in eliciting them. These issues are discussed in the present section, which is written in the form of notes referring to the headings used above.

The reason for referral

State in everyday language why the patient has been referred, e.g. 'Severe depression, failing to respond to drug treatment'.

The present illness

In an out-patient clinic, it is usually better to consider this item first because the patient probably wants to talk about it straight away. However, with in-patients the doctor may already have substantial information about the present illness, either from doctors dealing with the case before admission, or from relatives. In these circumstances the interviewer may find it better to begin with the family and personal history.

Always record which complaints have been volunteered by the patient, and which revealed by questioning. Record the severity and duration of each symptom, how it began and what course it has taken (increasing gradually; diminishing stepwise; staying the same; intermittent). Indicate which symptoms co-vary and which take an independent course (e.g. obsessional thoughts and rituals may have fluctuated together, whilst depressed mood may have been a recent addition). Any recent treatment should be noted, together with its apparent effects. When a drug has not been effective, note whether the patient took it in the required dosage.

Family history

Mental illness among parents or siblings suggests that the cause of illness may in part be hereditary. Because the family is the environment in which the patient grew up, the personality and attitudes of the parents are important. So are separations from the parents for any reason. Ask about the parents' relationship with one another, e.g. whether there were frequent quarrels. Enquire about separations, divorce, and remarriage. Rivalry between siblings may be important, as may favouritism towards one child by the parents. The occupation and social standing of the parents reflect the material circumstances of the patient's childhood.

Recent events in the family may have been stressful to the patient. Serious illness of either parent, or divorce of a sibling, are likely to be relevant problems in other family members. Finally, the family history may throw light on the patient's concerns about himself. For example, the death of an older brother from brain tumour may partly explain a patient's extreme concern about headaches.

Personal history

Pregnancy and birth: events in pregnancy are occasionally relevant, especially when the patient is mentally handicapped. An unwanted pregnancy may be followed by a poor relationship between mother and child. Similarly serious problems during delivery sometimes account for intellectual impairment.

Early development: few patients know whether they have passed through developmental stages normally. However, this information is more important if the patient is a child or adolescent, in which case the parents are likely to be interviewed routinely. This information may also be important in cases of mental handicap, when the parents or other relatives should be questioned and previous medical records should be obtained. (A summary of the main developmental milestones will be found in Chapter 20.)

Notes should also be made of any prolonged periods of separation from the mother, for example through illness. The effects of such separations vary considerably (see Chapter 20) and it is important to ask an appropriate informant whether the patient was emotionally upset at the time and, if so, for how long.

Health in childhood: there is little point in recording minor childhood ailments such as uncomplicated chicken-pox; but it is appropriate to enquire about encephalitis or convulsions, any illness leading to prolonged admission to hospital, or prolonged disability.

Early neurotic traits: it is conventional to enquire about such symptoms as fears, sleep-walking, shyness, stammering, and food fads. However, there is no evidence that these behaviours in childhood are precursors of neurosis in adult life.

Schooling: the school record not only gives an indication of intelligence and scholastic achievements, but also reflects social development. The type of school and examination results should be noted. The interviewer should also ask whether the patient had friends and was popular; whether he played games, and with what success; and how he got on with teachers. Similar questions are asked about **higher education**.

Occupational history: information about the present job helps the interviewer to understand the circumstances of the patient's life and judge whether he is under stress at work. A list of previous jobs is mainly relevant to the assessment of personality. If the patient has had many jobs, it is important to ask why he left each one. Repeated dismissals may reflect an awkward, aggressive, or otherwise abnormal personality (though there are, of course, many other reasons for repeated sackings). When each job is inferior to the last, it is necessary to consider declining efficiency caused by chronic mental illness or by alcohol abuse. Information about relationships with colleagues, senior and junior, helps to assess personality.

When the patient has served in the Armed Forces, or worked abroad, details should be obtained, and an enquiry made about tropical disease later in the history.

Menstrual history: it is usual to enquire about the age of menarche and how the patient first learnt about menstruation. These questions were more important in earlier times when ignorance about sexual matters was widespread and the unexpected onset of periods in an unprepared girl could give rise to lasting anxieties. In Britain today, this rarely happens except among some immigrant groups. When interviewing immigrants to this country, or when working in other countries, the interviewer may find the answers more informative. Questions about current menstrual function should be asked in all relevant cases. Dysmenorrhoea, menorrhagia, and premenstrual tension should be identified and amongst women in middle life the menopause should be noted. The date of the last period should also be noted.

Marital history: the interviewer should enquire about previous lasting relationships with the opposite sex and about the present marital relationship. Sexual relationships are considered in the next section: in this part of the history it is the personal aspects that are considered. Frequent broken relationships before marriage may reflect abnormalities of personality. A previous relationship may determine the patient's attitude to the present marriage; for example, when a first marriage has ended in divorce because of the husband's infidelity, a woman may over-react to minor difficulties in her second marriage.

The spouse's occupation, personality, and state of health give information of obvious relevance to the patient's circumstances. Present difficulties can often be understood better by enquiring about each partner's original expectations of the marriage. It is also useful to ask about the sharing of decisions and responsibilities in the marriage. The dates of birth of the children, or of any miscarriages, may indicate whether marriage was forced by pregnancy.

Sexual history: it is traditional to begin the sexual history by asking how the patient acquired information about sexual matters. Such a question was more likely to give useful information in times when ignorance was more widespread than today.

In taking the sexual history, the interviewer should use common sense in deciding how much to ask the individual patient. For example, a detailed account of masturbation and sexual techniques may be essential when the patient is seeking help for sexual impotence, but the interviewer is often more concerned to find generally whether the patient's sexual life is satisfying or not. Only if there are problems need he enquire into all the details under this heading. Judgement must also be used about the optimal timing and amount of detail of questions about homosexuality.

Finally the interviewer should ask about methods of contraception and, when relevant, a woman's wishes about bearing children.

Children: pregnancy, childbirth, miscarriages, and induced abortions are important events sometimes associated with adverse psychological reactions in the mother. Information about the patient's children is relevant to present worries and the pattern of family life. Since children may be affected by the parent's illness, it is important to know whether a seriously depressed woman has the care of a baby, or whether a violent alcoholic man has children in the home. If admission to hospital is being considered for a woman patient, it is important to find out about dependent children and if necessary arrange for their care. This is obvious but sometimes overlooked.

Previous illness: previous medical or surgical treatment should always be asked about, and particularly careful inquiries made about previous mental illness. Patients or relatives may be able to recall the presenting symptoms of illness, and the main points about treatment. However, details of diagnosis and treatment can usually be obtained only from the doctors who treated the patient at the time. In psychiatry the nature of previous illness is an important guide to the present disorder, and it is nearly always appropriate to request information from other hospitals.

Present circumstances: questions about housing, finances, and the composition of the household help the interviewer to understand the patient's circumstances and to judge more clearly what aspects of his life are likely to be stressful and how illness may affect him. There can be no general rule about the amount of detail to elicit, and this must be left to common sense.

Assessment of personality

Aspects of a patient's personality can be judged by asking him for his own self-rating, by asking other people who know him well, and by observing his behaviour at interview. Mistakes can arise from paying too much attention to the patient's own assessment of his personality. Some people give an unduly favourable account of themselves; for example antisocial people may conceal the extent of their aggressive behaviour or dishonesty. Conversely, depressed patients often judge themselves too severely, as being for example ineffectual, selfish, or unreliable, an impression that is not confirmed by other people. It is therefore essential whenever possible to interview other informants.

Good indications of personality can often be obtained by asking the patient or others how he has behaved in particular circumstances. For example, if a patient says he is self-confident, it is useful to enquire how he behaves in particular situations when he has to convince other people or speak in public. Similarly, personality can often be assessed by asking about occasions when social roles are changing, such as leaving school, starting work, marrying, or becoming a parent.

When assessing a patient's personality from behaviour at interview, it is essential to allow for the possible effects of psychiatric illness. Thus, when depressed a normally self-possessed and sociable person may appear abnormally shy and lacking in self-confidence.

Whatever the source of information, it is important to assess the strengths in a patient's personality, as well as the weaknesses.

Enquiries about personality are most fruitful when they are systematic. The scheme outlined on p. 42 is widely used, and covers the most important areas of enquiry in clinical work. The points given below refer to patient-interviews, but can be adapted to informant-interviews.

The assessment begins with enquiries about **relationships** with friends and people at work. Is the person shy or does he make friends easily? Are his friendships close and are they lasting? **Leisure activities** can throw light on personality, not only by reflecting a person's interests but also by indicating his preference for company or solitude, and his levels of energy and resourcefulness.

Mood is considered next. The interviewer tries to find out whether the patient is generally cheerful or gloomy; whether he has marked changes of mood, and if so, how quickly they appear, how long they last, and if they follow life-events. The interviewer should also find out whether the patient shows emotions or hides them.

Character: the interviewer will already have gathered some impression of this while taking the personal history. Further information about the patient's character should be sought; for example, by asking whether he is: reserved, timid, shy, or self-conscious; sensitive or suspicious, resentful or jealous; irritable, impulsive, or quarrelsome; selfish or self-centred; lacking in confidence; strict, fussy, rigid, meticulous, punctual, or excessively tidy.

These are chiefly negative attributes of character but, as mentioned above, it is also important to ask about positive ones. It is not appropriate to go through a complete list with every patient; common-sense will indicate what to enquire about as the picture of the patient gradually builds up. It is good practice, however, with every patient to determine how resilient he is in the face of adversity.

Answers should not always be taken at face value; for example, when readiness to anger is asked about, the interviewer should not simply accept the answer that the patient never feels angry. Instead he should persist in questioning, for example by remarking that everyone feels angry at times and asking what makes the patient angry. The interviewer should also find out whether the patient expresses anger or bottles it up; and if the former, whether through angry words or violent acts. If the patient contains anger, he should be asked how he feels when he does so.

Attitudes and standards: in this part of the interview it is usual to ask about attitudes to the body, health, and illness, as well as religious and moral standards. The personal history will usually have provided general indications about these matters so that extensive questioning is seldom necessary.

Habits: this final section deals with habits of taking tobacco, alcohol, or drugs.

Mental state examination

In the course of history taking, the interviewer will have noted the patient's symptoms up to the time of the consultation. The mental state examination is concerned with the symptoms and behaviour at the time of the interview. Hence there is a degree of overlap between the history and the mental state, mainly in observations about mood, delusions, and hallucinations. If the patient is already in hospital, there will also be some overlap between mental state examination and the observations made by nurses and occupational therapists of his behaviour outside the interview room. The psychiatrist should pay considerable attention to these accounts from other staff, which are at times more revealing than the small sample of behaviour observed at mental state examination. For example, a patient may deny hallucinations at interview, but the nurses may notice him repeatedly talking alone as if replying to voices. On the other hand, mental state examination may reveal information not disclosed at other times, for example suicidal intentions in a depressed patient.

The following paragraphs describe the examination of the mental state. The symptoms and signs that are referred to here have been described in Chapter 1. These descriptions will be repeated only when there is a special reason to do so. Carrying out the mental state examination is a practical skill that can be learnt only by watching experienced interviewers and by practising repeatedly under supervision. As his skills increase, the trainee psychiatrist will benefit from reading the more detailed account by Leff and Isaacs (1978), and from studying the Present State Examination, a standardized scheme described by Wing *et al.* (1974).

The mental state examination follows the headings in Table 2.1.

Appearance and behaviour

Although the mental state examination is largely concerned with what the patient says, much can also be learnt from observing his appearance and behaviour.

Table 2.1. Summary of the mental state examination

Behaviour
Speech
Mood
Depersonalization, derealization
Obsessional phenomena
Delusions
Hallucinations and illusions
Orientation
Attention and concentration
Memory
Insight

The patient's **general appearance** and clothing repay careful observation. Self-neglect, as shown by a dirty unkempt look and crumpled clothing, suggests several possibilities including alcoholism, drug addiction, depression, dementia, or schizophrenia. Manic patients may wear bright colours, adopt incongruous styles of dress, or appear poorly groomed. Occasionally an oddity of dress may provide the clue to diagnosis: for example, a rainhood worn on a dry day may be the first evidence of a patient's belief that rays are being shone on her head by persecutors.

The interviewer should also note the patient's body build. An appearance suggesting recent weight loss should alert the observer to the possibility of physical illness, or of anorexia nervosa, depressive disorder, or chronic anxiety neurosis.

Facial appearance provides information about mood. In depression the most characteristic features are turning down of the corners of the mouth, vertical furrows on the brow, and a slight raising of the medial aspect of each brow. Anxious patients generally have horizontal creases on the forehead, raised eyebrows, widened palpebral fissures, and dilated pupils. Although depression and anxiety are especially important, the observer should look for evidence of the whole range of emotions, including elation, irritability, and anger; together with the unchanging 'wooden' expression of patients taking drugs with parkinsonian side-effects. The facial appearance may also suggest physical conditions such as thyrotoxicosis and myxoedema.

Posture and movement also reflect mood. A depressed patient characteristically sits leaning forwards, with shoulders hunched, the head inclined downwards and gaze directed to the floor. An anxious patient usually sits upright with head erect, often on the edge of the chair and with hands gripping its sides. Anxious people and patients with agitated depression are often tremulous and restless, touching their jewellery, adjusting clothing, or picking at the fingernails. Manic patients are overactive and restless.

Social behaviour is important. Manic patients often break social conventions and are unduly familiar to people they do not know well. Demented patients sometimes respond inappropriately to the conventions of a medical interview, or continue with their private preoccupations as if the interview were not taking place. Schizophrenic patients may behave oddly when interviewed; some are overactive and socially disinhibited, some withdrawn and preoccupied, and others aggressive. Patients with antisocial personality disorders may also appear aggressive. In recording abnormal social behaviour, the psychiatrist should give a clear description of what the patient actually does. He should avoid general terms such as 'bizarre', which are uninformative. Instead he should describe what is unusual.

Finally the interviewer should watch for certain uncommon **disorders of motor behaviour** encountered mainly in schizophrenia (see p. 28). These include stereotypes, posturing, negativism, echopraxia, ambitendence, and waxy flexibility. He should also look for tardive dyskinesia, a motor disorder seen chiefly in elderly patients, especially women, who have taken antipsychotic drugs for long periods (see p. 647). This disorder is characterized by chewing and sucking movements, grimacing, and choreo-athetoid movements affecting the face, limbs, and respiratory muscles.

Speech

How the patient speaks is recorded under this heading, whilst what he says is recorded later. The **rate and quantity** of speech are assessed first. Speech may be unusually fast as in mania, or slow as in depressive disorders. Depressed or demented patients may pause a long time before replying to questions and may then give short answers, producing little spontaneous speech. The same may be observed among shy people or those of low intelligence. The amount of speech is increased in manic patients and in some anxious patients.

Next the interviewer should consider the **patient's utterances**, keeping in mind some unusual disorders found mainly in schizophrenia. He should note whether any of the words are neologisms, that is private words invented by the patient, often to describe morbid experiences. Before assuming that a word is a neologism it is essential to make sure that it is not merely mispronounced or a word from another language.

Disorders of the **flow of speech** are recorded next. Sudden interruptions may indicate thought blocking but are more often merely the effects of distraction. It is a common mistake to diagnose thought blocking when it is not present (see p. 11). Rapid shifts from one topic to another suggest flight of ideas, while a general diffuseness and lack of logical thread may indicate the kind of thought disorder characteristic of schizophrenia (see p. 12). It can be difficult to be certain about these abnormalities at interview, and it is often helpful to record a sample of conversation for more detailed analysis.

Mood

The assessment of mood begins with the observations of behaviour described already, and continues with direct questions such as, 'What is your mood like?' or 'How are you in your spirits?'.

If **depression** is detected, further questions should be asked about: a feeling of being about to cry (actual tearfulness is often denied), pessimistic thoughts about the present, hopelessness about the future, and guilt about the past. Suitable questions are 'What do you think will happen to you in the future?' 'Have you been blaming yourself for anything?'.

Trainees are often wary of asking about suicide in case they should suggest it to the patient, but there is no evidence to warrant this reason for wariness. Nevertheless, it is sensible to enquire about suicide in stages, starting with the question 'Have you thought life is not worth living?' and if appropriate going on to ask: 'Have you wished you could die?' or 'Have you considered any way in which you might end your life?'.

Anxiety is assessed further by asking about physical symptoms and thoughts that accompany the affect. These are discussed in detail in Chapter 12; here we need only note the main questions. The interviewer should start with a general question such as 'Have you noticed any changes in your body when you feel anxious?', and then go on to specific enquiries about palpitations, dry mouth, sweating, trembling, and the various other symptoms of autonomic activity and muscle tension. To detect anxious thoughts, one can ask 'What goes through your mind when you are feeling anxious?'. Possible replies include thoughts of fainting, losing control, and going mad. Inevitably many of these questions overlap with inquiries about the history of the disorder.

Questions about **elation** correspond to those about depression; for example, 'how are you in your spirits?', followed if necessary by direct questions such as 'Do you feel unusually cheerful?'. Elated mood is often accompanied by ideas reflecting excessive self-confidence, inflated assessment of one's abilities, and extravagant plans.

As well as assessing the prevailing mood, the interviewer should find out **how mood varies** and whether it is appropriate. When mood varies excessively, it is said to be labile; for example, the patient appears dejected at one point in the interview but quickly changes to a normal or unduly cheerful mood. Any persisting lack of affect, usually called blunting or flattening, should also be noted.

In a normal person, mood varies in parallel with the main themes discussed; he appears sad while talking of unhappy events, angry while describing things that have annoyed him, and so on. When the mood is not suited to the context, it is recorded as incongruent; for example, if a patient giggles when describing the death of his mother. This symptom is often diagnosed without sufficient reason, so it is important to record specific examples. Further knowledge of the patient may later provide another explanation for the behaviour; for example giggling when speaking of sad events may result from embarrassment.

Depersonalization and derealization

Patients who have experienced depersonalization and derealization usually find them difficult to describe; patients who have not experienced them frequently misunderstand the question and give misleading answers. Therefore, it is particularly important to obtain specific examples of the patient's experiences. It is useful to begin by asking: 'Do you ever feel that things around you are unreal?' and 'Do you ever feel unreal or have the experience that part of your body is unreal?'. Patients with derealization often describe things in the environment as seeming artificial and lifeless; whilst those with depersonalization may describe themselves as feeling detached from their surroundings, unable to feel emotion, or as if acting a part. Some patients use illustrations to describe their experience, for example, 'as if I were a robot'; such descriptions should be distinguished carefully from delusions. If a patient has described these experiences he should be asked to explain them. Most cannot suggest a reason, but a few give a delusional explanation, for example that the feelings are caused by a persecutor (this should be recorded later under the heading of delusions).

Obsessional phenomena

Obsessional thoughts are considered first. An appropriate question is 'Do any thoughts keep coming into your mind, even though you try hard not to have them?'. If the patient says 'yes' he should be asked for an example. Patients are often ashamed of obsessional thoughts, especially those about violence or sexual themes, and persistent but sympathetic questioning may therefore be required. Before recording thoughts as obsessional, the interviewer should be certain that the patient accepts them as his own (and not implanted by someone or something else).

Some **compulsive rituals** can be observed, but others are private events (such as counting silently) which are detected only because they interrupt the patient's conversation. Appropriate questions are 'Do you have to keep checking activities that you know you have really completed?', 'Do you have to do things over and over again when most people would have done them only once?', and 'Do you have to repeat actions many times in exactly the same way?' If the patient answers 'yes' to any of these questions, the interviewer should ask for specific examples.

Delusions

A delusion is the one symptom that cannot be asked about directly, because the patient does not recognize it as differing from other beliefs. The interviewer may be alerted to delusions by information from other people or by events in the history. In searching for delusional ideas it is useful to begin by asking for an explanation of other symptoms or unpleasant experiences that the patient has described. For example, if a patient says that life is no longer worth living, he may also believe that he is thoroughly evil and that his career is ruined, though there is no objective evidence. Many patients hide delusions skilfully, and the interviewer needs to be alert to evasions, changes of topic or other hints of information being withheld. However, once the topic of the delusion has been uncovered, patients often elaborate on it without much prompting.

When ideas are revealed that may or may not be delusional, the interviewer must find out how strongly they are held. To do this without antagonizing the patient requires patience and tact. The patient should feel he is having a fair hearing. If the interviewer expresses contrary opinions to test the strength of the patient's beliefs, his manner should be enquiring rather than argumentative. On the other hand the interviewer should not agree with the patient's delusions.

The next step is to decide whether the beliefs are culturally determined convictions rather than delusions. This judgement may be difficult if the patient comes from another culture or is a member of an unusual religious group. In such cases any doubt can usually be resolved by finding a healthy informant from the same country or religion, and by asking him whether the patient's ideas would be shared by other people from that background.

Some **special forms of delusion** present particular problems of recognition. Delusions of thought broadcasting must be distinguished from the belief that other people can infer a person's thoughts from his expression or behaviour. In eliciting such delusions an appropriate question is 'Do you believe that other people know what you are thinking, even though you have not spoken your thoughts aloud?'. A corresponding question about delusions of thought insertion is: 'Have you ever felt that some of the thoughts in your mind were not your own but were put there from outside?'. A suitable question about delusions of thought withdrawal is 'Do you ever feel that ideas are being taken out of your head?'. In each case, if the patient answers 'Yes', detailed examples should be sought.

Delusions of control present similar difficulties to the interviewer. It is appropriate to ask 'Do you ever feel that some outside force is trying to take control of you?' or 'Do you ever feel that your actions are controlled by some person or thing outside you?'. Since these experiences are far removed from the normal, some patients misunderstand the question and answer 'yes' when they mean a religious or philosophical conviction that man is controlled by God or the devil. Others think the questions refer to the experience of being 'out of control' during extreme anxiety; some schizophrenic patients say 'yes' when they have heard commanding voices. Positive answers must therefore be followed by further questions to eliminate these possibilities.

Finally, the reader is reminded of the various **categories of delusion** described in Chapter 1, namely: persecutory, grandiose, nihilistic, hypochondriacal, religious, and amorous delusions together with delusions of reference, guilt, unworthiness, and jealousy. The interviewer should also distinguish between primary and secondary delusions, and should look out for the experiences of delusional perception and delusional mood that may precede or accompany the onset of delusions.

Illusions and hallucinations

When asked about hallucinations, some patients take offence because they think the interviewer regards them as mad. Enquiries should therefore be made tactfully, and common-sense judgement used to decide when it is safe to omit them altogether. Questions can be introduced by saying: 'Some people find that, when their nerves are upset, they have unusual experiences'. This can be followed by enquiries about hearing sounds or voices when no one else is within earshot. Whenever the history makes it relevant, corresponding questions should be asked about visual hallucinations, or those of taste, smell, touch, and deep bodily sensations.

If the patient describes hallucinations, certain further questions are required depending on the type of experience. The interviewer should find out whether the patient has heard a single voice, or several; if the latter, whether the voices appear to talk to each other about the patient in the third person. This experience must be distinguished from that of the patient who hears actual people talking in the distance and believes they are discussing him (delusion of reference). If the patient says the voices are speaking to him (second person hallucinations) the interviewer should find out what they say and, if the words are experienced as commands, whether the patient feels they must be obeyed. It is important to record examples of the words spoken by hallucinatory voices.

Visual hallucinations should be distinguished carefully from visual illusions. Unless the hallucination is experienced at the time of the interview, this distinction may be difficult because it depends on the presence or absence of a visual stimulus which has been misinterpreted.

The interviewer must also distinguish dissociative experiences from hallucinations. The former are described by the patient as the feeling of being in the presence of another person or a spirit with whom he can converse. Such experiences are reported by people with hysterical personality, though not confined to them; they are encouraged by some religious groups, and have little importance in diagnosis.

Orientation

This is assessed by asking about the patient's awareness of time, place, and person. If the question of orientation is kept in mind throughout the interview, it may not be necessary to ask specific questions at this stage in the examination because the interviewer will already know the answers.

Specific questions begin with the day, month, year, and season. In assessing the replies, it is important to remember that many healthy people do not know the exact date, and that understandably patients in hospital may be uncertain about the day of the week, particularly if the ward has the same routine every day. When enquiring about orientation in place, the interviewer asks what sort of place the patient is in (such as a hospital ward or an old people's home). Questions are then asked about other people such as the spouse or the ward staff; for example, who they are and what their relationship to the patient is. If the patient cannot answer these questions correctly, he should be asked about his own identity.

Attention and concentration

Attention is the ability to focus on the matter in hand. Concentration is the ability to sustain that focus. Whilst taking the history, the interviewer should look out for evidence of attention and concentration. In this way he will have already formed a judgement about these abilities before reaching the mental state examination. Formal tests add to this information and provide a semi-quantitative indication of changes as illness progresses. It is usual to begin with the **serial sevens test**. The patient is asked to subtract 7 from 100 and then take 7 from the remainder repeatedly until this is less than seven. The time taken is recorded, together with the number of errors. If poor performance seems to be due to lack of skill in arithmetic, the patient should be asked to do a simpler subtraction, or to say the months of the year in reverse order. If mistakes are made with these, he can be asked to give the days of the week in reverse order.

Memory

Whilst taking the history, questions will have been asked about everyday difficulties in remembering. During the examination of mental state, tests are given of immediate, recent, and remote memory. None is wholly satisfactory and the results should be assessed alongside other information about the patient's ability to remember and, if there is doubt, supplemented by standardized psychological tests.

Short-term memory is assessed by asking the patient to repeat sequences of digits that have been spoken slowly enough for him reasonably to be expected to register them. An easy short sequence is given first to make sure that the patient understands the task. Then five different digits are presented. If the patient can repeat five correctly, six are given, and then seven; if he cannot repeat five digits, the test is repeated with a different sequence of five. A normal response from a person of average intelligence is to repeat seven digits correctly. The test also involves concentration, so it cannot be used to assess memory if tests of concentration are definitely abnormal.

Next the interviewer assesses the patient's ability to learn new information and reproduce it straight away (to make sure it has been registered correctly) and then to remember. The interview continues on other topics for five minutes before recall is tested. A healthy person of average intelligence should make only minor errors. Some interviewers also give one of the sentences introduced by Babcock (1930) to test memory, for example 'one thing a nation must have to become rich and great is a large secure supply of wood'. Three repetitions of such a sentence are usually enough for correct immediate reproduction by a healthy young person. However, the test does not satisfactorily discriminate patients with organic brain disorder from healthy young people or from patients with depressive disorder (Kopelman 1986), and its use is not recommended.

Memory for **recent events** is assessed by asking about news items from the last day or two, or about events in the patient's life that are known to the interviewer (such as the ward menus on the previous day). Questions about news items should be adapted to the patient's interests, and should have been widely reported in the media.

Remote memory can be assessed by asking the patient to recall personal events or well-known public items from some years before, such as the birth dates of the patient's children or grandchildren (provided of course that the latter are known to the interviewer), or the names of earlier political leaders. Awareness of the **sequence of events** is as important as the recall of individual items.

When a patient is in hospital, important information about memory is available from observations made by nurses and occupational therapists. These observations include how fast the patient learns the daily routine and the names of staff and other patients; and whether he forgets where he has put things, or where to find his bed, the sitting room, and so on.

For elderly patients, the standard questions about memory in the clinical interview discriminate poorly between those who have cerebral pathology and those who do not. For these patients there are **standardized ratings of memory** for recent personal events, past personal events, and general events (Post 1965), which allow a better assessment of severity.

Standardized psychological tests of learning and memory can help in diagnosis and provide a quantitative assessment of the progression of memory disorder. One useful example is the Wechsler logical memory test (Wechsler 1945) in which the patient has to recall the contents of a short paragraph immediately and after 45 minutes. The score is based on the number of items recalled. Kopelman (1986) found this test to be a good discriminator between patients with organic brain disease on the one hand, and healthy controls and patients with depressive disorders on the other.

Insight

When insight is assessed, it is important to keep in mind the complexity of the concept (see Chapter 1). By the end of the mental state examination, the interviewer should have a provisional estimate of how far the patient is aware of the morbid nature of his experiences. Direct questions should then be asked to assess this awareness further. These questions are concerned with the patient's opinions about the nature of his individual symptoms; for example, whether he believes that his extreme feelings of guilt are justified or not. The interviewer should also find out whether the patient believes himself to be ill (rather than, say, persecuted by his enemies); if so, whether he thinks that the illness is physical or mental; and whether he sees himself as needing treatment. The answers to these questions are important because they determine, in part, how far the patient is likely to collaborate with treatment. A note that merely records 'insight present' or 'no insight' is of little value.

Some difficulties in mental state examination

Apart from the obvious problem of examining patients who speak little or no English—a problem which requires the help of an interpreter—several difficulties arise commonly.

The unresponsive patient

The doctor will encounter occasional patients who are mute, or stuporose (conscious but not speaking or responding in any way). He can then only make observations of behaviour; but this can be useful if done properly.

It is important to remember that some stuporose patients change rapidly from inactivity to over-activity and violence. It is therefore wise to have help at hand when seeing such a patient. Before deciding that the patient is mute, the interviewer should allow adequate time for reply and should try a variety of topics. He should also find out whether the patient will communicate in writing. Apart from the observations of behaviour described earlier in this chapter, the examiner should note whether the patient's eyes are open or closed; if open, whether they follow objects, move apparently without purpose, or are fixed; if closed, whether the patient opens them on request, and, if not, whether he resists attempts at opening them.

A physical examination including neurological assessment is essential in all such cases. Also certain signs found in catatonic schizophrenia should be sought, namely waxy flexibility of muscles and negativism (see Chapter 9).

In such cases it is essential to interview an informant who can give a history of the onset and course of the condition.

Over-active patients

Some patients are so active and restless that systematic interviewing is difficult. The interviewer may have to limit his questions to a few that seem particularly important, and to base his conclusions mainly on observations of the patient's behaviour and spontaneous utterances. However, if the patient is being seen for the first time during an emergency consultation, some of his over-activity may be a reaction to other people's attempts to restrain him. In such a case a quiet but confident approach by the interviewer often calms the patient enough to allow more adequate examination.

The patient who appears confused

When the patient gives a history in a muddled way, or if he appears perplexed or frightened, the interviewer should test cognitive functions early in the interview. If there is evidence of impaired consciousness, the interviewer should try to orientate the patient and to reassure him, before starting the interview again in a simplified form. In such cases every effort should be made to interview another informant.

Special investigations

Special investigations vary according to the nature of the patient's symptoms and the differential diagnosis. No single set of routine investigations is essential for every case, but for patients in hospital it is reasonable to do routine tests of the urine and to arrange estimations of haemoglobin, erythrocyte sedimentation rate, white blood cells, electrolytes, and urea. In the past the Wasserman reaction for syphilis was carried out routinely, but this practice has declined. The recent increase in cases of primary and secondary neurosyphilis is a reason for performing appropriate tests whenever there is the slightest reason to suspect tertiary infection. Other investigations are reviewed in the chapters on individual syndromes, particularly the section on organic psychiatry.

Physical examination

When patients attend as day-patients or become in-patients, the psychiatrist becomes responsible for their physical as well as their mental health, and he should conduct a thorough physical examination. When out-patients are seen, they are usually referred by a general practitioner or another specialist, who has often carried out the appropriate physical examination. Moreover, the care of such patients is usually shared between the psychiatrist and the other doctor. However, the psychiatrist should always determine what physical examination is relevant; he should then carry it out himself, or ensure that it has been done adequately by the referring doctor, or in certain cases arrange for another doctor to complete it. The latter course may be appropriate, for example, when the referral is made by a consultant physician who knows the patient well.

How extensive the physical examination should be must be judged in every case on the basis of diagnostic possibilities. However, the psychiatrist is most likely to be concerned with examination of the central nervous system (including its vascular supply) and the endocrine system. This does not, of course, imply that physical examination should be limited to these systems and, as indicated above, any patient admitted to hospital should certainly have a full routine examination.

Additional neurological examination when an organic syndrome is suspected

When an organic syndrome is suspected a routine neurological examination should be performed. In this section it is assumed that the reader has some knowledge of clinical neurology; those without such knowledge are referred to a standard textbook of neurology, such as *Brain's Diseases of the nervous system* (Walton 1985). Further information about tests of parietal lobe function will be found in the monograph of Critchley (1953). These tests do not help in the localization of disorders of the frontal or temporal lobes, which are diagnosed mainly from the history (see Chapter 11). The neurology of psychiatric disorders has been reviewed by Pincus and Tucker (1985).

Language abilities

Partial failure of language function is called **dysphasia**. Language may be affected in its expression or reception, or both, and in either its spoken or written form. Gross disorders of language function will have been noted when taking the history and mental state. Special tests will reveal less severe degrees of dysfunction. Before conducting them, tests for **dys-arthria** should be done by giving difficult phrases such as 'West Register Street' or a tongue twister.

Receptive aspects of language ability are tested in several ways. The patient can be asked to read a passage of appropriate difficulty, or failing this, individual words or letters. If he can read the passage, he is asked to explain it. Comprehension of spoken language is tested by asking a patient to listen to speech. Thus, he can be asked to explain what has been heard or to respond to simple commands, for example, by pointing to named objects.

Expressive aspects of language are tested by asking the patient to speak and write. He can be asked to talk about his work or hobbies, and then to name objects (for example, pen, key, watch, and component parts of these objects) and parts of the body. Next he can be asked to write a brief passage to dictation, and then to make up and write a passage (for example about the members of his family). If he cannot do these tests he should be asked to copy a short passage.

Language disorders point to the left hemisphere in right-handed people. In left-handed patients localization is less certain but in many it is still the left hemisphere. The type of language disorder gives some further guide to localization: expressive dysphasia suggests an anterior lesion, and receptive dysphasia a posterior lesion; mainly auditory aphasias suggest a lesion towards the temporal region, whilst mainly visual aphasias suggest a more posterior lesion.

Construction abilities

Apraxia is inability to perform a volitional act even though the motor system and sensorium are sufficiently intact for the person to do so. Apraxia can be tested in several ways. **Constructional** apraxia is tested by asking the patient to make simple figures with matchsticks (a square, triangle, cross) or to draw them. He can also be asked to draw a bicycle, house or clock face. **Dressing** apraxia is tested by asking the person to put on his clothes. **Ideomotor** apraxia is tested by asking him to perform increasingly complicated tasks to command, ending for example with touching the right ear with the left middle finger, while placing the right thumb on the left elbow.

Constructional apraxia, especially if the patient fails to complete the left side of figures, suggests a right-sided lesion in the posterior parietal region. It may be associated with other disorders related to this region, namely sensory inattention and anosognosia.

Agnosias

Agnosia is the inability to understand the significance of sensory stimuli even though the sensory pathways and sensorium are sufficiently intact for the patient to be able to do so. Agnosia cannot be diagnosed until there is good evidence that the sensory pathways are intact and that consciousness is not impaired. Several kinds of agnosia are tested. **Astereognosia** is failure to identify three-dimensional form; it is tested by asking the patient to identify objects placed in his hand while his eyes are closed. Suitable items are keys, coins of different sizes, and paper clips. **Atopognosia** is failure to know the position of an object on the skin. In **finger agnosia** the patient cannot identify which of his fingers has been touched when he has his eyes shut. Right–left confusion is tested by touching one hand or ear and asking the patient which side of the body has been touched. **Agraphognosia** is failure to identify letters or numbers 'written' on the skin. It is tested by tracing numbers on the palms with a closed fountain pen or similar object. **Anosognosia** is failure to identify functional deficits caused by disease. It is seen most often as unawareness of left-sided weakness and sensory inattention after a right parietal lesion.

Agnosias point to lesions of the association areas around the primary sensory receptive areas. Lesions of *either* parietal lobe can cause contralateral astereognosia, agraphognosia, and atopognosia. Sensory inattention and anosognosia are more common with right parietal lesions. Finger agnosia and right–left disorientation are said to be more common with lesions of the dominant parietal region.

Psychological assessment

In the past, clinical psychologists were largely concerned with the assessment of patients by standardized tests. Nowadays they are more concerned with treatment, and with assessment in the form of quantified observation of the patient's behaviour.

Many standardized tests are available. For the clinician the most useful are tests of intelligence and of higher neurological functions. Other tests are still in use but have less general value; for example, those of personality, 'brain damage', and thought disorder. In this section a knowledge of the principles of psychological testing is assumed; no detailed account will be attempted here. When psychological testing is an important part of assessment it will be mentioned in the chapters on clinical syndromes. At this stage a few general comments are appropriate.

In general adult psychiatry it is not necessary to have an accurate assessment of every patient's intelligence. If a patient seems to be of borderline subnormal intelligence, or if his psychological symptoms appear to be a reaction to work beyond his intellectual capacity, **intelligence tests** are essential. Such tests together with standard **tests of reading** ability are also essential in child and adolescent psychiatry (see Chapter 20) and in the assessment of mentally retarded patients (see Chapter 21).

In the past, much use was made of **'tests of brain damage'** in the diagnosis of possible organic syndromes. The recent advent of computerized axial tomography has reduced the need for such indirect ways of assessing diffuse cerebral pathology, although **specific neuropsychological tests** are still of some value as pointers to specific lesions of the frontal or parietal cortex. Such tests are also valuable in measuring the progression of deficits caused by disease. Further discussion of these issues will be found in Chapter 11.

Personality tests have some value in clinical research, but contribute little to everyday clinicial practice because usually more can be learnt from the clinical assessment described earlier in this chapter. Projective tests such as the Rorschach test are not recommended because their validity has not been established.

Tests of thought disorder were developed to improve the accuracy of diagnosis of schizophrenia, but they proved unsuccessful. However, they are occasionally helpful in charting the progression of thought disorder.

Standardized **rating scales of behaviour** are among the most useful applications of psychometric principles in everyday clinical practice. When no ready-made rating scale is available, a clinical psychologist can often devise *ad hoc* ratings that are sufficiently reliable to chart the effects of treatment in the individual patient. For example, in measuring the progress of a depressed in-patient, a scale could be devised for the nurses to rate to show how much of the time he was active and occupied. This could be a five-point scale, in which the criteria for each rating referred to behaviours (such as playing cards or talking to other people) appropriate to the individual patient.

Psychological principles are also used to make a **behavioural assessment**. This is a detailed account of the component elements of a patient's disorder (for example, in a phobic state the elements of anticipatory anxiety, avoidance behaviour, and coping strategies); and their relationship to stimuli in the environment (for example, heights) or more general circumstances (for example, crowded places), or internal cues (for example, awareness of heart action). A detailed description of this kind can aid diagnosis and provide a basis for behavioural treatment.

Special kinds of interview

Interviewing relatives

In psychiatry, interviews with one or more close relatives of the patient are highly important. Generally such interviews are used to obtain additional information about the patient's condition; sometimes they are used to involve the relative in the treatment plan, and sometimes to enlist his help in persuading the patient to comply with treatment.

A history from a relative or close friend is essential when the patient is suffering from a mental illness or personality disorder severe enough to impair his ability to give an unbiased and accurate account. In less severe disorders, a relative can still help by giving another view of the patient's illness and personality. For example, a relative is sometimes more able than the patient to date the onset of illness accurately, especially if it was gradual. A relative can also give a useful indication of how disabling the illness is and how it affects other people. Finally, when it is important to know about the patient's childhood, an interview with a parent or older sibling is important.

With few exceptions, the patient's permission should be obtained before interviewing a relative. Exceptions occur when the patient is a child (the referral usually being initiated by the parents), and when adult patients present as emergencies and cannot give a history because mute, stuporose, confused, violent, or extremely retarded. In other cases, the doctor should explain to the patient that he wishes to interview a relative to obtain additional information needed for diagnosis and treatment. He should emphasize that confidential information given by the patient will not be passed to the relative. If any information needs to be given to a relative, for example about treatment, the patient's permission should be obtained. It is important to remember that relatives may misunderstand the purpose of the interview. Some assume that demands will be made on them; for example the married daughter of an elderly demented woman may think that she will be asked to take her mother into her own small home. Other relatives expect to be blamed for the patient's illness; for example, the parents of a young schizophrenic may expect the doctor to imply that they have failed as parents. It is important for the interviewer to be sensitive to such ideas, and, when appropriate, to discuss them in a reassuring way. He should always begin the interview by explaining its purpose.

Adequate time should be allowed for the interview; relatives are likely to be anxious, and time is needed to put them at ease, gather facts, and impart any necessary information.

The interview will enable the doctor to discover whether the relatives are having any problems as a result of the patient's illness. If they need help, the doctor can contact their general practitioner. However, he should not become involved in the relative's problem to an extent that conflicts with his primary duty to his patient.

After the interview the psychiatrist should not let the patient know what the relative has said unless the latter has given permission. It is important to seek permission if the relative has revealed something that should be discussed with the patient; for example, an account of excessive drinking previously denied by the patient. However, if the relative is unwilling that information should be passed on, this must be respected by the doctor; for example a wife may fear violent retaliation from her husband. When the relative is unwilling in this way, the psychiatrist should try to find ways of enabling the patient to reveal the behaviour himself in a further interview.

Problems sometimes arise when someone other than the nearest relative telephones the psychiatrist about the patient. Information should not be given over the telephone, even if the doctor is certain of the caller's identity. Instead the patient should be consulted and, if he agrees, an interview arranged. The psychiatrist must never allow a conspiratorial atmosphere to develop in which he conceals conversations with family members or takes sides in their disputes.

Family interviews at home

It is sometimes appropriate to add to information about the patient's social circumstances by visiting the home, or arranging for a psychiatric nurse or a social worker to do so. Such a visit often throws new light on the patient's home life. It can sometimes lead to a more realistic evaluation of the relationship between family members than can be obtained from interviews in hospital. Before arranging a visit the psychiatrist should if possible talk to the general practitioner, who often has first-hand knowledge of the family and their circumstances from home visits over the years. If another member of the staff is going to make the visit, the psychiatrist should discuss the purpose of the visit with him.

Emergency consultations

When time is limited and an immediate decision is required about diagnosis and management, it may be possible to obtain an outline history. However short the time, it is essential to obtain a clear account of the presenting symptoms, including their onset, course, and severity. A knowledge of the major clinical syndromes will then guide the interviewer to enquiries about other relevant symptoms, including those which arise in organic brain syndromes. Recent stressful events should always be asked about, together with any previous physical or mental illness. An account of previous personality is important, though it may be difficult to obtain unless there are relatives or close friends present. Habits regarding alcohol and drugs are especially important.

The family and personal history will often have to be covered quickly by asking a few salient questions. Throughout the interview the psychiatrist should be thinking which questions need to be asked immediately and which deferred until later.

A brief but relevant physical examination should be carried out unless already performed by another doctor.

If the above points are borne in mind when conducting an emergency consultation, common sense coupled with a sound knowledge of the major clinical syndromes should prove a satisfactory guide.

Interviewing in primary care

Much of a general practitioner's work is concerned with the identification of minor psychiatric disorders among patients presenting with a combination of physical and mild psychological symptoms. A useful brief method of identifying psychiatric disorders has been described by Goldberg and Huxley (1980). It focuses on the emotional symptoms encountered most commonly in general practice, and takes account of faults in interviewing that were found by watching general practitioners at work.

In these brief interviews the first few minutes are extremely important. However short the time, it is essential to give the patient an adequate opportunity to express his problem. Family doctors sometimes omit this because they assume the patient has come back for further advice about a previous problem. Sometimes they start questioning too early, with the result that opening questions may be answered as if they were social pleasantries (for example 'How are you feeling now?'—'Fine thanks'). On the other hand the doctor should not sit in silence reading his previous notes, as the patient may then begin to feel ill at ease and become unable to reveal his real concerns. The interview can begin with an open question such as 'What have you noticed wrong?', and then proceed mainly by prompts and clarifying questions. As in a longer interview, the doctor should be as alert to non-verbal behaviour as he is to the spoken word.

The next task is to understand clearly the nature of the symptoms. In general practice, the presenting complaint is often physical even when the disorder is psychiatric. The patient should always be allowed adequate time to describe the complaint in his own words before questions are asked. Thus a complaint of headache should not be followed immediately by questions about the side of the head on which it is felt. Instead the patient should be encouraged to describe the symptom in more detail. It may then become apparent that he has a tight feeling over the brows rather than a painful headache. Although this may seem obvious, it was found to be a common cause of error in Goldberg and Huxley's study of interviews in general practice.

For any complaint that may have psychological causes Goldberg and Huxley put forward a simple scheme of assessment with four components: the patient's general psychological adjustment, the presence of anxiety and worries, symptoms of depression, and the psychological context. General psychological adjustment is assessed by asking about fatigue, irritability, poor concentration, and the feeling of being under stress. To enquire into anxiety and worries the interviewer asks about physical symptoms as well as tension, phobias, and persistent worrying thoughts. Symptoms of depression are covered next, including persistent depressive mood, tearfulness, crying, hopelessness, self-blame, thoughts that life is unbearable, ideas about suicide, early morning waking, diurnal variation of mood, weight loss, and loss of libido. Of these Goldberg and Huxley found that general practitioners were most likely to overlook questions concerned with depressive thoughts.

Often the family doctor already knows his patient's psychosocial circumstances, and can therefore omit some of the questions required in an interview with a new patient. However, he should think systematically about the patient's work, leisure, marriage, and other relationships, and should ask any questions needed to bring his knowledge up to date.

An interview of this kind can be conducted within the short time available for first consultations in general practice. Usually a conclusion can be reached by the end of the interview. If not, a preliminary plan can be made, and a later interview arranged for completion of a full psychiatric history and mental state examination.

Case notes

The importance of case notes

Good case records are important in every branch of medicine. In psychiatry they are even more vital because there is a large amount of information collected from a variety of sources. Unless material is recorded clearly, with facts separated from opinions, it is difficult to think clearly about clinical problems and to make appropriate decisions about treatment. Equally it is important to summarize the information in a way that allows essential points to be grasped readily by someone new to the case. Case notes are not just an *aide mémoire* for a doctor's own use, but an essential source of information for others who may see the patient in the future. So they must be legible, and well thought out.

It is important to remember the medico-legal importance of good case records. On the rare occasions when a psychiatrist is called upon to justify his actions in the coroner's court, at a trial, or after a complaint lodged by a patient, he will be greatly assisted by good case notes. The psychiatrist should remember that in certain circumstances case notes can be called upon by lawyers acting for patients.

The admission note

When a patient is admitted to hospital urgently, the doctor may have limited time for the interview. It is then particularly important to select the right topics to elicit and record. The admission note should contain at least (i) a clear account of the reasons for admission; (ii) any information required for a decision about immediate treatment; and (iii) any relevant information that will not be available later, including details of the mental state on admission and information from any informant whose presence at a later date cannot be relied upon. The account of the mental state should include well-chosen verbatim extracts to illustrate phenomena such as delusions or flight of ideas. If there is time, a systematic history should be added. However, it is a common mistake among trainees to spend too much time on details that are not essential to immediate decisions and can be taken next day, while failing to record details of mental state that may be transitory and yet of great importance to final diagnosis.

The admission note should end with a brief statement of a provisional plan of management. This plan should be agreed with the senior nurses caring for the patient at the time.

Progress notes

Progress notes should not be written in such general terms as to be of little value when the case is reviewed later. Instead of recording merely that the patient feels better or is behaving more normally, the note should state in what ways he feels better (for example, less despondent or less preoccupied with thoughts of suicide) or is less disturbed in behaviour (for example, no longer so restless as to be unable to sit at table throughout a meal).

Progress notes should also refer to treatment. Details of drug treatment often go unrecorded in the progress notes, presumably because they appear on the prescription sheet. However, when a patient's progress is reviewed, it is much more convenient to have the timing and dosage of medication recorded alongside the mental state and behaviour. Psychological and social treatment should also be noted. A verbatim account of a psychotherapy session is difficult to write and seldom of value in management. Instead, notes should be made of the main themes of therapeutic interviews, together with any relevant observations of the patient's response. At intervals, an additional note can be made summarizing progress made in the course of several sessions.

A careful note should also be made of any information or advice given by the doctor to the patient or his relatives. This should enable anyone giving advice later to know whether or not it differs from what was said before, so that an appropriate explanation can be given.

Observations of progress are made not only by doctors, but also by nurses, occupational therapists, clinical psychologists, and social workers. As a rule, these other members of staff keep separate notes for their own use, but it is desirable that important items of information are also written in the medical record.

A careful note should be kept of decisions reached at ward rounds and case conferences, and on any other occasions when the management of the patient is discussed with the consultant or his deputy. It is particularly important to set out clearly the plans made for the patient's further care on discharge from hospital.

The case summary

This section can best be understood by referring to the specimen case summary on pp. 68–9.

The case summary is usually written in two parts. The first is completed within a week of the patient's admission. It has two main purposes. First, after extensive history taking has been completed, it is a useful exercise to select the salient features of the case. Second, the Part I summary is valuable to any doctor called to see the patient when the usual psychiatrist is not available. The items included in the first summary are all those from 'Reason for referral' to 'On examination' in the specimen summary.

The Part II summary is usually prepared within a day or two of the patient's discharge; it complements the Part I summary by adding special investigations and all subsequent items in the specimen summary. The whole summary is important if the patient becomes ill again, especially if he is under the care of another psychiatrist.

Summaries should be brief but comprehensive. They should be written in telegraphic style and laid out in a standard form that makes it easy for other people to find particular items. It is sometimes appropriate to omit particularly confidential details, noting instead that relevant information will be found in the case history. The Part I summary seldom occupies more than one and a half sides of a typed page, while the Part II summary is about half a page in length. A longer summary often means that the case has not been understood clearly.

Some of the items in the summary call for comment. The reason for referral should be a brief statement avoiding technical terms; for example it might read: 'having been found wandering at night in an agitated state, shouting about God and the devil'; rather than 'for treatment of schizophrenia'. The description of personality is often the most difficult section to complete briefly but informatively. However, with practice it is usually possible to list well-chosen words and phrases which bring the person to life. This part of the summary is important and repays considerable thought.

If no abnormality is found on physical examination there is no need to make a separate entry for each system; it is usually sufficient to enter a single statement that routine physical examination showed no abnormality. However, when the mental state is recorded, a comment should be made under each heading whether or not any abnormality has been found.

When possible, the entry under diagnosis should use the categories of the current edition of the *International classification of disease* (or equivalent system in countries not using this). (See p. 87.) It may, however, be necessary to add some additional comment to convey the complexities of an unusual case. If the diagnosis is uncertain, alternatives should be given, with an indication of the likelihood of each.

The summary of treatment should indicate the main treatments used, including the dosage and duration of any medication. The prognosis should be stated briefly but as definitely as possible. Statements such as 'prognosis guarded' are of little help to anyone. Unless the doctor commits himself more firmly he will be unable to learn from comparing his predictions with the actual outcome. At the same time, it is appropriate to note how certain the writer is about the prognosis and why any uncertainties have arisen; for example: 'The depressive symptoms are not likely to recur in the next year provided the patient continues taking drugs. The subsequent course is uncertain because it depends on the course of her son's leukaemia'.

The plan for further treatment should specify not only what is to be done but also who is to do it. The roles of the hospital staff and of the family doctor should be made clear.

Following is an example of a widely used method of recording the case summary.

Example of a case summary

Consultant: Dr A	Admitted 27.6.81.
Registrar: Dr B	Discharged 4.8.81.

Mrs C. D. Date of birth 7.2.50

Reason for referral Increasingly low in mood and inactive despite out-patient treatment.

Family history *Father* 66, retired gardener, good physical health, mood swings; poor relationship with patient. *Mother* 57, housewife, healthy, convinced spiritualist; distant relationship. *Sibling* Joan, 35, divorced, healthy. *Home* materially adequate, little affection. *Mental illness* father's brother in hospital 4 times: 'Manic depression'.

Personal history *Birth and early development* normal. *Childhood health* good. *School* 6–16 uneventful; made friends. *Occupations* 16–22 shop assistant. *Marital* several boyfriends; married at 22, husband 2 years older, lorry driver. Unhappy in last year following husband's infidelity. *Children* Jane, 7, well; Paul, 4, epileptic. *Sexual* satisfactory until last year. *Menses* no abnormality. *Circumstances* council house; financial problems.

Previous illness Aged 20, appendicectomy. Aged 24 (postnatal) depressive illness lasting 3 weeks.

Previous personality Few friends; interests within the family; variable mood: worries easily, lacks self-confidence, jealous; no obsessional traits; no conventional religious beliefs but shares mother's interest in the supernatural. Drinks occasionally; non-smoker. Denies drugs.

History of present illness For six weeks, since learning of husband's infidelity, increasingly low-spirited and tearful, waking early, inactive, neglecting children.

Eating little. Low libido. Believes herself to be in contact with dead grandmother through telepathy. Progressive worsening despite amitriptyline 125 mg per day for three weeks.

On examination *Physical* n.a.d. *Mental* dishevelled and distraught. *Talk* slow, halting, normal form. Preoccupied with her unhappy state and its effect on her children. *Mood* depressed, with self-blame, hopelessness but no ideas of suicide. *Delusions* none. *Hallucinations* none. *Compulsive phenomena* none. *Orientation* normal. *Attention and concentration* poor. *Memory* not impaired. *Insight* thinks she is ill but believes she cannot recover.

Special investigations Haemoglobin and electroytes n.a.d.

Treatment and progress Amitriptyline increased to 175 mg/day; graded activities; joint interviews with husband to improve marital relationship. Advice from social worker to husband about management of financial problems. Progressive improvement in hospital with three weekends at home before final discharge. Amitriptyline reduced to 100 mg per day at time of discharge.

Condition on discharge Not depressed but still uncertain about future of marriage.

Diagnosis Depressive disorder.

Prognosis Depends on further progress with marital problems. If these improve, the short-term prognosis is good. However, vulnerable to further depressive illness in the long term.

Further management 1. Continue amitriptyline 100 mg for 6 months (prescriptions from hospital). 2. Out-patient attendance to continue marital interviews (first appointment 14.8.81). 3. Review progress and return to GP's care in 3 months.

Formulation

A formulation is a concise assessment of the case. Unlike a summary, it is a discussion of alternative ideas about diagnosis, aetiology, treatment, and prognosis, and of the arguments for and against each alternative. A good formulation is based on the facts of the case and not on speculation, but it may contain verifiable hypotheses about matters that are uncertain at the time of writing. A formulation is concerned not only with disease concepts, but also with the understanding of how the patient's lifelong experiences have influenced his personality and his ways of reacting to adversity.

There is more than one way of setting out a formulation, and the following is an approach recommended by the authors. The formulation begins with a concise statement of the essential features of the case. This should seldom be more than two or three sentences; for example: 'Mrs Jones is a 60-year-old divorced woman with depressed mood and sleep disturbance which started after an operation for cancer of the bowel and which have not responded to out-patient treatment'.

The differential diagnosis is considered next. This should be a list of reasonable possibilities in the order of their probability. The writer should avoid listing every conceivable diagnosis however remote. A note is made of the evidence for and against each diagnosis, with an assessment of the balance. At the end, the writer's conclusion about the most probable diagnosis should be stated clearly.

Aetiology comes next. The first step is to identify predisposing, precipitating, and maintaining causes. The reasons for any predisposition are then considered, usually in chronological order to show how each factor may have added to those that went before. For example, a family history of manic-depressive psychosis suggests a genetic predisposition to similar illness; in a particular case this may have been added to by the death of the patient's mother when he was a child, and increased further by adverse influences in a children's home.

After aetiology the conclusions about diagnosis and aetiology should be summarized with a list of outstanding problems and any further investigations needed. Next a concise plan of treatment is outlined. This should mention social measures as well as psychological treatment and medication, together with the role of nurses and occupational therapists.

Finally a statement is made about prognosis. This is often the most difficult part of the formulation. As with the summary, it is wrong to avoid commitment by writing down a vague statement. It is better to make a firm prediction; for example, 'These depressive symptoms should recover quickly in hospital but are likely to recur if her husband begins to drink heavily again'. If his prediction is proved wrong the doctor can learn by comparing it with the actual outcome, but nothing can be learnt from a non-committal statement.

Example of a formulation

(*Note*: this formulation refers to the same hypothetical case that was presented above in an example of a summary. By comparing the two, the reader can appreciate the difference between the material selected for each.)

Mrs C.D. is a 31-year-old married woman who for six weeks has been feeling increasingly low-spirited and unable to cope at home, despite out-patient treatment with antidepressant drugs.

Diagnosis

Depressive disorder As well as feeling low-spirited, Mrs C.D. has woken unusually early, felt worse in the morning and lost her appetite. She has little energy or initiative. She blames herself for being a bad mother and believes that she cannot recover. The only feature apparently against this diagnosis—her belief that she is in contact with her dead grandmother—is discussed below.

Schizophrenia Mrs C.D.'s belief that she is in contact with her dead grandmother was present before she became ill. It relates clearly to her own and her mother's interest in spiritualism. It is an overvalued idea not a delusion. She has no first-rank symptom of schizophrenia.

Personality disorder Although Mrs C.D. has mood variations from mild depression to an energetic cheerful state, these are not sufficiently intense to constitute a cyclothymic personality disorder.

Conclusions Depressive disorder.

Aetiology The symptoms appear to have been *precipitated* by news of her husband's infidelity. She was *predisposed* to react severely to this news by the insecure and jealous traits in her personality. She also appears to be predisposed to develop a depressive disorder in that (a) she became depressed after the birth of her first child (b) she is subject to mood variations (c) her father suffers similar, but more extreme, mood variations and his brother has been four times admitted to hospital for treatment of a manic-depressive disorder.

The depressive disorder may have been *maintained* in part by continuing quarrels with the husband and by worry about debts he has incurred. Her knowledge of her sister's divorce and subsequent unhappiness has added to her concerns about the future of her own marriage.

Treatment The pattern of symptoms of the depressive disorder suggest it is likely to respond to amitriptyline given in adequate dosage. The few side-effects experienced with 125 mg per day may indicate a lower than average blood concentration. The dose should be increased to 175 mg per day. Joint interviews with the patient and her husband are needed to attempt to resolve the marital problems. (It appears that she has a genuine wish for a reconciliation.) The husband should be advised by the social worker about the steps he can take to deal with his debts.

Prognosis If the marital problems improve the immediate prognosis is good. However, the several predisposing factors noted above indicate that she may develop further depressive disorder particularly at times when she encounters further stressful events.

Problem lists

A problem list is a useful addition to the formulation in cases with complicated social problems. Such a list makes it easier to identify clearly what can be done to help the patient, and to monitor progress in achieving agreed objectives of treatment.

The use of a problem list can be shown with two examples. The first is a

Problem	Action	Agent	Review
1. Frequent quarrels with husband	Joint interviews	Dr A	3 weeks
2. Three-year old son retarded in speech	Assessment	General practitioner	1 week
3. Housing said to be damp and unsatisfactory	Visit housing department of local authority	Patient	2 weeks
4. Sexual dysfunction (?secondary to 1 above)	Defer		

list (see above) that might be compiled for a young married woman who had taken a small overdose impulsively and had no psychiatric disorder or definite personality disorder.

As progress is made in dealing with the problems in this list, new ones may be added or existing ones modified. For example, after a few joint interviews it might appear that the patient's sexual difficulties are a cause of the marital problem rather than a result, and that counselling about sexual matters should be carried out. Item 4 would then be amended appropriately. Likewise if the assessment of the child by the general practitioner were to confirm speech delay, an appointment for a specialist opinion might follow.

It is often appropriate to draw up the list with the patient so that he understands which problems can be changed and what he must do himself to bring this about.

Similar lists can be a valuable aid to the review of cases during ward rounds. For this purpose, an important component of therapy is likely to be the treatment of mental disorder, often by drugs. Although such treatment can be shown on the same sheet as other problems, it should he separated clearly from them, as in the list on the following page drawn up for a 45-year-old depressed woman.

The life chart

A life chart is a way of showing the time relations between episodes of physical and mental disorder and potentially stressful events in the patient's life. It is often useful when the history is long and complicated.

Problem	Action	Agent	Review
1. Depressive disorder	Amitriptyline 150 mg/day	Dr A	3 weeks
2. Loneliness (children now grown up)	Seek paid or voluntary work	Patient and social worker	5 weeks
3. Shy and awkward in company	Social skills training group	Psychologist and nurse	4 weeks
4. Heavy irregular periods	Gynaecological opinion	Dr A	1 week

The chart has three columns, one for life events, and one each for physical and mental disorder. Its rows represent the years in the patient's life.

Completion of a life chart requires detailed enquiry into the timing of events, and this may clarify the relationships between stressors and the onset of illness, and also between physical and mental disorders. For example in the case of a recurrent illness previously thought to be provoked by stressful events, the chart may show it has run a regular course and that comparable events have occurred at other times without consequent illness. In another case, the chart may provide convincing evidence of a relationship between stressful events and illness.

Letters to general practitioners

When a letter is written to a general practitioner, whether after an out-patient assessment or on discharging a patient from hospital, the first step is to think what the general practitioner already knows about the patient, and what questions he asked on referral. If the family doctor's referral letter outlined the salient features of the case, there is no need to repeat them in reply. When the patient is less well known to the general practitioner, more detailed information should be given; it is then often appropriate to use subheadings (family history, personal history, etc.) so that information can be found readily if needed later.

Similarly, if the diagnosis given in the referral letter is correct, it is only necessary to confirm it; otherwise the reasons for the diagnosis should be outlined.

Treatment and prognosis are dealt with next. When discussing treatment, the dosage of drugs should always be stated. The psychiatrist should indicate whether he has issued a prescription, how long a period it covers, and whether he or the general practitioner are to issue any subsequent prescriptions. If psychotherapy, behaviour therapy, or social work are planned, the letter should name the therapist or agent concerned and indicate what profession he belongs to (for example, supportive psychotherapy from Mr Smith, hospital social worker). The date of the patient's next visit to hospital should be stated, so that the general practitioner knows whether to see the patient himself in the meantime.

At the time of discharge from in-patient or day-patient treatment, it is often appropriate to telephone the general practitioner to discuss subsequent management before the discharge letter is written. This telephone discussion ensures that the division of responsibilities is acceptable to the family doctor. If this is not done, the plans formulated may be well-intentioned but inappropriate.

Further reading

Engel, G. L. and Morgan, W. K. (1973). *Interviewing the patient*, pp. 26–79. W. B. Saunders, London.

Hollander, M. and Wells, C. E. (1980). Medical assessment in psychiatric practice. In *Comprehensive textbook of psychiatry* (4th edn) (eds. H. I. Kaplan and B. J. Sadock), Vol. I, pp. 543–49. Williams and Wilkins, Baltimore.

Institute of Psychiatry (1973). *Notes on eliciting and recording clinical information.* Oxford University Press, Oxford.

Leff, J. P. and Isaacs, A. D. (1978). *Psychiatric examination in clinical practice.* Blackwell, Oxford.

Pincus, J. H. and Tucker G. J. (1985). *Behavioural neurology* (3rd edn). Oxford University Press, New York.

3 Classification in psychiatry

In psychiatry, classification attempts to bring some order into the great diversity of phenomena encountered in clinical practice. Its purpose is to identify groups of patients who share similar clinical features, so that suitable treatment can be planned and the likely outcome predicted. Most systems of classification are based on diagnostic categories, such as schizophrenia or affective disorder. Diagnosis is the process of allocating a disorder to a diagnostic category. The great majority of psychiatrists agree that diagnostic classification is essential in psychiatry, but some dissent from this view.

In general medicine, classification is fairly straightforward. Most conditions can be classified on the basis of aetiology (for example pneumococcal or viral pneumonia) and of structural pathology (lobar or bronchopneumonia). Some general medical conditions are not yet classifiable in this way (such as migraine or trigeminal neuralgia); they are therefore classified solely on symptoms. Psychiatric disorders are mainly analogous to the second group. Some psychiatric disorders have an indisputable physical aetiology (such as phenylketonuria, mongolism, or general paralysis of the insane); but most can be classified only on symptoms.

This chapter begins with a brief discussion of the concept of mental illness. Then an outline is given of the basic principles that underlie most systems of classification, and the system used in this book is summarized. Certain contentious issues are reviewed; first, objections to psychiatric classification in itself, and second the question of categorical versus non-categorical classification. Next, an account is given of methods for achieving greater diagnostic agreement between psychiatrists. This leads to a description of individual systems of classification, including the main international systems. Finally, guidelines are given on classification in everyday clinical practice.

The concept of mental illness

In everyday speech the word 'illness' is used loosely. In psychiatric practice the term 'mental illness' is also used with little precision. To produce a good definition of mental illness is surprisingly difficult. In everyday clinical practice this difficulty does not matter much except in relation to certain legal issues such as compulsory admission to hospital. In forensic psychiatry, the definition of mental illness is important in relation to fitness to plead, criminal responsibility, and similar issues.

It is easy to understand why the concept of mental illness does not loom large in ordinary practice. The psychiatrist is not directly concerned with a concept of such generality. He is more interested in making sense of the wide-ranging phenomena encountered in psychiatry, so that he can plan treatment rationally and predict outcome. It turns out that the best way of doing so is to start with the basic data (symptoms and signs) and to group them into syndromes, that is constellations of symptoms that occur together frequently, and have implications for treatment and prognosis. The psychiatrist habitually works from the particular to the general, and not vice versa.

None the less, the concept of mental illness is intellectually interesting, and, as noted above, it has legal implications. For these reasons an outline of the main arguments will be given here.

Many attempts have been made to define mental illness (see Wootton 1959), but little progress has been made. A common approach is to examine the concept of illness in general medicine, and to look for any analogies with mental illness. In general medicine, an important distinction is made between disease and illness. Disease refers to objective physical pathology; illness refers to subjective awareness of distress or limitation of function. A person can have a disease without being ill, as in well-controlled diabetes; or he can be ill without having a disease, as in loss of a limb by trauma. However, this distinction has little bearing on psychiatric disorders, since most of them have no demonstrable physical pathology. Most psychiatric disorders are best regarded as illnesses.

Continuing the analogy with general medicine, mental illness could be defined in three different ways: absence of health; presence of suffering; and pathological process, whether physical or psychological.

Illness of any kind can be defined as the absence of health. This changes the emphasis of the problem, but does not solve it, because health is even more difficult to define. For example, the World Health Organization defined health as, 'a state of complete physical, mental and social well-being, and not merely the absence of disease or infirmity'. As Lewis (1953*b*) rightly commented, 'a definition could hardly be more comprehensive than that, or more meaningless'. Many other definitions of health have been proposed, all equally unsatisfactory (see Wootton 1959).

The second approach is to define illness by the presence of suffering. This ancient idea has some practical value, since it defines a group of people likely to consult doctors. Its disadvantage is that it cannot be applied to everyone who would usually be regarded as ill in everyday terms. For example, patients with mania may feel unusually well and not experience suffering, though most people would regard them as mentally ill.

Thirdly, mental illness can be defined by reference to pathological process. Some extremists such as Szasz (1960) take the view that illness can be defined only in terms of physical pathology. Since most mental disorders have no demonstrable physical pathology, on this view they are not illnesses. Szasz takes the further step of asserting that most mental disorders are therefore not the province of doctors. This kind of argument can be sustained only by taking an extremely narrow view of pathology, and it is incompatible with the available evidence. Thus, there are genetic and biochemical grounds for supposing that schizophrenia and depressive disorders may have a physical basis, though not in the form of gross structural pathology (see pp. 237 and 292).

Mental illness can also be defined in terms of psychopathology. Such a view was taken by Lewis (1953*b*), who suggested that illness could be characterized by 'evident disturbance of part functions as well as general efficiency'. In psychiatry part functions refer to perception, memory, learning, emotion, and other such psychological functions. A disturbance of the part function of perception would be an illusion or hallucination.

Several writers (Lewis 1953*b*; Wootton 1959) have warned strongly against defining mental illness in terms of socially deviant behaviour alone. The argument is often made that someone must have been mentally ill to commit a particularly cruel murder or abnormal sexual act (the word 'sick' is often used in this context). Although such antisocial behaviour may be highly unusual, there is no justification for equating it with mental illness. Moreover, if mental illness is inferred from socially deviant behaviour alone, political abuse may result. For example, opponents of a political system may be confined to psychiatric hospitals simply because they do not agree with the authorities.

From the above examples, it can be seen that mental illness is difficult to define. As already mentioned, the concept of mental illness need not be defined for most purposes, but the law requires psychiatrists to diagnose the presence or absence of 'mental illness' in relation to compulsory admission to hospital and certain court procedures. Faced with this task, most psychiatrists begin by separating mental handicap and personality disorder from mental illness, as explained in the next section. Whether implicitly or explicitly, they usually invoke Lewis's concept of part-functions to define mental illness; they diagnose mental illness if there are delusions, hallucinations, severe alterations of mood, or other major disturbances of psychological functions. In practice, most psychiatrists allocate psychiatric disorders to diagnostic categories, such as schizophrenia, affective disorders, organic mental states, and others; by convention, they agree to group these diagnostic categories together under the rubric mental illness. Problems may arise with certain abnormalities of behaviour such as abnormalities of sexual preference or drug abuse. For the reasons given above, these deviant behaviours are not usually regarded as mental illnesses, though they are deemed suitable for treatment by doctors.

The concept of mental illness is exceedingly complicated, and in a brief space only a few of the issues can be outlined. Readers seeking more information are referred to papers by Lewis (1953*b*), Wootton (1959), Farrell (1979), and Häfner (1987), and the book by Roth and Kroll (1987).

The need for classification

Classifications are needed in psychiatry, as in medicine, in order that doctors and others can communicate easily about the nature of patients' problems and about prognosis and treatment, and in order that research can be conducted with comparable groups of patients. The use of schemes of psychiatric classification has been criticized as inappropriate, or even harmful. Such criticisms have diminished as particular syndromes have been shown to respond to specific treatments.

Among psychiatrists, the main critics of classification have been psychotherapists (for example Menninger 1948), whose work is concerned more with neurotic and personality disorders than with the whole range of psychiatric disorder. Psychotherapists tend to make two main criticisms. The first is that allocating a patient to a diagnostic category distracts from the understanding of his unique personal difficulties. The second is that individual patients do not fit neatly into the available categories. Although these criticisms are important, they are arguments only against the improper use of classification. The use of classification can certainly be combined with consideration of a patient's unique qualities, indeed it is important to combine the two because these qualities can modify prognosis and need to be taken into account in treatment. Also, whilst it is not possible to classify a minority of disorders, this is not a reason for abandoning classification for the majority. Some sociologists have suggested that to allocate a person to a diagnostic category is simply to label deviant behaviour as illness (e.g. Scheff 1963; Lemert 1951). They argue that such labelling serves only to increase the person's difficulties. There can be no doubt that terms such as epilepsy or schizophrenia attract social stigma, but this does not lessen the reality of disorders that cause suffering and require treatment. These disorders cannot be made to disappear simply by ceasing to give names to them.

Psychosis and neurosis

Some systems of classification include categories of neurosis and psychosis. The term **psychosis** refers broadly to more severe forms of mental illness such as organic mental disorders, schizophrenia, and affective disorder. Numerous criteria have been proposed to define the term more precisely. Greater severity of illness is an obvious criterion, but the conditions that fall into this group can occur in mild as well as severe forms. Lack of insight is often suggested as a criterion for psychosis, but insight is itself difficult to define (see p. 33). A more straightforward criterion is the inability to distinguish between subjective experience and reality, as evidenced by hallucinations and delusions. Since none of these three criteria is easy to apply, the term psychosis is unsatisfactory. However, it is not only the difficulty of definition that makes it undesirable to use the term psychosis. There are two other reasons: first, the conditions embraced by the term have little in common; and second, it is less informative to classify a disorder as psychosis than it is to classify it as a particular disorder within the rubric of psychosis—for example, schizophrenia.

Although psychosis has little value as a category in a scheme for classifying mental disorders, it is still in everyday use as a convenient term for disorders which cannot be given a more precise diagnosis because insufficient evidence is available; for example, when it is still uncertain whether a disorder is schizophrenia or mania. Similarly it is useful to retain such terms as 'psychotic disorders not elsewhere classified' (in DSMIIIR), and 'acute or transient psychotic disorders' (in ICD10 draft). Finally, the adjectival form psychotic is in general use, for example in the terms psychotic symptom (generally meaning delusions, hallucinations, and excitement), and antipsychotic drug (meaning a drug that controls these symptoms).

The term **neurosis** refers to mental disorders that are generally less severe than the psychoses, and characterized by symptoms closer to normal experience (for example, anxiety). The history of the term is referred to on p. 154; at this point we are concerned with its value in classification. The objections to the term neurosis are similar to the objections to the term psychosis. First, neurosis is difficult to define (see p. 155); second, the conditions it embraces have little in common; third, more information can be conveyed by using a more specific diagnosis such as anxiety disorder or obsessional disorder, than by calling the condition a neurosis. A final objection is put forward in the manual to DSMIII, namely that neurosis has been widely used with an aetiological meaning in psychodynamic writings. It is true that the term has been so used, and such usage is historically unjustified (see p. 154). If this misuse were the only objection to the use of the term neurosis, it would be appropriate to ensure correct usage rather than abandon the term. Nevertheless, the term neurosis is not used in the American systems of classification DSMIII and DSMIIIR. In ICD10 (draft) it is retained in the adjectival form in the rubric 'neurotic, stress-related, and somatoform disorders'. However, like psychosis the term neurosis continues to be used in everyday clinical practice as a convenient term for disorders that cannot be assigned to a more precise diagnosis.

Types of classification

Categorical classification

Traditionally psychiatric disorders have been classified by dividing them into **categories**, which are supposed to represent discrete entities. The categories have been defined in terms of the symptom-patterns and the course and outcome of the different disorders. Such categories have proved useful in both clinical work and research. However, three objections are often raised against them. First, there is uncertainty about the validity of categories as representing distinct entities. Second, many systems of classification do not provide adequate definitions and rules of application, so categories cannot be used reliably. Third, many psychiatric disorders do not fall neatly within the boundaries of a category, but are intermediate between two categories; for example, schizoaffective disorder, which is intermediate between schizophrenia and affective disorder. Recently multivariate statistical techniques have been used in attempts to define categories more clearly. The results have been interesting, but so far not conclusive.

Categorical systems often include an implicit **hierarchy** of categories. If two or more diagnoses are made, it is often conventional (though not always made explicit) that one takes precedence. For example, organic mental disorders take precedence over schizophrenia. Foulds (1976) suggested that this hierarchical approach should be made an explicit basis of psychiatric classification. Foulds proposed a hierarchy of 'personal illness', of which the classes (in order of increasing priority) are: dysthymic states; neurotic symptoms; 'integrated delusions'; and 'delusions of disintegration'. According to Foulds, a high-priority condition could be accompanied by the symptoms of a condition of lower priority, but only the higher priority condition need be diagnosed. Although ingenious, this system has not been widely adopted.

Dimensional classification

Dimensional classification rejects the use of separate categories. In the past if was advocated by Kretschmer and other psychiatrists. Recently it has been strongly promoted by the psychologist Eysenck, who argues that there is no evidence to support the traditional grouping into discrete entities. Instead Eysenck (1970b) proposed a system of three dimensions: psychoticism, neuroticism, and introversion–extraversion. Patients are given scores which locate them on each of these three axes. For example, in the case of someone who would be assigned to hysteria in a categorical system, Eysenck's theory predicts that he would have high scores on the axes of neuroticism and extraversion, and a low score on the psychoticism axis. Subsequent research has not confirmed specific predictions of this kind, but the example brings out the principles.

The three dimensions were established by various procedures of multi-variate analysis. They are attractive in theory, but it should be remembered that they depend considerably on the initial assumptions and the choice of methods. The dimension of 'psychoticism' bears little relation to the concept of psychosis as generally used. For example, artists and prisoners score particularly highly on this dimension. The dimensions of neuroticism and introversion–extraversion have been useful in research, but in clinical practice they are difficult to apply to the individual patient.

The multiaxial approach

In one sense, the term multiaxial can be applied to the three dimensions just described. However, the term is usually applied to schemes of classification in which two or more separate sets of information (such as symptoms and aetiology) are coded. In 1947 Essen-Möller proposed that clinical syndrome and aetiology should be coded separately. It would then be possible to identify cases with a similar clinical picture on the one hand, and those with a similar aetiology on the other (Essen-Möller 1971). Such a scheme should avoid the unreliability of schemes in which clinical picture and aetiology can be combined in the definition of a single category, such as reactive depression.

Several multiaxial models have been proposed. In adult psychiatry, this kind of model has been adopted in DSMIIIR (see p. 88). In child psychiatry, wide use is now made of a modification of a five-axis system proposed by a WHO working party (Rutter *et al.* 1975*a*, see Chapter 20). Multiaxial systems are attractive, but there is an obvious danger that they will be so comprehensive and complicated as to be difficult for everyday use (see Williams 1985).

The basic categories for classification in psychiatry

Several categorical systems of classification have been used in psychiatry, but they contain the same basic categories (see Table 3.1). The first category is **mental retardation**, that is, impairment of intellectual functioning present continuously from early life. The second category is **personality**

Table 3.1. The basic classification

Mental retardation
Personality disorder
Mental disorder
Adjustment disorder
Other disorders
Developmental disorders
Other disorders specific to childhood

disorder, that is, dispositions to behave in certain abnormal ways present continuously since early adult life. The third category is **mental disorder**, that is, abnormalities of behaviour or psychological experience with a recognizable onset after a period of normal functioning. To qualify for a diagnosis of mental disorder, the abnormalities of experience or behaviour have to reach a certain level of severity. Disorders that fail to meet this criterion and that occur in relation to stressful events or changed circumstances are called **adjustment disorders**. A fifth category is required for other disorders that do not fit into the first four groups; for example, abnormalities of sexual preference, and drug dependence. The last two categories are for disorders of childhood; the sixth for disorders of development, the seventh for other kinds of disorder specific to this time of life.

The reliability of diagnosis

Diagnosis is the process of identifying a disease and allocating it to a category on the basis of symptoms and signs. Systems of classification are obviously of little value unless psychiatrists can agree with one another when they attempt to make a diagnosis. In the past thirty years there has been increasing interest in the extent and causes of diagnostic disagreement between psychiatrists (see Kendell 1975). Early studies consistently showed poor diagnostic reliability. In Philadelphia, Ward *et al.* (1962) concluded that overall disagreement was made up of the following elements: inconsistency in the patient, 5 per cent; inadequate interview technique, 33 per cent; inadequate use of diagnostic criteria, 62 per cent. The last two factors will be discussed in turn. (See Spitzer and Williams 1985 for a review of the process of diagnosis.)

Interviewing technique

Psychiatrists vary widely not only in the amount of information they elicit at interview, but also in their interpretation of the information. Thus, a psychiatrist may or may not elicit a phenomenon, and he may or may not regard it as a significant symptom or sign. Variations have been found between groups of psychiatrists trained in different countries, and between individual psychiatrists in the same country. When shown filmed interviews, American psychiatrists reported many more symptoms than did British psychiatrists (Sandifer *et al.* 1968). Presumably this reflected differences in training between the two countries.

Differences in eliciting symptoms can be reduced if psychiatrists are trained to use standardized interview schedules, such as the Present State Examination (PSE) (Wing *et al.* 1974); the Schedule of Affective Disorder and Schizophrenia (SADS), which covers both the present illness and past history (Endicott and Spitzer 1978); and the National Institute of Mental Health Diagnostic Interview Schedule (DIS). Non-specialists can also be trained to use these schedules. The point of such schedules is that first they specify sets of symptoms that must be enquired about, and secondly, they define the symptoms and give instructions on rating their severity.

Criteria for diagnosis

International studies have compared the diagnostic criteria used by different psychiatrists. For example in the US–UK Diagnostic Project, American and British psychiatrists were shown the same video-taped clinical interviews, and asked to make diagnoses (Cooper *et al.* 1972). Compared with those in London, psychiatrists in New York diagnosed schizophrenia twice as often, and mania and depression correspondingly less often. Further investigation suggested that New York was not typical of North America, and that diagnostic practice in some other places in the United States and in Canada was closer to British practice.

A second study, the International Pilot Study of Schizophrenia, was carried out in nine countries (World Health Organization 1973): Colombia (Cali); Czechoslovakia (Prague); Denmark (Aarhus); England (London); India (Agra); Nigeria (Ibadan); Taiwan (Taipei); USA (Washington); and USSR (Moscow). Psychiatrists in all these countries carried out lengthy interviews which included the Present State Examination. The psychiatrists made their own diagnoses and these were compared with those of the PSE computer program, CATEGO. There was substantial agreement between seven of the centres, but Washington and Moscow differed from the rest. In Washington, the findings confirmed the findings of the US–UK project described above. The Moscow psychiatrists also appeared to have an unusually broad concept of schizophrenia; this apparently reflected a particular local emphasis on the course of disorder as a diagnostic criterion.

In a third, less elaborate study, diagnostic practices were compared in France, Germany, and Great Britain (Kendell *et al.* 1974). Agreement was closest between German and British psychiatrists. French psychiatrists were notably different in diagnosing manic-depressive disorder much less frequently. Diagnostic unreliability can be reduced by providing a clear definition of each category in a diagnostic scheme. Each definition should specify discriminating symptoms rather than characteristic symptoms. **Discriminating symptoms** are those that may occur in the defined syndrome but seldom in other syndromes. Discriminating symptoms are important in diagnosis but may be of little concern to patients and relatively unimportant in treatment. An example is the delusion that thoughts are being inserted into the mind, a symptom that seldom occurs except in schizophrenia. **Characteristic symptoms** occur frequently in the defined syndrome but occur in other syndromes as well. Such symptoms may be important to the patient and relevant in planning treatment, but do not help in diagnosis. An example is thoughts of suicide, which occur in depressive disorders but also in other conditions.

Diagnostic criteria can be descriptive statements, as in the draft of ICD10, or more precise operational criteria, as in DSMIIIR. Operational definitions were originally suggested by the philosopher Carl Hempel, and were incorporated in an important report to the WHO on ways of overcoming the problems of diverse national classifications (Stengel 1959). The term **operational definition** in this context means the specification of a category by a series of precise inclusion and exclusion statements. Inclusion criteria can be of two types. **Conjunctive criteria** are requirements that must all be satisfied for inclusion of something in the category. **Disjunctive criteria** are requirements of which one or more, but not all, have to be satisfied for inclusion. The first detailed set of rules was drawn up by Feighner *et al.* (1972) in the United States, who provided specific inclusion and exclusion criteria. A similar approach was adopted in the Research Diagnostic Criteria (Spitzer *et al.* 1978), and in the American system DSMIII, which is described later in this chapter. When criteria of this kind are used, a substantial number of patients may not fit into any of the designated categories, and may have to be allocated to an 'atypical' category. In some kinds of research, this atypical group may not matter, but it can be a problem in everyday clinical practice.

Diagnosis by computer

Computer diagnosis ensures that the same rules will be applied to every case. Computer programs to generate diagnoses have been based either on a logical decision-tree or on statistical models. A decision-tree program evaluates a sequence of yes/no answers, and so successively narrows the diagnosis. It thus resembles differential diagnosis in clinical practice. Spitzer and Endicott (1968) first used this procedure to develop the program DIAGNO. Later Wing and colleagues (1974) developed the program CATEGO, for use with the Present State Examination.

CATEGO has proved valuable in epidemiological studies of major and minor psychiatric disorders, and comparison data are now available from a variety of patient groups and normal populations.

In the alternative statistical approach, data are collected from a sample of patients whose diagnoses are known. A scheme of classification is then devised from this database by statistical methods. Whereas the decision-tree method follows a sequence of arbitrary rules that underlie ordinary clinical practice, this second method estimates the probability that a given patient's symptoms match the symptoms of previously diagnosed patients.

The validity of schemes of classification

Whilst the unreliability of diagnosis can be reduced by the measures just described, a scheme of classification must also be valid. Even if different interviewers can be trained to reach high levels of agreement in making diagnoses, little has been achieved unless the diagnostic categories have some useful relationship to the disorders met in clinical practice. To be valid, a scheme of classification should have categories that fit well with clinical experience (face validity). The categories should also be able to predict the outcome of psychiatric disorders (predictive validity); ideally they should also point to associations between psychiatric disorders and independent variables, such as biochemical measures (construct validity).

So far little progress has been made towards establishing the validity of existing schemes of classification [see Spitzer and Williams (1985) for a discussion of reliability and validity in diagnosis].

Other features of schemes of classification

Two other features contribute to the value of a system of classification: its coverage and its ease of use. Coverage refers to the extent to which a scheme has categories for all the disorders that are encountered in clinical practice.

Individual systems of classification

In the history of psychiatric classification, an outstanding contribution was made by the German psychiatrist Emil Kraepelin whose work was based on detailed clinical observations and follow-up studies. In successive editions of his famous textbook, he refined the distinction between organic and functional psychoses, and further divided the latter into dementia praecox (later called schizophrenia) and manic depressive illness.

In European countries systems of classification still remain largely within Kraepelin's framework. The two main exceptions are Scandinavia and

France. In Scandinavia much emphasis is placed on the concept of **psychogenic** or **reactive psychoses**, which are said to have paranoid, depressive, or confusional symptoms, or sometimes a mixture of all three (see Strömgren 1985; Cooper 1986).

In French psychiatry, classification is based on a combination of psychopathology and elements of existential philosophy (see Pichot 1984). Certain diagnostic categories in France differ from those in Europe and North America. They include two special categories: ***Bouffée délirante***—the sudden onset of a delusional state with trance-like feelings of short duration and good prognosis. Although this condition may develop into schizophrenia, it is clearly separated from acute schizophrenia and acute manic depressive illness (see Chapter 9). ***Délires chroniques***—conditions which, in the ICD system, would be classified as 'Persistent delusional disorders'; they are separated from schizophrenia, a diagnosis which, in France, is used only when there is definite evidence of deterioration of personality. The *délires chroniques* are subdivided into the 'non-focused' in which several areas of mental activity are affected, and the 'focused' with a single delusional theme. The latter include several conditions such as erotomania, described in Chapter 10.

In the 1920s and 1930s American views on psychiatric classification diverged widely from those in Europe. Psychoanalysis and the teaching of Adolf Meyer directed American psychiatry towards a predominant concern with the uniqueness of individuals rather than with their common features. At the same time, diagnostic concepts were increasingly based on presumed psychodynamic mechanisms.

Recently in the United States attitudes towards psychiatric classification have changed considerably. An important first step was the introduction of strict criteria for classification in research, as described above (Feighner *et al.* 1972). This step was followed by the thorough work that led to the new American scheme, DSMIII.

Classification in developing countries

Classifications developed in Europe and North America have not proved entirely satisfactory in developing countries where behavioural disturbances can be different. In developing countries acute psychotic symptoms may present particular difficulties of diagnosis; they are often atypical and raise doubt as to whether they represent separate entities or merely variations of syndromes seen in developed countries. Investigation of these issues is difficult for outsiders who may not appreciate important cultural factors or the varying use of language to describe emotions and behaviour. For further information about the cultural aspects of classification see Fabrega 1987; Leff 1981; Murphy 1982; Simons and Hughes 1985; and Yap 1951).

The International Classification of Diseases (ICD)

Mental disorders were not included in the International Classification of Disease until its sixth edition. This first scheme for mental disorders was widely criticized. As a preliminary to a major revision of the scheme, a survey of principles of classification in different countries was carried out (Stengel 1959), and wide variations were found. Stengel recommended a new approach based on operational definitions and supported by a glossary, but not linked to any theories of aetiology.

The eighth edition of the International Classification (ICD8) was published in 1965. It made some progress towards solving the earlier problems but was still unsatisfactory in several ways. It contained too many categories, and allowed alternative codings for some syndromes. This probably reflected an endeavour to make the scheme widely acceptable. The glossary to ICD8 was not published until 1972. Meanwhile glossaries had been published in America and Great Britain (General Register Office 1968). Neither of these glossaries was detailed enough; they both contained internal inconsistencies, and they disagreed with one another.

Before preparation of the next edition, ICD9, several WHO working parties examined the principles and practice of classification (see Kendell 1975). A new descriptive glossary (based on the British glossary to ICD8) was drawn up (World Health Organization 1978). Improvements were made in the classificatory scheme, particularly in the sections on organic disorders, childhood disorders, and psychiatric disorders associated with physical illness. However, ICD9 still remained a compromise, no doubt because it aimed to be widely acceptable. It also lacked detailed rules of application. As Kendell (1975) pointed out, depressive disorders could be classified in several alternative ways which were mutually incompatible. Despite these shortcomings, ICD9 had some success in encouraging greater uniformity of classification in different countries. ICD10 is described below.

The Diagnostic and Statistical Manual (DSM)

In 1952 the American Psychiatric Association published the first edition of the Diagnostic and Statistical Manual (DSM I) as an alternative to ICD6 (which, as mentioned above, had been widely criticized). DSMI was influenced by the views of Adolf Meyer and Karl Menninger, and its simple glossary reflected the prevailing acceptance of psychoanalytic ideas in the United States. In 1965 work began on DSMII, in which both psychoanalytic and Kraepelinian ideas were represented.

The third edition, DSMIII, was published in 1980. It had been prepared with great care. Advisory committees had prepared detailed drafts, obtained opinions from 550 clinicians, and subjected the results to field tests. DSMIII was intended to provide a comprehensive classification with clear criteria for each diagnostic category.

There were five main innovations in DSMIII. First, operational criteria were provided for each diagnosis, with rules for the inclusion and exclusion of cases. Second, a multiaxial classification was adopted, which had five axes: I—clinical syndromes and 'conditions not attributable to mental disorder that are the focus of attention and treatment'; II—personality disorders; III—physical disorders and conditions; IV—severity of psychosocial stressors; and V—highest level of adaptive functioning in the last year. The third innovation was that the nomenclature was revised and some syndromes regrouped: for example, the terms neurosis and hysteria were discarded, and all affective disorders were grouped together. The fourth change was that the classification relied less on psychodynamic concepts; and the fifth was that duration of illness was introduced in some places as one of the criteria for diagnosis.

The production of DSMIII was an important achievement. It was influential in the United States, and many of its features have been incorporated in the draft of the World Health Organization classification, ICD10. Inevitably, some of the changes have been criticized, for example the rule restricting the diagnosis of schizophrenia to illnesses lasting more than six months. [For a discussion of DSMIII see Kendell (1983); Mezzich *et al.* (1985)].

DSMIIIR

DSMIIIR has been produced as an interim scheme to remedy some of the faults of DSMIII while the work of producing a full revision (DSMIV) is undertaken. The main categories in DSMIIIR are shown in Table 3.2. The most important changes are as follows. First, the multiaxial classification has been revised so that axis V now refers to global assessment of functioning. Second, some of the diagnostic hierarchies of DSMIII have been removed. For example, in DSMIII a patient with symptoms of both panic disorder and major depression was diagnosed as having only major depression, the panic attacks being regarded as associated symptoms; whereas in DSMIIIR, both diagnoses are made. In DSMIIIR, two kinds of hierarchy are retained: Organic Mental Disorder pre-empts the diagnosis of any disorder that could produce part of the symptomatology (for example, it pre-empts major affective disorder); and schizophrenia pre-empts other disorders in the same way (for example, it pre-empts dysthymic disorder). Third there have been some changes in the conditions coded on Axis II. In DSMIII Specific Development Disorder and Personality Disorder were coded on this axis; in DSMIIIR Pervasive Developmental Disorder and Mental Retardation are also coded on Axis II. The fourth change is that a new rubric has been introduced for sleep disorders. The fifth is that many points of detail have been revised; for example, in

Table 3.2. Main categories in DSMIIIR

Disorders usually first evident in infancy, childhood, or adolescence.
Organic mental disorders
Psychoactive substance use disorders
Schizophrenia
Delusional (paranoid) disorder
Psychotic disorders not elsewhere classified
Mood disorders
Anxiety disorders
Dissociative disorders and somatoform disorders
Sexual disorders
Sleep disorders
Factitious disorders
Impulse disorders not elsewhere classified
Adjustment disorder
Psychological factors affecting physical conditions
Personality disorders (coded on Axis II)

the criteria for diagnosing panic disorder, where the requirement for three spontaneous panic attacks within three weeks has been changed to four attacks in four weeks. Although this kind of detailed change may refine diagnosis, the altered criteria make it difficult to compare the results of epidemiological studies or clinical trials when one study has employed DSMIII and the other DSMIIIR. When the justification for change is not strong (as in the above example concerning panic disorder), the disadvantages of changing may outweigh the advantages.

The new International Classification

The World Health Organization has worked with psychiatric organizations in many countries to develop a tenth edition of the fifth chapter of the International Classification (ICD10), and this edition is now available as a final draft. The main categories in this draft are shown in Table 3.3.

ICD10 makes use of many of the conceptual and taxonomic advances incorporated in DSMIII. It includes three main elements:

1. An account of the multiaxial system and of the syndromes.
2. A glossary that will be printed in the main volume of ICD10. This will have a layout similar to the glossary and guide to ICD9, containing nomenclature and a brief summary of clinical features and notes on differential diagnosis.
3. Diagnostic criteria for research. This will be a separate version of the

classification with diagnostic criteria in the form of precise operational criteria.

The draft of ICD10 is similar in many ways to DSMIIIR, but the clinical descriptions and diagnostic guidelines are less detailed and less restrictive. There are some important differences from DSMIIIR in the nomenclature and in the grouping of disorders, and in some areas significant conceptual differences, such as in the definition of schizophrenia. The main headings of ICD10 (draft) are listed in Table 3.3. It does not contain the distinction, made in ICD9, between neurosis and psychosis; but, unlike DSMIIIR, it retains the term neurotic in the heading 'Neurotic, stress-related and somatoform disorders'.

Guidance will be given on equivalence of diagnoses between ICD10 and ICD9, and between ICD10 and DSMIIIR. There will also be provision for some national variation in the application of ICD10; and it is hoped to allow this variation while retaining the ability to collect comparable international data on the broader categories of mental disorder.

In this book differences between ICD10 (draft) and DSMIIIR will be discussed in the chapters on clinical syndromes.

Table 3.3. The main categories in the draft of ICD10

Organic, including symptomatic, mental disorders
Mental and behaviour disorders due to psychoactive substance use
Schizophrenia, schizotypal states, and delusional disorders
Mood (affective) disorders
Neurotic, stress related, and somatoform disorders
Physiologic dysfunction associated with mental and behavioural factors
Abnormalities of adult personality and behaviour
Mental retardation
Developmental disorders
Behavioural and emotional disorders with onset usually occurring in childhood or adolescence

---

Comparison of DSMIIIR and ICD10 (draft)

The two systems share several categories. Both contain rubrics for disorders of childhood and adolescence, organic mental disorders, disorders due to psychoactive substance use, and mood disorders. Of the differences, one arises because in ICD10 two categories—developmental disorders, and mental retardation—are used for conditions which appear under the single rubric 'developmental disorder' in DSMIIIR (where it is coded on Axis II). Most of the other differences arise because DSMIIIR uses a larger number of discrete categories to classify conditions which appear under a smaller number of more general rubrics in ICD10 (draft).

In some cases the broader categories of ICD10 correspond directly to a group of categories in DSMIIIR. Thus the single ICD10 rubric 'neurotic, stress-related, and somatoform disorder' corresponds to the four DSMIIIR categories anxiety disorder, somatoform disorder, dissociative disorder, and adjustment disorder. Also, the single ICD10 rubric 'schizophrenia, schizotypal states, and delusional disorders' corresponds to the three DSMIIIR categories schizophrenia, delusional disorder, and 'psychotic disorders not elsewhere classified'. In other cases the correspondence is less exact. These issues will be discussed in later chapters, where the relevant syndromes are described, but two examples will be given at this point. The first example concerns the DSMIIIR category sexual disorders, which includes sexual dysfunctions and paraphilias. In the draft of ICD10, sexual dysfunction appears (with other conditions) under the rubric 'psychological dysfunction associated with mental or behavioural factors', and paraphilias (referred to by the term 'abnormalities of sexual preference') appear under 'abnormalities of adult personality and behaviour'. The second example concerns the two other conditions (eating disorders and sleep disorders) listed under the above ICD10 rubric 'psychological dysfunction associated with mental or behavioural factors'. In DSMIIIR eating disorders are listed under 'disorders usually first evident in infancy, childhood, or adolescence', and sleep disorders have a separate rubric of their own.

Classification in this book

In this book both DSMIIIR and the draft of ICD10 classifications are discussed in chapters dealing with clinical syndromes; priority is often given to DSMIIIR as the more established system at present. As in other textbooks, disorders are grouped in chapters for convenience and ease of understanding. The headings of these chapters do not always correspond exactly with the terms used in DSMIIIR and ICD10; any difference usually means that the heading more appropriately summarizes the scope of the chapter.

In DSMIIIR, the term mental disorder is used instead of the term mental illness. It is defined as 'a clinically significant behaviour or psychological syndrome or pattern that occurs in a person and that is associated with present distress (a painful symptom) or disability (impairment of one or more important areas of functioning) or with a significantly increased risk of suffering death, pain, disability, or an important loss of freedom. In addition, this syndrome or pattern must not be merely an expectable response to a particular event, eg. the death of a loved one.'

ICD10 draft also uses the term mental disorder instead of mental illness. The same practice is followed in this book. (See Table 3.4.)

Classification in everyday practice

This subject was considered briefly in the section on formulation (p. 69). It is discussed in more detail here.

A classification is made after the history and examination of mental state have been completed. The first step is to review the pattern of the symptoms occurring in the past month (as reported by the patient and any other informants) and of the symptoms and signs elicited by mental state examination. Then an attempt is made to match this pattern to one or more of the diagnostic categories in the system of classification used. Reference is made if necessary to the definitions and rules of application provided by the scheme. In practice, only a small number of categories need be considered, the rest being obviously inapplicable. An important distinction needs to be made between characteristic symptoms and discriminating symptoms (see p. 84).

In attempting to match a patient's pattern of symptoms and signs to a diagnostic category, problems may arise when most symptoms fit well but one or two are incongruous. For example, a patient may have depressed mood, morbid self-blame, early morning waking, and diurnal mood variation—all symptoms typical of a depressive disorder. In addition the patient may have the delusion that people talk about him on television—a typical symptom of schizophrenia. When this kind of incongruity occurs, the clinician should review the case thoroughly and search for other evidence of the alternative syndrome. If only a single incongruous symptom is found among many that are congruous, generally the diagnostic category remains unchanged.

This kind of problem can sometimes be resolved by looking at the diagnostic category longitudinally was well as cross-sectionally. The process described so far is cross-sectional; that is, allocation to a category is based on present mental state and the history of symptoms in the past few weeks. The longitudinal approach deals with the nature and course of a disorder since it first began. For example, the present symptoms can be compared with those of any previous episodes of disorder. If it is found that the patient described above had had two previous episodes of clear-cut affective disorder, and no episodes of schizophrenia, then the clinician will more readily discount the current atypical symptom (the delusion of being talked about on television). If there have been two episodes of definite schizophrenia, the opposite conclusion will be justified. The time-course of previous illness is also informative; a history of intermittent episodes with complete recovery between them occurs more often with

Table 3.4. Classification of mental disorders in this book
(Major headings only)

Organic mental disorders
Delirium
Dementia
Amnestic syndrome

Psychoactive substance use disorder

Schizophrenic disorders (and related disorders*)

Delusional (paranoid) disorders

Mood (affective) disorders
Depressive disorders
Manic disorder

Neurotic disorders*
Minor emotional disorders*
Anxiety disorders
Obsessive-compulsive disorder
Somatoform disorders
Dissociative disorders
Post-traumatic stress disorder

Adjustment disorders

Personality disorders

Other disorders
Gender and sexual disorders
Factitious disorders

Disorders of infancy, childhood, or adolescence
Developmental disorders
Conduct disorders*
Emotional disorders*

Mental retardation

---

* Terms not used in DSMIIIR

affective disorder than with schizophrenia. These principles can, of course, be applied to other differential diagnoses.

When discussing diagnostic classification at a ward round or in a written formulation, the best practice is to list the possible categories, and then briefly review the evidence for and against each. The list might be, for example: depressive disorder; schizophrenia; organic disorder. Evidence 'for' consists of discriminating symptoms and a typical time-course of the illness; evidence 'against' includes absence of essential symptoms, presence of incongruous symptoms, and an atypical time-course. The reader may find it helpful to refer to the example of a formulation on p. 70.

Further reading

American Psychiatric Association (1987). *Diagnostic and statistical manual of mental disorders* (3rd edn, revised). American Psychiatric Association, Washington D.C.

Kendell, R. E. (1975). *The role of diagnosis in psychiatry*. Blackwell Scientific Publications, Oxford.

Lewis, A. J. (1953). Health as a social concept. *British Journal of Sociology* **4**, 109–24. Reprinted in Lewis, A.J. (1967). *The state of psychiatry*, pp. 179–94. Routledge and Kegan Paul, London.

Spitzer R. L. and Williams, J. B. W. (1987). Classification in psychiatry. In *Comprehensive textbook of psychiatry* (4th edn). (ed. H. I. Kaplan and B. J. Sadock). Williams and Wilkins, Baltimore.

Tischler, G., ed. (1987). *Diagnosis and classification in psychiatry*. Cambridge University Press, Cambridge.

World Health Organization (1981). *Current state of diagnosis and classsification in the mental health field*. World Health Organization, Geneva.

Wootton, B. (1959). *Social science and social pathology*, Chapter 7, pp. 203–26. George Allen and Unwin, London.

4 Aetiology

Psychiatrists are concerned with aetiology in two ways. First, in everyday clinical work, they try to discover the causes of the mental disorders presented by individual patients. Second, in seeking a wider understanding of psychiatry, they are interested in evidence about aetiology obtained from clinical studies, community surveys, or laboratory investigations. Correspondingly, the first part of this chapter deals with some general issues about aetiology in the assessment of the individual patient. The second part deals with the various scientific disciplines that have been applied to the study of aetiology.

When the clinician assesses an individual patient, he draws on a common fund of knowledge about aetiology built up from the study of groups of similar patients, but he cannot understand the patient in these terms alone. He must also use everyday insights into human nature. For example, in assessing a depressed patient, the psychiatrist should certainly know what has been discovered about the psychological and neurochemical changes accompanying depressive disorders, and what evidence there is about the aetiological role of stressful events and genetic predisposition. At the same time he will need intuitive understanding to recognize that this particular patient feels depressed because he has been told that his wife has cancer.

Common-sense ideas of this kind are nearly always an important part of aetiological formulation in psychiatry, but they must be used carefully if superficial explanation is to be avoided. Aetiological formulation can be done properly only if certain conceptual problems are clearly understood. These problems can be illustrated by a case-history.

For four weeks a 38-year-old married man became increasingly depressed. His symptoms started soon after his wife left him to live with another man.

In the past the patient's mother had received psychiatric treatment on two occasions, once for a severe depressive disorder, and once for mania; on neither occasion was there any apparent environmental cause for the illness. When the patient was 14 years old, his mother went away to live with another man, leaving her children with their father. For several years afterwards the patient felt rejected and unhappy but eventually settled down. He married and had two children, aged thirteen and ten at the time of his illness.

Two weeks after leaving home, the patient's wife returned, saying that she had made a mistake and really loved her husband. Despite her return the patient's symptoms persisted and worsened. He began to wake early, gave up his usual activities, and spoke at times of suicide.

In thinking about the causes of this man's symptoms, the clinician would first draw on knowledge of aetiology derived from scientific enquiries. Genetic investigations have shown that, if a parent suffers from mania as well as depressive disorder, a predisposition to depressive disorder is particularly likely to be transmitted to the children. It is therefore possible that this patient received the predisposition from his mother. Clinical investigation has also provided some information about the effects of separating children from their mothers. In the present case the information is not helpful because it refers to people who were separated from their mothers at a younger age than the patient. On scientific grounds there is no particular reason to focus on the departure of the patient's mother; but intuitively it seems likely that this was an important event. From everyday experience it is understandable that a man should feel sad if his wife leaves him; and he is likely to feel even more distressed if this event recapitulates a similar distressing experience in his own childhood. Therefore, despite the lack of scientific evidence, the clinician would recognize intuitively that the patient's depression is likely to be a reaction to the wife's departure.

The same sort of intuitions might suggest that the patient would recover when his wife came back. In the event he did not recover. Although his symptoms seemed understandable when his wife was away, they no longer seem so after her return.

This simple case-history illustrates the following aetiological issues: the complexity of causes in psychiatry: the classification of causes; the concept of stress; the concept of psychological reaction; and the roles that intuition and scientific knowledge should play in aetiology. These problems will be considered in turn.

The complexity of causes in psychiatry

In psychiatry, the study of causation is complicated by two problems. Both of these problems are met in other branches of medicine, but to a lesser degree.

The first problem is that causes are often *remote in time* from the effects they produce. For example it is widely believed that childhood experiences partly determine the occurrence of neuroses in adult life. It is difficult to test this idea because the necessary information can only be gathered either by studying children and tracing them many years later, which is difficult; or by asking adults about their childhood experiences, which is unreliable.

The second problem is that a *single cause* may lead to *several effects*.

For example, deprivation of parental affection in childhood has been reported to predispose to antisocial behaviour, suicide, depressive disorder and several other disorders. Conversely, *a single effect* may arise from *several causes*. The latter can be illustrated either by different causes in different individuals, or by multiple causes in a single individual. For example, mental handicap (single effect) may occur in several children, but the cause may be a different genetic abnormality in each child. On the other hand depressive disorder (single effect) may occur in one individual through a combination of causes, such as genetic factors, adverse childhood experiences, and stressful events in adult life.

The classification of causes

A single psychiatric disorder, as just explained, may result from several causes. For this reason, a scheme for classifying causes is required. A useful approach is to divide causes chronologically into predisposing, precipitating, and perpetuating.

Predisposing factors

These are factors, many of them operating from early life, that determine a person's vulnerability to causes acting close to the time of the illness. They include genetic endowment and the environment *in utero*, as well as physical, psychological, and social factors in infancy and early childhood. The term **constitution** is often used to describe the mental and physical make-up of a person at any point in his life. This make-up changes as life goes on, under the influence of further physical, psychological, and social influences. Some writers restrict the term constitution to the make-up at the beginning of life, whilst others also include characteristics acquired later (this second usage is adopted in this book). The concept of constitution includes the idea that a person may have a predisposition to develop a disorder (such as schizophrenia) even though the latter never manifests itself. From the standpoint of psychiatric aetiology, one of the important parts of the constitution is the personality.

When the aetiology of an individual case is formulated, the **personality** is always an essential element. For this reason the clinician should be prepared to spend considerable time in talking to the patient and to people who know him, in order to build up a clear picture of his personality. This assessment often helps to explain why the patient responded to certain stressful events, and why he reacted in a particular way. The obvious importance of personality in the individual patient contrasts with the small amount of relevant scientific information so far available. In the evaluation of personality, therefore, it is particularly important to acquire sound clinical skills through supervised practice.

Precipitating factors

These are events that occur shortly before the onset of a disorder and appear to have induced it. They may be physical, psychological, or social. Whether they produce a disorder at all, and what kind of disorder, depends partly on constitutional factors in the patient (as mentioned above). Physical precipitating factors include, for example, cerebral tumours or drugs. Psychological and social precipitants include personal misfortunes such as the loss of a job, and changes in the routine of life such as moving home. Sometimes the same factor can act in more than one way; for example, a head injury can induce psychological disorder either through physical changes in the brain or through its stressful implications to the patient.

Perpetuating factors

These factors prolong the course of a disorder after it has been provoked. When planning treatment, it is particularly important to give attention to these factors. The original predisposing and precipitating factors may have ceased to act by the time the patient is seen, but the perpetuating factors may well be treatable. For example, in their early stages many psychiatric disorders lead to secondary demoralization and withdrawal from social activities, which in turn help to prolong the original disorder. It is often appropriate to treat these secondary factors, whether or not any specific measures are carried out.

The concept of stress

Discussions about stress are often confusing because the term is used in two ways. First, it is applied to events or situations, such as working for an examination, that may have an adverse effect on someone. Second, it is applied to the adverse effects that are induced, which may be psychological or physiological change. In considering aetiology it is advisable to separate these components.

The first set of factors can usefully be called **stressors**. They include a large number of physical, psychological, and social factors, in the environment that can produce adverse effects. The term is sometimes extended to include events that are not experienced as adverse at the time, but may still have adverse long-term effects. For example intense competition may produce an immediate feeling of pleasant tension, though it may sometimes lead to unfavourable long-term effects.

The effect on the person can usefully be called the **stress reaction** to distinguish it from the provoking events. This reaction includes autonomic responses (such as a rise in blood pressure), endocrine changes (such as the secretion of adrenalin and noradrenalin), and psychological responses (such as a feeling of being keyed-up).

The concept of a psychological reaction

As already mentioned, it is widely recognized that psychological distress can arise as a reaction to unpleasant events. Sometimes the association between event and distress is evident; for example, when a man becomes depressed after the death of his wife. In other cases, it is far from clear whether the psychological disorder is really a reaction to an event or whether the two have coincided fortuitously; for example, when a man becomes depressed after the death of a distant relative. Jaspers (1963, p. 392) suggested three criteria for deciding whether a psychological state is a reaction to a particular set of events. First, there must be events that seem adequate in severity and closely related in time to the onset of the psychological state. Secondly, there must be a clear connection between the nature of the events and the content of the psychological disorder (in the example just given, the man should be preoccupied with ideas concerning his distant relative). Thirdly, the psychological state should begin to disappear when the events have ceased (unless, of course, it can be shown that perpetuating factors are acting to maintain it). These three criteria are quite useful in clinical practice, though they can be difficult to apply in many cases (particularly the second criterion).

Understanding and explanation

As already mentioned, aetiological statements about individual patients must combine knowledge derived from research on groups of patients, with intuitions derived from everyday experience. These two ways of making sense of psychiatric disorders have been called, respectively, **Erklären** and **Verstehen** by Jaspers (1963, p. 302). In everyday German, these terms mean 'explanation' and 'understanding' respectively, and they are usually translated as such in English translations of Jaspers' writing. However, Jaspers used them in a special sense. He used *Erklären* to refer to the sort of causative statement that is sought in the natural sciences. It is exemplified by the statement that a patient's aggressive behaviour has occurred because he has a brain tumour. Jaspers used *Verstehen* to refer to psychological understanding, or the intuitive grasp of a natural connection between events in a person's life and his psychological state. In colloquial English, this could be called 'putting oneself in another person's shoes'. It is exemplified by the statement, 'I can understand why the patient became angry when his wife was insulted by a neighbour'.

These distinctions are reasonably clear when we consider an individual patient. Confusion sometimes arises when attempts are made to generalize from insights obtained in a single case to widely applicable principles. Understanding may then be mistaken for explanation. Jaspers suggested that some psychoanalytic ideas are special kinds of intuitive understanding that are derived from the detailed study of individuals, and then applied generally. They are not explanations that can be tested scientifically. They are more akin to insights into human nature that can be gained from reading great works of literature. Such insights are of great value in conducting human affairs. It would be wrong to neglect them in psychiatry, but equally wrong to confuse them with statements of a scientific kind.

The aetiology of a single case

A discussion of how to make an aetiological formulation was given in Chapter 2 (p. 69). An example was given of a woman in her thirties who had become increasingly depressed. The formulation showed how aetiological factors can be grouped under the headings of predisposing, precipitating, and perpetuating factors. It also showed how information from scientific investigations (in this case genetics) can be combined with an intuitive understanding of personality and the likely effects of family problems on the patient. The reader may find it helpful to re-read the formulation on p. 70 before continuing with this chapter.

Approaches to aetiology

Before considering the contribution that different scientific disciplines can make to psychiatric aetiology, attention needs to be given to the kinds of aetiological model that have been employed in psychiatry. A model is a device for ordering information. Like a theory, it seeks to explain certain phenomena, but it does so in a broad and comprehensive way that cannot readily be proved false.

Reductionist and non-reductionist models

Two broad categories of explanatory model can be recognized. Reductionist models seek to understand causation by tracing back to simpler and simpler earlier stages. Examples are the medical model described below, and the psychoanalytic model. This type of model can be exemplified by the statement that the cause of schizophrenia lies in a disordered neurotransmission in a specific area of the brain.

Non-reductionist models try to relate problems to wider rather than narrower issues. The explanatory models used in sociology are generally of this kind. In psychiatry, this type of model can be exemplified by the statement that the cause of schizophrenia lies in the family to which the patient belongs: he is only the most conspicuous element in a disordered group of people.

It is unlikely that psychiatric aetiology can be understood by using either of these models exclusively. Different types of disorder are likely to require different kinds of explanation.

The 'medical model'

Several models are used in psychiatric aetiology, but the so-called medical model is the most prominent. It represents a general strategy of research that has proved useful in medicine, particularly in studying infectious diseases. A disease entity is identified in terms of a consistent pattern of symptoms, a characteristic clinical course and specific post-mortem findings. When an entity has been identified in this way, a set of necessary and sufficient causes is sought. In the case of tuberculosis, for example, the necessary cause is the tubercle bacillus, but it is not by itself sufficient. The tubercle bacillus in conjunction with either poor nutrition or low resistance is sufficient cause.

This medical model has also been useful in psychiatry, though not for all conditions. It is most relevant to organic syndromes, the best example being general paralysis of the insane, which is caused by syphilitic infection of the brain. It is least appropriate to the neuroses, which seem more like an exaggeration of normal psychological reactions to events. Nowadays the medical model might be better named the organic model, particularly because general medicine now adopts a broader aetiological framework including the idea that some disorders are quantitative variations from the normal.

The behavioural model

Some of the disorders that psychiatrists are called upon to treat do not fit readily into the medical model. These disorders include hysteria, sexual deviations, deliberate self-harm, the abuse of drugs and alcohol, and repeated acts of delinquency. The behavioural model is an alternative way of comprehending these disorders. In this model the disorders are explained in terms of factors that determine normal behaviour: drives, reinforcements, social and cultural influences, as well as internal psychological processes such as attitudes, beliefs, and expectations. The behavioural model predicts that there will not be a sharp distinction between the normal and the abnormal but a continuous graduation. This can be a useful way of considering many conditions seen by psychiatrists.

Although the behavioural model is mainly concerned with psychological and social causes, it does not exclude genetic, physiological, or biochemical aetiologies. This is because normal patterns of behaviour are partly determined by genetic factors, and psychological factors such as reinforcement have a basis in physiological and biochemical mechanisms. Also, the behavioural model employs both reductionist and non-reductionist explanations. For example, abnormalities of behaviour can be explained in terms of abnormal conditioning (a reductionist model), or in terms of a network of social influences (a non-reductionist model). For a review of the various models used in psychiatric aetiology the reader is referred to McHugh and Slavney (1986).

The contribution of scientific disciplines to psychiatric aetiology

Among the disciplines that have contributed to knowledge of psychiatric aetiology the main groups are: clinical studies and epidemiology; genetics, biochemistry, pharmacology, physiology, and neuropathology; experimental psychology, ethology, and psychoanalysis. In this section each group is discussed in turn, and the following questions are asked: What sort of problem in psychiatric aetiology can be answered by each discipline? How, in general, does each discipline attempt to answer the questions? Are there any particular difficulties in applying its methods to psychiatric disorders?

Clinical descriptive investigations

Before reviewing more elaborate scientific approaches to aetiology, attention is drawn to the continuing value of simple clinical investigations. Psychiatry was built on such studies. For example the view that schizophrenia and the affective disorders are likely to have separate causes depends ultimately on the careful descriptive studies and follow-up enquiries carried out by earlier generations of psychiatrists.

Only two examples can be given here of the many clinical investigations that have contributed in important ways to knowledge. Both are from the British literature but similar examples could have been chosen from the literature of continental Europe or America.

Anyone who doubts the value of clinical descriptive studies should read the paper by Aubrey Lewis on 'melancholia' (Lewis 1934). The paper describes a detailed investigation of the symptoms and signs of 61 cases of severe depressive disorder. It provided the most complete account in the English language, and it remains unsurpassed. It is an invaluable source of information about the clinical features of depressive disorders untreated by modern methods. Lewis's careful observations drew attention to unsolved problems including the nature of retardation, the relation of depersonalization to affective changes, the presence of manic symptoms, and the validity of the classification of depressive disorders into reactive and endogenous groups. None of these problems has yet been solved completely, but the analysis by Lewis was important in focusing attention on them.

The second example is the clinical follow-up study by Roth (1955). Elderly psychiatric patients were classified on the basis of their symptoms into five diagnostic groups: affective disorder, late paraphrenia, acute or subacute delirious states, senile dementia, and arteriosclerotic dementia. These groups were found to differ in their course. Two years later, about two-thirds of the patients with affective psychoses had recovered; about four-fifths of those with senile dementia and almost as many with arteriosclerotic dementia had died; over a half of the patients with paraphrenia were alive but still in hospital; and of those with acute confusional states, half had recovered and half had died. These findings confirmed the value of the original diagnoses, and refuted the earlier belief that affective and paranoid disorders in old age were part of a single degenerative disorder that could also present as dementia. This investigation clearly illustrates how careful clinical follow-up can clarify issues about aetiology.

Although many opportunities for this kind of research have been taken already, it does not follow that clinical investigation is no longer worthwhile. For example, a more recent clinical study describing the syndrome of bulimia nervosa has aetiological implications (Russell 1979). Well-conducted clinical enquiries are likely to retain an important place in psychiatric research for many years to come.

Epidemiology

Epidemiology is the study of the distribution of a disease in space and time within a population, and of the factors that influence this distribution. Its concern is with disease in groups of people, not in the individual person.

In psychiatry, epidemiology attempts to answer three main kinds of question: what is the prevalence of psychiatric disorder in a given population at risk; what are the clinical and social features of syndromes or forms of behaviour; and what factors may be important in aetiology?

Studies of **prevalence** can be useful for the planning of psychiatric services. Studies of **syndromes** can be useful for clinical practice; for example, epidemiological studies have shown that the risk of suicide is greatest in elderly males with certain characteristics, such as living alone, abusing drugs or alcohol, suffering from physical or mental illness, and having a family history of suicide.

Epidemiological studies of **aetiology** have been concerned with predisposing and precipitating factors, and with the social correlates of mental illness. Amongst predisposing factors, the influence of heredity has been examined in studies of families, twins and adopted people, as described in the later section on genetics. Other examples are the influence of maternal age on the risk of Down's syndrome; the psychological development of premature babies in later life; and the psychological effects of parental loss during childhood. Studies of precipitating factors include life events research, which is described in the following section on the social sciences.

There have been numerous studies of the **social correlates** of psychiatric disorder. In the United States, for example, Hollingshead and Redlich (1958) found that schizophrenia was eleven times more frequent in social class V than in social class I. In itself this finding throws no light on aetiology, but it suggests studies of other factors associated with social class (for example, poor housing). It also raises questions about the interpretation of associations; for example, do schizophrenics drift into the lower social classes when they become disabled, or were they in the lower social classes before the disorder began? Several epidemiological studies have focused on place of residence. Generally, high rates of schizophrenia have been found amongst people living in districts with poor housing and a large proportion of single-person households; whilst high rates of manic-depressive psychosis and neurosis have been found amongst those living in more prosperous districts (see, for example, Hare 1956*b*). Such results are difficult to interpret, since it is not clear whether they are directly due to the neighbourhood environment, or to other factors such as heredity, methods of child rearing, patterns of marriage, or the drift of mentally ill people into poor neighbourhoods.

The basic concept of epidemiology is that of **rate**, or the ratio of the number of instances to the numbers of people in a defined population. Instances can be episodes of illness, or people who are ill or have been so. Rates may be computed on a particular occasion (**point prevalence**), or over a defined interval (**period prevalence**). Other concepts include **inception rate**, which is based on the number of people who were healthy at the beginning of a defined period but became ill during it; and **lifetime expectation**, which is based on an estimate of the number of people who could be expected to develop a particular illness in the course of their whole life. In **cohort studies**, a group of people are followed for a defined period of time to determine the onset or change in some characteristic with or without previous exposure to a potentially important agent (for example, lung cancer and smoking).

Three aspects of method are particularly important in epidemiology—defining the population at risk; defining a case; and finding cases. It is essential that the population at risk be accurately defined. Such a population can be all the people living in a limited area (for example a country, island, or catchment area); or a subgroup chosen by age, sex or some other potentially important defining characteristic.

Defining a case is the central problem of psychiatric epidemiology. It is relatively easy to define a condition such as Down's syndrome, but until recently it has been difficult to define cases of affective disorder or schizophrenia. A major advance has been the development of standardized techniques for defining, identifying, rating, and classifying mental disorders. An example is the Present State Examination (Wing *et al.* 1974), and the associated computer programme CATEGO. This standardized interview was used, for example, in the International Pilot Study of Schizophrenia (see p. 280). As well as showing some differences in diagnostic practices (referred to on p. 83), the study showed that disorders meeting strict criteria for schizophrenia occurred in a wide variety of cultures—a finding which must be explained by any aetiological theory of this condition.

For case-finding, two methods are used. The first is to enumerate all cases known to medical or other agencies (declared cases). Hospital admission rates may give a fair indication of rates of major mental illnesses, but not of alcoholism or phobias. Moreover, hospital admission rates are influenced by many extraneous variables, such as the geographical accessibility of hospitals, attitudes of doctors, admission policies, and the law relating to compulsory admissions. The second method is to search for both declared and undeclared cases in the community. In community surveys, the best technique is often to use two stages: preliminary screening to detect potential cases with a self-rated questionnaire such as the General Health Questionnaire (Goldberg 1972), followed by detailed clinical examination of potential cases with a standardized psychiatric interview.

The social sciences

Many of the concepts used by sociologists are relevant to psychiatry. It has been noted (p. 104) that the concepts of social class and subculture have been informative in epidemiological studies in which a higher prevalence of schizophrenia has been found in the lower social classes. The concepts of stigma and labelling have been useful in analysing the handicaps of people with chronic mental illness who are living in the community; and the effects of in-patient treatment have been understood better by considering hospitals as institutions that can affect the behaviour of those who stay in them. The concept of social deviance has been useful in the study of delinquent behaviour among adolescents. Finally the concept of illness behaviour has been of value when examining the psychological consequences of physical illness.

Unfortunately, some of these potentially fruitful ideas have been used uncritically, for example in the suggestion that mental illness is no more than a label for socially deviant people—the 'myth of mental illness'. This development points to the obvious need for sociological theories to be tested by collecting appropriate data in the same way as other theories are tested.

Some of the concepts of sociology overlap with those of social psychology, for example, attribution theory (which deals with the way in which people interpret the causes of events in their lives, and ideas about self esteem). An important part of research in sociology, the study of life events, uses epidemiological methods (see below).

Transcultural studies

Studies in different societies have drawn attention to an important distinction. Biologically determined features of mental disorder are likely to be similar in different cultures, whilst psychologically and socially determined features are likely to be dissimilar. Knowledge of these variations is important in understanding the aetiology of mental disorder in individuals from immigrant groups. Thus the 'core' symptoms of schizophrenia are present in patients from widely different societies (see p. 280), but the symptoms of the less severe forms of anxiety disorder and depressive disorders differ considerably. For example in India, patients with anxiety disorders are especially likely to complain of bodily symptoms rather than emotional symptoms.

The study of life events

Epidemiological methods have been used in social studies to examine associations between illness and certain kinds of events in a person's life. Wolff studied the morbidity of several hundred people over many years and found that episodes of illness clustered at times of change in the person's life (see Wolff 1962). Rahe and his colleagues attempted to improve on the highly subjective measures used by Wolff (Rahe *et al.* 1967; Holmes and Rahe 1967). They used a list of 41 kinds of life change (e.g. of work, residence, finance, and family relationships) and weighted each one according to its apparent severity, for example 100 for the death of a spouse, 13 for a spell of leave for a serviceman.

As these last two examples show, the changes could be desirable or undesirable, and within or outside the person's direct control. In a study of men serving in the United States Navy, Rahe *et al.* (1970) found that those with the highest scores on the list of life changes developed more illnesses of all kinds. This finding suggested that the risk of illness was greater at a period of life change than at an uneventful time.

In subsequent studies the term life events has been commonly used. Research workers have modified the earlier methods in five ways:

(1) in order to reduce memory distortion, limits are set to the period over which events are to be recalled;

(2) efforts are made to date the onset of illness accurately;

(3) attempts are made to exclude events that are not clearly independent of the illness, for example losing a job because of poor performance;

(4) events are characterized in terms of their nature (for example, losses or threats) as well as their severity; and

(5) data are collected with a semi-structured interview, and improved rating methods are used.

A further development, due largely to the work of Brown and Harris (1978), is the idea that whilst not acting as stressors, some circumstances can make a person more vulnerable to stressful life events, and other circumstances can protect against them. For example, it is held that, among women, vulnerability is increased by having the care of small children, and decreased by having a confidant who can share problems.

This idea of protective factors has been used to explain the observation that some people do not become ill even when exposed to severe adversities—a finding that is particularly evident in studies of the effects of adverse family factors on children (see Rutter 1985*b*). There are, however, two major difficulties about the ideas of vulnerability factors and protective factors., First, if the findings are accepted there could be wholly different explanations for them, such as genetic or psychological differences between individuals. Second, the findings can be disputed on two kinds of grounds—technical and conceptual. The technical grounds are concerned with the validity of measures and the appropriateness of the statistical procedures. The conceptual grounds are concerned with the uncertainties of making a sharp distinction between protective and vulnerability factors on the one hand, and stressors on the other. Thus a confiding marriage has been treated as a protective factor, but divorce as a stressor. At present the notions of protective and vulnerability factors are attractive but still controversial (see, for example, Tennant and Bebbington 1978; Paykel 1983).

Even if the results of studies of life events are accepted, their importance may be less than at first appears. For example in one study (Paykel *et al.* 1969), events involving the loss or departure of a person from the immediate social field of the respondent ('exit events') were reported in 25 per cent of patients with depressive disorders but only 5 per cent of controls. This difference was significant at the 1 per cent level and appears impressive but Paykel (1978) has questioned its real significance, and carried out the following calculation.

The incidence of depressive disorder is not accurately known, but if it is taken to be 2 per cent for new cases over a six-month period, then a hypothetical population of 10 000 people would yield 200 new cases.

Paykel's study showed that exit events occurred to 5 per cent of people who did not become cases of depressive disorder; therefore, in the hypothetical population, exit events would occur to 490 of the 9 800 people who were not new cases. Amongst the 200 new cases, exit events would occur to 25 per cent, that is, 50 people. Thus the total number of people experiencing exit events would be 490 plus 50, or 540, of whom only 50 (less than 1 in 10) would develop depressive disorders. Hence the greater part of the variance in determining depressive disorder must be attributed to something else. Subsequent studies have given further reasons for caution. For example, in a community study, Henderson *et al.* (1982) found that antecedent life stress accounted for only about 4 per cent of the variance of scores on the General Health Questionnaire.

Migration and psychiatric disorder

Moving to another country, or even to an unfamiliar part of the same country, is a life change that has been suggested as a cause of mental disorder. Immigrants have been shown to have higher rates of mental disorder than similar people who remained in their own country. For example, in a well-known study Ødegaard (1932) found higher rates of schizophrenia among Norwegian-born immigrants who lived in the United States than among the population of Norway. (This study is also considered on p. 304). This finding may indicate that migration is a cause of mental disorder, but it can be explained in another way. Thus, amongst people who migrate, personal characteristics may make them unsettled in their country of origin, and may also predispose to mental disorder. Whilst Ødegaard's study compared migrants with people remaining in the country of origin, other studies have compared migrants with the native-born population of the new country. The latter studies are even more difficult to interpret, because higher rates of mental disorder among the migrants might reflect generally higher rates in their country of origin (that is, amongst those staying at home as well as those moving away). Alternatively, a higher rate among migrants might not reflect migration in itself, but a fall in their social class due to, for example, difficulty in finding work. As explained above, rates of certain psychiatric disorders are higher among people of lower social class. A further complexity is that different groups migrate for different reasons. For example, Europeans may move to America for economic reasons, whilst the Vietnamese migrated to escape from war. For all these reasons, it is not surprising that there is no simple relationship between migration and mental disorder (see Leff 1981 for a review).

Genetics

Genetic investigations are concerned with three issues—the relative contributions of genetic and environmental factors to aetiology; the mode of inheritance of disorders that have a hereditary basis; and the mechanisms of inheritance. In psychiatry, important advances have been made with the first two issues; but so far little progress has been made with the third.

Research methods in genetics are of three broad kinds: population and family studies, cytogenetics, and molecular genetics. Population and family studies are mainly concerned with estimating the contribution of genetic factors and the mode of inheritance; whilst cytogenetics and molecular genetics provide information about mechanisms of inheritance. To date, genetic research in psychiatry has relied mainly on methods of population genetics. For detailed accounts of the topics in this section, see McGuffin (1984), and Cloninger *et al.* (1985).

The contribution of genetic factors

Methods of population genetics are used to assess risk in three groups of people—families, twins, and people who have been adopted. In **family-risk studies** the investigator determines the risk of a psychiatric condition among the relatives of affected persons, and compares it with the expected risk in the general population. (The affected persons are usually referred to as index cases or **probands**). Such studies require a sample selected in a strictly defined way. Moreover, among the relatives it is not sufficient to ascertain the current prevalence of a psychiatric condition, because some of the population may go on to develop the condition later in life. For this reason, investigators use corrected figures known as **expectancy rates** (or morbid risks).

Family risk studies have been used extensively. Examples will be found in the chapters on affective disorders (see p. 237) and schizophrenia (see p. 292). Since these studies cannot distinguish between inheritance and the effects of family environment, they are the least satisfactory way of determining the genetic contribution. They are useful chiefly in pointing to the need for other kinds of investigation.

In **twin studies** the investigator seeks to separate genetic and environmental influences by comparing concordance rates in uniovular (monozygous, or MZ) and binovular (dizygous, or DZ) twins. Such studies depend crucially on the accurate determination of zygosity. If concordance for a psychiatric disorder is substantially higher in MZ twins than in DZ twins, a major genetic component is presumed. More precise estimates of the relative importance of heredity and environment can be made by comparisons between MZ twins reared together, and MZ twins reared apart from early infancy. A high concordance between MZ twins reared apart is strong evidence for a genetic aetiology. An example of such studies will be found in the chapter on schizophrenia (see p. 294).

Adoption studies provide another useful method of separating genetic and environmental influences. These studies are concerned with children who, since early infancy, have been reared by non-related adoptive parents. Two main comparisons can be made. First, the frequency of the disorder can be compared between two groups of adopted people: those whose biological parents had the illness, and those whose biological parents did not have it. If there is a genetic cause, the rate will be greater in the former. Secondly, in the case of adopted people who have a psychiatric disorder, the frequency of the disorder can be compared between the biological parents and the adoptive parents. If there is a genetic cause, the rate will be greater in the former. Such studies may be affected by a number of biases, such as the reasons why the child was adopted, non-random assignment of the children on socioeconomic status, and the effects on adoptive parents of raising a difficult child. An example is provided by the studies of schizophrenia reviewed on p. 294.

The mode of inheritance

This is assessed by using special statistical methods to test the fit of pedigree or family data with alternative models of inheritance. Usually four models are considered: the single major locus model, which may be dominant, recessive, or sex-linked, and a mixed model of major genes operating together. Attempts to study psychiatric disorders in this way have generally led to equivocal results, despite considerable research particularly on schizophrenia and affective disorder.

Linkage studies

Linkage studies seek to identify the locus of a gene on the chromosomes by studying the extent to which it co-segregates with a 'marker' gene. Genetic markers are readily identifiable characters with known single modes of inheritance and two or more common alleles (alternative genes). They include blood groups, human leucocyte antigens (HLA), and certain physiological abnormalities (for example, colour blindness). Large family pedigrees are studied to determine to what extent two genes 'stick together', departing from Mendel's law of independent assortment. From this, using appropriate mathematical techniques, it can be estimated how closely the gene loci are likely to be linked on a chromosome. Many such studies have been carried out with psychiatric disorders but so far no linkage has been found with a marker of this kind.

Linkage studies work best when there is an established mode of inheritance for the disorder, and high penetrance (i.e. nearly all those who carry the gene develop the disorder). Neither schizophrenia nor affective disorders are of this kind, and the value of linkage studies is likely to be limited. Among disorders of interest to psychiatrists, this method has so far been applied successfully only to Huntington's chorea (see p. 366), a condition due to a dominant gene with complete penetrance (provided subjects are followed up to a sufficient age). As mentioned below, recent advances in molecular genetics are likely to greatly increase the scope for linkage analysis.

Cytogenetic studies

These studies are concerned with identifying structural abnormalities in chromosomes and associating them with disease. In psychiatry the most important example concerns Down's syndrome (mongolism). In this condition two kinds of abnormality have been detected: in the first kind there is an additional chromosome (trisomy): in the second kind the chomosome number is normal, but one chromosome is unusually large because a segment of another chromosome is attached to it (translocation) (see p. 843). Other examples involve the X and Y chromosomes. In Turner's syndrome there is only one sex chromosome (XO); while in three other syndromes there is an extra one—XXY (Klinefelter's syndrome), XXX, and XYY.

Molecular genetics

It seems likely that advances in cell and molecular biology will contribute to knowledge of psychiatric aetiology. These advances stem from technical innovations. The first is the discovery of bacterial enzymes called **restriction endonucleases**, which cut DNA at sites with particular base sequences. The second advance is in techniques for reproducing fragments of human DNA by inserting them into bacterial plasmids (small circular pieces of DNA in bacteria) and encouraging the bacteria to reproduce. Techniques of this kind have been used to develop **genomic libraries**, i.e. bacterial cultures which contain almost the whole of the human genome. The third advance is the construction of **gene probes**, that is short sequences of DNA, either from the genome or copied from messenger RNA. Copies are made by employing enzymes from tumour viruses that reverse the normal sequence, in which RNA is made from DNA. It is possible to incorporate radioactive bases into the short DNA sequences thereby allowing a sequence to be identified; and because DNA sequences stick to sequences that are similar, the radioactive fragment can be used to search for and label a specific base sequence in mixtures of DNA which have been separated by electrophoresis. This procedure is called **gene mapping**.

These new techniques can be used in several ways. Human DNA shows many harmless variations in its base sequences. These variations may either provide new sites for restriction endonucleases, or remove existing ones. By changing the sites at which the enzymes cut the DNA, the variations lead to alterations in the length of cut fragments. For this reason these harmless variations in base sequence are called **restriction fragment length polymorphisms**. Because they are scattered throughout the human genome, they can be used as markers for linkage studies and it has been estimated that if two to three hundred were identified, it would be possible to obtain linkages for any genetic trait. This could be done without any knowledge of the biochemical basis of the genetic trait. (The Huntington's chorea gene was localized in this way.) By using additional technical procedures it is sometimes possible to isolate the particular gene that is responsible for the pathological state.

Restriction enzyme technology has also made possible the definition of chromosome deletions and rearrangements that are too small to be identified by microscopy. Such studies may increase knowledge of the causes of mental handicap.

Another approach which may have particular relevance to psychiatry is to isolate messenger RNAs which are expressed only in the nervous system. It is possible to identify from these RNAs not only the gene products but also the genes involved—a kind of reverse genetics. A number of genes for regulatory functions within the nervous system have already been cloned and sequenced, including those for the acetylcholine receptor and sodium channels. Gene probes are also being used to search for viral DNA in the brains of patients with degenerative diseases of the nervous system, including Alzheimer's disease.

At present these approaches cannot be applied to polygenic disorders, and schizophrenia may be of this kind. However, in the long term, it may be possible to learn more about these disorders by using novel approaches. In these approaches, 'candidate genes' would be identified; these are genes that might be involved in an abnormality of brain metabolism that can be identified in the disorder. Then a search would be made for restriction fragment length polymorphisms that are associated with the disease, and finally the relation of the two would be examined. This approach has already produced information about abnormal lipid metabolism in coronary artery disease. Other developments promise to increase knowledge of the control of development in the nervous system, and the causes of developmental defects. For an excellent review of this complex and developing area of research the reader should consult Weatherall (1986).

Biochemical studies

These studies can be directed either to the causes of disease, or to the mechanisms by which disease produces its effects. The methods of biochemical investigation are too numerous to consider here, and it is assumed that the reader has some knowledge of them. The main aim here is to consider some of the problems of using biochemical methods to investigate psychiatric disorder.

The first problem is that the living human brain in not accessible to detailed biochemical study by ethically acceptable methods. Moreover, because most psychiatric disorders do not lead to death (other than by suicide), post-mortem material is not widely available except among the elderly. Even indirect studies are difficult. Concentrations of substances in lumbar cerebrospinal fluid have an uncertain relationship to their concentrations in the brain. Concentrations in blood are even more indirectly related to those in the brain, and concentrations in the urine are more remote still.

The second problem is that in animals there is no obvious parallel to mental disorder in man. Attempts have been made to find models for behaviour seen in mental disorder, for example by subjecting animals to extreme stress, but none is convincing. As pointed out in the next section, the most useful biochemical studies in animals are those linked with pharmacological investigations.

The third problem is that even when biochemical changes have been found in mental disorder, it is difficult to know whether they are causal. They could be the result of alterations in diet or activity secondary to the disorder, to the effects of the drugs used in treatment, or to stress responses to the experimental procedure. Moreover, even if the biochemical changes are connected with the disorder itself, they may still be effects rather than causes.

Some of the findings of biochemical research are given in subsequent chapters, especially those on affective disorders and schizophrenia. At this point a few examples will be given of the different kinds of investigation. **Post-mortem studies of the brain** provide the most direct evidence of chemical changes within it. Unfortunately, interpretation of the findings is difficult because it must be established that any changes in the concentrations of neurotransmitters or enzymes did not occur after death. Moreover, because psychiatric disorders do not lead to death directly, the ultimate cause of death is another condition (often bronchopneumonia, or the effects of a drug overdose) that could have caused the observed changes in the brain. Even if this possibility can be ruled out, it is still possible that the chemical findings are the results of treatment rather than of disease. For example, in schizophrenic patients the density of dopamine receptors has been found to be increased in the nucleus accumbens and caudate nucleus (Owen *et al.* 1978). This finding might be interpreted as supporting the hypothesis that schizophrenia is caused by changes in dopamine function in these areas of the brain. The finding could equally be the result of long-term treatment with antipsychotic drugs, which block dopamine receptors and might lead to a compensatory increase of receptors. Owen *et al.* provided some evidence against this alternative when they demonstrated similar changes in two patients who had apparently never received antipsychotic drugs; but the point is still unsettled. In any case, even if it is eventually possible to rule out the effects of treatment, it must still be shown that the observed changes in receptors are not merely a compensatory mechanism to balance a primary disorder in another neurotransmitter system.

Even more serious problems arise when attempts are made to infer changes in the brain from **studies of cerebrospinal fluid, blood, and urine**. There are scientific doubts whether changes in the composition of lumbar c.s.f. represent changes in the brain. There are also ethical limitations on the circumstances when c.s.f should be obtained from psychiatric patients. Ingenious attempts have been made to infer biochemical events in the brain from measurements of substances in the blood. For example, it is known that the rate of synthesis of brain 5-hydroxytryptamine (5-HT) depends on the concentration of tryptophan in the brain; and that the latter is in turn largely determined by the concentration of unbound tryptophan in plasma. Findings of lowered free plasma tryptophan among depressed patients have therefore been interpreted as supporting the hypothesis that depressive disorder is characterized by—and may be the result of—low concentrations of 5-HT at crucial sites in the brain. Subsequent work has not confirmed these original findings consistently (see Green and Costain 1979). Even if the findings were to be confirmed, it would be hazardous to draw conclusions about events in the brain from such indirect evidence. The real advances that have followed investigations of blood and urine have been in the study not of mental disorder but of mental subnormality. A number of rare metabolic disorders have been identified which are associated with serious forms of mental retardation. Phenylketonuria is the best known example. In these disorders, metabolites in blood and urine do give an accurate reflection of biochemical processes in the brain (see Chapter 21).

Recently, novel methods of studying biochemical events in the living brain have become available and have been used in some studies of psychiatric disorders. These methods include nuclear magnetic resonance (NMR) spectroscopy, single photon emission computerized tomography (SPECT), and positron emission tomography (PET). These techniques are developing quickly. At the time of writing (1988) NMR spectroscopy can yield information about energy metabolism in the brain but the technique is limited by its insensitivity relative to PET. SPECT can be used to study the distribution in the brain of substances labelled with radioactive tracers; and PET can give information about cerebral blood flow and metabolism by using short-lived isotopes of oxygen. PET can also provide information about receptor sites in the brain by using other radiolabelled ligands. For example, methylspiperone labelled with ^{11}C has been used to study dopamine receptor affinity in schizophrenic patients; no abnormality was found but this could be due to methodological problems (Herold *et al.* 1985). If these techniques can be made more sensitive and their range extended, they may provide non-invasive ways of studying biochemical abnormalities in the living brain. At present, their use is limited to special research centres because of the cost of equipment; this limitation applies particularly to PET, which requires access to a cyclotron to make the necessary short-lived isotopes. For further information the interested reader should consult Trimble (1986).

Pharmacology

The study of effective treatment of disease can often throw light on aetiology. In psychiatry, because of the great problems of studying the brain directly, research workers have studied the actions of effective psychotropic drugs in the hope that the latter might indicate the biochemical abnormalities in disease. Such an approach must, of course, be used cautiously. If an effective drug blocks a particular transmitter system, it cannot be concluded that the disease is caused by an excess of that transmitter. The example of parkinsonism makes this clear; anticholinergic drugs modify the symptoms but the disease is due to a deficiency in dopaminergic transmission, not an excess of cholinergic transmission.

It is assumed here that the general methods of neuropharmacology are familiar to the reader, and attention is focused on the particular difficulties of using them in psychiatry. There are two main problelms. First, most psychotropic drugs have more than one action, and it is often difficult to decide which is relevant to the therapeutic effects. For example, although lithium carbonate has a large number of known pharmacological effects, it has so far been impossible to find one that explains its remarkable effect of stabilizing the mood of manic-depressive patients.

The second difficulty arises because the therapeutic effects of many psychotropic drugs are slow to develop, while most pharmacological effects identified in the laboratory are quick to appear. For example, it has been suggested that the beneficial effect of antidepressant drugs depends on alterations in the re-uptake of transmitter at presynaptic neurons. However, changes in re-uptake occur quickly, while the therapeutic effects are usually delayed for about two weeks.

Recent studies in animals have concentrated on changes that occur in brain neurotransmitter receptors during long-term psychotropic drug treatment. These changes are interesting because the time course is similar to that of the development of therapeutic effects. Also, antidepressant treatments that have different pharmacological effects when first given may, after repeated administration, produce similar effects on neurotransmitter receptor. Thus it appears that the late effects of both antidepressant drugs and electroconvulsive shock are to produce a common change in postsynaptic noradrenergic receptors, a change which may be important in mediating the antidepressant effect. [See Charney *et al.* (1981) for a review.]

Other pharmacological studies in animals and humans have identified subtypes of receptor for many of the classical neurotransmitters, and these subtypes seem to have distinct functional roles. It is possible that drugs could be developed which would affect the particular receptor subtypes, thereby reducing side-effects (see, for example, Peroutka *et al.* 1986).

Endocrinology

Endocrine studies can be employed directly to relate concentrations of circulating hormones to disease states. For example, plasma levels of free and total cortisol are high in depressed patients because cortisol is produced at an increased rate (see Sachar 1982). This cortisol production might be secondary to the stressful experience of being ill, or it might be part of the causation of the depression. Tests of endocrine regulation have been used in an attempt to distinguish these possibilities. For example, some patients with a depressive disorder show an abnormal response to dexamethasone. This glucocorticoid normally suppresses the output of cortisol and its effect is greatest if given about midnight, when the 'programme' for the next day's output of cortisol is determined. In normal subjects, this suppression lasts throughout the following day, but in some depressed patients it is less sustained. This difference can be interpreted as showing that some depressed patients have an abnormality in the control mechanisms for cortisol production rather than a simple increase in the circulating concentration of the hormone. However, the abnormality is not confined to depressive disorders and its significance is not clear. [See Braddock (1986) for a review.]

The secretion of some hormones is controlled by mechanisms involving neurotransmitters. Neuroendocrine challenge tests have been developed in which a particular monoamine pathway is stimulated with a specific drug and the subsequent hormone response determined in plasma. This procedure acts as a dynamic test of the monoamine system, and in patients with psychiatric disorders it has revealed more abnormalities than measurement of basal hormone output has demonstrated. For example, a reliable finding in depressed patients is a blunted growth hormone response to the noradrenergic agonist, clonidine. However, such an abnormality is not easy to interpret. While it may indicate that depressed patients have decreased brain noradrenergic function, it could also be attributed to a generalized deficiency in growth hormone release, or perhaps be secondary to a particular feature of depressive disorder, such as sleep disturbance (for a review see Checkley 1980).

Physiology

Physiological methods can be used to investigate the cerebral and peripheral disorders associated with disease states. Several methods have been used: studies of cerebral blood flow, particularly in chronic organic syndromes; electroencephalographic (EEG) studies; and a variety of psychophysiological methods, including measurements of pulse rate, blood pressure, blood flow, skin conductance, and muscle activity. These psycho-physiological measures can be interpreted in at least two ways. The first interpretation is straightforward. The data are used as information about the activity of peripheral organs in disease; for example, to determine whether electromyographic (EMG) activity is increased in the scalp muscles of patients who complain of tension headaches. The second interpretation depends on the assumption that peripheral measurements can be used to infer changes in the state of arousal of the central nervous system. Thus increases in skin conductance, pulse rate, and blood pressure are taken to indicate greater 'arousal'.

Much use has been made of EEG techniques in psychiatric research. Routine EEG recordings have aided the study of the relationships between epilepsy and psychiatric disorders, but otherwise have not been very useful. More recently visual, auditory, and somatosensory evoked potentials have been studied. Because the exact significance of these forms of electrical activity is not understood, the findings have been most valuable when they have shown differences in activity between the two sides or different areas of the brain in patients, rather than generalized differences in response between patients and normal subjects. For example Cooper *et al.* (1985) found that, compared with healthy people, schizophrenic subjects more often show abnormalities in the lateralization of somatosensory evoked cortical potentials.

Neuropathology

Neuropathological studies attempt to answer the question whether a structural change in the brain (localized or diffuse) accompanies a particular kind of mental disorder. In the past, many post-mortem investigations were carried out on the brains of patients who had suffered from schizophrenia or affective disorders. No changes were found. It was therefore assumed that these mental disorders were disorders of function rather than of structure (hence the name functional psychosis is sometimes used as a collective name for these conditions). Recent neurochemical studies (mentioned above) can be regarded as a logical extension of this kind of enquiry, but at a different level of organization.

Neuropathological investigations have an obvious application to the aetiology of dementia. Another important finding has been the post-mortem identification of lesions of the mamillary bodies in the brains of patients who had the amnestic syndrome. In this syndrome there is no general dementia, but profound disorder of memory (see p. 354).

Experimental and clinical psychology

A characterictic feature of the psychological approach to psychiatric aetiology is the idea of a continuity between the normal and the abnormal.

This idea leads to investigations that attempt to explain psychiatric abnormalities in terms of processes determining normal behaviour. An example is research into learning mechanisms as causes of neuroses (see Chapter 6).

A second characteristic of the psychological approach is its concern with the interaction between the person and his environment. The psychological approach differs from the social approach in being concerned less with environmental variables, and more with the person's ways of processing information coming from the external environment and from his own body. Some of these ideas will become clearer when coping mechanisms are discussed later in this section.

A third characteristic of psychological research into mental disorder is an emphasis on factors maintaining abnormal behaviour. Psychologists are less likely to regard behaviour disorders as resulting from internal disease processes, and more likely to assume that persisting behaviour is maintained by reinforcement. This has led, for example, to research findings suggesting that some abnormal behaviour of chronic schizophrenic patients is maintained by social reinforcement, and that some anxiety neuroses are maintained by avoidance of situations that provoke anxiety.

Experimental psychology, more than neurochemistry or neurophysiology, makes use of broad theoretical schemes. Familiar examples are operant and Pavlovian conditioning. Such schemes can be used to provide a framework for experimental work, and to construct plausible explanations of neurotic disorders (for example, Mowrer 1950). So far these schemes have not proved particularly useful. It has been more fruitful to apply to psychiatric problems some of the less elaborate theoretical constructs of psychology. One useful application is concerned with **coping mechanisms**. This term has been applied to certain ways in which people deal with changes in their environment. It is used in a narrow sense and a wide sense. Thus, some psychologists limit the word to those responses to a stressor that reduce any stress reaction that might otherwise ensue. Others apply it more widely to any response whether or not it reduces the stress reaction.

Coping mechanisms have two components: internal events and observable behaviour. After bereavement a person's coping mechanisms might be: first, a return to former religious beliefs (an internal mechanism) and second, joining a social club to combat loneliness (an observable behaviour). Research into coping mechanisms is much concerned with the ways in which meaning is attached to events. The same event, for example a change of job, can be seen as a threat by one person and as a challenge by another. It is presumed that the meaning attached to an event by a person is an important determinant of his response to it.

To date, in the study of psychiatric problems, psychology has been more successful in the use of experimental methods than in the application of theoretical constructs. This kind of experimental approach to patients, sometimes known as experimental psychopathology, has been referred to already (p. 2).

Ethology

Ethology is concerned with the observation and description of behaviour, particularly behaviour that appears to be innate. Ethology has contributed indirectly to psychiatric aetiology by suggesting simple techniques of observation that have been valuable in studying the behaviour of children. Another contribution has been the study of critical periods of development, during which the learning of a particular behaviour takes place more readily than at any other time.

Ethological studies of primates have examined the effects of separating infants from their mothers. When the primate mother is removed and the environment remains otherwise unchanged, the infant first makes frequent distress calls and then becomes active, apparently searching for her. Soon this activity decreases and the infant shuffles about in a hunched posture, calling less often. If the mother is returned to the infant, the two usually unite immediately. The infant's hunched posture soon disappears, and within two weeks he is as active as before the separation. When the separation is longer, the infant takes longer to readjust after its mother returns. Comparable methods of observation have been used to study human infants and young children (see, for example, Blurton-Jones 1972).

Other studies have examined ways in which emotional bonds develop between infant and mother in the first years of life, and the long-term effects on behaviour of disturbing this relationship, e.g. by isolating the infant from its mother for a time. Not surprisingly, there are both parallels and differences between animals and humans, but the methods and concepts developed in this work with animals have proved valuable in the study of human infants. [For a concise account of aspects of ethology relevant to psychiatry see Hinde (1985).]

Psychoanalysis

The method of investigation used in psychoanalysis differs from the methods considered so far in that is was developed specifically for the study of psychiatric disorders. It arose from clinical experiences and not from work in the basic sciences. Psychoanalysis is characterized by a particularly elaborate and comprehensive theory of both normal and abnormal mental functioning. Compared with experimental psychology, it is much more concerned with the irrational parts of mental activity. Because psychoanalytic theory provides a comprehensive range of explanations for clinical phenomena, it has a wide appeal. However, the features that make it all-embracing also make it impervious to scientific testing.

Freud originated psychoanalytic theory, but many other workers contributed to it or constructed alternative theories. This section refers only to Freud's theory and not to the contributions of these other analysts, which are described elsewhere in the book. This section also focuses on the basic ideas of psychoanalysis; hypotheses about particular syndromes are discussed in other chapters.

It is recommended that this account be supplemented by reading some of Freud's original writings, for example the New Introductory Lectures or the papers cited in the reading list at the end of this chapter. It is also valuable to study a critical evaluation of psychoanalytic theory (for example, Farrell 1981 or Dalbiez 1941).

Most of the data of psychoanalytic enquiry are obtained in the course of psychoanalytic treatment. They consist of an account given by the patient of his thoughts, fantasies, and dreams, together with his memories of childhood experiences. By adopting a passive role, the analyst tries to ensure that material of the interviews is the result of the patient's free associations, and not of his own preconceptions. The analyst also interprets some of the patient's statements and behaviour in terms of analytic theory. In analytic writings it is sometimes difficult to distinguish clearly between the patient's statements and the analyst's interpretations.

As pointed out earlier in this chapter, an important distinction can be made between understanding and explanation. In the sense of this distinction psychoanalysis is a highly elaborate form of understanding which seeks to make psychiatric disorders more intelligible. It does not lead to explanatory hypotheses that can be tested experimentally— although attempts have been made to test some of the low-level hypotheses (see Fisher and Greenberg 1977).

Farrell (1981) has pointed out that psychoanalysis is an example of a broad theory of a kind found in other branches of knowledge. Such theories can be useful in science by providing a framework within which other ideas can be developed. Darwin's theory of evolution is an example of a useful theory of this kind. To be useful, such theories must be able to incorporate new observations as they come along. Darwinian theory survives partly because it has proved compatible with later observations from genetics and from work on the fossil record. On the other hand, psychoanalytic theory has not proved compatible with advances in the neurosciences in such a satisfactory way. Its present status is more akin to that of the insights into human nature provided by great creative writers. These insights succeed in deepening our understanding of man, but they are not part of scientific knowledge. Psychiatrists need a wide understanding of human nature. They can achieve it from some of the ideas of psychoanalysis, but they can also achieve it from great works of literature.

At this point a summary will be presented of the main features of Freud's theory. The summary is too short to do full justice to Freud's ideas, but long in relation to the space devoted to some other methods of enquiry.

Many of the ideas in the theory were current before Freud began his psychological studies (see Sulloway 1979) but he succeeded in combining them ingeniously. A central feature was Freud's elaborate concept of the unconscious mind. He supposed that all mental processes originated there. Some of these processes were allowed to enter the conscious mind freely (for example, sensations), some not at all (the unconscious proper), and some occasionally (most memories, which made up the 'preconscious'). The unconscious mind, according to Freud, had three characteristics that were important in the genesis of neurosis: it was divorced from reality; it was dynamic in that it contained powerful forces; and it was in conflict with the conscious mind. These three characteristics will be discussed in turn.

The unconscious mind was divorced from reality in several ways. It contained flagrant contradictions and paradoxes, and it tended to telescope situations and fantasies that were widely separated in time. These features were well illustrated, in Freud's view, by dream-analysis. He believed that the manifest content of a dream (what the dreamer remembered) could be analysed back to a latent content, which was an infantile wish. The sleeper was thought to perform 'dream work' to translate the latent to the manifest content. He did this by using a series of mechanisms such as: condensation (several images fused into one); displacement (of feelings from an essential to non-essential features of an object); and secondary elaboration (rear-rangement of the assembled elements). Freud attached importance to this dream theory because he supposed the composition of neurotic symptoms to be like that of dreams, though with greater secondary elaboration.

Secondly the unconscious mind was dynamic; that is, it contained impulses that were kept in equilibrium by a series of checks and balances. In Freud's early writings, these impulses were regarded as entirely sexual. Later he placed more emphasis on aggressive impulses. Sexual wishes were supposed to be active even in infancy, receding by about the age of four and then remaining latent until re-emergence at puberty. In Freud's view, psychosexual development not only began early but was long and complicated. The first stage of organization was oral; that is the sexual drive was activated by stimulation of the mouth by sucking and touching with the lips. The second stage was anal, that is the drive was activated by expelling or retaining faeces. Only in the third stage did the genitals become the primary source of sexual energy. Sometimes these stages were not passed through smoothly. The libido (the energy of the sexual instincts) could become fixated (partially arrested) at one of the early stages. When this happened the person would tend to engage in infantile patterns of behaviour or regress to such patterns under stress. In this way the point of fixation determined the nature of any neurosis that developed later in life.

As libido developed, not only was it activated in these three successive ways, but its object was also supposed to change. Self-love came first, to be followed in both boys and girls by love of the mother. Next, still in infancy, boys focused their sexual wishes more intensely upon the mother while developing hostile feelings towards the father (the Oedipus complex). Girls developed the reverse attachments. These attachments came to an end through repression of sexual impulses. As a result the capacity to feel shame and disgust developed and the child passed into the latency period. Finally, at puberty the sexual impulses emerged again, and were directed into relationships with other adults.

The third aspect of the unconscious mind was its struggle against the conscious mind. This conflict was regarded as giving rise to anxiety that could persist throughout life and generate neurotic symptoms. One of Freud's lasting contributions was his idea that anxiety could be reduced by a variety of defence mechanisms, which could be discerned at times in the behaviour of healthy people. These mechanisms are considered on pp. 34–5.

Freud's ideas have had considerable influence in certain countries. In Great Britain most psychiatrists take the view (which is shared by the authors of this book) that some of the basic ideas are useful in understanding patients, for example the ideas about defence mechanisms; but that the details of the theory are generally unhelpful, either as an aetiological explanation of clinical syndromes or as a guide to practice. Much of the theory is expressed in an elaborate series of metaphors which, as explained above, cannot be subjected to verification.

It is stressed again that it is impossible to do justice to Freud's theories in the space of this chapter, and it is important to read some of his original papers.

Relationship of this chapter to the psychiatric syndromes

This chapter has reviewed several diverse approaches to aetiology. It may be easier for the reader to put these approaches in perspective when reading the chapters on the different psychiatric syndromes. A useful first step would be to read the section on the aetiology of depression on pages 237–51.

Further reading

Farrell, B. A. (1981). *The standing of psychoanalysis*. Oxford University Press, Oxford.

Freud, S. (1981). *From the history of an infantile neurosis (the 'wolf man').* Reprinted in Penguin Freud Library, Vol. 9, pp. 227–366. Penguin, Harmondsworth.

Freud, S. (1924*a*). *Neurosis and psychosis.* Reprinted in Penguin Freud Library. Vol. 10, pp. 209–18. Penguin, Harmondsworth.

Freud, S. (1924*b*). *The loss of reality in neurosis and psychosis.* Reprinted in Penguin Freud Library, Vol. 10, pp. 219–29. Penguin, Harmondsworth.

Freud, S. (1916–17). *Introductory lectures on psychoanalysis.* Reprinted in Penguin Freud Library, Vol. 1. Penguin, Harmondsworth.

Henderson, A. S. (1988). *An introduction to social psychiatry.* Oxford University Press, Oxford.

Jaspers, K. (1963). *General psychopathology* (trans, J. Hoenig and M.W Hamilton) pp. 301–11 (The psychology of meaning); 355–64 (The basic law of psychological understanding); and 383–99 (Pathological psychogenic reactions). Manchester University Press, Manchester.

Shepherd, M. (ed.) (1985). *The scientific foundations of psychiatry.* Cambridge University Press, Cambridge.

Weatherall, D. J. (1986). *The new genetics and clinical practice.* (2nd edn). Oxford University Press, Oxford.

5 Personality disorder

The term personality refers to enduring qualities of an individual shown in his ways of behaving in a wide variety of circumstances. All doctors should be able to assess personality so that they can predict how patients are likely to behave when ill. The psychiatrist shares this general concern about the personality of his patients but his interests go further. This is because among psychiatric patients personality not only determines how they react when ill; it can also prepare the ground for illness and can sometimes be mistaken for illness.

Features of personality make some people more vulnerable to develop emotional disorder when experiencing stressful events. Thus when faced with difficulties, a person who has always worried about minor problems is more likely to develop an anxiety disorder than a person who is less prone to worry. With this degree of vulnerability in the personality, abnormal behaviour occurs only in response to stressful events. In more abnormal personalities, unusual behaviour occurs even in the absence of stressful events. At times, these anomalies of behaviour may be so great that it is difficult to decide, solely on the patient's state at the time, whether they are due to personality or to mental disorder.

The conceptual distinction between personality and mental disorder is valuable in everyday clinical practice, but it is not always easy to make. Central to the concept is the duration of the unusual behaviour in question. If the person previously behaved normally and then begins to behave abnormally, he is said to have a mental disorder. If his behaviour has always been as abnormal as it is now, he is said to have a personality disorder. The distinction is easy when behaviour changes quickly (as in an acute manic disorder), but difficult when it changes slowly (as in some cases of schizophrenia).

Some German psychiatrists (for example, Jaspers 1963) added a third criterion, that illness arises from causes within the person and is not a reaction to circumstances. This led, in turn, to the idea that conditions clearly provoked by stressful events should not be regarded as illness but as reactions of the personality. Although there is some merit in this idea, it can no longer be sustained because recent research shows that stressful events also occur before the onset of some conditions (such as schizophrenia) that were regarded as illnesses rather than reactions by the earlier authors.

The assessment of personality

Although assessment has been discussed in Chapter 2, two points need to be mentioned again. The first is that judgements of personality of the kind made in everyday life should not be applied to patients. If we meet a new colleague at work, we are likely to judge his personality largely from his behaviour in the first few weeks of meeting him. We assume that this represents his habitual way of behaving. Occasionally we are wrong; for example, the new colleague may have been more guarded than he usually is. Generally, however, this sort of everyday assessment is accurate.

The personality of patients cannot be judged in the same way. It is a common mistake to place too much weight on the pattern of behaviour observed in the ward or in the out-patient clinic where behaviour is likely to reflect a combination of personality and mental disorder. Personality can be judged only from reliable accounts of past behaviour.

The second point concerns psychological tests. It is tempting to suppose that they give better information about personality than the clinician can obtain from interviews with the patient and informants. This is not so, because most personality tests are affected by the presence of mental disorder, and because they measure traits that are seldom important in clinical practice. In the assessment of personality there is no substitute for careful interviewing of the patient and other informants.

The concept of abnormal personality

Some personalities are obviously abnormal: for example those of violent and sadistic people who repeatedly harm others and show no remorse. It is, however, impossible to draw a sharp dividing line between the normal and the abnormal. Indeed, it is even difficult to decide what criterion should be used to make this distinction. Two criteria have been suggested, the first statistical and the second social. On the statistical criterion, abnormal personalities are quantiative variations from the normal, and the dividing line is decided by a cut-off score. In principle, this scheme is attractive, as it parallels the approach used successfully in defining abnormalities of intelligence. It has obvious value in research where tests are required to measure personality in groups of patients. However, in clinical work with individual patients it is of limited value.

The second approach can also be applied to a scheme in which abnormal personalities are regarded as quantitative variations from the normal. However, the arbitrary dividing line is determined by social criteria rather than by a statistical cut-off. The criteria are that the individual suffers from his own personality or that other people suffer from it. Thus someone with an abnormally sensitive and gloomy personality suffers himself, while a person who is emotionally cold and aggressive makes other people suffer. Although such criteria are subjective and lack the precision of the first approach, they correspond well with the realities of clinical practice and they have been adopted widely.

Given the conceptual problems involved, it is hardly surprising that it is difficult to frame a satisfactory definition of abnormal personality. The definition in the International Classification of Diseases is not without difficulties but is widely accepted: 'deeply ingrained maladaptive patterns of behaviour recognizable by the time of adolescence or earlier and continuing through most of adult life, although often becoming less obvious in middle or old age. The personality is abnormal either in the balance of its components, their quality and expression or in its total aspect. Because of this . . . the patient suffers or others have to suffer and there is an adverse effect on the individual or on society'.

It is important to recognize that people with abnormal personalities may have favourable as well as unfavourable traits. No matter how abnormal the personality, enquiries should always be made about positive features as well as unfavourable ones. These are particularly important in planning treatment.

How ideas about abnormal personality developed

The concept of abnormal personality in psychiatry can be traced back to the beginning of the nineteenth century when the French psychiatrist Pinel described '*manie sans délire*'. Pinel applied this term to patients who were prone to unexplained outbursts of rage and violence but were not deluded (at that time delusions were regarded as the hallmark of mental illness; and *délire* is the French term for delusion). Presumably this group of patients included not only those who could now be regarded as having antisocial personality, but also mentally ill patients who were not deluded, for example some with mania. [See Kavka (1949) for a translation of the relevant section of the second edition of Pinel's book, first published in 1801.]

Although other writers, such as the American Benjamin Rush (1830), were interested in similar clinical problems, it was an English physician who took the next important step forward. In 1835, J. C. Prichard, senior physician to the Bristol Infirmary, published his *Treatise on insanity and other disorders of the mind*. After referring to Pinel's *manie sans délire*, he suggested a new term, **moral insanity**, which he defined as a 'morbid perversion of the natural feelings, affections, inclinations, temper, habits, moral dispositions and natural impulses without any remarkable disorder or defect of the intellect or knowing or reasoning faculties and in particular without any insane delusion or hallucination' (Prichard 1835, p. 6). Although this description included the violent patients described by Pinel, Prichard clearly had a wider group in mind, since he added: 'a propensity to theft is sometimes a feature of moral insanity and sometimes it is its leading if not its sole characteristic' (p. 27). Prichard's category of moral insanity, like Pinel's *manie sans délire*, may have included affective disorders, for he wrote (p. 18): 'a considerable proportion among the most striking instances of moral insanity are those in which a tendency to gloom or sorrow is the predominant feature', and furthermore: 'a state of gloom and melancholy depression occasionally gives way . . . to the opposite condition of praeternatural excitement' (p. 19).

It is clear that Prichard also included patients who would now be regarded as having antisocial personality disorder. Thus he wrote (p. 23) 'eccentricity of conduct, singular and absurd habits, a propensity to perform the common actions of life in a different way from that usually practised, is a feature of many cases of moral insanity but can hardly be said to contribute sufficient evidence of its existence. When however such phenomena are observed in connection with a wayward and intractable temper with a decay of social affections, an aversion to the nearest relatives and friends formerly beloved—in short, with a change in the moral character of the individual, the case becomes tolerably well marked'.

Later in the nineteenth century, it became understood that mental illness could occur without delusions, and that affective disorders and schizophrenia were separate entities. Nevertheless, the concept of moral insanity continued, although with a more restricted meaning. Thus it was applied by Henry Maudsley to someone described as having 'no capacity for true moral feeling—all his impulses and desires, to which he yields without check, are egoistic, his conduct appears to be governed by immoral motives, which are cherished and obeyed without any evident desire to resist them' (Maudsley 1885, p. 171). Maudsley commented on the current dissatisfaction with the term moral insanity, which he referred to as 'a form of mental alienation which has so much the look of vice or crime that many people regard it as an unfounded medical invention' (p. 170).

The next step towards modern ideas was the introduction by Koch (1891) of the term **psychopathic inferiority** to denote this same group of people with marked abnormalities of behaviour in the absence of mental illness or intellectual impairment. Later, the word inferiority was replaced by personality to avoid the judgemental overtones. Kraepelin at first shared the general doubt about the best way to classify these people, and it was not until the 8th edition of his textbook that he finally adopted the term **psychopathic personality** and devoted a long chapter to it. He described seven separate types: excitable, unstable, eccentric, liars, swindlers, antisocial, and quarrelsome.

A further step was taken by another German psychiatrist, Schneider. Whereas Kraepelin's seven types of psychopathic personality included only those causing inconvenience, annoyance or suffering to other people, Schneider extended the concept to include those causing suffering to themselves and not necessarily to others. He included for example people with markedly depressive or insecure characters. In Schneider's usage psychopathic personality covered the whole range of abnormal personality, not just antisocial personality. In this way the term came to have two meanings: the wider meaning of abnormal personality of all kinds, and the narrower meaning of antisocial personality.

Confusion about the term psychopathic personality does not end with Schneider's broader definition. Two other usages call for attention. The first originates in the work of the Scottish psychiatrist Sir David Henderson, who in 1939 published an influential book *Psychopathic states*. In this he began by defining psychopaths as people who, although not mentally subnormal, 'throughout their lives or from a comparatively early age, have exhibited disorders of conduct of an antisocial or asocial nature, usually of a recurrent or episodic type which in many instances have proved difficult to influence by methods of social, penal and medical care or for whom we have no adequate provision of a preventative or curative nature'. So far this corresponds to the familiar narrow definition of psychopathic personality. However, Henderson extended his definition by referring to three groups of psychopaths: the predominantly aggressive, the predominantly passive or inadequate, and the creative. This division had the effect of widening the concept once again. The predominantly aggressive group includes not only those who are repeatedly aggressive, but also those prone to suicide, drug addiction, and alcohol abuse. The group of passive and inadequate personalities includes unstable, hypochondriacal and sensitive people, pathological liars, and those with a schizoid nature. The group of creative psychopaths is so wide as to be of little value; thus the examples given by Henderson included T. E. Lawrence and Joan of Arc, who were both creative in different ways but had little in common. In retrospect, Henderson's main contribution was to draw attention to the inadequate personalities.

Yet another variation in the meaning of the term psychopathic was introduced in the 1959 Mental Health Act for England and Wales. In this Act, psychopathic disorder was defined in Section 4(4) as: 'a persistent disorder or disability of mind (whether or not including subnormality of intelligence) which results in abnormally aggressive or seriously irresponsible conduct on the part of the patient, and requires or is susceptible to medical treatment'. This definition returns to the central idea of aggressive or irresponsible acts that cause suffering to other people. However, the definition is unsatisfactory because it includes the requirement for or response to treatment—criteria that may be administratively convenient but cannot be justified logically. Not surprisingly, many difficulties have attended the use of this definition. (More recent mental health legislation is discussed in the Appendix.)

The two meanings of psychopathic personality—the wider meaning of all abnormal personality, and the narrower meaning of antisocial personality—persist to the present day. Because of this ambiguity, this textbook avoids the term, and uses personality disorder and antisocial personality to denote the wide and narrow senses respectively.

The classification of abnormal personalities

Before considering how abnormal personalities can be classified, it is important to realize that each category in any classification scheme represents an ideal type which few patients fit exactly. To quote Schneider (1950) 'Any clinician would be greatly embarrassed if asked to classify into appropriate types the psychopaths (that is abnormal personalities) encountered in any one year. There are only a few cases in which one of the characteristic types of description or combinations can be applied without further qualification. Human beings resist precise measurement and, unlike the phenomena of disease, abnormal individuals cannot be classified neatly in the manner of clinical diagnosis.'

Two main approaches to classification have been used. The first is purely descriptive, using terms such as weak-willed and aggressive. The second is both descriptive and aetiological, for it labels abnormal personalities by reference to a syndrome of mental disorder that they partly resemble. For example, personalities characterized by eccentricity and emotional coldness are called schizoid, because these features resemble some of those found in schizophrenic patients, and because it has been suggested that the personality and the mental disorder illness share a common cause. Both approaches have been incorporated in the International Classification of Diseases, where the descriptive terms impulsive and histrionic are used alongside the aetiological term schizoid.

In Table 5.1, the classification of personality disorders in the draft of ICD10 is compared with that in DSMIIIR. The two schemes are broadly similar, the differences being of two kinds: the use of different names for similar types of personality disorder, and the inclusion in DSMIIIR of three types that do not appear in ICD10—and in ICD10 of one that does not appear in DSMIIIR. The differences in nomenclature are:

(1) the use in ICD10 (draft) of the term dyssocial to describe the personality disorder referred to as antisocial in DMSIIIR (in this book the term antisocial is used);

(2) the use in ICD10 (draft) of anankastic as the preferred term for the personality disorder called obsessive-compulsive in DSMIIIR; and

(3) the use in ICD10 (draft) of anxious as the preferred term for the personality disorder called avoidant in DSMIIIR.

Table 5.1. Classification of personality disorders

ICD10 (draft)	DSMIIIR*
Paranoid	Paranoid
Schizoid	Schizoid
	Schizotypal
Dyssocial	Antisocial
Impulsive	Borderline
Histrionic	Histrionic
	Narcissistic
Anankastic (obsessive-compulsive)	Obsessive-compulsive
Anxious (avoidant)	Avoidant
Dependent	Dependent
Other	Passive-aggressive

* The order of listing has been altered slightly to facilitate comparison between the schemes.

Four categories of abnormal personality are found in only one of the systems. (All four are described in this chapter). ICD10 (draft) contains one such category: impulsive personality disorder (described in this chapter on p. 136). DSMIIIR contains three such categories: schizotypal (see p. 137); borderline (see p. 137); and passive aggressive (see p. 138).

Although it is necessary to classify abnormal personalities for the purpose of collecting statistics, it is often better in everyday clinical work to give a brief description of the main features of the personality. Examples of such a description are: sensitive, lacking in self-confidence and prone to worry unreasonably; or abnormally aggressive, with little evidence of feelings for other people or of remorse. Above all the clinician should avoid the error which Jaspers (1963) called 'pseudo-insight through terminology'. In other words, he should not be misled into thinking that, because he has assigned a personality to an ICD category, he understands any more about the patient.

Clinical features of abnormal personalities

This section contains an account of the abnormal personalities that appear in the International Classification of Diseases. This is followed by a brief review of the additional or alternate classes used in DSMIIIR. Although the account given here follows the broad scheme of the International Classification of Diseases, the various kinds of abnormal personality are not described in the same order. Instead obsessional and histrionic personality disorders are discussed first, because they can be related most easily to observations of people in everyday life.

Obsessive-compulsive personality disorder

Obsessive-compulsive personality disorder is the term used in DSMIIIR. In ICD10 (draft) the preferred term for this personality disorder is **anankastic** following the usage of Kahn (1928). The only advantage of this term is that it avoids the erroneous implication of an inevitable link between this type of personality and obsessional disorders. (People with this kind of personality are also liable to develop anxiety and depressive disorders.)

Before describing obsessive-compulsive personality disorder, it is useful to review the expression of obsessional traits in someone with a normal personality. Such a person is dependable, precise, and punctual. He sets high standards and keeps to social rules. He is determined and persists at his tasks, despite difficulties. His moods are stable so that he can be relied upon to be the same from day to day. However, even within a normal personality, these qualities have another side; at times determination may give way to obstinacy, precision to preoccupation with unimportant detail, and high moral standards to bigotry. Moreover the qualities that make for stable moods can be expressed as a humourless approach to life.

In obsessive-compulsive personality disorder, these features are more extreme. One of the most striking is a lack of adaptability to new situations. The person is rigid in his views and inflexible in his approach to problems. Change upsets him and he prefers a safe routine that he knows. Such a person lacks imagination and fails to take advantage of opportunities. The qualities that make for reliability in a normal personality, are expressed in an obsessive-compulsive personality disorder as an inhibiting perfectionism that makes ordinary work a burden and leaves the person immersed in trivial detail. High moral standards are exaggerated to become painful guilty preoccupation with wrongdoing, which stifles enjoyment. People with this disorder seem without humour, ill at ease when others are enjoying themselves, moralistic in their opinions, and judgemental in their attitudes. They are often mean to the point of being miserly and do not enjoy giving or receiving gifts.

Indecision is another prominent feature of such people. They find it hard to weigh up the advantages and disadvantages of new situations; they delay decisions, and often ask for more and more advice. They fear making mistakes, and after deciding they worry lest the choice was wrong.

Sensitivity to criticism is a related feature of this personality. There is an undue concern about other people's opinions, and an expectation of being judged as harshly as they judge themselves.

Outwardly, such people often show little emotion. However, they are given to smouldering and unexpressed feelings of anger and resentment, often provoked by other people who have interfered with their routine of life. Such angry feelings may be accompanied by obsessional thoughts and images of an aggressive kind, even in those who do not develop the full syndrome of an obsessional disorder.

Histrionic personality disorder

This term is used in both ICD10 (draft) and DSMIIIR. The important features of this kind of personality are self-dramatization, a craving for novelty and excitement, and a self-centred approach to personal relationships.

In a normal personality, minor histrionic traits can be socially advantageous. People with such traits make lively, engaging company, and are popular guests; they do well in amateur dramatics, and are entertaining public speakers. They tend to wear their emotions on their sleeves and are easily moved to joy or tears, but the feelings soon pass.

When these qualities are exaggerated in histrionic personality disorder, they become less acceptable. The person dramatizes himself as a larger than life character; he seems to be playing a part, incapable of being himself. He often seems unaware that other people can see through his defences. Instead of the enjoyment of novelty found in a person with histrionic personality traits, in histrionic personality disorder there is a restless search for new experiences, coupled with short-lived enthusiasms, readiness to boredom and craving for novelty. The tendency to be self-centred may be greatly exaggerated in histrionic personality disorder. The person lacks consideration for others, appearing to think only of his own interests and enjoyment. He appears vain, inconsiderate, and demanding and may go to extreme lengths to force other people to fall in with his wishes. Emotional 'blackmail', angry scenes, and demonstrative suicide attempts are all part of the stock-in-trade of such a person. He displays emotions readily, exhausting others with tantrums of rage or dramatic expressions of despair. He seems to feel little of the emotions he expresses; he recovers quickly and often seems surprised that other people are not prepared to forget the scenes as quickly as he is himself.

With these qualities is combined a capacity for self-deception that can at times reach astounding proportions. The person goes on believing himself to be in the right when all the facts show that he is not. He is able to maintain elaborate lies long after other people have seen through them. This pattern of behaviour is observed in its most extreme form in 'pathological liars' and swindlers.

Some of these qualities are normal in children, particularly the transient enthusiasms, the easy change from laughter to tears, the enjoyment of make-believe and the egocentricity. This had led some psychiatrists to apply the term immature to this type of personality. However, the term is imprecise and is best avoided.

In histrionic personality disorder, the sexual life is also affected. Especially in women there is often sexual provocation combined with frigidity. They engage in displays of affection and are flirtatious, but they are often incapable of deep feelings and may fail to reach orgasm.

Schneider applied the term **attention-seeking psychopaths** to a particular group of people with histrionic personality disorder. Such people constantly strive to seem more than they are, and make unreasonable demands on others.

Paranoid personality disorder

This term is used in both ICD10 (draft) and DSMIIIR. The central features of this kind of abnormal personality are suspiciousness and sensitivity. As already mentioned, minor obsessional and histrionic traits can add socially desirable qualities to a normal personality. There is no such positive side to paranoid traits. Even when these traits form only a small part of the personality, they add a distrust that goes beyond ordinary caution and a sensitivity to rebuff that is a handicap to social relationships. In the paranoid personality disorder, this suspiciousness can be shown in several ways. The person may be constantly on the look out for attempts by others to get the better of him, to deceive him or play tricks on him. He may doubt the loyalty of other people and be unable to put his trust in them. As a result, he appears touchy and suspicious. He does not make friendships easily and may avoid involvement in groups. He may be perceived by other people as secretive, devious, and self-sufficient to a fault. He seems to have little sense of humour or capacity for enjoyment. Such personality traits are fertile grounds for jealousy. (See also Chapter 10.)

People with paranoid personalities appear argumentative and stubborn. Presented with a new proposal, they are overcautious and look for ways in which it might be designed to harm their own interests. Some engage in litigation that is prolonged long after any non-paranoid person would have abandoned it.

An important feature of the paranoid personality is a strong sense of self-importance. The person often has a powerful inner conviction that he is unusually talented and capable of great achievements. This idea is maintained, in the face of modest accomplishments, by paranoid beliefs that other people have prevented him from fulfilling his real potential, that he has been let down, tricked, swindled, or deceived. Sometimes, these self-important ideas are crystallized round a central overvalued idea that persists for many years.

Sensitivity is another important aspect of the paranoid personality.

People of this kind readily feel shame and humiliation. They take offence easily and see rebuffs where none are intended. As a result, other people find them difficult, prickly and unreasonable. Both Schneider (1950) and Kretschmer (1927) used the term **sensitive** to describe such a person. Kretschmer also described how, when faced with a deeply humiliating experience, such people develop suspicious ideas that can easily be mistaken for persecutory delusions. These 'sensitive ideas of reference' are considered further in Chapter 10.

The affective personality disorders

Some people have life-long disorders of mood regulation. They may be persistently gloomy (depressive personality disorder), or habitually in a state of inappropriate elation (hyperthymic personality disorder). A third group alternate between these two extremes (cycloid or cyclothymic personality disorder). These types of personality disorder have been described for many years, and are readily recognized in clinical practice. However, they do not appear in either ICD10 (draft) or DSMIIIR. This is because both systems classify these disorders under disorders of mood rather than disorders of personality, that is as 'persistent affective states' (cyclothymia or dysthymia) in ICD10, or as cyclothymia in DSMIIIR. People with **depressive personality disorder** seem to be always in low spirits. They take a persistently gloomy view of life, anticipating the worst outcome of every event. They brood about their misfortunes and worry unduly. They often have a strong sense of duty. They show little capacity for enjoyment and express dissatisfaction with their lives. Some are irritable and bad tempered.

People with **hyperthymic personality disorder** are habitually cheerful and optimistic and show a striking zest for living. They may also show poor judgement, and may be uncritical and hasty in coming to conclusions. Their habitual cheerfulness is often interrupted by periods of irritability, especially when their aims are frustrated. This kind of personality is seldom so extreme as to cause suffering. A few contentious people in this group were called pseudo-querulants by early German authors.

People with **cycloid personality disorder** alternate between the extremes of depressive and hyperthymic described above. This instability of mood is much more disruptive than either of the others. Such people pass through periods in which they are highly cheerful, active, and productive. At these times they take on additional commitments at work and in their social lives. Eventually the mood changes. Instead of confident optimism, there is a gloomy defeatist approach to life. Energy is reduced. Activities taken up with so much relish in the phase of elated mood, are now felt to be a burden. In this phase, different but equally unwise decisions may be made, and opportunities that could be managed are refused. In time, there is a change either to a normal mood or back to a further state of mild elation.

Schizoid personality disorder

This term is used in both ICD10 (draft) and DSMIIIR. In this disorder, the person is introspective and prone to engage in fantasy rather then take action. He is emotionally cold, self-sufficient, and detached from other people. The name schizoid was suggested by Kretschmer (1936), who held that there is an aetiological relationship between this kind of personality and schizophrenia (see Chapter 9). However, the two are not associated invariably, and the term should be used descriptively without implying any causal relationship with schizophrenia.

The most striking feature is lack of emotional warmth and rapport. People with this disorder appear detached, aloof and humourless, and seem incapable of expressing affection or tenderness. As a result, they do not make intimate friendships and often remain unmarried. They show little concern for the opinions of other people and pursue a lonely course through life. Their hobbies and interests are solitary and are more often intellectual than practical.

These people tend to be introspective. Their inner world of fantasy is often extensive but it lacks emotional content. They are more likely to be concerned with intellectual problems than with ideas about other people.

If the disorder is extreme, the individual is seen as cold, callous, seclusive, ill at ease in company, and without friends. Lesser degrees of the same traits, appearing as part of a normal personality, may confer advantages in some ways of life. For example, some forms of academic work may be carried out more effectively by a person who can detach himself from social activities for long periods, and can concentrate in a detached and unemotional way on intellectual problems.

Antisocial personality disorder

In ICD10 (draft) this personality disorder is called dyssocial. The preference of this book is for the term antisocial, which appears in DSMIIIR. People with this disorder show a bewildering variety of abnormal features. Several attempts have been made to identify an essential core to the disorder. The most useful of these recognizes four features: failure to make loving relationships, impulsive actions, lack of guilt, and failure to learn from adverse experiences.

The failure to make loving relationships is accompanied by self-centredness and heartlessness. In its extreme form there is a degree of callousness that allows the person to inflict cruel, painful, or degrading acts on others. This lack of feeling is often in striking contrast to a superficial charm, which enables the person to make shallow and passing relationships. Sexual activity is carried on without evidence of tender feelings. Marriage is often marked by lack of concern for the partner, and sometimes by physical violence. Many marriages end in separation or divorce.

The characteristic impulsive behaviour is often reflected in an unstable work record marked by frequent dismissals. It is also shown in the whole pattern of life, which seems to lack any plan or persistent striving towards a goal.

This impulsive behaviour, coupled with a lack of guilt or remorse, is often associated with repeated offences against the law. Such offences begin in adolescence with petty acts of delinquency, lying, and vandalism; many of them show a striking indifference to the feelings of other people, and some include acts of violence or callous neglect. Often the behaviour is made more extreme by the effects of alcohol or drugs.

People with sociopathic personality make seriously inadequate parents, and may neglect or abuse their children. Some have difficulty in managing their finances or in organizing family life in other ways.

Vivid descriptions of antisocial personality disorder are contained in Cleckley's book *The mask of sanity* first published in 1941. These still make valuable reading (Cleckley 1964.)

Impulsive personality disorder

People with this kind of personality disorder cannot control their emotions adequately, and are subject to sudden unrestrained outpourings of anger. These outbursts are not always confined to words, but may include physical violence leading at times to serious injury. Unlike people with antisocial personalities, who also exhibit explosions of anger, this group do not have other difficulties in their relationships. This disorder is recognized in ICD10 (draft) but not in DSMIIIR.

Avoidant personality disorder

These people are persistently anxious. They are ill at ease in company, fearing disapproval or criticism, and worrying that they will be embarrassed. They are cautious about new experiences and meeting people they do not know, and timid in the face of everyday hazards. As a result they have few close friends and avoid social demands such as taking new responsibilities at work. These people differ from schizoid personalities because they are not emotionally cold; indeed they crave the social relationships that they cannot attain. In ICD10 (draft) the term anxious personality disorder is preferred, with 'avoidant' as an accepted alternative.

Dependent personality disorders

This kind of personality disorder is recognized in both ICD10 (draft) and DSMIIIR. People with this disorder appear weak-willed and unduly compliant, falling in passively with the wishes of others. They lack vigour and show little capacity for enjoyment. They avoid responsibility and lack self-reliance. Some dependent people are more determined, but achieve their aims by persuading other people to assist them, whilst protesting their own helplessness.

If married, such people may be protected from the full effects of their personality by support from a more energetic and determined spouse who is willing to make decisions and arrange activities. Left to themselves, some drift down the social scale and others are found among the long-term unemployed and the homeless.

Other categories of abnormal personality

This section is concerned with several descriptions of personality disorder that are included in the American scheme (DSMIIIR) but not in the International Classification of Diseases.

Schizotypal personality disorder

The term schizotypal is used in DSMIIIR to denote a personality disorder characterized by social anxiety; inability to make close friendships; eccentric behaviour; oddities of speech (for example speech that is vague and excessively abstract); inappropriate affect; suspiciousness; ideas (but not delusions) of reference; other odd ideas (for example, ideas about telepathy and clairvoyance that are not normal in the culture); and unusual perceptual experiences (such as the sensing of the presence of a dead person by a person who is not recently bereaved). It has been suggested by the authors of DSMIIIR that this kind of personality is related to schizophrenia. More evidence is needed before this kind of personality is accepted as a separate category for diagnostic purposes.

Narcissistic personality disorder

People with this disorder are characterized by a grandiose sense of self-importance and by a preoccupation with fantasies of unlimited success, power, and intellectual brilliance. They crave attention from other people but show few warm feelings in return. They exploit others and seek favours that they do not return. Most people of this kind could be classified as having histrionic personality disorders, and others seem to fit into the group of antisocial personalities. Intermediate forms are inevitable in any scheme of classification of personality, and there seems to be no strong reason at present for assigning an additional category to people with these characteristics.

Borderline personality disorder

The term borderline has been used in psychiatry in two ways. The first describes symptoms and behaviours that are thought to be genetically related to schizophrenia. These conditions are considered on p. 291. The second usage refers to a kind of personality disorder. Until recently this personality disorder was not clearly defined; the central idea was that the person was 'unstable' but this instability was usually described in psychodynamic terms such as weak ego functions.

Spitzer *et al.* (1979) suggested objective criteria for the diagnosis of borderline personality disorder, and similar criteria are now incorporated in DSMIIIR in which borderline personality disorder is characterized by eight features, five of which are required to make the diagnosis. These features are: unstable relationships, impulsive behaviour that is harmful to the person (for example, reckless spending, uncontrolled gambling, binge-eating, or stealing), variable moods, undue anger, recurrent suicidal threats or behaviour, uncertainty about personal identity, persistent feelings of boredom, and 'efforts to avoid real or imagined abandonment'. The category is broad, encompassing several abnormal aspects of personality that can be classified in other ways. Indeed many of the people who meet the DSMIII criteria also meet criteria for histrionic, narcissistic, and antisocial personality disorder (Pope *et al.* 1983). It is therefore too early to be certain whether this category represents a separate group of abnormal personalities.

Passive-aggressive personality disorder

This term is applied to a person who, when demands are made upon him for adequate performance, responds with some form of passive resistance, such as procrastination, dawdling, stubbornness, deliberate inefficiency, pretended forgetfulness, and unreasonable criticism of people in authority.

Sjöbring's classification

Sjöbring devised a scheme which has been widely used in Scandinavia but not elsewhere. The reader may encounter this scheme in some of the important Scandinavian monographs published in English. The classification uses three dimensions to characterize personality, adding a fourth for intelligence (which is called **capacity**). The first of the three dimensions is **stability**. This resembles introversion–extraversion. A superstable person is cold, introverted, and interested in ideas, whilst a substable one is warm, sociable, and active. The second dimension is **solidity**. A supersolid person is dependable, deliberate, and self-possessed, whilst a subsolid one is inconstant, quick, and subjective in judgements. The third dimension is **validity**. A supervalid person is venturesome, expansive, and self-confident, whilst a subvalid person is retiring, cautious, and easily worried. The interested reader will find an account of this scheme in English in the paper by Sjöbring (1973).

Terms to avoid

Two commonly used terms should be avoided. Both tend to be used when the doctor has not thought clearly enough about the precise nature of his patient's difficulties. The first is **inadequate personality**, a term often employed in a pejorative way. In place of this term, it is better to specify precisely the ways in which the person is inadequate to the demands of life. Such a specification will lead to more constructive ideas about helping the person to cope better.

The second is **immature personality**, a vague term which implies a non-specific discrepancy between the patient's behaviour and his chronological age. In place of this term, it is better to specify the exact nature of this immaturity, whether it is in social relationships, or the control of emotions, or willingness to take responsibility, or elsewhere. This precise description of the patient's problems is more likely to lead to a constructive approach than the mere labelling of the personality as immature.

Epidemiology

Until recently there was little information about the frequency of personality disorders in the general population. However, information on antisocial personality disorder has recently come from a large community survey in three sites in the USA—Baltimore, Newhaven, and St Louis (Robins *et al.* 1984). In each site over 3000 people were interviewed, using DSMIII criteria. The lifetime prevalence was between 2.1 and 3.3 per cent. The rates were higher in people aged 25–44 than in older people. Older people should have lifetime rates as high as or higher than those of younger people, because they have passed through as much or more of the period of risk. The findings are thus anomalous. Possibly, the older people were less willing or less able to recall relevant information than were the younger ones.

Aetiology

Since little is known about the factors accounting for normal variations in personality, it is not surprising that knowledge about the causes of personality disorder should be incomplete. Research is made difficult by the long interval between potentially relevant events in early life, and the time when disorder comes to attention in the adult. It might be expected that the more extreme the disorder, the more obvious its causes would be. In keeping with this expectation, there is more information about antisocial personality disorder than about the other disorders. Nevertheless it is more convenient to begin by considering what is known about these other disorders.

General causes of personality disorder

Genetic causes

Although there is some evidence that normal personality is partly inherited, there is little evidence about the genetic contribution to personality disorders. Investigations of normal variations are illustrated by the work of Shields (1962), who studied 44 pairs of monozygotic twins, some of whom had been separated at birth. On personality tests, the scores of pairs of twins brought up apart were as similar as those of pairs of twins reared together, suggesting a substantial genetic influence. It has been suggested (for example, by Mayer-Gross *et al.* 1969) that personality disorders are merely extremes of genetic variation. However, there is no direct evidence to test this hypothesis.

It has been suggested that schizotypal personality disorder is related genetically to schizophrenia. Kendler *et al.* (1981) found some support for this idea in a study of adoptees: more of the biological relatives of schizophrenic adoptees had this kind of personality than did relatives of controls. However, Torgersen (1984) started with 44 probands with schizotypal personality disorder, looked for schizophrenia in the co-twins, and found no cases.

A second question is whether schizotypal personality has its own genetic basis (unrelated to schizophrenia). There is little evidence on this point but Torgersen (1984) found an excess of schizotypal personality disorder among the co-twins of probands with schizotypal personality disorder, suggesting a genetic contribution of aetiology.

Body build

The idea that body build is related to temperament is illustrated by the common belief that fat men are jolly. Kretschmer (1936) attempted to study the association scientifically. He described three types of body build: **pyknic** (stocky and rounded), **athletic** (with strong development of muscles and bones), and **asthenic** or **leptosomatic** (lean and narrow). Kretschmer suggested that pyknic build was related to the cyclothymic type of normal personality, and to the cycloid type of abnormal personality (cyclothymes are variable in mood). Asthenic build was thought to be related to the schizothymic type of normal personality and the schizoid type of abnormal personality (schizothymes are cold, aloof, and self-sufficient). Kretschmer's findings must be viewed cautiously because he made subjective judgements of personality and did not use statistics.

Sheldon *et al.* (1940) repeated these studies using more quantitative methods. Instead of assigning physique to one of three types, he rated it along three dimensions. **Endomorphy** signified 'predominance of soft roundness'; **mesomorphy** 'predominance of muscle, bone, and connective tissue', and **ectomorphy** 'predominance of linearity and fragility'. After elaborate measurements each person was given a score that indicated his position on the three dimensions: thus 711 indicated extreme endomorphy, whilst 444 indicated the midpoint on all three dimensions. Sheldon also attempted to rate personality objectively, but unfortunately chose dimensions that are no longer in general use. **Viscerotonia** denoted relaxation and enjoyment of comfort; **somatotonia** denoted assertiveness and energy; while **cerebrotonia** indicated strong inhibitory controls and a tendency to choose symbolic expression instead of action (Sheldon *et al.* 1942).

Sheldon's efforts at more precise measurement did not reveal any simple relationship between body build and personality. Interest in the subject has declined in recent years. In any case, even if such an association were to be proved, its significance would be difficult to explain. The most likely link would presumably be through genetic causes of both variables.

Relation to mental illness

As already mentioned, Kretschmer suggested not only a relationship between personality and body build, but also an association between personality and mental illness. On this view, some disorders of personality are partial expressions of a process—most probably genetic—that causes illness. Schizoid personalities are conceived as part way to schizophrenia, and cycloid personalities as part way to manic depressive psychosis. Although this theory is without convincing support, it lingers on in the names cycloid and schizoid. There could be some less specific genetic connection between mental disorder and personality disorder, as suggested by reports of an increased frequency of various kinds of personality abnormality among relatives of schizophrenic patients (see p. 295) and of patients with manic-depressive disorder (see p. 239).

Psychological theories

Although it is generally agreed that upbringing must affect the development of normal personality, little is known about the extent and nature of its influence in shaping abnormal personalities. This lack of information has allowed many rival theories of psychological development to flourish. Because none of these offers a satisfactory explanation of disorders of personality, only a brief account will be given of the two widely adopted schemes and reference made to some other theories. For further information on these theories, the reader is referred to Hall and Lindzey (1980).

Freud's theories: In this scheme, emphasis is placed on events in the first five years of life. It is supposed that crucial stages of development (oral, anal, and genital) must be passed through successfully if personality development is to proceed normally (see Chapter 4). Certain predictions are made about the effects of failure at particular stages; for example, that serious difficulties at the anal stage will result in an obsessional personality disorder. The scheme allows for some modifications of personality at a later age through identification with people other than the parents, but these are thought to be less important than the earlier influences.

The scheme is comprehensive and flexible enough to enable clinicians to construct a retrospective explanation of many of the personality disorders that they encounter among their patients. Some patients are helped by an understandable explanation of their problems. However, the scheme is unsatisfactory as a scientific account of abnormal personality because this same flexibility makes it impossible to generate crucial tests of the hypotheses.

Jung's theory is difficult to grasp because he chose to explain it in a particularly abstruse kind of metaphor. However, the scheme resembles Freud's in placing the greatest emphasis on internal psychic events rather than social influences. Unlike Freud, Jung thought of personality development as a life-long process. Indeed he referred to events in the first part of life as merely 'fulfilling one's obligations', and applied this term to severing ties with parents, finding a spouse, and starting a family. Jung was more concerned with changes that occur later and reach completion only when a person is ready to face death.

Other theories: **Adler** in his individual psychology rejected the idea of libido development and proposed, instead, that personality develops through efforts to compensate for feelings of inferiority. The **neo-Freudians**, Fromm, Horney, and Sullivan, emphasized social factors in development rather than the biologically determined stages in Freud's scheme, though the three authors had different opinions about the details of this social development. **Erikson's** scheme was essentially similar to Freud's in its early stages, though the nomenclature was different. Erikson placed more emphasis on events in adolescence, to which Freud gave little importance.

None of these schemes provides a convincing explanation for the personality disorders described in this chapter, so they will not be elaborated further.

Studies of childhood influences on personality development

Even in young infants, marked differences can be seen in such characteristic activities as patterns of sleeping and waking, approach and withdrawal from new situations, the intensity of emotional responses, and span of attention. Although these differences have been shown to persist into the childhood years, they do not seem to be closely related to adult personality traits (see Berger 1985.)

Considerable attention has been given to the effects on personality development of disturbances in parent–child relationships, particularly maternal deprivation. However, although such deprivation has been proposed as a cause of antisocial personality (see p. 146), there is no convincing evidence that it leads to other kinds of personality disorder.

Causes of antisocial personality

Genetic causes

There are no satisfactory twin studies directly concerned with the inheritance of antisocial personality. Some indirect evidence was provided by Lange (1931), who studied 13 pairs of monozygotic pairs in which one of each pair had committed a criminal offence. Of the 13 co-twins, as many as ten had offended. Moreover in one of the three discordant pairs, the proband had committed his offence after a head injury. On the other hand, among 17 pairs of binovular twins of the same sex, in which the proband was a criminal, only two co-twins had offended. As criminal behaviour cannot itself be inherited, the results of this study presumably reflect the inheritance of certain kinds of personality, including antisocial disorders. Lange reported that the personalities of the MZ twins were usually similar; for example, both were explosive and excitable, or both were weak-willed and shy; while DZ twins did not resemble each other so much in their personalities.

These striking findings must be viewed cautiously because the study had methodological shortcomings. The numbers were small and the selection of cases may have been biased. However, similar conclusions were reached from part of a larger study carried out in America by Rosanoff *et al.* (1934). In a study of 340 twin pairs they identified those in which at least one had offended in adult life. Among the 33 monozygous pairs, 22 had co-twins who had offended. Among the 23 dizygous pairs, only three had a criminal co-twin.

Another source of evidence is the study of people separated from antisocial parents by adoption at birth. Conflicting results have been obtained from such investigations, perhaps because the criterion of antisocial behaviour (usually criminal convictions) was subject to many influences other than those of personality.

Cadoret (1978*b*) attempted to study 190 adoptees who had been separated at birth from parents who showed persistent antisocial behaviour. He examined those adoptees who had been reared in a permanent home, and compared them with a control group of adoptees whose parents were not antisocial. The findings must be accepted cautiously because about 30 per cent of the subjects refused to be interviewed. Of the adult descendants of antisocial parents, 22 per cent had been diagnosed as having antisocial personality, while none of the descendants of controls had this diagnosis. This was true irrespective of whether the biological father or mother had shown antisocial behaviour. However, among the offspring, antisocial behaviour disorder was diagnosed more often in men than women. (Cadoret also found an increased rate of hysteria among the women, and suggested that this condition might be an alternative expression of the same genetic endowment.) These findings did not appear to be accounted for by differences in the families of adoption. However, in the sample as a whole, the number of antisocial symptoms in the offspring was related to psychiatric problems in the adoptive parents. Two other investigations support this evidence that the adopted children of antisocial biological parents have an increased rate of antisocial behaviour (Crowe 1974; Cadoret *et al.* 1975).

Other studies start with a group of adoptees who have shown antisocial behaviour. These studies show an excess of antisocial behaviour in the biological parents of the adoptees as compared with the biological parents of children who are not antisocial (Schulsinger 1982). However, the number of cases is not great. Thus in Schulsinger's study of 57 biological parents of antisocial adoptees, only four showed antisocial personality disorders. Even when a wide definition of antisocial personality disorder was adopted which included criminality, alcoholism, and hysterical personality traits, the figure was still only 14.

Chromosomal abnormalities

These have been suggested as an occasional cause of abnormally aggressive behaviour, following the discovery that about 3 per cent of patients in a maximum security hospital had the XYY karyotype (Jacobs *et al.* 1965). Since this report first appeared it has become known that the incidence of the XYY karyotype in the general population is higher than was thought at the time. The number found in the special hospital, though rather high, is much less remarkable than had originally been supposed.

Cerebal pathology and cerebal maturation

People with antisocial personality seem so different from normal people, and so similar in their behaviour to some patients who have suffered injuries to the brain, that organic causes have been suggested. There is no convincing direct evidence linking antisocial personality in adult life with brain injury in childhood. However, it has been suggested that antisocial behaviour in childhood can be caused by minor degrees of damage to the brain ('minimal brain dysfunction'): and there is evidence linking antisocial behaviour in childhood with antisocial personality in adult life. Taken together, these observations might provide indirect evidence of an association between damage to the brain in childhood and antisocial personality in adult life. However, while there is fairly strong evidence for a continuity between behaviour disorders in childhood and antisocial personality in adult life (see p. 768), there is only weak evidence that minimal brain dysfunction is a cause of behaviour disorder in childhood (see p. 769).

A related view is that antisocial personality disorder might result from delay in the development of the brain. Electroencephalographic abnormalities consistent with maturational delays have been reported in people with antisocial personalities. For example, Hill (1952) carried out an uncontrolled study of 194 antisocial and aggressive people, none of whom had epilepsy. Three patterns of abnormality were found, all of which could have arisen from maturational defects. The most frequent were bilateral excess of slow waves (theta activity) and foci of 3–5 cycles per second activity in the posterior temporal regions. Both kinds of abnormality were usually bilateral but, if not, were more often on the right. The abnormalities were less frequent among the older subjects. Williams (1969) confirmed these findings in a study of 333 men convicted of violent offences of whom 206 had been habitually aggressive, whilst 127 were known to have had only a single aggressive outburst usually in response to provocation. After exclusion of subjects with mental subnormality, epilepsy, or a previous head injury, 57 per cent of the habitually aggressive group had abnormal EEGs as against only 12 per cent of the single outburst group. Abnormalities were found most often in the anterior temporal region. Williams speculated that these abnormalities might indicate a primary disorder in the reticular activating system or limbic mechanisms. He concluded that disturbed cerebral physiology was an important predisposing cause of the propensity to seriously aggressive behaviour, though single outbursts were usually provoked by environmental factors.

The idea that cerebral disorder can contribute to repeated aggressive behaviour, especially when there is no adequate provocation, was developed further by Bach-y-Rita *et al.* (1971) who described an **episodic dyscontrol syndrome**. They regarded this as a disorder with more than one organic cause, and in their original series they included some patients with epilepsy. In a further study, Maletzky (1973) studied 22 men, excluding any who had evidence of epilepsy, pathological intoxication, schizophrenia, or acute drug reactions. All had the pattern of episodic violent behaviour described by Bach-y-Rita *et al.*, 14 having seriously injured a victim (who was often a family member) and five having killed. A sequence of aura, headache, and drowsiness was often described, and 12 patients reported amnesia for the episode. The frequency of these occurrences varied from one a day to a few in a year, with a median of four a month. Even small amounts of alcohol appeared to make the episodes more likely, and the authors suggested that benzodiazepines might have a similar effect. 'Soft' neurological signs were reported among the patients, and abnormal EEG findings, usually in the temporal regions, were reported in 14. No long-term follow-up was carried out, but from clinical experience the author suggests the syndrome may improve with age. Maletzky also reported striking improvements during treatment with phenytoin, but no placebo controls were used and so it is impossible to assess this finding. It remains uncertain whether the episodic dyscontrol syndrome is a separate entity, or merely represents a small group of patients with undiagnosed epilepsy coupled with an unusually aggressive personality.

Childhood behaviour problems and antisocial personality

Important associations have been found between behaviour problems in childhood and antisocial personality disorder in adult life. Robins (1966) followed 524 people who, as children 30 years before, had attended a child guidance clinic. Among those whose behaviour in childhood had been seriously antisocial, a substantial minority had persistent antisocial behaviour in adult life. Most of the adults with antisocial personality disorder had shown this behaviour as children. (This contrasted with the generally good prognosis of neurotic symptoms in childhood, see p. 166.) The outcome was particularly poor if, in childhood, several different antisocial behaviours co-existed, and if antisocial acts were repeated. Stealing among boys and sexual delinquency among girls had a poor prognosis.

The effects of upbringing

Two departures from the normal pattern of upbringing have to be considered: separation from parents, and disordered behaviour in the parents.

In 1944 Bowlby suggested, on the basis of an uncontrolled retrospective study of 44 young delinquents, that separation of a young child from its mother leads to a personality characterized by antisocial behaviour and failure to form close relationships. Later these ideas were expanded in an influential book *Forty-four juvenile thieves* (Bowlby 1946). This work stimulated much research into the immediate and long-term effects of separating children from their mothers, and the general conclusions of the studies are referred to on p. 779. In relation to the aetiology of antisocial personality disorder, it can be said first that the effects of separation from the mother are much more varied than Bowlby originally suggested, and not all children are affected adversely. Second, the original ideas suggested a unitary process—maternal deprivation—but in reality the effects of separation depend on many things: the age of the child, his previous relationship with his mother (and father), and the reasons for the separation. These last two points lead to the second kind of departure from the normal pattern of upbringing.

Two kinds of evidence point indirectly to the importance of the parents' behaviour and of enduring family relationships as causes of antisocial personality disorder. First, work on separation has highlighted the observation that when parents part, there have usually been months of tension and arguments which could themselves affect the child's development. The second line. of evidence is in two parts: the first, reviewed in an earlier paragraph, links behaviour disorder in childhood with antisocial personality disorder in later life. The second indicates that the behaviour of parents is an important cause of childhood behaviour disorders. For example Rutter (1972) showed that the association between separation and antisocial disorder in sons is determined by dysharmony in the marriage. Taken together these pieces of indirect evidence point quite strongly to the importance of the effects of upbringing as a cause of antisocial personality disorder.

Learning theory

Several authors have suggested that antisocial personality results from a failure of social learning. Scott (1960) proposed a broad scheme which is based on common-sense considerations rather than experimental evidence, but does provide a useful framework for the clinician. He suggested four ways in which repeated antisocial behaviour could develop. First, a person may acquire behaviour contrary to generally accepted standards through growing up in an antisocial family. Second, he may have had no opportunity to learn because he was not presented with consistent rules of behaviour in the family. Third, he may have learnt antisocial behaviour as a way of overcoming some emotional problem; for example, a young man who feels inferior with women may adopt aggressive behaviour to hide this. Fourth, the learning process itself may have been abnormal. This last idea has been developed by Eysenck (1970a), who suggested that antisocial personality disorder is more likely to develop in people who condition slowly and so fail to learn normal social behaviour. However, this broad explanation takes no account of the complexities of social learning, and cannot explain why people with antisocial personality may learn other behaviour patterns normally.

The prognosis of personality disorders

Just as small changes occur in normal personalities with increasing age, so abnormal personalities may become rather less abnormal as the person grows older. There is little factual information about the outcome of personality disorders, and virtually all of it concerns antisocial disorders. In the American follow-up study by Robins mentioned above, information was collected about people with persistent antisocial behaviour in early adult life. During the later follow-up about a third of them had improved as judged by the number of arrests and contacts with social agencies, but still had problems in relationships as shown by hostility to wives and neighbours. They also had an increased rate of death by suicide. Research in England showed that, amongst offenders with antisocial personalities whose first offences were aggressive, subsequent offences were not predominantly aggressive (Gibbens *et al.* 1959). This accords with a general impression among clinicians that antisocial people over the age of 45 present fewer problems of aggressive behaviour, but continue to have problems of personal relationship.

The management of personality disorders

It is said that people cannot change their natures, all they can do is change their situations. Although this refers to normal personalities, much the same holds for disordered personality. There has been some progress in finding ways of effecting small changes in disorders of personality, but management still consists largely of helping the person to find a way of life that conflicts less with his character. It is also true that personality does not become fixed in many people until their mid-twenties.

Assessment

As always in psychiatry, thorough assessment is the first step in management. Information from independent informants, which should be sought in every psychiatric assessment, is particularly important when personality disorder is being considered.

In assessing someone with a personality disorder, it is less useful to attach a single diagnostic label than to describe the main features of his character. This description should refer to his strengths and his weaknesses, because treatment attempts to build on favourable features as well as modify unfavourable ones. The patient's circumstances must be examined with equal care, with particular attention to any that regularly provoke undesirable behaviour. This last step is often overlooked to the patient's detriment. Aggressive people are not aggressive in all circumstances, nor are shy and self-conscious people ill at ease in every social encounter. To find out what provokes undesirable behaviour, there must be detailed observation over several weeks to discover any recurring patterns. This method is often useful for people with antisocial personalities, as they appreciate a practical approach.

Such enquiries may show that specific factors are making abnormal behaviour worse. For example, a man with an anankastic personality may need encouragement to move to a job with less responsibility for the work of other people, who have lower standards than his own. A man with an antisocial personality may be provoked into anger when he feels rejected by women. Sometimes the enquiries suggest that attention should be given to a problem which was not apparent at first. For example, the man just described may provoke rejection by his own clumsy approach to women. He might be helped by counselling and social skills training directed to this clumsiness.

General measures of treatment

The aims of treatment should be modest, and considerable time should be allowed to achieve them. Drugs have little part to play in the management of personality disorders. Anxiolytic drugs or major tranquillizers may be given for short periods at times of unusual stress, but they should not be maintained for long because their benefits are likely to decline and anxiolytics may induce dependency. Clinical experience suggests that treatment with lithium carbonate reduces the mood variations of some people with cyclothymic personality disorders, though there is no convincing evidence from clinical trials to confirm this opinion. If the use of lithium carbonate is considered, it should be preceded by a long period of observation to make sure that the mood changes are not responses to life events that could be modified. (See p. 671 for further advice about the use of lithium carbonate.)

Psychotherapy is most likely to help young people who lack confidence, have difficulty in making relationships, and are uncertain about the direction their lives should take. Such people must be highly motivated to work at solving their problems by examining their attitudes and emotions. Psychotherapy is least likely to help people with antisocial personality disorders, although some are helped by special forms of large group treatment in a therapeutic community. (This form of treatment is considered below.)

For most patients with personality disorder, psychotherapy is not indicated, but supervision and support are often beneficial. This can be given by a doctor, though many patients can be managed equally well by an experienced social worker or psychiatric nurse. For antisocial personalities several years of supervision may be required. For other kinds of personality disorder useful readjustments can often be effected over a period of months. Some antisocial people are put on probation after breaking the law, and this can sometimes provide useful external control when their motivation for treatment is poor at the start.

Whatever the nature of the disorder, the treatment plan aims to bring about limited changes in the patient's circumstances so that he has less contact with situations that provoke his difficulties, and more opportunity to develop the assets in his personality. It is essential to attempt to build a trusting relationship so that the patient can talk openly and learn from his mistakes. The patient will certainly experience setbacks, and at these times the therapist should avoid any suggestion of failure. Often progress can be made only by a series of small steps whereby the patient gradually moves nearer to a satisfactory adjustment. Often these steps can be taken most effectively when setbacks occur, since it is then most likely that the patient will be willing to face his real problems. The therapist should also help the patient to develop more satisfying relationships, for example by taking part in leisure interests, pursuing further education, or joining clubs.

When the disorder is of the antisocial kind, the patient should be seen over a long period, but not at short intervals. Indeed for some patients frequent visits only lead to undue dependency and a consequent worsening of their dificulties. Even if little progress is made, a supportive and watchful relationship can often prevent the accumulation of additional problems until some fortuitous change in the patient's life brings about some improvement.

It should also be recognized that there is no point in persisting with endless 'supportive' sessions that bring no benefit. No matter how skilful the treatment, some patients will not benefit, and the therapist should not be disheartened by this.

Psychotherapy for personality disorders

General issues

Treatment by dynamic psychotherapy is much the same for personality disorders as for neuroses. It can be carried out individually or in groups (see Chapter 18).

In the individual treatment of personality disorders, there are some differences in emphasis from the treatment of neuroses. There is less emphasis on the reconstruction of past events and more on the analysis of current behaviour. In so-called character analysis there is detailed examination of the ways a person relates to others, copes with external difficulties and deals with his own feelings. The approach is more directive than in the classical methods of analysis for neurotic symptoms, although the analysis of transference remains an important element. To emphasize any discrepancies between the patient's habitual ways of relating to others and his real life situation, the therapist has to reveal more of himself than is usual in classical analysis. At the same time the analysis of countertransference (the therapist's emotional attitudes to the patient) can be an important guide to the likely reactions of other people to the patient.

Hysterical personality disorder

Murphy and Guze (1960) have given an interesting account of the difficulties that can arise in the treatment of hysterical personalities. They describe direct and indirect demands that patients can place on the doctor. Direct demands include unreasonable requests for medication, repeated seeking for assurances of continuing help, telephoning at unreasonable times, and attempts to impose impractical conditions on treatment. Indirect demands include seductive behaviour, threats of dangerous actions such as drug overdoses, and repeated unfavourable comparisons of the present treatment with any received in the past. The doctor has to be alert for the first signs of such demands, and should clearly set limits by indicating how much of the patient's behaviour he is prepared to tolerate. This must be done before the patient's demands become too great.

Obsessional personality disorder

People with obsessional personality disorders often express great eagerness to please the therapist. However, this kind of personality disorder does not, as a rule, respond well to psychotherapy, and unskilled treatment can lead to excessive morbid introspection that leaves the person worse rather than better.

Schizoid personality disorder

The schizoid person's tendency to avoid close personal contacts makes any kind of psychotherapy difficult. A patient of this kind often drops out after a few sessions; if he does stay, he tends to intellectualize his problems, and to question the scientific status of the treatment. The therapist has to try gradually to penetrate these intellectual defences and to help the patient recognize his emotional problems. Only then can the therapist begin to explore ways of dealing with them. At best it is a slow process, and one that often fails.

Borderline personality disorder

These people do not respond well to exploratory psychotherapy, indeed attempts at treatment may worsen their emotional control and increase their impulsive actions. It is usually better to employ supportive treatment, directing any attempts at change to practical goals in dealing with everyday problems.

Psychological treatment for antisocial personality disorder

Individual psychotherapy

Most psychiatrists agree that individual psychotherapy seldom helps patients with antisocial personalities, and that the conduct of the interviews is often made difficult by their behaviour. Schmideberg (1947) is exceptional in reporting good results from a form of psychotherapy in which patients are confronted repeatedly and directly with evidence of their own abnormal behaviour. If such treatment is effective at all, it is only with therapists who have a particularly forceful and robust personality.

Small group therapy

If one person with an antisocial personality disorder joins a conventional therapeutic group, it seldom helps him and often disrupts the treatment of the others. On the other hand, groups composed entirely of antisocial patients can sometimes be run more constructively. This requires skill and experience, together with a determination to set limited goals and to encourage group members to share responsibility and help each other. This kind of treatment should not be undertaken without special training (see Whiteley 1975).

The therapeutic community

The principles of the therapeutic community are outlined in Chapter 18. The method has been used for antisocial personalities since the work of Jones (1952) at the Social Rehabilitation Unit at Belmont Hospital, later called The Henderson Hospital. In such a unit, antisocial patients live and work together, and meet several times a day for group discussions in which each person's behaviour and feelings are examined by the other group members. Frank discussion is encouraged and patients are required to consider their own behaviour and the effect it has on other people. These discussions often take place with much outpouring of emotion including anger. It is hoped that, by repeatedly facing these issues, patients will gradually learn to control their antisocial behaviour and adopt more acceptable ways of dealing with their feelings and relationships. Rapoport (1960) has described four aspects of treatment that may be important in bringing about change: permission to act on feelings without the usual social restraints; sharing of tasks and responsibilities; group decision-making to involve patients in making rules as well as breaking them; and confrontation of each person with the effects his actions have on others. No controlled study has been carried out and opinions about the value of this treatment are divergent. One- to two-year follow-up studies have reported improvement rates of 40–60 per cent, depending on whether the criterion for improvement was general social functioning, employment or reconviction (see Taylor 1966).

Other group regimes

In contrast to communities in which patients are given freedom to learn from their mistakes, Craft (1965) has advocated a more authoritarian regime for people who have antisocial personality disorder combined with subnormality of intelligence and who become more disturbed when treated in a therapeutic community.

Stürup (1968) described the application of therapeutic community principles to offenders who had committed violent crimes or serious sexual offences, and were detained on indefinite sentences in the the Herstedvester Detention Centre in Denmark. At Grendon Prison in England similar principles have been applied to the care of prisoners who have committed less serious offences and are not serving an indefinite sentence. In neither case has any controlled enquiry been possible. Hence it is difficult to evaluate Stürup's report (1968, p. ix) that 90 per cent of offenders passing through his unit committed no further offences.

Further reading

Hall, C. S., Lindzey, G., Loehlin J. C., and Marosevitz, J. (1985). *Introduction to theories of personality*. John Wiley, New York.

Lewis, A. (1974). Psychopathic personality: a most elusive category. *Psychological Medicine* **4**, 133–40.

Schneider, K. (1950). *Psychopathic personalities* (trans. M. W. Hamilton). Cassell, London.

Vaillant, G. E. and Perry, J. C. (1985). Personality disorders. In *Comprehensive textbook of psychiatry* (4th edn) (ed. H. I. Kaplan, and B. J. Sadock), Chapter 21. Williams and Wilkins, Baltimore.

6 Neurosis: part I

The word neurosis is widely used as a collective term for psychiatric disorders that have three things in common. First, they are functional disorders, that is they are not accompanied by organic brain disease. Second, they are not psychoses, i.e. the patient does not lose touch with external reality however severe the condition. Third, they differ from personality disorders in having a discrete onset rather than a continuous development from early adult life. These criteria delineate a broad group of conditions including specific syndromes, such as anxiety disorders and obsessional disorders, and less clearly differentiated states such as minor affective disorders and adjustment reactions. This chapter is concerned with the neuroses in general and with the less differentiated states; the following chapter reviews the specific syndromes.

The word neurosis is in common use in everyday psychiatric practice as a convenient collective term for these disorders. However, for reasons that were discussed on p. 79, the category neurosis is less satisfactory as a formal component of a system of classification. As explained on p. 79, the class of neuroses has been removed from the American system of classification. Nevertheless for the purposes of a textbook, it is still useful to draw together a number of common issues under the chapter heading of neurosis, as has been done here.

Terminology

Readers who are studying the neuroses for the first time may be confused by the terms neurosis, functional nervous illness, character neurosis, psychoneurosis, and abnormal emotional reaction. The term **neurosis** was used in 1772 by the Edinburgh physician Cullen to denote conditions arising from a 'generalised affection of the nervous system', that did not seem, at the time, to be caused by either localized disease or febrile illness. In other words, neuroses were regarded as disorders of the nervous system for which no physical cause could be found. The term necessarily included conditions such as migraine that are now within the subject matter of neurology (see Tuke 1892), as well as the disorders now regarded as neuroses. Used in this sense, neurosis was synonymous with the term **functional nervous illness**, which persisted until the 1930s.

Freud did not accept this negative view of neuroses as disorders of unknown aetiology. Like many other physicians of his time, he held that many forms of neurosis had clear psychological causes. He therefore called them **psychoneuroses**, a grouping that included hysteria, anxiety hysteria (roughly equivalent to the modern concept of agoraphobia), and obsessional neuroses. At first anxiety disorders were excluded from the psychoneuroses but were later added, so that the term psychoneurosis became synonymous with neurosis. As Freud tried to find causes for the psychoneuroses, he concluded that many originated in the processes that also determine the development of personality. This line of reasoning led to the term **character neurosis** to denote personalities that appeared to have origins similar to those presumed for the neuroses, even though the person might have no neurotic symptoms at the time. The term character neurosis is confusing and its use is not recommended.

Psychoanalysts were not the only clinicians to notice a clear relationship between neuroses and personality. Some German psychiatrists, notably Jaspers and Schneider, thought of neuroses as reactions to stress occurring in people with abnormal personalities. If this view is accepted, there is no need to think of neuroses as separate entities; it is only necessary to describe the personality from which the reaction arises. This approach led to the term **abnormal emotional reaction**, as a substitute for neurosis. As will be explained later, it is generally useful to think of neurosis as a reaction of a particular kind of personality to stress. However, the relationship between the type of personality and the type of reaction is not simple. Thus obsessional personalities may react with an anxiety disorder or a depressive disorder as much as with an obsessional disorder. Conversely hysteria may occur in people who do not have a histrionic personality.

It is important to make a clear distinction between individual neurotic symptoms such as anxiety or obsessions, and neurotic syndromes such as anxiety disorder or obsessional disorder. Individual neurotic symptoms occur in many psychiatric disorders, but the syndromes are unique combinations of symptoms. This distinction is reasonably clear for the main neurotic syndromes—anxiety disorder, obsessional disorder, and conversion and dissociative disorders. It is much less clear for hypochondriasis and depersonalization; some psychiatrists believe that these occur only as symptoms of another psychiatric syndrome, and that there is no primary hypochondriacal disorder or depersonalization disorder.

It was explained on p. 79 that the term neurosis was discarded from the American system of classification DSMIII. One reason for this change is that, as noted above, the term neurosis has been used widely by psychoanalysts, and as a result some psychatrists now associate it with psychoanalytic theories of aetiology. The authors of DSMIII did not wish to adopt these aetiological theories and so chose to abandon the term neurosis. However, as explained earlier, the term neurosis was in use long before Freud developed his theories, and to the present authors it is more appropriate to retain the word but use it in its historically correct sense, that is to denote disorders and not aetiology. [For a more detailed discussion of these issues, see Gelder (1986*a*).]

Classification

Table 6.1 shows how neurosis and related disorders are classified in DSMIIIR and ICD10 (draft). The two schemes are broadly similar but certain differences should be noted. The first difference, which is not shown in Table 6.1, is that in DSMIIIR there is no single rubric for these disorders. As explained already the term neurosis is not employed, and instead three separate headings are used: anxiety disorder, dissociative disorder and somatoform disorder. ICD10 (draft) brings the conditions listed in Table 6.1 together under the rubric 'neurotic, stress-related, and somatoform disorders'.

The second difference between DSMIIIR and ICD10 (draft) is in the classification of anxiety disorders. In DSMIIIR this category includes not only phobias, generalized anxiety, and panic disorders but also obsessive-compulsive disorder, and post-traumatic stress disorder. In ICD10 (draft) obsessive-compulsive disorder and anxiety disorder are classified separately, and post-traumatic stress disorder appears under a rubric of 'reactions to catastrophic stress', which also includes acute stress reactions and adjustment disorder.

The third difference between DSMIIIR and ICD10 is in the classification of the disorders formerly known as hysteria (a term which is avoided in both classifications). In DSMIIIR these disorders are divided into dissociative and somatoform disorders. The same terms are used in ICD10 (draft) but with different meanings. Thus the category of dissociative disorder in DSMIIIR broadly corresponds to 'dissociative disorders of memory, awareness, and identity' in ICD10 (draft), although there is one difference, namely that depersonalization disorder is classified under dissociative disorder in DSMIIIR but has a separate rubric in ICD10 (draft). ICD10 (draft) has a second group of dissociative disorders: those involving movement and sensation. This category includes what in the past has been called conversion hysteria, and in DSMIIIR these conditions are known as conversion disorder. In DSMIIIR conversion disorder appears under the rubric somatoform disorder, together with somatization disorder, body dysmorphic disorder, hypochondriasis, somatoform pain disorder, and undifferentiated somatoform disorder. Corresponding categories appear under somatoform disorder in ICD10 (draft).

The fourth difference is that ICD10 (draft) still retains the term neurasthenia, which is still used frequently in some countries, though rarely in the USA or the United Kingdom.

Table 6.1. Classification in ICD10 (draft) and DSMIIIR*

DSMIIIR	ICD10 (draft)
Anxiety disorders	*Phobic disorders*
Agoraphobia without history of panic disorder	Agoraphobia
Social phobia	Social phobia
Simple phobia	Specific phobia
	Other anxiety disorders
Panic disorder without agoraphobia	Panic disorder (episodic anxiety)
Panic disorder with agoraphobia	
Generalized anxiety disorder	Generalized anxiety disorder
	Mixed anxiety and depressive disorder
Obsessive-compulsive disorder	*Obsessive-compulsive disorder†*
	Reactions to catastrophic stress
	Acute stress reactions
Post-traumatic stress reaction	Post traumatic stress reaction
	Adjustment disorder
Dissociative disorders	*Dissociative disorders of memory, awareness, and identity*
Psychogenic amnesia	Psychogenic amnesia
Psychogenic fugue	Psychogenic fugue
	Psychogenic stupor
Multiple personality disorder	Multiple personality
Possession/trance disorder	Trance and possession states
Depersonalization disorder	
Somatoform disorders	*Dissociative disorders of movement and sensation*
Conversion disorder	Psychogenic disorder of voluntary movement
	Psychogenic convulsions
	Psychogenic anaesthesia and sensory loss
	Other dissociative disorder
	Somatoform disorders
Somatization disorder	Multiple somatoform disorder (Briquet's syndrome)
Body dysmorphic disorder	Undifferentiated multiple somatoform disorder

Table 6.1. Classification in ICD10 (draft) and DSMIIIR* (*cont.*)

DSMIIIR	ICD10 (draft)
Hypochondriasis	Hypochondriacal syndrome
	Psychogenic autonomic dysfunction
Somatoform pain disorder	Pain syndrome without specific organic cause
	Other neurotic disorders
	Neurasthenia
	Depersonalization–derealization syndrome

* The order of DSMIIIR has been altered to allow comparisons to be made more easily.
† subdivided.

In this book, neuroses and related disorders are discussed in three chapters, and the arrangement of sections is shown in Table 6.2.

The classification of minor depressive disorders

Some of the less severe forms of depressive disorder have features that meet the criteria for neurosis. They have no organic basis, seem to result from stressors acting on a predisposed personality, and do not include features (often called psychotic) such as hallucinations and delusions. Moreover, many of them include prominent anxiety symptoms, and some have other kinds of neurotic symptom as well. For this reason, minor depressive disorders have sometimes been classified as depressive neuroses or neurotic depression. The arguments for and against the use of these terms are discussed in the chapter on affective disorders (p. 228).

Before leaving the subject of minor depressive disorders two other points need to be made. The first was referred to by Mapother (1926) and Lewis (1956), who considered that anxiety neuroses cannot be separated clearly from depressive disorders. Most psychiatrists now accept that this distinction can be made among the more severe forms seen in psychiatric practice. However, the distinction cannot be made easily among the mild and transient disorders seen in general practice. The second issue is whether conditions presenting initially as undoubted anxiety neuroses or depressive disorders remain distinct as time passes. Information about this is incomplete but it appears that definite anxiety neuroses seldom turn into depressive disorders (Schapira *et al.* 1972), even though their course is often interspersed with brief episodes of depressive symptoms lasting for weeks or months (Clancy *et al.* 1978). There is no comparable information about the long-term course of the minor depressive disorders that could

Table 6.2. Arrangement of sections in this book

(a) *Considered in this chapter*
Minor affective disorder
Acute reactions to stress
Adjustment disorder
Post-traumatic stress disorder

(b) *Considered in Chapter 7*
Anxiety disorders
Obsessive compulsive disorder
Dissociative and conversion disorders
Depersonalization disorder

(c) *Considered in Chapter 12*
Somatization disorders
Hypochondriacal disorder

be diagnosed as neurotic depression, but clinical experience suggests that they too continue in the original pattern.

Neurasthenia and psychasthenia

Although no longer in general use in most countries, the term neurasthenia is important in the history of psychiatry, and a brief account is appropriate here. The term was first employed in 1869 by Beard in America to describe a syndrome of mental and physical fatigue, poor appetite, irritability, insomnia, poor concentration, and headache in the absence of specific disease. Beard recognized that similar symptoms could arise from chronic disease, wasting fevers, and parturition. The term came to be used in a wide sense, and neurasthenia was discussed at length in many textbooks of the late nineteenth and early twentieth century. Ross included the term in the first edition of his well-known book *The common neuroses* published in 1923; by the time the second edition was prepared in 1937, Ross had discarded the term on the grounds that most cases were anxiety states.

Originally the cause of neurasthenia was thought to be nervous exhaustion resulting from overwork, and treatment included a sequence of rest and planned activity, usually coupled with tonics and sometimes with electrical stimulation applied to the feet and head. Later, overwork was discounted as an important cause, and constitutional factors and psychological precipitants were emphasized instead.

Recent investigations in general practice (see Goldberg and Huxley 1980) have shown that complaints of fatigue and irritability commonly accompany those of anxiety and mild depression. Whilst it is no longer fashionable to call this pattern of symptoms neurasthenia, these recent observations show that the clinical phenomena described by Beard can still be detected today.

Janet used the related term psychasthenia to denote anxiety and obsessional disorders. The word psychasthenia was used to emphasize that the cause was to be thought of as psychological rather than physiological (see Janet 1909).

The epidemiology of the neuroses

Neurotic disorders can occur at three 'levels'—individual symptoms; minor neurotic disorders; and specific neurotic syndromes. Individual neurotic symptoms may be experienced by normal people from time to time. In a minor neurotic disorder (otherwise minor emotional disorder), a variety of neurotic symptoms occur together without any one predominating; this disorder is commonly seen in general practice. In specific neurotic syndromes, one type of symptom predominates; these disorders are more often seen in psychiatric practice.

Epidemiological methods have been used to estimate the frequency of disorder at each of these levels. In such studies, it is important to use standardized methods of observation. Thus, if general practitioners are simply asked to report the frequency of minor emotional disorders among their patients, their estimates vary as much as ninefold (Shepherd *et al.* 1966). Objective estimates reveal that this is not mainly due to any real difference in frequency. Instead it relates to differences in the doctors' ability to detect such disorders, and to variation in diagnostic practices especially when physical and emotional symptoms occur together. In general, family doctors detect emotional disorders more readily among women, the middle aged, separated and widowed (Goldberg and Huxley 1980).

At the first 'level', epidemiological studies show that **individual neurotic symptoms** are exceedingly common in the general population; for example, 815 in every 1000 people in New York reported some neurotic symptoms (Srole *et al.* 1962).

Estimates of the frequency of minor neurotic disorders show wide variation, ranging from lifetime prevalence rates of 18 per 1000 for men and 27 per 1000 for women (in a Danish survey by Fremming 1951); to 79 per 1000 for men and 165 per 1000 for women (in a Swedish investigation by Hagnell 1966). One-year prevalence rates vary even more (see Carey *et al.* 1980). Looked at in another way, neuroses probably form about two-thirds of the psychiatric cases seen in general practice (Shepherd *et al.* 1966). Among chronic neuroses inception rates are greater in the first half of life, exceeding recovery rates up to the age of 35 (Shepherd and Gruenberg 1957). There is also general agreement that the most frequent symptoms of these minor neurotic disorders are anxiety, depression, irritability, insomnia, and fatigue. [See Goldberg and Huxley (1980) for a review of the evidence.]

The prevalence of **individual neurotic syndromes** is considered in the next chapter where these disorders are described. At this stage, the relative frequencies of these syndromes should be noted: anxiety neuroses and mild depressive states are generally found to be more common than either hysteria or obsessional neuroses; and mild depression is especially common amongst women (see, for example, Bille and Juel-Nielsen 1968).

The population of neurotic patients consists of some who experience brief reactions to stress and others who have chronic disorders. Although it is not possible to draw a sharp dividing line between the two, it appears that amongst new cases of minor neurotic disorders about two-thirds recover within six months (Goldberg and Blackwell 1970; Hagnell 1970) while only about 4 per cent last as long as three years (Hagnell 1970). (The question of prognosis will be taken up again later.)

It is not surprising that in developing countries the incidence and prevalence of the neuroses is even more difficult to estimate. The few reported investigations suggest that rates in the community are comparable to those found in Britain and the United States. However, fewer patients reach general practitioners and psychiatric clinics [see German (1972) for a review; also the study of African students by German and Arya (1969)].

Minor emotional disorders

This is a broad term used to denote disorders that are met commonly in general practice but seldom referred to psychiatrists (see Goldberg and Huxley 1980). Whilst the psychiatric literature contains many descriptions of differentiated neurotic syndromes, there are few accounts of these minor states. One of the best descriptions has been given by Goldberg *et al.* (1976) who studied 88 patients from a general practice in Philadelphia. As shown in Table 6.3 these authors found that complaints of anxiety and worry were most frequent, but that despondency and sadness were almost as common. Mostly these complaints occurred together, and it was not possible to assign primacy to one or the other.

Somatic symptoms were present in about half the cases, and excessive concern with bodily functions in about a quarter. Some of these somatic symptoms are autonomic features of anxiety, but it is not fully understood why these and other bodily sensations should so often be the focus of the patients' concern when consulting practitioners. Some patients may emphasize somatic complaints because they expect them to be received more sympathetically than emotional complaints. Understandably some patients may also want to ensure that the doctor makes a thorough search

Table 6.3. *Relative frequency of 12 common symptoms in 88 patients diagnosed as having mental disorder in general practice*

Anxiety and worry	82
Despondency, sadness	71
Fatigue	71†
Somatic symptoms*	52
Sleep disturbance	50
Irritability	38
Excessive concern with bodily function	27
Depressive thoughts, inability to concentrate	21
Obsessions and compulsions	19
Phobias	11
Depersonalization	6

* Only those precipitated, exacerbated, or maintained by psychological factors.
† Not all the same patients who complain of despondency and sadness.
Source: Goldberg *et al.* (1976).

for physical illness before their symptoms are regarded as psychological. Whatever the reason, it is no new phenomenon, as shown by the lengthy coverage of physical symptoms of neurosis in many older textbooks on neuroses (see, for example, Déjerine and Gauckler 1913).

In the patients studied by Goldberg *et al.* (1976), complaints of sleep disturbance were also common, particularly difficulty in getting off to sleep and restlessness during the night. (Complaints of early waking suggest that the condition may be the early stage of depressive disorder requiring antidepressant medication, rather than a neurosis.) About a fifth of the patients complained of obsessional thoughts and mild compulsions. Definite phobic symptoms were less common than either of these although mild phobias are of course very common among normal people. Complaints of fatigue and irritability were also frequent (Table 6.3), and often accompanied by poor concentration and lack of enjoyment. As mentioned earlier, these symptoms were grouped together as neurasthenia in the past.

The more frequent somatic complaints of patients with minor neurotic disorders are as follows. Complaints related to the digestive system include feelings of abdominal discomfort or distension, and preoccupations with the effects of certain foods in producing indigestion or flatulence. There may also be complaints of poor appetite, nausea, epigastric pain, weight loss or difficulty in swallowing, and discomfort in the left iliac fossa. Complaints related to the cardiovascular system include palpitations, precordial discomfort, and worries about heart disease. Other complaints include aching in the neck, shoulders, and back. Headaches are commonly described as tightness and pressure, or a dull constant ache, or throbbing. Pain may have other regional localization. All these symptoms require a thorough search for physical disease before it is concluded that they are part of a minor neurotic disorder.

The nature of complaints differs among people from different cultures, and in the same society at different times. Interested readers should consult Déjerine and Gauckler (1913) for an account of the somatic symptoms presented by neurotic patients in France at the beginning of the century; and Ndetei and Muhangi (1979) for a description of the complaints of physical symptoms that are frequent among Africans with minor psychiatric disorder.

Reactions to stress

Acute reactions to stress

This term describes transient disorders of any severity or nature occurring in people free from mental disorders, in response to exceptionally stressful circumstances such as a natural catastrophe, battle, or an extreme crisis in relationships. The term is used for disorders that subside within hours or a few days. More prolonged reactions would be described as adjustment reactions if mild, or post-traumatic stress disorders (late sequelae of stress) if severe. The clinical picture of acute reactions to stress is varied, with some combination of agitation, autonomic signs of anxiety, restricted response to surroundings, apparent disorientation, stupor and fugue. The only treatment required is an opportunity to talk about the stressful events, with a few doses of an anxiolytic drug in severe cases.

Adjustment reactions

This term is used to describe mild or transient disorders lasting longer than acute reactions to stress and occurring in people previously free from mental disorder. The symptoms are varied, with some combination of worry, anxiety, depression, poor concentration, irritability, and aggressive behaviour. These disorders are generally reversible and usually last only a few months. They are closely related in time and content to the stressor, examples of which are bereavement, migration or separation. The diagnosis can also be applied to emotional reactions to disablement, for example after a stroke or a road accident. The essential point is that the reaction is understandable and in proportion to the severity of the stressful experience, and does not outlast the period of time that seems reasonable for adaptation to the change. Treatment is by brief psychotherapy designed to help the patient come to terms with the new situation, and make full use of his remaining assets.

Post-traumatic stress disorder

This term denotes an intense and usually prolonged reaction to intense stressors such as natural catastrophes (e.g. earthquakes, floods, and fires), man-made disasters (e.g. the effects of war or persecution), or personal assault (e.g. mugging or rape). By convention this category, unlike acute stress reactions or adjustment reactions, can be diagnosed in people who have a history of mental disorder before the stressful events.

The term is used when the reaction is characterized by recurrent distressing dreams or intrusive recollections of the original stressful events, coupled with avoidance of reminders of those events, and symptoms indicating increased arousal (e.g. irritability, insomnia, and poor concentration). Some patients also describe an inability to remember the events at will (despite the vivid intrusive recollections at other times), feelings of numbness or detachment, and diminished interest in everyday activities.

This kind of prolonged response to intense stressors has been recognized for many years. The recently renewed interest results partly from the study in the United States of servicemen returning from the Vietnam war. In the past, similar clinical pictures among soldiers have been called *combat neurosis*. Similar effects of a peacetime disaster have been described, for example in a well-known account of the aftermath of a serious fire at the Coconut Grove nightclub in America (Adler 1943).

Post-traumatic stress disorder is said to be more frequent in childhood and old age than at other times of life, and among people with previous psychiatric disorder than among those with no such history (Andreasen 1985). In many disasters the victims suffer physical injury, and this may increase the likelihood of a prolonged psychological reaction, particularly when the injury is to the head. The reaction generally begins soon after the stressful event, but its onset may be delayed for a few days or occasionally longer. Most cases recover within six months but an important minority persist for years.

Because of the possibility of injury to the brain during some kinds of stressful experience, assessment should include appropriate neurological examination as well as careful evaluation of the previous personality and psychiatric history. Immediate treatment is an anxiolytic drug and an opportunity to ventilate emotion. Further treatment employs supportive psychotherapy and strong encouragement to resume normal activities.

The aetiology of neuroses

This section deals with general causes of neurosis. Factors specific to the aetiology of individual neurotic syndromes are considered in the next chapter.

Genetic influences

There appear to be genetic determinants of the tendency to develop neurosis as measured by psychological tests of neuroticism (see Shields 1976 for a review). The tendency of the autonomic nervous system to react to stressors, as measured by the rate of habituation of galvanic skin responses (Lader and Wing 1966), is also in part determined genetically. Both kinds of tendency are thought to reflect a general predisposition to develop neurosis. Studies of the families of patients with neuroses point to the same conclusion. Thus, increased rates of neurosis have been found among close relations of neurotic patients (for example, by Brown 1942; and Slater 1943), and twin studies have shown higher concordance for neurosis among monozygous than dizygous twins. For example, Slater and Shields (1969) found overall concordance for neurosis of 40 per cent in 62 monozygous twins, and 15 per cent in 84 dizygous twins, suggesting a moderate genetic influence. [For a review, see Slater and Shields (1969).]

Influences in childhood

Upbringing

It is widely supposed that early experiences play an important part in the development of neurosis in adult life. However, this idea is largely speculative because scientific proof would require concurrent study of large numbers of people exposed to different kinds of life experience in childhood, and subsequent study of these people into adult life. Although some long-term follow-up investigations of children have been carried out (see p. 768), they have not included the detailed information about the child's early experience that is required to answer this question.

In the absence of relevant longitudinal studies, two related issues will be considered; the relationship of neurotic traits and neuroses in childhood to adult neuroses, and psychoanalytic theories of aetiology.

Neurotic traits

So-called neurotic traits in childhood include thumb sucking, nail biting, childhood fears, faddiness about food, stammering, and bed-wetting. None by itself is of pathological significance. The first four in this list are usually transient habits with little significance for later development. Stammering and bed-wetting may last longer but usually cease as the child grows older; and the few persistent cases are as likely to have been associated in childhood with antisocial behaviour as with neurotic symptoms (see Rutter 1972). Even when several neurotic traits occur together in childhood, there is no evidence that they predict neurosis in adult life. There is certainly no reason to think that adult neurosis is prevented by treating these problems in childhood. (For further discussion of neurotic traits see p. 780.)

Neurotic syndromes in childhood

In an important follow-up study of 500 adults who as children had attended a child guidance clinic 30 years previously, Robins (1966) found they had no more neurosis in adult life than did a suitably chosen control group. Other follow-up investigations have confirmed that most neurotic children grow up to be free from psychiatric disorders (see Graham 1986). In the few cases where childhood neurosis is followed by adult mental disorder, the latter usually takes the form of a neurosis or a depressive disorder (Pritchard and Graham 1966). These persistent cases may have a greater genetic component, while the transient cases may be more reactive to circumstances. It should be noted that most adults with neuroses have no history of child guidance attendance in childhood.

[See Robins (1970) for a review of follow-up studies of childhood disorders.]

Psychoanalytic theories

These theories were outlined in Chapter 4. Their contribution to understanding the aetiology of neurosis is, in the authors' view, not substantial, and will not be considered at length. Two aspects will be discussed briefly: the evolution of Freud's ideas, and the general nature of his explanation of the origins of neurosis. Apart from theories of aetiology, some of Freud's early papers contain vivid clinical descriptions of neurotic syndromes, which are strongly recommended to the reader [for example Freud (1895 *a, b*); Freud (1893–5)].

The evolution of Freud's ideas about the aetiology of neurosis is described in his autobiographical study (Freud 1935). These ideas originated in work with Breuer, which led Freud to conclude that hysteria was caused by a disorder of sexual function. In 1895 he postulated two kinds of disturbance causing separate kinds of neurosis. First, direct 'toxic' effects of suppressed sexual function caused anxiety neurosis and neurasthenia (which he called 'aktuel' neuroses); second, mental effects of suppressed sexual function caused hysteria, anxiety hysteria (agoraphobia), and obsessional neurosis. Before long, the idea of aktuel neurosis was abandoned, and all neuroses were thought to have psychological causes in the form of suppressed memories of disturbing events. Freud's attempts to elicit the supposed suppressed memories met with resistance in some patients, and this resistance led him to postulate an active process keeping the memories from consciousness. He called this process 'repression'. Later Freud concluded that some apparent memories were not recollections of actual events, but fantasies. Nevertheless these fantasies were thought to be important in aetiology. Thus he wrote: 'neurotic symptoms were not related directly to actual events but to phantasies embodying wishes and psychical reality was of more importance than material reality' (Freud 1935, p. 61).

Whilst developing these ideas about the cause of the neuroses, Freud was constructing two other hypotheses. One was about the organization of the mind, the other about normal mental development in childhood (see p. 119). He incorporated these ideas in several further revisions of his theory of neurosis.

In general terms, all versions of Freud's theory of the aetiology of neurosis have three components. First, it is proposed that anxiety is the central symptom of all neuroses; other symptoms arise secondarily through the action of mechanisms of defence (see p. 34), which act to reduce this anxiety. Second, anxiety arises when the ego fails to deal on the one hand with the mental energy reaching it from the id, and on the other hand with the demands of the super-ego. Third, neuroses orginate in childhood from a failure to pass normally through one or other of the three postulated stages of development, oral, anal, and genital. Readers who wish to know more about Freud's theories of neurosis should consult Fenichel (1945).

Personality

The influences of childhood factors referred to above can be thought of as predisposing to neurosis in adult life by affecting the development of personality. In general terms the importance of personality appears to be related inversely to the severity of the stressful events at the time when the neurosis begins. Thus people with normal personalities may develop neuroses when subjected to extremely stressful events, as in the war neuroses (Sargant and Slater 1940) but those who develop comparable symptoms in response to everyday problems generally have some predisposition of personality.

The relevant predisposing features of personality are of two kinds: a general tendency to develop neurosis, and a specific predisposition to exhibit a neurosis of a particular kind (for example an obsessional neurosis). Only the general tendency is considered here; specific predispositions will be considered in relation to neurotic syndromes (in the next chapter).

The most important attempt to measure general predisposition to neurosis (neuroticism) was made by Eysenck (1957). He linked neuroticism on the one hand with variations in capacity for conditioning and learning, and on the other hand with variations in autonomic reactivity. These ideas have been generally confirmed by experimental studies, and Eysenck's questionnaire measure of neuroticism is widely used in clinical investigations. Eysenck's ideas are discussed further in the next section.

Neuroses as faulty learning

Learning theories propose mechanisms by which experiences in childhood and later life give rise to neurosis. The theories are of two kinds. The first kind, exemplified by the writings of Mowrer (1950) and Dollard and Miller (1950), accepts some of the aetiological mechanisms proposed by Freud and attempts to account for them in terms of learning mechanisms. For example repression is equated with avoidance learning, emotional conflict with approach–avoidance conflict, and displacement with association learning. Although these parallels are interesting, the approach has not led to a major advance in the understanding of neurosis.

The second kind of theory rejects Freudian ideas, and attempts to explain neurosis directly in terms of concepts derived from experimental psychology. In this approach, anxiety is regarded as a drive state, while the other symptoms are thought to be learned behaviours reinforced by their effects in reducing this drive. This formulation has to overcome the objections that learned behaviour extinguishes quickly unless reinforced, whilst neurotic behaviour can persist for years without obvious reinforcement. Mowrer (1950) tried to resolve this 'neurotic paradox' by proposing a **two-stage theory**: first, neutral stimuli becomes sources of anxiety through classical conditioning; second, avoidance responses reduce this anxiety. This secondary reduction of anxiety is thought to reinforce and thereby perpetuate neurotic behaviour. Eysenck (1976) suggested a related explanation, the **'incubation effect'**. This idea is based on the observation that conditioned stimuli that do not produce a drive are subject to extinction (as in Pavlov's bell-salivation experiments), whilst conditioned stimuli that produce a drive are not extinguished by repetition; instead they are enhanced. This enhancement is called incubation. Eysenck proposed that in neuroses the relevant conditioned stimuli produced anxiety which acts as a drive, causing incubation, and prolonging the disorder.

As noted above (p. 167) Eysenck has linked the learning theory of neurosis with personality variables. He proposes that neuroticism reflects autonomic reactivity, that is a readiness to respond to stressors by developing anxiety. He suggests that a second variable, introversion–extraversion, reflects the ease with which inhibition builds up during learning. People with little tendency to inhibition (introverts) are supposed to be more responsive to social conditioning in childhood and more likely to develop anxiety, phobic, and obsessional disorders later in life. People with much tendency to inhibition (extroverts) are less responsive to conditioning, and are more likely to develop hysteria or antisocial behaviour in adult life. Although intellectually satisfying, this theory is not well supported by the results of investigations of patients. [See Gossop (1981) for a review.]

Causes in the environment

It is commonly supposed that **poor living conditions** can predispose to neurosis, either directly or through their effects on family life. If this supposition is correct, people who move from poor to better housing should experience fewer neuroses. Two well-known studies examined this possibility. Taylor and Chave (1964) investigated people moving from poor urban conditions to a new town; Hare and Shaw (1965) studied people moving from an old to a new housing estate in the same town. In neither investigation was the rate of neurosis reduced after the move. A possible explanation is that the beneficial effect of better housing is cancelled by the adverse effect of greater social isolation in new surround-ings. [The relationship between mental health and living conditions has been reviewed in the book edited by Freeman (1984).]

Another suggested cause of neurosis is **noise**; for example, the noise of aircraft. A causal relationship is suggested by the finding that near to a large airport, people who complain most of noise tend to have more neurotic symptoms than other people. This finding might indicate that noise causes neurosis, but it is equally possible that intolerance to noise is a symptom of neurosis caused by something else. Several investigations have examined this issue (Jenkins *et al.* 1981; Meecham and Smith 1977; Tarnopolsky *et al.* 1980); whilst the evidence is not conclusive, it seems unlikely that noise is an important cause of neurosis.

It has been suggested that some kinds of **working conditions** cause neurosis. This possiblity was studied extensively during the Second World War when it was concluded that work requiring constant attention but little initiative or responsiblity (such as repetitive machine work) can cause neurosis (Fraser 1947). More recent studies have shown that men on paced assembly lines report more neurotic symptoms than do comparable men who have more control over their rate of work (Broadbent and Gath 1979; Broadbent 1981). Taken alone this finding could be due to the selective movement of healthy people away from more unpleasant types of work. However, in other circumstances it has been shown that the same person has more neurotic symptoms when working in more stressful conditions. Thus, student nurses have been studied in different kinds of wards; they reported more symptoms when working in conditions they judged more stressful and less satisfying (Parkes 1982). It seems fair to conclude that stressful conditions of work can play a part in causing neurosis.

Prolonged **unemployment** is associated with increased reporting of minor affective symptoms (Banks and Jackson 1982). The explanation for this finding may be that unemployment causes these symptoms, or that people prone to develop such symptoms are less likely to find work. Warr and Jackson (1985) suggested that the second explanation was improbable, because they found that the severity of symptoms soon after the loss of a job did not predict length of subsequent unemployment. If unemployment is a cause of minor affective disorder, the effect might be related to loss of self-esteem and social role, to financial problems, or to increased emotional conflicts within the family. These factors are discussed further in the next section. [The relationship between employment and mental disorder has been reviewed by Smith (1985).]

Life events

Some general issues about research on life events were discussed on pp. 106–8; in this section we are concerned only with the role of life events in the aetiology of neurosis. It is known that patients with one kind of neurosis, minor affective disorder, report more life events in the three months before the onset of the disorder than are reported in the same period by controls (Cooper and Sylph 1973). However, as explained on p. 108, many people experience adverse events without developing psychiatric disorder.

People may differ in their responsiveness to life events for three reasons. First, the same event may have different meanings for different people. These differences in meaning presumably reflect previous experience; for example a family separation may be more stressful to an adult who has suffered separation in childhood. The second reason is that there may be protective influences in the social environment. For example, in a study of depressive disorders Brown and Harris (1978) found that women with close confiding relationships were more able to tolerate life events. The size of this protective effect is uncertain. Thus in a study of minor neurosis, Henderson *et al.* (1982) concluded that social network factors of this kind were less important than Brown and Harris supposed. It is not possible to decide with certainty between these alternative views because social relationships cannot be measured with sufficient precision. The third reason is that people differ in the personal qualities that enable them to withstand stressors. Little is known about these qualities—often called resilience—but it may be possible to define them by studying people who cope particularly well with stressors.

Causes in the family

It has been suggested that neurosis is an expression of emotional disorder within a whole family, not just a disorder in the person seeking treatment (the 'identified patient'). Although family problems are common among neurotic patients, their general importance is almost certainly overstated in this formulation, since emotional difficulties in other family members may be the result of the patient's neurosis rather than its cause. A study by Kreitman *et al.* (1970) illustrates this point. Compared with wives of controls, wives of neurotic men were found to have higher neuroticism scores and more neurotic symptoms; and these symptoms were more frequent in longer marriages, suggesting that they resulted at least in part from living with a neurotic husband. Such an interaction may be increased by the tendency of neurotic men to spend more time with their wives and less in outside social activities (Kreitman *et al.* 1970; Henderson *et al.* 1978).

Conclusion

The aetiology of neuroses is still not understood clearly. In the most general terms, the evidence is consistent with the idea that neuroses arise when stressful factors in a person's life outweigh both his capacity to deal with them and his supportive relationships. Both the capacity to withstand stress and predisposition to neurosis arise partly from inheritance and partly from upbringing. How upbringing has this effect, and what events in childhood are particularly important, are questions on which there is much speculation but little factual information. However, there is now fairly general agreement that early childhood is not the only important period in the development of predisposition to neurosis. Among stressors, family relations are important but factors related to employment may play a part as well. As mentioned earlier, factors determining whether a person develops a particular kind of neurosis will be considered in the next chapter.

The prognosis of neurosis

This section is concerned with general factors that affect the prognosis of all kinds of neuroses, and also with the outcome of the particular neurotic disorders considered in this chapter.

General issues

The prognosis of neuroses as a group has to be considered in relation to 'level' in the medical services at which they are identified. Among people aged 20–50 with neuroses identified in community surveys, about half recover in three months (Hagnell 1970; Tennant *et al.* 1981*a*). Among people with neuroses attending general practitioners, about half recover within a year (Mann *et al.* 1981), the others remaining unchanged for many months longer. Of those referred for psychiatric out-patient or in-patient treatment, only about half achieve a satisfactory adjustment even within four years (Greer and Cawley 1966). Looked at in another way,

Goldberg and Huxley (1980, p. 104) calculated from the data of Harvey Smith and Cooper (1970) that recent onset cases seen in general practice have a turnover of 70 per cent per year, and chronic cases a turnover of 3 per cent per year.

Death rate is increased by a factor of 1.5 to 2.0 among out-patients with neuroses and 2.0 to 3.0 among in-patients (Sims 1978). The main causes of these deaths are suicide or accident, but other causes are more frequent than expected, possibly because of early failure to diagnose primary physical disease which is causing secondary emotional disorder.

Of the neurotic disorders considered in this chapter, **acute reactions to stress** are, by definition, brief; they contribute substantially to the high turnover of cases described above. By definition, **adjustment disorders** are also of generally good prognosis, lasting a few weeks or months, though a minority last longer. **Post-traumatic stress disorders** have a similar course, though an important minority are prolonged. Of the **minor affective disorders**, about half improve within three months, and three quarters within six months (Catalan *et al.* 1984).

It is not easy to predict the outcome for individual patients with neurosis, but the following tend to be associated with a worse prognosis: symptoms initially severe; social problems likely to persist; lack of social support and friendships (Huxley *et al.* 1979; Cooper *et al.* 1969); and an abnormal personality (Mann *et al.* 1981).

Assessment

When any patient with a neurosis is assessed it is essential to make sure that no primary cause has been overlooked, such as physical disease, depressive disorder, schizophrenia, or dementia. The relative probability of these disorders varies according to the age of the patient. Even if there is no evidence of a primary cause when the patient is first examined, it should always be considered again if there is no improvement in the neurosis after adequate treatment. In weighing up the likelihood of physical disease, it should always be remembered that stressful events are commonplace, and their presence does not exclude the possibility of primary organic disease. This is particularly important in middle-aged patients who have not had a neurosis before and (as described in the next chapter) in any patient with symptoms suggesting a conversion or dissociative disorder.

The search for organic disease requires a thorough history and physical examination, together with appropriate investigations. What is appropriate varies with the age of the patient, the nature of the symptoms, and any clues from the history. If, after appropriate investigation, a degree of uncertainty remains, it is important to make a note of it; the diagnosis should be recorded as provisional and subject to review after a suitable interval. Depressive disorder, dementia, and schizophrenia should also be excluded by careful enquiry about relevant signs and symptoms (described in the chapters on each of these conditions).

When it is as certain as possible that the patient is free from organic disease, affective disorder, schizophrenia, and dementia, the next step is to assess the need for treatment of the neurosis. In deciding this, attention should be paid to the severity of the symptoms, how long they have been present, the likelihood that any causative stress will persist, and the patient's personality. At one extreme, the neurosis is likely to recover quickly without treatment if the symptoms are mild, have been present for only a few weeks, and began when temporary stressful events were present; or if the patient's personality is normal.

Management

The following principles apply to all neurotic disorders. Treatment is in three parts: treatment to relieve symptoms, steps to solve problems, and measures to improve relationships.

When **symptoms** are mild, supportive interviews are as effective as anxiolytic drugs (Catalan *et al.* 1984). In more severe cases an anxiolytic drug may be required for a few days to calm the patient and restore sleep, but this prescription should not be prolonged. It is not necessary to abolish all anxiety; a certain amount may motivate the patient to bring about changes in his life. (Supportive psychotherapy is discussed on pp. 704–5, and the use of anxiolytic drugs on pp. 634–9.)

Whenever possible, **problems** should be solved by the patient and not by other people, though relatives should be encouraged to play a part when appropriate. However, when problems are overwhelming or prolonged, the help of a doctor, nurse, or social worker may be needed. Thus Shepherd *et al.* (1979) found that social work was effective in two-thirds of chronic neuroses seen in general practice. Even in such cases the patient should still be encouraged to take a part in identifying the relevant problems, considering what can be done about each one, and deciding the order in which they should be tackled. In this way he will be better equipped to help himself in the future. When problems cannot be resolved the patient should be helped to come to terms with them.

Although many patients who develop minor neurotic disorders have only temporary problems, others have more prolonged **social difficulties**. Some lack friends in whom they can confide, or have few enjoyable activities. Such people should be encouraged to join a club or, in the case of a housewife who is lonely at home, take part-time paid or voluntary work. For most patients, such normal pursuits are better than those involving other people who are ill. For a few, however, a psychiatric social club or a day centre may be the only way of establishing social contact. For some patients with chronic neuroses, lack of social contacts result from long-standing difficulties in social relationships, and a proportion of these patients can be helped by one of the methods of psychotherapy described in Chapter 18.

Further reading

Fischer-Homberger, E. (1983). Neurosis. In *Handbook of psychiatry* (ed. M. Shepherd and O. Zangwill), Vol. 1. Cambridge University Press, Cambridge.

Goldberg, D. and Huxley, P. (1980). *Mental illness in the community*. Tavistock, London.

Shepherd, M., Cooper, B., Brown, A. C. and Kalton, G. (1981). *Psychiatric illness in general practice*, (2nd edn, with new material by M. Shepherd and A. Clare). Oxford University Press, Oxford.

Slater, E. and Slater, P. (1944). A heuristic theory of neurosis. *Journal of Neurology, Neurosurgery and Psychiatry* 7, 49–55.

7 Neurosis: part II

Anxiety disorders

Anxiety disorders are abnormal states which have the physical and mental symptoms of anxiety as their main clinical features, and which are not secondary to organic brain disease or to another psychiatric disorder. It is usual to classify anxiety disorders further but there is, unfortunately, an important disagreement in the major systems of classification as to how this should be done. This disagreement was noted on p. 156 when the general classification of neuroses was considered. It will now be explained more fully.

The first difference between the two systems of classification is that obsessional disorders are included under the rubric anxiety disorders in DSMIIIR, but not in ICD10 (draft). It is true that anxiety is one of the symptoms of obsessional disorders, and this suggests a relationship between the latter and anxiety disorders. However, obsessional disorders differ in important ways from other disorders with anxiety as a dominant feature, and for this reason they are considered separately in this book (though placed immediately after the anxiety disorders to help readers using DSMIIIR).

Under the rubric anxiety disorders, both DSMIIIR and the draft of ICD10 have another rubric, phobic disorder, for states with prominent phobic symptoms. However, in DSMIIIR some phobic states are classified under another heading. These are states with agoraphobic symptoms and panic attacks which are classified under panic disorders (another sub-group under anxiety disorders) rather than under phobic disorders.

In this chapter anxiety disorders are considered under headings which broadly conform to DSMIIIR and to the draft revision of ICD10 (see Table 7.1). Any differences from these schemes will be noted. For the purposes of description, it is convenient to start with generalized anxiety disorders. (One of the conditions listed in Table 7.1, post-traumatic stress disorder, has already been considered in Chapter 6.)

Clinical picture

Generalized anxiety disorders have psychological and physical symptoms. The **psychological symptoms** are the familiar feeling of fearful anticipation that gives the condition its name, irritability, difficulty in concentration,

Table 7.1. Classification of anxiety disorders and related conditions

DSMIIIR*	ICD10 (draft)
	Phobic disorders
Simple phobia	Simple phobia
Social phobia	Social phobia
Agoraphobia without a history of panic disorder	Agoraphobia
Panic disorder with agoraphobia	
	Other anxiety disorders
Panic disorder without agoraphobia	Panic disorder
Generalized anxiety disorder	Generalized anxiety disorder
	Mixed anxiety depressive disorder
Obsessive-compulsive disorder	Obsessive-compulsive disorder
Post-traumatic stress disorder	Post-traumatic stress disorder

* To aid comparison, the order of listing has been modified.

sensitivity to noise, and a feeling of restlessness. Patients often complain of poor memory when they are really experiencing the effects of failure to concentrate; if there is true memory impairment a careful search should be made for an organic syndrome. Repetitive worrying thoughts form an important part of generalized anxiety disorder. These thoughts are often provoked by awareness of autonomic overactivity; for example, a patient who feels his heart beating fast may worry about having a heart attack. Thoughts of this kind may prolong the condition.

The **appearance** of a person with a generalized anxiety disorder is characteristic. His face looks strained, with a furrowed brow; his posture is tense; he is restless and often tremulous. The skin looks pale, and sweating is common especially from the hands, feet, and axillae. Readiness to tears, which may at first suggest depression, reflects a generally apprehensive state.

The **physical symptoms and signs** of a generalized anxiety disorder result from either over-activity in the sympathetic nervous system or increased tension in skeletal muscles. The list of symptoms is long, and is conveniently grouped by systems of the body. Symptoms related to the *gastrointestinal tract* include dry mouth, difficulty in swallowing, epigastric discomfort, excessive wind caused by aerophagy, borborygmi, and frequent or loose motions. Common *respiratory symptoms* include a feeling of constriction in the chest, difficulty in inhaling (which contrasts with the expiratory difficulty in asthma), and overbreathing and its consequences (which are described below). *Cardiovascular symptoms* include palpitations, a feeling of discomfort or pain over the heart, awareness of missed beats, and throbbing in the neck. Common *genito-urinary symptoms* are increased frequency and urgency of micturition, failure of erection, and lack of libido. Women may complain of increased menstrual discomfort and sometimes amenorrhoea. Complaints related to the functions of the *central nervous system* include tinnitus, blurring of vision, prickling sensations, and dizziness (which is not rotational).

Other symptoms may be related to *muscular tension*. In the scalp this is felt as headache, typically in the form of constriction or pressure, which is usually bilateral and often in the frontal or occipital region. Tension in other muscles may be experienced as aching or stiffness, especially in the back and shoulders. The hands may tremble so that delicate movements are impaired. However, the use of the electromyogram has shown that such symptoms cannot be due solely to muscle tension. Scalp muscle tension is not always greater in patients who have 'tension headaches' than in controls who do not; and in the same patient it is not always greater during headaches than at other times (Martin and Mathews 1978).

It is important to remember that any of these physical symptoms may be the presenting complaint, particularly in general practice. Patients may, for example, complain of palpitations or headaches rather than of anxiety feelings. This presents problems of differential diagnosis that are discussed in the next section.

In generalized anxiety disorders *sleep* is disturbed in a characteristic way. On going to bed the patient lies awake worrying; when at last he falls asleep, he wakes intermittently. He often reports unpleasant dreams. Occasionally he experiences 'night terrors', in which he wakes suddenly feeling intensely fearful, sometimes remembering a nightmare, and sometimes uncertain why he is so frightened. In the morning he often feels unrefreshed. Early waking with inability to sleep again is much less common in the patient with a generalized anxiety disorder than in the patient with a depressive disorder. Therefore early waking should always suggest the possibility that anxiety symptoms are secondary to a depressive disorder.

Overbreathing is breathing in a rapid and shallow way which results in a fall in the concentration of carbon dioxide in the blood. The resultant symptoms include dizziness, tinnitus, headache, a feeling of weakness, faintness, numbness and tingling in the hands and feet and face, carpo-pedal spasms, and precordial discomfort. There is also a feeling of breathlessness, which may prolong the condition. When a patient has unexplained bodily symptoms, the possibility of persistent overbreathing should always be borne in mind. The diagnosis can usually be made by watching the pattern of breathing. If there is doubt, blood gas analysis should decide the matter in acute cases, though the findings may be normal in chronic cases. A helpful account of the condition is given by Hibbert (1984*b*).

Some of these symptoms and signs can be studied objectively with physiological recordings. Although often valuable in research, such recordings are of little help to the clinician who can learn all he needs from a careful history. The measures include sweat gland activity measured by galvanic skin responses, pulse rate, muscle blood flow, and electromyographic activity. Further information can be found in the review by Lader (1975).

Some patients with generalized anxiety disorder experience *panic attacks*. This term denotes sudden episodes of severe anxiety with marked physical symptoms and extreme apprehension (see p. 193). Some panic attacks are caused by involuntary hyperventilation, others result from an increase of anxiety in patients with an already high level of general anxiety. The rest are unexplained (spontaneous).

Patients with generalized anxiety disorder usually have *other symptoms*, notably depressive symptoms but also obsessional symptoms and depersonalization. However, these symptoms are not a major feature of the syndrome.

Differential diagnosis

Generalized anxiety disorders must be distinguished from other psychiatric disorders and from physical illnesses. Anxiety symptoms can occur in all psychiatric illnesses, but in some there are likely to be particular diagnostic difficulties. For example, anxiety is a common symptom of the syndrome of **depressive disorder**; conversely the syndrome of anxiety neurosis often includes some depressive symptoms. The two syndromes can usually be distinguished by the relative severity of the symptoms and by the order in which these appeared. Information on these two points should be obtained from a relative or other informant as well as from the patient. A serious diagnostic error is to mistake the agitation of a severe depressive disorder for a generalized anxiety disorder. This mistake will seldom be made if every anxious patient is asked about symptoms of a depressive disorder including depressive thinking and suicidal ideas.

In **schizophrenia** the patient sometimes complains of anxiety before other symptoms are recognized. However, the correct diagnosis can often be made by asking every anxious patient what he thinks is the cause of his symptoms. In reply, a schizophrenic patient may reveal delusional ideas. **Presenile** or **senile dementia** occasionally comes to notice because the person is complaining of anxiety. When this happens, the clinician may overlook an accompanying memory disorder or dismiss it as the result of poor concentration. Memory should therefore be assessed appropriately in every patient presenting with anxiety. Occasionally a patient dependent on **drugs or alcohol** reports that he is taking these substances to relieve anxiety, either because he wishes to deceive the doctor or because he genuinely mistakes symptoms of drug withdrawal for anxiety. If the patient reports that anxiety is particularly severe on waking in the morning, this should suggest the possiblity of alcohol dependence (withdrawal symptoms being most likely at this time, though it should be remembered that anxiety symptoms occurring as part of a depressive disorder are also worse at this time of day).

Some **physical illnesses** present with anxiety symptoms. In making a diagnosis, they should be considered when no obvious psychological cause can be found and when the personality is normal. Again, some diagnoses may be difficult to make. For example, in *thyrotoxicosis* the patient is irritable and restless, and there is tremor and tachycardia. Anxious patients should therefore be examined for an enlarged thyroid, atrial fibrillation, and exophthalamos. If there is any doubt, thyroid function tests should be arranged. *Phaeochromocytoma* and *hypoglycaemia* should be considered when the anxiety symptoms are episodic. In other physical illness, anxiety is sometimes the presenting symptom because the patient fears that the early symptoms portend fatal illness. This is particularly likely when the patient has a special reason to fear a serious illness, for example, because a relative or friend has died after developing similar symptoms. It is good practice to ask an anxious patient whether he knows anyone who has had similar symptoms.

The opposite diagnostic error can also be made. Thus generalized anxiety disorders with prominent physical symptoms can easily be mistaken for physical disease. The patient may then be subjected to unnecessary investigations that only make him more anxious. Such mistakes will be less common if the doctor remembers the diversity of anxiety symptoms; palpitations, headache, frequency of micturition, and abdominal discomfort can all be the primary complaint of an anxious patient. The correct diagnosis depends on finding other symptoms of generalized anxiety disorder; on enquiring carefully about the order in which symptoms appeared when the illness developed; and on asking about the order in which symptoms are experienced during an attack, for example in a paroxysm of tachycardia, does awareness of rapid heart action come before or after the feelings of anxiety? These issues are discussed further on p. 415.

Epidemiology

One month and one year prevalence rates range from 25 to 64 per 1000 (see Weissman and Merikangas 1986).

Aetiology

Genetic causes

Anxiety disorders are more frequent—about 15 per cent—among the relatives of patients with anxiety disorders than in the general population—about 3 per cent (Brown 1942; Noyes *et al*. 1978). Stronger evidence for a genetic aetiology was obtained by Slater and Shields (1969) in a study of 17 monozygous and 28 dizygous twin pairs, each containing a proband with an anxiety disorder. Forty-one per cent of the monozygous co-twins had an anxiety disorder, compared with only four per cent of the dizygous co-twins.

Personality

Whilst generalized anxiety disorders often occur in people with anxiety-prone personalities (see p. 136), they also arise in people of normal personality and in those with other kinds of personality disorder, notably the obsessional and asthenic types. Measurements of 'neuroticism' (see p. 167) are high in people who are prone to develop generalized anxiety disorder.

Stressful events

Clinical observations indicate that generalized anxiety disorders often begin in relation to stressful events, and become chronic when social problems persist. However, there have been no satisfactory studies specifically directed to the aetiological role of 'life events' in generalized anxiety disorder.

Psychoanalytic theories

These theories suppose that anxiety is experienced when the ego is overwhelmed by excitation. Freud suggested that this excess energy has three possible sources: the outside world (realistic anxiety), the id (neurotic anxiety), and the super-ego (moral anxiety). Breakdown is more likely when the ego has been weakened by developmental failure in childhood. Another part of psychoanalytic theory supposes that anxiety is experienced for the first time during the process of birth (primary anxiety). It is thought that the child is overwhelmed by stimulation at the very moment of separation from its mother. It has been suggested that this may explain why separation can provoke anxiety. This idea that separation is an important cause of neurotic anxiety (in the Freudian sense of this term) has been elaborated by Bowlby (1969).

Taken literally, ideas of energy flowing between compartments of the mind are impossible to reconcile with modern knowledge from the neurosciences. Viewed as metaphors representing the instinctual part of man in conflict with his social training and his conscience, they reflect everyday experience but add little to it.

Conditioning and cognitive theories

Conditioning theories propose that generalized anxiety disorders arise when fear responses become attached to previously neutral stimuli. They explain the tendency to develop these conditioned anxiety responses in terms of an inherited predisposition which is also reflected in an excessive lability of the autonomic nervous system. (For a review of these theories and the possible neural substrates for anxiety responses see Gray 1971.)

Cognitive theories propose that generalized anxiety disorders persist because of the way patients think about their symptoms. Patients with generalized anxiety disorder often fear that rapid heart beating indicates serious heart disease, or dizziness foreshadows a stroke, or depersonalization is evidence of incipient madness. Such fears lead to further anxiety, which in turn increases the symptoms that provoked the fears; thus a vicious circle is set up.

Prognosis

Most generalized anxiety disorders that are of recent onset recover quickly. Of those lasting for more than six months, about 80 per cent are present three years later despite efforts at treatment (Kedward and Cooper 1966). Poor prognosis is associated with severe symptoms and with syncopal episodes, agitation, derealization, hysterical features, and suicidal ideas (Kerr *et al.* 1974). The prognosis of anxiety disorders with mainly physical symptoms can be judged from a follow-up study of 'effort syndrome' by Wheeler *et al.* (1950). Although most patients had a good social prognosis, nine out of ten still had some symptoms 20 years later. Whilst this finding supports the clinical impression that patients who attribute their symptoms to physical causes are less easy to help than those who recognize the emotional basis for their disorder, it may also reflect the limitations of treatment at the time of the study. Thus, in a more recent study of medical patients with anxiety disorder, two-thirds were found to have improved substantially or recovered within six years (Noyes and Clancy 1976).

Although some generalized anxiety disorders persist for several years, they do not change their form. On follow-up, the rates of schizophrenia and manic-depressive disorder found in patients with generalized anxiety disorders are no greater than in the general population (Greer 1969; Kerr *et al.* 1974). On the other hand, brief depressive episodes occur repeatedly among many patients who have long-standing anxiety disorders (Clancy *et al.* 1978). It is often during one of these episodes that patients seek further treatment.

Treatment

Supportive measures

For most generalized anxiety disorders anxiolytic drugs need not be prescribed. Discussion with the doctor and reassurance are usually sufficient. Interviews need not be lengthy provided the patient feels that he has the doctor's undivided attention, and that his problems have been understood sympathetically. A clear explanation should be given of any physical symptoms of anxiety; for example, that palpitations are an exaggeration of a normal reaction to stressful events and not a sign of heart disease. The patient should be helped to deal with or come to terms with any relevant social problems. Anxiety is prolonged by uncertainty and a clear plan of treatment helps to reduce it. (Supportive therapy is discussed on p. 704.)

Behavioural and cognitive treatments

Provided the generalized anxiety disorder is not severe, relaxation training may be helpful. If relaxation is practised regularly, the effects can equal those of anxiolytic drugs, but many patients fail to persevere. Training in a group may improve motivation, and some patients do better when relaxation is part of yoga exercises.

Patients who hyperventilate can be helped in two ways. An immediate treatment is to rebreathe expired air from a bag in order to increase the concentration of carbon dioxide in the alveolar air. This rebreathing is also an effective way of demonstrating the connection between symptoms and hyperventilation. When the connection has been made clear, patients can practise controlled breathing at first under supervision and then at home.

As explained on p. 181, symptoms often persist because patients worry about them. For these patients, a combination of relaxation training and cognitive procedures is usually effective (Butler *et al*. 1987). This treatment—anxiety management—is described on p. 736.

Treatment with drugs

The use of drugs for generalized anxiety disorders should be selective. Drugs can be used to bring symptoms under control quickly, while the effects of other measures are awaited. Drugs may be needed in the minority of patients who do not improve with other measures. There is a general tendency to prescribe drugs too often and for too long, and this should be avoided.

Anxiolytic drugs are discussed on p. 634. In generalized anxiety disorders a long-acting benzodiazepine is appropriate, for example diazepam in a dose ranging from 5 mg twice daily in mild cases to 10 mg three times daily in the most severe. Anxiolytic drugs should seldom be prescribed for more than a few weeks because of the risk of dependence when given for longer. The risk of dependence is particularly great with barbiturates and their use should be avoided.

Beta-adrenergic antagonists are discussed on p. 637. For patients with generalized anxiety disorders, they have a limited use for controlling severe palpitations that do not respond to anxiolytics. Care should be taken to observe the contraindications for the use of these drugs and in other ways to follow the advice given on p. 637.

Tricyclic antidepressants and related compounds can be used to treat anxiety disorders in three circumstances. First, they can be used when symptoms of an existing generalized anxiety disorder have been aggravated by a concurrent depressive disorder. Second, since they are less likely than benzodiazepines and related drugs to be followed by dependence, tricyclic antidepressants can be used for their direct anxiolytic action in cases where there is some risk of dependence. Third, antidepressant drugs can be used in generalized anxiety disorders with frequent panic attacks (part of the group called panic disorder in DSMIII). For this purpose imipramine is usually recommended (Klein 1964). When used in this way imipramine should be started in very small doses to avoid side-effects of insomnia, restlessness, and an unpleasant feeling of agitation. The initial dose may need to be as low as 10 mg per day, increased by 10 mg every three days to 50 mg per day, and then increased by 25 mg every 5–7 days until a dose of 150 mg per day is reached. Higher doses of imipramine may be required; Zitrin *et al.* (1983) used doses over 200 mg per day, but such high doses should be prescribed only to physically fit patients and even then cautiously in view of the side-effects of the drug (see p. 657).

Monoamine oxidase inhibitors have also been used for the three purposes just described. Their effects in generalized anxiety disorders were first described by Sargant and Dally (1962). Because they interact with some drugs and foodstuffs, monoamine oxidase inhibitors should be reserved for cases in which other drugs have been tried without success. Monoamine oxidase inhibitors are discussed on p. 661.

Phobic anxiety disorders

Phobic anxiety disorders have the same core symptoms as generalized anxiety disorders, but these symptoms occur only in particular circumstances. In some phobic disorders these circumstances are few and the patient is free from anxiety for most of the time; in other cases, many circumstances provoke anxiety, but even so there are situations in which no anxiety is experienced. Two other features characterize phobic disorders: the person *avoids* circumstances which provoke anxiety, and he experiences *anticipatory anxiety* when there is the prospect of encountering such circumstances. The circumstances provoking anxiety include situations (for example, crowded places), 'objects' (for example, spiders) and natural phenomena (for example, thunder). For clinical purposes it is usual to recognize three principal phobic syndromes: simple phobia, social phobia, and agoraphobia. These syndromes will be described next, and some less common phobic syndromes will be mentioned later in this section.

Although these three syndromes are widely recognized, phobic disorders are classified differently in ICD10 (draft) and DSMIIIR. In ICD10 (draft) phobic disorders are not subdivided. In DSMIIIR, three subgroups are included: simple phobia, social phobia, and agoraphobia. However, agoraphobic patients who experience more than an arbitrarily determined number of panic attacks (four in four weeks, or one followed by a month of persistent fear of having another) are removed from the phobic disorders and classified as panic disorders. The reasons why panic attacks are given this importance are discussed on p. 193.

Simple phobia

In this type of disorder, a person is inappropriately anxious in the presence of a particular object or situation, which he or she tends to avoid. The whole range of anxiety symptoms (see p. 175) maybe experienced in the presence of the object or in the situation. The tendency to avoid the stimulus is strong, and in most cases there is actual avoidance. The prospect of meeting the object or entering the situation causes anticipatory anxiety; for example, a person who fears storms may become anxious when the sky is overcast. Simple phobias are often characterized by adding the name of the stimulus; for example, spider phobia. In the past it was common practice to use terms such as arachnophobia (instead of spider phobia) or acrophobia (instead of phobia of heights). This practice is not helpful.

Among adults, the life time **prevalence** of simple phobias has been estimated, using DSMIIIR criteria, as between 4 and 15 per cent for men and 9 and 26 per cent for women (Robins *et al.* 1984).

Aetiology Most simple phobias of adult life are a continuation of childhood phobias. In childhood, simple phobias are common (see p. 784). By early teenage years most of these childhood fears have been lost, but a few persist into adult life. Why the few persist is not certain except that, not surprisingly, the most severe of these phobias are likely to last the longest. The psychoanalytic explanation is that phobias that persist are not related to the obvious stimulus but a hidden source of anxiety. In the terms used in this theory, the source of anxiety is excluded from consciousness by repression, and attached to the manifest object by displacement.

A minority of simple phobias begin in adult life, in relation to a highly stressful experience; for example, a phobia of horses may follow a dangerous encounter with a bolting horse.

The **differential diagnosis** of simple phobic disorder is seldom difficult. The possiblity of an underlying depressive disorder should always be kept in mind, since some patients seek help for long-standing simple phobias when a depressive disorder makes them less able to tolerate their phobic symptoms. The **prognosis** of simple phobia in adult life has not been studied systematically. Clinical experience suggests that simple phobias persisting from childhood to adult life continue for many years, whilst those starting in adult life after stressful events have a better prognosis.

Treatment is with the exposure form of behaviour therapy (see p. 728).

Social phobia

In this disorder a person is inappropriately anxious in situations in which he is observed and could be criticized. He tends to avoid such situations, and if he enters them he does not engage in them fully; for example he avoids making conversation, or sits in a place where he is least conspicuous. Anxiety is also felt in anticipation of entering the situations. The situations include, for example, restaurants, canteens and dinner parties; seminars, board meetings and other places where it is necessary to speak in public; and occasions when some minor action is open to scrutiny, e.g. signing a cheque in front of other people. The symptoms are those of an anxiety disorder, complaints of blushing and trembling being particularly frequent. Socially phobic people are often preoccupied with the idea of being observed critically, though aware that the idea is groundless (Amies *et al.* 1983). Some patients take alcohol to relieve the symptoms of anxiety, and alcohol abuse is more common in social phobias than in other phobias.

Social phobias are about equally frequent in men and women. In one survey the six months' **prevalence** was estimated at about 1–2 per cent in men aged 18–64 and about 1–4 per cent among women [Weissman and Merikangas (1986)]. In its **course**, the condition usually begins between the ages of 17 and 30. The first episode occurs in some public place without any apparent reason. Subsequently anxiety occurs in similar places. The episodes gradually become more severe, and avoidance increases.

The **differential diagnosis** includes generalized anxiety disorder, (distinguished by the pattern of situations in which anxiety occurs), depressive disorder (distinguished by examination of the mental state) and schizophrenia. Patients which schizophrenia may avoid social situations because of persecutory delusions; patients with social phobia know that their insistent ideas of being observed are untrue. Social phobia must be distinguished from personality disorders characterized by life-long shyness and lack of self-confidence; the phobia has a recognizable onset and shorter history. Finally, a distinction needs to be made between social phobia and **social inadequacy**. The latter is a primary lack of social skills with secondary anxiety; it is not a phobic disorder but a type of behaviour that occurs in personality disorders and schizophrenia, and among people of low intelligence. Its features include hesitant, dull and inaudible diction, inappropriate use of facial expression and gesture, and failure to look at other people in conversation (see Bryant *et al.* 1976 for a more detailed account).

The **aetiology** of social phobia is not well understood. Most social phobias begin with a sudden episode of anxiety in circumstances like those which become the stimulus for the phobia. A reasonable suggestion is that the subsequent development of phobic symptoms is due to a combination of conditioning and abnormal cognitions. The principal abnormal cognition, which has been called 'fear of negative evaluation', is an undue concern that other people will be critical. Whether this cognition precedes the disorder or develops with it is unknown, but in either case it is likely to increase and perpetuate the phobic anxiety. Social phobia usually begins in late adolescence, when young people are expanding their social contacts and are particularly concerned about the impression they are making on other people. It is possible that social phobias occur particularly among people in whom these concerns are pronounced; however, there is no evidence on which to decide the matter. [See Amies *et al.* (1983) for a more detailed discussion.]

The **treatment** of social phobia is *cognitive behaviour therapy*, in which exposure to feared situations (see p. 735) is combined with anxiety management (see p. 736). The relapse rate is lower after this combined treatment than after exposure alone (Butler *et al.* 1984).

Anxiolytic drugs have a small part to play in the treatment of social phobia. They can be used to help the patients to cope with social encounters that are particularly likely to recur often. They can also be used briefly to reduce symptoms until behavioural treatment has its effect. If cognitive behaviour therapy is not effective, psychotherapy may help some patients, particularly those whose social phobia is associated with pre-existing problems in personal relationships.

For a review of social phobia see Liebowitz *et al.* (1985).

Agoraphobia

Clinical features

Agoraphobic patients are anxious when they are away from home, or in crowds, or in situations they cannot leave easily. In these circumstances the symptoms are those of any anxiety disorder (see p. 175), but other symptoms such as depression, depersonalization, and obsessional thoughts are more frequent in agoraphobia than in other phobic disorders.

Two groups of **anxiety symptoms** are more marked in agoraphobia than in other kinds of phobic disorder. First, *panic attacks* are more frequent, whether in response to environmental stimuli or arising spontaneously. In DSMIIIR, cases with more than four panic attacks in four weeks are classified as panic disorder with agoraphobia; the origins of this convention are discussed on p. 192. Second, *anxious cognitions* about fainting and loss of control are frequent among agoraphobic patients.

Many **situations** provoke anxiety and avoidance, but they fall into a characteristic pattern. They include buses and trains, shops and supermarkets, and places that cannot be left suddenly without attracting attention, such as the hairdresser's chair or a seat in the middle of a row in a place of entertainment. As the condition progresses, patients avoid more and more of these situations until in severe cases they may be more or less confined to their homes (the 'housebound housewife syndrome'). Apparent variations in this pattern are usually due to certain factors that can reduce symptoms. For example, most patients are less anxious when accompanied by a trusted companion and some are helped even by the presence of a child or pet dog. Such effects may suggest, erroneously, that the behaviour is histrionic.

Anticipatory anxiety is a common symptom. In severe cases this anxiety appears hours before the person enters the feared situation, adding to the patient's distress, and sometimes misleading doctors into thinking that the anxiety is generalized rather than phobic.

Other symptoms include depressive symptoms, depersonalization, and obsessional thoughts. Depressive symptoms are common, and often seem to be consequent upon the limitations to normal life caused by anxiety and avoidance. Depersonalization was at one time thought to signify a subgroup of agoraphobia with a special cause. Thus Roth (1959) described the *phobic anxiety depersonalization syndrome* and suggested that it might result from a disorder of the temporal lobes. Subsequent work has not supported this view.

An association has been reported between agoraphobia and *prolapse of the mitral valves*. For example, Kantor *et al.* (1980) reported that 44 per cent of agoraphobic women had prolapse of the mitral valves. Such findings have not been confirmed by subsequent studies.

The **onset and course** of agoraphobia differ in several ways from those of phobic neuroses. Most cases begin in the early or middle twenties, though there is a further period of high onset in the mid-thirties. Both these ages are later than the average ages of onset of simple phobias (childhood) and of social phobias (mostly late teenage years or early twenties; see Marks and Gelder 1966). Typically, the first episode occurs while the person (more often a woman, see below) is waiting for public transport or shopping in a crowded store. Suddenly she becomes extremely anxious without knowing why, feels faint, and experiences palpitations. She rushes away from the place and goes home or to hospital, where she recovers rapidly. When she enters the same or similar surroundings, she becomes anxious again and makes another hurried escape.This sequence recurs over the next weeks and months; the panic attacks are experienced in more and more places, and a habit of avoidance follows. It is unusual to discover any serious immediate stress that could acount for the first panic attack, though some patients describe a background of serious problems (e.g. worry about a sick child); in a few cases the symptoms begin soon after a physical illness or childbirth.

As the condition progresses, agoraphobic patients become increasingly dependent on the spouse or other relatives for help with activities, such as shopping, that provoke anxiety. The consequent demands on the spouse often lead to arguments, but serious marital problems are no more common among agoraphobics than among other people of similar social background (Buglass *et al.* 1977).

Differential diagnosis

Agoraphobia has to be distinguished from generalized anxiety disorder, social phobic disorder, depressive disorder, and paranoid disorder. When DSMIIIR is used, the cases described here as agoraphobia are divided into those with *panic disorder* (diagr.osed as panic disorder with agoraphobia) and those without (diagnosed as agoraphobia without a history of panic disorder).

A patient with *generalized anxiety disorder* may experience increased anxiety in public places, but (unlike the agoraphobic patient) does not describe other situations in which anxiety is absent, and does not show the avoidance pattern characteristic of agoraphobia. In severe cases the distinction may be difficult to make on the basis of current psychiatric state, but the history of the development of the disorder will usually point to the correct diagnosis. Agoraphobia can be confused with *social phobia* because many patients with agoraphobia feel anxious in social situations and some social phobics avoid crowded buses and shops. Detailed enquiry into the present pattern of avoidance and the development of the disorder will usually settle the point. Agoraphobic symptoms can occur in a *depressive disorder* but after careful history taking and mental state examination the diagnosis is seldom in doubt. It is important not to overlook a recent depressive disorder superimposed on a long-standing agoraphobic disorder (see treatment below). Occasionally a patient with a *paranoid disorder* avoids going out and meeting people in shops and other places. There may then be a superficial resemblance to agoraphobia, but this is dispelled if examination of the mental state reveals delusions of persecution or of reference that account for the behaviour.

Epidemiology

Using DSMIIIR criteria, the six-month prevalence of agoraphobia was estimated as about three per cent in two sites in the United States, and about six per cent in a third; the corresponding life time prevalences were about six per cent and about ten per cent (Robins *et al.* 1984, Weissman and Merikangas 1986). In all three sites the prevalence among women was about twice that in men. For seriously disabling agoraphobia, Agras *et al.* (1969) found a point prevalence of about one per thousand.

Aetiology

Theories of aetiology of agoraphobia have to explain why the initial anxiety attacks occur, and why they spread and recur persistently. The two problems will be considered in turn.

There are three explanations for the initial anxiety attacks. The *psychoanalytic* hypothesis proposes unconscious mental conflicts, related to unacceptable sexual or aggressive impulses. However, the only evidence for this hypothesis derives from psychoanalytic interviews with selected patients. (For a more detailed account see Mathews *et al.* 1981.) The *cognitive* hypothesis proposes that the anxiety attacks develop in people who are unreasonably afraid of minor physical symptoms (for example palpitations which are misinterpreted as evidence of serious heart disease). Although such fears are found in patients with established agoraphobia, it is not known whether they predate the disorder or are a consequence of it. The *'biological'* hypothesis proposes that the anxiety attacks result from a failure of normal inhibitory mechanisms in brain areas that control anxiety. This theory is considered under panic disorder on p. 193.

The spread and persistence of anxiety responses can also be explained in more than one way. It is reasonable to suggest that learning mechanisms are important: conditioning could account for the association of anxiety with more and more situations, whilst avoidance learning could account for the subsequent tendency to avoid. Although this explanation seems logical, there is no evidence that agoraphobic patients learn more readily than patients who have panic attacks without becoming agoraphobic. *Personality* may be important: agoraphobic patients are often described as dependent, and prone to avoid rather than confront problems. This dependency could have arisen from over-protection in childhood, which is reported more often by agoraphobics than by controls. However, from such retrospective reports it is not clear whether the dependency was present before the onset of the agoraphobia (see Mathews *et al.* 1981 for a review). Furthermore Buglass *et al.* (1977) found no difference between agoraphobics and controls in history of separation anxiety or of other indices of dependency. It has been suggested that agoraphobia, once started, could be maintained by family problems. However, in a well-controlled study, Buglass *et al.* (1977) found no evidence that agoraphobics had more family problems than controls. Clinical observation suggests that symptoms are sometimes prolonged by overprotective attitudes of other family members. However, this feature is not found in all cases.

Prognosis

Agoraphobia lasting for one year is found to have changed little at five year follow-up (Marks 1969). Brief episodes of depressive symptoms often occur in the course of chronic agoraphobia.

Treatment

In early cases, patients should be encouraged strongly to return to the situations they are avoiding, since avoidance seems to prolong the disorder. The treatment of choice is a form of *behaviour therapy* combining exposure to phobic situations with training in coping with panic attacks (see p. 735). Compared with exposure alone, this combination gives better long-term effects, including substantial and lasting changes in avoidance behaviour, and a reduction in both phobic anxiety and panic attacks (Cohen *et al.* 1984). However, most patients continue to experience mild anxiety in the situations in which symptoms were originally most severe (see Mathews *et al.* 1981). The prognosis for this kind of treatment is better in patients with good marital relationships before treatment (Monteiro *et al.* 1985).

The role of drugs is secondary to that of behaviour therapy. *Anxiolytic drugs* should be given only for a short time and only for a specific purpose such as helping the patient to undertake an important engagement before behavioural treatment has taken effect. *Antidepressant* drugs may be needed to treat concurrent depressive syndrome (see under 'prognosis' above). These drugs are also reported to have a therapeutic effect in agoraphobic patients who are not depressed (e.g. Zitrin *et al.* 1983), possibly by a direct effect on panic attacks (see p. 195). However, Marks *et al.* (1983) did not find a therapeutic effect of imipramine in patients who were not depressed. *Monoamine oxidase inhibitors* (p. 661) have also been reported to reduce agoraphobic symptoms (Sargant and Dally 1962). In the treatment of agoraphobia, a high rate of relapse has been reported when imipramine (Zitrin *et al.* 1983) or monamine oxidase inhibitors (Tyrer and Steinberg 1975) are stopped, even after many months of treatment.

Other phobic disorders

These disorders are not listed separately in either of the major schemes of classification, but are of sufficient clinical interest to warrant consideration here. They include the following phobias:

(i) Of dental treatment

About 5 per cent of adults have fears of the dentist's chair, which can become so severe that all dental treatment is avoided and serious caries develop (see Gale and Ayer 1969; Kleinknecht *et al.* 1973).

(ii) Of excretion

Patients with these phobias either become anxious and unable to pass urine in public lavatories, or have frequent urges to pass urine with associated dread of incontinence. Such patients often arrange their lives so as never to be far from a lavatory. A few have comparable symptoms centred around defecation.

(iii) Of vomiting

Some patients fear that they may vomit in a public place, often a bus or train; in these surroundings they feel anxious and nauseated. A smaller group have repeated fears that other people will vomit in such places.

(iv) Fear of flying

Anxiety during aeroplane travel is, of course, common. A few people have such intense fear that flying is impossible and they seek treatment. This fear occurs occasionally among pilots who have had an accident while flying.

(v) Space phobia

In this syndrome described by Marks (1981), the central feature is a fear of falling made worse by the absence of any immediate source of support. It therefore appears especially in open spaces. It has a superficial resemblance to agoraphobia, but starts later (mean age 55 years), is seldom accompanied by anxiety or depression, does not respond to behaviour therapy, and is often accompanied by evidence of neurological or cardiovascular disorder.

(vi) Of illness

Illness phobias are more closely related to obsessional thoughts than to the other phobic disorders. The patient experiences repeated fearful thoughts that he might have cancer, venereal disease, or some other serious illness. Such fears may be associated with avoidance of hospitals, but are not otherwise specific to situations.

Panic disorder

Although the diagnosis of panic disorder was not used until introduced in DSMIII in 1980, cases fitting this rubric have been described under a variety of names for more than a century. The central feature is the occurrence of panic attacks, that is, sudden attacks of anxiety in which physical symptoms predominate and are accompanied by fear of a serious consequence such as a heart attack. In the past these symptoms have been referred to as irritable heart, Da Costa's syndrome, neurocirculatory asthenia, disorderly action of the heart, and effort syndrome. These early descriptions assumed that patients were correct in fearing a disorder of cardiac function. Some later authors suggested psychological causes but it was not until the Second World War (when interest in this condition revived) that Wood (1941) convincingly showed it to be a form of anxiety disorder. From then until 1980 patients with panic attacks were classified as having either generalized or phobic anxiety disorders. In 1980 the authors of DSMIII introduced a new diagnostic category, panic disorder, which included patients whose panic attacks occurred with or without generalized anxiety, but excluded those whose panic attacks appeared in the course of agoraphobia. In the later DSMIIIR, all patients with frequent panic attacks are classified as having panic disorder whether or not they have agoraphobia. (Agoraphobia without panic attacks has a separate rubric.) The category panic disorder did not appear in ICD9; it does appear in the draft ICD10, but (unlike DSMIII) is not applied to agoraphobic patients. Although the description of panic disorder in this book concerns the later more restricted group, it largely applies to the wider group as well.

Clinical features

The symptoms of a panic attack are listed in Table 7.2. Not every patient has all these symptoms. (For the diagnosis of a panic disorder, DSMIIIR requires at least four of the symptoms in at least one attack of panic.) Important features of panic attacks are that anxiety builds up quickly, the response is severe, and there is fear of a catastrophic outcome. In DSMIIIR the diagnosis is made when panic attacks occur unexpectedly (i.e. not in response to a known phobic stimulus), and when more than four attacks have occurred in four weeks, or one attack has been followed by four weeks of persistent fear of another attack. The arbitrary nature of these criteria should be noted.

Differential diagnosis

Panic attacks occur in generalized anxiety disorders, phobic anxiety disorders (most often agoraphobia), depressive disorders, and acute organic disorders. In DSMIIIR panic disorder can be diagnosed when these disorders are present but, in the United Kingdom it is the custom not to diagnose panic disorder in the presence of these other disorders.

Table 7.2. Symptoms of a panic attack (from DSMIIIR)

Shortness of breath and smothering sensations
Choking
Palpitations and accelerated heart rate
Chest discomfort or pain
Sweating
Dizziness, unsteady feelings or faintness
Nausea or abdominal distress
Depersonalization or derealization
Numbness or tingling sensations
Flushes or chills
Trembling or shaking
Fear of dying
Fears of going crazy or of doing something uncontrolled

Epidemiology

Recent epidemiological studies have used criteria similar to those of DSMIIIR by including cases with repeated panic attacks whether or not accompanied by agoraphobia. Using these criteria the six months' prevalence of panic disorder is about 6–10 per 1000 (Von Korff *et al.* 1985); the lifetime prevalence is estimated to be about 7–20 per 1000 in people aged 18–65 (Robins *et al.* 1984). The prevalence in women is about twice that in men. Von Korff *et al.* (1985) also estimated the prevalence of panic attacks that were too mild or too infrequent to meet criteria for panic disorder: the six months' prevalence was about 30 per 1000. No sharp cut-off was found for panic attacks meeting or not meeting the criteria for panic disorders; instead there seemed to be a continuous variation. [For a review, see Weissman and Merikangas (1986).]

Aetiology

There are three main hypotheses about the origin of panic disorder. The first proposes a biochemical abnormality, the second hyperventilation, and the third a cognitive abnormality. Each will be briefly considered in turn. [For a more detailed discussion see Gelder (1986*b*).]

The *biochemical hypothesis* is reflected in the term 'endogenous anxiety' which has been proposed for these cases. The hypothesis is based on three sets of observations. First, chemical agents such as sodium lactate and yohimbine can induce panic attacks more readily in patients with panic disorder than in healthy people. Second, panic attacks are reduced by the drug imipramine. Third, there is some evidence that panic disorder occurs more often among relatives, suggesting a genetic basis (Crowe *et al.* 1983). Twin studies support this idea but the numbers studied are too small for a definitive conclusion. The findings of these family and twin studies may indicate only that severe anxiety disorders (marked by panic attacks) have a greater genetic loading than milder ones—a pattern that is found in genetic studies of other disorders.

A specific biochemical mechanism has been proposed, namely inadequate functioning of the presynaptic alpha-adrenoceptors that normally damp down the activity of the presynaptic neurone at noradrenergic synapses. Although this hypothesis can account for the effects of yohimbine in provoking panics (Charney *et al.* 1984), and could account for the effects of imipramine, it is not firmly established. In particular it is not known whether, in patients with panic disorder, abnormal responses to drugs such as yohimbine were present before the panics began.

The *hyperventilation hypothesis* is based on the observation that in some people, voluntary over-breathing produces symptoms like those of a panic attack (Hibbert 1984*b*). The hypothesis is that 'spontaneous' panic attacks result from involuntary hyperventilation. However, although some panics appear to originate, or to be exacerbated, in this way, hyperventilation has not been shown to be a general cause of panic disorder.

The *cognitive hypothesis* is based on the observation that fears about serious physical or mental illness are more frequent in patients with panic attacks than in anxious patients without panic attacks (Hibbert 1984*a*). The hypothesis is that, in panic disorder, there is a spiral in which anxiety leads to physical symptoms which in turn activate fears of illness and more anxiety (see Clark 1986). These observations suggest a cognitive treatment for panic disorder (see pp. 195 and 736).

Course and prognosis

Little is known about the course and prognosis of panic disorder. Recent follow-up studies have generally included patients with panic attacks and agoraphobia as well as patients with panic disorder alone. Earlier studies used categories such as effort syndrome. One study of effort syndrome found that 90 per cent still had symptoms 20 years later, though most had a good social outcome (Wheeler *et al.* 1950). In a more recent study of patients with panic disorder (diagnosed with DSMIII criteria) mortality rates from unnatural causes and, among men, from cardiovascular disorders were found to be higher than average (Coryell *et al.* 1982).

Treatment

Apart from supportive measures and attention to any causative personal or social problems, treatment is either with drugs or cognitive therapy.

Benzodiazepines are not generally as effective in patients with frequent panic attacks as they are in generalized anxiety. Recently a high-potency drug alprazolam has been claimed to be particularly effective. However, in one study in which comparable doses were used, alprazolam was found to be no more effective than diazepam in reducing panic attacks (Dunner *et al.* 1986). The use of the antidepressant drug **imipramine** for patients with panic attacks was introduced by Klein (1964). The first effect of the drug in these patients is often to produce an unpleasant feeling of apprehension, sleeplessness, and symptoms of increased sympathetic activity such as palpitations. For this reason small doses are used at first. One regime is 10 mg per day for three days, increasing by 10 mg every three days to 50 mg per day, and then by 25 mg per week to 150 mg per day. If symptoms are not then under control, further increments of 25 mg may be given to a maximum of 175–225 mg per day depending on the size of the patient and provided he is physically fit. Before high doses are given, an ECG should be done if there is any doubt about cardiac function. Full dosage is continued for three to six months. A relapse rate of up to 30 per cent has been reported after stopping imipramine in patients whose panic disorder was accompanied by phobias (Zitrin *et al.* 1978). For further information about the use of imipramine and other tricyclic drugs see pp. 655–61.

Recently a technique of **cognitive therapy** has been used to reduce fears of the physical effects of anxiety, on the assumption that such fears prolong the disorder. Common fears are that palpitations indicate an impending heart attack, or that dizziness indicates impending loss of consciousness. The relevant symptoms are induced by voluntary means— usually hyperventilation but occasionally in other ways such as exercise— and it is explained that the symptoms of a panic attack have an equally benign origin. This demonstration is followed by further explanation of the origin of the feared symptoms, and questioning of the patient's beliefs about them. Substantial improvement in symptoms has been reported in uncontrolled investigations of this treatment (for example, Clark *et al.* 1985) but controlled studies are needed before the treatment can be evaluated fully.

Transcultural variations of anxiety disorders

Koro is seen amongst men in South-west Asia, more commonly among the Chinese. The Cantonese people call it *Suk-Yeong*, which means shrinking of the penis. The patient experiences episodes of acute anxiety, lasting from 30 minutes to a day or two, in which he complains of palpitations, sweating, pericardial discomfort, and trembling. At the same time he is convinced that his penis will retract into the abdomen, and that when this process is complete he will die. Most episodes occur at night, sometimes after sexual activity. Patients may tie the penis to an object, or ask another person to hold the organ. This belief is not a delusion but resembles the conviction held by some Western patients during a panic attack that the heart will be damaged and they will die. (See Yap 1965 for a more detailed account.)

In other cultures less extreme variations of anxiety disorders are seen in which the presenting symptoms are more often somatic than mental. Leff (1981) has pointed out that this difference in symptomatology parallels the different vocabulary that is available for describing anxiety in the corresponding languages. Thus, in several African, Oriental, and American Indian languages there is no word for anxiety; instead a phrase denoting bodily experience is used. For example, in Yoruba, an African language, the phrase is 'the heart is not at rest'.

Obsessive-compulsive disorder

A useful general description of obsessive-compulsive disorder is contained in ICD9 where it is characterized as a state in which

the outstanding symptom is a feeling of subjective compulsion—which must be resisted—to carry out some action, to dwell on an idea, to recall an experience, or to ruminate on an abstract topic. Unwanted thoughts which intrude, the insistency of words or ideas, ruminations or trains of thought are perceived by the patient to be inappropriate or nonsensical. The obsessional urge or idea is recognized as alien to the personality but as coming from within the self. Obsessional actions may be quasi-ritual performances designed to relieve anxiety, e.g. washing the hands to deal with contamination. Attempts to dispel the unwelcome thoughts or urges may lead to a severe inner struggle, with intense anxiety.

Clinical picture

Obsessive-compulsive disorders are characterized by obsessional thinking, compulsive behaviour, and varying degrees of anxiety, depression, and depersonalization. Obsessional and compulsive symptoms are decribed on pp. 22–4, but the reader may find it helpful if the main features are repeated here.

Obsessional thoughts are words, ideas, and beliefs recognized by the patient as his own, that intrude forcibly into his mind. Because they are usually unpleasant, attempts are made to exclude them. It is the combination of an inner sense of compulsion and of efforts at resistance that characterize obsessional symptoms, but the amount of resistance is the more variable of the two. Obsessional thoughts may take the form of single words, phrases, or rhymes; they are usually unpleasant or shocking to the patient, and may be obscene or blasphemous. **Obsessional images** are vividly imagined scenes, often of a violent or disgusting kind, involving for example abnormal sexual practices.

Obsessional ruminations are internal debates in which arguments for and against even the simplest everyday actions are reviewed endlessly. Some **obsessional doubts** concern actions that may not have been completed adequately, such as turning off a gas tap or securing a door; others concern actions that may have harmed other people, for example, driving a car past a cyclist might have caused him to fall off his bicycle. Sometimes doubts are related to religious convictions or observances ('scruples')—a phenomenon well known to those who hear confession.

Obsessional impulses are urges to perform acts, usually of a violent or embarrassing kind; for example, leaping in front of a car, injuring a child, or shouting blasphemies in church.

Obsessional rituals include both mental activities, such as counting repeatedly in a special way or repeating a certain form of words; and repeated but senseless behaviours, such as washing the hands 20 or more times a day. Some of these have an understandable connection with obsessional thoughts that precede them, for example repeated handwashing and thoughts of contamination. Other rituals have no such connection; for example, routines concerned with laying out clothes in a complicated way before dressing. Some patients feel compelled to repeat such actions a certain number of times; if this cannot be achieved, they have to start the whole sequence again. Patients are invariably aware that their rituals are illogical, and usually try to hide them. Some fear that their symptoms are a sign of incipient madness, and are greatly helped by reassurance that this is not so.

Both obsessional thoughts and rituals inevitably lead to slow performance of everyday activities. However, a minority of obsessional patients are afflicted by extreme **obsessional slowness** that is out of proportion to other symptoms (Rachman 1974).

Obsessional thoughts and compulsive rituals may worsen in certain situations; for example, obsessional thoughts about harming other people often increase in a kitchen or other place where knives are kept. Because patients often avoid such situations, there may be a superficial resemblance to the characteristic pattern of avoidance found in a phobic anxiety disorder. It is partly for this reason that obsessional thoughts with fearful content (such as thoughts about knives) have been called **obsessional phobias**.

Anxiety is an important component of obsessive-compulsive disorders. Some rituals are followed by a diminution of anxiety, whilst others are followed by increased anxiety (Walker and Beech 1969). It is because anxiety is such a prominent symptom that these conditions are classified as anxiety disorders in DSMIIIR.

Obsessional patients are often **depressed**. In some, this seems to be an understandable reaction to the obsessional symptoms, but others have recurring depressive mood swings that arise independently. A proportion of obsessional patients also report **depersonalization**.

The **obsessional personality** is described in Chapter 5. It is important to realize that obsessional personality and obsessive-compulsive disorders do not have a simple one-to-one relationship. Obsessional personality is over-represented among patients who develop obsessive-compulsive disorder, but about a third of obsessional patients have other types of personality (Lewis 1936*b*). Moreover, people with obsessional personality are more likely to develop depressive disorders than obsessive-compulsive disorders (Pollitt 1960).

Differential diagnosis

Obsessive-compulsive disorders have to be distinguished from other disorders in which obsessional symptoms occur. The distinction from **generalized anxiety disorder, panic disorder**, or **phobic disorder** should seldom be difficult provided that a careful history is taken and the mental state is examined thoroughly. The course of obsessive-compulsive disorder is often punctuated by periods of depression in which the obsessional symptoms increase; when this happens the depressive disorder may be overlooked. **Depressive disorders** may also present with obsessional symptoms; it is particularly important to bear these conditions in mind because they usually respond well to antidepressant treatment. Obsessive-compulsive disorder is occasionally difficult to distinguish from **schizophrenia**, especially when the degree of resistance is doubtful, the obsessional thoughts are peculiar in content (for example, mingling sexual and blasphemous themes), or the rituals are exceptionally odd. In such cases it is important to search for schizophrenic symptoms, and to question relatives carefully about other aspects of the patient's behaviour. Obsessional symptoms are found occasionally in **organic cerebral disorders** and were especially common after the encephalitis lethargica epidemic in the 1920s.

Epidemiology

Obsessive-compulsive disorders are less frequent than anxiety neuroses. Estimates of one-year prevalence vary from 0.1–2.3 per 1000 (see Carey *et al.* 1980). A recent American study (using DSMIII criteria) found a lifetime prevalence of 2–3 per cent (Robins *et al.* 1984). Men and women are probably affected equally.

Aetiology

Healthy people experience occasional intrusive thoughts, some of which are concerned with sexual, aggressive, and other themes similar to those of obsessional patients (Rachman and Hodgson 1980). It is the frequency, intensity, and above all the persistence of obsessional phenomena that have to be explained.

Genetics

Obsessive-compulsive disorders have been found in about 5–7 per cent of the parents of patients with these disorders (Rüdin 1953; Brown 1942); although low, this rate is higher than in the general population. These findings could, of course, reflect environmental as well as genetic causes. Twin studies would help to identify the genetic component, but too few cases have been reported to allow firm conclusions. Whilst the genetic evidence for obsessive-compulsive disorders is uncertain, obsessional personality traits can be accounted for largely by genetic influences (Murray *et al.* 1981).

Relation to schizophrenia

The few reported cases of schizophrenia following obsessive-compulsive disorders (for example, Stengel 1945) can probably be explained by coincidence. Follow-up investigations clearly show that typical obsessional patients seldom develop features of schizophrenia (Kringlen 1965).

Organic factors

The clinical features of some severe obsessive-compulsive disorders are so difficult to explain in psychological terms that organic brain disorder has been suggested as the cause. Further evidence for an organic cause was the frequency of obsessional symptoms in patients after the epidemic of encephalitis lethargica in the 1920s. However, in most obsessional patients there is no convincing evidence of disease of the central nervous system.

Early experience

It is uncertain what part early experience plays in the aetiology of obsessive-compulsive disorders. Obsessional mothers might be expected to transmit symptoms to their children by imitative learning. However, the children of patients with obsessive-compulsive disorder have an increased risk of non-specific neurotic symptoms, but not of obsessional symptoms (Cowie 1961).

Psychoanalytic theories

Freud (1895*a*) originally suggested that obsessional symptoms result from repressed impulses of an aggressive or sexual nature. This idea fits with the turbulent sexual fantasies of many obsessional patients, and with their restraints on their own sexual and aggressive impulses. Freud also proposed that obsessional symptoms occur as a result of regression to the anal stage of development. Although this idea has not been confirmed by objective evidence, it is consistent with the obsessional patient's frequent concerns over excretory functions and dirt. Freud's ideas draw attention to the aggressive quality of many of the symptoms. However, as a causal explanation of obsessive-compulsive disorder it is not convincing.

Learning theory

It has been suggested that obsessional rituals are the equivalent of avoidance responses, but as a general explanation this cannot be sustained because anxiety increases rather than decreases after some rituals (Walker and Beech 1969). A useful review of this and other aspects of aetiology is given by Rachman and Hodgson (1980).

Prognosis

About two-thirds of cases improve by the end of a year. Cases lasting more than a year usually run a fluctuating course, with periods of partial or complete remission lasting a few months to several years (see Pollitt 1957). Prognosis is worse when the personality is obsessional and symptoms severe (Kringlen 1965), and when there are continuing stressful events in the patient's life. Severe cases may be exceedingly persistent; for example, in a study of obsessional patients admitted to hospital, Kringlen (1965) found that three-quarters remained unchanged 13–20 years later.

Treatment

In treatment, it is important to remember that obsessive-compulsive disorder often runs a fluctuating course with long periods of remission. The patient's evident distress often seems to call for vigorous treatment, but if the natural course of the condition is kept in mind, the doctor will avoid the common error of over-treating it. It is also essential to remember that depressive disorder often accompanies obsessive-compulsive disorder, and that effective treatment of the depressive disorder often leads to improvement in the obsessional symptoms. For this reason, in every patient presenting with obsessive-compulsive disorder, a thorough search should be made for depressive disorder.

Treatment should begin with an explanation of the symptoms, and if necessary with reassurance that they are not an early sign of madness (a common concern of obsessional patients). Obsessional patients often involve other family members in their rituals, so in planning treatment it is essential to interview relatives and encourage them to adopt a firm but sympathetic attitude to the patient.

Drugs

Anxiolytic drugs give some short-term symptomatic relief but should not be prescribed for more than a few weeks at a time. If anxiolytic treatment is needed for more than a month or two, small doses of a tricyclic antidepressant or a major tranquillizer are sometimes of value. Any coincident depressive disorder should be treated with an antidepressant drug in full dosage. It has been reported that one tricyclic antidepressant, clomipramine, has a specific action against obsessional symptoms (Capstick 1975) but a controlled clinical trial (Marks *et al.* 1980) indicated that the drug effects are modest and occur only in patients with definite depressive symptoms.

Behaviour therapy

Obsessional rituals usually improve with a combination of response prevention and exposure to any environmental cues that increase them (see Chapter 18 for a description of these treatments). About two-thirds of patients with moderately severe rituals can be expected to improve substantially but not completely (Boulagouris 1977; Rachman and Hodgson 1980). When rituals are reduced by this treatment, the accompanying obsessional thoughts usually improve as well.

Behavioural treatment is considerably less effective for obsessional thoughts occurring without rituals. The technique of thought-stopping has been used for many years but there is no good evidence that it has a specific effect. Indeed Stern *et al.* (1973) found an effect which did not differ from that of thought-stopping directed to irrelevant thoughts.

Psychotherapy

We have noted that obsessive-compulsive disorder runs a fluctuating course and may improve eventually whatever treatment is given. Until recovery, supportive interviews can benefit patients by providing continuing hope. Joint interviews with the spouse are indicated when marital problems seem to be aggravating the symptoms. However, exploratory and interpretative psychotherapy seldom help. Indeed some obsessional patients are made worse because these procedures encourage painful and unproductive rumination about the subjects discussed during treatment.

Psychosurgery

The immediate results of psychosurgery for severe obsessive-compulsive disorder are often striking, with a marked reduction in tension and distress. It has not been proved, however, that the long-term prognosis is improved, since no prospective controlled trial has been carried out. In a retrospective survey, Tan *et al.* (1971) studied 24 leucotomized patients, of whom 23 had undergone a bimedial operation. Compared with retrospectively chosen controls, the operated patients improved more in obsessional symptoms and social handicap over the next five years; post-operative personality changes were slight. For other forms of operation only uncontrolled assessments were available. Göktepe *et al.* (1975) followed

18 patients for two years after subcaudate tractotomy, and reported that seven recovered and eight improved. Mitchell-Heggs *et al.* (1976) followed 27 patients for 16 months after limbic leucotomy and reported that 7 recovered and 11 improved substantially. However, these periods of follow-up are much too short to allow definite conclusions.

In the absence of information from controlled studies, it is only justifiable to consider brain surgery when it has been demonstrated repeatedly in the individual patient that all other methods have failed. Even then surgery should be considered only when the obsessive-compulsive disorder has persisted unchanged for many years. Psychosurgery should not be used unless there has been a year of vigorous in-patient or day-patient treatment including both antidepressant drugs and behavioural treatment. If this practice is followed, the operation will be undertaken very rarely indeed. If the operation is done at all, it should probably be followed by a vigorous programme of behavioural therapy.

Conversion and dissociative disorders

Until recently these disorders were generally referred to as hysteria. A change of terminology has been suggested mainly because the word hysteria is used in everyday language to denote extravagant behaviour, and it is confusing to use the same word for the different phenomena of the syndrome considered here.

The two major systems of classification have adopted different conventions. In DSMIIIR the terms conversion and dissociative disorder are used, the former to denote disorders in which physical symptoms are the prinicipal manifestations of the disorder, the latter referring to mainly psychological manifestations such as amnesia and multiple personalities. In ICD10 (draft) both kinds of manifestation are called dissociative disorders, with a subdivision into dissociative disorders of movement and sensation (corresponding to dissociative disorders in DSMIIIR).

In this chapter the word hysteria is used occasionally as a convenient collective term for conversion and dissociative disorders, but otherwise the latter terms are preferred.

Conversion or dissociative symptoms and syndromes

A conversion or dissociative symptom is one that suggests physical illness but occurs in the absence of physical pathology and is produced unconsciously rather than deliberately. There are two obvious difficulties with this concept. First, physical pathology can seldom be excluded with complete certainty when a patient is first seen. The second difficulty is that it may be impossible to be certain that the symptoms are produced by unconscious mechanisms. Uncertainty about diagnosis can often be overcome only by waiting for follow-up information; until this is available the diagnosis of conversion or dissociative disorder has to be provisional, to be reviewed as new evidence becomes available. Uncertainty about the extent to which symptoms arise from unconscious mechanisms is even more difficult to resolve because, as explained on p. 209, there often seems to be a mixture of conscious and unconscious mechanisms.

Conversion and dissociative symptoms can occur in several psychiatric disorders. They are, of course, the main features of conversion and dissociative disorders but they also occur in anxiety, depressive, and organic mental disorders. It is important to recognize this and search carefully for other symptoms of these primary disorders before concluding that conversion symptoms indicate a conversion disorder or that dissociative symptoms indicate a dissociative disorder.

In this chapter the term psychogenic is used in places as a convenient way of referring to individual symptoms without using the term hysteria, for example the term psychogenic paralysis is used instead of hysterical paralysis. This usage follows that in ICD10 (draft).

Clinical picture

General considerations

Although conversion and dissociative symptoms are not produced deliberately, they represent the patient's ideas about illness. Sometimes the symptoms imitate those of a relative or friend who has been ill. Sometimes they originate in the patient's own experience of ill health; for example dissociative memory loss may appear in someone who has had a previous head injury. The reproduction of disease will be least accurate in people who know least about it, such as children and the mentally retarded, and most accurate in people with special knowledge, such as those working in a hospital. As a rule, there are obvious discrepancies between signs and symptoms of conversion and dissociative disorder and those of organic disease; for example, the pattern of anaesthesia does not correspond to the anatomical innervation of the part. Thorough physical examination is therefore essential in every case.

The symptoms of conversion and dissociative disorder usually confer some advantage on the patient. For this reason, following Freud, these disorders have been said to produce **secondary gain** (the primary gain is that anxiety arising from a psychological conflict is excluded from the patient's conscious mind). Thus a woman may be spared the care of an elderly relative if she develops a conversion disorder with paralysis of the arm. Although characteristic of conversion and dissociative disorders, secondary gain is not confined to it; people with physical illness sometimes gain some advantage from their misfortunes. A woman with paralysis of the arm due to organic cause may be pleased to be spared from nursing an elderly relative. Secondary gain is also seen at times in other neuroses; for example, an agoraphobic woman may receive more attention from her husband when she cannot go out. It follows that although secondary gain is an important feature of conversion and dissociative disorder, it cannot be used to support the diagnosis.

Patients with conversion and dissociative symptoms often show less than the expected amount of distress, a state sometimes called *'belle indiffér-ence'* following French writers of the nineteenth century. This is not the same as the attitude of stoical patients who do not allow themselves to show distress. The patient with a conversion disorder may be unconcerned by his symptoms, but often shows exaggerated emotional reactions in other ways. In keeping with this, in a small series of patients with conversion disorder, Lader and Sartorius (1968) found exceptionally high levels of autonomic arousal.

Disorders of movement

These disorders include paralysis of voluntary muscles, tremor, tics, and disorders of gait. When a limb with psychogenic **paralysis** is examined, the lack of movement is often seen to result from simultaneous action of flexors and extensors. If no muscle activity follows a request to move the part, other tests usually show that the muscles are capable of reacting when the patient's attention is directed elsewhere. The pattern of paralysis does not conform to the innervation of the part. Appropriate changes in reflexes are not present; in particular the plantar response always remains flexor. Wasting is absent except in chronic cases, when disuse atrophy may occasionally be seen. With this exception, muscle wasting strongly suggests an organic cause. Similarly, although the limbs may be held in the flexed position, true contractures are uncommon. Psychogenic **disorders of gait** are usually of a striking kind that draws attention to the patient and are worse when he is observed. The pattern does not resemble any described in known neurological conditions. Although dramatic unsteadiness may appear when balance is tested, it often disappears when the patient's attention is directed elsewhere.

Typically, psychogenic **tremor** is coarse and involves the whole limb. It worsens when attention is drawn to it, but so do many tremors with neurological causes. Choreo-athetoid movements with organic cause are easily mistaken for psychogenic symptoms. Disease of the nervous system should always be considered carefully before diagnosing any abnormal movement as psychogenic.

Psychogenic **aphonia** and **mutism** are not accompanied by any disorder of the lips, tongue, palate, or vocal cords, and the patient is able to cough normally. They are usually more extreme than corresponding conditions caused by organic lesions.

Disorders of sensation

Sensory symptoms include anaesthesiae, paraesthesiae, hyperaesthesiae, and pain, as well as deafness and blindness. In general, the sensory changes are distinguished from those in organic disease by a distribution that does not conform to the known innervation of the part, by their varying intensity, and by their response to suggestion. The last point must be used cautiously in diagnosis because, among suggestible patients, sensory symptoms with an organic cause may also respond to suggestion. **Hyperaesthesiae** are usually felt in the head or abdomen, and may be described as painful or burning. Though it is often said that extravagant descriptions support a psychogenic origin for such symptoms, this is not a safe diagnostic point because patients with histrionic personalities may describe symptoms of organic disease in equally florid terms. The diagnosis of **psychogenic pain** should be made only after a thorough search for organic causes (psychogenic pain is discussed further in Chapter 12).

Psychogenic **blindness** may take the form of a concentric diminution of the visual field ('tunnel vision') but other patterns of field defect occur as well. The blindness is not accompanied by changes in pupillary reflexes, and there may be indirect evidence that the person can see; for example, avoidance of bumping into furniture. The findings of perimetry are variable, whilst visual evoked responses are normal. Similar considerations apply to psychogenic **deafness**.

Psychogenic **convulsions** can usually be distinguished from epilepsy in three ways. The patient does not become unconscious, though he may be inaccessible; the pattern of movements does not show a regular and stereotyped form of seizure; there is no incontinence, cyanosis, or injury, and the tongue is not bitten. Also electroencephalographic findings are normal. Occasionally it is difficult to distinguish between complex partial seizures (temporal lobe epilepsy) and psychogenic convulsions, but the introduction of continuous EEG monitoring has made this less difficult. The older term **hystero-epilepsy** should not be used because it is ambiguous. If there is evidence of a true seizure disorder with electrographic abnormality, the diagnosis is epilepsy even if additional psychogenic features are present.

Gastrointestinal symptoms include complaints of abdominal discomfort, flatulence, and regurgitation. Repeated **vomiting** may be a symptom of emotional disturbance and is sometimes classified as psychogenic. This diagnosis should be made only after thorough investigation to exclude physical causes. In any case, psychogenic vomiting is a poorly understood condition, and is sufficiently unlike other manifestations of hysteria as to be appropriately considered separately. **Globus hystericus** has been shown by cine-radiology to be frequently caused by an abnormality in the physical mechanism of swallowing, or by oesophageal reflux or other disease affecting the oesophagus (Delahunty and Ardran 1970). It is a diagnosis that should be made exceedingly rarely, and then only after thorough physical investigation.

Briquet's syndrome

This name was suggested by a group of psychiatrists in St Louis to denote patients who have multiple physical symptoms starting before the age of 30 and lasting for many years, but without evidence of physical disease. The intention is to define patients in whom organic disease is clearly excluded and a psychogenic aetiology is undoubted. To make diagnosis more reliable, there is a list of 37 symptoms from which 15 must be present to make the diagnosis. None of these symptoms should be explained adequately by physical disease, injury, or the effects of medication, alcohol, or other drugs (Perley and Guze 1962). This criterion, together with the requirement of a history lasting many years, can be used to define a restricted group whose prognosis is more certain than the rest (Guze *et al.* 1986), but it excludes many patients for whom the diagnosis of conversion or dissociative disorder has to be considered. The name is derived from a nineteenth century French physician who wrote an important monograph on hysteria (Briquet 1859), although he did not describe the exact syndrome now referred to by his name.

Mental symptoms

Psychogenic **amnesia** starts suddenly. Patients are unable to recall long periods of their lives and sometimes deny any knowledge of their previous life or personal identity. A proportion of those who present in this way have concurrent organic disease, especially epilepsy, multiple sclerosis, or the effects of head injury (Kennedy and Neville 1957). These organic cases have similar symptoms to the psychogenic cases, and are also likely to start suddenly. Moreover, patients with organic disease may be as suggestible as those without it, and may recover their memory just as well.

In a psychogenic **fugue** the patient not only loses his memory but also wanders away from his usual surroundings. When found he usually denies all memory of his whereabouts during the period of wandering, and may also deny knowledge of his personal identity. Fugues also occur in epilepsy, severe depressive disorders, and alcoholism. They may also be associated with suicide attempts. Many patients who present in fugue give a history of seriously disturbed relationships with their parents in childhood, and many others are habitual liars (Stengel 1941).

Pseudodementia is a more extensive disorder with abnormalities of memory and behaviour that at first seem to indicate generalized intellectual impairment. Simple tests of memory are answered wrongly but in a way that strongly suggests the correct answer is in the patient's mind. It is often difficult to be certain how much of the behaviour is deliberately produced. However, the same clinical picture is sometimes associated with organic brain disease, epilepsy, or schizophrenia. (The term pseudo-dementia is also applied in a different sense to the apparent dementia of depressed elderly patients.)

The **Ganser syndrome** is a rare condition that has four features: the giving of 'approximate answers', psychogenic physical symptoms, halluci-nations, and apparent clouding of consciousness. It was first described among prisoners (Ganser 1898) but is not confined to them. The term 'approximate answers' denotes answers (in response to simple questions) that are plainly wrong and strongly suggest that the correct reply is known. Thus a patient who is asked how many legs a chicken has, might reply three; and when asked to add two and two might answer five. When hallucinations are present, they are usually visual and may be of an elaborate kind. The obvious advantage that a prisoner can gain from illness, coupled with the approximate answers, often suggests a crude form of malingering. However, the condition is maintained so consistently that unconscious mental mechanisms are generally thought more likely. Others have suggested that the syndrome is an unusual form of psychosis (see Whitlock 1961). An organic mental disorder should be excluded, particu-larly when muddled thinking and visual hallucinations are part of the clinical picture.

In psychogenic **stupor**, the patient shows the characteristic features of stupor. He is motionless and mute, he does not respond to stimulation, but he is aware of his surroundings. Before diagnosing psychogenic stupor, it is essential to exclude other possible causes, namely schizophrenia (p. 273), depressive disorder (p. 222) and mania (p. 225), and organic brain disorder.

In **multiple personality** there are sudden alterations between two pat-terns of behaviour, each of which is forgotten by the patient when the other is present. Each 'personality' is a complex and integrated scheme of emotional responses, attitudes, memories and social behaviour, and the new one usually contrasts strikingly with the patient's normal state. The condition is rare, though in the past it was probably fostered by the interest of doctors. Even rarer are cases in which there are more than two personalities. Striking examples of multiple personality have been described by Morton Prince (1908) and in the book *The three faces of Eve* (Thigpen *et al.* 1957). Like psychogenic memory disorder, these cases may have their basis in organic disease of the central nervous system (Lewis 1953*a*). Such states sometimes occur in the course of magical or religious rites; they seem to result from unconscious mechanisms rather than from conscious stimulation. When similar states occur in schizophrenia and temporal lobe epilepsy, they are classified under this primary diagnosis and not under psychogenic disorder.

Related syndromes

Epidemic hysteria

Occasionally dissociative or conversion disorders spread within a group of people as an 'epidemic'. This happens occasionally in men, but most often in closed groups of young women, for example in a girls' school, a nurses' home, or a convent. Usually anxiety has been heightened by some threat to the community, such as the possibility of being involved in an epidemic of actual physical disease already present in the neighbourhood. Typically, the epidemic starts in one person who is highly suggestible, histrionic, and a focus of attention in the group. This first case may be provoked by actual physical illness in an acquaintance or by general apprehension. Gradually other cases appear, first in the most suggestible then, as anxiety mounts, among those with less predisposition. The symptoms are variable but fainting and dizziness are common. Outbreaks among schoolchildren have been reported by Benaim *et al.* (1973) and Moss and McEvedy (1966). Some writers believe that the 'dancing manias' of the Middle Ages may have been hysterical epidemics in people aroused by religious fervour.

Variations in other cultures

Certain patterns of unusual behaviour are found in particular cultures. They have been regarded in the past as variants of hysteria, but they may have more than one cause. **Latah**, which is found among women in Malaya (Yap 1951), usually begins after a sudden frightening experience. The patient shows echolalia and echopraxia and is abnormally compliant in other ways. **Amok** has been described among men in Malaya (Van Loon 1927). It begins with a period of brooding, which is followed by violent behaviour and sometimes dangerous use of weapons. Amnesia is usually reported afterwards. Probably such cases are not all of one kind, some being manic, some schizophrenic, and others post-epileptic. **Arctic hysteria** is seen among the Eskimo (Gussow 1963), more often in the women. The affected person tears off her clothing, screams and cries, runs about wildly, and may endanger her life by exposure to cold. Sometimes the behaviour is violent. The relationship of this syndrome to hysteria is not firmly established, and there may be more than one cause. These and other cultural variations of hysteria have been described by Kiev (1972); Leff (1981); and Simons and Hughes (1985).

Differential diagnosis

There are three ways in which physical disease may be wrongly diagnosed as a dissociative or conversion disorder. First, the symptoms may be those of physical disease that has not yet been detected; for example, an undiagnosed tumour of the oesophagus causing difficulty in swallowing. Second, undiscovered brain disease may, in some unknown way, 'release' hysterical symptoms; for example, a small tumour in the frontal or parietal lobe, or an early dementia. Third, physical disease may provide a non-specific stimulus to hysterical elaboration of symptoms by a patient of histrionic personality. Some of these problems require further discussion.

Dissociative and conversion disorders have to be distinguished from the many physical illnesses that produce similar symptoms. The greatest difficulty arises with **organic diseases of the central nervous system**. The first step is to determine the exact form of the symptoms and signs, and to compare them carefully with those arising from known neurological diseases, such as cerebral tumours and diffuse cerebral pathology, including GPI. Such diseases can not only produce specific symptoms (for example of parietal lobe dysfunction) that can be mistaken for those of conversion or dissociative disorders. They may also 'release' a psychogenic syndrome—especially an amnesia or fugue. Dissociative disorders may also be difficult to distinguish from **partial complex seizures** (temporal lobe epilepsy), in which unusual disorders of behaviour can occur (see Chapter 11). These points should be considered afresh each time such behaviour occurs in a patient who has more than one episode of symptoms.

Many mistakes in diagnosis arise because dissociative and conversion disorders are confused with the extravagant behaviour of a **histrionic (or hysterical) personality** (p. 132). When distressed, people with this kind of personality display emotions readily, and tend to react in a demonstrative way that attracts attention. They respond in the same way to physical illness as to other events in their life—by exaggeration. Such over-reaction to organic disease can be mistaken for the wholly psychological dissociative or conversion disorders. Exaggeration of physical symptoms is sometimes called 'hysterical overlay' or 'functional overlay' (see p. 412). Similarly the histrionic personality can put its stamp on psychiatric disorder and histrionic behaviour can occur in depressive disorders, anxiety disorders, and many other conditions.

The distinction between dissociative and conversion disorders and **malingering** should be considered particularly among prisoners, military servicemen, or others who may consciously feign illness either to avoid something unpleasant or to gain compensation. The distinction is difficult because some patients add conscious embellishments to the core of unconsciously produced hysterical symptoms. This happens most often when the patient believes that his doctor is sceptical about his complaint. Unlike hysterical symptoms, the complaints of malingerers can rarely be sustained continuously; for this reason, discreet and prolonged observation will usually provide valuable information.

Diagnostic errors will be minimized if four other points are taken into account. First, **age** is important. Conversion and dissociative disorders seldom appear for the first time after the age of 40, presumably because most predisposed patients have already encountered problems severe enough to provoke the reaction at an earlier age. Second, conversion and dissociative disorders are **provoked by stress**. If no stress can be found the diagnosis is in serious doubt. It is therefore important to question other informants, since the patient may not reveal stressful circumstances of which he feels ashamed. On the other hand it is essential to remember that finding stressors does not prove the diagnosis of conversion or dissociative disorder, because they often precede physical illness as well. The third point concerns **secondary gain**. If none can be found, the diagnosis of conversion of dissociative disorder must be in serious doubt. However, as already noted, secondary gain does not prove the diagnosis, because patients sometimes extract advantage from physical illness as well as from emotional disorder. The fourth point is that **hysterical indifference** can seldom be judged reliably, and should be given little weight in diagnosis.

Related syndromes

Although hysterical symptoms are primarily the result of unconscious mechanisms, some degree of conscious elaboration is often present. There are three syndromes in which the conscious element appears to be relatively more important: compensation neurosis, hospital addiction (Munchausen syndrome), and artefactual lesions of the skin. These syndromes are considered in Chapter 12.

Epidemiology

The lifetime prevalence of conversion and dissociative disorder in the general population is difficult to determine but is probably between 3 and 6 per 1000 for women, and substantially lower for men (see Carey *et al.* 1980). Clinical experience suggests that most cases of the neurosis begin before the age of 35, and few new cases appear after 40, although hysterical symptoms commonly occur as part of some other disorder well beyond this age.

Aetiology

Before reviewing modern ideas about aetiology, it is instructive to consider briefly some of the explanations proposed in the past (more complete accounts are given by Veith (1965) and Ellenberger (1970).

Hysteria was recognized in the Ancient World. Among the physicians of Ancient Greece, it was thought to result from movement of the uterus from its normal position (hence the name of the condition). By the second century AD Galen rejected this idea, suggesting instead that the abnormality was an undue retention of uterine secretions. The theory of uterine pathology was generally held until the sixteenth century, when Willis (1621–1675) suggested that hysteria arose from a disorder of the brain (see Dewhurst 1980). By the early nineteenth century, although the importance of predisposing constitutional and organic causes was known, strong emotions were recognized as provoking causes. Later Charcot, a distinguished French neurologist, stressed the importance of strong emotions in producing hysteria in predisposed people. He based this belief partly on the observation that in susceptible patients phenomena resembling hysterical symptoms could be induced by hypnosis. He also believed that hysterical attacks went through a characteristic sequence of changes, but these changes were subsequently recognized as resulting from suggestion brought about by his own powerful personality.

The interest of the French school was continued by Charcot's pupil, Pierre Janet, who described a narrowing of the field of conscious awareness in patients with hysteria, and proposed that this narrowing might account for both their suggestibility and their symptoms (see Janet 1894).

Psychoanalytic theories of hysteria began with Freud's visit to Charcot in the winter of 1895–6 [See Sulloway (1979) for an interesting account of this period in Freud's life.] Freud developed his ideas with Breuer in a paper 'On the psychical mechanisms of hysterical phenomena' (1893). In the subsequent monograph *Studies in hysteria* (1895), Breuer and Freud wrote 'hysterics suffer mainly from reminiscences' (Standard Edition, Vol. 2, p. 7); that is from the effects of emotionally charged ideas lodged in the unconscious at some time in the past. This idea was central to their theory. Symptoms were explained as the combined effects of repression and the 'conversion' of psychic energy into physical channels in some way that was never fully explained. These ideas have been widely accepted, despite the difficulty in testing them directly.

Genetics

The few genetic studies have been inconclusive. Ljungberg (1957) studied first degree relatives of 281 patients, of whom almost half had hysterical disturbances of gait and a further fifth had hysterical fits. He found rates of hysteria in the relatives, 2.4 per cent among males and 6.4 per cent among females, that were probably higher than in the general population. A twin study by Slater (1961) did not support a genetic aetiology, since no concordance was found between identical twins, one of whom had hysteria.

Organic disease

As already noted, hysteria is sometimes associated with organic disease of the nervous system. However, it can undoubtedly occur in the absence of such pathology.

Hysteria as a reflex mechanism

From experience of treating acute hysterical reactions in wartime, Kretschmer (1961) suggested that they are preformed instinctive reactions of the nervous system to excessive stress. He believed that such reactions normally subside quickly, but can be prolonged in two ways. First, they may be deliberately cultivated by someone who wishes to take advantage of the symptoms. Second, by a supposed neurological mechanism, behaviour that is frequently repeated becomes habitual (or 'slips into a groove' to use Kretschmer's phrase). Although these ideas have never been substantiated, they differ from other theories in drawing attention to the apparent mixture of voluntary and involuntary causes in many cases of hysteria.

Prognosis

Among dissociative and conversion disorders of recent onset seen in general practice or hospital emergency departments, most recover quickly. However, those that last longer than a year are likely to persist for many years more. Thus Ljungberg (1957) found that, among patients who still had symptoms after a year, half still had them after ten years.

It has already been noted that organic disease is often missed among these patients. In a well-known study, Slater and Glithero (1965) followed up a series of patients who had been referred to a specialist neurological hospital and diagnosed as having hysteria (those with 'hysterical overlay' in known physical disease were excluded). They found that about a third of the patients developed a definite organic illness within 7–11 years, and a further third developed depression or schizophrenia. Although this study teaches an important lesson, it must be remembered that the patients were unrepresentative in being referred to a neurological hospital.

Treatment

For acute dissociative and conversion disorders seen in general practice or hospital casualty departments, treatment by reassurance and suggestion is usually appropriate, together with immediate efforts to resolve any stressful circumstances that provoked the reaction. For cases that have lasted more than a few weeks, more active treatment is required. The general approach is to focus on the elimination of factors that are reinforcing the symptoms, and on the encouragement of normal behaviour. It should be explained to the patient that he has a disability (as in remembering, or moving his arm) which is not caused by physical disease but by psychological factors. It is often helpful to explain the disorder as due to a blocking of the psychological process between, for example, the patient's intention to move his arm and the nervous mechanisms that bring about movement. He should then be told that if he tries hard to regain control, he will succeed. If necessary, he can be offered help in doing this, usually in the form of physiotherapy. Attention is then directed away from the symptoms and towards problems that have provoked the disorder. The hospital staff should show concern to help the patient, and this is best done by encouraging self-help. It is important not to make undue concessions to the patient's disability; for example, a patient who cannot walk should not be provided with a wheelchair, and a patient who has collapsed on the floor should be encouraged to get up but not assisted to his feet. To achieve these ends, there must be a clear plan so that all members of staff adopt a consistent approach to the patient.

Abreaction

This can be brought about by hypnosis or by intravenous injection of small amounts of amylobarbitone. In the resulting state, the patient is encouraged to relive the stressful events that provoked the disorder and to express the accompanying emotions. These methods have been used successfully in the treatment of acute dissociative and conversion disorders arising in soldiers in wartime (see Chapter 18). They are of much less value in civilian life, where more gradual methods will allow the patient to take reponsiblity for overcoming his symptoms and for finding solutions to problems that evoked them.

Psychotherapy

Patients with dissociative and conversion disorders usually appear to respond well to exploratory psychotherapy concerned with their past life, and they often produce striking memories of childhood sexual behaviour and other problems apparently relevant to dynamic psychotherapy. However, it is seldom fruitful to explore these ideas at length. Usually such exploration serves only to deflect attention from the patient's current difficulties, and may lead to over-dependence and transference reactions that are difficult to manage.

Other treatments

Medication has no part to play in the treatment of these conditions, unless they are secondary to a depressive disorder or anxiety disorder requiring treatment in its own right. Specific methods of **behaviour therapy** are also of little value. The use of operant conditioning methods has been reported, for example, in the treatment of psychogenic blindness (Parry Jones *et al.* 1970) but there is no evidence that these or other techniques are more effective than suggestion.

Subsequent care

With simple treatment most patients with dissociative and conversion disorders improve, unless there is a strong motivation to remain ill, as in compensation cases. Those who do not improve should be reviewed thoroughly for undiscovered physical illness. All patients, whether improved or not, should be followed carefully for long enough to exclude any organic disease that might not have been detected. Six months to a year will usually be needed, but if a condition such as multiple sclerosis has to be excluded, a much longer follow-up may be required. This must be done discreetly and tactfully in order to identify any symptoms suggestive of organic disease without perpetuating the psychological problems. The general practitioner is often best placed to undertake this.

Depersonalization disorder

Depersonalization disorder is characterized by an unpleasant state of disturbed perception in which external objects or parts of the body are experienced as changed in their quality, unreal, remote or automatized. The patient is aware of the subjective nature of this experience. The symptom of depersonalization is quite common as a minor feature of other syndromes but depersonalization disorder is uncommon.

In DSMIIIR depersonalization disorder is classified under dissociative disorder, together with the various dissociative states that have been considered in the last section. In ICD9 it has a separate place, which it is likely to retain in ICD10.

Clinical picture

As well as describing feelings of being unreal and experiencing an unreal quality to perceptions, patients say that their emotions are dulled and their actions feel mechanical. They no longer experience strong emotions such as love, hatred, anger, or pleasure; paradoxically they complain that this lack of feeling is extremely unpleasant. Insight is retained into the subjective nature of their experiences.

In depersonalization disorder, these symptoms are intense, and are accompanied by mild anxiety, mild depression, *déjà vu*, and changes in the experience of passage of time. Some patients complain of sensory distortions affecting not the whole body but a single part, such as the head, the nose, or limbs, which may be described as feeling as if made of cotton wool. Two-thirds of the patients are women. The symptoms usually begin suddenly, often during relaxation after intense physical exercise or psychological stimulation (Shorvon *et al.* 1946). The onset is often in adolescence or early adult life, the condition starting before the age of 30 in about half the cases (Shorvon *et al.* 1946). Once established, the disorder often persists for years, though with periods of partial or complete remission.

Differential diagnosis

Before diagnosing depersonalization disorder, a primary disorder must be carefully sought, such as an organic syndrome (including temporal lobe epilepsy), schizophrenia, depressive disorder, obsessional disorder, conversion or dissociative disorder and generalized and phobic anxiety disorders. Severe and persistent depersonalization symptoms also occur with schizoid personality disorder. Most patients who present with depersonalization will be found to have one of these other disorders; the primary syndrome is rare.

Aetiology

The more careful the search for a primary disorder, the fewer cases of primary depersonalization disorder will be identified. Ackner (1954*a,b*) studied a series of patients and found that all could be allocated to organic, depressive, anxiety, or hysterical syndromes, or to schizoid personality disorder. Apart from the possible association with schizoid personality disorder no definite constitutional factors have been identified. Lader (1969) suggested that the symptoms represent a restriction of sensory input that serves to reduce intolerably high levels of anxiety. He reported a striking example in a patient who was undergoing physiological recordings at the time. Since many cases begin when the patient is relaxed or tired, this mechanism, if it is important, cannot be invariable.

Prognosis

Most cases are secondary, and have the prognosis of the primary condition. The uncommon primary depersonalization disorder has not been followed systematically; clinical experience indicates that, if it lasts for more than a year, it has a poor long-term prognosis.

Treatment

Since most depersonalization disorders are secondary, treatment should usually be directed to the primary condition. In the small group of primary depersonalization disorders, a trial of an anxiolytic drug is worthwhile because a few patients are helped in this way. If there is a response, the benefits of continued prescribing have to be balanced against the risk of dependency on the drug. Otherwise drugs have no part in treatment. Behavioural treatment is ineffective. Psychotherapy has no specific value, but the patients, who often suffer extreme distress, may be helped by supportive interviews. Common-sense measures are also needed to reduce stressful events in their lives. However, the doctor has to accept that he can do little to relieve the symptoms of primary depersonalization disorders; for many patients the only help is encouragement to tolerate their symptoms while continuing as normal a life as possible. These patients often make repeated demands for additional treatment, but despite their obvious suffering it is important to resist the temptation to heap one ineffective measure on another.

Hypochondriasis

In this book, hypochondriasis is considered in Chapter 12 (Psychiatry and Medicine).

Further reading

Ackner, B. (1954). Depersonalization. *Journal of Mental Science* **100**, 838–53, 854–72.

Breuer, J. and Freud, S. (1895). *Studies on hysteria.* Reprinted as Vol. 3 of Pelican Freud Library. Penguin Books, Harmondsworth.

Lewis, A. J. (1936). Obsessional illness. In *Inquiries in psychiatry*, Chapter 7. Routledge and Kegan Paul, London.

Marks, I. M. (1987). *Fears, phobias, and rituals.* Oxford University Press, New York.

Merskey, H. (1979). *The analysis of hysteria.* Baillière Tindall, London.

8   Affective disorders

The affective disorders are so called because one of their main features is abnormality of mood. Nowadays the term is usually restricted to disorders in which this mood is depression or elation, but in the past some authors have included states of anxiety as well (for example Lewis 1956). In this book, anxiety states are described in Chapter 7.

It is part of normal experience to feel unhappy at times of adversity. The *symptom* of depressed mood is a component of many psychiatric syndromes and is also found commonly in certain physical diseases, for example in glandular fever. In this chapter, we are concerned neither with normal feelings of unhappiness nor with depressed mood as a symptom of other disorders, but with the *syndromes* known as depressive disorders. The central features of these syndromes are depressed mood, pessimistic thinking, lack of enjoyment, reduced energy, and slowness. Of these, depressed mood is usually, but not invariably, the most prominent symptom. The other elements are variable enough to suggest that there is not one disorder but several.

Similar considerations apply to states of elation. A degree of elated mood is part of normal experience at times of good fortune. Elation can also occur as a *symptom* in several psychiatric syndromes, though it is less widely encountered than depressed mood. In this chapter we are concerned with a *syndrome* in which the central features are over-activity, mood change, and self-important ideas. The mood change may be towards elation or towards irritability. This syndrome is called mania. In the past it was usual to restrict the term mania to severe cases, and to give the name hypomania to less severe cases. As there is no agreed dividing line between mania and hypomania, this book uses only the term mania and severity is indicated by adding mild, moderate, or severe.

Clinical features

Depressive syndromes

The clinical presentations of depressive syndromes are so varied that they cannot be described fully in a short space. In the following account disorders are grouped by their severity. The account begins with a description of the clinical features of depressive disorders of moderate severity, and continues with a description of severe disorders. Certain important variants of these moderate and severe disorders are then described. Finally the special features of the least severe depressive disorders are outlined.

In depressive disorders of moderate severity, the central features are low mood, lack of enjoyment, pessimistic thinking, and reduced energy, all of which lead to impaired efficiency. The patient's **appearance** is characteristic. Dress and grooming may be neglected. The facial features are characterized by a turning downwards of the corners of the mouth and by vertical furrowing of the centre of the brow. The rate of blinking may be reduced. The shoulders are bent, and the head inclined forwards so that the direction of gaze is downwards. Gestural movements are reduced. It is important to note that some patients maintain a smiling exterior despite deep feelings of depression.

Psychomotor retardation is frequent (though as described later some patients are agitated rather than slowed up). The retarded patient walks and acts slowly. Slowing of thought is reflected in the patient's speech; there is a long delay before questions are answered, and pauses in conversation may be so long that they would be intolerable to a non-depressed person.

The **mood** of the patient is one of misery. This mood does not improve substantially in circumstances where ordinary feelings of sadness would be alleviated—for example, in pleasant company or after hearing good news. Moreover the mood may be experienced as different from ordinary sadness. Patients sometimes speak of a black cloud pervading all mental activities. Some patients can conceal this mood change from other people, at least for short periods. Some try to hide their low mood during clinical interviews, making it more difficult for the doctor to detect.

Anxiety is also frequent though not invariable in moderately severe depressive disorder. (As described later, it is common in some less severe depressive disorders.) Another common symptom is **irritability**, which is the tendency to respond with undue annoyance to minor demands and frustrations. **Agitation** is a state of restlessness which is experienced by the patient as inability to relax, and seen by an observer as restless activity. When it is mild the patient is seen to be plucking at his fingers and making restless movements of his legs; when it is severe, he cannot sit for long but paces up and down.

Lack of interest and enjoyment is frequent, though not always complained of spontaneously. The patient shows no enthusiasm for activities and hobbies that he would normally enjoy. He feels no zest for living and no pleasure in everyday things. He often withdraws from social encounters. **Reduced energy** is characteristic (though sometimes associated with a degree of physical restlessness that can mislead the observer). The patient feels lethargic, finds everything an effort, and leaves tasks unfinished. For example, a normally houseproud woman may leave the beds unmade and the dirty plates on the table. Understandably, many patients attribute this lack of energy to physical illness.

A group of symptoms often called **biological** is important. They include sleep disturbance, diurnal variation of mood, loss of appetite, loss of weight, constipation, loss of libido, and, among women, amenorrhoea. These symptoms are frequent but not invariable in depressive disorders of moderate degree. (They are less usual in mild depressive disorders, but particularly common in the severe disorders.) Some of these symptoms require further comment.

Sleep disturbance in depressive disorders is of several kinds. Most characteristic is early morning waking, but delay in falling asleep and waking during the night also occur. Early morning waking occurs two or three hours before the patient's usual time; he does not fall asleep again, but lies awake feeling unrefreshed and often restless and agitated. He thinks about the coming day with pessimism, broods about past failures, and ponders gloomily about the future. It is this combination of early waking with depressive thinking that is important in diagnosis. It should be noted that some depressed patients sleep excessively rather than wake early, but they still report waking unrefreshed.

In depressive disorders, **weight loss** often seems greater than can be accounted for merely by the patient's **lack of appetite**. In some patients the disturbances of eating and weight are towards excess—they eat more and gain weight; usually it seems that eating brings temporary relief to their distressing feelings.

Pessimistic thoughts ('depressive cognitions') are important symptoms, which can be divided into three groups. The first group is concerned with the *present*. The patient sees the unhappy side of every event; he thinks that he is failing in everything he does and that other people see him as a failure; he no longer feels confident, and discounts any success as a chance happening for which he can take no credit.

The second group of thoughts is concerned with the *future*. The patient expects the worst. He forsees failure in his work, the ruin of his finances, misfortune for his family, and an inevitable deterioration in his health. These ideas of hopelessness are often accompanied by the thought that life is no longer worth living and that death would come as a welcome release. These gloomy preoccupations may progress to thoughts of, and plans for, **suicide**. It is important to ask about these ideas in every case. (The assessment of suicidal risk is considered further in Chapter 13.)

The third group of thoughts is concerned with the *past*. They often take the form of unreasonable guilt and self-blame about minor matters; for example, a patient may feel guilty about past trivial acts of dishonesty or of letting someone down. Usually these events have not been in the patient's thoughts for years but, when he becomes depressed, they flood back into his memory accompanied by intense feelings. Preoccupations of this kind strongly suggest depressive disorder. Some patients have similar feelings of guilt but do not attach them to any particular event. Other memories are focused on unhappy events; the patient remembers occasions when he was sad, when he failed, or when his fortunes were at a low ebb. These gloomy memories become increasingly frequent as the depression deepens.

Complaints about **physical symptoms** are common in depressive disorders. They take many forms but complaints of constipation and of aching discomfort anywhere in the body are particularly common. Complaints about any pre-existing physical disorder usually increase and hypochondriacal preoccupations are common.

Several **other psychiatric symptoms** may occur as part of a depressive disorder, and occasionally one of them dominates the clinical picture. They include depersonalization, obsessional symptoms, phobias, and hysterical symptoms such as fugue or loss of function of a limb. Complaints of **poor memory** are also common; they result from poor concentration, and if the patient is encouraged to make a special effort, it can usually be shown that retention and recall are not impaired. Sometimes, however, the apparent impairment of memory is so severe that the clinical presentation resembles that of dementia. This presentation, which is particularly common in the elderly, is sometimes called **depressive pseudodementia** (see p. 617).

Masked depression

The term 'masked depression' is sometimes used for cases where depressive mood is not conspicuous. Although there is no reason to think that these cases form a separate syndrome, the term is useful in drawing attention to a mode of presentation that is easily missed. Masked depression is discussed in the chapter on general hospital psychiatry. Here it should be noted that diagnosis depends on a careful search for the other features of depressive disorder, especially sleep disturbance, diurnal mood variation, and depressive cognitions. Masking is most likely to occur with mild or moderate disorders, but it occasionally occurs with severe disorders.

Severe depressive disorder

As depressive disorders become more severe, all the features just described occur with greater intensity. In addition, certain distinctive features may occur in the form of delusions and hallucinations; the disorder is then sometimes called **psychotic depression**.

The **delusions** of severe depressive disorders are concerned with the same themes as the non-delusional thinking of moderate depressive disorders. These themes are: worthlessness, guilt, ill-health and, more rarely, poverty. Such delusions have been described in Chapter 1, but a few examples may be helpful at this point. A patient with a *delusion of guilt* may believe that some dishonest act, such as a minor concealment in making a tax return, will be discovered and that he will be punished severely and humiliated. He is likely to believe that such punishment is deserved. A patient with *hypochondriacal delusions* may be convinced that he has cancer or venereal disease. A patient with a *delusion of impoverishment* may wrongly believe that he has lost all his money in a business venture. *Persecutory delusions* also occur. The patient may believe that other people are discussing him in a derogatory way, or about to take revenge on him. When persecutory delusions are part of a depressive syndrome, typically the patient accepts the supposed persecution as something he has brought upon himself. In his view, he is ultimately to blame.

Perceptual disturbances may also be found in severe depressive disorders. Sometimes these fall short of true hallucinations ('pseudohallucinations', see Chapter 1). In a minority of cases definite hallucinations occur; they are usually auditory, and take the form of voices addressing repetitive words and phrases to the patient. The voices seem to confirm his ideas of worthlessness (for example, 'you are an evil man; you should die'), or to make derisive comments, or urge the patient to take his own life. A few patients experience visual hallucinations, sometimes in the form of scenes of death and destruction.

Cotard's syndrome is a particular form of severe depressive disorder, described by a French psychiatrist (Cotard 1882). The characteristic feature is an extreme kind of nihilistic delusion (sometimes called by the French name *délire de négation—délire* meaning delusion in this context). Patients with this syndrome carry nihilism to its extreme. For example, a patient may complain that his bowels have been destroyed so that he will never pass faeces again. Another may assert that he is penniless and without any prospect of having money again. A third may be convinced that his whole family has ceased to exist. Although the extreme nature of these symptoms is striking, such cases do not appear to differ in important ways from other severe depressive disorders.

Agitated depression

This term is applied to depressive disorders in which agitation is prominent. As already noted, agitation occurs in many severe depressive disorders, but in agitated depression it is particularly severe. Agitated depression is seen more commonly among the middle-aged and elderly than among younger patients. However, there is no reason to suppose that agitated depression differs in other important ways from the other depressive disorders.

Retarded depression

This name is sometimes applied to depressive disorders in which psychomotor retardation is especially prominent. There is no evidence that they represent a separate syndrome. Therefore if the term is used at all, it should be in a purely descriptive sense. In its most severe form, retarded depression shades into depressive stupor.

Depressive stupor

In severe depressive disorder, slowing of movement and poverty of speech may become so extreme that the patient is motionless and mute. Such depressive stupor is rarely seen now that active treatment is available. The description by Kraepelin (1921, p. 80) is of particular interest. 'The patients lie mute in bed, give no answer of any sort, at most withdraw themselves timidly from approaches, but often do not defend themselves from pinpricks . . . They sit helpless before their food, perhaps, however, they let themselves be spoonfed without making any difficulty . . . Now and then periods of excitement may be interpolated.' This description draws attention to an important feature of the condition—interruption by periods of excitement when the patient is overactive and noisy. Kraepelin commented that recall of the events taking place during stupor was sometimes impaired when the patient recovered. Nowadays, the general view is that on recovery patients are able to recall nearly all the events taking place during the period of stupor (see, for example, Lishman 1978). It may be that in some of Kraepelin's cases there was clouding of consciousness (possibly related to inadequate fluid intake, which is common in these patients).

Mild depressive disorder

It might be expected that mild depressive disorders would present with symptoms similar to those of the depressive disorders described already, but with less intensity. Sometimes this is so, the patient complaining of low mood, lack of energy and enjoyment, and poor sleep. However, in mild depressive disorder there are frequently other symptoms that are found less often in severe disorders. These symptoms can be broadly characterized as 'neurotic', and they include anxiety, phobias, obsessional symptoms and, less often, hysterical symptoms. Although anxiety may be a symptom in all degrees of depressive disorder, it can be just as severe in the mild disorders as in the severe ones. This finding has suggested to many people that these mild depressive disorders are not just a minor variant of the moderate and severe cases but a separate syndrome. Because of the nature of the additional symptoms, this syndrome has been called **neurotic depression**.

Apart from the 'neurotic' symptoms found in some cases, mild depressive disorders are characterized by the expected symptoms of low mood, lack of energy and interest, and irritability. There is sleep disturbance, but not the early morning waking that is so characteristic of more severe depressive disorders. Instead there is more often difficulty in falling asleep and periods of waking during the night, followed usually by a period of sleep at the end of the night. 'Biological' features (poor appetite, weight loss, and low libido) are not usually found. Although mood may vary during the day, it is usually worse in the evening than in the morning. The patient may not be obviously dejected in his appearance, or slowed in his movement. Delusions and hallucinations are not encountered.

In their mildest forms these cases shade into the minor affective disorders considered in Chapter 6. As described later, they pose considerable problems of classification. Many of these mild depressive disorders are brief, starting at a time of personal misfortune and subsiding when fortunes have changed or a new adjustment has been achieved. However, some cases persist for months or years causing considerable suffering even though the symptoms do not increase.

Mania

As already mentioned, the central features of the syndrome of mania are elevation of mood, increased activity, and self-important ideas. When the mood is elevated, the patient seems cheerful and optimistic, and he may have a quality described by earlier writers as infectious gaiety. However, other patients are irritable rather than euphoric, and this irritability can easily turn to anger. The mood often varies during the day, though not with the regular rhythm characteristic of many severe depressive disorders. In patients who are elated, not uncommonly high spirits are interrupted by brief episodes of depression.

The patient's clothing often reflects his prevailing mood in its bright colours and ill-assorted choice of garments. When the condition is more severe, his appearance is often untidy and dishevelled. Manic patients are **over-active**. Sometimes their persistent over-activity leads to physical exhaustion. Manic patients start many activities but leave them unfinished as new ones catch their fancy. Their **speech** is often rapid and copious as thoughts crowd into their minds in quick succession. When the disorder is more severe, there is **flight of ideas** (see p. 11) with such rapid changes that it is difficult to follow the train of thought. **Sleep** is often reduced. The patient wakes early feeling lively and energetic; often he gets up and busies himself noisily, to the surprise of other people. **Appetite** is increased and food may be eaten greedily with little attention to conventional manners. **Sexual desires** are increased and behaviour may be uninhibited. Women sometimes neglect precautions against pregnancy, a point calling for particular attention when the patient is of childbearing age.

Expansive ideas are common. The patient believes that his ideas are original, his opinions important, and his work of outstanding quality. Many patients become extravagant, spending more than they can afford on expensive cars or jewellery. Others make reckless decisions to give up good jobs, or embark on plans for hare-brained and risky business ventures.

Sometimes these expansive themes are accompanied by **grandiose delusions**. The patient may believe that he is a religious prophet or destined to advise statesmen about great issues. At times there are delusions of persecution, the patient believing that people are conspiring against him because of his special importance. Delusions of reference and passivity feelings also occur. Schneiderian first-rank symptoms (see Table 9.3) have been reported in about 10–20 per cent of manic patients (Carpenter *el al.* 1973). Neither the delusions nor the first-rank symptoms last long—most disappear or change in content within days.

Hallucinations also occur. They are usually consistent with the mood, taking the form of voices speaking to the patient about his special powers or, occasionally, of visions with a religious content.

Insight is invariably impaired. The patient may see no reason why his grandiose plans should be restrained or his extravagant expediture curtailed. He seldom thinks himself ill, or in need of treatment.

Most patients can exert some **control** over their symptoms for a short time, and many do so when the question of treatment is being assessed. For this reason it is important to obtain a history from an informant whenever possible. Henry Maudsley expressed the problem well: 'Just as it is with a person who is not too far gone in intoxication, so it is with a person who is not too far gone in acute mania; he may on occasion pull his scattered ideas together by an effort of will, stop his irrational doings and for a short time talk with an appearance of calmness and reasonableness that may well raise false hopes in inexperienced people' (Maudsley (1879), p. 398).

Carlson and Goodwin (1973) have described three stages of mania which, while not in any way distinctly separated from one another, may help the reader to judge the pattern of symptoms in mild, moderate, and severe cases. In **mild** cases there is increased physical activity and speech; mood is labile being mainly euphoric but giving way to irritability at times; ideas are expansive and the patient often spends more than he can afford; sexual drive increases. In **moderate** cases, there is marked over-activity and pressure of speech which seems disorganized; the euphoric mood is increasingly interrupted by periods of irritability, hostility, and depression; grandiose and other preoccupations may pass into delusions. In **severe** cases, there is frenzied over-activity, thinking is incoherent, delusions become increasingly bizarre and hallucinations are experienced. It should be emphasized that this description is merely a guide, and there is no invariable sequence.

Mixed affective states

Depressive and manic symptoms sometimes occur at the same time. Patients who are over-active and over-talkative may be having profoundly depressive thoughts. In other patients mania and depression follow each other in a sequence of rapid changes; for example, a manic patient may become intensely depressed for a few hours and then return quickly to his manic state. These changes were mentioned in early descriptions of mania by Griesinger (1867), and have been re-emphasized in recent years, for example by Kotin and Goodwin (1972).

Manic stupor

In this unusual disorder, the patient is mute and immobile. However, his facial expression suggests elation and on recovery he describes having experienced a rapid succession of thoughts typical of mania. The condition is rarely seen now that active treatment is available for mania. Hence an earlier description by Kraepelin (1921, p. 106) is of interest: 'The patients are usually quite inaccessible, do not trouble themselves about their surroundings, give no answer, or at most speak in a low voice . . . smile without recognisable cause, lie perfectly quiet in bed or tidy about at their clothes and bedclothes, decorate themselves in an extraordinary way, all this without any sign of outward excitement.' On recovery, patients can remember the events that occurred during their period of stupor. The condition may begin from a state of manic excitement, but at times it is a stage in the transition between depressive stupor and mania.

Periodic psychoses

Some bipolar disorders recur regularly with intervals of only weeks or months between episodes. In the nineteenth century these regularly recurring disorders were designated *folie circulaire* (circular insanity) by the French psychiatrist Falret (1854). Nowadays they are often referred to as periodic psychoses. The latter term is not entirely satisfactory because some writers use it in a different way to include other disorders such as recurrent schizophrenic illnesses, unusual syndromes like periodic catatonia (see Chapter 9), and the recurring atypical psychoses to which Leonhard (1957) gave the name cycloid psychoses (see p. 290).

Bereavement

A recently bereaved person experiences symptoms closely resembling those of depressive disorders. Freud's theory of the aetiology of depressive illness was based on this similarity. For this reason it is convenient to describe the clinical features of bereavement here, even though they are usually part of normal experience rather than a pathological reaction. There are three stages. The first is characterized by a lack of emotional reaction ('numbness') and a feeling of unreality that lasts from a few hours to several days. In this stage, the bereaved person does not accept fully that the death has taken place. In the second stage, the person feels sad, weeps, sleeps badly, and loses appetite. He often experiences motor restlessness and difficulty in concentrating and remembering. About a third of bereaved people feel guilty about failures to do enough for the deceased, and about a fifth blame other people. Many have the experience at some time that they are in the presence of the dead person and about one in ten report brief hallucinations (Clayton 1979). In the third stage, these symptoms subside gradually, and the person accepts the new situation. It is important to note that certain features found fairly commonly in depressive disorders are much less frequent after bereavement, notably suicidal thoughts, retardation, and guilt about past actions in general as opposed to specific failures to do enough for the deceased. However, the bereaved complain more of physical symptoms (Parkes and Brown 1972).

Clayton *et al.* (1974) found that 35 per cent of a sample of recently bereaved widows over the age of 62 met the criteria of Feighner *et al.* (1972) for a depressive disorder. Among men, there is an increased rate of death from cardiovascular causes in the year after the death of the spouse (Rees and Lutkins 1967). It has been suggested that several factors increase the probability that grief will be unusually intense or prolonged. These factors include:

(1) the circumstances of the death—when it is sudden or unexpected, or takes place in a way that results in blame for the survivor;

(2) the relationship of the survivor to the dead person—when this is the parent of a dead child, the young child of a dead parent, or an adult in a dependent relationship with the deceased;

(3) characteristics of the survivor—insecure, unable to express feelings easily, still adjusting to a previous loss;

(4) the social circumstances of the survivor—without contact with organized religion, caring for dependent children.
[See Parkes (1985) for a review.]

Classification of depressive disorders

There is no general agreement about the best method of classifying depressive disorders. Three broad approaches have been tried. The first attempts to base classification on aetiology; the second on symptoms; and the third on the course of the disorder. This section describes each of these approaches in turn, before indicating how depressive disorders are classified in ICD10 and DSM IIIR. Finally, in this section it is suggested that for clinical purposes classifying depressive disorders is less useful than describing them systematically, and a descriptive scheme is proposed.

Classifications based on aetiology

Reactive and endogenous depression

According to this scheme, depressive disorders can be classified on the basis of aetiology into two groups—endogenous and reactive (less commonly called exogenous). In endogenous disorders, symptoms are caused by factors within the individual person, and are independent of outside factors. In reactive disorders, symptoms are a response to external stressors. The distinction between endogenous and reactive causes is unsatisfactory because it produces categories that are not mutually exclusive but overlapping. For this reason, the endogenous-reactive distinction was judged to be of little use in classification by many influential psychiatrists, notably Mapother (1926), Lewis (1934, 1936a, 1938),and Curran (1937). For example, Lewis (1934) wrote, 'every illness is a product of two factors—of the environment working on the organism—whether the constitutional factor is the determining influence or the environmental one, is never a question of kind, never a question to be dealt with as either/or'. Nowadays most psychiatrists agree that it is pointless to try to allocate depressive syndromes exclusively to endogenous or reactive categories; in seeking to understand the aetiology of individual cases, the relative contributions of both endogenous and reactive factors must be carefully weighed. Neither ICD10 nor DSMIIIR contains categories of reactive or endogenous depression.

The reactive-endogenous classification of depressive disorders carries a further complication. Many supporters of this classification maintain that the two aetiological categories are associated with characteristic patterns of symptoms. Thus endogenous disorders are said to be characterized by loss of appetite, weight loss, constipation, reduced libido, amenorrhoea and early morning waking (the 'biological' symptoms mentioned above, p. 219). Reactive disorders are said to be characterized by a pattern of anxiety, irritability, and phobias. The latter three symptoms are also used in another system of classification (described on p. 229) to distinguish neurotic from psychotic depressive disorders. In this way, confusion has arisen between two systems of classification, the reactive–endogenous classification (based on aetiology but incorporating symptoms as well), and the neurotic–psychotic classification (based only on symptoms). Some authors make no sharp distinction between the two systems (see, for example, Kiloh *et al.* 1972).

Recently further doubt has been cast on the combined aetiological–symptom approach to classification. Quantitative studies have found no definite relationship between stressful life events and type of symptom in depressive disorder (see, for example, Paykel *et al.* 1984).

Primary and secondary depression

This scheme, which is also based on aetiology, was introduced mainly for research purposes. The aim was to exclude cases of depression that might be caused by another disorder. This exclusion was attempted by applying the term 'secondary' to all cases with a history of previous non-affective psychiatric illness (such as schizophrenia or anxiety neurosis), or of alcoholism, medical illnesses or the taking of certain drugs (such as steroids). At first it was suggested (Guze *et al.* 1971) that primary and secondary depressive disorders might differ in prognosis and response to treatment. No such difference has been found, nor is there any convincing evidence for a difference between the two groups in the pattern of symptoms (see, for example, Weissman *et al.* 1977). Therefore, although this classification may have some value for research, it has little value for the clinician.

Occasionally clinicians encounter secondary mania, which arises, for example, after operations or treatment with steroids. In secondary mania, the average age of onset is later than in primary mania, and a family history of bipolar disorder is less likely. (See Krauthammer and Klerman (1978) for a review of the evidence.]

Classification based on symptoms

Neurotic and psychotic depressions

As already explained, certain symptoms are frequently more intense in the mild depressive disorders than in the severe disorders. This difference in symptom intensity has led to the suggestion that there are two distinct forms of depressive disorder, neurotic and psychotic. In recent years, this hypothesis has been pursued by statistical means. Standardized information gathered either from case-notes or by interviewing is subjected to some form of multivariate analysis. The results have been contradictory. In a series of papers, Roth and his colleagues in Newcastle held that two separate syndromes could be distinguished (Kiloh and Garside 1963; Carney *et al.* 1965). However, Kendell (1968) did not confirm this distinction, but found evidence for a unimodal distribution of cases.

The problems surrounding these issues are made more difficult by the imprecise use of the term psychotic. In one sense, this term means a disorder in which there is evidence of loss of contact with reality, usually in the form of hallucinations or delusions. However, in the literature on depressive disorders, the term has also been applied to cases with so-called biological symptoms, namely early morning waking, weight loss, poor appetite, impaired libido, and diurnal variation.

Another problem is that it is exceedingly difficult to collect data that could not have been affected by the preconceptions of the doctors assessing the patients. Thus, interviewers who believe that there are two separate syndromes may be more likely to elicit symptoms that confirm this hypothesis and less likely to elicit symptoms that do not. Indeed Kendell (1968) has produced evidence that such a bias does operate. Until this problem is overcome, the case for separate neurotic and psychotic syndromes must remain unproven.

Classification by course and time of life

Unipolar and bipolar disorders

Kraepelin was guided by the course of illness when he brought together mania and depression as a single entity. He found that the course was essentially the same whether the disorder was manic or depressive, so he put the two together in a single category of manic-depressive psychosis. This view was widely accepted until 1962 when Leonhard *et al.* suggested a division into three groups: patients who had had depressive disorder only (**unipolar depression**); those who had had mania only (**unipolar mania**); and those who had had both depressive disorder and mania (**bipolar**). Nowadays it is the usual practice not to use the term unipolar mania, but to include all cases of mania in the bipolar group, on the grounds that nearly all patients who have mania eventually experience a depressive disorder.

In support of the distinction between unipolar and bipolar disorders, Leonhard described differences in heredity and personality between the groups. However, it is generally agreed that the two groups differ neither in their symptoms when depressed nor in their response to treatment (with the possible exception of lithium therapy—see p. 254). There must be some overlap between the two groups, because a patient classified as having unipolar depression at one time may have a manic disorder later. In other words the unipolar group inevitably contains some bipolar cases that have not yet declared themselves. Despite this limitation, the division into unipolar and bipolar cases is probably the most useful classification proposed so far since it has some implications for treatment (see p. 264).

Seasonal affective disorder

Some patients repeatedly develop a depressive disorder at the same time of year. In some cases this timing reflects extra demands placed on the person at a particular season of the year, either in his work or in other aspects of his life. In other cases there is no such cause and it has been suggested (e.g. by Rosenthal *et al.* 1984) that they are related in some way to the changes in the seasons, for example in the length of daylight. Although these seasonal affective disorders are characterized mainly by the time at which they occur, some symptoms are said to occur more often than in other affective disorders. These symptoms are hypersomnia, and increased appetite with craving for carbohydrate.

The most common pattern is onset in autumn or winter, and recovery in spring or summer. This pattern has led to the suggestion that shortening of daylight is important, and to attempts at treatment by exposure to bright artificial light during hours of darkness. It has been reported that symptoms are reduced after three to four days of this treatment, though they generally relapse soon after it is stopped (Rosenthal *et al.* 1984). This effect seems to be due to the extra light rather than the accompanying reduction in sleep (sleep deprivation can reduce depressive symptoms in some patients—see p. 257) Such changes might to be due to placebo effect but this explanation is made less likely by the observation that the effect of bright light is greater than that of dim illumination (Kripke *et al.* 1983; Rosenthal *et al.* 1984, 1985). However, it has also been reported that extra light given in daytime hours is as effective as extra light given in hours of darkness (Wehr *et al.* 1986). This finding casts doubt on the idea that these disorders are caused by the shortage of daylight hours, and corrected by adding to them. Speculations that the improvements are related to the known effect of light in supressing the nocturnal secretion of melatonin are not supported by strong evidence.

Involutional depression

In the past, depressive disorders starting in middle life were thought to be a separate group, characterized by agitation and hypochondriacal symptoms. It was suggested that they might have a distinct aetiology, such as involution of the sex glands, or some kind of relationship with schizophrenia. Family studies do not support the idea of a separate group. Thus, among the relatives of patients with so-called involutional depression, the frequency of affective disorders is increased but there is no excess of involutional disorders (early onset disorders being just as frequent). Similarly, the rate of schizophrenia among relatives is not increased (see Slater and Cowie 1971, p. 86; Stenstedt 1952).

Senile depression

In the past, elderly patients with depression were also regarded as a separate group. However, there is no evidence that classification by age of onset is useful either in clinical work or research.

Classification in ICD and DSM

The main categories in the sections on affective disorders in DSMIIIR and the draft of ICD10 are shown in the Table 8.1. Broad similarities are evident, together with some differences. The similarities are first that both systems contain categories for single episodes of affective disorder as well as categories for recurrent episodes. The second is that both recognize mild but persistent mood disturbances in which there is either a repeated alternation of high and low mood (cyclothymia) or a sustained depression of mood insufficient to meet the criteria for manic or depressive disorder, and lasting longer than a manic depressive episode (dysthymia or depressive neurosis).

The principal difference between the two schemes is that ICD10 (draft) contains two categories additional to those in DSMSIIIR. The first of these categories is for 'other mood disorders', which is a residual category for mood disorders not meeting the criteria for any of the other categories. This rubric therefore corresponds to 'depressive disorders not otherwise specified' in DSMIIIR. The second difference is that in ICD10 (draft) schizoaffective disorders are classified under affective disorders, while in DSMIIIR they appear under a different rubric ('psychotic disorders not elsewhere classified'). In this book schizoaffective disorders are also considered separately from affective disorders—with schizophrenia in Chapter 9. Finally, the reader should note some of the terms used in DSMIIIR. *Mood syndrome* is a group of mood and other symptoms occurring together for a minimum period of time (specified as two weeks for a depressive syndrome and a 'distinct period' for a manic episode). A mood syndrome can occur in a schizoaffective disorder or an organic mental disorder, as well as an affective disorder. The term *mood episode* is restricted to mood syndromes occurring in the absence of either an organic disorder or a 'non-mood' psychotic disorder (that is schizophrenia, schizoaffective disorder, or delusional disorder). The term *mood disorder* refers to a sequence of mood episodes. Mood disorders are further classified as depressive ('major depression') or bipolar.

The term *dysthymia* appears in both systems but with somewhat

Table 8.1. The classification of affective disorders

ICD10 (draft)	DSMIIIR
Manic episode	*Manic episode*
Depressive episode severe mild	*Major depressive episode*
Bipolar affective disorder currently manic currently depressed currently mixed in remission	*Bipolar disorders* manic depressed mixed cyclothymia
Recurrent depressive disorders severe mild variable	*Depressive disorders* major depression, single episode major depression, recurrent dysthymia (depressive neurosis)
Persistent affective states cyclothymia dysthymia	
Other mood (affective) disorders other affective episode other recurrent affective disorders other persistent affective states	*Depressive disorders* *not otherwise specified*
Schizoaffective disorders schizomanic disorder schizodepressive disorder	
Affective disorders not otherwise specified	

different meanings. In DSMIIIR it is used to denote a chronic disturbance of mood for most of each day and on most days, occurring for at least two years (or for one year in the case of children or adolescents) and coupled with a change of appetite (diminished or increased) or sleep (insomnia or hypersomnia), reduced energy, low self-esteem, hopelessness, difficulty in making decisions, and poor concentration. When this condition is apparently a consequence of another condition such as anorexia nervosa, anxiety disorder or chronic physical illness it is called *secondary dysthymia*. In ICD10 (draft) the requirement of a diagnosis of dysthymia is that there

Table 8.2. A systematic scheme for the description of affective disorders

The episode	
severity	mild, moderate, or severe
type	depressive, manic, mixed
special features	with neurotic symptoms
	with psychotic symptoms
	with agitation
	with retardation or stupor
The course	unipolar or bipolar
Aetiology	predominantly reactive
	predominantly endogenous

are days or weeks of 'comparative normality' between periods of mood change. The duration of the disturbance ('several years') is not specified as precisely as in DSMIIIR, and the symptoms are described in less detail, though the central features are similar, namely low mood, feeling of tiredness, lack of enjoyment, and poor sleep.

Classification and description in everyday practice

Although neither DSMIIIR nor the draft of ICD10 is entirely satisfactory, it seems unlikely that any further rearrangement of descriptive categories will be better. The solution will come only when we have a better understanding of aetiology. Meanwhile, either ICD or DSMIIIR should be used for statistical returns. For research, cases are best classified by a standardized scheme such as RDC or PSE CATEGO (see p. 84). For most clinical purposes, it is better to *describe* disorders systematically than to classify them. This can be done for every case by referring to the severity, the type of episode, and the course of the disorder, together with an evaluation of the relative importance of endogenous and reactive causation.

This scheme is shown in Table 8.2. The **severity** of the episode is described as mild, moderate or severe. The **type** of episode is described as depressive, manic, or mixed. Any **special features** are noted, namely neurotic symptoms, psychotic symptoms, agitation, retardation, or stupor.

The **course** of the disorder is characterized as unipolar or bipolar. If the term bipolar is used descriptively, it is logical to restrict it to cases that have had both manic and depressive episodes. However, it has become conventional to record all cases with a manic episode as bipolar even if there has been no depressive disorder, on the grounds that (a) most manic patients develop a depressive disorder eventually; (b) in several important ways manic patients resemble patients who have had both types of episode. This convention is followed in this textbook.

Finally the predominant **aetiology** is noted, remembering that all cases have both endogenous and reactive causes.

Differential diagnosis

Depressive disorders have to be distinguished from normal sadness, and from other psychiatric disorders, namely neuroses, schizophrenia, and organic brain syndromes. As already explained on p. 217, the distinction from normal sadness is made on the presence of other symptoms of the syndrome of depressive disorder.

Mild depressive disorders are sometimes difficult to distinguish from **anxiety neuroses**. This point is also discussed in Chapter 6; here it need only be observed that accurate diagnosis depends on assessment of the relative severity of anxiety and depressive symptoms, and on the order in which they appeared. Similar problems arise when there are prominent **phobic** or **obsessional** symptoms, or when there are hysterical conversion symptoms with or without histrionic behaviour. In each case, the clinician may fail to identify the depressive symptoms and so prescribe the wrong treatment.

As cases with mixed anxiety and depressive symptoms are common, it can be asked whether anxiety and depressive disorders can really be distinguished from one another. In a follow-up study of 66 patients with anxiety disorders and 45 patients with depressive disorders, differences were found in the course of the two conditions over an average period of nearly four years (Kerr *et al.* 1972; Schapira *et al.* 1972). Of the 66 patients originally diagnosed as having anxiety disorders 24 (40 per cent) relapsed and all but one developed a further anxiety disorder. Of those originally diagnosed as having depressive disorders, 12 (26 per cent) relapsed and all but two developed a further depressive disorder. Moreover, features predicting relapse in the two groups were different, a finding that was strongly against the hypothesis that all the cases were really manifestations of the same disorder.

The differential diagnosis from **schizophrenia** depends on a careful search for the characteristic features of this condition (see Chapter 9). Difficult diagnostic problems arise when the patient has persecutory delusions but here again the distinction can usually be made on careful examination of the mental state and on the order in which symptoms appeared. Particular difficulties also arise when symptoms characteristic of depressive disorder and of schizophrenia are found in equal measure in the same patient; these so-called schizoaffective disorders are discussed on p. 288.

In middle and late life, depressive disorders are sometimes difficult to distinguish from **dementia** (chronic organic brain syndrome) because some patients with depressive symptoms complain of considerable difficulty in remembering. In depressive disorders, difficulty in remembering occurs because poor concentration leads to inadequate registration. The distinction between the two conditions can often be made by careful memory testing (if necessary by a clinical psychologist), though it can be extremely difficult. If memory disorder does not improve with recovery of normal mood, an organic brain syndrome is probable (see also p. 618).

Manic disorders have to be distinguished from: schizophrenia; organic brain disease involving the frontal lobes (including brain tumour and general paralysis of the insane); and states of brief excitement induced by amphetamines. The diagnosis from **schizophrenia** can be most difficult. In manic disorders auditory hallucinations and delusions can occur, including some that are characteristic of schizophrenia such as delusions of reference. However, these symptoms usually change quickly in content, and seldom outlast the phase of overactivity. When there is a more or less equal mixture of features of the two syndromes, the term schizoaffective (sometimes schizomanic) is often used. This term is discussed further in Chapter 9.

An **organic brain lesion** should always be considered, especially in middle-aged or older patients with expansive behaviour and no past history of affective disorder. In the absence of gross mood disorder, extreme social disinhibition (for example, urinating in public) strongly suggests frontal lobe pathology. In such cases appropriate neurological investigation is essential.

The distinction between mania and excited behaviour due to **drug abuse** depends on the history and an examination of the urine for drugs before treatment with psychotropic drugs is started. Drug-induced states usually subside quickly once the patient is in hospital (see Chapter 17).

The epidemiology of affective disorders

It is difficult to determine the prevalence of depressive disorder partly because different investigators have used different diagnostic definitions. Many studies in the United States have been concerned not with the syndrome of depression, but with depressive symptoms arising in any circumstances (see Weissman and Klerman 1978). Such data are of little value because of the failure to distinguish between depressive symptoms as part of another syndrome (for example schizophrenia), and depressive symptoms as part of a depressive disorder. Recently in both the United States and the United Kingdom the use of standardized diagnostic schedules has led to advances. These schedules include the Present State Examination (Wing *et al.* 1974), and the Research Diagnostic Criteria (Spitzer *et al.* 1978) with its supplementary Schedule for Affective Disorders and Schizophrenia (Endicott and Spitzer 1979).

Depressive **symptoms** are common, as shown by reported point prevalences of between 13 and 20 per cent of the population. They are more frequent among women, the lower socioeconomic groups, and the divorced or separated (see Boyd and Weissman 1982).

The information about depressive **syndromes** concerns bipolar cases (in which mania has occurred at some time) and unipolar cases. Bipolar cases are more reliably identified, but even so estimates of their incidence and prevalence vary substantially. A review of the evidence suggests that the lifetime risk for bipolar disorder is less than 1 per cent, and the annual incidence between 9 and 15 per 100 000 for men and between 7 and 30 per 100 000 for women (Boyd and Weissman 1982). Estimates of the ratio of women to men differ, but it is generally agreed to lie between 1.3:1 and 2:1 (Krauthammer and Klerman 1979).

For major depressive disorders the lifetime prevalence is about 6 per cent in surveys in the United States. Estimates of the annual **incidence** vary from about 80 to 200 per 100 000 among men and from about 250 to 7800 per 100 000 women. The point prevalence in industrialized countries is between 1.8 and 3.2 cases per 100 for men and between 2.0 and 9.3 per 100 for women (see Boyd and Weissman 1982). The reasons for increased rates among women are uncertain. The increase could be due in part to a greater readiness in women to admit depressive symptoms, but such selective reporting is unlikely to be the whole explanation. It is possible that some depressed men abuse alcohol and are diagnosed as alcoholic rather than depressed, thus underestimating the true number of depressive disorders. However, misdiagnosis of this kind is unlikely to account for the whole of the difference.

Bipolar disorders begin on average in the mid-twenties, unipolar disorders in the late thirties. Bipolar disorders are more frequent in the upper social classes, but unipolar disorders have not been found linked to any social class (see Weissman and Boyd 1985).

It has been suggested that, among African people, depressive disorders are uncommon and the symptom of guilt occurs infrequently (eg. Carothers 1947). In two Ugandan villages, however, a survey using standardized methods of assessment found the frequency of depressive disorder to be actually somewhat higher than in south London, and guilt to be a frequent symptom (Orley and Wing 1979).

The aetiology of affective disorders

There have been many different approaches to the aetiology of affective disorders. In this section, consideration is first given to the role of genetic factors and of childhood experience in laying down a predisposition to affective disorder in adult life. Next an account is given of stressors that may provoke affective disorders. This is followed by a review of psychological and biochemical factors through which predisposing factors and stressors might lead to affective disorders. In all these topics, investigators have paid more attention to depressive disorders than to mania. In this chapter, more space is given to aetiology than in most others in this book; the purpose is to show how several different kinds of enquiry can be used to throw light on the same clinical problem.

Genetic causes

Genetic causes have been studied mainly in moderate to severe cases of affective disorder, rather than in milder cases (those called 'neurotic depression' by some investigators). Most family studies have shown that parents, siblings, and children of severely depressed patients have a morbid risk of 10–15 per cent for affective disorder, as against 1–2 per cent in the general population. It is also generally agreed that there is no excess of schizophrenia among the relatives of depressed probands.

Twin studies suggest strongly that these high rates within families are largely due to genetic factors. Thus, from a review of seven twin studies, Price (1968) concluded that the concordance rates for manic-depressive psychosis were 68 per cent for monozygotic twins reared together (97 pairs), 67 per cent for monozygotic twins reared apart (12 pairs), and 23 per cent for dizygotic twins (119 pairs). Similar percentages were reported in studies from Denmark (Bertelsen *et al.* 1977).

Studies of adoptees also point to a genetic aetiology. Cadoret (1978*a*) studied eight children, each born to a parent with an affective disorder and then adopted by a healthy couple. Three of the eight developed an affective disorder, as against only eight of 118 adoptees whose biological parents either suffered from a different psychiatric disorder or were healthy. In a study of 29 adoptees who had suffered from a bipolar affective disorder, Mendlewicz and Rainer (1977) found psychiatric disorder in 31 per cent of their biological parents (mainly but not exclusively affective illnesses), as against only 12 per cent of adoptive parents. In a study of 71 Danish adoptees previously treated for a major affective disorder Wender *et al.* (1986) found a significantly increased frequency of similar disorders among the biological relatives but not among the adoptive relatives (comparing each group of relatives with the corresponding relative of healthy adoptees).

So far no distinction has been made between cases with depression only (unipolar disorders) and those with a history of mania (bipolar disorders). Leonhard *et al.* (1962) were the first to present evidence that bipolar disorders were more frequent among the families of bipolar probands than among the families of unipolar probands. Several subsequent investigations (reviewed by Nurnberger and Gershon 1982) have confirmed this finding. However, these studies have also shown that unipolar cases are frequent in the families of both unipolar and bipolar probands; it seems that unipolar disorders do not 'breed true' as the bipolar disorders seem to do (see, for example, Angst 1966). Bertelsen *et al.* (1977) report higher pairwise concordance rates among bipolar (74 per cent) than among unipolar (43 per cent) monozygotic twins, again suggesting a stronger genetic influence in bipolars.

The few genetic studies of 'neurotic depression' have found increased rates of both neurotic and other kinds of depressive disorder in families. However, when twins have been studied, similar concordance rates have been found among monozygotic and dizygotic pairs. This is the finding whether concordance is defined by the presence of 'neurotic' depression in the co-twin or, more broadly, as any kind of depressive disorder in the other twin. These findings suggest that the main cause of the increased incidence of depressive states in the families of 'neurotic depressives' is other than genetic (see McGuffin and Katz 1986).

There are conflicting theories about the **mode of inheritance** because no simple genetic model fits the frequencies of cases observed among family members of different degrees of relationship to the proband. Most family studies of depressive disorders have shown more affected women than men, suggesting sex-linked inheritance perhaps with a dominant but incompletely penetrant gene. However, the many reports of transmission from father to son (see Gershon *et al.* 1975) argue against this mode of transmission. This is because sons must inherit the X chromosome from the mother, since only the father can provide the Y chromosome.

Attempts to find **genetic markers** for affective disorder have not been successful. Linkages have been reported between affective disorder and colour blindness, Xg blood group, and certain HLA antigens, but none has been confirmed (see Gershon and Bunney 1976; also Nurnberger and Gershon 1982). Recently, techniques of molecular genetics have been used to look for linkage between identifiable genes and manic-depressive disorder in the members of large families. A study from North America of an Old Order Amish kinship suggested linkage with two markers on the short arm of chromosome 11, namely the insulin gene, and the cellular oncogene *Ha-ras-1* (Egeland *et al.* 1987). This position is interesting because it is close to the gene controlling the enzyme tyrosine hydroxylase, which is involved in the synthesis of catecholamines, substances that have been implicated in the aetiology of affective disorder (see p. 246). However this linkage with the insulin and *Ha-ras-1* markers was not confirmed in an Icelandic kinship studied by Hodgkinson *et al.* (1987), or in three families in North America studied by Detera-Wadleigh *et al.* (1987). The potential of this kind of study is high but much more work will be required before the general significance of findings can be assessed. The studies to date do however point to the important possibility that more than one genetic mechanism may be capable of producing the clinical picture of severe depressive disorder.

Some family studies have shown increased rates of other psychiatric disorders among the families of probands with affective disorder. This finding has led to the hypothesis that these other psychiatric disorders might be aetiologically related to affective disorder, an idea expressed in the name '**depressive spectrum disease**'. So far these claims have not been confirmed. Helzer and Winokur (1974) reported an increase of alcoholism among the relatives of male manic probands, but Morrison (1975) found such an association only when the probands had both alcoholism and depressive disorder. Similarly Winokur *et al.* (1971) reported an increased rate of antisocial personality disorder ('sociopathy') among the male relatives of probands whose depressive disorders had started before the age of 40. This finding was not confirmed by Gershon *et al.* (1975).

Physique and personality

Kretschmer (1936) proposed that patients of **pyknic body build** (thickset and rounded) were particularly prone to affective illness. Subsequent investigations using objective measurements have not shown any strong association of this kind (von Zerssen 1976).

Kraepelin (1921) suggested that people with **cyclothymic personality** (i.e. those with repeated and sustained mood swings) were more prone to develop manic-depressive disorder. Subsequently Leonhard *et al.* (1962) reported this association to be stronger among patients with bipolar disorders than among those with unipolar disorders. However, when personality was assessed without knowledge of the type of illness, bipolar patients were not found to have mainly cyclothymic personality traits (Tellenbach 1975).

No single type of personality seems to predispose to unipolar depressive disorders; in particular depressive personality disorder has no such associ-ation. Clinical experience suggests that the most relevant personality features are obsessional traits and readiness to develop anxiety. Presum-ably these features are important because they influence the way in which people respond to stressful life events. Unfortunately most reported investigations of personality in depressed patients are of little value because measurements were made when the patients were depressed. Assessments of patients who are currently depressed may not accurately reflect the premorbid personality.

Early environment

Maternal deprivation

Psychoanalysts have suggested that childhood deprivation of maternal affection through separation or loss predisposes to depressive disorders in adult life. Epidemiologists have attempted to discover what proportion of adults with depressive disorder have experienced parental separation or loss in childhood. Nearly all these studies have methodological defects. Their results are contradictory; of fourteen studies reviewed by Paykel (1981), seven confirm the hypothesis and seven do not. Other investigations have shown that the death of a parent is associated with disorders other than depressive disorders; for example, psychoneurosis, antisocial personality, and alcoholism (see Paykel 1981). At present, therefore, the association between childhood parental loss and later depressive disorder is uncertain. If it exists at all, it is weak and may be non-specific.

Relationships with parents

When assessing a depressed patient, it is difficult to determine retrospectively what kind of relationship he had in childhood with his parents. The patient's recollection of the relationship may be distorted by many factors, including the depressive disorder itself. These problems make it difficult to decide the aetiological importance of reports that, compared with normal controls or patients with severe depressive disorders, patients with mild depressive disorders (neurotic depression) remember their parents as having been less caring and more over-protective (Parker 1979).

Precipitating factors

Recent life events

It is an everyday clinical observation that depressive disorders often follow stressful events. However, several other possibilities must be discounted before it can be concluded that stressful events cause the depressive disorders that succeed them. First, the association might be coincidental. Secondly, the association might be non-specific; there might be as many stressful events in the weeks preceding other kinds of illness. Thirdly, it might be spurious; the patient might have regarded the events as stressful only in retrospect when seeking an explanation for his illness, or he might have experienced them as stressful only because he was already depressed at the time.

In recent years, research workers have tried to overcome each of these difficulties. The first two problems—whether the events are coincidental or whether any association is non-specific—require the use of control groups suitably chosen from the general population and from people with other illnesses. The third problem—whether the association is spurious—requires two other approaches. The first approach (Brown *et al.* 1973*b*) is to separate events that are undoubtedly independent of illness (such as losing a job because a whole factory closes) from events that may have been secondary to the illness (such as losing a job when no-one else is dismissed). The second approach (Holmes and Rahe 1967) is to assign a rating to each event according to the consensus view of healthy people about its stressful qualities.

By these methods, an excess of life events has been shown in the months before the onset of depressive disorder (Paykel *et al.* 1969; Brown and Harris 1978). However, an excess of similar events has also been shown to precede suicide attempts, and the onset of neurosis and schizophrenia. To estimate the relative importance of life events in each condition, Paykel (1978) applied a modified form of the epidemiological measure of relative risk. He found that the risk of developing depression increased sixfold in the six months after experiencing markedly threatening life events. The comparable increase for schizophrenia was two- to fourfold, and for attempted suicide sevenfold. Brown used another estimate, 'the brought forward time' (Brown *et al.* 1973*a*), and came to similar conclusions.

Are any particular kinds of events more likely to provoke a depressive disorder? Because depressive symptoms are part of the normal response to bereavement, it has been suggested that loss by separation or death might be particularly important. However, research shows that not all people with depressive symptoms report losses. For example, Paykel (1982) reviewed 11 studies that reported specifically on recent separations. In six of these studies depressives reported more separation than the control groups, suggesting some specificity; however, in five studies depressives did not report an excess of separations. Looked at the other way round, amongst people who experience loss events only about 10 per cent develop a depressive disorder (Paykel 1974). So far, therefore, the evidence does not point to any great specificity in the events that can provoke depressive disorder.

It is less certain whether mania is provoked by life events. In the past, mania was thought to arise entirely from endogenous causes. However, clinical experience suggests that a proportion of cases are precipitated, sometimes by events that might have been expected to induce depression, for example bereavement.

Predisposing life events

It is a common clinical impression that the events immediately preceding a depressive disorder act as a 'last straw' for a person who has been subjected to a long period of adverse circumstances such as an unhappy marriage, problems at work or unsatisfactory housing. Brown and Harris (1978) divided predisposing events into two kinds. The first are prolonged stressful circumstances which can themselves cause depression as well as adding to the effects of short-term life events. Brown and Harris gave the name *long-term difficulties* to these circumstances. The second kind of predisposing circumstance does not itself cause depression problems, instead it acts only by increasing the effects of short-term life events. This kind of circumstance is known as a *vulnerability factor*. In fact the distinction between the two kinds of circumstance is not clear-cut. Thus long continued marital problems (a long-term difficulty) are likely to be associated with a lack of a confiding relationship, and the latter has been identified by Brown as a vulnerability factor.

Brown and Harris studied working-class women living in Camberwell in London, and found three circumstances acting as vulnerability factors: having the care of young children, not working outside the home, and having no one to confide in. They also found that events in the past increased vulnerability, namely loss of the mother by death or separation before the age of 11.

Brown's four factors have not been supported consistently by subsequent enquiries. In a study in a rural community in the outer Hebrides, Brown was able to confirm only one of his four factors at a significant level, namely having three children aged under 14 years (Brown and Prudo 1981). One other study confirmed this last finding (Campbell *et al.* 1983) but three others did not (Solomon and Bromet 1982; Costello 1982; Bebbington *et al.* 1984). Another vulnerability factor—the lack of someone to confide in (lack of 'intimacy')—has received more support; Brown and Harris (1986) cites eight studies that confirm it, and two that do not. On the present evidence, therefore, Brown's interesting idea that particular circumstances of life increase vulnerability cannot be accepted in full. Although a reported lack of an intimate relationship seems to increase vulnerability to depressive disorder, this finding can be interpreted in three ways. First, it might show that a lack of opportunities to confide makes people more vulnerable. Second, it might indicate that depressed people have a distorted perception of the degree of intimacy they achieved before becoming depressed. Third, it might show that an underlying cause results in both difficulty in confiding in others and vulnerability to depression.

Recently attention has turned from these external factors to an intrapsychic factor, low self-esteem. Brown has suggested that vulnerability factors might act in part by lowering self-esteem, and intuitively, this seems likely to be important. However, it is difficult to measure self-esteem and its role as a predisposing factor is not yet established by research findings. [For reviews of the evidence for and against the vulnerability model see Brown and Harris (1986), and Tennant (1985).]

The effects of physical illness

Associations between physical illness and depressive disorder are described in Chapter 11. Here it should be noted that some conditions appear particularly likely to be followed by depression; for example influenza, glandular fever, parkinsonism, and certain endocrine disorders. It has been held that some operations, notably hysterectomy and sterilization, are followed by a depressive disorder more often than would be expected by chance. However, these clinical impressions have not been confirmed by prospective studies (Gath *et al.* 1982a; Cooper *et al.* 1982). It is likely that many physical illnesses can act as non-specific stressors in provoking depressive disorders, but that a few have specific effects. Mania has occasionally been reported in association with physical illnesses (for example cerebral neoplasm and virus infections), medication, (notably steroids), and surgery [see Krauthammer and Klerman (1978) for a review of the evidence]. However, no aetiological conclusions can be drawn from these diverse associations.

It should be mentioned here that the puerperium (although not an illness) is associated with an increased risk of affective disorder (see pp. 466–9).

Psychological theories of aetiology

These theories are concerned with the psychological mechanisms by which recent and remote life experiences can lead to depressive disorders. Most of the literature on this subject fails to distinguish adequately between the symptom of depression and the syndrome of depressive disorder.

Psychoanalysis

The psychoanalytic theory of depression began with a paper by Abraham in 1911, and was developed by Freud in 1917 in a paper called 'Mourning and melancholia'. Freud drew attention to the resemblance between the phenomena of mourning and the symptoms of depressive disorders, and suggested that their causes might be similar. It is important to note that Freud did not suppose that all severe depressive disorders necessarily had the same cause. Thus he commented that some disorders 'suggest somatic rather than psychogenic affections' and indicated that his ideas were to be applied only to those 'whose psychogenic nature was indisputable' (1917, p. 243). Freud suggested that, just as mourning results from loss by death, so melancholia results from loss of other kinds. Since it was apparent that not every depressed patient had suffered an actual loss, it was necessary to postulate a loss of 'some abstraction' or internal representation, or in Freud's terms the loss of an 'object'.

Freud pointed out that depressed patients often appear critical of themselves, and he proposed that this self-accusation was really a disguised accusation of someone else for whom the patient 'felt affection'. In other words, depression was thought to occur when feelings of love and hostility were present at the same time (ambivalence). When a loved 'object' is lost the patient feels despair; at the same time any hostile feelings attached to this 'object' are redirected against the patient himself, as self-reproach.

In addition to these mechanisms of reaction, Freud also put forward predisposing factors. He proposed that the depressed patient regresses to an earlier stage of development, the oral stage, at which sadistic feelings are powerful. Klein (1934) developed this idea by suggesting that the infant must acquire confidence that, when his mother leaves him, she will return even when he has been angry. This proposed stage of learning was called the 'depressive position'. Klein suggested that if this stage is not passed through successfully, the child will be more likely to develop depression in adult life.

Further important modifications of Freud's theory were made by Bibring (1953) and Jacobson (1953). They suggested that loss of self-esteem is of central importance in depressive disorders. They also proposed that self-esteem depends not only on experiences at the oral stage, but also on failures at later stages of development. However, although low self-esteem is certainly part of the syndrome of depressive disorders, there is no clear evidence about its frequency before the illness began. Nor has it been shown that low self-esteem is more common among people who subsequently develop depressive disorders than among those who do not.

According to psychodynamic theory, mania is a defence against depression; this is not a convincing explanation of most cases.

For a review of the psychoanalytic literature on depression, see Mendelson (1982).

Learned helplessness

This explanation of depressive disorders is based on experimental work with animals. Seligman (1975) originally suggested that depression develops when reward or punishment is no longer clearly contingent on the actions of the organism. When animals are exposed to experimental situations in which they cannot control punishing stimuli, they develop a behavioural syndrome known as 'learned helplessness'. The features of this syndrome bear some resemblance to those depressive disorders in man, notably reduced voluntary activity and reduced intake of food. The original hypothesis has been broadened by stating that depression results when 'highly desired outcomes are believed improbable or highly aversive outcomes are believed probable and the individual expects that no response (of his) will change their likelihood' (Abrahamson *et al.* 1978, p. 68). This work has attracted considerable attention, perhaps as a result of the name 'learned helplessness' rather than as a result of scientific strength.

Separation experiments in animals

Arising from the suggestion that the loss of a loved person may be a cause of depressive disorders, there have been numerous experiments on the effects of separation in primates. Most of these experiments are concerned with the separation of infants from their mothers, rather than the separation of adults from one another. As such they are of uncertain relevance to man, since depressive disorders may never occur in young children (see Chapter 20). Nevertheless the studies may be of some importance to understanding the effects of separating human infants from their mothers. In a particularly careful series of experiments, Hinde and his colleagues studied the effects of separating infant rhesus macaques from their mother (see Hinde 1977). These experiments confirmed earlier observations that separation causes distress to both infant and mother. After an initial period of calling and searching, the infant becomes less active, eats and drinks less, withdraws from encounters with other monkeys, and has an appearance resembling that of a sad human being. Hinde and his co-workers have shown that this response to separation depends on many other variables including the 'relationship' of the pair before separation.

In contrast with these effects of removing infants from their mothers, adolescent monkeys separated from their peer group showed no clear stage of 'despair' but instead greater exploratory behaviour (McKinney *et al.* 1972). Moreover, when five-year-old monkeys were taken away from their family group, reactions were observed only when they were housed alone, and not when they were housed with other monkeys, some of whom they knew already (Suomi *et al.* 1975). Therefore, although much can be learnt by studying separation in primates, it would be unwise to use the available data to support an aetiological theory of depressive disorders in man.

Cognitive theories

Most psychiatrists regard the gloomy thoughts of depressed patients as secondary to a primary disturbance of mood. However, Beck (1967) has suggested that these 'depressive cognitions' may be the primary disorder, or at least powerful factors in aggravating and perpetuating the disorder. Beck divides depressive cognitions into three components. The first is a stream of 'negative' thoughts, for example 'I am a failure as a mother'. The second is a set of expectations, for example that a person cannot be happy unless everyone likes him. The third is a series of 'cognitive distortions', of which four examples can be given: 'arbitrary inference', drawing a conclusion when there is no evidence for it and even some against it; 'selective abstraction', focusing on a detail and ignoring more important features of a situation; 'overgeneralization', drawing a general conclusion on the basis of a single incident; and 'personalization', relating external events to oneself in an unwarranted way.

Beck suggests that a person who habitually adopts such ways of thinking will be more likely to become depressed when faced with minor problems. For example, a rebuff would be more likely to lead to depression in a person who thinks that he needs to be liked by everyone, concludes arbitrarily that the rebuff means he is disliked, focuses on this event despite other evidence that he is generally popular, and draws these general conclusions from this single incident. (It can be seen from this example that the varieties of cognitive distortion are not entirely distinct from one another.)

As yet there is a lack of evidence that these mechanisms are present in people before the onset of depressive disorder; or that these mechanisms are more frequent in people who subsequently develop depressive disorders than in those who do not.

Biochemical theories

The monoamine hypothesis

This hypothesis supposes that depressive disorder is due to an abnormality in a monoamine neurotransmitter system at one or more sites in the brain. In its early form, the hypothesis suggested a changed provision of the monoamine; more recent elaborations postulate alterations in receptors as well as in the concentrations or the turnover of the amines [see, for example, Garver and Davis (1979)]. Three monoamine transmitters have been implicated: 5-hydroxytryptamine (5-HT), noradrenalin, and dopamine. The hypothesis has been tested by observing three kinds of phenomena: the metabolism of neurotransmitters in patients with affective disorders; effects of amine precursors and antagonists on measurable indices of the function of monoamine systems (usually neuroendocrine indices); and the pharmacological properties shared by antidepressant drugs. The evidence from these three kinds of investigation will now be considered in relation to the three kinds of transmitter: 5-HT, noradrenalin, and dopamine.

Indirect evidence about *5-HT function* in the brains of depressed patients has been sought by examining cerebro-spinal fluid (CSF). On balance, the evidence is for reduced concentrations of 5-hydroxyindolacetic acid (5-HIAA), the main metabolite of 5-HT formed in brain [see, for example, Van Praag and Korf (1971)]. The simple interpretation of these findings is that brain 5-HT function is also reduced. There are, however, several difficulties about such an interpretation. First, when CSF is obtained by lumbar puncture, it is uncertain what proportion of the metabolites of 5-HT originate in the brain rather than the spinal cord. Second, changed concentrations may simply reflect alternations in the transport of metabolites out of CSF. This possibility can be partly excluded by giving large doses of probenecid which interferes with such transport: the results of this procedure are against a simple change in transport. Interpretation seemed to be made more difficult by the observation that low or normal concentrations were found in mania, whereas raised concentrations had been expected on the grounds that mania was the opposite of depression. However, the existence of mixed affective disorders (p. 225) indicates that this original expectation was too simple. A further difficulty for the original hypothesis is that low concentrations of 5-HIAA persist after clinical recovery (see Coppen 1972). This finding might indicate that low 5-HT function is a 'trait' present in people who are prone to develop depressive disorders, and not just a 'state' found only during episodes of illness.

Measurements of 5-HT have been made in the brains of depressed patients who have died, usually by suicide. Although this is a more direct test of the monoamine hypothesis, the result are difficult to interpret for two reasons. First, the observed changes may have taken place after death. Second, the changes may have been caused before death but by factors other than the depressive disorder; for example, by anoxia, or by drugs used in treatment or taken to commit suicide. These limitations may explain why some investigators have reported lowered concentrations of 5-HT in the brain stem of depressed patients (for example, Lloyd *et al.* 1974), whilst others have not (for example Cochran *et al.* 1976). Recently 5-HT receptors have been shown to be of more than one kind, and it has been reported that one type—5-HT_2 receptors—are increased in the frontal cortex of suicide victims (Mann *et al.* 1986) (an increase in receptors could be a response to a reduction in the amount of the transmitter).

The functional activity of 5-HT systems in the brain has been assessed by giving a substance that stimulates 5-HT function and by measuring a neuroendocrine response that is controlled by 5-HT pathways—usually the release of prolactin. 5-HT function has been enhanced by intravenous infusions of L-tryptophan—a precursor of 5-HT—or by oral doses of fenfluramine, which releases 5-HT and blocks its re-uptake. The prolactin response to both these agents is reduced in depressed patients (see Cowen and Anderson 1986; Heninger *et al.* 1984). This suggests reduced 5-HT function, provided that the other mechanisms involved in prolactin release are working normally (a point that has not been fully established).

If 5-HT function is reduced in depressive disorders, L-tryptophan should have therapeutic effects and antidepressant drugs should share the property of increasing 5-HT function. Some workers have reported that L-tryptophan has antidepressant effects (for example Coppen and Wood

1978), but the effect is not a strong one. Antidepressant drugs affect 5-HT functions; indeed this finding is the main origin of the 5-HT hypothesis of the cause of depressive disorder. However, the effects are complex: most of these drugs decrease the number of 5-HT_2 binding sites, a finding that does not easily fit the hypothesis that 5-HT function is lowered in depressive disorders and should therefore be increased, not decreased, by antidepressant drugs. However, when repeated electric shocks are given to animals in a way that mimics the application of ECT to patients, the consequence is an increase of 5-HT_2 binding sites (see Green and Goodwin 1986).

It has to be concluded that the evidence for the 5-HT hypothesis is fragmentary and contradictory.

What is the evidence for an abnormality in *noradrenergic function*? The results of studies of the noradrenalin metabolite 3-methoxy-4-hydroxy-phenylethylene glycol (MHPG) in CSF of depressed patients are conflicting, but there is some suggestion that the metabolite is reduced (see Van Praag 1982). In post-mortem brain, measurements have not revealed a consistent abnormality in the concentration of noradrenalin (see Cooper *et al.* 1986). The growth hormone response to clonidine has been used as a neuroendocrine test of noradrenergic function. Several studies have shown a reduced response in depressed patients, suggesting a defect in post-synaptic noradrenergic receptor (see Checkley *et al.* 1986). Antidepressant drugs have complicated effects on noradrenergic receptors, and tricyclic drugs have the additional property of reducing the re-uptake of noradrenalin by presynaptic neurones. One effect, which is shared with ECT, is a reduction in the number of beta-noradrenergic binding sites in the cortex—an effect which might be primary, or a secondary compensation for increased noradrenalin turnover (see Green and Goodwin 1986). It is difficult to assess the overall effect of these drugs on noradrenergic synapses. In healthy volunteers there is some evidence that transmission is first increased (presumably by re-uptake block) and returns to normal, probably due to the effect on postsynaptic receptors (Cowen and Anderson 1986). If confirmed, this finding will be difficult to reconcile with the idea that antidepressant drugs act by increasing reduced noradrenergic function in depressive disorders.

There is little evidence of an abnormality of *dopaminergic function* in depressive disorder. The main metabolite of dopamine, homovanillic acid (HVA), has not been shown to be consistently reduced in CSF, and no significant changes in dopamine concentrations have been reported in post-mortem brains of depressed patients. Neuroendocrine testing does not reveal consistent changes suggestive of abnormalities of dopaminergic function, and it is generally agreed that the precursor L-dopa has no specific antidepressant effect.

It to be concluded that we do not yet understand the biochemical disorder in depressed patients, or the way that effective drugs correct it.

In any case, it is dangerous to argue from the effects of drugs to the biochemical basis of disease. Anticholinergic drugs relieve the symptoms of parkinsonism but the underlying fault is a deficiency of dopaminergic function not an excess of cholinergic function. This example is a reminder that transmitter systems interact in the nervous system, and that the monoamine hypotheses of depressive disorder are based on considerable over-simplification of the events at synapses in the central nervous system.

Endocrine abnormalities

These abnormalities are important in aetiology for three reasons. First, some disorders of endocrine function are followed by depressive disorders more often than would be expected by chance, suggesting a causative relationship. Second, endocrine abnormalities found in depressive disorder suggest that there may be a disorder of the hypothalamic centres controlling the endocrine system. Third, endocrine changes are regulated by hypothalamic mechanisms, which in turn are partly controlled by monoamine systems; hence endocrine changes might reflect abnormalities in monoamine systems. These three lines of enquiry will be considered in turn.

Cushing's syndrome is sometimes accompanied by depression or elation; and Addison's disease and hyperparathyroidism by depression. Endocrine changes may possibly account for depressive disorders occurring premenstrually, during the menopause and after childbirth. These clinical associations are discussed further in Chapter 12. Here it need only be noted that none has so far led to a better understanding of the causes of affective disorder.

Much research effort has been concerned with abnormalities in the control of cortisol in depressive disorders. In about half of patients whose depressive disorder is at least moderately severe, plasma cortisol is increased. Despite this patients do not show clinical features of excess production of cortisol, possibly because the number of glucocorticoid receptor sites is reduced (Whalley *et al.* 1986). In any case, excess cortisol production is not specific to depressed patients for similar changes occur in drug-free manic and schizophrenic patients (Christie *et al.* 1986). A more important finding is that the diurnal pattern of secretion is altered in depressed patients. An increased secretion of cortisol could arise because the experience of being ill acted as a stressor; but such an explanation is unlikely because stressors do not alter the diurnal pattern. In depressed patients cortisol secretion is abnormal in that it remains high throughout the afternoon and evening, whereas in normal subject it falls to a lower level. Another finding is that between 20 and 40 per cent of depressed patients do not show the normal suppression of cortisol secretion induced by giving the powerful synthetic corticosteroid dexamethasone about midnight. However, not all cortisol hypersecretors are dexamethasone resistant. These abnormalities seem to occur mainly in depressive disorders with 'biological' symptoms, but they are not detected in all such cases, nor are they associated with any single clinical feature. Moreover, abnormalities in the dexamethasone suppression test are not confined to affective disorders; they have been reported also in mania, chronic schizophrenia, and dementia (see Braddock 1986).

Other neuroendocrine functions have been studied in depressed patients. The responses of luteinizing hormone and follicle-stimulating hormone to gonadotrophin-stimulating hormone are usually normal. However the responses of prolactin and of thyroid-stimulating hormone to thyrotrophin-stimulating hormone are abnormal in up to half of depressed patients—the proportion depending on the sample and the methods of assessment (see Amsterdam *et al.* 1983).

Water and electrolytes

There have been several reports of changes in water and electrolytes in depressive disorders and mania. Thus 'residual sodium' (more or less equivalent to intracellular sodium) has been reported to be increased in both conditions (Coppen and Shaw 1963; Coppen *et al.* 1976). There have also been reports of changes in erythrocyte membrane sodium-potassium ATPase, such that active transport of sodium and potassium increases on recovery from mania and depressive disorders (Naylor *et al.* 1973, 1976). Such findings are of some interest because they could reflect an abnormality of the mechanisms subserving nerve conduction. However, much more needs to be known before aetiological hypotheses can be constructed.

Conclusion

The **predisposition** to develop mania and severe depressive disorders has important genetic determinants. There is no convincing evidence that this inherited predisposition is modified in important ways by specific childhood experiences of the kind postulated by psychoanalysts. Nevertheless, adverse early experience may play a part in shaping features of personality which in turn determine whether, in adult life, certain events are experienced as stressful. If such a predisposition exists, it is not expressed as a single personality type that is invariably associated with affective disorder, but in several different kinds of personality.

The **precipitating** causes are stressful life events and certain kinds of physical illness. Some progress has been made in discovering the types of event that provoke depression and in quantifying their stressful qualities. Such studies show that loss is an important precipitant, but not the only one. The effects of particular events may be modified by a number of background factors that may make a person more vulnerable, for example caring for several small children without help, and not having someone to confide in. As noted in the preceding paragraph the impact of potentially stressful events also depends on personality factors.

Two kinds of **mechanism** have been proposed to explain how precipitating events lead to the phenomena observed in depressive disorders. The first mechanism is psychological and the second biochemical. The two sets of mechanism are not necessarily mutually exclusive, for they may represent different levels of organization of the same pathological process. The psychological studies are at an early stage. Abnormalities have been shown in the thinking of depressed patients, and they may play a part in perpetuating depressive disorder. However, there is no convincing evidence that they induce it. The biochemical theory is based largely on the response of depressive disorders to treatment with drugs. Many studies give some general support to the hypothesis of a biochemical abnormality, but they have not identified it.

Course and prognosis

In considering course and prognosis it is convenient to deal with bipolar and unipolar disorders separately, because more information is available about the bipolar cases.

Bipolar disorders

As explained earlier, in these disorders there has been at least one episode of mania, irrespective of whether or not there has been a depressive disorder. The mean age of **onset** is about 30 years, though there is wide variation, some cases starting in the late teens, and a few in late life. Angst *et al.* (1973) reported that almost 90 per cent of cases began before the age of 50.

The natural **course** of manic episodes can be judged from reports written before the introduction of modern treatment. According to Kraepelin (1921, p. 73) 'while occasionally attacks run their course within a few weeks or even a few days, the great majority extend over many months. Attacks of two or three years duration are very frequent; isolated cases may last longer, for ten years or more'. In 1945, before phenothiazines had been introduced, Lundquist reported an average duration of 13 months. These estimates contrast with the average duration of under three months reported by Angst *et al.* in 1973. Among patients who have repeated manic attacks, the length of each episode does not seem to alter systematically in the later attacks (Angst *et al.* 1973).

It is generally agreed that nearly all manic patients **recover** eventually. Before modern treatment was available, about 5 per cent of manic disorders persisted for several years (Lundquist 1945; Stendstedt 1952). Nowadays, many of these lasting cases can be kept under control with prolonged medication. Manic illnesses often **recur**, and subsequent depressive disorder is frequent. The proportion of patients who have only a single episode of mania is wholly uncertain, estimates varying from as many as 50 per cent (Kraepelin 1921; Lundquist 1945) to as few as 1 per cent (Angst *et al.* 1973). Nowadays it is often difficult to decide whether there is a succession of illnesses or a single illness interrupted by periods of partially successful treatment. According to Angst *et al.* (1973) the length of remission between episodes of illness becomes shorter up to the third attack, but does not change after that.

Unipolar depressive disorders

The age of **onset** varies so widely that a mean is not informative. The **course** of the episode is equally variable. Kraepelin (1921, p. 97) wrote that 'the duration of the attack is usually longer than in mania; but it may likewise fluctuate between a few days and more than a decade. The remission of the morbid phenomena invariably takes place with many fluctuations . . .'. Studies that have included both unipolar and bipolar disorders have not revealed consistent differences between them in rates of **recovery** (see Tsuang *et al.* 1979). Among a group of patients treated at university hospitals in the USA, as many as 21 per cent had not recovered after two years, and most of these unrecovered patients had experienced severe depressive symptoms throughout this time (Keller *et al.* 1984). In this group of patients (whose median age was 38 years), age did not predict outcome. It is generally agreed, however, that among unipolar depressives most young patients recover eventually from the episode, though not all elderly patients do so.

Depressive disorders and suicide

Of people who have suffered a severe depressive disorder at any time, between 11 and 17 per cent will eventually commit suicide (Fremming 1951; Helgason 1964; Pitts and Winokur 1964). There is not enough information to decide the relative risks of suicide in unipolar and bipolar disorders.

Treatment

This section is concerned with the effectiveness of various forms of treatment. *Details of treatment with drugs and ECT are given in Chapter 17* which should be consulted before reading this section. Advice on the selection of treatments and the day-to-day care of patients is given in the section on management.

Antidepressant drugs

In an important study by the Medical Research Council (Clinical Psychiatry Committee 1965), the therapeutic effects of imipramine, phenelzine, ECT, and placebo were compared in 250 patients suffering from moderately severe depression. At the end of four weeks ECT was the most effective of these four treatments. After three months ECT and imipramine were equally effective, about two-thirds of the patients in both treatment groups having improved. Phenelzine was no more effective than placebo, about one-third of the patients in both these groups having improved. Other controlled trials have also shown imipramine to be more effective than placebo in moderately severe depressive disorders (for example Ball and Kiloh 1959). However, controlled trials also indicate that the value of imipramine in less severe 'neurotic' depressive disorders is less certain (Rogers and May 1975). Comparisons between the many tricyclic antidepressant drugs now available have not shown any important difference in their therapeutic effects, although there are some worthwhile differences in their side-effects (see, for example, Wechsler *et al.* 1965). These differences in side-effects are explained in Chapter 17, and are referred to in the section on 'management' later in this chapter (p. 260).

Comparative studies have shown that monoamine oxidase inhibitors are less effective than tricyclic antidepressants for moderate to severe depressive disorders. In mild cases with neurotic symptoms they are probably about as effective as tricyclics, provided that they are given for long enough and in sufficient dose. Thus for phenelzine the effect may take up to six weeks to appear and the dose may need to be increased beyond 45 mg per day to 60 mg or even 75 mg. There is still some doubt whether monoamine oxidase inhibitors have a specific antidepressant rather than an anxiolytic effect. However, work by Rowan *et al.* (1982) suggests that in high doses they are antidepressant. These authors found that phenelzine given for six weeks at doses increasing progressively to 60–75 mg a day was as effective in the treatment of mild depression as amitryptyline in doses increasing to 150–187.5 mg/day. Both drugs were more effective than placebo. These therapeutic effects have to be balanced against the many interactions of the monoamine oxidase inhibitors with foodstuffs and other drugs (see Chapter 17). It is therefore recommended that MAOI drugs should never be the first choice of treatment for any depressive disorder. If they are used it should only be for less severe chronic depressive disorders with prominent anxiety symptoms which have not responded to a full trial of a cyclic antidepressant drug.

It has been reported that, in cases resistant to treatment with a tricyclic or MAOI, the effect of a combination of the two drugs is greater than that of either given alone in corresponding dosage. This claim has not been proved, indeed two clinical trials have failed to confirm it (Young *et al.*

1979; Razani *et al*. 1983). However, it can be argued that neither trial was concerned with patients known to be resistant to single drugs (the patient group to whom combined treatment is most often given). If the combined treatment is used, it is essential to follow the precautions described on p. 263.

Lithium

This section is concerned with lithium only as a treatment for depressive disorders. Its use in prevention is considered later. Some studies suggest that, for depressive disorder without obvious precipitants ('endogenous depression'), lithium has antidepressant effects comparable to those of a tricyclic drug (for example Mendels *et al*. 1972; Watanabe *et al*. 1975; Worrall *et al*. 1979). However, other studies have not confirmed these effects (for example; Fieve *et al*. 1968; Stokes *et al*. 1971) or have obtained equivocal results (Goodwin *et al*. 1969). So it seems that if lithium has a therapeutic effect in the acute stage of depressive disorders, it is not a powerful effect. Hence there is no justification for using lithium in this way except perhaps when other measures have failed. Even the latter use is doubtful; there are few reports that lithium is effective in patients who have not responded to antidepressants (for example, Bennie 1975).

It has been reported that the therapeutic effects of tricyclic antidepressants can be increased if lithium is added (e.g. Lingjaerde *et al*. 1974). An important finding was that, in patients who did not respond to tricyclic antidepressants alone, improvement occurred when lithium was added (e.g. Heninger *et al*. 1983*b*). As yet the evidence for these potentiating effects of lithium is incomplete. There have been reports about similar results from combining lithium and an MAOI in patients unresponsive to MAOI alone (e.g. Zall *et al*. 1968; Price *et al*. 1985). Further double-blind controlled trials are required before the specific effects of these combined treatments can be evaluated. (Combined treatment with triiodothyronine and an antidepressant is discussed on p. 263).

Carbamazepine

This drug was introduced as an anti-convulsant. It has since been reported to have anti-manic effects (see p. 258). Carbamazepine is reported to have antidepressant properties as well (e.g. Post *et al*. 1986), but there is not yet enough evidence from controlled trials to assess the size and clinical importance of this effect.

Electroconvulsive therapy

This treatment is described in Chapter 17, where its unwanted effects are also considered. The present section is concerned with evidence about its therapeutic effects in depressive disorders. As mentioned above, an important clinical trial organized by the Medical Research Council (MRC

Drug Trials Subcommittee 1981) showed that ECT was more effective than imipramine or placebo after four weeks of treatment for depressive disorders. Marked improvement was found in 71 per cent of ECT-treated patients, 52 per cent of imipramine-treated patients, and 39 per cent of placebo-treated patients. However, at 6 months follow-up, marked improvement was found in equal numbers of patients in the ECT and imipramine-treated groups. Similar percentage improvements were obtained by Greenblatt *et al.* (1964) for active treatments (76 per cent for ECT; 49 per cent for imipramine) but the percentage improvement for placebo treatment (46 per cent) was as great as for imipramine. In another trial Kiloh *et al.* (1960) found an 89 per cent response to ECT compared with an 11 per cent response to placebo. These and other results have led to the firm conclusion that ECT is more effective than placebo, and more rapid in action than tricyclic antidepressants (Royal College of Psychiatrists 1977; Wechsler *et al.* 1965).

The studies considered so far used placebo tablets, with the result that the trials could not be double-blind. Other studies have used a placebo form of ECT, namely, the usual procedure including an anaesthetic but with the sole omission of electric shock. The results of several trials generally agree that the full procedure is more effective than this 'placebo ECT', although the placebo response varies between trials, just as it does in antidepressant drug trials. The trials also agree that the difference in effects between the full procedure and 'placebo ECT' is greatest at about four weeks after treatment, and disappears by about 12 months (see Johnstone *et al.* 1980; Lambourn and Gill 1978; West 1981; Brandon *et al.* 1984; Gregory *et al.* 1985). When Janicak *et al.* (1985) combined data from several studies they found a response rate of about 70 per cent for ECT and 40 per cent for 'placebo ECT'. One study did not find the full procedure more effective (Lambourn and Gill 1978); this study used unilateral brief pulse ECT, which is thought on other grounds to be less effective than unilateral or bilateral sine-wave ECT (see p. 681).

Clinicians generally agree that the therapeutic effects of ECT are greatest in severe depressive disorders, especially those with marked weight loss, early morning wakening, retardation and delusions. Studies by Carney *et al.* (1965), Hobson (1953), and Mendels (1965) confirmed this view, and identified certain features predicting an unfavourable response to ECT, namely, poor premorbid adjustment, neurotic traits, and fluctuating course, and hypochondriacal and histrionic features. However, these predictors are not specific to ECT; they resemble those for response to imipramine (Kiloh *et al.* 1962). From the trials comparing full ECT with 'placebo-ECT', it appears that delusions and (less strongly) retardation are the features separating patients responding to full ECT from placebo responders (Brandon *et al.* 1984; Clinical Research Centre 1984). Deluded depressed patients have also been reported to respond better to ECT than to tricyclic antidepressants (Perry *et al.* 1982), suggesting that ECT may be the treatment of choice for these patients.

Psychotherapy

The psychological treatments mainly used for depressive disorders can be divided into supportive methods, dynamic psychotherapy, 'interpersonal' methods, and cognitive therapy. **Supportive treatment** is part of the management of every depressed patient; it is intended to sustain him until other treatments have their effects, or natural recovery occurs. **Dynamic psychotherapy** is intended to have a specific therapeutic effect. Opinions differ about its value. Arieti (1977) suggests that it has a role in the treatment of most cases of depression, including severe cases. Other clinicians restrict the use of dynamic psychotherapy to the less severe cases. There have been a few attempts to evaluate treatment, and they have been concerned with group and marital therapy. They suggest that these two forms of psychotherapy may be valuable in reducing social difficulties that might lead to relapse, rather than in bringing about an early resolution of the depressive symptoms. In a comparison of weekly group therapy, imipramine and placebo, Covi *et al.* (1974) found that only the drug produced significantly more symptomatic improvement than the placebo. Friedman (1975) compared weekly marital therapy with amitriptyline, placebo, and minimal contact, over 12 weeks. He found that amitriptyline led to the most change in symptoms, but psychotherapy led to more beneficial changes in marital relationships.

'Interpersonal psychotherapy'

This is a systematic and standardized treatment approach to personal relationships and life problems. Weissman *et al.* (1979) reported that the effects of interpersonal therapy on the symptoms of moderately severe depressive disorders were equal to those of amitriptyline and greater than those of minimal treatment. Drug treatment had more effect on sleep disturbance, appetite, and somatic complaints; while interpersonal therapy had more effect on depressed mood, guilt, suicidal ideas, interests, and work. The drug effects began in the first week, the effects of psychotherapy only after 4–8 weeks (DiMascio *et al.* 1979). 'Endogenous' depression appeared less likely to respond to psychotherapy alone, while 'situational' depression responded equally well to drugs or psychotherapy (Prusoff *et al.* 1980).

Cognitive therapy

Results comparable to those of interpersonal psychotherapy have been reported with the use of cognitive therapy. For depressive disorder, the essential aim of this treatment is to modify patients' ways of thinking about life situations and about the depressive symptoms (see p. 736 for further information). Clinical trials indicate that for unipolar depressive disorders of moderate severity, the results of cognitive therapy are about equal to those of antidepressant drug treatment (Rush *et al.* 1977; Blackburn *et al.* 1981 and Murphy *et al.* 1984). When cognitive therapy is combined with antidepressant drugs, the outcome appears to be no better than with either treatment alone (Murphy *et al.* 1984). These findings are of great interest, for they challenge exclusively biochemical theories of depressive disorder. However, for most clinical purposes, treatment with antidepressant drugs are the first choice because they are well tested and less time-consuming. If cognitive therapy were shown to be effective for drug-resistant patients, its value would be great, but so far this has not been demonstrated.

Sleep deprivation

Several studies suggest that short-term changes can be brought about in a proportion of severe depressive disorders by keeping the patients awake for long periods. This interesting finding seems paradoxical because most depressed patients sleep badly. At present this procedure cannot be regarded as a practical form of treatment, but rather as a subject for further study [see Roy and Bhanji (1976) for a review.]

Treatment of mania

Antipsychotic drugs such as chlorpromazine and haloperidol usually bring the symptoms of acute mania under rapid control, although sometimes very large doses are needed (see p. 651). *Lithium carbonate* is also effective but the therapeutic response usually occurs only in the second week of treatment, and is therefore slower than the response to antipsychotic drugs. Controlled comparisons of lithium carbonate with chlorpromazine (for example, Prien *et al.* 1972) and haloperidol (for example, Garfinkel *et al.* 1980) indicate that both these drugs are superior to lithium in producing rapid control of overactivity. Otherwise the balance of evidence is that their effects are not obviously different (see Goodwin and Zis 1979).

Before neuroleptic drugs were introduced, *ECT* was often used to treat mania. The frequency of application of ECT was usually greater for mania than for depressive disorders, and it was often once or more than once a day (Kalinowsky and Hoch 1947, p. 173). ECT ceased to be used for mania when clinical experience showed neuroleptics to be more effective. There has been no report, however, of a satisfactory prospective trial comparing the two treatments. One study suggests that the effects of ECT in acute mania may be equivalent to those of lithium carbonate (Small *et al.* 1986), and some clinicians continue to advocate ECT for the minority of manic patients whose disturbed behaviour is not controlled by large doses of antipsychotic drugs.

Recently, the antiepileptic drug *carbamazepine* has been reported to have anti-manic effects similar to those of chlorpromazine (Okuma *et al.* 1981).

Prevention of relapse and recurrence

Strictly speaking, *relapse* refers to the worsening of symptoms after an initial improvement during the treatment of a single episode of affective disorder; *recurrence* refers to a new episode following a period of complete recovery. Treatment to prevent relapse should be called *continuation treatment*; and treatment to prevent recurrence should be called *preventative* (or prophylactic) treatment. In practice, however, it is not always easy to maintain the distinction between these two kinds of treatment because a drug that is given at first to prevent relapse is often used subsequently to prevent recurrence.

For *unipolar depressive disorders*, continuation treatment for six months with tricyclic antidepressant has been shown to reduce the relapse rate (Mindham *et al.* 1973; Paykel *et al.* 1975*b*). Another study demonstrated that relapse occurs frequently unless antidepressant drugs are continued for four to five months after the patient has been free from even mild depressive symptoms (Prien and Kupfer 1986). If antidepressant drugs are continued for even longer, as preventative treatment, they reduce the risk of recurrences (Medical Research Council 1981; Glen *et al.* 1984). Lithium carbonate can be used for the same purpose; however, for unipolar patients, the tricyclic antidepressant imipramine has been found to be more effective than lithium in preventing recurrences.

For *bipolar patients* continuation treatment with lithium is as effective as imipramine in preventing further depressive disorder, and more effective in preventing manic recurrences (Prien *et al.* 1973; Prien and Kupfer 1986). When the index illness is mania, lithium carbonate reduces both relapses and recurrences (Coppen *et al.* 1971). *Practical details of lithium prophylaxis are described on p. 671.*

Recently, *carbamazepine* has been reported to have preventative effects in manic disorders (Okuma *et al.* 1981) and, moreover, to be effective in some patients who do not respond to lithium (Post *et al.* 1983). These reports have not been fully evaluated, but it is reasonable to try carbamazepine for patients with frequently recurring affective disorders that do not respond to lithium. (See p. 676 for further information about the use of carbamazepine.)

Social factors may also contribute to relapse. Unhappy marriage seems to be one important factor (Kerr *et al.* 1974), and a particularly relevant feature of the marriage is criticism of the patient by the spouse. Thus, relapse has been shown to be predicted by a high frequency of critical comments during an interview at the time of the original illness (Vaughn and Leff 1986; Hooley *et al.* 1986). It is possible that intervention to reduce the relative's critical attitude might lower relapse rate, just as it does in schizophrenia (see p. 313), but this has not yet been demonstrated for depressive disorders.

Assessment of depressive disorders

The steps in assessment are (a) to decide whether the diagnosis is depressive disorder; (b) to judge the severity of the disorder, including the risk of suicide; (c) to form an opinion about the causes; (d) to assess the patient's social resources; and (e) to gauge the effect of the disorder on other people.

Diagnosis depends on thorough history taking and examination of physical and mental state. It has been discussed earlier in this chapter. Particular care should be taken not to overlook a depressive disorder in the patient who does not complain spontaneously of being depressed ('masked depression'). It is equally important not to diagnose a depressive disorder simply on the grounds, of prominent depressive symptoms; the latter could be part of another disorder; for example, an organic syndrome caused by a cerebral neoplasm. It should also be remembered that certain drugs can induce depression (see p. 424).

The **severity** of the disorder is judged from the symptoms. Considerable severity is indicated by 'biological' symptoms, and hallucinations and delusions, particularly the latter two. It is also important to assess how the depressive disorder has reduced the patient's capacity to work, or engage in family life and social activities. In this assessment the duration and course of the condition should be taken into account as well as the severity of the present symptoms. Not only does the length of history affect prognosis, it also gives an indication of the patient's capacity to tolerate further distress. A long continued disorder, even if not severe, can bring the patient to the point of desperation. The risk of **suicide** must be judged in every case (the methods of assessment are described on pp. 486–8).

Aetiology is assessed next, with reference to precipitating, predisposing, maintaining, and pathoplastic factors. No attempt need be made to allocate the syndrome to an exclusively endogenous or reactive category; instead the importance of external and internal causes should be evaluated in every case.

Provoking causes may be psychological and social (the 'life events' discussed earlier in this chapter) or they may be physical illness and its treatment. In assessing such cases, it is good practice to enquire routinely into the patient's work, finances, family life, social activities, general living conditions, and physical health. Problems in these areas may be recent and acute, or may take the form of chronic background difficulties such as prolonged marital tension, problems with children, and financial hardship.

The patient's **social resources** are considered next. Enquiries should cover family, friends, and work. A loving family can help to support a patient through a period of depressive disorder by providing company, encouraging him when he has lost confidence, and guiding him into suitable activities. For some patients, work is a valuable social resource, providing distraction and comradeship. For others it is a source of stress. A careful assessment is needed in each case.

The **effects** of the disorder **on other people** must be considered carefully. The most obvious problems arise when a severely depressed patient is the mother of young children who depend on her. This clinical observation has been confirmed in objective studies which have demonstrated that depressive disorder in either parent is associated with emotional disorder in the children (see Keller *et al.* 1986). It is important to consider whether the patient could endanger other people by remaining at work; for example, as a bus driver. When there are depressive delusions, it is necessary to consider what would happen were the patient to act on them. For example, severely depressed mothers may occasionally kill their children because they believe them doomed to suffer if they remain alive.

The management of depressive disorders

This section starts with the management of a patient with a depressive disorder of moderate or greater severity. The first question is whether the patient requires in-patient or day-patient care. The answer depends on the severity of the disorder and the quality of the patient's social resources. In judging severity, particular attention should be paid to the risk of suicide (or any risk to the life or welfare of family members, particularly dependent children) and to any failure to eat or drink that might endanger the patient's life. Provided that these risks are absent most patients with a supportive family can be treated at home, even when severely depressed. Patients who live alone, or whose families cannot care for them during the day, may need in-patient or day-patient care.

If the patient is to remain out of hospital, the next question is whether he should continue to work. If the disorder is mild, work can provide a valuable distraction from depressive thoughts and a source of companionship. When the disorder is more severe, retardation, poor concentration, and lack of drive are likely to impair performance at work, and such failure may add to the patient's feelings of hopelessness. In severe disorders there may be dangers to other people if the patient remains at his job.

The next step is to decide whether physical treatment is required. **ECT** will seldom be the first measure and will usually be considered only for patients already admitted to hospital. The only indication for ECT as a first measure is the need to bring about improvement as rapidly as possible. In practice this applies to two main groups of patients: those who refuse to drink enough to maintain an adequate output of urine (including the rare cases of depressive stupor); and those who present a highly dangerous suicidal risk. Occasionally this indication also applies to a patient who is suffering such extreme distress that the most rapid form of treatment is deemed justifiable. Such cases are rare. It should be remembered that the effects of ECT differ from those of antidepressant drugs in great rapidity of action rather than in the final therapeutic result.

The need for **antidepressant drug treatment** should be considered next. This treatment is indicated for most patients with a depressive syndrome of at least moderate severity, and particularly those with 'biological' symptoms. (*The management of antidepressant drug treatment is considered further on p. 659.*) One of the tricyclic antidepressants should be chosen unless there are special reasons to avoid the cardiovascular and other side-effects, in which case a drug with fewer side-effects such as mianserin may be chosen (see p. 658). *The dosage of these drugs, the precautions to be observed in using them, and the instructions to be given to patients, are described in Chapter 17.* Here it is only necessary to emphasize again the importance of explaining to the patient that, although side-effects will appear quickly, the therapeutic effect is likely to be delayed for up to three weeks. During this time patients should be seen to provide support; those with the more severe disorders may need to be seen every two or three days, and the others once a week. During this time it is important to make sure that the drugs are taken in the prescribed dose. Patients should be warned about the effects of taking alcohol. They should be advised about driving, particularly that they should not drive while experiencing sedative side-effects or any other effects that might impair their performance in an emergency.

If after a reasonable time antidepressant drug treatment has not succeeded the dose should be increased gradually to the maximum advised by the manufacturers, provided that there are no severe unwanted effects (see also Chapter 17). If the patient's condition worsens despite adequate treatment as an out-patient, day-hospital or in-patient care should be considered. Such a change is often followed by improvement even though the dose of drugs has not changed, presumably because the patient has been removed from a stressful environment.

For every patient, the need for suitable **activity** should be considered. Depressed patients give up activities and withdraw from other people. In this way they become deprived of social stimulation and rewarding experiences, and their original feelings of depression are increased. It is important to make sure that the patient is occupied adequately, though he should not be pushed into activities where he is likely to fail because of slowness or poor concentration. Hence there is a fairly narrow range of activity that is appropriate for the individual depressed patient, and the range changes as the illness runs its course. If the patient remains at home, it is important to discuss with relatives how much the patient should be encouraged to do each day. If he is in hospital the question should be decided in collaboration with nurses and occupational therapists. Relatives may also need to be helped to accept the disorder as an illness, and to avoid criticizing the patient.

The need for **psychological treatment** should also be decided in every case. All depressed patients require support, encouragement, and a thorough explanation that they are suffering from illness, not moral failure. If the depressive disorder is mainly a reaction to life problems and is not severe, discussion and counselling should be started. However, if the depressive disorder is severe, too much discussion of problems at an early stage only increases the patient's feeling of hopelessness. The more depressed the patient, the more the psychiatrist should take over problems for him in the early days of treatment. Later the psychiatrist should encourage the patient to resume responsibility for his own affairs as he recovers.

Any therapy directed to self-examination rather than to problem-solving is seldom appropriate for the acutely depressed patient, as it is likely to make the disorder worse. During intervals between acute episodes, such therapy may be valuable for patients who have recurrent depressive disorders caused largely by their ways of reacting to life events.

Resistant cases

If a depressive disorder does not respond within a reasonable time to a chosen combination of antidepressant drugs, graded activity, and psychological treatment, the plan should be reviewed. The first step is to check once more that the patient has been taking his medication in full amount. If he has not, the reasons should be sought. He may be convinced that no treatment can help, or may find the side-effects unpleasant. The diagnosis should also be reviewed carefully, and a check made that important stressful life events or continuing difficulties have not been overlooked.

If this enquiry reveals nothing, antidepressants should be continued in full dosage: there is no value in changing to another drug unless side-effects are preventing full dosage of the original preparation. Supportive interviews should be continued and the patient reassured that depressive disorders almost invariably recover in the end whether or not treatment can speed up this process. Meanwhile, provided that the patient is not too depressed, any problems that have contributed to his depressed state should be discussed further. In resistant cases it is particularly important to watch careully for developing suicidal intentions. If serious depression persists, ECT should be considered; clinical experience suggests that ECT is sometimes effective in patients who have not responded to full doses of antidepressant drugs, but this impression has not been tested in an adequate clinical trial. If after a thorough trial of single antidepressant drug no improvement is observed, combined drug treatment can be considered: either a cyclic antidepressant with an MAOI, or a cyclic antidepressant with lithium, or an MAOI with lithium. The combined use of a tricyclic antidepressant and MAOI has been advocated for many years but, as explained on p. 253, its value is not supported by controlled trials. If it is employed, the prescriber should watch carefully for side-effects. Although the combination can give rise to hypertension, hyperpyrexia, delirium, seizures, and coma, these serious effects seem to arise mainly with high doses and to be more frequent with the sequence MAOI followed by added tricyclic, than with the reverse sequence (see Ananth and Luchins 1977). Therefore the sequence MAOI followed by added tricyclic should be avoided. The sequence tricyclic followed by added MAOI seems to be safe, though its efficacy is uncertain (Razani *et al.* 1983). In practice, it is best to stop previously prescribed antidepressants for at least a week, and then start the two drugs again in sequence starting with small doses of each one, and watching carefully for side-effects as the doses are increased cautiously. Of the drugs that can be combined, phenelzine and isocarboxazid among the MAOIs, and amitriptyline among the tricyclics may be less likely to cause side-effects. [See Ananth and Luchins (1977) for a review of combined tricyclic and MAOI treatment.]

Combined treatment with lithium and either a tricyclic antidepressant or MAOI was introduced more recently. Preliminary reports and clinical experience suggest a striking response in some resistant depressive disorders (see p. 254). Until there is more substantial evidence from controlled trials, this combined treatment should be regarded as experimental, to be tried cautiously for selected patients, starting with small doses and watching carefully for side-effects as well as signs of improvement.

It has been reported that some patients who have not responded to imipramine or amitriptyline improve promptly when 1-triiodothyronine is added. This improvement is unlikely to be a pharmacokinetic effect because it is not accompanied by a change in plasma concentrations of the antidepressant drug. So far the evidence in support of this practice is not convincing, but the combination appears safe and can be tried in resistant cases when other measures have failed (see Goodwin *et al.* 1982).

When considering the use of these combined treatments, it should be remembered that although therapy should be vigorous, most depressive disorders recover eventually; it may be better in some cases to look after the patient carefully while awaiting spontaneous recovery than to treat with drug combinations whose effects are still somewhat uncertain. Before prescribing any of these combinations for the first time it is appropriate to consult someone who has experience of their use to discuss practical points.

Less severe cases

Not every depressive disorder requires treatment with antidepressant drugs. If the condition is of mild to moderate severity and clearly a reaction to stressful life events, treatment should be mainly psychological and social. The patient should be encouraged to talk about his feelings and to discuss his problems. If provoking factors can be altered, he should be encouraged to think of suitable means for changing them; if they cannot be altered, he should be helped to come to terms with his new situation. Help towards acceptance is particularly important after bereavement or other kinds of loss. Bereaved patients need time to talk about their ideas and feelings so that they no longer feel the pain of separation but can begin to cherish things of lasting value in the relationship.

Amongst patients with mild depressive disorders of reactive origin, a history of several weeks poor sleep is common. A hypnotic drug, given for a few days, often helps to start the process or recovery, but such treatment should not be prolonged. If the depressive symptoms do not respond to adequate social and psychological measures, and if there are symptoms indicating a likely response to medication (see p. 255), antidepressants should not be withheld. However, a frequent error is to prescribe antidepressants for many months to patients who have symptoms clearly related to life problems, and who did not show any response to medication in the first place.

Prevention of relapse and recurrence

After recovery, the patient should be followed-up for several months either by the psychiatrist or by the family doctor. If the recovery appears to have been brought about by an antidepressant drug, the drug should usually be continued at two-thirds to half the therapeutic dose for about six months. At follow-up interviews, a careful watch should be kept for signs of relapse. Relatives should be warned of the possibility of relapse and asked to report any signs of returning illness.

If the patient has had both manic and depressive illnesses in the past, and if recurrences have been frequent, lithium prophylaxis should be considered carefully, weighing possible advantages against the risks (see Chapter 17). If the depressive disorder was related to self-imposed stressors such as overwork, or unduly complicated social relationships, the patient should be encouraged to change to a life-style less likely to lead to further episodes of illness. These readjustments may be helped by psychotherapy, which may be individual, marital, or group therapy.

The assessment of mania

In the assessment of mania, the steps are those already outlined for depressive disorders. They are: (a) decide the diagnosis, (b) assess the severity of the disorder, (c) form an opinion about the causes, (d) assess the patient's social resources, and (e) judge the effect on other people.

Diagnosis depends on a careful history and examination. Whenever possible, the history should be taken from relatives as well as from the patient because the patient may not recognize the extent of his abnormal behaviour. Differential diagnosis has been discussed earlier in this chapter; it is always important to remember that mildly disinhibited behaviour can result from frontal lobe lesions (such as tumours or GPI) as well as from mania.

Severity is judged next. For this purpose it is essential to interview another informant. Manic patients are often able to exert self-control during an interview with a doctor, and then behave in a disinhibited and grandiose way immediately afterwards (see p. 224). At an early stage it is easy to be misled and to miss the opportunity to persuade the patient to enter hospital before he causes long-term difficulties to himself, for example ill-judged decisions or unjustified extravagance.

Usually the **causes** of a manic disorder are largely endogenous, but it is important to identify any life events that may have provoked the onset. Some cases follow physical illness, treatment by drugs (especially steroids) or operations.

The patient's **resources** and the **effect of the illness** on other people are assessed along the lines already described for depressive orders. Even for the most supportive family, it is extremely difficult to care for a manic patient at home for more than a few days unless the disorder is exceptionally mild. The patient's responsibilites in the care of dependent children or at work should always be considered carefully.

The management of manic patients

The first decision is whether to admit the patient to hospital. In all but the mildest cases, admission is nearly always advisable to protect the patient from the consequences of his own behaviour. If the disorder is not too severe, the patient will usually agree to enter hospital after some persuasion. When the disorder is more severe, compulsory admission is likely to be needed.

The immediate treatment is usually with an antipsychotic drug. Haloperidol is a suitable choice, chlorpromazine a more sedating alternative. The first dose should be large enough to bring the abnormal behaviour under rapid control. At this stage it is better for the patient to be somewhat over-sedated than to be left over-active, irritable, and interfering with other people. In emergencies, the first dose may need to be given by intramuscular injection (see p. 651 for further advice about the use of antipsychotic drugs in urgent cases).

The subsequent dosage should be adjusted frequently to take account of the degree of over-activity. The doctor should visit the ward repeatedly until the patient's condition has been brought under control. During this early phase, it is important for all staff to avoid angry confrontations which often arise because the patient makes unreasonable demands that cannot be met. It is often possible to avoid an argument by taking advantage of the manic patient's easy distractability; instead of refusing his demands, it is better to delay until his attention turns to another topic that he can be encouraged to pursue.

As soon as the patient is well enough to co-operate, tests of renal and thyroid function are carried out, so that the results are available if lithium treatment should be required later. Practices vary about the use of lithium. Some psychiatrists continue to use haloperidol or chlorpromazine through-out the manic episode, and reserve lithium for prophylactic treatment. Others start lithium as soon as the acute symptoms are under control, though taking precautions not to introduce it when the dose of haloperidol is high (because occasional interactions have been reported, see p. 670). The use of lithium rather than haloperidol at an early stage sometimes has the advantage of leaving the patient more alert; possibly it also has the advantage of making a depressive disorder less likely to follow.

Progress can be judged not only by the mental state and general behaviour, but also by the pattern of sleep and by the regaining of any weight lost during the illness. As progress continues, antipsychotic drug treatment is reduced gradually. However, it is important not to discontinue the drug too soon, otherwise relapse may occur with a return of all the original problems of management.

As explained already (p. 257), ECT was used to treat mania before antipsychotic drugs were introduced, but evidence about its effectiveness is still not available. It is appropriate to consider the treatment for the unusual patients who do not respond to drugs even when given in such high doses that intolerable side-effects are produced. In such cases clinical experience suggests that ECT is sometimes followed by a reduction in symptoms sufficient to allow treatment to continue with smaller doses of drugs. This practice should be reconsidered if new evidence from clinical trials becomes available.

Whatever treatment is adopted, a careful watch should be kept for symptoms of depressive disorder. It should be remembered that transient but profound depressive mood change, accompanied by depressive ideas, its common among manic patients. The clinical picture may also change rapidly to a sustained depressive disorder. If either change happens, the patient may develop suicidal ideas. A sustained change to a depressive syndrome is likely to require antidepressant drug treatment unless the disorder is mild.

The practical aspects of using lithium to prevent further episodes are discussed on pp. 666–73. There are two aspects of prophylaxis that require emphasis. First, patients should be seen and plasma lithium measured, at regular intervals. Second, some patients stop of their own accord because they fear the drug may have harmful long-term effects, or because it makes them feel 'flat'. The risk of stopping lithium is that it may lead to relapse. With carefully supervised follow-ups, the chances of relapse can be reduced substantially, though lesser degress of mood change often continue.

Further reading

Brown, G. W. and Harris, T. (1978). *Social origins of depression*. Tavistock, London.

Kraepelin, E. (1921). *Manic-depressive insanity and paranoia* (trans. R. M. Barclay), pp. 1–164. Churchill Livingstone, Edinburgh. (Reprinted in 1976 by Arno Press, New York.)

Lewis, A. J. (1930). Melancholia: a clinical survey of depressive states. *Journal of Mental Science* **80**, 277–378. (Reprinted in Lewis, A. J. (1967). *Inquiries in psychiatry*, pp. 30–117. Routledge and Kegan Paul, London.)

Lewis, A. J. (1938). States of depression: their clinical and aetiological differentiation. *British Medical Journal* 2, 875–8. (Reprinted in Lewis, A. J. (1967). *Inquiries in psychiatry*, pp. 133–140. Routledge and Kegan Paul, London.)

Paykel, E. S. (ed.) (1982) *Handbook of affective disorders*. Churchill Livingstone, Edinburgh.

9 Schizophrenia and schizophrenia-like disorders

Of all the major psychiatric syndromes, schizophrenia is much the most difficult to define and describe. The main reason for this difficulty is that, over the past 100 years, many widely divergent concepts of schizophrenia have been held in different countries and by different psychiatrists. Radical differences of opinion persist to the present day. If these conflicting ideas are to be made intelligible, it is useful to start with a simple comparison between two basic concepts—acute schizophrenia and chronic schizophrenia. Such a comparison can pave the way for description of the many varieties of clinical picture encountered in clinical practice, and for discussion of the main theories and arguments about schizophrenia. Accordingly, after a brief section on epidemiology, this chapter describes the features of 'typical' acute and chronic syndromes. The reader should bear in mind that these will be idealized descriptions, but it is useful to oversimplify at first before introducing controversial issues.

Essentially, in acute schizophrenia the predominant clinical features are delusions, hallucinations, and interference with thinking. Features of this kind are often called 'positive' symptoms. Some patients recover from the acute illness, whilst others progress to the chronic syndrome. By contrast, the main features of chronic schizophrenia are apathy, lack of drive, slowness, and social withdrawal. These features are often called 'negative' symptoms. Once the chronic syndrome is established, few patients recover completely.

Most of the disagreements about the diagnosis of schizophrenia are concerned with the acute syndrome. The criteria for diagnosis are concerned with both the pattern of symptoms and the course of the disorder. There are disagreements about both the range of symptoms that are required, and about the length of time that these symptoms should have been present, in order to make the diagnosis. This point is illustrated later in the chapter when the criteria for diagnosis in DSMIII and ICD10 (draft) are discussed.

Epidemiology

Estimates of the incidence and prevalence of schizophrenia depend on the criteria for diagnosis and the population surveyed (problems of diagnosis are discussed on p. 276). The annual **incidence** is probably between 0.1 and 0.5 per 1000 of the population. Thus Wing and Fryers (1976) found a rate of between 0.11 and 0.14 per 1000 for first contact with services in Camberwell, London; whilst Häfner and Reimann (1970) reported a rate of 0.54 per 1000 in Mannheim. The incidence varies with age, the highest rates occurring in young men and 35 to 39-year-old women.

The **lifetime risk** of developing schizophrenia is probably between 7.0 and 9.0 per 1000 of the population (see Jablensky 1986). In island communities, for example, cohort studies gave rates of 9.0 per 1000 on a Danish island (Fremming 1951) and 7.0 per 1000 in Iceland (Helgason 1964).

The **point prevalence** of schizophrenia in European countries is probably between 2.5 and 5.3 per 1000 (see Jablensky 1986). Collaborative studies by the World Health Organization have shown that the prevalence of schizophrenia, when assessed in comparable ways, is similar in different countries (Jablensky and Sartorius 1975). The similarities are greatest when Schneider's first-rank symptoms (see p. 279) are used as diagnostic criteria (Jablensky *et al.* 1986).

There are exceptions to this general uniformity of rates. Böök (1953) reported a high annual prevalence (11 per 1000) in the extreme north of Sweden. High rates have also been reported from north-west Yugoslavia and western Ireland, and among Catholics in Canada and the Tamils of southern India (see Cooper 1978). Conversely, a low prevalence of 1.1 per 1000 has been reported among the Hutterites, an Anabaptist sect in the United States (Eaton and Weil 1955).

These reported differences in prevalence may have more than one cause. First, they may reflect differences in diagnostic criteria. Second, they may be affected by differences in migration. For example, people predisposed to schizophrenia may stay in the remote north of Sweden because they are more able to tolerate extreme isolation; whilst those predisposed to schizophrenia may leave a Hutterite community because they are less able to tolerate a close-knit society. The third reason, which is related to the second, is that prevalence rates may reflect differences in methods of case-finding. It is possible that Eaton and Weil's findings may be partly explained by such differences of method, since a study in Canada found no differences between Hutterite and other areas in admission rates for schizophrenia (Murphy 1968). Also, a further study in western Ireland (NiNuallain *et al.* 1987) did not confirm a high incidence. Finally, it is important to note that differences in prevalence are not necessarily accounted for by any differences in the duration of illness.

Epidemiological studies of the demographic and social correlates of schizophrenia are considered later under aetiology.

Clinical features

The acute syndrome

Some of the main clinical features are illustrated by a short description of a patient. A previously healthy 20-year-old male student had been behaving in an increasingly odd way. At times he appeared angry and told his friends that he was being persecuted; at other times he was seen to be laughing to himself for no apparent reason. For several months he had seemed increasingly preoccupied with his own thoughts. His academic work had deteriorated. When interviewed, he was restless and awkward. He described hearing voices commenting on his actions and abusing him. He said he believed that the police had conspired with his university teachers to harm his brain with poisonous gases and take away his thoughts. He also believed that other people could read his thoughts.

This case history illustrates the following common features of acute schizophrenia: prominent persecutory ideas with accompanying hallucinations; gradual social withdrawal and impaired performance at work; and the odd idea that other people can read one's thoughts. In describing the features of schizophrenia here, it is assumed that the reader has read the description of symptoms and signs in Chapter 1. Reference will be made to that chapter in the following account.

In **appearance and behaviour** some patients with acute schizophrenia are entirely normal. Others seem awkward in their social behaviour, preoccupied and withdrawn, or otherwise odd. Some patients smile or laugh without obvious reason. Some appear to be constantly perplexed. Some are restless and noisy, or show sudden and unexpected changes of behaviour. Others retire from company, spending a long time in their rooms, perhaps lying immobile on the bed apparently preoccupied in thought.

The **speech** often reflects an underlying **thought disorder**. In the early stages, there is vagueness in the patient's talk that makes it difficult to grasp his meaning. Some patients have difficulty in dealing with abstract ideas (a phenomenon called concrete thinking). Other patients become preoccupied with vague pseudoscientific or mystical ideas.

When the disturbance is more severe two characteristic kinds of abnormality may occur. **Disorders of the stream of thought** include pressure of thought, poverty of thought, and thought blocking, which are described on p. 11. Thought withdrawal (the conviction that one's thoughts have been taken away) is sometimes classified as a disorder of the stream of thought, but it is more usefully considered as a form of delusion (see p. 20).

Loosening of association denotes a lack of connection between ideas. This may be detected in illogical thinking ('knight's move') or talking past the point (*Vorbeireden*). In the severest form of loosening the structure and coherence of thinking is lost, so that utterances are jumbled (word salad or verbigeration). Some patients use ordinary words in unusual ways (paraphrasias or metonyms), and a few coin new words (neologisms).

Abnormalities of mood are common, and of three main kinds. First, there may be sustained abnormalities of mood such as anxiety, depression, irritability, or euphoria. Secondly, there may be blunting of affect, sometimes known as flattening of affect. Essentially this is sustained emotional indifference or diminution of emotional response. Thirdly, there is incongruity of affect. Here the emotion is not necessarily diminished, but it is not in keeping with the mood that would ordinarily be expected. For example, a patient may laugh when told about a bereavement. This third abnormality is often said to be highly characteristic of schizophrenia, but different interviewers often disagree about its presence.

Auditory hallucinations are among the most frequent symptoms. They may take the form of noises, music, single words, brief phrases, or whole conversations. They may be unobtrusive or so severe as to cause great distress. Some voices seem to give commands to the patient. Some patients hear their own thoughts apparently spoken out loud either as they think them (*Gedankenlautwerden*) or immediately afterwards (*écho de la pensée*). Some voices seem to discuss the patient in the third person. Others comment on his actions. As described later, these last three symptoms have particular diagnostic value.

Visual hallucinations are less frequent and usually occur with other kinds of hallucination. **Tactile, olfactory, gustatory**, and **somatic** hallucinations are reported by some patients; they are often interpreted in a delusional way, for example hallucinatory sensations in the lower abdomen are attributed to unwanted sexual interference by a persecutor.

Delusions are characteristic. Primary delusions (see p. 15) are infrequent, and difficult to identify with certainty. Delusions may originate against a background of so-called primary delusional mood—*Wahnstimmung* (see p. 17). Persecutory delusions are common, but not specific to schizophrenia. Less common but of greater diagnostic value are delusions of reference and of control, and delusions about the possession of thought. The latter are delusions that thoughts are being inserted into or withdrawn from one's mind, or 'broadcast' to other people (see p. 20). These important symptoms are considered further on pp. 279 and 281.

In acute schizophrenia **orientation** is normal. Impairment of **attention** and **concentration** is common, and may produce apparent difficulties in remembering, though **memory** is not impaired. So-called delusional memory occurs in a few patients (see p. 17).

Insight is usually impaired. Most patients do not accept that their experiences result from illness, but usually ascribe them to the malevolent actions of other people. This lack of insight is often accompanied by unwillingness to accept treatment.

Schizophrenic patients do not necessarily experience all these symptoms. The clinical picture is variable, as described later in this chapter. At this stage the reader is referred to Table 9.1, which lists the most frequent symptoms found in one large survey.

Table 9.1. The most frequent symptoms of acute schizophrenia (World Health Organization 1973)

Symptom	Frequency (%)
Lack of insight	97
Auditory hallucinations	74
Ideas of reference	70
Suspiciousness	66
Flatness of affect	66
Voices speaking to the patient	65
Delusional mood	64
Delusions of persecution	64
Thought alienation	52
Thoughts spoken aloud	50

The chronic syndrome

In contrast to the 'positive' symptoms of the acute syndrome, the **chronic syndrome** is characterized by thought disorder and by 'negative' symptoms of under-activity, lack of drive, social withdrawal, and emotional apathy. The syndrome can be illustrated by a brief example. A middle-aged man lives in a group home and attends a sheltered workshop. He spends most of his time alone. He is usually dishevelled and unshaven, and cares for himself only when encouraged to do so by others. His social behaviour seems odd and stilted. His speech is slow, and its content vague and incoherent. He shows few signs of emotion. For several years this clinical picture has changed little except for brief periods of acute symptoms which are usually related to upsets in the ordered life of the hostel.

This description illustrates several of the negative features of what is sometimes called schizophrenic defect state. The most striking feature is diminished **volition**, that is a lack of drive and initiative. Left to himself, the patient may be inactive for long periods, or may engage in aimless and repeated activity. He withdraws from social encounters and his behaviour may deteriorate in ways that embarrass other people. A few patients neglect themselves to the point of incontinence.

A variety of **motor disturbances** occur, but most are uncommon. They are outlined here because they are the only symptoms of schizophrenia not described in Chapter 1.

Disorders of motor activity are often called **catatonic**. In the past a separate syndrome of catatonia was recognized, but nowadays the symptoms more often occur individually than as a distinct syndrome. **Stupor** and **excitement** are the most striking catatonic symptoms. A patient in stupor is immobile, mute, and unresponsive, although fully conscious. Stupor may change (sometimes quickly) to a state of uncontrolled motor activity and excitement.

Occasionally schizophrenic patients show a disorder of muscle tone called **waxy flexibility** (or *flexibilitas cerea*). The patient allows himself to be placed in an awkward posture which he then maintains apparently without distress for much longer than most people could achieve without severe discomfort. This phenomenon is also called **catalepsy** (a term that is also used to describe similar phenomena in patients who have been hypnotized). Some patients themselves take up odd and uncomfortable postures and maintain them for long peroids. At times these postures have obvious symbolic significance (for example, crucifixion). Occasionally a patient lies for a long period with his head raised a little above the pillow (the so-called psychological pillow). Healthy people would experience extreme discomfort if they tried to do the same.

Various disorders of movement occur in schizophrenia (see Manschreck *et al.* 1982). A **stereotypy** is a repeated movement that does not appear to be goal directed. It is more complex than a tic. The movement may be repeated in a regular sequence; for example, rocking forwards and backwards or rotating the trunk.

A **mannerism** is a normal goal-directed movement that appears to have social significance but is odd in appearance, stilted and out of context; for example a repeated hand movement resembling a military salute. It is often difficult to decide whether an abnormal movement is a stereotypy or a mannerism, but the distinction is of no diagnostic importance.

Ambitendence is a special form of ambivalence in which a patient begins to make a movement but, before completing it, starts the opposite movement; for example putting the hand back and forth to an object but without reaching it. *Mitgehen* is moving a limb in response to slight pressure on it, despite being told to resist the pressure (the last point is important). Mitgehen is often associated with forced grasping, which is repeated grasping (despite instructions to the contrary) at the interviewer's outstretched hand. In **automatic obedience** the patient obeys every command, though he has first been told not to do so. These disorders are described in more detail by Hamilton (1984).

Social behaviour may deteriorate. For example, some patients collect and hoard objects, so that their surroundings become cluttered and dirty.

Others break social conventions by talking intimately to strangers, or shouting obscenities in public.

Speech is often abnormal, showing evidence of **thought disorder** of the kinds found in the acute syndrome described above. **Affect** is generally blunted; when emotion is shown, it is often incongruous. **Hallucinations** are common, again in any of the forms occurring in the acute syndrome.

Delusions are often systematized. In chronic schizophrenia, delusions may be held with little emotional response. For example, patients may be convinced that they are being persecuted but show neither fear nor anger. Delusions may also be 'encapsulated' from the rest of the patient's beliefs. Thus a patient may be convinced that his private sexual fantasies and practices are widely discussed by strangers; his remaining beliefs may be normal, and his working and social life well preserved.

Orientation is normal. **Attention** and **concentration** are often poor. **Memory** is not generally impaired though some patients have difficulty in giving their age correctly (this is sometimes called 'age disorientation'). **Insight** is impaired; the patient does not recognize that his symptoms are due to illness and is seldom fully convinced of the need for treatment.

The symptoms and signs are combined in many ways so that the clinical picture is variable. The reader is referred to Table 9.2 which shows the range and frequency of the symptoms and behavioural abnormalities found in one survey of chronic schizophrenic patients.

Variations in the clinical picture

As anticipated in the introduction to this chapter, so far an account has been given of the typical features of acute and chronic syndromes. Such an account makes description easier, but it is an oversimplification. Two points need to be stressed. First, different features may predominate within a syndrome; for example, in the acute syndrome, one patient may have predominantly paranoid delusions, and another mainly thought disorder. Second, some patients have features of both the acute and the chronic syndromes. Clinicians have attempted to identify various clinical subtypes, and these will be described later in the chapter.

Depressive symptoms in schizophrenia

It has been recognized since the time of Kraepelin that depressive symptoms occur commonly in schizophrenia, both in the acute and the chronic stages. More recently these clinical observations have been confirmed by using standardized methods of assessment (World Health Organization 1973).

There are several reasons why depressive symptoms may be associated with schizophrenia. First, they may be a side-effect of antipsychotic

Table 9.2. Behavioural characteristics of chronic schizophrenic patients in rank order of frequency

Characteristic	Per cent
Social withdrawal	74
Under-activity	56
Lack of conversation	54
Few leisure interests	50
Slowness	48
Over-activity	41
Odd ideas	34
Depression	34
Odd behaviour	34
Neglect of appearance	30
Odd postures and movements	25
Threats or violence	23
Poor mealtime behaviour	13
Socially embarrassing behaviour	8
Sexually unusual behaviour	8
Suicidal attempts	4
Incontinence	4

From Creer and Wing (1975).

medication; this is not the full explanation, since depressive symptoms occur in patients not receiving drugs. Alternatively, a kinetic side-effect of medication may be interpreted wrongly as depressive retardation. Second, depressive symptoms may be a response to recovery of insight into the nature of the illness and the problems to be faced. Again this may happen at times, but it does not provide a convincing general explanation. Third, depression may be an integral part of schizophrenia. In a study of patients after the acute onset of schizophrenia, Knights and Hirsch (1981) found depression to be most common in the acute phase, decreasing during the following three months. They concluded that depression is a symptom of schizophrenia, although it may be recognized only after more striking symptoms have improved [see Hirsch (1986a), and Johnson (1986) for reviews.]

Water intoxication in schizophrenia

A few chronic schizophrenic patients drink excessive amounts of water, thus developing a state of 'water intoxication' characterized by polyuria and hyponatraemia (Vieweg *et al.* 1985). When severe this condition may give rise to seizures, coma, and visceral and cerebral oedema. Some patients die. The reasons for this behaviour cannot be explained by the patients, and has not been uncovered by investigation.

Factors modifying the clinical features

The amount of **social stimulation** has a considerable effect on the clinical picture. Understimulation increases 'negative' symptoms such as poverty of speech, social withdrawal, apathy, and lack of drive. Over-stimulation precipitates 'positive' symptoms such as hallucinations, delusions, and restlessness. Modern treatment is designed to avoid understimulation, and as a result 'negative' features including catatonia are less frequent than in the past.

The **social background** of the patient may affect the content of some symptoms. For example, religious delusions are less common now than a century ago (Klaf and Hamilton 1961). **Age** also seems to modify the clinical features of schizophrenia. In adolescents and young adults, the clinical features often include thought disorder, mood disturbance, and considerable disruption of behaviour. This 'hebephrenic' picture (described on p. 287) has been thought to reflect the effect of the disease process on a personality still developing. With increasing age, paranoid symptomatology is more common and the effects on personality are less marked (the 'paranoid type' of schizophrenia).

Low intelligence also affects the clinical features. Patients of subnormal intelligence usually present with a less complex clinical picture sometimes referred to as 'pfropfschizophrenie' (described in Chapter 21, p. 831).

Diagnostic problems

The development of ideas about schizophrenia

Some of the diagnostic problems encountered today can be understood better with some knowledge of the historical developments of ideas about schizophrenia.

In the nineteenth century, one view was that all mental disorders were expressions of a single entity which Griesinger called *Einheitpsychose* (unitary psychosis). The alternative view, which was put forward by Morel in France, was that mental disorders could be separated and classified. Morel searched for specific entities, and argued for a classification based on cause, symptoms, and outcome (Morel 1860). In 1852 he gave the name *démence précoce* to a disorder which he described as starting in adolescence and leading first to withdrawal, odd mannerisms and self-neglect, and eventually to intellectual deterioration. Not long after, Kahlbaum (1863) described the syndrome of catatonia, and Hecker (1871) wrote an account of a condition he called hebephrenia (an English translation has been published by Sedler 1985). **Emil Kraepelin** (1855–1926) derived his ideas from study of the course of the disorder as well as the symptoms. His observations led him to argue against the idea of a single psychosis, and to propose a division into dementia praecox and manic depressive psychosis. This grouping brought together as subclasses of dementia praecox the previously separate entities of hebephrenia and catatonia.

Kraepelin's description of dementia praecox appeared for the first time in 1893, in the 4th edition of his textbook, the account being expanded in subsequent editions (see Kraepelin 1897 for a translation of the description in the 5th edition). He described the illness as occurring in clear consciousness and consisting of 'a series of states, the common characteristic of which is a peculiar destruction of the internal connections of the psychic personality. The effects of this injury predominate in the emotional and volitional spheres of mental life' (Kraepelin 1919, p. 3). He originally divided the disorder into three subtypes (catatonic, hebephrenic, and paranoid) and later added a fourth (simple). Kraepelin separated paraphrenia from dementia praecox, on the grounds that it started in middle life and seemed to be free from the changes in emotion and volition found in dementia praecox.

It is commonly held that Kraepelin regarded dementia praecox as invariably progressing to chronic deterioration. However, he reported that, in his series of cases, 13 per cent recovered completely (though some relapsed later), and 17 per cent were ultimately able to live and work without difficulty.

Eugen Bleuler (1857–1959) was the Director of Burghölzli Clinic and Professor of Psychiatry in Zurich. He based his work on Kraepelin's, and in his own book wrote 'the whole idea of dementia praecox originates with Kraepelin' (Bleuler 1911, p. 1). He also acknowledged the help of his younger colleague, C. G. Jung, in trying to apply some of Freud's ideas to dementia praecox. Compared with Kraepelin, Bleuler was concerned less with prognosis and more with the mechanisms of symptom formation. It was Bleuler who proposed the name **schizophrenia** to denote a 'splitting' of psychic functions, which he thought to be of central importance.

Bleuler believed in a distinction between fundamental and accessory symptoms. Fundamental symptoms included disturbances of associations, changes in emotional reactions, a tendency to prefer fantasy to reality, and autism (withdrawal from reality into an inner world of fantasy). It is interesting that, in Bleuler's view, some of the most frequent and striking symptoms were accessory (secondary); for example, hallucinations, delusions, catatonia, and abnormal behaviours. Bleuler was interested in the psychological study of his cases, but did not deny the possibility of a neuropathological cause for schizophrenia. Compared with Kraepelin, Bleuler took a more optimistic view of the outcome, but still held that one should not 'speak of cure but of far reaching improvement'. He also wrote:

'as yet I have never released a schizophrenic in whom I could not still see distinct signs of the disease, indeed there are very few in whom one would have to search for such signs' (Bleuler 1911, pp. 256 and 258). Since Bleuler was preoccupied more with psychopathological mechanisms than with symptoms themselves, his approach to diagnosis was less precise than Kraepelin's.

Kurt Schneider (1887–1967) tried to make the diagnosis more reliable by identifying a group of symptoms characteristic of schizophrenia, but rarely found in other disorders. Unlike Bleuler's fundamental symptoms, Schneider's symptoms were not supposed to have any central psychopathological role. Thus Schneider (1959) wrote: 'Among the many abnormal modes of experience that occur in schizophrenia, there are some which we put in the first rank of importance, not because we think of them as basic disturbances, but because they have this special value in helping us to determine the diagnosis of schizophrenia. When any one of these modes of experience is undeniably present and no basic somatic illness can be found, we may make the diagnosis of schizophrenia . . . Symptoms of first rank importance do not always have to be present for a diagnosis to be made'. (The last point is important.) Schneider's first-rank symptoms are considered more fully by Mellor (1982). They are listed in Table 9.3. Some of these symptoms are included in the diagnostic criteria for schizophrenia used in DSMIIIR and ICD10 (draft) (see pp. 283–6).

Several German psychiatrists tried to define subgroupings within schizophrenia. **Karl Kleist**, a pupil of the neurologist Wernicke, looked for associations between brain pathology and different subtypes of psychotic illness. He accepted Kraepelin's main diagnostic framework, but used careful clinical observation in an attempt to distinguish various subdivisions within schizophrenia and other atypical disorders. He then attempted to match these subtypes to specific kinds of brain pathology (Kleist 1928, 1930). This attempt was ingenious but not successful.

Leonhard continued this approach of careful clinical observation, but did not pursue Kleist's interest in cerebral pathology. He published a complicated classification which distinguishes schizophrenia from the 'cycloid' psychoses, which are a group of non-affective psychoses of good outcome (Leonhard 1957). Cycloid psychoses are described later in this chapter. Leonhard also divided schizophrenia into two groups. The first group is characterized by a progressive course, and is divided into catatonias, hebephrenias, and paraphrenias. Leonhard gave this group a name which is often translated as '**systematic**'. The second group, called **non-systematic**, is divided into affect-laden paraphrenia, schizophasia, and periodic catatonia. **Affect-laden paraphrenia** is characterized by paranoid delusions and the expression of strong emotion about their content. In **schizophasia** speech is grossly disordered and difficult to understand. **Periodic catatonia** is a condition with regular remissions; during an episode

Table 9.3. Schneider's symptoms of the first rank

Hearing thoughts spoken aloud
'Third person' hallucinations
Hallucinations in the form of a commentary
Somatic hallucinations
Thought withdrawal or insertion
Thought broadcasting
Delusional perception
Feelings or actions experienced as made or influenced by external
  agents

akinetic symptoms are sometimes interrupted by hyperkinetic symptoms. Originally Leonhard's views had little impact outside his own country of East Germany, but recently an increasing concern with the heterogeneity of schizophrenia has led to a wider interest in his system of classification and particularly the concept of cycloid psychoses. Further information can be found in the accounts by Hamilton (1984) and Ban (1982).

Scandinavian psychiatrists have been influenced by Jaspers' distinction between process schizophrenia and reactive psychoses. In the late 1930s **Langfeldt**, using follow-up data on patients in Oslo, proposed a distinction between **true schizophrenia**, which had a poor prognosis, and **schizophreniform states**, which had a good prognosis (see Langfeldt 1961). True schizophrenia was defined narrowly and was essentially similar to Kraepelin's dementia praecox. It was characterized by emotional blunting, lack of initiative, paranoid symptoms, and primary delusions. Schizophreniform states were described as often precipitated by stress and frequently accompanied by confusional and affective symptoms. Langfeldt's proposed distinction between good and bad prognosis cases has been influential but, as explained later, other psychiatrists have not found that his criteria predict prognosis accurately (see p. 289).

In Denmark and Norway cases arising after stressful events have received much attention. The terms reactive psychosis or psychogenic psychosis are commonly applied to conditions which appear to be precipitated by stress, are to some extent understandable in their symptoms, and have a good prognosis. They were first described by Wimmer (1916). See also, Strömgren (1968, 1986); Faergeman (1963); and Cooper (1986).

International differences in diagnostic practices

By the 1960s there were wide divergences in the criteria for the diagnosis of schizophrenia. In Britain and continental Europe, psychiatrists generally employed Schneider's approach, using typical symptoms to identify a narrowly delineated group of cases. In the United States, on the other hand, interest in psychodynamic processes led to diagnosis on the basis of mental mechanisms, and to the inclusion of a much wider group of cases.

First admission rates for schizophrenia were much higher in the United States than in the United Kingdom. This discrepancy prompted two major cross-national studies of diagnostic practice. The **US-UK Diagnostic Project** (Cooper *et al.* 1972) showed that the diagnostic concept of schizophrenia was much wider in New York than in Britain. In New York the concept included cases that were diagnosed as depressive illness, mania, or personality· disorder in Britain. The **International Pilot Study of Schizophrenia** (IPSS) was concerned with the diagnosis of schizophrenia in nine countries (World Health Organization 1973). The main finding was that similar criteria were adopted in seven of the nine countries: Colombia, Czechoslovakia, Denmark, India, Nigeria, Taiwan, and the United Kingdom. Broader criteria were used in the United States and the USSR. Despite these differences it was found, by using standard diagnostic techniques, that a core of cases with similar features could be identified in all the countries. In France, schizophrenia is not defined in Kraepelian terms. It is regarded as a chronic disorder with an onset before the age of 30. The diagnosis is made largely on symptoms, especially those proposed by Bleuler, which are referred to as 'dissociation' and 'discordance'. The term *bouffée délirante* is used for a sudden onset syndrome of good prognosis (see Pichot 1982, 1984).

In the USSR the concept of schizophrenia has been developed by Snezhnevsky. The definition is based mainly on the course of the disorder and much less on the symptoms. Three main subdivisions are recognized: continuous, periodic, and shift-like (a mixture of the first two). The concept is unusually broad and appears to cover conditions which elsewhere would be regarded as personality disorder or mere eccentricity.

In the USA and several other countries, the introduction of DSMIII has led to a much narrower definition of schizophrenia than that described above.

Reasons for diagnostic inconsistencies

To agree about the diagnosis of schizophrenia, clinicians must first agree about the symptoms that make up the syndrome, about the criteria for deciding whether these symptoms are present, and about the length of time that these features must last before the diagnosis can be made. The criteria for diagnosing the various symptoms of schizophrenia were discussed in Chapter 1. Here we consider the other two issues.

The narrower the range of symptoms that are accepted as diagnostic of schizophrenia, the more reliable the diagnosis. However, a narrow definition may exclude cases that are aetiologically related—this problem cannot be settled until we know more about the causes of schizophrenia. An example of a well-known narrow definition is that requiring the presence of Schneider's first-rank symptoms (Table 9.3). The use of this criterion leads to high reliability in diagnosis [though not to effective prediction of outcome (Brockington 1986)]. However, first-rank symptoms can occur in cases that otherwise meet generally agreed diagnostic criteria for mania. Of the first rank symptoms, 'third person' hallucinations seem to be least discriminating (Mellor 1982). Both ICD10 (draft) and DSMIIIR use wider definitions of schizophrenia, including other symptoms as well as Schneider's first-rank symptoms.

There is disagreement about the duration of symptoms required before schizophrenia can be diagnosed. ICD10 (draft) requires one month, DSMIIIR six months. Both periods are arbitrary. The longer time is more likely to identify patients with a poor prognosis but the importance of prognosis in defining schizophrenia is not yet clear. [For reviews of this topic, the reader is referred to Brockington (1986), Pfohl and Andreasen (1986), and Andreasen (1987).]

'Standardized diagnoses'

An important example of a standardized diagnosis is CATEGO, a computer program designed to process data from a standard interview known as the Present State Examination (see Wing *et al.* 1974). The programme incorporates diagnostic rules which give a series of standard diagnoses. The narrowest syndrome (S+) is diagnosed mainly on the symptoms of thought intrusion, broadcast or withdrawal; delusions of control; and voices discussing the patient in the third person or commenting on his actions.

The **Feighner Criteria** were developed in St Louis to identify patients with a poor prognosis. They include symptomatic criteria that are less precise than those in CATEGO, and a criterion of six months of continuous illness. They also require the exclusion of cases meeting diagnostic criteria for affective disorder, drug abuse, or alcoholism. The criteria are reliable but restrictive, leaving many cases without a diagnosis. Patients with a poor prognosis are identified well (probably because of the criterion of six months' continuous illness). These criteria have been widely used in research.

The **Research Diagnostic Criteria** (RDC) were developed from those of Feighner by Spitzer *et al.* (1978). The main difference is in the length of history required before the diagnosis of schizophrenia can be made: two weeks, instead of the six months in Feighner's criteria. A structured interview, the Schedule of Affective Disorders and Schizophrenia (SADS), has been developed for use with RDC. Both Feighner's criteria and the RDC influenced the development of DSMIIIR (see Table 9.5 for the criteria in DSMIIIR).

'Symptomatic schizophrenia'

If the symptoms of schizophrenia occur with organic disease of the central nervous system, the condition is generally referred to as an organic brain syndrome. Alternatively, this combination is sometimes referred to as 'symptomatic schizophrenia'. Certain organic conditions that can produce a secondary schizophrenic syndrome are discussed elsewhere in this book. They include: **temporal lobe epilepsy** (complex partial seizures) (p. 390), **encephalitis** (p. 374), **amphetamine abuse** (p. 551), and **alcohol abuse** (p. 520). In addition, a schizophrenic syndrome can occur post partum (p. 467) and in the post-operative period (p. 472).

Classification in DSMIIIR and ICD

The classification of schizophrenia and schizophrenia-like disorders is summarized in Table 9.4.

Table 9.4. Classification of schizophrenia and schizophrenia-like disorders in ICD10 (draft) and DSMIIIR*

ICD10 (draft)	DSMIIIR
Schizophrenia	*Schizophrenia*
Paranoid	Paranoid
Hebephrenic	Disorganized
Catatonic	Catatonic
Undifferentiated	Undifferentiated
Residual	Residual
Post-schizophrenic depression	
Other schizophrenia	
Unspecified schizophrenia	
Schizotypal states	
Schizotypal disorder	
Simple schizophrenia	
	Schizoaffective disorder†
Persistent delusional disorders	*Delusional (paranoid) disorder*
Delusional disorder (paranoia)	
Other persistent delusional	
disorders	
Acute or transient psychotic	
disorders	
Acute delusional episode	
Psychogenic delusional disorder	*Brief reactive psychosis*

Schizophrenia-like episode	*Schizophreniform disorder*
Other (undifferentiated) acute psychotic episode	
Induced delusional disorder	*Induced psychotic disorder*
Other non-organic psychotic disorder	
Non-organic psychoses not otherwise specified	*Psychotic disorder not otherwise specified*

* The order of categories in the two systems has been changed slightly to show their comparable features more clearly.
† In ICD10 (draft) schizoaffective disorder appears under mood disorders.

Table 9.5. Criteria for schizophrenia in DSMIIIR

A. Characteristic psychotic symptoms of the active phase. Either (1), (2) or (3) [for at least one week (or less if symptoms successfully treated)]:

(1) two of the following:

  (a) delusions;

  (b) prominent hallucinations (throughout the day for several days or several times a week for several weeks and each hallucinatory experience is not limited to a few brief moments);

  (c) incoherence or marked loosening of associations;

  (d) catatonic behaviour;

  (e) flat or grossly inappropriate affect.

(2) bizarre delusions (i.e. involving a phenomenon that the individual's subculture would regard as totally implausible, e.g. thought broadcasting, or being controlled by a dead person);

(3) prominent hallucinations [as defined in (1b) above] of a voice with content having no apparent relation to depression or elation, or a voice keeping up a running commentary on the individual's behaviour or thoughts, or two or more voices conversing with each other.

B. During the course of the disturbance, functioning in such areas as work, social relations, and self-care is markedly below the highest

Table 9.5. Criteria for schizophrenia in DSMIIIR (*cont.*)

level achieved prior to the disturbance (or with onset in childhood or adolescence, failure to achieve expected level of social development).

C. Major depressive or manic syndrome, if present during the active phase of the disturbance (symptoms in A), was brief relative to the duration of the disturbance.

D. Continuous signs of disturbance for at least six months. The six-month period must include an active phase (of at least one week) during which there were psychotic symptoms characteristic of Schizophrenia (symptoms in A), with or without a prodromal or residual phase, as defined below.

Prodromal phase: A clear deterioration in functioning before the active phase of disturbance, not due to a disturbance in mood or to a Psychoactive Substance Abuse Disorder, and involving at least two of a list of symptoms (included in the original but not reproduced here).

Residual phase: Following the active phase of the disturbance, persistence of at least two of a list of symptoms (included in the originals but not here) and not due to a disturbance in mood or to a Psychoactive Substance Use Disorder.

E. Not due to any Organic Mental Disorder.

F. If a history of Autistic Disorder, the additional diagnosis of schizophrenia is made only if prominent delusions or hallucinations are also present.

DSMIIIR

In this classification **schizophrenia** is defined in terms of the symptoms in the acute phase, and also of the course, for which the requirement is continuous signs of disturbance for at least six months (Table 9.5). The acute symptoms are divided into three sets. None of the first set corresponds to Schneider's first-rank symptoms. The second set consists of 'bizarre' delusions which would seem implausible to other members of the same sub-cultural group. The examples given are thought-broadcasting, and being controlled by a dead person (both of these correspond with Schneider's first-rank symptoms). The third set are special kinds of auditory hallucinations: a voice giving a running commentary on the person's thoughts or actions; and two or more voices conversing with each other. The latter two types of auditory hallucinations fit Schneider's first-rank criteria. Schizophrenia is divided into five subtypes: catatonic, disorganized (corresponding to hebephenic in ICD), paranoid, undifferentiated, and residual.

In DSMIIIR schizophrenia is distinguished from two other major categories: '**Delusional (paranoid) disorder**' (discussed in the next chapter) and the mixed group of '**Psychotic disorders not elsewhere classified**.'

ICD10 (draft)

This classification is more complicated than DSMIIIR and requires more explanation. It groups together schizophrenia, schizotypal states, and delusional disorder in a single section (Table 9.4). Schizoaffective disorder is not classified under schizophrenia but under the rubric 'mood disorder'.

The ICD10 definition of **schizophrenia** places more reliance than DSMIIIR on first rank symptoms, and requires only one month's duration (Table 9.6). There are several subtypes; these differ most obviously from DSMIIIR in including a category of post-schizophrenic depression.

Schizotypal states are of two types: schizotypal disorder and simple schizophrenia. **Schizotypal disorder** refers to eccentric behaviour, and unusual thinking and affect resembling those seen in schizophrenia but without definite and characteristic schizophrenic anomalies. The manual for ICD10 (draft) does not recommend this category for general use because it is 'not clearly demarcated either from simple schizophrenia or from schizoid or paranoid personality disorders'. The writers of the manual comment that schizotypal states are probably genetically related to schizophrenic disorders (World Health Organization 1987, p. 46). It may be doubted, however, whether the evidence for this statement is strong enough to support a separate grouping in the diagnostic scheme. In **simple schizophrenia** there is insidious development of negative symptoms without delusions and hallucinations (see p. 287). **Delusional disorders** are divided into persistent and brief types. Each type is further subdivided. Persistent delusional disorders are of two kinds: delusional disorder (paranoia); and other persistent delusional disorders. The former is characterized by persistent single or multiple delusions without other symptoms; the latter by persistent delusions accompanied by 'hallucinatory voices or by schizophrenic symptoms which are insufficient to meet criteria for schizophrenia'.

The **acute** or **transient psychotic disorders** are divided into the following four subtypes. **Acute delusional episode** is broadly synonymous with *bouffée délirante* (p. 86), and with cycloid psychosis (p. 290). It is essentially a paranoid disorder which develops rapidly (usually within days) and resolves within a few weeks or months. **Psychogenic delusional disorder**, a term synonymous with psychogenic psychosis (p. 86), is a brief disorder arising in close temporal connection with stressful events. **Schizophrenia-like episode** is a disorder meeting diagnostic criteria for schizophrenia but lasting less than one month. The fourth subtype is '**other**

Table 9.6. Symptomatic criteria for schizophrenia in ICD10 (draft)

The normal requirement for a diagnosis of schizophrenia is symptoms belonging to any one of the groups (1), (2), or (3) below, or symptoms from at least two of the groups (4), (5) and (6). (The six groups are reproduced verbatim from ICD10 draft.) A further requirement is that symptoms should have been clearly present for most of the time during a period of one month or more.

(1) Thought echo, thought insertion or withdrawal, thought broadcasting, delusional perception;

(2) delusions of control, influence or passivity; or bizarre delusions of other kinds;

(3) hallucinatory voices giving a running commentary on the patient's behaviour, or discussing him between themselves, have a similar significance, as do almost any hallucinatory voices which continue for weeks or months on end;

(4) apart from the characteristic kinds of delusions mentioned above, delusional ideas of any content may be suggestive of the diagnosis, if accompanied by hallucinations in any modality. However, clearly defined delusions and hallucinations are not always present, particularly in chronic conditions. The diagnosis will then often depend on establishing the presence of 'negative' symptoms such as:

(5) blunting or incongruity of emotional responses, increasing apathy, paucity of speech; and

(6) breaks or interpolations in the train of thought. Although these various deficits are equally characteristic of schizophrenia, depression or neuroleptic drugs can sometimes produce a very similar clinical picture.

(undifferentiated) acute psychotic episode', which is a residual category of acute and brief psychotic disorders that do not meet the criteria for the other three subtypes.

It can be seen that there are broad similarities in the two major schemes of classification, ICD10 (draft) and DSMIIIR. Nevertheless, the differences of detail show how arbitrary are many of the criteria for making the diagnosis of schizophrenia.

Subtypes of schizophrenia

The variety of the symptoms and course of schizophrenia has led to several attempts to define subgroups. This section is concerned only with the traditional subgroups of hebephrenic, catatonic, paranoid, and simple schizophrenia.

Patients with **hebephrenic** schizophrenia often appear silly and childish in their behaviour. Affective symptoms and thought disorder are prominent. Delusions are common, and not highly organized. Hallucinations also are common, and not elaborate. **Catatonic schizophrenia** is characterized by motor symptoms of the kind described on p. 273 and by changes in activity varying between excitement and stupor. Hallucinations, delusions, and affective symptoms occur but are usually less obvious. In **paranoid schizophrenia** the clinical picture is dominated by well-organized paranoid delusions. Thought processes and mood are relatively spared, and the patient may appear normal until his abnormal beliefs are uncovered. **Simple schizophrenia** is characterized by the insidious development of odd behaviour, social withdrawal, and declining performance at work. Since clear schizophrenic symptoms are absent, simple schizophrenia is difficult to identify reliably, and ICD10 (draft) recommends that the diagnosis should be 'made sparingly, if at all'.

With the possible exception of paranoid schizophrenia, these 'subgroups' are of doubtful validity. Some patients present symptoms of one group at one time, and then symptoms of another group later. There is some genetic evidence for separating cases with the paranoid picture (see Kendler and Davis 1981) but not enough to recommend doing so in everyday clinical work. Catatonic symptoms are much less common now than 50 years ago, perhaps because of improvements in the social environment in which patients are treated. Other explanations are possible; for example, organic syndromes may have been included in some earlier series (see Mahendra 1981).

The four subgroups described above cannot be clearly distinguished in clinical practice, and no support was found for them in the International Pilot Study of Schizophrenia (World Health Organization 1973).

Schizophrenia-like disorders

Whatever definition of schizophrenia is adopted, there will be cases that resemble schizophrenia in some respects and yet do not meet the criteria for diagnosis. Schizophrenia-like disorders can be divided into four groups: (a) delusional or paranoid disorders; (b) brief disorders; (c) disorders accompanied by prominent affective symptoms; (d) disorders without all the required symptoms for schizophrenia. The latter three groups will be discussed below: **delusional or paranoid disorders** are discussed in the next chapter.

(a) Brief disorders

DSMIIIR uses **'brief reactive psychosis'** for a syndrome lasting not more than a month, apparently precipitated by stress and with prominent emotional turmoil (see Table 9.4). **Schizophreniform psychosis** is a syndrome similar to schizophrenia (meeting criteria A and C) which lasts less than six months and does not meet the criteria for brief reactive psychosis.

Draft ICD10 has a collective term **'acute or transient psychotic disorder'**, which has three specific subtypes and a fourth undifferentiated (Table 9.4). The first is for brief disorders without marked antecedent stressors; these are called **acute delusional episodes**. The terms *bouffée délirante* and *cycloid psychosis* are given as synonyms. The requirements for the diagnosis of the second subtype—*psychogenic delusional disorder*—are: unequivocal evidence of mental trauma preceding the onset of symptoms by no more than four weeks; prominent delusions the content of which relates to the stressors; a mood congruent with the person's interpretation of the stressors; absence of blunting of affect; and full remission usually within weeks and not beyond three months. (The last requirement means that the diagnosis is often made in retrospect.) The stressful events may be of a kind that would affect most people, or may be of particular significance to an individual. The third subtype, *schizophrenia-like episode*, is a non-commital term for cases meeting the symptom criteria for schizophrenia but lasting less than a month. Such cases could turn out to be schizophrenia or acute delusional episodes depending on the subsequent course. The fourth subtype, for cases that do not fit the other three, is called *other acute psychotic episodes*.

(b) Disorders with prominent affective symptoms

Some patients have a more or less equal mixture of schizophrenic and affective symptoms. As mentioned earlier, such patients are classifed under *schizoaffective disorder* in both DSMIIIR and ICD10. However, this subgroup is grouped with schizophrenia in DSMIIIR, and with mood disorder in draft ICD10. In this book the former convention is followed. As mentioned earlier, ICD10 (draft) also has a specific subtype of post-schizophrenic depression.

Schizoaffective disorder   This term has been used in several distinct ways (Tsuang and Simpson 1984). It was first applied by Kasanin (1933) to a small group of young patients with severe mental disorders 'characterised by a very sudden onset in a setting of marked emotional turmoil with a distortion of the outside world. The psychosis lasts a few weeks and is followed by recovery.' DSMIIIR requires that there should have been 'disturbance during which at some time there is either a major depressive or manic syndrome concurrent with symptoms from the group A criteria of schizophrenia (see Table 9.5), and that the symptoms do not meet the criteria for schizophrenia or for organic mental disorder. Draft ICD10 is similar. It specifies that the diagnosis 'should only be made where *both* definite schizophrenic and definite affective symptoms are equally prominent and present simultaneously'. There are two subtypes; **schizomanic disorder** and **schizodepressive disorder**.

(c) Disorders without all the required symptoms for schizophrenia

A difficult problem is presented by cases with symptoms which resemble those of schizophrenia but fail strict criteria for diagnosis, and which endure for years. There are three groups. The first group consists of people who from an early age have behaved oddly and shown features seen in schizophrenia; for example, ideas of reference, persecutory beliefs, and unusual styles of thinking. When long-standing, these disorders can be classified as personality disorders as in DSMIIIR (**schizotypal personality disorder**, see p. 137), or with schizophrenia as in ICD10 (**schizotypal disorder**). Because of a suggested close relationship to schizophrenia, these disorders have also been called **latent schizophrenia**. They have, for example, been reported as more frequent in the families of schizophrenic patients than in other families, suggesting a possible genetic relationship (see p. 295). The second group is of people who develop symptoms after a period of more normal development. There is a gradual development of social withdrawal, lack of initiative, odd behaviour and blunting of emotion. These 'negative' symptoms are not accompanied by any of the 'positive' symptoms of schizophrenia such as hallucinations and delusions. Such cases are classified as **simple schizophrenia** in ICD10 (draft); in DSMIIIR they have to be classified as schizotypal personality disorder. The third group is of patients who have shown the full clinical picture of schizophrenia in the past but no longer have all the symptoms required to make the diagnosis. These cases are classified as **residual schizophrenia** in both DSMIIIR and ICD10 (draft).

Some other notable terms

Schizophreniform states

As mentioned earlier, this term was applied by Langfeldt (1961) to good prognosis cases as distinct from 'true' schizophrenia. The main features of schizophreniform states were the presence of a precipitating factor; acute onset; clouding of consciousness; and depressive and hysterical features. Although Welner and Strömgren (1958) confirmed the better outcome of schizophreniform cases, recent work has cast considerable doubt on the predictive value of Langfeldt's criteria. It is unfortunate that DSMIIIR uses the term schizophreniform quite differently to describe a condition identical to schizophrenia but with a course of less than six months.

Cycloid psychoses

Kleist introduced the term cycloid marginal psychoses to denote functional psychoses which were neither typically schizophrenic nor manic depressive. Leonhard (1957) developed these ideas by describing three forms of cycloid psychosis which are distinguished by their predominant symptoms: these conditions are all bipolar and are described as having a good prognosis and leaving no chronic defect state. The first is **anxiety elation psychosis**, in which the prominent symptom is a mood change. At one 'pole' anxiety is associated with ideas of reference and sometimes with hallucinations. At the other 'pole' the mood is elated, often with an ecstatic quality. The second is **confusion psychosis**, in which thought disorder is the prominent symptom, and the clinical picture varies between excitement and a state of underactivity with poverty of speech. The third is **motility psychosis**, in which the striking changes are in psychomotor activity. These syndromes are described briefly by Hamilton (1984) and in detail by Leonhard (1957). In practice, it is difficult to distinguish them from schizophrenia (see Perris 1974).

Type I and Type II schizophrenia

For many years a distinction has been made between positive and negative symptoms of schizophrenia. Recently there has been renewed interest in defining negative symptoms and using them as an alternative approach to subtyping (Crow 1980, 1985; Andreasen 1982). There is no complete consensus on the specification of negative symptoms but it is generally agreed that they include poverty of speech, affective blunting, lack of volition, impaired attention, and social withdrawal. Crow and his colleagues have described two syndromes. Type I is said to have an acute onset, mainly positive symptoms, and good social functioning during remissions. It has a good response to neuroleptics, with biochemical evidence of dopamine over-activity. In contrast, Type 2 is said to have an insidous onset, mainly negative symptoms, and poor outcome. It has a poor response to neuroleptics without evidence of dopamine over-activity. In Type 2 there is evidence of structural change in the brain (especially ventricular enlargement). (Cognitive, biochemical and neurological aspects of schizophrenia are considered later in this chapter.) In practice, although some patients can be recognized to have the Type I syndrome, those with Type II are much less common, and most patients show a mixture of Type I and II symptoms. For example, Farmer *et al.* (1987)

found no 'pure' Type II patients in a series of 35 chosen to represent typical cases of chronic schizophrenia.

Gjessing's syndrome

Gjessing (1947) described a rare disorder in which catatonic symptoms recurred in phases. He also found changes in nitrogen balance, which were not always in phase with the symptoms. Gjessing believed that there were underlying changes in thyroid function and that the disorder could be treated successfully with thyroid hormone. The condition, if it exists, is exceedingly rare.

Borderline disorders

In the United States there has been much interest in states intermediate between schizophrenia and the neuroses and personality disorders. The term 'borderline states' has been applied to them, but is used in several different ways (see Dahl 1985; Tarnopolsky and Berelowitz 1987). There have been three main usages. In the first, a borderline state is regarded as an independent entity which is wholly distinct from all other diagnostic categories. The main features have not been defined precisely, but include anger, difficulty in relationships, and lack of self-identity. In the second usage, a borderline state is a mild expression of schizophrenia. This usage resembles Bleuler's concept of latent schizophrenia; it also covers the 'schizophrenia spectrum' referred to in some genetic studies (see p. 295) and the concept of pseudoneurotic schizophrenia (Hoch and Polantin 1949). In the third usage, the term 'borderline' is applied to a form of personality abnormality characterized by impulsive, unstable relationships; inappropriate anger; identity disturbance; unstable mood; and chronic boredom.

The lack of precise descriptive criteria makes these diagnostic categories of doubtful value. If patients with so-called borderline states are studied carefully, most can be diagnosed as having personality disorder, schizophrenia, or affective disorder. In doubtful cases, follow-up often strengthens the diagnosis.

Differential diagnosis

Schizophrenia has to be distinguished mainly from organic syndromes, affective disorder, and personality disorder. Among younger patients the most relevant **organic diagnoses** are drug-induced states and temporal lobe epilepsy. Among older patients, various brain diseases must be excluded. For example, an acute brain syndrome could be mistaken for schizophrenia; the same holds for dementia, particularly with prominent persecutory delusions. Some diffuse brain diseases can present a schizophrenia-like picture in the absence of neurological disorder; the most important example is general paralysis of the insane (see Chapter 11). In seeking to exclude such organic disorders, it is important to obtain a thorough history, mental state examination, and physical examination with particular reference to neurological abnormalities. There must be careful observation for clouding of consciousness, memory deficit, and other symptoms and signs which are not characteristic of schizophrenia. The distinction between **affective disorder** and schizophrenia depends on the degree and persistence of the mood disorder, the relation of any hallucinations or delusions to the prevailing mood, and the nature of the symptoms in any previous episodes. Differential diagnosis from **personality disorder** can be very difficult when insidious changes are reported in a young person. Prolonged lengthy observation for first-rank symptoms may be required.

Aetiology

Before reviewing evidence on the causation of schizophrenia, it may be helpful to outline the main areas of inquiry. Of the **predisposing** causes, genetic factors are most strongly supported by the evidence, but it is clear that enviromental factors play an important part as well. The nature of these environmental factors is uncertain. Neurological damage around the time of birth has been suggested, and so have psychological influences. For both the evidence is indirect and incomplete. Research on **precipitating** causes has been concerned with life events and physical illness. Although such precipitants seem to have an effect, the size of the effect is uncertain. Among **perpetuating** factors social and family influences seem important; however they are not considered in this section but in the later section on course and prognosis.

   Investigation of **mediating mechanisms** has concentrated on psychological processes such as arousal, attention, and thinking; and on biochemical disorders, in which interest has been encouraged by advances in psycho-pharmacology.

Genetics

The genetic study of schizophrenia has been directed towards three questions: (i) is there a genetic basis? (ii) is there a relationship between clinical form and inheritance? (iii) what is the mode of inheritance? These three questions will be considered in turn. [Readers requiring a more detailed account are referred to Kendler (1986) and Murray *et al.* (1986).]

(i) Is there a genetic basis?
Family studies

The first systematic family study of dementia praecox was carried out in Kraepelin's department by Ernst Rüdin, who showed that the rate of

Table 9.7. Approximate lifetime expectancy of developing schizophrenia for relatives of schizophrenics

Relationship	Risk (per cent)	
	Definite cases only	Definite and probable cases
Parents	4.4	5.5
All siblings	8.5	10.2
Siblings (one parent schizophrenic)	13.8	17.2
Children	12.3	13.9
Children (both parents schizophrenic)	36.6	46.3
Half siblings	3.2	3.5
Nephews and nieces	2.2	2.6

Adapted from Shields (1980).

dementia praecox was higher among the siblings of probands than in the general population (Rüdin 1916). Another comprehensive study of families was conducted by Kallman (1938), whose sample of schizophrenic probands numbered more than a thousand. He found increased rates not only among the probands' siblings but also among their children. Table 9.5 (p. 284) shows approximate risks for various degrees of kinship to a schizophrenic patient. More recent research has used better criteria for diagnosis in probands and relatives, and better ways of selecting the probands (see Weissman *et al.* 1986). These improved methods yield estimates of a life-time risk of about 5 per cent among first-degree relatives of schizophrenics, compared with 0.2–0.6 per cent among first-degree relatives of controls (see Kendler 1986). These findings suggest a familial aetiology but do not dis- tinguish between the effects of genetic factors and those of the family environment. To make this distinction twin and adoption studies are required.

An additional important finding in family studies is that rates of affective disorder are not generally increased in the families of schizophrenics, suggesting that the two disorders do not have a common familial cause.

Twin studies

These studies compare the concordance rates for schizophrenia in monozygotic (MZ) and dizygotic (DZ) twins. The methodological problems of such studies have been considered already (see p. 109).

The first substantial twin study was carried out in Munich by Luxenberger (1928), who found concordance in 11 of his 19 MZ pairs and none of his 13 DZ pairs. Although this finding for DZ pairs casts doubt on the selection of the sample, other workers (for example Kallmann 1946; Slater 1953) confirmed that concordance was higher among MZ than DZ pairs.

Subsequent investigations using improved methods have led to similar results. In these studies concordance rates in MZ pairs have varied considerably, but they have always been higher than the concordance rates in DZ pairs (Gottesman and Shields 1972; Kringlen 1967; Tienari 1968; Fischer 1973). Representative figures for concordance are about 50 per cent for MZ pairs and about 17 per cent for DZ pairs (Shields 1978). These studies have been criticized for failing to use reliable diagnostic criteria. However, re-analysis of some of the cases using better diagnostic methods yields similar results: 47 per cent concordance for MZ, and 14 per cent for DZ twins (McGuffin *et al.* 1984; Kendler 1986). It might be expected that studies of MZ twins discordant for schizophrenia would reveal some environmental factors relevant to aetiology. A few such factors have been reported, for example low birth-weight and poor family relationships, but no conclusive findings have emerged (see Pollin and Stabenau 1968).

A more precise estimate of the relative importance of genetic and environmental factors can be obtained by comparing MZ twins reared together with MZ twins separated at birth and reared apart. The concordance rates are quite similar for the two groups, suggesting a major genetic contribution (Shields 1978).

Adoption studies

Heston (1966) studied 47 adults who had been born to schizophrenic mothers and separated from them within three days of birth. As children they had been brought up in a variety of circumstances, though not by the mother's family. At the time of the study their mean age was 36. Heston compared them with controls who were matched for circumstances of upbringing, but whose mothers had not been schizophrenic. Amongst the offspring of schizophrenic mothers, five were diagnosed as schizophrenic, as against none of the controls. There was also an excess of antisocial personality and neurotic disorders among the children of schizophrenic mothers. The age-corrected rate for schizophrenia among the index cases was comparable to that among non-adopted children with one schizophrenic parent. In this investigation, no account was taken of the fathers.

Further evidence has come from a series of studies started in 1965 by a group of Danish and American investigators. The work has been carried out in Denmark, which has national registers of psychiatric cases and adoptions. In a study of children separated from schizophrenic mothers at an average age of six months, the findings confirmed those of Heston described above (Rosenthal *et al.* 1971). The major project (Kety *et al.* 1975) employed a different design. Two groups of adoptees were identified: 33 who had schizophrenia, and a matched group who were free from schizophrenia. Rates of disorder were compared in the biological and adoptive families of the two groups of adoptees. The rate for schizophrenia was greater among the biological relatives of the schizophrenic adoptees than among the relatives of controls, a finding which supports the genetic hypothesis. Furthermore, the rate for schizophrenia was not increased amongst couples who adopted the schizophrenic adoptees, suggesting that environmental factors were not of substantial importance. The reverse situation was studied by Wender *et al.* (1974), who found no increase in schizophrenia amongst adoptees who had normal biological parents and a schizophrenic adoptive parent (see Kety 1983).

The Danish investigators viewed schizophrenia as a spectrum of illnesses with four divisions: (i) process schizophrenia; (ii) reactive schizophrenia; (iii) borderline schizophrenia; and (iv) schizoid states. The last three are sometimes referred to collectively as schizophrenia spectrum disease. The adoption-study findings reported above were for process schizophrenia, but the investigators also reported an excess of schizophrenia spectrum disease in biological relatives. These data have been re-analysed using DSMIII criteria for diagnosis, and an excess of schizophrenia and schizotypal personality disorder has been confirmed among the biological relatives of schizophrenic probands (see Kendler and Gruenberg 1984).

Adoption studies cannot rule out environmental causes in the adoptive family; but they indicate that, if there are such environmental causes, they act only on genetically predisposed children.

Is there a relationship between clinical form and inheritance?

Early family studies of hebephrenic, catatonic, and paranoid subtypes showed that they did not breed true to type. However, there was a somewhat lower risk of schizophrenia in the relatives of patients with the paranoid form (see Kendler and Davis 1981). There is also a lower risk of schizophrenia among the relatives of probands with 'good-prognosis' illnesses. Shields (1978) suggests that the milder the illness is, the more heterogeneous the aetiology.

It has been suggested that schizoaffective disorder results from a genetic predisposition to both schizophrenia and affective disorder. This idea is not supported by studies of families in which one parent had schizophrenia, and the other an affective illness.

What is the mode of inheritance?

The genetic evidence does not permit definite conclusions about the mode of inheritance. There are three main theories (see Murray *et al.* 1986; Kendler 1986).

1. Monogenic

As the ratios of the frequencies of schizophrenia among people with different degrees of relationship with the proband do not fit any simple Mendelian pattern, it is necessary to propose modifying factors. Slater (1958) suggested a dominant gene of variable penetrance.

2. Polygenic

This theory proposes a cumulative effect of several genes (see, for example, Gottesman and Shields 1967). This model is less precise than the monogenic theory and even more difficult to test.

3. Genetic heterogeneity

Monogenic and polygenic theories assume that schizophrenia is a single disease. Heterogeneity theories explain the observed patterns of inheritance by proposing that schizophrenia is a group of disorders. Several attempts have been made to test these hypotheses, but the results have been ambiguous and will remain so until a definite biological or genetic marker is identified.

Molecular genetic studies

To date (1988) the results of such studies have been contradictory (see Lander 1988), but their potential is considerable (see p. 111).

Other constitutional factors

Perinatal factors

It has been suggested that factors acting around the time of birth may contribute to the aetiology of schizophrenia. In support of this idea, there is indirect evidence from studies of three kinds of factor: birth complications, birth order, and season of birth.

As evidence for birth complications, retrospective studies of schizophrenic patients report more obstetric complications than do studies of normal controls (Woerner *et al.* 1973). Also in studies of identical twins discordant for schizophrenia, it was found that the affected twin more often had a complicated birth (Pollin and Stabenau 1968). These findings could indicate that one causal factor is a minor degree of brain damage resulting from obstetric complications.

Schizophrenia has been reported as more frequent among the younger members of large sibships (Farina *et al.* 1963). The reason for this finding is unknown, but a greater frequency of birth complications could be the linking factor.

Schizophrenia is more frequent among people born in the winter than among those born in the summer (Hare 1975). The reason is unknown but it might be related to higher rates of infectious diseases in the winter. This idea is consistent with the speculation that virus diseases of the brain in early life could contribute to the aetiology of schizophrenia (see below).

The difficulty of interpreting the effects of factors such as birth order, season of birth, and birth complications is that they may all interact with other factors, such as maternal age and social conditions. Also there are all the usual problems of retrospective enquiry.

'High-risk' research

In 1968 Mednick and Schulsinger reported a study of 207 children who were interviewed and assessed for cognitive disturbance in 1962, when they were aged 8–12 years. Their galvanic skin responses were measured, their school reports were examined, and their parents were questioned. The subjects were reassessed 18 years later in 1980 (Parnas *et al.* 1982), when they were aged 26–30 years. Thirteen had developed schizophrenia (CATEGO diagnoses), 29 had 'borderline schizophrenia', and five had died by suicide. Of the measures made on the first occasion, those predicting schizophrenia on the second were: poor rapport at interview; social isolation or disciplinary problems mentioned in school reports; reports by the parents that the person had been passive as a baby and had shown short attention span as a child; and fast recovery of galvanic skin responses.

Those who developed 'borderline schizophrenia' had been found on the first occasion to show poor rapport at interview but the reports of their teachers and parents had not mentioned the abnormalities reported by the teachers and parents of those who subsequently developed schizophrenia. [Readers seeking further information about these studies are referred to *Schizophrenia Bulletin* (1987).]

Personality

Several early writers including Bleuler (1911) commented on the frequency of abnormalities of personality preceding the onset of schizophrenia. Kretschmer (1936) proposed that both personality type and schizophrenia were related to the asthenic type of body build. He suggested a continuous variation between normal personality, schizoid personality (see p. 135), and schizophrenia. He regarded schizoid personality as a partial expression of the psychological abnormalities that manifest in their full form in schizophrenia. Such ideas must be treated with caution since it is difficult to distinguish between premorbid personality and the prodromal phase of a slowly developing illness.

It has been suggested that schizophrenia is associated with another kind of personality, called *schizotypal* in DSMIIIR. This kind of personality has been described already (on p. 137); briefly it is characterized by social isolation, odd ideas and speech, and a tendency to experience ideas of reference, illusions and depersonalization.

Cutting (1985) reviewed studies of the frequency of premorbid schizoid personality among schizophrenics and found the average rate to be 26 per cent. Other kinds of abnormal personality were reported, on average, in 16 per cent. Without comparable assessments of control groups in most of the studies, it is not possible to assess the significance of these percentages.

Despite these reservations it seems probable that abnormal personality is common among people who later became schizophrenic. This may indicate a specific aetiological relationship, or a non-specific vulnerability to stressful events. It is emphasized that many schizophrenics have no obvious disorder of personality before the onset of the illness, and that only a minority of people with schizoid personalities develop schizophrenia.

Neurological abnormalities

Clinicians have often detected signs of minor neurological abnormality in schizophrenic patients. Although it is possible that some of these signs resulted from coincidental neurological disease, they might reflect the causative process. Research is concerned with four issues: non-localizing ('soft') neurological signs; possible abnormalities of the corpus callosum and cerebellum; evidence of ventricular enlargement; and neuropathology. Each will be considered in turn.

'**Soft signs**' (neurological signs without localizing significance) have been reported in many studies. Rochford *et al.* (1970) found them in about 65 patients examined before starting drug treatment. Pollin and Stabenau (1968) found at least one sign in nearly three-quarters of a series of schizophrenics. It is generally found that the commonest abnormalities are in stereognosis, graphaesthesia, balance, and proprioception. It has been suggested that these abnormalities reflect defects in the integration of proprioceptive and other sensory information (see Cox and Ludwig 1979; Quitkin *et al.* 1976).

Thickening of the **corpus callosum** has been reported in brains from a small number of schizophrenic patients (Rosenthal and Bigelow 1972). There have also been reports of functional abnormalities in schizophrenics suggesting impairment of inter-hemispheric transfer and therefore callosal function (for example, Carr 1980). This work needs to be replicated [see Wyke (1982) for a review of evidence on how function is integrated between the two hemispheres].

Cerebellar atrophy detected by CT scan has also been reported in schizophrenic patients (for example, by Heath *et al.* 1979). Yates *et al.* (1987) confirmed this finding but observed that evidence of cerebellar atrophy is equally frequent in the CT scans of patients with affective disorder.

Ventricular enlargement in schizophrenia was first reported from studies using air-encephalography (for example, Haug 1962). Using computerized tomographic (CT) scanning, which provides a non-invasive alternative, Johnstone *et al.* (1976) found significantly larger ventricles in seventeen elderly institutionalized schizophrenics than in eight normal controls. Subsequent studies have found that ventricular enlargement in schizo-phrenics is not correlated with length of hospital stay, length of illness, or current or past dosage of antipsychotic drugs (e.g. Weinberger *et al.*

1980*a*,*b*). Andreasen *et al.* (1982) reported that patients with enlarged ventricles had more 'negative' symptoms than other schizophrenics, but this finding was not confirmed by Farmer *et al.* (1987). It might be expected that ventricular enlargement would be associated with cognitive impairment, but this association was not found by Owens *et al.* (1985) or Farmer *et al.* (1987). Instead there is some evidence of an association between enlarged ventricles and poor premorbid educational and social adjustment (Weinberger *et al.* 1980*a*,*b*), suggesting that the cerebral abnormality causing the large ventricles may have been present before the schizophrenia began. This suggestion is also supported by the finding of ventricular enlargement in patients examined soon after the onset of schizophrenia.

Thus there is not yet enough evidence to decide the significance of the findings of enlarged ventricles. Recently, imaging by nuclear magnetic resonance (NMR) has been used but so far no new findings have emerged.

Neuropathology. In the past, many investigators searched for gross pathological changes in the brains of schizophrenic patients but with few exceptions found none. Exceptions were the reports by Southard (1910) of 'internal hydrocephalus' (ventricular enlargement), and by Alzheimer (1897) of cell loss and gliosis in the cerebral cortex. Recently, interest in the neuropathology of schizophrenia has revived because of the findings of enlarged ventricles described above. Brown *et al.* (1986) compared post-mortem brains of patients with schizophrenia and of patients with affective disorder. After controlling for age, sex, and year of birth, the investigators found that the brains of schizophrenics had lateral ventricles that were larger in the anterior and the temporal horn sections, with thinner parahippocampal (i.e. medial temporal) cortices. This last finding which was also reported by Bogerts *et al.* (1985), is of particular interest because the results of other kinds of study suggest links between schizophrenia and pathological changes in the temporal lobes (see p. 398).

Associations with neurological disorders

Patients with chronic temporal lobe epilepsy have an increased risk of developing schizophrenic symptoms (see p. 398), and so do patients with Huntington's chorea (see p. 367). An association of schizophrenia with brain injury was described by Achté *et al.* (1969), but was not apparent in patients described by Lishman (1968). From a review of published work, Davison and Bagley (1969) concluded that neurological conditions associated with schizophrenia have the common feature of affecting the temporal lobe.

Abnormalities of brain physiology

Recent investigations have been mainly concerned with electrical activity of the brain and with cerebral blood flow.

Compared with normal people, schizophrenic patients generally have increased amounts of theta activity, fast activity, and paroxysmal activity in their EEG. The significance of these findings is unknown. Studies of evoked potentials have also shown more abnormalities among schizophrenics than among normal subjects, but no single abnormality is present in all patients (see, for example, Connolly *et al.* 1983; Morstyn *et al.* 1983).

Recent studies have used positron emission tomography (PET) to measure cerebral glucose metabolism (with 18-fluro-deoxyglucose). Some of these studies have found a reduction in the ratio of glucose consumption in the frontal compared with the posterior cortex. This finding, sometimes called *hypofrontality*, corresponds to evidence of reduced cerebral blood flow in the frontal lobes (see Weinberger and Kleinman 1986). The significance of these findings is in doubt particularly as they were not confirmed in a study of patients with recent onset schizophrenia who had not received antipsychotic medication (Sheppard *et al.* 1983).

Left hemisphere dysfunction

Several forms of indirect testing have been used to decide whether there is a disorder of left hemisphere function in schizophrenia. Psychological tests of left hemisphere function are abnormal in schizophrenia, but right-sided and bilateral abnormalities have been reported as well (see Andreasen 1986). Tachistoscopic presentation of visual stimuli has given evidence of left hemisphere dysfunction in one experiment but not in five others (see Cutting 1985, p. 156). Dichotic listening experiments have shown a right ear disadvantage pointing to left hemisphere dysfunction (e.g. Colbourn and Lishman 1979). All these experiments are subject to numerous confounding influences, and their results do no more than suggest the possibility of greater abnormality in the left than in the right cerebral hemisphere. [See Gur (1986) for a review.]

The virus hypothesis

Symptoms like those of schizophrenia occur occasionally in the course of known virus infections of the brain, notably as a rare late consequence of encephalitis lethargica (see p. 374). The discovery of delayed effects of some neurotropic viruses (slow viruses) suggested that schizophrenia might be a late effect of an infection in infancy or in prenatal life. The evidence for this idea is slight. Crow *et al.* (1979c) reported a virus-like agent in the CSF of schizophrenic patients, but this finding has not been confirmed. Subsequently Crow (1983) suggested that the virus, acquired before birth or in the germ-line from an affected patient, might enter the genome (a provirus). Under certain circumstances proviruses can become active and cause pathological changes (Crow 1984). This ingenious hypothesis is so far unsupported by evidence.

Psychodynamic theories

Freud's theory of schizophrenia was stated most clearly in his 1911 analysis of the Schreber case (see p. 326) and in his 1914 paper 'On narcissism: an introduction'. According to Freud, in the first stage libido was withdrawn from external objects and attached to the ego. The result was exaggerated self-importance. Since the withdrawal of libido made the external world meaningless, the patient attempted to restore meaning by developing abnormal beliefs. Because of libidinal withdrawal, the patient could not form a transference, and therefore could not be treated by psychoanalysis. Although Freud developed his general ideas considerably after 1914, he elaborated his original theory of schizophrenia but did not replace it.

Melanie Klein believed that the origins of schizophrenia were in infancy. In the 'paranoid–schizoid position' the infant was thought to deal with innate aggressive impulses by splitting both his own ego and his representation of his mother into two incompatible parts, one wholly bad and the other wholly good. Only later did the child realize that the same person could be good at one time and bad at another. Failure to pass through this stage adequately was the basis for the later development of schizophrenia.

Hartmann (1964) and other writers developed Freudian ideas about schizophrenia in another way. They took the view that defects in the ego result in problems in the defence and 'neutralization' of libido and aggression. Yet a different approach was taken by Sullivan, who explained schizophrenia in terms not of a withdrawal of libido but rather of interpersonal difficulties. Recent psychodynamic views on aetiology and treatment have been discussed by Arieti (1974).

The family as a cause of schizophrenia

Two kinds of theory have been proposed about the family as a cause of the onset of schizophrenia: deviant role relationships, and disordered communication (see Liem 1980). The different role of the family in determining the *course* of established schizophrenia is discussed later (p. 312).

Deviant role relationships

The concept of the 'schizophrenogenic' mother was suggested by the analyst Fromm-Reichmann in 1948. In a comparison of the mothers of schizophrenic patients, neurotic patients, and normal controls, Alanen (1958, 1970) found that mothers of schizophrenics showed an excess of psychological abnormalities. He suggested that these abnormalities might be an important cause of the child's schizophrenia. Lidz and his colleagues (Lidz and Lidz 1949; Lidz *et al.* 1965) used intensive psychoanalytic methods to study the families of 17 schizophrenic patients, of whom 14 were in social classes I or II. There was no control group. Two types of abnormal family pattern were reported: (i) 'marital skew', in which one parent yielded to the other's (usually the mother's) eccentricities, which dominated the family; (ii) 'marital schism' in which the parents maintained contrary views so that the child had divided loyalties. It was suggested that these abnormalities were the cause rather than the result of the schizophrenia. Investigations by other clinicians have not confirmed these findings (see Sharan 1965; Ferreira and Winter 1965). Even if they were confirmed, the abnormalities in the parents could be an expression of genetic causes or secondary to the disorder in the patient. These and other speculations about the causative role of family relationships have had the unfortunate consequence of inducing unjustified guilt in parents.

Disordered family communication

Research on disordered communication in families originated from the idea of the **double bind** (Bateson *et al.* 1956). A double bind is said to occur when an instruction is given overtly, but contradicted by a second, more covert instruction. For example, a mother may overtly tell her child to come to her, whilst conveying by manner and tone of voice that she rejects him. A further element is said to be that there is no escape from the situation in which the contradictory injunctions are received. According to Bateson, double binds leave the child able to make only ambiguous or meaningless responses. Bateson further supposed that schizophrenia develops when this process persists. The theory is ingenious but not supported by evidence [see Leff (1978) for a more detailed discussion].

Wynne and his colleagues suggested that different patterns of disordered communication occurred among the parents of schizophrenics (Wynne *et al.* 1958). These investigators first gave projective tests to such parents, and identified 'amorphous communications' ('vague, indefinite, and loose') and 'fragmented communications' ('easily disrupted, poorly integrated, and lacking closure'). In a further study using blind interpretation of these tests, the investigators found more of these disordered communications in parents of schizophrenics than in parents of neurotics (Singer and Wynne 1965). In an independent replication, Hirsch and Leff (1975) found a similar but smaller difference between parents of schizophrenic patients and controls. These workers pointed out that such differences might simply be explained by a tendency for the parents of the schizophrenic patients to make more utterances in response to the projective tests. However, when Singer and Wynne's data were re-analysed to allow for number of utterances, some significant differences still remained between parents of schizophrenics and controls.

Subsequent attempts to test Wynne's hypothesis have used more elaborate methods such as observing family communication during the performance of a task (see Liem 1980; Wynne 1981). So far the hypothesis must be judged as not proven. Even if Wynne's findings are substantiated, it remains possible that the abnormalities are a reaction to, rather than the cause of, schizophrenia in the family member. Neither Wynne's theory nor any other theory of disordered communication can give a satisfactory explanation why it is unusual for more than one child in a family to develop schizophrenia.

Social factors

Culture

If cultural factors are important in the aetiology of schizophrenia, differences in the incidence of the disorder might be expected in countries with contrasting cultures. As explained already (p. 269), the incidence rates of schizophrenia are remarkably similar in widely different places, and the possibly exceptional rates are in areas (northern Sweden and north-western Yugoslavia) with cultures that do not differ much from others in the Western world. Rates in countries with contrasting cultures (for example, Nigeria and India) are similar to those in the West. It is not certain, however, how far the numbers of cases in developing countries are made up from brief psychoses rather than schizophrenia (see Stevens 1987; Jablensky 1987).

Occupation and social class

Several studies have shown that schizophrenia is over-represented among people of lower social class. In Chicago, for example, Hollingshead and Redlich (1958) found both the incidence and the prevalence of schizophrenia to be highest in the lowest socioeconomic groups. At first, these findings were thought to be of aetiological significance, but more recent evidence suggests that they could be a consequence of schizophrenia. For instance, Goldberg and Morrison (1963) found that schizophrenics were of lower social status than their fathers and that the change had usually occurred after the illness began.

Place of residence

Faris and Dunham (1939) studied the place of residence of mentally ill people in Chicago, and found that schizophrenics were over-represented in the disadvantaged inner city areas. This distribution has been confirmed in other cities, including Bristol (Hare 1956a) and Mannheim (Häfner and Reimann 1970). Faris and Dunham suggested that unsatisfactory living conditions caused the schizophrenia. However, the findings can be explained equally plausibly by the occupational and social decline described above, or by a search for social isolation by people about to develop schizophrenia. A search for isolation would be consistent with the finding that schizophrenics in disadvantated areas usually live alone, not with their families (Hare 1956*b*).

Migration

High rates of schizophrenia have been reported among migrants (see, for example, Malzberg and Lee 1956). In a study of Norwegians who had migrated to Minnesota, Ødegaard (1932) found that the inception rate for schizophrenia was twice that of Norwegians in Norway. The reasons for these high rates are not clear, but they are probably due mainly to a disproportionate migration of people who are unsettled because they are becoming mentally ill. The effects of a new environment may also play a part in provoking illness in predisposed people. Thus 'social selection' and 'social causation' may both contribute to an excess of schizophrenia among migrants [see Murphy (1977) for a review].

Social isolation

Schizophrenics often live alone, unmarried, and with few friends (see, for example, Hare 1956*b*). A retrospective study comparing schizophrenics with controls (Clausen and Kohn 1959) suggested that the pattern of isolation began before the illness, sometimes in early childhood. Schizophrenics who were not isolated in early life, were not isolated as adults.

Conclusion

From the epidemiological evidence, it is uncertain whether schizophrenia is evoked by living in a disadvantaged neighbourhood. On balance it seems more likely that people who are developing schizophrenia tend to move into areas providing solitary and unsatisfactory accommodation (see Cooper 1978).

Precipitating factors

Physical illness and childbearing

When schizophrenia follows closely on physical illness or childbearing the association seems usually to be due to general stressful psychological and physiological factors rather than to any specific causative agent.

Associations between neurological disorders and schizophrenia have been described (see p. 299) but as explained already, these appear to be predisposing rather than precipitating causes.

Psychosocial stresses

Life stresses have often been put forward as precipitants of schizophrenia, but few satisfactory studies have been carried out. In one of the most convincing studies, Brown and Birley (1968) used a standardized procedure to collect information from 50 patients newly admitted with a precisely datable first onset or relapse of schizophrenia. By comparison with a control group, the rate of 'independent' events in the schizophrenics was increased in the three weeks before the onset of the acute symptoms. (Independent events are those that could not be the result of illness—see p. 107.) When the events (which included moving house, starting or losing a job, and domestic crises) were compared with events preceding depression, neurosis, and suicide attempts, they were found to be non-specific. As a rough guide to the size of the effect, Paykel (1978) calculated that experiencing a life event doubles the risk of developing schizophrenia over the subsequent six months. Other workers have confirmed these findings both for first episodes and for relapse of schizophrenia (Jacobs *et al.* 1974; Jacobs and Myers 1976).

Mediating mechanisms

In research on the aetiology of schizophrenia, much attention has been given to mediating mechanisms. These are not 'ultimate' causes of schizophrenia in the same sense that genetic predisposition or early environment might be; nor are they precipitating factors. They are best thought of as central abnormalities that form a link between such causal factors and the phenomena of schizophrenia.

Psychological mediating mechanisms

'Arousal'

Much attention has been paid to autonomic measures such as skin conductance and pulse rate in schizophrenic patients. The results have been inconsistent, some workers reporting increased activity, and others reporting no differences from normal subjects [see Neale and Oltmans (1980) for a review]. The results of studies of autonomic activity and of EEG activity have been interpreted as indicating arousal in the central nervous system. Viewed in this way the results suggest that some but not all schizophrenics are over-aroused, and that this abnormality is more frequent among the more socially withdrawn chronic patients (see Lader 1975; also Venables and Wing 1962). Venables and his colleagues have reported asymmetries in autonomic responses which they interpret as evidence for a disorder of left hemispheric function possibly related to the hippocampus (see Venables 1977). However, these findings have not been confirmed.

The literature on arousal in schizophrenia is difficult to interpret, because different investigators work with different subgroups of patients (or do not specify the characteristics of patients), and because some of the reported effects could be due to medication.

Perception and attention

Disorders of **perception** are common in schizophrenia. Patients may describe perceptions as being more vivid, less real, or altered in shape or size. Psychological testing shows deficits indicating excessive attention to the detail of sensory input rather than to the overall impression or 'gestalt'.

Disorders of **attention** in schizophrenia include difficulty in focusing and maintaining attention, and in shifting its focus. Psychological investigations have not determined the cause of these difficulties, which some authors regard as secondary to abnormalities in arousal.

[For a review of studies of attention and perception in schizophrenia, see Cutting (1985), Chapters 8 and 14.]

Thought disorder

Many attempts have been made to characterize the abnormal thinking of people with schizophrenia. For example, Goldstein and Scheerer (1941) suggested that schizophrenics have difficulties in using abstract ideas, an abnormality which is often referred to as concrete thinking. This suggestion has not been confirmed by further research, and the usual clinical test of abstract thinking—the interpretation of proverbs—has been shown to be unreliable (Andreasen 1977).

Other research has used the concept of 'over-inclusiveness', which has been defined as 'the inability to conserve conceptual boundaries with the result that there is an incorporation of irrelevant ideas' (Cameron 1938). Payne and his colleagues, using object sorting tests, have shown that some schizophrenics classify objects in unusual and idiosyncratic ways (see Payne 1962).

A third approach to schizophrenic thought disorder uses Kelly's personal construct theory (Kelly 1955). Bannister (1962) suggested that schizophrenics had an abnormally loose construct system which could be measured with the repertory grid. He also suggested that abnormal constructs might have developed through repeated invalidations of the patient's previous attempts to make sense of the world, perhaps as a result of disordered family communication experienced in childhood. The available evidence does not support this theory.

Current research is more concerned with the nature of the disorders in schizophrenic language (see Wyke 1980). Small but significant differences have been found between the speech of schizophrenics and that of normal people, the main difference being reduced ability to convey an intended meaning. This is an interesting approach but so far it has not increased knowledge about aetiology.

Biochemical and psychopharmacological factors

Many findings of early biochemical investigations turned out to be the result of unusual diet or medication rather than of schizophrenia itself. Recent studies have usually attempted to control these extraneous variables. Several hypotheses have been suggested, but most attention has been paid to those concerned with **serotonergic** transmission, **transmethylation**, and **dopaminergic** transmission.

Woolley and Shaw (1954) suggested that *serotonergic transmision* in the brain might be diminished in schizophrenia. However, subsequent post-mortem brain studies have not revealed any consistent abnormality of serotonin or its metabolite 5-hydroxyindolacetic acid (Crow *et al.* 1979*a*).

Transmethylation

Mescaline, a hallucinogen, is a methylated substance with a chemical relationship to dopamine and noradrenalin. Osmond *et al.* (1952) suggested that abnormal methylated metabolites might be formed in the brain and might produce the psychological symptoms of schizophrenia. A basic weakness of the theory is that the effects of mescaline do not closely resemble schizophrenia. Some support for this theory apeared to be provided by the finding of a methylated substance in the urine of some schizophrenics (Friedhoff and van Winkle 1962). However, this compound (3,4-dimethoxyphenylethylamine) proved to be inactive in human beings, and was subsequently found to be excreted by normal subjects living in the same conditions as the schizophrenic patients, and to be dietary in origin (see Green and Costain 1981).

Recent attempts to identify methylated metabolites have centred on the indoleamine *N*-dimethyltryptamine, which can be identified in the tissues, blood, and urine of schizophrenic patients. This substance is also present in people with other mental disorders, so any specific relationship to schizophrenia is doubtful (see Rodnight *et al.* 1977).

The dopamine hypothesis

Two lines of research have converged on the transmitter dopamine. The first concerns amphetamine which, among other actions, releases dopamine at central synapses. Amphetamine also induces a disorder indistinguishable from schizophrenia in some normal people, and worsens schizophrenic symptoms. The second approach starts from the finding that the various antipsychotic drugs share dopamine blocking effects. Carlsson and Lindquist (1963) showed that such drugs increase dopamine turnover. This effect was interpreted as a feedback response of the presynaptic neurone to blockade of postsynaptic dopamine receptors. There is now much additional evidence that antipsychotic drugs block postsynaptic dopamine receptors. They also antagonize dopamine-sensitive adenylcyclase; and the extent to which this effect is produced *in vitro* by the different antipsychotic drugs correlates closely with their clinical potency (Miller *et al.* 1974). Further it has been shown that α-flupenthixol, an effective dopamine antagonist, has significant antipsychotic activity; whilst the β-isomer, which lacks receptor-blocking properties, is therapeutically inert (Johnstone *et al.* 1978).

Although the evidence is strong that dopamine is central to the action of antipsychotic drugs, evidence for the corollary—that dopamine metabolism is abnormal in schizophrenia—is weak. The antipsychotic drugs do not have effects specific to schizophrenia; they are equally effective in mania. Also, it is important to recall the analogy of parkinsonism (mentioned on p. 115). In this condition, anticholinergic drugs have therapeutic effects even though the biochemical lesion is not an excess of acetylcholine but a deficiency in dopaminergic neurones due to selective degeneration.

More direct evidence comes from biochemical studies of post-mortem brains from schizophrenic patients. There are reports of increased dopamine receptor density in the caudate nucleus putamen and nucleus accumbens (Owens *et al.* 1978); of increased concentrations of dopamine in the amygdala of the left hemisphere, with smaller increases in the caudate nucleus (Reynolds 1983); and of increases of the peptides cholecystokinin, somatostatin, and vasoactive polypeptide in the limbic regions [these peptides are usually associated with dopaminergic neurones (Ferrier *et al.* 1983).]

Positron emission tomography provides a way of investigating dopamine receptor binding in the brain of living patients by using appropriately labelled dopamine receptor ligands (see Sedvall *et al.* 1986). There is a report that D2 dopamine receptor densities in the caudate nuclei of both sides were greater in schizophrenic patients than normals, and this abnormality was present in small groups of patients who had never received neuroleptic drugs (Wong *et al.* 1986). However, this finding was not confirmed by Farde *et al.* (1987). More work will be needed before definite conclusions can be reached about dopamine function in untreated schizophrenic patients.

Conclusion

There is strong evidence for genetic causes. There is good reason to think that stressful life events often provoke the disorder; the events appear to be non-specific and are similar to those which precede affective disorders. There have been several attempts to find factors in early life that might increase vulnerability to schizophrenia in later years. One set of observations concerns minor neurological disorder, possibly secondary to birth injury. Another set concerns the way parents communicate with their children. Neither set is convincing. Psychological studies have succeeded in characterizing some of the abnormalities found in schizophrenia but so far they have not increased knowledge of causation. In established cases of schizophrenia, it is possible that exacerbations are related to events that increase an already high level of arousal. Although a biochemical disorder has long been suspected, no convincing evidence has been found. Dopamine receptors are blocked by drugs that control schizophrenic symptoms, but there is no compelling evidence that activity of dopaminergic systems is the central disorder in schizophrenia.

Course and prognosis

Although it is generally agreed that the outcome of schizophrenia is worse than that of most psychiatric disorders, there have been surprisingly few long-term follow-up studies of schizophrenic patients. Fewer still have included satisfactory criteria for diagnosis, samples of adequate size, and outcome measures that distinguish between symptoms and social adjustment. It is generally accepted that there are wide variations in outcome. This variation can be explained in three ways: first, schizophrenia may be a single condition with a course that is modified by extraneous factors; second, schizophrenia may consist of separate subtypes with different prognoses; third, the good prognosis cases may not be schizophrenia but some other condition. The second and third explanations have already been discussed; the rest of this section is concerned with the first explanation.

It is essential to distiguish between data from studies of first admissions to hospital, and data from investigations that study second or subsequent admissions, or give no information on this point (see Harding *et al.* 1987 for a review of outcome). When successive reports are studied, it appears that prognosis may have improved since the beginning of the century. Kraepelin (1919) concluded that only 17 per cent of his patients in Heidelberg were socially well-adjusted many years later. In 1932, from the same clinic Mayer-Gross reported social recovery in about 30 per cent of patients after 16 years. By 1966, Brown *et al.* reported social recovery in 56 per cent of patients after five years. Against this, in a study of patients identified as schizophrenic in a single centre between the early years of the century and 1962, Ciompi (1980) found little change in the proportion with a good or fair social outcome. Schizophrenics have a mortality substantially higher than that of the general population. The excess is contributed to by a variety of natural causes and by suicide (Allebeck and Wisledt 1986). All studies with prolonged follow-up report that up to 10 per cent of schizophrenics die by suicide (see Roy 1982).

An important long-term study was carried out by Manfred Bleuler (1972, 1974) who personally followed up 208 patients who had been admitted to hospital in Switzerland between 1942 and 1943. Twenty years after admission, 20 per cent had had a complete remission of symptoms and 24 per cent were severely disturbed. Bleuler considered that these proportions had changed little since the introduction of modern treatments although advances in drug and social treatments had substantially benefitted patients whose illnesses had a fluctuating course. When social adjustment was examined, a good outcome was found in about 30 per cent of the whole group, and in 40 per cent of those who had originally been first admissions. When full recovery had occurred, it was usually in the first two years and seldom after five years of continuous illness. Bleuler's diagnostic criteria were narrow, and his findings suggest that the traditional view of schizophrenia as a generally progressive and disabling condition must be reconsidered. Nevertheless, 10 per cent of his patients suffered an illness of such severity that they required long-term sheltered care. When the illness was recurrent, usually each subsequent episode resembled the first in its clinical features.

Bleuler's conclusions are broadly supported by Ciompi's larger but less detailed study of long-term outcome in Lausanne (Ciompi 1980). The study was based on the well-kept records of 1642 patients diagnosed as schizophrenic from the beginning of the century to 1962. The average follow-up was 37 years. A third of the patients were found to have a good or fair social outcome. Symptoms often became less severe in the later years of life. Huber *et al.* (1975) reported similar findings from a 22-year follow-up study of 502 patients in Bonn. (See Harding *et al.* 1987 for a review of outcome.)

There have been several attempts to find satisfactory predictors of the outcome of schizophrenia (see Stephens 1978). Langfeldt (1961) identified a set of criteria and reported them to be successful. However, in the International Pilot Study of Schizophrenia (World Health Organization 1979), tests were made of the predictive value of several sets of criteria based on symptoms, including Langfeldt's criteria, Feighner's diagnostic criteria, and others. All these symptom criteria proved to be largely unsuccessful at predicting outcome at two years (Strauss and Carpenter 1974), or five years (Strauss and Carpenter 1977). The best predictors of poor outcome appear to be the criteria used for diagnosis in DSMIII, in part though not entirely because they stipulate that the syndrome should have been present for six months before the diagnosis can be made (Helzer *et al.* 1983).

In the IPSS study, the investigators went on to test other clinical and social criteria. When 47 putative predictors were combined they accounted for less than 38 per cent of the variance of the two-year outcome; this percentage was made up of 11 per cent attributable to socio-demographic

Table 9.8. Factors predicting the outcome of schizophrenia

Good prognosis	Poor prognosis
Sudden onset	Insidious onset
Short episode	Long episode
No previous psychiatric history	Previous psychiatric history
Prominent affective symptoms	Negative symptoms
Older age at onset	Younger age at onset
Married	Single, separated, widowed, divorced
Good psychosexual adjustment	Poor psychosexual adjustment
Good previous personality	Abnormal previous personality
Good work record	Poor work record
Good social relationships	Social isolation
Good compliance	Poor compliance

variables, 14 per cent to past history, and 13 per cent to features of the most recent episode of illness.

Clinicians should therefore be cautious when asked to predict the outcome of individual cases. The factors listed in Table 9.8 are generally agreed to be a moderately useful guide.

So far this discussion has been concerned with factors operating before or at the onset of schizophrenia. An account will now be given of factors acting after the illness has become established.

Social environment and course

Cultural background

Recent international studies suggest that the incidence of schizophrenia is similar in different countries, but that the course and outcome are not similar. In a 12-year follow-up study of 90 patients in Mauritius, Murphy and Raman (1971) observed a better prognosis than that reported in the United Kingdom by Brown *et al.* (1966). More Mauritian patients were able to leave hospital and return to a normal way of life. Nearly two-thirds were classified as socially independent and symptom-free at follow-up as compared with only half of the English sample.

Comparable differences were reported at two-year follow-up in the International Pilot Study of Schizophrenia (World Health Organization 1979). Outcome was better in India, Columbia, and Nigeria than in the other centres. This finding could not be explained by any recorded differences in the initial characteristics of the patients. There remains the possibility of selection bias; for example, in these three countries it may be that patients with acute illness are more likely to be taken to hospital than patients with illness of insidious onset (see Stevens 1987). A more recent study designed to overcome these objections also found a more favourable course of illness in less developed countries (see Jablensky 1987; Jablensky *et al.* 1986).

Life events

As explained above (p. 305), some patients experience an excess of life events in the three weeks before the onset of acute symptoms of schizophrenia. This applies not only to first illnesses but also to relapses (Brown and Birley 1968). It seems likely therefore that patients exposed to many life events will have a less favourable course.

Social stimulation

In the 1940s and 1950s clinicians recognized that among schizophrenics living in institutions many clinical features were associated with an unstimulating environment. Wing and Brown (1970; Brown *et al.* 1966) investigated patients at three mental hospitals. One was a traditional institution, another had an active rehabilitation programme, and the third had a reputation for progressive policies and short admissions. The research team devised a measure of 'poverty of the social milieu' which took into account: little contact with the outside world, few personal possessions, lack of constructive occupation, and pessimistic expectations on the part of ward staff. Poverty of social milieu was found to be closely related to three aspects of the patients' clinical condition: social withdrawal, blunting of affect, and poverty of speech. The causal significance of these social conditions was strongly supported by a further survey of the same hospitals four years later. Improvements had taken place in the environment of the hospitals, and these changes were accompanied by corresponding improvements in the three aspects of the patients' clinical state.

While an understimulating hospital environment is associated with worsening of the so-called clinical poverty syndrome, an over-stimulating environment can precipitate florid symptoms and lead to relapse. Since factors in a hospital environment play an important part in determining prognosis, it seems likely that similar factors are important to patients living in the community.

Family life

Brown *et al.* (1958) found that, on discharge from hospital, schizophrenics returning to their families generally had a worse prognosis than those entering hostels. Brown *et al.* (1962) found that relapse rates were greater in families where relatives showed 'high expressed emotion' by making critical comments, expressing hostility, and showing signs of emotional over-involvement. In such families the risk of relapse was greater if the patients were in contact with their close relatives for more than 35 hours a week. The work was confirmed and extended when Leff and Vaughn (1981) investigated the interaction between 'expressed emotion' in relatives and life events in the three months before relapse. The onset of illness was associated either with a high level of expressed emotion or with an independent life event. In an investigation using psycho-physiological methods Sturgeon *et al.* (1984) reported an association between expressed emotion in a close relative and the level of autonomic arousal recorded in the patient, suggesting that such arousal may be a mediating variable.

Vaughn and Leff (1976) suggested an association between expressed emotion in relatives and the patient's response to antipsychotic medication. Among patients who were spending more than 35 hours a week in contact with relatives showing high emotional expression, the relapse rate was 92 per cent for those not taking antipsychotic medication, and only 53 per cent for those taking antipsychotic medication. Among patients taking antipsychotic drugs and spending less than 35 hours in contact with high emotional expression relatives, the relapse rate was as low as 15 per cent. In this study patients had not been allocated randomly to the treatment conditions. However, a further study (Leff *et al.* 1982; Leff *et al.* 1985*a*) strongly suggests that high emotional expression has a causal role. Twenty-four families were selected in which a schizophrenic patient had high contact with high emotional expression relatives. All patients were on maintenance neuroleptic drugs. Half of the families were randomly assigned to routine out-patient care. The other half took part in a programme including education about schizophrenia, relatives' groups, and family sessions for relatives and patients. The relapse rate was significantly lower in this group than in the controls at nine-month and two-year follow-up. Apart from providing further evidence of the importance of relatives' expressed emotion in relapse, this study showed the effectiveness of combined social intervention and drug treatment.

A study in California confirmed these conclusions, although in another study MacMillan *et al.* (1986) could not replicate the findings. Nevertheless a subsequent study in India found the same relationship between high emotional expression among relatives and high rate of relapse. However, high emotional expression was less frequent among relatives of the Indian schizophrenics than among relatives of British schizophrenics. This finding might help to explain the better outcome reported in Indian 'first-contact' patients (Leff *et al.* 1987). [Research on family treatment has been reviewed by Leff (1985*a*).]

Neuroleptics, given as maintenance treatment, appear to reduce the effect of stressors (life events, and high emotional involvement of relatives) in producing relapse (Leff *et al.* 1985*b*). There is also some evidence that special kinds of psychological treatment can reduce the effects of such stressors (Leff 1985; Hogarty *et al.* 1986).

Conclusion

Degree of social stimulation may be a common factor explaining the relationships between outcome of schizophrenia and different cultures, life events, changes in the social environment, and the emotional involvement of relatives. Too much stimulation appears to precipitate relapse into positive symptoms, while understimulation leads to worsening of negative symptoms. An intervening mechanism could be the degree of autonomic arousal.

Effects of schizophrenia on the family

With the increasing care of patients in the community rather than in hospital, difficulties have arisen for some families. Relatives of schizophrenics describe two main groups of problems (Creer 1978). The first group relates to social withdrawal: schizophrenic patients do not interact with other family members; they seem slow, lack conversation, have few interests, and neglect themselves. The second group relates to more obviously disturbed and socially embarrassing behaviour, such as restlessness, odd or uninhibited social behaviour, and threats of violence.

Creer found that relatives often felt anxious, depressed, guilty, or bewildered. Many were uncertain how to deal with difficult and odd behaviour. Further difficulties arose from differences in opinion between family members, and more commonly from a lack of understanding and sympathy among neighbours and friends. The effects on the lives of such relatives were often serious. Unfortunately, in Great Britain and other countries community services for chronic schizophrenic patients and their relatives are often less than adequate (see Johnstone *et al.* 1984).

Treatment

The treatment of schizophrenia is concerned with both the acute illness and chronic disability. In general, the best results are obtained by combining drug and social treatments, while methods aimed at providing psychodynamic insight are unhelpful.

This section is concerned with the evidence from clinical trials about the efficacy of various forms of treatment. A later section on management deals with the use of these treatments in everyday clinical practice.

The history of insulin-coma therapy is a warning that clinical impressions about the value of treatment can be misleading. Insulin-coma therapy was widely used for many years until Ackner and Oldham (1962) showed that coma induced by barbiturates produced equally good results. This finding indicated that the therapeutic benefits were probably due to non-specific factors including intensive care by enthusiastic staff. [See Hirsch (1986*a*) and Kane (1987) for reviews of treatment.]

Antipsychotic drugs

Treatment of acute schizophrenia

The effectiveness of antipsychotic medication in the treatment of acute schizophrenia has been established by several well-controlled, double-blind studies. For example, the NIMH collaborative project (Cole *et al.* 1964) compared chlorpromazine, fluphenazine, and thioridazine with placebo. Three-quarters of the patients receiving antipsychotic treatment for six weeks improved, whatever the drug, whilst a half of those receiving placebo worsened. Drug treatment has most effect on the positive symptoms of schizophrenia, such as hallucinations and delusions, and least effect on the negative symptoms. The sedative action is immediate but the antipsychotic effect develops more slowly, sometimes taking up to two to three weeks.

The various antipsychotic drugs do not differ in therapeutic effectiveness, although their side-effects vary (see p. 644). There is generally little to be gained by exceeding a maximum dose equivalent to about 900 mg of chlorpromazine a day (see Davis *et al.* 1980; a table of dose equivalents appears on p. 651). The exception to this rule is that higher dosages are sometimes required to achieve a sedative effect in acutely ill patients. In emergencies, when rapid response is required, a high potency neuroleptic such as haloperidol is preferable. For the acute illness there is no proven way of distinguishing patients who require medication if they are to improve from those who would improve without medication (Davis *et al.* 1980).

Treatment after the acute phase

Since the original demonstration by Pasamanick *et al.* (1964), many controlled trials have shown the effectiveness of continued oral and depot therapy in preventing relapse (see Hirsch *et al.* 1973; Leff and Wing 1971). It has also become clear that some chronic schizophrenics do not respond even to long-term medication, and that others remain well without drugs. Unfortunately there has been no success in predicting which patients benefit from such treatment. Since long-continued antipsychotic medication may lead to irreversible dyskinesias (see p. 647), it is important to know how long such treatment needs to be given. There is still no clear answer to this question, but Hogarty and Ulrich (1977) reported that, over a three-year period, maintenance antipsychotic medication was two and a half to three times better than the placebo in preventing relapse. There is a widespread clinical impression that, in preventing relapses of schizophrenia, depot injections are more successful than continued oral medication. However, Schooler *et al.* (1980) found that depot injections offered no such advantage. According to Davis *et al.* (1980), in the long-term management of schizophrenia there is no difference in the usefulness of the various antipsychotic drugs available.

Interaction of maintenance treatment and social treatment

Since both medication and social casework appear effective in the management of schizophrenia, it is reasonable to enquire whether the two kinds of treatment interact. Hogarty *et al.* (1974) studied the use of 'major role therapy' (i.e. social case-work) with and without drugs. Given alone, social casework had only a small effect in reducing relapse rate; combined with medication, it had a larger effect. This difference may have occurred partly because patients took their drugs more regularly when seeing social workers, but such an effect seems unlikely to be the whole explanation. In a study of the effect of adding day hospital treatment to continued medication, Linn *et al.* (1979) found that day care conferred extra benefit on patients when it was of low intensity and based on occupational therapy, but not when it included more active treatments such as group therapy.

Antidepressants and lithium

As already explained, symptoms of depression occur commonly in the syndrome of schizophrenia (p. 274). Since it is not easy to distinguish between depressive symptoms and apathy, it is difficult to assess the effects of antidepressant medication in chronic schizophrenia. As yet there has been no satisfactory clinical trial.

The value of lithium in treating schizophrenia is uncertain. Occasional beneficial effects could be due to the treatment of schizoaffective cases. There is some evidence that lithium has a therapeutic action in this diagnostic group. In two small trials, Brockington *et al.* (1978) found that chlorpromazine was more effective than lithium for schizodepressive patients (that is, those satisfying criteria for both depressive disorder and schizophrenia). However, lithium and chlorpromazine were equally effective for patients with 'schizomania'. [For a review of the evidence on the treatment of affective symptoms in schizophrenia see Hirsch (1986*a*).]

ECT

In the treatment of schizophrenia, the traditional indications for ECT are catatonic stupor and severe depressive symptoms accompanying schizophrenia. The effects of ECT are often rapid and striking in both these conditions. Nowadays ECT is seldom used for other presentations of schizophrenia, although there is some evidence that it is rapidly effective in acute episodes (Taylor and Fleminger 1980).

Psychotherapy

In the past, individual psychotherapy was used quite commonly for schizophrenia, though much more in the United States than in Britain. Evidence from clinical trials is scanty but it does not support the use of psychotherapy. An investigation by May (1968) found that psychotherapy had little benefit, but the treatment was short and provided by relatively inexperienced psychiatrists. Apart from the lack of convincing evidence that intensive individual psychotherapy is effective in schizophrenia, there may be some danger of the treatment causing over-stimulation and consequent relapse (see Mosher and Keith 1980).

Many kinds of group therapy have been used to treat schizophrenia. When the results have been compared with routine hospital treatment, the general finding in the better controlled evaluations has been that group therapy is of little benefit in the acute stage of the disorder (see Mosher and Keith 1980). Indeed clinical experience strongly suggests that small group therapy is likely to make some acutely ill patients worse, and to confer little or no benefit after the acute stage.

Work with relatives

There have been few controlled studies of intensive family therapy in the treatment of schizophrenia. They were all concerned with short interventions for acute illness, and all found slight benefits from the treatment (see Mosher and Keith 1980).

The work on emotional expression reviewed above (see p. 312) suggests that counselling should be beneficial to families, especially when directed to reducing specific problems. It also seems sensible to offer advice to families about practical matters, although it would be difficult to evaluate the effectiveness of such advice.

Behavioural treatment

The results of behavioural treatment for schizophrenia have not been fully evaluated. Most of the reported results could be due to receiving increased attention. **Individual methods** include social skills training (see Wallace *et al.* 1980; Liberman *et al.* 1986).

Token economies also use positive and negative reinforcement to alter behaviour but they are applied to all the patients in a ward rather than to a single patient. Rewards may be praise and interest, but it is usual to give tokens that can be used to purchase goods or privileges (hence the name of the treatment). Such systems can change the behaviour of regressed chronic patients. However, a clinical trial showed that the effects are due mainly to the graded and systematic approach rather than to the use of reinforcers (Baker *et al.* 1974). Unfortunately many patients relapse when they move from a token economy to a new environment in which there is not the same system of rewards. For this reason, and because there are potential ethical problems about the use of reward systems of this kind, the methods are not used widely.

Assessment

Assessment begins with differential diagnosis, which is particularly concerned with the exclusion of organic disorder (especially a drug-induced state), affective disorder, and personality disorder. In practice, the main difficulty is often to elicit all the symptoms from a withdrawn or suspicious patient. This procedure may require several psychiatric interviews as well as careful observations by the nursing staff. The differential diagnosis from affective disorder can be particularly difficult and may require prolonged observation for discriminating symptoms of schizophrenia.

While the psychiatric diagnosis is being confirmed, a social assesment should be carried out. This includes assessment of the patient's previous personality, work record, accommodation and leisure pursuits, and especially the attitudes to the patient of relatives and any close friends. The doctor or social worker can proceed with this enquiry while an evaluation of the patient's social functioning in the ward is made by nurses and occupational therapists.

Psychological testing

In the assessment of schizophrenia, formal psychological testing seldom adds much to clinical observation. In the past, projective tests such as the Rorschach and Thematic Apperception Tests were used to examine thought processes, but they are unreliable and lack validity. More recent tests using the repertory grid and sorting procedures are more reliable but rarely help much if the mental state has been carefully examined. Standardized tests of personality are less useful than a thorough history from an informant who knows the patient well.

While there is little place for psychometric assessment in diagnosing schizophrenia, the clinical psychologist has a valuable role in making quantitative assessments of specific abnormalities of behaviour as a basis for planning and evaluating social rehabilitation.

Management

Success in management depends on establishing a good relationship with the patient so that his co-operation is enlisted. It is often difficult to establish a working relationship with chronic patients who are paranoid or emotionally unresponsive, but with skill and patience progress can usually be made. It is important to make plans that are realistic, especially for the more handicapped patient. Over-enthusiastic schemes of rehabilitation may increase the patient's symptoms and (if he lives in the community) place unacceptable burdens on relatives.

The acute illness

Treatment in hospital is usually needed both for first episodes of schizophrenia and for acute relapses. Hospital admission allows a thorough assessment, and provides a secure environment for the patient. It also gives a period of relief to the family, who have often experienced considerable distress during the period of prodromal symptoms of the illness (see Johnstone *et al.* 1986).

There are important advantages in a few days of observation without drugs, although some acutely disturbed patients may require immediate treatment. A drug-free period allows thorough assessment of the patient's mental state and behaviour as described above. It also shows whether mental abnormalities and disturbed behaviour are likely to improve simply with change of environment. If they do not improve, an antipsychotic drug should be prescribed, the dose depending on the severity of the symptoms. There is a wide choice of drugs (see p. 644) but the clinician should become thoroughly familiar with a few. For acutely disturbed patients, the sedating effects of chlorpromazine are valuable.For less over-active patients, trifluoperazine is an alternative with less sedative action. Although these drugs need be given only once a day for their (delayed) antipsychotic effects, it is often appropriate to prescribe them in divided doses. In this way their immediate sedating effects can operate at the times when the patient is most disturbed. The timing and dosage should be reviewed frequently with the ward staff, and adjusted to changes in the patient's condition. At this stage, oral medication is usually given, although occasional intramuscular doses may be needed for acutely disturbed behaviour. If there are doubts whether the patient is swallowing tablets, the drug can be given as a syrup. Other phenothiazines are equally effective, but have no particular advantages unless there are problems with individual sensitivities or side-effects (see p. 644 for further advice about the use of antipsychotic drugs).

After the first few days, medication is continued at a constant daily amount for several weeks, with a gradual transfer to twice daily dosage or a single dose at night. Antiparkinsonian drugs should be prescribed if parkinsonian side-effects are troublesome, but they need not be given routinely. Symptoms of excitement, restlessness, irritability, and insomnia can be expected to improve within days. Affective symptoms, delusions, and hallucinations respond more slowly, often persisting for six to eight weeks. Lack of improvement at this stage suggests inadequate dosage or failure to take the drugs prescribed, but a few cases resist all efforts at treatment. Once there is undoubted evidence of sustained improvement, dosage can be reduced cautiously while careful watch is kept for any return of symptoms. This reduced dose is continued for a further period (see below).

During the early days of treatment, the doctor will have taken histories from the patient, relatives, and other informants, so as to build up a picture of the patient's previous personality, premorbid adjustment and social circumstances, and any precipitants of illness. By the time symptomatic improvement has taken place, the doctor should have formulated a provisional plan for continuing care. Although it is difficult to predict the long-term prognosis at this stage, a judgement has to be made about the likely immediate outcome. This judgement is based on the degree and speed of response to treatment, and on the factors listed in Table 9.8. The aim is to decide how much aftercare patients will require, and to make realistic plans accordingly.

After-care of 'good prognosis' patients

After a first episode of schizophrenia, patients judged to have a good immediate prognosis have two principal needs for treatment following discharge from hospital. The first is to take medication in reducing dosage for at least three months. The second is to be given advice about avoiding obviously stressful events. The patient should be seen regularly as an outpatient until a few months after medication has been stopped and symptoms have ceased. Thereafter, a cautiously optimistic prognosis can be given, but the patient and his family should be warned to consult a doctor immediately if there is any suggestion of the condition returning.

The after-care of the 'poor prognosis' patients without major social handicaps

When it is judged that further relapse is likely, continuing care will be required, and this will probably include prophylactic medication. It is often better to give such medication by injection (for example, as fluphenazine or flupenthixol decanoate), since some patients fail to take oral medication regularly over long periods. The dosage, which should be the minimum required to suppress symptoms, can be determined by cautiously varying its size and frequency while observing the patient's clinical state (see p. 650). Some patients show little response to continued antipsychotic medication even in high doses. For such patients medication should not be given continuously, but only for acute relapses (for which it generally remains active).

It is uncertain how long such prophylactic treatment with neuroleptics should be continued. The treatment should be reviewed at least once a year, taking into account side-effects as well as symptoms. Medication should be withdrawn if tardive dyskinesia occurs (see p. 647), otherwise a balance has to be struck between benefits and adverse effects.

Whether maintenance drug therapy is given or not, the patient should be seen regularly to review his mental state and social adjustment. When necessary he should be advised to avoid stressful situations and helped to reduce the amount of time spent with the family if it is emotionally arousing. Help may also be required in finding a suitable occupation. Community psychiatric nurses can undertake most treatment of this kind, and social workers can help with those measures not involving the administration of medication. The most difficult problem in continuing management is likely to be the patient's tendency to withdraw from treatment.

Patients with chronic handicap

When patients have poor social adjustment and behavioural defects characteristic of chronic schizophrenia, they require more elaborate after-care. They should be identified as early as possible so that long-term plans can be made for both rehabilitation in hospital and resettlement outside hospital. Maintenance drug therapy plays an important part, but the main emphasis is on a programme of rehabilitation tailored to the needs of the individual patient.

It can be expected that the least handicapped patients will live more or less independently. For the rest, sheltered work and accommodation are likely to be needed. The essential requirements are a management plan that focuses on one or two aspects of behaviour disorder at any one time, and a consistent approach between the members of staff carrying it out.

Despite the present emphasis on treatment outside hospital, early rehabilitation in hospital has significant advantages because it allows greater consistency of approach over the whole of the patient's day. Wards organized mainly for the treatment of acute illness are often too stimulating for chronic schizophrenics in need of rehabilitation. Hence it is appropriate to set aside a special area for rehabilitation. Treatment can be based either on the principles of a therapeutic community or on those of behavioural management. These two approaches produce similar results, and are compatible with one another (Hall 1983).

Most handicapped patients are able to live outside hospital albeit in sheltered provisions. A minority require long-term care in hospital. The components of a community service for these patients are described in

Chapter 19. Success depends less on physical provisions than on well-trained staff who have tolerant attitudes and the capacity to obtain satisfaction from work that produces small improvements over long periods.

When a patient has persisting abnormalities of behaviour, particular attention needs to be given to the problems of his family. Relatives may be helped by joining a voluntary group and meeting others who have learnt to deal with similar problems. They also need to know that professional help will be provided whenever problems become too great. Advice is needed about the best ways of responding to abnormal behaviour, and about the expectations they should have of the patient. Such advice is often given best by community nurses who have experience of treating chronic schizophrenia patients in hospital as well as in the community. Social workers also have a part to play in advising and helping relatives.

The violent patient

Over-activity and disturbances of behaviour are common in schizophrenia. Though often feared by laymen, major violence towards others is uncommon. Homicide is rare. Self-mutilation is more frequent, and about one schizophrenic patient in ten dies by suicide. These self-harmful behaviours may be associated with delusions of control, persecutory delusions or auditory hallucinations (see p. 271).

General management for the potentially violent patient is the same as for any other schizophrenic, although a compulsory order is more likely to be needed. While medication is often needed to bring disturbed behaviour under immediate control, much can be done by providing a calm, reassuring, and consistent environment in which provocation is avoided. A special ward area with an adequate number of experienced staff is much better than the use of heavy medication.

Threats of violence should be taken seriously, especially if there is a history of such behaviour in the past, whether or not the patient was ill at the time. The danger usually resolves as acute symptoms are brought under control, but a few patients pose a continuing threat. The management of violence is considered further in Chapter 22.

Further reading

Bleuler, E. (1911). (English edition 1950). *Dementia praecox or the group of schizophrenias*. International University Press, New York.

Cutting, J. (1985). *The psychology of schizophrenia*. Churchill Livingstone, Edinburgh.

Hamilton, M. (1984). *Fish's schizophrenia*. Wright, Bristol.

Kraepelin, E. (1986). Dementia praecox, (pp. 426–41 of the 5th edn of *Psychiatrie*. Barlta, Leipzig). Translated in: *The clinical roots of schizophrenia concept* (ed. J. Cutting and M. Shepherd). Cambridge University Press, Cambridge.

Kraepelin, E. (1919). *Dementia praecox and paraphrenia*. Churchill Livingstone, Edinburgh.

Wing, J. K. and Brown, G. W. (1970). *Institutionalism and schizophrenia*. Cambridge University Press, Cambridge.

10 Paranoid symptoms and paranoid syndromes

Introduction

The term 'paranoid' can be applied to symptoms, syndromes, or personality-types. Paranoid symptoms are delusional beliefs which are most commonly persecutory but not always so. Paranoid syndromes are those syndromes in which paranoid symptoms form part of a characteristic constellation of symptoms, such as pathological jealousy or erotomania (described later). Paranoid personalities are those personalities in which there is excessive self-reference and undue sensitiveness to real or imaginary humiliations and rebuffs, often combined with self-importance, combativeness, and aggressiveness. The term paranoid is descriptive and not diagnostic. If we recognize a symptom or syndrome as paranoid, this is not making a diagnosis, but it is a preliminary to doing so. In this respect it is like recognizing stupor or depersonalization.

Paranoid syndromes present considerable problems of classification and diagnosis. The reasons for this can be understood by dividing them into two groups. In the first group, paranoid features occur in association with a primary mental illness, such as schizophrenia, affective disorder, or an organic mental disorder. In the second group, paranoid features occur, but no other primary disorder can be detected—the paranoid features appear to have arisen independently. In this book, following the DSMIIIR and ICD10 classifications, the term delusional disorders is applied to this second group. It is this second group that has given rise to difficulties and confusion over classification and diagnosis. For example, there has been much argument as to whether these conditions are an alternative form of schizophrenia, or a stage in the evolution of schizophrenia, or a quite separate entity. It is because these problems arise frequently in clinical practice that a whole chapter is devoted to them.

This chapter begins with definitions of the commonest paranoid symptoms, and then reviews the causes of such symptoms. Next comes a short account of paranoid personality. This is followed by discussion of primary psychiatric disorders, such as organic mental states, affective disorders, and schizophrenia, with which paranoid features are frequently associated. These primary illnesses are dealt with elsewhere in the book, but the focus here is on differentiating them from delusional disorders. These disorders are then reviewed, with particular reference to paranoia and paraphrenia. These latter terms are considered against their historical background. Next, an account is given of a number of distinctive paranoid symptoms and syndromes, some of which are fairly common and some exceedingly rare. This chapter finishes with a description of the assessment and treatment of patients with paranoid features.

Paranoid symptoms

In the introduction it was pointed out that the commonest paranoid delusions are persecutory. The term paranoid is also applied to the less common delusions of grandeur and of jealousy, and sometimes to delusions concerning love, litigation, or religion. It may seem puzzling that such varied delusions should be grouped together. The reason is that the central abnormality implied by the term paranoid is a morbid distortion of beliefs or attitudes concerning relationships between oneself and other people. If someone believes falsely or on inadequate grounds that he is being victimized, or exalted, or deceived, or loved by a famous person, then in each case he is construing the relationship between himself and other people in a morbidly distorted way.

The varieties of paranoid symptom are discussed in Chapter 1, but the main ones are outlined here for convenience. The following definitions are derived from those in the glossary to the Present State Examination (PSE; see Wing *et al.* 1974).

Ideas of reference are held by people who are unduly self-conscious. The subject cannot help feeling that people take notice of him in buses, restaurants, or other public places, and that they observe things about him that he would prefer not to be seen. He realizes that this feeling originates within himself and that he is no more noticed than other people, but he cannot help the feeling all the same, quite out of proportion to any possible cause.

Delusions of reference consist of a further elaboration of simple ideas of self-reference, and the person does not recognize that the ideas are false. The whole neighbourhood may seem to be gossiping about the subject, far beyond the bounds of possibility, or he may see references to himself on the television or in newspapers. The subject may hear someone on the radio say something connected with some topic that he has just been thinking about, or he may seem to be followed, his movements observed, and what he says tape-recorded.

Delusions of persecution. The subject believes that someone, or some organization, or some force or power is trying to harm him in some way; to damage his reputation, to cause him bodily injury, to drive him mad or to bring about his death.

The symptom may take many forms, from the direct belief that people are hunting him down, to complex and bizarre plots with every kind of science fiction elaboration.

Delusions of grandeur. The glossary of the PSE proposes a division into delusions of grandiose ability, and delusions of grandiose identity.

The subject with delusions of *grandiose ability* thinks he is chosen by some power, or by destiny, for a special mission or purpose, because of his unusual talents. He thinks he is able to read people's thoughts, or that he is particularly good at helping them, that he is much cleverer than anyone else, that he has invented machines, composed music, or solved mathematical problems beyond most people's comprehension.

The subject with delusions of *grandiose identity* believes that he is famous, rich, titled, or related to prominent people. He may believe that he is a changeling and that his real parents are royalty.

The causes of paranoid symptoms

When paranoid symptoms occur in association with a primary organic, affective, or schizophrenic illness, the main aetiological factors are those determining this primary illness. The question still arises as to why some people develop paranoid symptoms, whilst others do not. It has usually been answered in terms of premorbid personality and of factors causing social isolation.

Many writers including Kraepelin have held that paranoid symptoms are most likely to occur in patients with premorbid personalities of a paranoid type (see next section). Modern studies of so-called late onset paraphrenia have supported these views (see Chapter 16, p. 621). Thus Kay and Roth (1961) found paranoid or hypersensitive personalities in over half of their group of 99 such patients.

Freud (1911) proposed that, in predisposed people, paranoid symptoms could arise through the defence mechanisms of denial and projection. He held that a person does not consciously admit his own inadequacy and self-distrust, but projects them on to the outside world. Clinical experience generally confirms this idea. If one examines paranoid patients, one often finds an inner dissatisfaction associated with a sense of inferiority, and with self-esteem and ambition which are inconsistent with achievement.

Freud also held that paranoid symptoms could arise when denial and projection were being used as defences against unconscious homosexual tendencies. These ideas were derived from his study of Daniel Schreber, the presiding judge of the Dresden appeal court (see Freud 1911). Freud never met Schreber, but read the latter's autobiographical account of his paranoid illness (now generally accepted to be paranoid schizophrenia), together with a report by Weber, the physician in charge. Freud held that Schreber could not consciously admit his homosexuality, so the idea 'I love him' was dealt with by denial and changed by a reaction formation to 'I hate him'; this was further changed by projection into 'it is not I who hate him, but he who hates me', and this in turn became transformed to 'I am persecuted by him'. Freud believed that all paranoid delusions could be represented as contradictions of the idea 'I (a man) love him (a man)'. He went so far as to argue that delusions of jealousy could be explained in terms of unconscious homosexuality; the jealous husband was unconsciously attracted to the man whom he accused his wife of loving. In this case the formulation was 'it is not I who love him; it is she who loves him'. At one time these ideas were widely taken up, but nowadays they gain little acceptance. They are certainly not supported by clinical experience.

Kretschmer (1927) also believed that paranoid disorders were more likely in people with predisposed or 'sensitive' personalities. In such people a precipitating event could induce what Kretschmer called sensitive delusions of reference (*sensitive Beziehungswahn*), occurring as an understandable psychological reaction.

Apart from psychological factors within the patient, social isolation may also lead to the emergence of paranoid symptoms. As mentioned later in this chapter, prisoners in solitary confinement, refugees, and migrants may be prone to paranoid developments, although the evidence on this is conflicting.

Social isolation can also be produced by deafness. In 1915, Kraepelin pointed out that chronic deafness could lead to paranoid attitudes. Houston and Royse (1954) found an association between deafness and paranoid schizophrenia, whilst Kay and Roth (1961) found hearing impairment in 40 per cent of late onset paraphrenics. However, it should be remembered that the great majority of deaf people do not become paranoid. [See Corbin and Eastwood (1986) for a review of the association of deafness and paranoid disorders in the elderly.]

Paranoid personality disorder

The concept of personality disorder was discussed in Chapter 5, and paranoid personality disorder was briefly described there. It is characterized by extensive sensitivity to setbacks and rebuffs, suspiciousness and a tendency to misconstrue the actions of others as hostile or contemptuous, and a combative and inappropriate sense of personal rights. It is implied in the DSMIIIR and ICD10 (draft) definitions that paranoid personality embraces a wide range of types. At one extreme is the painfully shy, timid youth who shrinks from social encounters and thinks everyone disapproves of him. At the other is the assertive and challenging man who flares up at the least provocation. Many grades lie between these two extremes.

Because of the implications for treatment, it is important to distinguish these paranoid personalities from the paranoid syndromes to be described later. The distinction can be very difficult to make. Sometimes the one shades into the other in the course of a single life history, as exemplified by the life of the philosopher Jean Jaques Rousseau. The basis for making the distinction is that in paranoid personalities there are no delusions but only dominant ideas, and no hallucinations. Separating paranoid ideas from delusions calls for considerable skill. The criteria for doing so are given in Chapter 1.

Primary psychiatric disorders with paranoid features

As mentioned in the introduction to this chapter, paranoid features occur in association with primary mental disorders. This association occurs commonly in clinical practice. As the primary disorders are described at length in other chapters, they are mentioned only briefly here.

Organic mental states

Paranoid symptoms are common in delirium. Impaired grasp of what is going on around the patient may give rise to apprehension and misinterpretation, and so to suspicion. Delusions may then emerge which are usually transient and disorganized; they may lead to disturbed behaviour, such as querulousness or aggression. Examples are drug-induced states. Similarly, paranoid delusions may occur in dementia, arising from any cause, including trauma, degenerations, infections, metabolic and endocrine disorders (see Chapter 11).

In clinical practice it is important to remember that in elderly patients with dementia, paranoid delusions may appear before any intellectual deterioration is detectable.

Affective disorders

Paranoid delusions not uncommonly occur in patients with severe depressive illness. The latter is often characterized by guilt and retardation, and by 'biological' features such as loss of appetite and weight, sleep disturbance, and reduced sex drive. These disorders are commoner in middle or later life. In depressive illness, the patient typically accepts the supposed activities of the persecutors as justified by his own guilt or wickedness, but in schizophrenia he often resents them bitterly. It is sometimes difficult to determine whether the paranoid features are secondary to depressive illness, or whether depressed mood is secondary to paranoid symptoms arising from another cause. Primary depression is likely if the mood changes have occurred earlier and are of greater intensity than the paranoid features. The distinction is important, as it may indicate whether antidepressant medication or phenothiazines should be prescribed.

Paranoid delusions also occur in manic patients. Often the delusions are grandiose rather than persecutory—the patient claiming to be extremely wealthy or of exalted rank or importance.

Paranoid schizophrenia

Paranoid schizophrenia has been described in Chapter 9. In contrast with the hebephrenic and catatonic forms of schizophrenia, the paranoid form usually begins later in life—in the thirties rather than in the twenties. The dominant feature of paranoid schizophrenia is delusions that are relatively stable over time. The delusions are frequently of persecution, but may also be of jealousy, exalted birth, Messianic mission, or bodily change. They may be accompanied by hallucinatory voices which sometimes but not invariably have a persecutory or grandiose content.

It is important to consider the differential diagnosis of paranoid schizophrenia from other paranoid conditions. The criteria for the diagnosis of schizophrenia in DSMIIIR and the draft of ICD10 were described on p. 282. In cases of doubt, the diagnosis of schizophrenia rather than delusional disorder is suggested if the paranoid delusions are particularly odd in content (often referred to by psychiatrists as bizarre delusions). If the delusions are grotesque, then there may be no room for doubt. For example, a middle-aged woman became convinced that a Cabinet Minister was taking a special interest in her, and was promoting her well-being. She believed that he was the pilot of an aeroplane that flew over her house shortly after noon each day. She therefore waited in her garden each day, and threw a large red beach-ball into the sky when the plane flew over. She maintained that the pilot always acknowledged this action by 'waggling the wings' of the plane. When the delusions are less extreme than this, a judgement as to how bizarre they are must be arbitrary.

There are two other diagnostic points. First, in schizophrenia delusions are more likely to be fragmented and multiple, rather than systematized and unitary. Secondly, paranoid schizophrenics often have hallucinations that seem to be totally unrelated to their delusions; whereas patients with paranoid conditions other than schizophrenia frequently have no hallucinations, or else hallucinations that are closely connected with their delusions. These criteria would help to support the diagnosis of paranoid schizophrenia, but would not in themselves justify a confident diagnosis.

Schizophrenia-like syndromes

Paranoid syndromes are common in several schizophrenia-like syndromes discussed in Chapter 9. These include the DSMIIIR categories of **brief reactive psychosis**, and **schizophreniform disorder**; and the draft ICD10 categories grouped under the heading **acute** or **transient psychotic disorders**.

Delusional disorders

DSMIIIR uses '**delusional (paranoid) disorder**' for a disorder with 'persistent, non-bizarre delusion that is not due to any other mental disorder'. Draft ICD10 has a rather similar category of **persistent delusional disorders**.

Historical background: paranoia and paraphrenia

These two terms have played a prominent part in psychiatric thought. Much can be learnt from reviewing the conceptual difficulties associated with these terms. For this reason, their history will be traced in some detail, starting with paranoia.

The term **paranoia**, from which the modern adjective paranoid is derived, has a long and chequered history (see Bynum 1983). It has probably given rise to more controversy and confusion of thought than any other term used in psychiatry. A comprehensive review of the large literature, which is mostly German, has been provided by Lewis (1970).

The term paranoia came into special prominence in the last quarter of the nineteenth century, but its origins are much older. The word paranoia is derived from the Greek *para* (beside) and *nous* (mind). It was used in ancient Greek literature to mean 'out of mind', that is, of unsound mind or insane. This broad usage was revived in the eighteenth century. However, in the mid-nineteenth century, German psychiatrists became interested in conditions that were particularly characterized by delusions of persecution and grandeur. The German term '*verrücktheit*' was often applied to these conditions, but eventually was superseded by paranoia. There were many different conceptions of these disorders. The main issues can be summarized as follows:

1. Did these conditions constitute a primary disorder, or were they secondary to a mood disorder or other disorder?
2. Did they persist unchanged for many years, or were they a stage in an illness which later manifested deterioration of intellect and personality?
3. Did they sometimes occur in the absence of hallucinations, or were hallucinations an invariable accompaniment?
4. Were there forms with good prognosis?

As early as 1863 Kahlbaum raised these issues, when he classified paranoia as an independent or primary delusional condition, which would remain unchanged over the years.

Kraepelin had a strong influence on the conceptual history of paranoia, although he was never comfortable with the term, and his views changed strikingly over the years (see Kendler and Tsuang 1981). In 1896 he used the term only for incurable, chronic, and systematized delusions without severe personality disorder. In the sixth edition of his textbook (see Kraepelin 1904) he wrote:

The delusions in dementia praecox are extremely fantastic, changing beyond all reason, with an absence of system and a failure to harmonize them with events of their past life; while in paranoia the delusions are largely confined to morbid interpretations of real events, are woven together into a coherent whole, gradually becoming extended to include even events of recent date, and contradictions and objections are apprehended and explained (p. 199).

In later descriptions Kraepelin (1912, 1919) used the distinction made by Jaspers (1913) between personality development and disease process. He proposed paranoia as an example of the former, in contrast to the disease process of dementia praecox. In his final account, Kraepelin (1919) developed these ideas by distinguishing between dementia praecox, paranoia, and a third paranoid psychosis, paraphrenia. Dementia praecox has an early onset and a poor outcome ending in mental deterioration, and was fundamentally a disturbance of affect and volition. Paranoia was restricted to patients with the late onset of completely systematized delusions, and a prolonged course usually without recovery but not inevitably deteriorating. An important point was that the patients did not have hallucinations. Kraepelin regarded paraphrenia as lying between dementia praecox and paranoia; in paraphrenia, the patient had unremitting systematized delusions, but did not progress to dementia. The main difference from paranoia was that the patient with paraphrenia had hallucinations.

Bleuler's concept of the paranoid form of dementia praecox (which he later called paranoid schizophrenia) was broader than Kraepelin's (Bleuler 1906, 1911). Thus Bleuler did not regard paraphrenia as a separate condition, but as part of dementia praecox. On the other hand he accepted Kraepelin's view of paranoia as a separate entity, but he differed from Kraepelin in maintaining that hallucinations could occur in many cases. Bleuler was particularly interested in the psychological development of paranoia; at the same time he left open the question of whether paranoia had a somatic pathology.

From this time, two main themes were prominent in the history of paranoia. The first theme was that paranoia was distinct from schizophrenia, and mainly psychogenic in origin. The second theme was that paranoia was part of schizophrenia.

Two celebrated studies of individual cases supported the first theme, the psychogenic origins of paranoid delusions. Gaupp (1914) made an intensive study of the diaries and mental state of the mass murderer Wagner who murdered his wife, four children, and eight other people, as part of a careful plan to revenge himself on his supposed enemies. Gaupp concluded that Wagner suffered from paranoia in the sense described by Kraepelin, as described above. At the same time, he believed that Wagner's first recognizable delusion developed as a psychogenic reaction. The second study, mentioned earlier in the chapter, was Freud's analysis of the memoirs of Schreber. Freud called this a case of paranoia, although Schreber's illness conformed much more to the clinical picture of schizophrenia than to any of the prevailing notions of paranoia.

The most detailed argument for psychogenesis was put forward by Kretschmer (1927) in his monograph, *Der sensitive Beziehungswahn*. Kretschmer believed that paranoia should not be regarded as a disease, but as a psychogenic reaction occurring in people with particularly sensitive personalities. Many of Kretschmer's cases would nowadays be classified as suffering from schizophrenia.

In 1931, Kolle put forward evidence for the second theme, that paranoia is part of schizophrenia. He analysed a series of 66 patients, with so-called paranoia, including those diagnosed by Kraepelin in his Munich clinic. For several reasons, both symptomatic and genetic, Kolle came to the conclusion that so-called paranoia was really a mild form of schizophrenia. Considerably less has been written about **paraphrenia**. However, it is interesting that Mayer (1921), following up Kraepelin's series of 78 paraphrenic patients, found that 50 of them had become schizophrenic. He found no difference in original clinical presentation between those who became schizophrenic and those who did not. Since then paraphrenia has usually been regarded as late onset schizophrenia of good prognosis. Kay and Roth (1961) used the term 'late paraphrenia' to denote paranoid conditions in the elderly which were not due to primary organic or affective illnesses. These authors found that a large majority of their 99 patients had the characteristic features of schizophrenia (see Chapter 10).

Modern classifications do not use separate categories for early and late onset schizophrenia.

Modern usage: DSMIIIR and ICD10

In DSMIIIR, Delusional (paranoid) disorder replaces the traditional category of paranoia (see Munro 1987). The criteria require 'non-bizarre delusions of at least one month's duration' and that 'auditory or visual hallucinations, if present, are not prominent'. There are five specific sub-types : persecutory, jealous, erotomanic, somatic, and grandiose. The somatic form covers the disorder sometimes referred to as Monosymptomatic hypochondriacal psychosis (Munro 1980). Delusional disorder appears to be rare, to occur predominantly in mid-life and to have a prolonged course (see Kendler and Tsuang 1981; Kendler 1982). The classification of paranoid disorders in DSMIII has been reviewed by Kendler (1987).

ICD10 (draft) gives a similar definition for the principal category of a persistent delusion disorder which is termed Delusional disorder (paranoia). However, the symptoms must have been present for at least six months rather than the one month required in DSMIIIR and the subtypes are not specified.

The essence of the modern concept of delusional disorder is that of a permanent and unshakeable delusional system, developing insidiously in a person in middle or late life. This delusional system is encapsulated, and there is no impairment of other mental functions. The patient can often go on working, and his social life may sometimes be maintained fairly well. In clinical practice, cases conforming strictly to the definitions are rare. The term paraphrenia does not appear in DSMIIIR or ICD10 (draft). The term is little used in modern psychiatric practice. The authors of this book do not recommend its use because it appears to denote a condition which can best be regarded as paranoid schizophrenia of late onset and good prognosis.

Special paranoid conditions

Certain paranoid conditions are recognizable by their distinctive features. They can be divided into two groups—those with special symptoms and those occurring in special situations. The special symptoms include jealous, erotic, and querulant delusions and also the delusions associated with the names of Capgras and Fregoli. The special situations include intimate relationships (*folie à deux*), migration, and imprisonment. Many of these symptoms have been of particular interest to French psychiatrists (see

Pichot 1982, 1984). None, apart from 'Induced psychosis', is recognized as a separate category in DSMIIIR or the draft of ICD10.

Among the conditions with special symptoms, pathological jealousy will be described first and in the greatest detail because of its importance in clinical practice. It is probably the most common, and is often dangerous.

Pathological jealousy

In pathological (or morbid) jealousy, the essential feature is an abnormal belief that the marital parter is being unfaithful. The condition is called pathological because the belief, which may be a delusion or an overvalued idea, is held on inadequate grounds and is unaffected by rational argument. Pathological jealousy has been reviewed by Shepherd (1961), and by Mullen and Maack (1985).

The belief is often accompanied by strong emotions and characteristic behaviour, but these do not in themselves constitute pathological jealousy. A man who finds his wife in bed with a lover may experience extreme jealousy and may behave in an uncontrolled way, but this should not be called pathological jealousy. The term should only be used when the jealousy is based on unsound evidence and reasoning.

Pathological jealousy has often been described in the literature, generally in reports of one or two cases. Various names have been given to it, including sexual jealousy, erotic jealousy, morbid jealousy, psychotic jealousy, and the Othello syndrome. The main sources of information are surveys of patients with pathological jealousy carried out by Shepherd (1961), Langfeldt (1961), Vauhkonen (1968), and Mullen and Maack (1985). Shepherd examined hospital case notes of 81 patients in London, and Langfeldt did the same for 66 patients in Norway; Vauhkonen made an interview study of 55 patients in Finland; and Mullen and Maack examined the hospital notes of 138 patients.

The frequency of pathological jealousy in the general population is unknown. However, the condition is not uncommon in psychiatric practice and most full-time clinicians probably see one or two cases a year. They merit careful attention, not only because of the great distress they cause within marriages and families, but also because they may be highly dangerous.

All the evidence suggests that pathological jealousy is commoner in men than women. In the three surveys mentioned above, the male to female ratios were: 3.76:1 (Shepherd); 1.46:1 (Langfeldt): and 2.05:1 (Vauhkonen).

Clinical features

As indicated above, the main feature is an abnormal belief in the partner's infidelity. This may be accompanied by other abnormal beliefs; for example, that the spouse is plotting against the patient, trying to poison him, taking away his sexual capacitites, or infecting him with venereal disease.

The mood of the pathologically jealous patient may vary with the underlying disorder, but often it is a mixture of misery, apprehension, irritability, and anger.

The behaviour of the patient is often characteristic. Commonly there is intensive seeking for evidence of the partner's infidelity; for example, by searching in diaries and correspondence, and by examining bed-linen and underwear for signs of sexual secretions. The patient may follow the spouse about, or engage a private detective to spy on her. Typically the jealous person cross-questions the spouse incessantly. This may lead to violent quarrelling and paroxysms of rage in the patient. Sometimes the partner becomes exasperated and worn out, and is finally goaded into making a false confession. If this happens, the jealousy is inflamed rather than assuaged.

An interesting feature is that the jealous person often has no idea as to who the supposed lover may be, or what kind of person he may be. Moreover, he may avoid taking steps that could produce unequivocal proof one way or the other.

The behaviour of patients with pathological jealousy may be strikingly abnormal. A successful City businessman carried a brief case that contained not only his financial documents but also a machete for use against any lover who might be detected. A carpenter installed an elaborate system of mirrors in his house so that he could watch his wife from another room. A third patient avoided waiting alongside another car at traffic lights, in case his wife in the passenger seat might surreptitiously make an assignation with the other driver.

Aetiology

In the surveys described above, pathological jealousy was found to be associated with a range of primary disorders. The frequencies varied, depending on the population studied and the diagnostic scheme used. For example, paranoid schizophrenia (or paranoia or paraphrenia) was reported in 17–44 per cent of patients; depressive illness in 3–16 per cent; neurosis and personality disorder in 38–57 per cent; alcoholism in 5–7 per cent; and organic disorders in 6–20 per cent. Primary organic causes include exogenous substances such as amphetamine and cocaine, but more commonly a wide range of brain disorders, including infections, neoplasms, metabolic and endocrine disorders, and degenerative conditions.

The role of personality in the genesis of pathological jealousy should be stressed. It is often found that the patient has a pervasive sense of his own inadequacy. There is a discrepancy between his ambitions and his attainments. Such a personality is particularly vulnerable to anything that may threaten this sense of inadequacy, such as loss of status or advancing age. In the face of such threats, the person may project the blame on to others, and this may take the form of jealous accusations of infidelity. As mentioned earlier, Freud believed that unconscious homosexual urges played a part in all jealousy, particularly the delusional kind. He held that this could occur when such urges were dealt with by repression, denial, and reaction formation. However, none of the three surveys mentioned above found any association between homosexuality and pathological jealousy.

Many writers have held that pathological jealousy may be induced by the onset of erectile difficulties in men or sexual dysfunction in women. In their surveys, Langfeldt and Shepherd found little or no evidence of such associations. Vauhkonen however reported sexual difficulties in over half the men and women in his series, but his sample was drawn partly from a marriage guidance clinic.

The prognosis depends on a number of factors, including the nature of any underlying psychiatric disorder, and the patient's premorbid personality. There is little statistical evidence on prognosis. Langfeldt followed up 27 of his patients after 17 years, and found that over half of them still had persistent or recurrent jealousy. This confirms a general clinical impression that the prognosis is often poor.

Risk of violence

Although there is no direct statistical evidence of the risks of violence in cases of pathological jealousy, there is no doubt that it can be highly dangerous. Mowat (1966) made a survey of homicidal patients admitted to Broadmoor hospital over several years, and found pathological jealousy amongst 12 per cent of men and 15 per cent of women. In Shepherd's series of 81 patients with pathological jealousy, three had shown homicidal tendencies. In addition to homicide, the risk of physical injury inflicted by jealous patients is undoubtedly considerable. In Mullen and Maack's (1985) series, few of the 138 patients had received criminal convictions but a quarter had threatened to kill or injure their partner and 56 per cent of men and 43 per cent of women had been violent to or threatened the supposed rival.

Assessment

The assessment of a patient with pathological jealousy should be painstaking and thorough. Full psychiatric assessment of the patient is essential and the spouse should be seen alone at first, and with the patient afterwards.

The spouse may give a much more detailed account of the patient's morbid beliefs and actions than can be elicited from the patient. The doctor should try to find out tactfully how firmly the patient believes in the partner's infidelity, how much resentment he feels, and whether he has contemplated any vengeful action. What factors provoke outbursts of resentment, accusation, and cross-questioning? How does the partner respond to such outbursts by the patient? How does the patient respond in turn to the partner's behaviour? Has there been any violence so far? It so, how was it inflicted? Has there been any serious injury?

In addition to these enquiries, the doctor should take a detailed marital and sexual history from both partners. It is also important to diagnose any underlying psychiatric disorder, as this will have implications for treatment.

Treatment

The treatment of pathological jealousy is often difficult, because the jealous person may regard it as obtrusive, and may show little compliance. Adequate treatment of any underlying disorder such as schizophrenia or affective illness is a first requisite. In cases where the underlying diagnosis is uncertain, a phenothiazine such as chlorpromazine may be beneficial.

Psychotherapy may be given to patients with neurotic or personality disorders. The aims may be to reduce tensions by allowing the patient (and spouse) to ventilate feelings. Behavioural methods have also been advocated (Cobb and Marks 1979). These include encouraging the partner to produce behaviour that reduces jealousy, for example by counter-aggression or refusal to argue, depending on the individual case.

If there is no response to out-patient treatment, or if the risk of violence is high, in-patient care may be necessary. Not uncommonly, however, the patient appears to improve as an in-patient, only to relapse on discharge.

If there appears to be a risk of violence, the doctor should warn the spouse. In some cases, the safest procedure is to advise separation. This is embodied in an old axiom that the best treatment for pathological jealousy is geographical.

Erotic delusions (De Clérambault's syndrome)

De Clérambault (1921; see also 1987) proposed that a distinction should be made between paranoid delusions and delusions of passion. The latter differed in their pathogenesis and in being accompanied by excitement. They also had a sense of purpose: 'patients in this category whether they display erotomania, litigious behaviour, or morbid jealousy all have a precise aim in view from the onset of the illness, which brings the will into play from the beginning. This constitutes a distinguishing feature of the illness'. This distinction is of historical interest only, as it is not made nowadays. However, the syndrome of erotomania is still known as De Clérambault's syndrome. It is exceedingly rare (see Enoch and Trethowan 1979 for futher information). Although erotomania is usually a disorder of women, Taylor *et al.* (1983) have reported four cases in a series of 112 men charged with violent offences.

In erotomania, the subject, usually a single woman, believes that an exalted person is in love with her. The supposed lover is usually inaccessible, being already married, of much higher social status, or famous as an entertainer or public figure. According to De Clérambault, the infatuated woman believes that it is the 'object' who first fell in love with her, that he is the more in love, or even the only one who is in love. She believes that she has been specially chosen by this man of high standing, and that it was not she who had made the initial advances. She derives satisfaction and pride from this belief. She is convinced that the 'object' cannot be happy or a complete person without her.

The patient often believes that the 'object' is unable to reveal his love for various reasons, that he is withheld from her, has difficulties in approaching her, has indirect conversations with her, and has to behave in a paradoxical and contradictory way. The woman may be a considerable nuisance to the 'object' who may complain to the police and the courts. Sometimes the patient's delusion remains unshakeable, and she invents explanations for the 'object's' paradoxical behaviour. She may be extremely tenacious and impervious to reality. Other patients turn from a delusion of love to a delusion of persecution. They become abusive, and make public complaints about the 'object'. This was described by De Clérambault as two phases, hope followed by resentment.

Probably most patients with erotic delusions are suffering from paranoid schizophrenia. Sometimes there is insufficient evidence to make a final diagnosis at the time, and they can be classified as erotomanic delusional disorder in DSMIIIR.

Querulant delusions and reformist delusions

Querulant delusions were the subject of a special study by Krafft-Ebing in 1888. Patients with this kind of delusion indulge in a series of complaints and claims lodged against the authorities. Closely related to querulant patients are paranoid litigants who undertake a succession of lawsuits; they become involved in numerous court hearings, in which they may become passionately angry and make threats against the magistrates. Baruk (1959) described 'reformist delusions', which are centred on religious, philosophical, or political themes. People with these delusions constantly criticize society, and sometimes embark on elaborate courses of action. Their behaviour may be violent, particularly when the delusions are political. Some political assassins fall within this group. It is extremely important that this diagnosis is made on clear psychiatric grounds rather than political grounds (see Bloch and Chodoff 1981).

Capgras delusion

Although there had been previous case reports, the condition now known as Capgras syndrome was well described by Capgras and Reboul-Lachaux in 1923 (see Serieux and Capgras 1987). They called it *l'illusion des sosies* (illusion of doubles). Strictly speaking it is not a syndrome but a single symptom, and it is better termed the *delusion* (rather than illusion) of doubles. The patient believes that a person closely related to him has been replaced by a double. He accepts that the misidentified person has a great resemblance to the familiar person, but still believes they are different people. It is an extremely rare condition. It is more common in women than in men and is usually associated with schizophrenia or affective disorder. A history of depersonalization, derealization or *déjà vu* is common. The misidentified person is usually the patient's spouse or another relative. It has been said that in most cases there is strong evidence of an organic component as shown by the clinical features, psychological testing, and radiological studies of the brain (see Christodoulou 1977). However, a review of 133 published cases concluded that more than a half were schizophrenic; 31 cases had proven physical illness (Berson 1983).

Fregoli delusion

This is usually referred to as the Fregoli syndrome, and derives its name from an actor called Fregoli who had remarkable skill in changing his facial appearance. The condition is even rarer than the Capgras delusion. It was originally described by Courbon and Fail in 1927. The patient identifies a familiar person (usually someone he believes to be his persecutor) in various other people he encounters. He maintains that, although there is no physical resemblance between the familiar person and the others, nevertheless they are psychologically identical. This symptom is usually associated with schizophrenia. Here again the clinical features, psychological testing, and radiological examination of the brain have been said to suggest an organic component in the aetiology (Christodoulou 1976).

Paranoid conditions occurring in special situations

An account will now be given of these conditions, beginning with induced psychosis.

Induced psychosis (*folie à deux*)

An induced psychosis is a paranoid delusional system which appears to have developed in a person as a result of a close relationship with another person who already has an established and similar delusional system. The delusions are nearly always persecutory. In DSMIIIR these cases are classified as Induced psychotic disorder; in the draft of ICD10, as Induced delusional disorder (*folie à deux*). The frequency of induced psychosis is not known, but it is rare. Sometimes more than two people are involved, but this is exceedingly rare.

The condition has occasionally been described in two people who are not family relations, but 90 per cent or more of reported cases are members of the same family. Usually there is a dominant partner with fixed delusions who appears to induce similar delusions in a dependent or suggestible partner, sometimes after initial resistance. Generally the two have lived together for a long time in close intimacy, often in isolation from the outside world. Once established, the condition runs a chronic course.

Induced psychosis is more common in women than in men. Gralnick (1942) studied a series of patients with *folie à deux* and found the following combinations in order of frequency: two sisters, 40; husband and wife, 26; mother and child, 24; two brothers, 11; brother and sister, 6; father and child, 2; not related, 9.

The principles of treatment are the same as for other paranoid conditions (p. 342). It is usually necessary to advise separation of the affected people. This sometimes leads to disappearance of the delusional state but not invariably, improvement being more likely in the recipient than in the inducer. Induced psychosis is comprehensively reviewed by Enoch and Trethowan (1979).

Migration psychoses

It might be expected that people migrating to foreign countries would be likely to develop paranoid symptoms because their appearance, speech, and behaviour attract attention to them. Ødegaard (1932) found that rates for schizophrenia (including paranoid schizophrenia) were twice as high amongst Norwegian-born immigrants to the United States as amongst the general population of Norway. However, the explanation of the finding appeared to be not so much that emigration was a pathogenic experience as that pre-psychotic Norwegians were more likely than others to emigrate. Astrup and Ødegaard (1960) later found that hospital first admission rates for psychotic illness in general were significantly lower amongst people who had migrated inside their own country than amongst those who stayed where they were born. The authors suggested that migration within one's own country might be a natural step for enterprising young people, whilst migrating abroad was likely to be a much more stressful experience. To this extent they favoured the environmental hypothesis.

Studies of immigrants are difficult to interpret. If one controls for factors such as age, social class, occupational status, and ethnic group, it becomes doubtful whether there is a significant association between migration and rates of mental illness (Murphy 1977). The highest rates of mental disorder have been reported in refugees whose migration was enforced (Eitinger 1960). However, such people may have been exposed to persecution, in addition to the experiences of losing their homeland and readjusting to another country.

Prison psychosis

The evidence about imprisonment is conflicting. The work of Birnbaum (1908) suggests that isolation in prison and especially solitary confinement may lead to paranoid disorders that clear up when the prisoners are allowed to mix with others. Eitinger (1960) reported that paranoid states were not uncommon in prisoners of war. However, Faergeman (1963) concluded that such developments were rare even amongst the inmates of concentration camps.

Cultural psychoses

It appears that in some developing countries there is a high incidence of transient and acute psychotic states, in which paranoid features commonly occur. Some of these acute states may be due to organic causes, such as tropical infections. Because of the conditions of observation, information about these disorders is incomplete. [A useful review has been provided by Leff (1981).]

Paranoid symptoms: assessment and diagnosis

In the assessment of paranoid symptoms there are two stages, the recognition of the symptoms themselves and the diagnosis of the underlying condition.

Sometimes it is obvious to everyone that the patient has persecutory ideas or delusions. At other times recognition of paranoid symptoms may be exceedingly difficult. The patient may be suspicious or angry. He may offer little speech, simply staring silently at the interviewer, or he may talk fluently and convincingly about other things, whilst steering away from delusional ideas or beliefs, or denying them completely. Considerable skill may be needed to elicit the false beliefs. The psychiatrist should be tolerant and impartial. He should present himself as a detached but interested listener, who wants to understand the patient's point of view. He should show compassion and ask how he can help, but without colluding in the delusions or giving promises that cannot be fulfilled. Tact is required to avoid any argument which may cause the patient to take offence. Despite skill and tact, experienced psychiatrists may interview a patient for a long time without detecting the morbid thoughts.

If apparently false beliefs are disclosed, before concluding that they are delusions, it may be necessary to check the patient's statements against those of an informant and to ensure that the patient has had an opportunity to recognize the falsity of his beliefs. As with all apparent delusions, they must be judged against the cultural background, since the patient may hold a false belief which is generally held by his own group.

If paranoid delusions are detected, the next step is to diagnose the underlying psychiatric disorder. This means looking for the diagnostic features of organic mental states, schizophrenia and affective disorders, which are described in other chapters.

It is important to determine whether any persecutory or jealous delusions are likely to make the patient behave dangerously, by trying to kill or injure his supposed persecutor. This calls for close study of the patient's personality and the characteristics of his delusions and any associated hallucinations. Hints or threats of homicide should be taken seriously, in the same way as for suicide. The doctor should be prepared to ask tactfully about possible homicidal plans and preparations to enact them. In many ways the method of enquiry resembles the assessment of suicide risk, 'Have you ever thought of doing anything about it?' 'Have you made any plans?' 'What might prompt you to do it?'

Sometimes a patient with persecutory delusions does not know the identity of a supposed persecutor, but may still be dangerous. For example, an overseas visitor in his early twenties was seen in a psychiatric emergency clinic. Careful enquiry revealed that he believed that unidentified conspirators were trying to kill him, and that his life was in imminent danger. When asked if he had taken any steps to protect himself, he said he had made a brief trip to Brussels to buy a pistol, which he was now carrying. When asked what he might do with the gun, he said he was waiting until 'the voices' told him to shoot someone.

The assessment of dangerousness is further discussed in Chapter 22. The most reliable guideline is that the risk of violence is greatest in patients with a history of previous violence.

The treatment of patients with paranoid symptoms

In the management of patients with paranoid symptoms, both psychological and physical measures should be considered.

Psychological management is frequently difficult. The patient may be suspicious and distrustful, and may believe that psychiatric treatment is intended to harm him. Even if he is not suspicious, he is likely to regard his delusional beliefs as justified, and to see no need for treatment. Considerable tact and skill are needed to persuade patients with paranoid symptoms to accept treatment. Sometimes this can be done by offering to help non-specific symptoms, such as anxiety or insomnia. Thus a patient who believes that he is surrounded by persecutors may agree that his nerves are being strained as a result, and that this nervous strain needs treatment.

It is usually necessary at an early stage to decide whether to admit the patient for in-patient care. This may be indicated if the delusions are causing aggressive behaviour or social difficulties. In assessing such factors, it is usually best to consult other informants, and to obtain a history of the patient's behaviour in the past. If voluntary admission is refused, compulsory admission is often justified to protect the patient or other people, although this is likely to add to the patient's resentment.

During treatment the psychiatrist should strive to maintain a good relationship. He should be dependable, and should avoid provoking resentment by letting the patient down. He should show compassionate interest in the patient's beliefs, but without condemning them or colluding in them.

Patients with paranoid delusions may be helped by psychological support, encouragement, and assurance. Interpretative psychotherapy and group psychotherapy are unsuitable because suspiciousness and hypersensitivity may easily lead the patient to misinterpret what is being said.

Treatment by medication may be indicated for a primary psychiatric illness, such as schizophrenia, affective disorder, or an organic mental state. In paranoid states with no detectable primary disorder, symptoms are sometimes relieved by antipsychotic medication, such as trifluoperazine, chlorpromazine, thioridazine, or haloperidol, the choice of drug and dosage depending on the patient's age, physical condition, degree of agitation, and response to previous medication. Probably the commonest reason for failure of treatment is that patients do not take their medication because they suspect it will harm them. It may then be necessary to prescribe a long-acting preparation such as fluphenazine decanoate. In some patients the dosage can be reduced or stopped later without ill-effects, whilst in others it must be maintained for long periods of time. This can only be discovered by trial and error.

Further reading

Hirsch, S. R. and Shepherd, M. (eds) (1974). *Themes and variations in European psychiatry*. John Wright, Bristol. See following sections: Strömgren, E. Psychogenic psychoses; Gaupp, R. The scientific significance of the case of Ernst

Wagner; and The illness and death of the paranoid mass murderer schoolmaster Wagner: a case history; Kretschmer, E. The sensitive delusion of reference; Baruk, H. Delusions of passion; Ey, H., Barnard, P. and Brisset, C. Acute delusional psychoses (Bouffées délirantes).

Kendler, K. S. (1987). Paranoid disorders in DSMIII: a critical review. In *Diagnosis and classification in psychiatry* (ed. G. L. Tischler). Cambridge University Press, Cambridge.

Lewis, A. (1970). Paranoia and paranoid: a historical perspective. *Psychological Medicine* **1**, 2–12.

Shepherd, M. (1961). Morbid jealousy: some clinical and social aspects of a psychiatric symptom. *Journal of Mental Science* **107**, 687–753.

11 Organic psychiatry

The term 'organic psychiatry' is applied to a diverse group of topics that are only loosely related to one another. First and foremost, the term is used to denote psychiatric disorders that arise from demonstrable structural disease of the brain, such as brain tumours, injuries, or degenerations. Secondly, it is applied to psychiatric disorders that arise from brain dysfunction which is clearly caused by disease outside the brain, such as myxoedema. By convention, the term also includes epilepsy, which is sometimes but not always associated with psychiatric disorder, and which may or may not be associated with a structural lesion in the brain. Finally, sleep disorders are generally included in organic psychiatry.

By convention, organic psychiatry excludes mental retardation, even though the latter is sometimes associated with demonstrable brain disease. Also excluded are the various biochemical disorders, such as disturbances of catecholamine metabolism, which may be present in a number of psychiatric syndromes. These biochemical disorders are referred to elsewhere in this book as mediating mechanisms.

This chapter is divided into three main parts. The first part describes the main organic psychiatric syndromes encountered in psychiatric practice and outlines the principles of assessment and treatment of these syndromes. It is recommended that the reader give detailed attention to this part of the chapter at an early stage.

The second part reviews the specific physical conditions that give rise to the psychiatric syndromes described in part one. Inevitably these conditions are numerous and diverse. It may be advisable for the reader to cover them quickly at a first reading, and to refer to them again in detail as they are met in clinical practice.

Part three deals with epilepsy and sleep disorders. For convenience, this part also includes movement disorders even though only two—Parkinson's disease and Wilson's disease—are associated with psychiatric syndromes.

Additional information on all these topics can be found in the valuable textbook on organic psychiatry by Lishman (1987). Reference to a textbook of neurology is also recommended.

Organic psychiatric syndromes

Organic psychiatric syndromes can be subdivided on three criteria. The first criterion is whether the impairment of psychological functioning is generalized or specific. Generalized impairment affects cognition, mood, and behaviour globally. Specific impairment affects just one or two functions, such as memory, thinking, perception, or mood.

The second criterion is whether the syndrome is acute or chronic. As explained below, the clinical features of an acute syndrome may differ radically from those of a chronic syndrome.

The third criterion is whether the underlying dysfunction of the brain is generalized or focal. Generalized dysfunction of the brain may result, for example, from raised intracranial pressure, whereas focal dysfunction may arise from a tumour in the temporal lobe (though such a lesion may also cause generalized dysfunction).

In this chapter, organic psychiatric syndromes are divided into three simple groups: acute generalized psychological impairment; chronic generalized psychological impairment; and specific psychological impairment. It can be seen that these groups are based on the first two criteria above.

The first group (acute generalized psychological impairment) is *delirium*. The most important clinical feature is impairment of consciousness. The underlying brain dysfunction is generalized, and the primary cause is often outside the brain; for example, anoxia due to respiratory failure.

The second group (chronic generalized psychological impairment) is referred to as *dementia*. The main clinical feature is generalized intellectual impairment, but there are also changes in mood and behaviour. The underlying brain dysfunction is generalized. The primary cause is usually within the brain, and often a degenerative condition, such as Alzheimer's disease.

The third group (specific psychological impairment) may take the form of a specific impairment of memory, thinking, perception, or mood. It may also include personality change or a schizophrenia-like picture. In some of these conditions, but not all, focal lesions in the brain can be demonstrated.

Classification of organic psychiatric syndromes

The classification of organic disorders is broadly similar in DSMIIIR and the draft of ICD10, the main difference being that only ICD10 contains specific categories for Pick's, Creutzfeldt–Jakob's, Huntington's, and Parkinson's diseases (see Table 11.1). Both classifications adopt a modification which was originally introduced in DSMIIIR. This modification is to extend the concept of organic disorder beyond disorders with cognitive impairment to include disorders without cognitive impairment but with other psychological symptoms, notably affective symptoms, believed to be due to underlying cerebral pathology.

Table 11.1. Classification of organic mental disorders

DSMIIIR	ICD10 (draft)*
Dementias arising in the senium and presenium	*Organic, including symptomatic mental disorders*
Primary degenerative dementia of the Alzheimer type, senile onset	Dementia in Alzheimer's disease, senile onset
Primary degenerative dementia of the Alzheimer type, presenile onset	Dementia in Alzheimer's disease, presenile onset
Multi-infarct dementia	Dementia in cerebrovascular disease
	Vascular dementia of acute onset
	Multi-infarct (predominantly cortical) vascular dementia
	Multi-infarct (predominantly sub-cortical) vascular dementia
Senile dementia not otherwise specified	Dementia associated with other disorders
Presenile dementia not otherwise specified	In Pick's disease
	In Creutzfeldt–Jakob disease
	In Huntington's disease
	In Parkinson's disease
	Other
Organic mental disorders associated with Axis III physical disorders or conditions, or whose aetiology is unknown	
Delirium	Delirium other than alcoholic
Dementia	
Amnestic disorder	Organic amnestic syndrome other than alcoholic
Organic delusional disorder	Organic delusional state
Organic hallucinosis	Organic hallucinosis
Organic mood disorder	Organic depressive state
	Organic manic state
Organic anxiety disorder	Organic anxiety state
	Emotionally labile state
Organic personality disorder	Organic personality disorder
Organic mental syndrome not otherwise specified	Post-encephalitic syndrome
	Post-concussional syndrome
	Other organic disorder

* The order of listing has been altered slightly to fascilitate comparison with DSMIIIR

In both systems of classification, the three main organic mental syndromes are delirium, dementia, and amnestic syndrome. These three syndromes are described separately in the first part of this chapter. Other organic syndromes are referred to later in the chapter under various medical conditions. For example, organic mood disorder is referred to under Cushing's syndrome; organic anxiety state under hyperthyroidism and phaeochromocytoma, and organic personality syndrome under frontal lobe disorder.

Delirium

Delirium is characterized by impairment of consciousness. It is a common accompaniment of physical illness, occurring in about 5 to 15 per cent of patients in general medical or surgical wards, and about 20 to 30 per cent of patients in surgical intensive care units (Lipowski 1980a). Most cases recover quickly, so despite their frequency only a few are seen by psychiatrists.

Historical background

In the past the word 'delirium' was used in two ways. Until the early nineteenth century it was generally used to denote a disorder of thinking. Later it was used to denote an organic brain disorder with impaired consciousness and the associated symptoms (see Berrios 1981b for a review).

In 1909 Karl Bonhoeffer, professor of psychiatry in Berlin, defined delirium as the stereotyped manifestation of acute brain failure. He proposed several different 'exogenous reactions'—or distinct psychiatric syndromes resulting from the effects of agents or disorders outside the brain. These proposed reactions included delirium, hallucinosis, epileptic excitement, twilight state, and amentia (which in Bonhoeffer's scheme meant a syndrome of incoherent thinking). Since the early part of the twentieth century, the last three syndromes have been discarded; the first two have been retained, but are now applied to the effects of both cerebral and extracerebral disorders. [See Cooper (1986).]

In the past, the term delirium has been used in a variety of ways but in DSMIIIR and the draft of ICD10 it is used as a synonym for the acute organic sydrome.

The term *confusional state* has also been applied to acute organic psychiatric syndromes. This term is unsatisfactory because the word confusion properly refers to muddled thinking. The latter is an important symptom of acute organic disorders, but is not confined to them. It is unsatisfactory to name a syndrome by a symptom of low specificity.

Clinical features

The most important feature is impairment of consciousness, though it is not always the most obvious. It often varies in intensity through the day and is usually worse at night. It is recognized by slowness, poor concentration, and uncertainty about the time of day. Lishman (1987) has summarized the main features as: 'slight impairment of thinking, attending, perceiving, and remembering, in other words as mild global impairment of cognitive processes in association with reduced awareness of the environment'. Occasionally it is difficult to establish whether consciousness is impaired. After recovery, memory is poor for the period of impaired consciousness, a point which may allow retrospective diagnosis in previously doubtful cases.

Apart from impaired consciousness, the other features vary widely between different patients, and in the same patient at different times. The features are often influenced by the patient's personality; for example, ideas of persecution are more likely in a person who is habitually suspicious and touchy. Lipowski (1980*b*) distinguished two patterns of presentation: in the first, the patient is restless and oversensitive to stimuli, and has psychotic symptoms; in the second, he is lethargic and quiet, and has few psychotic symptoms.

The patient's **behaviour**, as Lipowski's distinction implies, may take the form of overactivity, irritability, and noisiness; or else of inactivity, slowness, reduced speech, and perseveration. In either case, repetitive purposeless movements are common.

Thinking is slow and muddled but often rich in content. Ideas of reference and delusions (often persecutory) are common, but are usually transient and poorly elaborated.

Visual perception may be distorted. Illusions, misinterpretations, and visual hallucinations are frequent, and may have a fantastic content. Tactile and auditory hallucinations also occur.

Changes in **mood** such as anxiety, depression, or lability are common. Some patients are frightened and agitated, whilst others are perplexed. Experiences of depersonalization and derealization are also reported by some patients. **Disorientation** in time and place is an invariable and important feature. Disturbance of **memory** affects registration, retention, and recall, and new learning is impaired. As mentioned above, on recovery there is usually amnesia for most of the illness. **Insight** is impaired. [See Cutting (1987) for a description of the clinical features of delirium.]

Aetiology

The main causes of delirium are shown in Table 11.2. The condition appears particularly in association with: increasing age; anxiety; sensory

Table 11.2. Some causes of delirium

1. Drug intoxication
   e.g. anticholinergics, anxiolytic-hypnotics, anticonvulsants, digitalis, opiates, laevo-dopa, also some industrial poisons

2. Withdrawal of alcohol and drugs
   alcohol, anxiolytic-sedatives

3. Metabolic failures
   uraemia, liver failure, respiratory failure, cardiac failure, disorders of electrolyte balance

4. Endocrine causes: hypoglycaemia

5. Systemic infection:
   e.g. exanthemata, septicaemia, pneumonia

6. Intracranial infection
   encephalitis, meningitis

7. Other intracranial causes
   space occupying lesions, raised intracranial pressure

8. Head injury

9. Nutritional and vitamin deficiency
   thiamine, nicotinic acid, B_{12}

10. Epileptic:
    epileptic status, post-ictal states

under- or over-stimulation; drug dependence; and brain damage of any kind. Wolff and Curran (1935) showed that the clinical picture, as noted above, is much influenced by previous experience and personality. Engel and Romano (1959) showed that the severity of the clinical state was related to the degree of impairment of brain function as reflected by abnormal rhythms in the EEG.

The assessment, diagnosis, and treatment of acute organic psychiatric syndromes are described later in this chapter.

Dementia

Dementia is a generalized impairment of intellect, memory, and personality, with no impairment of consciousness. It is an acquired disorder, as distinct from amentia which is present from birth. Although most cases of dementia are irreversible, a small but important group are remediable.

[See Berrios (1987) for an account of the history of the concept of dementia.]

Clinical features

Dementia usually presents with impairment of memory. Other features include change in personality, mood disorder, hallucinations, and delusions. Though dementia generally develops gradually, it often comes to notice after an exacerbation caused by either a change in social circumstances or an intercurrent illness.

Again the clinical picture is much determined by the patient's premorbid personality. For example, in some patients, neurotic traits become exaggerated. People with good social skills may maintain a social facade despite severe intellectual deterioration, whilst those who are socially isolated or deaf are less likely to compensate for failing intellectual abilities.

Behaviour is often disorganized, inappropriate, distractable, and restless. There are few signs of interest or initiative. Changes in personality may manifest as antisocial behaviour, which sometimes includes sexual disinhibition or shoplifting. In middle-aged or elderly people any social lapse that is out of character should always suggest an organic cause.

Goldstein (see 1975) described the ways in which behaviour can be affected by the cognitive defects. Typically there is a reduction of interests ('shrinkage of the milieu'), rigid and stereotyped routines ('organic orderliness') and, when the person is taxed beyond restricted abilities, a sudden explosion of anger or other emotion ('catastrophic reaction').

As dementia worsens patients care for themselves less well and neglect social conventions. Behaviour becomes aimless, and stereotypies and mannerisms may appear. Eventually, the patient becomes disorientated, incoherent, and incontinent of urine and faeces.

Thinking slows and becomes impoverished in content. There may be concrete thinking, reduced flexibility, and perseveration. Judgement is impaired. False ideas, often of a persecutory kind, gain ground easily. In the later stages thinking becomes grossly fragmented and incoherent. Disturbed thinking is reflected in the quality of **speech**, in which syntactical errors and nominal dysphasia are common. Eventually the patient may utter only meaningless noises or become mute.

In the early stages, changes of **mood** may include anxiety, irritability, and depression. As dementia progresses emotions and responses to events become blunted, and sudden mood changes may occur without apparent cause.

Disorders of **cognitive function** are salient features. Forgetfulness is usually early and prominent, but may sometimes be difficult to detect in the early stages. Difficulty in new learning is generally the most conspicuous sign. Memory loss is more obvious for recent than for remote events. Patients often make excuses to hide these memory defects, and some confabulate. Other cognitive defects include impaired attention and concentration. Disorientation for time, and at a later stage for place and person, is almost invariable once dementia is well established.

Insight is lacking into the degree and nature of the disorder.

Subcortical dementia

In 1974 Albert and his colleagues introduced the term subcortical dementia to denote intellectual deterioration seen in progressive supranuclear palsy. The meaning of the term has been extended to cover a syndrome of slowing of cognition, difficulty with complex intellectual tasks, and affective disturbance without impairment of language, calculation, or learning. Possible causes of subcortical dementia include Huntington's chorea, Parkinson's disease, Wilson's disease, and multiple sclerosis. In contrast, Alzheimer's disease is usually regarded as an example of cortical dementia. So far, a clear distinction between the two forms of dementia has not been convincingly established (see Whitehouse 1986; Cummings 1986).

Aetiology

Dementia has many causes, of which the most important are listed in Table 11.3. The aetiology of dementia in the elderly is discussed separately in Chapter 16. Among elderly patients degenerative and vascular causes predominate, but at other ages no subgroups predominate. The clinician should therefore keep in mind the whole range of causes when assessing a patient, and should take care not to miss any that might be partly or wholly arrested by treatment, such as an operable cerebral neoplasm, cerebral syphilis, or normal pressure hydrocephalus.

Individual causes in the list should be familiar to the reader from general medical training. If necessary, a textbook of medicine should be consulted. Several of the conditions listed are described in detail later in this chapter. Alzheimer's disease is described in the chapter on psychiatry of the elderly (p. 611).

The assessment, diagnosis and treatment of dementia are also discussed later.

So far the two main generalized organic psychiatric syndromes (acute and chronic) have been described. An account will now be given of the third group of syndromes, in which there is impairment of specific psychological functions.

Table 11.3. Some causes of dementia

Degenerative	Senile dementia,* Alzheimer's disease, Pick's disease, Huntington's chorea, Parkinson's disease, Creutzfeldt–Jakob disease,† normal pressure hydrocephalus,‡ multiple sclerosis
Intracranial space occupying lesions	Tumour, subdural haematoma
Traumatic	Severe single head injuries, repeated head injury in boxers and others
Infections and related conditions	Encephalitis of any cause, neurosyphilis, cerebral sarcoidosis
Vascular	Multi-infarct dementia, occlusion of the carotid artery, cranial arteritis
Metabolic	Sustained uraemia, liver failure, remote effects of carcinoma or lymphoma; renal dialysis
Toxic	Alcohol, poisoning with heavy metals (lead, arsenic, thallium)
Anoxia	Anaemia, post-anaesthesia, carbon monoxide, cardiac arrest, chronic respiratory failure
Vitamin lack	Sustained lack of B_{12}, folic acid, thiamine

* See Chapter 16.
† Possibly infective, see p. 368
‡ Cause uncertain, see text.

Organic psychiatric syndromes with specific psychological dysfunctions

In this group, as explained earlier, psychological impairment is partial rather than general; that is, a limited number of specific functions are affected, such as memory, thinking, perception, or mood. Affective syndromes occur, depressive disorders being more common than mania. A schizophrenia-like syndrome can arise in association with brain disease (described later in this chapter). Personality disorder is another highly important complication (also described later).

In some of these conditions, but not all, focal lesions in the brain are demonstrable. Examples will now be given of syndromes due to focal brain damage, starting with the amnestic syndrome, which is the most distinctive.

The amnestic syndrome

The amnestic syndrome (otherwise known as the amnesic or dysmnesic syndrome) is characterized by a prominent disorder of recent memory and by disordered time-sense, in the absence of generalized intellectual impairment. The psychological disorder has been reviewed by Lishman (1987). The condition usually results from lesions in the posterior hypothalamus and nearby midline structures, but occasionally it is due to bilateral hippocampal lesions.

Korsakov, a Russian neuropsychiatrist, described a chronic syndrome in which memory deficit was accompanied by confabulation and irritability (Korsakov 1889). His patients also suffered from peripheral neuropathy. They either abused alcohol or developed the syndrome in association with puerperal sepsis or an infection causing persistent vomiting. It is therefore likely that they were suffering from thiamine deficiency. Nowadays peripheral neuropathy is not regarded as an essential feature of the amnestic syndrome, and vitamin deficiency is not regarded as the only cause.

The term Korsakov's syndrome has been used in more than one way, sometimes to denote a combination of symptoms, at other times to denote pathology as well as symptoms. Now the term usually implies impairment of memory and learning out of proportion to impairment of other cognitive functions. Confabulation may be present but is not an essential feature.

The term Wernicke–Korsakov syndrome is also used, for example by Victor *et al.* (1971). This term is used because the chronic amnestic syndrome often follows an acute neurological syndrome described by Wernicke in 1881. The main features of this acute syndrome are impairment of consciousness, memory defect, disorientation, ataxia, and opthalmoplegia. At post-mortem examination Wernicke found haemorrhagic lesions in the grey matter around the third and fourth ventricles and the aqueduct. More recent investigation has shown that lesions occur in these same anatomical sites in both the acute Wernicke syndrome and the chronic Korsakov syndrome.

In DSMIIIR, the amnestic syndrome is defined by impairment of both short- and long-term memory, not occurring exclusively during the course of delirium, and without the general loss of intellectual abilities required for a diagnosis of dementia. In addition to these criteria, the draft of ICD10 requires a history or objective evidence of an insult to, or disease of the brain, and the absence of a defect of immediate recall as tested for example by the digit span.

Clinical features

The central feature of the amnestic syndrome is a profound impairment of recent memory. The patient can recall events immediately after they occur, but cannot do so a few minutes or hours afterwards. Thus on a test of digit span, recall is good in the first few seconds, but impaired ten minutes later. New learning is grossly defective, but remote memory is relatively preserved. There is some evidence that the disorder may not be entirely an inability to lay down memories, but may also be a failure to recall established memories—possibly because of interference from irrelevant memories (Warrington and Weiskrantz 1970). One consequence of this profound disorder of memory is an associated disorientation in time.

Gaps in memory are often filled by confabulating. The patient may give a vivid and detailed account of recent activities all of which, on checking, turn out to be inaccurate. It is as though he cannot distinguish between true memories and the products of his imagination or the recollection of events from times other than those he is trying to recall. Such a patient is often suggestible; in response to a few cues from the interviewer, he may give an elaborate account of taking part in events that never happened. Confabulation is not a feature of the amnestic syndrome associated with bilateral hippocampal lesions.

Other cognitive functions are relatively well preserved. The patient seems alert and able to reason or hold an ordinary conversation, so that the interviewer is often surprised when the extent of the memory disorder is revealed. However, the disorder is not limited entirely to memory; some emotional blunting and lack of volition are often observed as well.

Aetiology and pathology

Alcohol abuse, the most frequent cause, seems to act by causing a deficiency of thiamine. Several other causes also seem to act through thiamine deficiency; for example, gastric carcinoma and severe dietary deficiency. As mentioned above, Korsakov described cases due to persistent vomiting in puerperal sepsis and typhoid fever, but these diseases are rarely seen today. At post mortem such cases generally have haemorrhagic lesions in the mamillary bodies, the region of the third ventricle, the periaqueductal grey matter, and parts of certain thalamic nuclei. The mamillary bodies (Brierly 1966) or the medial dorsal nucleus of the thalamus (Victor 1964) are the structures most often involved.

Other causes involve the brain directly and not through thiamine deficiency. The brain areas listed above may be damaged by vascular lesions, carbon monoxide poisoning, or encephalitis; and by tumours in the third ventricle. Another cause is bilateral hippocampal damage due to surgery. When the syndrome is due to causes other than thiamine deficiency, patients seem less likely to show confabulation and more likely to retain insight into the memory disorder.

Course and prognosis

Victor *et al.* (1971) studied 245 patients who had developed an acute Wernicke–Korsakov syndrome, most of whom had histories of many years of alcohol abuse. There was a 17 per cent death rate in the acute stage. All except 4 per cent of cases presented with Wernicke's encephalopathy. Eighty-four per cent of those who were followed up developed a typical amnestic syndrome. Once established there was no improvement in a half, complete recovery in a quarter and partial recovery in the rest. The best predictors of a better prognosis are a short history before diagnosis, and little delay between diagnosis and the start of a replacement treatment in cases due to thiamine deficiency.

Rarely an improvement occurs in cases due to causes other than alcoholism; for example, carbon monoxide poisoning or thiamine deficiency due to simple malnutrition. Sometimes the amnesia is progressive, as in cases with slowly expanding brain tumours.

Other psychiatric syndromes due to focal brain damage

An account will now be given of other 'focal' syndromes that are relevant to psychiatry. The many forms of dysphasia, agnosia and dyspraxia will not be described, as they are part of neurology; they are to be found in the textbook on organic psychiatry by Lishman (1987) or one of the standard textbooks of neurology.

Frontal lobe syndrome

Frontal lobe damage has distinctive effects on temperament and behaviour which are generally referred to as personality change. In **behaviour** the patient is disinhibited, over-familiar, tactless, and over-talkative. He makes jokes and engages in pranks (a feature sometimes referred to in the literature by the German word *Witzelsucht*). He may make errors of judgement, commit sexual indiscretions, and disregard the feelings of others. The **mood** is generally one of fatuous euphoria. **Concentration** and **attention** are reduced. Measures of formal intelligence are generally unimpaired, but special testing may show deficits in abstract reasoning. **Insight** is impaired.

Encroachment of a frontal lobe lesion on the motor cortex or deep projections may result in contralateral spastic paresis or dysphasia. Other possible signs are optic atrophy on the same side as the frontal lobe lesion, anosmia, a grasp reflex, and, if the lesion is bilateral, incontinence of urine [see Blumer and Benson (1975) for further information about personality change after frontal lobe injury.]

Parietal lobe

Compared with lesions of the frontal or temporal lobe, lesions of the parietal lobe are less likely to induce psychiatric changes (Lishman 1987), but they do cause various neuropsychological disturbances which are easily mistaken for hysteria. Lesions of the non-dominant parietal lobe cause visuo-spatial difficulties. Lesions of the dominant lobe are associated with dysphasia, motor and dressing apraxias, right–left disorientation, finger agnosia, and agraphia (see p. 59). These clinical features present in various combinations, some of which are designated as syndromes (see a textbook of neurology). If these conditions are not to be misdiagnosed, thorough neurological assessment is required. Important signs may include cortical sensory loss and sensory inattention and agraphaesthesia. There may also be evidence of a mild contralateral hemiparesis.

Temporal lobe

Although some temporal lobe lesions are asymptomatic, there is usually impairment of intellectual function especially with a lesion on the dominant side. There may be personality change resembling that of frontal lobe lesions, though more often accompanied by intellectual deficits and neurological signs. With chronic temporal lobe lesions another kind of personality change is characterized by emotional instability and aggressive behaviour.

Temporal lobe lesions may cause epilepsy, and also an increased risk of a schizophrenia-like psychosis (see p. 398). Unilateral temporal lobe lesions produce specific learning impairments (in right-handed people verbal on the left, non-verbal on the right). Rare bilateral lesions of medial temporal lobe structures can produce an amnestic syndrome. An important neurological sign of a deep temporal lobe lesion is a contralateral homonymous upper quandrantic visual field defect due to interference with the visual radiation. Sometimes a deep lesion causes a mild contralateral hemiparesis. Dominant lesions may produce language difficulties.

Occipital lobe

Occipital lobe lesions may cause complex disturbances of visual recognition which are easily misdiagnosed as hysterical. Complex visual hallucinations can also occur and may be mistaken for signs of non-organic mental illness. The visual fields should be examined thoroughly and tests carried out for visual agnosias.

The corpus callosum

Corpus callosum lesions typically extend laterally into both hemispheres. They then produce a picture of severe and rapid intellectual deterioration, with localized neurological signs varying with the degree of extension into the frontal or occipital lobes or the diencephalon.

Diencephalon and brainstem

With lesions of midline structures, the most characteristic features are the amnestic syndrome, hypersomnia and the syndrome of 'akinetic mutism'. There may also be progressive intellectual deterioration; emotional lability with euphoria and abrupt outbursts of temper; excessive eating; and endocrine signs of pituitary disorder.

The assessment of suspected organic psychiatric disorder

Any suspicion of an organic disorder should lead to detailed questioning about intellectual function and neurological symptoms. It is particularly important to interview other informants. The mode of onset and progression of symptoms should be determined in detail. An appropriate physical examination is essential.

Special investigations

With every patient the psychiatrist should use his judgement about the extent of the special investigations required. The aim should be to perform the minimum of investigations that will allow accurate diagnosis. A common basic routine for every patient is: haemoglobin and ESR; blood urea and electrolytes; urinary sugar and protein. Serology for syphilis used to be routine, but in the recent past was often omitted because of the decrease in cerebral syphilis. Its current use is discussed on p. 57. No single serological test is wholly satisfactory. The best combination is a reagin test together with the *Treponema pallidum* haemagglutination assay test.

Automated biochemistry now makes more extensive screening of blood samples possible, though experience is needed to interpret the results. If on clinical grounds there is the least suspicion of physical disorder or if any of the screening tests is abnormal, the clinician should judge what further investigations are required. They are likely to include: MSU microscopy; urine analysis for drugs and, in some cases, porphyrins; liver function tests; serum calcium and phosphate; thyroid function (T_4, T_3, TSH); serum B_{12}; and red cell folate. Also chest and lateral skull X-rays should be considered.

Further investigations

A review of the clinical findings and the results of this first round of investigations will usually indicate whether organic disorder can be excluded or special investigations are needed. The latter may include antero-posterior and basal skull X-rays, CT scan, EEG, and further laboratory investigations. Psychological tests may be required at this stage. Some of these investigations will now be considered in more detail.

Skull X-ray

As already noted, in the absence of physical signs a single lateral film is usually adequate. When indicated antero-posterior and basal views should be added. Possible findings include: abnormalities of the vault (such as overgrowth, osteolysis, abnormal vascular markings), intracranial calcification, changes in the sella turcica, the shift of a calcified pineal and unsuspected fractures.

Computerized tomography

Computerized tomography ('CT scanning') has increasing importance in the diagnosis of both focal and diffuse cerebral pathology. In the United Kingdom the current practice is that CT scans are not requested routinely for all psychiatric patients. Instead they are requested if there is any suspicion of organic brain disease in patients up to late middle age, or if there is any suggestion of a focal brain lesion in the elderly (radiological investigation of the elderly is further discussed in Chapter 16). Jacoby (1981) has reviewed the value of CT scanning in dementia and depressive disorders. Nuclear magnetic resonance (NMR) scanning has not been shown to have specific applications to the study of organic psychiatric disorder.

Electroencephalography

The EEG has an important but limited role in diagnosis. It must be interpreted skilfully. Apart from standard recordings, there are more elaborate techniques such as recordings during sleep or sleep deprivation, and ambulatory monitoring over 24 hours. The value of the EEG in diagnosis is limited by its sensitivity to minor physiological changes (such as level of wakefulness, blood sugar, and acid–base fluctuations) and to most psychotropic drugs. The EEG may be abnormal in some disorders generally thought to be without any organic pathology, namely antisocial personality disorder and some cases of schizophrenia. Conversely, normal records do not exclude cerebral pathology. Despite these problems, the EEG is sometimes helpful in localizing a space occupying or other focal lesion. Now that these aims can generally be achieved better with the CT scan, the main use of the EEG is in the management of epilepsy.

Further physical investigation

Psychiatrists who have the appropriate neurological skills may go on to perform a lumbar puncture or order further special imaging procedures. However, it is usually more appropriate to seek the opinion of a neurologist or general physician before doing more specialized investigations.

Psychological testing

Psychometric tests depend on the patient's co-operation but can be valuable when given by an experienced tester. They may help in localizing lesions in certain sites; for example, the parietal lobe. Even when interpreted skilfully, they discriminate poorly between organic and functional disorders. They are of more value in monitoring changes in psychological functioning over time, and in assessing patterns of disability as a basis for planning rehabilitation. Some of the most frequently used tests will now be considered briefly.

(1) *Wechsler Adult Intelligence Scale* (WAIS). This is a well-standardized test providing a profile of verbal and non-verbal abilities. Analysis of subscores can provide useful information for diagnosis. It is often said that organic impairment is indicated by a discrepancy between performance IQ (as an estimate of current capacity) and verbal IQ (as an estimate of previous capacity), but there is no strong evidence to support this view. Usually the more specific tests mentioned below are more helpful in diagnosis, but the WAIS is useful for screening.

(2) *Perceptual functions, especially spatial relationships*. This kind of test is exemplified by the Benton Revised Visual Retention Test, which requires the patient to study and reproduce ten designs. Parallel versions of the test are available, thus allowing serial testing.

(3) *New learning as a test of memory*. There are many new word learning tasks, for example the Walton-Black Modified Word Learning Test and the Paired Associate Learning Test, both of which give a useful quantitative estimate of memory impairment.

(4) *Specific tests*. Examples of specific tests are the Wisconsin Card Sorting Test for frontal lobe damage, and the Token Test for receptive language disturbance.

(5) *Dementia scales*. Strictly speaking these are not single psychometric tests but combinations of several tests. Examples are the Kendrick Battery and the Clifton Assessment Procedures for the Elderly (CAPE). Further information about the use of psychological tests in neuropsychiatry is provided by Lishman (1987).

(6) *Screening interviews*. Standardized procedures for assessing cognitive state are useful for screening groups of patients, and for monitoring progress. In interpreting the results, it is essential to take account of

previous education and achievement. The most widely used interview is the Mini Mental State Examination devised by Folstein *et al.* (1975).

Aspects of differential diagnosis

Organic or functional?

Usually there is little difficulty in distinguishing between organic and functional disorders, but occasionally the one may be mistaken for the other. Thus an organic disorder may sometimes be misdiagnosed as functional if the patient has abnormalities of personality that modify the clinical presentation; for example, by adding prominent depressive or paranoid features. Conversely, a functional disorder may be misdiagnosed as organic if there is apparent cognitive impairment; for example, a patient with a depressive disorder may complain of poor memory and 'confusion'. Of the two kinds of misdiagnosis, to miss an organic disorder is of course more serious. It is therefore vital that the psychiatrist should be constantly vigilant to the possibility of an organic psychiatric disorder. The first requirement is to take a full history and make a thorough examination of the physical and mental state. Certain features call for alertness. For example, complaints of physical symptoms should always be taken seriously, and suitable questions should be asked about their nature and time of onset. If psychiatric symptoms are not psychologically understandable, enquiry should always be directed to a possible primary organic disorder.

In making the distinction between organic and functional disorders, several principles should be borne in mind. The first concerns three modes of presentation—as hysteria (used here as a collective term for conversion and dissociative disorders), as episodic disturbed behaviour, and as depression. Hysteria should not be diagnosed unless there is an adequate psychological explanation for it, and unless every symptom has been adequately investigated. This principle holds even for patients with a previous history of hysteria. Brain disease may present with symptoms that resemble those of hysteria; this is likely for example with the parietal lobe lesions described above. Another point is that hysterical symptoms (such as global amnesia) may be 'released' by organic brain disease (see p. 212)

In a patient with a previously stable personality unexplained episodes of disturbed behaviour suggest organic brain disease. Possible causes include epilepsy, early dementia, and transient global amnesia; and extracerebral conditions such as hypoglycaemia, porphyria, or other metabolic disorders.

Finally, it should always be borne in mind that depressed mood may be the first manifestation of organic brain disease. Certain symptoms need to be analysed with particular care. For example, muscular weakness must be differentiated from the psychological experience of 'feeling weak', a distinction that is important in the diagnosis of myasthenia gravis. Another principle is that certain symptoms should arouse suspicion of an organic lesion; for example, visual hallucinations, or complaints of 'confusion', or any complaint that would be unusual in a functional disorder, such as ataxia and incontinence.

As mentioned above, a functional disorder may be misdiagnosed as organic if there is apparent cognitive impairment. The term 'pseudo-dementia' is applied to patients who have a functional disorder and show intellectual impairment resembling that of organic disease. Pseudodementia is most common in elderly depressed patients (see p. 618). In diagnosing pseudodementia from true dementia, it is important to know which symptoms developed first, since in functional disorders other psychological symptoms precede the apparent intellectual defects. Hence it is important to interview other informants to determine the precise mode of onset. [See Kopelman (1987) for a review of this topic.]

Acute or chronic?

In making the differential diagnosis, it is sometimes difficult to distinguish between an acute and a chronic organic psychiatric syndrome. This difficulty usually arises becase a clear history is lacking. It should be remembered that an acute syndrome may be superimposed on a long-standing dementia; such an event may obscure the diagnosis, or alternatively may draw attention to the underlying chronic disorder. The characteristic features of the acute and chronic syndromes have been described above. In distinguishing the acute syndrome, the most helpful features are: impairment of consciousness, perceptual abnormalities, disturbed attention, poor sleep, and thinking that is disorganized but rich in content.

Differential diagnosis of stupor

This condition, which is discussed on p. 32, requires specific mention. The main psychiatric causes are severe depression, schizophrenia, and rarely hysteria and mania. Organic causes are relatively uncommon in cases seen in psychiatric practice (Johnson 1984). They include focal lesions in the posterior diencephalon or upper midbrain (e.g. tumours, especially craniopharyngiomas; infarction, meningitis, and epilepsy) and a number of extracerebral causes (e.g. uraemia, hypoglycaemia, electrolyte and fluid disturbance, endocrine disorder, alcohol and drug intoxication). Diagnosis can usually be made on the history and examination. An EEG and CT scan can be helpful in distinguishing between organic and psychogenic causes. [See Lishman (1987) for a review of the differential diagnosis of stupor and Berrios (1981a) for a history of the concept of stupor.]

Diagnosis of the cause

A final aspect of differential diagnosis is to identify the cause of an organic psychiatric syndrome. If the cause is not readily apparent, the history and findings on physical and mental examination should be reviewed. Careful enquiry should be made about any history of head injuries, fits, alcohol or drug abuse, and recent physical illness. Dietary deficiency should be considered if the patient is elderly or of low intelligence. It is important to enquire about the symptoms of raised intracranial pressure (headaches, vomiting and visual disturbance), as well as those suggesting a focal lesion in the brain. Physical examination should be directed towards signs of disease in other systems as well as the nervous system. Any appropriate investigations should then be arranged.

The management of acute organic syndromes

The fundamental treatment is directed to the physical cause. General measures are necessary to relieve distress, and to prevent behaviour that might lead to accidents or other difficulties affecting the patient or other people. Amongst these general measures, the most important are to reduce the patient's anxiety, and to avoid too much or too little sensory stimulation.

Apart from good nursing care, the patient should be given repeated explanations of his condition. Disorientation and misinterpretation of the environment can be reduced by a calm and consistent approach, and by avoiding too many changes in the staff caring for the patient. If possible relatives and friends should visit the patient frequently; it is good practice to explain the patient's condition to them, and to advise them how to reassure and orientate the patient. There are many advantages in nursing the patient in a quiet single room. At night, the room should have enough light to enable him to know where he is; on the other hand it is desirable to avoid the high levels of illumination found in some intensive care units because it is important to ensure adequate sleep.

Drug treatment

In general it is important to give as few drugs as possible, and to avoid any that may increase impairment of consciousness. Nevertheless, medication often has an important role. Over-active, frightened, and disturbed patients may require medication to control distress and prevent accidents. There are two main requirements. First, during the daytime it may be necessary to calm the patient without inducing drowsiness. Second, at night it may be necessary to help him to sleep. For the first purpose (calming by day), the drug of choice is an antipsychotic drug such as haloperidol, which calms without causing drowsiness, hypotension, or cardiac side-effects. The effective daily dose usually varies between 10 and 60 mg. If necessary, the first dose of 2 mg to 10 mg can be given intramuscularly. Chlorpromazine and other phenothiazines are also widely used, but their usefulness is limited by their side-effects, such as hypotension and sedation. Chlorpromazine should be avoided when there is liver disease, or when the organic state may be due to withdrawal from alcohol (since chlorpromazine can increase the risk of seizures). Although benzodiazepines may be appropriate at night to promote sleep, they should be avoided in the daytime because their sedative effects may make the patient more disoriented. However, they may be used by day if there is liver failure, since they are unlikely to provoke hepatic coma. Chlormethiazole is often used to treat alcohol withdrawal states; this should be done only under close supervision in hospital since if further alcohol is taken, a dangerous interaction can occur (see p. 640).

The management of dementia

If possible the cause should be treated. Otherwise management begins with an assessment of the degree of disability and the social circumstances of the patient. The plan of treatment should seek to improve functional ability as far as possible, relieve distressing symptoms, make practical provisions for the patient, and support his family.

Plans for long-term care should make clear the part to be played by the doctors, nurses, and social workers. This applies whether the patient is living in hospital or outside. For certain conditions there are some benefits from carrying out the first stage of rehabilitation in special units; for example, dementia caused by head injury or by a stroke. It should be remembered that personality change and restlessness at night cause particular difficulties for the family.

Drugs

There is no specific drug treatment for dementia, and medication can be used only to alleviate certain symptoms. For example, anxiety may be treated by a benzodiazepine or a phenothiazine such as chlorpromazine or thioridazine. At night a benzodiazepine or a sedating phenothiazine may be useful. Patients with cognitive impairment may be unusually sensitive to antipsychotic drugs, so the first doses should be small. If the patient is over-active or deluded or hallucinated, a phenothiazine may be appropriate, but care is needed to find the optimal dose. If the patient has depressive symptoms, a trial of antidepressant medication is worthwhile even in the presence of dementia.

Behavioural methods

Much rehabilitation is based on the analysis of problems and the setting of goals. Behavioural methods share these principles but add specific procedures to modify particular aspects of behaviour. Recently these methods have been directed to improving deficits of memory, for example by the use of lists and reminders, and by practice (see Godfrey and Knight 1987). There is insufficient evidence on which to judge their value.

Specific physical conditions giving rise to mental disorders

Primary dementia

Among the important causes of dementia are intrinsic degenerative diseases of the central nervous system presenting in middle or late life. The dementias arising from these diseases are sometimes called primary dementias. The commonest examples are those occurring in old age, namely Alzheimer's disease and multi-infarct dementia, which are discussed in Chapter 16.

The category of **presenile dementia** was introduced in 1894 by Binswanger and later included in Kraepelin's classification. Nowadays the term presenile is usually taken to mean younger than 65 years of age. It includes Alzheimer's disease of presenile onset, and Pick's disease and Huntington's chorea.

Follow-up studies have shown that it is not easy to make an accurate diagnosis of presenile dementia. For example, Ron *et al.* (1979) studied 51 patients between 5 and 15 years after a confident diagnosis of presenile dementia had been made. Follow-up information led to rejection of the original diagnosis in almost a third of the cases. Accurate diagnosis depends on careful history taking together with mental and physical examination. In doubtful cases, admission for observation is often informative. A non-organic diagnosis is suggested by a history of affective disturbance, ability to learn in everyday activities or in psychological tests, and marked inconsistencies in performance. [See Horn (1987) for a review of primary dementia.]

Alzheimer's disease

Alzheimer's disease is described in the chapter on psychiatry of the elderly (p. 611).

Pick's disease

This disease, which was described by Pick in 1892, is much less common than Alzheimer's disease. It appears to be inherited as an autosomal dominant (Sjögren *et al.* 1952). The gross pathology is circumscribed asymmetrical atrophy of the frontal or temporal lobes accompanied by a lesser degree of general atrophy. The gyri are said to have a characteristic brownish 'knife blade' atrophy. There is severe neuronal loss in the outer layers of the atrophic cortex with proliferation of astrocytes and fibrous gliosis.

Although the onset may be at any adult age, most cases start between 50 and 60 years. Women are affected twice as often as men. There are no specific clinical features to separate Pick's disease from Alzheimer's, and the distinction is generally made at autopsy, not in life. None the less it is sometimes said that the presenting symptoms of Pick's disease are changes in character and social behaviour more often than memory disturbance. There is loss of inhibition (sometimes affecting sexual behaviour) deterioration of conventional manners, and sometimes marked loss of drive. These features correspond to the predominant pathology in the frontal lobes, and to a lesser extent temporal lobes. Parietal lobe features and extrapyramidal symptoms are less common. The condition is progressive with death after 2–10 years. [See Heston *et al.* (1987) for a review of the genetics and natural history of Pick's disease.]

Huntington's chorea

This was described in 1872 by George Huntington, a New England physician. Since then epidemiological studies have shown that the condition occurs in many countries; the estimated prevalence varies widely, the average being about 4–7 per 100 000 (see, for example, Oliver 1970). Men and women are affected in equal numbers. The pathological changes mainly affect the frontal lobes and the caudate nucleus. Neuronal loss, which is most marked in the frontal lobes, is accompanied by gliosis. The basal ganglia are strikingly atrophied.

Clinical features

Huntington's chorea usually begins at an age between 25 and 50, the mean being in the forties (Minski and Guttman 1938). A rare juvenile form has been reported. The onset of neurological and psychiatric symptoms may be several years apart. Neurological signs precede psychiatric symptoms in just over half the cases. The early neurological signs are choreiform movements of the face, hands, and shoulders. These movements are sudden, unexpected, aimless, and forceful. They are associated with dysarthria and changes in gait. Patients often attempt to disguise an involuntary movement by following it with a voluntary movement in the same direction. Gradually, abnormal movements become increasingly obvious with gross writhing contortions and ataxia. Patients begin to drop objects and later to fall over. Extrapyramidal rigidity and epilepsy also occur, especially in younger patients. Eventually walking, eating, and even sitting become difficult or impossible.

Memory is less affected than other aspects of cognitive function and insight is often retained until a late stage. In the early stage distractability is characteristic, and in the later stages apathy. Psychiatric symptoms of all types occur at an early stage but depressive symptoms are particularly frequent. Folstein *et al.* (1983) have argued that there is a specific association between Huntington's chorea and affective disorder. A schizophrenia-like state with persecutory delusions also occurs. Cognitive impairment usually occurs late in the course except in the rare cases of juvenile onset. It may at first consist of focal rather than generalized deficits. The cognitive impairment usually progresses slowly. The expectation of life is variable but the average is probably 13–16 years. When the onset is late patients often survive for many years and may die of other causes. Suicide is a frequent case of death; among Huntington's chorea patients living in the community the suicide rate is 7 per cent (Reed and Chandler 1958).

Surveys have shown that the first diagnosis is wrong in at least a third of cases. Common wrong diagnoses are various psychiatric disorders, especially schizophrenia, Alzheimer's dementia, and various disorders of movement including chorea. Interviews with wives (Hans and Koeppen 1980) and a postal survey of relatives (Barette and Marsden 1979) have confirmed that family members suffer much personal distress. Their first reaction is usually disbelief, followed by resentment and hostility. Most family members say they would prefer to have known the diagnosis earlier and to have had an opportunity for genetic counselling. Social problems and alcoholism are frequent in these families (Dewhurst *et al.* 1970).

Aetiology

Huntington's chorea is normally inherited as an autosomal dominant, although sporadic cases have been described. The dominant inheritance suggests an inborn error of metabolism. Perry *et al.* (1973) were the first to report decreased concentrations of gamma-aminobutyric acid (GABA), a neuro-inhibitory transmitter, in the caudate nucleus. Later work has shown decreased GABA biosynthesis and increased dopamine concentrations in parts of the basal ganglia.

Management

In general, the treatment is similar to that of other dementing disorders. For the specific control of choreiform movements, phenothiazines and butyrophenones have been reported as effective. It is uncertain whether they act as non-specific tranquillizers or through their specific effect on the dopamine systems. Pallidectomy and thalamotomy have also been used for the involuntary movements; some success has been reported in younger patients, but there is a risk of worsening the dementia or causing neurological side-effects.

Prevention

From surveys of family members it appears that, at a time of life when they are likely to become parents, only a few know about the risks of any future children being affected. There is disagreement as to how far families should be told and how strongly they should be advised against having children. Carter *et al.* (1983) found a considerable decline in births after non-directive genetic counselling.

The recent finding by Gusella *et al.* (1983) of a polymorphic DNA marker for Huntington's chorea makes possible a predictive test. The use of such a test raises the ethical questions that have to be considered with other genetic markers for inherited disease (see Crauford and Harris 1986).

Creutzfeldt–Jakob disease

This uncommon disorder was described by Creutzfeldt in 1920 and independently by Jakob in 1921. It is a rapidly progressive degenerative disease of the nervous system characterized by intellectual deterioration and various neurological deficits including cerebellar ataxia, spasticity, and extrapyramidal signs. Evidence for an infective agent followed the discovery that the rare neurological disease kuru, which is pathologically similar, can be transmitted. In 1968 Gibbs *et al.* were able to transmit Creutzfeldt–Jakob disease by inoculation of brain biopsy homogenate to a chimpanzee, an observation that has been frequently repeated. The nature of the transmissible agent remains uncertain but it is often referred to as a 'slow virus'. It could provide a model for other chronic neurological diseases.

Precautions should be taken to avoid contamination with blood from these patients. Essentially they involve extra care in handling samples of blood or tissue from these patients.

Normal pressure hydrocephalus

In this variety of hydrocephalus there is no block within the ventricular system (Hakim and Adams 1965). Instead there is an obstruction in the subarachnoid space such that cerebral spinal fluid can escape from the ventricles but is prevented from flowing up over the surface of the hemispheres. There is marked hydrocephalus with a generally normal or even low ventricular pressure (though sometimes with episodes of high pressure).

The characteristic features are progressive memory impairment, slowness, marked unsteadiness of gait, and later urinary incontinence. The condition is more common in the elderly but sometimes occurs in middle life. Often, no cause for the obstruction can be discovered although there may be a history of subarachnoid haemorrhage, head injury, or meningitis. It is most important to be alert to the possibility of this syndrome and to differentiate the condition from the primary dementias, or possibly from depressive disorder with mental slowness. Treatment is a shunt operation to improve the circulation of cerebrospinal fluid. The results are difficult to predict. The dementia may improve but generally it does not (see Lishman 1987).

Head injury

The psychiatrist is likely to encounter two main kinds of patients who have suffered a head injury. First, there is a small number of patients with serious and lasting psychological sequelae, such as persistent defect of memory. Second, there is a larger group with emotional symptoms and anergia; these symptoms are less obvious and may be easily overlooked, but they often cause persistent disability. [See Brooks (1984) for a general review of head injury.]

Acute psychological effects

Impairment of consciousness occurs after all but the mildest closed injuries, but is less common after penetrating injuries. The cause is uncertain but is probably related to rotational stresses within the brain. On recovery of consciousness, defects of memory are usually apparent. The period of **post-traumatic amnesia** is the time between the injury and the resumption of normal continuous memory. The duration of post-traumatic amnesia is closely correlated with: first, neurological complications such as motor disorder and dysphasia, and persistent deficits in memory and calculation; second, psychiatric disability and generalized intellectual impairment; and third, change of personality after head injury. The period of **retrograde amnesia** is the time between the injury and the last clearly recalled memory *before* the injury. It is not a good predictor of outcome.

After severe injury there is often a prolonged phase of delirium, sometimes disordered behaviour, mood disturbance, hallucinations, delusions, and disorientation.

Chronic psychological effects

Damage to the brain is of central importance in determining chronic psychological effects. Other factors are important, particularly the premorbid personality, and also environmental factors such as type of job, amount of social support available, and whether there is a compensation claim.

Lishman (1968) found that the site and extent of brain damage after penetrating injuries were related to the mental state one to five years later. The amount of tissue destruction was related both to intellectual impairment and 'organic' psychological symptoms such as apathy, euphoria, poor judgement, and disinhibition. Neurotic symptoms were not related to the amount of damage. Lishman's study suggested that cognitive disorder was particularly associated with parietal and temporal damage (especially on the left side). Affective disorders were more common after frontal lobe injury.

Lasting cognitive impairment

When head injuries are followed by post-traumatic amnesia of more than 24 hours, they are likely to give rise to persisting cognitive impairment proportional to the amount of damage to the brain. After a closed injury, the impairment is usually global, and varies in severity from obvious dementia to slight defects that only become apparent during intellectually demanding activities. After a penetrating or other localized injury, there may be only focal cognitive defects but some evidence of general impairment is usually found. Less severe head injury, followed by only transient loss of consciousness, can cause diffuse brain damage and be followed by cognitive impairement (see Boll and Barth 1983).

Slow improvement usually takes place over months or years. For example Miller and Stern (1965) followed 100 patients with severe head injuries for an average of 11 years and found substantial improvement over this period. Some patients had improved greatly despite pessimistic medical reports written 3 years after the injury. Presumably these findings reflect the slow education of intact brain tissue. Dementia out of keeping with the severity of the injury should suggest subdural haematoma, normal pressure hydrocephalus, or a coincidental degenerative process.

Personality change

Personality change is common after severe head injury, and particularly likely after frontal lobe damage. There may be irritability, loss of spontaneity and drive, some coarsening of behaviour, and occasionally reduced control of aggressive impulses. These changes may improve gradually, but when present often cause serious difficulties for the patient and his family.

Emotional symptoms

Emotional symptoms may follow any kind of injury. It is uncertain whether after head injury they are a non-specific response or a specific result of brain damage. The main predictors of emotional distress are the extent of the injury, the patient's personality, and social circumstances (see Brooks 1984). Any compensation proceedings or litigation may also be significant (see p. 475)

A minority of patients describe a syndrome of post-traumatic emotional disorder. The main features are anxiety, depression and irritability, often accompanied by headache, dizziness, fatigue, poor concentration, and insomnia. Lewis (1942) examined prolonged neurotic reactions among soldiers with head injuries, and concluded that they occurred in 'much the same person as develops a psychiatric syndrome anyway'. In a study of patients who were making claims for compensation, Miller (1961) found no relation between the severity of head injury and the extent of neurotic symptoms. In his study of penetrating injuries, Lishman (1968) found no demonstrable relationship between extent of brain damage and the main symptoms of the post-traumatic syndrome. It can be concluded that a vulnerable personality is the main aetiological factor in emotional problems after head injury [see Trimble (1981) for a review.]

Schizophrenia-like and affective syndromes

It is difficult to draw firm conclusions about the incidence of schizophrenia-like syndromes after head injury. Achté *et al.* (1969) studied 3552 Finnish soldiers aged 22–26 years after head injury, and found that the rate of schizophrenia-like syndromes was well above expectation. In an extensive review of schizophrenia-like syndromes associated with organic disorders of the central nervous system, Davison and Bagley (1969) confirmed this finding and concluded that it could not be explained by chance. These authors suggested that trauma can sometimes be of direct aetiological significance, and not merely a precipitating factor. There is some evidence (for example Achté *et al.* 1969) that head injury is associated with paranoid and affective psychoses, but it is less convincing. It is generally agreed that the risk of suicide is substantially increased among head-injured patients, though the reason is not clear.

Social consequences of head injury

The physical and psychosocial consequences of head injury for the patient often place a heavy burden on relatives. Many relatives experience severe distress and have to make substantial changes in their everyday lives. Family life is particularly affected if the patient shows personality change. Rehabilitation should take account of this burden on families and include help for them (see Brooks 1984; Livingston *et al.* 1985).

Treatment

A plan for long-term treatment should be made as early as possible after head injury. Planning begins with a careful assessment of three aspects of the problem. The first is the degree of physical disability. It has been shown by prospective study that early assessment of the extent of neurological signs provides a useful guide to the likely pattern of long-term physical disability (Bond 1975). Second, any neuropsychiatric problems should be assessed and their future course anticipated. Third, a social assessment should be made.

Treatment includes physical rehabilitation, to which the clinical psychologist can sometimes contribute behavioural techniques. If there are associated psychiatric disorders, the psychiatrist has an occasional role in treatment. Practical and social support are needed for the family. Any problems of compensation and litigation should be settled as quickly as possible. Ideally, continuing help should be provided by a special team. [See Brooks (1984) and Livingston (1986) for reviews of the treatment of head injury.]

Boxing and head injury

For many years there has been dispute about the significance of 'punch drunk' states after repeated minor head injury in the boxing ring. There have been numerous published reports of a characteristic syndrome, but most of the findings could be due to biased selection of cases with coincidental neurological disease. However, in an important study of a random sample of 224 retired professional boxers, Roberts (1969) found that 37 had a characteristic syndrome related to the extent of exposure to head-injury during boxing. The principal features were dysarthria, slowness of movement, unsteadiness of gait, intellectual impairment and personality change in the form of irritability and lack of drive. Johnson (1969) reported that morbid jealousy occurred in some cases. When the syndrome is fully developed, there are cerebellar, pyramidal, and extrapyramidal signs as well as intellectual disorientation. The condition usually progresses until retirement from the ring, but only occasionally progresses afterwards. Cerebral atrophy has been shown radiologically. Corsellis *et al.* (1973) examined the post-mortem brains of ex-boxers and found excessive loss of cortical neurones and neurofibrillary degeneration. The psychiatrist should bear this condition in mind as an occasional cause of dementia.

Intracranial infections

Neurosyphilis

So far the recent increase in primary and secondary syphilis has not been accompanied by an increase in neurosyphilis. Although uncommon, neurosyphilis is important to recognize as a cause of mental symptoms because it is treatable. Of every twelve patients with neurosyphilis approximately five have general paresis, four meningovascular syphilis, and three tabes dorsalis. Of these groups general paresis (General Paralysis of the Insane; GPI) is the most important to psychiatrists. Neurosyphilis is so variable in presentation that there is a case for testing the serology of all patients admitted to psychiatric wards. If this practice is not followed, serological tests should certainly be performed for all psychiatric patients with symptoms or signs suggesting organic brain disease. If serology is positive, treatment with penicillin is required. The administration of such treatment is complicated for several reasons, including the risk of Herxheimer reactions. It is therefore advisable to obtain a neurologist's collaboration in the management.

General paresis

The identification of general paresis and the discovery of its cause were important landmarks in the history of psychiatry because they stimulated a search for organic causes of other psychiatric syndromes. A further important discovery was that one cause could give rise to many different kinds of clinical picture [see Hare (1959) for a historical review.]

General paresis is three times more common in men than women. It usually starts between the ages of 30 and 50. The time from infection to symptoms is generally thought to be between 5 and 25 years, with an average of 10 to 15 years. General paresis often presents with minor emotional symptoms or evidence of personality changes such as moodiness, irritability, or apathy, which precede evidence of intellectual impairment. About half the patients present more urgently, often with a striking lapse of social conduct such as indecent exposure, or sometimes with a seizure.

In the past, an expansive and grandiose clinical picture was frequently described. Nowadays, the most striking symptoms are usually those of dementia. Since the condition was first described, patients with a depressive clinical picture seem to have become relatively more common; they were found, for example, in about a quarter of one series (Dewhurst 1969). Such patients have the symptoms of a depressive disorder, evidence of dementia, and delusions that may be of an extreme melancholic content. Less common presentations resemble mania or schizophrenia. Many other combinations of psychiatric symptoms can occur, so it is important to keep the diagnosis in mind when assessing any unusual psychiatric state. Neurological examination usually reveals abnormalities, most often Argyll Robertson pupils, tremor, and dysarthria. As the disease progresses there is increasing dementia, spastic paralysis, ataxia, and seizures. In untreated cases death usually occurs within four to five years. If treatment is given early, the condition usually remits; if treatment is given in established cases, progression of the disease can generally be halted.

Encephalitis

Encephalitis may be due either to a primary viral disease of the brain or to a complication of bacterial meningitis, septicaemia, or a brain abscess. Many viral causes have been identified, of which herpes simplex is the most common in the United Kingdom. Encephalitis sometimes occurs after influenza, measles, rubella, and other infectious diseases, and also after vaccination.

In the acute stage headache, vomiting, and impaired consciousness are usual, and seizures are common. There may be an acute organic psychiatric syndrome. Rarely encephalitis presents with predominant psychiatric symptoms. However, the psychiatrist is more likely to see the complications that follow the acute episode; these may include prolonged anxiety and depression, dementia, personality change, or epilepsy. In childhood encephalitis may be followed by behaviour disorders (see Lishman 1987).

Encephalitis lethargica (epidemic encephalitis)

A small outbreak of encephalitis lethargica was first reported in 1917 by Von Economo at the Vienna Psychiatric Clinic (Von Economo 1929). The condition increased in the 1920s. By the 1930s it had largely disappeared, although possibly rare sporadic cases still occur. The acute stage was usually characterized by somnolence and opthalmoplegia. The chronic sequelae were of most interest to the psychiatrist. Parkinsonism was a disabling complication, and oculogyric crises were particularly striking. Another disabling sequel was personality change towards more antisocial behaviour. Some patients developed a clinical state resembling schizophrenia. Davison and Bagley (1969) analysed 40 of these schizophrenia-like cases from the literature, and found that they had fewer schizophrenic family members than did schizophrenic probands.

Mental symptoms were commonly associated with parkinsonism. Some Parkinsonian patients had marked slowing and apathy. Sacks (1973) has given a vivid description of such cases, and the striking but temporary improvements brought about in some by L-dopa.

Benign myalgic encephalomyelitis

This is a rare condition which occurs in epidemics. It is sometimes called Royal Free Disease because of a notable outbreak in 1955 at the Royal Free Hospital in London. The common features of the various outbreaks are fatigue, headache, myalgia, paresis, mental symptoms, low or absent fever, and no mortality; at the onset there may also be sore throat and gastrointestinal symptoms. The severity of the symptoms contrast with the lack of neurological signs and lack of evidence for an infective agent. The sequelae include prominent psychological symptoms.

McEvedy and Beard (1970) suggested that most if not all the cases in the Royal Free epidemic were examples of epidemic hysteria. Against this view, it has been argued that common features occurring in widely dispersed outbreaks suggest an organic basis, even if some cases have hysterical features (Acheson 1959; Ramsay 1973). At present, there is insufficient evidence to settle the argument and it is possible that two separate conditions exist, with similar symptoms, the one organic the other psychiatric. [See Dawson (1987) for a review of the syndrome.]

Cerebral abscess

A cerebral abscess may present rapidly and obviously with headache, epileptic seizures, papilloedema, and focal signs. On the other hand, a cerebral abscess may develop insidiously, and may then be mistaken for a psychiatric disorder. It is vital that the psychiatrist should always be alert to such a possibility. For example, the diagnosis of cerebral abscess should always be considered when depressive symptoms are accompanied by mild confusion and fever, especially when the patient seems generally ill. In such cases papilloedema often appears late and there may be few other neurological signs. Radiological studies using CT scan are likely to be important. The primary focus of infection is usually outside the brain and difficult to detect; common sites include the mastoid, middle ear and nasal sinuses, and chronic suppurative lung disease. Penetrating head injury is another cause.

Tuberculous meningitis

Nowadays, tuberculous meningitis is uncommon and notoriously difficult to diagnose. The psychiatrist occasionally encounters the condition when it presents with apathy, irritability, and 'personality change'. Pyrexia, neck stiffness, and clouding of consciousness are often late to appear, and should therefore be looked for repeatedly.

Cerebrovascular disease

Cerebrovascular accident

Amongst people who survive a cerebrovascular accident, just over half return to a fully independent life. The rest suffer some loss of independence because of disabilities that may be psychological as well as physical. The psychological changes are often the more significant, and many patients do not return to normal life even after physical disability has ceased to be a serious obstacle.

Cognitive defects

A single stroke can cause dementia and other deficits of higher cortical function such as dysphasia and dyspraxia, which may handicap the patient to a degree that is often underestimated by doctors. After a first stroke repeated small strokes may lead to progressive dementia.

The separate condition of multi-infarct dementia is described under psychiatry of the elderly (p. 614).

Personality change

Irritability, apathy, or lability of mood may occur. Inflexibility in coping with problems is common and may be seen in extreme form as a 'catastrophic reaction'. Such changes are probably due more to associated widespread arteriosclerotic vascular disease than to a single stroke; they may continue to worsen even though the focal signs of a stroke are improving.

Mood disturbance

Depressed mood is a common reaction to the handicap caused by a stroke. It may contribute to the apparent intellectual impairment and is often an important obstacle to rehabilitation. It is not certain that depressed mood is more common after stroke than after other disabling illnesses in elderly people. Depression is not associated with the size of the brain lesion, and only weakly with the degree of intellectual impairment. It has been argued (Robinson *et al.* 1984; Robinson *et al.* 1986*b*) that depression is associated with lesions in the anterior part of the left hemisphere. However, there is as yet no conclusive proof and it seems equally likely that depression after stroke is caused by social and psychological factors [see House (1987*b*) for a review]. Treatment of depressive symptoms depends mainly on an active rehabilitation programme with help for both the patient and the family. Severe and persistent depressive symptoms may respond to treatment with a tricyclic antidepressant, but the drug should be given cautiously because side-effects are frequent.

Other problems

Psychological problems include denial, excessive invalidism, poor motivation, and disturbed behaviour. Ability to work, enjoy leisure, and take part in other social activities may be reduced. Many relatives are anxious or otherwise distressed, and the degree of distress is not directly related to the extent of the patient's physical disability (Wade *et al.* 1986; Carnwarth and Johnson 1987).

Treatment

Although rehabilitation is used widely, it probably has little effect on the physical recovery of most stroke patients (Lind 1982). However, rehabilitation can improve psychological well-being and reduce social problems. It is not agreed whether rehabilitation should be provided in specialist units (see Garraway 1985).

Subarachnoid haemorrhage

A high incidence of mental disorder has been reported after subarachnoid haemorrhage. In a study of 261 patients after subarachnoid haemorrhage, Storey (1967, 1970) found that 40 per cent had organic psychiatric defects on simple clinical testing. Adverse personality changes were also common, although suprisingly relatives reported personality improvement in 13 per cent of patients with bleeds from anterior aneurysms. Significant depressive symptoms were reported in 14 per cent. [For a review of psychiatric aspects of subarachnoid haemorrhage see Lishman (1987).]

Subdural haematoma

The psychiatrist should remember that subdural haematoma is not uncommon after falls associated with chronic alcoholism. The symptoms may then be easily overlooked or misdiagnosed. Acute haematomas may cause coma or fluctuating impairment of consciousness, and are often associated with hemiparesis and oculomotor signs. The psychiatrist is more likely to see the chronic syndromes, in which patients present with headache, vague physical complaints, and fluctuating consciousness, but often few localizing neurological signs. If there is any suspicion of a subdural haematoma, radiological investigation is required. Treatment is by surgical evacuation, which may reverse the symptoms in some chronic cases, but leaves many others with continuing deficits.

Other neurological conditions

Cerebral tumours

Many cerebral tumours cause psychological symptoms at some stage, and a significant minority first present with such symptoms. Psychiatrists are most concerned with slow growing tumours in brain areas that produce psychological effects but few neurological signs, for example frontal meningiomas. The nature of the psychological symptoms depends not only on the site of the tumour but also on the presence or absence of raised intracranial pressure. The rate of tumour growth is also important; fast-growing tumours with raised intracranial pressure can present as an acute organic syndrome, whilst less rapidly growing tumours are more likely to cause cognitive defects. The nature of the psychological symptoms is also much affected by the patient's personality. It should be remembered that focal lesions can give rise to one of the specific syndromes discussed already (p. 353); these may take the form of personality change or may be mistaken for neurotic symptoms.

In psychiatric practice, cerebral tumours are easily overlooked unless the psychiatrist is constantly alert. Unexplained 'changes in personality' are particularly suspicious.

Transient global amnesia

This syndrome is important in the differential diagnosis of episodes of unusual behaviour. It occurs in middle or late life. It is characterized by abrupt episodes, lasting several hours, in which there is a global loss of recent memory. The patient apparently remains alert and responsive but usually appears bewildered by his inability to understand his experience. There is impairment of new learning but not of other cognitive functions, and the patient may be able to continue a set task or find his way around. There is complete recovery, but with amnesia for the episode. The aetiology is obscure but the prognosis good (see Fisher and Adams 1964).

Patients with this condition often present as emergencies to general practitioners and casualty officers. Doctors who are not familiar with the syndrome may misdiagnose it as a hysterical fugue.

Multiple sclerosis

In its early stages, multiple sclerosis is often difficult to diagnose, and the physical symptoms may be erroneously diagnosed as conversion or dissociative disorder, thereby adding to the patient's distress. Psychological symptoms also occur early in the disorder, and may occasionally be the presenting feature. In the established disease, psychological symptoms are common. Surridge (1969) found mood abnormality in 53 per cent of 108 patients with multiple sclerosis as against 13 per cent of controls with muscular dystrophy. Half of these patients with mood abnormalities were depressed, and half euphoric. Depression often occurred early, apparently as a reaction to the neurological symptoms. However, the extent of the mood disturbance was not closely related to the amount of neurological abnormality. Euphoria was more frequent in patients with intellectual impairment. Some patients show marked denial of their disability.

Occasionally, a rapidly progressive dementia occurs early in the disease. In most cases, however, intellectual deterioration is less severe and progresses slowly, though dementia is common in the late stages of the disease. Psychometric testing shows that, in the early stages, well-practised verbal skills are often preserved despite deficits in problem solving, dealing with abstract concepts, memorizing, and learning (see Ron 1986*b*).

Multiple sclerosis places heavy burdens on patients' families, especially when it causes disablement (see Miles 1979).

Endocrine disorders

Hyperthyroidism

In hyperthyroidism, there are always some psychological symptoms, including restlessness, irritability, and distractability, which may be so marked as to resemble anxiety disorder. In the past, acute organic psychiatric syndromes were observed as part of a 'thyroid crisis', but with modern treatment they are rare. Schizophrenia or affective disorders occur in a few patients, but may be coincidental.

The differential diagnosis between thyrotoxicosis and anxiety disorder depends on a history of distinctive symptoms and on physical examination. Discriminating symptoms of the thyrotoxicosis are preference for cold weather and weight loss despite increased appetite. The most discriminating signs of thyrotoxicosis are a palpable thyroid, sleeping pulse above 90 beats per minute, atrial fibrillation, and tremor. T_4 and T_3 should be measured.

As mentioned above, an acute organic psychiatric syndrome is now uncommon, but mild degrees of memory impairment can often be demonstrated if specially looked for [Whybrow and Hurwitz (1976)]. Occasionally, delirium occurs soon after the start of treatment with antithyroid drugs.

Occasionally, a functional psychosis begins in association with thyrotoxicosis. The nature of the association between the two conditions has long been of interest. As long ago as 1909, Packard studied 82 cases reported in the literature and concluded that thyrotoxicosis was a precipitant rather than a fundamental cause. Packard's conclusion is generally held today. It is probable that there is no specific psychosis associated with thyrotoxicosis; the clinical picture may be of depressive disorder, mania, or schizophrenia, although modified at times by the psychological effects of hyperthyroidism.

Alexander (1950) considered that thyrotoxicosis was a psychosomatic disorder (in the sense of a physical disorder induced by psychological factors) but this is not supported by evidence (see Weiner 1977).

Hypothyroidism

Lack of thyroid hormones invariably produces mental effects. In early life, it leads to retardation of mental development. When thyroid deficiency begins in adult life, it leads to mental slowness, apathy, and complaints of poor memory. These effects are important to psychiatrists because they easily lead to a mistaken diagnosis of dementia or a depressive disorder.

The symptoms of hypothyroidism are less distinctive than those of thyrotoxicosis. They include poor appetite and constipation, generalized aches and pains, and sometimes angina. Occasionally, these psychiatric symptoms are the first evidence of myxoedema. On psychiatric examination, actions and speech are found to be slow, and thinking may be slow and muddled. Since these features are non-specific, myxoedema must be differentiated from dementia on the basis of its physical signs: distinctive facial appearance with non-pitting oedematous swelling and receding hair line; deep coarse voice; dry rough skin and lank hair; slow pulse, and delayed tendon reflexes.

In determining the cause of hypothyroidism, it is important to remember that lithium therapy may be a cause (see p. 668). Measurements of TSH help to distinguish primary thyroid disease (in which TSH is high) from pituitary causes (in which TSH is low).

Asher (1949) coined the phrase 'myxoedematous madness' to denote serious mental disorders associated with thyroid deficiency in adult life. There is no single form of psychiatric disorder specific to hypothyroidism. The commonest is an acute or subacute organic syndrome. Other patients develop a slowly progressive dementia or more rarely there may be a serious depressive disorder or schizophrenia. Paranoid features are said to be common in all the conditions.

Replacement therapy usually reverses the organic features provided that the diagnosis has not been long delayed. A severe depressive disorder may also require antidepressant medication or ECT. Tonks (1964) reported that patients with organic syndromes have a better prognosis than those with the clinical picture of an affective or schizophrenic disorder.

Addison's disease (hypoadrenalism)

Psychological symptoms of withdrawal, apathy, fatigue, and mood disturbance are frequent and appear early. Hence, Addison's disease may be misdiagnosed as dementia. When he first described the disease in 1868, Thomas Addison commented that memory disorder was common. Subsequent observations confirm this view; for example, Michael and Gibbons (1963) reported memory disorder in three-quarters of a series of patients. Addisonian crises are accompanied by the features of an acute organic psychiatric syndrome. The diagnosis is usually apparent because the patient is obviously unwell, cold, and dehydrated, with low blood pressure and signs of failing circulation. Occasionally a depressive or schizophrenic picture coincides with Addison's disease, but less commonly than in Cushing's syndrome (see Lishman 1987).

Cushing's syndrome (hyperadrenalism)

Emotional disorder is common, as Cushing noted in his original description, and Michael and Gibbons (1963) reported emotional disorder in about half their cases. Cushing's disease usually comes to attention because of physical symptoms and signs, and any psychiatric disorders are usually encountered as complications in known cases. The physical signs include moon-face, 'buffalo hump', purple striae of the thighs and abdomen, hirsutes, and hypertension. Women are usually amenorrhoeic and men often impotent.

Depressive symptoms are the most frequent psychiatric manifestations of Cushing's syndrome. Paranoid symptoms are less common and appear mainly in patients with severe physical illness (Cohen 1980; Kelly *et al.* 1985). The severity of the depressive symptoms is not related closely to plasma cortisol concentrations, and premorbid personality and stressful life events appear to predispose to the development of the affective disorder. Nevertheless, psychological symptoms usually improve quickly when the medical condition has been controlled. A few patients develop a severe depressive disorder with retardation, delusions, and hallucinations. Even these severe disorders generally improve when the endocrine disorder is brought under control. A textbook of medicine should be consulted for information about endocrine treatment.

Corticosteroid treatment

The psychiatric symptoms induced by corticosteriod treatment might be expected to be identical to those of Cushing's syndrome, but they are not entirely the same. When the symptoms are not severe, euphoria or a mild manic syndrome is more common than depressive symptoms. When they are severe, they take the form of depressive disorder, as in Cushing's syndrome (see Ling *et al.* 1981).

Sometimes corticosteroid treatment induces an acute organic syndrome in which paranoid symptoms may be prominent. The severity of the mental disorder is not associated with the dosage. It appears that patients with a history of previous mental disorder are not specially prone to develop the psychological complications of cortisone treatment.

Less severe symptoms usually improve when the dose is reduced. A severe depressive disorder may require treatment with antidepressant medication, or a manic disorder with antipsychotic drugs. Lithium prophylaxis should be considered for patients who need to continue steroid treatment after an affective disorder has been brought under control.

Rapid withdrawal of corticosteroids may cause lethargy, weakness, and joint pain. Delirium may follow the withdrawal of long-standing treatment for systemic lupus erythematosus and rheumatoid arthritis. A minority of patients become psychologically dependent on corticosteroids, and strongly resist withdrawal.

Phaeochromocytoma

Phaeochromocytomas are a rare and easily overlooked cause of episodic attacks of anxiety. They are tumours, usually benign, arising from the chromaffin cells of the adrenal medulla or ectopically in relation to the sympathetic ganglia. They secrete adrenalin and noradrenalin either continuously or paroxysmally, causing attacks characterized by palpitations, blushing, sweating, tremulousness, and violent headaches, together with hypertension and tachycardia. Intense anxiety is usual in the attacks. Occasionally there is an episode of confusion. Between attacks blood pressure is usually continuously raised. The attacks may be precipitated by physical exertion or occasionally by emotion.

Diagnosis depends on the demonstration of increased concentrations of catecholamines in the blood or urine, or of their metabolites in the urine. For further information about the syndrome and its treatment the reader should consult a textbook of medicine.

Acromegaly

In acromegaly, apathy and lack of initiative are common, but other psychiatric symptoms are uncommon. Depression sometimes occurs, but it may be a psychological reaction to the physical symptoms rather than a direct effect of the hormonal disturbance.

Hypopituitarism

Psychological symptoms are usual. From a survey of the literature, including his own series of cases, Kind (1958) concluded that 90 per cent of patients with hypopituitarism had some psychological symptoms, whilst half had severe symptoms. The main symptoms were depression, apathy, lack of initiative, and somnolence. Sometimes cognitive impairment is severe enough for hypopituitarism to be misdiagnosed as dementia. Another possible misdiagnosis is mild depressive disorder. In the differential diagnosis from anorexia nervosa, hypopituitarism is distinguished by loss of bodily hair and by the absence of weight phobia. Psychological symptoms usually respond well when hypopituitarism is treated by replacement therapy.

Hyperparathyroidism

Psychological symptoms are common and apparently related to the raised blood level of calcium (Petersen 1968). Depression, anergia, and irritability are the most frequent symptoms. Cognitive impairment also occurs. An acute organic psychiatric syndrome may develop as part of a 'parathyroid crisis'. A few patients first present with psychiatric symptoms, whilst many patients report, in retrospect, that they experienced mild anergia and low spirits for years before definite symptoms appeared (see de Alarcón and Franchesini 1984).

Hyperparathyroidism should be considered when prolonged neurotic or minor intellectual symptoms are accompanied by thirst and polyuria. Mental symptoms usually recover after removal of a parathyroid adenoma, but there may be episodes of hypocalcaemia after the operation, giving rise to anxiety and sometimes tetany.

Hypoparathyroidism

Hypoparathyroidism is usually due to removal of or damage to the parathyroid glands at thyroidectomy, but a few cases are idiopathic. The main symptoms are tetany, ocular cataracts, and epilepsy. Denko and Kaelbling (1962) reviewed the literature on hypoparathyroidism and concluded that at least half the cases attributable to surgery had psychiatric symptoms, usually in the form of acute organic psychiatric syndromes. In idiopathic cases of hypoparathyroidism chronic psychiatric syndromes are more common. Less frequent complications are depression, irritability and nervousness ('pseudoneurosis'). Bipolar affective disorder and schizophrenic disorders are rare (see Lishman 1987) and may be coincidental. The diagnosis is made on the characteristic physical symptoms and measurement of serum calcium.

Insulinomas

These usually present between the ages of 20 and 50. There is generally a long history of transient but recurrent attacks in which the patient behaves out of character, often in an aggressive and uninhibited way. At times the clinical features may resemble those of almost any psychiatric syndrome. The important diagnostic clue is the recurrence of attacks. Usually the patient cannot remember what happened during an attack.

Diagnosis depends on demonstrating a low blood glucose concentration during or immediately after an attack. In doubtful cases, the advice of a physician should be obtained [see Marks and Rose (1965) and Lishman (1987) for further information].

Metabolic disorders

Liver disease

The psychiatric features of liver failure are sometimes known as hepatic encephalopathy. The clinical picture is an acute organic psychiatric syndrome (Summerskill *et al.* 1956), together with flapping tremor of the outstretched hands, facial grimacing, and fetor hepaticus. As in other acute organic syndromes, there may be hallucinations and confabulation. The condition may progress to coma, and there is a substantial mortality.

Acute porphyria

The classification of the porphyrias is complex and need not be detailed here (for a full account, the reader should consult a textbook of medicine). In Britain, the commonest form is the acute intermittent type, which is an inborn error of metabolism inherited through a dominant autosomal gene with incomplete penetrance. Acute porphyria is important to the psychiatrist because it may resemble hysteria, an acute organic reaction, or a functional psychosis. McAlpine and Hunter (1966) suggested that acute porphyria caused the madness of George III; although their arguments were scholarly and ingenious, they are open to substantial doubt.

Acute intermittent porphyria occurs at any age from puberty onwards, but is most common in the third decade. The clinical picture is variable, but the typical symptoms are: acute abdominal pain, pain in limbs or back, nausea and vomiting, tachycardia, headaches, and severe constipation. Seizures occur in 20 per cent of cases. There may be a peripheral neuropathy which is predominantly motor. There is often a history of laparotomies without abnormal findings.

Psychiatric symptoms occur during the attack in a quarter to three-quarters of cases, and at times dominate the clinical picture (Ackner *et al.* 1962). They include depression, restlessness, and disturbed behaviour. Emotions are often labile. There may be an acute organic syndrome with impaired consciousness or eventually coma. Delusions and hallucinations often occur.

Attacks may be precipitated by acute infection, alcohol, anaesthesia, and certain drugs, notably barbiturates, the contraceptive pill, dichloralphenazone, and methyldopa.

The **diagnosis** is made by the detection of porphobilinogen and D-amino laevulinic acid in the urine. Porphyria is not common, but is often missed when it presents in psychiatric practice. It should be considered whenever there is a long history of intermittent physical and psychological complaints.

There is no specific **treatment**. The main aim is prevention of attacks by avoiding precipitants. Most attacks improve without residual defects. A few patients are handicapped by persistent peripheral neuropathy or muscular wasting. Occasionally abnormal mental states are prolonged.

Cerebral anoxia

Cerebral anoxia can be divided into four categories: **anoxic** (respiratory failure, asphyxia, the effects of high altitude); **anaemic** (blood loss and carbon monoxide poisoning); **stagnant** (cerebral vascular disease, peripheral circulatory failure, cardiac failure, cardiac arrest and arrythmias); and **metabolic** (hypoglycaemia, cyanide poisoning). The clinical picture depends substantially on the cause, but most forms of anoxia are temporary and present with impairment of consciousness which may be accompanied by muscular twitching or tremor and epileptic fits. Afterwards there is a dense amnesic gap but usually no permanent consequences. In a small proportion of patients who have had severe anoxia, there may be permanent memory deficits and neurological symptoms.

Carbon monoxide poisoning

The psychiatrist has an interest in both the causes and the effects of carbon monoxide poisoning. In the past carbon monoxide poisoning was usually the result of deliberate self-harm with domestic gas supplies. Household gas no longer contains substantial amounts of carbon monoxide, but car exhaust fumes do and are sometimes used for self-poisoning.

After carbon monoxide poisoning, the course is variable. Milder cases recover over days or weeks. Recovery of consciousness is often followed by an organic psychiatric syndrome; this clears up leaving an amnestic syndrome, which in turn gradually improves. Extrapyramidal and other neurological signs occur at an early stage, and then resolve. In more severe cases there is a characteristic period of partial recovery, followed by relapse with a return of an acute organic syndrome and extrapyramidal symptoms. Occasionally death occurs at this stage. Some patients are left with permanent extrapyramidal symptoms, or become demented.

The frequency of these complications is uncertain. Shillito *et al.* (1936) surveyed 21 000 cases of carbon monoxide poisoning in New York City and found few lasting problems. In contrast Smith and Brandon (1973) made a detailed study of 206 cases from a defined area. They followed up 74 patients for an average of three years: 8 patients had sustained gross neurological damage; 8 patients had died; of those alive at follow-up, 8 had improved, 21 had shown personality deterioration, and 27 reported memory impairment.

Vitamin deficiency

Severe chronic malnutrition is accompanied by psychological changes such as apathy, emotional instability, cognitive impairment, and occasional delusions or hallucinations. These symptoms are well-known among prisoners of war (see, for example, Helweg-Larsen *et al.* 1952). In peace time severe malnutrition with deficiency of several vitamins as well as protein and calories is common in some parts of the world. The psychological changes are usually reversed in adults when a normal diet is resumed. However, children may have permanent changes. Even in developed countries there are groups of people who lack balanced diets and are at special risk of deficiency; they include the aged, the chronically mentally ill, the mentally handicapped, alcoholics, and patients with chronic gastro-intestinal diseases.

Vitamin B deficiency

Thiamine deficiency

Chronic depletion of thiamine leads first to fatigue, weakness, and emotional disturbance. Eventually it causes beri-beri, which is characterized by peripheral neuropathy, cardiac failure, and peripheral oedema. More acute and severe depletion of thiamine may lead to Wernicke's encephalopathy and thereby to the amnestic syndrome (see p. 354).

Nicotinic acid deficiency

In established pellagra, disorientation and confusion may progress to outbursts of excitement and violence. Depression is often conspicuous and a paranoid hallucinatory state is sometimes seen. In these cases response to treatment with nicotinic acid is often dramatic.

More acute and severe nicotinic acid depletion leads to an acute organic psychiatric syndrome. Cogwheel rigidity and grasping and sucking reflexes are said to be characteristic. This clinical picture may occur in elderly malnourished patients and in alcoholics.

Vitamin B_{12} deficiency

Severe pernicious anaemia due to deficiency of gastric intrinsic factor causes the classical picture of subacute combined degeneration of the cord accompanied by anaemia (macrocytic and megaloblastic) and a progressive dementia. In less advanced cases there is depression and lethargy. There may also be impairment of memory which improves after treatment with B_{12} (Shulman 1967).

It has been suggested that the dementia and other psychological symptoms may occur before the characteristic physical features. Surveys have often shown that low serum B_{12} levels are common among psychiatric patients. However, it is highly likely that such findings can be explained by a poor diet consequent upon psychiatric disorder, rather than by B_{12} deficiency as a causal factor. Clinical experience indicates that it is unusual to diagnose B_{12} deficiency for the first time in a patient with early dementia. When B_{12} deficiency is found, replacement therapy rarely leads to improvement in dementia. It is reasonable to measure serum B_{12} in any unexplained acute or chronic organic psychiatric syndrome, but there is no justification for its routine estimation in all psychiatric patients.

Folic acid deficiency

Among the elderly and among psychiatric patients of all ages, it is common to find folic acid deficiency of dietary origin, but it is difficult to assess its causal significance, if any. Low serum concentrations of folate and low red cell levels are unusually common in epileptic patients, probably as a result of anticonvulsant medication. It has been suggested that these deficiencies may account for some of the psychological symptoms of epileptic patients, but at present the evidence is not convincing.

Overall there is little evidence that folate deficiency is an important cause of psychiatric disorder. Routine screening is not justified, although measurement of red cell folate may occasionally be appropriate when investigating an unexplained organic psychiatric disorder. If the folate is low, replacement therapy can be tried, though without great expectation of success.

Toxic disorders and side-effects of drugs

Table 11.4 lists drugs that are most likely to give rise to psychiatric side-effects. In addition to this list it is important to remember alcohol, drugs of addiction, psychotropic medication, and steroid therapy (all discussed

Table 11.4. Drugs with psychological side-effects

Antiparkinsonian agents	
Anticholinergic drugs (benzhexol, benztropine, procyclidine)	Disorientation, agitation, confusion, visual hallucinations
Laevodopa	Acute organic syndrome, depression, psychotic symptoms
Antihypertensive drugs	
Reserpine	Depression
Methyldopa	Tiredness, weakness, depression
Sympathetic blockers	Impotence, mild depression
Digitalis	Disorientation, confusion, and mood disturbance
Diuretics	Weakness, apathy, and depression (due to electrolyte depletion)
Analgesics	
Salicylamide	Confusion, agitation, amnesia
Phenacetin	Dementia with chronic abuse
Antituberculous therapy	
Isoniazid	Acute organic syndrome and mania
Cycloserine	Confusion, schizophrenia-like syndrome

elsewhere in this book). The rare syndromes associated with heavy metals, such as lead, arsenic, and mercury are reviewed by Lishman (1987), and in the larger medical textbooks.

Electrolyte and body fluid disorders

Various electrolyte and fluid disorders can cause mental symptoms, usually but not invariably in the form of an acute organic syndrome. In Table 11.5 the main psychological disturbances are listed, and certain important physical symptoms and signs are shown in brackets. (Other physical features of the various disorders will be found in a textbook of medicine.) The role of hypomagnesaemia is at present uncertain. Calcium metabolism was mentioned earlier in relation to parathyroid conditions (p. 383); it is of particular interest because there seems to be a close relationship between the concentration of serum calcium and the extent of the mental changes (Petersen 1968; de Alarcón and Franchesini 1984)

Table 11.5. Psychological symptoms of electrolyte disorders

Sodium depletion	Weakness, dizziness, sweating Lassitude, apathy Progression to an acute organic syndrome and coma (low blood pressure, abdominal pain)
Potassium depletion	Lethargy, apathy, anorexia, constipation, depression, anxiety Rarely an acute organic syndrome (Paralytic ileus, muscle weakness, ECG changes)
Potassium excess	Weakness, lethargy and confusion (cardiac arrhythmia)
Hypercalcaemia	Depression and acute organic syndrome
Hypocalcaemia	Depression and acute organic syndrome (cramps, tetany)
Alkalosis	Apathy, disorientation, acute organic syndrome (paraesthesia; tetany)
Acidosis	Impaired consciousness (rapid respiration)

Epilepsy

The psychiatrist is likely to meet four kinds of problem in relation to epilepsy; differential diagnosis (particularly of atypical attacks, aggressive behaviour, and sleep problems); the treatment of the psychiatric and social complications of epilepsy; the treatment of epilepsy itself in patients who consult him; and the psychological side-effects of anticonvulsant drugs. Reviews of these problems and of other aspects of epilepsy can be found in the tests by Laidlaw *et al.* (1988), Reynolds and Trimble (1981), and Pedley and Meldrum (1983, 1985, 1986).

Types of epilepsy

To understand the psychiatric aspects of epilepsy, it is necessary to know how epilepsy is classified and what the clinical features are of its common forms. It is useful to remember that the term **ictus** refers to seizure itself and is characterized by abnormal electrical activity. The **aura** is nothing more than a simple partial seizure, and may therefore be complete seizure or the first stage in which consciousness is preserved. It should be

Table 11.6. Classification of seizures

---

1. *Partial seizures or seizures beginning focally*
   Simple motor or sensory (without impaired consciousness)
   Complex partial (secondarily generalized; with impaired consciousness).

2. *Generalized seizures without focal onset.*
   Tonic–clonic convulsion
   Myoclonic, atonic
   Absences

3. *Unclassified*

---

distinguished from **prodromata**, symptoms which sometimes precede the seizure.

The International League against Epilepsy drew up the original version of the classification of seizures (Gastaut 1969), which is now in general use in a slightly revised version (Dreifuss *et al.* 1981). Traditional terms such as **petit mal** and **grand mal** are not used because of their ambiguity. The scheme is elaborate, and the outline shown in Table 11.6 is much simplified. The principal distinction is between partial seizures which start focally, and generalized seizures which are generalized from the beginning. Since focal seizures often become generalized, a description of the initial stages of the attack is of the greatest importance in the use of this diagnostic scheme.

Simple partial seizures

This group includes Jacksonian motor seizures and a variety of sensory seizures in which the phenomena are relatively unformed. Consciousness is not impaired. These seizures may secondarily become generalized, with impaired consciousness.

Complex partial seizures

This category replaces the earlier categories of 'psychomotor' seizures and 'temporal lobe epilepsy'. These seizures arise most commonly in the temporal lobe but may have other focal origins. Those originally in the frontal lobe are particularly likely to be misdiagnosed as psychiatric disorder (Williamson and Spencer 1986). They are often preceded by a simple partial seizure which lasts for a few seconds and may take the form of hallucinations of smell, taste, vision, hearing, or bodily sensation. The patient may also experience intense disturbances of thinking, perception, or emotion. Consciousness is impaired.

The clinical features of complex partial seizures are summarized in Table 11.7. (A detailed description is given by Daly 1975.) An important

Table 11.7. Clinical features of complex partial seizures

Consciousness	Impaired
Autonomic and visceral	'Epigastric aura', dizziness, flushing, tachycardia, and other bodily sensations
Perceptual	Distorted perceptions, *déjà vu*, visual, auditory, olfactory, and somatic hallucinations
Cognitive	Disturbances of speech, thought, and memory
Affective	Fear and anxiety
Psychomotor	Automatisms, grimacing and other bodily movements, repetitive or more complex stereotyped behaviour

point is that in an individual patient the sequence of events in the seizure tends to be the same on each occasion. A particularly common feature is the 'epigastric aura', a sensation of churning felt in the stomach and spreading towards the neck. Patients often have great difficulty in describing these phenomena.

The whole ictal phase lasts up to one or two minutes. During this phase and the post-ictal phase the subject appears out of touch with his surroundings and may show automatisms. After recovery, only the aura may be recalled. Status epilepticus of two kinds may occur, a prolonged single seizure or a rapid succession of brief seizures. In such cases a prolonged period of automatic behaviour and amnesia may be mistaken for a hysterical fugue or other forms of psychiatric disorder.

Generalized tonic–clonic seizure

This is the familiar epileptic seizure with a sudden onset, tonic and clonic phases, and a final period of several minutes in which the patient is unrousable. Most tonic–clonic seizures are secondary to a seizure of another type.

Myoclonic, atonic

There are several types of generalized epilepsy with predominantly motor symptoms, such as widespread myoclonic jerks or drop attacks. They are unlikely to present problems to the psychiatrist.

Absences

There are several clinical types, all of which have impaired consciousness as the cardinal feature. The attack starts suddenly without an aura, lasts for seconds and ends abruptly. There are no post-ictal abnormalities. Motor symptoms or simple automatisms are often present. The simple absence seizure ('*petit mal*') is rather less common. For a number of purposes including treatment, it is important to distinguish between absence seizures and the less florid forms of complex partial seizures. The latter often begin with an aura, last longer, and are followed by slow return to recovery. An EEG may be required to make the distinction with certainty.

Epidemiology

In the United Kingdom, surveys in general practice have shown the prevalence of epilepsy to be at least 4–6 per 1000. The inception rate is highest in early childhood, and there are further peaks at adolescence and over the age of 65. In a few cases starting in childhood, epilepsy is associated with mental handicap. [For a review of the epidemiology of epilepsy see Sander and Shorvon (1987).]

Aetiology

Many causes of epilepsy are known and their frequency varies with age. In the newborn, birth injury, congenital malformations, metabolic disorders, and infections are the most common. In the elderly, the most common causes are cerebrovascular disease, head injury, and degenerative cerebral disorder. In at least a half of patients no cause is found after full investigation; in such cases genetic factors appear to be of greater significance than in those with demonstrable pathology.

Seizures can occur as a result of drug therapy, but many neurologists would not diagnose them as epilepsy on the grounds that the latter must have a primary origin in the brain. Amongst the psychotropic drugs chlorpromazine is implicated most often, and amitriptyline and imipramine less often. Sudden withdrawal of substantial doses of any drug with antiepileptic properties may be followed by seizures. The withdrawal of large doses of diazepam and alcohol are the commonest examples among psychiatric patients.

The diagnosis of epilepsy

Epilepsy is essentially a clinical diagnosis which depends upon detailed accounts of the attacks given by witnesses as well as by the patient. The rest of the history, the physical examination, and special investigations are concerned with aetiology. The extent of investigation is guided by the initial findings, the type of attack, and the patient's age. Only an outline

Table 11.8. Differential diagnosis of epilepsy

Organic
  Syncope
  Hypoglycaemia
  Transient ischaemic attacks
  Migraine
  Sleep disorders, especially night terrors

Non-organic
  Temper tantrums
  Breath holding
  Hyperventilation
  Hysteria
  Panic attacks
  Schizophrenia
  Aggressive outburst in unstable personality
  Night terrors

---

can be given here; for a full account the reader is referred to a textbook such as that by Laidlaw *et al.* 1988.

An EEG can confirm but cannot exclude the diagnosis of epilepsy. It is more useful in determining the type of epilepsy and site of origin. The standard recording may be supplemented by sleep recording, ambulatory monitoring, and split-screen video techniques.

Since epilepsy is often erroneously diagnosed in children and adults (Jeavons 1983), it is important to keep in mind the differential diagnoses (Table 11.8). Particular difficulty may be experienced in distinguishing complex forms of epilepsy from certain kinds of psychiatric disorder, of which hysteria is the most important and difficult. Features that suggest hysteria are an unusual or variable pattern of attacks, occurrence only in public, and absence of autonomic signs or changes in reflexes. Factors that point strongly to epilepsy are tongue-biting, incontinence, definite loss of consciousness, and sustaining injury during the attack. Epilepsy is often considered in the diagnosis of aggressive outbursts but is a rare cause (Treiman and Delgado-Escueta 1985). If the diagnosis remains uncertain, closer observation in hospital should be considered (though seizures often stop when the patient is in hospital). [See Fenton (1986) and Lowman and Richardson (1987) for reviews of the differential diagnosis between epilepsy and psychiatric disorder.]

If an epileptic patient has an abnormal personality and shows aggressive outbursts, it is sometimes difficult to decide whether the latter are due to epileptic automatism or simply an expression of personality disorder (see p. 396).

Social aspects of epilepsy

The person with epilepsy is often at a social disadvantage. In a survey of epileptic patients in general practice, Pond and Bidwell (1960) found that half had experienced serious difficulties with work. Many patients suffer more from the misconceptions and prejudices of other people about epilepsy than from the condition itself. Problems arise in school, at work, and in the course of family life. Marriage prospects may be affected. In the care of people with epilepsy it is important to attempt to reduce these misunderstandings, and to support the patient and his family (see Laidlaw *et al.* 1988; Reynolds and Trimble 1981).

In Britain legislation about driving is less restrictive than it used to be. To obtain a driving licence the patient must have had at least two years with no fits whilst awake, whether or not he is still taking antiepileptic drugs. Those who suffer fits only whilst asleep may have a licence if this pattern has been present for at least three years.

Psychiatric consequences of epilepsy

As mentioned already, it used to be thought that people with epilepsy suffered an inevitable deterioration of personality. This belief has been repeatedly disproved, but continues as a popular misconception that causes much unnecessary distress. However, there are several important ways in which epilepsy predisposes to psychiatric disturbance. [For reviews see Hermann and Whitman (1984).]

Prevalence

In their survey of epileptic patients in general practice, Pond and Bidwell (1960) found that nearly 30 per cent had conspicuous psychological difficulties, 7 per cent had had in-patient psychiatric care, and 10 per cent were educationally subnormal. Temporal lobe disorders were especially associated with psychological disability. Edeh and Toone (1987) used modern methods of case definition and found a high prevalence in general practice. Psychiatric disorder was more common in those with both temporal lobe and other focal epilepsy. In their Isle of Wight survey of schoolchildren aged between 5 and 14, Graham and Rutter (1968) diagnosed psychiatric disorder in 7 per cent of non-epileptic children, 30 per cent of those with uncomplicated epilepsy, and nearly 60 per cent of those with epilepsy complicated by evidence of brain damage. However, the precise nature of this association remains uncertain.

Clinical features

A classification of the psychiatric consequences of epilepsy is shown in Table 11.9.

Table 11.9. Associations between epilepsy and psychological disturbance

---

1. Psychiatric disorder associated with the underlying cause

2. Behavioural disturbance associated with the seizure
   Pre-ictal
   Ictal
   Post-ictal

3. Inter-ictal disorders
   Cognitive
   Personality
   Sexual behaviour
   Crime
   Emotional disorder
   Psychoses

Psychiatric disorder associated with the underlying cause

The underlying cause of epilepsy may contribute to intellectual impairment or personality problems, especially if there is extensive brain damage. Epilepsy is common in the mentally retarded (see Chapter 21).

Behavioural disturbance associated with the seizure

Increasing tension, irritability, and depression are sometimes apparent as prodromata for several days before a seizure. Transient confusional states and automatisms may occur during seizures (especially complex partial seizures) and after seizures (usually those involving generalized convulsions, and complex partial seizures). Less commonly, non-convulsive seizures may continue for days or even weeks (absence status and complex partial status). An abnormal mental state may be the only sign of this condition (Stores 1986) and the diagnosis is easily overlooked (see *Lancet* 1987a).

Inter-ictal disorders

There is no convincing evidence of a direct relationship between epilepsy and psychiatric disturbance occurring between seizures. However there are several indirect associations.

Cognitive function

In the nineteenth century it was widely believed that epilepsy was associated with an inevitable decline in intellectual functioning. Subsequently, investigations tended to support this belief, but the findings were misleading because they were based on residents in institutions. Early research was also unsatisfactory because it was retrospective, and therefore unable to distinguish between dementia that progressed over time, and lifelong intellectual retardation (see Brown and Reynolds 1981). Nowadays it is established that relatively few people with epilepsy show cognitive changes.

When intellectual changes do occur, the significant aetiological factors are likely to be: brain damage; poor concentration and memory during periods of abnormal electrical activity; and the adverse effects of anti-epileptic drugs given in high doses or even in doses optimal for the control of seizures (especially barbiturates).

A few epileptic patients show a progressive decline in cognitive function. In such cases careful investigation is required to exclude the progression of an underlying neurological disorder, toxic drug levels, and repeated non-convulsive epileptic status.

Learning problems are more common in children with epilepsy than in non-epileptic children (Stores 1981). Apart from the factors listed above, possible causes include poor school attendance, and the general social difficulties of being epileptic. When intellectual deterioration occurs in children, it may be due to medication, or the underlying pathological process causing the seizures, or the seizures themselves (Ellenberg *et al.* 1986; Corbett *et al.* 1985).

Personality

As already explained, nineteenth-century writers suggested that seizures cause personality deterioration. Early in the twentieth century, it was held that epilepsy and personality changes resulted from some common under-lying abnormality. The 'epileptic personality' was said to be characterized by egocentricity, irritability, religiosity, quarrelsomeness, and 'sticky' thought processes. It is now recognized that these ideas arose from observations of severely affected people with brain disease living in institutions. Surveys of people with epilepsy living in the community have shown that only a minority have serious personality difficulties. Even when they occur, such personality problems show no distinctive pattern (see Tizard 1962; Fenton 1983). For example there is little evidence to support an association between epilepsy and aggressiveness (Treiman and Delgado-Escueta 1985). It has been suggested that abnormalities of personality are mainly associated with temporal lobe lesions (see, for example, Pond and Bidwell 1960; Guerrant *et al.* 1962).

When personality disorder does occur, social factors probably play an important part in aetiology. These factors include the social limitations imposed on the epileptic, his own embarrassment, and the reactions of other people. It is also possible that brain damage sometimes contributes to the development of personality disorder.

Sexual dysfunction

Sexual dysfunction is probably more common in epileptics than in non-epileptics. This is thought to apply particularly to patients with temporal lobe foci. Possible causes include the general social maladjustment of some epileptics and the effects of antiepileptic medication (see Toone 1985).

Epilepsy and crime

Nineteenth-century writers such as Lombroso thought that crime was far more common among epileptic than among non-epileptic people. It is now well established that there is no such close association between epilepsy and crime.

In a survey of the prison population of England and Wales, Gunn (1977*a*) found the proportion of people with epilepsy to be 7–8 per 1000, which is probably greater than in the general population. Prisoners with epilepsy were no more aggressive than other prisoners, but they had a greater rate of psychiatric disturbance. There was no relationship between epilepsy and the type of crime. The explanation for the disproportionate number of epileptics in prison is not known; it may be that the social difficulties of epileptics lead them into more conflict with the law. For general reviews see Gunn (1977*a*); Treiman and Delgado-Escueta (1985).

Gunn and Fenton (1971) carried out a survey of special hospitals and concluded that crimes committed during epileptic automatisms are extremely rare. This conclusion, which has important medico-legal implications, is supported by evidence from other countries (see *Lancet* 1981 and p. 868).

Emotional disorder

In Pond and Bidwell's (1960) general practice survey, half the epileptic patients with psychological problems (15 per cent of the total number) were thought to suffer from emotional disorder. There was no evidence that these disorders had a distinctive pattern. Since this survey was carried out before the introduction of standardized diagnostic methods it is not possible to compare the findings with the prevalence of emotional disorder in the general population. Mild unhappiness is probably much more common than formal psychiatric disorder.

Inter-ictal psychoses

The nature of inter-ictal psychoses is controversial. Some writers have suggested that psychotic disorder is less common in people who suffer from epilepsy than in the general population (the antagonism hypothesis); others have argued the opposite view, that such illnesses are more common in epilepsy (the affinity hypothesis). It is still not possible to reach definite conclusions but most recent research has concentrated on possible associations between certain forms of epilepsy and schizophrenia-like disorders.

Inter-ictal disorders resembling schizophrenia

Hill (1953) and Pond (1957) defined a 'chronic paranoid hallucinatory psychosis' associated with temporal lobe epilepsy. The clinical picture closely resembled that of schizophrenia except that affective responses were preserved. Slater and his colleagues (1963) collected 69 patients with unequivocal epilepsy who developed an illness diagnosed as schizophrenia. Almost all these patients suffered from temporal lobe epilepsy, and although there was no control group, the authors argued that this association was unlikely to have been due to chance. Like Hill and Pond, these authors reported that normal affective responses were usually preserved. They also found that some cases progressed towards a more 'organic' clinical picture. A family history of schizophrenia was usually lacking. The psychosis usually began many years after the onset of epilepsy, in patients with a normal premorbid personality.

There has been continuing dispute as to whether or not there is a specific association between temporal lobe epilepsy and schizophrenia. It now seems likely that there is an association between temporal lobe epilepsy and chronic paranoid–hallucinatory conditions, though the noso-logical status of the latter is uncertain.

A complicating factor is that epilepsy arising in the temporal lobe can be due to damage elsewhere in the brain. Sometimes a patient's history suggests widespread brain damage involving areas other than the temporal lobe. On the other hand pathological studies more often show discrete focal lesions in the temporal lobes (Lishman 1987).

Inter-ictal affective disorders

The relationship of epilepsy to affective disorder has been studied less thoroughly than its relationship to schizophrenia. Few attempts have been made to separate the syndrome of depressive disorder from common depressive symptoms. Nevertheless, depressive disorder is probably the commonest psychiatric condition in people with epilepsy (see Trimble 1985).

Suicide and deliberate self-harm

Suicide is four times more frequent among people with epilepsy than among the general population (Sainsbury 1986) and deliberate self-harm is six times as frequent (Hawton *et al.* 1980). The association has been reviewed by Barraclough (1987).

Treatment

The drug treatment of epilepsy is summarized in Chapter 17. For a more detailed account of the care of epileptic patients a textbook of epilepsy should be consulted (for example, Laidlaw *et al.* 1988). Here it is only necessary to emphasize the importance of distinguishing between peri-ictal and inter-ictal psychiatric disorders. For peri-ictal psychiatric disorders, treatment is aimed at control of the seizures. For inter-ictal psychiatric disorders, the treatment is the same as it would be for a non-epileptic patient, though it should be remembered that many psychotropic drugs can increase seizure frequency. Emotional arousal can do the same.

Sleep disorders

Psychiatrists may be asked to see patients whose main problem is either difficulty in sleeping or, less often, excessive sleep. Many patients who sleep badly complain of tiredness during the day and mood disturbance. Although prolonged sleep deprivation leads to some impairment of intellectual performance and disturbance of mood, loss of sleep on occasional nights is of little significance. The daytime symptoms of people who sleep badly are probably related more to the cause of their insomnia (often a depressive disorder or anxiety disorder) than to the insomnia itself. Wakefulness in infants is discussed on p. 781.

Table 11.10 shows the DSMIIIR classification of sleep disorders. The ICD10 classification is simpler, but has similar headings. [Sleep disorders have been reviewed by Gulleminault and Mandini (1984), Parkes (1985), and Kales *et al.* (1987).]

Insomnia

There is a wide variation in reported estimates of the prevalence of insomnia, depending on the definition of insomnia and on the population studied. Rates of 10 per cent to 20 per cent are usual, but rates of 30 per cent have been reported (see, for example, Mellinger *et al.* 1985). Insomnia is mostly secondary to other disorders, notably painful physical conditions, depressive disorders, anxiety disorders, and dementia. It also occurs with excessive use of alcohol or caffeine. Sleep may be disturbed for several weeks after stopping heavy drinking of alcohol. In about 15 per cent of cases of insomnia, no cause can be found ('primary insomnia'). People vary in the amount of sleep they require, and many who complain of insomnia are probably having enough sleep without realizing it.

Usually the diagnosis of insomnia has to be based on the account given by the patient. EEG and other physiological recordings in a sleep

Table 11.10. Classification of sleep disorders

Insomnia Disorder (*Disorders of the initiation and maintenance of sleep: DIMS)
Insomnia related to another mental disorder
Insomnia related to a physical condition or medication
Primary insomnia

Hypersomnia (*Disorders of excessive Somnolence: DOES)
Hypersomnia related to another mental disorder
Hypersomnia related to a physical condition or medication use
    (includes narcolepsy or sleep apnoea)
Primary hypersomnia

Sleep–wake schedule disorder
*Transient
    (a) Time zone change ('jet-lag')
    (b) 'Work shift' changes
Sleep–wake schedule disorder, Frequently changing type
Sleep–wake schedule disorder, Advanced or Delayed type
Sleep–wake schedule disorder, Disorganized type

Parasomnias
Sleep-walking disorder
Sleep terror disorder
Dream anxiety disorder

---

* Items marked with an asterisk are commonly used terms, but do not appear in DSMIIIR.

laboratory are occasionally helpful when there is continuing doubt about the extent and nature of the insomnia. These observations often show that, despite the patient's complaint, sleeping time is within the normal range.

If insomnia is secondary to another condition, the latter should be treated. When no cause can be found it is probably useful to encourage regular habits and exercise, and discourage over-indulgence in tobacco, caffeine, and alcohol. Training in relaxation (see p. 728) helps some patients. Although it may sometimes be justifiable to give a hypnotic for a few nights, demands for prolonged medication should be resisted. This is because withdrawal of hypnotics may lead to insomnia as distressing as the original sleep disturbance. Continuation of hypnotics may be associated with impaired performance during the day, tolerance to the sedative effects, and dependency. The use of hypnotic drugs is described further on p. 639.

Hypersomnia

Narcolepsy

Narcolepsy usually begins between the ages of 10 and 20 years, though it may start earlier. Onset is rare after middle age. Narcolepsy is more frequent among males. Cataplexy (sudden temporary episodes of paralysis with loss of muscle tone) occurs in most cases, but sleep paralysis and hypnagogic hallucinations occur in only a quarter of patients. Cataplexy may start at the same time as the narcolepsy, or after it; it is rare for it to precede the sleep disorder. There is a family history of narcolepsy in about a third of patients, and in occasional families the disorder appears to be transmitted as an autosomal dominant. Almost all cases of narcolepsy have the HLA type DR2, compared with about a quarter of the general population; the significance of this association is not understood, though it points to a genetic origin, and links it with chromosome 6. Many aetiological theories have been advanced [see Parkes (1985) for a review] but none is convincing.

Psychiatric aspects of narcolepsy Strong emotions sometimes precipitate cataplexy but apparently not narcolepsy. Patients with narcolepsy often have secondary emotional and social difficulties, and their difficulties are increased by other people's lack of understanding. Schizophrenia-like mental disorders, often with no family history of schizophrenia, have been reported to occur more frequently in patients with narcolepsy than in the general population (Davison 1983). The reason for this association is not known [see Roy (1976) for a review of psychiatric aspects of narcolepsy].

Management The EEG is helpful in diagnosis of narcolepsy. Night-time sleep is often abnormal with an unusually early onset of REM sleep, frequent periods of wakefulness, and many shifts of phase. Narcoleptic attacks by day are sometimes accompanied by REM sleep, though not always. In the multiple sleep latency test, the subject is given the opportunity to fall asleep four to five times at two-hour intervals during the day. The test is positive if the time taken to fall alseep is repeatedly less than ten minutes (see Gulleminault and Mandini 1984).

There is no really satisfactory treatment. Patients should be encouraged to follow a regular routine with planned short periods of sleep during the day. If stressful events seem to provoke attacks, efforts should be made to avoid them. Regular dosage with amphetamine or methylphenidate has some effect in reducing narcoleptic attack but little effect on cataplexy. These drugs have to be given in high doses that lead to side-effects and problems of dependency. (These problems are discussed on p. 673).

Tricyclic antidepressants do not affect the sleep disorder but may reduce the frequency of cataplexy. Some authors suggest the combined use of tricyclics and amphetamines, but this combination is better avoided if possible because of the risk of hypertensive effects. [See Parkes (1985) for further information about narcolepsy and its treatment.]

Other hypersomnias

In other hypersomnias, episodes of sleep are more gradual in onset and usually longer lasting than attacks of narcolepsy. The daytime drowsiness causes difficulties at work (see Parkes 1985). The more common causes are idiopathic hypersomnolence and sleep apnoea. Kleine–Levin syndrome is a very rare cause.

Idiopathic hypersomnolence   This is the most prevalent of the primary hypersomnias. Patients complain that they are unable to wake completely until several hours after getting up. During this time they feel confused and maybe disorientated ('sleep drunkenness'). They usually report prolonged and deep night-time sleep. Almost half have periods of daytime automatic behaviour, the aetiology of which is obscure. Most patients respond well to small doses of CNS stimulant drugs (see Roth *et al.* 1972).

Sleep apnoea   This syndrome consists of daytime drowsiness together with periodic respiration and excessive snoring at night. It is usually associated with upper airways obstruction. The typical patient is a middle-aged overweight man who snores loudly. Treatment consists of relieving the cause of the respiratory obstruction or obesity. Continuous positive pressure ventilation using a face mask is often effective.

The Kleine–Levin syndrome   This consists of episodes of somnolence and increased appetite, often lasting for days or weeks and with long intervals of normality between them. Patients can always be roused from the daytime sleep, but are irritable on waking and occasionally aggressive; some are muddled and experience depression, hallucinations, and disorientation. Although the combination of appetite disorder and sleep disturbance suggests a hypothalamic disorder, there is no convincing evidence about the aetiology.

Sleep–wake schedule disorders

Fatigue and transient difficulties in sleeping accompany changes in bodily rhythms after travel across time zones or changes in shift work. Regular changes of shift or the irregular alternation of night work and days off may lead to chronic problems of poor sleep, fatigue, impaired concentration, and an increased liability to accidents.

Parasomnias

Nightmares (Dream anxiety disorder) A nightmare is an awakening from REM sleep to full consciousness with detailed dream recall. Children experience nightmares with a peak frequency around the ages of five or six years. Nightmares may be stimulated by frightening experiences during the day, and frequent nightmares usually occur during a period of anxiety (see Kales *et al.* 1987).

Night terror disorder Night terrors are much less common than nightmares. They are sometimes familial. The condition begins in child-hood and usually ends there but occasionally persist into adult life. A few hours after going to sleep the child, whilst in stage three to four non-REM sleep, sits up and appears terrified. He may scream and usually appears confused. There are marked increases in heart and respiratory rates. After a few minutes the child slowly settles and returns to normal calm sleep. There is little or no dream recall. Benzodiazepines and imipramine have been shown to be effective in preventing night terrors (see Kales *et al.* 1987), but their prolonged use should be avoided.

Sleep-walking disorder Sleep-walking is an automatism occurring during deep non-REM sleep, usually in the early part of the night. It is most common between the ages of 5 and 12 years, and 15 per cent of children in this age group walk in their sleep at least once. Occasionally the disorder persists into adult life. Sleep-walking may be familial.

Most children do not actually walk, but sit up and make repetitive movements. Some walk around, usually with their eyes open, in a mechanical manner but avoiding familiar objects. They do not respond to questions and are very difficult to wake. They can usually be led back to bed. Most episodes last a few seconds or minutes, but rarely as long as an hour.

As sleep-walkers can occasionally harm themselves, they need to be protected from injury. Doors and windows should be locked and danger-ous objects removed. Benzodiazepines may be helpful (see Kales *et al.* 1987).

Movement disorders

Parkinson's disease

It is because dementia occurs in patients with Parkinson's disease that movement disorders are considered in this chapter. Estimates of the prevalence of this association vary widely. It has been reported that the frequency of dementia is greater than chance (Mindham *et al.* 1982) but the magnitude of the increased risk is still not certain. It has been suggested that the dementia is 'subcortical'; that is, due to a lack of activated inputs to the cortex from lower centres, rather than to primary cortical pathology (see p. 352).

The association of Parkinson's disease with depression is well established but the cause is not understood. Depression can often be understood as an appropriate response to the limitations of an unpleasant disease. Mindham (1970 *et al.*) found a highly significant correlation between the severity of the signs of Parkinson's disease and the intensity of the depressive symptoms. However, depression is not always a reaction to disability because it sometimes precedes physical symptoms. Moreover it is more frequent in parkinsonism than in other disabling conditions. Also, although laevodopa reduces the motor symptoms of Parkinson's disease, the frequency of depressive episodes seems to be increased when it is used. [Whitlock (1986*b*) has reviewed the psychiatric aspects of Parkinson's disease.]

Drugs used to treat parkinsonism may cause organic mental disorders. Anticholinergic drugs may cause excitement, agitation, delusions, and hallucinations. Laevodopa is associated with an acute organic syndrome as well as the depressive symptoms. Stereotactic surgery for the treatment of tremor is often followed by transient deficits in cognitive function and rarely by lasting cognitive impairment.

Spasmodic torticollis

In this rare condition there are repeated, purposeless movements of the head and neck, or sustained abnormal positions, or both. There is always some element of muscle spasm (a point of distinction from tics). The onset is usually between the ages of 30 and 50 years. The course may vary but it is usually a slow progression over many years. It is not certain whether the causes are organic, psychogenic or a combination of the two [see Lishman (1987) and Martin (1982) for reviews of the evidence]. Treatment is unsatisfactory. Approaches have ranged from psychotherapy to surgery to the affected muscles, but there is no evidence that any is effective.

Writer's and occupational cramps

In the writer's cramp, attempts at handwriting are accompanied by painful spasms of the muscles controlling fine movements of the fingers. The spasms often begin as soon as the pen is gripped. The patient can learn to write with the other hand, but sometimes this too becomes affected. Related activities such as holding a paintbrush are not usually affected.

Occupational cramps are similar disorders in which a particular motor skill is impaired. They occur for example in pianists, violinists, telegraph-ists, and typists. They usually begin in middle life, and the prognosis is poor. Attempts have been made to explain the aetiology in terms of psychodynamic, organic, and learning theories, but without success. The poor response to any psychological treatment suggests an organic element in the aetiology, but so far none has been found.

Whatever the type of cramp, a common-sense behavioural approach to treatment is probably as effective as any other. For example, patients with writer's cramp can be taught to relax and then write for gradually increasing periods; first letters, then words and sentences. A form of aversion therapy has been used whereby a special pen delivers a small shock whenever the pressure of the writing fingers is too great. This therapy gives unsatisfactory results and it is not recommended.

Tics

Tics are purposeless, stereotyped, and repetitive jerking movements occurring most commonly in the face and neck. They are much more common in childhood than in adult life, though a few cases begin up to 40 years of age. The peak of onset is about seven years, and the onset is often at a time of emotional disturbance. They are especially common in boys. Most sufferers have just one kind of abnormal movement, but a few people have more than one (multiple tics). Like almost all involuntary movements, tics are worsened by anxiety. Tics can be controlled briefly by voluntary effort, but this results in an increasingly unpleasant feeling of tension. Many tics occurring in childhood last only a few weeks; others last longer, but 80–90 per cent of cases improve within five years. A few cases become chronic. [The subject of tics has been reviewed by Corbett and Turpin (1985).]

Gilles de la Tourette syndrome

This condition was described first by Itard in 1825 and subsequently by Gilles de la Tourette in 1895. The main clinical features are multiple tics beginning before the age of 16, together with vocal tics (grunting, snarling, and similar ejaculations). About half the people affected show coprolalia (uttering obscenities), and a few show echolalia. There may be stereotyped movements such as jumping and dancing. The tics usually precede the other features (Corbett *et al.* 1969). Associated features include over-activity, difficulties in learning, emotional disturbances, and social problems.

The frequency of the condition is about 1 to 5 per 10 000 population. It is 3 to 4 times commoner in males, and the mean age of onset is 5–6 years (Shapiro *et al.* 1978)

Studies of families suggest that Gilles de la Tourette syndrome and multiple tics (without vocal tics) are expressions of the same basic condition.

Aetiological explanations have been proposed in terms of psychogenic, developmental, and learning theories, but none of them is convincing. The condition is aggravated by emotional influences, but this does not prove an emotional aetiology. Despite the lack of structural pathology, an organic cause is now thought most likely, possibly involving neurotransmission in the basal ganglia.

Many treatments have been tried. Haloperidol appears to be the most satisfactory, but the side-effects can be a disadvantage. There is not enough follow-up information to indicate the prognosis, but clinical impressions suggest that the outcome is generally poor. [For a review of the syndrome see Corbett and Turpin (1985).]

Drug-induced disorders of movement

These disorders are discussed in Chapter 17, p. 646.

Further reading

Bonhoeffer, K. (1909). Exogenous psychoses. In Hirsch, S. R. and Shepherd, M. (ed.) (1974). *Themes and variations in European psychiatry*. John Wright, Bristol.

Hales, R. E. , and Yudofsky S. C. (eds.) (1987). *Textbook of Neuropsychiatry*. American Psychiatric Press, Washington, DC.

Laidlaw, J., Richens, A. and Oxley, J. (eds.) (1988). *A textbook of epilepsy* (3rd edn). Churchill Livingstone, Edinburgh.

Lishman, W. A. (1987). *Organic psychiatry* (2nd edn). Blackwell, Oxford.

Wolff, H. G. and Curran, D. (1935). Nature of delirium and allied states. *Archives of Neurology and Psychiatry* **35**, 1175–1215.

12   Psychiatry and medicine

Introduction

Physical disorders and psychiatric disorders commonly occur together in the general population, in patients who consult general practitioners, and in those referred to psychiatrists, physicians, surgeons, and other specialists.

In a study of a randomly chosen sample of the *general population*, Eastwood and Trevelyan (1972) found a positive association between psychiatric and physical disorder.

In *general practice*, surveys have consistently found that patients identified as suffering from psychiatric illness have high rates of physical morbidity (for example, Shepherd *et al.* 1966).

In *psychiatric practice*, physical illness has been found to occur commonly among psychiatric out-patients (Koryani 1979). In a study of 200 consecutive in-patients admitted to a general hospital psychiatric in-patient unit with district responsibilities, Maguire and Granville-Grossman (1968) found that 67 had a concurrent physical illness. Of these 67 patients, 33 had not been previously diagnosed as physically ill, and 18 required transfer to specialist medical care. The incidence of physical disorder increased with increasing age.

In medicine and surgery, numerous studies have found associations between physical and psychiatric disorders among both in-patients and out-patients. In medical wards, for example, surveys have shown that over a quarter of in-patients have psychiatric disorders. The frequency and nature of these disorders depend on the age and sex of the patients and on the type of ward. For example, affective and adjustment disorders are more common in younger women, whilst organic mental disorders are more common in the elderly, and drinking problems in younger men. Psychological problems are frequent in certain departments, notably emergency clinics, and gynaecological and medical out-patient clinics. Organic mental disorders are frequent in geriatric wards, and drinking problems in liver units. [See Mayou and Hawton (1986) for a review of the prevalence of psychiatric disorder in general hospitals.]

That psychiatric disorder may interfere with recovery from physical illness was suggested by the results of Querido (1959) who studied 1630 patients in a general hospital the found that medical outcome seven months later was significantly worse in patients who had had the most psychiatric symptoms at the time of the original illness. It is of course possible that the original physical illness had been more serious in the patients who originally had the most psychiatric symptoms.

Psychiatric disorder in medical and surgical wards often goes undetected. In a survey of medical wards in an English hospital, Maguire *et al.* (1974) found that half the psychiatric morbidity had not been recognized by physicians or nurses. Subsequent studies have confirmed that many affective and organic disorders and most drinking problems are not detected among patients in general hospitals (see Mayou and Hawton 1986). It is important for several reasons that these psychiatric disorders should not be missed. Severe conditions are likely to need psychiatric treatment, and may carry a risk of suicide. Moderately severe disorders may also require treatment, and if persistent may delay recovery from the physical illness. Even mild disorders may cause suffering which could be alleviated.

Whether psychiatric treatment should be provided by a specialist or non-specialist depends on the severity of the psychiatric disorder. Severe disorders are likely to require treatment by a psychiatrist. Moderate and mild disorders can usually be treated by a physician, surgeon, or general practitioner with a sound basic knowledge of psychiatry.

In discussing the associations between physical and psychiatric disorder, it is useful to recognize the five types listed below:

1. Psychological factors as causes of physical illness.

2. Psychiatric disorders presenting with physical symptoms.

3. Psychiatric consequences of physical illness:
   (a) organic disorders (see also Chapter 11);
   (b) functional disorders.

4. Psychiatric and physical disorder occurring together by chance.

5. Physical complications of psychiatric problems:
   (a) deliberate self-harm;
   (b) alcohol and other substance abuse;
   (c) eating disorders.

The first three types of association are discussed in this chapter. The fourth type needs no discussion. Among associations of the fifth type, eating disorders are discussed here, whilst deliberate self-harm and substance abuse are reviewed in Chapters 13 and 14 respectively.

Psychological factors as causes of physical illness

In the nineteenth century it was widely accepted that psychological factors can play a part in the aetiology of physical illness (see Tuke 1872). In the twentieth century psychoanalysts, including Ferenczi, Groddeck, and Adler, suggested that Freud's theory of conversion hysteria could be applied to physical illnesses, and they presented case studies to support this idea. From these beginnings there emerged the body of theory and practice known as psychosomatic medicine, in which the term psychosomatic was used in a much narrower aetiological sense than that first used in the early nineteenth century by Heinroth (see Bynum 1983). Contributions to ideas on psychosomatic medicine also came from research by Pavlov on conditioning, by Cannon on the visceral response of animals to rage and fear, and by Wolf and Wolff on human psychological response to emotion. [See Weiner (1977) for a review of early literature on psychosomatic medicine.]

Against this background, psychosomatic theory held that emotional changes in human beings were accompanied by physiological changes and, if these emotional changes were persistent or frequent, pathological physical changes could follow. Once physical pathology was established, psychological factors could help to maintain or aggravate it, or to trigger relapses. It was also assumed that physical conditions induced in this way would improve if the psychological disturbance improved, either spontaneously or as a result of psychological treatment.

These early ideas were taken up enthusiastically in some places, notably the United States. Two main theories developed. The first held that *specific* types of emtional conflict or personality structure could cause specific physical pathology, the second that *non-specific* stressors could contribute to pathology in organs that were vulnerable for some other reason.

Two prominent exponents of the first theory were Franz Alexander and Flanders Dunbar. Alexander, a German-born psychoanalyst who migrated to the USA, proposed that there were seven psychosomatic diseases: bronchial asthma, rheumatoid arthritis, ulcerative colitis, essential hypertension, neurodermatitis, thyrotoxicosis, and peptic ulcer (see Alexander 1950). Dunbar founded the American Psychosomatic Society, and published a substantial survey of her own and other clinicians' observations in the book *Emotion and bodily changes* (see Dunbar 1954). She described specific personality types which she believed were associated with specific disorders. This view persists today in the concept of Type A behaviour and ischaemic heart disease (see p. 447). In support of the second theory (that non-specific psychological stressors lead to physical ilness in consititutionally predisposed people) different writers proposed different intervening processess, such as psychophysiological (Wolf and Wolff 1947), behavioural (Mahl 1953), and hormonal factors (Selye 1950). [These theories and the relevant research have been reviewed by Weiner (1977).]

Subsequent developments

These ideas about psychosomatic medicine were most influential in the years between 1930 and the late 1950s. Subsequently there developed a more general approach to the psychological causation of physical illness. It became apparent that many findings reported in the earlier psychosomatic literature were based on faulty research. For example, observations were often made on biased samples of patients, notably those selected by physicians for referral to psychiatrists; often there were no control groups; and methods of psychological assessment were subjective and unstandardized. Above all, most of the work was retrospective in that the clinician saw patients with established physical diseases, and tried to determine whether certain emotional conflicts, personality characteristics, or stressful events had preceded the onset of those diseases.

More recent theories are more modest and accept that physical illness has multiple causes. For instance, Engel and his colleagues maintain that a particular emotional disturbance can induce physical pathology, but they apply it to a wider group of physical diseases than the seven psychosomatic diseases proposed by Alexander (see Engel 1962). They believe that people are particularly likely to become physically ill if they develop a 'giving-up, given-up complex' in response to actual or threatened 'object loss'. This 'complex' is a combination of depressed mood, 'helplessness' and 'hopelessness'. To Engel 'helplessness' and 'hopelessness' are 'the greatest degree of disorganization in reponse to stress'. In helplessness, there are feelings of 'being left out, let down and deserted, but the individual considers himself neither responsible nor capable of doing anything about it, instead feeling that help must be provided from an outside source'. On the other hand, in hopelessness, the feelings include 'more despair, futility, "nothing left", the self-judgement that one is completely responsible for the situation leads to the feeling that there is nothing he or anyone can do to overcome the feelings or change the situation' (Engel 1962, pp. 174–5).

Clinicians will recognize the state of demoralization described by Engel as a common and important reaction to physical illness which may hinder psychological adjustment. However, there is no convincing evidence that it is of causal significance in either the onset or course of physical disease.

Nemiah and Sifneos (1970) have suggested that a cause of psychosomatic illness may be 'alexithymia', which consists of inability to recognize and describe feelings, difficulty in discriminating between emotional states and bodily sensations, and inability to fantasize. Although these characteristics are recognizable in clinical practice, it has not been established that they constitute a syndrome, or that they are specifically associated with physical disorder (see Taylor 1984 for a review).

Research has also focused on more objective study of the role of stressful life events in precipitating physical illness. Most early workers identified life events with the Schedule of Recent Experience (Holmes and Rahe 1967) or a modification of it, a method which had some limitations. (See p. 106 for a review of the methodology of research on life events.) Although improved methods have been used in more recent research, it is too early to draw firm conclusions. If life events have a role in the aetiology of physical illness, it is likely to be as 'triggers' or precipitants rather than as 'formative' causes (see Creed 1984; Craig and Brown 1984).

Other work has dealt with the *psychological mechanisms* through which emotions could induce physical changes. Originally Wolf and Wolff (1947) studied a patient with a gastric fistula and found that emotional changes were accompanied by characteristic changes in the colour, motility, and secretory activity of the stomach mucosa. Subsequent research by others had focused on neuroendocrine mechanisms and immune processes (see Dorian and Garfinkel 1987). All these investigations show that emotion can be accompanied by psychological changes, but they do not yet show whether or how such changes can result in pathological conditions. [see Weiner (1977) and Lipowski (1985) for reviews of the extensive literature on this subject.]

Treatment

Franz Alexander believed that the psychosomatic diseases would clear up or improve in response to psychological treatment. There have been many reports of individual patients with asthma, peptic ulcer, or ulcerative colitis who appeared to get better physically after psychotherapy. These reports do not prove that psychological treatment affected the outcome, and are not supported by the few clinical trials that have been completed (see Karasu 1979). A more rewarding application of psychological techniques may be in the modification of behaviours that predispose to physical disease; for example, smoking, over-eating, and excessive drinking.

Some patients with physical disorders, do of course, need psychiatric treatment for psychological disorders arising in response to physical illnesses. This is the subject of a later section.

Conclusion

Most psychiatrists no longer accept the principles of traditional psycho-somatic medicine. There is no reason for separating a subgroup of so-called psychosomatic disorders. It it is doubtful whether psychological factors can lead to the initial onset of physical disease, though they may cause relapse or aggravation of such disease.

Psychiatric disorder presenting with physical symptoms

General considerations

Bodily symptoms without significant physical cause occur frequently in the general population, and in people attending general practices (Goldberg and Huxley 1980) and general hospitals (Mayou and Hawton 1986). Most of the bodily symptoms are transient, and not related to psychiatric disorder; most improve with medical advice and reassurance. The minority that persist are difficult to treat; a small and highly atypical proportion of them are seen by psychiatrists (Barsky and Klerman 1983).

Psychiatric disorders presenting with physical symptoms are heterogeneous and difficult to classify. The word **hypochondriasis** has been used generally for all psychiatric disorders with prominent somatic symptoms, and specifically for a narrow diagnostic category described later in the chapter [see Kenyon (1965) for a historical review]. The term **somatization** is now generally preferred, but unfortunately it also is used in more than one way: as a psychological mechanism underlying the formation of somatic symptoms; and as a DSMIII subcategory of somatoform disorder.

The precise mechanisms underlying somatization are poorly understood (Barsky and Klerman 1983). It is probable that most symptoms arise in part from the misinterpretation of normal bodily sensations, trivial physical complaints, or autonomic symptoms of anxiety. Social and psychological factors may predispose to somatization or reinforce it: examples include previous experience of friends and relatives, over-concern by members of the patient's family, and cultural differences in the extent to which distress is expressed in bodily rather than psychological terms.

Somatization is a feature of many psychiatric disorders (see Table 12.1) but is most frequently associated with adjustment, mood and anxiety disorders (e.g. Katon *et al.* 1984) and depressive disorder (Kenyon 1964). There are particular problems in the nosology of disorders in which there are few psychological symptoms (Cloninger 1987) now grouped together in both DSMIII and ICD10 as Somatoform disorders. There are also cultural differences in the ways doctors interpret symptoms. Thus, when the same patients were assessed by Chinese and American psychiatrists, the former were likely to diagnose neurasthenia and the latter depressive disorder (Kleinman 1982).

Table 12.1. Classification of psychiatric disorders which can present with somatic symptoms*

DSMIIIR
Adjustment disorder (Chapter 6)
   adjustment disorder with physical complaints

Mood (affective) disorders (Chapter 8)

Anxiety disorders (Chapter 7)
   Panic disorder
   Obsessive-compulsive disorder
   Generalized anxiety disorder
   Post-traumatic stress disorder

Somatoform disorders
   Somatization disorders
   Conversion disorder (or hysterical neurosis, conversion type)
   Somatoform pain disorder
   Hypochondriasis (or hypochondriacal neurosis)
   Body dysmorphic disorder
   Undifferentiated somatoform disorder
   Somatoform disorder NOS

Dissociative disorders (or Hysterical neurosis, dissociative type)
   (Chapter 7)

Schizophrenic disorders (Chapter 9)

Delusional (paranoid) disorders (Chapter 10)

Psychoactive substance use disorders (Chapter 14)

Factitious disorders
   With physical symptoms
   With physical and psychological symptoms
   Factitious disorders NOS

Malingering (V code)   *(continued overleaf)*

Management

The treatment of somatization disorders presents two general problems to the psychiatrist. The first is to ensure that he and other doctors have a consistent approach. The second is to make sure the patient understands that his symptoms are not due to physical illness but are nevertheless being taken seriously.

   To these ends the physician should explain clearly the purpose and results of all investigations, and the likely value of psychological assess-

Table 12.1. Classification of psychiatric disorders which can present with somatic symptoms* (*cont.*)

Draft ICD 10
Reaction to severe stress and adjustment disorders
    Acute stress reaction
    Post-traumatic stress disorder
    Adjustment disorder

Mood (affective) disorders

Other anxiety disorders

Dissociative disorders

Somatoform disorders
    Multiple somatoform disorder
    Undifferentiated multiple somatoform disorder
    Hypochondriacal syndrome (hypochondriasis, hypochondriacal
    neurosis)
    Psychogenic autonomic dysfunction
    Pain syndrome without organic cause
    Other psychogenic disorders of sensation, function and behaviour

Other neurotic disorders
    Neurasthenia

Schizophrenia, schizotypal states and delusional disorders

Mental and behavioural disorders due to psychoactive substance use

---

* Some disorders are considered in other chapters. For these disorders, the chapter
  number is given in brackets in the DSMIIIR classification.

ment. The psychiatrist should be aware of the result of physical investigations, and the explanation and advice given to the patient by other clinicians.

Assessment

Many patients are reluctant to accept that their somatic symptoms may have psychological causes and that referral to a psychiatrist may be appropriate. Hence the clinician should adopt a tactful and sensitive approach. As noted above, it is important to discover the patient's views about the causes of his symptoms and to discuss them seriously. The patient should be made aware that the doctor believes his symptoms to be real. Physicians and psychiatrists should work together to achieve a consistent approach. The usual principles of history taking and assessment should be applied, though the interview may need to be adapted to suit the patient. Attention should be directed to any of the patient's thoughts and behaviours that accompany the physical symptoms, and to the relatives' reactions. It is important to obtain information from other informants as well as from the patient.

A point about diagnosis needs emphasis. When a patient has unexplained physical symptoms, a psychiatric diagnosis should be made only on positive grounds. It should not be assumed that such symptoms are psychological origin merely because they occur in relation to stressful events. Such events are common and may coincide with physical disease which, while not yet identifiable, is far enough advanced to produce symptoms. For the diagnosis of psychiatric disorder, the same strict criteria should be used for the physically ill as for the physically healthy.

Treatment

Many patients with somatic complaints seek repeated medical investigation and reassurance. When all necessary investigations have been carried out, the patient should be told clearly that no further investigation is required. This information should be given with a combination of authority and willingness to discuss the investigation and their results. After this explanation, the aim should be to combine psychological management with treatment of any associated physical disorder.

It is important to avoid arguments about the causes of the symptoms. Amongst patients who do not fully accept psychological causes for their symptoms, many are willing to accept that psychological factors may influence their perception of these symptoms. Such patients may then accept guidance on learning to live more positively with their symptoms. Explanation and reassurance are usually effective in cases of recent onset. In chronic cases, however, reassurance is seldom helpful; sometimes repeated reassurance may even reinforce complaint behaviour (see Salkovskis and Warwick 1986).

Specific treatments should be based on a formulation of the individual's difficulties. They include antidepressant medication and specific behavioural techniques such as anxiety management and cognitive therapy.

Somatoform disorders

Somatization disorder

In DSMIIIR the essential feature of this disorder is multiple somatic complaints of several years' duration, beginning before the age of 30. Diagnosis requires a minimum of 13 such complaints from a list of 25, which symptoms should not be due to organic pathology or pathophysiologic mechanisms and should not occur only in panic attacks. These complaints have caused 'the individual to take medicine (other than aspirin), see a doctor, or alter his life style'. A similar syndrome was originally proposed by a group of psychiatrists in St Louis, USA (Perley and Guze 1962). It was regarded as a form of hysteria and was named Briquet's syndrome after the nineteenth century French physician who wrote an important monograph on hysteria (although he did not describe the exact syndrome to which his name was given.)

The St Louis group holds that there is a familial association between somatization disorder in females and sociopathy and alcoholism in their male relatives. The group believes that follow-up studies and family studies show somatization disorder to be a single stable syndrome (Guze *et al.* 1986). However, there must be doubts about these views because amongst some patients diagnosed as having somatization disorders some fulfil criteria for other DSMIII diagnoses (Liskow *et al.* 1986) The prevalence of somatization disorder is unknown but it is much more common in women than men. The course is fluctuating and the prognosis poor (see Cloninger 1986). The disorder is difficult to treat, but continuing care by one doctor with only a minimum of essential investigations can reduce the patient's use of health services and may improve his functioning state (see Smith *et al.* 1986).

Conversion disorder

Conversion symptoms are common among people attending doctors. Conversion disorder, as defined in DSMIIIR and ICD10 (draft), is much less common, accounting for 1 per cent of admissions to hospital (see Mayou and Hawton 1986) though acute conversion syndromes, such as amnesia, difficulty in walking, and sensory complaints, are seen regularly in emergency departments. In this book, conversion disorder and its management are described on pp. 202–8. The related chronic pain syndromes are considered later in this chapter (p. 434).

Somatoform pain disorder

This is a an exclusion category for patients with chronic pain which is not caused by any physical or specific mental disorder (see Williams and Spitzer 1982). DSMIIIR states that 'the predominant disturbance is at least six months' preoccupation with pain; and that either, after appropriate evaluation, no organic pathology or pathophysiological mechanism has been found to account for the pain, or that when there is related organic pathology, the pain or resulting social or occupational impairment is grossly in excess of what would be expected from the physical findings'. Pain syndromes are discussed more fully on p. 433.

Hypochondriasis

In DSMIIIR hypochondriasis is defined as 'preoccupation with a fear or belief of having a serious disease based on the individual's interpretation of physical signs of sensations as evidence of physical illness. Appropriate physical evaluation does not support the diagnosis of any physical disorder that can account for the physical signs or sensations or for the individual's unrealistic interpretation of them. The fear of having, or belief that one has a disease, persists despite medical reassurance.' The definition goes on to exclude patients with panic disorder or delusions, and requires a duration of at least six months.

In the past, there has been dispute as to whether hypochondriasis is a separate diagnostic category. Gillespie (1928) and others reported that a primary neurotic syndrome of hypochondriasis was common in psychiatric practice. From a review of the case notes of patients given this diagnosis at the Maudsley Hospital, Kenyon (1964) found that most patients appeared to have an underlying depressive disorder and he suggested that there was no reason to retain the concept of a primary syndrome of hypochondriasis. However, this conclusion was based on patients admitted to a specialist psychiatric hospital. Most psychiatrists working in general hospitals believe that a few patients with chronic physical symptoms are best regarded as cases of hypochondriasis, as defined in DSMIIIR or draft ICD10.

Dysmorphophobia

The syndrome of **dysmorphophobia** was first described by Morselli (1886) as 'a subjective description of ugliness and physical defect which the patient feels is noticeable to others'. The typical patient with dysmorphophobia is convinced that some part of the body is too large, too small, or misshapen. To other people the appearance is normal, or there is a trivial abnormality. In the latter case, it may be difficult to decide whether the preoccupation is disproportionate. The common complaints are about the nose, ears, mouth, breasts, buttocks, and penis, but any part of the body may be involved. The patient may be constantly preoccupied with and tormented by his mistaken belief. It seems to him that other people notice and talk about his supposed deformity. He may blame all his other difficulties on it: if only his nose were a better shape, he would be more successful in his work, social life, and sexual relationships.

Some patients with this syndrome meet diagnostic critera for other disorders. Thus Hay (1970b) studied twelve men and five women with the condition, and found the eleven had severe personality disorder, five schizophrenia, and one a depressive illness. In the patients with a psychiatric disorder the preoccupation is usually delusional; in those with personality disorder it is usually an overvalued idea (see McKenna 1984).

The severe cases described in the psychiatric literature are infrequent, but less severe forms of dysmorphophobia are more common, especially in plastic surgery and dermatology clinics. DSMIIIR introduced a new category, **body dysmorphic disorder**, for those in whom dysmorphophobia does not seem to be secondary to any other psychiatric disorder. It denotes 'a preoccupation with some imagined defect in appearance' which 'is not of delusional intensity'. The separate validity of this syndrome has not yet been established.

Treatment of dysmorphophobia is often difficult. Any accompanying psychiatric disorder should be treated in the usual way, and counselling provided for any occupational, social, or sexual difficulties. It should be explained tactfully that there is no real deformity, and that some people develop mistaken beliefs about their appearance; for example, through misinterpreting overheard remarks. Some patients are helped by such reassurance and continued support, but many do not change.

Cosmetic surgery is often said to be contraindicted for these patients unless there is a major deformity, but some patients with minor physical abnormalities are greatly helped by surgery (Hay and Heather 1973). A small proportion remain very dissatisfied after such operations. Selection for surgery is difficult and requires careful assessment of the patient's expectations [see Frank (1985) for a review].

Factitious disorder

The DSMIIIR category Factitious disorder covers the 'intentional production or feigning of physical and psychological symptoms which can be attributed to a need to assume the sick role'. It has subdivisions for patients with psychological symptoms only, those with physical symptoms only, and those with both. An extreme form of this disorder is commonly known as the Munchausen syndrome (see below). Unlike malingering, factitious disorder does not bring any external rewards such as financial compensation.

Reich and Gottfried (1983) described 41 cases, of whom 30 were women. Most had worked in occupations related to medicine. There were four principal clinical groups: self-induced infections, simulated specific illnesses with no actual disorder, chronic wounds, and self-medication. Many were willing to accept psychological assessment and treatment.

Common syndromes of factitious disorder include dermatitis artefacta (Sneddon 1983), pyrexia of unknown origin, bruising disorders (Ratnoff 1980) and brittle diabetes (Schade *et al.* 1985). Psychological syndromes include feigned psychosis (Hay 1983), and feigned grief over fictitious bereavement. [See Folks and Freeman (1985) for a review of factitious disorder.]

Munchausen syndrome

Asher (1951) suggested the term Munchausen syndrome for the patient who is 'admitted to hospital with apparent acute illness supported by a plausible or dramatic history. Usually his story is largely made up of falsehoods; he is found to have attended and deceived an astounding number of hospitals; and he nearly always discharged himself against advice after quarrelling violently with both doctors and nurses. A large number of scars is particularly characteristic of this condition.'

The Munchausen syndrome occurs mainly in early adult life and in men. The presenting symptoms may be of any kind, including psychiatric symptoms. They are accompanied by gross lying (pseudologia fantastica), which includes the giving of false names, and invented medical histories (see King and Ford 1988). There may be self-inflicted wounds or infections. Patients frequently demand major analgesics. They may obstruct efforts to obtain information about themselves and may interfere with diagnostic investigations.

They invariably discharge themselves prematurely. When further information is obtained, it often reveals many recurrent previous simulated illnesses.

Such patients suffer from profound disorder of personality, and often report major deprivation and disturbance in early life. The prognosis is uncertain but appears to be poor; indeed, there are few reports of successful treatment.

Munchausen syndrome by proxy

Meadow (see 1985) has described a form of child abuse in which parents give false accounts of symptoms in their children, and may fake the signs. They seek repeated medical investigations and needless treatment for the children. The signs reported most commonly are neurological signs, bleeding, and rashes. Some children collude in the production of symptoms and signs. Hazards for the children include disruption of education and social development. The prognosis is probably poor, and some children may progress to the adult Munchausen syndrome (Meadow 1985).

Malingering

Malingering is the fraudulent simulation or exaggeration of symptoms. In DSMIIIR it is classified on Axis V, and is said to differ from factitious disorder in that external incentives motivate symptom production, whereas in factitious disorder there are no external incentives but a psychological need for the sick role. Malingering occurs most often among prisoners, the military, and people seeking compensation for accidents. Before malingering is diagnosed, there should always be a full medical examination. When the diagnosis is certain, the patient should be informed tactfully of the results of the evaluation and the conclusion. He should be encouraged to deal more appropriately with any problems that led to the symptoms, whilst adopting some face-saving measures that may help.

Psychiatric consequences of physical illness

Introduction

Organic mental disorder may occur in the course of many serious physical illnesses or surgical procedures, especially among the elderly. Delirium, dementia, and the organic disorders associated with specific medical conditions are discussed in Chapter 11. This section is concerned only with emotional disorders consequent upon physical illness.

No clear dividing line can be drawn between normal and abnormal emotional reactions to physical illness. It is not surprising that physically ill people often feel anxious or depressed, and sometimes angry. Most of these emotions are mild and transient, but some are intense or lasting, and some amount to affective disorders. It is impressive, however, that many patients cope with even severe physical illness with little distress.

Physical illnesses may activate psychological defence mechanisms (see p. 34). The commonest of these is probably denial. As a temporary defence against anxiety, denial can be valuable; for example, immediately after the diagnosis of a potentially fatal illness, the patient's denial of the prognosis may allow him to continue with everyday life. If prolonged, however, denial may be maladaptive, leading to delay in obtaining treatment, lack of collaboration in treatment, or failure to safeguard the financial interests of the family. Whenever a physically ill patient appears to respond inappropriately to his circumstances, the clinician should consider whether this response can be understood in terms of denial or the other defence mechanisms referred to on p. 34.

Coping and adaptation

The term **coping** has been applied to describe psychological processes evoked by acute stressful events (Lazarus 1966), whilst **adaptation** is a more appropriate term for psychological processes in reponse to chronic illness. Coping behaviours may be adaptive or maladaptive. On the evidence of clinical observations the common types of coping behaviour were divided by Lipowski into denial, vigilance, avoidance, and tackling (see Lipowski 1985). The related term coping strategy is sometimes used to refer to behaviours such as seeking information, looking for alternative sources of satisfaction, or social withdrawal. Such terms are often used in clinical practice, but their value in research has so far been limited by the lack of precise definitions.

Sick role and illness behaviour

Sociologists have pointed out that the impact of physical illness on a person is affected by social forces and that illness has social consequences.

According to Parsons (1951) society bestows a **sick role** on people who have been accepted as ill. Parsons suggested that this role had four components: exemption from normal social responsibilites; the right to care and help for others; an expectation that the sick person will desire to recover; and an obligation to seek and co-operate with appropriate treatment. The original formulation was theoretical and its practical applications were limited. However, the term sick role is now used in a looser sense to cover the many social advantages and disadvantages of illness.

Mechanic (see 1978) suggested the descriptive term **illness behaviour** for the social aspects of being ill. He defined it as 'the ways in which given symptoms may be differently perceived, evaluated and acted (or not acted) upon by different kinds of persons'. Illness behaviour includes consulting doctors, taking medicines, seeking help from relatives and friends, and giving up various activities. Such behaviours often depend more on perceptions of illness and circumstances than on the presence of disease. This view of illness has been influential in emphasizing the social aspects of response to illness and its treatment.

Quality of life

Physical illness and disability may have widespread effects upon a patient's adjustment in work, leisure, and family life. Patients vary in their capacity for social adjustment; most manage well but a few develop social handicaps out of proportion to the severity of the illness. In contrast, a few patients find advantages in physical illness; for example, as an excuse to avoid responsibilities, or as an opportunity to reconsider their way of life and improve its quality. Sexual function is often affected by physical illnesses, of which the most important are listed in Table 12.2. This topic is discussed further on p. 569.

Determinants of psychological and social responses to illness

Some physical conditions and treatments (see Table 12.3) and some drugs (see Table 12.4) cause symptoms resembling those psychiatric disorder (for example malaise and fatigue). They may also precipitate psychiatric disorder.

Certain factors increase the risk of serious psychiatric disorders developing in the physically ill. Patients are more vulnerable if they have had a previous psychiatric disorder or a life-long inability to deal with adversity, or if they have a disturbed home life (see Campbell 1986) or an otherwise unsatisfactory social background (see Lipowski 1985). Certain kinds of physical illness are more likely to provoke serious psychiatric consequences. These include life-threatening illnesses, and illnesses requiring lengthy and unpleasant treatment such as radiotherapy or renal dialysis,

Table 12.2. Some medical conditions associated with impaired sexual function

---

Endocrine disorder
  Diabetes
  Hypogonadism
  Hypopituitarism

Cardiovascular disorders
  Myocardial infarction

Respiratory failure

Chronic renal failure

Neurological disorders
  Spinal cord damage
  Damage to higher centres

Pelvic surgery

Disabling arthritis

Medication
  Anticholinergic drugs
  Hormones
  Psychotropic drugs (phenothiazines, antidepressants)
  Antihypertensive drugs
  Diuretics
  L-Dopa
  Indomethacin

---

or mutilating treatment such as mastectomy. A physical illness is more likely to have adverse psychological consequences if its effects are particularly significant to the patient's life; for example, arthritis of the hands of a pianist.

Psychological symptoms induced directly by physical illness

The main types of psychological symptom are shown in Table 12.3 along with some of the physical disorders that can induce them. Because all the symptoms listed in the table are commonly encountered in ordinary psychiatric practice, the psychiatrist must always be on the look-out for undetected physical illness in his patients. The physical conditions listed in Table 12.3 are considered further in the part of this chapter dealing with individual syndromes.

Table 12.4 lists some commonly used drugs which can produce psychi-

Table 12.3. Some organic causes of common psychiatric symptoms

Depression	Carcinoma, infections, neurological disorders including dementias, diabetes, thyroid disorder, Addison's disease, SLE
Anxiety	Hyperthyroidism, hyperventilation, phaeochromocytoma, hypoglycaemia, neurological disorders, drug withdrawal
Fatigue	Anaemia, sleep disorders, chronic infection, diabetes, hypothyroidism, Addison's disease, carcinoma, Cushing's syndrome, radiotherapy
Weakness	Myasthenia gravis, McArdle's disease and primary muscle disorder, peripheral neuropathy, other neurological disorders
Episodes of disturbed behaviour	Epilepsy, hypoglycaemia, phaeochromocytoma, porphyria, early dementia, toxic states, transient global amnesia
Headache	Migraine, giant cell arteritis, space-occupying lesions
Loss of weight	Carcinoma, diabetes, tuberculosis, hyperthyroidism, malabsorption

atric symptoms. Whenever psychological symptoms are found in a medical or surgical patient, the possibility should be considered that they have been induced by medication. [See Davies (1987) for detailed information on the adverse effects of drugs.]

Psychiatric disorder induced directly by physical illness

Some physical illnesses can directly induce not only organic mental disorders (discussed in Chapter 11), but also affective disorders, both depressive and manic (Krauthammer and Klerman 1978). These physical illnesses include infectious diseases (p. 460), neurological disorders (p. 378), endocrine disorders (p. 379), malignant diseases (p. 462), and connective tissue disorders (p. 459). Similar effects can be induced by the drugs used to treat these physical disorders. [Whitlock (1982) has reviewed these conditions in detail.]

Acute physical illness is sometimes followed by a paranoid disorder, for which there is no clear evidence of psychological or physical causation. Suspicion and resentment are often directed to the hospital staff and the

Table 12.4. Some drugs with psychiatric side-effects

Delirium	CNS depressants (hypnotics, sedatives, alcohol, antidepressants, neuroleptics, anticonvulsants, antihistamines), Anticholinergic drugs, Beta-blockers, Digoxin, Cimetidine
Psychotic symptoms	Hallucinogenic drugs, Appetite suppressants, Sympathomimetic drugs, Beta-blockers, Corticosteroids; L-Dopa, indomethacin
Mood disorder Depression	Antihypertensive drugs, Oral contraceptives, Neuroleptics, Anticonvulsants, Corticosteroids, L-Dopa
Elation	Antidepressants, Corticosteroids, Anticholinergic drugs, Isoniazid
Behavioural Disturbance	Benzodiazepines, Neuroleptics

patient's relatives. There is no clouding of consciousness. Response to antipsychotic medication is good (Cutting 1980).

Psychiatric disorder induced indirectly by physical illness

In the physically ill, the commonest psychiatric disorders are emotional disorders, which occur in 10–30 per cent of patients with severe physical illnesses. Most of these emotional disorders can be diagnosed as DSMIII adjustment disorders, but specific anxiety and affective disorders are also common. Other non-organic psychiatric disorders are infrequent. Anxiety is more common with acute physical illness, depression with chronic physical illness.

Management of psychiatric disorder associated with physical illness

Assessment is similar to that for any psychiatric disorder, except that it requires knowledge of the nature and prognosis of the physical illness. The psychiatrist must be aware that certain symptoms, such as tiredness and malaise, may be features of both physical and psychiatric disorders. He must also be able to distinguish severe psychiatric conditions, such as anxiety or depressive disorders, from normal emotional responses to physical illness and its treatment. This distinction can be based partly on clinical experience of the reactions of other patients with similar illness, and partly on eliciting symptoms that seldom occur in normal distress (such as hopelessness, guilt, loss of interest, and severe insomnia). Although emotional distress is inevitable in physical illness, it can be reduced by support, appropriate reassurance, advice, information, and practical help. Emotional distress amounting to psychiatric disorder can normally be treated successfully with standard psychiatric methods, including drugs, simple psychotherapy, and cognitive behavioural methods. These treatments will be discussed next.

Drug therapy

Hypnotic and anxiolytic drugs are valuable for short periods at times of great distress, particularly during admission to hospital. The indications for antidepressants are probably the same as those for patients who are not physically ill, but there have been too few satisfactory trials to establish the precise indications for medically ill patients with depression (see Popkin *et al.* 1985). Attention should be paid to possible side-effects and drug interactions before prescribing for medically ill patients.

Counselling and psychotherapy

Counselling and brief psychotherapy should include education about the patient's physical illness, and a willingness to discuss practical issues. Group therapy is often recommended but is difficult to organize and not always popular with the patients most in need of help.

Cognitive and behavioural methods

Much medical management uses a common-sense approach, such as giving advice on work, leisure, social life, and exercise. There is probably ample scope for formal cognitive behavioural methods, such as anxiety management. There are many case reports of such methods, but few clinical trials (mainly limited to chronic pain).

Psychiatric and physical disorders occurring together by chance

Psychiatric and physical disorders often arise independently of one another, and then interact. Psychiatric disorder may affect the patient's response to physical symptoms and increase the problems of medical management. Conversely, physical illness may exacerbate psychiatric symptoms. It is not uncommon for patients and doctors to ascribe all the psychiatric symptoms entirely to the physical illness and its effects, rather than to independent psychological and social factors that may be important.

Classification in DSMIIIR and ICD10 (draft)

Several categories in the DSMIIIR and ICD10 (draft) apply to patients who present to physicians or surgeons rather than to psychiatrists. As shown in Table 12.5 these categories are broadly similar in the two classifications, though the groupings are somewhat different and there are minor differences in nomenclature.

Most of the conditions listed in Table 12.5 are discussed elsewhere in this chapter or in the chapter on organic psychiatry. DSMIIIR has a rubric **psychological factors affecting physical conditions**, which is intended to cover the group of psychosomatic disorders described earlier in this chapter. The definition specifies the time relationships between the psychological factors and the physical disorder, the presence of demonstrable organic pathology, and the exclusion of somatoform disorder.

DSMIIIR includes an axis V code, **non-compliance with medical treatment** for which there is no ICD equivalent. ICD10 (draft) has a category of Somatoform disorder named **psychogenic autonomic dysfunction**. The definition states 'the symptoms are presented by the patient as if they were due to physical disorder in a system or organ which is largely or completely under autonomic control, i.e. the cardiovascular, gastrointestinal, and respiratory systems'. Examples include hyperventilation, cardiac neurosis, and gastric neurosis. Such categories are unlikely to prove useful.

The psychological care of the dying patient

This section is mainly concerned with patients who are dying slowly, especially from cancer. Surveys have shown that these patients often have significant depressive or anxiety symptoms. Among patients dying in hospital, for example, it has been reported that up to a half have such symptoms. Guilt and anger are also common, either in association with depressive symptoms or without them. Guilty ideas are often concerned with the demands that the patient must inevitably make on the family. Anger may be obvious or hidden; although evoked by the patient's plight, it is often displaced on to doctors, nurses, and relatives who are trying to help him. Acute organic syndromes are also common.

These symptoms have both physical and psychological causes. The physical causes are important and include dyspnoea, nausea, vomiting, and pain. There is a particularly strong association between dyspnoea and anxiety. Some of the drugs used to treat physical illness may cause depression (see Table 12.4). The psychological causes are obvious but often overlooked. Depression can be understood as a form of mourning for the impending loss of friends and family and of the patient's own

Table 12.5. Classification in DSMIIIR and ICD10 (draft)

DSMIIIR	ICD10 (draft)
Disorders usually first evident in infancy, childhood, or adolescence	*Behavioural and emotional disorders with onset usually occurring in childhood or adolescence*
Eating disorders	Eating disorder (other than Pica)
Tic disorders	Tic disorders
Organic mental disorders	*Organic, including symptomatic, mental disorders*
Dementias arising in the Senium and Presenium	
Psychoactive Substance-Induced Organic Mental Disorder	
Organic mental disorder associated with Axis III physical disorders, or whose aetiology is unknown	
Psychoactive substance use disorder	*Mental and behaviour disorders due to psychoactive substance use*
Anxiety disorder	*Neurotic, stress-related, and somatoform disorders*
Post-traumatic stress disorder	*Post-traumatic stress disorder*
Somatoform disorder	*Somatoform disorders*
Sleep disorder	
Factitious disorder	
Adjustment disorder with physical complaints	
Sleep and arousal disorders	*Psychological and behavioural factors associated with disorder or diseases classified elsewhere*
V codes Non-compliance with medical treatment	

future. Anxiety is an understandable reaction to the uncertainties ahead and the possibility of pain, disfigurement, and incontinence. Patients are often made anxious by the thought that they may be abandoned by their friends, relatives, or doctors.

These reactions are more common among dying patients who are young, and less frequent in those who are elderly. They depend on the patient's personality and his beliefs about an after-life. They are also increased when the patient has poor communication with the staff looking after him, or with his relatives. Poor communication is more common than it need be because staff or relatives are often uncertain how to speak to the dying. Such uncertainty is greater if the patient, relatives, and staff do not know exactly who has been told what about the diagnosis and prognosis. In these circumstances, relatives may draw back from the patient, so increasing his feelings of fear and despair.

Kübler-Ross (1969) was one of the first psychiatrists to talk to a large number of dying patients and to attempt to describe their needs. She described phases of psychological adjustment to impending death. Although the phases do not always occur in the same sequence, and some may not be experienced at all, they are a useful guide to reactions that may be met. The phases are: denial and isolation; anger; 'bargaining' (partial acceptance but immediate problems still denied); depression; and acceptance.

Dying patients use various psychological defence mechanisms against overwhelming emotion. The three commonest mechanisms are denial, dependency, and displacement. **Denial** is usually the first reaction to being told that the illness is fatal. This reaction may lead to an initial period of calm. Afterwards denial usually diminishes and the patient gradually comes to terms with the problems facing him. Even so, denial may return at times when there are signs that the disease is progressing. As a result, a patient may behave for a time as if he understands the nature of his illness, and may later behave as if unaware of it. A degree of **dependency** is appropriate at certain stages of treatment, but it may be exaggerated to the point of giving up responsibility and making undue demands on other people. As mentioned above, **displacement** occurs when the dying patient directs anger inappropriately at other people.

Management

The aim is to bring about what Hackett and Weissman called an appropriate death, which means that 'the person should be relatively free from pain, should operate on as effective a level as possible, should recognize and resolve remaining conflicts, should satisfy as far as possible remaining wishes and should be able to yield control to others in whom he has confidence' (Hackett and Weissman 1962).

For success in these aims the first requirement is adequate treatment of physical symptoms. The second requirement is to make a good relationship with the patient so that he feels able to talk freely about the illness and his feelings. If the doctor encourages the patient to lead the discussion, it is seldom difficult to know how much to say about diagnosis and prognosis. If the patient does not indicate a desire to be given information about approaching death, it is usually better to withhold it until he is more prepared to receive it. On the other hand if he wants to know the prognosis, prevarication will only make him feel that he cannot trust those who are caring for him. The decision as to what should be said is less difficult than is usually supposed. It is useful to remember that most patients become aware that they are dying whether they are told or not.

Psychotropic medication has a limited but important part in the treatment of the dying. Anxiolytic drugs may be given for short periods to relieve extreme distress. Antidepressant drugs should be prescribed when there is a persistent depressive disorder that does not respond to psychological measures.

It should not be forgotten that relatives also need information, advice, and an opportunity to talk about their feelings. They should be helped to understand the reasons for the patient's anger or other reactions that may cause them distress.

Most problems of the dying are better dealt with by hospital staff or the general practitioner than by a psychiatrist. Sometimes care is best provided in hospices where it is possible to offer close attention to detail that can improve the dying person's quality of life. Specialized nurses can assist the general practitioner care for people at home [see Corr and Corr (1985) for a review]. Referral to a psychiatrist is appropriate for patients with severe psychiatric symptoms or disturbed behaviour (usually due to an acute organic syndrome). In one terminal care unit about a sixth of admissions were referred to a psychiatrist (Stedeford and Bloch 1979). The referred patients had four main types of problem: (i) difficulty in talking to relatives and doctors about the illness; (ii) difficulties in accepting social restrictions, making appropriate plans, and taking decisions about their illness and everyday lives; (iii) difficulties in accepting the effects of the illness on the pattern of family life; (iv) long-term problems (personality and family problems) that had been present long before the physical illness [see Patterson (1977) for a review.]

Consultation and liaison psychiatry

These terms refer to two separate ways of conducting psychiatric work in a general hospital. In consultation work, the psychiatrist is available to give an opinion on patients referred to him by physicians and surgeons. In liaison work he becomes a member of a medical or surgical team, takes part in ward rounds and clinical meetings and offers advice about any patient to whose care he feels able to contribute. The liaison psychiatrist also tries to help other staff to deal with day-to-day psychological problems encountered in their work, including the problems of patients whom he does not interview himself. One of the aims of liaison psychiatry is to teach staff working in general hospitals about assessment and management. In the consultation approach it is implicitly assumed that the staff possess these skills. In practice most psychiatrists work in a way that combines elements of the two approaches. To use consultation well requires close personal contact between the psychiatrist and the physician.

Most psychiatrists working in general hospitals now do combine both approaches, undertaking consultations but also trying to establish close working relationships with medical and nursing staff.

In North American general hospitals up to five per cent of all admissions are referred to psychiatrists. In Britain and many other countries, smaller proportions are referred and most are for the assessment of emergencies including deliberate self-harm (see p. 413). Consultation and liaison units vary considerably in their size and organization. Some are staffed entirely by psychiatrists, and others by a team of psychiatrists, nurses, social workers, and clinical psychologists. In some countries, clinical psychologists provide a separate behavioural medicine service. Some services have in-patient beds for patients who are both medically ill and psychiatrically disturbed. [See Lipowski (1985) for reviews of the development and practice of consultation and liaison.]

Consultation

Consultation has two parts: assessment of the patient and communication with the doctor making the referral. Assessment is not essentially different from that of any other patient referred for a psychiatric opinion, but depends particularly on the patient's physical state and his willingness to see a psychiatrist. On receiving the referral request the psychiatrist makes sure that the referring doctor has discussed psychiatric referral with the patient. Before interviewing the patient the psychiatrist reads the relevant medical notes and asks the nursing staff about the patient's mental state and behaviour. He finds out what treatment the patient is receiving, and if necessary consults a reference book about the side-effects of any drugs not well known to him.

When starting to interview the patient, the psychiatrist makes clear the purpose of the consultation. It may be necessary to discuss the patient's anxieties about seeing a psychiatrist and to explain how the interview may contribute to the treatment plan. Next an appropriately detailed history is obtained and the mental state examined. Usually the physical state is already recorded in the notes, but occasionally it will be necessary to extend the examination of the nervous system. It is essential for the psychiatrist to have a full understanding of the patient's physical condition. At this stage it may be necessary to ask further questions of the ward staff or social worker, to interview relatives, or to telephone the family doctor and enquire about the patient's social background and any previous psychiatric disorder.

The psychiatrist usually keeps separate full notes of the examination of the patient and of interviews with informants. His entry in the medical notes should differ from conventional psychiatric case-notes (see Garrick and Stottard 1982). The entry should be brief and free of jargon, and should contain only essential background information. It should omit confidential information as far as possible and should concentrate on practical issues, including answering the questions raised by the referring doctor. When an opinion is entered in the medical notes, the principles are similar to those adopted in writing to the general practitioner (see p. 73). It is important to make clear the nature of any immediate treatment that is recommended, and who is to carry it out. If the assessment is provisional until other informants have been interviewed, the psychiatrist should state when the final opinion will be given. It is often appropriate to discuss the proposed plan of management with the consultant, ward doctor, or nurse in charge, before writing a final opinion. In this way the psychiatrist can make sure that his recommendations are feasible and acceptable, and that he has answered the relevant questions about the patient. The note should be signed legibly, and should tell the ward staff where he or a deputy can be found should further help be required.

Recommendations about treatment are similar to those for a similar psychiatric disorder in a physically well patient. When psychiatric drugs are prescribed, attention should be paid to the possible effects of the patient's physical state on their metabolism and excretion; and to any possible interactions with other drugs prescribed for the physical illness. A realistic assessment should be made of the amount of supervision available on a medical or surgical ward; for example, for a depressed patient with suicidal ideas. No undue demands should be made, but with support from a psychiatrist the nursing staff can manage most brief psychiatric disorders that arise in a general hospital. [For reviews of the methods of consultation see Lipowski (1985); Glickman (1980).]

Psychiatric emergencies

The successful management of a psychiatric emergency depends greatly on the initial clinical interview. The aims are to establish a good relationship with the patient, elicit information from the patient and other informants, and observe the patients behaviour and mental state.

Although the pressures on the doctor in an emergency often make it difficult to follow this systematic approach, time can be saved and mistakes avoided if the assessment is as complete as the circumstances permit, and a calm and deliberate approach is adopted.

If the patient is actually or potentially violent, it is essential to arrange for adequate but unobtrusive help to be available. If restraint cannot be avoided, it should be accomplished quickly by an adequate number of people using the minimum of force. Staff should always avoid attempting single-handed restraint. Physical contact (including physical examination) should not be be attempted unless the purpose has been clearly understood by and agreed with the patient. Extreme caution is, of course, required with a patient thought to possess any kind of offensive weapon.

Emergency drug treatment of disturbed or violent patients

For a patient who is frightened, diazepam (5–10 mg) may be useful. For a more disturbed patient, rapid calming is best achieved with 2–10 mg of haloperidol injected intramuscularly and repeated, if necessary, every half hour or every hour, up to a maximum of 60–100 mg in 24 hours (depending upon the patient's body size and physical condition). Chlorpromazine (75–150 mg intramuscularly) is a more sedating alternative to haloperidol, but more likely to cause hypotension. When the patient is calm, haloperidol may be continued in smaller doses usually three to four times a day and preferably by mouth, using a syrup if the patient will not swallow tablets. The dosage depends on the patient's weight and on the initial response to the drug. Careful observations by nurses of the physical state and behaviour are necessary during this treatment. Extrapyramidal side effects may require treatment with an antiparkinsonian drug.

Patients who refuse to accept advice about treatment

Patients may be unwilling to accept their doctors' advice for many reasons. Commonly it is because they are frightened or angry, or do not understand what is happening; occasionally the cause is a mental illness that interferes with the patient's ability to make an informed decision. It has to be accepted that some patients will refuse treatment even after a full and rational discussion of the reasons for carrying it out; and it is, of course, a right of a conscious, mentally competent adult to do so. However, in many countries (including the United Kingdom), it is accepted that the doctor in charge of the patient does have the right to give immediate treatment in life-threatening emergencies when he cannot obtain the patient's consent. If this has to be done, opinions should be obtained from medical and nursing colleagues, and, if possible, from the patient's relatives. Detailed records should be kept of the reasons for the decision. It is essential for all doctors to know the law about these matters in the country in which they are practising.

If a patient has a mental disorder that impairs the ability to give informed consent, it may be appropriate to use legal powers of compulsory assessment and treatment, even though the powers for compulsory treatment of a mental disorder do not give a right to treatment of concurrent physical illness. This is because successful treatment of the psychiatric disorder may result in the patient giving informed consent for the treatment of the physical illness.

Genetic counselling

Genetic counselling about the risks of hereditary disease is mainly given to couples contemplating marriage or planning or expecting a child. The scope of counselling has been enlarged by increasing understanding of genetic mechanisms and by improved methods for identifying carriers and for making prenatal diagnoses. It includes providing information about risks, helping family members to cope with worries caused by the diagnosis, and enabling them to take well-informed decisions about family planning and treatment. Genetic counselling is usually provided by the staff of genetic clinics, but there is also a need for counselling by family doctors (Lipkin *et al.* 1986).

The nature of the advice varies with the type of genetic risk. Especially difficult issues are raised by new methods which make it possible to identify carriers for Huntington's chorea before they have developed symptoms (see p. 366). It should be remembered that receiving information about risk can be very distressing, especially for parents who have experienced a previous abnormal pregnancy.

After giving information about the nature of the disorder, the counsellor should discuss alternative actions with the couple. These actions include effective contraception (including sterilization) and, for an increasing number of conditions, prenatal diagnosis with the opportunity for termination. The parents should be aware that awaiting prenatal diagnosis can be distressing. Unfortunately, counselling is more effective in imparting knowledge than in changing behaviour and many couples ignore warnings that future children will be at high risk.

A review of syndromes

Pain

Pain is the commonest symptom encountered in medical and surgical practice. In general practice, pain is a common presenting symptom of emotional disorder (Bridges and Goldberg 1985). In psychiatric practice, pain is reported by about one-fifth of in-patients and over a half of out-patients (Merskey and Spear 1967). Pain is associated with several psychiatric disorders, including depressive, anxiety and conversion disorders, and the condition termed somatoform pain disorder in DMSIIIR.

The **assessment** of a patient presenting with pain of unknown cause should include an appropriate examination and investigation of possible physical causes. When these are negative it should be remembered that not uncommonly physical illness presents with pain before it can be detected in other ways. The psychiatric assessment of these cases should include a full description of the pain and the circumstances in which it occurs, and of any symptoms suggestive of a depressive or other psychiatric disorder.

The **treatment** of a psychiatric disorder associated with pain is along the usual lines. Particular skill is often required to maintain a working relationship with the patient who may be unwilling to accept a psychological basis for his symptoms. At the same time, any underlying physical disorder should be treated, and adequate analgesics provided. [Psychological aspects of pain are reviewed in a book edited by Sternbach (1986).]

Chronic pain

The treatment of chronic pain is difficult, and is now often provided in specialized pain clinics. Many patients attending these clinics have serious organic disease, but others have insufficient or no organic pathology to account for the severity of their pain. Some patients (with or without physical pathology) have depressive disorders (Tyrer 1986; Katon *et al.* 1985). This finding has led some psychiatrists to argue that a variant of depressive disorder—'pain-prone disorder'—occurs in patients who have pain but no clear depressive symptoms (Blumer and Heilbronn 1982). There is no convincing evidence for this idea, and it is more likely that such patients show 'learned pain behaviour', that is a form of illness behaviour in which complaints of pain are reinforced by family and other social factors (see Pilowsky and Spence 1975; Blackwell *et al.* 1984; Tyrer 1986). Chronic pain often imposes large demands on family life (Payne and Norfleet 1986).

The management of chronic pain should be individually planned (see Turk and Rudy 1987) and consistent. It should co-ordinate all aspects of medical care and involve the patient's family. Any physical causes must be treated. Antidepressant medication is sometimes effective even in patients who have no evidence of a depressive disorder. Behavioural treatment can be useful, although many chronic pain patients lack the necessary motivation to make full use of it. Such treatment aims to reduce social reinforcement of maladaptive behaviour, and to encourage the patient to seek ways to ovecome his disabilities (see Linton 1986; Keefe *et al.* 1986; Keefe and Gil 1986; Blackwell *et al.* 1984).

Specific pain syndromes

Some specific pain syndromes are discussed in other sections of this book, namely atypical chest pain (see p. 450), abdominal pain (see p. 454), diabetic neuropathy (see p. 446) and phantom limb pain (see p. 473). Other conditions in which psychological factors may be important are pelvic pain in women, post-herpetic pain, fibrositis (Wolfe 1986), headache, and facial pain. The two latter are discussed here as examples.

Headache and facial pain   Patients with chronic or recurrent headache are more likely than those with acute headache, to be seen by psychiatrists. There are many physical causes of headache, notably migraine, which affects about one in ten of the population at some time of their life (see Marsden 1983).

Many patients attending neurological clinics have headaches for which no physical cause can be found. The commonest is the so-called 'tension' headache, which is usually described as a dull generalized feeling of pressure or tightness extending around the head. It is frequently of short duration and relieved by analgesia or a good night's sleep, but may occasionally be constant and unremitting. A proportion of patients describe clear depressive symptoms and others anxiety in relation to obvious life stresses.

Amongst patients with headaches for which no physical cause can be found, most can be reassured by investigation and explanation (Fitzpatrick and Hopkins 1981). Some patients with persisting headache, even without psychiatric symptoms, respond to some form of psychiatric treatment, such as antidepressants, psychotherapy, or cognitive behavioural methods. [See Blanchard (1986) for a review.]

Facial pain also has many physical causes but there are two overlapping syndromes which may have psychological causes (Feinmann and Harris 1984). The more common is temporo-mandibular dysfunction (Costen's syndrome, facial arthralgia) a dull ache around the temporomandibular joint, which usually presents to dentists. 'Atypical' facial pain is a deeper aching or throbbing pain which is more likely to present to neurologists. Patients with these symptoms are often reluctant to see a psychiatrist but several trials suggest that antidepressants can relieve symptoms, even when there is no evidence of a depressive disorder (Feinmann *et al.* 1984). In other cases, cognitive-behavioural methods are effective (Feinmann and Harris 1984).

Table 12.6. DSMIIIR criteria for anorexia nervosa

---

1. Refusal to maintain body weight over a minimal normal weight for age and height, e.g. weight loss leading to maintenance of body weight 15 per cent below expected; failure to make expected weight gain during period of growth, leading to body weight 15 per cent below expected.

2. Intense fear of becoming obese, even when underweight.

3. Disturbance in the way in which one's body weight, size, or shape is experienced, e.g. the individual claims to 'feel fat' even when emaciated, believes that one area of the body is 'too fat' even when obviously underweight.

4. In females, absence of at least three consecutive menstrual cycles when otherwise expected to occur (primary or secondary amenorrhoea). (A woman is considered to have amenorrhoea if her periods occur only following hormone, e.g. estrogen, administration.)

Disorders of eating

Psychogenic vomiting

Psychogenic vomiting is chronic and episodic vomiting without an organic cause which commonly occurs after meals and in the absence of nausea. It should be distinguished from the more common syndrome of bulimia nervosa, in which self-induced vomiting is accompanied by abnormal ideas about body weight and shape. Psychogenic vomiting appears to be more common in women than in men and usually presents in early or middle adult life. It is reported that psychotherapeutic and behaviour treatments can be helpful [see Morgan (1985) for a review].

Anorexia nervosa

Anorexia nervosa was described and named in 1868 by the physician William Gull, who emphasized psychological causes, the need to restore weight, and the role of the family.

The DSMIIIR criteria are listed in Table 12.6. The main clinical features are a body weight below the standard weight, an intense wish to be thin and, in women, amenorrhoea. Most patients are young women (see epidemiology below). The condition usually begins in adolescence, most often between the ages of 16 and 17. It generally begins with ordinary efforts at dieting in a girl who is somewhat overweight at the time. The central psychological features are over-valued ideas about body and shape and weight, a fear of being fat and a relentless pursuit of a low body weight. The patient has a distorted image of her body, believing herself to be too fat even when severely underweight. This distorted image has been confirmed by measurements of the actual and perceived size of the body (see Garner 1981). It explains why many patients do not want to be helped to gain weight.

The pursuit of thinness may take several forms. Patients generally eat little and show a particular avoidance of carbohydrates. They may set themselves daily calorie limits (often between 600 and 1000 calories). Some try to achieve weight loss by induced vomiting, excessive exercise, and purging. Patients are often preoccupied with thoughts of food, and sometimes enjoy cooking elaborate meals for other people. Ten to 20 per cent of patients with anorexia nervosa admit to stealing food, either by shop-lifting or in other ways. In various series reported by British psychiatrists, up to half the patients had episodes of uncontrollable over-eating, sometimes called binge-eating or bulimia. This behaviour becomes more frequent with increasing age. During binges the patients may eat large amounts of foods usually avoided, such as a whole loaf of bread with jam and butter. After over-eating they feel bloated and may induce vomiting. Binges are followed by remorse and intensified efforts to lose weight. If other people encourage them to eat, patients are often resentful; they may hide food or vomit secretly as soon as the meal is over.

Amenorrhoea is an important feature. It occurs early in the development of the condition and in about a fifth of cases it precedes obvious weight loss. Some cases first come to medical attention with amenorrhoea rather than eating disorder.

Depressive symptoms, lability of mood, and social withdrawal are all common. In women and men lack of sexual interest is usual. [Anorexia nervosa is reviewed in the book by Garfinkel and Garner (1982), and by Fairburn and Hope (1988).]

Physical consequences

A number of important symptoms and signs are secondary to starvation, including sensitivity to cold, constipation, low blood pressure, bradycardia, and hypothermia. In most cases, amenorrhoea is probably secondary to weight loss but as mentioned above in a few cases amenorrhoea is the first symptom. Investigations may show leucopenia, and abnormalities of water regulation. Vomiting and abuse of laxatives may lead to hypokalaemia and alkalosis. These abnormalities may cause epilepsy or rarely, death from cardiac arrhythmia. Hormonal abnormalities also occur: growth hormone levels are raised; plasma cortisol is increased and its normal diurnal variation lost; levels of gonadotrophin are reduced. Thyroxine and

TSH are usually normal but triiodothyronine (T_3) may be reduced (see Mitchell 1986).

Epidemiology

Case register estimates of incidence in Britain and the United States range from 0.37 to 4.06 per 100 000 population per year. Reported incidence rates have increased recently, but it is uncertain whether they reflect a real increase or a greater awareness of the condition (Szmukler 1985).

It is difficult to determine the true prevalence of anorexia nervosa because many people with the condition deny their symptoms. Surveys have suggested prevalence rates of 1–2 per cent among schoolgirls and female university students. Many more young women may have amennorrhoea and less weight loss than that required for the diagnosis of anorexia nervosa (Crisp *et al.* 1976). Amongst anorexic patients seen in clinical practice only 5–10 per cent are male. The onset of anorexia nervosa in females is usually between the ages of 16 and 17, and seldom after the age of 30; in males the peak onset is earlier, about the age of 12. The condition is more common in the upper than lower social classes, and is rarely seen in non-Western countries or in the non-white population of Western countries.

Aetiology

Anorexia nervosa appears to result from a combination of individual predisposition and social factors that encourage dieting. Once the disorder is started, the response of the family may help to perpetuate it.

Genetics

Among the female siblings of patients with established anorexia nervosa, 6 to 10 per cent suffer from the condition (Theander 1970), as against the 1 to 2 per cent found in the general population of the same age (see above). This increase might be due to family environment or to genetic influences. Holland *et al.* (1984) found a much greater concordance in MZ than in DZ twins.

Hypothalamic dysfunction

In anorexia nervosa there is profound disturbance of weight regulation. In some cases amenorrhoea begins before weight loss. This combination suggests a primary disorder of hypothalamic function, since it can occur with structural lesions of the hypothalamus. However, post-mortem studies have not revealed any regular occurrence of hypothalamic lesions in anorexia nervosa. The occasional occurrence of amenorrhoea before weight loss has been interpreted as evidence for a primary hypothalamic-pituitary abnormality. The balance of evidence now suggests that most of the endocrine and metabolic abnormalities are secondary to starvation. [See Mitchell (1986) for a review of the endocrine abnormalities in anorexia nervosa.]

Social factors

Surveys show that many schoolchildren and college students diet at one time or another. Concern about body weight is more frequent, and anorexia nervosa more prevalent, in the middle and upper social classes. There is also a high prevalence of anorexia nervosa in occupational groups who are particularly concerned with weight, such as ballet students (Garner and Garfinkel 1980).

Individual psychological causes

Bruch (1974) was one of the first writers to suggest that a disturbance of body image is of central importance in anorexia nervosa. She supposed that patients are engaged in 'a struggle for control, for a sense of identity and effectiveness with the relentless pursuit of thinness as a final step in this effort'. She also suggested three predisposing factors: dietary problems in early life; parents who are preoccupied with food; and family relationships that leave the child without a sense of identity. Crisp (1977) proposed that, while anorexia is at one level a 'weight phobia', the consequent changes in body shape and menstruation can be regarded as a regression to childhood and an escape from the emotional problems of adolescence. It is often said that psychosexual immaturity is characteristic of patients with anorexia nervosa. In a study of the sexual attitudes and knowledge of 31 female anorexics aged 15–33, Beumont *et al.* (1981) found that a considerable number were anxious or uninformed about sexual matters, but others appeared normal or near normal. These findings are difficult to evaluate in the absence of a control group, but psychosexual problems did not appear to be characteristic of the group as a whole.

Causes within the family

Disturbed relationships are often found in the families of patients with anorexia nervosa, and some authors have suggested that they have an important causal role. Minuchin *et al.* (1978) held that a specific pattern of relationships could be identified consisting of 'enmeshment, overprotectiveness, rigidity and lack of conflict resolution'. They also suggested that the development of anorexia nervosa in the patient served to prevent dissension within the family. From a study of 56 families in which one member had anorexia nervosa, Kalucy *et al.* (1977) concluded that the other family members had an unusual interest in food and physical appearance, and that the families were unusually close knit to an extent that might impede the patient's adolescent development. Neither these studies nor others in the literature have shown convincingly that such patterns of behaviour precede the illness or differ significantly from the patterns in families of normal adolescents.

Course and prognosis

In its early stages, anorexia nervosa often runs a fluctuating course, with exacerbations and periods of partial remission. The long-term prognosis is difficult to judge because most published series are either based on selected cases or are incomplete in their follow-up. Outcome is very variable. The only long-term outcome study (Theander 1985) found that the disorder ran a chronic course over many years, and that at least 18 per cent of patients died as a direct result of the disorder or from suicide. More recent accounts of outcome over short periods indicate a slightly better prognosis with a lower mortality. About a fifth of patients make a full recovery, and another fifth remain severely ill; the remainder show some degree of chronic or fluctuating disturbance. Although weight and menstrual function usually improve, eating habits often remain abnormal, and some patients become overweight while others develop bulimia nervosa.

The only established factor predictive of outcome is the length of illness at presentation. It is often said that late age of onset is associated with a bad prognosis. However, it is evident that many patients whose illness begins in early adolescence also have a poor outcome (see Smith 1982). [For a review of outcome studies and of predictive studies, see Szmukler and Russell (1986).]

Assessment

Most patients with anorexia nervosa are reluctant to see a psychiatrist, so it is important to try to establish a good relationship. A thorough history should be taken of the development of the disorder, the present pattern of eating and weight control, and the patient's ideas about body weight. In the mental state examination, particular attention should be given to depressive symptoms. More than one interview may be needed to obtain this information and gain the patient's confidence. The parents or other informants should be interviewed whenever possible. It is essential to perform a physical examination, with particular attention to the distribution of body hair (normal in anorexia nervosa, abnormal in pituitary failure), the degree of emaciation, signs of vitamin deficiency, and the state of the peripheral circulation. A search should also be made for evidence of any other wasting disease, such as malabsorption, endocrine disorder, or cancer. Electrolytes should be measured if there is any possibility that the patient has been inducing vomiting or abusing purgatives.

Management

Starting treatment   Success largely depends on making a good relationship with the patient so that a clear approach to weight control is possible. It should be made clear that the maintenance of an adequate weight is an essential first priority. It is important to agree a definite dietary plan but not to become involved in wrangles about it. At the same time, it should be emphasized that weight control is only one aspect of the problem, and help should be offered with psychological problems.

Educating the patient and family about the disorder and its treatment is important. Admission to hospital is often needed if the patient's weight is dangerously low (for example, less than 65 per cent of standard weight), if weight loss is rapid, or if there is severe depression. It is also indicated if out-patient care has failed. Less serious cases may be treated as out-patients. [See Hsu (1986) for a review.]

Restoring weight   The patient's admission should be on the understanding that she will stay in hospital until her agreed target weight has been reached. The target has usually to be a compromise between the ideal weight (from height and weight tables) and the patient's idea of what her weight should be. A balanced daily diet of at least 300 calories is provided as three or four meals a day. Successful treatment depends on expert care, with clarity about aims and methods, firmness, and understanding. Eating must be supervised by a nurse, who has two important roles: to reassure the patient that she can eat without the risk of losing control over her weight; and to be firm about agreed targets and ensure that the patient does not induce vomiting or take purgatives. In the early stages, it is often best for the patient to remain in bed in a single room while nurses maintain close observation. It is reasonable to aim for a weight gain of between a half and one kilogram each week. Treatment usually lasts between 8 and 12 weeks. Some patients demand to leave hospital before their treatment is finished, but with patience the staff can usually persuade them to stay.

Behavioural principles are sometimes used. The usual approach is to remove privileges when the patient enters hospital, and to restore them gradually as rewards for weight gain. Suitable privileges include having visitors, newspapers, books, radio, or television for agreed periods of time. It is essential that the patient should agree freely to the programme before it starts, and should feel free to withdraw whenever she wishes. These methods have been described more fully by Garfinkel and Garner (1982). They have not been shown convincingly to give better results than a general programme of the kind described above (which leads to satisfactory weight gain in hospital in about four patients out of five).

Rarely the patient's weight loss is so severe as to pose an immediate threat to life. If such a patient cannot be persuaded to enter hospital, compulsory admission has to be used.

The role of psychotherapy   Many forms of psychotherapy have been tried. It is generally agreed that intensive psychoanalytic methods are not helpful. Clinical experience suggests that there is some value in simple support measures directed to improving personal relationships and increasing the patient's sense of personal effectiveness. In recent years, family therapy has been advocated (for example by Minuchin *et al.* 1978). Although problems in family relationships are common in anorexia nervosa, there is no convincing evidence that the general use of family therapy improves the outcome. If this therapy is used, it should be for selected cases in which family problems seem particularly relevant and the family members are willing to join in treatment. Another alternative is cognitive therapy, which aims to identify and modify abnormal cognitions about eating, weight, and shape. Many patients and families find self-help groups valuable.

Bulimia nervosa

Bulimia refers to episodes of uncontrolled excessive eating, sometimes called 'binges'. As mentioned above, the symptom of bulimia occurs in some cases of anorexia nervosa. Although the syndrome of bulimia nervosa was described by Russell (1979) as an 'ominous variant' of anorexia nervosa, it is known to occur without preceding anorexia nervosa. The syndrome has two prinicipal components. The first is an intractable urge to over-eat. The second is self-induced vomiting to prevent weight gain, sometimes accompanied by the abuse of purgatives. Patients with this syndrome are usually of normal weight. Most patients are female and they often have normal menses (see Table 12.7 for the DSMIIIR criteria).

Patients have overvalued ideas about shape and weight resembling those in anorexia nervosa, together with a profound loss of control over eating. Episodes of bulimia may be precipitated by stress or by the breaking of self-imposed dietary rules, or may occasionally be planned. In the episodes enormous amounts of food are consumed; for example, a loaf of bread, a whole pot of jam, a cake, and biscuits. This voracious eating takes place alone. At first it brings relief from tension, but relief is soon followed by guilt and disgust. The patient then induces vomiting, which at first is often brought about by putting fingers in the throat, but later can usually be done at will. There may be many episodes of bulimia and vomiting each day.

Depressive symptoms are more common than in anorexia nervosa, and

Table 12.7. DSMIIIR criteria for bulimia nervosa

1. Recurrent episodes of binge-eating (rapid consumption of a large amount of food in a discrete period of time).

2. During the eating binges there is a feeling of lack of control over the eating behaviour.

3. The individual regularly engages in either self-induced vomiting, use of laxatives, strict dieting, fasting, or vigorous exercise in order to prevent weight gain.

4. A minimum average of two binge-eating episodes per week for at least three months.

5. Persistent over-concern with body shape and weight.

probably are secondary to the eating disorder. A few patients appear to suffer from a depressive disorder requiring antidepressant drugs. [See Fairburn and Hope (1988) for a review of bulimia nervosa.]

Physical consequences

Repeated vomiting leads to several complications. Potassium depletion is particularly serious, resulting in weakness, cardiac arrythmia, and renal damage. Urinary infections, tetany, and epileptic fits may occur. The teeth become pitted in a characteristic way by the acid gastric contents.

Epidemiology

The prevalence of bulimia nervosa is not certain, but it is most common in young women, and may occur in up to 10 per cent of this age group. Surveys indicate that self-induced vomiting is also commonly used as a way of controlling weight by women who do not have bulimia (Cooper and Fairburn 1983). Bulimia nervosa has only been identified in developed countries.

Prognosis

This is uncertain, since there have been no long-term studies. It is probable that abnormal eating habits persist for many years, but that they vary in severity.

Management

The assessment of bulimia nervosa is similar to that described for anorexia nervosa, but is easier because a good working relationship can often be established. It is necessary to assess the patient's physical state, and to identify any depressive disorder that might benefit from treatment with antidepressant drugs. Out-patient treatment is usually possible, and admission to hospital is indicated only if there are severe depressive symptoms or physical complications, or if out-patient treatment has failed.

The most extensively studied *psychological treatment* is a cognitive behavioural therapy which seeks to make patients responsible for controlling their own eating. Patients attend as out-patients several times a week, keep records of their food intake and episodes of vomiting, and attempt to identify and avoid any environmental stimuli or emotional changes that regularly precede the urge to overeat.

Treatment with *antidepressant medication* should be reserved for patients with definite disorder. [See Fairburn (1987) for a review of treatment. See Fairburn and Hope (1988) for a general review of bulimia nervosa.]

Obesity

By convention, obesity is diagnosed when body weight exceeds standard weight by 20 per cent. When weight excess is greater than 30 per cent, the risk of cardiovascular disorder is increased.

Most obesity is probably caused by a combination of constitutional and social factors that encourage overeating. Psychological causes do not seem to be of great importance in most cases, but psychiatrists are sometimes asked to see obese people whose excessive eating seems to be determined by emotional factors. Overweight people often have low self-esteem and social confidence; otherwise they generally show no more psychological disturbance than the general population, although a few have serious psychiatric problems. Little is known about psychological aspects of obesity in infancy or childhood [for a review see Woolston (1987)].

Treatment

Mildly obese people may need nothing more than advice about diet. The moderately obese require closer supervision (see Wadden and Stunkard 1985). It is important to be aware that many obese people do not eat generally more than other people, and that aiming at an 'ideal' weight is unrealistic and even inappropriate. The long-term results of all kinds of reducing diet are disappointing, whether supervised by a doctor or not (Stunkard and McClaren-Hume 1959). Dieting may be associated with affective symptoms (Smoller *et al.* 1987). Weight groups, whether supervised or self-help, produce short-term benefit but do not improve long-term results. The same holds for appetite-suppressing drugs (see Stunkard 1980). Behavioural methods usually include self-monitoring, the changing of eating habits and attitudes, increasing exercise, and social support. In controlled trials it has been found that regaining weight is less frequent after these methods than after other treatment (see Stunkard 1980; Forreyt *et al.* 1981).

For the grossly obese, surgical procedures are sometimes used, including jaw-wiring and bypass operations. Jaw-wiring is often followed by rapid weight gain when the wiring is removed. Jejuno-ileal bypass results in sustained weight loss which seems to be due to reduced food intake rather than continued malabsorption. Metabolic complications are common after the operation, but psychological benefits seem to be considerable (Castelnuovo-Tedesco *et al.* 1982). Gastric reduction operations have fewer complications but are technically more difficult. The psychological and social outcomes of surgery are good but careful selection and prolonged follow-up are required. [For reviews of outcome see Stunkard *et al.* (1986). For reviews of obesity in general see *Annals of Internal Medicine* (1985).]

Diabetes mellitus

Diabetes is a chronic condition requiring prolonged medical supervision and informed self-care, and it is hardly surprising that many physicians emphasize the psychological aspect of treatment (Tattersall 1981).

Psychological factors and diabetic control

Diabetes mellitus has sometimes been included among the so-called psychosomatic disorders, but there is no convincing evidence that psychological factors evoke the disease. None the less psychological factors are highly important because they influence the control of established diabetes, and it is now generally accepted that good control of blood glucose is the single most important factor in preventing long-term complications. Psychological factors can impair control in two ways. First, stressful experience can lead directly to endocrine changes (Kemmer *et al.* 1986). Second, many diabetics show poor self-care and compliance with medical advice, and this is an important cause of 'brittle' diabetes (Tattersall 1985). Psychological factors also limit the use of new methods of diabetic control, such as insulin pumps, which require expert and conscientious self-care.

Problems of being diabetic

For the diabetic person, psychological and social problems may be caused by restrictions of diet and activity, the need for careful self-care, and the possibility of serious physical complications such as vascular disease and impaired vision. Although most diabetic patients adapt well to the limitations of their illness, an important minority have difficulties in their work, leisure, and social activities. Psychiatric problems include depression and anxiety (see Wilkinson 1987). There may be an increased prevalence of eating disorders amongst adolescent and young adult diabetic women (Rodin *et al.* 1986). Psychiatric distress is probably most common in diabetics with severe medical complications, such as loss of sight, renal failure, and vascular disease. Pregnancy is a particularly difficult time for diabetic women, since there may be difficulties in control of the diabetes and increased risks of miscarriages and fetal malformations (see Tattersall 1981; Bradley 1985).

Sexual problems are believed to be common among diabetics. Two kinds of impotence occur in the men. First there is psychogenic impotence of the kind found in all chronic debilitating diseases. The second kind is more common in diabetes and is said to be characteristic of it. It may predate other features of the disease and is thought to be associated with pelvic autonomic neuropathy, although vascular and endocrine factors may also contribute (McCulloch *et al.* 1984).

Organic psychiatric syndromes

An **acute organic syndrome** is a prodromal sign of diabetic (hyperglycaemic) coma. It may present as an episode of disturbed behaviour, and the onset may be abrupt or insidious. The prodromal physical symptoms include thirst, headaches, abdominal pain, nausea, and vomiting. The pulse is rapid and blood pressure low. Dehydration is marked and acetone may be smelt on the breath. Another cause of an acute organic syndrome is hypoglycaemia (see below).

Mild **cognitive impairment** is not uncommon among chronic diabetics (Bale 1973; Perlmutter *et al.* 1984). It may be caused by recurrent attacks of hypoglycaemia or by cerebral arteriosclerosis. A more severe dementia is sometimes associated with cerebrovascular disease.

Psychiatric intervention

In addition to clear advice (see Assal *et al.* 1985) and well planned and sympathetic medical cover (see Tattersall 1981) there is a limited role for specialist psychological intervention. The latter includes the treatment of any depressive disorder, and behavioural methods to improve diabetic control and to relieve associated psychological and social problems (see Wing *et al.* 1986). Tricyclic antidepressants may be helpful in relieving the pain of diabetic neuropathy (see Young and Clarke 1985). [Principles of management in children are described by Lindsay (1985).]

Hypoglycaemia

This condition is usually induced by therapeutic insulin (when the patient has too much insulin or not enough food). Other syndromes occur as a result of an insulin secreting tumour of the pancreas, or of alcoholism or liver disease. Common psychological features of acute hypoglycaemia include anxiety and other abnormalities of mood, restlesness, irritability, aggressiveness, and behaving as if drunk. Physical symptoms include hunger and palpitations. Common physical signs are flushing, sweating, tremor, tachycardia, and ataxic gait. Occasionally other neurological signs occur. Severe episodes may proceed to hypoglycaemic coma. Hypoglycaemia is important in the differential diagnosis of psychiatric disorders, but it is easily missed.

Cardiovascular disorders

Ischaemic heart disease

For many years, it has been assumed that emotional disorder predisposes to ischaemic heart disease (Osler 1910). Dunbar (see 1954) described a 'coronary personality'. Such ideas are difficult to test because only prospective studies can separate psychological factors present before the heart disease from the psychological effects of being ill. Recent research has concentrated on several groups of possible risk factors including chronic emotional disturbance, social and economic disadvantage, overwork, or other chronic stress, and the Type A behaviour pattern (see Jenkins 1982; Weiss *et al.* 1984; Steptoe 1985). The best established of these factors is the Type A behaviour pattern, which is defined as hostility, excessive competitive drive, ambitiousness, a chronic sense of urgency, and a preoccupation with deadlines (Friedman and Rosenman 1959). There have been two large prospective studies of the Type A behaviour pattern. The Western Collaborative Group studied over 3000 men aged 29 to 59 working in ten Californian companies, and followed them up for eight to nine years (Rosenman *et al.* 1975). The other study was based on a sample from over 5000 men and women aged 29–62 living in the town of Framingham, Massachusetts (Haynes *et al.* 1980). These subjects were initially free from cardiovascular disease, and were followed up for eight years. In both studies rates of ischaemic heart disease proved to be twice as high in Type A subjects as in other subjects. Although Type A behaviour has been widely accepted to be an independent risk factor for ischaemic heart, recent evidence has cast doubt on this conclusion. Most studies have failed to find an association between Type A behaviour and extent of coronary artery disease. Such prospective studies have failed to confirm a clear association between Type A and mortality or evidence of coronary artery disease on angiography. Some of the discrepancies may be due to the lack of standard criteria for defining Type A behaviour and to the breadth of the concept. Most current research has preferred to concentrate on more precisely defined psychological factors such as depression or hostility [see Dimsdale (1988) for a review].

Trials of primary and secondary prevention have largely concentrated on changing risk factors such as smoking, diet, and lack of physical activity (see *Lancet* 1982*b*). Attempts have also been made to alter Type A behaviour. Thus the Stanford Heart Disease Prevention programme attempted to alter two behavioural characteristics: 'hostility' and 'time urgency'. The study was based on male volunteers who had experienced a heart attack. An experimental group of 600 patients received monthly group therapy, and a control group of 600 were simply seen by a cardiologist. In the experimental group, the frequency of Type A behaviour was reduced, and the re-infarction rate was 7 per cent compared with 14 per cent among the controls (Friedman *et al.* 1982). It is not known whether at the end of the treatment there were differences between the two groups in exercise, smoking or other risk factors that might have mediated these effects (see Johnston 1985).

Angina

Angina is often precipitated by emotions such as anxiety, anger, and excitement. It can be a frightening symptom and some patients become over-cautious, despite reassurance and encouragement to resume normal activities. Angina may be accompanied by atypical chest pain and breathlessness caused by anxiety or hyperventilation. There is often little relationship between objectively measured exercise tolerance and the patient's complaints of chest pain and limitation of activity (see Mayou 1986).

Medical treatment combined with regular and appropriate exercise can be highly effective in combating these problems. Some patients are helped to regain confidence by individually planned behavioural programmes.

Myocardial infarction

Patients often meet the early symptoms of myocardial infarction with denial, and consequently delay seeking treatment. In the first few days in hospital, acute organic mental syndromes and anxiety symptoms are common (see Cay 1984), and emotional distress may be an important cause of arrhythmias and sudden death (Lown 1982).

Survivors of cardiac arrest may suffer cognitive impairment. When mild, such impairment often manifests later as personality change or behavioural symptoms, and can then be mistaken for an emotional response to illness (Reich *et al.* 1983). When patients return home from hospital, they commonly have depressive symptoms (such as fatigue, insomnia, and poor concentration), and excessive concern and caution about somatic symptoms. Most patients overcome these early problems and return to a fully active life. A few suffer persistent emotional distress and social disability out of proportion to their physical state, often accompanied by atypical somatic symptoms. Such problems are more common in patients with the following features: long-standing psychiatric or social problems; over-protective families; a myocardial infarction that ran a complicated course (Mayou 1979).

Attempts have been made to reduce these psychological problems with various forms of rehabilitation (Razin 1982), in which the most important component is probably early mobilization. Other components include exercise training, education programmes, and group therapy. Exercise training has been widely used but is probably not particularly effective in reducing psychological problems, despite common beliefs to the contrary (Mayou *et al.* 1981; Taylor *et al.* 1986; Stern and Cleary 1982). Individual and group psychotheraphy seem to have only a limited value (see Johnston 1985). It is important to provide appropriate and individually planned care for the small minority of patients with persistent depression or other emotional or social problems. Tricyclic antidepressants should be used with care because of cardiac side-effects.

Cardiac surgery

Coronary artery surgery for the relief of angina is one of the commonest forms of major surgery. It is highly successful in relieving angina, but after the operation up to a quarter of the patients report persistent anxiety or depression and limitation of everyday activities. The outcome is least satisfactory amongst patients who before operation have severe emotional distress or respond over-cautiously to angina. Early neuropsychiatric symptoms are usual but most improve rapidly [see Mayou (1986) for a review].

Essential hypertension

Brief changes in blood pressure occur in the course of temporary emotional states. It has been suggested that prolonged emotional changes can lead to sustained hypertension (for example Alexander 1950) but the evidence is still unconvincing (see Weiner 1977) although there is some indirect evidence from animal experiments. For example, Henry *et al.* (1967) found that rats became hypertensive if kept in crowded conditions. In humans, there have been studies of people working in stressful occupations. Cobb and Rose (1973) found hypertension to be more common among air traffic controllers than in the general population. Theorell and Lind (1973) studied middle-aged men and reported that those with more responsible jobs had higher blood pressure. Attempts have also been made to relate hypertension to neurotic conflicts or personality type, but the findings have not been convincing. [See Mann (1986) for a review.]

Complaints of headache, dizziness, and fatigue are common among hypertensive patients who know they are hypertensive but not among those who do not know (Kidson 1973). However, awareness does not necessarily lead to such consequences. In a screening programme, Mann (1977) combined telling patients the diagnosis with giving them psychological support, and found no adverse effects (Mann 1977).

There is still uncertainty about the best treatment for the many people with mild hypertension. Such people comply poorly with drug treatment (Winickoff and Murphy 1987). Some hypotensive drugs cause depression, notably reserpine, beta-blockers, and clonidine. These problems have led to the use of psychological methods to replace drugs. So far the most effective approach seems to be a combination of meditation and relaxation, practised at home (Patel 1975). The potential value of such methods for the population at large is uncertain. [See Mann (1986) for a review of the psychological aspects of hypertension.]

Atypical cardiac symptoms

During the American Civil War, Da Costa (1871) described a condition which he called Irritable Heart. This syndrome consisted of a conviction that the heart was diseased, together with palpitations, breathlessness, fatigue, and inframammary pain. This combination has also been named 'disorderly action of the heart', 'effort syndrome', and 'neurocirculatory asthenia'. The symptoms were originally thought to indicate a functional disorder of the heart. More recently they have been attributed to mitral value prolapse, but such an association seems unlikely.

Atypical chest pain, in the absence of heart disease and often associated with complaints of breathlessness and palpitations, is very common among patients in primary care and in cardiac out-patient clinics. Most patients with this condition are reassured by thorough assessment, but a significant minority continue to complain of physical and psychological symptoms and to limit their everyday activites. Follow-up studies of patients with chest pain and normal coronary angiograms have consistently found subsequent mortality and cardiac morbility to be little greater than expectation, but persistent disability to be common (Bass and Wade 1984).

The commonest psychiatric causes of atypical chest pain are hyperventilation, anxiety, and panic disorders: less common causes are depressive disorder and hypochondriasis. Many patients have chest pain which is due not to psychiatric disorder but to non-cardiac physical causes that have been misconstrued. Cognitive behavioural treatments are often effective in the management of anxiety and hyperventilation. Depressive disorder should be treated with antidepressant medication.

Respiratory disorders

Breathlessness arising from many respiratory and cardiac disorders may be exacerbated by psychological factors. Breathlessness can also be entirely psychological in origin (see p. 177); for example, hyperventilation associated with anxiety disorders).

Asthma

Alexander (1950) suggested that asthma is caused by unresolved conflicts about dependency, but there is no satisfactory evidence for this idea. Explanations in terms of learning theory are equally unsupported (see Steptoe 1984). There is more convincing evidence that emotions such as anger, fear, and excitement can provoke and exacerbate individual attacks in patients with established asthma. It has been reported that evidence of chronic psychological and family problems is more common in severely asthmatic children who die of asthma than in other children with severe asthma (Strunk *et al.* 1985).

Perhaps surprisingly, among asthmatic children the prevalence of psychiatric morbidity is little greater than in the general population of children (Graham and Rutter 1970). However, when psychological problems occur in children they can add to management problems.

Attempts have been made to treat asthma with psychotherapy and behavioural therapy but there is no convincing evidence that these treatments are better than simple advice and support (see Steptoe 1984). Individual and family treatment can be useful for the minority of asthmatic children in whom psychological factors are important (see Graham 1986).

Chronic bronchitis

Chronic obstructive airways disease impairs the quality of life and is often associated with anxiety and depression (McSweeney *et al.* 1982). It also causes hypoxaemia which may lead to cognitive impairment (Grant *et al.* 1982; Prigatano *et al.* 1984). Some patients complain of breathlessness out of proportion to their physical disorder (Burns and Howell 1969), which may respond to psychological intervention. In everyday clinical practice breathing exercises, general physical exercise, and social support all appear to improve morale and reduce disability (see Rosser and Guz 1981). Pulmonary rehabilitation programmes providing exercise training and behavioural methods are increasingly available (Make 1986).

Cystic fibrosis

In the past cystic fibrosis had a very poor prognosis for life, and consequently there were severe psychological effects on the child and family. Recently the prognosis has much improved and the children experience emotional disturbance and behavioural problems with no greater frequency than children with other chronic physical illnesses (see Graham 1986). Adults with cystic fibrosis have to cope with chronic physical disability, substantially impaired fertility, and the risk that any child born to them has a one in forty chance of having the disease (see Office of Health Economics 1986*a*).

Renal disorders

Uraemia

Uraemia causes an acute organic psychiatric syndrome characterized by drowsiness and fluctuating consciousness; there may be episodes of disturbed behaviour in up to a third of cases. Intellect may be impaired (see Osberg *et al.* 1982). These symptoms are not closely related to the urea concentration in the plasma, probably because electrolyte disturbances and failure to excrete drugs also contribute to the aetiology.

Chronic renal failure

The treatment of end-stage renal failure is stressful to patients, families, and hospital staff. Symptoms of anxiety or depression occur in about half the patients. There is probably an increased risk of suicide. Impaired capacity to work, reduced physical activity, marital problems, and sexual dysfunction are common. These psychosocial difficulties add to the management problems and affect the course of the medical illness (see House 1987*a*) and survival (Hussebye *et al.* 1987). Comparisons of dialysis patients with transplantation patients suggest that the latter have a better quality of life with fewer handicaps. Among dialysis patients, those treated at home report fewer problems than those treated in hospital. Continuous ambulatory peritoneal dialysis is less restricting than haemodialysis but is not medically suitable for many patients with renal failure. (Evans *et al.* 1985; Simmons *et al.* 1986).

End-stage renal failure in children may considerably restrict the quality life for themselves, their siblings, and their parents (see Winterborn 1987). Although some children with end-stage renal failure have emotional difficulties, many manage remarkably well, as do their families (Fielding *et al.* 1985).

In many renal units a liaison psychiatrist works closely with staff and patients. Psychiatric help is mainly sought for mood disorders, difficulties in accepting renal failure or its treatment, and disruptive or unco-operative behaviour. [See House (1987a) for an account of psychosocial problems and how they are related to the type of treatment for the renal problem.]

Haemodialysis

Psychological problems include cognitive deficits associated with uraemia, anaemia, drug toxicity, and other physical complications. Other organic disorders are an acute psychiatric syndrome associated with dialysis disequilibrium, and a rare dialysis dementia probably due to the aluminium content of the perfusion fluid. Depression and anxiety are common. Symptoms such as lethargy, insomnia, and poor concentration may be due to either physical or psychological causes. Impotence is common, and often psychologically determined.

Psychological and social factors can cause difficulties in management, particularly when dialysis is carried out in the patient's home. The patient's capacity to cope may be influenced by his emotional state, personality, and understanding of the treatment. Within the family, the willingness and ability to help in treatment is important, and so is the quality of family relationships. General social and financial circumstances are also important.

Renal transplantation

After receiving a kidney transplant, most patients are better physically and psychologically than they were before the operation. There is often a striking improvement in their sense of well-being, both physical and mental, and their sexual functioning and in ability to work. Neverthe-less psychological problems often occur. Problems of transplant rejection or threatened rejection are common, and frequently associated with con-siderable depression and anger. Psychological problems may also occur in association with immunosuppressive drugs, steroids in high dosage, and antihypertensive drugs. [See Levy (1986) for a review of renal transplantation.]

Gastrointestinal disorders

Gastrointestinal symptoms are often an expression of psychiatric disorder. Complaints of poor appetite, abdominal pain, and constipation can all be due to psychological causes, especially depressive disorders and anxiety neuroses. In addition to the conditions reviewed in this section, the following conditions are discussed elsewhere: eating disorders (p. 436), alcoholic gastritis (p. 515), carcinoma of pancreas (p. 462) and bowel (p. 456).

Oesophageal symptoms

The condition known as **Globus hystericus** (difficulty in swallowing or a persistant feeling of a lump at the level of the upper oesophageal stricture) has often been classified as hysterical. However, cineradiology has shown that there is frequently abnormality in the oesophageal mechanisms involved in swallowing (Delahunty and Ardran 1970). A psychological diagnosis should never be made until a physical cause has been thoroughly excluded by gastroenterological investigation.

Abdominal pain

Unexplained abdominal pain is frequent among patients in medical and gastroenterology clinics and wards (see Eisendrath *et al.* 1986). Such pain may be psychologically determined. For example, amongst patients undergoing appendicectomy, psychiatric symptoms have been reported as more frequent in those with normal than in those with abnormal appendices (Creed 1981). The prognosis for psychologically determined abdominal pain is uncertain, but some patients have persistent pain (Drossman 1982). Abdominal pain is also common in children (see p. 785).

Food allergy syndrome

In recent years, the medical profession has recognized food allergy as a disorder. However, many patients erroneously attribute psychological symptoms to this cause. For example, amongst patients attending allergy clinics but not found to have food allergy, many complain of psychological and bodily symptoms (especially hyperventilation), which they attribute to food. Such patients tend to be dissatisfied with medical opinion, and to reject any psychological explanation or treatment. [See Rix *et al.* (1984); Royal College of Physicians and the British Nutrition Foundation (1984).]

Peptic ulcer

It has long been held that mental activity can affect the stomach [see Weiner (1977) for a review]. Peptic ulcers have been produced in animals by electrical stimulation of the hypothalamus. If rats are allowed varying degrees of control over electric shock, the less control they have the more likely they are to develop ulcers (see Ader 1976). In human subjects, the direct effect of emotion of the gastric mucosa has been observed in patients with gastric fistulae, such as the patient Tom who was described by Wolf and Wolff (1947).

Alexander (1950) suggested that 'the repressed longing for love is the unconscious psychological stimulus directly connected with the psychological processes leading finally to ulceration'. Although there is no support for such psychosomatic theories, some observations suggest that psychological factors may play a part in the aetiology of peptic ulcer. For example, it has been reported that gastric and duodenal ulcers are more common at times of environmental stress, such as wartime bombing; and recent research indicates that patients with duodenal ulcers report more chronic background difficulties than do control subjects (see Tennant 1988 for a review).

There is no evidence that specific psychological treatment is beneficial in the treatment of peptic ulcer.

Ulcerative colitis

Because no physical cause has been found for ulcerative colitis, some authors have suggested that psychological factors can lead to its initial onset; on these grounds, Alexander (1950) included the disease among his group of psychosomatic disorders. In some patients with ulcerative colitis, clinical experience suggests that psychological stressors can provoke relapses of the established illness. There is, however, no scientific evidence for the role of psychological or social factors in initiating the illness or provoking relapses.

Although many psychological and social problems have been described in association with ulcerative colitis (Feldman *et al.* 1967) most patients seem to adapt well to this unpleasant disease (Hendriksen and Binder 1980). Karush *et al.* (1977) carried out a controlled trial comparing combined psychotherapy and medical treatment, with medical treatment alone. They reported a better outcome after the combined treatment, but there are serious doubts about their diagnostic criteria, matching of controls, and assessment of outcome. Many patients benefit from the provision of information and encouragement, but it is doubtful whether more elaborate psychological treatment is helpful in most cases. [See Drossman (1986) for a review.]

Crohn's disease

There is no convincing evidence that psychological factors contribute to onset or relapse in Crohn's disease. However, the unpredictable, fluctuating, and chronic course of the disease means that it often affects the quality of life greatly (Meyers *et al.* 1980). Psychiatric symptoms are common (Helzer *et al.* 1984). Most patients report an improvement in quality of life and psychological symptoms after surgery.

Colostomy and ileostomy

Several bowel diseases require surgical treatment that results in a temporary or permanent stoma. Psychiatric morbidity seems to be greater after this treatment than after other bowel surgery, and is probably more frequent in patients with cancer than in those with other conditions. Amongst patients with a stoma, about half report post-operative depression or other psychiatric symptoms, which mostly improve over a few months. Other common problems (which may be persistent) are social and leisure activities, embarrassment about possible leakage of bowel contents, and sexual difficulties (Thomas *et al.* 1984, 1987). Patients with stomas are often helped by practical advice from other stoma patients who have made a good adjustment.

Irritable bowel syndrome

The irritable bowel syndrome is abdominal pain or discomfort, with or without an alteration of bowel habits, persisting for longer than three months in the absence of any demonstrable organic disease. The condition is common in gastroenterology clinics, and also amongst people who have not consulted a doctor (Thompson and Heaton 1980). It is uncertain whether the condition is related to intestinal motility disorder, dietary fibre deficiency, food intolerance, or bile acid malabsorption. Research has proved little evidence of an association with life events, social factors, or psychiatric symptoms (Sammons and Karoly 1987; Creed and Guthrie 1987). However, psychological and social factors may increase the likelihood of referral to a gastroenterology clinic, and may make management more difficult.

Successful treatment depends upon careful assessment, followed by clear explanation and reassurance. There is no effective medical treatment, but counselling and behavioural methods can be helpful in reducing excessive anxiety or disability [see Ford (1986) for a review] and in the management of somatic symptoms. The long-term prognosis for abdominal pain and changed bowel habit is often good.

Sensory disorders

Deafness

Deafness may develop before speech is learnt (prelingual deafness) or afterwards. Profound early deafness interferes with speech and language development, and with emotional development (Thomas 1981). When patients with this condition leave school at sixteen, they are on average eight years behind children with normal hearing. Prelingually deaf adults often keep together in their own social groups and communicate by sign language. They appear to develop behaviour problems and social maladjustment more often than emotional disorder. For the management of such problems, special knowledge is required of the practical problems of deafness (see Denmark 1985).

Deafness of later onset has less severe effects then those just described (see Thomas 1981). However, the acute onset of profound deafness can be extremely distressing, whilst milder restriction of hearing may cause depression and considerable social disability.

Kraepelin suggested that deafness was an important factor in the development of persecutory delusions. This idea was supported by Kay *et al.* (1976), who carried out a large survey of elderly patients with chronic paranoid hallucinatory illnesses, and found a high prevalence of deafness among them (see p. 621). It is not known whether there is any association between deafness and paranoid disorders in younger patients. This subject has been reviewed by Cooper (1984) and by Corbin and Eastwood (1986).

Tinnitus

Tinnitus is very common, but few sufferers consult doctors or complain that the condition prevents a normal life (Hawthorne and O'Connor 1987). Some patients are helped by medicine and treatment, whilst others are helped by devices which mask tinnitus with a more acceptable sound.

Behavioural methods can enable people to accept their tinnitus and to minimize their social handicaps (see Hallam *et al.* 1984; Jakes *et al.* 1986).

Blindness

Although it imposes many difficulties, blindness in early life need not lead to abnormal psychological development in childhood (see Ammerman *et al.* 1986; Graham 1986) or to unsuccessful later development. In previously sighted people the later onset of blindness causes considerable distress. Initial denial and subsequent depression are common, as are prolonged difficulties in adjustment. For accounts of blindness as a cause of psychiatric disorder see Cooper (1984), and Corbin and Eastwood (1986).

Skin disorders

Alexander (1950) included 'neurodermatitis' among the psychosomatic disorders. Psychological causes have been suggested for many skin conditions including urticaria, lichen simplex, atopic dermatitis (Faulstich and Williamson 1985), psoriasis, alopecia areata, and pruritus (see Whitlock 1976). The evidence for psychological causation is not strong. However, psychiatric disorders are common among people with established skin disease. Patients with conspicuous skin disorders such as acne, psoriasis and eczema often describe the considerable effects on their social lives resulting from embarrassment and lack of confidence (Jowett and Ryan 1985). A small minority fail to come to terms with their disability and suffer considerable emotional distress.

Primary psychiatric disorder may present to the dermatologist as dysmorphophobia, illness fears, pruritis, delusions of parasite infestation, and factitious disorder (Cotterill 1981; Sheppard *et al.* 1986). For example, patients with dysmorphophobia (see p. 417) may complain of supposed hair loss or abnormality of the appearance of the skin, where little or no abnormality is apparent to the doctor.

Factitious skin disorders include dermatitis artefacta, which is the name for self-inflicted skin lesions, usually areas of superficial necrosis. Most patients with this condition are young women, many of whom have abnormal personalities, though there is no single personality type. The condition persists for many years in about a third of cases. Recovery is usually associated with a change in life circumstances rather than with treatment (see Sneddon and Sneddon 1975; Gupta *et al.* 1987*a,b*). Another factitious skin disorder is self-induced purpura.

Some patients, particularly middle-aged to elderly women, present to dermatologists with delusions about parasites or other objects in the skin (Ekbom's syndrome). These delusions are usually encapsulated; they are sometimes associated with a depressive disorder, but more often constitute a monosyptomatic paranoid disorder (Berrios 1985). A few respond to antipsychotic drugs such as pimozide, but generally the prognosis is poor (see Munro 1980).

A less common but important condition is **trichotillomania** which is the irresistible urge to pull hairs from the scalp. The hair-pulling is often denied by the patient. Most cases start in adolescence, though children are occasionally affected. Women are more commonly affected than men.

Some cases start at a time of stress and last only a few months, others continue for years. Usually the scalp hair is pulled out, but eyelashes, eyebrows, axilary, and pubic hair may be removed. Hairs may be pulled out in tufts or one by one. Some patients save the hair and eat it, a practice that can lead to hair ball in the stomach or to intestinal obstruction. Trichotillomania may be associated with a variety of psychiatric disorders. It may also be an isolated symptom, which sometimes responds to behavioural treatment. It is difficult to treat and has a poor prognosis except when the onset is in early childhood (see Krishnan *et al.* 1985).

Connective tissue disorders

Rheumatoid arthritis

Rheumatoid arthritis was one of Alexander's psychosomatic disorders, but there is no convincing evidence that psychological factors are important in its aetiology (see Weiner 1977; Koehler 1985). As with other physical illnessess, psychological abnormalities have often been described, but they are most likely to be the result rather than the cause of the illness, or simply coincidental. Attempts to describe a characteristic premorbid personality have been equally unsatisfactory. Reports that psychological stressors can precipitate the onset or relapse of the disease are unconvincing.

It is not surprising that this painful chronic disorder is associated with anxiety and depressive symptoms, and with limitation of work, leisure, family life, and sexual function. Emotional problems are particularly severe in juvenile patients. Physicians treating rheumatoid arthritis spend much of their time in treating the patients' psychological reactions to the illness, and in attempting to improve compliance with treatment and to minimize psychological handicaps. Psychological interventions can help to improve compliance, control pain (Skevington 1986), treat affective disorders, and reduce psychosocial handicaps. Methods include anxiety management, cognitive therapy, counselling and the use of self-help support groups [see Anderson *et al.* (1985), Lerman (1987) for reviews].

Systemic lupus erythematosus

Psychiatric disorders are common in the course of systemic lupus erythematosus, though seldom the first manifestation. They include acute and chronic organic syndromes, other psychoses, and emotional disorders. Most of these disturbances last less than six weeks but some recur.

Cognitive impairment is common in patients with active or inactive systemic lupus erythematosus (see Carbotte *et al.* 1986). The course of the psychiatric symptoms usually follows that of other features of the physical disease. The treatment of the psychiatric symptoms is mainly that of the primary condition. Prolonged treatment with steroids in high doses can cause psychological symptoms in some patients [see Lishman (1987) and Lim *et al.* (1988) for further information].

Infections

Prolonged depressive disorder is likely to follow certain infectious diseases, particularly infectious hepatitis, influenza and brucellosis. Investigations of the last two suggest that prolonged depressive disorder is more likely in people who have experienced previous psychological difficulties (see Whitlock 1982). In one study, a series of psychological tests was completed by 600 people who subsequently developed Asian influenza. Delayed recovery from the influenza was no more common among people whose initial illness had been severe, but it was more frequent among those who had obtained more abnormal scores on the psychological tests before the illness (Imboden *et al.* 1961).

Sexually transmitted disease

Amongst patients attending clinics for sexually transmitted disease (STD), 20–30 per cent have psychiatric disorders, whether or not venereal disease is diagnosed (Mayou 1975). Catalan *et al.* (1981) reported that over a fifth of males and a quarter of females attending an STD clinic were experiencing sexual dysfunction and that most would have liked further help for this problem.

Apart from HIV infection, genital herpes is probably the most emotionally distressing sexually transmitted disease, because it often causes intense discomfort and threatens the danger of transmission in pregnancy (see Van der Plate and Aral 1987; Levenson *et al.* 1987).

It should be borne in mind that patients occasionally present with severe fears of venereal disease, which persist despite reassurance; these fears are mainly related to depressive disorder.

HIV infection

The nature of the physical symptoms, the relentless progressive course, and the reactions of other people all mean that emotional distress is common in patients with HIV infection. Such distress is the more likely because high-risk groups (homosexuals, haemophiliacs, and drug abusers) may have other reasons for psychological problems. In addition, there are neuropsychiatric complications of HIV infection (Levy *et al.* 1988). Even so, many patients with AIDS manage to lead relatively normal lives for substantial periods.

Most people undergoing diagnostic HIV antibody testing suffer anxiety or depression. This response is usually transient in people with a negative test result, but can be severe and lasting in those with a positive result. Alcohol and substance abuse are common in this group and acute and subacute brain syndromes have been described at this stage.

For those who are HIV positive but not suffering from AIDS or other symptoms, there are problems of facing uncertainty about the future, as well as the restrictions imposed by unfavourable public attitude: such people, both children and adults, may have considerable psychiatric and social problems.

Many of those who develop AIDS suffer neurological and psychiatric symptoms. Various acute and subacute syndromes are described, of which the most frequent is a syndrome of subacute encephalitis. Delirium may also be due to opportunistic infection or to cerebral malignancy.

Chronic impaired cognitive function seen in between one quarter and one third of AIDS patients is associated with headaches, depression, seizures, progressive dementia, and peripheral neuropathy. HIV infection can also result in neurological symptoms and dementia in those who do not have AIDS (Navia and Price 1987).

It is too early to be certain about the implications of the HIV epidemic for psychiatric services. Psychiatrists should be involved in planning services to provide general support and counselling, together with symptomatic treatment for neuropsychiatric complications. It is not yet known what facilities may be required for AIDS patients who develop dementia. [See Catalan (1988) for a review.]

Post-viral syndromes

Symptoms of depression, fatigue, and malaise are believed to be common following viral infections such as influenza, hepatitis, and infectious mononucleosis, but there is little information on the epidemiology or nature of the association. In the last few years there has been a very considerable increase in the numbers of people presenting to doctors with fatigue and emotional symptoms which they believe are consequences of viral infections. Numerous viruses, including Epstein–Barr virus (see Straus 1987) have been incriminated but the significance of organic causes remain uncertain. It is probable that in some instances the aetiology is psychological and that in other cases with organic causes, psychological factors contribute to the clinical features (see David *et al.* 1988).

Cancer

Aetiology

It is not surprising that cancer patients have emotional reactions to the disease. Some writers have also suggested the opposite relationship—that psychological factors play a part in the aetiology of cancer. This suggestion is not convincing because it is based on research with severe limitations of method, including reliance on retrospective accounts and on subjective or non-standardized methods of assessment (see Fox 1978). Instead of studying the role of psychological factors in the onset of cancer, other workers have examined the influence of these factors on the course and outcome of cancer. Greer *et al.* (1979) reported that the prognosis of breast cancer was better in patients who reacted to their illness by denial or who had 'a fighting spirit' than in patients who reacted in other ways. Research with animals has indicated that the rate of tumour growth may be increased in animals exposed to stressful situations that are only partially under their control. This finding suggests the possibility that endocrine or immunological mechanisms may be identifiable through which emotion could affect the prognosis of malignancy.

It has been suggested that depressive symptoms may be a precursor of cancer in various sites. The issue remains unproved (see Evans *et al.* 1974), and there is a need for further studies of representative samples of patients. One association may be important. In a study of patients with carcinoma of the pancreas, Fras *et al.* (1967) found that 76 per cent had psychiatric symptoms, mainly depressive; in almost half of these patients, depression had preceded the onset of physical symptoms and signs such as abdominal pain, weakness, jaundice, and weight loss.

Psychological consequences of cancer

Generally the psychological consequences of cancer are the same as the psychological reactions to any serious physical illness. Some patients delay seeking medical help because of fear or denial of symptoms (see Greer 1985). Learning the diagnosis of cancer may cause shock, anger, and disbelief as well as anxiety and depression. The risk of suicide is increased in the early stages. Depressed mood is common throughout the course of cancer (Noyes and Kathol 1986) but the commonest DSMIIIR psychiatric diagnosis is adjustment disorder (see Derogatis *et al.* 1985). Both the advance and the recurrence of cancer are often associated with increased psychiatric disturbance, which may result from worse physical symptoms, such as pain and nausea, from fear of dying, or from the development of organic brain symptoms.

Several kinds of treatment for cancer may cause psychological disorder. Emotional distress is particularly common after mastectomy (see p. 464) and mutilating surgery (see Greer 1985). Radiotherapy causes nausea, fatigue, and emotional distress (Forester *et al.* 1985). Chemotherapy often causes malaise and nausea, and anxiety about chemotherapy may cause anticipatory nausea. The latter occurs before the beginning of a new course of treatment and may be so severe as to prevent continuation. Anxiety management and other behavioural methods are often effective for this condition (see Burish and Carey 1986).

Organic mental disorder may arise from brain metastases, which originate most often from carcinoma of the lung, but also commonly from tumours of the breast, alimentary tract, prostate, and pancreas, as well as melanomas. Occasionally brain metastases produce psychiatric symptoms before the primary lesion is discovered. Organic mental disorder is sometimes induced by certain kinds of cancer in the absence of metastases, notably by carcinoma of the lung, ovary, or stomach. The mechanism is unkown (see Lishman 1987).

Close family relatives of cancer patients may experience psychological problems, which may persist even if the cancer is cured (Naysmith *et al.* 1983). Nevertheless many patients and relatives make a good adjustment to cancer. The extent of their adjustment depends partly on the information they receive. Some doctors are reluctant to tell patients that the diagnosis is cancer, but most patients prefer to know the diagnosis and how it will affect their lives. The problem is particularly difficult when the patient is a child; even then it is probably better to tell the child the diagnosis unless there are particular reasons against it. Various psychiatric interventions can be helpful, including counselling, social support groups (Taylor *et al.* 1986), cognitive and behavioural treatments [see Watson (1983) for a review of psychological intervention], and antidepressant medication.

Although psychological problems in patients with cancer can often be helped, many remain undetected. One solution is to provide educational programmes, counselling, or group therapy for all patients even if they do not report problems.

However, it seems more appropriate to select suitable patients (Maguire *et al.* 1980), particularly as there is some evidence that counselling may occasionally increase distress in vulnerable patients who have denied their anxieties. The patients most likely to need psychological treatment include those with a history of previous psychiatric disorder or poor adjustment to other problems, and those who lack a supportive family. Examples of programes based on early identification and selective treatment have been described by Worden and Weissman (1984), Maguire (1985), and Stam *et al.* (1986). In addition to the types of cancer described below, several other cancers are referred to elsewhere in this book, viz. carcinoma of the pancreas (see p. 462), carcinoma of the colon (see p. 456) and brain tumours (see p. 378). Psychiatric aspects of cancer surgery to the head and neck have been reviewed by Shapiro and Kornfeld (1987).

Breast cancer

About a quarter of patients undergoing mastectomy or other treatments develop depression or anxiety of clinical severity within eighteen months (Fallowfield *et al.* 1986). Affective symptoms are especially common after a recurrence, and during radiotherapy (Hughson *et al.* 1987) and chemotherapy. Other responses to mastectomy are low self-esteem, embarrassment about disfigurement, and marital and sexual problems (Maguire *et al.* 1978). There is no evidence that psychiatric morbidity is any less after conservative treatment by lumpectomy and radiotherapy than after mastectomy (Fallowfield *et al.* 1987). Careful follow-up to detect and treat patients with psychiatric complications is probably more useful than counselling given routinely. Antidepressants and cognitive-behavioural treatment are useful when there are specific indications [see Maguire (1985) for a review].

Childhood malignancy

This also presents special problems. The child often reacts to the illness and its treatment with behaviour problems (Carr-Gregg and White 1987). Many parents react at first with shock and disbelief, taking months to accept the full implications of the diagnosis. About one mother in five develops an anxiety neurosis or depressive disorder during the first two years of treatment of childhood leukaemia, and other family members may also be affected. In the early stages of the illness parents are usually helped by advice about practical matters, and later by information to discuss their feelings, which often include guilt (see Maguire 1983; Van Dongen-Melman and Sanders-Woudstra 1986). Adult survivors of cancer in childhood or adolescence appear to be at risk of social difficulties (Teta *et al.* 1986).

Psychiatric aspects of obstetrics and gynaecology

Pregnancy

Psychiatric disorder is more common in the first and third trimesters of pregnancy than in the second (see Wolkind and Zajicek 1981). In the first trimester, unwanted pregnancies are associated with anxiety and depression. In the third trimester there may be fears about the impending delivery, or doubts about the normality of the fetus. Psychiatric symptoms in pregnancy are more common in women with a history of previous psychiatric disorder and probably also in those with serious medical problems affecting the course of pregnancy, such as diabetes. Although minor affective symptoms are common in pregnancy, serious psychiatric disorders are probably less common than in non-pregnant women of the same age (Pugh *et al.* 1963).

Amongst women who have chronic psychological problems when not pregnant, some report improvement in these problems during pregnancy, whilst others require extra psychiatric care. The latter are often late or poor attenders at antenatal care, thus increasing the risk of obstetric and psychiatric problems. Abuse of alcohol, opiates, and other substances should be strongly discouraged in pregnancy, especially in the first trimester when the risk to the fetus is greatest (see p. 516).

During pregnancy great care must be taken in the use of psychotropic drugs, because of the risk of fetal malformations, impaired growth, and prenatal problems (see Loudon 1987). Pharmacokinetics may be altered. Benzodiazepines should be avoided throughout pregnancy and during breast-feeding because of the danger of depressed respiration and withdrawal symptoms in the neonate. Lithium should be stopped throughout the first trimester of pregnancy but can be restarted later if there are pressing reasons; it should again be stopped at the onset of labour. Mothers taking lithium should not breast feed (see Robinson *et al.* 1986*a*). It is preferable to avoid using tricyclic antidepressants or neuroleptics during pregnancy unless there are compelling clinical indications.

Hyperemesis gravidarum

About half of all pregnant women experience nausea and vomiting in the first trimester. Some authors have suggested that these symptoms, as well as the severe condition of **hyperemesis gravidarum**, are primarily of psychological aetiology. There is, however, no reason to doubt that physiological factors are of primary importance, although psychological factors may substantially influence the severity and course of the symptoms (see Katon *et al.* 1980).

Pseudocyesis

Pseudocyesis is a rare condition in which a woman believes she is pregnant when she is not, and develops amenorrhoea, abdominal distension, and other changes similar to those of early pregnancy. The condition is commoner in younger women. Pseudocyesis usually resolves quickly once diagnosed, but some patients persist in believing that they are pregnant. Recurrence is common (see Drife 1987; Small 1986).

Couvade syndrome

In this syndrome, the husband of the pregnant woman reports that he is himself experiencing some of the symptoms of pregnancy. This condition may occur in the early months of the woman's pregnancy, when the man complains usually of nausea and morning sickness and often of toothache. These complaints usually resolve after a few weeks (see Bogren 1983).

Unwanted pregnancy

Until 1967, psychiatrists in Britain were often asked to see pregnant women who were seeking a therapeutic abortion on the grounds of mental illness. Since 1967 the laws has allowed therapeutic abortion on the grounds of likely damage to the health of the mother and also of her children. The provisions now make it generally more appropriate for decisions to be made by the family doctor and the gynaecologist, without involving a psychiatrist. However, psychiatric opinions are still sought at times, not only about the grounds for termination of pregnancy but also for an assessment of the likely psychological effects of termination in a particular patient.

Spontaneous abortion

In a recent study, 67 women were interviewed four weeks after spontaneous abortion, and 32 (48 per cent) of them were PSE cases as defined by the Present State Examination (a rate four times higher than in the general population of women). All the women were diagnosed as suffering from depressive disorder. Many women showed features typical of grief. Depressive symptoms were more frequent in women with a history of previous spontaneous abortion (Friedman and Gath 1988).

Therapeutic abortion

Greer *et al.* (1976) followed up 360 women 18 months after termination of first trimester pregnancies by vacuum aspiration. Each patient received brief counselling before termination. Compared with ratings before termination, at follow-up there were significant improvements in psychiatric symptoms, guilt, and interpersonal and sexual adjustments. Adverse psychiatric and social consequences were rare.

Post-partum mental disorders

These disorders can be divided into maternity blues, puerperal psychosis, and chronic depressive disorders of moderate severity.

Maternity blues

Amongst women delivered of a normal child, between a half and two-thirds experience brief episodes of irritability, lability of mood, and episodes of crying. Lability of mood is particularly characteristic, in the form of rapid alternations between euphoria and misery. The symptoms reach their peak on the third or fourth post-partum day. Patients often speak of being 'confused', but tests of cognitive function are normal. Although frequently tearful, patients may not be feeling depressed at the time, but tense and irritable (Yalom *et al.* 1968; Kennerley and Gath 1986).

Maternity blues is more frequent among primigravida. It is not related to complications at the delivery or to the use of anaesthesia. 'Blues' patients have often experienced depressive symptoms in the last trimester of pregnancy; they are also more likely to give a history of premenstrual tension (see Nott *et al.* 1976; Davidson 1972 for evidence on these points).

Both the frequency of the emotional changes and their timing suggests that maternity blues may be related to readjustment in hormones after delivery. Oestrogens and progesterone both increase greatly during late pregnancy and fall precipitously after childbirth. Changes also occur in adrenal steriods but they are complicated by associated changes in corticosteroid binding globulin. Yalom *et al.* (1968) suggested that changes in oestrogen or progesterone might be related to the blues, but this suggestion has not been confirmed (Nott *et al.* 1976). Bower and Altschule (1956) suggested that changes in corticosteroids might be important, but there is no direct evidence to support this view. At present the cause of maternity blues remains unknown.

No treatment is required because the condition resolves spontaneously in a few days. [For a review of maternity blues, see Kennerley and Gath (1986).]

Puerperal psychosis

In the nineteenth century, puerperal and lactational psychoses were thought to be specific entities that were distinct from other mental illnesses (for example Esquirol 1845; Marcé 1858). Later psychiatrists such as Bleuler and Kraepelin regarded the puerperal psychoses as no different from other mental illnesses. This latter view is widely held today on the grounds that puerperal psychoses generally resemble other psychoses in their clinical picture (see below).

The **incidence** of puerperal psychoses has been estimated in terms of admission rates to psychiatric hosptial (for example, Pugh *et al.* (1963); Kendell *et al.* 1987). The reported rates vary, but a representative figure is one admission per 500 births. This incidence is substantially above the expected rate for non-puerperal women of the same age. Puerperal psychoses are more frequent in primiparous women, those who have suffered previous major psychiatric illness, those with a family history of mental illness, and probably in unmarried mothers. There is no clear relationship between psychosis and obstetric factors (Kendell 1985). The onset of puerperal psychosis is usually within the first one to two weeks after delivery, but rarely in the first two days.

The early onset of puerperal psychoses has led to speculation that they might be caused by hormonal changes such as those discussed above in relation to the blues syndrome. There is no evidence that hormonal changes in women with puerperal psychoses differ from those in other women in the early puerperium. Hence if endocrine factors do play a part, they probably act only as precipitating factors in predisposed women (see Swyer 1985).

Three types of **clinical picture** are observed: acute organic, affective, and schizophrenic. Organic syndromes were common in the past, but are now much less frequent since the incidence of puerperal sepsis was reduced by antibiotics. Nowadays affective syndromes predominate. Dean and Kendell (1981) found that 80 per cent of cases were affective, and that the proportion of manic disorders was unusually high. Though less common than affective disorders, schizophrenic illnesses were much more frequent than the expected rate. As mentioned above, the clinical features of these syndromes are generally regarded as being much the same as those of corresponding non-puerperal syndromes. The exceptions are that affective features are probably more common in puerperal schizophrenic disorders; and that disorientation and other organic features are more common in both the schizophrenic and the affective disorders.

In the **assessment** of patients with puerperal psychosis, it is important to ascertain their ideas concerning the baby. Severely depressed patients may have delusional ideas that the child is malformed or otherwise imperfect. These false ideas may lead to attempts to kill the child to spare it from future suffering. Schizophrenic patients may also have delusional beliefs about the child; they may be convinced for example that the child is abnormal or evil. Again such beliefs may point to the risk of an attempt to kill the child. Depressed or schizophrenic patients may also make suicide attempts.

Treatment is given according to the clinical syndrome, as described in other chapters. For in-patient care, the ward should have facilities for a separate nursery where the child can be nursed at times when the mother is too ill to care for him. The layout of the ward should enable staff to observe the mother closely while she is with the baby. The nursing staff should have experience in the care of small babies as well as in psychiatry. Since the mental state may change quickly in puerperal psychosis, the psychiatrist should visit frequently to re-examine the patient. These arrangements are demanding for a while, but the risk to the child does not usually last long if treatment is vigorous.

For patients with depressive disorders of marked or moderate severity, ECT is usually the best treatment, because it is rapidly effective and enables the mother to resume the care of her baby quickly. For less urgent depressive disorders, antidepressant medication may be tried first. If the patient has predominantly schizophrenic features, a phenothiazine may be tried; if there is no definite improvement within a few days, ECT should be given as well as the phenothiazine.

Most patients recover fully from a puerperal psychosis, but a few (mostly schizophrenics) remain chronically ill (Protheroe 1969). After subsequent childbirth the recurrence rate for depressive illness in the puerperium is 15–20 per cent. According to Protheroe (1969), amongst women who have suffered a puerperal depressive illness, at least half will later suffer a depressive illness that is not puerperal.

Puerperal depression of mild or moderate severity

Less severe depressive disorders are much more common than the puerperal psychoses. Estimated rates vary, but are mainly within the range 10 to 15 per cent (see Kendell 1985). These depressive disorders usually begin after the first two weeks of the puerperium. Tiredness, irritability, and anxiety are often more prominent than depressive mood change, and there may be prominent phobic symptoms.

Clinical observation suggests that these disorders are often precipitated in vulnerable mothers by the psychological adjustment required after childbirth, as well as by the loss of sleep and hard work involved in the care of the baby. Previous psychiatric history and recent stressful events appear to be important aetiological factors. Paykel *et al.* (1980) assessed a series of women with mild clinical depression about six weeks post-partum, and found that the strongest associated factor was recent stressful life events. Previous history of psychiatric disorder, younger age, early post-partum blues, and a group of variables affecting poor marital relationship and absence of social support were also notable.

Most patients recover after a few months. Pitt (1968) found that about 4 per cent of all delivered women were still depressed twelve months after delivery. Using case register data from south-east London, Kendell *et al.* (1976) found there were two peaks of psychiatric consultation among women after childbirth—one about 3 months and the other 9 to 12 months after delivery.

Cooper *et al.* (1988) examined 483 pregnant women six weeks before the expected date of delivery, and re-examined them three, six, and twelve months after childbirth. At all stages of assessment, the point prevalence of psychiatric disorder was no higher than in a matched sample of women from the general population. There was no evidence that the post-natal psychiatric disorder differed either diagnostically or in duration from psychiatric disorders arising at other times.

In treatment, psychological and social measures are usually as important as antidepressant drugs.

Menstrual disorders

Premenstrual syndrome

This term denotes a group of psychological and physical symptoms starting a few days before the onset, and ending shortly after the onset, of a menstrual period. The psychological symptoms include anxiety, irritability, and depression; the physical symptoms include breast tenderness, abdominal discomfort, and a feeling of distension.

The estimated frequency of the premenstrual syndrome in the general population varies widely from 30 per cent to 80 per cent of women of reproductive age (see Clare 1985). There are several reasons for this wide variation in reported rates. First, there is a problem of definition. Mild and brief symptoms are frequent premenstrually and it is difficult to decide when they should be classified as premenstrual tension. Second, information about symptoms is often collected retrospectively by asking women to recall earlier menstrual periods. Third, description of premenstrual symptoms appears to vary according to whether or not the subject knows that the enquiry is concerned specifically with premenstrual syndrome.

The aetiology is uncertain. Physical explanations have been based on ovarian hormones (oestrogen excess; progesterone lack); pituitary hormones; disturbed fluid and electrolyte balance. None of these theories has been proved. Dalton (1964) has particularly argued that the premenstrual syndrome is caused by oestrogen–progesterone imbalance, but the evidence on this point remains inconclusive (Clare 1985). Various psychological explanations have been based on possible associations of the syndrome with neuroticism or with individual or public attitudes towards menstruation. These ideas are also unproven.

The syndrome has been widely treated with progesterone, and also with oral contraceptives, bromocriptine, diuretics, and psychotropic drugs. There is no convincing evidence that any of these is effective, and treatment trials suggest a high placebo response (up to 65 per cent). Psychological support and encouragement may be as helpful as medication. [For reviews see Clare (1985); Rubinow and Roy-Byrne (1984); Osofsky and Blumenthal (1985); Gath and Iles (1988).]

The menopause

In addition to the physical symptoms of flushing, sweating, and vaginal dryness, menopausal women often complain of headache, dizziness, and depression. It is not certain whether depressive symptoms are more common in menopausal women than in non-menopausal women. Weissman and Klerman (1978) concluded that there is no such increase in symptoms at the menopause. Nevertheless, amongst patients who consult general practitioners because of emotional symptoms, a disproportionately large number of women are in the middle age-group that spans the menopausal years (Shepherd *et al*. 1966).

In a community survey of over 500 women aged 35–59, it was found that both psychiatric symptoms and the personality dimension of neuroticism were associated with vasomotor symptoms (flushes and sweats) but not with the cessation of menstruation (Gath *et al*. 1987).

Depressive and anxiety-related symptoms at the time of the menopause could have several causes. Hormonal changes have often been suggested, notably deficiency of oestrogen. In some countries, notably the USA, oestrogen has been used to treat emotional symptoms in women of menopausal age, but the results are uncertain. Psychiatric symptoms at this time of life could equally well reflect changes in the woman's role as her children leave home, her relationship with her husband alters, and her own parents become ill or die.

The results of trials of treatment with oestrogens have been disappointing. It seems wisest to treat depressed menopausal women with methods that have been shown to be effective at any other time of life [see Osborn (1984) for a review].

Hysterectomy

Several retrospective studies have indicated an increased frequency of depressive disorder after hysterectomy (e.g. Barker 1968). A recent prospective investigation using standardized methods showed that patients who are free from psychiatric symptoms before hysterectomy seldom develop them afterwards; some patients with psychiatric symptoms before hysterectomy lose them afterwards, but others do not (Gath *et al*. 1982*a*,*b*). It is likely that these persisting cases (those with symptoms before and after surgery) are identified in the retrospective studies, and lead to the erroneous conclusion that hysterectomy causes depressive disorder. This finding provides a general warning about inferring the effects of treatment from the results of retrospective investigations.

Sterilization operations

Similar considerations apply to these procedures. Retrospective studies have suggested that sterilization leads to psychiatric disorder, sexual dysfunction, and frequent regrets after the operation. A recent prospective enquiry has shown that the operation does not lead to significant psychiatric disorder; sexual relationships are more likely to improve than worsen, and definite regrets are reported by fewer than one patient in twenty (Cooper *et al.* 1982).

Psychiatric aspects of surgical treatment

Pre-operative mental state and early outcome

It is a matter of everyday observation that patients about to undergo surgery are often anxious. Many investigators have looked for relationships between psychological state before surgery and post-operative psychological state or rate of recovery. For example, one influential study (Janis 1958) reported that patients who were anxious before surgery were likely to be excessively anxious afterwards; those who were moderately anxious were least anxious afterwards; whilst those who were least anxious before were likely to be inappropriately angry and resentful afterwards. Other investigators have not confirmed these findings, but have found a linear relationship between anxiety before and after surgery.

Cohen and Lazarus (1973) compared two groups of patients with different attitudes to forthcoming surgery: a 'vigilant' group who sought information about the operation, and an 'avoidant' group who preferred not to know. Contrary to the authors' expectation, the vigilant group fared worse post-operatively as judged by the number of days they stayed in hospital, and by the reporting of minor complications. Most other research shows, as would be expected, that those who show more general ability to cope with stress suffer less post-operative problems (see Johnston 1986).

Many, but not all studies of psychological preparation for surgery have shown that intervention can reduce post-operative distress and problems, especially if it includes cognitive coping techniques rather than mere information (see Ridgeway and Mathews 1982).

Post-operative mental state and adjustment

Delirium is common after major surgery (see Lipowski 1980*a*; Tune and Folstein 1986) and is associated with old age, pre-operative mental and physical state, type of surgery, and post-operative physical complications and medication. The treatment of post-operative mental disorders is the same as that of similar mental disorders occurring at other times (see Rogers and Reich 1986).

There may be long-term problems of adjustment to mutilating surgery, for instance some surgery for cancer (see p. 463). Some patients fail to obtain optimal benefits from successful curative surgery, such as hip replacement and coronary artery surgery (see p. 449).

Psychiatric aspects of various types of surgery are described in the sections on cancer, and gynaecological, gastrointestinal, renal and heart disease. General and specific aspects of psychiatry and surgery have been reviewed by Milano and Kornfeld (1984). [Psychological aspects of organ transplantation have been reviewed by Beidel (1987). Plastic surgery and limb amputation are reviewed below.]

Plastic surgery

People with physical deformities often suffer teasing, embarrassment, and distress, which may markedly restrict the lives of adults (Harris 1982) and children (Hill-Beuf and Porter 1984). In patients who are psychiatrically healthy, reconstructive plastic surgery generally gives good results. Even when there is no major objective defect, cosmetic surgery to the nose and face, breast or other parts of the body is usually successful (Khoo 1982; Hay and Heather 1973; Hay 1970*a*). Nevertheless full psychological assessment and discussion before plastic surgery are necessary (Connolly and Gipson 1978; Hay 1970*a*) because the outcome is likely to be poor in patients who have unrealistic expectations, delusions, or a history of dissatisfaction with previous surgery. As explained in the section on dysmorphophobia, such patients are likely to be left with a greater sense of grievance after cosmetic surgery (see Frank 1985).

Limb amputation

Limb amputation has different psychological consequences for young and for elderly people (see Frank *et al.* 1984). Young amputees, such as those losing a leg in military action or a road accident, characteristically show denial at first, and later experience depression and phantom limb pains which slowly resolve. In contrast, older subjects usually undergo amputation after prolonged medical and surgical problems associated with vascular disease. Such patients do not commonly experience severe immediate emotional distress (Parkes 1978). However, they often describe phantom limb pain, and show helplessness, difficulty with their prosthesis, and general functional incapacity disproportionate to their physical state (Sherman *et al.* 1987). Amputation is reviewed by Lundberg and Guggenheim (1986).

Blood disorders

Leukaemia

Leukaemia in children and adults, especially in acute form, causes great distress to patients and their families. Chemotherapy and its side-effects are often extremely unpleasant (see p. 463), and behavioural treatments may help to reduce anxiety and anticipatory nausea. Neuropsychological sequelae of treatment have been reported in 42 per cent of children reassessed six or more years after successful treatment of acute lymphoblastic leukaemia (Wheeler *et al.* 1988).

Lymphomas

Although they have a better prognosis than other cancers, Hodgkin's disease and non-Hodgkin's lymphoma can cause substantial psychiatric and social morbidity, especially when the diagnosis is learnt during the course of treatment. These effects can be lessened by frank discussion of the diagnosis and treatment with patients and relatives (Lloyd *et al.* 1984; Devlen *et al.* 1987).

Haemophilia

Amongst patients with haemophilia, surveys have shown that emotional reactions and chronic handicaps are common and disturbing to family life (Lineberger 1981; Klein and Nimorwicz 1982). New methods of treatment have greatly reduced the significance of bleeding episodes but led to HIV infection in many sufferers (see p. 460).

Muscle diseases

Muscular dystrophy

Muscular dystrophy is the most common progressive muscle disease in childhood and is inherited as a sex-linked recessive gene. Diagnosis is often delayed. Parents are often severely distressed by this delay and by the ways in which information is given (Firth 1983). They need information about the illness and its course, and about the genetic implications.

There is a tendency for boys with this condition to be of less than average intelligence. The progressive physical handicaps lead to increasing restrictions and social isolation, with consequent boredom, depression, and anger. The children require considerable help and support for their families and others. The illness is extremely distressing for parents (see Witte 1985).

Myasthenia gravis

Myasthenia gravis presents with weakness and fatigue. It is not uncommon for the diagnosis to be delayed because the symptoms suggest psychiatric disorder, especially if there is a history of previous psychological problems. For some patients it is difficult to adjust to a regular schedule of medication. Clinical neurologists have reported that the physical symptoms may be precipitated and aggravated by emotional influences (see Lishman 1987).

Accidents

Psychological factors, including overt psychiatric illness, are important causes of accidents at home, at work, and on the roads. Psychiatric reasons for accident proneness include: in children, over-activity and conduct disorders; in young adults, alcohol and drug abuse and mood disorders; and in the elderly, organic mental disorders. In the UK it has been estimated that over a quarter of drivers involved in road traffic accidents have impaired driving because of alcohol, drugs, illness, or emotional distress, (Cremona 1986).

Emotional symptoms are common following accidents, especially those in which there is a head injury. Such symptoms are not closely related to the severity of the accident or to the physical injuries. Occasionally accident victims describe the clinical features of post-traumatic stress disorder (see p. 164).

Compensation neurosis

Compensation neurosis (or accident neurosis) is a term used for psychologically determined physical or mental symptoms occurring when there is an unsettled claim for compensation. From his experience as a neurologist, Miller (1961) drew attention to the frequency of a psychological basis for persistent physical disability after industrial injuries and road accidents. He emphasized the role of the compensation claim in prolonging symptoms and suggested that settlement was followed by recovery. Miller pointed to the role of a previously vulnerable personality, and argued that this is not a reason for denying compensation to the person 'any more than treating the pre-existence of a thin skull in the case of fracture' (see p. 371).

In fact there is little satisfactory evidence on the prevalence and course of psychological symptoms after accidents, or on any link between such

symptoms and compensation proceedings (see Weighill 1983). Few accident victims claim compensation, and even fewer become involved in
prolonged litigation. For example, amongst patients with mild head
injuries, several studies found no association between prolonged psychological consequences and court proceedings or hope of compensation (see
Boll and Barth 1983).

It has usually been assumed that settlement of a compensation claim is
followed by improvement. This assumption was not supported by a follow-
up of 35 subjects who had severe somatic symptoms, for which it was
agreed that there was no adequate demonstrable physical basis. One to
seven years after compensation, little recovery was found in this group
(Tarsh and Royston 1985).

[For guidance on writing a psychiatric report for compensation proceedings, see Hoffman (1986).]

Spinal cord injury

It appears that most of the psychological problems apparent in hospital
and immediately after discharge resolve rapidly. Most recent follow-up
studies have found that the majority of patients are not psychologically
disturbed a year or so later (see Richards 1986; Frank *et al.* 1987).

Burns

Psychological and social problems may contribute to the causation of
burns in children and adults (see Welch 1981). For example, burns in
children are associated with over-activity and mental retardation, and also
with child abuse and neglect. In adults, burns are associated with deliberate self-harm, alcohol and drug abuse, and dementia. Severe burns and
their protracted treatment may cause severe psychological problems.
Hamburg *et al.* (1953) described three stages. In the first, lasting days or
weeks, denial is common. The most frequent psychiatric disorders are
organic syndromes. At this stage, the relatives often need considerable
help. The intermediate stage is prolonged and painful; here denial recedes
and emotional disorders are more common. Patients need to be helped to
withstand pain, to express their feelings and gradually accept disfigurement. In the final stage the patient leaves hospital and has to make further
adjustments to deformity or physical disability and the reaction of other
people to his appearance.

There are conflicting reports about the numbers of patients who have
persistent emotional difficulties in adjusting after burns. Andreasen and
Norris (1972) found persistent difficulties in about a third, but other
workers have reported higher figures (see Welch 1981). It is generally
agreed that the outcome is worse in patients with burns affecting the

appearance of the face. Such patients are likely to withdraw permanently from social activities. These patients need considerable support from the staff of the burns unit, but only a minority require psychiatric referral [see Tucker (1986) for a review].

Further reading

Kaplan, H. I. and Sadock, B. J. (1985). *Comprehensive textbook of psychiatry* (4th edn). Williams and Wilkins, Baltimore.
Lipowski, Z. J. (1985). *Psychosomatic Medicine and Liaison Psychiatry*. Plenum, New York.

13 Suicide and deliberate self-harm

In recent years a large proportion of admissions to medical wards has been people who have deliberately taken drug overdoses or harmed themselves in other ways. It has become clear that only a small minority of these patients intend to take their lives; the rest have other motives for their actions. Equally, only a minority are suffering from psychiatric disorder; the rest are facing difficult social problems. Psychiatrists are often called upon to identify and treat the minority with suicidal intent or psychiatric disorder, and to provide appropriate help for the rest.

In order to assess such patients properly, the psychiatrist must understand the differences between people who commit suicide (completed suicide), and those who survive after taking an overdose or harming themselves (deliberate self-harm). At this early stage in the chapter, it may be helpful to give a brief outline of the differences between the two.

In general, compared with people who harm themselves and survive, those who commit suicide are more often male, and are usually suffering from a psychiatric disorder. They plan their suicidal acts carefully, take precautions against discovery, and use dangerous methods. By contrast, amongst those who harm themselves and survive, a large proportion carry out their acts impulsively in a way that invites discovery and is unlikely to be dangerous. The two groups are not distinctly separate; they overlap in important ways. This point should be borne in mind throughout this chapter.

The chapter begins with an account of those who die by suicide. After this we describe people whose overdoses of drugs or self-injury do not result in death. Each section starts with a description of the behaviour, its epidemiology and its causes. We then consider assessment, management, and prevention.

Suicide

The act of suicide

People who take their lives do so in different ways. In England, drug overdoses account for about two-thirds of suicides among women and about a third of those among men (Morgan 1979). The drugs used most often are analgesics and antidepressants; barbiturates were often used until recently, but are less common now. In the 1978 Registrar General's Report carbon monoxide accounted for about a third of deaths by poisoning among men but less than 5 per cent among women. Nowadays carbon monoxide poisoning arises mainly from car exhaust fumes; until it was made less toxic, domestic gas was a frequent cause. The remaining deaths are by a variety of physical means: hanging, shooting, wounding; drowning, jumping from high places, and falling in front of moving vehicles or trains (Symonds 1985). Violent methods, especially shooting, are more common in the United States than in Britain.

Most completed suicides have been planned. Some patients save drugs obtained from a series of prescriptions; others use drugs that can be bought without a prescription, such as aspirin. Precautions against discovery are often taken; for example, choosing a lonely place or a time when no one is expected.

In most cases a warning is given before committing suicide. In a survey in the United States, interviews were held with relatives and friends of people who had committed suicide. It was found that suicidal ideas had been expressed by over two-thirds of the deceased, and clear suicidal intent by rather more than a third. Often the warning had been given to more than one person (Robins *et al.* 1959). In a similar study of people who had committed suicide, Barraclough *et al.* (1974) found that two thirds had consulted their general practitioner in the previous month, and 40 per cent had done so in the previous week. A quarter had been psychiatric out-patients at the time, of whom half had seen a psychiatrist in the week before their suicide.

Amongst people committing suicide, about one in six leaves a suicide note (see Shneidman 1976). The content of the note varies; some ask for forgiveness, whilst others are accusing or vindictive, drawing attention to failings in relatives or friends. Such vindictive notes are more often left by younger people. Older people often express concern for those who remain alive (Capstick 1960).

The epidemiology of suicide

Accurate statistics about suicide are difficult to obtain. In England and Wales, official figures depend on the verdicts reached in coroners' courts, and comparable procedures are used in other countries. Such figures are affected by several sources of error. Occasionally it is uncertain whether a death is caused by suicide or murder. Much more often it is difficult to decide whether death was by suicide or accident. In many cases of uncertainty, the verdict will depend on legal criteria. In England and Wales there is a strict rule that suicide must be proved by evidence; if there is doubt an open or accidental verdict must be returned. In some other countries; less stringent criteria are used.

For these reasons, it is not surprising that official statistics appear to underestimate the true rates of suicide. In Dublin, psychiatrists ascertained four times as many suicides as the coroners did (McCarthy and Walsh 1975) and similar discrepancies have been reported from other places (see for example, Litman *et al.* 1963). Amongst people whose deaths are recorded as accidental, many have recently been depressed or dependent on drugs or alcohol, thus resembling people who commit suicide (Holding and Barraclough 1975). For this reason, some investigators try to estimate suicide rates by combining official figures for suicide, accidental poisoning and undetermined causes. For the purpose of comparing suicide rates between different countries, this procedure makes little difference since the rank ordering is not affected significantly by using it (Barraclough 1973).

The suicide rate in the United Kingdom (less than 10 per 100 000 per year) is in the lower range of those reported in Western countries but still accounts for one per cent of all deaths. Recently, the highest rates have been reported in Hungary (about 40 per 100 000 per annum) and the German Democratic Republic (36 per 100 000). Among the lowest rates are those of Spain (about 4 per 100 000) and Greece (about 3 per 100 000). Rates are generally lower in Roman Catholic countries. It is not certain how variations in suicide rates reflect variations in reporting rather than real differences in the frequency of suicide. However, indirect evidence for real differences between nations in suicide rates was put forward by Sainsbury and Barraclough (1968). They showed that within the United States the rank order of suicide rates among immigrants from eleven different nations was similar to the rank order of national rates within the eleven countries of origin.

Changes in suicide rates.

Over the years since 1900, suicide rates in Great Britain have changed substantially at different times. During both world wars, recorded rates for men and women fell, but it is not certain whether this fall reflected a true change or the difficulties of ascertaining causes of death in war time. There were also two periods when rates were unusually high. The first, 1932–3, was a time of economic depression and high unemployment; the second, between the late 1950s and the early 1960s, was not so. Another unusual period was 1963–74, when rates declined in England and Wales but not in other European countries (except Greece) or in North America (see Sainsbury 1986). The reasons for this fall are not clear. Since 1975, the rates in England and Wales have risen again, especially among men, and there has been a particular increase in suicide by vehicle exhaust gas, hanging, and suffocating (McClure 1984*b*). Similar changes have occurred in Scotland (McLoone and Crombie 1987). The overall increase of suicide is made up of a large increase in the 15–35 year age group, and a decrease in the 45 to 65-year-olds (Platt 1987). The most striking increase is among men aged 25–35. It has been suggested that these variations might reflect different rates in cohorts of people born at different times, rather than factors acting on all age groups at the time the figures were collected. However, this suggestion was not confirmed in a recent study in England and Wales (Murphy *et al.* 1986). The true explanation for these changing rates is still unknown.

Variations with the seasons

In England and Wales, for every decade since 1921–30 suicide rates have been highest in the months of April, May, and June. A similiar pattern has been found in other countries in the northern hemisphere. In the southern hemisphere a similar rise occurs during the spring and early summer, even though these seasons are in different months of the year. The reason for these fluctuations is not known.

Variations according to personal characteristics

In both men and women, suicide rates increase with age. At all ages, the rate is higher in men than women. Suicide rates are lowest among the married, and increase progressively through the never married, widowers, and widows, and divorced. Rates are higher in social class V (unskilled workers) and social class I (professional) than in the remaining social classes. Suicide rates in the elderly have decreased recently but are still much higher than in younger people. Among the elderly, suicide is particularly associated with depressive disorder, physical illness, and social isolation (Blazer 1986).

Variations according to place of residence

Suicide rates in cities used to be higher than those in the country. In recent years this difference has grown less and for men it has reversed (Adelstein and Mardon 1975). Within large cities rates vary among different kinds of residential area. The highest rates are reported from areas in which there are many inhabitants of boarding houses, and many immigrants and divorced people. The common factor appears to be social isolation (Sainsbury 1955). Compared with the general population, people who have committed suicide are more likely to have been divorced, unemployed, or be living alone (Sainsbury 1955; Whitlock 1973*a*,*b*).

The causes of suicide

Social causes

In 1897, Durkheim published an important book in which he proposed a relationship between suicide and social conditions (see Durkheim 1951).

He divided suicides into three main categories. **Egotistic suicide** occurred in individuals who had lost their sense of integration within their social group, so that they no longer felt subject to its social, family, and religious controls. **Anomic suicide** occurred in individuals who lived in a society that lacked 'collective order' because it was in the midst of major social change or political crisis. **Altruistic suicide** occurred in individuals who sacrificed their lives for the good of the social groups, thus reflecting the influence of the group's identity. Durkheim's views have been influential even though it now seems that he overemphasized social factors at the expense of individual causes. Sainsbury's work on social isolation, referred to above, follows directly from Durkheim's ideas.

Sometimes the means of suicide and its timing seems to be influenced by another suicide that has attracted attention in a community or received wide publicity in newspapers or on television (see Eisenberg 1986). For example, a widely publicized case of suicide by burning with lighted petrol, was followed by several similar acts of suicide (Ashton and Donnan 1981).

Medical causes

Mental disorders are a most important cause of suicide. In several studies interviews have been held with doctors, relatives, and friends of people who have committed suicide, and detailed histories have been compiled about the deceased. These studies indicate that, amongst those who die from suicide, about nine in every ten have some form of mental disorder at the time of death (Robins *et al.* 1959; Barraclough *et al.* 1974). The most frequent of these mental disorders are depressive disorders and alcoholism.

The importance of **depressive disorders** is confirmed by findings that rates of suicide are increased among depressed patients (Fremming 1951; Pokorny 1964). Depressed patients who die by suicide cannot be distinguished from other depressed patients by their symptoms (Fawcett *et al.* 1987). However, they differ in having made more previous suicide attempts (Barraclough *et al.* 1974), and being more often single, separated, or widowed (Pitts and Winokur 1964) and older (Robins *et al.* 1959). The risk is also greater among men than women (Pitts and Winokur 1964).

Alcoholism is the second most frequent psychiatric disorder among those who die from suicide, being present in at least 15–25 per cent of cases (Robins *et al.* 1959; Barraclough *et al.* 1974; Murphy 1986). Follow-up studies of alcoholics confirm this high risk of suicide. Thus among alcoholics who had received psychiatric treatment in hospital, the incidence of suicide over a five-year follow-up was about 80 times that of the general population (Kessell and Grossman 1965). The risk is greatest among older men with a long history of drinking, a definite depressive illness and previous suicidal attempts. It is also increased among those whose drinking has caused physical complications, marital problems, difficulties at work, or arrests for drunkenness offences (see Miles 1977). **Drug-dependent** patients also have an increased suicide risk (James 1967). Thus among 133 young people who committed suicide in California, 55 per cent had as the principal psychiatric diagnosis, substance abuse. Usually the abuse was long-standing and involved more than one substance (Fowler *et al.* 1986).

Personality disorder is detected in a third to a half of people who commit suicide (Seagar and Flood 1965; Ovenstone and Kreitman 1974). This group tends to be younger, to come from broken homes, and to live in a subculture in which violence and alcohol or drug abuse is common. Personality disorder probably combines with other causes to increase the risk of suicide. In their study, Barraclough *et al.* (1974) found personality disorder in about half the alcoholics and a fifth of the depressed patients who had died by suicide. In **chronic neuroses** there is also an increased risk of suicide (Sims 1973). **Schizophrenia** accounts for only about three per cent of suicides, but when treating a schizophrenic patient, the risk should be borne in mind. In schizophrenia, suicide is more likely among young men early in the course of the disorder, particularly when there are depressive symptoms.

Chronic painful physical illness is associated with suicide (Robins *et al.* 1959), especially among the elderly (Sainsbury 1962). The risk of suicide among **epileptics** is about four times that in the general population (Sainsbury 1986; Barraclough 1987). The risk is also high among patients on dialysis, and those with disease of the nervous system or cancer (Whitlock 1986*a*).

The suicide rate is higher after **deliberate self-harm** (see p. 492).

Conclusion

The associations between suicide and the various factors mentioned above do not, of course, establish causation. Nevertheless they point to the importance of two sets of interacting influences: amongst social factors, social isolation stands out; whilst amongst medical factors, depressive disorders, alcoholism, and abnormal personality are particularly prominent.

'Rational' suicide

Despite the findings reviewed above, there can be no doubt that suicide is occasionally the rational act of a mentally healthy person. Moreover mass suicides have been described among groups of people, and it is unlikely that they were all suffering from mental disorder. An example was the religious community at Jonestown, in which a large number of people died together by taking poison (Rosen 1981). Nevertheless, in the clinical assessment of someone who is talking of suicide, it is a good rule to assume that his suicidal inclinations are influenced by an abnormal state of mind.

If this assumption is correct—as it usually will be—the patient's urge to suicide is likely to diminish with recovery from the abnormal mental state. Even if the assumption is wrong (that is, if the patient is one of the few who have reached a rational decision to die) the doctor should still try to protect him from harming himself. Given more time for reflection, most people with suicidal intent change their intentions. For example, they may discover that death from a cancer need not be as painful as they believed. Hence they may change a decision that was made rationally but on false premises.

Special groups

Children and young adolescents

Accurate estimation of suicide rates is even more difficult for children than for adults. However, suicide is known to be rare in children. In a survey of official records in England and Wales of all known suicides occurring between 1962 and 1968 amongst children under the age of 14, Shaffer (1974) found none in those aged under 12. In several countries there is clear evidence of a recent marked increase in suicide by older adolescents; in some countries, notably the USA, there has also been an increase among younger children (see Eisenberg 1986). These increases may be due to many factors, including an increase in the number of broken homes, changing attitudes to suicide and to deliberate self-harm, and media publicity.

In the 12- to 14-year-old group, more boys than girls commit suicide. Boys are more likely to use violent methods of suicide such as hanging or shooting, and girls to take drug overdoses. There are international differences in methods, use of firearms being specially common in the USA. Among children seen by child psychiatrists, most who threaten suicide do not carry it out. Nevertheless, of the children who died by suicide in Shaffer's series, almost half had previously talked about, threatened, or attempted suicide.

Little is known about factors leading to suicide in childhood. Shaffer (1974) reported that suicidal behaviour and depressive disorders were common among the parents and siblings, and that children who died by suicide had usually shown antisocial behaviour. Shaffer distinguished two groups of children. The first comprised children of superior intelligence who seemed to be isolated from less educated parents. Many of their mothers were mentally ill. Before death, the children had seemed depressed and withdrawn, and some had stayed away from school. The second group consisted of children who were impetuous, prone to violence, and resentful of criticism.

Little is known of the consequences of child or adolescent suicide on surviving family members, but it is likely to be profound. [See Hawton (1986) for a review of suicide in adolescence.]

Older adolescents and young adults

Between the years 1972 and 1983, suicide rates among 15 to 24-year-olds increased. In most European countries the increase has been greater among males than females (Platt 1987). The causes are uncertain but may include increased abuse of alcohol, unemployment (see p. 495), and more family disruption due to rising rates in divorce.

University students

In the 1950's it was reported that suicide rates were high among male students in some universities. Rook (1959) reported that the rate was 22 per 100 000 among Cambridge male undergraduates compared with 6 per 100 000 in males aged 20–24 in the general population. Rook also presented evidence that the rates were high in the universities of Oxford and London. The reasons for these high rates are uncertain, though it has been suggested that loneliness and pressures of work might be important. Accurate data are difficult to obtain but it seems that the present rates among British undergraduates may still be high, though lower than in 1959 (Hawton *et al.* 1978). In the USA, it has been reported that suicide rates among students at Harvard and Yale are not raised (Eisenberg 1980).

Doctors

The suicide rate among doctors is greater than that in the general population, but there are no consistent findings of differences between medical specialties (see Roy 1985; Arnetz *et al.* 1987). Many reasons have been suggested, such as the ready availability of drugs, increased rates of addiction to alcohol and drugs, the extra stresses of work, reluctance to seek treatment for depressive disorders, and the selection into the medical profession of predisposed personalities. Whatever the true reasons, it is clear that the profession could do useful preventive work within its own ranks.

Suicide pacts

In suicide pacts, two people agree that at the same time each will take his own life. Completed pacts are uncommon. Cohen (1961) reported that completed pacts account for one in 300 of all completed suicides, while Parry-Jones (1973) estimated that there are about twice as many uncompleted suicide pacts as completed ones. Suicide pacts have to be distinguished from cases where murder is followed by suicide (especially when one person dies but the other is revived), or where one person aids another person's suicide without intending to die himself. The law deals with such cases by the provisions of the Homicide Act of 1957 and the Suicide Act of 1961. Under the Suicide Act a survivor who took an active part in the death of the other person is guilty of aiding and abetting suicide. Under the Homicide Act, a survivor who took an active part in the death of the other person is guilty of manslaughter. In practice, all cases are reviewed carefully, but not all are followed by prosecution. Of survivors found guilty, many are dealt with by probation (Parry-Jones 1973).

The psychological causes for these pacts are not known. It seems paradoxical that suicide, an act that is so often associated with social isolation, should be carried out with another person. Usually there is a particularly close relationship between the two members of the pact. In Parry-Jones's series, half the pacts were between lovers; however, in this study at least one person from each pair survived and had been prosecuted, so the finding may not be representative.

According to Rosenbaum (1983), the initiator is usually a mentally ill man who influences a woman who is not mentally ill. There appears to be considerable cultural variations in the nature of suicide pacts (Fishbain and Aldrich 1985). [The subject has been reviewed by Rosen (1981).]

The assessment of suicidal risk

General issues

Every doctor should be able to assess the risk of suicide. The first requirement is a willingness to make tactful but direct enquiries about a patient's intentions. The second is an alertness for the general factors that signify an increased risk.

Asking a patient about suicidal inclinations does not make suicidal behaviour more likely. On the contrary, if the patient has already thought of suicide he will feel better understood when the doctor raises the issue, and this feeling may reduce the risk. If a person has not thought of suicide before, tactful questioning will not make him behave suicidally. [For a review of general issues see Hawton and Catalan (1987); Hawton (1987).]

Assessing risk

The most obvious warning sign is a **direct statement of intent**. It is now well recognized, but cannot be repeated too often, that there is no truth in the idea that people who talk of suicide do not enact it. On the contrary, two-thirds of those who die by suicide have told someone of their intentions. The greatest difficulty arises with people who talk repeatedly of suicide. In time their statements may no longer be taken seriously but may be discounted as threats intended to influence other people. However, some repeated threateners do kill themselves in the end. Just before the act, there may be a subtle change in their way of talking about dying, sometimes in the form of oblique hints that need to be taken more seriously than the original open statements.

Risk is also assessed by considering the factors that have been found in surveys to be associated with suicide (see p. 481 above). Older patients are more at risk, as are the lonely and those suffering from chronic painful illness. **Depressive disorders** are highly important especially when there is severe mood change, with insomnia, anorexia, and weight loss (Barraclough *et al.* 1974). It is important to remember that suicide may occur during recovery from a depressive disorder in patients who previously, when more severely depressed, had thought of the act but had lacked the energy and initiative to carry it out. **Hopelessness** is a predictor of subsequent as well as immediate suicide. In a 10-year follow-up study of patients with suicidal ideas admitted to hospital, hopelessness was found to be an important determinant of suicide at some time in the 10 years (Beck *et al.* 1985*b*).

Other associations

As noted earlier there is an increased risk of suicide with alcohol dependence, especially when associated with physical complications or severe social damage; drug dependence; epilepsy; and abnormal personality. Suicidal schizophrenics are difficult to recognize; few give a warning or show any obvious mood change, but a history of previous self-harm is an important pointer.

Completing the history

When these general risk factors have been assessed, the rest of the history should be evaluated. The interview should be conducted in an unhurried and sympathetic way that allows the patient to admit any despair or self-destructive intentions. It is usually appropriate to start by asking about current problems and the patient's reaction to them. Enquiries should cover losses, both personal (such as bereavement or divorce) and financial, as well as loss of status. Information about conflict with other people and social isolation should also be elicited. Physical illness should always be asked about, particularly any painful condition in the elderly.

In assessing previous personality, it should be borne in mind that the patient's self-description may be coloured by depression. Whenever possible, another informant should be interviewed. The important points include mood swings, impulsive or aggressive tendencies, and attitudes towards religion and death.

Mental state examination

The assessment of mood should be particularly thorough and cognitive function must not be overlooked. The interviewer should then assess suicidal intent. It is usually appropriate to begin by asking whether the patient thinks that life is too much for him, or whether he no longer wants to go on. This can lead to more direct questions about thoughts of suicide, specific plans, and actions such as saving tablets. It is important always to remember that severely depressed patients occasionally have homicidal ideas; they may believe that it would be an act of mercy to kill other people, often the spouse or a child, to spare them intolerable suffering. Such homicidal ideas must not be missed, and should always be taken extremely seriously.

The management of the suicidal patient

General issues

Having assessed the suicidal risk, the clinician should make a treatment plan and try to persuade the patient to accept it. The first step is to decide whether the patient should be admitted to hospital or treated as an out-patient or day-patient. This decision depends on the intensity of the suicidal intentions, the severity of any associated psychiatric illness, and the availability of social support outside hospital. If out-patient treatment is chosen the patient should be given a telephone number with which he can, at all times, obtain help if feeling worse. Frustrated attempts to find a doctor can be the last straw for a patient with suicidal inclinations.

If the suicidal risk is judged to be significant, in-patient care is nearly always required. An occasional exception may be made when the patient lives with reliable relatives, but only if these relatives wish to care for the patient themselves, understand their responsibilities, and are able to fulfill them. Such a decision requires an exceptionally thorough knowledge of the patient and his problems. If hospital treatment is essential but the patient refuses it, admission under a compulsory order will be necessary. The method of arranging this in England and Wales is outlined in the Appendix.

Management in hospital

The obvious first requirement is to prevent the patient from harming himself. This depends on adequate staffing, vigilance, and good communications. At times special nursing arrangements may be required so that the patient is never left alone. It is essential that a clear policy should be stated for each patient and understood by all the staff. For example, it should be clearly specified whether the patient is to be kept in pyjamas, how closely a member of staff is to remain at hand, and whether potentially dangerous objects such as scissors are to be removed. The policy should be drawn up as soon as the patient is admitted, and agreed between the doctor and the nursing staff. It should be carefully reconsidered at frequent intervals until the danger passes. It is especially important that any changes in policy should be made clear when staff change between shifts.

When intensive supervision is needed for more than a few days, increasing difficulties may arise. Patients under constant obversation may become irritated and resentful, and may evade supervision. Staff should be aware of such problems, and treatment of any associated mental illness should not be delayed. If the patient has a severe depressive disorder, the rapid action of ECT may be required (see Chapter 8).

Appropriate physical treatment should be accompanied by simple psychotherapy. However determined the patient is to die, there is usually some small remaining wish to go on living. If doctors and nurses adopt a caring and hopeful attitude, these positive feelings can be encouraged and the patient can be helped towards a more realistic and balanced view of his future. At the same time he can be helped to see how an apparently overwhelming accumulation of problems can be dealt with one by one.

However carefully patients are managed, it will happen occasionally that a patient dies by suicide despite all the efforts of the staff. The doctor then has an important role in supporting other staff, particularly any nurses who have come to know the patient well through taking part in constant observation. Although it is essential to review every suicide carefully to determine whether any useful lessons can be learnt, this review should never become a search for a culprit.

The relatives

When a patient has died by suicide, the relatives require not only the support that is appropriate for any bereaved person, but also help with particular difficulties. In a study by Barraclough and Shepherd (1976) the relatives usually reported that the police conducted their enquiries in a considerate way, but nearly all found the public inquest distressing. The subsequent newspaper publicity caused further grief reactivating the events surrounding the death and increasing any feelings of stigma. Sympathetic counselling is likely to help relatives with these difficulties.

Suicide prevention

As reported above, many people who commit suicide contact their doctors shortly beforehand. Most have a psychiatric illness, and four-fifths are being treated with psychotropic drugs—though not always with the most appropriate drug or the optimal dosage. These findings suggest a need to improve skills of doctors in identifying high-risk patients and in planning their treatment. On the other hand, many depressed patients are treated successfully by general practitioners. It would be wrong therefore to suggest that the solution to the problem lies wholly in better training of doctors, though the latter might make a contribution.

Suicide prevention centres

In the United States, suicide prevention centres staffed by clinicians have been developed in many cities, starting in Los Angeles in 1958. It is difficult to assess their efficacy. Miller *et al.* (1984) found that suicide rates among young women decreased in areas with prevention centres, while they were increasing elsewhere. On the other hand, an analysis of the results of another published study of these centres failed to show that they reduced suicide rates in the communities that they served (Dew *et al.* 1987). A common finding is that many of the contacts with the centres (which are made by telephone) do not relate to suicide; and those that do relate to suicide appear to be of low risk. For this reason it has been suggested that the centres might be better called crisis intervention centres.

The Samaritan organization

This organization was founded in London in 1953 by the Reverend Chad Varah. People in despair are encouraged to contact a widely publicized telephone number. The help offered ('befriending') is provided by non-professional volunteers who are trained to listen sympathetically without attempting to take on tasks that are in the province of a doctor or social worker.

There is some evidence that amongst people who phone the Samaritans, the suicide rate in the ensuing year is higher than in the general population (Barraclough and Shea 1970). This suggests that the organization is attracting an appropriate group of people, but it also raises the question of the efficacy of the help offered.

To examine this problem, Bagley (1968) compared suicide rates in 15 pairs of towns in England and Wales. One of each pair was served by the Samaritans, the other was a similar kind of town except that it had no Samaritan branch. The results appeared to show lower rates of suicide in the towns served by the Samaritans. This finding was not confirmed by another study of similar design, but with improved matching of the towns (Jennings *et al.* 1978). It seems therefore that the effectiveness of the Samaritans has not been proved. The methodological problems involved may be too great to allow the issue to be decided conclusively. Even so, whether or not they prevent suicide, the Samaritans appear to perform a useful role by providing for the needs of many lonely and despairing people.

Deliberate self-harm

Introduction

Before the 1950s little distinction was made between people who killed themselves and those who survived after an apparent suicidal act. Stengel (1952) identified epidemiological differences between the two groups, and proposed the terms 'suicide' and 'attempted suicide' to distinguish the two forms of behaviour. He supposed that a degree of suicidal intent was essential in both groups; in other words, those who survived were failed suicides. These ideas were developed in an important monograph (Stengel and Cook 1958).

In the 1960s it was proposed that suicidal intent should no longer be regarded as essential, because it was recognized that most 'attempted suicides' had 'performed their acts in the belief that they were comparatively safe; aware, even in the heat of the moment, that they would survive their overdosage, and be able to disclose what they had done in good time to ensure rescue' (Kessel and Grossman 1965). For this reason, Kessel proposed that 'attempted suicide' should be replaced by 'deliberate self-poisoning' and 'deliberate self-injury'. These terms were chosen to imply that the behaviour was clearly not accidental, without any assumption whether the desire for death was present. By the end of the 1960s, these ideas were widely accepted.

Kreitman and his colleagues introduced the term 'parasuicide' to refer to 'a non-fatal act—in which an individual deliberately causes self injury or ingests a substance in excess of any prescribed or generally recognised therapeutic dose' (Kreitman 1977, p. 3). Thus, the term parasuicide excludes the question whether death was a desired outcome. Although 'parasuicide' has been used quite widely, 'self-poisoning' and 'self-injury' are retained by some workers. Morgan (1979) suggested the term deliberate self-harm (sometimes abbreviated to DSH) to provide a single term covering deliberate self-poisoning and deliberate self-injury. It has been objected that the term deliberate self-harm is sometimes a misnomer because the act is not invariably harmful (even though done in the knowledge that it might cause harm). In fact, no single term is wholly satisfactory. In this chapter, the term deliberate self-harm will be used rather than parasuicide.

The distinction between suicide and deliberate self-harm is not absolute. There is an important overlap. Some people who had no intention of dying succumb to the effects of an overdose. Others who intended to die are revived. Moreover, many patients were ambivalent at the time, uncertain whether they wished to die or live.

It should be remembered that among patients who have been involved in deliberate self-harm, the suicide rate in the subsequent twelve months is about a hundred times greater than in the general population. For this reason and other reasons to be given later, deliberate self-harm should not be regarded lightly.

The act of deliberate self-harm

The drugs used in deliberate self-poisoning

In the United Kingdom, about 90 per cent of the cases of deliberate self-harm referred to general hospitals involve a drug overdose, and most of them present no serious threat to life. The most commonly used drugs are **anxiolytic drugs** and the **non-opiate analgesics** such as salicylates and paracetamol. In recent years paracetamol has been used increasingly; it is particularly dangerous because it damages the liver (Davidson and Eastham 1966) and may lead to the delayed death of patients who had not intended to die. It is especially worrying that this drug is often taken by younger patients who are usually unaware of the serious risks (Gazzard *et al.* 1976). **Antidepressants** are taken in about a fifth of cases; in large amounts they may cause cardiac arrhythmias or convulsions. In the 1950s **barbiturates** were commonly used in deliberate self-poisoning; such usage is much less frequent nowadays following the general reduction in the prescribing of these drugs. Amongst all cases of deliberate self-harm about half the men and a quarter of the women take alcohol in the six hours before the act (Morgan *et al.* 1975).

Methods of deliberate self-injury

Deliberate self-injury accounts for 5–15 per cent of all deliberate self-harm presenting to general hospitals in Britain (Hawton and Catalan 1987). The commonest method of self-injury is laceration, usually of the forearm or wrists; it accounts for about four-fifths of the self-injuries referred to a general hospital (see Hawton and Catalan 1987). Self-laceration is discussed separately below. Other forms of self-injury are jumping from heights or in front of a train or motor vehicle, shooting, and drowning. These violent acts occur mainly among older people who intended to die (Morgan *et al.* 1975). They are more common in North America than in Britain.

Deliberate self-laceration

There are three forms of deliberate self-laceration: deep and dangerous wounds inflicted with serious suicidal intent, more often by men; self-mutilation by schizophrenic patients (often in response to hallucinatory voices) or by transsexuals; and superficial wounds that do not endanger life. Only the last group will be described here.

The patients are mostly young. Generally they have severe personality problems characterized by low self-esteem, impulsive or aggressive behaviour, unstable moods, difficulty in interpersonal relationships, and a tendency to abuse alcohol and drugs. Sexual identity problems have also been reported in association with self-laceration (Simpson 1976).

Usually increasing tension and irritability precede self-laceration, and are then relieved by it. Some patients say that the lacerations were inflicted during a state of feeling detached from their surroundings and of experiencing little or no pain. The lacerations are usually multiple, and made with glass or a razor blade on the forearms or wrists. Generally, some blood is drawn and the sight of this is often important to the patient. Some patients cause other injuries as well, for example by burning with cigarettes or by inflicting bruises. After the act, the patient often feels shame and disgust. A difficult problem can be presented by psychiatric in-patients, especially adolescents, who lacerate themselves in imitation of others (Walsh and Rosen 1985). [A useful review is given by Simpson (1976).]

The epidemiology of deliberate self-harm

During the 1960s and early 1970s there was a substantial increase in cases of deliberate self-harm admitted to general hospitals. Among women, deliberate self-harm is now the most frequent single reason for admission to a medical ward, and among men it is second only to ischaemic heart disease.

Accuracy of statistics

The official statistics for the incidence of deliberate self-harm are likely to be less than the true rates, because not all cases are referred to hospital. For example, a survey in Edinburgh suggested that hospital referral rates underestimated the frequency of deliberate self-harm by at least 30 per cent (Kennedy and Kreitman 1973). Another reason for inaccuracy in rates is wide variation in the definition and identification of deliberate self-harm.

Trends in the last two decades

In the early 1960s a substantial increase in deliberate self-harm began in most Western countries (see Weissman 1974; Wexler *et al.* 1978). In the United Kingdom, the rates of admission to general hospitals increased about fourfold in the ten years up to 1973 (Kreitman 1977; Bancroft *et al.* 1975). The rates continued to increase more slowly in the mid-1970s, but have been falling since the late 1970s, especially among young women (Alderson 1985). The reasons for the decline are unknown, as there has been no change in most of the social factors associated with deliberate self-harm, and unemployment has been rising. One explanation for this decline in England and Wales may be a decrease in the prescribing of psychotropic drugs, which could be used in self-poisoning.

Variations according to personal characteristics

Deliberate self-harm is more common among younger people, the rates declining sharply in middle age. In all but the very old, the rates are 1.5–2.1 times higher for **women**; particularly high rates are found among females aged 15–30 years. The peak age is older for men than for women. For both sexes rates are very low under the age of 12 years. Deliberate self-harm is more prevalent in the lower **social classes**. There are also differences related to **marital status**; the highest rates for both men and women are among the divorced, and high rates are also found among teenage wives and younger single men and women (Bancroft *et al.* 1975; Holding *et al.* 1977).

Variations according to place of residence

High rates are found in areas characterized by high unemployment, overcrowding, many children in care, and substantial social mobility (Buglass and Duffy 1978; Holding *et al.* 1977)

Causes of deliberate self-harm

Precipitating factors

Compared with the general population, people who deliberately harm themselves experience four times as many stressful life problems in the six months before the act (Paykel *et al.* 1975*a*). The events are various but a recent quarrel with a spouse, girlfriend, or boyfriend is particularly common (Bancroft *et al.* 1977). Other events include separations from or rejection by a sexual partner, the illness of a family member, recent personal physical illness, and a court appearance.

Predisposing factors

The precipitating events often occur against a background of long-term problems concerning marriage, children, work, and health. In one study. (Bancroft *et al.* 1977) about two-thirds of patients had some kind of marital problem; half the men had been involved in an extramarital relationship, and a further quarter said that their wives had been unfaithful. Among the unmarried, a similar proportion have difficulties in their relationships with sexual partners. Among men, unemployment is frequent: in a study in Bristol, one-third of men who deliberately harmed themselves were unemployed (Morgan *et al.* 1975), and in Edinburgh the proportion was nearly a half (Holding *et al.* 1977). Generally such findings from interviews with individual patients agree with the findings from epidemiological studies of neighbourhoods; for example, that deliberate self-harm is more frequent in areas with high rates of unemployment. Kreitman *et al.* (1969) have suggested that a kind of social contagion may operate in such areas, so that people become more likely to harm themselves if they know someone else who has done so.

A background of poor physical health is common (Bancroft *et al.* 1975). This applies particularly to epileptics, who are found in the deliberate self-harm population about six times more frequently than would be expected (Hawton *et al.* 1980).

Finally, there is some evidence that early parental loss through bereavement or a history of parental neglect or abuse is more frequent among cases of deliberate self-harm (see Hawton and Catalan 1987).

Psychiatric disorder

Amongst patients who deliberately harm themselves, many have affective symptoms falling short of a full psychiatric syndrome (Newson-Smith and Hirsch 1979*a*; Urwin and Gibbons 1979), but few have severe or sustained psychiatric disorder. This is in marked contrast to cases of completed suicide (see p. 482). Personality disorder is more common, being found in about a third to a half of self-harm patients (Kreitman 1977).

Dependence on alcohol is common (as in completed suicide), the frequencies in different series varying between 15 and 50 per cent among men, and 5 and 15 per cent among women.

In a large series of people who deliberately harmed themselves, about half had consulted a general practitioner, psychiatrist or social worker, or another helping agency, in the previous week (Bancroft *et al.* 1977).

Unemployment

The recent increase in unemployment in all Western countries has focused attention on a possible association with deliberate self-harm. Amongst men who deliberately harm themselves, the proportion of unemployed has been increasing in recent years, and the rate for deliberate self-harm is greater with greater length of unemployment. However, unemployment is related to many other social factors associated with deliberate self-harm and there is no evidence that unemployment is a direct cause. Little is known about any association between deliberate self-harm and unemployment among women. [See Platt (1986) for a review.]

Motivation and deliberate self-harm

The motives for deliberate self-harm are usually mixed and difficult to identify for certain. Even if the patient knows his own motives, he may try to hide them from other people. For example, someone who has taken an overdose in frustration and anger may feel ashamed and say instead that he wished to die. In the study, amongst patients who said they intended to die, only about half were judged by psychiatrists to have had true suicidal intentions (Bancroft *et al.* 1979). Conversely, someone who truly intended to kill himself may deny it. For this reason, more emphasis should be placed on a common-sense evaluation of the patient's actions leading up to self-harm, than on his subsequent account of his own motives.

Despite this limitation, useful information has been obtained by questioning groups of patients about their motives. Only a few say that the act was premeditated. About a quarter say they wished to die. Some say that they are uncertain whether they wanted to die or not; others that they were leaving it to 'fate' to decide; and others that they were seeking unconsciousness as a temporary escape from their problems. Another group admit that they were trying to influence someone; for example that they were seeking to make a relative feel guilty for failing them in some way (Bancroft *et al.* 1979). This motive of influencing other people was first emphasized by Stengel and Cook (1958) who described the act of attempted suicide (as it was then called) as 'calling forth action from the human environment'. This behaviour has since been referred to as 'a cry for help'. Although some acts of deliberate self-harm result in increased help for the patient, others may arouse resentment, particularly if they are repeated (see Hawton and Catalan 1987).

The outcome of deliberate self-harm

This section deals with the risk that the act of self-harm will be repeated, and second with the risk that the patient will die by suicide on some later occasion.

The risk of repetition

Repetition rates are based on groups of patients, some of whom have received psychiatric treatment after the act. Reported rates vary between about 15 and 25 per cent in the year after the act (Kreitman 1977). There are three broad patterns. First, some patients repeat only once; second, some repeat several times but only during a limited period of continuing problems; and third a small group repeat many times over a long period as a habitual response to stressful events.

Several studies agree that the following factors distinguish patients who repeat self-harm from those who do not: previous deliberate self-harm, previous psychiatric treatment, a personality disorder of the antisocial type, a criminal record, and alcohol or drug abuse. Lower social class and unemployment are also predictors (see Kreitman 1977). These factors are summarized in Table 13.3 (p. 500).

The risk of completed suicide

Among people who have intentionally harmed themselves the risk of later suicide is much increased. For example, in the first year afterwards, the risk of suicide is about 1–2 per cent, which is 100 times that of the general population (Kreitman 1977). An eight-year follow-up showed that, amongst patients who were previously admitted with deliberate self-harm, about 2.8 per cent eventually take their own lives and about twice the expected number die from natural causes (Hawton and Fagg 1983). Looked at in another way, in a third to a half of completed suicides, there is a history of previous deliberate self-harm (see Kreitman 1977).

Among people who deliberately harm themselves, the risk of eventual suicide is greater in those with other risk factors for suicide. Thus the risk is greater among older patients who are male, depressed, or alcoholic (see Kreitman 1977). A non-dangerous method of self-harm does not necessarily indicate a low risk of subsequent suicide, but the risk is certainly higher when violence or dangerous drug overdoses have been used.

In the weeks after deliberate self-harm, many patients report changes for the better. Those with psychiatric symptoms often report a decrease in their intensity (Newson-Smith and Hirsch 1979*a*). Improvements may results from help provided by psychiatrists and other professionals, or from improvements in relatives' attitudes and behaviour. Some patients, however, fare much worse and repeatedly harm themselves within months of the first act; and some relatives are unsympathetic and even hostile.

The assessment of patients after deliberate self-harm

General aims

Assessment is concerned with three main issues: the immediate risk of suicide; the subsequent risks of further deliberate self-harm or of suicide; and any current medical or social problems. The assessment should be carried out in a way that encourages the patient to undertake a constructive review of his problems and of the ways he can deal with them himself. This encouragement of self-help is important, because many patients are unwilling to be seen again as out-patients.

Usually the assessment has to be carried out in an accident and emergency department or a ward of a general hospital, in which there may be little privacy. Whenever possible, the interview should be in a side room so that it will not be overheard or interrupted. If the patient has taken an overdose, the interviewer should first make sure that the patient has recovered sufficiently to be able to give a satisfactory history. If consciousness is still impaired, the interview should be delayed. Information should also be obtained from relatives or friends, the family

Table 13.1. Circumstances suggesting high suicidal intent

Planning in advance
Precautions to avoid discovery
No attempts to obtain help afterwards
Dangerous method
'Final acts'

doctor, and any other person (such as a social worker) already attempting to help the patient. Wide enquiry is important because sometimes information from other sources differs substantially from the account given by the patient. [See Hawton and Catalan (1987) for a review.]

Specific enquiries

The interview is directed to five questions: (1) What were the patient's intentions when he harmed himself? (2) Does he now intend to die? (3) What are the patient's current problems? (4) Is there a psychiatric disorder? (5) What helpful resources are available to this patient? Each will be considered in turn.

1. *What were the patient's intentions when he harmed himself?* As mentioned already, patients sometimes misrepresent their intentions. For this reason the interviewer should reconstruct, as fully as possible, the events that led up to the act of self-harm. He will need to find the answers to five subsidiary questions (see Table 13.1).

(a) Was the act **planned** or carried out on impulse? The longer and more carefully the plans have been made, the greater the risk of a fatal repetition.

(b) Were **precautions** taken against being found? The more thorough the precautions, the greater the risk of fatal repetition. Of course, events do not always take place as the patient expected; for example a husband may arrive home later than usual because of an unexpected delay. In such circumstances, it is the patient's reasonable expectations that count.

(c) **Did the patient seek help?** Serious intent can be inferred if there were no attempts to obtain help after the act.

(d) **Was the method dangerous?** If drugs were used, what were they and what amount was taken? Did the patient take all the drugs available to him? If self-injury was used, what form did it take? (As noted above, the more dangerous the method the greater the risk of a further suicide attempt.) Not only should the actual risk be assessed, but also the risk anticipated by the patient, which may be inaccurate. For example, some people wrongly believe that paracetamol overdose is harmless or that benzodiazepines are dangerous.

(e) **Was there a 'final act'** such as writing a suicide note or making a will? If so, the risk of a further fatal attempt is greater.

By reviewing the answers to these questions, the interviewer makes a judgement of the patient's intentions at the time of the act. A similar approach has been formalized in Beck's suicide intent scale (Beck *et al.* 1974*b*) which gives a score for the degree of intent.

2. *Does the patient now intend to die?* The interviewer should ask directly whether the patient is pleased to have recovered or wishes that he had died. If the act suggested serious suicidal intent, and if the patient now denies such intent, the interviewer should try to find out by tactful questioning whether there has been a genuine change of resolve.

3. *What are the current problems?* Many patients will have experienced a mounting series of difficulties in the weeks or months leading up to the act. Some of these difficulties may have been resolved by the time the patient is interviewed; for example, a husband who has planned to leave his wife may now have agreed to stay. The more that serious problems remain, the greater the risk of a fatal repetition. This risk is particularly strong if there are problems of loneliness or ill-health. The review of problems should be systematic and should cover the following: intimate relationships with the spouse or another person; relations with children and other relatives; employment, finance, and housing; legal problems; social isolation, bereavement, and other losses. Drug and alcohol problems can be considered at this stage or when the psychiatric state is reviewed.

4. *Is there psychiatric disorder?* It should be possible to answer this question from the history and from a brief but systematic examination of the mental state. Particular attention should be directed to depressive disorder, alcoholism, and personality disorder. Schizophrenia and dementia should also be considered, though they will be found less often.

5. *What are the patient's resources?* These include his capacity to solve his own problems; his material resources; and the help that others may provide. The best guide to the patient's ability to solve future problems is his record of dealing with difficulties in the past, for example the loss of a job, or a broken relationship. The availability of help should be assessed by asking about the patient's friends and confidants, and about any support he may be receiving from his general practitioner, social workers or voluntary agencies.

Is there a continuing risk of suicide?

The interviewer now has the information required to answer this important question. In summary, he reviews the answers to the first four questions outlined above, namely: (a) Did the patient originally intend to die? (b) Does he intend it now? (c) Are the problems which provoked the act still

Table 13.2. Factors predicting suicide after deliberate self-poisoning

---

Evidence of serious intent*

Depressive disorder
Alcoholism or drug abuse
Antisocial personality disorder

Previous suicide attempt(s)

Social isolation
Unemployment
Older age group
Male sex

---

* See Table 13.1.

present? and (d) Is he suffering from a mental disorder? He also decides what help other people are likely to provide after the patient leaves hospital (question 5 above). Having reviewed the individual factors in this way, the interviewer compares the patient's characteristics with those found in groups of people who died by suicide. These characteristics are summarized in Table 13.2.

Is there a risk of further non-fatal self-harm?

The predictive factors which have been outlined already (see p. 496), are summarized in Table 13.3. The interviewer should consider all the points in turn before making a judgement about the risk. Using their own six-item scale (slightly different from Table 13.3) Buglass and Horton (1974) gave a score according to the number of items that were present in each case. Patients with a score of zero had a five per cent chance of repeating the act in the next year, while those with a score of five or more had an almost 50 per cent chance.

Table 13.3. Factors predicting the repetition of deliberate self-poisoning*

Previous deliberate self-harm
Previous psychiatric treatment
Antisocial personality disorder
Alcohol or drug abuse
Criminal record
Low social class
Unemployment

---

* See Kreitman and Dyer (1980).

Is treatment required and will the patient agree to it?

If the patient is actively suicidal, the procedures are those outlined in the first part of this chapter (see p. 488). About 5–10 per cent of deliberate self-harm patients require admission to a psychiatric unit for further management; most need treatment for depressive disorders or alcoholism, but a few require only a brief respite from overwhelming domestic stress. The best methods of treating the remaining patients are less certain. A quarter to a third are probably best referred to general practitioners, social workers, or others who may already be involved in their case. Many patients (up to half) may benefit from out-patient care, usually problem-orientated counselling for personal problems rather than treatment for psychiatric disorder. Many patients refuse the offer of out-patient help; their care should be discussed with the general practitioner before they are allowed home. It is useful to provide an emergency telephone number enabling patients to obtain immediate advice or an urgent appointment in any further crisis.

Special problems

Mothers of young children

Mothers of young children require special consideration because of the known association between deliberate self-harm and child abuse (Roberts and Hawton 1980). It is important to ask about the mother's feeling towards her children, and to enquire about their welfare. In the United Kingdom information about the children can usually be obtained from the general practitioner, who may ask his health visitor to investigate the case.

Children and adolescents

Despite problems of case definition and identification, it appears that there has been a striking increase in the frequency of deliberate self-harm amongst children and adolescents in many parts of the developed world. Deliberate self-harm is rare but not unknown among pre-school children (Rosenthal and Rosenthal 1984); it becomes increasingly common after the age of 12. It is more common amongst girls except at younger ages. The commonest method is drug overdosage which is usually not dangerous, though occasionally life-threatening. The more dangerous methods of self-injury are more frequent amongst boys. Epidemics of deliberate self-harm occasionally occur amongst adolescents in hospitals and other institutions.

It is difficult to determine the motivation of self-harm in young children, especially as a clear concept of death is not usually developed until around the age of 12. It is probable that only a few of the younger children have any serious suicidal intent. Possibly their motivation is more often to communicate distress, escape from stress, or manipulate other people.

Deliberate self-harm in children and adolescents is associated with histories of broken homes, family psychiatric disorder, and child abuse. It is often precipitated by social problems such as difficulties with parents, boyfriends, or school work (see Hawton and Catalan 1987). Hawton (1986) described three main groups: those with acute distress about problems of less than a month's duration, but without behavioural disturbance; those with chronic psychological and social problems, but without behavioural disturbance; and those with chronic psychological and social problems, and also behavioural disturbance such as stealing, truancy, drug taking, or delinquency.

For most children and adolescents, the outcome of deliberate self-harm is relatively good, but an important minority continue to have social and psychiatric problems, and to repeat acts of deliberate self-harm. A poor outcome is associated with poor psychosocial adjustment, a history of previous deliberate self-harm, and severe family problems. There is a significant risk of suicide amongst adolescents, especially boys (see Hawton 1986).

When children harm themselves, it is better for them to be assessed by child psychiatrists rather than members of the adult services for deliberate self-harm. Treatment is usually directed towards the family. In the case of adolescents, treatment largely follows the general principles of management described in this chapter.

Who should assess?

In 1968 a British Government report recommended that all cases of deliberate self-harm should be assessed by a psychiatrist (Central Health Services Council 1968). The intention was to make sure that patients with depressive and other psychiatric disorders should be identified and treated, and that appropriate assistance should be given for other psychological and social problems. It is likely that a large proportion of the patients at that time were suffering from psychiatric disorder. The increase of cases since then has been made up mainly of younger patients in whom serious psychiatric disorders are less frequent. Such patients usually require assessment and counselling for social problems, rather than diagnosis and treatment of psychiatric disorders.

In England and Wales, a recent government report (Department of Health and Social Security 1984) recognized that such assessments could be carried out equally well by trained staff other than psychiatrists, as long as psychiatrists provide training and supervision, and interview any patients who may have a psychiatric disorder. It has been shown that if they receive appropriate additional training, junior medical staff (Gardner *et al.* 1977), psychiatric nurses (Hawton *et al.* 1979), and social workers (Newson-Smith and Hirsch 1979*b*) can all assess these patients as well as psychiatrists. It is emphasized that when a nurse or social worker makes the assessment a psychiatrist reviews the question of psychiatric disorder.

For patients admitted to medical beds after deliberate self-harm, the best policy seems to be that the local consultant physicians and psychiatrists should agree who is to make the assessments and who will take the final responsibility for decisions about management. In this way each hospital can adopt the policy that makes the most effective use of the available medical, nursing, and social work staff.

Management

As indicated above, the assessment procedure divides patients into three groups. About ten per cent need immediate in-patient treatment in a psychiatric unit, and about a quarter require no special treatment because their self-harm was a response to temporary difficulties and carried little risk of repetition. This section is concerned with the remaining two-thirds for whom some out-patient treatment may be appropriate.

The main aim of such treatment is to enable the patient first to resolve the difficulties that led up to the act of self-harm, and second to deal with any future crisis without resorting to further self-harm. The main problem is that, once they have left hospital, many patients are disinclined to take part in any treatment.

The treatment is psychological and social. Drugs are seldom required, but a small minority of patients require antidepressant medication. It is more often necessary to withdraw drugs for which there is no clear indication. The starting-point of treatment is the list of problems compiled during the assessment procedure. The patient is encouraged to consider what steps he should take to resolve each of these problems, and to formulate a practical plan for tackling them one at a time. Throughout this discussion, the therapist tries to persuade the patient to do as much as possible for himself.

Many cases are associated with interpersonal problems. It is often helpful to interview the other person involved, at first alone, and then in a few joint interviews with the patient. This procedure may help to resolve problems that the couple have been unable to discuss on their own.

When deliberate self-harm follows a bereavement or other kind of loss, a different approach is needed. The first step should be sympathetic listening while the patient expresses his feelings of loss. Then the patient is encouraged to seek ways of gradually rebuilding his life without the lost person. Appropriate measures will depend on the nature of the loss—whether it was through death, or the break-up of a marriage, or the end of another relationship. Again, the emphasis should be on self-help.

Some special problems of management

Patients refusing assessment After deliberate self-harm, some patients refuse to be interviewed, and others seek to discharge themselves before the assessment is complete. In such cases it is essential to gather as much information as possible from other sources, in order to exclude serious suicidal risk of psychiatric disorder before letting the patient leave hospital. Occasionally detention under a compulsory order is appropriate.

Frequent repeaters Some patients take overdoses repeatedly at times of stress. Often the behaviour seems intended to reduce tension or gain attention. However, when overdoses are taken repeatedly, relatives often become unsympathetic or even overtly hostile, and staff of hospital emergency departments angry and bewildered. These patients usually have a personality disorder and many insoluble social problems, but neither counselling nor intensive psychotherapy is usually effective. It is helpful if all those involved in management agree a clear plan whereby the patient is rewarded for constructive behaviour. An opportunity for continuing support by one person should be arranged. However, whatever help is arranged, the risk of eventual death by suicide is high.

Delayed complications When someone has taken an overdose of certain substances, notably paracetamol or paraquat, the risk of late medical complications should be borne in mind. If the overdose seems to have been impulsive and without suicidal intent, the problem may not at first seem serious; but later there may be severe, possibly fatal medical complications.

Deliberate self-laceration The management of self-laceration presents many problems. The patient often has difficulty in expressing his feelings in words, and so formal psychotherapy is seldom helpful. Simple efforts to gain the patient's confidence and increase his self-esteem are more likely to succeed. An attempt should also be made to find an alternative method of relieving tension, for example through vigorous exercise. Anxiolytic drugs are seldom helpful and may produce disinhibition. If drug treatment is needed to reduce tension, a phenothiazine is more likely to be effective (see Hawton and Catalan 1987).

The results of treatment

As already indicated, the treatment of deliberate self-harm has two aims. The first is to help the patient to deal with the social and emotional problems that led up to the act. The second is to prevent further acts of self-harm.

Two retrospective studies suggested that psychiatric intervention might be effective in reducing the repetition of deliberate self-harm. Greer and Bagley (1971) reported that, if patients received no psychiatric attention before discharge from hospital, they made more attempts at deliberate self-harm in the next 18 months than those who had been assessed or treated by a psychiatrist. These findings held even when allowances were made for characteristics correlated with the risk of repetition. Kennedy (1972) used a general practice survey to identify deliberate self-harm patients who had not been referred to the Edinburgh Regional Poisoning Treatment Centre. At one-year follow-up, he found that this group had repeated deliberate self-harm more often than patients who had been admitted to the Centre where psychiatric assessment and treatment were available. The disadvantages of both studies were that they were retrospective; hence the groups of patients could not be adequately matched, and the treatment provided could not be clearly described.

Prospective studies have compared different treatments for deliberate self-harm patients, but no study has included a no-treatment group. In a study of patients who had harmed themselves at least twice, Chowdhury *et al.* (1973) compared a usual follow-up service with an augmented service which included intensive follow-up home visits for defaulters and provided a continuously accessible on-call team. At six-month follow-up, there were no differences between the two groups in rates of repeated deliberate self-harm. The experimental group showed a slightly greater improvement in psychological symptoms, and a significantly greater improvement in handling problems of finance, housing, and employment. In a study of problem-orientated counselling, Hawton *et al.* (1981) found no difference in outcome between patients treated at home and those treated in an out-patient clinic. In another study, Hawton *et al.* (1987) found no overall difference in outcome between patients treated at an out-patient clinic and those receiving routine care from their general practitioner. However, women with interpersonal difficulties improved more with clinic treatment. Gibbons *et al.* (1978) compared task-centred social casework with routine treatment; they found no difference in rates of repetition of deliberate self-harm, even though the groups receiving social work improved more in social adjustment.

It seems, therefore, that additional treatments of the kinds described do not reduce the overall risk of repeated self-harm. It may still be useful to deal with social problems, since many of them would have required attention even if the patient had not harmed himself.

Primary prevention

If prevention after the first episode of self-harm is so difficult, can primary prevention be achieved? Three main strategies have been suggested: reducing the availability of means of self-harm; encouraging the work of agencies that try to help people with social and emotional problems; and improving health education.

Reducing the means

It has been suggested that psychotropic drugs should be prescribed more cautiously, especially for patients whose affective symptoms are a reaction to life problems. Drugs may not help these patients but may merely provide the opportunity to take an overdose when the problems increase. Two factors should be weighed against this argument: up to a third of people who take deliberate drug overdoses use drugs originally prescribed for a person other than the patient: and another quarter use drugs that can be bought without prescription, notably analgesics some of which are particularly dangerous in overdosage.

This last consideration has led to suggestions that, if any non-prescribed drug is dangerous in overdose, it should be sold in strip or blister packets to prevent people taking large amounts on impulse; or a small quantity of emetic should be added. It has also been suggested that paracetamol, one of the most dangerous analgesics, should be available only on prescription (e.g. Gazzard *et al.* 1976).

Encouraging helping agencies

This at first appears sensible but, on closer enquiry, may be unlikely to help. In one study it was found that about three-quarters of patients taking deliberate overdoses already knew about the Samaritans and many were also aware of the social services provided in their area (Bancroft *et al.* 1977). Their overdoses were taken impulsively without thought about ways of obtaining help.

Education

Education about the dangers of drug overdoses and discussions of common emotional problems might be provided for teenagers. However, in the absence of any evidence that such measures reduce deliberate self-harm, there is an understandable reluctance to introduce them in schools.

Further reading

Hawton, K. and Catalan, J. (1987). *Attempted suicide: a practical guide to its nature and management* (2nd edn). Oxford University Press, Oxford.
Kreitman, N. (ed) (1967). *Parasuicide*. John Wiley, London.
Morgan, H. G. (1979). *Death wishes? The understanding and management of deliberate self harm*. John Wiley, London.
Roy, A. (ed.) (1986) *Suicide*. Williams and Wilkins, Baltimore.

14 The abuse of alcohol and drugs

The phrase 'psychoactive use disorder' is used in ICD and DSM to refer to conditions arising from the abuse of alcohol, psychoactive drugs, and other chemicals such as volatile solvents. In this chapter, problems related to alcohol will be discussed first, under the general heading of alcohol abuse; problems related to drugs and other chemicals will be discussed second under the general heading of abuse of psychoactive substances.

Classification of disorders due to the use of alcohol and other psychoactive substances

The two classification systems, ICD10 (draft) and DSMIIIR, use similar categories but group them in different ways. Both schemes recognize the following disorders: intoxication, abuse (divided into harmful and hazardous use in ICD10 draft), dependence syndrome, withdrawal states, psychotic states induced by drugs (in DSMIIIR these are divided into delusional disorder and hallucinosis), dementia, amnestic syndrome, and residual states (personality change and 'flashbacks').

In ICD10 (draft) the first step in classification is to specify the drug that is involved: this provides the primary diagnostic category. To this is added the type of mental disorder, thereby producing a secondary classification with an additional code. In this system any kind of disorder can, in principle, be attached to any drug—though in practice certain disorders do not develop with individual drugs. The scheme in DSMIIR is different in two main ways. First, organic mental conditions induced by drugs appear in different parts of the classification from dependence and abuse. The first are classified under the rubric organic mental disorders, the other two appear together under the rubric psychoactive substance use disorders. Second, for each drug separate categories are provided for the disorders that can occur when it is taken. This scheme has the advantage of providing special categories for conditions that are peculiar to a particular drug, for example idiosyncratic intoxication with alcohol, alcohol withdrawal, delirium, and post-hallucinogen perceptual disorder. The disadvantage of this scheme is that it is rather cumbersome. However, the list of disorders in

DSMIIR (shown in Table 14.3) provides a useful summary of the conditions described in this chapter (though dependence to nicotine is not considered here).

Table 14.1. Classification of disorders due to the use of alcohol and psychoactive drugs, (i) types of disorder

ICD10 (draft)	DSMIIR
Intoxication	Intoxication
Hazardous use	Abuse
Harmful use	
Dependence syndrome	Dependence
Withdrawal state	Uncomplicated withdrawal
	Withdrawal with delirium
Psychotic state	Delusional disorder
	Hallucinosis
Dementia	Dementia
Amnestic syndrome	Amnestic syndrome
Residual state	Personality disorder
Unspecified	Other

Table 14.2. Classification of disorders due to the use of alcohol and psychoactive drugs, (ii) types of drug

ICD10 (draft)	DSMIIR*
Alcohol	Alcohol
Tobacco	Nicotine
Opioids	Opioids
Cannabinoids	Cannabis
Sedative/hypnotic	Sedative/hypnotic
	Anxiolytic
Cocaine	Cocaine
Other stimulants	Amphetamine
Hallucinogens	Hallucinogens
Others (includes solvents)	Phencyclidine and similar drugs
	Inhalants
	Caffeine
	Others
Multiple drugs	Polysubstance

* The order of entries in the classification has been attached to show parallels with ICD10.

Table 14.3. Classification of disorders due to alcohol and
psychoactive drugs, (iii) full classification in DSMIIIR

(a) Psychoactive substance dependence due to:
Alcohol
Amphetamine
Cannabis
Hallucinogens
Inhalants
Nicotine
Opioids
Phencyclidine and similar drugs
Sedative/hypnotic/anxiolytics
Polysubstances

(b) Psychoactive substance abuse due to:
Alcohol
Amphetamine
Cannabis
Hallucinogens
Inhalants
Opioids
Phencyclidine and similar drugs
Sedative/hypnotic/anxiolytics

(c) Psychoactive substance-induced organic mental disorders due to:
Alcohol
    Intoxication
    Idiosyncratic intoxication
    Uncomplicated withdrawal
    Withdrawal delirium
    Hallucinosis
    Amnestic disorder
    Dementia

Amphetamine
    Intoxication
    Withdrawal
    Delirium
    Delusional disorder

Caffeine
    Intoxication

Cannabis
  Intoxication
  Delusional disorder

Cocaine
  Intoxication
  Withdrawal
  Delirium
  Delusional disorder

Hallucinogen
  Hallucinosis
  Delusional disorder
  Mood disorder
  Post-hallucinogen perceptual disorder

Inhalants
  Intoxication

Nicotine
  Withdrawal

Opioid
  Intoxication
  Withdrawal

Phencyclidine and similar arylcyclohexamines
  Intoxication
  Delirium
  Organic mental disorder not otherwise specified

Sedative/Hypnotic/Anxiolytic
  Intoxication
  Withdrawal
  Withdrawal delirium
  Amnestic disorder

Other psychoactive substance
  Intoxication
  Withdrawal
  Delirium
  Dementia
  Amnestic syndrome
  Delusional disorder
  Hallucinosis
  Mood disorder
  Anxiety disorder
  Personality disorder

Definitions

Intoxication refers to psychological and physical changes brought about by a psychoactive substance, disappearing when that substance is eliminated from the body. The nature of the psychological changes varies with the person as well as with the drug; for example, some people intoxicated with alcohol become aggressive, others maudlin. The term *hazardous use* is used in ICD10(draft) to denote use that carries a high risk of future damage to physical or mental health, but has not yet led to these effects. The term *harmful use* means use that is already causing harm to health. Together, hazardous and harmful use constitute *abuse*. The term *dependence syndrome* refers to certain physiological and psychological phenomena induced by the repeated taking of a physical substance: these include a withdrawal state (see below) and a strong desire to take the drug. Other features, varying in importance with different drugs, include tolerance (see below) to the effects of the drug, progressive neglect of alternative sources of satisfaction, and persistent use despite evidence of harmful consequences. *Tolerance* is a state in which, after repeated administration, a drug produces a decreased effect, or increasing doses are required to produce the same effect. A *withdrawal state* is a group of symptoms and signs occurring when a drug is reduced in amount or withdrawal, and lasting for a limited time. The term *residual state* describes physiological or psychological changes occurring when a drug is taken and after it has been withdrawn, and persisting after the drug has been eliminated and any withdrawal state has subsided.

Alcohol abuse

Terminology

In the past, the term alcoholism was generally used in medical writing. Although the word is still widely used in everyday language, it is unsatisfactory as a technical term because it has more than one meaning. It can be applied to habitual alcohol consumption that is deemed excessive in amount according to some arbitrary criterion. Alcoholism may also refer to damage, whether mental, physical, or social, resulting from such excessive consumption. In a more specialized sense, alcoholism may imply a specific disease entity that is supposed to require medical treatment. On the other hand, to speak of 'an alcoholic' often has a pejorative meaning, suggesting behaviour that is morally bad.

For most purposes it is better to use four more specific terms: excessive consumption of alcohol; alcohol-related disability; problem drinking; and alcohol dependence. These terms will be explained later, but at this stage they can be defined briefly. *Excessive consumption* of alcohol refers to a daily or weekly intake of alcohol exceeding a specified amount. *Alcohol-related disability* refers to any mental, physical, or social harm resulting from excessive consumption. *Problem drinking* is drinking that incurs alcohol-related disability, but has not yet advanced to alcohol dependence. *Alcohol dependence* refers to a state in which there is a syndrome of mental or physical disturbance when the drug is withdrawn. The term alcoholism, if it is used at all, should be regarded as a shorthand way of referring to some combination of these four conditions. However, since these specific terms have been introduced recently, the term alcoholism has to be used in this chapter when referring to much of the literature. Before explaining these specific terms further, it is appropriate to examine the moral and the medical models of alcohol abuse.

The moral and medical models

According to the **moral model**, if someone drinks too much, he does so of his own free will, and if his drinking causes harm to himself or his family, his actions are morally bad. The corollary of this attitude is that public drunkenness should be punished. In many countries, this is the official practice; public drunks are fined, and if they cannot pay the fine, they go to prison. Many people now believe that this approach is too harsh and unsympathetic. Whatever the humanitarian arguments, there is little practical justification for punishment, since there is little evidence that it influences the behaviour of excessive drinkers.

According to the **medical model**, a person who abuses alcohol is sick rather than wicked. Although it had been proposed earlier, this idea was not strongly advocated until 1960, when Jellinek published an influential book, *The disease concept of alcoholism*. The disease concept embodies three basic ideas. The first is that some people have a specific vulnerability to alcohol abuse. The second idea is that excessive drinking progresses through well-defined stages, at one of which the person can no longer control his drinking, (Glatt 1976; Keller 1976). The third idea is that excessive drinking may lead to physical and mental disease of several kinds. While the latter is true, it seems illogical to say that the abuse of alcohol is itself a disease because it can lead to other diseases.

One of the main consequences of the disease model is that attitudes towards excessive drinking become more humane. Instead of blame and punishment, medical treatment is provided. The disease model also has certain disadvantages. By implying that only certain people are at risk, it diverts attention from two important facts. First, *anyone* who drinks a great deal for a long time may become dependent on alcohol. Second, the best way to curtail the abuse of alcohol may be to limit consumption in the whole population, and not just among a predisposed minority.

The syndrome of alcohol dependence

In 1977, a group of investigators sponsored by the World Health Organization recommended the term *alcohol dependence syndrome* to describe a group of symptoms arising in some people when they stop drinking alcohol (Edwards *et al.* 1977*a*). This syndrome has been well described by Victor and Adams (1953) who found that relative or absolute withdrawal was followed by a state of tremulousness, transient hallucinations, epileptic fits, and delirium tremens. Soon after this, Isbell *et al.* (1955) gave large quantities of ethyl alcohol to 10 healthy ex-morphine addicts for periods of between 7 and 87 days. Four patients who dropped out early in the experiment developed tremulousness, nausea, sweating, and insomnia. Of the six patients who drank over 48 days two had epileptic fits and three had delirium tremens on withdrawal.

As described by Edwards *et al.* (1977*b*), there are seven essential elements in the alcohol dependence syndrome:

(i) *The feeling of being compelled to drink.* The dependent drinker is aware of being unsure that he can stop drinking once started. If he tries to give up alcohol, he experiences a craving for it.

(ii) *A stereotyped pattern of drinking.* Whereas the ordinary drinker varies his intake from day to day, the dependent person drinks at regular intervals to relieve or avoid withdrawal symptoms.

(iii) *Primacy of drinking over other activities.* For the dependent drinker alcohol takes priority over everything else, including health, family, home, career, and social life.

(iv) *Altered tolerance to alcohol.* The dependent drinker is relatively unaffected by blood levels of alcohol that would incapacitate a normal drinker. Since he can 'hold his drink', he may persuade himself that alcohol is no problem to him. This is a false argument, because increasing tolerance is an important sign of increasing dependence. In the late stages of dependence, tolerance falls and the dependent drinker becomes incapacitated after only a few drinks.

(v) *Repeated withdrawal symptoms.* Withdrawal symptoms occur in people who have been drinking heavily for years and who maintain a high intake of alcohol for weeks at a time. The symptoms follow a drop in blood concentration. They characteristically appear on waking, after the fall in concentration during sleep.

The earliest and commonest feature is acute tremulousness affecting the hands, legs, and trunk ('the shakes'). The sufferer may be unable to sit still, hold a cup steady, or do up buttons. He is also agitated and easily startled, and often dreads facing people or crossing the road. Nausea, retching, and sweating are frequent. If alcohol is taken, these symptoms may be relieved quickly; if not, they may last for several days.

As withdrawal progresses, misperceptions and hallucinations may occur, usually only briefly. Objects appear distorted in shape, or shadows seem to move; disorganized voices, shouting, or snatches of music may be heard. Later there may be epileptic seizures, and finally after about 48 hours delirium tremens may develop (see below).

(vi) *Relief drinking.* Since they can stave off withdrawal symptoms only by further drinking, many dependent drinkers take a drink on waking. In most cultures, early morning drinking is diagnostic of dependency.

With increasing need to stave off withdrawal symptoms during the day, the drinker typically becomes secretive about the amount consumed, hides bottles or carries them in a pocket. Rough cider and cheap wines may be drunk regularly to obtain the most alcohol for the least money.

(vii) *Reinstatement after abstinence.* A severely dependent person who drinks again after a period of abstinence is likely to relapse quickly and totally, returning to his old drinking pattern within a few days.

The syndromes become established most often in the mid-forties for men, and a few years later for women (Royal College of Psychiatrists 1979). However, it is now occurring increasingly among teenagers, and it is sometimes seen for the first time in elderly people after retirement. Once established, the syndrome usually progresses steadily and destructively, unless the patient stops drinking or manages to bring it under control.

Alcohol-related disabilities

This section describes the different types of damage, physical, psychological, and social, that can result from excessive drinking. A person who suffers from these disabilities may or may not be suffering from the dependence syndrome.

Physical damage

Excessive consumption of alcohol may lead to physical damage in several ways. First, it can have a direct toxic effect on certain tissues, notably the brain and liver. Second, it is often accompanied by poor diet which may lead to deficiency of protein and B vitamins. Third, it increases the risk of accidents, particularly head injury. Fourth, it is accompanied by general neglect which can lead to increased susceptibility to infection.

Physical complications of excessive drinking occur in several systems of the body. **Alimentary disorders** are common, notably damage to the liver, gastritis, peptic ulcer, oesophageal varices and carcinoma, and acute and chronic pancreatis. Damage to the liver, including fatty infiltration, hepatitis, cirrhosis, and hepatoma, is particularly important. The rate of cirrhosis appears to be increasing. Thus, in a 20-year prospective study of cirrhosis in Birmingham, Saunders *et al.* (1981) found that the annual incidence rate for all cases of cirrhosis almost tripled between 1959 and 1975, whilst the proportion due to alcohol rose from one-third to two-thirds. Similar increases have been reported from most other European countries (see Walsh 1982, p. 47).

For a person dependent on alcohol, the risk of dying from liver cirrhosis is almost 10 times greater than the average (Williams and Davis 1977). On the other hand, only about 10 per cent of alcohol-dependent people develop cirrhosis. Recent work suggests that vulnerability to alcohol-induced liver disease may be influenced by genetic factors, for there is an association with the histocompatibility (HLA) antigens AW32, B8, B13, B27 and B37 (see Eddleston and Davis 1982). Conversely, HLA–A28 may be associated with a protective effect. However, no single HLA antigen is uniformly associated with the development of alcoholic liver disease (Faizallah *et al.* 1982). There is also a suggestion that patterns of drinking may influence the risk of certain forms of liver disease. Thus in Scotland, alcoholic hepatitis occurred in two-thirds of a group of continuous heavy drinkers, as against one-third of binge-drinkers (Brunt *et al.* 1974).

Excess alcohol consumption also damages the **nervous system**. Neuropsychiatric complications are described later; other neurological conditions include peripheral neuropathy, epilepsy, and cerebellar degeneration. The latter is characterized by unsteadiness of stance and gait, with less effect on arm movements or speech. Rare complications are optic atrophy, central pontine myelinolysis, and *Marchiafava–Bignami syndrome*. The latter syndrome results from widespread demyelination of the corpus callosum, optic tracts, and cerebellar peduncles. Its main features are dysarthria, ataxia, epilepsy, and marked impairment of consciousness; in the more prolonged forms there are dementia and limb paralysis [see Lishman (1981) for a review]. Head injury is common in alcohol-dependent people. Thus, in a large series of men arrested for public drunkenness in London, nearly a quarter had a history of head injury resulting in unconsciousness (Gath *et al.* 1968).

Other physical complications of excessive drinking are too numerous to detail here. Examples include anaemia, myopathy, episodic hypoglycaemia, haemochromatosis, cardiomyopathy, vitamin deficiencies, and tuberculosis. They are described in textbooks of medicine, for example, the *Oxford textbook of medicine* (Weatherall *et al.* 1987).

Not surprisingly, the **mortality rate** is increased in excessive drinkers. In the United Kingdom the overall rate is about twice the expected level, whilst for women aged between 15 and 39 it is 17 times greater (Adelstein and White 1976). Similar findings have been reported in the United States (Schmidt and de Lindt 1972), and in Sweden (Peterson *et al.* 1980). Even allowing for the fact that heavy drinkers tend to be heavy smokers, alcohol itself it almost certainly responsible for a substantial part of this increased mortality.

Damage to the fetus

Recently evidence has been presented that a **fetal alcohol syndrome** occurs in some children born to mothers who drink excessively. In France, Lemoine *et al.* (1968) described a syndrome of facial abnormality, small stature, low birth-weight, low intelligence, and psychological over-activity. In Seattle, USA, a series of reports confirmed this general clinical picture (Jones and Smith 1973; Hanson *et al.* 1976). It is a limitation of this research that both studies were retrospective.

In a large prospective study in France (Kaminski *et al.* 1976), women who drank above 400 ml of wine per day (or equivalent of other drinks) were not found to have babies with higher rates of congenital malformation or neonatal mortality. However, the women had more than the expected number of stillbirths, and their babies' birth-weights were lower. Compared with other mothers, those who drank excessively were older, more often unmarried, of lower social status and of greater parity, and they smoked more. They also had more bleeding in early pregnancy. When allowance was made for these factors, the authors still found that alcohol independently affected birth weight, placental weight, and stillbirths.

Other research on this subject has been reviewed by Kessel (1977*b*) and Abel (1984). It seems fair to conclude that, among the offspring of some mothers who drink excessively, there is a syndrome of the kind mentioned above but that it occurs infrequently and only when the mother has been drinking very heavily indeed during pregnancy. Impaired growth, low intelligence, and dysmorphic features have been found ten years after the initial diagnosis (Streissguth *et al.* 1985). When mothers drink excessively, though less heavily than this, their infants appear to have lower birth-weights and stature than others, but the differences are not great. Because mothers who drink excessively have more of the other known high-risk factors, such as smoking, malnutrition, and social handicaps, it is not certain that all the effects described are due directly to alcohol.

Available evidence does not make it possible to specify a safe level of drinking for pregnant mothers. Until more is known it seems best to follow the advice of the US Surgeon General that pregnant women should not drink alcohol (Surgeon General 1981).

Psychiatric disorders

Alcohol-related psychiatric disabilities fall into four groups: intoxication phenomena; withdrawal phenomena; chronic or nutritional disorders; and associated psychiatric disorders (see Cutting 1979).

(i) Intoxication phenomena

In DSMIIIR the term **alcoholic idiosyncratic intoxication** is applied to maladaptive marked changes in behaviour such as aggression occurring within minutes of taking an amount of alcohol insufficient to induce intoxication in most people (the behaviour being uncharacteristic of the person). In the past, these sudden changes in behaviour were called **pathological drunkenness**, or *mania à potu*, and the descriptions emphasized the explosive nature of the outbursts of aggression. There is doubt whether behaviour of this kind really is induced by small amounts of alcohol. Maletzky (1976) gave intravenous infusions of alcohol to 23 men who gave a history of pathological drunkenness. Fifteen developed aggressive behaviour but they did so only when the blood alcohol level was substantially raised (see Coid 1979 for a review).

Memory blackouts or short-term amnesia are frequently reported after heavy drinking. At first the events of the night before are forgotten, even though consciousness was maintained at the time. Such memory losses can occur after a single episode of heavy drinking in people who are not dependent on alcohol; if they recur regularly, they indicate habitual heavy drinking. With sustained excessive drinking, memory losses may become more severe, affecting parts of the daytime or even whole days.

(ii) Withdrawal phenomena

The general **withdrawal syndrome** has been described earlier under the heading of alcohol dependence. Here we are concerned with the more serious psychiatric syndrome of delirium tremens.

Delirium tremens

This occurs in people whose history of excessive drinking extends over several years. There is a dramatic and rapidly changing picture of disordered mental activity, with clouding of consciousness, disorientation in time and place, and impairment of recent memory. Perceptual disturbances include misinterpretations of sensory stimuli and vivid hallucinations which are usually visual, but sometimes in other modalities. There is severe agitation, with restlessness, shouting, and evident fear. Insomnia is prolonged. The hands are grossly tremulous and sometimes pick up imaginary objects, and truncal ataxia occurs. Autonomic disturbances include sweating, fever, tachycardia, raised blood pressure, and dilatation of pupils. Blood testing shows leucocytosis, a raised ESR and impaired liver function. Dehydration and electrolyte disturbance are characteristic.

The condition lasts three or four days, the symptoms being characteristically worse at night. If often ends with deep prolonged sleep from which the patient awakens with no symptoms and little or no memory of the period of delirium.

(iii) Toxic or nutritional conditions

These include **Korsakov's psychosis** and **Wernicke's encephalopathy**, which are described in the chapter on Organic Psychiatry (Chapter 11), and **alcoholic dementia**, which is described next.

Alcoholic dementia   In the past there has been disagreement whether excessive alcohol intake can cause dementia. This doubt may have arisen because patients with general intellectual defects have been wrongly diagnosed as having Korsakov's psychosis (Cutting 1978). However, it is now generally agreed that chronic alcohol abuse can cause dementia.

Recently, attention has shifted to the related question of whether chronic alcohol abuse can cause brain atrophy. This question has been studied mainly by radiographic methods, originally air encephalography (Brewer and Perrett 1971), and subsequently computed tomography. Both techniques show enlarged ventricles and widened sulci in a third to two-thirds of alcoholic patients (e.g. Fox *et al.* 1976; Carlen *et al.* 1978; Bergman *et al.* 1980). Such changes have been reported among alcoholics who have been abstinent for an average of seven months (Ron *et al.* 1980; Lishman *et al.* 1980). However, longitudinal studies suggest a gradual improvement with more prolonged abstinence (Carlen *et al.* 1978; Ron *et al.* 1982).

Neuropathological studies can provide more direct evidence of cerebral atrophy. Few have been reported. In one study, comparing 25 alcoholics with 44 controls, measurements of the 'pericerebral space' (which represents the space between brain and skull) were greater in the alcoholics. This was true of those without pathological signs of Wernicke's encephalopathy as well as those with such signs (Harper and Kril 1985).

If cerebral atrophy does occur in excessive drinkers, it is not necessarily due solely to a direct toxic effect of alcohol on the brain. Part or all of the effect might be secondary to liver disease, and an association has been reported between the latter and cerebral atrophy (e.g. Acker *et al.* 1982; Harper and Kril 1985). Such an association might indicate that, as a consequence of liver disease, cerebral atrophy is caused in some way by interference with the supply of nutrients to the brain. However, the association could also arise because people who are vulnerable to the effects of alcohol on the liver are also vulnerable to its effects on the brain.

In any case, the association was not confirmed by Lee *et al.* (1979) in a study of young alcoholic men.

Atrophy of the vermis of the cerebellum has been found at autopsy in about a third of patients with chronic alcoholism (Harper and Kril 1985). (The corresponding clinical evidence of cerebellar dysfunction was referred to on p. 515).

Studies of this kind suggest that alcoholic dementia is more common than was previously supposed, and it should be searched for carefully in every problem drinker. Older patients appear to be more at risk than younger ones with a similar length of heavy drinking; and those who have been drinking without respite seem to be more at risk than people who have periods in which they reduce their drinking [see Ron (1977) and Thomas (1986) for reviews].

(iv) Associated psychiatric disorders

Personality deterioration

As the patient becomes more and more concerned with the need to obtain alcohol, there is increasing self-centredness, a lack of consideration for others, and a decline in standards of conduct. Responsibilities at home and work are evaded, and behaviour may become dishonest and deceitful.

Affective disorder

The relationship between alcohol consumption and mood is complex. On the one hand some depressed patients drink excessively in an attempt to improve their mood; on the other hand excess drinking may induce persistent depression or anxiety (Gibson and Becker 1973; Woodruff *et al.* 1973).

Suicidal behaviour

Suicide rates amongst alcoholics are higher than among non-alcoholics of the same age. Kessel and Grossman (1965) found that 8 per cent of alcoholics admitted for treatment killed themselves within a few years of discharge. Reports from a number of countries suggest that 6 per cent to 20 per cent of alcoholics end their lives by suicide (Ritson 1977). Suicide among alcoholics is discussed further on p. 482.

Impaired psychosexual function

Erectile dysfunction and delayed ejaculation are common. These difficulties may be worsened when drinking leads to marital estrangement, or if the wife develops a revulsion for intercourse with an inebriated partner.

Pathological jealousy

Possibly as a result of sexual dysfunction, excessive drinkers may develop the delusion that the partner is being unfaithful. This syndrome of pathological jealousy is described on p. 334. Although it is a striking complication, delusional jealousy is less common than a non-delusional suspicious attitude to the spouse.

Alcoholic hallucinosis

This is characterized by auditory hallucinations, usually voices uttering insults or threats, occurring in clear consciousness. The patient is usually distressed by these experiences, appearing anxious and restless.

There has been considerable controversy about the aetiology of the condition. Some follow Kraepelin and Bonhöffer in regarding it as organically determined; others follow Bleuler in supposing that it is related to schizophrenia.

Benedetti (1952) made a retrospective survey of 113 cases of alcoholic hallucinosis and divided them in 90 cases of less than six months' duration (acute cases) and the remaining chronic group. Among the former he found no evidence of a link with schizophrenia as judged by family history. However, he did find evidence of an organic cause, in that about half had experienced memory disorders. Despite this the condition cleared up without residual defect. Among the cases that had lasted six months, nearly all went on for much longer, despite abstinence. Half developed the typical picture of schizophrenia, and half developed amnesic syndromes or dementia. In their family histories, these chronic patients were intermediate between the acute cases and typical schizophrenic patients. Of course, this study cannot tell us whether these patients would have developed schizophrenia if they had never taken alcohol.

Some authors have held that alcoholic hallucinosis is not essentially different from the hallucinations occurring in excessive drinkers in the 24–48 hours after alcohol withdrawal (Knott and Beard 1971). It is true that auditory hallucinations may occur in simple withdrawal states (Hershon 1977) and may accompany the visual hallucinations of delirium tremens (Gross *et al.* 1971). However, they are fleeting and disorganized, in contrast to the persistent organized voices experienced in alcoholic hallucinosis.

Cutting (1978) has concluded that there is a small group of patients who have a true alcoholic hallucinosis, but that many of those who receive this diagnosis have depressive symptoms or first-rank symptoms of schizophrenia. Clinical experience also points to this conclusion.

Social damage

Excessive drinking is liable to cause profound social disruption particularly in the family. **Marital and family tension** is virtually inevitable (Orford 1979). The divorce rate amongst heavy drinkers is high; and the wives of such men are likely to become anxious, depressed, and socially isolated

(Wilkins 1974); the husbands of 'battered wives' frequently drink heavily; and some women admitted to hospital because of self-poisoning blame their husband's drinking. The home atmosphere is often detrimental to the children, because of quarrelling and violence, and a drunken parent provides a poor role model. Children of heavy drinkers are at risk of developing emotional or behaviour disorders, and of performing badly at school.

At **work**, the heavy drinker often progresses through declining efficiency, lower grade jobs, and repeated dismissals to lasting unemployment. There is also a strong association between **road accidents** and alcohol abuse. In the United Kingdon, a third of drivers killed on the road have blood alcohol levels above the statutory limit; in the hours around midnight the figure rises to 50 per cent; and on Saturday night to 75 per cent (Department of the Environment 1976). In one series, a third of drivers arrested for driving under the influence of alcohol had raised gamma-glutamyl-transpeptidase activity, suggesting chronic alcohol abuse (Dunbar *et al.* 1985). The toll of road accident deaths involving alcohol is particularly high in the young (Havard 1977).

Excessive drinking is also associated with **crime**, mainly petty offences, such as larceny, but also fraud, sexual offences, and crimes of violence including murder. Studies of recidivist prisoners in England and Wales have shown that many of them had serious drinking problems before imprisonment. This is particularly so for men on short sentences (Edwards *et al.* 1971). It is not easy to know how far alcohol causes the criminal behaviour and how far it is just part of the life-style of the criminal. This question is discussed further on p. 867.

Excessive alcohol consumption and problem drinking

Having described alcohol dependence and alcohol-related disabilities, we are now in a position to explain the terms excessive alcohol consumption and problem drinking. The concept of **excessive alcohol consumption** can be defined in relation to a significant risk of developing alcohol dependence and alcohol-related disability, and expressed in units of alcohol. We have seen that there is reason to suppose that anyone may become dependent on alcohol if he or she drinks a sufficiently large amount for long enough. Unfortunately, no exact threshold can be specified, because relevant data from research are inadequate.

According to the Royal College of Physicians (1987, p. 108) 'safe levels' are up to 21 units per week for men and up to 14 units per week for women provided that the whole amount is not taken in one bout, and provided there are occasional drink-free days. The same report suggests that 'hazardous' levels are between 21–49 units per week for men, and 14–35 units per week for women. 'Dangerous' levels are above these limits. According to the Royal College of Psychiatrists (1986 p. 137), 'evidence suggests that the potential for personal harm increases greatly above 50 units of alcohol per week for men (400 g alcohol) and 35 units per week for women (280 g alcohol)'. The report goes on to recommend that consumption should be 'well below these limits'.

The term **problem drinker** has been proposed to refer to people whose repeated heavy drinking causes alcohol-related disability (Department of Health and Social Security 1978*a*). A problem drinker may or may not be dependent on alcohol.

Before the terms excessive alcohol consumption and problem drinking can be considered, it is necessary to explain the units in which alcohol consumption is assessed. In everyday life, this is done by referring to conventional measures such as pints of beer or glasses of wine. These measures have the advantage of being widely understood, but they are imprecise because both beers and wines vary in strength (see Table 14.4). Alternatively, consumption can be measured as the amount of alcohol (expressed in grams). This measure is precise, and useful for scientific work, but difficult for many people to relate to everyday measures. For this reason, the concept of a unit of alcohol has been introduced for use in health education. A unit can be related to everyday measures for it corresponds to half a pint of beer, one glass of table wine, one conventional glass of sherry or port, and one single bar measure of spirits. It can also be related to amounts of alcohol (see Table 14.4); thus on this measure a can of beer (450 ml) contains nearly 1.5 units, a bottle of table wine contains about 7 units, a bottle of spirits about 30 units, and one unit is about 8 g of alcohol.

Epidemiological aspects of excessive drinking

Epidemiological methods can be applied to the following questions concerning excessive drinking:

1. What is the annual per capita consumption of alcohol for a nation as a whole; how does this vary over the years and between nations?

2. What are the drinking habits of different groups of people within a defined population?

3. How many people in defined population are problem drinkers?

Table 14.4. Alcohol content of some beverages

Beverages	Approximate alcohol content (per cent)	Grams alcohol per conventional measure	Units of alcohol per conventional measure (approximate)
1. *Beers and cider*			
Ordinary beer	3	16 per pint 12 per can	2 per pint 1.5 per can
Strong beer	5.5	32 per pint 24 per can	4 per pint 3 per can
Extra strong beer	7	40 per pint 32 per can	5 per pint 4 per can
Cider	4	24 per pint	3 per pint
Strong cider	6	32 per pint	4 per pint
2. *Wines*			
Table wines	8–10	8 per glass 56 per bottle	1 per glass 7 per bottle
Fortified wines (sherry, port, vermouth)	13–16	8 per measure 120 per bottle	1 per measure 15 per bottle
3. *Spirits* (whisky, gin, brandy, vodka)	32	8–12 per single measure* 240 per bottle	1–1.5 per measure* 30 per bottle

Adapted from the Royal College of Physicians (1987, p. 6).
* Somewhat larger measures are used in Scotland and Northern Ireland (12 gram).

4. How does problem drinking vary with such characteristics as sex, age, occupation, social class, and marital status?

Unfortunately, we lack reliable answers to these questions, partly because different investigators have used different methods of defining and identifying heavy drinking and 'alcoholism', and partly because excessive drinkers tend to be evasive about the amounts they drink and the symptoms they experience.

In Great Britain, the average consumption of alcohol per person over the age of 15 years, for the year 1983, was equivalent to almost 9 litres of absolute alcohol, made up of an average of 138 litres (243 pints) of beer, 12 litres of wine, 7 litres of cider, and 5 litres of spirits, with the rest derived from home-brewed beverages (see Royal College of Physicians 1987, p. 20).

This amount of alcohol consumed in Britain has increased substantially in the post-war period. Thus the percentage rise in consumption per capita from 1950 to 1979 has been estimated as 63 per cent (Walsh, 1982, p. 21). Similar increases have occurred in 20 of 21 European countries. The only decrease (of 7 per cent) was reported in France, a country in which alcohol consumption was exceptionally high in 1950 (at 22 litres of absolute alcohol per person aged 15 or above, per annum). Increases of over 300 per cent were reported from Germany and The Netherlands (Walsh 1982, p. 21).

These changes should be seen in a historical perspective. In Great Britain between 1860 and 1900 the consumption of alcohol was about 10 litres of absolute alcohol per head of population over 15 years old. Consumption then fell until the early 1930s (reaching about 4 litres per person over 15 years per annum). Consumption then increased slowly until the 1950s when it began to rise more rapidly (see Royal College of Psychiatrists 1986, p. 107).

These changes have been accompanied by alterations in the kinds of alcoholic beverages consumed. In Britain in 1900, beer and spirits accounted for most of the alcohol drunk; in 1980, the consumption of wine had risen about four times and accounted for almost as much of the consumption of alcohol as did spirits—though most alcohol was still consumed as beer (see Royal College of Physicians 1987, p. 20).

The drinking habits in different groups

Surveys of drinking behaviour generally depend on self-reports, a method that is open to obvious errors. Enquiries of this kind have been conducted in London (Edwards *et al.* 1972), in Scotland (Dight 1976), and in England and Wales (Wilson 1980), as well as in the United States (see Lex 1985).

Such studies show that the highest consumption of alcohol is generally amongst young men who are unmarried, separated, or divorced. Indeed, Dight (1976) found that 3 per cent of the population, mostly single men in their late teens or twenties, were responsible for 30 per cent of all alcohol consumption in Scotland. In recent years consumption amongst women has risen (Shaw 1980).

The prevalence of problem drinking

This can be estimated in three ways: from hospital admission rates; by the use of Jellinek's formula; and by surveys in the general population.

Hospital admission rates

These give an inadequate measure of prevalence because a large proportion of problem drinkers do not enter hospital. In the United Kingdom psychiatric admissions for alcohol problems account for 10 per cent of all psychiatric admissions. In France, Germany, and Eire the figure is almost 30 per cent. In the United Kingdom there has been a 30-fold increase in psychiatric hospital admission rates for problem drinking in the past 30 years, but this may reflect changes more in the provision of services than in prevalence.

Jellinek's formula

This was proposed to overcome the difficulties in estimating the numbers of alcoholics. Jellinek proposed that the frequency of cirrhosis of the liver should be used as an indirect measure. The formula proposed was $R \ (PD)/K$, in which D is the number of cirrhosis deaths in a given year and place: P is the percentage of such deaths due to alcoholism: K is the percentage of all alcoholics with complications who die from cirrhosis: R is the ratio of all alcoholics to alcoholics with complications. On the basis of long-term trends and mortality rates in different populations, it was assumed that the relationship between problem drinking and cirrhosis was fairly constant (Jolliffe and Jellinek 1941). Using the Jellinek formula, in 1951 the World Health Organization made its well known estimate that there were 350 000 alcoholics in England and Wales.

The Jellinek formula has been much criticized (e.g. Popham 1956; Brenner 1959), mainly on the grounds that the supposed constants K, P, and R are subject to change. Jellinek (1959) himself suggested that the formula should be abandoned, and this is now widely accepted.

General population surveys

One method is to ascertain cases of problem drinking by seeking information from general practitioners, social workers, probation officers, health visitors, and other agents who are likely to come in contact with heavy drinkers (Prys Williams and Glatt 1966). Another approach is the community survey in which samples of people are asked about the amount they drink and whether they experience symptoms. For example, in the London suburb of Camberwell, Edwards *et al.* (1972) questioned 928 people and found 25 'problem drinkers' and five who were alcohol dependent.

Problem drinking and population characteristics

Sex

For many years in the United Kingdom, the ratio of male to female 'alcoholics' has been five to one. Recently it seems that alcohol problems have increased substantially, and perhaps disproportionately, amongst women (Shaw 1980). Thus convictions for drunkenness and for drunken driving offences have risen more rapidly in women than men (though this may be due to changes in arrest policy) and so have hospital admissions for alcohol problems (see Smith 1981; Eagles and Besson 1985).

Age

We have seen that the heaviest drinkers are men in their late teens or early twenties. There has been disturbing evidence of increasing drinking and drunkenness amongst adolescents. In England and Wales, convictions for drunkenness in people aged under 16 more than doubled between 1964 and 1976. High levels of drunkenness were found in a study of over 7000 English adolescents (Hawker 1978) whilst evidence of serious drinking problems was found amongst a large proportion of 15- to 16-year-olds in Scotland (Plant *et al.* 1982).

Occupation

The risk of problem drinking is much increased among several occupational groups: chefs, kitchen porters, barmen, and brewery workers, who have easy access to alcohol; executives and salesmen who entertain on expense accounts; actors and entertainers; seamen; and journalists and printers. Doctors are another important group with an increased risk of problem drinking, and they are often particularly difficult to help (see Murray 1976; Rawnsley 1984).

The causes of drinking and alcohol dependence

Despite much research, surprisingly little is known about the cause of excessive drinking and alcohol dependence. At one time it was supposed that certain people were particularly predisposed, either through personality or an innate biochemical anomaly. Nowadays this simple notion of specific predisposition is no longer held. Instead problem drinking is thought to result from a variety of interacting factors, which can be divided into individual factors and those in society.

Individual factors

Genetic factors

Some excessive drinkers have a family history of excessive drinking and, compared with excessive drinkers who do not have such a family history, they develop dependence at an earlier age and more severely. These findings apply particularly to men, the evidence about women being less certain (Latcham 1985). If these findings are partly the result of genetic factors (rather than social influences in the family) rates of excessive drinking should be higher in monozygotic (MZ) than dizygotic (DZ) twins, but the results of MZ/DZ comparisons are conflicting (see Goodwin 1985). However, some support for a genetic explanation comes from investigations of adoptees. In an adoption study in Denmark, drinking problems were nearly four times more likely in the adopted-away sons of 'alcoholic' biological parents than in the adopted-away sons of non-alcoholic biological parents (Goodwin *et al.* 1973). Similar findings have been reported from America (Cadoret and Gath 1978), and Sweden (Bohman 1978). Such studies suggest a genetic mechanism but do not indicate its nature.

Further analysis of the Swedish adoption data suggest two separate kinds of inheritance. In some cases there appears to be a large genetic component in aetiology, with severe 'alcoholism' passing from fathers to sons, the women seldom being affected. In other cases, there appears to be a smaller genetic component, with milder drinking problems affecting both men and women in the family (Cloninger *et al.* 1981; Bohman *et al.* 1981). This work needs confirmation.

If a genetic component to aetiology were confirmed, it would still be necessary to discover the mechanism. The latter might be biochemical, involving the metabolism of alcohol, or psychological, involving personality. [See Goodwin (1985) for a review of genetic factors in 'alcoholism'.]

Biochemical factors

Several possible biochemical factors have been suggested, including abnormalities in alcohol dehydrogenase or in neurotransmitter mechanisms. So far there is no firm evidence that any biochemical factors play a causal role.

Learning factors

It has been reported that children tend to follow their parents' drinking patterns (Hawker 1978), and that from an early age boys tend to be encouraged to drink more than girls (Jahoda and Cramond 1972). Nevertheless, it is not uncommon to meet people who are abstainers although their parents drank heavily. It has been suggested that learning processes may contribute in a more specific way to the development of alcohol dependence through the repeated experience of withdrawal symptoms. On this view, relief of withdrawal symptoms by alcohol may act as a reinforcer for further drinking.

Personality factors

Little progress has been made in identifying personality factors that contribute to alcohol dependence. In clinical practice it is common to find that alcohol problems are associated with chronic anxiety, a pervading sense of inferiority, or self-indulgent tendencies. However, many people with personality problems of this kind do not resort to excessive drinking.

It seems likely that if personality is important it is because it increases vulnerability to other causal factors.

Psychiatric disorder

Although not a common cause of problem drinking, psychiatric disorder should always be borne in mind, as it may be treatable. Some patients with depressive disorders take to alcohol in the mistaken hope that it will alleviate low mood. Those with anxiety states, including social phobias, are also at risk. Alcohol dependence occasionally occurs in patients with brain disease or schizophrenia.

Alcohol consumption in society

In recent years there has been increasing interest in the idea that rates of alcohol dependence and alcohol-related disability are related to the general level of alcohol consumption in a society. Previously it had been supposed that levels of intake amongst excessive drinkers were independent of the amounts taken by moderate drinkers. The French demographer Ledermann (1956) challenged this idea, proposing instead that the distribution of consumption within a homogeneous population follows a logarithmic normal curve. If this is the case, an increase in the average consumption must inevitably be accompanied by an increase in the number of people who drink an amount that is harmful.

The mathematical details of Ledermann's work have been heavily criticized (for example, Miller and Agnew 1974; Duffy 1977). None the less there are striking correlations between average annual consumption in a society and several indices of alcohol-related damage among its members (see Smith 1981). For this reason, despite the criticisms of Ledermann's work, it is now widely accepted that the proportion of a population drinking excessively is largely determined by the average consumption of that population.

What then determines the average level of drinking within a nation? Economic, formal, and informal controls must be considered. The **economic control** is the price of alcohol. There is now ample evidence, from the United Kingdom and other countries, that the real price of alcohol profoundly influences a nation's drinking (see, for example, Nielsen and Sorensen 1979). Also heavy drinkers as well as moderate drinkers reduce their consumption when the tax on alcohol is increased (see Kendell *et al.* 1983).

The main **formal controls** are the licensing laws. It is difficult to be sure how these affect drinking behaviour, because results in different countries have been conflicting. For example, in Finland in 1969 a new law led to greatly increased availability of alcohol in restaurants, cafés, and shops. This was followed by a 47 per cent increase in consumption. In Scotland recent relaxation of licensing hours did not apparently lead to a large increase in consumption, but increasing the availability of alcoholic drinks in shops seemed to be associated with greater consumption (see Royal College of Psychiatrists 1986, p. 117).

Informal controls are the customs and moral beliefs in a society that determine who should drink, in what circumstances, at what time of day, and to what extent. Some communities seem to protect their members from alcoholism despite general availability of alcohol; for example, among Jews, drinking problems are uncommon even in countries with high rates in the rest of the community.

Recognition of the problem drinker

Only a small proportion of problem drinkers in the community are known to specialized agencies (Edwards *et al.* 1973), and many opportunities to detect problem drinkers are missed. When special efforts are made to screen patients in medical and surgical wards, between 10 and 30 per cent are found to have serious drinking problems, the rates being highest in accident and emergency wards (for example, Barcha *et al.* 1968; Jarman and Kellet 1979; Holt *et al.* 1980).

Problem drinking often goes undetected because excessive drinkers conceal their drinking. However doctors and other professionals often do not ask the right questions. It should be a standard practice to ask all patients—medical, surgical, and psychiatric—about their alcohol consumption. It is useful to ask four questions: Have you ever felt you ought to cut down on your drinking? Have people annoyed you by criticizing your drinking? Have you ever felt guilty about your drinking? Have you ever had a drink first thing in the morning (an 'eye-opener') to steady your nerves or get rid of a hangover? These questions are known as 'CAGE', from the initial letters of the words cut, annoyed, guilty, and eye-opener. Two or more positive replies are said to identify problem drinkers (Mayfield *et al.* 1974). Some patients will give false answers, but others find these questions provide an opportunity to reveal their problems.

The next requirement is for the doctor to be suspicious about 'at risk' factors. In general practice, problem drinking may come to light as a result of problems in the marriage and family, at work, with finances, or the law (Hore and Wilkins 1976). The wife may complain of the husband's boastfulness, lack of consideration, sexual dysfunction, or aggressiveness towards herself and the children. The problem drinker is likely to have many more days off work than the moderate drinker, and repeated absences on Monday are highly suggestive. The occupations at risk (see p. 526) should also be remembered.

In hospital practice, the problem drinker may be noticed if he develops withdrawal symptoms after admission. Florid delirium tremens is obvious, but milder forms may be mistaken for an acute organic syndrome for example in pneumonia or post-operatively.

In both general and hospital practice, 'at-risk' factors include physical disorders that may be alcohol-related. Common examples are gastritis, peptic ulcer, and liver disease, but others such as neuropathy and seizures should be borne in mind. Repeated accidents should also arouse suspicion. Psychiatric 'at risk' factors include anxiety, depression, erratic moods, impaired concentration, memory lapses, and sexual dysfunction. In all cases of deliberate self-harm, problem drinking should be considered.

If at-risk factors raise suspicion, or if the patient hints at a drink problem, the next step is to ask tactful but persistent questions to confirm the diagnosis. The doctor should find out how much the patient drinks on a typical 'drinking day', starting with the amount he takes in the second half of the day, and working back to the earlier part of the day. The patient should be asked how he feels if he goes without drink for a day or two and how he feels on waking. Gradually a picture can be built up of what and how much a patient drinks throughout a typical day. Similarly, tactful enquiry should be made about social effects of drinking, such as declining efficiency at work, missed promotion, accidents, lateness, absences, and extended meal breaks. The patient should be asked about any difficulties in relationship with the spouse and children. In this way, the patient may be led step by step to recognize and accept that he has a drinking problem which he has previously denied. Once this stage is reached, the doctor should be in a position to enquire about the typical features of dependency, and the full range of physical, psychological, and social disabilities described in preceding sections.

Laboratory tests

Several laboratory tests can be used to detect heavy drinkers, though none gives an unequivocal answer. This is because the more sensitive tests can give 'false positives' when there is disease of the liver, heart, kidneys, or blood, or if enzyme-inducing drugs have been taken, such as anticonvulsants, steroids, or barbiturates. However, abnormal values point to the possibility of alcohol abuse. Only the three most useful tests are considered here.

Gamma-glutamyl-transpeptidase (GGT)

Estimations of GGT in blood provide a useful screening test (Rosalki *et al.* 1970). The level is raised in about 80 per cent of problem drinkers, both men and women, whether or not there is demonstrable liver damage. The heavier the drinking, the greater the rise in GGT.

Mean corpuscular volume (MCV)

MCV is raised above the normal value in about 60 per cent of alcohol-dependent people, and more commonly in women than in men. If other causes are excluded, a raised MCV is a strong pointer to excessive drinking. Moreover, it takes several weeks to return to normal after abstinence.

Blood alcohol concentration

A high concentration does not distinguish between an isolated episode of heavy drinking and chronic abuse. If, however, a person is not intoxicated when the blood alcohol concentration is well above the legal limit of driving, he is likely to be unusually tolerant of alcohol. This tolerance suggests persistent heavy drinking. Alcohol is eliminated rather slowly from the blood and can be detected in appreciable amounts for 24 hours after an episode of heavy drinking.

The treatment of the problem drinker

Early detection

Early detection of problem drinking is important, because treatment of established cases is difficult, particularly when dependence is present. Many cases can be detected early by general practitioners, physicians, and surgeons when patients seek treatment for another problem. If counselling is given to such patients during their stay in a medical ward, their alcohol consumption is found to be reduced a year later (Chick *et al.* 1985).

The treatment plan

The assessment should include a full drinking history and an appraisal of current medical, psychological, and social problems. An intensive and searching enquiry often helps the patient gain a new recognition and understanding of his problem, and this is the basis of treatment. It is usually desirable to involve the husband or wife in the assessment, both to obtain additional information and to give the spouse a chance to unburden feelings.

An explicit treatment plan should be worked out with the patient (and spouse if appropriate). There should be specific goals and the patient should be required to take responsibility for realizing them. These goals should deal not only with the drinking problem, but also with any accompanying problems in health, marriage, job, and social adjustment. In the early stages they should be short-term and achievable; for example, complete abstinence for two weeks. In this way the patient can be rewarded by early achievement.

Longer-term goals can be set as treatment progresses. These will be concerned with trying to change factors that precipitate or maintain excessive drinking, such as tensions in the family. In drawing up this treatment plan, an important decision is whether to aim at total abstinence or at limited consumption of alcohol (controlled drinking).

Total abstinence versus controlled drinking

The disease model of alcoholism proposes that an alcohol-dependent person must become totally abstinent and remain so, since a single drink would lead to relapse. Alcoholics Anonymous have made this a tenet of their approach to treatment. In 1962 Davies reported that seven alcoholics who had failed to abstain when asked to do so, had nevertheless succeeded in drinking in a controlled and moderate way. This finding was confirmed by Orford and Edwards (1977) and in the influential American Rand report (Armor *et al.* 1976). Several writers have suggested that controlled drinking might be a suitable goal for people dependent on alcohol (Pattison 1966; Orford 1973; Clark 1976.) In 1973, Sobell and Sobell (1973*b*) tested the idea by randomly assigning patients to 'non-drinking' and 'controlled drinking' groups. They found no difference in outcome one year later. However, Ewing and Rouse (1976) did not confirm this finding. More recently a 29–34-year follow-up of Davies's original cases showed that all but two had relapsed into uncontrolled drinking (Edwards 1985).

The issue of abstinence versus controlled drinking remains unresolved. A prevalent view is that controlled drinking may be a feasible goal for people aged under 40, whose problem has been detected early, and who are not heavily dependent or damaged; whilst abstinence is the better goal for those aged over 40, who are heavily dependent and have incurred physical damage, and who have attempted controlled drinking unsuccessfully (Ritson 1982). If controlled drinking is to be attempted, then the doctor should advise the patient clearly about safe levels (see p. 521).

Withdrawal from alcohol

For patients with the dependence syndrome, withdrawal from alcohol is an important first stage in treatment which should be carried out carefully. In the less severe cases, withdrawal may be at home provided there is someone to look after the patient. The general practitioner or health visitor should visit daily to check the patient's physical state and supervise medication. However, any patient likely to have severe withdrawal symptoms should be admitted to hospital.

Sedative drugs are generally prescribed to reduce withdrawal symptoms. Chlormethiazole or chlordiazepoxide are often used. Chlormethiazole may be prescribed in either of two ways: flexibly according to the patient's symptoms, or on a fixed six-hourly regime of gradually decreasing dosage over six to nine days. It should not be prescribed for more than a few days because it can itself become a drug of dependence. Preparations and dosages of chlormethiazole are subject to revision, and before prescribing it the clinician should consult the current edition of the *British national formulary* or equivalent work of reference. Chlormethiazole should not be given to patients who may continue to take alcohol, since the combination may cause fatal respiratory depression. According to the severity of symptoms, chlordiazepoxide may be given in doses of 50 mg or 100 mg by intramuscular injection repeated if necessary in two to four hours. Oral dosage may be 40 to 100 mg daily in divided doses. If convulsions occur, large doses of chlordiazepoxide may be used. Vitamin supplements are often given, and in some countries anticonvulsants, glucose, and magnesium infusions are added. During the first five days, there should be a daily check on the patient's temperature, pulse, blood pressure, hydration, level of consciousness, and orientation.

Withdrawal from alcohol is the main purpose of so-called **detoxification units**. In some places these units are used mainly for chronic drunkenness offenders who have little prospect of progressing to a treatment programme. In other places patients come mainly from general practitioners and a substantial proportion move on to further treatment (see Hamilton *et al.* 1977; Arroyave *et al.* 1980).

Informing the patient

Information about the effects of heavy drinking is an important first stage in treatment. The information given should relate to the specific problems of the individual patient, both the problems that have occurred already and those likely to develop if drinking continues.

Psychological treatment

Group therapy

This is probably the most widely used treatment for problem drinkers. Regular meetings are attended by about 10 patients and one or more members of staff. The aim is to enable patients to observe their own problems mirrored in other problem drinkers and to work out better ways of coping with their problems. They gain confidence whilst members of the group jointly strive to reorganize their lives without alcohol. Group therapy is further discussed on pp. 710–14.

Supportive therapy

If group therapy is not available or not acceptable to the patient, individual psychological support may be provided by a psychiatrist or social worker. The aim is to help the patient to cope with problems in day-to-day living without drinking to excess. Supportive therapy is discussed on p. 704.

Behaviour therapy

Recently there has been increasing interest in behavioural methods which tackle drinking behaviour itself rather than underlying psychological problems. Patients may be shown films of themselves when drunk; taught to drink without gulping rapidly; and shown how to identify stimuli to drinking and find other ways of dealing with them. In a clinical trial of these methods Sobell and Sobell (1973*b*) found that outcome on many measures was better than with conventional methods. Much more evaluative work needs to be done before these time-consuming methods are brought into everyday practice.

Medication

Apart from the management of withdrawal discussed above, drug treatment plays only a small part in the management of excessive drinking. None the less drug treatment is described at some length here because it carries certain risks and may cause unpleasant side-effects. **Disulfiram** (Antabuse) is sometimes prescribed as a deterrent to impulsive drinking. It acts by blocking the oxidation of alcohol so that acetaldehyde accumulates. If the patient drinks alcohol he experiences unpleasant flushing of the face, headache, choking sensations, rapid pulse, and feelings of anxiety. The drug is not without risk, occasionally causing cardiac irregularities, and rarely cardiovascular collapse. It also has unpleasant side-effects in the absence of alcohol: a metallic taste in the mouth; gastrointestinal symptoms; dermatitis; peripheral neuropathy; urinary frequency; impotence; and toxic confusional states. Treatment with disulfiram should not be started until at least 12 hours after the last ingestion of alcohol. On the first day the patient is warned carefully about the dangers of drinking alcohol while taking the drug, and then given four tablets each of 200 mg and told not to take any alcohol whatever. The dosage is then reduced by one tablet a day over three days, the maintenance dose being half to one tablet a day.

Citrated calcium carbimide is used in the same way. Compared with disulfiram, it is more rapidly absorbed and excreted, induces a milder reaction with alcohol, and has fewer side-effects. Details of the dosage will be found in standard works of reference.

Some clinicians find these drugs valuable (see Costello 1975; Armor *et al.* 1976). In our view they have a limited use for a few patients and then only as an adjunct to other treatment. They are most suited to patients who are compliant in treatment, attend regularly, and have high expectations of improvement (Kitson 1977)—just the patients who are most likely to abstain without them.

Treatment in primary care

An Advisory Committee on Alcoholism (Kessel 1978) concluded that the treatment of alcoholism should be undertaken increasingly by primary care teams. General practitioners are well placed to provide early treatment and they are likely to know the patient and his family well. It is often effective if the general practitioner gives simple advice in a frank, matter-of-fact way, but with tact and understanding. This is followed by supportive treatment as described above. Barbor *et al.* (1986) reviewed published reports about this kind of treatment and concluded that they have a modest effect sufficient to recommend them as the first approach to the treatment of problem drinkers.

Other agencies concerned with drinking problems

Alcoholics Anonymous (AA)

This is a self-help organization which came to Britain from the USA in 1947. Members attend group meetings usually twice weekly on a long-term basis. In crisis they can obtain immediate help from other members by telephone. The organization works on the firm belief that abstinence must be complete. At present there are about 1200 groups in the United Kingdom.

Alcoholics Anonymous does not appeal to all problem drinkers because the meetings involve an emotional confession of problems. However, the organization is of great value to some problem drinkers, and anyone with a drink problem should be encouraged to try it. The activities of Alcoholics Anonymous are described by Robinson (1979).

Al-Anon

This is a parallel organization providing support for the spouses of excessive drinkers, and *Al-Ateen* does the same for their teenage children.

Councils on alcoholism

These are voluntary bodies that co-ordinate available services in an area and train counsellors. They advise problem drinkers and their families where to obtain help, and provide social activities for those who have recovered.

Hostels

These are intended mainly for homeless problem drinkers. They provide rehabilitation and counselling. Usually abstinence is a condition of residence.

Results of treatment

A number of investigations have combined results from different treatment centres. The Rand Report (Armor *et al.* 1976) describes a prospective study of 45 treatment centres in the USA, of which eight were followed for 18 months. Only a quarter of the patients remained abstinent for six months, and fewer than 10 per cent for 18 months. However, at 18 months 70 per cent of patients had reduced their consumption of alcohol. Patients with a better outcome had received more intensive treatment but the form of treatment made no difference.

In a controlled trial with 100 male alcoholics, Edwards *et al.* (1977*b*) compared simple advice with intensive treatment that included introductions to Alcoholics Anonymous, medication, repeated interviews, counselling for their wives, and, where appropriate, in-patient treatment as well. The advice group received a three-hour assessment together with a single session of counselling with the spouse present. The two groups were well matched. After 12 months there was no significant difference between them in drinking behaviour, subjective ratings, or social adjustment (see also Orford and Edwards 1977).

Probably outcome depends as much upon factors in the patient as upon the particular treatment. There is some disagreement as to what these factors are but the following generally predict a better prognosis whatever treatment is used: good insight into the nature of the problems; social stability in the form of a fixed abode, family support, and ability to keep a job; and ability to control impulsiveness, to defer gratification, and to form deep emotional relationships.

Prevention of alcohol dependence

In seeking to prevent problem drinking and alcohol dependence, two approaches are possible. The first is to improve the help and guidance available to the individual as already described. The second is to introduce social changes likely to affect drinking patterns in the population as a whole. It is with this second group that we are concerned here. Consumption in a population might be reduced by four methods:

1. *The pricing of alcoholic beverages*. Putting up the price of alcohol would probably reduce the consumption.

2. *Advertising*. Controlling or abolishing the advertising of alcoholic drinks might be another preventive measure, but there is little evidence that it would work. A total press and television ban in British Columbia made little difference (Smart and Cutler 1976). Moreover, there is a large alcohol problem in the Soviet Union, where there is no advertising in the Western sense.

3. *Controls on sale*. Another preventive measure might be to control sales of alcohol by limiting hours or banning sales in supermarkets. It is known that relaxation of restrictions led to increased sales in Finland and some other countries, but it does not follow that increased restrictions would reduce established rates of drinking.

4. *Health education*. It is not known whether education about alcohol abuse is effective. Little is known as to how attitudes are formed or changed. Although education about alcohol seems desirable, it cannot be assumed that classroom lectures or mass media propaganda would alter attitudes. Indeed Plant *et al.* (1985) concluded, from a follow-up study of teenagers, that education had no significant effect on their drinking habits.

Abuse of psychoactive substances

Epidemiology

Little is known for certain about the prevalence of different types of drug dependence. In the United Kingdom, information comes from several sources: criminal statistics, mainly based on offences involving the misuse of drugs and thefts from chemists shops; hospital admissions; Home Office statistics; and special surveys. Unfortunately none of these sources is satisfactory, since much drug use goes undetected.

Reported prevalence rates vary widely, partly because different methods of ascertainment have been used. However, a few findings are agreed. Rates are high in disadvantaged areas of large cities. Adolescents are at risk, particularly around school leaving age. Amongst attenders at drug dependence clinics in big cities, there is a high proportion of unemployed with few stable relationships and leading disorganized lives. On the other hand many young drug abusers remain in employment and their drug taking is a passing phase (Plant 1975).

The prevalence of drug abuse among people under 20 years of age rose steeply in the mid and late 1960s. It may have declined again in the 1970s but there is concern that it has increased again in the 1980s.

A study of heroin abuse in an English new town illustrates the way in which drug abuse spreads. De Alarcón (1969) studied paths of transmission by establishing the approximate date on which each heroin user had first injected the drug and the identity of the person who had provided it. At first, there were only a few heroin users and they had been initiated in other towns. They gradually initiated a small number of new cases in the town. Heroin abuse then spread rapidly from these 'new cases' to others. Two major 'transmission trees' were traced, one including 32 users who could be traced back to one original initiator, the other including 16 users.

Causes of drug abuse

There is no single cause of drug abuse. It is generally argued that three factors are important, namely availability of drugs, a vulnerable personality, and social pressures. Once regular drug-taking is established, pharmacological factors are important in determining dependence.

People can become dependent on drugs by three routes. The first is by taking drugs prescribed by doctors. In the first part of the twentieth century much of the known dependence on opiates and barbiturates in Western countries was of this kind; nowadays benzodiazepine dependence is often acquired in this way. The second route is by taking drugs that can be bought legally without prescription: nicotine is an obvious contemporary example, and in the nineteenth century much dependence on opioids arose from taking freely available remedies containing morphia (see Berridge and Edwards 1981). (Alcohol dependence is also acquired in this way, but we are not concerned here with that kind of abuse.) The third route is by taking drugs that can be obtained only from illicit sources ('street drugs').

Many drug users, particularly younger people taking non-prescribed drugs, appear to have some degree of **personality vulnerability** before taking drugs. They often seem to be without resources to cope with the challenges of day-to-day life, inconsistent in their feelings, and critical of society and authority as shown by a poor school record, truancy, or deliquency. Many of those who abuse drugs report depression and anxiety, but it is seldom clear whether these are the causes or the consequences of drug dependence. Some give a history of mental illness or personality disorder in the family. Some drug abusers come from severely **disorganized backgrounds**, and a history of childhood unhappiness is common. However, many people who abuse drugs show none of these features.

The risk of drug abuse is greater in societies which condone drug-taking. Within the immediate group, there may be **social pressures** for a young person to take drugs to achieve status.

Causes of drug dependence

Not all drug abusers become dependent on drugs. The causes of dependence are pharmacological and psychological. *Pharmacological* dependence develops quickly with opiates and probably more slowly with anxiolytics; it is does not appear to develop with cannabis or hallucinogenic drugs. The pharmacological mechanisms of dependence are not understood clearly but may involve changes in receptors on synapses (see Paton 1969). *Psychological* factors may operate through conditioning. It seems that some of the symptoms experienced as a drug is withdrawn are conditioned responses, established during previous episodes of withdrawal. Also some drugs such as opiates have reinforcing effects of their own, so that laboratory animals will work to obtain them as a reward.

Consequences of intravenous drug taking

Some drug abusers administer drugs intravenously in order to obtain a marked and rapid effect. The practice is particularly common with opioid abuse, but barbiturates, benzodiazepines, amphetamines, and other drugs may be taken in this way. Intravenous drug use has important consequences, some local, others general.

   Local effects include thrombosis of veins, infections at the injection site, and inadvertent damage to arteries. *General* effects are due to transmission of infection, especially when needles are shared. Examples include bacterial endocarditis, hepatitis, and AIDS.

Social consequences of drug dependence

There are three reasons why drug abuse has undesirable social effects. First, chronic intoxication may affect behaviour adversely, leading to unemployment, motoring offences, and family problems including neglect of children. Second, because illicit drugs are generally expensive, the abuser may cheat or steal to obtain money. Third, drug abusers often keep company with one another, and those with previously stable social behaviour may be under pressure to conform with a group ethos of antisocial or criminal activity.

Drug abuse in pregnancy and the puerperum

When a pregnant woman abuses drugs, the fetus may be affected. When drugs are taken in early pregnancy there is a risk of increased rates of fetal abnormality. When drugs are taken in late pregnancy, the fetus may become dependent on them. With heroin and related drugs, the risk of fetal dependence is great, and after delivery the neonate may develop serious withdrawal effects requiring skilled care. If the mother continues to take drugs after delivery the infant may be neglected. Intravenous drug use may lead to infection of the mother with AIDS or other conditions that can affect the fetus.

Diagnosis of drug dependence

It is important to diagnose drug dependence early, at a stage when tolerance may be less established and behaviour patterns less fixed, and the complications of intravenous use may not have developed. Before describing the clinical presentations of the different types of drugs, some general principles will be given. The psychiatrist who is not used to treating drug-dependent people should remember that he may be in the unusual position of trying to help a patient who is attempting to deceive him. Patients dependent on heroin may overstate the daily dose to obtain extra supplies for their own use or for sale to others. Also many patients take more than one drug but may not say so. It is important to try to corroborate the patient's account of the amount he takes by asking detailed questions about the duration of drug-taking, and the cost and source of drugs; by checking the story for internal consistency; and by external verification whenever possible.

Certain **clinical signs** lead to the suspicion that drugs are being injected. These include: needle tracks and thrombosis of veins, especially in the antecubital fossa; the wearing of long sleeves in hot weather; and scars. Intravenous use should be considered in any patient who presents with subcutaneous abscesses or hepatitis.

Behavioural changes may also suggest drug dependence. These include absence from school or work and occupational decline. The dependent person may also neglect his appearance, isolate himself from his former friends, and adopt new ones in a drug culture. Minor criminal offences, such as petty theft and prostitution may also be indicators.

Dependent people may come to medical attention in several ways. Some declare that they are dependent on drugs. Others conceal their dependency, asking for controlled drugs for the relief of pain such as renal colic or dysmenorrhoea. It is important to be especially wary of such requests from temporary patients. Others present with drug-related complications such as cellulitis, pneumonia, serum hepatitis, or accidents; or for the treatment of acute drug effects, overdose, withdrawal symptoms, or adverse reactions to hallucinogenic drugs. A few are detected during an admission to hospital for an unrelated illness.

Laboratory diagnosis

Whenever possible, the diagnosis of drug abuse should be confirmed by laboratory tests. Most drugs of abuse can be detected in the urine, the notable exceptions being cannabis and LSD. Urine specimens should be sent to the laboratory as quickly as possible. An indication should be given of the interval between the last admitted drug dose and the collection of the urine sample. The laboratory should be provided with as complete a list as possible of drugs likely to have been taken, including those prescribed as well as those obtained in other ways.

Prevention, treatment and rehabilitation: general principles

Because treatment is difficult, considerable effort should be given to **prevention**. For many drugs the most important preventative measure—restricting availability—depends mainly on government, not medical, policy. The reduction of over-prescribing by doctors is important, especially with benzodiazepines and other anxiolytic drugs. Health education is essential, and information about the dangers of drug abuse should be available to young people in the school curriculum and through the media. Another aspect of prevention is the identification and treatment of family problems that may contribute to drug-taking. In all these preventive measures, the general practitioner has a particularly important role.

When drug abuse has begun, treatment is more effective before dependence is established. At this stage, as at later stages, the essential step is to motivate the person to control his drug-taking. This requires a combination of advice about the likely effects of continuing abuse, and help with any concurrent psychological or social problems. If the person is associating with others who abuse drugs, he should be urged to leave them and establish new friendships and interests.

The main aim of the treatment of the drug-dependent person is the withdrawal of the drug of dependence. If this cannot be achieved, continued prescribing may be considered. In addition, psychological treatment and social support are required. At this point in the chapter, the general principles of treatment are outlined. In later sections, treatment specific to individual drugs will be considered.

In Britain, most drug-dependent patients are treated in clinics based on psychiatric units. In some large cities there are **special treatment centres** mainly for people dependent on narcotics. In-patient care is usually provided within the psychiatric unit of general hospitals, in psychiatric hospitals, or in therapeutic communities run by charitable organizations.

Treatment of physical complications

The complications of self-injection may need treatment in a general hospital. These complications include skin infections, abcesses, septicaemia, hepatitis-B, and AIDS. In some places more than half the intravenous drug users are reported to be HIV positive (see Moss 1987).

Principles of withdrawal

The withdrawal of misused drugs is sometimes called *detoxification*. Withdrawal is best carried out gradually with the patient in hospital. This advice applies to opiates and particularly to barbiturates (see below). Withdrawal from stimulant drugs can often be an out-patient procedure provided that the doses are not very large and that barbiturates are not taken as well. Nevertheless, the risk of depression and suicide should be remembered.

Drug maintenance

Some clinicians undertake to prescribe drugs to dependent people who are not willing to give them up. The usual procedure is to prescribe a drug which has a slower action (and is therefore less addictive) than the 'street' drug. Thus methadone is prescribed in place of heroin. When this procedure is combined with help with social problems and a continuing effort to bring the person to accept withdrawal, it is called **maintenance therapy**. It is important to realize that prolonged prescribing is not in itself therapeutic; it is the psychological and social measures which accompany the prescribing that justify the name of therapy. The rationale for this procedure is twofold. First, prolonged prescribing will remove the need for the patient to obtain 'street' drugs, and will thereby reduce the need to steal money and associate with other drug-dependent people. Second, social and psychological help will make the person's life more normal so that he will be more able to give up drugs eventually. This form of treatment is used particularly for heroin dependence.

If maintenance is used, it should be remembered that some drug-dependent people convert tablets or capsules into material for injection, a particularly dangerous practice. Also some of these people attend a succession of general practitioners in search of supplementary supplies of drugs. They may withhold information about attendance at clinics, or pose as temporary residents.

There is little good information about the outcome of long-term prescribing coupled with social support, compared with drug-free programmes. Much seems to depend on the personality of the drug user. Some patients who receive maintenance drugs achieve a degree of social stability, but others continue heavy drug abuse and deteriorate both medically and socially.

Some drug-dependent patients are helped by simple measures such as counselling. In many units, group psychotherapy is provided to help patients develop insight into personal and interpersonal problems. Some patients benefit from treatment in a therapeutic community in which there can be a frank discussion of the effects of drug taking on the person's character and relationships, within the supportive relationship of the group (see p. 719 for an outline of community therapy).

Rehabilitation

Many drug takers have great difficulty in establishing themselves in normal society. The aim of rehabilitation is to enable the drug-dependent person to leave the drug subculture, and develop new social contacts. Unless he can do this, any treatment is likely to fail.

Rehabilitation is often undertaken after therapeutic community treatment outlined in the previous paragraph. Patients at first engage in work and social activities in sheltered surroundings, and then take greater responsiblity for themselves in conditions increasingly like those of every day life. Hostel accommodation is a useful stage in this gradual process. Continuing social support is usually required when the person makes the transition to normal work and living.

Abuse of specific types of drug

Opioids

This group of drugs includes morphine, heroin, codeine, and synthetic analgesics such as pethidine, methadone, and dipipanone. The medical use of the drugs is mainly for their powerful analgesic actions; they are abused for their euphoriant effects. In the past morphine was abused widely in Western countries, but has been largely replaced as a drug of abuse by **heroin**, which has a particularly powerful euphoriant effect, especially when taken intravenously. Although some people take heroin intermittently without becoming dependent, dependence develops rapidly with regular usage especially when the drug is taken intravenously.

As well as euphoria and analgesia, these drugs produce respiratory depression, constipation, reduced appetite, and low libido. *Tolerance* develops rapidly, leading to increasing dosage. Tolerance does not develop equally to all the effects, and constipation often persists when other effects have diminished. When the drug is stopped, tolerance diminishes rapidly so that a dose taken after an interval of abstinence has greater effects than it would have had before the interval. This loss of tolerance can result in dangerous—sometimes fatal—respiratory depression when a previously tolerated dose is resumed after a drug-free interval, for example after a stay in hospital or prison.

Withdrawal symptoms rarely threaten the life of someone in reasonable health, though they cause great distress and so drive the person to seek further supplies. The withdrawal symptoms include: intense craving for the drug; restlessness and insomnia; pain in muscles and joints; running nose and eyes; sweating; abdominal cramps, vomiting and diarrhoea; pilo-erection; dilated pupils; raised pulse rate; and disturbance of temperature control. These features usually begin about six hours after the last dose, reach a peak after 36-48 hours, and then wane.

Methadone is approximately as potent, weight for weight, as morphine. It causes cough suppression, constipation, and depression of the central nervous system and of respiration. Pupillary constriction is less marked. The withdrawal syndrome is similar to that of heroin and morphine, but slower and less severe. Thus symptoms may begin only after 36 hours, and reach a peak after three to five days. For this reason, methadone is is often used to replace heroin in patients dependent on the latter drug.

The natural course of opiate dependence   Follow-up studies of opiate-dependent people indicate that after seven years only about a quarter to a third appear to be abstinent while between 10 and 20 per cent have died from causes related to drug taking (for example, Stimson *et al.* 1978; Chapple *et al.* 1972). Deaths are usually due to accidental over-dosage, often related to loss of tolerance after a period of enforced abstinence (Gardner 1970). In future, death rates of intravenous drug users are likely to rise as a result of infection with AIDS.

Abstinence is often related to changed circumstances of life; a point that is reflected in the report of 95 per cent abstinence among soldiers who returned to the USA after becoming dependent on opiates during service in the Vietnam War (Robins *et al.* 1974).

Prevention   Because dependence develops rapidly, and because treat-ment of dependent opiate-abuser is unsatisfactory, preventive measures (see p. 541) are particularly important with this group of drugs.

Treatment of crisis   Heroin-dependent people present in crisis to a doctor in three circumstances. First, when their supplies have run out, they may seek drugs either by requesting them directly, or by feigning a painful disorder. Although withdrawal symptoms are very unpleasant, so that the abuser will go to great lengths of obtain more drugs, they are not usually dangerous to an otherwise healthy person. Therefore, it is best to offer drugs only as the first step of a planned withdrawal programme. This programme is described in the following sections. In the United Kingdom, only specially licensed doctors may legally prescribe heroin or certain related drugs to a drug-dependent person as maintenance treatment. The relevant regulations are available within the Health Service, and are subject to revision from time to time.

The second form of crisis is drug overdose. This requires medical treatment, directed particularly to any respiratory depression produced by the drug.

The third form of crisis is an acute complication of intravenous drug usage such as local infection, necrosis at the injection site, or infection of a distant organ—often the heart or liver. Doctors in the United Kingdom are required (under the Misuse of Drugs Notification of Supply to Addicts Regulations 1973) to notify the names of people addicted to heroin and certain related drugs to the Chief Medical Officer of the Home Office. Doctors working in other countries are advised to find out the local legal requirements.

Planned withdrawal (detoxification) The severity of withdrawal symptoms depends on psychological as well as pharmacological factors. Therefore the psychological management of the patient during withdrawal is as important as the drug regime. The speed of withdrawal should be discussed with the patient to establish a timetable which is neither so rapid that the patient will not collaborate, nor so protracted that the state of dependence is perpetuated. During withdrawal, much personal contact is needed to reassure the patient; the relationship formed in this way can be important in later treatment.

When the dose is low, opioids can be withdrawn rapidly while symptomatic treatment is given for the more unpleasant withdrawal effects. These effects are usually abdominal cramps, diarrhoea, anxiety, and insomnia. They can be relieved with a combination of diphenoxylate (or 'Lomotil', which is diphenoxylate with atropine) and an anxiolytic–hypnotic such as chloromethiazole or a benzodiazepine. Since the last two drugs have a high potential for dependence they should be taken only under close supervision. The drug combination is usually given for three days: for example Lomotil two tablets six-hourly for 24 hours, followed by one tablet six-hourly for 48 hours; together with chlormethiazole twice daily (in the morning and at night) for three days. (Since the formulation of chlormethiazole varies in different countries, the precise dosage should be obtained from an appropriate work of reference.) Other drugs that have been used to reduce withdrawal symptoms include propranalol, thioridazine, and clonidine. [For information about clonidine in withdrawal, see Herbert *et al.* (1985).]

When the daily dose of heroin is high, it may be necessary to prescribe an opioid, reducing the dose gradually. This can be done most effectively if heroin is replaced by methadone, which has a more gradual action. The difficulty is to judge the correct dose of methadone because patients often lie about their dosage of heroin, either over-stating it in the hope of ensuring that the withdrawal regime will be gradual, or under-stating it in an attempt to avoid censure. Methadone should be given in a liquid form to be taken by mouth. In the United Kingdom, Methadone Mixture Drug Tariff Formula is convenient. The initial dose is normally between 20 mg and 70 mg per day depending on the patient's usual consumption. Doses above 40 mg per day should be given with great caution. Although 10 mg of pharmaceutical heroin is about equivalent to 10 mg of methadone, street heroin varies in potency in different places and at different times. Therefore advice about the equivalent dose of methadone should if possible be obtained from a doctor experienced in treating drug dependence. The dose should be reduced by about a quarter every two or three days, according to the patient's response. If withdrawal is to be done as an out-patient, the dose reduction should be smaller and the intervals longer to reduce the patient's temptation to seek additional supplies. An out-patient regime might last several weeks, nevertheless a clear time-limit should be set from the start. Withdrawal from high doses should not normally be done as an out-patient procedure.

Pregnancy and opioid dependence   The babies of opioid-dependent women are more likely than other babies to be premature and of low birth weight. Also they may show withdrawal symptoms after birth, including irritability, restlessness, tremor, and a high-pitched cry. These signs appear within a few days of birth if the mother was taking heroin, but are delayed if she was taking methadone, which has a longer half-life in the body. Low birth-weight and prematurity are not necessarily related directly to the drug since poor nutrition and heavy smoking are common among these women.

Later effects have been reported, these children being more likely, as toddlers, to be overactive and to show poor persistence. However, these late effects may result from the unsuitable family environment provided by these mothers rather than from a lasting effect of the intrauterine exposure to the drug. [For a review see Caviston (1987).]

Maintenance treatment for heroin dependence   If possible, patients should be withdrawn from drugs. If they refuse, maintenance treatment is used by some clinicians. The principle of this treatment has been explained on p. 542. Instead of heroin, methadone is prescribed as a liquid preparation formulated to discourage attempts to inject it: in the United Kingdom as Methadone Mixture Drug Tariff Formula containing 5 mg methadone hydrochloride per 5 ml. This preparation is not to be confused with the cough mixture properly referred to as methadone linctus. The maintenance dose is from 20 to 70 mg per day. Great care is needed in deciding the amount, and the higher dosage should never be given on the first occasion except to someone known to be heavily addicted.

Although some patients seem to acquire some social stability while taking maintenance methadone, the general value of this form of treatment has not been demonstrated convincingly, and is increasingly questioned. [See Gossop (1978) for a review.]

Therapeutic community methods These forms of treatment aim to produce abstinence by effecting a substantial change in the patient's attitudes and behaviour. Drug-taking is represented as a way of avoiding pre-existing personal problems, and as a source of new ones. Group therapy and communal living are combined in an attempt to produce greater personal awareness, more concern for others, and better social skills. In most therapeutic communities, some of the staff have previously been dependent on drugs, and are often better able than other staff to gain the confidence of the patients in the early stages of treatment.

Results of treatment

One British study (Gossop *et al.* 1987) concerned 50 people treated as in-patients for opiate dependence. All were drug-free on discharge from hospital; six months later 26 were abstinent, but of these three were in prison and two in hospital, so that just under half of those living outside an institution were apparently no longer taking opioids. A study of a therapeutic community treatment showed that those who stayed more than six months had a better outcome as judged by subsequent convictions for crime (Wilson and Mandelbrote 1978) and frequency of drug injection (Wilson 1978).

Anxiolytic and hypnotic drugs

The most frequently abused drugs of this groups are now the benzodiaze-pines. The most serious problems are presented by barbiturates; although more careful prescribing has limited the extent of their therapeutic use, they are available as 'street' drugs. Other drugs of this group currently abused include chlormethiazole, and glutethimide.

Barbiturates

Many people dependent on barbiturates take them by mouth. These people are usually middle-aged or elderly and they began taking the drug because it had been prescribed as a hypnotic. In recent years younger people have been using barbiturates intravenously, by dissolving capsules. These people generally take other intravenous drugs as well. Intravenous abusers favour short-acting barbiturates; for example, pentobarbitone or 'Tuinal' (a mixture of quinalbarbitone and amylobarbitone). In aqueous solution these drugs are highly irritant to tissues, causing periphlebitis, indolent abscesses, sloughing ulcers, and even gangrene. Patients with such complications not infrequently need surgical treatment varying from skin grafting to amputation. Overdosage amongst users is common, and difficult to treat.

Tolerance develops less rapidly to barbiturates than to opioids but when it develops it presents a particular danger. The danger is that tolerance to the sedating effect occurs to a greater extent than it does to the depressant effects on vital centres, so increasing the risk of inadvertent fatal overdosage.

Recognition of the abuser of barbiturates depends on a number of features. He may appear to be drunk, with slurred speech and incoherence. Dullness and drowsiness are common, and so is depression. Nystagmus is a valuable sign, which should always be sought. Pupillary size is not helpful. Younger intravenous users tend to be unkempt and dirty, and often appear malnourished. Blood levels are generally only useful in acute poisoning. Urine should be examined to investigate the possible simultaneous abuse of other drugs.

Prevention of dependence   It is essential that dependence on anxiolytic and hypnotic drugs is avoided by restricting precribing to small amounts taken for short periods. The patient should be told why long-term consumption is to be avoided.

Withdrawal   Abrupt withdrawal of barbiturates from a dependent person is highly dangerous. It may result in a mental disorder like that after alcohol withdrawal, and may lead to seizures and sometimes to death (see Isbell *et al.* 1950). The withdrawal syndrome may not appear at its severest for several days.

The syndrome begins with anxiety, restlessness, disturbed sleep, anorexia, and nausea. These may progress to vomiting, hypotension, pyrexia, tremulousness, major seizures, disorientation, and hallucinations—a picture similar to delirium tremens.

Withdrawal should nearly always be an in-patient procedure. If the patient has been taking a small dose of barbiturate, out-patient withdrawal may be considered but only if there is no history of epilepsy before drug abuse, or of recent anti-epileptic medication.

In the management of withdrawal, phenothiazines should be avoided as they may lower the fit threshold. Instead withdrawal can be initiated by giving enough pentobarbital in divided doses to maintain the patient between intoxication and withdrawal. Following this, dosage is reduced from 50 to 100 mg a day as long as withdrawal symptoms do not occur. An alternative is to use a benzodiazepine.

If slow withdrawal is to be attempted outside hospital, short-acting substitutes should be avoided because of the risk of abuse. Instead phenobarbitone should be given. An attempt should be made to calculate the patient's usual daily dosage allowing for all drugs with similar actions such as alcohol and benzodiazepines. For every 100 mg of a shorter acting barbiturate or its equivalent, a daily dose of 30 mg phenobarbitone should be given in divided dose, up to a maximum of 300 mg daily (exceptionally 400 mg). This is reduced progressively over 10–20 days, the patient being asessed every second or third day.

Maintenance treatment   This may be considered for some elderly patients who have taken barbiturates for a long time. The barbiturate is replaced by a benzodiazepine and continued efforts are made to reduce the dose gradually. In most cases withdrawal can be achieved eventually.

Benzodiazepines

These drugs were in use for many years before it became apparent that their prolonged use could lead to tolerance and dependence with a characteristic **withdrawal syndrome**. This syndrome includes: irritability, anxiety, sleep disturbance, increased perceptual sensitivity, and somatic symptoms such as tremor, sweating, palpitations, headache, and muscle pain (Peturrson and Lader 1984).

Dependence often results from prolonged medical use but may also result from the availability of benzodiazepines as 'street' drugs because of their euphoriant effects. The withdrawal syndrome closely resembles the anxiety symptoms for which the drugs are usually prescribed; hence if symptoms appear after the dose of benzodiazepine has been reduced, the doctor may revert to a higher dosage in the mistaken belief that these symptoms indicate a persistent anxiety disorder.

Treatment of dependence consists of gradual withdrawal combined with supportive counselling. Anxiety management (see p. 735) may be added for patients who cannot give up the drugs with simple measures alone.

[See Peturrson and Lader (1984) for further information about benzodiazepine dependence.]

Cannabis

Cannabis is derived from the plant *Cannabis sativa*. It is consumed either as the dried vegetative parts in the form known as marijuana or 'grass', or as the resin secreted by the flowering tops of the female plant. Cannabis contains several pharmacologically active substances of which the most powerful psychoactive member is delta-1-tetrahydrocannabinol. In some parts of North Africa and Asia, cannabis products are consumed in a similar way to alcohol in Western society. In North America and Britain the intermittent use of cannabis is quite widespread. It appears that most users do not take any other illegal drug, but some are given to high consumption of alcohol. **The effects** of the drug vary with the dose, the person's expectations and mood, and the social setting. Users sometimes describe themselves as 'high' but, like alcohol, cannabis seems to exaggerate the pre-existing mood whether exhilaration or depression. Users report an increased enjoyment of aesthetic experiences and distortion of the perception of time and space. There may be reddening of the eyes, dry mouth, tachycardia, irritation of the respiratory tract, and coughing. Cannabis intoxication presents hazards for car drivers.

Though a **withdrawal syndrome**, resembling that seen with benzodiazepines, has been reported after prolonged use of cannabis (Tunving 1985), the evidence for such a syndrome is not conclusive. Physical dependence does not seem to occur, though psychological dependence may develop. No serious **adverse effects** have been proved among intermittent users. Although there is no positive evidence of teratogenicity, cannabis has not been proved safe in the first three months of pregnancy. Inhaled cannabis smoke irritates the respiratory tract and is potentially carcinogenic.

It is not certain whether cannabis can cause a psychosis. Though an association between the two has been reported (e.g. Chopra and Smith 1974) it is not certain whether this association is causal or coincidental (see Edwards 1976). It is also said that chronic use of cannabis can lead to a state of apathy and indolence (an 'amotivational state'). However, an objective study of chronic cannabis users failed to demonstrate this (Beaubrun and Knight 1973). Cerebral atrophy has been reported in a few cannabis users (Campbell *et al.* 1971) but has not been confirmed in a subsequent investigation (Co *et al.* 1977).

For a review of the pharmacological and medical aspects of cannabis-taking see Graham (1976). The social and legal aspects are well reviewed in the report of the Advisory Committee on Drug Dependence (1968).

Stimulant drugs

These drugs include amphetamines, related substances such as phenmetrazine and methylphenidate, and fenfluramine. Cocaine, which has similar effects, is considered separately in the next section. Amphetamines have been largely abandoned in medical practice, apart from their use for the hyperkinetic syndrome of childhood (p. 795) and for narcolepsy (p. 401). Fenfluramine is used in the treatment of obesity.

In the past, most addiction to stimulant drugs arose from injudicious prescribing. Now these drugs are sought as 'street drugs' and used often intravenously to produce euphoria. Apart from their immediate effect on mood, the drugs produce over-talkativeness, over-activity, insomnia, dryness of lips, mouth and nose, and anorexia. The pupils dilate, the pulse rate increases, and blood pressure rises. With large doses there may be cardiac arrhythmia, and occasionally circulatory collapse.

Prolonged use of high doses may result in repetitive stereotyped behaviour, for example, repeated tidying. A **paranoid psychosis** indistinguishable from paranoid schizophrenia also may be induced by prolonged high doses. The features include persecutory delusions, auditory and visual hallucinations, and sometimes hostile and dangerously aggressive behaviour (Connell 1958). Usually the condition subsides in about a week, but occasionally it persists for months. It is not certain whether these prolonged cases are true drug-induced psychoses, schizophrenia provoked by the amphetamine or merely coincidental.

Tolerance is not marked and the **withdrawal** syndrome is not severe, consisting mainly of low mood and energy. Nevertheless, psychological **dependence** can develop quickly. Dependence on stimulant drugs may be recognized from the history of over-activity and high spirits alternating with inactivity and depression. Whenever amphetamine abuse is at all likely, a urine sample should be taken for analysis as soon as possible, and certainly before any phenothiazines are administered, since these drugs interfere with the assay for amphetamine.

Prevention depends on restriction of the drugs and careful prescribing. Doctors should be wary of newly arrived patients who purport to suffer from narcolepsy. **Treatment** of acute overdoses requires sedation and management of hyperpyrexia and cardiac arrhythmias. Most toxic symptoms, including paranoid psychoses, resolve quickly when the drug is stopped. An antipsychotic drug may be needed to control florid symptoms, but if this medication can be avoided the differential diagnosis from schizophrenia will be easier.

Apart from the mangement of these acute conditions, treatment consists of gradual withdrawal of the drug coupled with supportive interviews.

Cocaine

Cocaine is a central nervous stimulant with effects similar to those of amphetamines (described above). It causes strong psychological dependence. It is used by injection, by smoking, and by sniffing into the nostrils. The latter practice sometimes causes perforation of the nasal septum. In 'freebasing', chemically pure cocaine is extracted from the 'street' drug to produce a more powerful effect.

The clinical picture is of excitation, dilated pupils, tremulousness and sometime dizziness. In high doses cocaine can occasionally cause seizures and death from cardiac and respiratory arrest. Psychological effects, apart from excitement, include confusion and depression. A paranoid psychosis may occur, similar to that produced by amphetamines. Formication ('cocaine bugs'), a feeling as if insects are crawling under the skin, is experienced sometimes by cocaine abusers. (This symptom can also occur with amphetamine abuse.)

In the United Kingdom a doctor is required, under the Misuse of Drugs (Notification and Supply of Addicts) Regulations 1973, to notify the Chief Medical Officer of the Home Office if he attends a patient whom he considers to be addicted to cocaine.

Hallucinogens

Drugs of this type are sometimes known as *psychedelics* but we do not recommend this term because it does not have a single clear meaning. The term *psychomimetic* is also used, because the drugs produce changes that bear some resemblance to those of the functional psychoses. However, the resemblance is not close, so we do not recommend this term.

The synthetic hallucinogens include lysergic acid diethylamide (LSD), dimethyl tryptamine, and methyldimethoxyamphetamine. Of these drugs, LSD is encountered most often in the United Kingdom. Hallucinogens also occur naturally in some species of mushroom, and varieties containing psilocybin are consumed for their hallucinogenic effects.

The *physical actions* of LSD are variable. There are initial sympatho-mimetic effects: heart rate may increase and pupils dilate. However, overdosage does not seem to result in severe physiological reactions. There is no certain evidence linking conventional dosage with chromosomal or teratogenic abnormalities but it is nevertheless prudent that the drug be avoided during pregnancy.

The *mental effects* develop during the two hours after LSD consumption, and generally last from 8 to 14 hours. The most remarkable experiences are distortions or intensifications of sensory perception. There may be confusion between sensory modalities (synaesthesia), sounds being perceived as visual or movements experienced as if heard. Objects may seem to merge with one another or move rhythmically. The passage of time appears to be slowed and experiences seem to have a profound meaning. A distressing experience may be distortion of the body image, the person sometimes feeling that he is outside his own body. These experiences may lead to panic with fears of insanity. The mood may be exhilaration, distress, or acute anxiety. According to early reports, behaviour could be unpredictable and extremely dangerous, the user sometimes injuring or killing himself through behaving as if he were invulnerable. Recently there may have been some reduction in such adverse reactions, possibly because users are more aware of the dangers and take precautions to ensure support from other people during a 'trip'.

Whenever possible, adverse reactions should be managed by 'talking down' the user, explaining that the alarming experiences are due to the drug. If there is not time for this, a minor tranquillizer such as diazepam should be given. For severe intoxication, phenothiazines may be given, but are contraindicated if anticholinergic drugs (atrophine or phencyclidine PCP) have been taken as well. No withdrawal symptoms occur even when LSD has been taken regularly, and no physical dependence develops.

It has been argued that abuse of lysergide can cause long-term abnormalities in thinking or behaviour (Blacker *et al.* 1968), or even schizophrenia. The evidence for any such association is extremely dubious (see Strassman 1984). However, the 'flashback' is a recognized event; that is, the recurrence of psychedelic experience weeks or months after the drug was last taken. This experience may be distressing and occasionally requires treatment with an anxiolytic drug.

Phencyclidine

In its actions this drug is sufficiently different from the hallucinogens to require separate description. It can be synthesized easily, and is taken by mouth, smoked, or injected (see *British Medical Journal* 1980).

Small doses of this drug produce drunkenness, with analgesia of fingers and toes, and even anaesthesia. Intoxication with the drug is prolonged, the common features being agitation, depressed consciousness, aggressiveness and schizophrenia-like psychosis, nystagmus and raised blood pressure. With *high doses* there may be ataxia, muscle rigidity, convulsions, and unresponsiveness to the environment even though the eyes are wide open. EEG changes may be seen. Phencyclidine can be detected in the urine for 72 hours after it was last taken.

With serious *overdoses*, an adrenergic crisis may occur with hypertensive heart failure, cerebrovascular accident, or malignant hyperthermia. Status epilepticus may appear. Fatalities have been reported, due mainly to hypertensive crisis, but also to respiratory failure or suicide. Chronic use of phencyclidine may lead to aggressive behaviour accompanied by memory loss.

A phencyclidine *withdrawal syndrome* has been described, consisting of extreme craving, anergia, depression, and physical discomfort. These symptoms may be relieved by desimipramine (Tennant *et al.* 1981*b*).

Treatment of acute intoxication is symptomatic, according to the features listed above. Haloperidol, or diazepam, or both may be given. Chlorpromazine should be avoided because it is considerably less safe: it may also increase the anticholinergic effects of phencyclidine or any other drugs that may have been taken. [For a discussion of clinical management see Walker *et al.* (1981).]

Anticholinergic drugs

The belladonna alkaloids, which are naturally occurring anticholinergic drugs, have been used for centuries for their psychotropic effects. These effects include euphoria, visual hallucinations, and impaired consciousness, leading to coma and convulsions. Recently abuse of synthetic anticholinergic drugs, particularly benzhexol, has been reported (e.g. Cranshaw and Mullen 1984).

Solvent abuse

Solvent abuse started amongst adolescents in the USA in the 1950s. It came to attention in the United Kingdom in the early 1970s and is now causing serious concern (*Lancet* 1982a; Watson 1982).

The prevalence of solvent abuse in the United Kingdom is uncertain, but such abuse occurs mainly in boys aged 8–19, with a peak in those aged 13–15 (Sourindrin 1985). Most of the young people known to abuse solvents do so as a group activity, and only about five per cent are solitary abusers. In most of these cases, abuse is occasional and experimental, but in about 10 per cent it is daily and sustained over months or years (Watson 1982).

The substances abused are mainly solvents and adhesives (hence the name 'glue sniffing'), but also include many other substances such as petrol, cleaning fluid, aerosols of all kinds, agents used in fire extinguishers, and butane. Adhesives containing toluene and acetone are among the most frequently abused (Sourindrin and Baird 1984). Abuse is often associated with taking other illicit drugs, or with tobacco or alcohol consumption which can be heavy. The methods of ingestion depend on the substance; they include inhalation from tops of bottles, beer cans, cloths held over the mouth, plastic bags, and sprays.

If abuse is regular, psychological *dependence* can develop, but physical withdrawal symptoms are rare. With sustained use over 6–12 months, tolerance can develop.

The *clinical effects* are similar to those of alcohol consumption. The central nervous system is first stimulated and then depressed. The stages of intoxication are similar to those of alcohol: euphoria, blurring of vision, slurring of speech, inco-ordination, staggering gait, nausea, vomiting and coma. Compared with alcohol intoxication, solvent intoxication develops and wanes rapidly (within a few minutes, or up to 2 hours). There is early disorientation, and two-fifths of cases may develop hallucinations, which are mainly visual and often frightening. This combination of symptoms may led to serious accidents (see Watson 1982).

From a survey of young people referred to a child psychiatry clinic in London, Skuse and Burrell (1982) found that many chronic users reported transient symptoms of a *toxic psychosis*, which often had an affective component. These authors also reported that physical symptoms were common in chronic users, notably weight loss, nausea and vomiting, acute bronchospasm, and cardiac arrhythmias.

Certain substances have *neurotoxic effects*. Peripheral neuropathy is a frequently described consequence of some hexacarbons. For example, *n*-hexane and methylbutylketone are both metabolized to 2,5 hexane-dione, which causes neuropathy. Severe and disabling peripheral neuro-pathy has been described in teenagers abusing glues containing these substances (Korobkin *et al.* 1975). Abuse of toluene can result in impaired cerebellar function (Boor and Hurtig 1977). See Ron (1986*a*) for a review of the adverse effects of solvent abuse.

Solvent abuse can be fatal. Anderson *et al.* (1982) identified 140 deaths from volatile substance abuse in the United Kingdom over the period 1971–81. As many as 39 deaths were identified in 1981; these accounted for over 1 per cent of all deaths from all causes in males aged 10–19 years. The male–female ratio was 13 to 1. About half the deaths were due to the direct toxic effects of the solvent. The rest were due to trauma, asphyxia (plastic bag over head) or inhalation of stomach contents.

The *diagnosis* of acute solvent intoxication is suggested by several features: glue on the hands, face or clothes; chemical smell of the breath; rapid onset and waning of intoxication; disorientation in time and space. Chronic abuse is diagnosed mainly on an admitted history of habitual consumption, increasing tolerance, and psychological dependence. A suggestive feature is a facial rash ('glue-sniffer's rash') caused by repeated inhalation from a bag.

There is no specific *treatment* for solvent abuse. Favourable results have been reported in chronic or periodic abusers treated by means of family and individual work at a psychiatric hospital (Skuse and Burrell 1982). Some people advocate a strong publicity campaign against solvent abuse, but others maintain this might only make matters worse (*Lancet* 1982*a*).

Further reading

Edwards, G. (1982). *The treatment of drinking problems*. Grant McIntyre, London.

Edwards, G., and Busch, C. (eds.) (1981). *Drug problems in Britain: a review of ten years*. Academic Press, New York.

Hofman, F. G. (1983). *A handbook on drug and alcohol abuse: the biochemical aspects* (2nd edn). Oxford University Press, New York.

Royal College of Psychiatrists (1986). *Alcohol, our favourite drug: a new report of a special committee*. Tavistock, London.

Royal College of Physicians (1987). *Medical consequences of alcohol abuse: a great and growing evil*. Tavistock, London.

15 Problems of sexuality and gender

This chapter is concerned with four topics related to sexuality and gender: homosexual behaviour, sexual dysfunction, abnormalities of sexual preference, and disorders of gender identity. No account is given here of normal sexual physiology; the reader seeking further information on this is referred to a suitable account (for example Bancroft 1983). The clinician needs to be aware of the wide variations in sexual behaviour and in social attitudes towards this behaviour for two reasons. First, such awareness should help the clinician to avoid imposing his own attitudes on his patients. Second, it should help him to recognize that some forms of sexual behaviour are abnormal if they are habitually preferred to normal sexual intercourse, but are within normal limits if occasionally performed as minor variants of normal intercourse. A useful account of these subjects is given in the book by Ford and Beach (1952).

In this chapter homosexuality is discussed not because it is considered a disorder, but because homosexual people seek psychological help for problems associated directly or indirectly with their sexual orientation. Sexual dysfunction denotes impaired or dissatisfying sexual enjoyment or performance. Such conditions are common, and find an obvious place in this chapter. Abnormalities of sexual preference, although uncommon, take many forms and therefore require more space here than is justified by their clinical importance. The final part of this chapter deals with gender identity, which is a person's sense of being male or female. When this sense of identity is at variance with biological sex, the person is said to have a gender identity disorder.

Homosexuality

This term denotes erotic thoughts and feelings towards a person of the same sex and any associated sexual behaviour. Using a six-point scale to rate degree of homosexuality, Kinsey *et al.* (1948) estimated that 10 per cent of men were 'more or less exclusively homosexual' (rating 5 or 6) for at least three years, and that 4 per cent of men were exclusively homosexual throughout their lives. Kinsey *et al.* (1953) reported that four per cent of single women were persistently homosexual from the ages of 20 to 35, while Kenyon (1980) concluded that about one in 45 of the adult female population was predominantly homosexual.

People cannot be divided sharply into those who are homosexual and those who are heterosexual. There is a continuum, with exclusively heterosexual people at one extreme, and exclusively homosexual people at the other; between them are people who engage in varying degrees of both homosexual and heterosexual behaviour and relationships.

Homosexual behaviour in men

In men homosexual behaviour includes oral–genital contact, mutual masturbation, and, less often, anal intercourse. In these acts, the partners usually change roles; but with some couples one partner is always passive and the other always active. Relationships between homosexual men do not usually last as long as those between men and women, or those between lesbian couples.

Some exclusively homosexual men experience strong feelings of identity with other homosexuals and adopt the corresponding **social behaviour**, for example seeking the company of homosexual acquaintances in clubs or bars. A promiscuous minority seeks for a series of sexual partners in such places, or frequents public lavatories where it is know that other homosexuals will be found. A few homosexual men adopt an effeminate style of life, preferring work and leisure activities that would usually be undertaken by a woman. Some adopt exaggerated feminine mannerisms, and a small number like to dress in women's clothes (in which they may be mistaken for transsexuals or transvestites). However, most homosexual men do not behave in this way, and some are notably masculine in their social behaviour.

Homosexual men vary in **personality** as much as do other men. However, when homosexual is combined with a disorder of personality, the individual is particularly likely to run into difficulties with other people or with the law, and therefore more likely to be referred to a psychiatrist. Scott (1957) has suggested that homosexual men referred to psychiatrists can be divided into five groups. The first group comprises adolescents or mentally immature adults whose homosexual behaviour may be temporary. The second contains adults with normal personalities whose social adjustment is normal. The third is made up of those with disordered personalities, such as the effeminate and self-advertising, the inadequate and socially isolated, the resentful and antisocial (the latter may be aggressive and often exploit other homosexuals). The fourth group includes latent homosexuals whose overt sexual behaviour appears only at times of stress or depression, particularly in middle or later life. The fifth group contains those homosexuals who have severe sociopathic personality disorder, brain damage, or schizophrenia, and who may injure or otherwise damage their partners. Although anal intercourse is often the cause of marked social disapproval, it is not particularly associated with abnormal personality; Saghir and Robins (1973) report that most persistently homosexual men have experienced anal intercourse at some time.

Many homosexual men live as happily as those who are heterosexual, forming stable and rewarding relationships with a partner. For others, homosexuality leads to difficulties which change with increasing age. In adolescence there may be distress as sexual orientation is recognized for the first time, and a decision has to be made whether to follow or suppress homosexual feelings. As the person grows older sexual partnerships may become more difficult to arrange. With the approach of middle age there may be loneliness, isolation, and depression, particularly if the man has not previously established stable relationships built on friendships as well as sexual attraction. A few middle-aged homosexuals, finding it increasingly difficult to obtain sexual partners of their own age, turn towards teenage homosexual prostitutes. It is exceptional for these men to turn to prepubertal children; paedophiles are a separate group to be considered later in this chapter.

Homosexual behaviour in women

In women homosexual **sexual behaviours** include mutual masturbation, oral–genital contacts (cunnilingus), caressing, and breast stimulation. A small minority of women practice full body contact with genital friction or pressure (tribadism), or insertion of a vibrator or artificial penis into the vagina. Active and passive roles are usually exchanged, but one partner may prefer to take the more active role habitually. Other sexual practices such as sexual sadism occasionally occur with female homosexual practices. **Social behaviour** is usually unremarkable, but some homosexual women seek the kind of work and leisure activities usually associated with men. A few female homosexuals dress and behave in a masculine way. They are less likely than male homosexuals to frequent bars and public places.

As with males, there is a continuum between the exclusively heterosexual and the exclusively homosexual. Most female homosexuals engage in heterosexual relationships at some time, even though they obtain little satisfaction from them, and some marry. As a group, they are less promiscuous than homosexual men, more likely to form lasting relationships, and correspondingly less likely to suffer loneliness and depression in middle life (see Saghir and Robins 1973.)

All kinds of **personality** are represented among female homosexuals.

Legal aspects of homosexual behaviour

There are no laws specifically concerning homosexual behaviour between women. In England and Wales, homosexual behaviour between consenting males over the age of 21 in private is not an offence, but to attempt to obtain a partner in a public place breaks the law. The age for legal consent for homosexual intercourse is 21, whereas for the female partner in heterosexual intercourse it is 16.

Determinants of homosexual behaviour

It has long been supposed that homosexual behaviour is determined by **heredity**. This view was aparently confirmed when Kallmann (1952) reported 100 per cent concordance of homosexuality in 40 monozygotic male twin pairs, as against only 12 per cent concordance in 26 dizygotic twin pairs. Although this report of complete concordance between monozygotic pairs has not been confirmed, other investigators have found that monozygotic twins are more often alike in respect of homosexuality than are dizygotics (for example Heston and Shields 1968). Reports of female identical twins with a homosexual proband have been too few to allow any conclusions about inheritance of homosexuality among women. In neither male nor female homosexuals is there convincing evidence of abnormality in **sex chromosomes** or the **neuroendocrine system** (see Bancroft 1983 and Kenyon 1980 for reviews of this and other determinants). There have been studies of variations in body and build that might reflect constitutional differences between homosexual and heterosexual people, but no convincing differences have been found among men (Coppen 1959) or women (Kenyon 1968; Eisinger *et al.* 1972). It is interesting that although many animals engage in sexual activity with members of the same sex, there is apparently no evidence of exclusively homosexual behaviour in species other than humans.

Psychological and social determinants have also been investigated. Social anthropologists point out that the acceptance of homosexual behaviour varies widely in different societies. Ford and Beach (1952) reported that among 76 societies described in the literature, homosexuality was socially acceptable—at least for certain people—in 49 of them (64 per cent). Observations such as these suggest the social influences may play a part in determining how far homosexual impulses are expressed.

Many studies have been made of the **upbringing** of homosexual men. Bieber (1962) was amongst those who have concluded, on the basis of the patients' memories of childhood events, that homosexual men have commonly had a poor relationship with the father, or experienced prolonged absence of the father. Other psychoanalysts report that the mothers of homosexual men are overprotective or unduly intimate. Little weight can be placed on such retrospective accounts of the relationships of homosexual men with their parents. If there is any association with upbringing it is more likely to reflect some inhibition of the development of heterosexual behaviour than a specific determinant of homosexuality. In any case the reports were all based on patients seeking treatment. When Siegelman (1974) compared homosexual and heterosexual men all of whom had normal neuroticism scores, he found no evidence of abnormal parental behaviour.

In a study of homosexual women Wolff (1971) concluded that their mothers were rejecting or indifferent. Kenyon (1968) found that, compared with heterosexual women, more homosexual women reported a poor relationship with both mother and father; also a quarter of their parents had divorced (compared with 5 per cent in the controls). Some psychoanalysts suggest that female homosexuality results from failure to resolve unduly close relationships with the parents in early childhood, with the result that intimate involvement with men is frightening and women become the only possible object of love. There is no single convincing view on this question.

A useful way of uniting these different ideas is to suppose that young people develop with the capacity for both heterosexual and homosexual behaviour, and that various factors determine which behaviour develops more strongly. Heterosexual development might be *impeded by* repressive family attitudes towards sex, or by a general lack of self-confidence. Freudians suggest that it could also be impeded by unresolved castration anxiety. On the other hand, homosexual development might be *encouraged by* unusually close relationships with a friend of the same sex, especially when other social relationships have not developed well (see Bancroft 1975 for a full account of this scheme). None of these ideas is founded on convincing research evidence, but the general framework has some value in the assessment of a homosexual person who is seeking help.

Persistence of homosexual behaviour

In the absence of data from adequate follow-up studies, clinical experience must be used to predict whether homosexual behaviour will persist. Persistence appears to depend on the patient's age, the extent to which there has been any heterosexual interests, the person's own wish to change, and the external pressures acting upon him. People who have reached adult life without experiencing heterosexual feelings are unlikely to develop them later. It is useful to add an assessment of personality, bearing in mind that a worse outcome is suggested by antisocial traits or by any evidence of effeminate social behaviour. In general, the older the person, the less likely he is to change his sexual orientation.

Helping the homosexual

Homosexual men may consult doctors about five kinds of problem. The first concerns shy and sexually inexperienced young men who fear that they may be homosexual but in fact are not. The second is presented by young men who have realized, correctly, that they are predominantly homosexual, and are bewildered about the implications for their lives. The third concerns men who have bisexual inclinations and want to discuss ways of arranging their lives appropriately. The fourth is the problem of the established homosexual who becomes depressed or anxious because of personal or social difficulties arising from sexual relationships. In these four groups, the doctors' principal role is to help the patient to clarify his thoughts. More elaborate treatment is seldom required. The fifth kind of problem concerns the homosexual who is concerned about the possibility of being infected with AIDS or has been found to be HIV positive. Such a person may require counselling as well as suitable medical treatment.

Sometimes a homosexual person asks for help in modifying his sexual feelings and behaviour. It is difficult to help him bring about such changes but the person can assist this process by avoiding situations that stimulate his homosexual feelings, while at the same time seeking opportunities for social encounters with women. The patient should try to modify his mental preoccupations when alone; and also his fantasies during masturbation, since they are thought to be powerful reinforcers of sexual behaviour. Although psychoanalysis (Bieber 1962) and psychotherapy have been used in attempts to change sexual orientation, there is no convincing evidence that either has worthwhile effects. Aversion therapy has been used to suppress homosexual mental imagery but the results are not satisfactory (Bancroft 1974). Nowadays, behavioural treatment is concerned mainly with reducing anxiety, and with developing heterosexual behaviour patterns by methods similar to those for the treatment of sexual dysfunction (described earlier).

Homosexual women are less likely than men to seek advice about changing their sexual behaviour, and more likely to ask for help with problems arising in social relationships. These problems include feelings of depression or jealousy when a relationship with another homosexual woman is insecure. Many homosexual women also have a male partner and some are married. These women may seek advise about problems in the relationship with the man, or about dysfunction in heterosexual intercourse.

Masters and Johnson (1979) have offered treatment to both male and female homosexual couples who have stable social relationships but complain of inability to achieve a satisfactory sexual performance.

Classification of problems of sex and gender

In each of the two main systems of classification three categories are used, but the terms differ slightly. The categories are: (i) sexual dysfunction (in both systems); (ii) abnormalities of sexual preference (ICD10) or paraphilias (DSMIIIR); (iii) abnormalities of gender identity (ICD10) or gender identity disorders (DSMIIIR). However, although the three categories are considered together in this chapter, in ICD10 (draft), sexual dysfunction appears under a separate rubric ('physiological dysfunction associated with mental or behavioural factors') from the other two categories (which appear together under the rubric 'abnormalities of adult personality and behaviour'). In DSMIIIR there is another kind of separation. Thus two of the three categories (sexual dysfunctions and paraphilias) appear together under the rubric 'sexual disorder', while the third (gender identity disorder) is under the rubric 'disorders usually first evident in infancy, childhood, and adolescence'.

In both systems, the three main categories are classified further. In both DSMIIIR and ICD10 (draft), sexual dysfunctions are divided according to the stage of the sexual response that is mainly affected. Thus there are categories for disorders of sexual desire, sexual enjoyment, sexual arousal, orgasm, and ejaculation; and for vaginismus and dyspareunia. The terminology is slightly different in the two systems (see Table 15.1). DSMIIIR has more categories, and some disorders are divided into male and female kinds.

Abnormalities of sexual preference (paraphilias) are also subdivided in both ICD10 (draft) and DSMIIIR. In this case the nomenclature is very similar in the two systems (see Table 15.1). The only substantial difference is that DSMIIIR has a category for frotteurism, a condition which in ICD10 (draft) is a classified under 'other abnormalities of sexual preference'.

Abnormalities of gender identity (gender identity disorders in DSMIIIR) are also divided in a similar way. There is, however, one difference in nomenclature (see Table 15.1); and DSMIIIR has an additional category for gender identity disorder of childhood.

Sexual dysfunctions

In men, sexual dysfunction refers to repeated impairment of normal sexual interest and/or performance. In women, it refers more often to a repeated unsatisfactory quality to the experience; sexual intercourse can be completed, but without enjoyment (Bancroft *et al.* 1982). What is regarded as normal sexual intercourse, and therefore what is thought to

Table 15.1. Classification of problems of sexuality and gender

ICD10 (draft)	DSMIIIR
Sexual dysfunctions	*Sexual dysfunctions*
Lack or loss of sexual desire	Hypoactive sexual disorder
Lack of sexual enjoyment	Sexual aversion disorder
Failure of genital response	Female sexual arousal disorder
	Male erectile disorder
Orgasmic dysfunction	Inhibited female orgasm
	Inhibited male orgasm
Premature ejaculation	Premature ejaculation
Vaginismus	Vaginismus
Dyspareunia	Dyspareunia
Abnormalities of sexual preference	*Paraphilias*
Fetishism	Fetishism
Fetishistic transvestism	Transvestic fetishism
Exhibitionism	Exhibitionism
Voyeurism	Voyeurism
Paedophilia	Paedophilia
Sado-masochism	Sexual sadism/sexual masochism
Multiple abnormalities of sexual preference	Frotteurism
Other abnormalities of sexual preference	Paraphilias not otherwise specified
Abnormalities of gender identity	*Gender identity disorder*
Transsexualism	Transsexualism
Dual role transvestism	Gender identity disorder of adolescence and adulthood—non-transsexual type
	Gender identity disorder of childhood

be impaired or unsatisfactory, depends in part on the expectations of the two people concerned. For example, when the woman is regularly unable to achieve orgasm, one couple may regard it as normal, whilst another may ask for treatment. Problems of sexual dysfunction can be usefully classified into those affecting (1) sexual desire, (2) sexual enjoyment, (3) genital response (erectile impotence in men, failure of arousal in women),

(4) orgasm (premature or retarded ejaculation in men, orgasmic dysfunction in women). A fifth category includes problems such as pain on ejaculation, vaginismus, and dyspareunia. Sexual dysfunction is sometimes disclosed when the patient consults the doctor about another complaint. This presentation is more likely among women who complain of symptoms such as depression or poor sleep, and gynaecological symptoms such as vaginal discharge.

Prevalence of sexual dysfunctions

The prevalence among men is not known with certainty because surveys have failed to obtain a random sample or to characterize the dysfunctions clearly. Erectile dysfunction that is partial or temporary, rather than complete and permanent, is not uncommon, especially with increasing age. In a population survey, total and persisting erectile dysfunction was reported by 1.3 per cent of American men aged under 35, 6.7 per cent aged under 50, and 18.4 per cent aged under 60 (cumulative figures from Kinsey *et al.* 1948). Among men presenting for treatment of sexual dysfunction, erectile dysfunction is the most frequent complaint. The prevalence of *premature ejaculation* is not known exactly because it depends in part on the partner's expectations as well as her speed of response. Inhibited male orgasm appears to be less common; it was reported to Kinsey *et al.* (1948) by only 6 of 4108 men interviewed. However, among men attending a sex therapy clinic it was reported by 5 per cent (Hawton *et al.* 1986).

Among 436 women randomly selected for interview in a community survey, at least one kind of sexual dysfunction was reported by more than one in three. The most frequent sexual dysfunctions were *impaired sexual interest* (17 per cent) and *infrequent orgasm* (16 per cent). Eight per cent reported dyspareunia. Among women seeking help for sexual disorders, impaired sexual interest is described by about half and orgasmic dysfunction by about 20 per cent (Hawton 1985). In about a third of couples seen for treatment, both partners have a problem, usually low libido in the woman and premature ejaculation in the man. Sexual dysfunction is found in about 10 per cent of psychiatric out-patients (Swan and Wilson 1979).

Lack or loss of sexual desire

Complaints of diminished sexual desire are much more common among women than men. They often reflect general problems in the relationship between the partners. Sometimes there is a specific sexual problem, which may be due to longstanding inhibitions about sex, or to an apparent biological variation of sexual drive that cannot be modified.

Sexual desire is reduced during a depressive disorder. In most cases it returns to the previous level as the depressive disorder resolves, but in a few the impairment persists. This may explain why an increased frequency of previous depressive disorders has been reported among people with a current complaint of impaired sexual desire attending for treatment (Schreiner-Engel and Schiavi 1986).

Lack of sexual enjoyment (sexual aversion disorder)

Sexual enjoyment may be lacking or replaced by a positive aversion to genital contact. However, each major diagnostic system recognizes only one aspect of these problems. ICD10 (draft) has a category for lack of sexual enjoyment, defined as a lack of appropriate pleasure despite normal sexual responses and the experience of orgasm. DSMIIIR has a category for sexual aversion disorder, defined as persistent or extreme aversion to, and avoidance of, all or almost all genital sexual contact with a sexual partner.

Failure of genital response

Erectile dysfunction

This is the inability to reach an erection or to sustain it long enough for satisfactory coitus. It may be present from the first attempt at intercourse (primary) or develop after a period of normal function (secondary). In contrast to premature ejaculation, it is more common among older men. If a man has had more than one sexual partner, he should be asked whether the failure occurs with each partner or only with one. It is also important to find out whether erection occurs on waking or in response to masturbation; if they do, failure of erection with a partner is likely to be psychological rather than physiological in origin.

Failure of female arousal

Failure of vaginal lubrication is often secondary to lack of sexual interest. Other causes are anxiety about intercourse and inadequate sexual foreplay by the partner. From the time of the menopause, hormonal changes often lead to reduced vaginal secretions.

Orgasmic dysfunction

Inhibited male orgasm

This term refers to serious delay in ejaculation, or complete absence of it. Usually the delay occurs only during coitus, but it may also occur in masturbation. It is usually associated with a general psychological inhibition about sexual relations, but it may be caused by drugs such as antipsychotics or monoamine oxidase inhibitors.

Inhibited female orgasm

Orgasmic dysfunction in women may be related to the man's inexperience as well as the woman's capacity to reach orgasm. Whether it is regarded as a disorder depends on social attitudes and the expectations of the individual. Many women do not regularly achieve orgasm during intercourse. About 25 per cent of women have no orgasm during intercourse for the first year of marriage (Gebhard *et al.* 1970). In the past, absence of orgasm was not generally thought abnormal. Attitudes then changed, so that some women regarded themselves as abnormal although previously they would have been content with the intimacy of sexual relations without regular orgasm. Recently there has been some return to earlier attitudes.

Premature ejaculation

This term refers to habitual ejaculation before penetration or so shortly afterwards that the woman has not gained pleasure. It is more common among young than older men, especially during their first sexual relationships.

Vaginismus

This is spasm of the vaginal muscles which causes pain when intercourse is attempted. The spasm is usually part of a phobic response associated with fears about penetration, but occasionally it is the result of painful scarring after episiotomy. It is made worse by an inexperienced partner. The woman often reports that spasms start as soon as the man attempts to enter the vagina, and in severe cases it occurs when the woman attempts to introduce her own finger. Extreme cases of vaginismus may lead to non-consummation of marriage. So-called 'virgin wives' sometimes have extreme fears and guilt about sexual relationships rather than a specific fear of penetration. Some women with vaginismus are married to passive men who have low libido and who seem at times to be colluding with their wives' refusal to permit full sexual relations (see Dawkins 1961; Friedman 1962).

Dyspareunia

This is the term for pain on intercourse. Such pain has many causes. After partial penetration pain may result from impaired lubrication of the vagina, from scars or other painful lesions, or (as described above) from the muscle spasm of vaginismus. Pain on deep penetration strongly suggests pelvic pathology such as endometriosis, ovarian cysts and tumours, or pelvic infection, though it can be caused by impaired lubrication associated with low sexual arousal.

Other sexual dysfunctions

Pain on ejaculation

This problem is uncommon. The usual causes are urethritis or prostatitis, but sometimes no cause can be found.

Specific sexual fears

A few women are made extremely anxious by specific aspects of the sexual act, such as being touched on the genitalia, the sight or smell of seminal fluid, or even kissing. Despite these specific fears, they may still enjoy other parts of sexual intercourse.

Aetiology of sexual dysfunction

Factors common to many forms of sexual dysfunction

Sexual dysfunction arises from varying combinations of a poor general relationship with the partner, low sexual drive, ignorance about sexual technique, and anxiety about sexual performance. Other important factors are physical illness, depressive and anxiety disorder, medication, and alcohol or drug abuse. Some of these factors will now be considered.

Sexual drive varies between people but the reason for this is not known. Endocrine factors have been suggested because in the male the increasing sexual drive at puberty is related to an increased output of androgens. Also in the male, castration, treatment with oestrogens, or the administration of anti-androgenic drugs reduce sexual drive. However, no convincing association has been shown between androgens and low sexual drive in men seeking help for this problem. Thus, although Cooper *et al.* (1970) reported low urinary testosterone levels in men in whom erectile dysfunction had begun gradually and sexual drive had always been low, treatment with androgens does not usually increase sexual drive in men with normal endocrine function.

Androgens, given in small doses, increases the sexual drive of women (see Hawton 1985), though they are not used in treatment.

Ignorance about sexual technique can be a cause of sexual dysfunction in men and women, and can also lead to sexual dysfunction in the partner.

Anxiety is an important cause of sexual dysfunction. Sometimes anxiety is an understandable consequence of an earlier frightening experience such as a man's failure in his first attempt at intercourse, or a woman's experience of sexual abuse or assault. Sometimes the anxiety seems to relate to frightening accounts of sexual relationships received from parents or other people. Psychoanalysts suggest that anxiety about sexual relationships often originates from even earlier experiences, emphasizing in particular failure to resolve the oedipal complex in boys or the corresponding attachment to the father in girls. Such ideas are difficult to test.

Phsyical or psychiatric illness, and associated **treatment** can affect sexual performance. Many effects of treatment are obvious (for example, those of colostomy) but others, such as the side-effects of drugs, are not. Sexual dysfunctions sometimes appear to date from a period of abstinence associated with minor physical illness, pregnancy or childbirth, or from the debilitating effects of physical illness. Of the diseases that have a direct effect on sexual performance, diabetes mellitus is particularly important. Between a third and a half of **diabetic** men experience erectile dysfunction as a result either of neuropathy affecting the autonomic nerves mediating erection, or of vascular disorders. Impaired ejaculation also occurs. Some diabetic women may be affected in a corresponding way although this is less certain (see Fairburn 1981). Sexual dysfunction is reported after **myocardial infarction** but it may result from anxiety rather than from physical causes. Most other physical causes are self-evident. Nevertheless, doctors often fail to think of the sexual consequences of disease and the (often unexpressed) problems that result. For this reason the causes are listed in Table 15.2, despite their obviousness. A comprehensive account of the effects of physical illness on sexual function has been written by Kolodny *et al.* (1979).

Several **drugs** have side-effects that involve sexual function (see Table 15.3). The most important drugs are antihypertensives (especially adrenoceptor antagonists), and major tranquillizers (especially thioridazine). The role of oral contraceptives is still uncertain (see Hawton and Oppenheimer 1983). If they cause dysfunction, it is probably only in a minority. Anxiolytics, sedatives, and hormones have more effect on the sexual activity of men than of women. Apart from these prescribed drugs the excessive use of **alcohol** impairs sexual performance.

The aetiology of particular conditions

Male erectile disorder

Primary cases may occur through a combination of low sexual drive and anxiety about sexual performance. Secondary cases may arise from diminishing sexual drive in the middle-aged or elderly; loss of interest in the sexual partner; anxiety; depressive disorder; organic disease and its treatment.

Premature ejaculation

This is so common in sexually inexperienced young men that it may be regarded as a normal variation. When it persists, it is often because of fear of failure.

Table 15.2. Medical and surgical conditions commonly associated with sexual dysfunction*

Medical	
Endocrine	diabetes, hyperthyroidism, myxoedema, Addison's disease, hyperprolactinaemia
Gynaecological	vaginitis, endometriosis, pelvic infections
Cardiovascular	angina pectoris, previous myocardial infarction
Respiratory	asthma, obstructive airways disease
Arthritic	arthritis from any cause
Renal	renal failure with or without dialysis
Neurological	pelvic autonomic neuropathy, spinal cord lesions, stroke
Surgical	mastectomy colostomy; ileostomy oophorectomy episiotomy; operations for prolapse amputation

* Modified from Hawton and Oppenheimer (1983).

Table 15.3. Some drugs that may impair sexual function*

Alcohol	
Antihypertensives:	guanethidine, beta-adrenoceptor antagonists, methyl dopa
Antidepressants:	tricyclics, monoamine oxidase inhibitors
Anxiolytics and hypnotics:	benzodiazepines, barbiturates
Antipsychotics:	especially thioridazine
Anti-inflammatory drugs:	indomethacin
Anticholinergics:	e.g. probanthine
Diuretics:	bendrofluazide
Hormones	steroids, possibly oral contraceptives

* Modified from Hawton and Oppenheimer (1983).

Inhibited female orgasm

This arises from normal variations in sexual drive; poor sexual technique by the partner; lack of affection for him; tiredness, depressive disorder, physical illness, and the effects of medication.

Vaginismus

This has the psychological causes described above (p. 566).

Dyspareunia

This generally has physical causes (though it may result from vaginismus, or from failure of arousal and consequent lack of vaginal lubrication).

The assessment of a patient who presents with sexual dysfunction

Whenever possible the sexual partner should be interviewed as well as the patient. The two should be seen separately, and then together. The first step is to define clearly the **nature of the problem** as it appears to each partner. Details should not be omitted because the interviewer is too embarrassed to make full enquiries. Each of the partners should be asked, separately, whether the problem has occurred with other partners. The **origin and the course** of the dysfunction is recorded next. It is especially important to discover whether the problem has always been present or whether it started after a period of normal function. The general strength of sexual **drive** is assessed by asking about frequency of intercourse and masturbation, and about sexual thoughts and feelings of sexual arousal.

An assessment is next made of **knowledge** of sexual techniques, and then of anxieties about sex. At the same time, possible sources of misinformation and anxiety are considered by asking about the family's attitude to sex, the kind of sex education received by each partner, and the extent of sexual experience with other partners. Each partner should be asked about the sexual **technique** of the other.

Social **relationships** with the opposite sex are considered next. The interviewer should find out whether either partner is shy and socially inhibited. If the couple are husband and wife, or otherwise cohabiting, disharmony in their relationship should be enquired into carefully. If the couple lack a loving relationship in their everyday life, it is unlikely that they will achieve a fully satisfying sexual relationship. It is important to remember that some couples ask for help with sexual problems which are the result and not the cause of marital conflict. The interviewer should also find out why the patient has come for treatment at this time. The reason may be that the sexual problem has increased, but there may be another reason such as the spouse's threatening to leave.

Careful enquiry must also be made for evidence of **psychiatric disorder** in either partner, especially depressive illness, which might account for the sexual problem. Finally, questions are asked about **physical illness** and its **treatment** and, psychotropic medication, abuse of alcohol or drugs. If the general practitioner or another specialist has not already done so, a **physical examination** should be carried out (see Table 15.4). Appropriate

Table 15.4. Important points in the physical examination of men presenting with sexual dysfunctions (adapted from Hawton 1985)

General examination (Directed especially to evidence of diabetes mellitus, thyroid disorder and adrenal disorder)

Hair distribution
Gynaecomastia
Blood pressure
Peripheral pulses
Ocular fundi
Reflexes
Peripheral sensation

Genital examination
Penis: congenital abnormalities, foreskin, pulses, tenderness, plaques, infection, urethral discharge

Testicles: size, symmetry, texture, sensation

---

laboratory tests should be arranged; for example, fasting blood sugar, testosterone, and gonadotrophin levels in men with erectile dysfunction.

Treatment of sexual dysfunction

Before directing treatment to the sexual problem, it is important to consider whether the couple need marital therapy instead. If it is appropriate to focus treatment on the sexual problem, **advice and education** may be all that is needed. If **specific sex therapy** is appropriate it should be directed to both partners whenever possible. The usual approach, which owes much to the work of Masters and Johnson (1970), has four characteristic features. First, the partners are treated together. Second, they are helped to communicate better, through words and actions, about their sexual relationship. Third, they are taught the anatomy and physiology of sexual intercourse. Fourth, they are given a graded series of 'sexual tasks'. Masters and Johnson held that two other factors were important. The first was that treatment should be intensive; for example, seeing both partners every day for up to three weeks. The second was that treatment should be carried out by a man and a woman working as co-therapists. It has been shown that neither of these measures is essential. Bancroft and Coles (1976) found that good results were obtained when only one therapist saw couples, and when treatment was given once a week. Although the best results are obtained with the treatment of couples, useful help can often be given to a patient who has no regular partner. Such a patient can at least discuss his difficulties and possible ways of overcoming them. Discussion of this kind can sometimes help to overcome social inhibitions and so help to develop a relationship with someone of the opposite sex.

Communication is not only talking more freely about the problems each partner is experiencing; it is also concerned with increasing understanding of the other person's wishes and feelings. Some women believe that all men know instinctively how to please the female during intercourse. They interpret failure to please as due to lack of concern or affection rather than to ignorance. They do not realize that such failure might be overcome by a more frank expression of their own desires.

Education stresses the physiology of the sexual response. For example, the doctor explains the longer time needed for a woman to reach sexual arousal, and he emphasizes the importance of foreplay, including clitoral stimulation, in bringing about vaginal lubrication. Suitably chosen sex education books can reinforce the therapist's advice. Such counselling is often the most important part of the treatment of sexual dysfunctions.

Graded tasks begin with simple, tender physical contact. The couples are encouraged to caress any part of the other person's body except the genitalia, in order to give enjoyment (Masters and Johnson call this the 'sensate focus'). At a later stage, the couple may engage in mutual masturbation. Penetration is prohibited until the early stages have been completed. At every stage, both partners are encouraged to provide the experience most enjoyed by the other person, and they are strongly discouraged from checking on their own state of sexual arousal. Such checking is a common habit of people with sexual disorder, and has been called the 'spectator role'. Graded tasks are not only therapeutic on their own; they also help to uncover hidden fears or areas of ignorance that need to be discussed with the couple.

Special methods have been devised for certain problems. The so-called squeeze technique is used for premature ejaculation. When the man indicates that he is about to have an orgasm, the woman grips the penis for a few seconds and then releases it suddenly. Intercourse is then continued. A somewhat similar 'start-stop' method has been described in which the woman attempts to regulate the amount of sexual stimulation during intercourse.

Dynamic psychotherapy is used by some psychiatrists as their main method of treatment. The results are discussed in the next section.

Results of treatment

Directive methods of the kind described above are followed by a successful outcome in about a third of cases, and by worthwhile improvement in a further third (Bancroft and Coles 1976). Problems associated with low sexual desire are unresponsive and have a poor long-term outcome; other problems, especially vaginismus, generally do well. Outcome is better among patients who engage wholeheartedly in the early stages of treatment, but it is just as good in problems of long duration as in others (Hawton *et al.* 1986). There have been no controlled evaluations of psychotherapy for sexual dysfunction. In the few uncontrolled studies, patients were so highly selected that no general conclusions could be reached.

The use of **hormones** is not recommended, except for the occasional use of testosterone in hypogonadism. There is no convincing evidence that testosterone improves erectile dysfunction unless there is a gross endocrine disorder. Bromocriptine has been prescribed for erectile dysfunction on the doubtful premise that hyperprolactinaemia is associated with low libido erectile dysfunction. There is no convincing evidence that it is generally effective (for a review see Hawton 1980).

[See Bancroft *et al.* (1986) for a review of sex therapy research.]

Sexual dysfunction among the physically handicapped

Physically handicapped people have sexual problems arising from several sources: direct effects on sexual function, for example disease of the nervous system affecting the autonomic nerve supply; the general effects of tiredness and pain; fears about the effects of intercourse on the handicapping condition; and lack of information about the sexual activities of other people with the same disability. Much can be done to help disabled people by discussing the forms of sexual activity that are possible despite their disability; and, if appropriate, by adapting the methods already described for treating sexual dysfunction. [See Stewart (1978) and Crown (1978) for accounts of sexual problems among the disabled.]

Abnormalities of sexual preference (paraphilias)

The study of these disorders in the past

For centuries, abnormalities of sexual preference were regarded as offences against the laws of religion rather than conditions that doctors should study and treat.

The systematic study of these conditions began in the 1870s with the work of Krafft-Ebing, Hirschfeld, Schrenck-Notzing, and Havelock Ellis. Krafft-Ebing (1840–1902), a Professor of Psychiatry in Vienna, compiled an important systematic account in his book *Psychopathia sexualis,* which was first published in 1886 and later achieved twelve editions and translation into seven languages. In 1899 Magnus Hirschfeld founded a journal

(Jahrbuch für sexuelle Zwischenstufen) devoted to the study of abnormalities of sexual preference. Krafft-Ebing considered that these conditions were due mainly to hereditary causes, though the latter could be modified by social and psychological factors.

About the same time, Schrenck-Notzing developed psychological treatments for both sexual inadequacy and abnormalities of sexual preference, and reported striking successes from the use of therapeutic suggestion (Schrenk-Notzing 1892). In England, the study of sexual disorders was particularly associated with the name of Havelock Ellis (1859–1939).

Freud attempted to explain these conditions as failures of the developmental processes that he believed himself to have identified in normal children. Following this contribution, psychoanalysts have devoted much attention to abnormalities of sexual preference. As a result, most of the literature on these conditions is still in the psychoanalytic tradition; and until recently treatment of both abnormalities of sexual preference and sexual dysfunction has been largely centred on psychoanalytic principles. As described later, these approaches have not been successful either in explaining the conditions or in modifying them.

The concept of abnormal sexual preference

This concept has three aspects. The first aspect is social: the behaviour does not conform to some generally accepted view of what is normal. The accepted view is not the same in every society or at every period of history. For example, regular masturbation was regarded as abnormal by many medical writers in Victorian England. The second aspect concerns the harm that might be done to the other person involved in the sexual behaviour. Intercourse with young children or extreme forms of sexual sadism are examples. The third aspect is the suffering experienced by the person himself. This suffering is related to the attitudes of the society in which the person lives (for example, attitudes to cross-dressing); to conflict between his sexual urges and his own moral standards; and to his awareness of distress caused to another person by his sexual practices (for example a man's cross-dressing might distress his wife).

General considerations

Abnormalities of sexual preference may come to medical attention in various ways, and the doctor should be aware of the different modes of presentation.

A doctor may be consulted directly by the person with the abnormalities. He may also be asked to help by the spouse or other sexual partner, possibly because behaviour accepted in the past has now become so frequent that it can be tolerated no longer. Sometimes the problem is presented as sexual inadequacy, and the abnormality of sexual preferences is discovered only in the course of history taking.

A doctor may also be asked for an opinion about a patient charged with an offence arising from abnormalities of sexual preference. Offences of this kind include indecent exposure, the behaviour of a 'peeping Tom', the stealing of clothes by fetishists, appearing in public in clothes of the opposite sex, rape and assaults upon children, intercourse with willing children who are under age, and incest. With two exceptions these offences are discussed in the following paragraphs in relation to the corresponding abnormality of sexual preference. The exceptions are rape and incest, which are considered in Chapter 22, and the problem of pornography, discussed below.

There are different opinions about the extent to which doctors should attempt to alter abnormal sexual preferences. There seems to be no reason why doctors should not try to help people who wish to alter unusual patterns of sexual behaviour, but they should not try to impose treatment on people who do not want it. How to decide who really wants help is a difficult point that is taken up later in this chapter.

Pornography

It is not known whether pornographic publications merely provide a harmless outlet for sexual impulses that might otherwise be inflicted on another person; or whether they encourage such impulses and so increase sexual offences. Epidemiological studies have attempted to relate the numbers of sexual offences to changes in the law about pornography (as in Denmark), but they have given inconclusive results. Clinical studies of abnormalities of sexual preference suggest that fantasies experienced during sexual arousal and orgasm are reinforced by pornographic literature. This evidence is inconclusive because it is not known whether a person who has strong sexual fantasies is more likely to enact them. Moreover, for people with abnormal sexual preferences it is possible that pictorial material promotes solitary sexual release and so reduces the involvement of other people.

Without more definite evidence it seems appropriate that pornographic material relating sexual activity to violence or to children should not be available to young people whose sexual development is incomplete. The arguments for more general restrictions are that pornographic publications debase women, and possibly put children at risk of exploitation. These are important matters of public policy which like many other such policies have to be decided on limited evidence. In his dealings with his patients and their families, the doctor is more likely to be asked what effect pornographic material, discovered by a wife or parent, is likely to have on a husband or adolescent son. He should explain the different points of view, and indicate that the effects are likely to differ in different people.

If the doctor can interview the person concerned and review his sexual life thoroughly, he will usually be able to give some useful advice. Such advice should, if possible, extend to broader aspects of personal relationships and not merely to the effects of the pornographic material.

Abnormalities in the preference of sexual 'object'

These abnormalities involve a preference for something other than another adult person in the achievement of sexual excitement. The alternative 'object' may be inanimate, as in fetishism and fetishistic transvestism, or may be a child (paedophilia) or an animal (zoophilia). A second group of abnormalities of preference, involving variations in behaviour rather than the object, will be discussed later.

Fetishism

In sexual fetishism, inanimate objects are the preferred or only means of achieving sexual excitement. The disorder shades into normal sexual behaviour; it is not uncommon for men to be aroused by particular items of clothing, such as stockings, or by parts of the female body that do not usually have sexual associations.

Prevalence

As the sole or preferred means of sexual arousal, sexual fetishism is uncommon but no exact figures are available.

Description

Fetishism usually begins in adolescence. It occurs almost exclusively among men, although a few cases have been described among women (see, for example, Odlum 1955). Most fetishists are heterosexual but some are homosexual—20 per cent according to Chalkley and Powell (1986). The objects that can evoke sexual arousal are many and varied, but for each person there is usually a small number of objects or classes of objects. Among the more frequent are rubber garments, women's underclothes, and high-heeled shoes. Sometimes the object is an attribute of a person, for example lameness or deformity in a woman; or a part of the human body, such as the hair or foot. The texture and smell of objects is often as important as their appearance; for example, furs, velvet, rubber garments, and polished leather are often preferred. Contact with the object causes sexual excitement, which may be followed by solitary masturbation or by sexual intercourse incorporating the fetish if a willing partner is available.

Fetishists may spend much time seeking their desired object. Some buy them, and others steal—for example, underclothes from a washing line. A few men engage in a fetishistic behaviour with a prostitute. When the object is a particular attribute of a woman, many hours may be spent in searching for and following a suitable woman. Inanimate fetish objects are often hoarded; Hirschfeld recorded a striking example, the hoarding by one man of 31 pigtails of hair, each cut with scissors from women he had followed, and each labelled with the date and hour when it had been cut (Hirschfeld 1944).

Aetiology

There are several theories of fetishism but few facts. Fetishism has occasionally been reported in association with EEG evidence of temporal lobe dysfunction (Epstein 1961) or with frank epilepsy (Mitchell *et al.* 1954). There is no evidence of such associations in the majority of cases. Fetishism was the first sexual disorder for which a theory of association learning was put forward. Thus Binet (1877) suggested that it arose by a chance coming together of sexual excitation and the object that becomes the fetish object. Some experimental evidence for such a mechanism has been reported by Rachman (1966). Male volunteers were repeatedly shown pictures of boots followed immediately by sexually arousing pictures of women. After several pairings, the pictures of boots were also followed by sexual arousal. The suggestion that fetishism results from faulty imprinting (Wilson 1981) rests entirely on analogy. Imprinting apparently affects the sexual behaviour of birds, but there is no evidence that it does so in man.

Psychoanalysts suggest that sexual fetishism arises when castration anxiety is not resolved in childhood, and the man attempts to ward off this anxiety by maintaining in his unconscious mind the idea that women have a penis (Freud 1927). In Freud's words it is 'a token of triumph against the threat of castration and a protection against it'. In this view, each fetish is a symbolic representation of a phallus. Although some fetishes can be interpreted in this way, others require tortuous interpretations if the general hypothesis is to be sustained (see, for example, Stekel 1953). In any case the general idea does not convincingly explain the majority of cases.

The explanation that best fits clinical observations is that sexual fetishism arises when the expression of heterosexual impulses has been inhibited in some way. This inhibition might arise in a number of ways; for example, through shyness with women or irrational fears about sexual intercourse. Sexual arousal might then become associated by chance with something other than heterosexual ideas, and in this way conditioned responses could arise. This kind of explanation is not supported by direct evidence, but it is at least consistent with what facts are available.

Prognosis

In the absence of reliable follow-up data, the prognosis has to be based on clinical experience. In adolescents and young adults, fetishism is often transient, disappearing when satisfying heterosexual relationships have been established. The prognosis at all ages depends crucially on the extent of other friendships and sexual activities. Solitary single men without a sexual partner have a worse prognosis. The prognosis also depends on the frequency of the behaviour and the extent to which it has already broken social conventions and legal barriers.

Treatment

There are case-reports of treatment by psychoanalysis (see Nagler 1957) and by aversion therapy [see Kilmann (1982) for a review] but no controlled trials. Clinical experience indicates that the general measures outlined later in the chapter are as effective as any psychoanalytic or specific behavioural treatment.

Fetishistic transvestism

This condition, known as transvestic fetishism in DSMIIIR is repeated dressing in the clothes of the opposite sex to achieve sexual excitement. It varies from the occasional wearing of a few articles of clothing to complete cross-dressing. Some men who cross-dress are effeminate homosexuals or transsexuals. Almost all women who cross-dress are lesbian or transsexual and not fetishistic transvestists. For this reason, the description below is of the condition in men.

Prevalence

The prevalence of fetishistic transvestism is not known.

Description

Cross-dressing usually begins about the time of puberty. The person usually starts by putting on only a few garments, but as time goes by, he adds more until he is eventually dressed entirely in clothes of the other sex. Transvestists experience erections when cross-dressing and may masturbate. Later the clothes may be worn in public, at first underneath male outer garments but eventually without such precautions against discovery.

Most transvestists are heterosexual. Unlike the transsexuals described later, they have no doubt that they are really men. Exceptionally, after many years of cross-dressing, a few transvestists may begin to believe that they are women. Despite these transitional cases, transvestists differ in important ways from transsexualists. Transvestists are sexually aroused by cross-dressing and convinced they are of the correct gender; transsexuals experience no erotic pleasure from cross-dressing and are convinced that they are trapped in a body that is of the opposite sex to their real nature. Many transvestists are married; most of them hide the behaviour from their wives, but a few reveal it and persuade their wives to assist in obtaining clothes. Wives usually express distress and disgust if they discover their husband dressed as a woman, but a few appear to collude with the behaviour.

Aetiology

There is no evidence that the chromosomal sex or hormonal make-up of transvestists is abnormal (see Lukianowicz 1959). Despite a report of three cases in one family (Liakos 1967) transvestism is not familial and there is no evidence that it is inherited. Although occasional associations with temporal lobe dysfunction have been reported (Epstein 1960; Davies and Morgenstern 1960) there is no evidence of such an association in the majority. Suggestions (for example Allen 1969) that transvestism is an expression of repressed homosexuality do not accord with the clinical evidence that transvestists continue to have heterosexual interests for many years. Transvestism develops gradually from puberty, and since it is associated with sexual arousal, the aetiology is likely to resemble that proposed above for fetishism, namely an impediment to normal sexual development coupled perhaps with association learning. Some psychoanalysts (for example Fenichel 1945) have suggested that the transvestist is creating a 'phallic woman' (himself in women's clothes) to allay castration anxiety. The theory is not convincing.

Prognosis

In the absence of reliable information from follow-up of a representative group of transvestists, statements about prognosis must be based on clinical experience. Most cases appear to continue for years, becoming less severe as sexual drives decline in middle age or later. However there are wide variations in outcome, and the comments made earlier about the prognosis of fetishism apply here as well. As already noted, a minority of persistent transvestists develop the idea that they are women and continue to cross-dress without sexual arousal.

Treatment

There are some reports of psychoanalytic treatment (Rosen 1979) and aversion therapy (Marks and Gelder 1967) but no clinical trials. Cross-dressing can sometimes be supressed rapidly by aversion therapy. In the long term, however, general measures (described at the end of this chapter) are probably as effective as psychoanalysis or aversion therapy.

Paedophilia

Paedophilia is repeated sexual activity (or fantasy of such activity) with pre-pubertal children, as a preferred or exclusive method of obtaining sexual excitement. Males who have intercourse with young girls can be divided into two groups. An adolescent group have intercourse with girls who are only a few years younger than themselves and who are often at an age when sexual behaviour would be permitted in some other societies. With few exceptions, such adolescent males are of normal intelligence and background. The second group are older men who deliberately choose a sexual partner who is still a child.

The law on sexual intercourse with young people is complicated. Thus in England and Wales, girls under 16 cannot give legal consent to sexual intercourse; and young men under 21 cannot, as the law stands at present, consent to homosexual practices. However, if a girl is between 13 and 16 years old and the man is less than 24, and if he believes her to be over 16, then the girl's consent is a defence against a charge of unlawful sexual intercourse brought against the man. Paedophilia, however, involves relationships between an adult and a prepubertal child, rather than these borderlines of the legal age of consent.

Prevalence

Paedophilia is almost invariably a disorder of men. There is no reliable information about its prevalence. From the existence of child prostitution in some countries and the ready sale of pornographic material depicting sex with children, it appears that interest in sexual relationships with children is not rare. Nevertheless paedophilia, as an exclusive form of sexual behaviour, is probably uncommon.

Description

The paedophile usually chooses a child aged between 9 years and puberty. The child may be of the opposite sex (heterosexual paedophilia) or the same sex (homosexual paedophilia). Although the condition can begin at any age, most paedophiles seen by doctors are men of middle age. There is no evidence that paedophiles have changed their interests from adult to child partners as they grow older; usually the preference seems established from the start.

Paedophilia has to be distinguished from exhibitionism towards young girls (in which no attempt is made to engage in direct sexual contact). Sexual contact with children may also be sought by people with subnormal intelligence, dementia, and alcoholism. With younger children fondling or masturbation is more likely than full coitus, but some young children are injured by forcible attempts at penetration. Rare and tragic cases of sexual sadism occur. [Sexual abuse of children is described on p. 814.]

The child

Of the children involved in paedophilia, two-thirds have co-operated in sexual activity more than once with the same or another adult (Gibbens and Prince 1965). However, some of these children have apparently co-operated through fear rather than interest. A minority of the children are also promiscuous and steal, play truant, or run away from home, but most are not delinquent and come from well organized families. Gibbens and Prince thought that the mothers often showed an ambivalent attitude both to discipline and to the child's sexual development. The long-term effects of paedophilia on the child are not certain. In a follow-up of children who had experienced sexual activity with an adult, Bender and Grugett (1952) found there was no lasting maladjustment provided that the child had developed normally up to the time of the sexual experience. The effect on the child is probably much influenced by the reaction of the parents, and by how far the child is involved in legal proceedings (Mohr *et al.* 1964).

Aetiology

This is unknown. Paedophiles often have a marked incapacity for relationships with adults, and fears of relationships with women. The various aetiological theories are reviewed by Mohr *et al.* (1964).

Prognosis

In the absence of reliable information from follow-up studies, prognosis has to be judged in individual patients by the length of the history, the frequency of the behaviour, the absence of other social and sexual relationships and the strengths and weaknesses of the personality. Behaviour that has been frequently repeated is likely to persist despite efforts at treatment.

Treatment

Both group treatment (Hartman 1965) and behaviour therapy (Beech *et al.* 1971) have been tried, but there is no convincing evidence that either leads to good results in the majority of paedophiles. The general measures described at the end of this chapter should be tried, although good results should not be expected.

Other abnormalities in the preference of sexual object

Zoophilia

Zoophilia, otherwise called bestiality or bestiosexuality, is the use of an animal as a repeated and preferred or exclusive method of achieving sexual excitement. It is uncommon, and rarely encountered by doctors.

Necrophilia

In this extremely rare condition sexual arousal is obtained through intercourse with a dead body. Occasionally there are legal trials of men who murder and then attempt intercourse with the victim. No reliable information is available about the causes or prognosis of this extreme form of abnormal sexual preference.

Abnormalities in the preference of sexual act

The second group of abnormalities of sexual preference involves variations in the behaviour that is carried out to obtain sexual arousal. Generally the acts are directed towards other adults but sometimes children are involved (for example, by some exhibitionists).

Exhibitionism

Exhibitionism is the repeated exposing of the genitals to unprepared strangers for the purpose of achieving sexual excitement but without any attempts at further sexual activity with the other person. The name exhibitionsim was suggested by Lasègue (1877) and further clinical observations were reported by Krafft-Ebing in 1886 (see Krafft-Ebing 1924). The use of the term in this technical sense is to be distinguished from its everyday sense of extravagant behaviour to draw attention to oneself.

Prevalence

This is not known. Exhibitionists make up about one-third of sexual offenders referred for psychiatric treatment, and about a quarter of sexual offenders dealt with in the courts (Rosen 1979). Almost all are men, though there are rare women exhibitionists who repeatedly expose the breasts, or some, even rarer, who expose the genitalia.

Description

The act of exposure is usually preceded by a feeling of mounting tension. Exhibitionists characteristically seek to evoke a strong emotional reaction from the other person, generally surprise and shock. Some are satisfied by any evidence of being noticed, even laughter. Most exhibitionists choose places from which escape is easy, though a few choose places where they risk detection. Whatever the exact pattern of behaviour, the experience is one of the intense excitement and exhilaration at the same time. In some exhibitionists the preoccupation is persistent, in others it is episodic. As a broad generalization, two groups can be described. The first group includes men of inhibited temperament who struggle against their urges and feel much guilt after the act; they sometimes expose a flaccid penis. The second group includes men who have aggressive traits, sometimes accompanied by features of antisocial personality disorder. They usually expose an erect penis, often while masturbating. They gain pleasure from any distress they cause and often feel little guilt. About two-thirds of exhibitionists are married, and most are aged 20–40 (Gayford 1981).

Women often fear that the act of exposure will be followed by rape but it seems that exhibitionists seldom commit rape. However, some persistent exhibitionists make other, less serious physical advances to women (Rooth 1973). It has been suggested that exhibitionism and voyeurism are related to one another aetiologically, but exhibitionists seldom practise voyeurism (Rooth 1971). There is uncertainty about the relationship between exhibitionism and the making of *obscene phone calls* by men who talk to women about sexual activities while masturbating. It has been suggested (Tollison and Adams 1979) that these obscene callers are also exhibitionists, but it is not easy to identify them in order to study their psychopathology.

In Britain, if a man is brought to court because of exhibitionism, he is charged with the offence of *indecent exposure* (see Chapter 22, p. 884), for the definition of indecent exposure). About four-fifths of men charged with indecent exposure are exhibitionists (as defined at the beginning of this section).

Aetiology

There are several theories, all unsubstantiated. As in other sexual deviations, the first step must be to explain why heterosexual development has been inhibited. The same explanations have been put forward for this disorder as for the others we have described earlier in the chapter; namely, failure to resolve Oedipal conflict or a general inhibition of social relationships. The relationship between exhibitionists and their parents has been investigated retrospectively. Some exhibitionists describe unduly close relationships with their mothers and a poor relationship with ineffectual fathers (see Rickles 1950). As always with retrospective accounts, it is not certain how far these memories reflect the actual circumstances of the patient's upbringing. Also, many people describe similar experiences in childhood, but do not grow up to be exhibitionists. To the clinician, the most striking feature of many exhibitionists is a personality characterized by lack of assertion and a striking degree of passivity in everyday relationships.

Whatever the original cause of exhibitionism, it has been suggested that the behaviour is perpetuated by the reinforcing effects of sexual release during masturbation that often follows (Evans 1970). Exhibitionism may be self perpetuating in this way, but it is not a form of obsessive-compulsive behaviour as suggested by Rickles (1950). Although the exhibitionist may feel compelled to carry out his act, the phenomenon is not a compulsion in the technical sense of the term, nor is there any evidence that it is associated with obsessive-compulsive neurosis. In middle-aged or elderly people, the onset of exhibitionism should always suggest organic brain disease. Such organic disease presumably releases a reaction pattern that is preformed but has been previously inhibited.

Prognosis

There is no reliable information about prognosis. Clinical experience suggests a variable outcome. Men who exhibit only once do not fall within the definition of the disorder. In men who exhibit repeatedly but only at times of stress the prognosis depends on the likelihood of the stressors returning. Exhibitionists who repeat often are likely to persist for years despite treatment by psychiatrists or punishment by the courts. In keeping with these clinical impressions, the evidence from the courts is that the reconviction rate for indecent exposure is low after a first conviction but high after a second conviction. Although a history of exhibitionism is sometimes given by men who commit rape, the majority of exhibitionists do not go on to commit violent sexual acts nor do they interfere with children (Rooth 1973). A full account of exhibitionism is given by Rooth (1971).

Treatment

Associated psychiatric disorders such as depressive disorder, alcoholism or dementia should always be sought and treated appropriately if found. Many treatments have been tried specifically for exhibitionism, including psychoanalysis, individual and group psychotherapy (Witzig 1968), aversion therapy (Rooth and Marks 1974), and covert sensitization (Maletszky 1974, 1977). There is no satisfactory evidence that any of these treatments is effective for most cases. A practical approach combines counselling and behavioural techniques. Counselling deals with the exhibitionistic behaviour and with other problems in personal relationships, whilst behavioural techniques are concerned with self-monitoring to identify circumstances that trigger the behaviour. Cyproterone acetate has been used to reduce sex drive, but it is not recommended because of uncertain results and problems of long-term use (see p. 590). For a discussion of an eclectic approach to treatment see Rooth (1980).

Voyeurism

Many men are sexually excited by observing others engaged in intercourse. Voyeurism (occasionally called scopophilia), is observing the sexual activity of others repeatedly as a preferred means of sexual arousal. The voyeur also spies on women who are undressing or without clothes, but does not attempt sexual activity with them. Voyeurism is usually accompanied or followed by masturbation.

Voyeurism is a disorder of heterosexual men, whose heterosexual activities are usually inadequate. Although the voyeur usually takes great care to hide from the women he is watching, he often takes considerable risks of discovery by other people. Hence most voyeurs are reported by passers-by, not by the victim.

Aetiology

Among adolescents voyeuristic activities are not uncommon as an expression of sexual curiosity, but they are usually replaced by direct sexual experience. The voyeur continues to watch because he is shy, socially awkward with girls, or prevented from normal sexual expression by some other obstacle. Psychoanalytic explanations follow the general lines described above for other sexual disorders. Behavioural theories seek an explanation in terms of chance associations between a first experience of peeping and sexual arousai.

Prognosis

No reliable information is available.

Treatment

Psychoanalysis, group therapy (Witzig 1968) and counter-conditioning (Jackson 1969) have been used but, as no systematic trials have been reported, no conclusions can be drawn. It is doubtful whether any treatment is effective, but it is reasonable to try the general measures described later in this chapter.

Sexual sadism

Sadism is named after the Marquis de Sade (1774–1814) who inflicted extreme cruelty on women for sexual purposes. Sexual sadism is achieving sexual arousal, habitually and in preference to heterosexual intercourse, by inflicting pain on another person.

Prevalence

Inflicting pain or restraint in fantasy or practice is a not uncommon accompaniment of other forms of sexual behaviour. Sex-shops sell chains, whips, and shackles, while some pornographic magazines provide pictures and descriptions of sadistic sexual practices. Sexual sadism as a predominant sexual practice is probably uncommon but its frequency is not known.

Description

Beating, whipping, and tying are common forms of sadistic activity. Repeated acts are usually with a partner who is a masochist, or a prostitute who is paid to take part. Sadism may be a component of homosexual as well as heterosexual acts. Rare cases of sexual sadism towards animals have been reported (see Allen 1969). The acts may be symbolic, with little actual damage, some involving humiliation rather than injury. Sometimes serious and permanent injuries are caused. Extreme examples are 'lust murders', in which the killer inflicts serious and often ritually repeated injuries—usually stabbings and mutilations—on the genitalia of his victim. In these rare cases, ejaculation may occur during the sadistic act or later by intercourse with the dead body (necrophilia). Further information is given by Hirschfeld (1944).

Aetiology

This is not known. Psychoanalytical explanations draw attention to the association of loving and aggressive feelings that is supposed to exist in the young child's early relationship with his parents. Behavioural formulations rely on association learning. The two explanations are equally unsatisfactory.

Prognosis

There is no reliable information, but clinical experience suggests that once established the behaviour is likely to persist for many years.

Treatment

There are case reports of the use of behaviour therapy (for example Davison 1968) but no evidence from adequate clinical trials. In the absence of any proven treatment, men who have committed serious injury must be dealt with by legal means if there is risk of another offence. In deciding this issue it is wise to assume that treatment of any kind is unlikely to alter an established pattern of sadistic sexual behaviour. The risks must not be underestimated when potentially dangerous behaviour has been planned or has already occurred.

Sexual masochism

Sexual masochism is achieving sexual excitement, as a preferred or exclusive practice, through the experience of suffering. As a predominant activity, it differs from the common use of minor painful practices as an accompaniment to sexual intercourse. The condition is named after Leopold von Sacher-Masoch (1836–1905), an Austrian novelist, who described sexual gratification from the experience of pain.

Prevalence

Fantasies of being beaten or raped are common enough among males to create a demand for pornographic literature, and also for prostitutes who will help the man act out his fantasies. Established sexual masochism is probably uncommon though no exact information is available.

Description

The suffering may take the form of being beaten, trodden upon, bound or chained, or the enactment of various symbolic forms of humiliation; for example, dressing as a child and being punished. Masochism, unlike most other sexual deviations, occurs in women as well as in men, perhaps as a reflection of the more submissive role of the woman in normal sexual relationships. It may occur in homosexual as well as heterosexual relationships.

At times, the masochist may allow dangerous forms of assault upon himself, including strangulation, a practice that can increase sexual excitation through the resulting partial anoxia. Some solitary people seek sexual arousal from anoxia by covering the head with a plastic bag. This act is sometimes accompanied by fetishistic practices or cross-dressing. Occasionally this behaviour has resulted in death (see, for example, Johnstone *et al.* 1960).

Aetiology

This is not known. One theory is that, as a result of beatings delivered to pubertal children, sexual arousal becomes associated by chance with the experience of pain and humiliation. Psychoanalytic theory suggests that masochism is sadism turned inwards, and therefore explicable in the same way as sadism (see p. 586).

Prognosis

There is no reliable information about prognosis. Clinical experience suggests that, once established as a preferred form of sexual behaviour, masochism is likely to persist for many years.

Treatment

There are case reports of treatment by psychoanalysis (Stekel 1953) and behavioural treatment (Marks *et al.* 1965) but no satisfactory evidence from which to judge the effects of either.

Other abnormalities of preference of the sexual act

In **frotteurism** the preferred form of sexual excitement is applying or rubbing the male genitalia against another person, usually a stranger and an unwilling participant, in a crowded place such as an underground train. In **coprophilia**, sexual arousal is induced by thinking about or watching the act of defecation and this is the preferred sexual activity; in **coprophagia** arousal follows the eating of faeces. In **sexual urethism**, which occurs mainly in women, erotic arousal is obtained by stimulation of the urethra.

Urophilia refers to sexual arousal obtained by watching the act of urination, being urinated upon, or drinking urine. It was described at length by Havelock Ellis (1928) who named it **undinism**. The prevalence of these disorders is not known, but some are sufficiently common to demand provision from prostitutes. Further information will be found in Allen (1969) and Tollison and Adams (1979).

Assessment and management of abnormalities of sexual preference

In assessment, the first step is to **exclude mental illness.** Abnormal sexual preference is sometimes secondary to dementia, alcoholism, depressive illness, or mania. These illnesses probably release the behaviour in a person who has previously experienced the corresponding sexual fantasies but not acted on them. It is particularly important to look for mental illness when the abnormal sexual preference comes to notice for the first time in middle age or later.

Detailed enquiry is then made about the patient's sexual practices. It should be borne in mind that patients not uncommonly have more than one form of abnormal sexual preference. The extent and vigour of normal heterosexual interests, both in the present and in the past, are determined. Whenever possible, an interview should be arranged with the patient's regular sexual partner.

It is always important to find out what part the abnormal sexual preference is playing in the patient's life. Apart from being a source of sexual arousal, it may be a comforting activity that helps to ward off feelings of loneliness, anxiety, or depression. Unless other means are found to deal with such feelings, treatment may reduce the patient's abnormal sexual preference but worsen his emotional state.

Motives for seeking treatment

People who request treatment for sexual disorders often have mixed motives. Many consult a doctor because their sexual behaviour has become known to the spouse, another relative, or the police. Such people may have little wish to change and many of them prefer to be told that no treatment will help, so as to justify the continuation of their sexual practices. Sometimes people with abnormal sexual preferences seek help when they become depressed and feel guilty about the behaviour and its effects on other people. At these times of low mood, strong wishes for change may be expressed only to fade quickly as normal mood returns. Strong motivation is known to be important whether treatment is by psychoanalysis (Bieber 1962), psychotherapy (Ellis 1956), or behaviour therapy (Feldman and McCulloch 1979). It is therefore important to assess whether the expressed wishes for change will be maintained.

Planning treatment

The aim of treatment must be discussed with the patient: whether it is to control, or if possible give up, the behaviour; or to adapt better to the behaviour so that less guilt and distress are felt. In considering these aims, the doctor will sometimes have to take into account whether any psychological or even physical harm is being caused to other people, although his first concern must be for his patient. At this early stage it is important to make clear that, whatever the aim, treatment will require considerable effort on the part of the patient.

If the agreed aim is better adjustment, treatment will be by counselling designed to explore the patient's feelings, and to help him to identify the problems caused by his sexual practices and to find ways of reducing them. If the agreed aim is change, the first step is to find ways of encouraging ordinary heterosexual relationships. For this purpose, treatment is directed first to any anxieties that are impeding social relationships with the opposite sex. Attention is then directed to any detected sexual inadequacy using the methods outlined earlier in this chapter. In most cases, these two steps are the most important part of treatment.

The problems likely to arise from giving up the abnormal sexual behaviour are considered next. Some patients occupy much of their time in preparing for the sexual act (for example fetishists may spend many hours searching for a particular kind of women's underclothes). As already noted, the behaviour often becomes a way of warding off feelings of loneliness or despair. To safeguard against distress, the patient must be helped to develop leisure activities, seek new friends, and find other ways of coping with unpleasant emotions.

Only when these steps have been taken should attention be directed to ways of suppressing the unwanted sexual behaviour. Sometimes the preceding steps are enough to strengthen the patient's capacity to control himself, but additional help is often needed.

Masturbation fantasies appear to play an important part in perpetuating abnormal sexual behaviour. It is therefore important to encourage the patient to keep any abnormal fantasies out of mind during masturbation. If he cannot rid his mind of fantasies, he should be encouraged to modify them progressively, so that the themes become less and less sexually abnormal and increasingly concerned with ordinary heterosexual intercourse.

For men, antiandrogens have been used in an attempt to reduce sexual drive but this approach has limited value. Oestrogens may be tried if libido is strong, and if the continuation of the behaviour is likely to have serious consequences outweighing the risks of treatment. Oestrogens may be given as depot injections such as oestradiol undecylenate, or as an oestradiol implant. The therapy can cause breast enlargement and nodules, testicular atrophy, osteoporosis, and, rarely, breast tumours. For this reason antiandrogen drugs such as cyproterone acetate are sometimes used although it is still not clear how far their effects exceed the placebo response (see Wakeling 1979 for further information). Cyproterone can produce a reversible atrophy of the seminiferous tubules and its side effects include gynaecomastia, sedation, and depression.

Behavioural treatment may also be tried. Aversion therapy is no longer recommended, except possibly for temporary suppression of strong mental imagery while other steps are taken to enable the patient to suppress such imagery himself. Used in this way, aversion therapy is most effective for fetishism and transvestism. The main value of behaviour therapy is to encourage normal heterosexual behaviour, although the general methods described earlier in this chapter seem to be equally effective.

Many people with abnormal sexual preferences appear before the courts. Sanctions such as a suspended sentence or probation order can sometimes help the patient to gain control of his own behaviour. However, no doctor should agree to treat patients who are sent to him against their wishes.

Abnormalities of gender identity

Transsexualism

A transsexual person is convinced that he is of the sex opposite to that indicated by his external genitalia. In addition, he feels estranged from his body, has an overpowering wish to live as a member of the opposite sex, and seeks to alter his bodily appearance and genitalia to conform to those of the opposite sex. Most transsexuals are men. In the past the condition was called **eonism** because it was exemplified by the Chevalier d'Eon de Beaumont. In psychiatric literature, the condition was mentioned by Esquirol in 1838 and described in more detail by Krafft-Ebing in 1886 (see Krafft-Ebing 1924). More recently the description by Benjamin (1966) has directed the attention of doctors and the public to the condition.

Prevalence

Epidemiological data are understandably difficult to obtain. Wålinder (1968) estimated the prevalence amonst Swedish males to be 1 in 37 000 and among Swedish females to be 1 in 103 000. Hoenig and Kenna (1974) reported similar figures (1:34 000 and 1:108 000) in Great Britain. Most of those seeking medical help are men.

Description

(a) Among men. Patients report a strong conviction of belonging to the other sex, usually dating from before puberty. It is sometimes reported by the parents that in childhood the patients preferred the company and pursuits of girls, although such a history is not invariable (gender disturbance in children is referred to on p. 594).

By the time medical help is requested, most transsexuals have started dressing as women. In contrast to transvestists, they cross-dress to feel more like women, not to produce sexual arousal. (They also differ from those homosexuals who dress as women to attract other homosexuals.) For this purpose, make-up is worn and the hair is arranged in a feminine style; facial and body hair is usually removed by electrolysis. Transsexuals try to adopt feminine gestures and to alter the pitch of the voice, but few succeed wholly convincingly. Transsexuals also seek changes in social role. They apply for the kind of work that is usually done by women and they enjoy cooking and sewing. They do not show maternal interests. Sex drive is usually low and, unlike transvestists, these patients do not masturbate when cross-dressed. As Benjamin has written (1966 p. 21) 'the transvestist looks on his sex organ as an organ of pleasure, and the transsexual turns from it in disgust'.

There is no characteristic type of **personality**, but some transsexuals are self-centred, demanding, and attention-seeking; they are often particularly difficult to treat.

Many transsexual patients are greatly distressed by their predicament. Depression is common, and in one series 16 per cent had made suicide attempts (Wålinder 1967). About a third marry but, not surprisingly, about half of these become divorced (Roth and Ball 1964).

Transsexuals often ask the doctor for help in altering the appearance of the breasts and external genitalia. Usually the first requests are for oestrogens to enlarge the breasts. These requests are often followed by increasingly insistent demands for surgery to the breasts, for surgical castration and removal of the penis, and even for operations to create an artificial vagina. Such demands are usually made in a determined and persistent way, and are sometimes accompanied by threats of self-mutilation or suicide. Some patients do attempt to castrate themselves, and may maintain afterwards that the injury was accidental.

(b) Among women. Many women who appear to be transsexuals are really homosexuals. Transsexual women resemble transsexual men in having held since childhood a strong conviction that they 'occupy' a body of the wrong sex. Some seek to alter their body by mastectomy or hysterectomy, and a few hope for plastic surgery to create an artificial

penis. Transsexual women strive to be like men in dress, voice, gestures, and social behaviour, and in their choice of work and hobbies. They wish to have intercourse not with a lesbian, but in the role of male with a heterosexual partner.

Aetiology

Many ideas have been put forward to explain this puzzling condition but its cause remains unknown. Transsexuals have normal sex chromosomes, and there is no convincing evidence of a genetic cause. It has been suggested that abnormal acquisition of gender role might be relevant. However, there is no convincing evidence that transsexuals have been brought up in the wrong gender role.

It has been suggested that transsexualism might result from hormonal abnormalities during intrauterine development. There is some evidence that when pregnant rhesus monkeys are given large doses of androgens, their female infants behave more like males during play (Young *et al.* 1964). There is no direct parallel in man but it may be relevant that female children with the adrenogenital syndrome (involving exposure to large amounts of androgen before and after birth) have been reported to show rather boyish behaviour in childhood (Ehrhardt *et al.* 1968). Despite this, they have not been reported to grow up as transsexuals. Endocrine disorders have also been sought in adult transsexuals but no definite abnormality has been found. Wålinder (1967) found abnormal EEGs in 28 per cent of his patients. There is no other evidence of organic brain disorder among transsexuals.

In an interesting minority of patients, transsexualism begins after many years of transvestism. These patients start by cross-dressing to obtain sexual excitement, but the resultant arousal gradually diminishes. At the same time the patients gradually become convinced that they are women.

Prognosis

There is no reliable information about the prognosis of untreated transsexuals. Clinical experience suggests that once established the condition persists for many years, though it is not known whether it lasts beyond middle age. The rate of suicide among transsexuals is probably increased.

Treatment

Although transsexualism is undoubtedly a psychological disorder in a person whose body is normal, patients usually demand treatment directed to the body not the mind. The most rational treatment would be to alter the patient's conviction that he is of the wrong sex, but attempts to do so by psychotherapy rarely succeed. If treatment involving physical changes is offered, it should be done by carefully planned stages. The evident distress of these patients and their insistent demands should not be allowed to interfere with this plan. Many psychiatrists, including the authors, consider that physical changes are seldom appropriate and that in most cases it is better to use supportive psychotherapy. When other treatment is used it generally passes through the stages described in the following paragraphs.

A male transsexual usually has three aims: to take on a woman's appearance, to live as a woman, and to change his genitalia. For the first the beard is often removed by electrolysis. The man can learn to speak like a woman, and practise appropriate gestures and ways of walking and sitting. These changes in speech and movement are often particularly difficult, but social skills training with video-feedback may possibly aid them (Yardley 1976). Male patients usually seek breast enlargement, at first by oestrogens and later by mammoplasty. Neither treatment should be provided at an early stage, since suitable clothing can be used instead and the drugs are not without danger (see below).

If the patient persists in his intentions, he may try to live as a woman. He may then become sufficiently impressed by the problems of living as a woman as to modify his aims. If after a year the patient persists in demanding surgery and his personality is stable, he may be given a full explanation of what the operation entails. He must understand that no surgery can make a man into a woman; at best it can provide only a poor copy of the female body.

Oestrogen is sometimes given at this stage or earlier to produce some enlargement of the breasts and deposition of fat around hips and thighs. Minor side-effects include nausea and dizziness, while more serious risks are thrombosis and malignant breast tumours (Symmers 1968). Methyl testosterone has been prescribed to women transsexuals who wish to become male, but it carries the risk of liver damage.

If after these preliminaries the psychiatrist considers that the patient is one of the few who might benefit from surgery, the opinion of an experienced consultant surgeon can be sought. He will make the final decision about the indications for surgery and the type of operation, though with the psychiatrist's advice. In giving this it should be remembered that the late results of such surgery are uncertain.

More than a dozen follow-up studies have been reported, but only one included any kind of comparison group. This study (Meyer and Reter 1979) compared patients who received sex reassignment surgery with those who were refused surgery and therefore not really comparable. No study has compared the patients allocated randomly to surgery and non-surgery. The uncontrolled studies have shown improvement rates of about 60 per cent after sex reassignment surgery. In the comparative study of Meyer and Reter, a similar rate of improvement was found in unoperated controls. This finding should be interpreted with caution since only half the patients were assessed at follow-up, and the follow-up period was longer for operated patients. Nevertheless the improvement rate in unoperated patients is an important warning against uncritical acceptance of the value of surgery. The publicity given to a few successful cases should certainly not be given undue weight. For a review of outcome studies of sex reassignment surgery, see Abramowitz (1986). More information about the treatment is given by Green and Money (1969) and by Schapira *et al.* (1979).

Dual role transvestism

This term is used in ICD10 (draft) to describe people who wear clothes of the opposite sex but are neither fetishistic transvestites (seeking sexual excitement) nor transsexuals (wishing a change of gender and sexual role). Instead they enjoy cross-dressing in order to gain a temporary membership of the opposite sex.

Gender identity disorder of adolescence and adulthood— non-transsexual type

This term is used in DSMIIIR to denote people who have passed puberty and feel a persistent or recurrent discomfort or sense of inappropriateness about their assigned gender identity. They cross-dress persistently or repeatedly, or imagine themselves doing this, but are not sexually excited by these actions or fantasies; nor are they preoccupied with change in their primary or secondary sex characteristics.

Gender identity disorders in children

Parents more often seek advice about effeminate behaviour in boys than about masculine behaviour in small girls (it is not clear whether such behaviour in girls is less frequent or more socially acceptable). Effeminate boys prefer girlish games and enjoy wearing female clothing. The outcome amongst these boys is variable (Green and Money 1961); some develop normal male interests and activities, others continue their effeminate ways into adolescence. Further information is given by Green (1974).

Other aspects of sexual behaviour

Rape, incest, and pornography are discussed in Chapter 22 (Forensic Psychiatry).

Further reading

Bancroft, J. (1983). *Human sexuality and its problems*. Churchill Livingstone, Edinburgh.

Elstein, M. (1980). Sexual medicine. *Clinics in obstetrics and gynaecology*, Vol 7, No. 2. Saunders, London.

Ford, C. S. and Beach, F. A. (1952). *Patterns of sexual behaviour*. Methuen, London.

Hawton, K. (1985). *Sex therapy; a practical guide*. Oxford University Press, Oxford.

Kaplan, H. I. and Sadock, B. J. (eds.) (1985). Normal human sexuality and psychosexual disorders. In *Comprehensive textbook of psychiatry* (4th edn.), Vol. 1, Chapter 24. Williams and Wilkins, Baltimore.

16 Psychiatry of the elderly

Introduction

It is only in the past thirty years that the psychiatric care of the elderly has attracted special interest. This change of interest largely reflects the increasing numbers of old people in the population. In western Europe at the beginning of this century only 5 per cent of the population were aged over 65; now the figure is about 15 per cent, a third of whom are aged over 75. It is expected that the proportion of elderly people will continue to rise well into the next century, mainly because of an increase in the numbers of those aged over 85 years. Since the prevalence of mental disorder and particularly dementia increases with age, there has been a disproportionate increase in the demand for psychiatric care for the elderly. People aged over 65 now make up half of all long-stay psychiatric patients, and about a fifth of all the first admissions to psychiatric wards.

The demand for care will continue to rise in developed countries. Also developing countries, in which there are fewer of the elderly at present, will begin to experience problems of increasing numbers. While recognizing that greater numbers of the elderly are likely to mean more cases of psychiatric disorder, it should not be forgotten that most old people, even the very old, have good mental health.

Although the psychiatric disorders of the elderly have some special features, they do not differ substantially from the psychiatric disorders of younger adults. It is the needs of elderly psychiatric patients that set them apart from others. Indeed the practice of psychogeriatrics requires special psychiatric skills. It is for this reason that a separate chapter is devoted to the subject.

The chapter begins with a brief account of normal ageing. General principles of psychogeriatric care are discussed next, and then an account is given of different psychiatric syndromes in the aged.

Normal ageing

The ageing brain

The weight of the human brain decreases by approximately 5 per cent between the ages of 30 and 70 years, 10 per cent by the age of 80, and 20 per cent by the age of 90. Along with these changes, the ventricles enlarge and the meninges thicken. There is some loss of nerve cells, but this is minor and selective; more important is a decline in quantity of nerve processes. Senile plaques are increasingly common with advancing age. They are present in 80 per cent of healthy people aged 70 or more. In a smaller number there are neurofibrillary tangles and granulovacuolar degeneration. Ischaemic lesions are present in brains from half of normal subjects aged over 65. Biochemically there is evidence of decline in some neurotransmitter systems and changes in brain protein synthesis. Unfortunately the significance of many of these findings is not understood because of the difficulty of studying the relationships between post-mortem histology and brain function in life (see Perry and Perry 1982).

The psychology of ageing

Because old people are often unwell and have sensory impairments, it is difficult to decide what is psychologically normal in old age. It is commonly accepted that intellectual functions as measured with standard intelligence tests decline from mid-life, but there is considerable individual variation. The significance of the changes is uncertain, partly because the tests focus on new learning tasks, which tend to under-represent the value of experience. Deterioration of short-term memory is an obvious feature of aging but the true nature and extent of the defect is not clear. Slowness is another obvious characteristic of ageing, and it partly explains impaired performance on cognitive tests. Impairment of psychomotor tasks, which has been demonstrated repeatedly, appears to be due to changes in central rather than peripheral mechanisms. As well as these cognitive and motor changes there are important alterations in personality and attitudes, such as increasing cautiousness, rigidity, and 'disengagement' from the outside world. [See Birren and Sloane (1980), and Woods (1982) for further information about the psychology of normal ageing.]

Physical health

In addition to a general decline in functional capacity and adaptability with ageing, chronic degenerative conditions are common. As a result, the elderly consult their family doctors frequently and occupy a half of all general hospital beds. The demands are particularly large in those aged over 75. Medical management is often made more difficult by the presence of more than one disorder, by increased sensitivity to the side-effects of treatment, and by the frequency of psychiatric and social problems (see Kane 1985).

Sensory and motor disabilities are frequent among elderly people. In a study in Jerusalem (Davies and Fleischman 1981) difficulties in seeing were reported by 54 per cent of 70-74-year-olds, and by 69 per cent of those over 80. The corresponding figures for other disabilities were: difficulty in hearing, 34 per cent and 50 per cent; difficulty in walking 29 per cent and 62 per cent; difficulty in talking, 9 per cent and 22 per cent.

Studies by the World Health Organization show that although reported prevalences of these disorders differ somewhat in other countries, the figures from Jerusalem are fairly representative (Davies 1986).

Social circumstances

Almost all the elderly live at home; about a third are alone, about half are with their spouse, and about 10 per cent with their children. Many see families, friends, and neighbours regularly, but a quarter of those over 65 have no children to help them and a considerable number rarely have visitors. In an ageing population in which more middle-aged women work, there are fewer people to visit and help the elderly. The aged have poorer accommodation and lower incomes than younger people. A half of the aged are believed to be near the official definition of poverty, and many lack basic amenities such as adequate bathrooms and inside lavatories. These problems increase with increasing age. Although this picture of unsatisfactory social circumstances is typical of most Western countries it is not so everywhere. In some cultures (for example the Chinese), the elderly are esteemed and most can expect to live with their children. [See Kane (1985) for a review of the social circumstances of the elderly.]

General considerations

Until the mid-1950s understanding of the mental disorders of later life was largely based upon accounts written at the beginning of the century, when Kraepelin, Bleuler, and others described the presenile, senile, and arterio-sclerotic psychoses. At that time disorders with a predominantly affective picture were usually ascribed to a supposed underlying organic cause. Doubts about the evidence for such an organic cause, together with the success of new physical treatments, led to a re-examination of the problem. Using information from case-notes, Roth (1955) divided patients into five diagnostic groups, and assessed their outcome six months and two years after admission. He found that affective psychosis, late paraphrenia, and acute confusion had better prognoses than arteriosclerotic or senile psychoses. Roth also found that organic states appeared to be diagnosed more often in the United States than in Britain, and this finding was subsequently confirmed in a systematic comparison between the two countries (Copeland and Gurland 1985). Roth's investigation provided the basis for many subsequent studies of the epidemiology, clinical features, prognosis, and treatment of mental disorder in old age.

Epidemiology

In an area of Newcastle-upon-Tyne, Kay *et al.* (1964) carried out the first systematic prevalence study of psychiatric disorder amongst elderly people

Table 16.1. Estimated prevalence of psychiatric disorder*

Disorder	Prevalence in people aged 65 and over (%)	Ratio of patients living at home to those in institutions
Dementia (severe)	5.6	6:1
Dementia (mild	5.7	10:1
Manic-depressive	1.4	18:1
Schizophrenia (excluding long-stay hospital patients)	1.1	9:1
Neurosis and personality disorder	12.5	51:1
All disorder	26.3	14:1

* Adapted from Kay *et al.* (1964).

in the general population, including those living at home as well as those living in institutions. The findings, which are shown in Table 16.1 have been broadly replicated in subsequent surveys in Britain, North America, and Europe. There are problems of case definition and case finding for organic mental disorders (see Cooper and Bickel 1984). It is particularly difficult to distinguish mild dementia from the effects of normal ageing or from life-long poor cognitive performance due to low intelligence or lack of education. Nevertheless, it is generally agreed that about 5 per cent of people over the age of 65 suffer from moderate or severe dementia and that the prevalence rises to about 20 per cent of those over 85 (see Henderson 1986). Follow-up of the Newcastle group confirmed that patients with dementia had a poor prognosis; they were three times more likely than those in the other diagnostic groups to require admission to a hospital or an institution.

Other surveys have shown a high prevalence of psychiatric disorder among elderly people in sheltered accommodation and in hospital. A third of the residents in old people's homes have significant cognitive impairment. In general hospital wards a third to a half of the patients aged 65 or over suffer from some form of psychiatric illness (Mayou and Hawton 1986; Erkinjuntti *et al.* 1986).

It has frequently been reported that general practitioners are unaware of most of the psychiatric problems amongst elderly people living in the community. Williamson *et al.* (1964) found that general practitioners were unaware of 60 per cent of elderly patients with neurosis, 76 per cent with depression, and 87 per cent with slight to moderate dementia. Such findings presumably reflect both the difficulties of early diagnosis and unawareness by doctors of the benefits of early identification of mental disorder in the elderly. Moreover, the presentation of such disorders to general practitioners and psychiatrists is determined as much by social factors as by a change in the patient's mental state. For example, there may be a sudden alteration in the patient's environment, such as illness of a relative, or a bereavement. Sometimes, an increasingly exhausted or frustated family decide they can no longer continue to care for the old person. At other times there is an element of manipulation by relatives who are trying to rid themselves of an unwanted responsibility.

Epidemiology is discussed further when individual syndromes are considered later in this chapter. [A review of epidemiological methods and findings has been provided by Kay and Bergmann (1980) and by Eastwood and Corbin (1985).]

Services for the elderly

National policies for the provision of services for the elderly differ widely. In the USA emphasis has been placed on care in hospitals and nursing homes. In Europe, Canada, and Australasia there has been varying emphasis on social policies to provide sheltered accommodation and care in the community. In this section, the development of services in the United Kingdom will be described as an example.

After the Second World War, legislation was enacted in the United Kingdom making local authorities responsible for domiciliary, day, and residental services for the elderly. In the National Health Service the role of primary care was emphasized, and a new medical speciality of geriatric medicine was established to develop the special interest and skill necessary to provide adequate community and hospital care for old people. Specialist psychiatric services soon followed.

The government policy document *Services for mental illness related to old age* (Department of Health and Social Security 1972) divided elderly patients with psychiatric problems into three broad groups: 1. Patients who entered hospitals for the mentally ill before modern methods of treatment were available, and who have grown old in them; 2. Elderly patients with functional mental illness; 3. Elderly patients with dementia. ('Elderly' is usually taken to mean over 65 years of age.) The first group of old long-stay patients are mostly schizophrenics; they are usually cared for by general psychiatrists. Their numbers are being increased by the 'new long-stay' who, in their turn, will require some form of institutional care as they grow old (see Chapter 19). With the exception of these patients who have grown old in hospital, the specialist psychogeriatric services are usually responsible for all elderly psychiatric patients, whether their illness is functional or organic. The case for defining the speciality in this way, rather than confining it to the elderly demented, is twofold. First, there are special problems in the diagnosis and management of functional

Table 16.2. Recommended provisions for the elderly per 1000 total population over the age of 65*

Local hospital beds for continuing and relief care	2.5–3.0
District General Hospital beds for assessment and short-term care	included in general adult provisions
Psychiatric day hospital places	3.0
Geriatric hospital beds	10
Geriatric day hospital places	2
Residential care (Local Authority)	25

* See Department of Health and Social Security 1972, 1985; Health Advisory Service, 1983

illness in the elderly; second, staff morale can be maintained better if a proportion of recoverable cases is seen.

Government policy in Britain, more than in some other countries, emphasizes the importance of treatment in the community rather than in hospital (Department of Health and Social Security 1972, 1978b, 1985; Health Advisory Service 1983). In trying to achieve this goal, obstacles arise because of the administrative separation of health services, which are provided by central government, from social services and community facilities which are the responsibility of local authorities.

Table 16.2 lists the official recommendations for provision of hospital places and residential care. In most areas there are shortages of hospital beds, special accommodation, and staff. Also many elderly people require practical services, such as home help or day care, but are not receiving them. For example, among a random sample of 477 people aged 65 and over living at home, only about 10 per cent were receiving domiciliary services, although almost three times as many appeared to need them (Foster *et al.* 1976).

The organization of psychiatric services varies in different places, since it reflects the personal style of doctors in addition to local needs and national policies. Nevertheless, there are some general principles of planning (see Copeland 1984; Arie 1985; Levy and Post 1982). The aims of a service should be defined in relation to the age distribution of the population to be served, taking into account the extent of the services for this age group provided by general adult psychiatry teams. In general the aims should be: to maintain the elderly person at home for as long as possible; to respond quickly to medical and social problems as they arise; to ensure co-ordination of the work of those providing continuing care; and to support relatives and others who care for the elderly at home. There should be close liaison with the medical geriatric departments as well as the local authority social services. A multi-disciplinary approach should be adopted by a clinical team that includes psychiatrists, psychologists, community nurses, and social workers. Some members of the team should spend more of their working day in patients' homes and in general practices than in the hospital. The contributions of the several parts of the service will now be considered.

Primary care

In the United Kingdom, general practitioners with their health visitors and nurses deal with most of the problems of mentally ill old people without referring them to specialists. As already mentioned, general practitioners do not detect all the psychiatric problems of the elderly at an early stage (Williamson *et al.* 1964), nor do they always provide all the necessary long-term medical supervision. A review (Royal College of Physicians 1981) suggested that these problems are partly due to lack of awareness of the significance of psychiatric illness among the elderly and partly to the provision of a 'patient-initiated' style of service. There is also a need to improve communication between workers based in general practice and those working in the psychogeriatric services. Despite these problems, general practitioners and their teams are the most important group caring for the elderly in the United Kingdom.

Hospital care

The policy of the Department of Health and Social Security is for assessment in a District General Hospital, and for long-term and relief care in local hospitals. Nevertheless many elderly psychiatric patients are still treated in the wards of mental hospitals. However, the care provided is more important than the type of building in which it is given. The basic requirements are opportunities for privacy and the use of personal possessions, together with occupational and social therapy. Provided these criteria are met, long-term hospital care can be the best provision for very disabled patients.

Psychogeriatric assessment units

From a study in Belfast, Kidd (1962) concluded that extensive 'misplacement' of patients between geriatric and psychiatric hospitals led to poor treatment, prolonged stay, and unnecessary mortality. Subsequent studies have not confirmed this conclusion. For example, Copeland *et al.* (1975) found that 64 per cent of patients admitted to a geriatric hospital were psychiatrically ill, but only 12 per cent appeared to be wrongly placed and their outcome did not appear to be affected adversely. It seems that many patients can be cared for equally well in either type of hospital. Although the original findings of 'misplacement' have not been confirmed, they aroused concern that led to an official policy of developing joint psychogeriatric assessment units. When geriatricians and psychiatrists co-operate in making assessments before admission to hospital, there is little need for such units. Nevertheless, there are other advantages in having psychogeriatric beds in a general hospital close to medical services.

Day and out-patient care

In the 1950s day care began in geriatric hospitals. A few years later, the first psychiatric day hospitals for the elderly were opened. Psychiatric day hospitals should provide a full range of diagnostic services and offer both short-term and continuing care for patients with functional or organic disorders, together with support for relatives. These arrangements depend crucially on adequate transport facilities. In the United Kingdom, day care provisions by local authorities include day centres and social clubs. They can assist severely demented patients who do not require medical or nursing care.

Out-patients clinics have a smaller part to play in providing care for the elderly than for younger patients because assessment at home is particularly important for old people. However, they are convenient for the assessment and follow-up of younger mobile patients. There are advantages when these clinics are staffed jointly by medical geriatricians and psychogeriatricians.

Residential care

In Britain, under Part III of the National Assistance Act of 1948, local authorities are responsible for providing old people's homes and other sheltered accommodation. When the 1948 Act was passed, there was a legacy of large impersonal institutions (see Townsend 1962). Since then, accommodation has been provided in small units, but it has still proved difficult to achieve an acceptable standard of privacy, while encouraging independence and involvement in outside activities. In some homes there is no security of tenure, and residents who have to be admitted to hospital may find themselves homeless if discharged.

The average age of residents has risen steadily. They are more disabled physically and mentally than was originally intended, and about a third are forgetful and disorientated. It has been argued that the most severely ill should be cared for in separate specialist homes. However, as Meacher (1972) has pointed out, such segregation can have harmful effects, and it is now generally accepted that old people's homes should take some of the more seriously ill. To do so successfully requires a close working relationship between the staff of the home and those in primary care and specialist services. When specialist homes have been provided, they have often been used for 'difficult' patients rather than those who would benefit most from their provisions (see Wilkin *et al.* 1982). In the United Kingdom, much of the provision for long-term residential nursing care is in homes run by private health care organizations or voluntary bodies.

There is a need for special housing, conveniently sited and easy to run. Ideally an old person should be able to transfer to more sheltered accommodation if he or she becomes more disabled, without losing all independence or moving away from familiar places. In many communities in the United Kingdom, there is still not enough variety of accommodation offering a range of independence. Provisions of this kind are better in many parts of Europe, the USA, and Australasia (see Grundy 1987).

Other countries have different systems of care. Gurland *et al.* (1979) compared two random samples of patients living in institutions in New York and London. Both cities provided residential care for about 4 per cent of their elderly population. However, in New York 60 per cent of the places for the elderly were in large nursing homes staffed by nurses, whereas in London nearly two-thirds were in small residential units staffed by a warden and domestic helpers. Thus many elderly people with similar problems were receiving different forms of care in the two cities. For the elderly in Scandinavia there are considerably more hospital beds per unit of population than in Britain; there are also more residential places which are more varied and of better quality, and offer greater privacy and freedom of choice.

Domiciliary services

In addition to medical services, these domiciliary services include home helps, meals at home, laundry, telephone, and emergency call systems. In the United Kingdom, local authorities provide these services; they also support voluntary organizations and encourage local initiatives such as good neighbour schemes and self-help groups. Although these provisions are increasing, so are the numbers of those requiring them. In a random sample of nearly 500 people aged 65 and over living at home, Foster *et al.* (1976) found that 12 per cent were receiving domiciliary services but a further 20 per cent still needed them. Bergmann *et al.* (1978) have argued that if resources are limited, more should be directed to patients living with their families than to those living alone. This is because the former can often remain at home if they receive such help, while many of the latter require admission before long even when extra help is given.

Some general principles of assessment

In Britain most psychogeriatricians believe that the first assessment should normally take place in the elderly patient's home, where the patient's functioning can be assessed in its normal setting and other informants can be interviewed and social conditions observed. Since less than half of the patients assessed in this way are admitted to hospital, the home visit is an important opportunity to plan treatment with all those concerned. The answers to three general questions should be sought: (1) Can the patient be managed at home? (2) If so what additional help does the family need? (3) Can the patient manage his financial affairs?

During the assessment, emphasis should be put on the medical history and physical examination as well as a thorough formulation of social problems. Whenever possible the clinician should interview close relatives or friends, who can give information about the patient and may be involved in his continuing care. Such interviews are specially helpful when the patient has cognitive impairment. In every case, the reasons for the referral should be considered carefully, since many emergencies reflect changes in the attitudes of the family and neighbours to the patient's long-standing problems, rather than a change in his psychiatric state. In order to answer the three questions listed above, the clinician will need to elicit the following information:

1. The time and mode of onset of symptoms and their subsequent course.
2. Any previous medical and psychiatric history.
3. The patient's living conditions and financial position.
4. The patient's ability to look after himself. Any odd or undesirable behaviour that may cause difficulties with his neighbours.
5. The attitudes and availability of family and friends, and their ability to help.
6. Other services already involved in the patient's care.

Usually a diagnosis can be made and provisional plans formulated during the first home visit. Hospital admission may be required, either for investigation and treatment, or for social reasons. More often it is possible to arrange extra social or medical care in the patient's normal surroundings.

With these general points in mind, consideration can now be given to specific aspects of history taking, physical and mental examination, and psychological assessment.

History taking

Normally the problem should be discussed with the general practitioner before the patient is seen. If there is any likelihood of intellectual impairment in the patient, it is usually best to speak to relatives or other informants first. Details of the onset and time course of the symptoms are of particular value in differential diagnosis. Since a social formulation is important, the history should cover information about the patient's financial state and social circumstances, and about people who may be willing to help him. A description of the patient's behaviour over a typical 24-hour period is often helpful in eliciting symptoms and disabilities, and obtaining a detailed picture of the patient's way of life and the reactions of other people. Enquiry should also be made about hazards such as: poor heating; the capacity to handle fire, gas and electricity; wandering; and allowing strangers into the home.

Examination

A thorough physical examination should be carried out, including an appropriately detailed neurological assessment with particular attention to vision and hearing. The mental state examination should include a systematic assessment of cognitive functions. It may be necessary to test linguistic, visuo-spatial, and other higher cortical functions.

If the patient is admitted to hospital, systematic observations should be made of his behaviour on the ward. Schedules such as the Gresham Ward Questionnaire (Post 1965) provide a scheme for assessing memory for general events, past personal events, and recent personal events; a simple score for correct answers gives a useful indication of the severity of intellectual handicap.

Physical investigations

On admission to hospital, the minimum routine investigations are a full blood count, blood urea and electrolytes, urine analysis and culture, and chest X-ray. If physical illness is suspected, additional investigations may be required. In the case of very old patients with dementia, the clinician should use his judgement in deciding how far to pursue physical investigations when there are no clinical signs. If an organic diagnosis is suspected the following may be required: blood count and film, ESR, syphilis serology, thyroid function, electrolytes, urea and liver function, plasma calcium, vitamin B_{12}, chest X-ray, skull X-ray, ECG, and EEG. It is probably justified to arrange a CT scan only when there are specified indications. With older patients, especially when a reasonably confident clinical diagnosis can be made, elaborate investigations are seldom necessary.

Psychological assessment

In skilled hands, psychometric testing has a limited but important role (see Miller 1980a; Woods 1982). Common obstacles to testing are the patient's confusion, lack of motivation, or sensory handicaps, and his need for adequate time to become accustomed to the procedure. The two main uses of psychological assessment are to measure decline in cognitive function, and to differentiate between organic and functional illness. Measuring cognitive decline is difficult because there is seldom enough information about the patient's premorbid state. There is doubt about the common assumption that verbal tests indicate the premorbid level. Also reliance on previous educational and other achievement can be misleading.

Serial measurements can provide better evidence of decline, but the assessor must be aware of the test–retest reliability of his methods.

In making the diagnosis between organic and functional illness, verbal learning tests are the most helpful and design copying is also useful. In addition, the demonstration of focal abnormalities of higher cortical functions strongly suggests an organic disorder. It can be helpful to use a battery of tests, such as those introduced by Kendrick, which combine an object learning test and a motor task (see Gibson *et al.* 1980). For demented patients already in hospital, a careful description of their behaviour can also contribute to the assessment of disability and remaining skills (see Patterson and Jackson 1980).

Treatment

Essentially the psychiatric treatment of the elderly resembles that of other adults, but there are differences in emphasis. If practicable, treatment is generally preferable at home rather than in hospital, not only because most elderly people want to be at home, but also because they function best there. Home treatment requires a willingness on the part of the doctor to be flexible and responsive to changing needs, to arrange a plan with the family, to organize appropriate day care or help, and to admit to hospital should it become necessary.

Whenever possible, it is essential to treat the underlying cause of an organic mental disorder. Other physical disorders, however minor, should be actively treated, as this can also benefit the mental state. Mobility should be encouraged, and physiotherapy is often helpful. A good diet should be provided.

Use of drugs

Substantially more drugs are prescribed for the elderly than for younger people. Drug-induced morbidity is a major medical problem, partly because the pharmacokinetics of drugs are different in old people (see Royal College of Physicians 1984). Most problems arise with drugs used to treat cardiovascular disorders (hypotensives, diuretics, and digoxin), and those acting on the central nervous sytem (antidepressants, hypnotics, anxiolytics, antipsychotics, and antiparkinsonian drugs). It is essential to restrict the number of drugs to avoid harmful drug interactions, and prudent to start with small doses. Medication should be reviewed regularly and kept to a minimum.

Compliance with treatment is a problem in elderly patients, especially in those who live alone, have poor vision or are confused. The drug regime should be as simple as possible, medicine bottles labelled clearly and memory aids provided, and if possible drug taking should be supervised.

The patient's response should be watched carefully. In these aspects of treatment, as in many others, domiciliary nursing plays a vital part.

Despite the need for caution in prescribing, elderly patients should not be denied effective drug treatment, especially for depressive disorders. Antidepressant medication should be started cautiously and increased gradually. If patients do not respond, it is sometimes helpful to measure the plasma concentration of antidepressant as a guide to increasing the dose.

Many elderly people sleep poorly, and about 20 per cent of those aged over 70 take hypnotics regularly. In the elderly, hypnotic drugs often cause adverse side-effects, notable daytime drowsiness leading to confusion, falls, incontinence, and hypothermia. If a hypnotic is essential, the minimum effective dose should be used and the effects monitored carefully. Chlormethiazole, dichloralphenazone, and medium- or short-acting benzodiazepines are useful as hypnotics. Promazine is particularly useful in restless demented patients.

Electroconvulsive therapy

Although special caution is needed, ECT can be remarkably successful in treating serious depressive disorder in the elderly. In patients with cognitive impairment, ECT may be followed by temporary memory impairment and confusion, so that longer intervals between treatments are advisable. Before receiving ECT, physically frail patients should be assessed by an experienced anaesthetist.

Psychological treatment

Interpretative psychotherapy is seldom appropriate for the elderly. However, supportive therapy with clearly defined aims may be required, and joint interviews with the spouse are sometimes helpful.

There has been increasing interest in behavioural treatment of demented patients. Methods have been developed for training patients with problems in eating, continence, or social skills (see Whitehead 1984) and it can be useful to encourage patients with memory disorder to use memory aids such as notebooks and alarm clocks. Folsom (1967) described reality orientation therapy, which is intended to reduce confusion and improve behaviour. In this approach, basic information is given about orientation in time and place, and repeated on every contact with the patient. This technique is widely practised, though the results of evaluative studies are conflicting (Whitehead 1984). It may be that some patients are helped by certain of the techniques.

Social treatment

Some patients can achieve independence through measures to encourage self-care, social contacts, and domestic skills. More severely impaired patients can benefit from a humane, dignified environment in which individual needs are respected and each person retains some personal possessions. Disorientation can be reduced by the general design of the ward and the use of simple aids such as colour codes on doors. For those living at home, domiciliary occupational therapy may be helpful.

Support for relatives

Time should be spent with the family in discussion of problems and advice about care. Such support can help families to avoid some of the frustrations and anxieties of caring for elderly relatives. Practical help should include the organization of day care or holiday admissions, and a laundry and meal service to the home. If these steps are taken, many patients can remain in their own homes without imposing an unreasonable burden on their families. Community psychiatric nurses play essential roles in co-ordinating these services, supporting relatives, and providing practical nursing care. The first two roles can also be undertaken by social workers.

Delirium

Because delirium has physical causes, the patients are usually under the care of physicians or general practitioners. In a survey of patients admitted to medical geriatric wards, about a tenth were found to have delirium (Hodkinson 1973). The main predisposing factors were pre-existing dementia, defective hearing and vision, Parkinson's disease, and advanced age. The most frequent precipitating causes were pneumonia, cardiac failure, urinary infection, carcinomatosis, and hypokalaemia. The mortality is high [see Lipowski (1985) for a review].

The **clinical features** of delirium are discussed on p. 348. It should be remembered that amongst elderly patients impairment of consciousness, although invariable, is not always obvious—especially when the onset is gradual. This condition can be called a subacute organic syndrome; it is sometimes misdiagnosed as an irreversible dementia. In patients who have a preceding dementia, cognitive function can sometimes be affected by minor physical upsets, such as constipation, dehydration, or mild bronchitis. Since many of the causes of delirium are a threat to life, mortality is high. In a Newcastle survey of patients admitted to hospital with such syndromes, half were found to have died within two years of admission (Roth 1955).

The basic requirement in management is to search for and treat the underlying cause. Meanwhile, psychotropic drugs can provide valuable symptomatic relief. Long-acting benzodiazepines may increase confusion. Small doses of phenothiazine, such as promazine or thioridazine, or of haloperidol are usually effective without increasing confusion. The amount and timing of the dosage should be carefully determined for each patient, by reference to the *British national formulary* or a similar source. If a hypnotic is needed, chlormethiazole, dichloralphenazone, and medium or short-acting benzodiazepines are safe and effective.

Dementia in the elderly

In this book, the main account of the syndrome of dementia is given in Chapter 11, p. 350. The reader is referred to that chapter for a definition of dementia, and a description of its clinical features and treatment. This section is concerned only with dementia in the elderly.

Dementia in the elderly has been recognized since Esquirol described 'démence senile' in his textbook *Des maladies mentales* (see Esquirol 1838). Esquirol's description of the disorder was in general terms, but it can be recognized as similar to the present day concept (Alexander 1972). Kraepelin distinguished dementia from psychoses due to other organic causes, such as neurosyphilis; and he divided dementia into pre-senile, senile, and arteriosclerotic forms. In 1955, in an important follow-up study, Roth showed in the elderly that dementia differed from affective disorders and paranoid disorders in its poorer prognosis.

Dementia in old age can be divided into three groups according to aetiology and pathology:

1. Dementia of the Alzheimer type. This has the same pathological changes in the brain as pre-senile dementia of the Alzheimer type (pre-senile dementia is described in Chapter 11). It is the commonest kind of dementia in old age.
2. Multi-infarct dementia. As the name implies, this is due to multiple infarcts in the brain, resulting from vascular occlusions. It corresponds to the older category of arteriosclerotic dementia.
3. Dementia due to other causes. This group includes dementia resulting from a wide range of causes, such as neoplasms, infections, toxins, and metabolic disorders, some of which are reversible (see Larson *et al.* 1984; Marsden 1984).

This chapter is concerned only with groups 1 and 2. Group 3 is discussed in Chapter 11.

The clinical picture of dementia is much the same in all three groups. Some minor differences in clinical features are found fairly consistently, but they cannot always be relied on to differentiate between the three groups.

It is only recently that pathologists have distinguished the subgroups of dementia outlined above. For many years it was believed that vascular disease was the commonest cause of dementia. Doubt was cast on this belief when Corsellis (1962) reported that pathological changes of Alzheimer's disease were more common. This finding was subsequently confirmed by several workers. For example, in a careful clinicopathological study based on 50 successive post-mortems of demented patients, Tomlinson *et al.* (1970) found the following distribution of changes: definite Alzheimer type, 50 per cent; probable Alzheimer type, 16 per cent; definite arteriosclerotic, 12 per cent; probable arteriosclerotic, 6 per cent; both Alzheimer and arteriosclerotic, 8 per cent; no evident pathology, 8 per cent.

Alzheimer's disease

Prevalence of dementia

After reviewing the results of 20 surveys of dementia carried out in Europe, Japan, and North America, Henderson (1986) concluded that the prevalence of moderate and severe dementia is about 5 per cent of persons aged 65 years and over, and 20 per cent of those aged over 80 years. About 80 per cent of these demented people are in the community rather than institutions. The total number of demented people is increasing rapidly in developed countries as life expectancy improves (see also Jorm *et al.* 1987).

Clinical features

Although the clinical features of dementia have been described in Chapter 11, the features of Alzheimer's disease in the elderly are reviewed here briefly. This is because the condition is common and important, and because some of its features are characteristic (though not discriminating for diagnostic purposes).

Alzheimer's disease usually begins after the age of 70. In one large study, the mean age of onset was found to be 73 for men and 75 for women (Larsson *et al.* 1963). It occurs mainly in women. Death usually occurs within five to eight years of the first signs of the disease appearing. Doctors are seldom consulted until a later stage of chronic deterioration, or following a sudden worsening in relation to some other physical illness.

Presentation is often with minor forgetfulness, which is difficult to distinguish from normal ageing. The onset is usually insidious for the initial two to four years, with increasing memory disturbance and lack of spontaneity. Disorientation is normally an early sign and may be first evident when the subject is in unfamiliar surroundings, for example on holiday. The mood may be predominantly depressed, euphoric, flattened, or labile. Self-care and social behaviour decline although some patients maintain a good social façade despite severe cognitive impairment.

Patients are often restless and may wake at night, disorientated and perplexed. In the early stages, the clinical features are substantially modified by the premorbid personality, and any personality defects tend to be exaggerated.

In the later stages of the illness intellectual impairment and personality change are obvious, and language and visiospatial disorders are frequent. Focal signs of parietal lobe dysfunction (such as dysphasia or dyspraxia) may occur. Incidental physical illness may cause a superimposed delirium resulting in a sudden deterioration in cognitive function which may be permanent.

Pathology of Alzheimer's disease

As mentioned above, the pathological changes are the same in presenile and senile Alzheimer's disease. Grossly the brain is shrunken with widened sulci and enlarged ventricles. Histologically, there is some cell loss, particularly in the three outer cortical layers, together with proliferation of astrocytes, increased fibrous gliosis, and shrinkage of the dendritic tree. Silver staining shows senile plaques throughout the cortical and subcortical grey matter, and also neurofibrillary tangles and granulovacuolar degeneration. The limbic regions are particularly affected and the sensorimotor and occipital areas relatively spared. Electron microscopy shows that the senile plaques have a central core of amyloid surrounded by abnormal neurites; and that the neurofibrillary tangles are helically paired twisted filaments see (Perry and Perry 1982, Reisberg 1983; Roth and Iversen 1986).

It has been reported that the degree of cognitive impairment is closely related to the number of senile plaques, and less closely related to the number of neurofibrillary tangles (see Roth 1971).

Neurophysiological abnormalities have been found in the peripheral nerves as well as in the cerebral hemispheres, suggesting a possible widespread involvement of the nervous system (Levy *et al.* 1970).

Biochemistry

The outstanding feature is a change in the presynaptic cholinergic system of the cortex. Reduction of choline acetyl transferase was first shown by Bowen *et al.* (1976). Reduced synthesis of acetylcholine has been shown in biopsy tissue and found to be correlated both with the extent of cognitive impairment before death, and with the severity of pathological changes in the brain (Neary *et al.* 1986). Very low levels of acetylcholine have been found in the nucleus basalis of Meynert, a subcortical structure that is the major source of cholinergic innervation of the cortex.

Although cholinergic abnormalities have received most attention, there is growing evidence that other neurotransmitters are significantly affected (see Hardy *et al.* 1985). Noradrenalin and 5-hydroxytryptamine are reduced in many cortical and subcortical areas, and the peptide somatostatin is reduced within the cortex. The latter finding is of interest because, unlike the reduction in the other neurotransmitters, it is attributable to the loss of intrinsic cortical neurones rather than the loss of terminals of neurones, whose cell bodies are subcortical (Beal *et al.* 1986).

Are there subtypes of Alzheimer's disease?

Presenile and senile dementia are widely thought to be the same disorder because both are associated with neuritic plaques and neurofibrilliary tangles, and because they have similar neurochemical abnormalities. However, some workers have suggested that there are two types of Alzheimer's disease. Type 1 is said to be characterized by late onset, mild pathology without substantial cell loss, mild biochemical changes, and a slower course. Type 2 Alzheimer's disease is said to have an early onset, substantial cell loss, marked biochemical changes and a more rapid course. There are also more severe motor and parietal signs, and genetic factors are more obvious in Type 2. The greater cell loss in Type 2 includes the sub-cortical nuclei, especially the nucleus basalis of Meynert and the nucleus coeruleus. The biochemical disorder includes a marked decrease in cortical choline acetyl transferase. It is not certain whether the subtypes are discrete, or whether they represent different ends of a continuum (see Bondareff 1983; Jorm 1985).

Aetiology

In the large study mentioned above, Larsson *et al.* (1963) found evidence of a **genetic** basis for Alzheimer's disease of the elderly. This finding was confirmed by Heston *et al.* (1981) in a rigorous study of the relatives of 125 probands with Alzheimer's dementia proved by post-mortem histology. In this study the relatives also had an excess of Down's syndrome.

The evidence from population studies suggests that genetic factors are more important the earlier the onset of the disease. Pedigree studies of a small number of families suggest an inheritance consistent with autosomal dominance. However, it remains uncertain whether, as suggested by Breitner and Folstein (1984), there is a familial subtype of Alzheimer's disease with autosomal dominant inheritance (and characterized by aphasia, agraphia, and apraxia), or whether there is a continuum with greater genetic loading in those who develop the disease at an earlier age.

Recently molecular genetic techniques have been applied in Alzheimer's disease. Interest has been focused on chromosome 21 because of the association of Down's syndrome and Alzheimer's disease. Furthermore, in a study of four families with a probable autosomal dominant transmission, the gene responsible was located on chromosome 21 (St George-Hyslop *et al.* (1987). There has been considerable interest in the possibility that the responsible gene is that encoding for amyloid A4 precursor. This gene is found on chromosome 21, and amyloid A4 is found in plaques and tangles (see Anderton 1987). However, the responsible gene in several Alzheimer's disease families has been shown not to be that of the amyloid A4 precursor (Van Broeckhoven *et al.* 1987; Tanzi *et al.* 1987. Furthermore, there is considerable doubt as to whether amyloid A4 is the constituent of the paired helical filaments (see Anderton 1987). Finally, as discussed above, it is unclear whether any single gene is likely to be of major importance in the aetiology of most cases of Alzheimer's disease.

It has been suggested that excess **aluminium** may cause Alzheimer's disease. The evidence is of two kinds. In animal experiments, aluminium can induce the formation of agyrophilic tangles resembling the tangles found in the brain in Alzheimer's disease. In humans, aluminium silicate has been found in plaques in the brains of patients with Alzheimer's disease (Candy *et al.* 1986). It has also been argued that it is relevant that dialysis dementia (see p. 453) is associated with excess aluminium. The importance of these observations is uncertain: the concentrations of aluminium in the animal experiments is high; the aluminium found in tangles may be taken up secondarily; and the pathological changes in definite cases of aluminium toxicity do not resemble those of Alzheimer's disease (see Foncin and El Hachini 1986).

Other unconfirmed hypotheses are that the disease is caused by a slow virus of the type implicated in kuru and Creutzfeldt–Jakob disease (see, for example, Gibbs *et al.* 1968), or by abnormal immune mechanisms. [See Deary and Whalley (1988) for a review of aetiology.]

Multi-infarct dementia

In this condition, dementia is associated with multiple infarcts of varying size, mostly caused by thromboembolism from extracranial arteries (Hachinski *et al.* 1974). The term multi-infarct dementia (MID) has largely replaced the older term 'arteriosclerotic'. The condition is slightly more common in men than in women. The onset, which is usually in the late sixties or the seventies, may follow a cerebrovascular accident and is often more acute than in Alzheimer's disease. Emotional and personality changes may appear first, followed by impairments of memory and intellect that are characteristically fluctuating. Episodes of emotional lability and confusion are common, especially at night. Fits or minor episodes of cerebral ischaemia are usual at some stage.

The diagnosis is difficult to make with certainty unless there is a clear history of strokes or else definite localizing signs. Suggestive features are patchy psychological deficits, erratic progression, and relative preservation of the personality. On physical examination there are usually signs of hypertension and of arteriosclerosis in peripheral and retinal vessels, and there may also be neurological signs such as pseudobulbar palsy, rigidity, akinesia, and brisk reflexes.

Hachinski *et al.* (1975) devised a method, based on clinical features, for deriving an Ischaemia score to differentiate Alzheimer's disease from multi-infarct dementia. The method has attracted interest but its validity is not fully established (Liston and La Rue 1985).

The course of multi-infarct dementia is usually a stepwise progression, with periods of deterioration that are sometimes followed by partial recovery for a few months. About half the patients die from ischaemic heart disease, and others from cerebral infarction or renal complications. From the time of diagnosis the life-span varies widely but averages about four to five years—perhaps slightly longer than for Alzheimer's disease (Roth 1955).

In multi-infarct dementia the gross pathology is distinctive. There is localized or generalized brain atrophy and ventricular dilatation, with areas of cerebral infarction and evidence of arteriosclerosis in major vessels. On microscopy, multiple areas of infarction and ischaemia are evident. Tomlinson *et al.* (1970) found that the volume of damaged cerebral cortex at post-mortem was related to the degree of intellectual impairment shortly before death; usually no cognitive impairment was detectable until at least 50 ml of brain tissue had been affected.

In multi-infarct dementia biochemical studies have shown that there is no association between cognitive impairment and levels of choline acetyltransferase (Perry *et al.* 1978)—a distinguishing feature from dementia of the Alzheimer type. [For a review of the pathology see Perry and Perry (1982).]

The assessment of dementia in the elderly

The assessment of dementia in general is discussed in the chapter on organic psychiatry (p. 350). In the elderly, assessment follows the same principles.

Dementia has to be differentiated from acute organic syndromes, depressive disorders, and paranoid disorders. An acute organic syndrome is suggested by impaired and fluctuating consciousness, and by symptoms such as perceptual misinterpretations and hallucinations (see p. 349). Differentiation from affective disorders and paranoid states is discussed later in this chapter. It should be remembered that hypothryoidism may be mistaken for dementia.

In the assessment of dementia it is important to look for the treatable causes, although they are rare. They include, for example, deficiency of vitamin B_{12}, neurosyphilis, and operable tumours (see Chapter 11). The investigations listed earlier in this chapter are usually sufficient. As already mentioned, the intensity of investigation must be judged in relation to the patient's age and general debility.

The assessment should also include a thorough search for treatable, often minor, medical conditions that are associated rather than primary causes. Treatment of these conditions can reduce distress and disability (Wells 1978).

The principles of social assessment have been described earlier in the chapter (p. 604)

The treatment of dementia in the elderly

As implied above, the first concern must be to treat any treatable physical disorder. If the latter is the primary cause, the dementia may sometimes be reversible. If an acute organic mental state is superimposed on the dementia, the mental state may improve considerably with treatment of any associated physical disorder.

Whatever the cause of dementia, restlessness by day or night may be reduced by drugs such as promazine, thioridazine, or haloperidol, without causing serious side-effects. Reducing restlessness is an important first step when a family is worn down by caring for a confused and wandering patient. Antipsychotic drugs may also be required for paranoid delusions, and antidepressants for severe depressive symptoms.

For Alzheimer's disease it has been reported that drugs of four kinds may be of specific benefit. *Cholinergic* drugs, include precursors of acetylcholine such as choline and lecithin, stimulators of acetylcholine release such as piracetam, and inhibitors of acetylcholine hydrolysis such as physostigmine and tetrahydroaminoacridine (THA). *Vasodilators* include isoxsuprine, dihydroergotoxine, hydergine, (a mixture of ergot alkaloids), and cyclandelate. *Neuropeptides* include vasopressin and its papaverine analogues, which are given intranasally. Putative *enhancers of brain metabolism* include pentifylline, and pyritinol. There have been no satisfactory clinical trials showing specific effects of these substances in patients with Alzheimer's disease and their use is not recommended. [For a review of the evidence see Reisberg (1983); Davis and Mohs (1986); Roth and Iversen (1986).]

For multi-infarct dementia there are no specific measures apart from the control of blood pressure and, if indicated, surgical treatment of carotid artery stenosis.

Psychological and social treatment

For elderly demented patients the principles of psychological and social treatment follow those outlined in the chapter (p. 608). Whenever feasible, patients should continue to live in their own homes, particularly if they have someone to live with. Social care should be planned with all concerned—family, friends, general practitioner, and in most cases a community psychiatric nurse or social worker. Day care may be needed for the patient not only to provide supervision, occupation, and training, but also to relieve the family. Occasional hospital admissions may be indicated, to provide a holiday or tide over a crisis.

If the patient cannot be managed at home, residential care may be appropriate in an old people's home or other sheltered accommodation. Failing this, long-term care in hospital will be needed. For a review of the principles of management see Council on Scientific Affairs (1986).

Affective disorder

Depressive disorder

Depressive disorders are common in later life. The point prevalence for depression of clinical severity is about 10 per cent for those aged over 65, with 2-3 per cent being severe. For first depressive disorders of a severe kind, the highest incidence is between the ages of 50 and 65. First depressive illnesses become less common after the age of 60, but only become rare after the age of 80. The incidence of suicide increases steadily with age, and in the elderly suicide is usually associated with depressive disorder. There is evidence from population surveys that many depressive disorders in elderly patients are not detected by their general practitioners, or are regarded as normal ageing or mild dementia (Foster *et al.* 1976; Cooper and Bickel 1984). [See Swartz and Blazer (1986) for a review.]

Clinical features

There is no clear distinction between depressive disorders in the elderly and those in younger people, but symptoms are often more striking in the elderly. Post (1972) reported that a third of his depressed elderly patients had severe retardation and agitation. Depressive delusions concerning poverty and physical illness are common, and occasionally there are nihilistic delusions, such as beliefs that the body is empty, non-existent, or not functioning (see Cotard's syndrome, p. 221). Hallucinations of an accusing or obscene kind are frequent. A small proportion of retarded patients present with 'pseudodementia'; that is, they have conspicuous difficulty in concentration and remembering, but careful clinical testing shows there is no defect of memory function (see Bulbena and Burrows 1986). Depressive disorders in the elderly present in diverse ways and should always be considered when the patient has anxious, hypochondriacal, or confusional symptoms.

Course and prognosis

From accounts written before the introduction of ECT, it is clear that many depressive disorders lasted for years. Nowadays considerable improvement within a few months can be expected in about 85 per cent of admitted patients; the remaining 15 per cent do not recover completely. Long-term follow-up shows a less encouraging picture. Post (1972) reported that patients who recovered in the first few months fell into three groups: one-third remained completely well for three years; another third suffered further depressive disorders with complete remissions; and the remaining third developed a state of chronic invalidism punctuated by depressive disorders. From a one-year follow-up study of consecutive referrals of elderly in-patients and out-patients, Murphy (1983) reported a similar outlook. Poor outcome was associated with the severity of the initial illness with poor physical health and severe life events in the year. Another study (Murphy *et al.* 1988) found that depressed patients had a significantly higher mortality than matched controls and that the difference was not entirely due to differences in physical health between the groups when first seen. Despite this poor outlook for affective symptoms, only a small number of patients develop dementia (Roth 1955; Post 1972). As explained in the chapter on suicide and deliberate self-harm (p. 481), suicide is especially frequent in the elderly (see Blazer 1986; Lindsay 1986). Factors predicting a good prognosis are: onset before the age of 70, short duration of illness, good previous adjustment, absence of disabling physical illness, and good recovery from previous episodes.

Aetiology

In general the aetiology of depressive disorders in late life almost certainly resembles the aetiology of similar disorders in early life. Genetic factors are of less significance. For first degree relatives the risk is 4–5 per cent with elderly probands, as against 10–12 per cent with young and middle-aged probands (Stenstedt 1952). It might be expected that the loneliness and hardship of old age would be important predisposing factors for depression. Surprisingly, there is no convincing evidence for such an association (see Murphy 1982). Indeed Parkes *et al.* (1969) even found that the association between bereavement and mental illness no longer held in the aged.

Although neurological and other physical illnesses may have a slightly raised prevalence among depressed as against non-depressed elderly patients, there is no evidence that they have a specific aetiological role. Instead such illnesses appear to act as non-specific precipitants. [See Murphy (1986) for a review of aetiology.]

Differential diagnosis

The most difficult differential diagnosis is between depressive pseudo-dementia and dementia. It is essential to obtain a detailed history from other informants, and to make careful observations of mental state and behaviour. In depressive pseudodementia usually a history of mood disturbance precedes the other symtoms. On examination of mental stage, the depressed patient's unwillingness to answer questions can usually be distinguished from the demented patient's failure of memory. Psychological testing is often said to be useful, but it requires experienced interpretation and it usually adds little to skilful clinical assessment (Miller 1980*b*). At times, dementia and depressive illness coexist. If there is real doubt there is no harm in a trial of antidepressant treatment.

Less frequently, depressive disorder has to be differentiated from a paranoid disorder. When persecutory ideas occur in a depressive disorder, the patient usually believes that the supposed persecution is justified by his wickedness (see p. 221). Particular difficulty may occur with the small group of patients who suffer schizoaffective illness in old age (see below).

Treatment

The general principles of the treatment of depressive disorders are the same for adults of all ages. They are described in Chapter 8. With elderly patients it is especially important to be aware of the risk of suicide. Any intercurrent physical disorder should be treated thoroughly. Antidepressants are effective, but should be used cautiously (perhaps starting with half the normal dosage) and adjusted in relation to side-effects and response. It is probably wise to avoid the once-daily dosage now commonly used for younger patients; instead the drugs should be given two or three times a day. Although it is appropriate to start cautiously, it is equally important to avoid under-medication. As stressed earlier in this chapter, it should be remembered that the compliance of elderly patients is often poor. For severe and distressing agitation, life-threatening stupor, or failure to respond to drugs, ECT is usually appropriate. If the patient is unduly confused after ECT, applications should be given at longer intervals. If a patient has previously responded to antidepressants or ECT, but does not respond in the present episode, undetected physical illness is a likely cause. After recovery, antidepressant medication should be reduced slowly and then continued in a reduced dose for several months as in younger patients (see p. 661). A minority of patients require more prolonged maintenance treatment.

Mania

Mania accounts for between 5 and 10 per cent of affective illnesses in old age. Unlike depressive disorder, mania does not increase in incidence with age. The clinical picture nearly always combines depressive and manic symptoms, and the condition is frequently recurrent. Management is similar to that described for younger patients (p. 265). Lithium prophylaxis is valuable but the blood levels should be monitored with special care, and should be kept at the lower end of the therapeutic range used for younger patients. [Shulman (1986) has reviewed mania in old age.]

Schizoaffective disorder

In a study of patients aged over 60 admitted to hospital, Post (1971) found that 4 per cent had schizoaffective disorders (that is, disorders with a more or less equal mixture of the symptoms of schizophrenia and affective disorder), or they had a schizophrenic illness followed by an affective illness or vice versa. For these conditions, intermediate and long-term outcome were less favourable than for depressive disorder.

Neurosis and personality disorder

In later life, neurosis is seldom a cause for referral to a psychiatrist. In a survey in general practice, Shepherd *et al.* (1966) found that, after the age of 55, the incidence of new cases of neurosis declined; however, the frequency of consultations with the general practitioner for neurosis did not fall—presumably as a result of chronic or recurrent cases. From surveys in the community, however, it appears that after the age of 65 new cases of neurosis still appear, and that the prevalence of cases of at least moderate severity is about 12 per cent (see Kay and Bergmann 1980). Probably many of these new cases do not present to general practitioners or psychiatrists.

In most elderly patients presenting with neurosis, personality disorder is an important predisposing factor. Physical illness is a frequent precipitant, and retirement, bereavement, and change of accommodation also contribute (see Eastwood and Corbin 1985). Among the elderly, neurotic syndromes are usually of the non-specific kind, with symptoms of both anxiety and depression. Hypochondriacal symptoms are often prominent. Hysteria, obsessional neurosis, and phobic neurosis are less common.

Personality disorder causes many problems for elderly patients and their families. Paranoid traits may become accentuated with the social isolation of old age, sometimes to the extent of being mistaken for a paranoid state (see p. 621). Abnormal personality is one of the causes of the so-called '(senile squalor syndrome', in which elderly people become isolated and neglect themselves in filthy conditions. Gross self-neglect is often associated with both social isolation and physical disorder, and is associated with a high mortality after hospital admission. It is often difficult to decide when to intervene and when to use compulsory powers (Cybulska and Rucinski 1986). Criminal behaviour is rare in the elderly (Taylor and Parrott 1988).

The *treatment* of neuroses and personality disorders in old age is generally similar to that in younger adult life. It is essential to treat any physical disorder. Social measures are usually more important that psychological treatments, but psychotherapy and behavioural treatment should not be ruled out because of age alone.

Alcoholism and drug abuse

Reported prevalence rates for problem drinking among the elderly vary widely. Excessive drinking declines with increasing age but, whilst not a major problem, it is still significant among the elderly. These excessive drinkers are of two kinds: those who began in early life; and those who began in old age, often as a response to social or other stress (Zimberg 1983; Eastwood and Corbin 1985).

The prevalence of drug abuse has been little researched. It is difficult to distinguish between inadvertant and deliberate misuse. Excessive use of hypnotics and misuse of analgesics and laxatives are relatively common (see Eastwood and Corbin 1985).

Abuse and neglect of the elderly

Abuse and neglect of the elderly by other family members is often overlooked. Women are more often affected than men, and those who have physical illness or psychiatric disorder are most at risk. Abuse is usually by a relative and is often repeated. It may take the form of neglect or forced confinement, which may be shown in failure to thrive. Also, property may be misused (see O'Malley *et al.* 1983).

Schizophrenia and paranoid states in the elderly

In the assessment and management of schizophrenia and paranoid states, the same principles apply to elderly as to younger adult patients (see Chapters 9 and 10). In this book, paranoid syndromes are divided into those due to primary disorders (organic, schizophrenic, or affective) and a separate group called paranoid states which appear to be unrelated to any primary disorder (see p. 330). Since similar principles of treatment apply to schizophrenia and paranoid states in the elderly, the two conditions are dealt with together here.

All the paranoid syndromes outlined above occur in elderly patients, the commonest being those secondary to organic or affective disorders. In some patients, schizophrenia starts in early or mid-life and persists into old age. (See the discussion of long-term outcome of schizophrenia in

Chapter 9.) With increasing age, the symptoms become less florid, and the behaviour more subdued. In a few patients schizophrenia or a paranoid state occurs for the first time in late life. Many clinicians combine these two conditions (late onset schizophrenia and paranoid state) into a single group. For example, the term 'late paraphrenia' has been used for all paranoid syndromes of the elderly in which there is no evidence of organic or affective disorder. However, the draft of ICD10 and DSMIIIR use the same diagnostic criteria for the elderly as for younger patients.

Late paraphrenia was described by Kay and Roth (1961) on the basis of a clinical follow-up and genetic study of 99 patients. Females predominated over males in a ratio of about 7:1, and unmarried patients were significantly more common than in the general population. The clinical picture was characterized by many schizophrenia-like disorders of thought, mood, and volition; by relatively good preservation of intellect, personality and memory, and by conspicuous hallucinations. The course of the illness tended to be chronic, and the changes of schizophrenic type usually became more prominent. The authors concluded that the late paraphrenia must be regarded as the mode of manifestation of schizophrenia in old age. The condition is uncommon, accounting for about 10 per cent of first admissions among the elderly (Kay and Bergmann 1980; Eastwood and Corbin 1985), though possibly some less severe cases are regarded as eccentricity and not brought to medical attention.

Post (1966) did not use the term paraphrenia, but divided paranoid conditions of the elderly into the following groups: (a) schizophrenia with typical first rank symptoms; (b) schizophrenia with more understandable paranoid symptoms; (c) paranoid hallucinosis in which paranoid beliefs are based solely on pathological perceptions. These clinical groups are not specially useful because they do not differ in aetiology, social characteristics, or outcome.

Aetiology

In schizophrenia and paranoid states of the elderly, the same aetiological factors apply as in younger adults (pp. 292 and 326). However, certain causal factors may apply particularly in old age. Thus Kay and Roth (1961) found that, compared with patients with affective disorder, significantly more late paraphrenics were living alone at the onset of illness, and were 'socially isolated' as a result of deafness, abnormalities of personality, and lack of surviving relatives (Corbin and Eastwood 1986).

Differential diagnosis

Schizophrenia is diagnosed by the same criteria as in younger patients (see p. 282). In paranoid states, there are persecutory delusions, but no demonstrable underlying primary disorder. Both conditions have to be differentiated from organic mental disorders, affective disorders, and paranoid personality. In organic mental disorder, cognitive impairment is detectable and visual hallucinations are more likely. In affective disorder, the mood disturbance is more profound, and the persecutory delusions are usually associated with ideas of guilt. In paranoid personality there are lifelong suspiciousness and distrust, with sensitive ideas but no delusions (p. 327).

Treatment

In old age, the general principles of treatment are as described in Chapters 9 and 10. Out-patient treatment is sometimes suitable, but for adequate assessment an in-patient admission is usually required. Compulsory admission may be indicated at times. A few patients improve on admission, and remain well on discharge if social help is provided. Most patients require antipsychotic medication, usually with a phenothiazine, occasionally with a butyrophenone, and several studies indicate a good response (Eastwood and Corbin 1985). The dosage should be about half that for younger adults. If there are doubts about a patient's likelihood of continuing medication, and if there is no one to supervise, a depot preparation should be considered. Any treatable sensory deficit, such as deafness or cataract, should be attended to. Attendance at a day hospital or centre may be needed to ensure adequate supervision.

Further reading

Arie, T. (1985). *Recent advances in psychogeriatrics.* Churchill Livingstone, Edinburgh.

Birren, J. E. and Sloane, R. B. (1980). *Handbook of mental health and ageing.* Prentice Hall, Englewood Cliffs, New Jersey.

Levy, R. and Post, F. (1982). *The psychiatry of late life.* Blackwell Scientific Publications, Oxford.

Roth, M. (1955). The natural history of mental disorder in old age. *Journal of Mental Science* **101**, 281–301.

17 Drugs and other physical treatments

This chapter is concerned with the use of drugs, electroconvulsive therapy, and psychosurgical procedures. Psychological treatments are the subject of the next chapter. This separation, although convenient when treatments are described, does not imply that the two kinds of therapy are to be thought of as exclusive alternatives when an individual patient is considered; on the contrary many patients require both. In this book, the ways of combining treatments are considered in other chapters where the treatment of individual syndromes is discussed. It is important to keep this point in mind when reading this chapter and the next.

Our concern is with clinical therapeutics rather than basic psychopharmacology which the reader is assumed to have studied already. An adequate knowledge of the mechanisms of drug action is essential if drugs are to be used in a rational way, but a word of caution is appropriate. The clinician should not assume that the therapeutic effects of psychotropic drugs are necessarily explained by the pharmacological actions that have been discovered so far. For example, substantial delay in the effects of antidepressant and antipsychotic drugs suggests that their actions on transmitters, which occur rapidly, are only the first steps in a chain of biochemical changes.

This caution does not imply that a knowledge of pharmacological mechanisms has no bearing on psychiatric therapeutics. On the contrary, there have been substantial advances in pharmacological knowledge since the first psychotropic drugs were introduced in the 1950s, and it is increasingly important for the clinician to relate this knowledge to his use of drugs.

General considerations

The pharmacokinetics of psychotropic drugs

Before psychotropic drugs can produce their therapeutic effects, they must reach the brain in adequate amounts. How far they do so depends on their absorption, metabolism, excretion, and passage across the blood–brain barrier. A short review of these processes is given here. The reader who has not studied them before is referred to the monograph by Goldstein *et al.* (1974).

In general, psychotropic drugs are easily **absorbed** from the gut because most are lipophilic and are not highly ionized at physiological pH. Like other drugs, they are absorbed faster from an empty stomach, and in smaller amounts by patients suffering from intestinal hurry, malabsorption syndrome, or the effects of a previous partial gastrectomy.

Most psychotropic drugs are **metabolized** in the liver. This process begins as the drugs pass through the liver in the portal circulation on their way from the gut. This 'first-pass' metabolism reduces the amount of available drug, and is one of the reasons why larger doses are needed when a drug such as chlorpromazine is given by mouth than when it is given intramuscularly. The extent of this liver metabolism differs from one person to another. It is altered by certain other drugs which, if taken at the same time, induce liver enzymes (for example, barbiturates) or inhibit them (for example, monoamine oxidase inhibitors). Some drugs, such as chlorpromazine, actually induce their own metabolism, especially after being taken for a long time. Not all drug metabolites are inactive: for example, chlorpromazine is metabolized to a 7-hydroxy derivative which has therapeutic properties, as well as to a sulphoxide which is inactive. Because chlorpromazine, diazepam, and many other psychotropic drugs give rise to many metabolites, measurements of plasma concentrations of the parent drug are a poor guide to therapeutic activity.

Psychotropic drugs are **distributed** in the plasma, where most are largely bound to proteins; thus diazepam, chlorpromazine, and amitriptyline are about 95 per cent bound. They pass easily from the plasma to the brain because they are highly lipophilic. For the same reason they enter fat stores, from which they are released slowly long after the patient has ceased to take the drug.

Most psychotropic drugs and their metabolites are **excreted** mainly through the kidney. When kidney function is impaired, excretion is reduced and a lower dose of drug should be given. For basic or acidic drugs, renal excretion depends on the pH of the urine: for example amphetamine, a weak base, is excreted more rapidly when the urine is acid rather than alkaline. Lithium is filtered passively and then partly reabsorbed by the same mechanism that absorbs sodium. The two ions compete for this mechanism; hence reabsorption of lithium increases when that of sodium is reduced. Certain fractions of lipophilic drugs such as chlorpromazine are partly excreted in the bile, enter the intestine for the second time, and are then partly reabsorbed; that is, a proportion of the drug is recycled between intestine and liver.

Measurement of circulating drug concentrations

As a result of the mechanisms described above, plasma concentrations after standard doses of psychotropic drugs vary substantially from one patient to another. Tenfold differences have been observed with the antidepressant drug nortriptyline. It might be expected, therefore, that measurements of the plasma concentration of circulating drugs would help the clinician. There are several reasons why this is seldom the case. The most important reason is that the relationship between plasma concentration and clinical effects is variable. A second reason is that, as already noted, most psychotropic drugs are substantially bound to plasma proteins. Assays measure the total drug concentration but the free fraction is more important; and the ratio of free to bound drug varies in different patients. A third reason has also been mentioned above: many drugs have metabolites, some of which have therapeutic effects while others do not. Some assays are too specific, measuring only the parent drug but not its active derivatives; others are too general, measuring active and inactive metabolites alike. For these reasons it is only with the simplest psychotropic drug, lithium carbonate, that plasma concentrations are sufficiently useful to be measured routinely, and then only to avoid toxic effects.

As an alternative to these assays, measurements can be made of the pharmacological property thought to be responsible for the therapeutic effect. This has been tried with the neuroleptics by measuring dopamine receptor blocking activity. Such methods are still experimental.

Plasma concentrations vary throughout the day, rising immediately after the dose and falling at a rate that differs between individual drugs and individual people. The rate at which a drug level declines after a single dose varies from hours with lithium carbonate to weeks with slow release preparations of injectable neuroleptics. Knowledge of these differences allows more rational decisions about appropriate intervals between doses.

Drug interactions

When two psychotropic drugs are given together, one may interfere with or enhance the actions of the other. Interference may arise through alterations in absorption, binding, metabolism, or excretion; or by interaction between pharmacodynamic effects.

For psychotropic drugs, interactions affecting drug absorption are seldom important, although it is worth noting that absorption of chlorpromazine is reduced by antacids. Interactions due to protein *binding* are uncommon, although the chloral metabolite trichloracetic acid may displace warfarin from albumin. Interactions affecting drug *metabolism* are of considerable importance. Examples include the inhibition of the metabolism of sympathomimetic amines by monoamine oxidase inhibitors, and the increase in metabolism of chlorpromazine and tricyclic antidepressants by barbiturates which induce the relevant enzymes. Interaction affecting renal *excretion* are mainly important for lithium, the elimination of which is increased by acetazolamide, aminophylline, and sodium bicarbonate.

Pharmacodynamic interactions are exemplified by the antagonism of guanethidine and tricyclic antidepressants.

As a rule, a single drug can be used to produce all the effects required of a combination; for example, many tricyclic antidepressants have anti-anxiety effects. It is desirable to avoid combinations of psychotropic drugs whenever possible; if a combination is to be used, it is essential to know about possible interactions.

Drug withdrawal

Many psychotropic drugs do not achieve their full effects for several days and antidepressants may take up to three weeks. After drugs have been stopped there is often a comparable delay before their effects are lost. With some drugs, tissues have to readjust when treatment is stopped; this readjustment may appear clinically as a withdrawal syndrome. Among the psychotropic drugs, the hypnotics and anxiolytics are most likely to induce this kind of effect. After withdrawal of hypnotic drugs, readjustments are shown clinically as sleep disturbance and physiologically in an increase in rapid eye movement (REM) sleep. These changes occur, for example, when large doses of nitrazepam are stopped; withdrawal from smaller doses results in sleep disturbance without a rebound of REM (Adam *et al.* 1976). Unless the symptoms are recognized as due to drug withdrawal, it may be wrongly concluded from the sleep disturbance that the patient still needs a hypnotic. Withdrawal symptoms also occur when daytime benzo-diazepines are stopped abruptly (see p. 636).

General advice about prescribing psychotropic drugs

It is good practice to use well-tried drugs with therapeutic actions and side-effects that are thoroughly understood. The clinician should become familiar with a small number of drugs from each of the main groups—two or three antidepressants, two or three antipsychotics, and so on. In this way he can become used to adjusting the dosage and recognizing side-effects. (Recommendations about drugs of choice will be found in the later part of this chapter.) Well-tried drugs are usually less expensive than new preparations.

Having chosen a suitable drug, the doctor should prescribe it in adequate doses. He should not change the drug or add others without a good reason. In general, if there is no therapeutic response to one established drug, there is no likelihood of a better response to another taken from the same therapeutic group (provided that the first drug has been taken in adequate amounts). However, since the main obstacle to adequate dosage is usually side-effects, it is sometimes appropriate to change to a drug with a different pattern of side-effects—for example, from one tricyclic anti-depressant to another with fewer anticholinergic effects.

Some drug companies market tablets that contain a mixture of drugs: for example, tricyclic antidepressants with a small dose of a phenothiazine. These mixtures have little value. In the few cases when two drugs are really required, it is better to give them separately so that the dose of each can be adjusted independently.

Occasionally, drug combinations are given deliberately in the hope of producing interactions that will be more potent than the effects of either drug taken alone in full dosage (for example, a tricyclic antidepressant with a monoamine oxidase inhibitor). This practice, if it is to be used at all, should be carried out only by specialists because the adverse effects of combinations are much less easy to predict than those of single drugs.

When a drug is prescribed, it is necessary to determine the dose, the interval between doses, and the likely duration of treatment. The dose-ranges for commonly used drugs are indicated later in this chapter. Ranges for others will be found in the manufacturers' literature, the *British national formulary*, or a comparable work of reference. Within the therapeutic range, the correct dose for an individual patient should be decided after considering the severity of symptoms, and the patient's age, weight, and any factors that may affect drug metabolism (for example, other drugs being taken; or renal disease).

Next the interval between doses must be decided. Psychotropic drugs are often given three times a day, even though their duration of action is such that most can be taken once or twice a day without any undesirable fall in plasma concentations between doses. Less frequent administration has the advantage that out-patients are more likely to be reliable in taking drugs. In hospital, less frequent drug rounds mean that nurses have more time for psychological aspects of treatment. Some drugs, such as anxiolytics are required for immediate effects rather than continuous action; they should not be given at regular intervals but shortly before occasions on which symptoms are expected to be at their worst. The duration of treatment depends on the disorder under treatment; it is considered in the chapter dealing with clinical syndromes.

Before giving a patient a first prescription for a drug, the doctor should explain several points. He should make clear what effects are likely to be experienced on first taking the drug—for example, drowsiness or dry mouth. He should also explain how long it will be before therapeutic effects appear and what the first signs are likely to be—for example improved sleep after starting a tricyclic antidepressant. He should name any serious effects that must be reported by the patient, such as coarse tremor after taking lithium. Finally he should indicate how long the patient will need to take the drug. For some drugs such as anxiolytics, the latter information is given to discourage the patient from taking them for too long; for others, such as antidepressants, it is given to deter the patient from stopping too soon.

Compliance with treatment

Many patients do not take the drugs prescribed for them. This problem is greater when treating out-patients, but also occurs in hospital where some patients find ways of avoiding drugs administered by nurses.

If a patient is to comply with medication of any kind, he must be convinced of the need to take it, free from unfounded fears about its dangers, and aware how to take it. Each of these requirements presents particular problems when the patient has a psychiatric disorder. Thus, schizophrenic or seriously depressed patients may not be convinced that they are ill or they may not wish to recover. Deluded patients may distrust their doctors, and hypochondriacal patients may fear dangerous side-effects. Anxious patients often forget the prescribed dosage and frequency of their drugs. It is not surprising, therefore, that many psychiatric patients do not take their drugs in the prescribed way. It is important for the clinician to give attention to this problem. Time spent in discussing the patient's concerns is time well spent, for it often increases compliance. [For a comprehensive review of patients' compliance with treatment, see Haynes *et al.*(1979).]

The overprescribing of psychotropic drugs

In the last 30 years, many safe and effective drugs have been produced for the treatment of psychiatric disorders. Unfortunately, their proven value in severe conditions has led to unnecessary prescribing for mild cases that would recover without medication. Similarly, the safety of these drugs has sometimes encouraged prolonged prescribing when brief treatment would be more appropriate. These problems have arisen most often with drugs prescribed for insomnia, anxiety, and depressed mood. All three symptoms are important components of psychiatric illness, but in their mildest form they are also part of everyday life. The extent of usage of anxiolytic and antidepressant drugs was shown by a survey of all prescriptions issued in general practices serving 40 000 people (Skegg *et al.*1977). It was found that psychotropic drugs were prescribed more often than any others. Amongst patients registered in the practices, nearly 10 per cent of men and over 20 per cent of women received at least one prescription for a psychotropic drug during the course of a year. In women aged 45–49, one third received such a prescription.

While there are important implications about the amount of drugs consumed through these high rates of prescribing, it is equally important to remember that many prescribed drugs are not taken. Nicholson (1967) collected unused drugs from about 500 patients' houses in the course of six days. He recovered 36 000 tablets, of which nearly 5000 were sedatives and tranquillizers, over 2000 were hypnotics and 750 were antidepressants. Unused drugs are a danger to children and a potential source of self-poisoning either by the patient or by other people. For these reasons patients should not be given more drugs than they need, and care should be taken to enquire whether existing supplies have been used before prescribing more.

Prescribing for special groups

Children seldom require medication for psychiatric problems. When they do require it, doses should be adjusted appropriately by consulting an up-to-date work of reference (such as the *British national formulary*). For **elderly** patients, who are often sensitive to side-effects and may have impaired renal or hepatic function it is important to start with low doses.

There are special problems about prescribing psychotropic drugs in **pregnancy** because of the risk of teratogenesis. This risk, which varies between drugs, will be considered later in the chapter when the actions of the drugs are described. At this point, some general advice will be given. *Anxiolytic and sedative drugs* are seldom essential in early pregnancy, and psychological treatments can usually be used. If medication is needed benzodiazepines have not been shown to be teratogenic. If an *antidepressant drug* is required it is probably better to use long-established preparations such as imipramine and amitriptyline for which there is no evidence of a teratogenic effect after many years of use. Newer drugs, even if they have not been shown to be unsafe, should be avoided because there has been less time to accumulate evidence. It is seldom necessary to start *antipsychotic* drugs in early pregnancy. When a patient is already receiving them, the risk of relapse if the drugs are stopped must be weighed against the uncertainty about the teratogenic effects of the particular drug. So far there is no evidence that these drugs damage the fetus but as noted above, the degree of uncertainty must be greater with newer drugs than with those that have been used for many years. Therefore, it is wise to avoid these drugs in the first trimester whenever possible (see Edlund and Craig 1984). *Lithium carbonate* should not be started in early pregnancy but some patients become pregnant while taking the drug. There is evidence that lithium is associated with fetal abnormality, especially affecting the heart (see p. 670). This drug should be stopped and if necessary neuroleptic or tricyclic drugs used to control the affective disorder, since these may have a smaller risk. Mothers who are taking lithium at term should if possible stop the drug before delivery; and in any case no further doses should be taken during labour. Serum lithium concentrations should be measured frequently and the use of diuretics avoided.

Because it is difficult to be certain of the teratogenic potential of new psychotropic drugs, it is prudent to avoid them when possible in early pregnancy. It is also often appropriate to advise women of childbearing age who require psychotropics, to adopt a reliable method of contraception to avoid pregnancy until the need for the drug is over.

Psychotropic drugs should be prescribed cautiously to women who are **breast feeding**. Diazepam and other *benzodiazepines* pass readily into breast milk and may cause sedation and hypotonicity in the infant. *Neuroleptics* and *antidepressants* also enter breast milk although rather less readily than diazepam; *lithium carbonate* enters freely and serum concentrations in the infant can approach those of the mother so that breast feeding is contraindicated. [For reviews see *Drugs and Therapeutics Bulletin* (1983) and Loudon (1987).]

What to do if there is no therapeutic response

The first step is to find out whether the patient has been taking the drug in the correct dose. He may not have understood the original instructions, or may be worried that a full dose will produce unpleasant effects. Some patients fear they will become dependent if they take the drug regularly. Other patients may have little wish to take drugs for different reasons, schizophenics because they do not regard themselves as ill, and depressed patients because they do not believe they can be helped. If the doctor is satisfied that the drug has been taken correctly, he should find out whether the patient is taking any other drug (such as a barbiturate) which could affect the metabolism of the psychotropic agent. Finally, he should review the diagnosis to make sure that the treatment is appropriate before deciding whether to increase the dose.

The evaluation of psychotropic drugs

After being tested in animals, new drugs have to be evaluated for clinical use. This requires two stages. First, the drug is used cautiously at doses sufficient to give therapeutic effects without unwanted effects. Then, controlled clinical trials are carried out in which the drug is compared, under double-blind conditions, with a placebo or standard drug. Readers seeking information about the methodology of clinical trials are referred to Harris and Fitzgerald (1970). This section is concerned only with a few essential points that need to be kept in mind when reading a report of a trial of a new psychotropic drug. These points concern patients, treatments, and measurements.

Patients

In evaluating any clinical trial the clinician has to decide how far the selected patients are typical of all those who have the disorder (for example, schizophrenics are a diverse group) and how far they resemble the patients he wishes to treat (for example, chronic schizophrenics undergoing rehabilitation). Part of the selection procedure will have been reported by the research workers, but often other parts are not stated explicitly. Thus if a trial is restricted to hospital out-patients, it is necessary to consider what kinds of patients are likely to be referred to the particular hospital by the local general practitioners. For example, it might be important to know whether most patients with depressive disorders are referred, or only those who have not responded to adequate antidepressant treatment. If the latter, a hospital-based trial will be dealing with drug-resistant patients.

Important questions to consider are: How were diagnoses made and were standard and generally accepted diagnostic methods used? Of the patients originally referred to the trial, how many were rejected? Of those accepted, how many dropped out and were they replaced? Another important issue is how the patients would have fared without treatment. This question applies particularly to any trial not including a placebo condition. In such a trial, if patients treated with the new drug improve as much as those treated with a standard preparation, this may merely indicate that the patients selected for the investigation have a high rate of spontaneous recovery. A final point to check is whether allocation of patients to the various treatments has been random.

Treatments

The first questions concern dosage, intervals between doses, whether the same quantity of drugs was given to every patient, and whether additional drugs were allowed. It is important to decide whether the treatments were given for long enough. Nearly all clinical trials include precautions to ensure that neither patients nor staff can tell which treatment any one patient is receiving (the 'double-blind' trial). Identical tablets do not always achieve this aim because side-effects, such as dry mouth, tremor, or postural hypotension, can provide clues to the identity of one or more treatments. It is important therefore to study the frequency and pattern of side-effects reported by each group of patients.

It is also important to know what precautions have been taken to ensure that patients took the drugs prescribed for them. These precautions include counting any tablets remaining at the end of each treatment period; measuring blood plasma levels; and incorporating in the tablets a marker substance, such as riboflavine, that can be detected in urine more easily than the drug itself.

Measurements

When assessment methods are chosen for a clinical trial, a balance has to be struck between precision and reliability on the one hand, and clinical relevance on the other. Psychological test scores may be reliable and precise, but they seldom relate in a simple way to judgements made in everyday clinical work. Psychiatric rating scales are less reliable and precise but more relevant. It is important also to consider whether the assessments are sensitive within the range of changes to be expected in the trial: thus measures developed for use with severely depressed patients treated in hospital may not be appropriate for patients with minor depressive disorders in general practice. The timing of assessments should also be considered; for example, whether they began sufficiently early and were continued long enough. Finally the appropriateness of the statistical methods should be reviewed. If statistically significant changes are reported, it is important to decide whether they are big enough to justify a change to the new treatment.

The classification of drugs used in psychiatry

Drugs that have effects mainly on mental symptoms are called **psychotropic**. Psychiatrists often use two other groups of drugs: **antiparkinsonian** agents, which are employed to control the side-effects of some psychotropic drugs, and **antiepileptic drugs**.

The psychotropic drugs are divided into five groups (Table 17.1) **Anxiolytic** drugs reduce anxiety. They are sometimes called minor tranquillizers because they have a calming effect, though generally not powerful enough to calm severely ill schizophrenic or manic patients (drugs that calm such patients are sometimes called major tranquillizers). In large doses anxiolytics produce drowsiness; hence the drugs are sometimes referred to as anxiolytic-sedatives. In still larger doses they promote sleep, so that the anxiolytic group overlaps with the **hypnotic group**. **Antipsychotic** agents control some of the symptoms of schizophrenia, mania, and organic psychoses. As already noted, they are sometimes called major tranquillizers; and because of their side-effects they are also referred to as neuroleptics. The next group comprises **antidepressant** drugs, which relieve the symptoms of depressive disorders, although they do not affect the mood of healthy people. Drugs with the latter effect are called central nervous **stimulants;** they have little use in psychiatric practice.

Not all the drugs used in psychiatry fit into this scheme. Lithium carbonate has a moderate antidepressant effect (see p. 254) and controls the symptoms of mania, but its main use is to prevent relapses of these

Table 17.1. Classification of drugs used commonly in psychiatry

---

(a) *Psychotropic*
    Anxiolytic
    Hypnotic
    Antipsychotic
    Antidepressant
    Stimulant

(b) *Others*
    Antiparkinsonian
    Antiepileptic

---

conditions. Disulfiram and citrated calcium carbamide are used in the treatment of alcoholism; hormones and vitamins have some special uses; and antibiotics are used for cerebral syphilis and other bacterial infections of the brain. However the scheme of classification is useful, not least because it corresponds to that in the *British national formulary* which is a standard source of information about specific drugs.

The five main groups of drugs will now be reviewed in turn. For each group, an account will be given of therapeutic effects, pharmacology, principal compounds available, pharmacokinetics, unwanted effects (both those appearing with ordinary doses and the toxic effects of unduly high doses) and contraindications. General advice will also be given about the use of each group in everyday clinical practice, but specific applications to the treatment of individual disorders will be found in the chapters dealing with these conditions. Drugs that have a limited use in the treatment of a single disorder, for example disulfiram for alcohol problems, are discussed in the chapters dealing with the relevant clinical syndromes.

Anxiolytic drugs

Drugs that are anxiolytic in small doses produce drowsiness and sleep when given in large amounts. They are prescribed widely and often inappropriately. Before prescribing these drugs it is always important to seek the causes of anxiety and to try to modify them. It is also essential to recognize that a degree of anxiety can motivate patients to take steps to reduce problems that are causing it. Hence removing all anxiety in the short term is not always beneficial to the patient in the long run. Anxiolytics are most useful when given for a short time either to tide the patient over a crisis or to help him tackle a specific problem. Tolerance probably develops sooner or later to all anxiolytic sedatives. Because the benzodiazepines are now the most widely used anxiolytics, they will be considered first. Other compounds will then be described in less detail. When reading this section, it is important to keep in mind that psychological treatment can be used for anxiety(see p. 735).

Benzodiazepines

Pharmacology

Benzodiazepines are anxiolytic, sedative and, in large doses, hypnotic. They also have muscle relaxant and anticonvulsant properties. Their pharmacological actions are mediated through specific receptor sites located in a supramolecular complex with GABA receptors. Benzodiazepines enhance GABA neurotransmission thereby altering indirectly the activity of other neurotransmitter systems such as those involving noradrenalin and 5-HT.

Compounds available

Research in commercial laboratories has produced many variants on the basic benzodiazepine structure, but the resulting drugs are similar in their actions. The clinician needs only two compounds: one with a short action and one with a long action. The short-acting compounds, which include oxazepam, lorazepam, temazepam, and triazolam, are more appropriate when a brief action is required. As noted above, short-acting drugs seem particularly likely to cause dependency and should be prescribed with caution. Long-acting compounds, which include diazepam, chlordiazepoxide, nitrazepam, clobazam, and chlorazepate, are more appropriate when a sustained action is needed. An appropriate pair of drugs is lorazepam 3–10 mg per day in divided doses, and diazepam 6–30 mg per day in divided doses. It is conventional to use nitrazepam as a hypnotic, but it is generally more rational to use a shorter acting drug to avoid residual effects next day. Alprazolam is said to be more effective than other benzodiazepines for panic attacks, but this report has not been substantiated in a trial in which equivalent doses of alprazolam and another benzodiazepine have been compared (see p. 195).

Pharmacokinetics

Benzodiazepines are rapidly absorbed. They are highly bound to plasma proteins but, because they are lipophilic, pass readily into the brain. They are metabolized to a large number of compounds, many of which have therapeutic effects of their own: for example, temazepam and oxazepam are among the metabolic products of diazepam. Excretion is mainly as conjugates in the urine [see Schwartz (1973) for a review].

Unwanted effects

Benzodiazepines are well-tolerated. When they are given as anxiolytics, their main side-effects are due to the sedative properties of large doses, which can lead to ataxia and drowsiness (especially in the elderly) and occasionally to confused thinking. Minor degrees of drowsiness and of impaired co-ordination and judgement can affect driving skills and the operation of potentially dangerous machinery; moreover people affected in this way are not always aware of it (Betts *et al.*1972). For this reason, when benzodiazepines are prescribed, especially those with a longer action, patients should be advised about these dangers and about the potentiating effects of alcohol. The prescriber should remember that these effects are more common among elderly patients and those with impaired renal or liver function. Although in some circumstances benzodiazepines reduce tension and aggression, in certain doses they lead to a release of aggression by reducing inhibitions in people with a tendency to aggressive behaviour (DiMascio 1973). In this they resemble alcohol. This possible effect should be remembered when prescribing to women judged to be at risk of child abuse.

Toxic effects

Benzodiazepines have few toxic effects. Patients recover from large overdosages because these drugs do not depress respiration and blood pressure as barbiturates do. No convincing evidence of teratogenic effects has been reported, but it is wise to avoid prescribing in the first trimester of pregnancy unless there is a strong indication. Cerebral atrophy as judged by CT scan has been reported in some long-term benzodiazepine users, but it has not been shown to be an effect of the drug rather than an incidental finding (see Lader *et al.* 1984).

Drug interactions

Benzodiazepines, like other sedative-anxiolytics, potentiate the effects of alcohol and of drugs that depress the central nervous system.

Effects of withdrawal

It is now generally agreed that physical dependence develops after prolonged use of benzodiazepines. The frequency depends on the drug and the dosage, and has been estimated as between 5 and 50 per cent among patients taking the drugs for more than six months (see Hallstrom 1985). Dependence is associated with a withdrawal syndrome characterized by: apprehension, insomnia, nausea, and tremor, together with heightened sensitivity to perceptual stimuli. In severe cases epileptic seizures have been reported (see Petursson and Lader 1984). Since many of these symptoms resemble those of an anxiety disorder, it can be difficult to decide whether the patient is experiencing a benzodiazepine withdrawal syndrome or a recrudescence of the anxiety disorder for which the drug was prescribed originally (see Rodrigo and Williams 1986).

Withdrawal symptoms generally begin within two to three days of stopping a short-acting benzodiazepine and seven days of stopping a long-acting one. The symptoms generally last for three to ten days. Withdrawal symptoms seem more frequent after drugs with a short than a longer half-life (see Tyrer *et al.* 1981). If benzodiazepines have been taken for a long time, it is best to withdraw them gradually over several weeks (Committee on the Review of Medicines 1980). If this is done withdrawal symptoms can be minimized or avoided.

Other drugs used to treat anxiety

Beta-adrenoceptor antagonists

These drugs relieve some of the autonomic symptoms of anxiety, such as tachycardia, almost certainly by a peripheral effect (see Bonn *et al.* 1972). They are best reserved for anxious patients whose main symptom is palpitation or tremor that does not respond to benzodiazepines. An appropriate drug is propranolol in a dose of 40 mg three times a day. Contraindications are heart block, systolic blood pressure below 90 mm Hg, or a pulse rate less than 60 per minute; history of bronchospasm; metabolic acidosis, for example in diabetes; and after prolonged fasting, as in anorexia nervosa. Great caution is needed if there are signs of poor cardiac reserve. Beta-adrenoceptor antagonists precipitate heart failure in a few patients and should not be given to those with atrioventricular node block as they decrease conduction in the A-V node and bundle of His. They can cause severe bronchospasm and exacerbate both Raynaud's phenomenon and intermittent claudication. In diabetics they may cause hypoglycaemia. Some drugs interact with beta-blockers to increase these adverse effects. It is important, therefore, to find out what other drugs are being taken, and to consult a work of reference to find out whether interactions have been reported.

Phenothiazines

These are sometimes prescribed for their anxiolytic effects. In doses that do not lead to side-effects, they are generally no more effective than benzodiazepines. Nevertheless, as anxiolytics phenothiazines have a small place in the treatment of two groups of patients—those with persistent anxiety who have become dependent on other drugs, and those with aggressive personalities who respond badly to the disinhibiting effects of other anxiolytics.

Tricyclic antidepressants

These drugs are appropriate treatment for the anxiety that often accompanies a depressive disorder. Sometimes sedative tricyclics are used for their anxiolytic effects in patients who are not suffering from depressive illness. These drugs are also worth trying for patients with chronic anxiety states that have not responded to benzodiazepines. The use of imipramine in the treatment of panic attacks is described on p. 195.

Barbiturates and other sedative anxiolytics

In the past **barbiturates** were widely used as anxiolytics. Although effective they readily cause dependency and they should not be used for this purpose. The **sedative antihistamine** hydroxyzine is sometimes used as an anxiolytic but it has anticholinergic side-effects and no obvious advantage over benzodiazepines as an anxiolytic. **Propanediols** such as meprobamate also have no advantage over benzodiazepines, and are more sedative in doses needed to relieve anxiety.

Unwanted effects resemble those of the benzodiazepines and generally appear at doses nearer to the anxiolytic dose. Barbiturates may produce irritability, drowsiness, and ataxia. In large doses the **toxic effects** of sedative anxiolytics are to depress respiration and reduce blood pressure. This is particularly a problem with the barbiturates. The **interactions** of these drugs with others resemble those of the benzodiazepines. In addition, barbiturates interact with coumarin drugs and reduce their anticoagulant action. They also increase the metabolism of tricyclic antidepressants and tetracycline. The **effects of withdrawal** resemble the effects of withdrawing benzodiazepines, described above. After stopping barbiturates the effects are particularly marked in the form of psychological tension, sweating, tremor, irritability, and, after large doses, seizures. Hence barbiturates should not be stopped suddenly if the dose has been substantial.

Advice on management

Before an anxiolytic drug is prescribed the cause of the anxiety should always be sought. For most patients, attention to life problems, an opportunity to talk about their feelings, and reassurance from the doctor are enough to reduce anxiety to tolerable levels. If an anxiolytic is needed, it should be given for a short time—seldom more than three weeks—and withdrawn gradually. It is important to remember that dependency is particularly likely to develop among people with alcohol problems. If the drug has been taken for several weeks, the patient should be warned that he may feel tense for a few days when it is stopped.

The drug of choice is a benzodiazepine. A short-acting compound should be chosen if anxiety is intermittent, a long-acting one if anxiety lasts throughout the day. The prescriber should become familiar with one preparation from each group, preferably the least expensive, and should thoroughly understand its effects. The other drugs should be kept for the specific purposes outlined above: beta-adrenoceptor antagonists for control of palpitations and tremor caused by anxiety and not responding to benzodiazepines; phenothiazines for patients who respond badly to the disinhibiting effects of sedative-anxiolytics (for example, abnormally aggressive patients), or for patients who have become dependent upon them; and sedative tricyclics in small doses for persistent chronic anxiety unresponsive to other drugs. Monoamine oxidase inhibitors are anxiolytic, but should not be used as such because of the risks of interactions with other drugs and foodstuffs (see p. 663).

Hypnotics

Hypnotics are drugs used to improve sleep. Many anxiolytic sedatives also act as hypnotics, and they have been reviewed in the previous section. Hypnotic drugs are prescribed widely and often continued for too long. This reflects the frequency of insomnia as a complaint. Mendelson (1980) found that about a third of American adults reported disturbed sleep, and a third of these described it as a major problem. Insomnia is reported more often by women and by the elderly.

Pharmacology

The ideal hypnotic would increase the length and quality of sleep without residual effects the next morning. It would do so without altering the pattern of sleep and without any withdrawal effects when the patient ceased to take it. Unfortunately, no drug meets these exacting criteria. It is not easy to produce drugs that affect the whole night's sleep and yet have been eliminated sufficiently by morning to leave behind no sedative effects. Moreover the electrophysiological characteristics of sleep are altered while most drugs are being taken and for some nights after they have been stopped. Thus hypnotic drugs affect the pattern of the EEG; they suppress rapid eye movement (REM) sleep while they are taken, and lead to an increase of REM sleep up to several weeks after they have been stopped. These latter changes are often reflected in reports of disturbed sleep.

Compounds available

Nowadays the most commonly used hypnotics are benzodiazepines. In the past, barbiturates were prescribed most frequently, but are very rarely used now. Among the many other drugs available, chloral hydrate, chlormethiazole, and glutethimide are the commonest.

Of the **benzodiazepines**, nitrazepam, flurazepam, temazepam, and triazolam are commonly used as hypnotics. The first two are long-acting and more liable to produce hangover effects. The last two are short-acting drugs appropriate for initial insomnia. Any of the other benzodiazepines can be used as a hypnotic taken as a single dose at night. **Barbiturates** are conveniently divided into short-, medium-, and long-acting compounds. Only the medium-acting are suitable as hypnotics; the short-acting drugs are used for anaesthesia and the long-acting for epilepsy. Barbiturates available as hypnotics include amylobarbitone, amylobarbitone sodium, butobarbitone, and quinalbarbitone. In overdose, barbiturates are more dangerous than benzodiazepines because they more readily produce respiratory depression. Hence they are not recommended as hypnotics.

Other hypnotic drugs include **chloral hydrate**, which is sometimes prescribed for children and old people. It is a gastric irritant and should be diluted adequately. **Dichloralphenazone** is related to chloral but is less irritant. **Chlormethiazole edisylate** is a hypnotic drug with anticonvulsant properties. It is often used to prevent withdrawal symptoms in patients dependent on alcohol. For this reason it is sometimes thought, mistakenly, to be a suitable hypnotic for alcoholic patients. This belief is wrong because the drug is as likely as any other hypnotic drug to cause dependency. Although an effective hypnotic, **glutethimide** is toxic in overdosage and for this reason should not be prescribed except in small amounts (see *British Medical Journal* 1976).

Pharmacokinetics

The metabolism and excretion of benzodiazepines has been described already. Barbiturates, the other important group of hypnotics, vary somewhat in their patterns of metabolism and excretion. Long-acting barbiturates are more water-soluble and less lipid-soluble than the medium-acting compounds, and are therefore largely excreted unchanged through the kidneys. Medium-acting compounds are largely metabolized in the liver and subsequently excreted as conjugated hydroxyl compounds. Barbiturates induce the enzymes by which they are themselves metabolized; they also induce liver enzymes that metabolize other drugs (see below).

Unwanted effects

The most important unwanted effects of hypnotics are their residual effects. These are experienced by the patient on the next day as feelings of being slow and drowsy. Psychological tests of reaction time have shown deficits in the afternoon after a single bed-time dose of a barbiturate or long-acting benzodiazepine (e.g. Bond and Lader 1973). The person with these deficits is not always aware of them, which may be serious for work involving potentially dangerous machinery or for driving motor vehicles, trains, or aeroplanes. People who sleep badly often make similar complaints after a poor night in which they did not take hypnotics; but these subjective feelings are not accompanied by comparable impairments of performance on psychological tests. The complaints may reflect the cause of insomnia (for example, depression, or over-indulgence in alcohol on the previous day) rather than the loss of sleep itself.

Contraindications

Barbiturates and dichloralphenazone should not be given to patients suffering from acute intermittent porphyria.

Drug interactions

The most important interaction of hypnotic drugs is with alcohol. At first the two potentiate one another, sometimes to a dangerous extent. After prolonged usage, a degree of cross-tolerance develops; however, persistent abuse of alcohol may damage the liver and so increase sensitivity to hypnotic drugs by reducing their metabolism. With the longer-acting benzodiazepines the alcohol-potentiating effect may last well into the day after the drug was taken (Saario *et al.* 1975). Barbiturates increase the metabolism of other drugs including anticoagulants, tricyclic antidepressants, and tetracycline. The interaction between chlormethiazole and alcohol is particularly dangerous and can result in deaths from respiratory failure. For this reason there must be adequate supervision when the drug is used during withdrawal of alcohol. It should never be prescribed for alcoholics who continue to drink.

Advice on management

Before prescribing hypnotic drugs it is important to find out whether the patient is really sleeping badly and if so, why. Many people have unrealistic ideas about the number of hours they should sleep. For example, they may not know that length of sleep often becomes shorter in middle and late life. Others take 'cat naps' in the daytime, perhaps through boredom, and still expect to sleep as long at night. Some people ask for sleeping tablets in anticipation of poor sleep for one or two nights, for example when travelling. Such temporary loss of sleep is soon compensated by increased sleep on subsequent nights and any supposed advantage in alertness after a full night's sleep is likely to be offset by the residual effects of the drugs. If a drug is justifiable in these circumstances it should be a short-acting benzodiazepine.

Among the common causes of disturbed sleep are excessive caffeine or alcohol; pain, cough, pruritus, and dyspnoea; and anxiety and depression. When any primary cause is present, this should be treated, not the insomnia. If, after careful enquiry, a hypnotic appears to be essential, it should be prescribed for a few days only. The clinician should explain this to the patient, and should warn him that a few nights of restless sleep may occur when the drugs are stopped, but this restlessness will not be a reason for prolonging the prescription.

For children the prescription of hypnotics is not justified, except for the occasional treatment of night terrors and somnambulism. Hypnotics should also be prescribed with particular care for the elderly, who may become confused and get out of bed in the night perhaps injuring themselves. Many patients are started on long periods of dependency on hypnotics by the prescribing of 'routine night sedation' in hospital. Prescription of these drugs should *not* be routine; it should be a response only to a real need, and should be stopped before the patient goes home.

Antipsychotic drugs

This term is applied to drugs that reduce psychomotor excitement and control some symptoms of schizophrenia without causing disinhibition, confusion, or sleep. Alternative terms for these drugs are **neuroleptic, antischizophrenic,** and **major tranquillizer**. None of these names is wholly satisfactory. Neuroleptic refers to the side-effects rather than to the therapeutic effects of the drugs; major tranquillizer does not refer to the most important clinical action; and antischizophrenic suggests a more specific action than the drugs really possess. The term antipsychotic is used here because it appears in the *British national formulary*.

The main therapeutic uses of antipsychotic drugs are to reduce hallucinations, delusions, agitation and psychomotor excitement in schizophrenia, organic psychosis, or mania. The drugs are also used prophylactically to prevent relapses of schizophrenia. In 1952 the introduction of chlorpromazine led to substantial improvements in the treatment of schizophrenia and paved the way to the discovery of the many psychotropic drugs now available.

Pharmacology

Antipsychotic drugs share the property of blocking dopamine receptors. This may account for their therapeutic action, a suggestion supported by the close relationship between their potency in blocking dopaminergic mechanisms *in vitro* and their therapeutic strength. It is also supported by the finding that, of the two stereo-isomers of flupenthixol, the alpha isomer blocks dopamine receptors and is therapeutic, while the beta isomer does not block dopamine receptors and is not therapeutic (Johnstone *et al.* 1978). Both alpha and beta isomers block noradrenergic and cholinergic receptors. These anti-adrenergic and anticholinergic actions account for many of the side-effects of the drugs, while the antidopaminergic actions on basal ganglia are responsible for the extrapyramidal side-effects. Drugs that lead to fewer extrapyramidal side-effects have anticholinergic actions which appear to exert an 'in-built' antiparkinsonian activity.

Compounds available

A large number of antipsychotic compounds have been developed. Some, like chlorpromazine, are phenothiazines. They differ from one another in the nature of the side chain, for example, and the radical in the 2 position (see Table 17.2 for example). Others are thioxanthenes (for example thiothixine, flupenthixol), butyrophenones (for example haloperidol) (Table 17.3) or diphenylbutylpiperidines (for example pimozide). The various compounds differ more in their side-effects than in their therapeutic properties. An account of the relations between structure and function is given by Shepherd *et al.* (1968).

Phenothiazines fall into three groups, according to the side-chain attached to the 10 position R_2 in Table 17.2) Aminoalkyl compounds such as chlorpromazine are the most sedative and have moderate extrapyramidal side-effects. **Piperidine** compounds such as thioridazine have fewer extrapyramidal effects than this first group. **Piperazine** compounds such as trifluoperazine or fluphenazine are the least sedating and the most

Table 17.2.

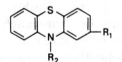

The basic phenothiazine structure

Type of compound	Example	R_1	R_2
Aminoalkyl	Chlorpromazine	—Cl	$- (CH_2)_3 - N \begin{smallmatrix} CH_3 \\ CH_3 \end{smallmatrix}$
Piperidine	Thioridazine	—SCH$_3$	$-CH_2-CH_2$ (piperidine ring with N—CH$_3$)
Piperazine	Trifluoperazine	—CF$_3$	$-(CH_2)_3 - N$ (piperazine) $N - CH_3$
	Fluphenazine	—CF$_3$	$-(CH_2)_3 - N$ (piperazine) $N - CH_2 - CH_2 OH$

Table 17.3. Two other antipsychotic drugs

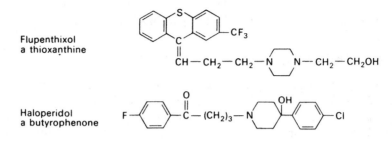

Flupenthixol
a thioxanthine

Haloperidol
a butyrophenone

likely to produce extrapyramidal effects. They are also the most potent therapeutically.

Thioxanthines are similar in structure to the phenothiazines (Table 17.2 and 17.3) differing only in the presence of a carbon rather than a nitrogen atom in the 10 position. Their properties are also similar to those of phenothiazines. **Butyrophenones** have a different base structure (Table 17.3). They have powerful antipsychotic effects and are highly likely to cause extrapyramidal side-effects, but have relatively little sedative effect. The **butylpiperidines,** of which pimozide is most often used in clinical work, are related in structure to the butyrophenones. Their most important difference is a longer half-life which allows once daily dosage.

The wide range of drugs now available can be seen from Table 17.4, which is not an exhaustive list. Fortunately, the clinician need acquaint himself with only a few of these drugs, as explained below.

Slow-release depot preparations are used for patients who need to take drugs to prevent relapse and cannot be relied on to take them regularly. These preparations include the esters fluphenazine enanthate, fluphenazine decanoate, flupenthixol decanoate, and clopenthixol decanoate; as well as fluspiriline. All except the latter are given in an oily medium. Fluspiriline is an aqueous suspension and has a shorter action than the others. Flupenthixol has been reported to have a mood-elevating effect, but this has not been proved.

Choice of drug

Of the many compounds available, the following are appropriate: chlorpromazine when a more sedating drug is required; trifluoperazine or haloperidol when sedation is undesirable; and fluphenazine decanoate when a depot preparation is required. Promazine or thioridazine is useful for elderly patients when it is desirable to reduce the risk of extrapyramidal and anticholinergic side-effects. For the treatment of mania, haloperidol is often preferred because it is less sedative than most phenothiazines.

Table 17.4. A list of antipsychotic drugs

Phenothiazines with:	*Butyrophenones*
(a) *Aliphatic side-chain*	Haloperidol
Chlorpromazine	Trifluperidol
Promazine	Spiroperidol
	Droperidol
(b) *Piperidine side-chain*	
Thioridazine	
Mesoridazine	
Pericyazine	*Diphenylbutylpiperidines*
Fluspiriline	Penfluridol
(c) *Piperazine side-chain*	
Trifluoperazine	
Perphenazine	*Azepines*
Fluphenazine	Clozapine
Prochlorperazine	
Thiopropazate	
	Indoles
	Oxypertine
Thioxanthines	Molindone
Thiothixene	
Flupenthixol	
Clopenthixol	*Substituted benzamides*
Chlorprothixene	Sulpiride
	Amine depletors
	Reserpine
	Tetrabenazine

Chlorpromazine and haloperidol can be given by intramuscular injection to produce a rapid calming effect in severely disturbed patients.

Pharmacokinetics

Antipsychotic drugs are well absorbed, mainly from the jejunum. They are largely metabolized in the liver. When they are taken by mouth, part of this metabolism is completed as they pass through the portal system on their way to the systemic circulation (first-pass metabolism). With chlorpromazine 75 per cent of the drug is metabolized in this way; with fluphenazine the proportion is even greater; while with haloperidol and pimozide it is less. The breakdown of chlorpromazine is complicated, about 75 metabolites having been detected in the blood or urine. The two principal metabolites are 7-hydroxychlorpromazine which is still therapeutically active, and chlorpromazine sulphoxide which is not. Combinations of active and inactive metabolites also occur with other antipsychotic drugs. They make it difficult to interpret the clinical significance of plasma concentrations; hence the latter are seldom used in everyday clinical work. Chlorpromazine induces liver enzymes that increase its own metabolism; the latter is also increased by barbiturates and some antiparkinsonian drugs (notably orphenadrine). Other drugs (paticularly imipramine and amitriptyline) reduce the metabolism of chlorpromazine by competing for relevant enzymes.

Unwanted effects

The many different antipsychotic drugs share a broad pattern of unwanted effects that are mainly related to their antidopaminergic, antiadrenergic, and anticholinergic properties (see Table 17.5). Details of the effects of individual drugs will be found in the *British national formulary* or a similar work of reference. Here an account is given of the general pattern, with examples of the side-effects associated with a few commonly used drugs.

Extrapyramidal effects

These are related to the antidopaminergic action of the drugs on the basal ganglia. As already noted, the therapeutic effects may also derive from the antidopaminergic action, though presumably at a site other than the basal ganglia. It is not surprising, therefore, that it has so far proved impossible to produce antipsychotic drugs with no extrapyramidal side-effects.

The effects on the extrapyramidal system fall into four groups. **Acute dystonia** occurs soon after treatment begins, especially in young men. It is observed most often with butyrophenones and with the piperazine group of phenothiazines. The main features are torticollis, tongue protrusion, grimacing and opisthotonus, an odd clinical picture which can easily be mistaken for histrionic behaviour. It can be controlled by biperiden lactate 2–5 mg given carefully by intramuscular injection, or in the most severe cases by slow intravenous injection. **Akathisia** is an unpleasant feeling of physical restlessness and a need to move, leading to an inability to keep still. It occurs usually in the first two weeks of treatment with neuroleptic drugs, but may begin only after several months. Akathisia is not reliably controlled by antiparkinsonian drugs but when occurring early in treatment it disappears if the dose is reduced. Occasional late cases have been described which do not respond quickly to a reduction in dose. It is difficult to differentiate these cases from tardive dyskinesia (Munetz and Cornes 1982).

The common side-effect is a **parkinsonian syndrome** characterized by

Table 17.5. Some unwanted effects of antipsychotic drugs

Antidopaminergic effects
  Acute dystonia
  Akathisia
  Parkinsonism
  Tardive dyskinesia

Antiadrenergic effects
  Postural hypotension
  Inhibition of ejaculation

Anticholinergic effects
  Dry mouth
  Reduced sweating
  Urinary hesitancy and retention
  Constipation
  Blurred vision
  Precipitation of glaucoma

Other effects
  Cardiac arrhythmias
  Weight gain
  Amenorrhoea
  Galactorrhoea
  Hypothermia

Sensitivity reactions
  See text

---

akinesia, an expressionless face, and lack of associated movements when walking, together with rigidity, coarse tremor, stooped posture, and in severe cases a festinant gait. This syndrome often takes a few weeks to appear after the drug has been taken and then sometimes diminishes even though the dose has not been reduced. The symptoms can be controlled with antiparkinsonian drugs. However, it is not good practice to prescribe antiparkinsonian drugs prophylactically as a routine, because not all patients will need them. Moreover, these drugs themselves have undesirable effects in some patients; for example, they occasionally cause an acute organic syndrome, and possibly increase the incidence of tardive dyskinesia.

This last syndrome, **tardive dyskinesia,** is particularly serious because, unlike the other extrapyramidal effects, it does not always recover when the drugs are stopped. It is characterized by chewing and sucking movements, grimacing, choreoathetoid movements, and possibly akathisia

(Barnes and Braude 1985). The latter usually affect the face but the limbs and the muscles of respiration may also be involved. The syndrome is seen occasionally among patients who have not taken antipsychotic drugs. Clinical observations suggest that it is much more common among those who have taken antipsychotic drugs for many years. However, a review by an American Psychiatric Association task force (1987) concluded that neither size of daily dose nor length of treatment is the main determinant. Tardive dyskinesia is more common among women, the elderly, and patients who have diffuse brain pathology [see Kane and Smith (1982) for a review of prevalence and risk factors]. In about half the cases, tardive dyskinesia disappears when the drugs are stopped. Estimates of the frequency of the syndrome vary in different series, but it seems to develop in 20–40 per cent of schizophrenic patients treated with long-term antipsychotic drugs (see Marsden and Jenner 1980). Whatever the exact incidence, the existence of this syndrome should be a deterrent to the long-term prescribing of antipsychotic drugs in large doses.

The *cause* of the syndrome is uncertain but it could possibly be supersensitivity to dopamine resulting from prolonged dopaminergic blockade. This explanation is consistent with the observations that tardive dyskinesia may be aggravated in three ways: frequently by stopping the antipsychotic drugs; by the action of anticholinergic antiparkinsonian drugs (presumably by upsetting further the balance between cholinergic and dopaminergic systems in the basal ganglia); and by L-dopa and apomorphine in some patients. However, there are other observations that do not readily fit this explanation.

Many *treatments* for tardive dyskinesia have been tried but none is universally effective. It is important, therefore, to reduce its incidence as far as possible by limiting long-term treatment and high doses to patients who really need them. At the same time a careful watch should be kept for abnormal movements in all patients who have taken antipsychotic drugs for a long time. If dyskinesia is observed, the antipsychotic drug should be stopped if the state of the mental illness allows this. Although the dyskinesia may at first worsen after stopping the drug, in many cases it will improve over several months. If the dyskinesia persists after this time, or if the continuation of antipsychotic medication is essential, a cautious trial can be made of a drug from one of the groups that have been reported, on the basis of clinical trials, to reduce the abnormal movements. A drug can be tried from each of the groups in turn. These groups include dopamine receptor antagonists such as haloperidol and pimozide, and dopamine-depleting agents such as tetrabenazine. [The reader is referred to MacKay and Sheppard (1979) for a review of the treatment of tardive dyskinesia; and to Marsden and Jenner (1980) for further information about the pathophysiology of this and other extrapyramidal side-effects of antipsychotic drugs and to Stahl (1986) for a review of the natural history of tardive dyskinesia.]

Antiadrenergic effects

These include postural hypotension with reflex tachycardia, nasal congestion, and inhibition of ejaculation. The effects on blood pressure are particularly likely to appear after intramuscular administration, and in the elderly whatever the route of administration.

Anticholinergic effects

These include dry mouth, urinary hesitancy and retention, constipation, reduced sweating, blurred vision, and rarely the precipitation of glaucoma.

Other effects

Cardiac arrhythmias are sometimes reported. ECG changes are more common in the form of prolongation of the QT and T wave blurring. Depression of mood had been said to occur, but this is difficult to evaluate because untreated schizophrenic patients may have periods of depression. Some patients gain weight when taking antipsychotic drugs, especially chlorpromazine. Galactorrhoea and amenorrhoea are induced in some women. In the elderly, hypothermia is an important unwanted effect. Some phenothiazines, especially chlorpromazine, increase the frequency of seizures in epileptic patients. Prolonged chlorpromazine treatment can lead to photosensitivity and to accumulation of pigment in the skin, cornea, and lens. Thioridazine in exceptionally high dose (more than 800 mg/day) may cause retinal degeneration. Rare adverse reactions include cholestatic jaundice and agranulocytosis.

These drugs have not been shown to be teratogenic but nevertheless they should be used cautiously in early pregnancy.

The neuroleptic malignant syndrome

This rare but serious disorder occurs in a small minority of patients taking neuroleptics, especially high potency compounds. Most reported cases have followed the use of neuroleptics for schizophrenia but in some cases the drugs were used for mania, depressive disorder, and organic mental disorders. The onset is usually but not invariably in the first ten days of treatment. The **clinical picture** includes the rapid onset (usually over 24–72 hours) of severe motor, mental, and autonomic disorders. The prominent *motor* symptom is generalized muscular hypertonicity. Stiffness of the muscles in the throat and chest may cause dysphagia and dyspnoea. The *mental* symptoms including akinetic mutism, stupor, or impaired consciousness. Hyperpyrexia develops with evidence of *autonomic* disturbances in the form of unstable blood pressure, tachycardia, excessive sweating, salivation, and urinary incontinence. In the blood, creatinine phosphokinase (CPK) levels may be raised, and the white cells increased. Secondary features may include pneumonia, thromboembolism, cardiovascular collapse, and renal failure. The mortality rate appears to be between 15 per cent (Kellam 1987) and 20 per cent (Caroff 1980). The syndrome lasts for one to two weeks after stopping an oral neuroleptic but may last two to three times longer after stopping long-acting preparations. Patients who survive are usually without residual disability.

The **differential diagnosis** includes encephalitis, and in some countries heat stroke. Before the introduction of antipsychotic drugs, a similar disorder was reported as a form of catatonia sometimes called acute lethal catatonia. The **cause** is unknown.

The condition can probably occur with any neuroleptic but in many reported cases the drugs used have been haloperidol or fluphenazine. The cause could be related to excessive dopaminergic blockade, though why this should affect only a minority of patients cannot be explained. **Treatment** is symptomatic: the main needs are to stop the drug, cool the patient, maintain fluid balance, and treat intercurrent infection. No drug treatment is certainly effective. Diazepam can be used for muscle stiffness. Dantrolene, a drug used to treat malignant hyperthermia, has also been tried. Bromocriptine, amantadine, and L-dopa have been used but with insufficient cases for a definite statement about their value. Some patients who developed the syndrome on one occasion have been given the drug again safely after the acute episode has resolved (see Caroff 1980). Nevertheless, if an antipsychotic has to be used again it is prudent to restart treatment cautiously with a low potency drug such as thioridazine, used at first in low doses. [For a review of the syndrome see Shalev and Munitz (1986), and Kellam (1987).]

Contraindications

There are few contraindications and they vary with individual drugs. Before any of these drugs is used, it is important to consult the *British national formulary* or a comparable work of reference. Contraindications include myasthenia gravis, Addison's disease, glaucoma, and evidence of present or past bone marrow depression; all of these conditions can be exacerbated by these drugs. For patients with liver disease chlorpromazine should be avoided and other drugs used with caution. Caution is also required when there is renal disease, cardiovascular disorder, parkinsonism, epilepsy, or serious infection.

Dosage

Doses of antipsychotic drugs need to be adjusted for the individual patient and changes should be made gradually. Doses should be lower for children, the elderly. patients with brain damage or epilepsy, and the physically ill. The dosage of individual drugs can be found in the *British national formulary* or a comparable work of reference or in the manufacturer's literature. An indication of the relative dosage of some commonly used drugs, taken by mouth is given in Table 17.6. Some practical guidance on the most commonly used drugs is given in the next section.

Table 17.6. Approximate relative dosage of some antipsychotic drugs*

Taken by mouth	
chlorpromazine	100
thioridazine	100
trifluoperazine	5
fluphenazine	2
haloperidol	2

* See Davis (1987).

Advice on management

Use in emergencies

Antipsychotic drugs are used to control psychomotor excitement, hostility, and other abnormal behaviour resulting from schizophrenia, mania, or organic psychosis. If the patient is very excited and particularly if he is abnormally aggressive, the first dose should be large enough to bring his behaviour under control. Chlorpromazine is useful because it has sedative side-effects and is less likely to result in acute dystonic reaction than drugs such as haloperidol. An appropriate dose for a healthy young adult is chlorpromazine 100–200 mg by mouth; or if a rapid action is essential, an intramuscular injection of 50 to 100 mg according to the weight of the patient and the degree of danger. An appropriate dose of haloperidol is 10–30 mg by intramuscular injection. When larger doses are given, a careful watch must be kept for hypotensive effects, and antiparkinsonian agents may be needed to prevent extrapyramidal effects. The doses stated above must be reduced appropriately for children and adolescents, older patients, the physically ill, people of small body size, and those who have taken too much alcohol. Thus for an elderly agitated patient 25 mg of chlorpromazine by mouth may be enough. The *British national formulary* or the maker's literature should be consulted before deciding the dose.

In the **management of the acutely disturbed patient,** there are several other practical points that can be dealt with conveniently here. Although it may not be easy in the early stages to differentiate between mania and schizophrenia as causes of the disturbed behaviour, it is necessary to try to distinguish them from organic mental states and from outburst of aggression in 'abnormal personalities. Among organic causes it is important to think of post-epileptic states, the effects of head injury, transient global amnesia, and hypoglycaemia. People with abnormal personalities may act highly abnormally when subjected to stressful events, especially if they have taken alcohol or other drugs. When over-active behaviour is secondary to an organic cause, it may be necessary to treat it symptomatically; but any drugs must be given cautiously, and the primary disorder should be treated whenever possible. If the patient has been drinking alcohol, the danger of potentiating the sedative effects of antipsychotic drugs should be remembered. Similarly antipsychotic drugs that may provoke seizures (for example chlorpromazine) should not be used for post-epileptic states.

In order to make a diagnosis, a careful history should be taken from an informant as well as the patient. It is unwise to be alone with a patient who has already been violent, at least until a diagnosis has been made. The interviewer should do his best to calm the patient. Provided that it seems safe and help remains at hand, he should disengage anyone who is restraining the patient physically. If medication is essential and the patient refuses to accept it, compulsory powers must be acquired by invoking the relevant part of the Mental Health Act (p. 901) before applying treatment. If, having obtained the necessary legal authority, a calming injection is required, the doctor should assemble enough helpers to restrain the patient effectively. They should act in a swift and determined way to secure the patient; half measures are likely to make him more aggressive. After the patient has become calmer, blood pressure should be monitored, particularly when the antipsychotic drug has been given by intramuscular injection. (See also p. 432.)

The treatment of the acute episode

When any necessary emergency measures have been taken, or from the beginning in less urgent cases, treatment with moderate doses of one of the less sedating antipsychotic drugs should be started. An appropriate prescription would be trifluoperazine 15 mg to 30 mg per day in divided doses, or haloperidol 10–15 mg per day in divided doses. The latter drug is often used for manic patients because it has less sedative side-effects. In the early stages of treatment the amount and timing of doses should be adjusted if necessary from one day to the next, until the most acute symptoms have been brought under control. Thereafter, regular twice-daily dosage is usually appropriate. A careful watch should be kept for acute dystonic reactions in the early days of treatment, especially when large doses are being used. Watch should also be kept for parkinsonian side-effects as treatment progresses; if they appear, an antiparkinsonian drug should be given (see next section). For the elderly or physically ill, appropriate observations of temperature and blood pressure should be made to detect hypothermia or postural hypotension.

If the disorder does not respond within a week to ten days, the dose should be increased progressively until either a therapeutic effect is obtained or troublesome side-effects appear. If the latter, it may be necessary to change to another drug with a different pattern of unwanted effects; for example, from chlorpromazine to haloperidol if the former has caused serious postural hypotension. Unwanted effects are the only reason for changing from one antipsychotic drug to another. If a full dose of one drug does not produce a therapeutic effect, it is unlikely that another drug will be more effective.

Treatment after the acute episode

Episodes of mania and acute organic mental disorders usually subside within weeks. On the other hand, schizophrenic patients often require treatment for many months or years. Such maintenance treatment can be a continuation, in a smaller dose, of the oral medication used to bring the condition under control. However, schizophrenic patients frequently fail to take their drugs regularly, and so delayed release depot preparations are often used. These are given by intramuscular injection. At the start of treatment a test dose is given to find out whether serious side-effects are likely with the full dose; for fluphenazine decanoate 12.5 mg is appropriate. The maintenance dose is then established by trial and error. It is likely to be between 25 and 50 mg every 2–4 weeks, and it is appropriate to begin with fluphenazine decanoate 25 mg every three weeks. It is important to find the smallest dose that will control the symptoms; since this may diminish with time, regular reassessment is needed of the remaining symptoms of illness and the extent of side-effects. It is not necessary to give antiparkinsonian drugs routinely; if they are needed it may be only for a few days after the injection of the depot preparation (when the drug plasma concentrations are highest).

Alternative sustained-action injectable preparations are flupenthixol decanoate and clopenthixol decanoate. It has been reported that the former leads to less depression of mood than fluphenazine preparations, but this report has not been substantiated.

[An informative review of the use of long-term antipsychotic treatment in psychiatry has been provided by Shepherd and Watt (1977).]

Antiparkinsonian drugs

Although these drugs have no direct therapeutic use in psychiatry, they are often required to control the extrapyramidal side-effects of antipsychotic drugs.

Pharmacology

Of the drugs used to treat idiopathic parkinsonism, the anticholinergic compounds are used for drug-induced extrapyramidal syndromes.

Preparations available

Many anticholinergic drugs are available and there is no rational reason for choosing any particular compound. Those most often used in psychiatric practice are the synthetic anticholinergics, benzhexol, benztropine mesylate, and procyclidine; and the antihistaminic, orphenadrine. Orphenadrine is said to have a mood-elevating effect. An injectable preparation of biperiden is useful for the treatment of acute dystonias.

Unwanted effects

In large doses, these drugs may cause an acute organic syndrome especially in the elderly. Their anticholinergic activity can summate with those of antipsychotic drugs so that glaucoma may be precipitated, or retention of urine in men with enlarged prostates. Drowsiness, dry mouth, and constipation also occur. These effects tend to diminish as the drug is continued. There is some evidence that these drugs increase the likelihood of tardive dyskinesia with prolonged antipsychotic treatment.

Drug interactions

Antiparkinsonian drugs can induce drug metabolizing enzymes in the liver, so that plasma concentrations of antipsychotic drugs are sometimes reduced.

Advice on management

As noted already, anticholinergic drugs should not be given routinely because they may increase the risk of tardive dyskinesia. It has also been pointed out that patients receiving injectable long-acting antipsychotic preparations usually require anticholinergic drugs for only a few days after injection, if at all. There have been reports of dependence on benzhexol, possibly resulting from a mood-elevating effect (see, for example, Harrison 1980). Benzhexol 5–15 mg per day in divided doses or orphenadrine 50–100 mg three times a day is appropriate for routine use.

Antidepressants

Antidepressant drugs have therapeutic effects in depressive illness, but they do not have immediate mood-stimulating effects of the kind produced by amphetamine. Two groups of drugs have been reported to have antidepressant properties. One consists of the tricyclic antidepressants and related compounds, the first of which, imipramine, was tested in clinical practice by Kuhn (1957). The second consists of the monoamine oxidase inhibitors; despite many years of use, their antidepressant effects are still debated. In this chapter tricyclic and related drugs are considered first; then the monoamine oxidase inhibitors; and finally L-tryptophan, a compound with more uncertain antidepressant properties.

Tricyclic and tetracyclic antidepressants

Pharmacology

Tricyclic antidepressants are so called because they have three linked rings to which a side-chain is attached. Their antidepressant properties depend on this central ring structure; their potency and sedative properties depend on variations in the side-chain. When a fourth ring is attached the compound is called tetracyclic. For the clinician these tetracyclic drugs can be regarded as further variants on the tricyclic structure rather than a separate group. Many tricyclic and tetracyclic drugs have been produced, mainly for commercial reasons. They do not differ importantly in their therapeutic effects although their different range of side-effects is sometimes useful for the clinician. It used to be thought that the therapeutic effect of these drugs was related to their common property of increasing the availability of noradrenalin or serotonin at receptors on postsynaptic neurones by blocking the re-uptake of these transmitters into presynaptic nerve terminals. However, this effect is not strong for some antidepressant drugs (for example, iprindole and mianserin), and in any case it takes place sooner than the therapeutic effect (which is generally delayed for up to two weeks or more). It is known that antidepressant drugs have further effects after blocking the re-uptake of transmitters. These effects include reduced sensitivity of alpha$_2$-adrenergic autoreceptors (stimulation of these receptors reduces the production of noradrenalin, and blocking them increases it), reduced post-synaptic beta-adrenergic sensitivity, and increased serotonergic function. The overall effect of these changes is difficult to judge. Thus, the therapeutic effect of these drugs cannot be explained despite many years of intensive research. [See Heninger *et al.*(1983*a*) for a review.]

Compounds available

The many compounds available are classified into tricyclics, tetracyclics, and other compounds. The tricyclics are divided further into aminobenzyls, dibenzylcycloheptanes, and aminostilbenes. However, the clinician is more concerned with pharmacological differences than with variations in structure, and the former are fewer in number. Despite some claims by manufacturers, there is no evidence that any drug acts more quickly than the rest.

'Standard' antidepressants

Amitriptyline has marked sedative effects as well as antidepressant properties. It is therefore an appropriate drug for the treatment of depressive disorder accompanied by anxiety or agitation. A sustained release preparation ('Lentizol') is available for use once a day, but amitriptyline is itself long-acting and can be given once a day. For this reason the use of sustained release formulations is not advised. **Imipramine** is a suitable alternative for retarded depression because it is less sedating than amitriptyline.

Other antidepressants

These include dothiepin, doxepin, iprindole, lofepramine, mianserin, fluoxetine, trazadone, and trimipramine. Of these, mianserin has fewer anticholinergic side-effects than amitriptyline and may be *less toxic to the heart*. Mianserin is therefore appropriate for the treatment of depressive disorder in patients with cardiac disease, though it has not been established that the antidepressant effect of the drug is as great as that of amitriptyline. Iprindole, lofepramine, trazodone, and perhaps doxepin may also have fewer cardiotoxic effects than imipramine. Fluvoxamine and fluoxetine are selective 5-HT uptake blockers. They may be less cardiotoxic (and less sedating) than the standard antidepressants but can cause nausea, anxiety, and anorexia. Convulsions have been reported in association with fluvoxamine, and it is prudent to avoid its use in patients with a history of epilepsy. Compounds that are *less sedative* than the standard antidepressants include desipramine, maprotiline, lofepramine, and nortriptyline.

Clomipramine, which has a strong effect on 5-HT uptake has been reported to have a specific *effect on obsessional symptoms* but the evidence is not convincing. The drug has been given by intravenous infusion but this practice is not recommended because it may lead to dangerous cardiac dysrhythmia.

Pharmacokinetics

Antidepressant drugs are rapidly absorbed, and extensively metabolized in the liver. They have a long action and need to be given only once a day. Patients differ widely in the extent to which they absorb and metabolize antidepressants; with nortriptyline, as mentioned earlier, tenfold differences in blood concentration have been reported after giving the same dose to different people. For this reason, dosage should always be adjusted according to the individual's clinical response and experience of side-effects. Measurements of plasma levels are of some value in patients who have not responded to the usual dosage. With nortriptyline there is some evidence that too high a dose as well as too low a dose is associated with poor response. (Asberg *et al.* 1971). However, this 'therapeutic window' has not been confirmed with amitriptyline (Coppen *et al.* 1978) and it may not apply generally. Concentrations in breast milk are similar to those in plasma.

Unwanted effects

These are numerous and important (see Table 17.7). They can be divided conveniently into five groups. **Autonomic:** dry mouth, disturbance of accommodation, difficulty in micturition leading to retention, constipation leading rarely to ileus, postural hypotension, tachycardia, increased sweating. Of these, retention of urine, especially in elderly men with enlarged prostates, and worsening of glaucoma are the most serious; dry mouth and accommodation difficulties are the most common. Iprindole and mianserin are least likely to produce these anticholinergic side-effects. **Psychiatric:** tiredness and drowsiness with amitriptyline and other sedative compounds; insomnia with imipramine; acute organic syndromes; mania may be provoked in manic-depressive patients. **Cardiovascular effects:** tachycardia and hypotension occur commonly. The electrocardiogram frequently shows prologation of PR and QT intervals, depressed ST segments and flattened T waves. Ventricular arrhythmias develop occasionally,

Table 17.7. Some unwanted effects of tricyclic antidepressant drugs

Autonomic (excluding cardiovascular)	dry mouth impaired accommodation difficulty in micturition constipation increased sweating
Cardiovascular	tachycardia hypotension ECG changes ventricular arrythmias
Neurological	fine tremor inco-ordination headache muscle twitching epileptic seizures peripheral neuropathy
Other	skin rashes cholestatic jaundice agranulocytosis

more often in patients with pre-existing heart disease. These effects may be less marked with mianserin, and trazodone. **Neurological:** fine tremor (commonly), inco-ordination, headache, muscle twitching, epileptic seizures in predisposed patients and, rarely, peripheral neuropathy. **Other:** allergic skin rashes, mild cholestatic jaundice, and rarely agranulocytosis. Mianserin has been associated, rarely, with depression of white blood cells (Committee on the Safety of Medicines 1981) and regular white cell counts have been recommended by the manufacturers. Teratogenic effects have not been recorded in women but antidepressant drugs should nevertheless be used cautiously in the first trimester of pregnancy.

Antidepressants should be withdrawn slowly. Sudden cessation may be followed by nausea, anxiety, sweating, and insomnia.

Toxic effects

In overdosage, tricyclic antidepressants produce a large number of effects, some extremely serious. Urgent expert treatment in a general hospital is therefore required, but the psychiatrist should know the main signs of overdosage. These can be listed as follows. The **cardiovascular** effects include ventricular fibrillation, conduction disturbances, and low blood pressure. Heart rate may be increased or decreased depending partly on the degree of conduction disturbance. The **respiratory** effects lead to respiratory depression. The resulting hypoxia increases the likelihood of cardiac complications. Aspiration pneumonia may develop. The **central nervous system** complications include agitation, twitching, convulsions, hallucinations, delirium, and coma. Pyramidal and extrapyramidal signs may develop. **Parasympathetic** effects include dry mouth, dilated pupils, blurred vision, retention of urine, and pyrexia. Most patients need only supportive care, but cardiac monitoring is important and arrhythmias require urgent treatment by a physician in an intensive care unit. Tricyclic antidepressants delay gastric emptying, and so gastric lavage is valuable for several hours after the overdose. Lavage must be carried out with particular care to prevent aspiration of gastric contents, if necessary by the insertion of a cuffed endotracheal tube before lavage is attempted.

Antidepressants and heart disease

The cardiovascular side-effects of tricyclic drugs noted above, coupled with their toxic effects on the heart when these drugs are taken in overdose, have led to the suggestion that tricyclic antidepressant drugs may be dangerous in patients with heart disease. The evidence is conflicting: a British drug monitoring system linked cardiac deaths with amitriptyline (Coull *et al.* 1970) but a similar system in the United States did not confirm such a link (Boston Collaborative Drug Surveillance Program 1972). Tricyclic antidepressants have anticholinergic and quinidine-like effects, and they decrease myocardial contractility. The drugs could therefore impair cardiac function. However, Veith *et al.* (1982) found no effect of tricyclic antidepressants on left ventricular function at rest or after exercise in depressed patients with chronic heart disease.

As noted above, it is possible that antidepressants without marked anticholinergic effects (such as mianserin or trazodone), are safer than other antidepressants, but this has not been proved. Orme (1984) concluded that any antidepressant drug is probably safe for patients with only mild heart disease, but tricyclic antidepressants should be used very cautiously for patients with severe heart disease, such as recent myocardial infarction, heart failure, or electrocardiographic evidence of bundle branch block or heart block.

Interactions with other drugs

The metabolism of tricyclic drugs is reduced competitively by phenothiazines and increased by barbiturates (though not by benzodiazepines). Tricyclic compounds potentiate the pressor effects of noradrenalin, adrenalin, and phenylephrine by preventing re-uptake (Boakes *et al.* 1973) and this is a potential hazard when local anaesthetics are used for dental surgery or other purposes. Tricyclic antidepressants also interfere with the effects of the antihypertensive agents bethanidine, clonidine, debrisoquine, and guanethidine. They do not, however, interact with the beta-adrenoceptor antagonists used to treat hypertension. Alternatively, mianserin can be used to treat depressed hypertensives for it interacts only with clonidine. Interactions of tricyclic drugs with monoamine oxidase inhibitors are considered later.

Contraindications

Contraindications include agranulocytosis, severe liver damage, glaucoma, and prostatic hypertrophy. The drugs must be used cautiously in epileptic patients, in the elderly, and after coronary thrombosis.

Management

The clinician should become familiar with two 'standard' drugs, one of which is more sedating than the other. Amitriptyline (more sedating) and imipramine (less sedating) fulfil these requirements and have been thoroughly tested in clinical trials. The doctor should also be familiar with a drug that has few anticholinergic side-effects and is less cardiotoxic than the rest; mianserin is one choice, although it is not yet certain whether its antidepressant properties are as great as those of amitriptyline. There is no value in changing from one tricyclic to another in the hope of producing a therapeutic effect when the first has failed, nor is there any value in giving more than one antidepressant drug at the same time (combinations of antidepressants and monoamine oxidase inhibitors are considered later). Equally there is nothing to be gained by using proprietary preparations containing a mixture of an antidepressant and a phenothiazine. Agitation can usually be controlled equally well by choosing a sedative antidepressant. If it necessary to supplement the latter with a phenothiazine, it is better to give the drugs separately so that doses can be adjusted independently.

If a depressed patient needs antihypertensive drugs, management is easier if the antihypertensive treatment can be a diuretic, a suitable beta adrenoceptor antagonist such as propranolol, or a combination or the two. If this cannot be done, blood pressure should be measured carefully at least once a week because tricyclics may interfere with the actions of other antihypertensives (see above). If necessary, the dose of the antihypertensive drugs should be adjusted. It is also important to continue measuring blood pressure and to be ready to readjust the antihypertensive dosage after the antidepressant drugs have been stopped.

Having selected a suitable antidepressant drug, it is most important to tell the patient that the therapeutic effect is likely to be delayed for up to two or three weeks although sleep may improve sooner. He should be told that side-effects will appear earlier than this, and that he may notice dry mouth, difficulty in accommodation, and constipation. An older patient should be warned about the effects of postural hypotension. Reassurance should be given that most of these effects are likely to grow less as the drug is taken for longer. Since the patient may feel worse from the side-effects of the drug before feeling any benefits from its therapeutic effects, he should be seen again after a week (or earlier if he is severely depressed). At this interview the doctor should find out what side-effects have appeared, and explain any that were not discussed on the first occasion. He should encourage the patient to continue taking the drug, and should reassess the severity of the depression.

The starting dose should be moderate; for example, amitriptyline 75–100 mg/day according to the urgency. If necessary this dose can be increased after about a week when the extent of the side-effects will have been observed. The whole dose of the antidepressant can usually be given at night, so that any sedative side-effects help the patient to sleep and the peak of other side-effects is less likely to be noticed. Doses must be reduced for elderly patients, those with cardiac disease, prostatism, or other conditions that may be exacerbated by the drugs, and those with disease of the liver or kidneys.

If after two or three weeks the depressive disorder has not responded, the drug should not be changed for another. Instead the doctor should try to find out why there has been no response. In doing this he should consider whether the patient has been taking the drugs in the correct dose, whether the diagnosis is correct, and what part social factors are playing in maintaining the condition. Poor compliance with antidepressant drug treatment is common. It often results from the depressed person's gloomy conviction that nothing can help him, from an unwillingness to suffer unpleasant side-effects, or from a fear that once started the drug will have to be taken indefinitely.

When a therapeutic effect has been achieved, the drug should be continued in full dose for at least six weeks. After this treatment a reduced dosage should usually be continued for a further six months (Mindham *et al.* 1973). If a relapse occurs when the dose is reduced, the former dosage should be reinstated for at least a further three months before lowering it cautiously for a second time.

Monoamine oxidase inhibitors

Although monoamine oxidase inhibitors have been used in psychiatry for many years, the exact nature of their therapeutic actions has not been established beyond doubt. They certainly have anxiolytic properties. They may have a specific antidepressant action as well, and this may be restricted to less severe depressive disorders. An antidepressant action has not been proved conclusively, and any improvement experienced by the patient could result from the anxiolytic effects of the drugs. Monoamine oxidase inhibitors have been reported to have therapeutic actions in phobic anxiety states (Sargant and Dally 1962) and anxiety disorders with panic attacks (Sheehan *et al.* 1980). One of these drugs, tranylcypromine, has a stimulant effect similar to that of amphetamine; this may account in part for the reputation gained by the whole group in the treatment of depressive disorders.

Against these modest therapeutic effects must be set a wide range of dangerous interactions with certain drugs and foodstuffs. These interactions are sufficiently serious that we recommend that monoamine oxidase inhibitors should never be used as a drug of first choice, but only after failure of adequate treatment with one of the tricyclic or similar antidepressant drugs. Even in these circumstances, monoamine oxidase inhibitors should be used infrequently. It is emphasized that these issues are still somewhat controversial.

Pharmacological actions

Monoamine oxidase inhibitors (MAOIs) inactivate enzymes that oxidize noradrenalin, 5-hydroxytryptamine, tyramine, and other amines which are widely distributed in the body as transmitters, or are taken in food and drink or as drugs. Monoamine oxidase exists in a number of forms that differ in their substrate and inhibitor specificities. The action of the drugs is not confined to the monoamine oxidases. The drugs also inhibit the hydroxylases in the liver which metabolize barbiturates, tricyclic antidepressants, phenytoin, and antiparkinsonian drugs. Inhibition of monoamine oxidase occurs rapidly, but when MAOIs are withdrawn it can take two weeks before the enzyme recovers its previous level of activity, so that dangers of drug interactions persist for this time. A full account of these important actions of the monoamine oxidase inhibitors will be found in a standard textbook of pharmacology.

Compounds available

Several compounds are available but, with the exception of tranylcypromine, there are few therapeutic differences between them. **Iproniazid** is the prototype of this group of drugs but its hepatotoxic effects make it unsuitable for general use in psychiatry. **Phenelzine** is the most widely used compound being less toxic to the liver than the others. **Isocarboxazid** is reported to have fewer side-effects than phenelzine, and can be useful for patients who respond to the latter drug but suffer from its side-effects of hypotension or sleep disorder. **Tranylcypromine** differs from the others in combining the ability to inhibit monoamine oxidase with an amphetamine-like stimulating effect which many patients welcome. Indeed the drug is partly metabolized to amphetamine. It is sometimes used in combination with trifluoperazine as the proprietary preparation 'Parstelin' (tranylcypromine 10 mg plus trifluoperazine 1 mg in each tablet) but there is no good reason to use this mixture. Some patients become dependent on the stimulant effect of tranylcypromine (see for example Griffin *et al.* 1981). Moreover, compared with phenelzine, it is more likely to give rise to hypertensive crises, though less likely to damage the liver. For these reasons, tranylcypromine should be prescribed with particular caution.

Pharmacokinetics

Monoamine oxidase inhibitors are absorbed quickly and distributed widely. Most are hydrazine derivatives and these are inactivated by acetylation of their side-chain in the liver. The speed of this acetylation varies between individual people in a way that is genetically determined. It has been reported that people who are slow acetylators respond better to the antidepressant effects of the drugs (Johnstone and Marsh 1973). The non-hydrazine compound of clinical interest, tranylcypromine, is metabolized rapidly and largely eliminated within 24 hours.

Unwanted effects

These include dry mouth, difficulty in micturition, postural hypotension, headache, dizziness, tremor, parasthesiae of the hands and feet, constipation, and oedema of the ankles. Hydrazine compounds can give rise to hepatocellular jaundice.

Interactions with foodstuffs and drugs

Foods and drink

Some foods contain tyramine, a substance that is normally inactivated by monoamine oxidases, mainly by those in the intestine and liver. When these enzymes are inhibited, tyramine is not broken down and is free to exert its hypertensive effects. These effects are due to the release of noradrenalin with consequent elevation of blood pressure. This may reach dangerous levels and occasionally result in a subarachnoid haemorrhage. Important early symptoms of such a crisis include a severe, usually throbbing, headache. The main foodstuffs to be avoided are extracts of meat and yeast, smoked or pickled fish, hung poultry or game and cheeses—especially camembert, brie, stilton, gorgonzola, cheddar, and some American processed cheeses. Chianti, some other red wines and some beers may also cause reactions. About four-fifths of reported interactions between foodstuffs and MAOI, and nearly all the deaths, followed the consumption of cheese (see McCabe 1986). Hypertensive crises are treated by blocking alpha adrenoceptors by parenteral administration of phentolamine, or if this drug is not available by intramuscular chlorpromazine. Blood pressure must be followed carefully.

Drugs

Patients taking monoamine oxidase inhibitors must not be given drugs of which the metabolism depends on enzymes that are affected by the MAOI. These drugs include sympathomimetic amines such as adrenalin, noradrenalin, amphetamine, and fenfluramine, as well as phenylpropanolamine and ephedrine (which may be present in proprietary cold cures). L-Dopa and dopamine may also cause hypertensive reactions. Antihypertensive drugs, such as methyldopa and guanethidine, and antihistamines are also affected. Local anaesthetics often contain a sympathomimetic amine and should also be avoided. Morphine, pethidine, procaine, cocaine, alcohol, barbiturates, and insulin can also be involved in dangerous interactions. Sensitivity to oral antidiabetic drugs is increased, with consequent risk of hypoglycaemia. The metabolism of barbiturates, phenytoin, and other drugs broken down in the liver may be slowed.

Tricyclic drugs also interact with monoamine oxidase inhibitors, occasionally giving rise to hyperpyrexia, restlessness, muscle twitching and rigidity, convulsions, and coma. When an MAOI is added to a tricyclic, and the dose of each drug is regulated carefully, such reactions are infrequent. Some clinicians make use of this combination, believing it to be more effective than either drug used alone. This practice is discussed further on p. 263. It is important to emphasize that the MAOI should be added to the tricyclic; it is not appropriate to give a tricyclic drug to a patient already receiving an MAOI because a serious interaction is more likely. If administered at all, combinations should be prescribed only by clinicians with experience of their use (gained under supervision by a more experienced person), and then only for patients who can be relied on to adhere strictly to the dosage schedules and to report side-effects. Imipramine, as well as clomipramine and other drugs with relatively specific effects on 5-HT uptake, should not be given with an MAOI (see White and Simpson 1981).

The possibility of interactions must be remembered when changing between tricyclic antidepressants and monoamine oxidase inhibitors. Tricyclics should not be given for two weeks after stopping an MAOI, otherwise interactions may occur. If tricyclics are given first (as done in combined treatment) no drug-free interval is required. This adds to the other reasons for always using a tricyclic as the first drug for depressive illness.

Contraindications

These include liver disease, phaeochromocytoma, congestive cardiac failure, and conditions which require the patient to take any of the drugs that react with MAOI.

Management

As explained earlier, monoamine oxidase inhibitors should not be prescribed as the first drug for the treatment of depressive disorders. If they are prescribed, the dangers of interactions with foods and other drugs must be explained carefully to the patient. A warning card should also be given because few patients remember the essential facts when given by word of mouth. A suitable card reproduced from the *British national formulary* is shown in Figure 17.1. Patients should be told to show this card to any doctor or dentist who is treating them. They should also be told not to buy any proprietary drugs, except from a qualified pharmacist, to whom the card should always be shown. If an MAOI has to be used, phenelzine is probably the best choice, starting in a dose of 15 mg twice a day and increasing cautiously to 15 mg four times a day. Although patients are often impressed by the amphetamine-like effects of tranylcypromine,

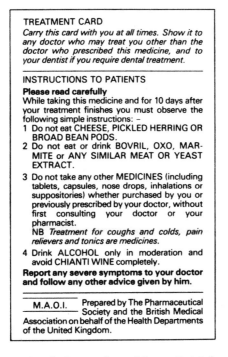

TREATMENT CARD

Carry this card with you at all times. Show it to any doctor who may treat you other than the doctor who prescribed this medicine, and to your dentist if you require dental treatment.

INSTRUCTIONS TO PATIENTS

Please read carefully
While taking this medicine and for 10 days after your treatment finishes you must observe the following simple instructions: –

1 Do not eat CHEESE, PICKLED HERRING OR BROAD BEAN PODS.

2 Do not eat or drink BOVRIL, OXO, MAR-MITE or ANY SIMILAR MEAT OR YEAST EXTRACT.

3 Do not take any other MEDICINES (including tablets, capsules, nose drops, inhalations or suppositories) whether purchased by you or previously prescribed by your doctor, without first consulting your doctor or your pharmacist.
NB *Treatment for coughs and colds, pain relievers and tonics are medicines.*

4 Drink ALCOHOL only in moderation and avoid CHIANTI WINE completely.

Report any severe symptoms to your doctor and follow any other advice given by him.

M.A.O.I.   Prepared by The Pharmaceutical Society and the British Medical Association on behalf of the Health Departments of the United Kingdom.

Fig. 17.1. Treatment Card. (Reproduced from *British national formulary*. Copyright BNF).

we do not recommend its use because some patients become dependent on this stimulant action.

If the drugs do not have a therapeutic effect, an interval of at least two weeks must be allowed before tricyclic antidepressants are substituted. MAOIs should be discontinued slowly.

Amine precursors

The hypothesis that the cerebral content of 5-hydroxytryptamine (5-HT) is lowered in depressive disorder has led to the therapeutic use of the precursors L-tryptophan and 5-HTP, which are capable of crossing the blood–brain barrier. These substances are sometimes given alone, but can be used in combination with an MAOI inhibitor (to reduce metabolism) or with the 5-HT uptake blocker clomipramine (given to increase the concentration of 5-HT in the synaptic cleft). Even with these combinations the evidence for an antidepressant effect of L-tryptophan or of 5-HTP is equivocal (see Baldessarini 1984). If either preparation is used, it should be as a therapeutic experiment for a patient who has failed to respond to adequate courses of other antidepressant treatments. (see p. 262).

Pharmacology

5-Hydroxytryptamine is synthesized from tryptophan by hydroxylation to 5-hydroxytryptophan (5-HTP) and then by decarboxylation. It is broken down by monoamine oxidase. L-Tryptophan is an essential amino acid which probably has no important pharmacological actions of its own. In particular it does not elevate mood in normal people.

Pharmacokinetics

Tryptophan is readily absorbed. It enters many metabolic reactions and is rapidly broken down by a pyrrolase in the liver to kynurenine and eventually nicotinic acid. The activity of this pyrrolase is increased by cortisol and oestrogens and by the inducing effect of L-tryptophan itself.

Compounds available

Tryptophan is available as a tablet containing 0.5 g of the drug together with 5 mg pyridoxine hydrochloride and 10 mg ascorbic acid (which are respectively cofactors in the decarboxylation and hydroxylation reactions). It has also been made up as a chocolate flavoured powder, intended to disguise the unpleasant taste of the large quantities of L-tryptophan.

Unwanted effects

L-Tryptophan has few unwanted effects except nausea and anorexia occurring soon after it is taken. It causes daytime drowsiness and can improve night time sleep if taken in the evening.

Advice on management

The lack of convincing evidence for a therapeutic effect indicates that the drug should not be used as the treatment of first choice for depressive illness. Its use may occasionally be worth considering for patients who have not responded to other treatments, but the clinician should not expect substantial effects.

Lithium

Lithium salts have been used in medicine for over a century, originally in the treatment of gout. In the 1940s they were employed as a substitute for sodium chloride for cardiac patients taking a salt-free diet. Toxic effects were frequent and the practice was abandoned. As a treatment for mania, lithium salts were first employed in 1949 by Cade in Australia. It was the work of Schou in Denmark that established the use of lithium carbonate in the treatment and prophylaxis of affective disorders.

The principal use of lithium is to prevent recurrence of mania and depressive disorders. It is also used as a treatment for acute episodes of mania. It may have an antidepressant effect but this is less sure; any such effect is certainly no greater than that of tricyclic drugs which are less toxic. Lithium carbonate has also been reported, on inadequate evidence, to reduce premenstrual tension. The evidence for the therapeutic effectiveness of lithium in depressive disorder is examined in the chapter dealing with the affective disorders (p. 254).

In animals lithium affects a number of transmitters and enzymes, although some of these actions have been observed only at lithium concentrations greater than those used in humans. It is not clear which of the many pharmacological actions of the lithium ion explains its therapeutic effects.

Pharmacokinetics

Lithium is rapidly absorbed from the gut and diffuses quickly throughout the body fluids and cells, displacing sodium and potassium and interfering with magnesium and calcium. Lithium moves out of cells more slowly than sodium. It is removed from plasma by renal excretion and by entering cells and other body compartments. There is therefore a rapid excretion of lithium from the plasma, and a slower phase reflecting its removal from the whole body pool. Lithium, like sodium, is filtered and partly re-absorbed in the kidney. When the proximal tubule absorbs more water, lithium absorption increases. Therefore dehydration causes plasma lithium concentrations to rise. Because lithium is transported in competition with sodium, more is reabsorbed when sodium concentrations fall. Thiazide diuretics increase sodium excretion without increasing that of lithium; hence they can lead to toxic concentrations of lithium in the blood.

Dosage and plasma concentrations

Because the therapeutic and toxic doses are close together, it is essential to measure plasma concentrations of lithium during treatment. Measurements should first be made after four to seven days; then weekly for three weeks; and then, provided that a satisfactory steady state has been achieved , once every six weeks. After an oral dose, plasma lithium levels rise by a factor of two or three within about four hours. For this reason, concentrations are normally measured twelve hours after the last dose, usually just before the morning dose which can be delayed if necessary for an hour or two. It is important to follow this routine because published information about lithium concentrations refers to the level twelve hours after the last dose, and not to the 'peak' reached in the four hours after that dose. If an unexpectedly high concentration is found it is important to find out whether the patient has inadvertently taken the morning dose before the blood sample was taken.

Until recently, the accepted range for prophylaxis was 0.7–1.2 mmol/1 measured 12 hours after the last dose. However, Srinivasan and Hullin (1980) proposed that these levels were unnecessarily high. They suggested that concentrations in the range 0.5–0.8 mmol/1 were sufficient for prophylaxis, and that higher levels were required only for treatment of acute illness. This view is now accepted by many. In the treatment of acute mania, plasma concentrations below 0.9 mmol/1 appear to be ineffective and a range of 0.9–1.4 mmol/1 is probably required (Prien *et al.* 1972). Serious toxic effects appear with concentrations above 2.0 mmol/1 though early symptoms may appear between 1.5–2.0 mmol/1.

Although it is conventional to measure concentrations 12 hours after the last dose, it is plausible to assume that any damage caused by the drug may depend on the highest level reached. For this reason, delayed release tablets have been introduced in an attempt to reduce the peak concentrations. However, it appears that the time-course of plasma levels resulting from these tablets is no different from that of lithium carbonate (see Srinivasan and Hullin 1980). It is prudent to give lithium in two doses a day rather than one, so that peak concentrations are less. An exception must be made for patients who take one dose reliably but consistently forget to take a second on the same day.

Unwanted effects

A mild diuresis due to sodium excretion occurs soon after the drug is started. Other common effects include tremor of the hands, dry mouth, a metallic taste, feelings of muscular weakness, and fatigue. **Later effects:** After the initial sodium diuresis, many patients develop poor renal concentrating ability, resulting in polyuria and polydipsia. A few patients develop a diabetes insipidus syndrome (see below). Polyuria can lead to dehydration (with the risk of lithium intoxication so that patients should be advised to drink enough water to compensate for the fluid loss). Some patients, especially women, gain some weight when taking the drug. Persistent fine tremor mainly affecting the hands is common; but coarse tremor suggests that the plasma concentration of lithium has reached toxic levels. Most patients adapt to the fine tremor; for those who do not, propranolol 10 mg t.d.s. often reduces the symptom. Occasional cases of partial hair loss have been reported, in the absence of hypothyroidism (Mortimer and Dawber 1984), and some of coarsening of the hair (McCreadie and Farmer 1985).

Thyroid gland enlargement occurs in about 5 per cent of patients taking lithium. The thyroid shrinks again if thyroxine is given while lithium is continued; and it returns to normal a month or two after lithium has been stopped (Schou *et al.* 1968). Lithium interferes with thyroid production and **hypothyroidism** occurs in up to 20 per cent of women patients (Lindstedt *et al.* 1977) with a compensatory rise in thyroid-stimulating hormone. Tests of thyroid function should be performed every six months to help in detecting these changes, but these intermittent tests are no substitute for a continuous watch for suggestive clinical signs particularly lethargy and substantial weight gain. If hypothyroidism develops and the reasons for lithium treatment are still strong, thyroxine treatment should be added.

Reversible **ECG changes** also occur. These may be due to displacement of potassium in the myocardium by lithium, for they resemble those of hypokalaemia, with T-wave flattening and inversion or widening of the QRS. Other changes include a reversible **leucocytosis** and occasional papular or maculopapular rashes. There is some uncertain evidence that prolonged treatment may lead to osteoporosis in women.

Long-term effects on the kidney: In 10 per cent of cases there is a persistent impairment of concentrating ability, and in a small number the syndrome of nephrogenic diabetes insipidus develops due to interference with the effect of antidiuretic hormone. This syndrome does not respond to antidiuretic treatments but usually recovers when the drug is stopped though there are reports of persisting cases (Simon *et al.* 1977). Structural changes have been reported in the kidneys of animals receiving toxic doses of lithium (Radomski *et al.* 1950) but these are much higher doses than the equivalent in humans. There have also been reports of tubular damage in patients on prolonged treatment (e.g. Herstbech *et al.* 1977). The incidence of pathological findings varies according to criteria for selection of the patients. Among those with impaired renal function, most show pathological changes in the tubules; in other patients about one in six show such changes (see Bendz 1983). Sclerotic glomeruli have also been reported, but glomerular function is seldom reduced. Glen *et al.* (1979) did not find increased mortality from renal disease in 784 patients who had taken lithium for many years, and there is no report of uraemia definitely attributable to lithium (Anonymous 1984). Hence it seems that, provided doses are kept below 1.2 mmol/1, there is no reason to expect renal damage in patients whose renal function is normal at the start. Nevertheless in the present state of knowledge it is wise to perform simple tests of renal function every six months (see below). Readers who require further information about the effects of lithium on the kidney should consult Myers *et al.* (1980).

Effects on memory are sometimes reported by patients, who complain especially of everyday lapses of memory such as forgetting well-known names. It is possible that this impairment of memory is caused by the affective disorder rather than by the drug itself. These subjective impressions of memory impairment are not matched by the results of psychological testing in patients on and off lithium (Smigman and Perris 1983).

However, with normal volunteers lithium has been shown to cause minor but reliably detectable memory deficits and to impair certain kinds of information processing (Glue *et al.* 1987).

Toxic effects

These are related to dose. They include ataxia, poor co-ordination of limb movements, muscle twitching, slurred speech, and confusion. They constitute a serious medical emergency for they can progress through coma and fits to death. If these symptoms appear, lithium must be stopped at once and a high intake of fluid provided, with extra sodium chloride to stimulate an osmotic diuresis. In severe cases renal dialysis may be needed. Lithium is rapidly cleared if renal function is normal so that most cases either recover completely or die. However, a few cases have been reported of permanent neurological damage despite haemodialysis (von Hartitzsch *et al.* 1972).

Lithium crosses the placenta. There are reports of increased rates of abnormalities in the babies of mothers receiving lithium in pregnancy. For example, a rate of 7 per cent has been reported, with most abnormalities affecting the baby's heart (Kallen and Tandberg 1983). The drug should therefore be avoided in the first trimester of pregnancy (see also Weinstein 1980). Lithium is secreted into breast milk to the extent that plasma lithium concentrations of breast-fed infants can be half or more of that in the maternal blood. Bottle feeding is a wise precaution in such cases.

Drug interactions

There have been several reports of serious toxic reactions when lithium is given with large doses of haloperidol in the treatment of acute mania (for example Cohen and Cohen 1974; Loudon and Waring 1976). These reactions consist of confusion, tremor, and signs of extrapyramidal and cerebellar dysfunction. Of the four cases reported by Cohen and Cohen, two were left with dementia and two with persistent dyskinesia. Other investigators have not found evidence of this syndrome among patients taking the two drugs. It has been suggested that the cases reported by Cohen and Cohen may have been due to coincidental encephalitis. However, Loudon and Waring conclude that there must be special caution when doses of haloperidol above 40 mg/day are combined with lithium concentrations greater than 1 mmol/1. Until more evidence is available this is a sensible precaution.

Thiazide diuretics can precipitate lithium toxicity, so they should not be given with lithium. If a patient taking lithium requires surgery involving a muscle relaxant, the anaesthetist should be informed in advance because the effect on muscle relaxants may be potentiated. Lithium should be stopped 48–72 hours before the operation (*Drugs and Therapeutics Bulletin* 1981*a*; Havdala *et al.* 1979).

Contraindications

These include renal failure or recent renal disease, current cardiac failure or recent myocardial infarction, and chronic diarrhoea sufficient to alter electrolytes. It is advisable not to use lithium for children or, as explained above, in early pregnancy. It should not be prescribed if the patient is judged unlikely to observe the precautions required for its safe use.

The management of patients on lithium

A careful routine of management is essential because of the effects of therapeutic doses of lithium on the thyroid and kidney, and the toxic effects of excessive dosage. The following routine is one of several that have been proposed and can be adopted safely. Successful treatment requires attention to detail, so the steps are set out below at some length.

Before starting lithium, a physical examination should be carried out including the measurement of blood pressure. It is also useful to weigh the patient. The urine should be examined for protein, sugar, and casts. Blood should be taken for estimation of electrolytes, urea, serum creatinine, haemoglobin, ESR, and a full blood count. When a particularly thorough evaluation is indicated, creatinine clearance is carried out, and 18-hour collection usually being adequate. Thyroid function tests are also necessary: T_4 as a screening test, followed by T_3, TSH, and FTI as indicated. (It is sensible to find out from a clinical pathologist or consultant endocrinologist, what tests are preferred locally.) If indicated, ECG, pregnancy tests, or lithium clearance should be done as well.

If these tests show no contraindication to lithium treatment, the doctor should check that the patient is not taking a thiazide diuretic. A careful explanation should then be given to the patient. He should understand the possible early toxic effects of an unduly high blood level; and also the circumstances in which this can arise—for example, during intercurrent gastroenteritis, renal infection, or the dehydration secondary to fever. He should be advised that if any of these arise, he should stop the drug and seek medical advice. It is usually appropriate to include another member of the family in these discussions. Providing printed guidelines on these points is often appropriate (either written by the doctor, or in one of the forms provided by pharmaceutical firms). In these discussions a sensible balance must be struck between alarming the patient by overemphasizing the risks, and failing to give him the information he needs to take a responsible part in the treatment.

Starting treatment: Lithium should normally be prescribed as the carbonate. Treatment should begin and continue with two doses 12 hours apart. The only exception is that, if the patient persistently forgets one of the doses, a single evening dose can be tried. If the drug is being used for prophylaxis, it is appropriate to begin with 750–1000 mg per day in divided doses, taking blood for lithium estimations every week and adjusting the dose until an appropriate concentration is achieved. For prophylaxis, a lithium level of 0.4–0.8 mmol/1 (in a sample taken 12 hours after the last dose) may be adequate, as explained above; if this is not effective, the previously accepted higher range of 0.7–1.2 mmol/1 should be used. In judging response, it should be remembered that it may take several months before lithium achieves its full effect.

As treatment continues lithium estimations should be carried out every six weeks. It is important to have some means of reminding patients and doctors about the times at which repeat investigations are required. If a doctor is treating many patients with lithium it is useful to keep a card index arranged in order of date to ensure that tests are not overlooked. Every six months, blood samples should be taken for electrolytes, urea, and creatinine, a full blood count, and the thryoid function tests listed above. The results should be recorded in tabular form in the patient's notes so that results of successive estimations can be compared easily. If two consecutive thyroid function tests a month apart show hypothyroidism, lithium should be stopped or L-thyroxine prescribed. Troublesome polyuria is a reason for attempting a reduction in dose, while severe persistent polyuria is an indication for specialist renal investigation including tests of concentrating ability. A persistent leucocytosis is not uncommon and is apparently harmless. It reverses soon after the drug is stopped.

While lithium is given, the doctor must keep in mind the rare interactions that have been reported with haloperidol (see above). It is also prudent to watch for toxic effects with extra care if other antipsychotic drugs are being taken or ECT is being given. If the patient requires an anaesthetic for any reason, the anaesthetist should be told that the patient is taking lithium; this is because, as noted above, there is some evidence that the effects of muscle relaxant may be potentiated.

Lithium is usually continued for at least a year, and often for much longer. The need for the drug should be reviewed once a year, taking into account any persistence of mild mood fluctuations which suggest the possibility of relapse if treatment is stopped. Continuing medication is more likely to be needed if the patient has previously had several episodes of affective disorder within a short time, or if previous affective disorders were so severe that even a small risk of recurrence should be avoided. Some patients have taken lithium continuously for 15 years or more, but there should always be compelling reasons for continuing treatment for more than five years.

When lithium is withdrawn suddenly, some patients become irritable and emotionally labile (King and Hullin 1983) and a few relapse, more often into mania than depression. Although the frequency of these changes is uncertain it is prudent to withdraw lithium gradually, over a period of a few weeks.

Central nervous stimulants

This class of drugs includes mild stimulants, of which the best known is caffeine, and more powerful stimulants such as amphetamine. Other mild stimulants include fencamfamin, meclofenoxate, and pemoline. These drugs have been advocated for the treatment of states of fatigue and senility, but their value for these purposes is doubtful. They are not suitable for the treatment of depressive disorders.

The most important of the poweful stimulants are the amphetamines. Although these drugs were much used in the past, they are no longer recommended because they readily give rise to dependence. They are certainly not appropriate for the treatment of depressive disorders. They have been used as appetite suppressants, but this is no longer appropriate. Their only remaining indication for adult patients is in the treatment of narcolepsy. (Their use in the hyperkinetic syndrome of childhood is discussed on p. 796.)

The remaining central nervous stimulant, cocaine, has even more potential for causing dependence. It has no uses in psychiatry but is still prescribed occasionally for terminally ill patients, often in combination with diamorphine or morphine.

The main **preparations** are dexamphetamine sulphate, given for narcolepsy in divided doses of 10 mg per day increasing to a maximum of 50 mg per day by steps of 10 mg each week; and methylamphetamine hydrochloride which has similar effects.

Unwanted effects: These include restlessness, insomnia, poor appetite, dizziness, tremor, palpitations, and cardiac arrhythmias. **Toxic effects** from large doses include disorientation and aggressive behaviour, hallucinations, convulsions, and coma. Persistent abuse can lead to a paranoid state similar to paranoid schizophrenia (Connell 1958). Amphetamines **interact** dangerously with monoamine oxidase inhibitors. They are **contraindicated** in cardiovascular disease and thyrotoxicosis.

Antiepileptic drugs

Antiepileptic drugs are sometimes called anticonvulsants, a name that is less appropriate because not all epileptic seizures are convulsive. The drugs are usually given prophylactically; a single seizure is not treated. However, when seizures are continuous (status epilepticus) or frequently repeated with recovery between (serial seizures) drugs are needed to arrest the condition. The psychiatrist should know about these drugs, not only because he may be called upon to treat patients with epilepsy but also because some of the drugs may cause behavioural disturbance.

Compounds available

A large number of compounds are used to treat epilepsy. The drugs in most common use can be classified on the basis of their chemical structure into hydantoins, barbiturates, succinimides, benzodiazepines, carbamazepine, and sodium valproate. However, these chemical differences are of little interest to the clinician who will find it more useful to classify the drugs according to the type of epilepsy for which they are most effective. Before considering such a classification, some comments are required on the main groups of drugs.

Hydantoins have been widely used since the introduction of phenytoin in 1938. This drug is the only one in general use today.

Barbiturates, introduced in 1912, were until recently the most widely prescribed antiepileptic drugs. Those used most often to treat seizure disorders are phenobarbitone and the closely related drug primidone.

Other compounds: *Carbamazepine* is chemically similar to the tricyclic antidepressant drugs, differing from imipramine only in its shorter side chain. This structure suggests that it might have an antidepressant action as well (see p. 254). *Sodium valproate* has a structure that is different from the other antiepileptics, being a branched chain carboxylic acid salt. *Sulthiame* is a sulphonamide derivative.

Choice of drug and type of seizure (Table 17.8)

In treating epilepsy, the choice of drug is based more on freedom from adverse effects than on any differences in effectiveness in controlling seizures. For partial (otherwise called focal) seizures, whether complex or simple in type, carbamazepine is the drug of choice and phenytoin or sodium valproate the main alternatives. Phenytoin has a narrow optimal dosage range for seizure control, and is more likely than carbamazepine to give rise to adverse effects. For tonic–clonic generalized seizures, the first choice lies between carbamazepine and sodium valproate. For absence seizures, sodium valproate is the first choice with ethosuximide as the alternative. Until recently myoclonic and atonic seizures did not respond well to antiepileptic drugs, but some can now be controlled with the newer drugs sodium valproate or clonazepam.

Table 17.8. Classification of seizures and drugs of choice

Type of seizure	First choice	Others
(a) Partial or focal (whether simple or complex)	Carbamazepine	Phenytoin or sodium valproate
(b) Generalized tonic–clonic	{ Carbamazepine or sodium valproate	Phenytoin
Absence seizures	Sodium valproate	Ethosuximide
Myoclonic and atonic	Sodium valproate	Clonazepam

Drugs used in status epilepticus

Diazepam, given intravenously, is the drug of first choice. Care must be taken to avoid respiratory depression and venous thrombophlebitis. As a rule, diazepam is not effective in status epilepticus when injected intra-muscularly, but it can be given effectively by rectal infusion when entry to a vein is difficult (Munthe-Kaas 1980). If diazepam fails, an intravenous infusion of chlormethiazole should be used. In the past paraldehyde was the mainstay of treatment, but until recently was out of fashion. It is now being used increasingly when diazepam fails. It can be given intramuscu-larly, rectally, or by intravenous infusion. If a plastic syringe is used, the drug must be given as soon as it has been drawn up. If status persists despite these measures, intravenous phenytoin, with ECG monitoring (because of the danger of cardiac arrhythmia), or phenobarbitone may be tried. These latter measures should not be taken without advice from a neurologist unless the circumstances are exceptional. Details of dosage will be found in the *British national formulary* or comparable handbooks; a useful discussion of the treatment of status epilepticus is given by Rimmer and Richens (1988).

Pharmacodynamics

It appears that antiepileptic drugs do not have a single common pharmaco-logical action that accounts for their therapeutic effects. Presumably they act in different ways and perhaps at different stages in the development of seizure activity; for example, phenobarbitone increases seizure threshold, whereas phenytoin appears to limit the propagation of the discharge. Until more is known about the mechanisms involved, the clinician gains little of practical value from a review of the pharmacodynamics of these drugs.

Pharmacokinetics

There are so many different antiepileptic drugs that many exceptions can be made to any generalization about them. Most are readily absorbed, the exception being phenytoin which is not very soluble in water and is absorbed in different amounts from different proprietary preparations. Most antiepileptic drugs are metabolized in the liver and excreted in the urine as the conjugated or free compound. Most have long actions. They can therefore be given once or twice a day provided that the dose is not so big that side-effects result from the peak level after a single dose. Carbamazepine is an exception and has to be given three times a day to many patients.

It is often useful to measure plasma concentrations because they are not always closely related to dose. Although this can be done for most of the commonly used drugs, it is most useful with phenytoin since the relationship between its dose and plasma concentration is particularly variable. Whichever drug is measured, it is necessary to find out how long after the last dose the sample should be taken—otherwise there may be difficulty in the interpretation of the results.

Unwanted effects

All antiepileptic drugs are potentially harmful and must be used with care. Because adverse effects differ between the many compounds in use, only general guidance can be given here. Before prescribing, it is important to study carefully a work of reference such as the *British national formulary* or the review paper by Jeavons (1970).

Phenytoin has many adverse effects. It commonly causes gum hypertrophy. Acne, hirsutism,and coarsening of the facial features are sufficiently frequent to demand caution in its use. In the nervous system cerebellar signs occur (ataxia, dysarthria, nystagmus) and indicate overdosage; among children intoxication may occur without these signs, and may therefore be missed. High plasma concentrations (above 40 mg/ml) may result in an acute organic mental disorder. According to Glaser (1972) phenytoin can cause an encephalopathy, of which one feature is an increase in seizure frequency. Uncommon haematological effects include a megaloblastic anaemia related to folate deficiency, leucopenia, thrombocytopenia, and agranulocytosis. Serum calcium may be lowered. Reynolds (1968) has suggested that mental side-effects of phenytoin are due to folate deficiency. However, the evidence for this is not convincing (see Richens 1976).

Carbamazepine has fewer unwanted effects. Drowsiness, ataxia, and diplopia develop if the plasma concentrations are too high; idiosyncratic effects include an erythematous rash, water retention, hepatitis, and leucopaenia or other blood dyscrasias. **Sodium valproate** has few adverse effects, the more common including potentiation of the effects of sedative drugs, gastrointestinal disturbance (often prevented by taking the drug with food, or by taking an enteric-coated preparation), and obesity. Thrombocytopenia, tremor, transient hair loss, and serious impairment of liver function have occurred occasionally. It has been recommended that liver function tests should be carried out before starting treatment (see *Drugs and Therapeutics Bulletin* 1981*a*) but this is still controversial. The unwanted effects of **phenobarbitone** in the treatment of epilepsy include drowsiness, irritability, and in larger doses slurred speech and ataxia. In children hyperactivity and emotional upset are frequent, and impaired learning and skin rashes can occur. For these reasons the drug should be avoided whenever possible.

The infants born to epileptic mothers appear to have a slightly increased incidence of congenital malformations including hare lip and cleft palate. These malformations may result from the use of anticonvulsants in pregnacy, but could perhaps be more related in some unknown way to the epilepsy itself. These possible risks have to be balanced against the risk of stopping the drugs in the individual patient.

Drug interactions

With so many different compounds in use it is difficult to make useful general statements about the interactions of antiepileptic drugs. It is important to remember that liver metabolism may play a major role in the elimination of these drugs, and this is increased by some compounds (notably phenobarbitone, phenytoin, primidone, and carbamazepine). Sulthiame inhibits the metabolism of phenytoin, phenobarbitone, and primidone. Also, some antiepileptic drugs accelerate the metabolism of other drugs, including the contraceptive pill (it may therefore be advisable to use another form of contraception). Antidepressants, anticoagulants, folic acid, vitamin D, and steroids are also affected, and in each case it may be necessary to increase the dose. For this reason, if the clinician is using an antiepileptic drug and is not already fully familiar with its effects, it is important to refer to a textbook of clinical pharmacology. This caveat applies equally to the use of carbamazepine to prevent recurrences of affective disorder (see p. 258).

Contraindications

These are few in number and depend on the particular drug. They should be checked carefully before prescribing a compound with which the doctor is not already familiar. It should be noted especially that phenobarbitone has a limited place in treating epilepsy, especially among children and psychiatric patients, because it frequently leads to disturbed behaviour. In patients who have renal or hepatic disease, antiepileptic drugs must be given cautiously.

Management

The psychiatrist is more likely to be involved in maintaining established treatment for a patient with epilepsy than in starting treatment for a newly diagnosed case. In some patients the epilepsy and the psychiatric disorder will be unrelated. Other patients will have psychiatric symptoms that are secondary to the epilepsy or its treatment. Adverse behavioural effects of treatment occur particularly with barbiturates but also with overdosage of any antiepileptic drug. The psychiatrist will usually be taking over treatment of an established condition from a general practitioner or neurologist, and he should normally discuss the case with them before making any changes. If the psychiatrist initiates treatment of a new case he should remember that the treatment is likely to continue for years; hence discussion with a specialist as well as the family doctor will usually be appropriate. Drug treatment is not indicated for a single seizure (though the cause must be investigated).

It is good practice to prescribe only one antiepileptic drug at a time and adjust its dose carefully. Sudden changes in dosage are potentially hazardous, for they may cause status epilepticus. The drug chosen should be known to be effective for the particular type of epilepsy presented by the patient (see above). If this first choice fails, a second can be tried, again given on its own. With the range of preparations now available it should be uncommon to combine two drugs, and most exceptional to use more than two. Whenever combinations are used, careful consideration must be given to possible interactions. It is particularly important to avoid the following combinations: sulthiame with phenytoin, since the former may increase phenytoin concentrations to toxic levels; phenobarbitone and primidone because the latter is broken down to phenobarbitone; sodium valproate and drugs such as clonazepam which are also sedative. Similarly it is important to review any drugs that are being prescribed for other purposes, and to decide whether they might interact with the antiepileptic drug.

Throughout treatment a careful watch should be kept for the particular side-effects of the drug in use. At the same time the doctor should make sure that the patient is continuing to comply with the dosage schedule. He should warn the patient about the dangers of suddenly stopping taking the tablets (an important cause of status epilepticus). If it becomes necessary to change from one drug to another, the new drug should be introduced gradually until its full dosage is reached. Only then should the old one be phased out.

Once an effective regime is established it should be continued until there has been freedom from seizures for at least two years. Plasma concentrations should be measured if there is poor control of seizures (since this poor control may be the result of too little drug or too much), or any change in neurological or behavioural state, or other signs suggesting drug intoxications. When drugs are eventually withdrawn this should be done gradually. In the United Kingdom epileptic patients may drive a private motor vehicle but not a public service or heavy goods vehicle, provided they have experienced no epileptic attacks for at least two years or epileptic attacks only while asleep during a period of at least three years. However, patients whose epilepsy can be controlled only at the expense of drowsiness should not drive. If there is doubt, advice should be obtained from a consultant with special experience in the treatment of epilepsy. [For a review of epilepsy and driving see O'Brien (1986).]

Electroconvulsive therapy

Convulsive therapy was introduced in the late 1930s on the basis of the mistaken idea that epilepsy and schizophrenia do not occur together. It seemed to follow that induced fits should lead to improvement in schizophrenia. However, when the treatment was tried it became apparent that the most striking changes occurred not in schizophrenia but in severe depressive disorders, in which it brought about a substantial reduction in chronicity and mortality (Slater 1951). At first, fits were produced either by using cardiazol (Meduna 1938) or by passing an electric current through the brain (Cerletti and Bini 1938). As time went by, electrical stimulation became the rule. The subsequent addition of brief anaesthesia and muscle relaxants made the treatment safe and acceptable.

Indications

This section summarizes the indications for ECT. Further information about the efficiency of the procedure will be found in the chapters dealing with the individual psychiatric syndromes.

ECT is a rapid and effective treatment for severe **depressive disorders.** In the Medical Research Council trial (Clinical Psychiatry Committee 1965) it acted faster than imipramine or phenelzine, and was more effective than imipramine in women and more effective than phenelzine in both sexes. (However, Greenblatt *et al.* 1964 did not find sex differences in response.) These findings accord with the impression of many clinicians, and with the recommendations of this book that ECT should be mainly used when it is essential to bring about improvement quickly.

The strongest indications are therefore an immediate high risk of suicide, depressive stupor, or danger to physical health because the patient is not drinking enough to maintain adequate renal function. Less strong indications are persistent severe depressive disorder despite an adequate trial of antidepressant drugs; and a depressive disorder causing extreme distress requiring rapid relief. ECT is also appropriate for some **puerperal depressive disorders** when it is important that the mother should return quickly to the care of her baby. In the past, ECT was used to control the symptoms of **mania.** Although effective drug treatment is now available, ECT is still used in exceptional cases that fail to respond to drugs (see p. 257). Clinical experience suggests that ECT can produce rapid changes in acute **catatonic schizophrenia** (though there have been no clinical trials to test this) and in the depressive form of **schizoaffective psychosis.** It is not indicated in other forms of schizophrenia. The use of ECT in these conditions is considered further in other chapters of this book. [The reader will find a useful short account of indications for ECT in the memorandum of the Royal College of Psychiatrists (1977) and a longer account in the review by Kendell (1981).]

Mode of action

The specific therapeutic effects of ECT must presumably be brought about through physiological and biochemical changes in the brain. The first step in identifying the mode of action must be to find out whether the therapeutic effect depends on the seizure; or whether other features of the treatment are sufficient, such as the passage of the current through the brain and the use of anaesthesia and muscle relaxants. Clinicians have generally been convinced that the patient does not improve unless a convulsion is produced during ECT procedure. This impression is strongly supported, though not proved beyond doubt, by the evidence of clinical trials. Thus less improvement is observed when the convulsion is shortened by lidocaine (Cronholm and Ottosson 1960) or when subconvulsive shocks are given (Miller *et al.* 1953). There is also less improvement when the shock is left out but the anaesthesia and all other aspects of the procedure remain the same (Brill *et al.* 1959; Robin and Harris 1962; Freeman *et al.* 1978). Slight reservations must remain because each of these investigations had some methodological problem. For example, in the study by Cronholm and Ottosson patients were not randomly allocated; whilst Robin and Harris used rating methods that were not wholly satisfactory. Taken together, however, the general weight of evidence points to the importance of the seizure. This conclusion is supported by the apparent therapeutic effectiveness of seizures produced by the drug flurothyl or 'Indoklon'. (Laurell 1970).

Several kinds of wave-form have been used to deliver the electric current used in ECT, and it is still uncertain which is best. Compared with sine-wave stimulation, brief pulse stimulation uses less energy to elicit a seizure. It has been suggested that brief pulse stimulation is followed by less memory loss immediately after ECT (e.g. Valentine *et al.* 1968). This finding has not been confirmed, and there seem to be no lasting differences in memory loss after the two kinds of stimulation (Warren and Groome 1984; Squire and Zouzounis 1986). Moreover, the antidepressant effect may be less after brief low energy pulses than after high-energy sine-wave stimuli, even though the two kinds of stimulation produce seizures of equal duration (Robin and deTissera 1982). The explanation for the reduced antidepressant effect may be that the seizure, although equal in length, is less intense after low energy stimulation. There is some indirect evidence for this idea in the finding that low energy stimulation leads to a smaller output of prolactin, which is thought to reflect seizure intensity (Robin *et al.* 1985). Experiments have been carried out with animals to identify changes in neurotransmitters after electrically induced seizures, administered in a schedule similar to that used for ECT. With this procedure, post-synaptic beta-adrenergic receptors decrease and 5-HT$_2$ receptors increase. The former change resembles that produced by antidepressant drugs, but the latter is opposite in direction (see Kellar and Stockmeier 1986). Postsynaptic sensitivity to dopamine also increases, as judged by neuroendocrine responses to apomorphine (Grahame-Smith *et al.* 1978). Although interesting, these findings are difficult to interpret because monoamine systems interact. For example, the effect of repeated convulsions in increasing 5-HT$_2$ receptors depends on intact noradrenergic projections (see Kellar and Stockmeier 1986).

Physiological changes during ECT

If ECT is given without atropine premedication, the pulse slows at first and then rises quickly to 130–190 beats a minute, falling to the original resting rate or beyond towards the end of the seizure before a final less marked tachycardia lasting several minutes. It is generally agreed that atropine abolishes both these periods of slowing, although a controlled trial by Wyant and MacDonald (1980) did not confirm this. If no muscle relaxant is given, there are corresponding changes in blood pressure; if a relaxant is given, blood pressure changes are less although systolic pressure can still rise to 200 mm Hg. Cerebral blood flow also increases by up to 200 per cent. If no atropine is given, transient cardiac arrhythmias occur during ECT in up to 70 per cent of patients; adequate doses of atropine reduce this substantially provided that the heart is healthy. More details of these physiological changes are given by Perrin (1961). There is an increased output of prolactin and neurophysin during and soon after the seizure (Whalley *et al.* 1982).

Unilateral or bilateral ECT

For many years the electric current used in ECT was always given through electrodes placed on opposite sides of the head. More recently it has been found that memory loss after ECT is less if both electrodes are placed over the non-dominant hemisphere. Since the effects of ECT appear to be due to the seizure, treatment should be equally effective with either electrode placements provided that a generalized seizure is induced. Until recently, there was no good evidence against this view. Indeed a review of 20 relevant studies by d'Elia and Raotma (1975) concluded that unilateral and bilateral electrode placements had the same antidepressant effect. However, three recent double-blind trials suggested that bilateral placement is more effective. The first showed more rapid recovery from depressive disorder after bilateral than after unilateral ECT (Gregory *et al.* 1985). The second showed a greater improvement at the end of treatment with bilateral ECT (Malitz *et al.* 1986). The third found a greater proportion of patients improved after six treatments with bilateral (81 per cent) than with unilateral ECT (56 per cent) (Abrams *et al.* 1983). The results of these and other trials are difficult to interpret because procedures varied in several ways. They differed in the number of applications of ECT given as a course of treatment, the type of stimulus and the amount of current used, and the criteria for deciding whether a convulsion had been produced. Also, Horne *et al.* (1985) found that unilateral electrode placement more often fails to induce a full seizure discharge (as judged by EEG monitoring) than does bilateral placement. When precautions were taken to overcome this failure, the investigators found no difference between uni- and bilateral ECT. For these reasons, it is still uncertain whether bilateral ECT is more effective than unilateral, but it is reasonable to prefer bilateral ECT when an urgent response is important (for example, in a patient with strong suicidal ideas) or when there is a poor response to the first few treatments of unilateral ECT. (The technique for determining handedness and electrode placement is described on p. 685.)

Unwanted effects after ECT

Subconvulsive shock may be followed by *anxiety* and *headache*. ECT can cause a brief retrograde *amnesia* as well as loss of memory for up to 30 minutes after the fit. If ECT is repeated at short intervals, this amnesia builds up; this does not usually happen when treatments are given two or three times a week. Some patients complain of *confusion, nausea,* and *vertigo* for a few hours after the treatment, but with modern methods these unwanted effects are mild and brief (Gomez 1975). These effects are less marked after unilateral ECT. A few patients complain of *muscle pain,* especially in the jaws, which is probably attributable to the relaxant. There have been a few reports of sporadic major *seizures* in the months after ECT (for example Blumenthal 1955) but these seizures may have had other causes. If they occur at all it is only during the first year after treatment.

Occasional *damage to the teeth, tongue, or lips* can occur if there have been problems in positioning the gag or airway. Poor application of the electrodes can lead to small electrical *burns*. Fractures, including *crush fractures* of the vertebrae, occurred occasionally when ECT was given without muscle relaxants. All these physical consequences are rare provided that a good technique of anesthesia is used and the fit is modified adequately. *Other complications* of ECT are rare and mainly occur in people suffering from physical illness. They include: arrhythmia, pulmonary embolism, aspiration pneumonia, and cerebrovascular accident. *Prolonged apnoea* is a rare complication of the use of muscle relaxants.

Memory disorder after ECT

As already mentioned, the immediate effects of ECT include loss of memory for events shortly before the treatment, and impaired retention of information acquired soon after the treatment. These effects are less after unilateral than after bilateral ECT, and the type of effect depends on the side of the head through which the current passes: electrode placement on the non-dominant side leads to selective impairment of non-verbal learning. These memory changes are experienced by nearly all patients receiving ECT, and they disappear within a few weeks of the end of the treatment.

Many patients fear that there will be lasting memory change, and some complain of it after ECT. However, studies have revealed no differences in performance on tests of memory given before ECT and a few weeks afterwards (Cronholm and Molander 1964). Also several studies have found no significant differences in memory tests between ECT treated patients and controls who had not received ECT (for example, Weeks *et al.* 1980; Johnstone *et al.* 1980). However, in a study of former patients who were complaining that they had suffered permanent harm to memory from ECT given in the past, Freeman *et al.* (1980) found that these patients did worse than controls on some tests in a battery designed to test memory. These patients also had residual depressive symptoms, so it is possible that continuing depressive disorder accounted for the memory problems. It seems reasonable to conclude that, when used in the usual way, ECT is not followed by permanent memory disorder except perhaps in a small minority; and that even in this group, it is still uncertain whether the impairment is due to the effects of ECT or to a continuation of the original depressive disorder.

The mortality of ECT

The death rate attributable to ECT was estimated to be 3–4 per 100 000 treatments by Barker and Barker in 1959. A survey of all ECT treatments given with anaesthesia in Denmark, found a similar rate of one death in 22 210 treatments, i.e. 4 to 5 per 100 000 treatments (Heshe and Roeder 1976). The risks are related to the anaesthetic procedure and are greatest in patients with cardiovascular disease. When death occurs it is usually due to ventricular fibrillation or myocardial infarction.

Contraindications

The contraindications to ECT are any medical illnesses that increase the risk of anaesthetic procedure by an unacceptable amount; for example respiratory infections, serious heart disease, and serious pyrexial illness. Other contraindications are diseases likely to be made worse by the changes in blood pressure and cardiac rhythm that occur even in a well modified fit; these include serious heart disease, recent coronary thrombosis, cerebral or aortic aneurysm, and raised intracranial pressure. Patients of African stock who might have sickle cell trait need additional care that oxygen tension does not fall. Extra care is also required with diabetic patients who take insulin. Although risks rise somewhat in old age, so do the risks of untreated depression and of drug treatment.

ECT should not be given to patients taking reserpine (see Crammer *et al.* 1982, p. 233), but it is not contraindicated by any other psychiatric medication. The anaesthetist must know when the patient is taking a monoamine oxidase inhibitor or lithium. It is, of course, wise to inform the anaesthetist of all the drugs taken by any patient who is to be anaesthetized.

Technique of administration

In this section we outline the technical procedures used at the time of treatment. Although the information in this account should be known, it is important to remember that ECT is a practical procedure that must be learnt by apprenticeship as well as by reading. [Much useful information is contained in a report to the Royal College of Psychiatrists by Pippard and Ellam (1981).]

ECT should be given in pleasant, safe surroundings. Patients should not have to wait where they can see or hear treatment given to others. There should be a recovery area separate from the room in which treatment is given, and adequate emergency equipment should be available including a sucker, endotracheal tubes, adequate supplies of oxygen, and, ideally, a defibrillator. The nursing and medical staff who give ECT should receive special training.

The first step in giving ECT is to put the patient at ease, and to check his identity. The case-notes should then be seen to make sure that there is a valid consent form. The drug sheet should be checked to ensure that the patient is not receiving any drugs, such as MAOIs, that might interfere with anaesthetic procedures. It is also important to check for evidence of drug allergy or adverse effects of previous general anaesthetics. The drug sheet should be available for the anaesthetist to see. If the patient is not well known to the psychiatrist and anaesthetist who are giving ECT, one or other should check for evidence of physical illness, especially recent cardiac disease. The next step is to make sure that nothing has been taken by mouth for at least five hours; then with the anaesthetist, to remove dentures and check for loose or broken teeth. Finally the record of any previous ECTs should be examined for evidence of delayed recovery from the relaxant (due to deficiency in pseudocholinesterase) or other complications.

Except in exceptional circumstances an anaesthetist should be present when ECT is given (though this cannot always be achieved in developing countries). Suction apparatus, a positive pressure oxygen supply, and emergency drugs should always be available. If possible, there should be a telephone in the room or nearby. A cardiac defibrillator is an added precaution although it is very rarely required [see Pippard and Ellam (1981)]; the anaesthetist's opinion should be sought about its provision. A tilting trolley is also valuable. As well as the psychiatrist and anaesthetist at least one nurse should be present.

Premedication with atropine is generally used to dry secretions and lessen the incidence of arrhythmias and vagal overstimulation. It is often given intravenously in a dose of 0.3–0.6 mg at the time of the anaesthetic. Sometimes it is given subcutaneously beforehand. In any case, the decision about the use of atropine and its route, timing, and dose should be decided by the anaesthetist. (The American Psychiatric Association's Task Force recommended methoscopolamine instead of atropine for ECT because it does not pass the blood–brain barrier. However, the evidence that the use of atropine increases confusion after ECT is not compelling.) The anaesthetist then administers an ultra-short-acting anaesthetic agent (often methohexitone) followed immediately by a muscle relaxant (often suxamethonium chloride) from a separate syringe, although the same needle can be used. The anaesthetist is responsible for the choice of drugs. He ensures that the lungs are well oxygenated before a mouth gag is inserted.

While the anaesthetic is being given, the psychiatrist checks whether unilateral or bilateral electrode placement has been prescribed for the patient. Handedness is used as a guide to cerebral dominance: it should be determined at least by asking which hand is used to catch and throw, and which foot to kick. In right-handed people the left hemisphere is nearly always dominant; in left-handed people either hemisphere may be dominant. Hence, if there is evidence that the patient is not right-handed, it is usually better to use bilateral electrode placements. In all cases the patient should be watched carefully after the first application of ECT. Marked confusion, especially with dysphasia, for more than five minutes after the return of consciousness suggests that the dominant side has been chosen inadvertantly. In such an event either the opposite side should be stimulated subsequently, or bilateral placement should be used instead. If there is any doubt about handedness, bilateral positioning should be chosen.

The skin is cleaned in the appropriate areas and moistened electrodes are applied. (If good electrical contact is to be obtained it is also important that grease and hair lacquer are removed by ward staff before the patient is sent for ECT.) While dry electrodes can cause skin burns, it is also important to remember that excessive moisture causes shorting and may prevent a seizure response. (This can happen more readily with unilateral placement because the electrodes are closer to one another.) Although enough muscle relaxant should have been given to ensure that convulsive movements are minimal, a nurse or other assistant should stand ready to restrain the patient gently if necessary. The electrodes are now secured firmly. For unilateral ECT the first electrode is placed on the non-dominant side, 4 cm above the mid-point between the external angle of the orbit and the external auditory meatus. The second is 10 cm away from the first, vertically above the meatus of the same side (see Fig 17.2). For bilateral ECT, electrodes are on opposite sides of the head, each 4 cm above the mid-point of the line joining the external angle of the orbit to the external auditory meatus—usually just above the hairline. The shock is now given.

Various **types of machine** are available to give the electric shock. Some machines give a bidirectional sinusoidal or modified sinusoidal wave-form, others a unidirectional stimulus. In Great Britain most machines are now of the latter type. So far, there is no certain reason for preferring one type of machine, for it is not certain whether it is the quantity of electricity delivered (the charge), the energy (work done), or the peak initial current that is important. [Useful information about these matters is provided in Appendix 6 to the monograph by Pippard and Elam (1981).] It is important to study the manufacturer's instructions for each machine, and to test and maintain the machine regularly to ensure that it is safe and delivering the correct amount of current. It is also important to have an up-to-date reserve machine.

Electrodes are either mounted together on a head-set, or held separately by the operator one in each hand. The latter arrangement makes it easier to obtain good contact with both electrodes.

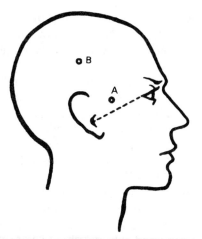

Fig. 17.2. Unilateral ECT. Electrodes are placed: A: 4 cm above midpoint between ear-hole and angle of eye; B: 10 cm further way above ear. [From Crammer, J., Barraclough, B., and Heine, B. (1982) *The use of drugs in psychiatry.* Gaskell, London.]

It is essential to observe carefully for **evidence of a seizure.** If satisfactory muscle relaxation has been achieved the seizure takes the following form. First the muscles of the face begin to twitch and the mouth drops open; then the upper eyelids, thumbs and big toes jerk rhythmically for about half a minute. It is important not to confuse these convulsive movements with muscle twitches due to the depolarization produced by suxamethonium. EEG monitoring has been used to check whether a seizure has been induced but the records can be difficult to interpret because of the muscle artefact produced by direct stimulation of the frontalis muscle. An alternative is to isolate one forearm from the effects of the muscle relaxant. This can be done by blowing up a blood pressure cuff to above systolic pressure before the relaxant is injected; this pressure is maintained during the period in which the seizure should occur, and then released. Seizure activity can then be observed in the muscles of the isolated part of the arm. When judging the appropriate cuff pressure it is important to remember that systolic pressure rises during the seizure; if the cuff is not at sufficient pressure the relaxant will pass into the forearm at this time.

After the seizure, the lungs are oxygenated thoroughly with an airway in place. The patient remains in the care of the anaesthetist and under close nursing observation until breathing resumes and consciousness is restored. During recovery, the patient should be turned on his side and cared for in the usual way for anyone recovering from an anaesthetic after a minor surgical procedure. A qualified nurse should be in attendance to supervise the patient and reassure him. Meanwhile the psychiatrist makes a note of the date, type of electrode placement, and drugs used, and amount of current, together with a brief description of the fit and any problems that have arisen. When the patient is awake and orientated, he should rest for an hour or so on his bed or in a chair.

If ECT is ever given to a day-patient, it is especially important to make certain that no food or drink has been taken before the patient arrives at the hospital. He should rest for several hours and should not leave until it is certain that his recovery is complete; he should leave in the company of a responsible adult, preferably by ambulance, and certainly not riding a bicycle or driving a car. The authors believe that it is always preferable to admit patients to hospital for ECT.

The most important problem, apart from those relating to the anaesthetic procedure, is failure to produce a clonic convulsion (a tonic jerk produced by the current must not be mistaken for a seizure). If it is certain that no seizure has appeared, checks should be made of the machine, electrodes, and contact with the skin. Also the possibility of shorting due to excess moisture on the scalp should be considered. If all these are excluded, the patient may have either an unusually high resistance to the passage of current through the extracranial tissues and skull, or a high convulsive threshold. The charge can then be increased by five joules and one further stimulus given. (It is not good practice to 'play safe' by giving larger doses to all patients, because the degree of memory impairment after treatment depends on the current used.)

Frequency and number of treatments

In Great Britain bilateral ECT is usually given once a week, although in urgent cases three applications may be used in the first week. If treatment is to be three times a week for more than the first week, unilateral ECT is preferable because it leads to less memory disorder.

Decisions about the length of a course of ECT have to depend on clinical experience since relevant information is not available from clinical trials. A course of ECT is usually from six to a maximum of twelve treatments. Progress should be reviewed at least once a week; there is usually little response until two or three treatments have been given, after which increasing improvement takes place. If the response is more rapid than this, fewer treatments may be given. If there has been no response after six to eight treatments, the course should usually be abandoned since it is unlikely that more ECT will produce useful change.

As some patients relapse after ECT, antidepressants should be started towards the end of the course to reduce the risk of relapse. In the past, 'maintenance' ECT was sometimes given every two to four weeks with the aim of preventing relapse. There is no evidence that this procedure is more effective than the prescription of antidepressant drugs, though it is sometimes resorted to in rare cases of intractable depressive disorder that have failed to respond to adequate doses of antidepressant drugs given singly or in combination.

Medico-legal issues including consent to ECT

Before a patient is asked to agree to ECT, it is essential to explain the procedure and indicate its expected benefits and possible risks (especially the possible effects on memory). The importance of this step is underlined by the finding (Freeman and Kendell 1980) that only one-fifth of patients receiving ECT thought that they had received adequate explanation. Many patients expect severe and permanent memory impairment after treatment and some even expect to receive unmodified fits. Once the doctor is sure that the patient understands what he has been told, the latter is asked to sign a standard form of consent. The patient should understand that consent is being sought for the whole course of ECT and not just for one treatment (although he can of course withdraw consent at any time). All this is the doctor's job—he should not delegate it to other staff.

If a patient refuses consent or is unable to give it because he is in a stupor or for other reasons, and if the procedure is essential further steps must be considered in the United Kingdom. The first is to decide whether there are grounds for invoking the appropriate section of the Mental Health Act (see Appendix). The section does not allow anyone to give consent on behalf of the patient, but it does establish formally that he is mentally ill and in need of treatment. In England and Wales the opinion of a second independent consultant is required by the Mental Health Act 1983. The requirements of the Act are outlined on p. 905. Readers working elsewhere should find out the relevant legal requirements. If the decision is made in this careful way, it is rare for patients to question the need for treatment once they have recovered. Instead most acknowledge that treatment has helped, and they understand why it was necessary to give it without their expressed consent.

Psychosurgery

Psychosurgery refers to the use of neurosurgical procedures to modify the symptoms of psychiatric illness by operating either on the nuclei of the brain or on the white matter. Psychosurgery began in 1936 with the work of Moniz whose operation consisted of an extensive cut in the white matter of the frontal lobes (**frontal leucotomy**). This extensive operation was modified by Freeman and Watts (1942) who made smaller coronal incisions in the frontal lobes through lateral burr holes. Although their so-called **standard leucotomy** was far from standardized anatomically, and although it produced unacceptable side-effects (see below), the procedure was widely used in Great Britain and other countries. There was enthusiasm for the intial improvements observed in patients, but this was followed by growing evidence of adverse effects including intellectual impairment, emotional lability, disinhibition, apathy, incontinence, obesity and epilepsy. This led to a search for more restricted lesions capable of producing the same therapeutic benefits without these adverse consequences. Some progress was made but at the same time advances in pharmacology made it possible to use drugs to treat the disorders for which surgery was intended.

There have been no controlled trials to test the value of these operations. If such surgery is used at all, it should be only after the most thorough and persistent attempts to produce improvement with other forms of treatment. If this is done, the requirement for psychosurgery will be extremely small. It is not easy to judge how widely the operations are used. A survey of neurosurgeons in the USA and Canada identified only 1039 such procedures for psychiatric disorders in the three years 1971–3 (Donnely 1978). A survey of the 44 neurological units in the British Isles showed that the number of these operations had declined from 158 per annum in 1974 to 119 in 1976, and that they had been performed for persistent depression, anxiety states, and obsessive-compulsive neurosis (Barraclough and Mitchell-Heggs 1978). The numbers have almost certainly fallen further since this survey.

Types of operation

As operations on the frontal lobe became anatomically less extensive, the most commonly used procedures in Great Britain became the restricted undercutting of the medial third of the orbital cortex, and a bimedial operation aimed at the fronto-thalamic bundle. At the same time it became clear that the frontal cortex has complex connections with the hypothalamus, temporal cortex, hippocampus, amygdala, and mamillary bodies. The surgical approach was therefore directed to some of these connections as well as to the frontal lobe.

Nowadays the older 'blind' operations have been replaced by stereotactic procedures that allow the lesions to be placed more accurately. These stereotactic operations are tractotomy, limbic leucotomy, and amygdalotomy. In **stereotactic tractotomy**, the target is the posterior part of the area incised in orbital undercutting. The lesion is produced by implanting radioactive yttrium 'seeds' (see Knight 1972). In **stereotactic limbic leucotomy** small bilateral lesions are placed in the lower medial quadrant of the frontal lobe to interrupt two of the fronto-limbic pathways, and in the cingulum (Richardson 1973). In **amygdalotomy** bilateral lesions are placed in the amygdala, usually in an attempt to control aggressive behaviour (see Small *et al.* 1977).

After the operation, there is usually a decline in anxiety and tension; other symptoms recover more slowly. It is important to carry out appropriate rehabilitation during the post-operative period. This will vary according to the condition being treated; for obsessional neurosis, a behavioural treatment is appropriate, while for depressive disorder a gradual programme of social rehabilitation is required.

Indications

There is no general agreement about these. Some clinicians consider that psychosurgery should never be used, others regard it as the treatment of choice for a few intractable disorders. Because no satisfactory controlled evaluation has been carried out, judgements have to be made on the uncertain basis of follow-up studies of patients subjected to one procedure. Patients treated by stereotactic subcaudate tractotomy have been followed by Ström-Olsen and Carlisle (1971) who reported on 210 patients, and by Göktepe *et al.* (1975) who reported on a further 208. In these two series the few schizophrenics changed little, while improvement rates were about 70 per cent for depressive disorders, 60 per cent for anxiety states, and 50 per cent for obsessional neuroses. However, the criteria of improvement were far from rigorous, and the lack of controls makes it impossible to decide how much improvement would have taken place without the operations.

Sixty-six patients treated with **stereotactic limbic leucotomy** were followed by Mitchell-Heggs *et al.* (1976) who concluded that this operation could benefit several kinds of patient. They reported improvement rates of 78 per cent for depressive disorders, 66 per cent for chronic anxiety neuroses, and 89 per cent for obsessional disorders, and 80 per cent in a small number of schizophrenics. Again methodological shortcomings make it difficult to interpret the significance of these findings.

Unwanted effects

The serious adverse effects of the early operations have been mentioned already. With modern stereotactic procedures, residual effects are far fewer but when they do occur they follow the same pattern of apathy, excessive weight gain, disinhibition, and epilepsy.

Management

In our experience, vigorous and persistent treatment with drugs and behavioural methods almost always leads to an acceptable remission in patients who might be considered for psychosurgery. A good rule is that the operation should never be carried out until the effects of several years of vigorous treatment have been observed. If this rule is followed, the operation will hardly be used. If the operation is to be considered at all, it should only be for chronic intractable obsessional disorder and severe chronic depressive disorders in older patients. There is no clear justification for psychosurgery for anxiety neuroses or schizophrenia. [For an account of a less conservative view the reader should consult Bartlett *et al.* (1981).]

Obsolete treatments

Continuous narcosis

Many psychiatric patients report sleeping badly for months, and some say that they desire a prolonged period of sleep. In continuous narcosis, this is provided by heavy and repeated sedation continued for several days at a time. The patient is kept asleep throughout the day as well as the night, being wakened only to eat and to evacuate the bladder and bowels. This procedure has been used for severe and chronic anxiety and obsessional neuroses, and it is often followed by a temporary period of relief. There is no evidence that the longer effects are better than those of less intensive treatment, and the method had fallen from general use. Sargant and Slater (1963) provide a detailed account.

Insulin coma therapy

This was introduced in the late 1930s by Sakel (1938) as a treatment for schizophrenia, and for many years was used extensively without controlled evaluation. Eventually Ackner and Oldham (1962) found that insulin coma therapy had no more therapeutic effect than repeated periods of unconsciousness produced by sedative hypnotics. In any case antipsychotic drugs were being introduced at the same time and proved to have powerful therapeutic effects. Insulin coma soon ceased to be used. The procedure was, essentially, to produce repeated hypoglycaemic comas with insulin and then reverse them after an interval by giving glucose. An account of the methods is given by Sargant and Slater (1963).

Modified insulin therapy

Many psychiatric patients lose weight during their illness. It has always been part of treatment to attempt to restore weight as psychological improvement occurs. During and after the Second World War a treatment became popular in which small doses of insulin were given to improve the appetite of patients with chronic anxiety neuroses with the hope that this would also improve their anxiety. Today it is considered more logical to bring about weight gain by treating the primary psychological disorder. Modified insulin treatment is no longer in general use, and is not recommended in this book. Those who wish to find out more should consult Sargant and Slater (1963).

Further reading

Barchas, J. D., Berger, P. A, Ciaranello, R. D., and Elliot, G. R. (1977). *Psychopharmacology.*Oxford University Press, New York.

Crammer, J., Barraclough, B., and Heine, B. (1982). *Use of drugs in psychiatry* (2nd edn). Gaskell, London.

Grahame-Smith, D. G., and Aronson, J. K. (1984). *Oxford textbook of clinical pharmacology and drug therapy*. Oxford University Press, Oxford.

Green A. R. and Costain D. (1981). *Pharmacology and biochemistry of psychiatric disorders*. John Wiley, Chichester.

Royal College of Psychiatrists (1977). Memorandum on the use of electroconvulsive therapy. *British Journal of Psychiatry* **131,**261–72.

Silverstone, T. and Turner, P. (1982). *Drug treatment in psychiatry* (2nd edn). Routledge and Kegan Paul, London.

18 Psychological treatment

This chapter is concerned with the various kinds of psychotherapy, behavioural and cognitive therapies, and with some related treatments such as relaxation. The subject is large, and it will be easier to follow if the reader's attention is drawn to certain points about the organization of the chapter and its relation to other parts of the book. First, it is recommended that this account be read in conjunction with the general advice about planning treatment in the previous chapter and about the provision of services in Chapter 19. Second, although this chapter includes general comments about the value of the different treatments, advice about the specific use of these treatments will be found in the chapters concerned with particular syndromes. Third, because the chapter has to cover many different techniques of treatment, it is not possible to consider each in detail. For this reason suggestions for further reading are given. Finally, and most important, it is emphasized that psychological treatments cannot be learnt by reading alone; it is necessary also to obtain appropriate and adequately supervised experience of some of the methods.

The first part of this chapter deals with psychotherapy and begins with some general considerations. First the main types of psychotherapy are listed, then an outline is given of simple psychotherapy of the kind that might be carried out by a psychiatrist early in his training. Next comes a review of features that are common to this simple kind of treatment and to other forms of psychotherapy, and by a brief review of research on this subject. Next comes a similar review of the forms of psychological treatment such as relaxation, autogenic training, abreaction, and hypnosis.

General considerations

Types of psychotherapy and general indications for their use

It is helpful to have a broad framework in which to place the many forms of psychotherapy. One practical scheme divides psychotherapy along two dimensions, the first concerned with the complexity of the procedures, and the second with the number of patients taking part. On the first dimension treatments can be divided into: simple psychotherapy which is appropriate in primary care; short or long-term supportive psychotherapy which can be provided by all psychiatrists; and special methods with are best provided by specialists in psychotherapy (see Skynner and Brown 1981). On the second dimension, treatments can be divided into psychotherapy with a single patient (individual psychotherapy), psychotherapy with couples, small group therapy, and large group therapy.

In primary care, psychotherapy may be considered either for patients with emotional problems of short duration, or for patients who need help in coming to terms with the effects of incurable illness, whether physical or mental. Some general practitioners with a special interest may undertake psychotherapy with other groups of patients, but most will consider referring patients with more difficult problems to a psychiatrist.

Psychiatrists are likely to use psychotherapy as the main treatment for younger patients with mild but recurrent depressive or anxiety symptoms arising mainly from intrapsychic problems such as persistent low self-esteem or from difficulties in interpersonal relationships. (Specific neurotic syndromes are more likely to respond to cognitive and behavioural methods.) General psychiatrists are likely to refer two kinds of difficult problems for psychotherapy: personality disorders characterized by schizoid or histrionic features, and more than usually complicated cases of the kind (outlined above) they would normally treat themselves. (In practice many patients suitable for treatment by a general psychiatrist receive psychotherapy from trainee psychiatrists under the supervision of a specialist therapist.)

On the choice between individual, group, marital, or family therapy, it can be said at this stage that individual therapy is more suitable for specific problems that can be the focus of short-term treatment. It is also appropriate for people who would feel unduly awkward in a group, either through shyness or through the nature of their problems (for example a sexual deviation). Otherwise, for patients whose problems mainly concern their relationships with other people, individual and group therapy are usually equally effective.

Marital therapy is appropriate when the emotional problems mainly reside in the relationship between the two partners of a marriage. Family therapy may be employed when the difficulties of an older child or adolescent reflect those of his parents. These preliminary generalizations are provided as a background to the chapter, but it will become evident that they frequently need to be modified.

What happens in psychotherapy?

It is difficult to give a concise answer to this question, because there are many different forms of psychotherapy. The basic elements can be illustrated in an outline of brief therapy of the kind that might be carried out by a psychiatrist over a few months with a patient whose problems were mainly in personal relationships.

After taking a full psychiatric history, in the first phase of treatment the therapist discusses with the patient what aspects of his problems are to be dealt with in treatment, what aims are realistic, and how long treatment will last. In this sort of treatment, between five and twenty sessions might be allocated depending on the complexity of the problems. The therapist emphasizes that the patient will be helped to find his own solutions to his problems; the therapist's role is not to provide the solutions but to help the patient towards them.

The patient is then asked to talk about one of the problems selected for consideration. He is encouraged to give specific examples of events that can be examined in detail with the intention of finding out how he thought, felt, and acted at the time. Various prompts and other interviewing techniques are required for this, but they are essentially similar to those described in Chapter 2. To encourage the patient to think aloud about his difficulties, the therapist says little. He encourages the patient to talk about emotionally painful subjects rather than avoid them, to review his own part in any difficulties that he ascribes to other people, and to look for common themes in what he is describing. At times the therapist helps the patient to look back on his life to see how present patterns of behaviour began. He asks him to consider whether behaviour that served a purpose in the past is continuing to the present, although no longer appropriate. Finally, he encourages the patient to consider alternative ways of thinking and behaving in situations that cause difficulties.

Throughout treatment, the therapist pays as much attention to the patient's non-verbal behaviour as to his words, because discrepancies between the two often point to problems that have not yet been expressed directly. He also watches for behaviour that suggests undue emotional attachment to the therapist. If such attachment is suspected, it is discussed with the patient. At the same time the therapist must be sensitive to his own emotional reactions to the patient, and make sure that he is neither over-involved nor rejecting. If he does have such feelings, he should try to find out why—if necessary through discussion with a colleague.

In the middle phase of treatment, the patient continues to talk about the problems he identified at the start and examines current examples. The therapist points out any patterns of behaviour that are being repeated, and relates them to the patient's account of childhood experiences. He also comments on the patient's emotional reactions during the interview.

As the end of treatment approaches, the patient should feel that he has a better understanding of the problems selected at the beginning, and should be more confident of dealing with them himself. At this stage the patient should no longer feel too dependent on the therapist, but it is often useful to ease the separation by arranging a few follow-up appointments spaced over two or three months.

Other forms of psychotherapy differ from this basic procedure in several ways. First, many long-term treatments begin in an unstructured way; the patient is simply asked to talk about anything that occurs to him, with the expectation that themes and goals will emerge later. Second, treatments differ in the number and kind of explanations offered by the therapist. In the simple kind of treatment just described, explanations are based mainly on common sense. In more intensive treatments, they are based on some theory of psychological development—for example, that of psychoanalysis. As a rule, formulations based on a theoretical framework are not presented to the patient *in toto*, but revealed piecemeal in the form of comments about the origins of his behaviour and feelings as they gradually emerge during the interviews. (These comments are one form of interpretation.) Third, treatments differ in how far attention is given to matters other than day-to-day experiences. In some treatments, fantasies in the form of dreams and paintings are used extensively to encourage the patient to examine aspects of his personality of which he was previously unaware. Fourth, treatments differ in the extent to which the relationship between patient and therapist is encouraged to develop into a transference, which can then be utilized to put the patient more in touch with his own feelings and reactions. (Transference is discussed further on p. 698.)

Common factors in psychotherapy

In all forms of psychotherapy, the therapist tries to help the patient to overcome emotional problems by a combination of *listening* and *talking*. In this process, listening is generally more important than talking because the main purpose is to help the patient to understand himself more clearly. For the patient, part of this process is thinking aloud, which is a good way to clarify ideas that have not been put into words before. It also helps the patient to become aware of links between aspects of feelings and behaviour that have previously been unrecognized.

Restoration of morale is an important part of psychotherapy because most of the patients who are treated have experienced repeated failures and become demoralized, losing the conviction that they can help themselves. *Release of emotion* may be helpful in the early stages of treatment if the patient is emotionally aroused, but it is not generally useful to repeat the process many times. The term abreaction refers to a procedure in which particularly intense and rapid release of feelings is encouraged.

All forms of psychological treatment include a *rationale* that makes the patient's disorder more intelligible. This rationale may be described in detail by the therapist (as in the behaviour therapies or short-term psychotherapy), or the patient may have to piece it together from partial explanations and interpretations (as in psychoanalytically-oriented treatments). Whatever the method of imparting the rationale, it has the effect of making problems more understandable and therefore gives the patient more confidence that he can solve his problems.

All psychotherapy contains an element of *suggestion*. In hypnosis this is deliberately cultivated as the main agent of change. In other treatments suggestion is removed as much as possible because its effects are generally not lasting.

Transference and counter-transference

Another component of psychotherapy, the relationship between patient and therapist, is present from the start and grows more important as treatment lasts longer or is carried out more frequently. Even in the shortest forms of psychotherapy this relationship forms the cornerstone of treatment, helping to sustain the patient through his difficulties and to motivate him to overcome his problems. As treatment progresses, the realistic relationship or 'treatment alliance' becomes more intense, and unrealistic elements are superimposed on it. These arise largely because the therapist listens more than he talks. As a result, the patient reveals personal problems that in other circumstances would be revealed not at all, or only to an intimate friend or close relation. The psychotherapist, on the other hand, tells the patient little about his own background or personal beliefs. The intimacy of the situation causes the patient to react to the therapist as if he were a close relation. The patient cannot correct his fantasies about the therapist by knowing what he is really like. As a result, the patient transfers to the therapist feelings and attitudes that were originally experienced in relation to other significant persons with whom he experienced a comparable intimacy in earlier life— usually the parents. It is for this reason that the process is called transference. When the therapist is conceived as a good figure, transference is said to be positive; when the therapist is conceived as a bad figure the transference is said to be negative. Similarly, the therapist has a role unlike that of his everyday relationships. He has to remain an impartial professional and yet be genuinely concerned about the patient's most intimate problems. Despite his training, the therapist cannot always achieve this combination of detachment and concern. He may then respond in a way that is not simply a reflection of the patient's personal qualities but also a displacement on to the patient of ideas and feelings related to other figures in the therapist's life. This process is called counter-transference.

Both transference and counter-transference can be impediments to treatment, but both can be turned to advantage. One disadvantage of transference is that it may induce behaviour that distracts from the main plan of treatment; for example, there may be attempts to prolong interviews, requests for extra appointments, and dramatic behaviours demanding urgent action, such as threats of suicide. Transference may also make it difficult to bring treatment to an end; there may be a recrudescence of symptoms that had improved, and demands for further treatment. If these behaviours are noticed early and discussed, difficulties can be prevented with the added advantage that the patient learns more about himself.

Counter-transference causes difficulties when the therapist becomes inappropriately involved in the patient's problems or is inappropriately angry with him. It too can be turned to advantage. If the therapist recognizes these feelings and examines how they have arisen, he will learn more about his patient and—equally important—about himself.

Transference and counter-transference are most developed in the intensive forms of treatment based on psychoanalysis, where transference is encouraged in order to use it therapeutically. However, it is important to realize that transference and counter-transference occur to some degree in every form of psychological treatment.

How modern psychotherapy developed

The use of psychological healing must be as old as the practice of medicine itself. Parallels are often drawn between aspects of modern psychotherapy and the ceremonials carried out in some of the ancient Greek temples of healing. However, the history of formal psychotherapy starts in the mid-nineteenth century. At that time, the most important developments concerned hypnosis, which came to the attention of doctors in Great Britain and France through the activities of Anton Mesmer. In England, it was a Manchester doctor, James Braid, who first properly detached hypnosis from mystical and superstitious practices. Braid suggested the name hypnosis in a book (Braid 1843) in which he attempted a physiological explanation drawing parallels between hypnosis and sleep. In contrast Alexander Bertrand, who worked in France, was more concerned with the psychological determinants of the hypnotic state.

At that time the main alternative form of psychotherapy was called persuasion, a treatment that relied on argument rather than suggestion. In contrast to hypnosis it did not set out to impress the patient and make him suggestible. Instead it relied on discussion of symptoms and other problems in ways that might help the patient to control them and become more self-reliant. The treatment was not based on any special theory of psychological development, but rather on the physician's good sense and understanding of people and disease.

Freud's interest in psychological treatment began with hypnosis. In Paris in 1886 he saw Charcot's demonstrations of hypnosis with hysterical patients. He tried the method with some of his own neurotic patients and at first was pleased by its success. He was not a particularly good hypnotist, however, and his early successes were not always repeated. He therefore began to modify the method. At first Freud used hypnosis to suppress symptoms (Greenson 1967) but by 1889, in the case of Emmy von N., he was employing it to release the emotion associated with repressed ideas. Remembering Bernheim's demonstration that patients could recall forgotten events under the influence of waking suggestion, Freud turned to this method instead, requiring his patients to shut their eyes while he placed his hands on the forehead (Breuer and Freud 1893–5, pp. 109 and 270). He soon found that it was equally effective for the patient to lie on a couch and talk freely while the therapist kept out of sight. This was the origin of *free association*. Freud used various methods to encourage the flow of associations, to comment on them, and to regulate the intensity of the relationship between patient and analyst. These methods made up the basic technique of psychoanalysis and subsequently of much psychotherapy. They are described briefly later in this chapter. [The interested reader is recommended to read one of the accounts written by Freud himself (for example, Freud 1923).]

As psychoanalysis developed, Freud built up the elaborate theory of mental development mentioned already in Chapter 3. Not all of his colleagues agreed with these ideas and some parted from him to form their own 'schools' of psychotherapy. A brief outline of some of these developments will now be given. [The reader will find more information in the books by Brown (1961) and Munroe (1955).]

Adler and Jung were the first important figures to leave Freud and develop their own theories. **Adler**, who left Freud in 1910, rejected the libido theory and emphasized instead the influence of social factors in development. In keeping with this, his therapeutic technique, known as *individual analysis*, attempts to bring about greater understanding of how the patient's life-style has developed, and also places considerable emphasis on current problems. Adler's theories lacked the ingenuity and interest of Freud's. His methods have never been used widely, although they laid the foundation for the development of the influential dynamic-cultural school of American analysts (see below).

While Adler emphasized the real problems in the patient's life, **Jung** was more concerned with the inner world of fantasy. As a result, his technique of psychotherapy relies more on the interpretation of unconscious material as represented in dreams and artistic production, although contemporary problems are by no means neglected. In interpreting these problems, reference is made not only to the past experience of the individual but also to aspects of the 'collective' unconscious which Jung believed to be common to all mankind (the archetypes). In contrast with Freudian analysis, in Jungian analysis the relationship between therapist and patient is less one-sided because the therapist is more willing to be active and to reveal information about himself.

Several other developments followed which were important in the evolution of psychotherapy. All shared the basic analytic technique; they differed mainly in their theories of mental development, and consequently in the kind of response made by the therapist to the patient's account of himself.

The so-called **dynamic-cultural** school of analysis shares some of Adler's concerns with social causes of neurosis. The most important figures in this movement were Karen Horney and Erich Fromm, two refugees from Nazi Germany who settled in the United States in the 1930s, and the American Harry Stack Sullivan. All three emphasized social factors in the development of personality and in the aetiology of neurosis; and all three considered that the stages of development, which Freud attributed to the unfolding of biological influences, were determined to a much greater extent by influences within the family.

Horney accepted Freud's idea that abnormal anxiety is the basis of all neuroses, that other symptoms represent mechanisms of defence acting to reduce the experience of this anxiety, and that the origins of neurosis are in childhood. Horney, however, rejected Freud's ideas about the origins of anxiety. She did not accept his theory of instinctual forces and the stages of libido development, and she particularly took issue with his view of the psychological development of women, including the notion of 'penis envy'. For Horney, anxiety was inevitable in childhood arising from the experience of being insignificant, helpless, and threatened. She held that anxiety is normally overcome by the experience of being brought up by loving parents. In some children who have not had this experience, anxiety persists, and defences develop against it. Horney's defences, which she called 'neurotic trends' are not identical with Freud's defence mechanisms: they include striving for affection, striving for power, and submissiveness. Horney also emphasized the social context outside the family, and pointed out that behaviour can be neurotic in one society but adaptive in another. For Horney, neurotic symptoms were not an essential feature of neurosis; the important features were the neurotic trends and the characteristic structure that grew around them. She summarized the difference between her treatment and Freud's method as follows: 'I differ from Freud in that after the recognition of the neurotic trends, while he primarily investigates their genesis I primarily investigate their actual functions and their consequences. My contention is that by working through the consequences the patient's anxiety is so much lessened and his relation to self and others so much improved, that he can dispense with the neurotic trends.' (Horney 1939, p.282).

Fromm also rejected Freud's theory of instinctual development in causing neurosis, and emphasized instead relationships between the individual and society. Fromm's account of psychopathology includes psychic mechanisms which are broadly similar to those of Freud but differ in important detail. They include: 'moral masochism' (a need to be helpless and dependent on others), 'sadism' (a need to exploit others or make them suffer), and 'automaton conformity' (excessive conformity with and submission to other people). Fromm accepted the importance of family influences in shaping character, but also drew attention to wider cultural influences that produce features of personality shared by all members of a society. Fromm was generally concerned more with social than with clinical issues, and partly for this reason his ideas have not had a great influence on therapy.

Fromm's views on character structure and the interaction between psychological and social factors are described in *The fear of freedom* (Fromm 1942).

Sullivan was also concerned with the patient's relationships with other people in adult life. For him, sexual problems were only one aspect of the patient's problems; they lacked the central importance ascribed to them in psychoanalysis. His treatment centred on the relationship between analyst and patient, and the discussion of everyday social encounters. In this process, patient and therapist were more equal than in Freudian analysis, and Sullivan preferred pointed questions and provocative statements to interpretations based on theory.

Melanie Klein enlarged on some of the biological and psychoanalytical aspects of Freud's theories. Her work has been influential among analysts in Britain, where it has grown into the '**object–relations**' school. Her developments of technique were particularly related to play therapy with children, in which she made extensive use of interpretations. Her ideas have also been applied to the treatment by psychotherapy of schizophrenia and severe ('psychotic') depression, but such a usage is not to be recommended—indeed it is generally contraindicated. An essential concept in Klein's theory is the 'object', a term that refers to a person who is emotionally important to the patient (for example a parent), and to an internal psychological representation of such a person. Klein's theory of personality is much concerned with the earliest development of the infant, with the way in which 'objects' are dealt with at this time, and with the instinctual feelings of love and hatred that accompany them. The theory has been described as 'fanciful projections of a theoretically based therapist' (Wolberg 1977, p. 186). However, a substantial group of psychotherapists use interpretations about object relations whilst employing a technique broadly similar to psychoanalysis. [For an outline of Klein's theories see Segal (1963); for an account of Klein's technique of analysis of children see Klein (1963).]

A further line of development can be traced to **Ferenczi**. By the early 1920s psychoanalysis, which began a a brief treatment, had grown increasingly long. Ferenczi tried to shorten it while keeping broadly within Freud's methods. He set time-limits to treatment, adopted a less passive role as therapist, and planned the way in which the main themes were to be dealt with in treatment. Many of these innovations have found their way into the brief psychotherapy used today.

The value of psychotherapy

Although in the practice of medicine our aim must be to use only treatments that have proved valuable in clinical trials, there are still many treatments that have not been evaluated in this way. Many surgical procedures in common use can be judged only on clinical grounds because they have not been subjected to comparative trial.

There are several reasons why a treatment continues to be used without a complete evaluation. Sometimes the treatment has been used for so long with such obvious benefit that it seems unethical to test it—for example appendicectomy. In other cases, the desired outcome of treatment is so complicated that it is difficult to devise valid and reliable ways of assessing it objectively; the use of physiotherapy for rheumatoid arthritis is an example. Psychotherapy is used largely on the basis of clinical opinion rather than scientific evaluation. One reason for this is the real problem of measuring the changes aimed at by psychotherapists (this and other research problems are discussed in a later section). Another reason is the belief, held by some clinicians, that the treatments are obviously beneficial. In reading this chapter, it is important to remember that many recommendations about the indications for various kinds of psychotherapy are based on clinical experience and therefore subject to revision when evaluative studies are carried out.

Individual psychotherapy

Brief psychotherapy

This kind of psychotherapy aims to produce limited but worthwhile changes within a short time—seldom more than six months and often considerably less. Because treatment is focused upon specific problems, the term *focal psychotherapy* is sometimes used.

The basic *procedures* of brief psychotherapy have been described already (see p. 695). They are mainly the techniques common to all kinds of psychotherapy (see p.696) rather than those specific to any of the 'schools' of therapy.

Indications

Brief psychotherapy is mainly helpful for patients who have difficulties in personal relationships but are free from serious disorder of personality.

Suitable patients are interested in gaining psychological understanding of their own behaviour, reasonably intelligent, and well motivated to change by their own efforts. Particularly suitable patients include those who have problems in relationships leading to unhappiness and anguish in the absence of a specific neurotic syndrome. Patients with obsessional or hypochondriacal neurosis are much less likely to respond to such brief treatment.

[An account of the eclectic type of brief psychotherapy is given by Garfield (1980), while accounts of brief psychoanalytical methods are given by Malan (1963), Sifneos (1972) and Davenloo (1980).]

Counselling

This is a particular form of brief psychotherapy. The term is used in a specific sense to refer to methods developed by Carl Rogers. In these methods the therapist takes a passive role, largely restricting his interventions to comments on the emotional significance of the client's utterances ('reflection of feelings'). Rogers believed that this limited procedure, together with the relationship between patients and therapist, was therapeutic.

The term counselling is also applied less specifically to other kinds of brief therapy with limited objectives, in which the therapist takes a more active role.

Supportive psychotherapy

Supportive psychotherapy is used to help a person through a time-limited crisis caused either by social problems or by physical illness. It is also employed to relieve the distress caused by prolonged physical or mental illness or physical handicap. It is often useful with patients who have serious disorders of personality that are unlikely to change with treatment.

Patients are encouraged to talk about their problems while the therapist listens sympathetically. The therapist offers advice, and may use suggestion deliberately in order to help the patients through a short-lived worsening of the symptoms. He may also arrange practical help. When the problem is insoluble or the illness chronic, he helps the patient to accept inevitable disability and to live as well as possible despite it.

Listening is an important part of supportive therapy. The patient should feel that he has the doctor's undivided attention and concern, and that his worries are being taken seriously. When supportive treatment is used in conditions of acute crisis, patients may be helped by the opportunity to release emotions. However, as noted above, it is not usually helpful to repeat this process frequently.

Explanation and advice is important, but it should be borne in mind that distressed patients often remember little of what they are told. Doctors often give information in language that is too complicated. Important points should be put simply and repeated often, and sometimes also put in writing so that the patient can study them at home.

Reassurance is valuable but premature reassurance can destroy the patient's confidence in the doctor. It should be offered only when the patient's concerns have been fully understood. Reassurance must be truthful, but if a patient asks about prognosis, it may be appropriate to give the most optimistic outcome of those that can be foreseen. If a patient finds he has been deceived, he will lose the basic trust on which all treatment depends. Even in the most difficult cases a positive approach can often be maintained by encouraging patients to build on their few remaining assets and opportunities.

Prestige suggestion: in supportive treatment, patients should be encouraged to take responsibility for their own actions and to work out solutions to their problems. Nevertheless there are times when it is appropriate for the doctor to use his authority as an expert to persuade the patient to take some necessary first step—for example, an anxious patient might be told confidently that he will be able to cope with a frightening social encounter. This kind of persuasion is called prestige suggestion. It is important to discuss the outcome in such a way that the patient sees himself rather than the doctor as having mastered the problem. Suggestion should be used sparingly; if the patient tries and fails, he may lose confidence not only in himself but also in his doctor.

The regulation of the **relationship** between patient and therapist is important in supportive therapy. Intense relationships develop easily when the patient has a dependent personality and the treatment is prolonged. If there is a real need for lengthy treatment, dependency should be directed to the staff of the hospital or general practice rather than to an individual member. In general practice, dependency may be shown by demands for repeat prescriptions long after any real need for the drugs has ceased, and by a dramatic increase in symptoms whenever the doctor tries to change the medication. [A useful account of these problems has been given by Balint *et al.* (1970).]

Supportive treatment is often mistakenly given to patients who do not benefit from it, or to those who would gain as much from the support of friends and relatives as from the time given by the doctor. It is essential not to abandon people with incurable illness, but support in a self-help group or at a day centre is often more appropriate than individual supportive psychotherapy given by a doctor. [A useful account of supportive treatment is given by Bloch (1986).]

Crisis intervention

The supportive treatment just described may help people to pass through a crisis unchanged. Crisis intervention attempts to use the crisis to bring about change and to impart better ways of dealing with future stress. For example, it may be used when there is an acute disruption of personal affairs such as the break-up of a marriage, or the sudden death of someone who is loved; or after natural disasters such as floods and earthquakes. The ideas of crisis intervention originated in the work of Lindemann (1944) and of Caplan (1961). Much has since been written about the subject and about the related idea of coping behaviour (see for example Lazarus 1966). The literature is made difficult by a rather obscure terminology, but the essential notions are straightforward. **Coping** refers to behaviour used to deal with a difficulty or threatened difficulty, and it can take four forms: **problem-solving behaviour** which is the satisfactory, adaptive form; **regression** which is the use of behaviours that were appropriate at an earlier time of life but are no longer adaptive; and **denial** and **inertia** which are self-explanatory. Viewed in another way, the response to a crisis can be thought of as passing through *four stages*: emotional arousal with efforts to solve the problem; if these fail, greater arousal and distress accompanied by disorganization of behaviour; then trials of alternative ways of dealing with the problem; finally, if there is still no resolution, exhaustion and abnormal behaviour called 'decompensation' (see Caplan 1961).

Although no two problems are exactly alike, it is useful to recognize four groups according to their themes (Bancroft 1986): **loss problems** which include the loss of a person through bereavement or separation, and the loss of a body-part or the function of an organ; **role changes** such as entering marriage, parenthood, or a new job with added responsibilities: **problems in relationships** such as those between sexual partners, or between parent and child; and **conflict problems**, usually difficulties in choosing between two equally undesirable alternatives.

Treatment starts by attempting to restore emotional arousal to a near normal level. This is because if emotional arousal is too high, problem-solving is interfered with; and if it is too low there is little motivation for change. To achieve an optimal level, reassurance and an opportunity to express emotions are usually enough, although anxiolytic drugs may be required for a few days. Patients are encouraged to help themselves, but early in treatment arrangements sometimes have to be made for them—for example, over the care of children.

The patient's problems and his assets are assessed carefully. He is encouraged to suggest alternative solutions and choose the most promising. The therapist's role is to encourage, prompt, and question. He does not formulate problems or suggest solutions directly but helps the patient to do so himself. One way of providing such help is to divide the patient's task into *seven stages* as suggested by Goldfried and Goldfried (1975): identify the problem, propose alternative solutions, rehearse each alternative until its implications are clear, choose one solution, define the steps needed, take these steps, check the result. In crisis intervention, an important aim is that the patient should recognize that he has learnt a general method that can be used for solving future problems. Treatment is usually short but intensive.

Indications

Clinical experience suggests that crisis intervention may be most valuable for well-motivated people with stable personalities who are facing major but transitory difficulties; in other words, those who are most likely to cope eventually on their own. The generally accepted indications have been mentioned already. They include emotional reactions or disturbed behaviour (for example, deliberate self-harm) arising in response to social crises such as the breakdown of marriage or other relationships, traumatic events such as rape or other forms of assault, severe disruptions in life such as unexpected bereavement, and natural disasters such as floods.

Brief psychotherapy and the general practitioner

In countries with well developed systems of primary care, most patients with neurotic or personality problems are treated by general practitioners. There are many opportunities for psychological treatment in general practice, but little time to carry it out. Treatment must therefore be brief. There are other limitations on the kinds of psychotherapy that are practicable. For example, the general practitioner should avoid the development of a relationship so intense that it will cause problems if the patient has to be treated for physical illness, or if other members of the same family need treatment.

The best known attempt to adapt psychotherapy to the conditions of general practice is the work of Balint and his colleagues, whose ideas have been influential in the training of family doctors in Great Britain. These ideas were based on psychoanalysis, which is perhaps least suited to the special conditions of general practice. Nowadays more attention is given to an eclectic approach that is not based on psychoanalytic theory (see Sowerby 1977).

Individual long-term psychotherapy

There are many different methods of long-term psychotherapy, each derived from a different theory of psychological development. All these treatments attempt to bring about lasting changes in the patient's emotions and habitual patterns of responding to people, a process often referred to as personality change. The indications for all the long-term psychotherapies are discussed at the end of this section, after the procedures themselves have been described. Since most of the procedures originate from it, psychoanalysis will be examined first.

Psychoanalysis

Psychoanalysis is the most time-consuming form of psychotherapy. Its practitioners receive lengthy training which involves personal analysis as well as supervised experience in treating patients. For these reasons and because results have not been shown to be better than those of shorter forms of treatment, psychoanalysis is not widely available as part of the health services of most countries.

In the basic psychoanalytic technique, the analyst tries to reveal as little as possible about himself, while encouraging the patient to talk freely about his own thoughts and feelings ('free association'). This is the 'basic rule' of analysis which, with dream analysis, is thought to allow access to unconscious processes. The analyst asks questions to make the material clearer, confronts the patient with any contradictions, and makes interpretations. Otherwise he remains relatively passive. As this procedure continues, the patient usually begins to avoid certain topics and may show other forms of **resistance** to treatment such as rejecting the therapist's interpretations.

Gradually the patient's behaviour and talk begin to give direct or indirect evidence that he is developing intense but distorted ideas and feelings about the analyst. These distortions result from the **transference** to the analyst of ideas and feelings related to earlier experiences in the patient's life. At the same time a **treatment alliance** develops, that is, a realistic approach between the patient and analyst reflecting the former's wish to achieve change. The development of transference is deliberately encouraged by the use of a couch and by seeing the patient frequently, sometimes as often as five days a week. At times the patient presents his ideas and feelings not in words (as he is meant to do) but in his behaviour within or outside the therapeutic sessions (**acting out**). Interpretations are made about this behaviour, and about other issues in treatment. At first **interpretations** are frequently rejected, sometimes because they are inaccurate, but also because ingrained habits of thought can be changed only slowly—they require repeated **working through**. As interpretations begin to be accepted the patient is said to gain **insight**. As treatment progresses the analyst's feelings towards the patient change in ways that are partly realistic and partly distorted by is own previous experiences (**counter-transference**).

Two of the concepts mentioned above—transference and counter-transference—have been explained on p. 698, but for completeness they will be considered again briefly.

Negative transference denotes the patient's hostile feelings to the therapist; whilst **positive transference** denotes the opposite feelings to the therapist, such as dependency, idealization, or erotic feelings. If transference develops to such an extent that many of the patient's neurotic problems are re-experienced in relation to the analyst, this is called the **transference neurosis**. The analysis of the latter is an essential part of treatment.

As already described, **counter-transference** refers to feelings of the therapist towards the patient that are unrealistic, and so an interference in treatment. In recent years the term has been extended to all the analyst's feelings towards the patient, whether unrealistic or not. According to Heimann (1950), some of these feelings provide the analyst with valuable insights into the patient's problems. [For an account of other basic concepts of psychoanalysis the reader is referred to Sandler *et al.* (1970a–e) or Greenson (1967).]

Psychoanalytically orientated psychotherapy

This treatment employs the basic concepts and methods of psychoanalysis but generally puts less emphasis on the development and analysis of the transference neurosis.

Treatment is shorter and less intensive than psychoanalysis (sessions are usually once a week) and aims to bring about less profound changes. The couch is used less often and the therapist takes a more active part. Some therapists set specific goals (which is not done in psychoanalysis), but otherwise the strategies of treatment are those of psychoanalysis. Readers who require a detailed account are referred to Wolberg (1977).

Other forms of long-term psychotherapy

These vary in the nature of the interpretations, in the relative emphasis put on present problems and early experience, and in the attention given to dreams. The variants of treatment proposed by Jung, Klein, and the neo-Freudians were referred to in the historical section earlier in this chapter. Readers who wish to obtain further information are referred to Munroe (1955).

Existential psychotherapy

This stems originally from the existential movement in philosphy. It is concerned with patients' ways of dealing with the fundamental issues of human existence—the meaning and purpose of life, isolation, freedom, and the inevitability of death. In this method of treatment, increased awareness of the self is more important than exploration of the unconscious, but many of the techniques are borrowed from brief psychoanalytic therapy. [An account of existential psychotherapy has been written by Yalom (1985).]

Results and indications

It is still uncertain how far the results of long-term psychotherapy are superior to those of shorter methods. In general the research literature supports the impression of experienced clinicians that patients who respond well to long-term therapy are highly motivated, at least of average intelligence, and free from schizophrenia, manic-depressive illness, or antisocial personality. [For a summary of the research literature, see Bloch (1979).] Clinical experience suggests that long-term therapy is more appropriate than shorter treatment for patients who have long lasting and complicted emotional difficulties, or delays in their personal development. In general, specific neurotic syndromes respond less well than disorders primarily affecting personal relationships. Some therapists have devised special techniques claimed to be suitable for schizophrenia (see Arieti 1974), but these are not generally recommended. Contraindications to long-term therapy include marked paranoid personality traits, and severe depressive personality disorder. Histrionic and schizoid personality disorders, while not contraindications, are particularly difficult to treat.

Small group psychotherapy

This section is concerned with psychotherapy carried out with a group of patients, usually about eight in number. Treatment in larger groups is considered later. Small group psychotherapy can be used with the intention of bringing about substantial change in symptoms, personal problems or difficulties in interpersonal relationships; as a form of supportive treatment; or to encourage limited adjustments to specific problems including those of disabling physical or mental illness.

The development of group psychotherapy

Group therapy is often said to originate from the work of Joseph Pratt, an American physician who used 'class methods' to treat patients with pulmonary tuberculosis (Pratt 1908). Pratt's classes had little resemblance to modern group therapy, for they combined supportive conversations with instruction about the effects of disease. A more obvious precursor of modern group psychotherapy is the work of J. L. Moreno, a Romanian who worked in Vienna before emigrating to the United States. Moreno also laid the foundations of psychodrama and sociometry (measurement of the social position of the members of a group). Trigant Burrow, an

American, experimented with analysis in small groups (Burrow 1927) and his combination of analytic enquiry and comment on each patient's 'social image' has an obvious similarity to modern group therapy. Despite these developments and others up to the 1940s, it was the experience of treating neuroses in wartime Britain that led to the full development of group therapy.

Pioneering steps were taken in the Northfield Military Hospital, where S. H. Foulkes developed group methods which he had first tried in his civilian practice in 1941 (see Foulkes and Lewis 1944). His method was based on psychoanalysis; the therapist or group leader was relatively passive, and much use was made of analytic interpretations (see Foulkes 1948 p. 136). A different approach was developed by W. R. Bion, a Kleinian analyst whose interest in groups also grew from wartime experience at the Northfield Hospital. His theory of group dynamics (see Bion 1961) was more elaborate than that of Foulkes. It has been criticized as being 'more interested in understanding the dynamics of groups than in elaborating an effective system of therapy' (Yalom 1975, p. 179). After the 1939–45 war, group therapy grew vigorously. Particularly in the United States many new methods were tried with an enthusiasm that was not generally matched by critical appraisal of the results. [A useful account of the history of group therapy is given by Taylor (1958).]

Therapeutic factors in small group treatments

Certain psychological processes take place when people meet repeatedly in a small group to discuss their problems. Processes that help people to resolve problems (therapeutic factors) include: the feeling of belonging to the group (**cohesiveness**), learning from the successes and mistakes of others (**interpersonal learning**), discovering that other people have similar problems (**universality**), regaining hope through being valued and helped by others (**altruism**), learning from other members' reactions to one's own social behaviour, copying the behaviour of others (**modelling**), and the opportunity to express strong emotions (**catharsis**). [Accounts of these therapeutic factors are given by Yalom (1975), Bloch *et al.* (1981) and Bloch and Crouch (1985). A general review of the field will be found in Brown and Pedder (1979).]

The principal varieties of group treatment

Dynamic-interactional methods

These are now the most widely used small group techniques. They concentrate on present problems in relationships, and how these problems are reflected within the group. The past is discussed only in so far as it helps to make sense of present problems. The therapist seeks to capitalize on the therapeutic factors mentioned in the preceding paragraph, and to help each person to correct his false assumptions about other people's views of him.

Group therapy of this kind goes through predictable **stages**. At first the group tends to depend too much on the therapist, asking for expert advice about everyday problems and about appropriate ways of behaving within the group. Before long, some patients miss meetings or come late, either because they are anxious about talking in the group, or because they are angry and resentful about lack of immediate progress. The second stage begins as the members get to know each other better and become used to discussing each other's problems. This is the stage in which most change can be expected. The therapist encourages the examination of current problems and relationships, and he comments on the dynamics of the group. In the last stage of treatment the problems of the most dependent members tend to dominate the rest. To avoid this imbalance, discussion of problems of termination should begin several weeks before the group is due to end. [A full account of these methods is given by Yalom (1975).]

Analytic group therapy

Analytic group therapy is essentially an adaptation of psychoanalysis to treatment in a group. Several varieties have been described. In the most important, **group analytic treatment**, each patient is considered as the meeting-point of relationships with other group members. Interpretations are made about these relationships and how they become intensified into transferences. Reference is also made to unconscious material that is inferred from the talk and behaviour of the individual members. The method has been described by Foulkes and Anthony (1957) and by de Maré and Kreeger (1974).

Transactional group therapy

Transactional group therapy, which derives mainly from the work of Berne (1966), attempts to increase the patients' understanding of their ways of relating to other people. Berne suggests that relationships have three components: remains of earlier relationships with parents, residues of childhood behaviour, and an adult level of interaction. Berne has written about these ideas in a popular style which has undoubtedly added to the appeal of the method. For example, in *Games people play* (1966) he describes patterns of interaction under titles such as 'see what you made me do' and 'if it weren't for you'. Each encapsulates a recurrent situation which most readers could recognize in their own lives or those of the people they know. Treatment passes through four stages: **structural analysis** designed to encourage each member of the group to recognize the three levels in himself; **transactional analysis** dealing with the ways in which group members relate to one another—for example as adult to adult, or parent to child; **game analysis** examining transactions between several people; and **script analysis**, a 'script' being a consistent pattern of interaction laid down in childhood and persisting into adult life.

Experiential group methods

Experiential group methods include encounter and sensitivity groups. There are many variations most of which originate from charismatic leaders. Indeed they often have the aura of a cult rather than a form of medical treatment. All these methods can be traced back to the **sensitivity groups** which began in the National Training Laboratories in the United States, and were intended to teach community workers about group process by direct experience in the short term. Another source of ideas was the work of Carl Rogers in the University of Chicago. From these beginnings, training groups (T groups) developed, in which people seeking 'personal awareness' (rather than treatment) are required to talk about their own experiences. This and other forms of experiential group share the basic requirement of unrestrained self-disclosure and a willingness to receive frank comments from other members of the group.

Encounter groups are essentially intense forms of experiential group. In some the 'encounter' is entirely verbal, though the words are usually very direct and emotive. Some forms include physical contact as well, for example touching, massage, and rearrangements of the body position of other participants. Other methods seek to intensify the group-members' experience by prolonging it ('**marathon**' groups) for a whole day or even longer without interruption except for meals and sleep. Another well-publicized variant is the **Gestalt therapy** of Perls (see Perls *et al.* 1951; and Fagan and Shepherd 1971). This is a complex method, but one characterisic procedure is to encourage each individual to personify parts of his mind and body in order to arrange an artificial dialogue between them. It is hoped that this will improve the person's self-knowledge.

Many people taking part in such encounter groups report finding them helpful, but it appears that emotional problems are increased in a minority of participants, notably those who had substantial emotional disorders at the start. Not surprisingly, the most direct and attacking methods seem the most likely to have these adverse effects (see Lieberman *et al.* 1973). Although these effects are most serious with encounter methods, it is possible that even the less intense experience of sensitivity training can have adverse effects on a minority of those taking part (Stone and Tieger 1971).

Action techniques

These overlap with some of the procedures used in encounter groups. In **psychodrama**, the group enacts scenes taken from the life of one of its members. These scenes usually reflect either current relationships or those of the family in which the person grew up. The enactment usually provokes strong feelings in the person represented, whilst other members often see a reflection of their own problems. Treatment usually begins with a 'warm up' to help participants feel less self-conscious. It ends with a discussion in which everyone takes part. The therapist often has one or more assistants who try to keep the action going without taking the lead. One technique, role-reversal, can sometimes be used profitably in other psychotherapy. Here the patient and another person enact an event from the patient's experience, but the role of the patient is played by the other person. In this way the patient may be helped to see his own behaviour more objectively and to understand other people's points of view.

Action techniques are used most often in combination with other group methods. For example, a few sessions of psychodrama can provide topics for discussion when a group using other methods is failing to make progress. Instead of building a drama round the personal experiences of one member, the action can be concerned with problems that the participants share, for example how to deal with authority. [An account of action techniques is given by Lewis and Streitfeld (1970).]

Indications

There is no evidence that the results of group therapy in general differ from those of long-term individual psychotherapy, or that the results of any one form of group therapy differ from those of the rest. In particular there is no evidence that encounter groups or action techniques are superior to other methods.

There are no specific proven indications for long-term group therapy (as opposed to long-term individual psychotherapy), but it is generally thought to be well suited to patients whose problems are mainly in relationships with other people rather than in specific symptoms. As in individual psychotherapy, results are better in patients who are young, well-motivated, able to express themselves fluently in words, and free from severe personality disorder. Groups are often suitable for patients with moderate degrees of social anxiety, presumably because they benefit from the opportunity to rehearse social behaviour. The contraindications are similar to those for long-term individual psychotherapy, with the additional point that a group should never include a solitary patient whose problem may cause him to be made an outsider (for example, deviant sexual behaviour).

Psychotherapy with couples and families

Marital therapy

Because the term marital therapy should, of course, be confined to treatment for a husband and wife, the term *couple therapy* is sometimes used to include people living together outside marriage. In this section the term marital therapy will be used because most of the reported work is with spouses. Treatment of this kind is usually given either because marital conflict appears to be the cause of emotional disorder in one of the partners, or because the marriage appears likely to break up and both partners wish to save it. (Family therapy, which is discussed later, differs in including one or more other family members, usually children.)

In the apparently simple step from treating an individual to treating a couple, there is an important conceptual issue This is the idea that the problem is not confined to one person but shared between marriage partners. The problem then centres on the way the partners interact, and treatment is directed to this interaction. It is generally assumed that a good marriage includes the sharing of values, concern for the welfare and personal development of the spouse, tolerance of differences, and an agreed balance of dominance and decision-making. However, to avoid imposing values, the clinician often adopts a 'target problem' approach, whereby the couple are required to identify the difficulties that they would like to put right. It is also helpful to the clinician in discussion with the patients to bear in mind the stages through which a marriage passes: first living together, then bringing up children, and finally readjusting when the children leave home.

The development of marital therapy

This therapy is a relatively recent development which, in Britain, owes much to the work of Henry Dicks. In his book *Marital tensions* Dicks (1967) proposed that psychoanalytic ideas were useful in understanding and treating marital problems. In the United States, an important influence was that of Bateson's group in Palo Alto who studied indirect modes of communication within families (see Haley 1963 and Watzlawick *et al.* 1968). Another development was the introduction of the behavioural principles described below.

Description of marital therapies

Analytic methods

These methods employ concepts from psychoanalysis. A central idea is that the behaviour of a married couple is largely determined, from the moment they choose each other, by unconscious forces. Each person selects a spouse who is perceived as completing unfulfilled parts of himself. When the selection is successful the couple complement one another, but sometimes one partner fails to live up to the (unconscious) expectations of the other. For example, a wife may criticize her husband for failing to show the independence and self-reliance that she lacks herself.

The aim of this kind of treatment is therefore to help each person to understand his own emotional needs and how they relate to those of the partner. Various combinations of patient and therapist are used. One therapist may see the two partners together; two therapists may see them together (each therapist having a primary concern with one of them); or separate therapists may see the patients separately, but meet regularly to co-ordinate their treatments. Opinions differ about the value of and indications for each of these methods. In marital therapy of this kind, the therapist takes a more active part than he would in the analytic treatment of a single patient. The therapist is also less likely to make interpretations about transferences towards himself, and more likely to comment on the relationship between the partners and how it reflects the childhood experience of each.

Transactional methods

In these methods, one or two therapists may take part but the partners are always seen together. The focus of treatment is on the hidden rules that govern the behaviour of the couple towards one another, on disagreements about who makes these rules, and on inconsistencies between these two 'levels' of interaction. These issues are discussed around conflicts arising in the everyday life of the couple, for example who decides where to go on holiday, and who decides who is to decide this. In this way it is hoped to arrive at a more balanced and co-operative relationship. [A lively account of the method has been given by Haley (1963).]

Behavioural methods

These use so-called operant-interpersonal techniques. The therapist first identifies the ways in which undesired behaviour between the couple is reinforced. He then asks each partner to say what alternative behaviours would be preferable in the other person. These behaviours must be described in specific terms; for example, 'talk to me for half an hour when you come in from work', rather than 'take more notice of me'. Each partner then has to agree a way of rewarding the other when the desired behaviour is carried out. This may simply be through the expression of approval and affection, or it may be by carrying out a behaviour that the partner desires. The latter is often called 'give to get'. Described as briefly as this, the treatment may seem a crude form of bargaining that is remote from a loving relationship. In practice it can enable a couple to co-operate and give up old habits of criticism and nagging, with a consequent improvement in their feelings for one another. [The method has been described by Stuart (1969).]

Eclectic methods

As well as these formal methods, there is an important place for simple treatment directed to specific problems as part of a wider plan of treatment. For example, many depressed patients have some marital difficulties that are contributing to their problems. A few sessions can then be undertaken with the couple, with attention to specific and limited goals.

Results and indications

Gurman (1979) reviewed the literature and found fairly strong evidence that marital therapy is better than no treatment, and that the behavioural form of marital therapy is followed by improvement in about 60 per cent of cases. Crowe (1973) compared a behavioural form of marital treatment with two other methods, one combining elements of systems theory and interpretation, the other a non-directive approach. The non-directive approach was followed by least improvement, but the other two did not differ in their effects. Clinical experience supports the value of the simple eclectic methods just described, particularly if incorporated in a wider plan of treatment.

Family therapy

Several family members take part in this treatment. Both parents are involved, together with one of the children whose problems brought the family to treatment in the first place. At times they are joined by other children or grandparents. The aim of treatment is to alleviate the problems that led to the disorder in the identified patient, rather than to achieve some ideal state of a healthy family.

Family therapy is a recent development dating from the 1950s. It can be traced to two sources: an influential book by Ackerman (1958) on *The psychodynamics of family life*, and the work on communication by Bateson and his colleagues (mentioned above).

Classification

According to Madanes and Haley (1977), a useful way of distinguishing between different forms of family therapy is as follows: some forms are concerned mainly with past events, others with the present; in some the therapist relies on interpretation, in others he suggests actions to be taken by the family; some have a general strategy of treatment whatever the presenting problem, others apply flexible tactics to the particular disorder; some insist that all members of the family have equal rights in treatment, others accept the usual divisions of authority between parents and children. It will be apparent that these differences lead to many different forms of therapy. Only four forms will be described here. The interested reader is referred to Skynner (1976).

Psychodynamic methods

These methods use concepts taken from the psychoanalytical treatment of individual patients. It is assumed that current problems in the family originate in the separate past experiences of its individual members, particularly those of the parents. The therapist's role is to give interpretations linking present behaviour with past experience. He also uses aspects of the relationship between himself and the different family members to throw light on their unconscious ideas and feelings. In keeping with psychoanalytical practices he is not directive. Ackerman's work is an important example of this form of treatment.

Communication and systems methods

These methods owe much to the work of Haley (1963), Satir (1967), and Minuchin (1974). The methods attempt to change the present, rather than explore the past. They assume that family problems can be traced to unspoken rules of behaviour, to disagreements about who makes these rules, and to distorted communication. The therapist's role is to expose the rules, to help the family to modify them, and to improve communication.

The above three authors describe somewhat different roles for the therapist. Satir's role is that of a teacher who instructs the members how to communicate. For Minuchin the role is that of a director of a play, who helps the family to try out ways of communicating with one another, thereby bringing to light the unspoken rules by which they interact. These rules are called the family structure, and the method is called **structural family therapy**. Haley sees the role more in terms of provoking the family into desirable actions and of helping them to set goals. He calls this approach **strategic therapy**. [The interested reader should refer to the book by Minuchin and Fishman (1981) or the article by Madanes and Haley (1977).]

Behavioural methods

These methods are based on the idea that the behaviour of each individual in the family is maintained by continuing social reinforcement from the others. It is also assumed that problems arise either when undesirable behaviour is unwittingly reinforced or when desirable behaviour is not rewarded. The therapist's role is to encourage family members first to specify desirable behaviours, and then to make contact with the others to organize more appropriate systems of reinforcement.

Eclectic approaches

In everyday clinical practice, especially with adolescents, there is a place for a simple short-term method designed to bring about limited changes in the family. For this purpose, it is appropriate to concentrate on the present situation of the family and to examine how the members communicate with one another. The number of family members who are to take part should be decided on practical rather than theoretical grounds; for example, some of the children may be too young, others may be away as students for much of the time. Sessions can be at varying intervals, perhaps weekly at first, and then every three weeks to allow the family time to work at the problems raised in treatment.

Indications and contraindications

Family therapy is used mainly in the treatment of problems presented by young people living with their parents. Skynner (1969) suggests that conjoint family therapy is most useful in two circumstances: when the parents cannot cope with the behaviour of a child or adolescent, or when the family is making one member a scapegoat for shared problems. If one member has a serious illness requiring treatment in its own right (for example a severe depressive disorder) family therapy may be combined with other treatment. For example, antidepressant medication can be given for the depressive disorder, whilst family therapy can be used for any family conflicts which appear to be prolonging the disorder. Similarly, family therapy may help in the treatment of anorexia nervosa after appropriate steps have been taken to restore weight. The use of special kinds of family treatment to reduce relapses in schizophrenia is described on pp. 313 and 317.

Other forms of psychotherapy

Therapy in large groups

This form of therapy is characteristic of therapeutic communities and also part of the daily programme of many psychiatric wards. Large groups usually include all the patients in a treatment unit together with some or all of the staff, the number varying from 20 to 50. At the simplest level, these groups allow patients to express problems of living together. At a more ambitious level, they can attempt to change their members. Change is attempted by presenting each member with examples of his disordered behaviour or irrational responses. At the same time support is provided by other members who share similar problems and opportunities for social learning. The group is sometimes made into a kind of governing body which formulates rules and seeks to enforce them. Because large groups can evoke much anxiety in patients and staff, care should be taken to prepare new members for the experience. It is also important to protect vulnerable people from attacks by other group members and to decide when patients are too unwell to participate.

Self-help groups

All the groups described so far are led by a professional therapist. Self-help groups are organized and led by patients or ex-patients who have learnt ways of overcoming or adjusting to their difficulties. The other group members benefit from this experience and from mutual support. There are self-help groups for people who suffer from many kinds of disorder; among the best known are Alcoholics Anonymous and Weight Watchers. Other self-help groups are helpful to patients with chronic physical conditions such as colostomy; to people facing special problems, such as single parents or those with a handicapped child; and to widows (Cruse Clubs). If they are well run, such self-help groups can be of considerable value.

Psychotherapy for children

The kinds of psychotherapy discussed so far do not lend themselves to the treatment of young children who lack the necessary verbal skills. In practice there are fewer difficulties than might be expected because many emotional problems of younger children are secondary to those of their parents, and it is often appropriate to direct psychotherapy mainly to the parents.

Some psychotherapists believe that it is possible to use the child's play as equivalent to the words of the adult in psychotherapy. **Klein** developed this approach extensively by making frequent analytic interpretations of the child's actions during play, and by attempting to relate these actions to the child's feelings towards his parents. Although ingenious, this approach is highly speculative since there is almost no evidence against which the interpretations can be checked. **Anna Freud** developed child psycho-therapy by a less extreme adaptation of her father's techniques to the needs of the child. She recognized the particular difficulty for child analysis of the child's inability or unwillingness to produce free associations in words. However, she considered that neither play with toys, nor drawing and painting, nor fantasy games could be an adequate substitute. More-over she cautioned against the use of uncontrolled play which may lead to the acting out of aggressive urges in a destructive way. Anna Freud accepted that for many disorders of development, non-analytic techniques could be helpful. These techniques include reassurance, suggestion, the giving of advice, and acting as a role model (an 'auxiliary ego'). However, for neurotic disorders in childhood, and for the many mixed disorders, she advocated analytic techniques to identify the unconscious content of the disorder, and interpret it in a way that strengthens ego functions. [A concise account of Anna Freud's views on child analysis is contained in Freud, A. (1966) Chapters 2 and 6.] In Britain most psychotherapy for children is eclectic; the therapist tries to establish a good relationship with the child and to learn about his feelings and thoughts, partly through the medium of play and partly by talking and listening. Child psychotherapy is discussed further in the chapter on child psychiatry (p. 776).

Research in psychotherapy

Although many investigations of psychotherapy have been carried out, definite results are few. This account is therefore brief. [Further information on the extensive research literature can be found in the review edited by Garfield and Bergin (1986).]

Until recently, psychotherapy research suffered from over-ambitious attempts to investigate complex problems, although the available methods of assessment were suited only to simple issues. An understandable wish to establish the value of psychoanalytically based treatments was provoked in part by Eysenck's challenging assertion that they had no therapeutic effect (Eysenck 1952). This problem cannot be answered until there are valid and reliable methods for the assessment of basic psychodynamic variables. Moreover, there is no unambiguous specification of psychoanalytical method that would allow one study to be replicated by another research team. No amount of complicated experimental design or elaborate statistics can overcome these fundamental problems.

For these reasons, psychotherapy research has been most informative when applied to simple forms of treatment. Work by two groups of investigators stands out as particularly successful: Carl Rogers's investigation of client-centred therapy (see, for example, Rogers and Dymond 1954), and enquiries into short-term therapies by a group at Johns Hopkins Hospital led by Jerome Frank (see Frank *et al.* 1978). These investigations and others in psychotherapy can be divided into studies of outcome and studies of the processes occurring in the therapy sessions.

Few well-conducted studies of the **outcome** of psychotherapy have been reported, and even they are often difficult to interpret. Untreated control groups are required if treatment effects are to be separated from spontaneous recovery. When a lengthy technique is being studied, controls are difficult to find because patients seeking treatment are unlikely to be willing to wait for a long time. Two approches have been taken to the evaluation of completed studies of outcome. The first, exemplified by the work of Luborsky *et al.* (1975), is to accept only investigations that reach certain minimal scientific standards. The second, adopted by Smith and Glass (1977), is to include all studies having a comparison group, and to subject them to a statistical analysis designed to yield a composite estimate of change. It turns out that the two approaches give similar results. In general, psychotherapy leads to greater change than is found in comparable patients who are untreated, but no differences can be detected between the results of different forms of psychotherapy.

Even this finding has to be qualified. Frank's research group found that the difference between treated and control groups grew less with the passage of time after treatment had ended, so that five years later no differences existed. The explanation appeared to be that the control groups continued to improve slowly for several years and eventually caught up with the treated patients. This suggested that psychotherapy had merely accelerated natural processes of change (Stone *et al.* 1961). This finding must be treated cautiously because the patients studied by Frank's group had disorders that were not severe or longstanding. For this reason the results may not apply to all patients treated with psychotherapy.

An important point in assessing any outcome study is that hidden selection processes operate before a patient is accepted for psychotherapy. This applies particularly to comparison between American and British studies. As Goldberg and Huxley (1980) point out, in Britain a patient with a psychiatric disorder has to pass through three 'filters' before he can be treated with psychotherapy. First, the patient has to decide that his problems are appropriate to take to a general practitioner. Secondly, the general practitioner must recognize that the problem requires treatment from a psychiatrist. Thirdly, the psychiatrist must decide to use psychotherapy rather than some other treatment. In the United States, one of these filters is often removed because patients refer themselves directly to psychiatrists. In England, Shepherd *et al.* (1966) have shown that general practitioners refer to psychiatrists only about 5 per cent of their patients with identified psychiatric disorder. This difference in referral methods is likely to alter substantially the types of patient receiving psychotherapy in the two countries, possibly resulting in less severe disorders reaching psychotherapists in the USA.

The investigations reviewed so far were designed to measure possible beneficial effects of psychotherapy. The idea that psychotherapy could harm some patients was first discussed fully in the book *Psychotherapy for better or worse* by Strupp, Hadley, and Gomes-Schwartz (1977) and soon afterwards in the review by Bergin and Lambert (1978). The latter authors found nine well-conducted investigations in which some worsening of symptoms seemed to have occurred in some patients. Clinical experience indicates that, when harm results from psychotherapy, it is usually in the form of excessive preoccupation with emotional problems, increase of symptoms, and 'acting out'.

Research into the **process** of psychotherapy has added little to the results of outcome studies. There have been several attempts to find which techniques and what aspects of the therapist's personality are associated with good results. Amongst investigators concerned with the personality of the therapist, Whitehorn and Betz (1954) reported that they could identify two types of therapist whose results differed when treating schizophrenic patients with psychotherapy. However, other workers have not confirmed these claims consistently (see Parloff *et al.* 1978). It has also been argued that the results of treatment vary with measurable qualities of empathy, warmth, and genuineness in the therapist (Truax and Carkhuff 1967). This notion too was not confirmed by others (see Shapiro 1976).

The study of patients who **drop-out** from treatment has been more fruitful. Dropping-out depends on factors in the patient, the therapist and the treatment (Frank *et al.* 1957). Patients who drop out are more likely to be of lower social class, less educated, less integrated into society, and less ready to talk about their feelings; to have persevered less in any previous treatment, and to be receiving a treatment that does not match their expectations.

The factors that determine whether patients stay in treatment are not necessarily the same as the factors that lead to improvement in patients who remain. Every psychiatrist knows of patients who have persisted for years with a treatment that has not helped them at all. According to Frank's group, the likelihood of patients dropping out of psychotherapy can be reduced by making their expectations about treatment more realistic (Hoehn-Sarik *et al.* 1964). Although such methods are attractive, their value is not firmly established. When Yalom *et al.* (1967) prepared patients in a similar way for group therapy, attendance did not improve, although the patients learnt more quickly what was required of them during group sessions.

Behaviour and cognitive therapies

The term **behaviour therapy** is applied to psychological treatments based on experimental psychology and intended to change symptoms and behaviour. Two other terms are used to describe these methods: **behaviour modification** is employed both as a synonym for behaviour therapy, and to refer to a particular group of procedures based on operant conditioning. **Behavioural psychotherapy** generally refers to behaviour therapies other than operant methods. The term **cognitive therapy** is applied to psychological treatments intended to change maladaptive ways of thinking and thereby bring about improvement in psychiatric disorders.

How behaviour therapy developed

Behaviour therapy can be traced to Janet's (see 1925) methods of **re-education**, which were used for disorders with a behavioural element. These early methods arose from practical experience rather than from any formal theory. It was the well-known experiments on conditioning by Pavlov and on reward learning by Thorndike and others (Thorndike 1913) that provided a theoretical basis for a treatment based on experimental psychology. The practical application of these findings can be traced to the experiments of Watson and Rayner (1920). These workers showed for example that, in a healthy child, fear responses could become associated with a previously neutral stimulus by Pavlovian conditioning. This experiment suggested that naturally occurring fears might be removed by comparable methods. However, although behaviourism continued as a dominant force in psychology throughout the 1920s and 1930s, especially in the United States, there were few applications to treatment except in the (now abandoned) use of aversion therapy for alcoholism.

The development of modern behaviour therapy dates from the 1950s when it grew from three separate beginnings. In England, psychologists working at the Maudsley Hospital applied learning principles to the treatment of individual patients, especially those with phobic disorders. In South Africa, Wolpe developed a treatment based on his experimental work with animals. He subsequently described it in an influential book *Psychotherapy by reciprocal inhibition* (Wolpe 1958). This book was a landmark because, for the first time, the clinician was offered a practical treatment procedure backed by a reasonably convincing theory and supported by results. The third strand of development began with Skinner's *Science and human behaviour* (1953) in which he argued that normal and abnormal behaviours are governed by the laws of operant conditioning and that similar principles could be used to change them. These beginnings explain the subsequent course of development of behaviour therapy in Britain and the United States. Wolpe's ideas were introduced to Britain by Eysenck (1960) and were soon adopted because they were easily assimilated to the methods which the Maudsley Hospital psychologists had started. In the United States, on the other hand, there was a vigorous development of methods based on operant conditioning.

How cognitive therapy developed

Cognitive therapy has had two distinct but related lines of development. The first has been from the work of a psychiatrist, A. T. Beck, who became dissatisfied with the results of psychoanalytic psychotherapy for depressed patients and sought an alternative approach. He was struck by the recurring themes in the thinking of depressed patients (for example, about personal failure), and suggested that these themes should be regarded as part of the primary disorder rather than secondary to either underlying unconscious conflicts or biochemical abnormalities. Beck went on to develop a treatment designed to alter these recurring thoughts (see p. 736).

The second line in the development of cognitive therapy has been from the work of psychologists who were dissatisfied with the behavioural approach to treatment developed from work on operant conditioning. The contribution of one of these psychologists, D. H. Meichenbaum, will serve as an example. He examined the thinking of people with minor emotional disorders, and noticed that certain kinds of recurrent thoughts were described frequently by these people (for example, thoughts about social embarrassment). He then set out to develop ways of controlling these thoughts (see p. 735). Subsequently the approach to treatment has been taken up by many other psychologists and by psychiatrists, and has been applied to conditions such as bulimia nervosa, panic attacks, and hypochondriasis. These applications will be discussed later in this chapter.

Cognitive and behavioural approaches to treatment

All psychiatric disorders have cognitive and behavioural components and, for the patient to recover, both elements must change. Behavioural treatment is directed to changing the behavioural component of psychiatric disorders, but for recovery to take place there must be a secondary change in cognitions. Equally, in successful cognitive treatment a primary change in cognitions must be followed by a secondary change in behaviour. This does not mean that cognitive and behavioural treatments are interchangeable: in many conditions it is more effective to initiate change in one way rather than the other. For example, in obsessional disorders with rituals and obsessional thoughts, improvement is greater when rituals are treated with behaviour therapy than when obsessional thoughts are treated with cognitive therapy. It is becoming clear, however, that in many disorders the best results are obtained by combining the two procedures. For example, in phobic disorders behaviour therapy often leads to an incomplete improvement, and the addition of cognitive therapy increases the change. Because these two kinds of procedure are often combined, the term cognitive behaviour therapy (abbreviated to CBT) is often used. In the following paragraphs some general principles of behavioural and cognitive treatment will be outlined. This account will be followed by brief descriptions of the main procedures devised to treat common psychiatric disorders.

Principles of behavioural treatment

In behavioural treatment, the therapist attempts to alter a prominent behavioural element in a psychiatric disorder by encouraging the patient to carry out an incompatible behaviour. For example, avoidance behaviour in phobic disorders is treated by encouraging the patient to enter situations he fears ('exposure'); and the inactivity and social withdrawal of depressed patients is treated by encouraging the patient to plan a series of pleasurable activities ('activity scheduling').

Although these simple procedures are central to behaviour therapy, it is not enough to instruct the patient to carry them out. This is because of two difficulties. First, patients are often unaware of all the occasions when the abnormal behaviour is present and consequently do not use the therapeutic behaviours at the right times. Second, the new behaviour has to be practised frequently and over a long period, and unless special steps are taken to maintain motivation, most patients do not persist for long enough. There are ways of overcoming each of these difficulties.

The extent and timing of the behaviour disorder can be determined by a thorough enquiry into the patient's day-to-day activities, supplemented by the analysis of a diary, kept by the patient, of the symptoms and of attempts to cope with them. This kind of enquiry is called a *behavioural analysis*. The analysis of social phobia can serve as an example: patients with this disorder usually do not know exactly what features of social encounters they are avoiding, saying only that they feel anxious in company. A behavioural analysis might establish that the patient is anxious only in specific aspects of social encounters, such as making eye-contact, or initiating conversation. Graduated exposure to these specific elements, taken one at a time, is more effective than attempts to return to social situations in a less planned way.

It is essential to overcome poor motivation if good results are to be obtained with behaviour therapy. Although most patients have a general wish to recover, they usually have inadequate motivation to practise specific behavioural procedures repeatedly for weeks or months. Lack of motivation often relates to previous unsuccessful attempts to control abnormal behaviour, and to consequent demoralization. Motivation can usually be restored by providing a clear explanation of the aims of treatment, and by explaining the differences between the proposed pro- gramme and the patient's previously unsuccessful attempts at overcoming problems. It is also useful to present each procedure as an experiment in which completion of the task will be valuable, whilst inability to complete it will not be a failure but an outcome providing new information about the disorder. This 'no-fail' approach is an important way of sustaining motivation.

Principles of cognitive treatment

In cognitive treatment, the therapist attempts to change one or more of the disordered ways of thinking that characterize the disorder; for example, the irrational fears of a phobic patient, or the unreasonably pessimistic ideas of a depressed patient. The aim is to change these ways of thinking directly with the expectation that other changes will follow. Several techniques are used to produce changes in thinking.

The first step is to identify the irrational ideas. Although patients can describe some of these ideas, they are usually unaware of others. These unacknowledged ideas are often particularly important in maintaining the disorder. Irrational ideas can usually be elicited by careful interviewing, in which the patient is asked about the reasons for his actions and his expectations about the outcome of events (the latter by asking, 'What would happen if you were to do that?'). Irrational ideas can also be identified by asking the patient to keep a daily record of thoughts experienced at times when the other symptoms increase (for example, what he was thinking as he began to feel more depressed?).

Next, an attempt is made to change the irrational ideas. Two kinds of technique are used, verbal and behavioural. It may at first seem paradoxical that behavioural procedures are part of cognitive therapy; however these techniques are used to bring about a primary change in thinking and not, as in behaviour therapy, in behaviour.

Verbal techniques are used in two ways: with guidance from the therapist in therapy sessions, and by the patient during everyday activities. The latter techniques must be easy to remember and possible to carry out at times of distress. They are of two kinds. First, there are techniques intended to interrupt cognitions (for example, an anxious patient's thoughts that he will die of a heart attack). These methods are forms of *distraction*, either focusing attention on the immediate environment (for example, by counting objects) or on a normal mental content (for example, mental arithmetic). Alternatively, a sudden sensory stimulus can be arranged, for example by snapping a rubber band on the wrist, a method sometimes called *thought stopping*. The second kind of technique is intended to neutralize the emotional effect of irrational thoughts. The patient repeats to himself an appropriate rational response to the irrational thought, for example 'my heart is beating fast because I am feeling anxious, not because I have heart disease'. Because it is difficult for the patient to give priority to reassuring thoughts at times when they are most needed, it is useful for him to carry a 'prompt card' on which the thoughts are written.

Techniques used by the therapist in treatment sessions are designed to alter intrusive cognitions by giving information, and questioning their logical basis. The therapist also identifies the patient's illogical ways of thinking which allow the intrusive thoughts to persist despite evidence that they are false. These *'logical errors'* include unjustified generalization from single instances to general rules, and focusing on evidence for the irrational ideas while failing to take account of evidence against them. The therapist also tries to identify irrational beliefs that make the patient more likely to experience anxiety or depression when he encounters minor problems. Beck (1976) has called these beliefs *'underlying assumptions'*. An example is the idea that to be happy a person must be successful in everything he does. Such a belief could make the patient more likely to feel depressed when he has a minor failure in his work or personal relationships.

Specific examples of cognitive techniques will be given later in the chapter.

Behavioural techniques

Relaxation training

The simplest behavioural treatment for generalized anxiety disorders is **relaxation training**. Jacobson (1938) originally described *progressive relaxation*, an elaborate procedure intended to bring about reduction of tonus in individual groups of skeletal muscles and to regulate breathing. Subsequent developments have simplified the procedure and shortened the period of training (see Bernstein and Borkovec 1973) and these simple methods are used in behaviour therapy. They can be learnt from tape-recorded instructions or in group sessions, thus reducing the time that each therapist has to spend with the patient. Relaxation can be practised at regular times of the day, or carried out in stressful situations. Usually treatment begins with the first, and progresses to the second.

There is a surprising lack of controlled studies of the efficacy of any of the forms of relaxation training. The most common uses are for anxiety disorders and insomnia but there is no satisfactory study comparing relaxation training with anxiolytic or hypnotic drugs. Clinical experience suggests first, that the various methods are about equally effective; and second, that when carried out persistently, their effects are equivalent to those of a moderate dose of a benzodiazepine drug. However, it is often difficult to persuade patients to practise diligently enough to produce these useful effects. If this happens, a combination of behavioural and cognitive procedures can be used (see p. 735).

Relaxation training has also been used in the treatment of mild hypertension (see p. 450), and in other conditions in which stressful events may worsen a physical disorder by producing excessive arousal. It has been shown to have specific effects in lowering blood pressure, which are greater than those of non-specific factors such as contact with the therapist (Brauer *et al.* 1979). [For a review of relaxation training see Glaister (1982).]

Exposure

Exposure techniques are used in the treatment of phobic disorders in which anxiety is combined with avoidance behaviour. For simple phobias, exposure techniques give good results when used alone. For social phobia and agoraphobia, exposure techniques are less effective when used alone and for this reason they are usually combined with cognitive procedures (see p. 727). In this section, exposure treatments are described. combined exposure and cognitive treatments are discussed on p. 735.

Exposure can be carried out in the actual situations that provoke anxiety (*'exposure in practice'*), or in the clinic by helping the patient to imagine these situations in a vivid way (*'exposure in imagination'*). In either procedure exposure can be gradual, starting with situations that provoke little anxiety and building up slowly through increasingly more difficult ones ('desensitization'); alternatively, exposure can be sudden, starting with situations that provoke severe anxiety ('flooding').

Desensitization in imagination was developed by Wolpe (1958). Treatment begins with the construction of a list of situations that provoke increasing amounts of anxiety—a *hierarchy*. Relaxation is taught, and used for two purposes. First, relaxation is used to reduce the anxiety response to imagining phobic situations, thereby making it easier to progress smoothly along the hierarchy. Originally it was thought important to neutralize completely the anxiety response to the phobic stimuli but it is now generally agreed that this is not essential. Second, relaxation is used to improve imagery, since relaxed patients can more easily imagine situations vividly. Until recently, desensitization was the most frequently used technique of behaviour therapy. As explained above, desensitization is now used mainly for simple phobias.

In **flooding treatment**, situations are identified which produce severe anxiety. Patients are encouraged to enter these situations or imagine them, and to continue doing so repeatedly until their fear response subsides. After this procedure, they experience less anxiety when entering the feared situation subsequently. **Implosion** is a variant of flooding in which particularly severe anxiety is induced by persuading the patient to imagine exceptionally frightening scenes. Both flooding and implosion cause some distress, and neither has been shown to produce better results than those of desensitization (see Gelder *et al.* 1973). For these reasons they are not recommended for routine use.

A combination of exposure techniques to improve motivation, and cognitive procedures has been called *programmed practice* (Mathews *et al.* 1981). It is described under cognitive therapy on p. 735.

Behavioural methods of obsessional neurosis

Obsessional neuroses do not respond well to relaxation or desensitization (see Rachman and Hodgson 1980). For obsessional rituals the best method of treatment is **response prevention**, which derives from the work of Meyer and Levy (1971). When the latter persuaded patients to refrain from carrying out rituals, at first there was an increase in distress, but with persistance the rituals and the distress subsequently diminshed. The method of Meyer and Levy required continuous supervision over the whole day. Subsequent work has shown that such intense supervision is unnecessary, except perhaps in the early treatment of the most severe cases. Once rituals have been brought under some degree of control in this way, patients are encouraged to practise keeping them under control whilst returning to environmental situations that usually make them worse. It is sometimes helpful to demonstrate what is required and encourage the patient to follow the example. In the case of hand-washing rituals, this might consist of holding a 'contaminated' object and then carrying out other activities without washing. This procedure is called **modelling** (see p. 733). Treatment often begins in hospital with much help from the therapist, but is is important that the patient should soon practise in his own home and take increasing responsibility for the procedure. Clomipramine has been recommended as an adjunct to response prevention, but there is no good evidence that it improves the results except for patients with depressive symptoms (Marks *et al.* 1980). When obsessional thoughts accompany rituals, they usually improve if the latter are treated successfully by response prevention. When obsessional thoughts occur without rituals, a cognitive procedure—thought stopping (see p. 736)—should be tried.

Assertiveness training

Assertiveness training is designed to encourage direct but socially acceptable expression of thoughts and feelings by people who are shy or socially awkward. The method was first described by Salter (1949) and developed by Wolpe (1958). The essence of the treatment is that patients enact social encounters in which a degree of self-assertion would be appropriate; for example, being ignored by a gossiping shop assistant. By a combination of coaching, modelling, and role-reversal, patients are encouraged to practise appropriate verbal and non-verbal behaviour. (The latter might take into account eye contact, facial expression, and posture.) [An account of these methods has been given by Rimm and Masters (1974).]

Social skills training

This technique derives from the work of Argyle and his colleagues (for example Trower *et al.* 1978), who regard social behaviour as a set of learnt skills that can be assessed and improved in certain ways. video recordings are used to define and rate elements of the patient's behaviour in standard social encounters. The patient is then taught more appropriate behaviour by a combination of direct instruction, modelling, video-feedback, and role reversal. Trower *et al.* have devised a procedure suitable for patients particularly lacking in social skills. The procedure can be applied to socially inadequate people and to patients with social deficits consequent upon schizophrenia, when it should be part of a more general programme of treatment. Socially anxious people are less likely to benefit from social skills training, since they do not usually lack social skills but are too anxious to put into practice the skills they possess (see Shaw 1979).

Self-control

All behavioural treatments encourage patients to learn to control their own behaviour and feelings. In self-control techniques such learning is the principal aim. The methods can be traced on the one hand to Goldiamond (1965) who suggested that operant conditioning methods should be used for this purpose, and on the other to Bandura (1969) who pointed out the importance of self-reward. Self-control treatments lack specific procedures directed to individual symptoms. Instead they attempt to increase the patient's ability to make common-sense efforts at altering his behaviour. For this reason they have usually been employed when the goals of treatment are obvious but the effort required to achieve them are great. Over-eating and excessive smoking are examples.

Two stages of treatment can be recognized: self-monitoring and self-reinforcement. **Self-monitoring** refers to keeping daily records of the problem behaviour and the circumstances in which it appears. Thus a patient who over-eats can be asked to record what he eats, when he eats it, and associations between eating and either stressful events or feeling states such as unhappiness. Keeping such records can itself act as a powerful stimulus to self-control, because patients often avoid facing the true extent of their problem and the factors that make it worse. Once the problem behaviour has been documented in this way the patient is required to start '**self-reinforcement**'; that is, he rewards himself in some way when he has controlled behaviour successfully. Thus a woman who is trying to diet might buy herself new shoes on reaching her target weight for the month. **Self-evaluation** refers to making records of progress, and this also helps to bring about change.

In self-control treatment the patient takes responsibility for his own treatment, and the therapist merely advises him. If the behaviour is found to be under the control of particular environmental stimuli, the patient is at first encouraged to avoid them. Thereafter he returns to them progressively in order to extend his control over his behaviour.

Contingency management

This group of procedures is based on the principle that, if behaviour persists, it is being reinforced by certain of its consequences, and if these consequences can be altered the behaviour should change. Likewise if some aspect of behaviour needs to be strengthened or made more frequent, this should be possible by increasing its reinforcing consequences. It is assumed that the relevant positive reinforcers are usually social. They include expressions of approval and disapproval from other people, and actions that are enjoyable and rewarding for the patient.

Contingency management has four stages. First, the behaviour to be changed is defined, and another person (usually a nurse, spouse, or parent) is trained to record it; for example a nurse might count the number of times a schizophrenic patient shouts obscene phrases in the ward. Second, the events that immediately follow (and presumably reinforce) the behaviour are identified. For example, nurses may unwittingly reinforce the behaviour by paying more attention to the patient when he shouts than when he is quiet. Third, alternative reinforcements are devised; these may be tokens that can be exchanged for privileges, signs of approval by other people, or some activity that the patient enjoys. Last, staff or relatives must be trained to provide these reinforcements immediately after the desired behaviour and to withold them at other times. As treatment progresses, records are kept of the frequency of the problem behaviours and of the behaviours to be encouraged. Although treatment is mainly concerned with the consequences of behaviour, some attention is also given to events that might be provoking it. For example, in a ward the abnormal behaviour of one patient may be provoked on each occasion by the actions of another patient. [A good account of the practical details of contingency.management is given by Rimm and Masters (1974).]

Contingency management can be arranged for individual patients, for couples or families (as in behavioural, marital, and family therapy), or for a group of patients living together in a ward or hostel. When reinforcement is mainly by tokens to be exchanged for privileges, the system is called a **token economy**. Ethical problems arise with token economies because it is often necessary to deprive patients of some amenity before it can be earned with tokens. If this amenity is something that the patient should have by right, there is ethical difficulty. It is sometimes difficult to decide whether a particular amenity is a right or privilege—for example, the opportunity to watch television.

Token economies often bring about useful changes in behaviour but these tend to disappear when the patient moves to new surroundings, at work or in the family. Relapse probably occurs because the patient starts meeting people who respond to him just as the staff originally did in hospital, taking more notice of him when his behaviour is abnormal. Such a setback can sometimes be avoided by training the other people to respond appropriately. [More information about the problems of achieving long-term changes is given by Keeley *et al.* (1976) and by Rimm and Masters (1974, Chapter 6).]

A further problem about token economy treatment is whether tokens have any specific effect. With chronic schizophrenic patients, Baker *et al.* (1974) found that the treatment was equally effective when the tokens were withheld. Hence it is likely that other features of the programme, particularly the careful planning of graduated goals, must be useful in themselves. If tokens have an effect it may be because they encourage staff to observe behaviour systematically, and not because they act as reinforcers for the patient's behaviour.

Contingency management has proved to be valuable as one component of treatment for mentally handicapped adults. It has also been used effectively for patients with schizophrenic defect states. Behaviour disorders in children have been treated by training parents to act as therapists; this approach has some value in improving the social behaviour of autistic children.

Other behavioural techniques

Modelling This is a method which requires the patient to imitate behaviour demonstrated by the therapist. Although given prominence in many books on behaviour therapy, it is not reviewed here. The reason is that, whilst it is an important aspect of learning especially in childhood (see Bandura 1962), modelling alone has not proved to be an effective treatment for adult psychiatric patients. It may, however, encourage some patients to begin using other more specific techniques. [Readers who wish to review the evidence are referred to Bandura (1971).]

Negative practice Negative practice derives from the work of Dunlap (1932) who suggested that tics, stammering, thumb-sucking, and nail-biting could be reduced when the patient deliberately repeated the behaviour. Some theoretical support for this idea is provided by experiments showing that inhibition accumulates during massed practice (Hull 1943); on repetition, reactive inhibition becomes associated with the behaviour, which is then reduced. Negative practice has been used mainly to treat tics. Although short-term improvement has been reported (for example, Walton 1961), there is no convincing evidence of sustained improvement.

The pad and bell method The pad and bell method is a special procedure, first developed in the 1930s for the treatment of enuresis. Two metal plates separated by a pad are placed under the sheets of the bed. If the child passes urine in his sleep, the pad becomes moist and its resistance falls, allowing electric contact between the metal plates which are wired to a battery and a bell. The noise of the bell wakes the child, who must then go to the lavatory to empty his bladder. After this has been repeated on several nights, the child does not pass urine in his sleep but wakens to empty the bladder. Eventually he sleeps through the night without being enuretic. The waking from sleep before passing urine can be understood as the result of classical conditioning. It is less easy to understand how the treatment leads to the child passing an uninterrupted dry night. [Readers who wish to know more about this treatment and its rationale are referred to Lovibond and Coote (1970). The method is mentioned again on p. 807.]

Biofeedback

In biofeedback techniques, patients attempt to gain control of bodily functions, such as blood pressure, over which they otherwise have little or no control. Such lack of control may occur with functions regulated by the autonomic nervous system and normally not under direct voluntary control, or with functions normally under voluntary control but no longer so because of injury or disease that has interfered with neural pathways.

The essentials of treatment are simple. A physiological monitor is used to provide information about the function to be controlled, and this information is presented to the person in an easily understood form such as a tone of varying pitch or a visual display. The person then tries to alter the display by regulating the function, for example by relaxing. Although plausible in theory, this technique does not add much to the ability that people already have to control autonomic functions. It can, however, be of some value when normal sensory information has been interfered with, for example after spinal injury (Brudny *et al.* 1974). Biofeedback of galvanic skin response or pulse rate has been used as an aid to relaxation training, but most patients can be taught to relax without this additional help. [For a fuller account of biofeedback, and a more positive assessment of its value, see Basmajian (1983) or Stroebel (1985).]

Aversion therapy

In this technique, negative reinforcement is used to help a patient suppress inappropriate behaviour that he wishes to control. There are two problems about the use of negative reinforcement, one technical and the other ethical. The technical problem is that the effects of negative reinforcement on behaviour are usually temporary. The ethical problem is that negative reinforcement requires the use of stimuli that are unpleasant or mildly painful, and agents with these effects are used in other circumstances as a form of punishment. Although there is a distinct difference between negative reinforcement used to help a person suppress behaviour that he wishes to control, and punishment for wrongdoing, it is nevertheless important to make sure that the boundary between the two is maintained. This is particularly important when aversion therapy is being considered for people with conditions such as disorders of sexual preference, which may be the subject of legal proceedings.

Nowadays, aversion therapy is seldom used because it has not been shown to produce better results than other, less unpleasant, treatments. In the 1940s, however, the procedures were used to treat alcohol dependence by classical conditioning, in which the sight, smell, and taste of alcohol were linked with nausea and vomiting induced by apomorphine. After early enthusiasm (Lemere *et al.* 1942) the method was given up because the uncertain results did not justify the unpleasantness of the procedure. In the 1960s aversion therapy was used to treat disorders of sexual preference, especially sexual fetishism. Mild electric shocks were used, with reinforcement conditions designed to produce operant conditioning (see Bancroft and Marks 1968). The treatment fell out of use as experience showed that comparable effects could be obtained in other ways (see p. 578). As a less distressing alternative, mental images of unpleasant situations were tried instead of externally applied aversive stimuli, a method known as '*covert sensitization*' (see Cautela 1967). However, this method has not been shown to have specific therapeutic effects.

Techniques for treating sexual dysfunction are described in Chapter 15.

Cognitive and cognitive-behaviour therapies

Most cognitive treatments include some behavioural elements, so the term cognitive-behaviour therapy is generally applicable.

Cognitive-behaviour therapy for phobic disorders

Although, as explained on p. 728, simple phobias can be treated effectively with exposure (a form of behaviour therapy), social phobia and agoraphobia respond better to a combination of cognitive and behavioural methods. Cognitive techniques are used to interrupt intrusive thoughts and neutralize their effects. Two kinds of intrusive thought are modified: concerns about the effects of being anxious ('fear of fear'), and concerns that other people will react unfavourably to the patient ('fear of negative evaluation'). In social phobia, fears of 'negative evaluation' are particularly important, whilst in agoraphobia more attention is given to 'fear of fear' (for example thoughts that the person will faint, die, or lose control). Treatment combines exposure, a thorough explanation of the physiology of anxiety, questioning the logical basis of the fears, and instruction in distraction techniques. (The method for questioning the basis of fears is described in the next section.)

Anxiety management for generalized anxiety disorders

This treatment combines relaxation training with an explanation of the origin of symptoms, and the teaching of techniques for controlling the anxiety provoked by intrusive thoughts. Anxious patients frequently misunderstand the significance of symptoms such as palpitations and dizziness, fearing for example that these symptoms indicate physical disease. A simple explanation is given of the physiology of the normal fear response and its relation to anxiety disorders. Patients are taught to reduce the effects of intrusive thoughts in two ways. The first method is distraction: for example the patient is encouraged to pay attention to objects in the environment instead of focusing on the thoughts. The second procedure is to repeat reassuring statements which negate the content of the intrusive thoughts: for example, in response to the thought that dizziness indicates incipient madness, the patient can repeat the thought that although anxious people often feel dizzy they do not go mad. Patients with chronic anxiety disorders usually respond well to anxiety management, and this response has been shown to persist at least six months (Butler *et al.* 1987). Further research is required before the longer-term results of this treatment can be assessed.

Techniques for anxiety disorder with panic attacks

Patients with frequent panic attacks have particularly strong convictions that specific physical symptoms of anxiety are evidence of serious physical disease (see p. 194). These convictions, which often relate to heart disease, create a vicious circle in which symptoms of anxiety such as tachycardia generate more anxiety. Provided panic attacks are not frequent, patients respond to anxiety management; but if the attacks are frequent an alternative treatment is needed. In one technique, physical symptoms like those feared by the patient are produced in a benign way (usually by voluntary hyperventilation) and their origin is pointed out; then the equally harmless cause of the patient's symptoms is explained. Most patients with panic disorder respond well to this simple procedure, and this improvement has been shown to last at least six months (Clark *et al.* 1985). More research is needed before long-term benefits can be assessed.

Thought stopping

Thought stopping is a particular form of distraction used to control obsessional thoughts. Because these thoughts are highly intrusive, an effective distracting stimulus has to be sudden and intense. It must also be easy for the patient to produce unobtrusively; one way is to snap an elastic band on the wrist. The use of this procedure in obsessional neurosis is discussed on p. 730.

Cognitive-behaviour therapy for depressive disorders

Cognitive therapy for depressive disorders is a complex procedure combining behavioural and cognitive techniques, with emphasis on procedures for changing ways of thinking.

The **behavioural components** of cognitive therapy are of two kinds. The first, '*an activity schedule*' is used because depressed patients are often inactive, and this inactivity may increase their depressed mood by depriving them of rewarding experiences and by allowing them to dwell on depressive ideas. Graduated activities are planned that are appropriate to the patient's interests and the severity of the disorder. The second kind of behavioural component, 'reality testing', consists of activities designed to challenge irrational ideas. These tasks have to be worked out for each patient, using the approach, 'let us find out what happens if you try to do this'.

The **cognitive components** of cognitive therapy initially include recording the occurrence of intrusive thoughts, interrupting these thoughts by distraction, and practising alternative reassuring thoughts (for example, 'because I think something, it is not necessarily true'). The next step is to identify illogical modes of thinking by questioning the patient about the reasoning behind the intrusive thoughts. Several kinds of distorted logic make it possible for maladaptive thoughts to persist. Common examples are generalizing too widely from single occurrences ('over-generalization'), focusing on one unfavourable aspect of a situation while ignoring other, favourable aspects ('selective abstraction'), and inappropriate self-blame for the consequences of other people's actions ('personalization'). [The terms in brackets are those used by Beck *et al.* (1979) to describe these ways of thinking.] When these errors of logic have been identified, they are pointed out repeatedly to the patient who is encouraged to recognize and correct them in everyday life.

Cognitive-behaviour therapy for bulimia nervosa

The **behavioural components** of this treatment are intended to re-establish more normal patterns of eating (three or four meals a day with no snacks between). Patients keep records of what they eat, when they eat, and when they induce vomiting or take laxatives. These procedures usually lead to some improvement, which is needed before cognitive procedures are introduced in the second stage of treatment.

There are several **cognitive components**. Interviewing and diary-keeping are used to identify intrusive thoughts. Distraction is used to interrupt these thoughts and alternative reassuring ideas are rehearsed as in the treatment of anxiety disorders. The logical basis of intrusive thoughts is challenged by pointing out inconsistencies. In bulimia nervosa some thoughts resemble those in depressive disorders (for example 'no-one likes me'), whilst others are characteristic of eating disorders (for example, 'gaining weight means losing control of myself'). The next step, as in depressive disorders, is to identify illogical ways of thinking that allow dysfunctional ideas to persist in the face of evidence to the contrary. The errors of logic are generally the same as those described above under depressive disorders.

Some problems in the use of behaviour and cognitive therapies

Multiple disorders

Patients often have more than one problem—for example, generalized anxiety with poor social skills. It is usually best to treat such problems one at a time. If improvement can be brought about in one aspect of the disorder, the patient usually feels more confident, and may be able to deal with the remaining problems without further help.

Combinations of behaviour therapy with psychotherapy

Although it might appear in theory that psychodynamic treatment could not be combined with behaviour therapy, in practice such a combination presents little difficulty. The patient must understand the purpose of each approach; for example, psychotherapy is given for his problems in intimate relationships, and behaviour therapy for an associated phobia. If the psychotherapy needs to be intensive, it may be difficult for one clinician to change from the more passive role of psychotherapist to the more directive role of behaviour therapist. Hence it is often appropriate to have two therapists.

Psychoanalysts expected that direct treatment of symptoms in either cognitive or behavioural therapy would lead to the appearance of other symptoms because underlying psychodynamic problems had not been affected. Clinical experience and the results of many follow-up studies have not confirmed this expectation.

Other forms of psychological treatment

Hypnosis

Hypnosis is a state in which a person is in a relaxed and drowsy state, and unusually suggestible. This enhanced suggestibility is shown by the possibility of inducing diminished sensitivity to painful stimuli, as well as vivid mental imagery, hallucinations, failures of memory, and 'age regression' (behaving as the person might have done when younger). Although this enhanced suggestibility is characteristic of hypnosis, it is not confined to it. Some susceptible subjects can produce the above phenomena in response to direct suggestion when in a state of full alertness (see, for example, Barber 1962). Indeed there seem to be no phenomena peculiar to the hypnotic trance.

Hypnosis can be induced in many ways. The main requirements are that the subject should be willing to be hypnotized and convinced that hypnosis will occur. Most procedures contain some combination of the following elements: relaxation and slowed respiration, a fixation point for attention (such as a moving object), rhythmic monotonous instructions, and the use of a graduated series of suggestions, for example that the arm will rise from the patient's side. The therapist uses the suggestible state either to implant direct suggestions of improvement or to encourage recall of previously repressed memories.

Indications

In psychiatry, hypnosis can be used in several ways. The first and simplest use, which requires only a light trance, is as a form of relaxation. For this purpose, has not been shown to be better than methods that leave patients with more control over their actions. The second use, which requires a deeper trance, is to enhance suggestion in order to relieve symptoms, especially those of hysteria. Although this procedure is often effective, at least in the short term, it has not been proved better than more gradual forms of suggestion with no trance. Moreover the sudden removal of symptoms by hypnosis is sometimes followed by an intense emotional reaction of anxiety or depression. The third use of hypnosis is as an aid to psychotherapy, by bringing about the recall of repressed memories, but there is no evidence that this improves the effects of treatment. For all these reasons the authors do not recommend the use of hypnosis in clinical psychiatry. [Readers seeking more information about hypnosis are referred to Wolberg (1977) for a brief account or Wolberg (1948) for an extended one.]

Autogenic training

This technique derives from the work of Oskar Vogt who, at the turn of the century, studied the psychophysiological changes brought about by hypnosis and auto-suggestion. Shortly afterwards, in 1905, Schultz developed from this work a clinical procedure known as autogenic training and used it to treat physical symptoms caused by emotional disorder (Schultz 1932).

In autogenic training, 'standard exercises' are used to induce feelings of heaviness, warmth, or cooling in parts of the body and to slow respiration. 'Meditative exercises' follow, in which colours or objects are imagined as vividly as possible. Practising these two kinds of exercises is supposed to induce changes in autonomic nervous activity that benefit patients with diverse disorders of the cardiovascular, endocrine, and urogenital systems as well as neuroses and habit disorders. It has not been established that autonomic changes after autogenic training differ substantially from those following simple relaxation, nor is there any good evidence about the therapeutic effects of the procedure. These methods have not been used widely in Britain or the United States, though they are employed more in Europe and Canada. [The interested reader is referred to the short account by Schultz and Luthe (1959).]

Techniques of meditation

In recent years a number of techniques of meditation have attracted popular attention, and some have been used to treat neurotic patients. Although the individual methods are based on different systems of belief, they have certain common features. First, they include some kind of instruction about relaxation and about the regulation of the speed and depth of breathing. Second, they include some mental process to direct the person's attention away from the external world and from the stream of thoughts that would otherwise occupy his mind. Often this requires concentration on a repeated word or phrase (a mantra). Third, emphasis is placed on setting aside from the day's activities periods when calm can be restored. Fourth, the person joins a group of people who believe strongly in the method and encourage each other to practise it. Such group pressure is often lacking from hospital-based programmes of relaxation or meditation, and this may explain why many hospital patients fail to persist with the exercises.

There is no satisfactory evidence about the value of these methods. Clinical experience indicates that the less extreme forms have some value for patients whose neurotic symptoms result from a style of life that is too stressful and hurried.

Abreaction

It has long been known that the unrestrained expression of emotion often leads to temporary relief of mental disorder. Such abreaction is part of many forms of religious healing and it has also been used in medicine. Since it is of most value in acute neuroses caused by extreme stress, its main use has been for war neuroses. After Sargant and Slater (1940) used abreaction in the treatment of acute neurosis in soldiers evacuated from Dunkirk, the method was widely employed in the front line of battle to bring rapid relief and so enable soldiers to return quickly to combat. In civilian practice, abreaction has much less value because comparable cases are seldom encountered in which acute symptoms are seen a few hours after emotional trauma. Abreaction can be brought about by strong encouragement to relive the traumatic events. This procedure can be facilitated by giving a sedative drug intravenously. The use of abreaction in peacetime is not recommended. [Those who are interested in the details of the procedure are referred to Sargant and Slater (1963).]

Further reading

Suggestions for further reading about specific methods of psychological treatment have been given in the course of this chapter. The following reading list concerns general issues about psychotherapy.

Bloch, S. (1986). *An introduction to the psychotherapies* (2nd edn). Oxford University Press, Oxford.

Brown, D. and Pedder, J. (1979). *Introduction to psychotherapy: an outline of psychodynamic principles and practice*. Tavistock Publications, London.

Frank, J. D. (1967). *Persuasion and healing*. Johns Hopkins Press, Baltimore.

Hawton, K., Salkovskis, P. M., Kirk, J. W., and Clark, D. M. (1989). *Cognitive behavioural approaches for adult psychiatric disorders: a practical guide*. Oxford University Press, Oxford.

Storr, A. (1979). *The art of psychotherapy*. Secker and Warburg with Heinemann Medical Books, London.

Wolberg, L. R. (1977). *The technique of psychotherapy*. Secker and Warburg with Heinemann Medical Books, London.

Yalom, I. (1985). *The theory and practice of group psychotherapy* (3rd edn). Basic Books, New York.

19 Psychiatric services

The last two chapters have dealt with the treatment of individual patients by physical and psychological methods. This chapter deals with the provision of specialist psychiatric and social services for whole populations. In the United Kingdom these services are provided by hospital authorities and by local government. It should be noted, however, that most patients with psychiatric disorder are treated by general practitioners, who refer to psychiatrists only about five per cent of their patients with psychiatric symptoms (Shepherd *et al.* 1966). The proportion of patients with minor emotional or neurotic symptoms referred to specialists is particularly small. In other countries, primary care is less established, and specialist services deal with a wider range of cases.

Psychiatric and social services can be divided into two groups: those for acute, and those for chronic patients. The provision of services for chronic patients presents the more difficult problems. Some of these problems are discussed in the chapters on disorders of old age (p. 600) and childhood (p. 775). This chapter is concerned with services for patients with disabling chronic psychiatric disorders.

Before describing the present services, an outline will be given of the historical development of provisions for psychiatric patients.

The historical background

Until the middle of the eighteenth century, there were hardly any special provisions for the mentally ill. In England, for example, the only hospital for the mentally ill was the Bethlem Hospital, founded in 1247. In continental Europe there was a similar lack, although in the Middle Ages hospitals in Spain were a notable exception (Chamberlain 1966). Nearly all mentally ill people lived in the community with some help from poor law provisions, or else they were in prison. In England the Vagrancy Act of 1744 made the first legal distinction between lunatics and paupers. In the eighteenth century private 'madhouses' (that is, places for the mentally ill) were developed mainly for mentally disordered people who could afford to pay, but also for some who were paupers supported by their parishes (Parry-Jones 1972). About the same time, a few hospitals or wards were established through private benefaction and public subscription. The lunatic ward at Guy's Hospital was founded in 1728, and this was followed by St. Luke's Hospital (1751) which was founded as an alternative to the overcrowded Bethlem

Hospital. In those days, just as nowadays, there were debates about the value of psychiatric wards in general hospitals (Allderidge 1979).

At the end of the eighteenth century, in Britain and other countries, public concern led to renewed efforts to improve the care of the mentally ill. In Paris Pinel gave an important lead in 1793, when he released patients who had previously been restrained in chains. Pinel went on to introduce other reforms leading to more humane care. In Britain William Tuke, a quaker philanthropist founded the Retreat at York in 1792. This provided 'moral' (that is, psychological) management based on respect for the patient, rather than the bleeding and purging favoured by most doctors at that time. At the Retreat there were pleasant surroundings, and adequate facilities for occupation and recreation. These enlightened principles were later described by William Tuke's grandson, Samuel, in *A description of the Retreat*, published in 1813.

Despite such pioneering efforts, in the early nineteenth century many mentally ill people lived as vagrants or as inmates of workhouses and gaols. Public concern was increased by reports of scandalously low standards of care in some of the private madhouses—though many continued to provide good care (see Parry-Jones 1972). In 1808 the County Asylum Act provided for the building of mental hospitals in each of the English counties, but little progress was made. In 1845 it was necessary to enact the Lunatics Act, this time requiring each county to build an asylum. When the first new asylums were built, they provided enough space for their patients, and their staff attempted to base treatment on moral management. This liberal approach was encouraged by the **non-restraint movement**, which began with the work of Gardiner Hill at the Lincoln Asylum in 1837, and was taken further at the Middlesex County Asylum, Hanwell, by John Conolly. In 1856 John Conolly published a significant book *The treatment of the insane without mechanical restraints*.

Unfortunately these liberal steps were soon followed by a new restrictive approach. More and more patients were being transferred to the new asylums from the community. Under the pressures of overcrowding and staff shortages, and increasing public intolerance of mental disorder moral management gave way to a custodial approach. This change was endorsed by the 1890 Lunacy Act, which amongst other things imposed restrictions on discharge from hospital. These custodial provisions continued into the twentieth century, and their legacy is still to be seen in the architecture of the large Victorian hospitals in which much modern psychiatry is practised. [See Jones (1972) and Rothman (1971) for accounts of psychiatric hospitals in Britain and the United States in the nineteenth century.]

In England an early indication for the return to liberal policies after the First World War was the opening in 1923 of the Maudsley hospital. This provided an out-patient service and voluntary in patient treatment in a hospital where teaching and research were pursued. In 1930, the Mental

Treatment Act repealed many of the restrictions imposed by the Lunacy Act of 1890, and allowed county asylums to accept patients for voluntary treatment. This 1930 Act also encouraged local government authorities to set up many more out-patient clinics and to establish after-care facilities. Not long after, the new optimism was encouraged by the introduction of treatments such as insulin coma (later abandoned) and ECT. At the same time, efforts were made to improve conditions in hospitals and to unlock previously locked wards.

After the 1939–45 war, several influences led to major changes in psychiatric hospitals. Social attitudes had become more sympathetic towards disadvantaged people. Amongst psychiatrists, wartime experience of treating battle neuroses had encouraged interest in the general treatment of neuroses. The advent of the National Health Service paved the way for a reorganization of medical services. In 1952 the introduction of chlorpromazine made it easier to control disturbed behaviour, and therefore easier to open wards which had been locked, and discharge more patients into the community. Vigorous efforts at rehabilitation helped patients by improving handicaps which resulted as much from years of institutional living as from mental illness. Day hospitals were set up, and hostels began to provide alternative accommodation on the community. As a result of all these changes, the numbers of patients in psychiatric hospitals began to fall substantially. Similar changes were introduced in other countries and were particularly rapid in the USA.

Whilst a large reduction in mental hospital beds was achieved, not all the early aims were realized in Britain or in other countries. Some patients simply could not manage in the community; of these, a proportion became vagrants or prison inmates. Others survived outside hospital but could not progress through the rehabilitation services. In many day hospital and rehabilitation services, patients attended for years without advancing further (see Jones 1972; Cross *et al.* 1972). It became clear that earlier views of the benefits of 'deinstitutionalization' had been over-optimistic and that services outside hospital were inadequate to provide the help needed by patients and their families.

Along with the changes in the care of major mental disorders there was an expansion in the out-patient treatment of neurotic disorders by new physical and psychological methods.

Psychiatric services have continued to expand with additional services for emotional disorders, for complications of alcohol and drug abuse, and for the psychiatric problems of children and the elderly. In contrast, services for mentally retarded people, which were previously part of psychiatry, have been increasingly transferred to the social services.

Recent developments

There have been five interwoven themes, of which the first three are considered further in this chapter. These five themes are:

1. Hospital care   In nearly all developed countries the numbers of psychiatric in-patients have fallen. Hospital admissions are mostly brief, and are increasingly to psychiatric units in general hospitals rather than to mental hospitals. Hospital out-patient and day-patient services have expanded greatly.

2. Community care   It is widely accepted that continuing care in the community, if feasible and adequate, is desirable for most chronic patients. However, there is no single agreed way of providing community care, and reality falls short of expectation almost everywhere.

3. Rehabilitation   This denotes all psychological and social provisions intended to help chronically handicapped patients to achieve their best level of social functioning. Rehabilitation was originally developed in mental hospitals to enable long-stay patients to resettle in the community. Now it is increasingly provided in the community as well.

4. The multi-disciplinary team   There are now not only more psychiatrists than ever before, but also more clinical psychologists and social workers. At the same time psychiatric nurses are acquiring specialist treatment skills, whilst an increasing range of voluntary groups are contributing to the care of psychiatric patients. Care is usually provided by multidisciplinary teams whose members work together to use their individual skills to the greatest effect. Unfortunately the good intentions of this approach are sometimes frustrated by professional rivalries.

5. Legal reform   As a result of changes in the management of chronic illness and of greater public concern for the rights of the individual, legal reforms have redefined and limited the uses of compulsory treatment. In some countries there is disagreement for political and ethical reasons about the role and methods of psychiatry, a recent example being the controversy that led to changes in Italy (see p. 751).

Chronically handicapped patients

With the exception of the elderly (who are not considered in this chapter), most people with chronic and seriously handicapping mental disorder are schizophrenics. Of the rest, some have chronic affective disorders or presenile dementia, whilst others have personality disorders resulting in, for example, aggressive behaviour or the abuse of alcohol or drugs. In addition to such primary psychiatric problems, many chronic psychiatric patients have physical disabilities as well, such as epilepsy, brain damage, or other physical illness.

Many chronically disabled psychiatric patients would formerly have been long-stay in-patients in mental hospitals, but now live in the community with their family or friends, or in hostels. In the community many continue to receive psychiatric or social care at day hospitals or day centres. There is, however, an important group who are not offered this care or are reluctant to use it. Some of this group live very limited lives with their families, whilst others find their way into lodging houses or prisons, or become vagrants without regular accommodation. Studies have shown that a large proportion of destitute people are mentally ill or alcoholic, or have personality disorders. Many move repeatedly from one form of accommodation to another, and some sleep rough at times (see Leach and Wing 1980; Lamb and Talbott 1986; Herzberg 1987).

People with chronic disabling mental illness suffer from three kinds of handicap (Wing and Morris 1981):

(1) **Impairments** directly due to psychiatric illness; for example, persistent hallucinations, social withdrawal, underactivity, and slowness;

(2) **Secondary social disadvantages**, such as unemployment, poverty and homelessness, as well as the stigma still attached to chronic psychiatric illness;

(3) **Adverse personal reactions** to illness and social disadvantage, such as low self-esteem, expectations of failure, and helplessness. Individual reactions vary greatly, depending on personality and premorbid experience, and on the reactions of others.

Only the first kind of handicap results from the illness alone. The second and third kinds are greatly affected by social circumstances. In the past, they were attributed to the effects of living in hospital for many years, and sometimes referred to as institutionalization or 'institutional neurosis' (Barton 1959). It is now clear that these handicaps are not solely attributable to the hospital, because similar handicaps can occur in the community, especially if the environment is unstimulating.

Wing and Furlong (1986) have listed five features of severe handicap which are particularly likely to cause problems in management: (a) risk of harm to self and others; (b) unpredictability of behaviour and liability to relapse; (c) poor motivation and capacity of self-management or performance of social roles; (d) lack of insight; and (e) low public acceptability.

The most severely handicapped group

Amongst the most severely chronically handicapped people, there is a sizeable group who need protection or shelter in hospital or in some suitable community alternative. In such an environment, they can live more contented lives, and they less often become disturbed in their behaviour. Broadly similar groups of this kind have been identified in Britain (Wing and Furlong 1986; Wing 1986), the USA (Bachrach 1986), and other countries (Häfner 1987*a*).

In Britain, the evidence comes from hospital statistics and epidemiological research. Hospital statistics show that the continuing decrease in the number of in-patients is mainly accounted for by a decrease in those who have been in hospital for more than five years, and that the numbers of patients in hospital for less than one year (short-stay) and for between one year and five years (medium long-stay) are relatively stable. In other words, despite admission and discharge policies intended to prevent prolonged admission (see Wing 1982, 1986), there has been a continuing recruitment of 'new' long-stay patients (recently admitted people who remain in hospital for longer than a year).

The problems and needs of 'new long-stay' patients have been defined from interviews with the patients, their relatives, and others caring for them. Mann and Cree (1976) studied 400 patients aged under 65, who had been resident for more than one to three years in 15 hospitals selected randomly from each of the health regions of England and Wales. Almost half the patients were chronic schizophrenics. The group as a whole were severely disabled. Almost a third were judged to need further in-patient care, and half of these seemed likely to need such care permanently. Other surveys, including those of families (Creer and Wing 1975) and of single homeless people (Leach and Wing 1980), show that other chronic patients at present in the community would benefit from long-term care.

General principles of service provision

Hospital care

The older mental hospitals were built at a time when the aim was long-term asylum rather than return to the community. All services were concentrated on a single site, which was often remote from centres of population. These large old mental hospitals have considerable disadvantages, mainly arising from their size and their isolation. Goffman (1961) argued that American State hospitals in the 1950s were 'total institutions', similar to other segregated communities isolated from everyday life, such as orphanages and prisons. He described such institutions as impersonal, inflexible, and authoritarian. Even then, British mental hospitals were in some ways different from those described by Goffman. Nevertheless, in a study of three British mental hospitals, Wing and Brown (1970) found that many were characterized by 'clinical poverty' and 'social poverty'. Most modern mental hospitals are very different: there are fewer patients; duration of stay is much shorter; and more active, individually planned treatment is provided in more stimulating surroundings.

The decrease in numbers of in-patients began in Britain in the 1950s and soon afterwards in several other countries, the reduction being particularly rapid in the United States. Although in-patient numbers have not fallen so much everywhere (for example, in Eire, Finland, and Sweden), almost all developed countries have substantially reduced in-patient numbers or plan to do so in the near future. In contrast, in Japan there has been an increase in the last 30 years from very few psychiatric beds to a proportion greater than in England and Wales (Häfner 1987*a*).

Care for acute illness

Although it has been claimed that newer methods of community care will largely eliminate the need for hospital care, there are strong reasons for admitting patients with acute illnesses to hospital, even when there is a good community service. These reasons were listed by Leff (1986):

1. Removal from a stressful environment.

2. Contact with skilled staff.

3. Shelter from the reactions of the public.

4. Supervision of medication.

5. Protection against self harm.

6. Containment of aggression.

7. Provision of graded activities.

8. Provision of a temporary home.

Hospital units providing care for acutely ill patients have to strike a balance between the patients' need for privacy and the staff's need to observe the patients. There should be small secure areas for disturbed patients; areas where patients can be private, and others where they can be with other people. There should be provisions for occupational therapy, for the practice of domestic skills, and for recreation. Outdoor space is also desirable.

Care for acute psychiatric illness is increasingly provided in general hospitals in Britain (Goldberg 1986), the United States (Schulberg 1984) and many other countries (Häfner 1987*b*). General hospital psychiatric units have the advantages of modern buildings, proximity to the area they serve, and lack of stigma. They also enable psychiatric staff to mix with colleagues in other branches of medicine. These units none the less have disadvantages, including the difficulties of providing adequate work rehabilitation, and of creating an informal environment suitable for psychiatric patients in a hospital designed primarily for the different needs of medical and surgical patients. It may be more satisfactory to have a separate psychiatric wing in the grounds of a general hospital.

Care for patients with chronic disorders

Patients with chronic disorders may require several kinds of in-patient care: acute treatment during relapse, short-term rehabilitation and, for a few of the most severely handicapped, long-stay (see Talbott and Glick 1986). Hospital staff therefore need the skills to deal with florid symptoms of relapsing patients as well as the negative symptoms of patients with chronic illness.

The basic requirements for in-patient units for long-stay patients are broadly similar to those for acute patients (Leff 1986), although they are best provided in buildings of a domestic type. They should have single bedrooms, areas for privacy and others for mixing with other people, and outdoor space. Sheltered work and recreational facilities need not be in the same building but should be within walking distance.

Partial hospital care

The first day hospital opened in Moscow in 1933 because of a shortage of hospital beds. The first formal programmes of day care were introduced in North America and Britain soon after the Second World War. Since then, there has been a rapid expansion of various forms of partial hospital care. Day hospitals were originally intended to provide acute care for those who did not need to be in-patients. Now they are used in many ways (see Katz 1985; *Lancet* 1987*b*). They vary in selection of patients and in the range of treatments provided. Some day hospitals accept mainly patients with disorders requiring treatment of an intensity midway between out-patient and in-patient care; for example, depressive disorders of moderate severity. Others are more concerned with the care of patients handicapped by chronic illness, particularly schizophrenia, many of whom attend regularly for long periods of a year or more (Gath *et al.* 1973).

Day care may be provided in a separate area within an in-patient unit, or in a different building within the same hospital, or on the community either in a purpose-built mental health centre or a converted house. The first of these arrangements—day care within an in-patient unit—has the advantage of continuity of care for patients who progress to day-patient care after an in-patient admission. [See Rosie (1987) for a review of partial hospitalization.]

Community care

'Community care' is now one of the most widely used terms in psychiatry, but there is little agreement about its precise meaning. The term has been applied to two distinct approaches to treatment. One is concerned with the treatment of major psychiatric disorder outside the hospital, whilst the other is concerned with the treatment and primary prevention of less severe psychiatric disorder which in the past would not have been managed by the psychiatric services. The two contrasting approaches are well illustrated by the development of community care in the United Kingdom and in the United States. Both approaches have principles in common: responsibility for a defined population; provision of treatment close to the patient's home; continuity of care; comprehensive services; and a multi-disciplinary team approach.

Developments in the United Kingdom illustrate the first alternative. Community care was originally developed to reduce the need for long-term hospital care for major psychiatric disorders. Nowadays, however, it provides for a wider group of patients. The main principles are:

(1) primary care for psychiatric disorder is provided by general practitioners and their teams;

(2) comprehensive specialist psychiatric services are provided within a defined area;

(3) psychiatric units offer treatment for acute illness, and facilities for those requiring long-term asylum;

(4) specialist psychiatric services are co-ordinated with those provided by general practitioners, local authority social services, and other organizations including voluntary groups and private nursing homes.

These general principles can be implemented in different ways, depending upon the resources and needs of local communities. They have been recommended to other European nations by the World Health Organization (1980).

In contrast, in the United States the main emphasis has been on a new system of community care which is separate from the original hospital-based system. This approach stemmed from an enthusiasm after the Second World War for crisis intervention and the possibility of primary prevention. The Federal Government established the Joint Commission on Mental Illness and Health which published a report in 1961 strongly criticizing the State hospital system. The Commission recommended that most treatment should be in the community, and that mental health centres should be set up for catchment areas throughout the country. Community Mental Health Centers (CMHC) were subsequently set up by Federal legislation. They have staff from several disciplines, and offer psychological and social care. They vary in aims and organization, but their main emphasis has usually been an acute intervention for psychosocial problems, rather than on care for chronic psychiatric disorders. Recently, however, the centres have provided more care for the severely ill and the elderly. The best form of organization for the centres is still controversial, and many local innovations have been tried (see Talbott 1985; Mechanic and Aiken 1987). Many psychiatrists in the United States have been dissatisfied with their limited role in the centres.

Most national programmes of community care have encountered problems of poor working relationships between different disciplines, professional isolation of individuals, and the difficulty of providing good training and supervision for staff. The most serious criticism of these national programmes is that they fail to provide adequate help for severely mentally ill patients and their families.

The effects of a rapid change to community care for psychiatric patients was recently shown in Italy. In 1978, the Italian Parliament passed Law 180, the aims of which were to dismantle the mental hospitals and replace them by a comprehensive system of community care. The scheme was based on the work of Franco Basaglia in hospitals in north-east Italy, and on the proposals of the professional and political movement he founded, *Psichiatria Democratica*. Law 180 prohibited admission to mental hospitals and required the establishment of psychiatric units in general hospitals and of community services in catchment areas. The consequences of this sudden change have been controversial. It is clear that in many areas the provision of new facilities has been inadequate. On the other hand, in places where the reforms have been properly implemented with good facilities in the general hospital and community, and with enthusiastic staff, the new provision has proved adequate for the whole range of psychiatric problems in the local population (see Tansella and Williams 1987).

Many other countries have found that a community-based service cannot be achieved by merely closing mental hospitals. There needs to be a gradual change to a well-planned, adaptable, and carefully maintained alternative system. The new provision can take many forms but countries with well-developed system of primary care are at a considerable advantage.

Rehabilitation

During the nineteenth century many mental hospitals experimented with occupational treatments, most of which were eventually discontinued. In the years after the First World War progressive hospitals made renewed efforts to help their patients to lead more active lives both in hospital and after discharge. After the Second World War, industrial and occupational therapies were used widely to help chronically disabled patients in the move from hospital to ordinary homes or sheltered accommodation (see Bennett 1983). At that time, most long-stay patients were suffering from handicaps that were largely due to years of institutional living, and were therefore responsive to vigorous new methods. In modern psychiatric hospitals, where the social environment is much improved, the disabilities of chronic patients are more often due to illness than to institutionalization, and therefore pose more difficult problems in rehabilitation.

Rehabilitation means all measures involved in helping handicapped people to attain their best level of social functioning, which for some people means a fully independent life, and for others (those with severe impairments) life-long support. Good rehabilitation requires skilled assessment of each patient's potential, a wide range of treatment methods, and continuity of care (see Watts and Bennett 1983; Anthony and Liberman 1986).

Planning rehabilitation

Rehabilitation must be tailored to the needs of the individual. It is essential to assess systematically each patient's assets and deficits (Wing and Morris 1981):

(1) persistent symptoms, both positive (such as hallucinations) and negative (such as lack of drive);

(2) unusual behaviour, especially if likely to be socially disapproved, for example, shouting obscenities;

(3) activities of daily living, such as the capacity to wash and dress;

(4) occupational or domestic skills, such as shopping and cooking;

(5) personal attitudes and expectations;

(6) social circumstances to which the patient is likely to return.

It may be helpful to supplement clinical evaluation with the use of standardized rating scales. At the end of the assessment, a rehabilitation plan is drawn up. There should be clear short-term and long-term aims, and the plan should specify: the order in which disabilities will be attended to; a 'key worker' to undertake the continuing care of the patient; the responsibilities of other members of the clinical team; the methods and facilities to be used, including the role of psychotropic medication; and ways of encouraging the patient to take part, and of rewarding him for doing so.

Treatment

Various treatment methods are required for any rehabilitation programme. These methods can be divided broadly into psychological, occupational, social, and residential. They are partly described later in this chapter, and partly in the chapter on psychological treatment. Care can be provided in a mental hospital, day hospital, or special rehabilitation centre. For patients resident in hospital, there are advantages in working away from the hospital and thus having a more normal pattern of daily activity.

Psychological methods Psychological methods range from individual supportive therapy to ward-based behavioural programmes including token economies (Hall 1983), and out-patient behavioural programmes including social skills training (Liberman *et al.* 1986).

Occupational methods This kind of rehabilitation confers several benefits. It can prepare patients for simple industrial work (Carstairs *et al.* 1956; Wing *et al.* 1964). It can also help to give some structure to the day, and to provide an opportunity for collaboration with other people. Payment for work can be an incentive, and good results can be a source of self-esteem. In recent years, as unemployment has increased among healthy people, the chances of employment for the handicapped have fallen. It is therefore less appropriate to direct rehabilitation mainly towards employment in normal industry. Instead activities such as gardening, crafts, home repairs, and cooking can provide a sense of achievement and prepare for constructive use of leisure time, with less risk of eventual failure.

Social methods Although handicapped people should be encouraged whenever possible to join social groups used by healthy people, some need special clubs and social centres where they can be with other people who have similar difficulties in coping with the demands of normal life.

Residential care As early as the thirteenth century, at Gheel in Belgium, arrangements were made for mentally disordered people to stay with local families. Nowadays the practice of boarding out works well in many parts of Europe and the United States, but it has not been widely adopted in Britain (Olsen 1979*a,b*).

In Britain, much residential care has been in hostels. In the 1950s the first hostels for psychiatric patients were intended to be half-way houses from which patients would soon move to more independent living.

However, experience quickly showed that many residents could not leave the half-way houses, which thus became long-term hostels (see Wing and Hailey 1972). This change should not be seen as a failure, since long-term hostels undoubtedly serve a useful purpose. For example, in a study of hostel residents, Hewett and Ryan (1975) found that half had remained in the hostel over two years and had reached a plateau in recovery; nevertheless most were working and had little behavioural impairment.

Most hostel residents can live fairly independent lives but a few severely disabled people require much additional care. This care may be provided in a more intensely staffed hostel either on a hospital site or elsewhere (Wyke 1982; Wing and Furlong 1986). This kind of hostel can provide the necessary care in a domestic setting, with provisions for day time occupation and for leisure hours.

Organization   Rehabilitation is usually provided by general psychiatrists but there is a need for psychiatrists with special expertise and responsibility for the development and management of rehabilitation services. Good working relationships are required to make the best use of the skills of staff from different disciplines and it is essential that there is a clearly identified 'key worker' for each patient.

Evaluation of psychiatric services

All services should be monitored routinely, and the effectiveness of the individual components of the service should be evaluated by research. There have been two main approaches: (a) studies of the utilization of services within defined populations; and (b) comparative trials in which patients are randomly allocated to different kinds of treatment, for instance, day hospital or in-patient care, or treatment by a doctor, social worker, or community psychiatric nurse.

Research on utilization of services

The most accurate answers can be obtained by the use of a case register, as shown by a series of reports describing the services in Camberwell, south London (Wing and Hailey 1972; Wing 1982). In areas without a register, much useful information on the efficacy of services can be obtained by a combination of good record keeping and simple operational research. Wing and Hailey (1972) suggested that an area service should be assessed by asking six basic questions:

1. How many patients are in contact with the service?

2. What are their needs and those of the relatives?

3. Are the services at present meeting these needs?

4. How many others, not in contact with the service, also have needs?

5. What new services, or modifications to existing services, are required to cater for unmet needs?

6. Having introduced them, are the needs met?

Other British examples of this approach are given in accounts of the development of a community-based service in north London (Leff 1986) and of a district general hospital-based service in north-west England (Goldberg 1986).

Comparative trials

Comparative trials of different types of care are time-consuming and difficult to carry out. As in any clinical trial patients must be selected appropriately and allocated to treatments randomly, the alternative treatments must be specified clearly, and the measures of outcome must be dependable. Some trials have shown that various kinds of day care can be as effective as in-patient care in the treatment of acute disorders, without imposing excessive burdens on families. Other trials have shown that, for acute disorders, brief in-patient care followed by day care or support at home can be as effective as more prolonged in-patient care, (see Braun *et al.* 1981). The most comprehensive studies (Stein and Test 1980; Hoult 1986) compared hospital admission with community care in the management of psychiatric problems from defined populations; the main finding was that community care was no more expensive, appeared to have clinical advantages, and was preferred by patients and families.

From these findings Mosher (1983) held that research 'comparing non-hospital with in-hospital treatment has found the former to be as good as or better than the latter, and usually cheaper'. Others believe this conclusion to be unfounded and maintain that there are patients for whom hospital admission is preferable (see Tantam 1985). They argue that all controlled evaluations have omitted the most seriously disturbed patients, have failed to compare community care with the best possible hospital alternative, and have ignored the consistent finding that there are always some patients initially treated in the community who eventually require admission. These critics also argue that it is unrealistic to expect to provide good community care by skilled therapists in every health district.

Evidence about the relative cost-effectiveness of community care and hospital care is difficult to interpret, and no final conclusions can be drawn (see Wilkinson and Pelosi 1987 for a review).

Controversy about the effectiveness of community as opposed to hospital care is unfortunate. It suggests that the two kinds of care are exclusive alternatives, but it is better to regard them as complementing one another in a system of care. Good domiciliary and local services can be effective and are often more acceptable to patients, but there are circumstances in which hospital admission can be more beneficial to acute and chronic patients (see p. 748 and p. 749).

The provision of psychiatric services in the United Kingdom

In the United Kingdom specialist services are divided into health authority and local authority services. Health authorities provide facilities for in-patients, day-patients, and out-patients. Local authorities provide day activities, and residential accommodation such as hostels and group homes. Each of these facilities will be discussed in turn. Although the general principles apply to all developed countries, there are many differences of detail in the ways in which provisions are made in different countries.

Service needs are conveniently expressed in relation to a notional population of 100 000. Estimates of service needs for England and Wales were set out in the Government White Paper 'Better services for the mentally ill' (Department of Health and Social Security 1975). These are summarized in Table 19.1. In interpreting these estimates, it should be borne in mind, that in the United Kingdom general practitioners make a major contribution to psychiatric care.

The estimated requirement for beds in a district general hospital psychitric unit was 50 per 100 000 population. Most of these beds would be for patients with acute disorders or exacerbations of chronic disorders, but this figure also includes accommodation for elderly people with functional illnesses. A further 30–40 beds per 100 000 are required for the 'elderly severely mentally infirm', most of whom are demented. A third category of patients requiring hospital accommodation is the 'new' long-stay patients who have begun to accumulate in long-stay wards in recent years, despite advances in community care. The number of hospital beds required for such patients was left undecided in this planning document; it depends in part on the provision of supervised hostel places in the community.

A more recent memorandum (Department of Health and Social Security 1985) contains more flexible extimates. The estimate for acute beds in a District General Hospital is now 35–50 per 100 000, depending upon local

Table 19.1. Summary of guidelines for services at district level. Rates per 100 000 population

	Facility	Beds	Day places
Hospital services	District general hospital psychiatric unit	50	65
	Accommodation for the elderly severely mental infirm	30–40	25–40
	Units for the 'new' long-stay	*	
Local authority services	Hostels	4–6	
	Long-stay accommodation	15–24	
	Day centres		60

* Still to be determined.
From 'Better services for the mentally ill'. Department of Health and Social Security (1975).

circumstances. There is no estimate of beds required for long-stay hospital patients, because it is recognized that the number depends upon the extent and pattern of community facilities. [See Hirsch (1987) for a review of the planning of beds and other resources in acute psychiatry.]

Hospital services

The Department of Health and Social Security has recommended that beds for acute cases should be provided on a District General Hospital site but in a separate block with its own 'external space' and entrance, and with accommodation on only the ground and first floor levels. In many areas, however, there are no general hospital units and psychiatry continues to be practised in old mental hospitals. It is still possible for the smaller of these hospitals to modernize their buildings and create a satisfactory environment. The Department of Health and Social Security recommends that at least one hospital in each catchment area should act as administrative base for the service. Out-patient clinics should be available at the District General Hospital and in other places easily accessible to patients.

Day hospital services have been discussed on p. 749.

Sometimes the requirements for a specialist service do not justify separate provision for each hospital district. It is then appropriate for a regional service to provide specialist in-patient or out-patient services for a larger populaton. Such regional units may be suitable for adolescents, drug-dependent patients, and potentially violent patients requiring secure accommodation.

Psychiatric services within the community

In Great Britain the policy is to develop out-patient, day-hospital, and crisis intervention services in local communities. There are various ways in which this can be done, but all require close collaboration with general practitioners, social services, and voluntary organizations.

Liaison with primary care services

An increasing number of psychiatrists spend some of their time working in primary care (Mitchell 1985). Surveys of psychiatrists and general practitioners have shown three main ways of working (Strathdee 1987). In the first, the psychiatrist replaces the general practitioner as the doctor of first contact ('replacement model'). This approach is unsuitable for the British system of general practice, in which the GP is invariably the doctor of first contact. In the second way of working, the psychiatrist holds an out-patient clinic in a general practitioner health centre ('increased throughput model'). The problem of this arrangement is that communication between the visiting psychiatrist and the general practice is not always good. In the third approach, the psychiatrist collaborates with the general practitioner in the hospital of patients ('liaison' model). This makes for good communication and allows the general practitioner to increase his psychiatric skills [see Shepherd *et al.* (1986) for reviews].

Community psychiatric nurses

In the 1950s and 1960s psychiatric nurses pioneered many developments in community care, particularly for chronic patients. A community psychiatric nursing service is now an essential part of a community psychiatric service. Some community psychiatric nurses work with general practitioners, and assist in the care of other disorders as well as the chronic. There have been few evaluations of the work of these nurses but it appears that they can manage major and minor psychiatric disorders effectively (Paykel *et al.* 1985). There is concern, however, that increasing involvement of community psychiatric nurses in treating patients with minor psychiatric disorders, may reduce the services for patients with major disorders (Wooff *et al.* 1986).

Residential accommodation

In a comprehensive service it is important to provide sheltered accommodation, both short-term and long-term, for mentally disordered people. Such accommodation is needed for patients who are well enough to live outside hospital but too handicapped to live on their own or with their families.

There are two kinds of hostel: short-stay hostels, sometimes known as half-way houses, which are intended for rehabilitation; and long-stay hostels for people who are unlikely to improve further (see Ryan 1979). As shown in Table 19.1, the Department of Health and Social Security recommends that, for a population of 100 000, there should be 4–6 short-stay places and 15–24 long-stay places.

The intensity of supervision varies in different kinds of residential accommodation. In the hostels just described, there may be supervision by visiting medical and nursing staff, and by a resident warden. For patients needing more supervision, more highly staffed 'hostel wards' are being developed within or close to hospitals. In these hostel wards, severely handicapped patients are encouraged to learn to care for themselves, with close supervision. It is hoped that this will enable patients to graduate to an ordinary staffed hostel, but it is not yet possible to judge the effectiveness of these arrangements (see Wing and Furlong 1986; Hyde *et al.* 1987).

Group homes provide accommodation for patients who need little supervision. They are particularly suitable for chronic schizophrenics who have become independent of the hospital but cannot live on their own or with their families. Group homes are ordinary houses in residential areas. Five or six patients live together, sharing domestic tasks according to their abilities. Community nurses visit regularly, but as much responsibility as possible is left to the residents. Success depends on discreet supervision and careful selection of patients who are to live closely together.

Local authority services

Local authorities are expected to provide services complementing those provided by the Health Service. There are three main types of service:

1. Social work.

2. Day care, including occupational therapy, sheltered workshops, day centres, and social clubs.

3. Residential care, including residential homes, hostels, and other sheltered housing.

Of these only day centres need to be discussed further.

Day centres

These complement day hospitals, but have more restricted aims. Instead of providing psychiatric treatment, they offer company for the lonely, occupation for the handicapped, and meals for people who have difficulty in shopping or cooking. Their staff is non-medical. As shown in Table

19.1, the Department of Health and Social Security recommends a provision of 60 day-centre places for a population of 100 000.

Services in developing countries

In developing countries, the prevalence and nature of psychiatric disorders is broadly similar to that in developed countries, but there is more psychiatric morbidity associated with untreated or inadequately treated physical illness. There are also differences in the presentation of illnesses. Specialist psychiatric resources are minimal in many of these countries and it is neither possible nor appropriate to establish all the psychiatric provisions which are available in the developed world. It is essential to identify priorities and make the maximum use of local facilities including, in some places, traditional healers.

The World Health Organization (1984) has identified four priorities: psychiatric emergencies; chronic major psychiatric illness; psychiatric problems associated with general medical care; and specific high risk groups (such as alcohol and drug abuse). The WHO have stressed the need for national, regional and local policies to provide care and training, largely via auxiliary workers, with little emphasis on the use of hospitals. Experience suggests that simple training in the management of emergencies and the use of a limited range of psychotropic drugs for major mental illness can be highly effective. Improved management of psychiatric problems seen in general medical care can also have substantial benefits.

Further reading

Jones, K. (1972). *A history of the mental health services.* Routledge and Kegan Paul, London.

Watts, F. N. and Bennett, D. H. (1983). *Theory and practice of psychiatric rehabilitation.* John Wiley, Chichester.

Wilkinson, G. and Freeman, H. (eds.) (1986). *The provision of mental health services in Britain: the way ahead.* Gaskell, London.

Wing, J. K. (ed.)(1982). *Long term community care:* experience in a London Borough. *Psychological Medicine Supplement* No. 2.

20 Child psychiatry

The practice of child psychiatry differs from that of adult psychiatry in several important ways. It is seldom that the child initiates the consultation with the clinician. Instead he is brought by adults—usually the parents—who think that some aspect of behaviour or development is abnormal. Much depends on the attitudes and tolerance of these adults, and how they perceive the child's behaviour. Healthy children may be brought to the doctor by over-anxious and solicitous parents or teachers, whilst in other circumstances severely disturbed children may be left to themselves. A related factor is that psychiatric problems in a child may be a manifestation of disturbance in other members of his family.

Another difference from adult psychiatry is that, in deciding what is normal and what is abnormal, greater attention must be paid to the stage of development of the patient and the duration of the disorder. For example repeated bed-wetting would be regarded as normal in a 3-year-old child but abnormal in a child aged 7.

The practice of child psychiatry differs from adult psychiatry in two other ways. First, children are generally less able to express themselves in words. Evidence of disturbance is therefore based more on observations of behaviour made by parents, teachers, and others. The assessment of these accounts requires skills in taking a developmental history, assessing behaviour, evaluating the emotional involvement of informants, and understanding the home and school background. Second, in the treatment of children less use is made of medication or other methods of individual treatment than in adult psychiatry. Instead the main emphasis is on changing the attitudes of parents, reassuring and retraining the child, and co-ordinating the efforts of others who can help him especially at school.

The first part of this chapter is concerned with a number of general issues concerning psychiatric disorder in childhood including its frequency, causes, assessment, and management. The second part of the chapter contains information about the principal syndromes encountered in the practice of child psychiatry. The chapter does not provide a comprehensive account of child psychiatry. It is an introduction to the main themes for the psychiatrist who is starting his specialist general training. It is expected that he will follow it by reading a specialist text such as the textbooks by Graham (1986) or one of those listed in the further reading at the end of the chapter. In this book, childhood mental retardation is dealt with in Chapter 21. This is a convenient arrangement but the reader should remember that many aspects of the study and care of mentally retarded children are closely related to child psychiatry.

Normal development

The practice of child psychiatry calls for knowledge of the normal process of development from a helpless infant into an independent adult. In order to judge whether any observed emotional, social, or intellectual functioning is abnormal, it has to be compared with the corresponding normal range for the age group. This section provides a summary of the main aspects of development that concern the psychiatrist. A textbook of paediatrics should be consulted for details of these developmental phases (for example, Illingworth 1980). A useful review of psychological and social development has been provided by Rutter (1980).

The first year of life

This is a period of rapid development of motor and social functioning. Three weeks after birth, the baby smiles at faces; selective smiling appears by six months, fear of strangers by eight months, and anxiety on separation from the mother shortly after.

Bowlby (1980) has emphasized the importance in the early years of life of a general process of **attachment** of the infant to the parents and of more selective emotional **bonding**. Although bonding to the mother is most significant, important attachments are also made to the father and other people who are close to the infant. Recent research has stressed the reciprocal nature of this process and the probable importance of the very early contacts between mother and new-born infant in initiating bonding (Rutter 1980).

By the end of the first year, the child should have formed a close and secure relationship with the mother. There should be an ordered pattern of sleeping and feeding; and weaning has usually been accomplished. The child has begun to learn about objects outside himself, simple causal relationships, and spatial relationships. By the end of the first year, the child enjoys making sounds and may say 'mama', 'dada', and perhaps one or two other words.

Year two

This is also a period of rapid development. The child begins to wish to please the parents, and appears anxious when they disapprove. He begins to learn to control his behaviour. By now, attachment behaviour should be well established. Temper tantrums occur, particularly if exploratory wishes are frustrated. These do not last long, and should lessen as the child learns to accept constraints. By the end of the second year he should be able to put two or three words together as a simple sentence.

Pre-school years (2 to 5 years)

This phase brings a rapid increase in intellectual abilities, especially in the complexity of language. Social development occurs as the child learns to live within the family. He begins to identify with the parents and to adopt their standards in matters of conscience. Social life develops rapidly as he learns to interact with siblings, other children, and adults. Temper tantrums continue, but diminish and should disappear before the child starts school. At this age, the child has much curiosity about the environment, and may ask a great number of questions.

In children aged 2 to 5, fantasy life is rich and vivid. It can form a temporary substitute for the real world, enabling desires to be fulfilled regardless of reality. Special objects such as teddy bears or pieces of blanket become important to the child. They appear to comfort and reassure the child, and help sleep. They have been called 'transitional objects'.

The child begins to learn about his own sexual identity. He realizes the differences between males and females in their appearance, clothes, behaviour, and anatomy. Sexual play and exploration are common at this stage.

According to psychodynamic theory, at this stage defence mechanisms develop to enable the child to cope with anxiety arising from unacceptable emotions. These defence mechanisms have been described on p. 34. They include repression, rationalization, compensation, and displacement.

Middle childhood (5 to 10 years)

By the age of 5, the child should understand his or her identity as boy or girl, and his position in the family. He has to learn to cope with school, and to read, write, and acquire numerical concepts. The teacher becomes an important person in the child's life. At this stage, the child gradually learns what he can achieve and what are his limitations. Defence mechanisms, conscience, and standards of social behaviour develop further. According to psychoanalytic theory, this is a period in which psychosexual development is quiescent (the latent period). This notion has been questioned [see, for example, Rutter (1971)] and it now seems that in the 5- to 10-year-old period sexual interest and activities are present, although they may be concealed from adults.

Adolescence

Adolescence is the growing-up period between childhood and maturity. Among the most obvious features are the physical changes of puberty. The age at which these changes occur is quite variable, usually between 11 and 13 in girls, and 13 and 17 in boys. The production of sex hormones precedes these changes, starting in both sexes between the ages of 8 and 10. Adolescence is a time of increased awareness of personal identity and individual characteristics. At this age, young people become self-aware, are concerned to know who they are, and begin to consider where they want to go in life. They can look ahead, consider alternatives for the future, and feel hope and despair. It is popularly but wrongly believed that emotional turmoil and alienation from the family are characteristic of adolescence (see p. 818).

Peer group relationships are important and close friendships often develop, especially amongst girls. Membership of a group is common, and this can help the adolescent in moving towards autonomy. Adolescence brings a marked increase in heterosexual interest and activity. At first, tentative approaches are made to the opposite sex. Gradually these become more direct and confident. In late adolescence, there is a capacity for affection towards the opposite sex, as well as sexual feelings. How far and in what way sexual feelings are expressed depends greatly on the standards of society and on rules in the family.

The classification of psychiatric disorders in children and adolescents

Both DSMIIIR and the draft of ICD10 contain a scheme for classifying the psychiatric disorders of childhood. Disorders of adolescence are classified partly with this scheme, and partly with the categories used in adult psychiatry.

Seven main groups of childhood psychiatric disorders are generally recognized by clinicians, and are supported by studies using multivariate analysis (see Quay and Werry 1986). Listed below are the terms used in this book for the seven groups, with some alternatives in brackets:

(1) Adjustment reactions;

(2) Pervasive developmental disorders (psychoses of childhood);

(3) Specific developmental disorders;

(4) Conduct (antisocial, or externalizing) disorders;

(5) Hyperkinetic (attention-deficit) disorders;

(6) Emotional (neurotic, or internalizing) disorders;

(7) Symptomatic disorders.

Many child psychiatric disorders cannot be classified in a satisfactory way by allocating them to a single category. Therefore multiaxial systems have been proposed. A widely adopted system has axes for: (i) clinical psychiatric syndromes; (ii) specific delays in development; (iii) intellectual level; (iv) medical conditions; and (v) abnormal social situations. [Further information is given by Rutter and Gould (1985).] This scheme is easy to use, and allows clinicians to record systematically the different kinds of information required in categorizing children's problems.

The DSMIIIR and ICD10 (draft) classifications for child psychiatric disorders are shown in Table 20.1. Both schemes are complicated, so only the main categories are shown in the table. (The first category in each scheme—mental retardation—refers to conditions described in Chapter 21). Both systems have categories for pervasive developmental disorders and specific developmental disorders, with the latter divided into disorders affecting speech and language, academic (or scholastic) skills, and motor skills. Both systems have categories for disorders of behaviour, which are divided into conduct disorder, attention-deficit (hyperkinetic) disorder, and (in DSMIIIR only) oppositional-defiant disorder. Both systems have a category for anxiety (emotional) disorder. DSMIIIR has separate categories for eating, elimination, and tic disorders. ICD10 (draft) has a separate category only for tic disorders; it classifies eating and elimination disorders (as well as sleep disorders, stuttering, and the form of rapid, often unintelligible speech known as cluttering) under 'other behavioural and emotional disorders'. [For further information about classification in child psychiatry, see Rutter and Gould (1985); Cantwell (1985).]

Epidemiology

Behavioural and emotional disorders occur frequently in the general population of children. Estimates vary according to the diagnostic criteria and other methods used, but it appears that rates in the developed countries are similar (Graham 1986). The limited evidence suggests that rates of emotional and behavioural disorders in developing countries are quite similar to those in developed ones. (There are, or course, particular

Table 20.1. Classification of childhood psychiatric disorders

DSMIIIR	ICD10 (draft)†
*Mental retardation**	*Mental retardation*
*Pervasive developmental disorders**	*Pervasive developmental disorders*
*Specific developmental disorders**	*Specific development disorders*
Language and speech disorder	Of speech and language
Academic skills disorders	Of scholastic skills
Motor skills disorder	Of motor function
Other developmental disorder	Mixed and other
Disruptive behaviour disorders	*Behavioural and emotional disorders with onset usually in childhood and adolescence*
Conduct disorder	*Conduct disorder*
Attention deficit–hyperactivity	*Hyperkinetic disorder*
Oppositional-defiant disorder	
Anxiety disorders of childhood and adolescence	*Emotional disorder* *Mixed disorder of conduct and emotion*
Eating disorders	—
Gender identity disorder	
Tic disorders	*Tic disorders*
Elimination disorders	*Other behavioural and emotional disorders (includes eating disorders)*
Other disorders of infancy and childhood and adolescence	

* Coded on Axis 2
† The order of entries has been altered somewhat to facilitate comparison with DSMIIIR

problems in comparing the prevalences of learning difficulties.) In Britain, the prevalence of child psychiatric disorder in ethnic minority groups has usually been found to be similar to that in the rest of the population. The exception is a high prevalence of conduct disorder found among West Indian girls (Rutter *et al.* 1974).

The frequency of psychiatric conditions varies with age. Richman *et al.*

(1982) reported that 7 per cent of 3-year-olds had symptoms amounting to a moderate or severe problem, and a further 15 per cent had mild problems such as disobedience. In the middle years of childhood, rates of psychiatric disorder vary in different kinds of areas, being twice as high in urban areas (about 25 per cent) than in rural areas (about 12 per cent) (Rutter *et al.* 1975*b*).

Evidence about mid-adolescence was provided by a four-year follow-up of the Isle of Wight Study described below (Rutter *et al.* 1976*a*). At the age of fourteen, the one-year prevalence rate of significant psychiatric disorder was about 20 per cent. Similar findings have been reported from other countries. Less is known about prevalence among older adolescents, but the rates are probably similar to those in mid-adolescence.

The most detailed findings come from a study of physical health, intelligence, education, and psychological difficulties in all the 10- and 11-year-olds attending state schools in the Isle of Wight—a total of 2199 children (Rutter *et al.* 1970*a*). Screening questionnaires were completed by parents and teachers. Children identified in this way were given psychological and educational tests and their parents were interviewed. The one-year prevalence rate of psychiatric disorder was about 7 per cent, the rate in boys being twice that in girls. There was no correlation with social class, but prevalence increased as intelligence decreased. Psychiatric disorder was associated with physical handicap and especially with evidence of organic brain damage. There was also a strong association between reading retardation and conduct disorder. Several years later the same methods were used to survey an inner London borough (Rutter *et al.* 1975*b,c*). It was found that the rates of all types of disorder were twice those in the Isle of Wight.

Referral to specialists

General practitioners spend much of their time advising and reassuring parents about their children, but only a small proportion of these consultations lead to referral to paediatric or child psychiatry clinics (Bailey *et al.* 1978). General practitioners are more likely to refer to a paediatrician developmental difficulties, physical symptoms with a probable psychological cause, and psychological complications of physical illness. Emotional and conduct disorders are more likely to be referred to a child psychiatry clinic. However, many of the cases referred are no more severe than those which the general practitioner deals with himself (see Gath *et al.* 1977).

Prognosis

Mild symptoms and behavioural or developmental problems are usually brief. However this is not so for the symptoms severe enough to be diagnosed as a childhood psychiatric disorder, which occur in 5–15 per cent of children. These conditions often persist for several years. Thus in the Isle of Wight Study three-quarters of children with conduct disorder and half of those with emotional disorders at age 10, were still handicapped by these problems four years later (Rutter *et al.* 1976*a*).

The prognosis for adult life can be established only by long follow-up, which is difficult to arrange. The outstanding study is that of Robins (1966) who followed people who had attended a child guidance clinic 30 years previously, and compared them with a control group who had attended the same schools but had not been referred to the clinic. She found that emotional disorders had a good prognosis. When these disorders did continue they usually took the form, in the adult, of neurosis or depression. By contrast, children with conduct disorder had a poor outcome. As adults they were likely to develop antisocial personality disorder or alcoholism, have problems with employment or marriage, or commit offences. More recent research has confirmed that the outcomes of neurotic and conduct disorders are very different. It has also shown that definite overactivity syndromes have a poor prognosis and psychoses a worse one (see Robins 1979*a*; Zeitlin 1986). Zeitlin examined the records of patients who had attended the same hospital for psychiatric treatment both as children and as adults. He found considerable continuity in the types of symptoms reported, especially when the original problems were depressive or obsessive symptoms or conduct disorders.

Aetiology

In discussing the causes of child psychiatric disorders, much the same principles apply as those described in the earlier chapter on the aetiology of adult disorders. In child psychiatry, there are fewer disease entities and more reactions to environmental factors, notably those in the family, school, and neighbourhood. Even more than in adult life, the determinants of childhood disturbance are usually multiple. In the following paragraphs four interacting groups of factors will be considered briefly. These are: inheritance; temperament; physical impairment, with special reference to brain damage; and environmental, family, social, and cultural causes. Aetiology is reviewed in the textbooks edited by Rutter and Hersov (1985), Quay and Werry (1986), and Graham (1986).

Inheritance

The hereditary factors of importance in child psychiatry are polygenic. They do not seem to control the disorders directly but rather the predisposition to develop some kinds of disorder. There are also wider influences acting through polygenic control of intelligence and temperament—though the evidence for this is less strong (McGuffin 1987).

Temperament and individual differences

In a longitudinal study in New York, Thomas *et al.* (1968) found that certain temperamental factors detected before the age of 2 might predispose to later psychiatric disorder. In the first two years, one group of children ('difficult children') tended to respond to new environmental stimuli by withdrawal, slow adaptation, and an intense behavioural response. Another group ('easy children') responded to new stimuli with positive approach, rapid adaptation, and a mild behavioural response. This group was less likely than the first to develop behavioural disorders later in childhood. The investigators thought that these early temperamental differences were determined both genetically and by enviromental factors. The validity of the methods in this study, and the significance of the findings, have been questioned (see Graham and Stevenson 1987).

Physical disease

Although serious physical disease of any kind can predispose to psychological problems in childhood, brain disorders are the most important. In the Isle of Wight Study about 12 per cent of physically ill children aged 10-11 years were classified as having psychiatric problems compared with about 7 per cent in the general population of the same age (Rutter *et al.* 1976*a*). The prevalence of psychiatric problems was 34 per cent in children with brain disorders. This high prevalence could not be explained by the adverse social factors known to be associated with the risk of brain disorder. Nor is it likely to have been due to physical disability as such because rates of psychiatric disorder are less in children equally disabled by muscular disorders. The rate of psychiatric disorder among children with brain damage is related to the severity of the damage, though not closely to the site. It is as common among brain-injured girls as boys, a finding which contrasts with the higher rate of psychiatric disorder among boys in the general population.

Minimal brain dysfunction

The observation that major brain damage in children can cause definite psychiatric disorder led to the hypothesis that smaller amounts of damage could account for otherwise unexplained disorders. This idea has a long history but recent ideas date from the studies of brain-injured children by Strauss and Lehtinen (1947), who described a variety of clinical features including over-activity, inattention, disordered conduct, and deficits in perception and learning. Later writers assumed that in children without neurological signs, over-activity and inattention resulted from minor brain pathology, which was referred to as minimal brain damage. When it became accepted that there were usually no demonstrable structural changes in the brain, the name minimal brain dysfunction was used.

Pasamanick and Knobloch (1966) suggested that there is 'a continuum of reproductive casualty'. By this they meant that reading disability, behaviour disorders, epilepsy, and mental handicap, might result from increasing degrees of brain disorder resulting from abnormalities of pregnancy or childbirth. These ideas were based in part on the observation that histories of abnormal pregnancy, prematurity, and asphyxia at birth are common among children attending psychiatrists (Pasamanick and Knobloch 1966). Such evidence is difficult to interpret because these factors are related to social disadvantage which might be the real cause of any psychiatric problems. The balance of evidence does not support the idea that minimal brain disorder is the cause of childhood psychiatric disorders [see Rutter (1982) and Shaffer (1985b) for reviews.]

Environmental factors

Family

As a child progresses from complete dependence on others to independence, he needs a stable and secure family background, with a consistent pattern of emotional warmth, acceptance, help, and constructive discipline. Prolonged separation from or loss of parents can have a profound effect on psychological development in infancy and childhood. Poor relationships in the family may have similar adverse effects.

The well-known work of Bowlby (1951) led to widespread concern with the effects of 'maternal deprivation'. Bowlby originally suggested that prolonged separation from the mother was a major cause of juvenile delinquency. Subsequently he argued that the early experience or threat of separation from the mother is associated with anxiety or depression in later years (Bowlby 1973, 1980). Since the original formulation of the consequences of maternal deprivation, it has become apparent that the effect of separation depends on many factors. These include: the age of the child at the time of separation, his previous relationship with his mother and father, and the reasons for the separation. It is also apparent that the various consequences of parental deprivation have different long-term effects. An unstimulating environment and lack of encouragement to learn in infancy is associated with educational underachievement in later years. Poor emotional attachments in early life may result in difficulties in social relationships.

The family factors most strongly associated with psychiatric disorder in the child include: discordant relationships, the illness or personality deviance of a parent, and large family size. Patterns of child rearing are not clearly related to psychiatric disturbance in the child except where they involve child abuse (see Rutter and Madge 1976).

Social and cultural factors

Although the family is undoubtedly the part of the child's enviroment with most effect on his development, wider social influences are important as well, particularly in the aetiology of conduct disorder. In the early years of childhood these social factors act indirectly through their influence on the patterns of family life. As the child grows older and spends more time outside the family, they have a direct effect as well. These factors have been studied by examining the associations between psychiatric disorder and type of neighbourhood and school.

Rates of childhood psychiatric disorder are higher in areas of social disadvantage. For example, as already noted (p. 767) the rates of both emotional and conduct disorder were found to be higher in a poor inner London borough than in the Isle of Wight. The important features of inner city life may be lack of play space, inadequate social amenities for teenagers, overcrowded living conditions, and lack of community involvement. Rates of child psychiatric referral and delinquency also vary between schools (Power *et al.* 1972; Gath *et al.* 1977). These differences do not seem to be due to the size of the school or the age of its buildings but rather to its social enviroment.

Psychiatric assessment of children and their families

The aims of assessment are to obtain a clear account of the presenting problem; to find out how this problem is related to the child's past development and his present life in its psychological and social context; and to plan treatment for the child and family.

The psychiatric assessment of children differs in several ways from that of adults. With children, it is often difficult to follow a set routine: a flexible approach to interviewing is required, though it is still important that information and observations are recorded systematically. Both parents should be asked to attend the assessment interview, and it is often helpful to have other siblings present. Time can be saved by asking permission to obtain information from teachers before the child attends the clinic. This information should be concerned with the child's behaviour in school and his educational attainments.

Child psychiatrists vary in their methods of assessment. All agree that it is important to see the family together at some stage. Some prefer to do this from the start. Others feel they can make a better assessment by first interviewing the parents and child separately, and then proceeding to a joint interview at which family interactions can be observed. If separate interviews are used, it may be advisable to start by seeing the adolescent patient on his own before seeing the parents. In the case of younger children the main informants are usually the parents, but children over the age of 6 should usually be seen on their own at some stage. In the special case of suspected child abuse, the interview with the child is, of course, particularly important. Whatever the problem, the parents should be made to feel that the interview is supportive and does not undermine their confidence.

Interviewing the parents

Parents should be encouraged to talk spontaneously before systematic questions are asked. The methods of interviewing are similar to those used in adult psychiatry (see Chapter 2). The items to be included in the history are listed in the scheme described by Graham (1986) which appears in the appendix to this chapter. Apart from factual information, the psychiatrist has to find out about feelings and attitudes.

The child

Because younger children may not be able or willing to express ideas and feelings in words, observations of their behaviour and interaction with the interviewer are especially important; with very young children, drawing and the use of toys may be helpful. With older children, it may be possible to follow a procedure similar to that used with adults.

It is essential to begin by establishing a friendly atmosphere and winning the child's confidence. It is appropriate to ask the child what he likes to be called. It is usually better to begin with a discussion of neutral topics such as pets, games, or birthdays before turning to the presenting problem. When a friendly relationship has been established, the child can be asked about the problem, his likes and dislikes, and his hopes for the future. It is often informative to ask what he would request if given three wishes. He may also be given the opportunity to express his concerns and feelings in paintings or play.

Observations of the child's behaviour and mental state should be recorded. The items to be included are listed in the appendix to this chapter (p. 823). When assessing the mental state it should be remembered that children who are seeing a psychiatrist for the first time may be silent and withdrawn; this behaviour should not be misinterpreted as evidence of depression. At some stage, preferably late in the consultation, a physical examination is usually performed, with particular attention to the central nervous system (see appendix). By the end of the interview an assessment should have been made of the child's development relative to other children of his age.

Ending the assessment

At the end of the assessment the psychiatrist should explain to the parents (and the child, depending on age) how he plans to proceed and whether he will be contacting other people involved, such as the general practitioner, teacher, or social worker. He should give clear information about any proposed treatment, and should encourage questions and discussion.

Psychological assessment

Measures of intelligence and educational achievement are often useful. Some of the more commonly used procedures are listed in Table 20.2. Some psychologists also use one or more of the many projective techniques. These are difficult to score and their validity has not been established. However, they sometimes provide a useful way of discovering the child's feelings about the members of his family and about other matters. Used in this way, they resemble clinical methods (for example, asking the child to make up a story) rather than psychological tests.

Other information

The most important additional informants are the child's teachers. They can describe his classroom behaviour, educational achievements, and relationships with other children. They may also make useful comments about the family and home circumstances. It is often helpful for a social worker to visit the home. This can provide useful information about material circumstances in the home, the relationship of family members, and the pattern of their life together.

Formulation

A formulation should be made in every case. This starts with a brief statement of the current problem. The diagnosis and differential diagnosis are discussed next. Aetiological factors are then considered. Any further assessment should be specified, a treatment plan drawn up, and the expected outcome recorded.

Table 20.2. Notes on some psychological measures in use with children and the mentally retarded

---

(a) Intelligence tests

Stanford–Binet intelligence scale	A revision of the original intelligence test; now seldom used. Provides mental age. Weighted to verbal abilities and this may result in cultural bias. More useful for middle-class patients and for low ability.
Wechsler intelligence scale for children—revised form (WISC-R)	Provides a profile of specific verbal and performance ability as well as IQ for children aged 6–14 years. Widely used and well standardized. Cannot be used for IQ below 40.
Wechsler pre-school and primary scale of intelligence (WPPSI)	A version of WISC for use with younger children (4–6.5 years) and with the mentally retarded.
British ability scales	Twenty-four sub-scales suitable for 2.5–17 years, and covering six areas: speed of information processing, reasoning, spatial imagery, perceptual matching, short-term memory, retrieval and application of knowledge. Analysis can be general or specific.
Goodenough–Harris drawing test	A brief test of non-verbal intelligence for children aged 3–10 years.

(b) Social development assessments

Vineland social maturity scale	The original development scale recently revised, which has psychometric limitations. Covers general self-help, self-help in dressing, self-help in eating, locomotion, communication, self-direction, social isolation, and occupation. Provides 'Social Age'.

Adaptive behaviour scales (Nihira)	Rating scales to evaluate abilities and habits in ten behavioural areas.
Gunzburg progress assessment charts	Provides a clear visual display of self-help, communication, social and occupational abilities.

(c) Other developmental assessment

Denver development scale	Assessments of gross and fine motor, language, and social development used for children up to two years of age.
Bayley scales of infant development	Range of items which can be scored on mental and psychomotor development indices. Comprehensive and reliable for ages two months to two and a half years.

(d) Educational attainment

Neale analysis of reading	Graded test of reading ability, accuracy, comprehension, and rate for age six upwards.
Schonell graded word reading test	The child reads words of increasing difficulty.
Schonell graded word spelling test	The child spells words of increasing difficulty.
Tests of mathematical ability	No satisfactory test. Arithmetic subtests of WISC-R, WPPSI and British ability scales.

Treatment

Although the members of the treatment team (doctor, social worker, and psychologist) have special skills, they do not confine themselves to their traditional professional roles when they work with children and families. Instead they take whatever part seems most likely to be helpful in the particular case. Child psychiatrists vary in their preferred method of working, including the use of co-therapy with other members of the team.

It is usual to adopt a family approach, and to maintain close liaison with other agencies involved with the child or his family. The child psychiatrist works closely with paediatricians, the child health and social services, teachers, and educational psychologists. Since many childhood problems are obvious at school or lead to educational difficulties, the child's teachers usually need to be involved in treatment. Teachers may require advice about the best way to manage behavioural disturbance; remedial teaching may be required; or some other change may be needed in the child's school timetable. Occasionally a change of school is indicated.

In the following sections, brief general descriptions are given of the main kinds of treatment. In the second part of the chapter further information is given about the management of individual disorders. Further information about treatment in child psychiatry can be obtained from Graham (1986) or one of the textbooks listed at the end of this chapter.

Drug treatment

Drugs have a limited but important place in child psychiatry. The main indications, which are discussed later in this chapter, are epilepsy, depressive disorders, obsessional disorders, over-activity syndromes, Gilles de la Tourette's syndrome, and occasionally nocturnal enuresis. In all cases dosages should be checked carefully in a standard reference book, paying attention to allowances required for the child's age and body weight.

Individual psychotherapy with the child

This originated in the separate methods developed by Anna Freud and Melanie Klein. These methods differed especially in the emphasis placed by the latter on the psychodynamic interpretation of the child's play. Nowadays lengthy intensive treatment of this kind is not used commonly. Instead most pychotherapy with children is brief and aims to help with current problems. The principal indications are emotional disorders and physical complaints related to important psychological factors.

The psychotherapist tries to make a warm and accepting relationship with the child. He uses this relationship to encourage the child to express feelings and to find alternative ways of behaving. Acceptance is important and criticism should be avoided, although this does not, of course, imply approval of every aspect of the child's behaviour. At first, the child often perceives the psychotherapist as an agent of his parents and expects him to share their attitudes. For this reason, it is advisable to delay discussion of the presenting problems until the child's confidence has been gained by talking about neutral things that interest him.

There have been few evaluations of individual psychotherapy for children. Psychotherapy is generally used for disorders with a good prognosis, and may shorten their course. Evaluations of child psychotherapy have been reported by Eisenberg *et al.* (1965), and Rosenthal and Levine (1971).

Family therapy

This is a specific form of treatment which should be distinguished from the general family approach to treatment described above. In family therapy the child's symptoms are considered as an expression of the functioning of the family, which is the primary focus of treatment. Several approaches have been used, based on behavioural or psychoanalytical systems, or communication or structural theories. These kinds of therapy are described on p. 711. In practice, most therapists adopt an eclectic approach.

The indications for family therapy are still debated. Such treatment may be appropriate when:

(1) the child's symptoms appear to be part of a disturbance of the whole family;

(2) individual therapy is not proving effective;

(3) family difficulties arise during another kind of treatment.

Family therapy may be contraindicated when the parents' marriage is breaking up, or the child's problems do not seem closely related to family function. It is important that a therapist's interest in family therapy should not prevent a thorough evaluation of the case and the use of other treatments when indicated. Uncontrolled studies of family therapy have led to claims that it has substantial effects. Controlled evaluations suggest more modest benefits for children with a wide range of emotional and behavioural disorders. Research on family therapy has been reviewed by Gurman *et al* (1986).

Group therapy

Group therapy can be used for the child or the parents. Older children and adolescents may be helped by the sharing of problems, discussions, and modelling that from part of group therapy. Parents may be helped by the opportunity to discuss shared problems of child management or other difficulties. The principles of group therapy are described in Chapter 18.

Behaviour therapy

Behavioural methods have several applications in child psychiatry. They can be used to encourage new behaviour by positive reinforcement and modelling. This is often done by first rewarding behaviour that approximates to the desired behaviour (shaping), before reinforcement in a more discriminating way. Thus with autistic and retarded children, shaping has been used for minor behaviour problems such as temper tantrums and refusal to go to bed, and for problems in toilet training. Punishment is not used in shaping because it is ethically unacceptable (and has only temporary effects). Instead efforts are made to identify and remove any factors in the child's environment that are reinforcing unwanted behaviour. It is often found that undesired behaviour is reinforced unwittingly by extra attention given to the child when the behaviour occurs. If the child is ignored at such times and attended to when his behaviour is more normal, beneficial changes often take place. More specific forms of behaviour therapy can be used for enuresis (see p. 733), or phobias. The principles resemble those which apply in adult psychiatry (see Chapter 18).

Social skills training in a group or in individual sessions is often used for children who have difficulty in relationships with other children or adults.

Occupational therapy

Occupational therapists can play a large part in assessment of the child's development, and in psychological treatment and measures to improve parent–child interaction.

Special education

Children attending as out-patients, as well as the smaller number who are day- or in-patients, often benefit from additional educational arrangements. Special teaching may be needed to remedy backwardness in writing, reading, and arithmetic which is common among children with conduct disorders.

Substitute care including fostering

This can be valuable for children whose symptoms result from a severely unstable home environment, or extreme parental rejection. The children considered for residential placement often have conduct disorders and severe educational problems. Removal from home should be considered only after every practical effort has been made to improve the circumstances of the family. Residential care can be arranged in a foster home, a children's home (in which a group of about ten children live in circumstances as close as possible to those of a large family), or a boarding school.

Hospital units

Admission to an in-patient unit is usually arranged for any of three reasons. First, the behaviour disorder may be too severe to treat in any other way: examples include severe hyperactivity, childhood psychosis, and school refusal resistant to out-patient treatment. Second, the child may be admitted for observation when the diagnosis is uncertain. Third, in-patient treatment is one way of providing a period away from a disturbing home enviroment, for example when there is gross over-protection.

Sometimes the mother is admitted as well as the child. This allows close observation of the way in which she responds to the child, for example in cases of child abuse. Once the nature of the problem is clear, the mother can be helped to overcome it by taking an increasing part in the child's care while both remain in hospital.

Day hospital treatment for children provides many of the advantages of in-patient care without removing the child from home. Unless there is any danger that the child may be abused, remaining at home has the advantage that relationships with other family members are maintained. Day care can also relieve the family from some of the stressful effects of managing an overactive or autistic child.

Review of syndromes

Problems of pre-school children and their families

It has been noted already that in the pre-school years children are learning several kinds of social behaviour. They are acquiring sphincter control. They are learning how to behave at mealtimes, to go to bed at an appropriate time, and to control angry feelings. They are also becoming less dependent. All these things are being learnt within the family. The psychiatric problems of pre-school children centre round these behaviours and they often reflect factors in the family as well as factors in the child. Many psychological problems at this age are brief, and can be thought of as delays in normal development. Most of these problems are treated by general practitioners and paediatricians. The more serious ones may be referred to child psychiatrists.

Prevalence

Richman *et al.* (1982) studied a sample of 705 families with a 3-year-old in a London borough. The most frequent abnormal behaviour items in these 3-year-olds were: bed-wetting at least three times a week (present in 37 per cent); wetting by day at least once a week (17 per cent); overactivity (14 per cent); soiling at least once a week (13 per cent); difficulty in settling at night (13 per cent); fears (13 per cent); disobedience (11 per cent); attention-seeking (10 per cent); and temper tantrums (5 per cent).

Whether these behaviours are reported as problems depends on the attitudes of the parents as well as on the nature, severity, and frequency of the behaviour. Richman *et al.* (1982) overcame this difficulty by making their own ratings of the extent of the problem. They based this assessment on the effects on the child's well-being and the consequences for the other members of the family. They used common-sense criteria to decide whether the problems were mild, moderate, or severe. Seven per cent of the 3-year-olds in their survey had behaviour problems of marked severity and 15 per cent had mild problems. The behaviours most often rated as problems were temper tantrums, attention-seeking, and disobedience.

Prognosis

As explained above, many psychological problems of pre-school children are brief. However, Richman *et al.* (1982) found that certain problems detected in 3-year-old children were still present at the age of 8; these problems included over-activity, conduct disorder, speech difficulty, effeminacy, and autism.

Aetiology

Aetiological factors are related to the stage of development, the child's temperament, and influences in the family. There are wide individual variations in the rate at which normal development proceeds, particularly in sphincter control and language acquisition. As noted above (p. 769) a child's temperamental characteristics are evident from the earliest weeks. These are capable of affecting the mother's response—how much time she spends with him, how often she picks him up, and so on. These maternal responses may in turn affect the child's development. Behaviour problems at this age are also associated with poor marital relationships, maternal depression, rivalry with siblings, and inadequate parental behaviour. [See Richman *et al.* (1982) for a review of the evidence.]

Some common problems

Temper tantrums

In toddlers occasional temper tantrums are normal, and only persistent or very severe tantrums are abnormal. The immediate cause is often unwitting reinforcement by excessive attention and inconsistent discipline on the part of the parents. When this arises it is often because the parents have emotional problems of their own or their relationship is unsatisfactory. Temper tantrums usually respond to kindly but firm and consistent setting of limits. In treatment it is first necessary to discover why the parents have been unable to set limits in this way. They should be helped with any problem of their own and also advised how to respond to the tantrums.

Sleep problems

The commonest sleep difficulty is wakefulness at night which is most frequent between the age of one and two years. About a fifth of children of this age take at least an hour to get to sleep or are wakeful for long periods during the night. Management depends on a detailed assessment of the problem and any other difficulties. When wakefulness is an isolated problem and not over-distressing to the family, it is enough to reassure parents about the prognosis. However, if treatment is needed because the sleep problem is seriously exhausting or distressing to the family, the most effective approach is behavioural (Richman *et al.* 1985). Hypnotic medication may be useful for special occasions but is unlikely to be effective in the long term. The handbook by Douglas and Richman (1984) is useful for parents.

Other difficulties such as nightmares, and night terrors are quite common among healthy toddlers but they seldom persist for long. They are discussed on p. 403.

When sleep disturbances are severe or persistent, two possible causes should be considered. First, the problems may have been made worse by physical or emotional disorders. Second, they may have been exacerbated by the parents' over-concern or inability to provide reassurance. If either of these causes is found, it should be treated. Otherwise it is usually sufficient to reassure the parents and the child.

Feeding problems

Minor food fads or food refusal are common in pre-school children, but do not usually last long. In a minority, the behaviour is severe or persistent, although not accompanied by signs of poor nourishment. When this happens it is often because the parents are over-attentive and obsessional, and unwittingly reinforce the child's behaviour. Treatment is directed to the parents' management of the problem. They should be encouraged to ignore the feeding problem and refrain from offering the child special foods or otherwise attempting to do anything unusual to persuade him to eat. Instead he should be offered a normal meal and left to decide whether to eat it or not.

Pica

This is the eating of items generally regarded as inedible, for example, soil, paint, and paper. Is it often associated with other behaviour problems. Cases should be investigated carefully because some are due to brain damage and mental retardation. Some are associated with emotional distress, which should be reduced if possible. Otherwise, treatment consists of common-sense precautions to keep the child away from the abnormal items of diet. Pica usually diminishes as the child grows older.

Assessment and treatment

In assessing problems in pre-school children, the psychiatrist usually has to rely largely on information from the parents. As noted already, it is important to distinguish between a primary disorder in the child, and one that reflects the difficulties of the mother or the entire family. It is necessary to make a careful assessment of the particular behaviour, the child's general level of development and the functioning of the family as a whole.

Apart from particular points noted already under the specific disorders, treatment includes counselling for the mother—and sometimes other family members as well—and advice about child-rearing. Little is known about the value of specific treatments. Behavioural methods are probably useful; language delays may benefit from educational measures; and occasionally medication is required to control extreme over-activity (see p. 796). It is often helpful to arrange for the child to spend part of the day away from the family in a playgroup or nursery school.

Emotional disorders

The diagnosis of emotional (neurotic, or internalizing) disorder is widely used in child psychiatry, where it has much the same meaning as neurotic disorder in adult psychiatry. The DSMIIIR and ICD10 (draft) classifications of these disorders are shown in Table 20.3. In each classification there are categories for separation anxiety and for phobic avoidance. DSMIIIR has a category (over-anxious disorder) for children who worry excessively. ICD10 (draft) has categories for children who are excessively wary of strangers or novel situations, and for those with persistent

Table 20.3. Classification of emotional disorders in childhood

ICD10 (draft)	DSMIIIR
Separation anxiety disorder	Separation anxiety disorder
Phobic disorder of childhood	Avoidant disorder of childhood
Social sensitivity disorder	Overanxious disorder
Sibling rivalry disorder	
Other emotional disorder	

emotional disturbance apparently related to rivalry or jealousy of an immediately younger sibling.

In addition to these categories, the following section refers to other childhood emotional disorders, namely dissociative and conversion disorders, obsessive-compulsive disorder, and depressive disorder. School refusal is also considered in this section.

Prevalence

Amongst childhood psychiatric disorders, emotional disorders are second in frequency only to conduct disorders. In their survey of 10-and-11-year-old children on the Isle of Wight, Rutter *et al.* (1970*a*) found a prevalence of 2.5 per cent in both boys and girls. This was about half the rate for conduct disorders. In their community survey of an Inner London borough, the prevalence rate was twice as high for both conditions (Rutter *et al* 1975*b*). In a survey of over 1000 children referred to a child psychiatric clinic in south-east London, one third were diagnosed as having emotional disorders (Gath *et al.* 1977).

The prognosis of most forms of emotional disorder is favourable. Even severe disorders usually improve without treatment leaving no residual symptoms. The exceptions are obsessive-compulsive disorders and depressive disorders, which more often have an unfavourable outcome. As noted already (p. 768), when childhood emotional disorder does persist into adult life, it is usually as a neurotic syndrome or an affective disorder.

Anxiety disorder

Children with this disorder are abnormally fearful. They cling to their parents, on whom they are over-dependent. They are timid with other children. They often have disturbed sleep with frequent nighmares. They may concentrate badly. Various bodily symptoms may be experienced, notably headaches and symptoms related to the alimentary system such as nausea, vomiting, abdominal pain, and bowel disturbance. Phobias and obsessional symptoms also occur.

Sometimes a separation anxiety disorder is precipitated by a frightening experience. This may be brief, such as admission to hospital, or prolonged (for example, conflict between the parents). In some cases it occurs in children who tend to react with excessive anxiety to everyday stressors, and are presumed to have an anxiety-prone temperament, possibly for genetic reasons. In other cases the child's anxiety is a response to chronically anxious or over-protective parents.

Children with separation anxiety disorders cling to their parents and demand attention. They may worry that an accident or illness may befall their parents. This kind of anxiety disorder is one cause of school refusal (see p. 787).

Children with over-anxious disorders worry excessively about stressful events such as examinations, or about taking part in activities with other children. They may have other anxiety symptoms including phobias, panic attacks, and somatic symptoms.

In treatment, account should always be taken of a range of possible aetiological factors, including stressful events, separation, and anxiety-prone temperament. Stressors should be reduced if possible, the child should be helped to talk about his worries, and where appropriate the family should be helped to understand how their own anxiety or over-protection effect the child. Anxiolytic drugs can help to relieve severe anxiety but they should be used for short periods only. When anxiety symptoms are worse in particular circumstances, the patient may benefit from the simple behavioural techniques used for phobias as described in the next section.

Phobic disorders

Minor phobic symptoms are common in childhood. They usually concern animals, insects, the dark, school, and death. The prevalence of more severe phobias varies with age. Severe and persistent fears of animals usually begin before the age of five, and nearly all have declined by the early teenage years. Some children fear social situations especially when they have to meet people they do not know well. In DSMIIIR this condition is called **avoidant disorder**. These children shy away from meeting strangers, and are embarrassed in company, blushing and remaining silent.

Most childhood phobias improve without specific treatment provided the parents adopt a firm and reassuring approach. For phobias that do not improve, simple behavioural treatment can be combined with reassurance and support. The child is encouraged to encounter feared situations in a graded way, as in the treatment of phobias in adult life. Psychotherapy has also been used but is not obviously more effective than simple behavioural treatment. A full account of childhood phobias can be found in Johnson (1985).

Somatization disorders

Children often complain of somatic symptoms when they are suffering from a psychiatric disorder. These complaints include abdominal pain, headache, cough, and limb pains. Most of these children are treated by family doctors. The minority referred to specialists are more likely to be sent to paediatricians than to child psychiatrists.

Of the symptoms, abdominal pain has been studied most thoroughly. Its estimated prevalence varies between 4 and 17 per cent of all children. It is a common reason for paediatric referral. In most cases, the pain is associated with headache, limb pains, and sickness (Apley and Hale 1973). Physical causes for the abdominal pain are seldom found and psychological ones are often suspected. Some abdominal pains are related to anxiety and, as discussed on p. 454, others have been ascribed to 'masked' depressive disorders. Others appear to be a direct symptomatic response to stressful events. Treatment is similar to that for other emotional disorders. Follow-up suggests that a quarter of cases severe enough to require investigation by a paediatrician develop chronic psychiatric problems.

Conversion disorder is more common in adolescence than in childhood, both as an individual illness and in its epidemic form (see p. 202). In childhood, symptoms are usually mild and seldom last long. The most frequent symptoms include paralyses, abnormalities of gait, and inability to see or hear normally. As in adults, such symptoms can occur in the course of organic illness as well as in an emotional disorder. Also as in adult psychiatry, physical symptoms are sometimes misdiagnosed as conversion disorder. For these reasons, the diagnosis of conversion disorder should be made only after the most careful search for organic disease.

Conversion disorder was encountered rarely in the Isle of Wight study of children in the community (Rutter *et al.* 1970*a*). Among children referred to paediatricians it has been reported in 3–13 per cent (see Rae 1977). In a survey of prepubertal children, Caplan (1970) found that conversion disorder was diagnosed in about 2 per cent of those referred to the Maudsley Hospital. In almost half of this 2 per cent, organic illness was eventually detected either near the time or during the four to eleven years' follow-up. Amblyopia was the symptom of organic disorder most likely to be misdiagnosed as psychogenic. As in adults, physical illness was more likely to be misdiagnosed as conversion disorder when physical signs were absent and an obvious emotional upset coincided with the onset of symptoms (Rivinus *et al.* 1975).

Conversion and other somatization disorders should be treated as early as possible. Delay may allow symptoms to become entrenched as secondary gains accumulate. Treatment is directed mainly to reducing any stressful circumstances and to encouraging the child to talk about the problem. Symptoms may subside with these measures, or may need management comparable to that used for conversion disorder in adults (see p. 212). See Goodyear and Taylor (1985) for further information about somatization disorders in childhood. Physiotherapy and behavioural methods may be valuable for motor symptoms (Dubowitz and Hersov 1976).

Obsessive-compulsive disorders

Obsessive-compulsive disorders are rare in childhood. However several forms of repetitive behaviour are common, particularly between the ages of four and ten. These repetitive behaviours include preoccupation with numbers and counting, the repeated handling of certain objects, and hoarding. Much of this behaviour cannot strictly be called compulsive, because the child does not struggle against it (see p. 22 for the definition of obsessional and compulsive symptoms). However, it is not certain how crucial this distinction is in childhood. It is also common for children to adopt rituals, such as avoiding cracks in the pavement or touching lamp-posts. Many children's games contain elements of shared ritual, and some of these brief solitary rituals also seem to be part of normal development. However, in some children rituals take up an increasing amount of the child's time—for example, re-checking school work many times or repeated hand-washing.

When severe and persistent obsessional thoughts or compulsive symptoms occur in childhood, they are often part of an anxiety or depressive disorder. True obsessional disorder is less common, and seldom appears in full form before late childhood, though the first symptoms may appear in early childhood. Onset may be acute or insidious. Obsessional children often involve their parents by asking them to take part in the rituals or give repeated reassurance about the obsessional thoughts.

Clinical observations suggest that less severe forms of the disorder have a generally good outcome, but severe forms have a poor prognosis. There is no satisfactory follow-up investigation of obsessional children, but adults with obsessional disorders often date the onset of their symptoms to childhood or adolescence.

When obsessional symptoms occur as part of an anxiety or depressive disorder, treatment is directed to the primary disorder. True obsessional disorders of later childhood are treated along similar lines to an anxiety disorder with the addition of behavioural methods (see p. 201). Clomipramine (see p. 201) may be effective in some cases. For a review of obsessional disorders in childhood, see Rapoport (1986).

Depressive disorders

Many children appear miserable in distressing circumstances, such as the serious illness of a parent, the death of a family member, or parental disharmony. Some of these children are tearful and lose interest and concentration. They may eat and sleep badly. Although such depressive symptoms are common in middle and late childhood, depressive disorders are infrequent. Thus Rutter *et al.* (1970*a*) found depressive disorders in only three of the girls and none of the boys among 2000 10-to-11-year-olds—though depressive symptoms were common as part of other disorders. Among 2303 14-year-olds, 35 had a depressive disorder (Rutter *et al.* 1976*a*). More recent estimates give somewhat higher figures: 1 per cent of children in middle childhood, and 2–5 per cent in mid-adolescence (see Graham 1986).

Some of the variation in estimates reflects differences in diagnostic criteria. Thus some psychiatrists maintain that depressive disorders are common in childhood on the grounds that such disorders present in a masked form with little or no depressed mood but with a wide variety of other symptoms including unexplained abdominal pains, headache, anorexia, and enuresis.

It is not unreasonable to suggest that in childhood, as in adult life, depressive disorders can come to light because of associated physical or behavioural symptoms. However, in children, as in adult life, the diagnosis of depressive disorder should be made only when there is clear evidence of the principal features of the syndrome (Kovacs and Beck 1977). Depressed mood is particularly important even though it may not be obvious at first. Depressive disorder should be distinguished clearly from depressive symptoms occurring as a component of an emotional or conduct disorder. Bipolar disorder does not occur before puberty.

Depressive disorders in childhood are treated by reducing distressing circumstances, and helping the child to talk about his feelings. Antidepressant drugs have been used to treat depressive symptoms in childhood but as yet no satisfactory clinical trial has been carried out. In general, these drugs should be reserved for older children with definite symptoms of a severe depressive disorder. For reviews of childhood depressive disorder see Ambrosini and Puig-Antich (1985) or Rutter *et al.* (1986).

School refusal

There are many causes of repeated absence from school. Physical illness is the commonest. A few children are deliberately kept at home by parents to help with domestic work or for company. Some are truants who could go to school but choose not to, often as a form of rebellion. An important group stay away from school because they are anxious or miserable when there. These are the school-refusers. The important distinction between truancy and school refusal was first made by Broadwin in 1932. Later, Hersov (1960) studied 50 school-refusers and 50 truants, all referred to a child psychiatric clinic. Compared with the truants, the school-refusers came from more neurotic families, were more depressed, passive, and overprotected, and had better records of school work and behaviour.

Prevalence

Temporary absences from school are extremely common but the prevalence of school refusal is uncertain. In the Isle of Wight school refusal was reported in rather less than 3 per cent of 10- and 11-year-olds with psychiatric disorder (Rutter *et al.* 1970*a*). It is commonest at three periods of school life, between 5 and 7 years, at 11 years with the change of school, and, especially at 14 years and older.

Clinical picture

At times, the first sign to the parents that something is wrong is the child's sudden and complete refusal to attend school. More often there is an increasing reluctance to set out, with signs of unhappiness and anxiety when it it time to go. Children complain of somatic symptoms of anxiety such as headache, abdominal pain, diarrhoea, sickness, or vague complaints of feeling ill. These complaints occur on school days but not at other times. Some children appear to want to go to school but become increasingly distressed as they get nearer to it. The final refusal can arise in several ways. It may follow a period of gradually increasing difficulty of the kind just described. It may appear after an enforced absence for another reason, such as a respiratory tract infection. It may follow an event at school such as a change of class. It may occur when there is a problem in the family such as the illness of a grandparent to whom the child is attached. Whatever the final sequence of events, the child is extremely resistant to efforts to return him to school and his evident distress makes it hard for the parents to insist that he goes.

Aetiology

Several causes have been suggested. Johnson *et al.* (1941) emphasized the general role of separation anxiety, a mechanism also stressed by Eisenberg (1958). More recent observations suggest that separation anxiety is particularly important in younger children. In older children there may be a true school phobia, that is a fear of certain aspects of school life, including travel to school, bullying by other children, or failure to do well in class. Other children have no specific fears but feel inadequate and depressed.

Prognosis

Clinical experience suggests that most younger children eventually return to school. However, a proportion of the most severely affected adolescents do not return before the end of the time for compulsory school attendance. There have been a few studies of the longer prognosis. Berg and Jackson (1985) followed up 168 teenage school-refusers who had been treated as in-patients. Ten years later, about a half still suffered from emotional or social difficulties or had received further psychiatric care. This study was concerned with severe cases and the general prognosis may be rather better.

Treatment

Except in the most severe cases, arrangements should be made for an early return to school. They should be discussed with the schoolteachers, who should be given advice about any difficulties that are likely to be encountered. It is often more satisfactory for someone other than the mother—for example, a social worker—to accompany the child to school at first. In a few cases a more elaborate graded behavioural plan is necessary. In the most severe cases admission to hospital may be required to reduce anxiety before a return to school can be arranged. Occasionally a change of school is appropriate.

In older children, any depressive disorder should be treated. It has been reported that antidepressants are effective for school refusal even when there is no depressive disorder, but this view is not generally accepted. In all cases, the child should be encouraged to talk about his feelings, and the parents given support. See Hersov and Berg (1980) and Berg (1984); for reviews of school refusal.

Conduct disorders

Conduct disorders, sometimes called externalizing disorders are character-ized by severe and persistent antisocial behaviour. They form the largest single group of psychiatric disorders in older children and adolescents. The prevalence of conduct disorders is difficult to estimate because the dividing line between them and normal rebelliousness is arbitrary. Rutter *et al.* (1970*a*) found the prevalence of 'antisocial disorder' to be about 3 per cent on the Isle of Wight; in a subsequent study in London about twice this rate was found (Rutter *et al.* 1976*b*). In a study of over 1000 children referred to a child guidance clinic in south-east London (a sample which excluded children referred for a court report) Gath *et al.* (1977) reported that conduct disorders made up one-third of the sample. Studies in the community, in psychiatric practice, and in the juvenile courts, all indicate that conduct disorders are more common in boys than girls (Rutter *et al.* 1970*a*; Gath *et al.* 1977).

Because conduct disorders vary widely in their clinical features, attempts have been made to classify them. One of the earliest classifications was into socialized, unsocialized, and over-inhibited groups (Hewett and Jenkins 1946). In DSMIIIR, conduct disorders are divided into: disorders of a group type, in which the behaviour occurs mainly as a group activity with peers; and conduct disorders of a solitary aggressive type, in which the behaviour is mainly aggressive and not carried out as a group activity. DSMIIIR also has a separate category, 'oppositional-defiant disorder', in which defiant, hostile, and negativistic behaviour begins at home but sometimes extends to other situations later. ICD10 (draft) has three corresponding subdivisions into socialized conduct disorder, unsocialized conduct disorder, and conduct disorders confined to the family context.

Clinical features

The essential feature is persistent abnormal conduct which is more serious than ordinary childish mischief. In the pre-school period the disorder usually manifests as aggressive behaviour in the house, often with over-activity. In later childhood it is usually first evident in the home as stealing, lying, and disobedience, together with verbal or physical aggression. Later, the disturbance is often evident outside the home as well, especially at school, as truanting, delinquency, vandalism, and poor school work, as well as reckless behaviour or alcohol and drug abuse.

In children above the age of seven years persistent stealing is abnormal. Below that age, children seldom have a real appreciation of other people's property. Many children steal occasionally, so that minor or isolated instances need not to be taken seriously. A small proportion of children present with sexual behaviour that incurs the disapproval of adults. In younger children, masturbation and sexual curiosity may be frequent and obtrusive. In adolescent girls, promiscuity is a particular problem. Although fire-setting is rare, it is obviously dangerous (see p. 888).

Aetiology

Conduct disorders are found commonly in children from unstable, inse-cure, and rejecting families living in deprived areas. Antisocial behaviour is frequent amongst children from broken homes, those from homes in which family relationships are poor and those who have been in residential care in their early childhood. Conduct disorders are also related to adverse factors in the wider social environment of the neighbourhood and school (Power *et al.* 1972; Rutter *et al.* 1975*c*; Gath *et al.* 1977).

As well as these environmental causes, certain factors in the child may predispose to conduct disorder. Adoption studies suggest that genetic factors may play a part in the aetiology of aggressive behaviour (Hutchings and Mednick 1974). Temperamentally difficult babies are more likely than easy babies to show behaviour problems in later childhood (see Graham and Stevenson 1987).

Children with brain-damage and epilepsy are prone to conduct disorder, as they are to other psychiatric disorders. An important finding in the Isle of Wight survey was a strong association between antisocial behaviour and specific reading retardation (see p. 802). It is not known whether antisocial behaviour and reading retardation result from common predisposing factors, or whether one causes the other. [See Rutter and Giller (1983) for a review of the aetiology of conduct disorder.]

Prognosis

Conduct disorders usually run a prolonged course in childhood (Rutter *et al.* 1976*b*). The long-term outcome varies considerably with the nature and extent of the disorder. Among people who had attended a child guidance clinic for conduct disorder in adolescence Robins (1966) found that almost half had some form of antisocial behaviour in adult life, and no cases of sociopathic disorder were found in adult life among those with diagnoses other than conduct disorder in adolescence. There are no good indicators of the long-term outcome of individual cases. The best available predictors seem to be the extent of the childhood antisocial behaviour and the quality of relationships with other people (Robins 1978). There is no convincing evidence that treatment affects the long-term outlook. However it is unfortunate that awareness of a poor long-term prognosis often leads to half-hearted attention to the immediate problems. It is reasonable to believe that in many cases immediate distress can be reduced. Moreover in some cases it is possible to modify adverse social and family factors and thereby improve the long-term outlook.

Treatment

Mild conduct disorders often subside without treatment other than common-sense advice to the parents. For more severe disorders, treatment is mainly directed to the family. It usually takes the form of social case-work or family therapy. Some families are difficult to help, especially where there is material deprivation, chaotic relationships, and poorly educated parents. A simple form of behaviour therapy is sometimes used, in which desirable behaviour is rewarded while undesirable behaviour is not reinforced. Group therapy, in which peer pressures are utilized, is sometimes helpful. If there are associated reading difficulties remedial teaching should be arranged. Medication is of little value.

The treatment of **truancy** requires separate consideration. A direct and energetic approach is called for. Pressure should be brought to bear upon the child to return to school, and if possible, support from the family should be enlisted. If other steps fail, court proceedings may need to be initiated. At the same time, an attempt should be made to resolve any educational or other problems at school. In all this it is essential to maintain good communications between clinician, parents, and teachers.

Occasionally residential placement may be necessary in a foster home, group home, or special school. This should be done only for compelling reasons. There is no evidence that institutional care improves the prognosis for conduct disorder.

Juvenile delinquency

Delinquency is not a psychiatric diagnosis but a legal category. However, juvenile delinquency may be associated with psychiatric disorder, especially conduct disorder. For this reason it is appropriate to interrupt this review of the syndromes of child psychiatry to consider juvenile delinquency. The majority of adolescent boys when asked to report their own behaviour, admit to offences against the law, and a fifth are convicted at some time (West and Farrington 1973); most of the offences are trivial. Amongst boys who are convicted only a half are reconvicted. Few continue to offend in adult life. Many more boys than girls are delinquent and the peak age of contact with the police is 15–16 years. In considering these figures it has to be remembered that crime statistics may be misleading. Nevertheless there seems to be substantial similarity in the characteristics of self-reported offenders and of convicted offenders (West and Farrington 1973).

Delinquency is often equated with conduct disorder. This is wrong, for although the two categories overlap, they are not the same. Many delinquents do not have conduct disorders or any other psychological disorder. Equally, many of those with conduct disorder do not offend. Nevertheless in an important group, persistent law-breaking is frequently preceded and accompanied by abnormalities of conduct, such as truancy, aggressiveness, attention-seeking, and by poor concentration.

Aetiology

The aetiology of juvenile delinquency overlaps with that of conduct disorder. However, somewhat greater emphasis must necessarily be given to social explanations since delinquency is defined by the provisions of the law and by the way it is operated. [For an extended review see Rutter and Giller (1983).]

Social factors

Delinquency is related to low social class, poverty, poor housing, and poor education. There are marked differences in delinquency rates between adjacent neighbourhoods which differ in these respects. Rates also differ between schools. Many social theories have been put forward to explain the origins of crime but none offers a completely adequate explanation.

Family factors

Many studies have found that crime runs in families. For example, about half of boys with criminal fathers are convicted, as compared with a fifth of those with fathers who are not criminals (see West and Farrington 1977). The reasons for this are poorly understood. They may include poor parenting and shared attitudes to the law.

Bowlby (1944) examined the characteristics of 'juvenile thieves' and argued that prolonged separation from the mother during childhood was a major cause of their problems. More recent work has not confirmed such a precise link (see p. 770). Although delinquency is particularly common among those who come from broken homes, this seems to be largely because separation often reflects family discord in early and mid-childhood (see Rutter and Madge 1976). Other family factors correlated with delinquency are large family size and child-rearing practices.

Factors in the child

Genetic factors appear to be of only minor importance in the aetiology of delinquency. They are certainly less significant than in the more serious criminal behaviour of adult life (see p. 865). The association of genetic factors with conduct disorder has been noted already. There are also important relationships between delinquency and slightly below average IQ as well as educational and reading difficulties (Rutter *et al.* 1976*b*). As noted above, there are at least two possible explanations for the latter finding. Temperament or social factors may predispose to both delinquency and the reading failure. Alternatively it is possible that reading difficulties result in frustration and loss of self-esteem at school and that these predispose to antisocial behaviour.

Physical abnormalities probably play only a minor role among the causes of delinquency even though brain-damage and epilepsy predispose to conduct disorder.

Assessment

When the child is seen as part of an ordinary referral and his delinquency is related to a psychiatric syndrome, the latter should be assessed in the usual way. Sometimes the child psychiatrist is asked to see a delinquent specifically to prepare a court report. In these circumstances, as well as making enquiries among the parents and teachers it is essential to consult any social worker or probation officer who has been involved with the child. Psychological testing of intelligence and educational achievements can also be useful. The form of the report is similar to that described in Chapter 22. It should include a summary of the history and present mental state together with recommendations about treatment.

Treatment

When considering the treatment of delinquent children and adolescents, the psychiatrist needs to know how the legal system works. In England and Wales the provisions are largely covered by the Children and Young Persons Act of 1969. This contains a wide range of provisions: fines, the requirement that the parent or guardian take proper control (see p. 908), supervision by a probation officer, a period at an attendance centre, or an order committing the child to the care of the local authority. It is also possible to make orders for compulsory treatment or to send older delinquents for fixed periods to detention centres or Borstals for custodial training. Since delinquent behaviour is common, mainly not serious, and usually a passing phase, it is generally appropriate to treat first offences with minimal intervention, coupled with firm disapproval. The same applies to minor offences that are repeated. For more serious recurrent delinquency a more vigorous response may be required. For this purpose a community-based programme is usually to be preferred, with the main emphasis on improving the family environment, reducing harmful peer group influences, helping the offender to develop better skills for solving problems, and improving educational and vocational accomplishments.

Since the main aim of the law as it applies to children and young persons is treatment rather than punishment or even deterrence, there has been extensive criminological research to determine the effectiveness of the measures used. The general conclusions are not encouraging. The risk of reconviction seems to be greater among children who have had any court appearance or period of detention than among children who have committed similar offences without any official action having been taken (see e.g. West and Farrington 1977). There have been many attempts to establish and evaluate forms of treatment that might be effective. One of the earliest, the Highfields Project, compared group treatment in a small well-staffed unit with the usual custodial sentence. Modest benefits were found for the former (Weeks 1958). A larger study, the PICO (Pilot Intensive Counselling Organization) project, found some evidence that 9 months' counselling was of more benefit to 'amenable' boys in a medium security unit than to more difficult and unco-operative boys (called 'non-amenable'). These and other studies suggest the need to match the type of treatment to the type of offender. Some delinquents seem to respond better to authoritative supervision, others to more permissive counselling. Unfortunately it is not yet possible to provide any satisfactory practical guidelines about the choice of treatment for the individual delinquent.

The results of an elaborate investigation known as the Community Treatment Project of the Californian Youth Authority (Warren 1973) showed that community treatment was generally at least as effective as institutional care. [See Rutter and Giller (1983) for a review.]

Over-activity syndromes

About a third of children are described by their parents as over-active, and 5–20 per cent of schoolchildren are so described by teachers. These reports encompass behaviour varying from normal high spirits to a severe and persistent disorder. In the past, the boundary of the behaviour disorder has been drawn differently in the United States and the United Kingdom. In the USA a wide definition was used and estimates of prevalence were higher (generally about 10 per 1000 children) than in the UK where a narrow definition led to estimates of about 1 per 1000 children (e.g. Rutter *et al.* 1970).

This section is concerned with the more severe forms of over-activity, which are called hyperkinetic syndrome in ICD10 (draft) and attention-deficit hyperactivity disorder in DSMIIIR. As explained below, the diagnostic criteria for these disorders differ and it is unlikely that agreed criteria will be reached until more is known about aetiology. It seems likely that the present terms are being applied to what is really a heterogeneous group of conditions (see Taylor 1986*a*; Cantwell 1983).

Hyperkinetic disorder

Clinical features

The cardinal features of this disorder are extreme and persistent restlessness, sustained and prolonged motor activity, and difficulty in maintaining attention. Children with the disorder are often impulsive, reckless, and prone to accidents. There are learning difficulties which result only partly from poor concentration. Minor forms of antisocial behaviour are common, particularly disobedience, temper tantrums, and aggression. However, these antisocial behaviours do not occur early and are not prominent. Mood fluctuates, but depressive mood is common.

Restlessness, over-activity, and related symptoms often start before school age. Sometimes the child was over-active as a baby, but more often significant problems begin when the child begins to walk: he is constantly on the move, interfering with objects, and exhausting his parents. (DSMIIIR requires a disturbance of at least six months before the diagnosis of attention-deficit conduct disorder can be made, and onset before the age of seven years).

Epidemiology

As noted above, estimates of prevalence of attention-deficit hyperkinetic disorder in the United States are about ten times higher than in the United Kingdom. This difference results from the use of wider diagnostic criteria in the USA. Another reason is that DSMIIIR allows multiple diagnoses so that a child can be diagnosed as having both attention-deficit hyperkinetic disorder and conduct disorder; in the United Kingdom only one diagnosis would be made. However, real differences in prevalence cannot be ruled out.

Aetiology

In the past hyperkinetic disorder was ascribed to 'minimal brain damage'. However, although several forms of brain pathology are associated with overactivity and poor concentration, there is no evidence that they cause hyperkinetic disorders. **Genetic factors** are suggested by studies of adopted children (see Cantwell 1975). It is possible that **social factors** increase an innate tendency to hyperactivity, since over-active behaviour is more frequent among young children living in poor social conditions (Richman *et al.* 1982). However, social factors are unlikely to be the sole cause of hyperkinetic disorder. **Lead intoxication** (Needleman *et al.* 1979) and **food additives** have been suggested as causes, but there is no convincing evidence for either (see Taylor, E. A. 1984).

Prognosis

The overactivity usually lessens as the child grows older, especially when it is mild and not present in every situation. It usually ceases by puberty. The prognosis for any associated learning difficulties is less good, while antisocial behaviour has the worst prognosis. When the overactivity is severe, accompanied by learning failure, or associated with low intelligence, the prognosis is poor and the condition may persist into adult life.

Treatment

A hyperactive child exhausts his parents, who need support from the start of treatment, particularly as it may be difficult to reduce the child's behaviour. The child's teachers need advice about management, which may include remedial teaching. Methods of behaviour modification may help to reduce the inadvertent reinforcement of over-activity by parents and teachers.

Stimulant drugs may be tried, especially when attention deficits are severe. The usual drug is methylphenidate. Dosage should be related to body weight. It is appropriate to start with 2.5 mg in the morning; adding after four days a further 2.5 mg at midday; and, depending on the response and side-effects, increasing cautiously to a maximum of 10 mg in the morning and 10 mg at midday for a five-year-old of average weight, (or a lower dose for a younger child). The side-effects include irritability, depression, insomnia, and poor appetite. With high doses there may be suppression of growth (see Barkley 1977). The drug may be needed for several months or even a year or more, and careful monitoring is essential. The drug may be stopped from time to time in an attempt to minimize side-effects and to confirm that medication is still needed. In clinical trials short-term benefits of the drug have been shown in about two-thirds of children with hyperkinetic syndrome (see Cantwell 1977; Barkley 1977), but the long-term benefits are uncertain. It seems best to reserve drug treatment for severe cases, which have not responded to other treatment. Surprisingly, there is no report of children treated in this way becoming addicted to the drug.

For a review of the hyperkinetic syndrome see Taylor, E. A. (1986).

Pervasive developmental disorders

Childhood autism

This condition was described by Kanner (1943) who suggested the name infantile autism, which is still widely used. However, the term childhood autism is used in ICD10 (draft) and autistic disorder in DSMIIIR.

The prevalence of autism is probably about 30–40 per 100 000 children: it is four times as common in boys as in girls (see Rutter 1985a).

Clinical features

In his original description, Kanner (1943) identified the main features, which are still used to make the diagnosis. The first was onset within the first two years of life (now usually extended to two and a half years) after a period of normal early development. The other features are described below.

Autistic aloneness is the inability to make warm emotional relationships with people. Autistic children do not respond to their parents' affectionate behaviour by smiling or cuddling. Instead they appear to dislike being picked up or kissed. They are no more responsive to their parents than to strangers. There is no difference in their behaviour towards people and inanimate objects. A characterisitc sign is gaze avoidance, that is the absence of eye to eye contact.

Speech and language disorder is another important feature. Speech may develop late or never appear. Occasionally, it develops normally until about the age of two years, and then disappears in part or completely. This lack of speech is a manifestation of a severe cognitive defect, which affects non-verbal communication as well. It is also shown in play; autistic children do not take part in the imitative games of the first year of life, and later they do not use toys in an appropriate way. They also show little imagination or creative play. As autistic children grow up, about half acquire some useful speech, although serious impairments usually remain, such as the misuse of pronouns and the inappropriate repeating of words spoken by other people (echolalia).

Obsessive desire for sameness is a term applied to stereotyped behaviour together with evidence of distress if there is any change in the environment. For example, autistic children may prefer the same food repeatedly, insist on wearing exactly the same clothes, or engage in repetitive games. They are often fascinated by spinning toys.

Bizarre behaviour and mannerisms are commonly found. Some autistic children engage in odd motor behaviour such as whirling round and round, twiddling their fingers repeatedly, flapping their hands, or rocking. Others do not differ obviously in motor behaviour from normal children.

Other features: autistic children may suddenly show anger or fear without apparent reason. They may be over-active and distractible; they may sleep badly, and soil or wet themselves. About 25 per cent of autistic children develop seizures, usually about the time of adolescence.

Kanner originally believed that the intelligence of autistic children was normal. Later research has shown that three-quarters have IQ scores in the retarded range and that this finding appears to represent true intellectual impairment (Rutter and Lockyer 1967). Some autistic children show areas of ability despite impairment of other intellectual functions (Hermelin and O'Connor 1983).

Aetiology

The cause of childhood autism is unknown. It seems likely that the central abnormality is cognitive, affecting particularly symbolic thinking and language (see Rutter 1983), and that the behavioural abnormalities are secondary to this cognitive defect. **Genetic** influences are probable since the condition is more frequent in the families of affected persons than in the general population. Also in a small study of twins, Folstein and Rutter (1971) found concordance for autism in four of eleven monozygotic pairs, as against none of ten dizygotic pairs.

Organic brain disorder is suggested by an increased frequency of complications of pregnancy and childbirth, and by an association with epilepsy (in 2 per cent of cases). Some patients have non-localizing neurological abnormalities ('soft signs').

Kanner (1943) originally suggested that the disorder was a response to **abnormalities in the parents** who were characterized as cold, detached, and obsessive. These ideas have not been substantiated (see Koegel *et al.* 1983), and any psychological abnormalities in the parents are likely to be a response to the problems of bringing up the child or, possibly, genetically determined.

A relationship between childhood autism and schizophrenia has been suggested, but the balance of evidence is that the two conditions are separate.

Prognosis

Between 10 and 20 per cent of children with childhood autism begin to improve between the ages of about four to six years and are eventually able to attend an ordinary school and obtain work. A further 10 to 20 per cent can live at home but need to attend a special school or training centre and cannot work. The remainder, at least 60 per cent, improve little and are unable to lead an independent life, most needing long-term residential care (Rutter 1970). Those who improve may continue to show language problems, emotional coldness, and odd behaviour. As noted already, a substantial minority develop epilepsy in adolescence.

Differential diagnosis

It is more usual to encounter partial syndromes than the full syndrome. These partial syndromes must be distinguished from **psychoses of childhood** arising after the age of 30 months (see below) and the rare syndrome of '**autistic psychopathy**' (see below).

Deafness should be excluded by appropriate tests of hearing. **Developmental language disorder** (see p. 804) differs from autism in that the child usually responds normally to people, and has good non-verbal communication. **Mental handicap** can be differentiated because although the child has general intellectual retardation he usually responds to other people in a more normal way than the autistic child. Compared with a mentally handicapped child of the same age the autistic child has more impairment of language relative to other skills.

Treatment

Treatment has three main aspects: management of the abnormal behaviour, arrangements for social and educational services, and help for the family. Individual psychotherapy has been used in the hope of effecting more fundamental changes but there is no evidence that it succeds. Nor is there evidence that any form of medication is effective in childhood autism except in short-term management of behaviour problems.

Behavioural methods using contingency management (see p. 731) may control some of the abnormal behaviour of autistic children and perhaps foster more normal development. This treatment is often carried out at home by the parents, instructed and supervised by a clinical psychologist. It is not known whether these methods have any lasting benefit, but in autism even temporary changes are often worthwhile for the patient and the family.

Most autistic children require special schooling. It is generally thought better for them to live at home and to attend special day schools. If the condition is so severe that the child cannot stay in the family, residential schooling is necessary, even though the characteristic social withdrawal may be increased by an institutional atmosphere. Educational and residential provisions are often best arranged through the services for the mentally retarded.

The family of an autistic child needs considerable help to cope with the child's behaviour, which is often bewildering and distressing. Although little can be done to treat many of these patients, the doctor must not withdraw from the family who need continuing support and repeated encouragement in their efforts to help the child to realize any potential for normal development. Many parents find it helpful to join a voluntary organization in which they can meet other parents of autistic children and discuss common problems. A general review of treatment is given by Rutter (1985*c*).

Autistic psychopathy

This rare condition was first described by Asperger (1944) and is sometimes called *Asperger's syndrome*. In ICD10 (draft) it is called *schizoid disorder of childhood*. The condition is characterized by abnormalities of social behaviour similar to those of childhood autism, with stereotyped and repetitive activites. It differs from autism in that there is no general delay or retardation of cognitive development or language. The disorder is about six times more common in boys than girls. The children develop normally until about the third year when they begin to lack warmth in their relationships and to speak in monotonous ways. They are solitary, spending much time in narrow interests and routines. They are often clumsy, eccentric, and without friends.

The *cause* of autistic psychopathy is unknown. Some cases may be minor variants of childhood autism, but most are probably separate. Usually the abnormalities persist into adult life. Most people with the disorder can work but few form successful relationships and marry. [See Graham (1986) for further information.]

Disintegrative disorder

In ICD10 (draft) this condition is called *childhood disintegrative disorder*. It begins after a period of normal development lasting longer than two and a half years. It resembles childhood autism in the marked loss of cognitive functions, abnormalities of social behaviour, and unfavourable outcome.

It is unclear how far the disorder is distinct from childhood autism. In DSMIIIR, no separate rubric is provided, and children with the above features are classified under pervasive developmental disorder.

Other childhood disorders

Dementia

Dementing disorders are rare in childhood. They result from organic brain diseases such as lipoidosis, leucodystrophy, or subacute sclerosing pan-encephalitis. Some of the causes are genetically determined and may affect other children in the family. The prognosis is variable. Many cases are fatal, others progress to profound mental retardation.

Schizophrenia

Schizophrenia is almost unknown before seven years of age and seldom begins before late adolescence. When it occurs in childhood, the onset may be acute or insidious. The whole range of symptoms occur that characterize schizophrenia in adult life (see Chapter 9.) Before symptoms appear, many of these children are odd, timid or sensitive, and show delayed speech development. Early diagnosis is difficult particularly when these non-specific abnormalities precede the characterisic symptoms. Antipsychotic drugs are used as in the treatment of adult schizophrenia, with appropriate reductions in dosage. The child's educational needs should be met and support given to the family. [See Tanguay and Cantor (1986) for a review of schizophrenia in childhood.]

Manic-depressive disorder

Depressive disorders in childhood have been considered already (p. 787). The typical picture of mania is rarely seen until late adolescence. It is possible that mania appears occasionally in a disguised form in younger adolescents, causing episodes of over-active and disturbed behaviour. (See p. 820.)

Specific developmental disorders

Both DSMIIIR and draft ICD10 contain categories for specific develop-mental disorders. The latter are circumscribed developmental delays which cannot be accounted for by another disorder. It is debatable whether these conditions should be classified as mental disorders at all, since many of the children have no other signs of psychopathology. For this reason DSMIIIR codes specific delays of development on a separate axis from that used to code psychiatric disorders.

Specific reading disorder

In DSMIIIR this condition is called *developmental reading disorder*. It is defined by a reading age well below (usually 1.5 to 2 standard deviations) the level expected from the child's age and IQ (see Yule 1967). Defined in this way, the disorder was found in about 4 per cent of 10-to-11-year-olds in the Isle of Wight and about twice that percentage in London [see Yule and Rutter (1985) for a review].

Clinical features

Specific reading disorders should be clearly distinguished from general backwardness in scholastic achievement owing to low intelligence or inadequate education. The child presents with a history of serious delay in learning to read, sometimes preceded by delayed acquisition of speech and language. Writing and spelling are also impaired, but development in other areas is not. Compared with children with general backwardness at school, those with specific reading retardation are much more often boys. They are also more likely to have minor neurological abnormalities. On the other hand, they are less likely to come from socially disadvantaged homes.

Aetiology

Aetiology is not known. The frequent occurrence of other cases in the family suggests a genetic cause but evidence is lacking. Because children with cerebral palsy and epilepsy have increased rates of specific reading disorder, it has been suggested that children with specific reading disorder but no obvious neurological disease might have minor neurological abnormalities. The evidence does not support this idea. The most likely cause appears to be disorder of brain maturation affecting one or more of the perceptual and language skills required in reading. This explantion is in keeping with the findings of difficulties in verbal coding and sequencing in many cases and of confusion between right and left—and with the general improvement with age.

Social factors may add to these psychological problems. Presumably borderline difficulties may lead to reading retardation among children brought up in a large family or poor school, where they receive little personal attention; but not among children brought up in better circumstances. Frequent changes of school and an illiterate home background are also associated with specific reading disorder, and could act in a similar way. As already noted, children with reading disorder have a high rate of conduct disorder.

Assessment and treatment

It is important to identify the disorder early. Assessment is carried out by an educational or clinical psychologist. Treatment is educational unless there are additional medical or behavioural problems requiring separate intervention. Sometimes associated behavioural problems are secondary to frustration caused by the reading difficulty; they improve when reading improves. Several educational approaches are used but it is most important to reawaken the interest of a child with a long experience of failure. Continued extra teaching and parental interest seem to be helpful but there is no good evidence that any one method of teaching is better than others (see Gittelman 1985).

Prognosis

Prognosis varies with the severity of the condition. About a quarter of children with a mild problem in mid-childhood achieve normal reading skills by adolescence. However, very few with severe problems in mid-childhood overcome them by adolescence. Whilst there is insufficient evidence to be certain what happens to these people as adults, those with substantial difficulties in adolescence seem likely to retain them (see Maughan *et al.* 1985).

Specific arithmetic disorder

In DSMIIIR this condition is called **developmental arithmetic disorder**. Difficulty with arithmetic is probably the second most common specific disorder. Little is known about it. There has been no study of its epidemiology although it is thought to be quite common. Although it causes less severe handicap in everyday life than reading difficulties, it can lead to secondary emotional difficulties while the child is at school.

The **causes** are uncertain. The existence of mathematical prodigies suggests that some of the abilities needed for mathematics might be inherited. If so, arithmetical difficulties might also be determined by heredity. However, it seems unlikely that there is a single cause. **Assessment** is usually based on the arithmetic sub-tests of the WISC and the WAIS and on specific tests. **Treatment** is by remedial teaching but it is not known whether it is effective. The **prognosis** is not known.

Specific motor disorder

Some children have delayed motor development, which results in clumsiness in school-work or play. In DSMIIIR this condition is called **developmental co-ordination disorder**. It is also known as clumsy child syndrome, or specific motor dyspraxia. The children can carry out all normal movements, but their co-ordination is poor. They are late in developing skills such as dressing, walking, and feeding. They tend to break things and are poor at handicrafts and organized games. They may also have difficulty in writing, drawing, and copying. IQ testing usually shows good verbal but poor performance scores.

These children are sometimes referred to a psychiatrist because of a secondary emotional disorder. An explanation of the nature of the problem should be given to the child, the family, and the teachers. Special teaching may improve confidence. It may be necessary to exempt the child from organized games or other school activities involving motor co-ordination. There is usually some improvement with time. [Further information is given by Cantwell and Baker (1985a) and Henderson (1987).]

Disorders of speech and language

Half of all children use words with meaning by 12.5 months and 97 per cent do so by 21 months. Half form words into simple sentences by 23 months (Neligan and Prudham 1969). Vocabulary and complexity of language develop rapidly during the pre-school years. However, when they start school, 1 per cent of children are seriously retarded in speech and 5 per cent have difficulty in making themselves understood by strangers. The process by which language is acquired is complex, and still not fully understood.

The most common cause of delay in the development of normal speech is mental retardation. Other important causes are deafness and cerebral palsy. Social deprivation can cause mild delays in speaking. Infantile autism is an important but infrequent cause. The remaining cases are attributed to the specific developmental speech and language delay described below [see Bishop (1987) for a review of causes]. Children with *developmental language disorder* have a marked delay in acquiring normal speech, in the absence of any primary cause. Two categories are recognized in DSMIIIR: receptive and expressive. The former have difficulty in understanding language. The latter appear to understand language but their own speech is hard to understand because the words are ill-formed. Children with expressive disorder have greater difficulty with longer words, with the ends of words, and with consonants.

Serious speech delay is often accompanied by other problems of development. It has obvious and important consequences for education and social development. Thorough early investigation is essential and should include both a detailed assessment of speech and language and a search for one of the causes mentioned above. Treatment depends partly on the cause but usually includes a programme of speech training carried out through play and social interaction. In milder cases this help is best provided at home by the parents who are given information on what to do. More severe difficulties are likely to require specialized help in a remedial class or a special school. The prognosis depends on the cause. [For a review of speech and language disorders see Cantwell and Baker (1985*b*).]

Elective mutism

In this condition, a child refuses to speak in certain circumstances although he does so normally in others. Usually speech is normal in the home but lacking in school. There is no defect of speech or language, only a refusal to speak in certain situations. Often there is other negative behaviour such as refusing to sit down or to play when invited to do so. The condition usually begins between three and five years of age, after normal speech has been acquired.

Clinically significant elective mutism is rare, probably occurring in about 1 per 1000 children. Assessment is difficult because the child often refuses to speak at the clinic so that diagnosis depends to a large extent on the parents' account. In questioning them it is important to ask whether speech and comprehension are normal at home. Although psychotherapy, behaviour modification, and speech therapy have been tried, there is no evidence that any treatment is generally effective. In some cases, elective mutism lasts for months or years. A 5–10-year follow-up of a small group showed that about half had improved (Kolvin and Fundudis 1981).

Stammering

Stammering (or stuttering) is a disturbance of the rhythm and fluency of speech. It may take the form of repetitions of syllables or words, or of blocks in the production of speech. Stammering is four times more frequent in boys than girls. It is usually a brief disorder in the early stages of language development. However, 1 per cent of children suffer from stammering after they have entered school.

The cause of stammering is not known, although many theories exist. Genetic factors, brain damage, and anxiety may all play a part in certain cases: it seems unlikely that all are caused in the same way. Stammering is not usually associated with a psychiatric disorder even though it can cause distress and embarrassment. Most children improve whether treated or not. Many kinds of treatment have been tried including psychotherapy and behaviour therapy, but none has been shown to be effective. The usual treatment is speech therapy.

Functional enuresis

Functional enuresis is the repeated involuntary voiding of urine occurring after an age at which continence is usual (usually 5 years), in the absence of any identified physical disorder. Enuresis may be **nocturnal** (bed wetting) or **diurnal** (during waking hours), or both. Most children achieve daytime and night-time continence by three or four years of age. Nocturnal enuresis is often referred to as **primary** if there has been no preceding period of urinary continence for at least one year. It is called **secondary** if there has been a preceding period of urinary continence for this period.

In Great Britain, the prevalence of nocturnal enuresis is about 10 per cent at five years of age, 4 per cent at eight years, and 1 per cent at fourteen years. Similar figures have been reported from the United States. Nocturnal enuresis occurs more frequently in boys. Daytime enuresis has a lower prevalence and is more common in girls than boys.

Nocturnal enuresis can cause great unhappiness and distress, particularly if the parents blame or punish the child. This unhappiness may be made worse by limitations imposed by enuresis on activities such as staying with friends or going on holiday.

Aetiology

Nocturnal enuresis occasionally results from physical conditions but more often appears to result from delay in maturation of the nervous system alone or in combination with environmental factors. There is some evidence for a genetic cause; about 70 per cent of children with enuresis have a first-degree relative who has been enuretic (Bakwin 1961). Also concordance rates for enuresis are twice as high in monozygotic as in dizygotic twins (Hallgren 1960).

There is evidence that enuresis can be related to anatomical or functional abnormalities of the bladder. More enuretic children have urinary infections than children of comparable age in the general population. It has also been reported that enuretic children have bladders that have a reduced capacity or function abnormally.

Although most children are free from psychiatric disorder, the proportion with psychiatric disorder is greater than that of other children. Psychological factors can contribute to aetiology; for example, unduly rigid toilet training, negative or indifferent attitudes of parents, and stressful events leading to anxiety in the child.

Assessment and treatment

A careful history and appropriate physical examination is required to exclude undetected physical disorder, particularly urinary infection, diabetes, or epilepsy; and to assess possible precipitating factors, and the child's motivation.

Psychiatric disorder should also be sought. If none is found, an assessment should be made of any distress caused to the child. An evaluation is made of the attitudes of the parents and siblings to the bed-wetting. Finally, the parents should be asked how they have tried to help the child.

Any physical disorder should be treated. If the enuresis is functional, an explanation should be given to the child and parents that the condition is common and the child is not to blame. It should be explained to the parents that punishment and disapproval are inappropriate and unlikely to be effective. The parents should be encouraged not to focus attention on the problem but to reward success without drawing attention to failure. Many younger enuretic children improve spontaneously soon after an explanation of this kind, but those over six years of age are likely to need more active measures.

Treatment begins with advice about restricting fluid before bedtime, lifting the child during the night, and the use of star-charts to reward success.

Children who do not improve with these simple measures may be treated with enuresis alarm methods (otherwise called the pad and bell method). Two perforated metal plates, separated by a cotton sheet, are incorporated in a low voltage circuit including a battery, a switch, and a bell or buzzer. The resistance of the cotton sheet prevents current from flowing in the circuit. When the bed is made, the plates are placed under the position in which the child's pelvis will rest. When the child begins to pass urine, the circuit is completed and the bell or buzzer sounds. The child turns off the switch, and rises to complete the emptying of the bladder. The bed is remade and a dry sheet is put between the metal plates before the child returns. Successful results probably depend on conditioning mechanisms, but they cannot be fully explained by classical conditioning; other learning mechanisms play a part, including social reinforcement from the parents for the child's successes (see Turner 1973).

The enuresis alarm seldom succeeds with children under the age of six, or those who are unco-operative. For the rest it is effective within a month in about 70–80 per cent of cases (see Shaffer *et al.* 1968), although about a third relapse within a year (Turner 1973). It is often difficult to persuade families to persist long enough with the treatment. It has been suggested that children with associated psychiatric disorder do less well than the rest even if they persist in treatment.

Enuresis can be treated with a tricyclic antidepressant, usually imipramine or amitriptyline. These drugs are given in a dose of 25 mg at night increasing to 50 mg if necessary. Their beneficial effect has been demonstrated in clinical trials. Most bed-wetters improve initially with complete relief in about a third. However, most also relapse when the drug is stopped. Because of this high relapse rate, the side-effects of tricyclics and the danger of accidental overdose, the drugs have a limited value in treating enuresis. They are most useful when it is important to control the enuresis for a short time—for example, when the child goes on holiday. [See Shaffer (1985a) for a review of enuresis and its treatment.]

Functional encopresis

Encopresis is the repeated voluntary or involuntary passing of faeces into inappropriate places after the age at which bowel control is usual, in the absence of known organic cause. DSMIIIR stipulates that the diagnosis should not be made unless the chronological and mental ages are greater than four years. Encopresis may be present continously from birth (primary) or start after a period of continence (secondary).

At the age of three years, 6 per cent of children are still incontinent of faeces at least once a week; at seven years the figure is 1.5 per cent. Among children over the age of three years, loss of bowel control is more often secondary to constipation, and true encopresis is less common. The condition is three to four times more frequent among boys than girls. [See Hersov (1985) for a review.]

Faeces may be passed into clothing, or deposited in inappropriate places such as the floor of the living room. Children who soil their clothes may deny what has happened and try to hide the dirty clothing. Some children smear faeces on walls or elsewhere. Most of these children have associated psychological problems of various kinds.

Aetiology

Repeated faecal soiling may be secondary to chronic constipation which may be associated with several causes, including: mental retardation; conditions that cause pain on defecation (for example, anal fissure); and Hirschsprung's disease. The causes of true encopresis are less understood. In some cases, parental attitudes to toilet-training seem important. Some parents have unrealistic expectations about the age at which control can be achieved, and are unduly punitive; others fail to adopt a consistent approach. Emotional disorder is common among children with encopresis, and may sometimes be a contributory cause. For example, soiling some-times begins after an upsetting event such as the illness of a parent, or the birth of a sibling. In other cases, soiling develops when the child has a poor relationship with one or both parents and appears to be rebelling.

Assessment and treatment

The first step is to exclude physical causes of chronic constipation (see above), and joint assessment by a paediatrician and psychiatrist is often helpful for this purpose. The next step is to assess parental attitudes and emotional factors in the child.

Treatment begins with finding out what the child thinks and feels about the problem, and providing him with explanation and reassurance. The parents also need reassurance and explanation. The most successful approach is usually a behavioural programme in which the child is encouraged to sit on the toilet for about 10 minutes after each meal, and is rewarded for doing this and for succeeding in passing a motion into the toilet. When there are associated emotional problems or conflicts with the parents, individual or family psychotherapy may be helpful. When out-patient treatment fails, the child may respond to behavioural management in hospital. If the child is admitted, the parents need to be closely involved to reduce the risk of relapse when the child returns home.

Prognosis

Whatever the cause, it is unusual for encopresis to persist beyond the middle teenage years, although associated problems (especially aggressive behaviour) may continue. When treated, most cases improve within a year (see Graham 1986).

Child abuse

In recent years, the concept of child abuse has been widened to include the overlapping categories of physical abuse (non-accidental injury), emotional abuse, sexual abuse, and neglect. Most of the literature on child abuse refers to developed countries, rather than to developing countries in which children commonly face poor nutrition and other hardships such as severe physical punishment, abandonment, and employment as beggars and prostitutes.

The term *fetal abuse* is sometimes applied to various behaviours detrimental to the fetus, including physical assult and the taking by the mother of substances likely to cause fetal damage. *Munchausen's syndrome by proxy* is the name given to illness in children which has been fabricated by the parents. It is discussed on p. 419. [For reviews of child abuse the reader is referred to Mrazek and Mrazek (1985) and Bankowski and Carballo (1986).]

Physical abuse (non-accidental injury)

Estimates of the prevalence of physical abuse vary with the criteria used. A survey of children under four years of age in an English county suggested an annual rate of one per 1000 children for injuries of such severity that there was evidence of bone fracture or bleeding around the brain (Baldwin and Oliver 1975). Less severe injury is much more frequent but often does not come to professional attention.

Clinical features

Parents may bring an abused child to the doctor with an injury said to have been caused accidentally. Alternatively relatives, neighbours, or other people may become concerned and may report the problem to the police, social workers, or voluntary agencies. The most common forms of injury are multiple bruising, burns, abrasions, bites, torn upper lip, bone fractures, subdural haemorrhage, and retinal haemorrhage. Suspicion of physical abuse should be aroused by the pattern of the injuries, a previous history of suspicious injury, unconvincing explanations, delay in seeking help, and incongruous parental reactions. The psychological characteristics of abused children vary but include fearful responses to the parents, other evidence of anxiety or unhappines, and social withdrawal. Such children often have low self-esteem, and may be aggressive.

Aetiology

Child abuse is more frequent in neighbourhoods in which family violence is common; schools, housing, and employment are unsatisfactory; and there is little feeling of community.

In parents the factors associated with child abuse include: youth, abnormal personality, psychiatric disorder, lower social class, social isolation, disharmony and breakdown in marriage, and a criminal record. When a parent has psychiatric disorder it is most often a personality disorder; only a few parents have disorders such as schizophrenia or affective disorder. Many parents give a history of having themselves suffered abuse or deprivation in childhood. Although child abuse is much more common in families with other forms of social pathology, it is certainly not limited to such families. Risk factors in the children include premature birth, early separation, need for special care in the neonatal period, congenital malformations, chronic illness, and a difficult temperament. In abusing families relationships between the parents are harsher and colder than in matched controls (Jones and Alexander 1987).

Management

Doctors and others involved in the care of children should always be alert to the possibility of child abuse. They need to be particularly aware of the risks to children who have some of the characteristics described above, or are cared for by parents with the predisposing factors listed there.

Doctors who suspect abuse should refer the child to hospital and inform a paediatrician or casualty officer of their suspicions. In the hospital emergency department, in-patient admission should be arranged for all children in whom non-accidental injury is suspected. The parents should be told that admission is necessary to allow further investigations. If the parents refuse admission, it may be necessary in England and Wales to apply to a magistrate for a Place of Safety order; similar action may be appropriate in other countries. During admission assessment must be thorough and include photographs of injuries and skeletal X-rays. Radiological examination may show evidence of previous injury or, occasionally, of bone abnormalities such as osteogenesis imperfecta. CT scan may be needed if subdural haemorrhage is suspected. All findings must be fully documented.

Once it has been decided that non-accidental injury is probable senior doctors should talk to the parents. Other children in the family should be seen and examined. The subsequent procedure will vary according to the administrative arrangements in different countries. In the United Kingdom, the Social Services staff should be notified so that they can organize a case conference for the exchange of information and opinions between various representatives of hospital and community. It may be decided to put the child's name on a child abuse register, thereby making the Social Services Department responsible for visiting the home and checking the problem regularly.

In some cases, the risk of returning the child to the parents is too great and separation is required. If the parents do not agree to separation, a care order can be sought by the Social Services Department. When abuse is severe, prolonged, or permanent, separation may be necessary, and parents may face criminal charges. From known cases of injury or death in children returned to their parents, it is vitally important that most careful assessment be made before physically abused children are returned to the parents, and that close supervision be kept when they are returned.

Countries vary in the requirements and procedures for reporting and monitoring possible physical abuse in children. Generally better methods are being introduced and there is increasing willingness to intervene even against parents' wishes.

Prognosis

Children who have been subjected to physical abuse are at high risk of further problems. For example, the risk of further severe injury is probably between 10 and 30 per cent (see Graham 1986), and sometimes the injuries are fatal. Abused children are likely to have subsequent high rates of physical disorders, delayed development, and learning difficulties. There are also increased rates of behavioural and emotional problems in later childhood and adult life even when there has been earlier therapeutic intervention (Lynch and Roberts 1982). As adults, many former victims of abuse have difficulties in rearing their own children. The outcome is better for abused children who can establish a good relationship with an adult and can improve their self-esteem; and for those without brain damage (Rutter 1985*b*; Lynch and Roberts 1982).

Emotional abuse

The term emotional abuse usually refers to persistent neglect or rejection sufficient to impair a child's development. However, the term is sometimes applied to gross degrees of over-protection, verbal abuse, or scapegoating which impair development. Emotional abuse often accompanies other forms of child abuse.

Emotional abuse has various effects on the child, including failure to thrive physically, impaired psychological development, and emotional and conduct disorders (see Rutter 1985*b*; Garbarino *et al.* 1986). Diagnosis depends on observations of the parents' behaviour towards the child, which may include frequent belittling or sarcastic remarks about him during the interview. One or both parents may have a disorder of personality, or occasionally a psychiatric disorder. The parents should be interviewed separately and together, to discover any reasons for the abuse of this particular child; he may, for example, fail to live up to their expectations, or may remind them of another person who has been abusive to one of them. The parents' mental state should also be assessed.

Treatment

In treatment, the parents should be offered help with their own emotional problems, and with their day-to-day interactions with the child. It is often difficult to persuade parents to accept such help. If the parents reject help, and if the effects of emotional abuse are serious, it may be necessary to involve the Social Services and to consider the steps described above for the care of children suffering physical abuse. The child may need individual help.

Child neglect

Child neglect may take several forms including: emotional deprivation, neglect of education, physical neglect, lack of appropriate concern for physical safety, and denial of necessary medical or surgical treatment. These forms of neglect may lead to physical or psychological harm.

Child neglect is more common than physical abuse, and it may be detected by various people including relatives, neighbours, teachers, doctors, or social workers. Child neglect is associated with adverse social circumstances, and is the most common reason for a child to need foster care (Fanshel 1981).

Non-organic failure to thrive and deprivation dwarfism

Paediatricians recognize that some young children fail to thrive for no apparent organic cause. In children under three, this condition is called non-organic failure to thrive (NOFTT); in older children it is called psycho-social short stature syndrome (PSSS) or deprivation dwarfism.

Non-organic failure to thrive is caused by the deprivation of food and close affection. There is usually evidence of problems in the parent-child relationship since the child's early infancy; these problems include rejection and, in extreme cases, expressed hostility towards the child. The infant may present either with recent weight loss or a weight persistently below the third percentile for chronological age. Height (or length) may be reduced. Head circumference may eventually be affected and there may be cognitive and developmental delay. The infant may be irritable and unhappy, or in more severe cases lethargic and resigned. There is a clinical spectrum ranging from infants with mild feeding problems to those with all the severe features described above (Skuse 1985). If treated with food and care, the infants usually grow and develop quickly (Kempe and Goldbloom 1987).

'Deprivation dwarfism' was first reported in 1967 by Powell *et al.* They described 13 children with abnormally short stature, unusual eating patterns, retarded speech development, and temper tantrums. Since this original account, the syndrome has been widely recognized. Although short in stature, the children may be of normal weight or even slightly overweight for their height. In severe cases the head circumference is reduced. Emotional and behavioural disorders occur and may include food searching, scavenging, and hoarding (McCarthy 1981). There is often cognitive and developmental delay. There is usually a history of deprivation or of psychological maltreatment. Away from the deprived environment, these children eat ravenously, sometimes until they vomit through over-indulgence.

In treating either syndrome the first essential is to ensure the child's safety, which often means admission to hospital. Subsequently some children can be managed at home, some need foster-care. Some parents can be helped to understand their child's needs, and to plan for them; other parents are too hostile to be helped. If help is feasible, it should be intensive and should probably focus on changing patterns of parenting (e.g. Kempe and Goldbloom 1987). It is unusual for the parents to be psychiatrically ill, but some have severe post-partum depression or other psychiatric disorder.

With both syndromes, the prognosis for severe cases is poor for psychological development and physical growth. The mortality rate is significant (Oates *et al.* 1985). Many children have to be placed permanently in foster care. Milder cases have a better outcome, especially if recognized early.

Deprivation dwarfism is especially resistent to family rehabilitation, and the child's subsequent development may be disappointing (Oates *et al.* 1985).

Sexual abuse

The term sexual abuse refers to the involvement of children in sexual activities which they do not fully comprehend and to which they cannot give informed consent, and which violate generally accepted cultural rules. The term covers various forms of sexual contact with or without varying degrees of violence. The term also covers some activities not involving physical contact, such as posing for pornograhic photographs or films. The abuser is commonly known to the child and usually a member of the family (incest).

Prevalence

The prevalence of sexual abuse has been estimated from criminal statistics or from surveys, but differences in definition and thoroughness of reporting making it difficult to interpret published figures. It is agreed that children are more often female, and the offenders usually male. Retrospective studies suggest that between 20 and 50 per cent of women recall some experience of abuse in childhood (Peters *et al.* 1986). These figures include a wide range of abusive experiences, ranging from relatively minor touching experiences to repeated intercourse.

Clinical features

The presentation of child sexual abuse depends on the type of sexual act and the relationship of the offender to the child. Children are more likely to report abuse when the offender is a stranger. Sexual abuse may be reported directly by the child or a relative, or it may present indirectly with unexplained problems in the child, such as physical symptoms in the urogenital or anal area, pregnancy, behavioural or emotional disturbance, or precocious or otherwise inappropriate sexual behaviour. In adolescent girls running away from home or unexplained suicidal attempts should raise the suspicion of sexual abuse. When abuse occurs within the family, marital and other family problems are common (Furniss *et al.* 1984).

Effects of sexual abuse

Early emotional consequences of sexual abuse include anxiety, fear, depression and anger, together with reactions to any unwanted pregnancy, and inappropriate sexual behaviour. It is not certain how common these reactions are, or how they relate to the nature and circumstances of the abuse. Long-term effects are said to include depressed mood, low self-esteem, self-harm, difficulties in relationships, and sexual maladjustment. In assessing these long-term effects, it should be remembered that sexual abuse often occurs in families with severe and chronic problems which are likely to have adverse long-term consequences. [See Alter-Reid *et al.* (1986); Browne and Finkelhor (1986); and Conte (1985) for reviews of sexual abuse.]

Aetiology

There is little reliable information about sexual abuse. It occurs in all socioeconomic groups, but is more frequent among socially deprived families. Finkelhor (1984) suggests there are several of preconditions which make sexual abuse more likely: deviant sexual motivation, impulsivity, a lack of conscience, a lack of external restraints (for example, cultural tolerance), and a lack of resistance by the child (through insecurity, ignorance, or other causes of vulnerability).

Assessment

It is important to be ready to detect sexual abuse and to give serious attention to any complaint by a child of being abused in this way. It is also important not to make the diagnosis without adequate evidence, which requires social investigation of the family as well as psychological and physical examination of the child. The child should be interviewed sympathetically and encouraged to describe what has happened: drawings or toys may help younger children to give a description (Jones and MacQuiston 1988). It is often appropriate to carry out a physical examination, including inspection of the genitalia and anal region, and, if intercourse may have taken place within 72 hours, the collection of specimens from the genital and other regions (Kingman and Jones 1987).

Treatment

The initial management and the measures to protect the child are similar to those for physical abuse (see p. 810). However, there are particular difficulties involved in intervening with families in which sexual abuse has occurred. These include a marked tendency to deny the seriousness of the abuse and of other family problems, and deviant sexual attitudes and behaviour of all family members including other children (Furniss *et al.* 1984; Mrazek and Mrazek 1985). In addition, the sexually abused child often has a highly abnormal sexual development which requires individual help (Jones 1986).

Suicide and deliberate self-harm

Both deliberate self-harm and suicide are rare amongst children less than 12 years of age (though more common in adolescence—see p. 484). These problems are discussed in the chapter on suicide and deliberate self-harm pp. 484 and 501).

Gender identity disorders

Effeminacy in boys

Some boys prefer to dress in girls' clothes and to play with girls rather than boys. Some have an obvious effeminate manner and say they want to be girls. There is no evidence of any endocrine basis for these behaviours. Possible family influences include the encouragement of feminine behaviour by the parents, a lack of boys as companions in play, a girlish appearance, and the lack of an older male with whom the child can identify. However, many children experience these influences without being effeminate. It is difficult to know how far intervention is appropriate. Associated emotional disturbance in the child may require help, and it may be useful to investigate and discuss any family behaviours which seem to be contributing to the child's behaviour. Effeminate behaviour in early childhood may proceed in adult life to homosexuality or bisexuality, transvestism, or personality problems (see Green 1985; Zuger 1984).

Tomboyishness in girls

In girls the significance of marked tomboyishness for future sexual orientation is not known. It is usually possible to reassure the parents, and sometimes necessary to discuss their attitudes to the child and their responses to her behaviour.

Psychiatric aspects of physical illness

The associations between physical and psychiatric disorders in children resemble those in adults (see Chapters 11 and 12). There are three main groups of association, which are met at least as frequently in paediatric as in child psychiatric practice. The first group comprises the psychological and social consequences of physical illness. The second consists of psychiatric disorders presenting with physical symptoms, for example abdominal pain and multiple tics. The third consists of physical complications of psychiatric disorders; for example, eating disorders, attempted suicide, and encopresis.

Most medical syndromes in children are discussed in the chapter on psychiatry and medicine (Chapter 12). In this section we consider some special problems in childhood. [See Graham (1986) for a detailed review.]

The consequences of physical illness

When physically ill, children are more likely than adults to develop delirium. A familiar example is delirium caused by febrile illness.

Some chronic physical illnesses have psychological consequences for the child. In the Isle of Wight study of children (Rutter *et al.* 1970a) the prevalence of psychiatric disorder was only slightly increased with physical illnesses that do not affect the brain (for example, asthma or diabetes); however, the prevalence was considerably higher with organic brain disorder or epilepsy. Chronic illness may impair reading ability and general intellectual development (Rutter *et al.* 1970a; Eiser 1986), and sometimes also self-esteem and ability to form relationships.

Effect on parents

Parents are inevitably distressed by learning that their child has a chronic disabling physical illness. The effects depend upon many factors, including the nature of the physical disorder, the temperament of the child, the parents' emotional resources, and the circumstances of the family. The parents may experience a sequence of emotional reactions like those of bereavement, and their marital and social lives may be affected.

Most parents eventually develop a warm, loving relationship with a handicapped child, and cope sucessfully with the difficulties. A few manage less well and may have unrealistic expectations, or may be rejecting or over-protective. [See reviews by Breslau *et al.* (1981); Romans-Clarkson *et al.* (1986).]

Effect on siblings

The brothers and sisters of children with physical problems may develop emotional or behavioural disturbances. They may feel neglected themselves, irritated by restrictions on their social activities, or resentful of having to spend much of their time helping to look after the handicapped child. Although some studies have shown more emotional and behavioural disturbances in siblings than would be expected by chance (Ferrari 1984; Breslau and Prabucki 1987), most siblings manage well and may even benefit through increased abilities to cope with stress and to show compassion for others.

Management

Everyone involved in the care of physically disabled children should be aware of the psychological difficulties commonly experienced by the children and their families. Doctors should be skilled in giving distressing information to families, and in providing advice and support (Graham 1986). Medical care should be well co-ordinated; for example, regular liaison between the paediatrician and the child psychiatrist is important. There should also be good communication with teachers and social workers, and others involved.

Children in hospital

The admission of a child to hospital has important psychological consequences for the child and family. For many years, most hospitals discouraged families from visiting children. Bowlby (1951) suggested that this separation could have adverse immediate and long-term psychological effects; he identified successive stages of protest, despair, and detachment in the child during admission to hospital. These ideas were influential. It is now general policy to encourage parents to visit and help in the care of their child. It is also recognized as important to prepare children for admission by explaining in simple terms what will happen, and by introducing members of staff who will care for them in hospital.

It has been shown that repeated admission to hospital in early or middle childhood is associated with behavioural and emotional disturbances in adolescence (see Rutter 1981). It is possible that these long-term consequences are being reduced with the improvements in hospital care mentioned above (Shannon *et al.* 1984).

Adolescence

There are no specific disorders of adolescence. However, special experience and skill are required to apply the general principles of psychiatric diagnosis and treatment to patients at this time of transition between childhood and adult life. It is often particularly difficult to distinguish psychiatric disorder from the normal emotional reactions of the teenage years. For this reason, this section begins by discussing how far emotional disorder is an inevitable part of adolescence.

Considerable changes—physical, psychosexual, emotional, and social—take place in adolescence. In the 1950s and 1960s it was widely assumed that these changes were commonly accompanied by emotional upset of such a degree that it could be considered a psychiatric disorder. Indeed, Anna Freud (1958) regarded 'disharmony within the psychic structure' as a 'basic' fact of adolescence. Others described alienation, inner turmoil, adjustment reactions, and identity crises as common features of this time of life. Recently a more cautious view has prevailed. Rutter *et al.* (1976*b*) have reviewed the evidence, including their own findings in 14-year-olds on the Isle of Wight. They concluded that rebellion and parental alienation are uncommon in mid-adolescence although inner turmoil, as indicated by reports of misery, self-depreciation, and ideas of reference, is present in about half of all adolescents. However, this turmoil seldom lasts for long and it usually goes unnoticed by adults. Among older adolescents rebellious behaviour is more common and many become estranged from school during their last year of compulsory attendance. Other problems include excessive drinking of alcohol and the use of drugs and solvents (discussed in Chapter 14); problems in relationships and sexual difficulties; and irresponsible behaviour in driving cars and motorcycles (see Bewley 1986; Spicer 1985).

Although psychiatric disorders are only a little more common in adolescence than in the middle years of childhood the pattern of disorder is markedly different, being closer to that of adults. In adolescence, the sexes are affected equally; anxiety is less common than in earlier years, while depression and school refusal are more frequent. [For a review of problems in adolescence and their treatment, the reader is referred to Steinberg (1982).]

Clinical features of psychiatric disorders in adolescence

Emotional disorders

Generalized anxiety states are less common in adolescence than in childhood. Social phobias begin to appear in early adolescence, agoraphobia in the later teenage years. School refusal is common between 14 years of age and the end of compulsory schooling, and at this age is often associated with other psychiatric disorders. Depressive symptoms are more common in adolescence than in childhood. In the Isle of Wight survey they were ten times more frequent among 14-year-olds than 10-year-olds. In adolescence, depressive mood is often less immediately obvious than anergy, 'alienation' from parents, withdrawal from social contacts with peers, and under-achievement at school.

Conduct disorders

About half the cases of conduct disorder seen in adolescents have started in childhood. Those which begin in adolescence differ in being less strongly associated with reading retardation and family pathology. Among younger children aggressive behaviour is generally more evident in the home or at school. Among adolescents it is more likely to appear outside these settings as offences against property. Truancy also forms part of the conduct disorders occurring at this age.

Manic and depressive disorder

Manic-depressive disorder is rare before puberty, but increases in incidence during adolescence. The classification and aetiology of this disorder are the same for adolescents as for adults, as described in Chapter 8. In adolescents the clinical features of depressive disorders are similar to those in adults, but less frequently include sleep disturbances, delusions, and hallucinations. Contrary to early beliefs, mania and bipolar illnesses are now thought to occur frequently in adolescence. From studies of adults it appears that the first episodes of these illnesses may manifest in adolescence as abnormal behaviour, which may be misdiagnosed.

The treatment of affective disorder is as described in Chapter 8, but with appropriate reductions in drug doses. Lithium is usually an effective prophylactic when the illness is recurrent. [See Ryan and Puig-Antich (1986) for a review of affective disorder in adolescence.]

Schizophrenia

Schizophrenia in adolescence is more common in boys than girls. Usually the diagnosis presents little difficulty. However, there may be difficulty in detecting characteristic symptoms, especially in patients whose main features are gradual deterioration of personality, social withdrawal, and decline in social performance. The prognosis may be good for a single acute episode with psychotic and florid symptoms, but is poor when the onset is insidious.

Eating disorders

Problems with eating and weight are common in adolescence. They are discussed in Chapter 12.

Suicide and deliberate self-harm

In recent years there has been a marked increase in suicide and deliberate self-harm among adolescents. These subjects are discussed in Chapter 13 (pp. 484 and 501).

Alcohol and substance abuse

There is evidence that the frequency of excessive drinking among adolescents is increasing. Most adolescent heavy drinkers seem to reduce their drinking as they grow older, but a few progress to more serious drinking problems in adult life.

Occasional drug taking is common in adolescence and is often a feature of group activities. Cigarette smoking and the use of cannabis are especially frequent. Solvent abuse is largely confined to adolescence and usually of short duration. Abuse of drugs such as amphetamines, barbiturates, opiates, and cocaine is less common but serious, since most drug-dependent people have experimented with these drugs during adolescence. Problems of substance abuse in adolescence are similar to those in adults, as described in Chapter 14. [See Hendren (1986) for a review of alcoholism and substance abuse in adolescents.]

Sexual problems

Concern about sexuality is normal in adolescence. Excessive worry about masturbation and sexual identity and orientation may lead to medical consultation. Sexual abuse is increasingly a cause of referral to psychiatrists.

It is probable that at least two-thirds of teenage pregnancies are terminated and some of the remainder are unwanted. There is a raised incidence of prenatal complications as compared with older mothers. Very young mothers frequently have substantial difficulties as parents and there is a poor outlook for many teenage marriages. The psychological and social problems of teenage pregnancy show that there is a need for access to continuing medical and social services during and after pregnancy (see Black 1986).

Assessment

There are special skills in interviewing adolescents. In general, younger adolescents require an approach similar to that used for children, while with older adolescents it is more appropriate to employ that used with adults. It must always be remembered that a large proportion of adolescents attending a psychiatrist do so somewhat unwillingly and also that most have difficulty in expressing their feelings in adult terms. The psychiatrist must therefore be willing to spend considerable time establishing a relationship with an adolescent patient. To do this, he must show interest in the adolescent, respecting his point of view and talking in terms he can understand. As in adult psychiatry it is important to collect systematic information and describe symptoms in detail, but with adolescents the psychiatrist must be prepared to adopt a more flexible approach to the interview.

It is usually better to see the adolescent before interviewing the parents. In this way, the psychiatrist makes it clear that he regards the adolescent as an independent person. Later, other members of the family may be interviewed, and the family seen as a whole. As well as the usual psychiatric history, particular attention should be paid to information about the adolescent's functioning at home, in school, or at work; and about his relationship with peers. A physical examination should be carried out unless the general practitioner has performed one recently and reported the results.

Such an assessment should allow allocation of the problem to one of three classes. In the first, no psychiatric diagnosis can be made and reassurance is all that is required. In the second, there is no psychiatric diagnosis but anxious parents or a disturbed family need additional help. In the third, there is a psychiatric disorder requiring treatment.

Treatment

Treatment methods are intermediate between those employed in child and adult psychiatry. As in the former, it is important to work with relatives and teachers. It is necessary to help, reassure, and support the parents and sometimes to extend this to other members of the family. This is especially important when the referral reflects the anxiety of the family about minor behavioural problems rather than the presence of a definite psychiatric disorder. However, it is also important to treat the adolescent as an individual who is gradually becoming independent of the family. In these circumstances, family therapy as practised in child psychiatry is usually inappropriate and may at times be harmful.

Services for adolescents

The proportion of adolescents in the population who are seen in psychiatric clinics is less than the proportion of other age groups. Of those referred, some of the less mature adolescents can be helped more in a child psychiatry clinic. Some of the older and more mature adolescents are better treated in a clinic for adults. Nevertheless for the majority the care can be provided most appropriately by a specialized adolescent service provided that close links are maintained with child and adult psychiatry services, and with paediatricians. There are no generally agreed principles for the organization of these units, or the treatment that they provide. Most units accept out-patient referrals not only from doctors, but also from senior teachers, social workers, and the courts. When the referral is non-medical the general practitioner should be informed and the case discussed with him. All adolescent units work with schools and Social Services although there is no one agreed way of arranging this. In-patient facilities are usually limited in extent. In Britian there are centres in each Health Service Region.

Appendix: History taking and examination in child psychiatry

The format and extent of an assessment will depend on the nature of the presenting problem. The following scheme is taken from the book by Graham (1986), which should be consulted for further information. Graham suggests that clinicians with little time available should concentrate on the items in bold type.

1. **Nature and severity of presenting problem(s). Frequency. Situations in which it occurs. Provoking and ameliorating factors. Stresses thought by parents to be important.**

2. Presence of other current problems or complaints.
   (a) Physical. Headaches, stomachaches. Hearing, vision. Seizures, faints, or other types of attacks.
   (b) Eating, sleeping, or elimination problems.
   (c) **Relationship with parents and sibs. Affection, compliance.**
   (d) Relationships with other children. Special friends.
   (e) Level of activity, attention span, concentration.
   (f) Mood, energy level, sadness, misery, depression, suicidal feelings. General anxiety level, specific fears.
   (g) Response to frustration. Temper tantrums.
   (h) Antisocial behaviour. Aggression, stealing, truancy.
   (i) **Educational attainments, attitude to school attendance.**
   (j) Sexual interest and behaviour.
   (k) Any other symptoms, tics, etc.

3. Current level of development.
   (a) Language: comprehension, complexity of speech.
   (b) Spatial ability.
   (c) Motor co-ordination, clumsiness.

4. Family structure.
   (a) Parents. Ages, occupations. **Current physical and emotional state**. History of physical or psychiatric disorder. Whereabouts of grandparents.
   (b) Sibs. Ages, presence of problems.
   (c) Home circumstances: sleeping arrangements.

5. Family function.
   (a) **Quality of parental relationship. Mutual affection. Capacity to communicate about and resolve problems. Sharing of attitudes over child's problems.**

(b) **Quality of parent–child relationship. Positive interaction: mutual enjoyment. Parental level of criticism, hostility, rejection.**
(c) Sib relationships.
(d) Overall pattern of family relationships. Alliance, communication. Exclusion, scapegoating. Intergenerational confusion.

6. Personal history
   (a) Pregnancy—complications. Medication. Infectious fevers.
   (b) Delivery and state at birth. Birth-weight and gestation. Need for special care after birth.
   (c) Early mother–child relationship. Postpartum maternal depression. Early feeding patterns.
   (d) Early temperamental characteristics. Easy or difficult, irregular, restless baby and toddler.
   (e) Milestones. Obtain exact details only if outside range of normal.
   (f) **Past illnesses and injuries. Hospitalizations.**
   (g) Separations lasting a week or more. Nature of substitute care.
   (h) Schooling history. Ease of attendance. Educational progress.

7. Observation of child's behaviour and emotional state.
   (a) **Appearance. Signs of dysmorphism. Nutritional state. Evidence of neglect, bruising, etc.**
   (b) **Activity level. Involuntary movements. Capacity to concentrate.**
   (c) **Mood. Expression or signs of sadness, misery, anxiety, tension.**
   (d) **Rapport, capacity to relate to clinician. Eye contact. Spontaneous talk. Inhibition and disinhibition.**
   (e) **Relationship with parents. Affection shown. Resentment. Ease of separation.**
   (f) Habits and mannerisms.
   (g) Presence of delusions, hallucinations, thought disorder.
   (h) Level of awareness. Evidence of minor epilepsy.

8. Observation of family relationships.
   (a) Patterns of interaction—alliances, scapegoating.
   (b) Clarity of boundaries between generations: enmeshment.
   (c) Ease of communication between family members.
   (d) Emotional atmosphere of family. Mutual warmth. Tension, criticism.

9. Physical examination of child.

10. Screening neurological examination.
    (a) Note any facial asymmetry.

(b) Eye movements. Ask the child to follow a moving finger and observe eye movement for jerkiness, inco-ordination.
(c) Finger–thumb apposition. Ask the child to press the tip of each finger against the thumb in rapid succession. Observe clumsiness, weakness.
(d) Copying patterns. Drawing a man.
(e) Observe grip and dexterity in drawing.
(f) Observe visual competence when drawing.
(g) Jumping up and down on the spot.
(h) Hopping.
(i) Hearing. Capacity of child to repeat numbers whispered two metres behind him.

Further reading

Graham, P. (1986). *Child psychiatry: a developmental approach*. Oxford University Press, Oxford.
Hersov, L. and Rutter, M. (1985). *Child psychiatry: modern approaches* (2nd edn). Blackwell, Oxford.
Quay, A. C. and Werry, J. S. (1986). *Psychopathological disorders of childhood* (3rd edn). John Wiley, New York.
Shaffer, D., Ehrhardt, A. A., and Greenhill, L. L. (1985). *The clinical guide to child psychiatry*. Free Press, New York.
Steinberg, D. (1982). *The clinical psychiatry of adolescence*. John Wiley, Chichester.

21 Mental retardation

Until recent years, most mentally retarded people lived in large hospitals under the care of doctors and nurses. Nowadays the educational and social care of the mentally retarded is generally undertaken by teachers and social workers, and most of the medical care by paediatricians and family doctors. Nevertheless the psychiatrist still has an important role, both in the organization of services and in the assessment and treatment of psychiatric disorders in mentally retarded children and adults. This chapter is therefore concerned with the organization of services and with psychiatric disorder in both children and adults. Many of the psychiatric problems of mentally retarded children are similar to those of children of normal intelligence; they will not be dealt with here but references will be made to the corresponding sections of the chapter on child psychiatry.

Terminology

Over the years several terms have been applied to people with intellectual impairment from early life. In the nineteenth and early twentieth centuries the word idiot was used for people with severe intellectual impairment, and imbecile for those with moderate impairment. The special study and care of such people was known as the field of mental deficiency. When these words came to carry stigma, they were replaced by the terms mental subnormality and mental retardation. In Great Britain the term mental handicap has recently been used increasingly and has been adopted by the Department of Health.

In this chapter the term mental retardation is used. This term is preferred because it is used in the draft of ICD10 and DSMIIIR, and also because the term mental handicap can lead to confusion between the different handicaps of the mentally retarded and of chronic schizophrenics.

The concept of mental retardation

A fundamental distinction has to be made between intellectual impairment starting in early childhood (mental retardation), and intellectual impairment developing later in life (dementia). In 1845 Esquirol made this distinction when he wrote:

Idiocy is not a disease, but a condition in which the intellectual faculties are never manifested; or have never been developed sufficiently to enable the idiot to acquire such an amount of knowledge as persons of his own age and placed in similar circumstances with himself are capable of receiving. (Esquirol 1845, pp. 446–7)

At the end of the nineteenth century a significant advance was made when methods of measuring intellectual capacity became available. Early in the twentieth century Binet's celebrated tests of intelligence provided quantitative criteria for ascertaining mental retardation. These tests also made it possible to identify mild intellectual retardation that might not be obvious otherwise (see Binet and Simon 1905). Unfortunately, those responsible for the mentally retarded began to assume that people with such mild degrees of intellectual impairment were socially incompetent and required institutional care (see Corbett 1978).

Similar views were reflected in the legislation of the time. In 1886 the Idiots Act had made a simple distinction between idiocy (more severe) and imbecility (less severe). In 1913 the Mental Deficiency Act added a third category for people who 'from an early age display some permanent mental defect coupled with strong vicious or criminal propensities in which punishment has had little or no effect'. As a result of this legislation, people of normal or near normal intelligence were admitted to hospital for long periods simply because their behaviour offended against the values of society. Although some of these people had 'strong vicious' propensities, others were girls whose repeated illegitimate pregnancies were interpreted as a sign of the 'criminal' propensities mentioned in the Act.

In the past the use of social criteria clearly led to abuse. Nevertheless, it is unsatisfactory to define mental retardation in terms of intelligence quotient alone. Social criteria must be included, since a distinction must be made between people who can lead a normal or near-normal life, and those who cannot. In practice the most useful modern definition is probably the one used by the American Association for Mental Deficiency (AAMD), which defines mental retardation as 'sub-average general intellectual functioning which originated during the development period and is associated with impairment in adaptive behaviour' (Heber 1981).

DSMIIIR defines mental retardation as a 'significantly sub-average general intellectual functioning', having an onset before the age of 18 and with 'concurrent deficits and impairments in adaptive behaviour, taking into account the person's age'. Like ICD, DSMIIIR has the following four subtypes: mild (IQ 50–70); moderate (IQ 35–49); severe (IQ 20–34); profound (IQ below 20).

Educationalists use other terms and these differ between Britain and the United States. In Britain, the terms are Educationally Subnormal

(ESN) and Severely Educationally Subnormal (ESN(S)). In the United States, three groups are recognized: Educable Mentally Retarded (EMR), Trainable Mentally Retarded (TMR), and Severely Mentally Retarded (SMR). [For a review see Clarke and Clarke (1983*b*)]

Epidemiology

In 1929, in an important survey of schoolchildren in six areas of Britain, E. O. Lewis found that the total prevalence of mental retardation was 27 per 1000, and the prevalence of moderate and severe retardation (IQ less than 50) was 3.7 per 1000. Subsequent studies in many countries have generally shown that, in the population aged 15–19, the prevalence of moderate and severe retardation is about 3.0 to 4.0 per 1000. Although the prevalence of moderate and severe retardation has changed little since the 1930s, the incidence of severe retardation has fallen by a third to a half. The prevalence has not changed because patients are living longer, particularly those with Down's syndrome. The incidence has fallen because antenatal and neonatal care have improved, and numbers of children born to mothers aged over 35 are smaller. The age distribution of severely retarded people in the population has been changing, so that the numbers of adults (particularly the middle-aged) have increased (see Graham 1986).

Tizard (1964) drew attention to the distinction between 'administrative' prevalence and 'true' prevalence. He defined administrative prevalence as 'the numbers for whom services would be required in a community which made provision for all who needed them'. It has become standard practice for district services to carry out local censuses in terms of administrative prevalence. If the true prevalence of all levels of retardation (IQ less than 70) is taken to be 20–30 per 1000 of the population of all ages, then the administrative prevalence is about 10 per 1000 of all ages. In other words, less than half of all retarded people require special provision. Administrative prevalence is greater in childhood and falls after the age of 16. This reduction results from continuing slow intellectual development and gradual social adjustment.

Because the definition of mental retardation is imprecise, and because it is difficult to identify psychiatric disorder among mentally retarded people, estimates of the prevalence of such disorder are likely to be inaccurate. It is, however, undoubtedly greater than in the general population (see Corbett 1985). Rates of psychiatric disorder are high among mentally retarded people in hospital, presumably because psychiatric disorder is a common reason for admission and because long-term institutional care may lead to behavioural disturbance. From the few general population studies, there is good evidence that the mentally retarded have high rates of psychiatric disorder and disturbed behaviour. In a survey of intellectually retarded children aged 9–11 years, Rutter *et al.* (1970*a*) found that almost a third were rated as 'disturbed' by their parents, whilst about 40 per cent were so rated by their teachers. These rates were three to four times higher than the rates among intellectually normal children. Corbett *et al.* (1975) found in an area of south-east London that rates for psychiatric disorder were particularly high among children with severe retardation; disturbed behaviour was detected in 43 per cent, childhood psychosis in 13 per cent, hyperkinetic syndrome in 12 per cent, severe stereotypies in 5 per cent, neurosis in 3 per cent, and conduct disorder in 9 per cent. In the United States, rather similar findings have been reported by Eaton and Menolascino (1982).

Among people with mild mental retardation the relative frequencies of psychiatric symptoms and syndromes do not differ significantly from those in people of normal intelligence. Among people with severe retardation, certain kinds of abnormal behaviour are unexpectedly frequent, including autism, hyperkinetic syndromes, stereotyped movements, pica, and self-mutilation.

Clinical features of mental retardation

General description

The most frequent manifestation of mental retardation is uniformly low performance on all kinds of intellectual task, including learning, short-term memory, the use of concepts, and problem-solving. Specific abnormalities may lead to particular difficulties. For example, lack of visuospatial skills may cause many practical difficulties such as inability to dress; or there may be disproportionate difficulties with language or social interaction, both of which are strongly associated with behaviour disorder. In the retarded child, the common behaviour problems of childhood tend to occur when he is older and more physically developed than the normal child and they last longer. Such behaviour problems usually improve slowly as the child grows older. At the same time, there is often some catching up in performance on intelligence tests.

Mild mental retardation (IQ 50–70)

People with mild retardation account for about four-fifths of the mentally retarded. Usually their appearance is unremarkable and any sensory or motor deficits are slight. Most people in this group develop more or less normal language abilities and social behaviour during the pre-school years, and their mental retardation may never be formally identified. In adult life most of them can live independently in ordinary surroundings, though they may need help with housing and employment, or when under some unusual stress.

Moderate retardation (IQ 35–49)

People in this group account for about 12 per cent of the mentally retarded. Most of them can talk or at least learn to communicate, and most can learn to care for themselves albeit with some supervision. As adults, they can usually undertake simple routine work and find their way about.

Severe retardation (IQ 20–34)

People with severe retardation account for about 7 per cent of the mentally retarded. In the pre-school years their development is usually greatly slowed. Eventually many of them can be trained to look after themselves under close supervision and to communicate in a simple way. As adults they can undertake simple tasks and engage in limited social activities. Among the severely retarded, a small number of 'idiots savants' have highly specific cognitive abilities that are normally associated with superior intelligence (Hermelin and O'Connor 1983).

Profound retardation (IQ below 20)

People in this group account for less than 1 per cent of the mentally retarded. Few of them learn to care for themselves completely. Some eventually achieve some simple speech and social behaviour.

Physical disorders among the mentally retarded

The most important physical disorders in the mentally retarded are sensory and motor disabilities, epilepsy, and incontinence. Severely retarded people (especially children) usually have such problems, often as multiple disorders. Only a third are continent, ambulant, and without severe behaviour problems; a quarter are highly dependent on other people. Among the mildly retarded, similar problems occur but less frequently, and determine whether special schooling is needed. Any **sensory disorders** add an important additional obstacle to normal cognitive development. It is known that about a fifth of mentally retarded children living in hospital have some defect of vision or hearing (see Department of Health and Social Security 1971). **Motor disabilities** are frequent, and include spasticity, ataxia and athetosis.

 Epilepsy is common among the mentally retarded, especially the severely retarded. Corbett *et al.* (1975) surveyed all the severely retarded children (whether in hospital or outside) originating from a London suburb. One-third of these children had experienced seizures at some time, and one-fifth had had at least one seizure in the year before the enquiry. Epilepsy is most common when mental retardation is due to cerebral damage, and uncommon when the retardation is due to chromosomal abnormalities. Epilepsy becomes less prevalent with increasing age, partly because those with severe cortical damage tend to die early, and partly because epilepsy tends to improve with age irrespective of intelligence level.

The types of epilepsy found in the mentally retarded are usually the same as those found in people of normal intelligence. However, certain rare syndromes are particularly associated with mental retardation. An example is infantile spasms in which seizures start in the first year and take the form of so-called salaam attacks with tonic flexion of the neck and body and movement of the arms outward and forward. The episodes last for a few seconds (see Corbett and Pond 1979). The condition has also been reported in association with autism.

Psychiatric disorders among the mentally retarded

All varieties of psychiatric disorder occur in the mentally retarded, but the symptoms are often greatly modified by low intelligence (Reid 1982; Corbett 1985). Certain symptoms, such as delusions, hallucinations, and obsessions seem to be different in people with severe retardation and limited language development. It is also difficult to detect symptoms when they are present, because the patient needs a minimum verbal fluency (probably at an IQ level of about 50) if he is to describe his experiences. Hence in diagnosing psychiatric disorder among the mentally retarded, more emphasis has to be given to behaviour and less to reports of mental phenomena than would be the case in people of normal intelligence. A short account will now be given of the major syndromes.

Schizophrenia

In the mentally retarded the clinical picture of schizophrenia is especially characterized by poverty of thinking. Delusions are less elaborate than in schizophrenics of normal intelligence. Hallucinations have a simple and repetitive content. It may be difficult to distinguish between the motor disorders of schizophrenia and the motor disturbances common among the retarded. It is difficult to make a definite diagnosis of schizophrenia when the IQ is below 45, but the diagnosis should be considered if there is a distinct worsening of intellectual or social functioning without evidence of an organic cause, especially if any new behaviour is odd and out of keeping with the patient's previous behaviour. When there is continuing doubt, a trial of antipsychotic drugs is often appropriate.

Some earlier psychiatrists (including Kraepelin) described a syndrome called '*Pfropfschizophrenie*'. This disorder was said to begin in mentally retarded children and adolescents and to be characterized by mannerisms and stereotypies. It now appears that these features were related more to severe mental retardation than to schizophrenia.

In mentally retarded patients the principles of treatment of schizophrenia are essentially the same as in patients of normal intelligence.

Affective disorder

When suffering from a **depressive disorder**, mentally retarded people are less likely than those of normal intelligence to complain of mood changes or to express depressive ideas. Diagnosis has to be made mainly on an appearance of sadness, changes in appetite and sleep, and on behavioural changes of retardation or agitation. Severely depressed patients with adequate verbal abilities may describe hallucinations or delusions. A few make attempts at suicide (which are usually poorly planned). **Mania** has to be diagnosed mainly on over-activity and behavioural signs such as excitement, irritability, and nervousness. The principles of treatment of affective disorders among the mentally retarded are essentially the same as among people of normal intelligence.

Neurosis

Neurotic disorders occur commonly among the less severely retarded, especially when they are facing changes in the routine of their lives. The clinical picture is often mixed. Conversion and dissociative symptoms may be florid. Treatment is usually directed more to bringing about adjustments in the patient's environment than to discussion of his problems.

Personality disorder

This is common among the mentally retarded. Sometimes it leads to greater problems in management than those caused by the retardation itself. The general approach is as described on p. 847, though with more emphasis on finding an environment to match the patient's temperament and less on attempts to bring about self-understanding (Reid and Ballinger 1987).

Organic psychiatric disorders

These are common among mentally retarded people. Disturbed behaviour due to delirium is sometimes the first indication of physical illness. Similarly a progressive decline in intellectual and social functioning may be the first indication of dementia. Both syndromes are more common at the extremes of life. The syndrome known as childhood disintegrative psychosis (p. 800) is a form of dementia occurring in early life, often associated with lipoidoses or other progressive brain pathology. As the life expectation of mentally retarded patients is increasing, dementia in late life is becoming more common. There is a particular association between Alzheimer's disease and Down's syndrome (see p. 842).

Autism and over-activity syndromes

Both are common among the mentally retarded. They are discussed in the chapter on child psychiatry (pp. 795 and 797) and will not be considered further here.

Behaviour disorders

Stereotyped or repetitive and apparently purposeless activities such as mannerisms, head banging, and rocking are common in the severely retarded, occurring in about 40 per cent of children and about 20 per cent of adults. Repeated self-injurious behaviour is less frequent but may be even more persistent (see Corbett 1985; Kirman 1987; Griffin *et al*. 1987). Many severely retarded children are overactive, distractable, and impulsive, but not to an extent that would indicate a diagnosis of over-activity syndrome. Other common disturbances are emotional lability (including temper tantrums), self-stimulation, pica (McLoughlin 1987), and undue dependency (see Quine 1986). When these problems are severe admission to hospital may be required, although institutional surroundings may make them worse. Offences against the law are seldom a serious problem [see p. 867, also Hunter 1979].

Sexual problems

Public masturbation is the most frequent problem. Some of the mentally retarded show a child-like curiosity about other people's bodies which can be misunderstood as sexual. In the past, much concern was expressed about the risk that mentally retarded people would have sexual intercourse and produce mentally handicapped children. It is now apparent that many kinds of severe retardation are not inherited; and those which are inherited are often associated with infertility. A more important concern is that, even if their children are of average intelligence, the severely mentally retarded are unlikely to make good parents. With modern contraceptive methods, the risk of unplanned pregnancy is much reduced [see Craft and Craft (1981) for further information].

Effects of mental retardation on the family

When a new-born child is found to be mentally retarded, the parents are inevitably distressed. Feelings of rejection are common but seldom last long. More often the diagnosis of mental retardation is not made until after the first year of life. The parents then have to make even greater changes in their hopes and expectations for the child. They often experience prolonged depression, guilt, shame, or anger. A few reject the child, while others become over-involved in its care, sacrificing other important aspects of family life. The majority achieve a satisfactory adjustment although the temptation to over-indulge the child remains. However well they adjust psychologically, the parents are still faced with a long prospect of hard work, frustration, and social problems. If the child also has a physical handicap, these problems are increased.

Ann Gath (1978) compared two groups of families, those with a Down's syndrome child at home, and matched controls with a normal child of the same age. Both were studied from the time of the child's birth. There were only small differences between the two groups of families in mental or physical health. Among the parents of the young children with Down's syndrome, a significant proportion gave evidence of marital disharmony but others felt that their relationship had been strengthened by looking after the affected child. It was concluded that 'despite the understandable emotional reaction to the fact of the baby's abnormality, most of the families in this study have adjusted well and two years later are providing a home environment that is stable and enriching for both the normal and handicapped children' (Gath 1978, p. 116). However it seemed likely that the siblings were often at some disadvantage because of the time and effort that had to be devoted to the retarded child.

Other investigators have surveyed the needs of the mothers of older mentally retarded children. Tizard and Grad (1961) compared two groups of families, those with a mentally retarded child living at home and those with a comparable child in an institution. The former were found to be preoccupied with the 'burden of care' for their child, while the latter were living nearly normal lives. Wilkin (1979) found that most mothers with a mentally retarded child living at home were much helped by their husbands but received little assistance from other people. Generally the mothers were pleased with the educational services provided for their retarded child, but were more critical of what they saw as lack of interest and expertise among doctors and social workers. Most of the mothers reported problems of a practical kind: two-thirds wanted help in looking after the child during the school holidays, and large proportions (about half) wanted day care during the week-end, baby-sitting in the evening, or help with transport. Brimblecombe (1979) also found that mothers with a mentally retarded child living at home were dissatisfied with the medical services and with the amount of practical help they received from hospitals and social services. Voluntary organizations were often judged more helpful. [For a review of the problems of families with a mentally retarded member see Bicknell (1982), and Byrne and Cunningham (1985).]

Table 21.2. Causes of mental retardation in a community survey*

	Per cent
Down's syndrome	26
Other inherited conditions or associated congenital malformations	19
Perinatal injury	18
Infections	14
Inherited biochemical errors	4
Others	4
Undiagnosable	15

* Corbett *et al.* (1975).

Aetiology of mental retardation

Introduction

Lewis (1929) distinguished two kinds of mental retardation: **subcultural** (the lower end of the normal distribution curve of intelligence in the population) and **pathological** (due to specific disease processes). In a study of the 1280 mentally retarded people living in the Colchester Asylum, Penrose (1938) found that most cases were due not to a single cause but to an interaction of inherited and environmental factors. Subsequent evidence has confirmed that mental retardation has multiple causes (see MacKay 1982). This finding applies particularly to mild mental retardation which is usually due to a combination of genetic and adverse environmental factors, and which is more common in the lower social classes. Among the severely retarded, however, post-mortem examination shows pathological conditions in the majority (Crome and Stern 1972). Several surveys have shown that most of these pathological conditions can be diagnosed in life, and two-thirds can be diagnosed before birth (Graham 1986). In may of these conditions, the primary cause of the pathology is unknown.

Corbett *et al.* (1975) studied all the severely mentally retarded children living in a defined area of London. They were able to make a diagnosis in 85 per cent. The distribution of the diagnoses is shown in Table 21.2.

It should be noted that increasing success in identifying specific causes does not remove the need to consider all the additional social and other factors in each case. Until recently, severe retardation was thought to be evenly distributed in the population; now, however, it is known to be more common in the lower social classes, possibly because preventive measures have been less effective there.

Table 21.3. The aetiology of mental retardation

Genetic
Chromosome abnormalities
    Down's syndrome
    Klinefelter's syndrome
    Turner's syndrome

Metabolic disorders affecting:
    amino acids (e.g. phenylketonuria, homocystinuria, Hartnup
       disease)
    the urea cycle (e.g. citrullinuria, aminosuccinic aciduria)
    lipids (Tay–Sachs, Gaucher's, and Niemann–Pick diseases)
    carbohydrate (galactosaemia)
    purines (Lesch–Nyhan syndrome)
    mucopolysaccahridoses (Hurler's, Hunter's, Sanfillipo's, and
       Morquio's syndromes)

Gross disease of the brain
    Tuberose sclerosis
    Neurofibromatosis

Cranial malformations
    Hydrocephalus
    Microcephalus

Antenatal damage
    Infections (rubella, cytomegalo virus, syphilis, toxoplasmosis)
    Intoxications (lead, certain drugs, alcohol)
    Physical damage (injury, radiation, hypoxia)
    Placental dysfunction (toxaemia, nutritional growth retardation)
    Endocrine disorders (hypothyroidism; hypoparathyroidism)

Perinatal
    Birth asphyxia
    Complications of prematurity
    Kernicterus
    Intraventricular haemorrhage

Post-natal damage
    Injury (accidental, child abuse)
    Lead intoxication
    Infections (encephalitis, meningitis)
Malnutrition

Inheritance

There is good evidence from family, twin, and adoption studies that polygenic inheritance is important in determining intelligence within the normal range, and that much mild mental retardation represents the lower end of the distribution curve of intelligence (see Rutter 1980). In severe retardation, genetic abnormalities are responsible for metabolic disorders and other anomalies that cause mental disorder (see Tables 21.3 and 21.4).

Social factors

Studies of the general population suggest that factors in the social environment may account for variation in IQ of as much as 20 points. The evidence comes from two kinds of enquiry (see Clarke *et al.* 1985; Rutter 1980). The first is epidemiological. Low IQ is related to lower social class, poverty, poor housing, and an unstable family environment. Such social factors may be the effects of low intelligence and do not necessarily exclude a genetic cause. Thus mentally retarded people might drift into an adverse social environment and bring up their children there.

The second source of evidence is from attempts to enrich the environment of deprived children in special residential care (see O'Connor 1968) and to provide special education. In one experiment, children from large and unsatisfactory institutions were transferred to small well-staffed children's homes or given more stimulating education. Twenty years later they were found to have higher IQs than those who remained in their original institutions as children (see Skeels 1966). More recent studies have confirmed that, for socially deprived children, well planned and prolonged intervention can be beneficial (see Clarke and Clarke 1985*a*).

Other environmental factors

These include intrauterine infection (such as rubella), environmental pollutants (such as lead), maternal alcoholism in pregnancy (see p. 516), severe malnutrition, and excessive irradiation to the womb (see Clarke and Clarke 1985). There seem to be vulnerable periods of brain development during which damage is particularly likely to follow exposure to such environmental hazards (see Davison 1984; Cowie 1980). Malnutrition in the first two years of life is probably the most common cause of retardation in the world as a whole, but is much less frequent in developed countries.

There is no doubt that severe **lead intoxication** can cause an encephalopathy with consequent intellectual impairment. It is much less certain whether the moderate levels of lead found in some British children (especially as a result of air pollution from lead additives in petrol) can cause intellectual retardation. It is known that children absorb lead more readily than adults and are therefore at greater risk from environmental pollution. However, most of the studies have been of children from poor homes, and it is impossible to be certain how far findings of low intelligence (compared with children in other areas) are due to slightly raised lead levels in their blood, and how far to social influences (see Smith 1986 for a review).

Table 21.4. Notes on some causes of mental retardation

Syndrome	Aetiology	Clinical features	Comments
Chromosome abnormalities (For Down's syndrome and X-linked retardation see text)			
Triple X	Trisomy X	No characteristic feature	Mild retardation
Cri du chat	Deletion in chromosome 5	Microcephaly, hyperteleorism, typical cat-like cry, failure to thrive	
Inborn errors of metabolism			
Phenylketonuria	Autosomal recessive causing lack of liver phenylalanine hydroxylase. Commonest inborn error of metabolism	Lack of pigment (fair hair, blue eyes). Retarded growth. Associated epilepsy, microcephaly, eczema, and hyperactivity	Detectable by post-natal screening of blood or urine. Treated by exclusion of phenylalanine from the diet during early years of life
Homocystinuria	Autosomal recessive causing lack of cystathione synthetases	Ectopia lentis, fine and fair hair, joint enlargement, skeletal abnormalities similar to Marfan's syndrome. Associated with thromboembolic episodes	Retardation variable. Sometimes treatable by methionine restriction
Galactosaemia	Autosomal recessive causing lack of galactose 1-phosphate uridyl transferase	Presents following introduction of milk into diet. Failure to thrive, hepatosplenomegaly, cataracts	Detectable by post-natal screening for the enzymic defect. Treatable by galactose-free diet. Toluidine blue test on urine
Tay–Sachs disease	Autosomal recessive resulting in increased lipid storage (the earliest form of the cerebro-macular degenerations)	Progressive loss of vision and hearing. Spastic paralysis. Cherry-red spot at macula of retina. Epilepsy	Death at 2–4 years
Hurler's syndrome (gargoylism)	Autosomal recessive affecting mucopolysaccharide storage	Grotesque features. Protuberant abdomen. Hepatosplenomegaly. Associated cardiac abnormalities	Death before adolescence

Lesch–Nyhan syndrome	X-linked recessive leading to enzyme defect affecting purine metabolism. Excessive uric acid production and excretion	Normal at birth. Development of choreo-athetoid movements, scissoring position of legs and self-mutilation	Can be diagnosed prenatally by culture of amniotic fluid and estimation of relevant enzyme. Post-natal diagnosis by enzyme estimation in a single hair root. Death in second or third decade from infection or renal failure. Self-mutilation may be reduced by treatment with hydroxytrytophan
Other inherited disorders			
Neurofibromatosis (Von Recklinghausen's syndrome)	Autosomal dominant inheritance	Neurofibromata, *café au lait* spots, vitiligo. Associated with symptoms determined by site of neurofibromata. Astrocytomas, menigioma	Retardation in a minority
Tuberose sclerosis (Epiloia)	Autosomal dominant (very variable penetrance)	Epilepsy, adenoma sebaceum on face, white skin patches, shagreen skin, retinal phakoma, subungual fibroma. Associated multiple tumours in kidney, spleen, and lungs	Retardation in about 70 per cent
Lawrence–Moon–Biedl syndrome	Autosomal recessive	Retinitis pigmentosa, polydactyly, sometimes with obesity and impaired genital function	Retardation usually not severe
Infection			
Rubella embryopathy	Viral infection of mother in first trimester	Cataract, microphthalmia, deafness, microcephaly, congenital heart disease	If mother infected in first trimester, 10–15 per cent infants are affected (infection may be subclinical)
Toxoplasmosis	Protozoal infection of mother	Hydrocephaly, microcephaly, intra-cerebral calcification, retinal damage, hepatosplenomegaly, jaundice, epilepsy	Wide variation in severity
Cytomegalovirus	Virus infection of mother	Brain damage. Only severe cases are apparent at birth	

Table 21.4. *continued*

Syndrome	Aetiology	Clinical features	Comments
Congenital syphilis	Syphilitic infection of mother	Many die at birth. Variable neurological signs. 'Stigmata' (Hutchinson teeth and rhagades often absent)	Uncommon since routine testing of pregnant women. Infant's WR positive at first but may become negative
Cranial malformations			
Hydrocephalus	Sex-limited recessive Inherited developmental abnormality, e.g. atresia of aqueduct, Arnold–Chiari malformation. Meningitis. Spina bifida	Rapid enlargement of head In early infancy, symptoms of raised csf pressure. Other features depend on aetiology	Mild cases may arrest spontaneously. May be symptomatically treated by CSF shunt. Intelligence can be normal
Microcephaly	Recessive inheritance, irradiation in pregnancy, maternal infections	Features depend upon aetiology	Evident in up to a fifth of institutionalized mentally retarded patients
Miscellaneous			
Spina bifida	Aetiology multiple and complex	Failure of vertebral fusion. *Spina bifida cystica* is associated with meningocele or, in 15–20%, myelomeningocele. Latter causes spinal cord damage, with lower limb paralysis, incontinence, etc.	Hydrocephalus in four-fifths of those with myelomeningocele. Retardation in this group
Cerebral palsy	Perinatal brain damage. Strong association with prematurity.	Spastic (commonest), athetoid and ataxic types. Variable in severity	Majority are below average intelligence. Athetoid are more likely to be of normal IQ
Hypothyroidism (cretinism)	Iodine deficiency or (rarely) atrophic thyroid	Appearance normal at birth. Abnormalities appear at 6 months. Growth failure, puffy skin, lethargy	Now rare in Britain. Responds to early replacement treatment
Hyperbilirubinaemia	Haemolysis, rhesus incompatibility, and prematurity	Kernicterus (choreoathetosis), opisthotonus, spasticity, convulsions	Prevention by anti-Rhesus globulin. Neonatal treatment by exchange transfusion

Birth injury

This is also important. Early studies estimated that clinically recognizable birth injuries accounted for about 10 per cent of mental retardation. Pasamanick and Knobloch (1966) extended this observation, by suggesting a 'continuum of reproductive casualty' in which mild subnormality is assumed to result from less obvious brain lesions sustained *in utero* or perinatally (see p. 769). Although this last idea is controversial, there is good evidence that prematurity and low birth weight are associated with mental retardation.

Specific causes of mental handicap

Many syndromes have been identified which are caused by single genes or chromosomal abnormalities. A large number of specific biochemical abnormalities have now been identified which account for the mental retardation. Table 21.3 summarizes many of the main causes, but is not exhaustive. Since these causes are rare, they will not be described in this chapter. Useful information about some of the less rare conditions is summarized in Table 21.4. Although these syndromes are still discussed in some textbooks of psychiatry, they are more likely to be dealt with by paediatricians than by psychiatrists. If the psychiatrist takes over the care of a patient suffering from any of these rare syndromes, he should work closely with the paediatrician and family doctor, and should acquaint himself with the up-to-date knowledge of the particular syndrome. Further information can be found in a standard textbook of paediatrics.

The **specific genetic syndromes** are sufficiently varied to require separate comment. Five groups may be recognized.

1. **Dominant conditions**. These are rare. Examples include the phako-matoses, including neurofibromatosis.

2. **Recessive conditions**. This is the largest group of specific gene disorders. It includes most of the inherited metabolic conditions, such as phenylketonuria, homocystinuria, and galactosaemia.

3. **Sex-linked conditions**. The prevalence of intellectual retardation is 25 per cent greater in males than in females. Lehrke (1972), was the first to suggest that the excess among males might be due to X-chromosome-linked causes. Recent research suggests that up to a fifth of intellectual handicap in males is due to X-linked causes (see Turner 1982). Several rare specific syndromes have been identified, for example glucose dehydrogenase deficiency and the Lesch–Nyhan syndrome. However, in most cases there is no metabolic abnormality. In many of these, usually referred to as cases of 'fragile X syndrome', the only clinical sign is enlargement of the testes. A marker is visible in the X chromosome in lymphocyte culture. Although most of the carrier females have normal

intelligence, many have learning difficulties and about 10 per cent have been reported to have mild mental retardation (Turner 1982; Baraitser 1986; Kinnell 1987).

4. **Chromosome abnormalities**. The most common is Down's syndrome. Sex-chromosome abnormalities, such as Klinefelter's syndrome (XXY), and Turner's syndrome (XO), may also cause retardation (see Ratcliffe 1982).

5. **Conditions with partial and complex inheritance** such as anencephaly. This group is poorly understood.

In this chapter, only the common condition of Down's syndrome will be described further.

Down's syndrome

In 1866, Langdon Down tried to relate the appearance of certain groups of patients to the physical features of ethnic groups. One of the groups had the condition originally called Mongolism, and now generally known as Down's sydrome. This condition is a frequent cause of mental retardation occurring in one in every 600–700 births. However, the incidence of Down's syndrome is decreasing because of reduced birth rates among older women, and increases in detection by amniocentesis with subsequent termination of pregnancy. The retardation is usually mild or moderate but can occasionally be severe.

The **clinical picture** is made up of a number of features any one of which can occur in a normal person. Four of these features together are generally accepted as strong evidence for the syndrome. The most characteristic signs are: (a) mouth—a small mouth and teeth, furrowed tongue, high-arched palate; (b) eyes—oblique palpebral fissures, epicanthic folds; (c) head—flat occiput; (d) hands—short and broad, curved fifth finger, single transverse palmar crease; (e) joints—hyperextensibility or hyperflexibility, hypotonia.

There are often other associated abnormalities. Congenital heart disease (especially septal defects) occurs in about 20 per cent. Intestinal abnormalities are common, especially duodenal obstruction. Hearing may be impaired

There is considerable variation in the degree of mental retardation; the IQ generally is between 20 and 50, and in 15 per cent it is above 50. Mental abilities usually develop fairly quickly in the first six to twelve months of life but then increase more slowly. The temperament of children with Down's syndrome is usually described as lovable and easy going. Many of them show an interest in music. Although there is little good epidemiological evidence, it is likely that behaviour problems are less frequent than in other forms of retardation (Gath and Gumley 1986).

In the past the infant mortality of Down's syndrome was high, but with improved medical care survival into adult life is more common. About a quarter of people with Down's syndrome now live beyond 50; signs of premature ageing appear and Alzheimer-like changes in the brain develop in middle life (Oliver and Holland 1986).

Aetiology

In 1959, Down's syndrome was found to be associated with the chromosomal disorder of trisomy (three chromosomes instead of the usual two). About 95 per cent of cases are due to trisomy 21. These cases result from failure of disjunction during meiosis and are associated with increasing maternal age. The risk of recurrence in a subsequent child is about 1 in 100. The remaining five per cent of cases of Down's syndrome are attributable either to translocation involving chromosome 21 or to mozaicism. The disorder leading to translocation is often inherited and the risk of recurrence is about 1 in 10. Mozaicism occurs when non-disjunction takes place in any cell division after fertilization. Normal and trisomic cells occur in the same person and the effects on cognitive development are particularly variable.

Causes of psychiatric disorder and behaviour problems in the mentally retarded

The diversity of psychiatric disorders among the mentally retarded makes it unlikely that they have a single aetiology. Several causes have to be considered: genetic, organic pathology, psychological, and social (see Corbett 1985).

There is no evidence that the same **genetic** abnormality causes mental retardation and psychiatric disorder. As noted already, most severely retarded people have some **organic brain pathology**, and so do a smaller number of those with moderate and mild retardation. As mentioned in the chapter on child psychiatry, in children of normal intelligence psychiatric disorder is associated with brain damage (see Rutter *et al.* 1970*a*). There is also a known association between cerebral pathology on the one hand and schizophrenia and affective disorders on the other (see Davison and Bagley 1969; Davison 1983). In mentally retarded patients, therefore, it is likely that some psychiatric disorders (including major psychiatric illnesses) are related to brain pathology. There is an especially close association between **epilepsy** and behaviour disorder in the mentally retarded. This applies particularly to hyperkinetic behaviour (see Corbett and Pond 1979). Such behaviour disorder may be due not only to the direct effects of epilepsy but also to the side-effects of anticonvulsant drugs (see p. 676).

Organic disorder cannot be the whole explanation, because the rate of mental disorder is increased in mentally handicapped people with no brain pathology. Other causes include **psychological** factors associated with mental handicap, particularly abnormalities of temperament, language difficulty, inability to acquire social skills, and educational failure. **Social** factors such as bereavement or a disrupted family are important in causing mental disorder and behaviour problems in the mentally retarded just as they are in patients of normal intelligence (see Rutter and Madge 1976).

It should not be forgotten that **iatrogenic** factors can contribute to the causes of psychiatric disorder among the mentally retarded. As mentioned above, these include the side-effects of drugs, especially those used to treat epilepsy, and also over- or understimulating environments within an institution.

The assessment of the mentally retarded

Severe retardation can usually be diagnosed in infancy, especially as it is often associated with detectable physical abnormalities or with retardation of motor development. The clinician should be cautious in diagnosing less severe mental retardation on the basis of delays in development. Although routine examination of a child may reveal signs of developmental delay suggesting possible mental retardation (see Illingworth 1980), confident diagnosis often requires a second opinion from a specialist. Full assessment has several stages: history taking, physical examination, developmental testing, behavioural assessment, and examination of the mental state. These will be considered in turn. Although this section is concerned mainly with the assessment of children, similar principles apply in adolescence and adult life.

History taking

In the course of obtaining a full history, particular attention should be given to any family history suggesting an inherited disorder, and to abnormalities in the pregnancy or the delivery of the child. Dates of passing developmental milestones should be ascertained (see p. 762). A full account of any behaviour disorders should be obtained.

Physical examination

A systematic physical examination should include the recording of weight, height, and head circumference. It is important to be alert for the physical signs of the many specific syndromes (see Table 21.4). The neurological examination should include particular attention to vision and hearing.

Developmental assessment

This assessment is based on a combination of clinical experience and standardized methods of measuring intelligence, language, motor performance, and social skills. Although the IQ is the best general index of intellectual development, it is not reliable in the very young. Table 20.2 lists some commonly used developmental tests (see p. 774)

Behavioural assessment

This is based on the observations by the clinical team of the patient's ability to care for himself, his social abilities including his ability to communicate, his sensory motor skills and any unusual behaviour.

Psychiatric assessment

This is directed not so much to the making of a diagnosis as to the formulation of relevant medical and social factors including the attitudes of people who might be involved in the patient's care. If the mentally retarded person has reasonable language ability, it is possible to carry out a standard psychiatric interview whilst making appropriate allowance for any difficulty in his concentration. When language is less well developed, an account has to be obtained mainly from informants. It is particularly important to obtain a complete description of any change from the usual pattern of behaviour. It is often necessary to ask teachers, hospital staff, or parents to keep records of behaviours such as eating, sleeping, and general activity. The interviewer should keep in mind the possible causes of psychiatric disorder outlined above, including unrecognized epilepsy.

Differential diagnosis

At the end of the assessment, the main diagnoses to be considered are: delayed maturation; deafness, blindness or other sensory defects; childhood psychosis; childhood autism; and states due to the side-effects of drugs. (Childhood psychosis and autism are described on p. 797.)

The care of the mentally retarded

A historical perspective

In the last few decades the aims and methods of care for the mentally retarded have been transformed. These changes and the remaining unsolved problems can best be understood in relation to the history of the development of services (see Corbett 1978).

The special treatment of the mentally retarded began with the remarkable efforts of Itard, physician-in-chief at the Asylum for the Deaf and Dumb in Paris, to train the 'wild boy' found in Aveyron in 1801. This child was thought to have grown up in the wild, isolated from human beings. Itard made great efforts to educate the boy, but after persisting for six years he concluded that the training had been a failure. Nevertheless his work had important and lasting consequences, one of which was the development of special educational methods for the mentally retarded. These methods were developed by Seguin, director of the School for Idiots at the Bicêtre in Paris, who in 1842 published his *Theory and nature of the education of idiots*. Seguin believed that the mentally retarded had latent abilities which could be encouraged by special training. He therefore devised an educational programme of physical exercises, moral instruction, and graded tasks (Seguin 1864, 1866). His ideas were particularly taken up in Switzerland and Germany. Another pioneer was the Swiss physician Guggenbühl who in 1841 founded at Abendberg the first special residential institution for the mentally retarded. Similar institutions were soon opened in other parts of Europe to provide a training that would enable their pupils to live as independently as possible. However it was recognized that some mentally retarded people needed long-term care.

At the end of the nineteenth century several influences led to a more custodial approach to the care of the mentally retarded. These influences included the development of the science of genetics, the beliefs embodied in the eugenics movement, and a general decrease in public tolerance of abnormal behaviour. In England and Wales, such ideas were reflected in the Mental Deficiency Act of 1913, which empowered local authorities to provide for the confinement of the intellectually and morally defective and imposed upon them a responsibility to provide training and occupation. As a result the total number of in-patients of this kind rose from 6000 in 1916 to 50 000 in 1939.

In the 1960s, the need for reform was recognized, partly because of changes that had already been effected in psychiatric hospitals (see p. 743), partly because of improved psychological research, partly because of campaigning by groups of parents, and partly because of public concern about the generally poor conditions in which the mentally retarded were housed. Surveys of hospitals for the retarded showed that the mean IQ of their patients was over 70. Many residents had only mild retardation, and many did not need hospital care. About the same time it was shown that simple training could help many patients, both the mildly and severely retarded (see O'Connor 1968). Further investigations showed the advantages of residential care in small homely units (Tizard 1964). However public concern was aroused less by these research findings than by a series of scandals about the conditions in hospitals for the mentally retarded. For example, Morris (1969) reported a survey of 33 subnormality hospitals. She described large isolated hospitals with dilapidated buildings that were overcrowded and squalid. They were poorly organized, and few of them had clear objectives for treatment. There were shortages of nursing and other staff (see Clarke *et al.* 1985).

The last 20 years have seen the acceptance in all developed countries (especially Scandinavia) of the need for methods of care with a less medical approach. Unfortunately, there have been divergent views about these methods, and resources have been inadequate and progress slow. In the United States, deinstitutionalization has been carried out at great speed with both successes and failures (Landesman-Dyer 1981). In Britain the problems and possible solutions have been set out in policy papers from the Department of Health and Social Security (1971, 1985).

Among the new concepts of care the main principle is 'normalization', an idea developed in Scandinavia in the 1960s. This term refers to the general approach of providing a pattern of life as near normal as possible (Nirje 1970). The least handicapped are brought up in their own homes and encouraged to lead almost independent lives as adults. For the few who enter hospital the accommodation and activities are designed to be as close as possible to those of family life. The concept of normalization has been greatly developed in the United States (see Wolfensberger 1980). The provisions required to achieve these aims have been described by Malin *et al.* (1980), and the Office of Health Economics (1986*b*). The following account relates particularly to the United Kingdom, but the principles are widely applicable.

The general provisions

For the care of the mentally retarded in a community the precise model matters less than the detail in which it is planned and the enthusiasm with which it is carried out. Good planning requires an estimate of the needs of the population to be served. Table 21.5 shows the estimated needs of a general population of 100 000 (see Kushlik and Blunden 1974; Tizard 1974). As a guide to the provision of services in any area, the figures can be modified in the light of any local information. Local case registers and linked developmental records are important.

The general approach is educational rather than medical. The team providing the care includes psychiatrists, psychologists, nurses, residential care staff, teachers, occupational therapists, physiotherapists, and speech therapists. Volunteers can often play a valuable part, and it is useful to encourage self-help groups for parents.

The family doctor and paediatrician are now mainly responsible for the early detection of mental retardation, but the child psychiatrist also plays

Table 21.5. Facilities required for the mentally retarded in a population of 100 000*

Children (aged 0–14 years)		
(a) *Mildly retarded:* See text		
(b) *Severely retarded:* Total number 90		
Accommodation	At home	60
	Residential care	30
Education	Special pre-school	10
	Special school	60
	Special care unit	10
	No schooling	10
Adults (aged over 14 years)		
Total number requiring care: 375		
Employment	Employable	180
	Sheltered workshop	140
	Neither	55
Accommodation	Employable: home	105
	hostel	75
	Not employable: home	45
	residential	150

* See Kushlik and Blunden (1974); Tizard (1974).

some part. Apart from this, the psychiatrist has three roles. The first is to help mentally retarded children and adults who have psychiatric problems. In this role he is most likely to be called upon at times of particular difficulty for the family. These are when the diagnosis is first made, when the child enters school, and when he leaves school. The second role is liaison between the medical, educational, and social services, all of which may be involved in the care of the individual patient. The third role is to give a lead in the planning of services.

The mildly retarded

The number of mildly retarded people in the population is not known accurately. Few need specialist services. Most are able to live with their families and to remain under the care of the family doctor. Some have additional problems, such as physical disability, minor emotional disorders, and psychiatric illness. A few mildly retarded children require fostering, boarding school placements, or residential care, either because of such additional problems or because of difficulties in the family. Mildly retarded adults may need support when they are facing extra problems;

for example, they may need help with housing and employment, or with the special problems of old age. Most can live at home or in a hostel and carry out sheltered work.

Severely retarded children

There are about 90 severely retarded children in a population of 100 000. Some require special services throughout their lives, and appropriate planning should begin as soon as the diagnosis is certain. About two-thirds can remain at home provided that their parents are taught how to care for them and are given appropriate practical assistance and emotional support. The practical help may include day care, or short stays in hospital or residential care when the parents need a holiday or when another family member is ill. About a quarter of severely retarded children living at home have behavioural problems, difficulty in walking, or incontinence. When the time comes for the child to attend school, account should be taken of such practical matters as the need for transport and for provisions in the holidays.

About one-third of severely retarded children need some form of residential care. About half of these have physical or behavioural problems or incontinence too great for the parents or hostel staff to manage. Even though such children need to live in hospital many can still attend a special school in the community.

Severely retarded adults

In the care of the mentally retarded it is often particularly difficult to arrange a smooth transition during adolescence from children's services to adult services that make best use of a combination of normal facilities and special provisions. Care at home becomes less easy to manage and less appropriate and residential provision is often preferable (which should be outside hospital if possible). At this stage the co-ordination of services passes from the school to the social services department. Provisions are required for sheltered work, day centres, and hostel accommodation (Brimblecombe 1985). Some severely retarded people will continue to need treatment for behaviour disorders, psychiatric illness, epilepsy, or physical disability. A few will need to remain in hospital.

Because of the marked increase in the life expectancy of severely retarded people, large unforeseen demands are now being placed on services, and it is difficult to predict the scale of future needs.

Specific services

An account will now be given of the main elements in a service for the mentally retarded. Use will be made of the following headings from the

Department of Health Report *Better services for the mentally handicapped* (1971).

(1) The prevention or early detection of mental handicap.

(2) The assessment of the mentally handicapped person's assets and disabilities, and their periodic re-assessment.

(3) Advice, support, and practical measures for families.

(4) Provision for education, training, occupation, or work appropriate for each handicapped person.

(5) Residential accommodation appropriate to the individual's needs.

(6) Medical, nursing, and other services for those who require them, as out-patients, day-patients, or in-patients.

1. Preventive services

In the United States, the President's Panel on Mental Retardation (1972) concluded that it would be possible to reduce the occurrence of mental retardation by 50 per cent before the end of the century. Recent experience suggests that this estimate is much too optimistic. Moreover such an aim could be achieved only for severe retardation, and then only in developed countries. For mild retardation, which has less discrete causes, reduction on such a scale is highly unlikely (see Clarke *et al.* 1985).

Primary prevention depends largely on genetic counselling, early detection of fetal abnormalities during pregnancy, and safe childbirth. Secondary prevention aims to prevent the progression of disability by either medical or psychological means. The latter include 'enriching' education and early attempts to reduce behavioural problems.

Genetic counselling

This begins with assessment of the risk of an abnormal child being born. Such an assessment is based on study of the family history and knowledge of the genetics of conditions that give rise to mental defect. The parents are then given an explanation of the risks and encouraged to discuss them. Most parents seek advice only after a first abnormal child has been born. Some do so before starting to have children because there is a mentally retarded person on one or other side of the family. (For a general account of genetic counselling, see p. 433.)

Prenatal care

This begins before conception by giving advice on diet, alcohol and smoking, and by providing immunization against rubella for girls who lack immunity. Some causes of mental retardation can now be diagnosed *in utero*. Amniocentesis, fetoscopy and ultrasound scanning of the fetus in the second trimester can reveal chromosomal abnormalities, most open neural tube defects, and about 60 per cent of inborn errors of metabolism.

Amniocentesis carries a small but definite risk, and so is usually offered only to women who have carried a previous abnormal fetus, women with a family history of congenital disorder, and those over 35 years of age.

Rhesus incompatibility is now largely preventable. Sensitization of a rhesus negative mother can usually be avoided by giving anti-D antibody. An affected fetus can be detected by amniocentesis and treated if necessary by exchange transfusion. For pregnant women with diabetes mellitus, special care can improve the outlook for the fetus. Further information about these aspects of care will be found in up-to-date textbooks of obstetrics and paediatrics.

Postnatal prevention

In Britain, all infants are routinely tested for phenylketonuria, and routine testing for hypothyroidism and galactosaemia is becoming increasingly common. Special intensive care units and improved methods of care for premature and low birth-weight infants can prevent mental retardation in some infants who previously would have suffered brain damage. However, the methods also enable the survival of some retarded children who would otherwise have died.

'Compensatory' education

This is intended to provide optimal conditions for the mental development of the retarded child. Such was the aim of the 'Head Start' programme in the United States, which provided extra education for deprived children. Its methods varied from nursery schooling to attempts to teach specific skills (see Rutter and Madge 1976). Many of the results were disappointing. A more intensive programme with similar aims has been carried out in Milwaukee (Heber and Garber 1975). Skilled teachers educated children living in slum areas whose mothers had a low IQ (under 75). This additional education started when the child was three months old and continued until school age. At the same time, the mothers were trained in a variety of domestic skills. These children were compared with control children of the same age who came from similar families but who had not received additional education and whose mothers had not been trained. At the age of four and a half, the trained children had a mean IQ 27 points higher than that of the controls. Although this study can be faulted because the selection of children was not strictly random, and because some of the changes in test scores could have been due to practice, the main findings probably stand. The findings show that substantial effort by trained staff can produce worthwhile improvement in children of low intelligence born to socially disadvantaged mothers. The findings also indicate a need to train the parents as well as the children.

Overall there is now good evidence that pre-school intervention can be effective (Lazar *et al.* 1982). [For a review see Clarke *et al.* (1985).]

2. Assessment

Severe retardation is usually obvious from an early age. Lesser degrees may become apparent only when the child starts school. Family doctors and teachers should be able to detect possible retardation, but a full assessment requires expert knowledge. Full assessment is often carried out in an assessment centre where the child can be observed in many different activities. The methods have been described earlier (p. 847).

Once mental retardation has been diagnosed, regular reviews are required. For the mentally retarded living in the community, these reviews will usually be carried out by paediatricians, teachers, and social workers. The psychiatrist's main responsibility is for patients resident in hospital or attending as outpatients.

It is important to arrange a thorough review when the child leaves school. This review should assess his need for further education, prospects for employment, suitability for a training centre, and requirements for day care. Mentally retarded adults also need to be assessed regularly to make sure that they are continuing to achieve their potential and still receiving appropriate care.

3. Help for families

Help for families is needed most when the diagnosis is first made. For worried parents it is not enough to give an explanation on just one occasion. They may need to be given an explanation repeatedly before they can absorb all its implications. Adequate time must be provided to explain the prognosis, indicate what help can be provided, and discuss the part the parents can play in helping their child to achieve his full potential.

Afterwards the parents need continuing support. When the child starts school, they should be kept informed about his progress. They should be given help with practical matters such as day care for the child during school holidays, baby-sitting, or arrangements for family holidays. In addition to practical matters, the parents need continuing psychological support.

Families are likely to need extra help when their mentally retarded child is approaching puberty or leaving school [see Brimblecombe (1979) for a more detailed account of these matters].

4. Education, training, and occupation

In 1929, the Mental Deficiency Committee made the following comment on schools for the mentally retarded:

If the majority of children for whom these schools are intended are to lead the lives of ordinary citizens . . . these schools must be brought into close relation with the public elementary school system and presented to parents not as something distinct and humiliating but as a helpful variation of an ordinary school.

Progress in achieving this aim has been slow and there are considerable variations in provisions between Health Regions. In 1970 the Education of Handicapped Children Act required Local Education Authorities to provide for the education and training of all mentally retarded children whether living in hospitals or in their own homes. In 1978 the Warnock Committee (Committee of Enquiry into the Education of Handicapped Children and Young People) recommended increased provisions for the special education of pre-school and school-age children. This Committee also emphasized the need for as many mentally retarded children as possible to be educated in ordinary schools, either in ordinary classes or in special classes but with social integration outside the classroom.

A subsequent Education Act (1981) required Local Authorities to identify handicapped children of all kinds and to make statements of need for them. Health Authorities are required to notify Local Authorities of handicapped children below school age.

Research has consistently shown the value of an early start. Such a start can be made in a special pre-school or playgroup, or occasionally in day care at a hospital. When normal school age is reached, the least handicapped children can attend remedial classes in ordinary schools. The others need to attend special schools 'for children with learning difficulties' (formerly called schools for the Educationally Subnormal). It is still not certain which retarded children benefit from ordinary schooling, and particularly whether the severely retarded do so. Education in an ordinary school offers the advantages of more normal social surroundings and the expectation of progress; but it carries the disadvantage of lack of special teaching skills and equipment, and the risk of the child not being accepted by the more able children.

Traditionally, education for the more severely retarded has been based on the sensory training methods started by Itard and Seguin (see p. 846). It is only recently that the content of the curriculum has been reconsidered. The first change was towards an approach similar to that of an ordinary primary school with an emphasis on self expression. However, methods of this kind may be inappropriate for the retarded. There is now an increasing use of a more structured approach to teaching and of behavioural methods in training.

Before retarded children leave school, they need reassessment and vocational guidance. Most of the mildly retarded are able to take normal jobs or enter sheltered employment. The severely retarded are likely to transfer to adult training centres. For some this transfer will be a stage in the progression towards normal employment, but for the majority it will be permanent. Adult training centres were originally intended to provide sheltered industrial work. It is now apparent that they should provide a wider range of activities if the abilities of each attender are to be developed as much as possible. Even for the minority of severely retarded people who require intensive supervision, care is usually provided better in a training centre than in a hospital. [For a review see Office of Health Economics (1986*b*).]

5. Residential care

It is now widely accepted that the mentally retarded should be looked after by their parents or if they are too heavy a burden for their parents, in small homely residential units. Support for this view came from an important study by Tizard (1964), who compared two groups of children who had moderate or severe mental retardation but no serious additional physical handicaps. One group was reared in a large hospital, and the other in a small residential unit where care was provided in small family-like groups. The children brought up in this small unit developed better verbal abilities, emotional relationships, and personal independence. Subsequently King *et al.* (1971) showed that local authority hostels (which are somewhat larger than the small units) had similar advantages over hospitals for the mentally retarded. King *et al.* suggested that the advantages of the hostels are due not only to their smaller size and better staffing, but also to their 'child-centred' approach. Studies such as those of Landesman-Dyer (1981) confirmed that merely moving mentally retarded children to smaller living units is not beneficial unless the staff encourage residents to live as normally as possible.

These findings are reflected in the report of the Committee of Enquiry into Mental Handicap Nursing and Care (the 'Jay Report' 1979). The report suggests that conventional nursing training is not an appropriate preparation for the general care of mentally retarded children. However, it is widely believed that trained hospital staff have a role to play in the care of the mentally retarded. This role is to treat the mentally retarded who have accompanying mental illness, severe behaviour disorder, epilepsy, important sensory defect or language impairment, and other severe physical problems.

In Britain, official policy is to replace existing large, isolated hospitals by smaller units in the community they serve. Various alternatives have been proposed. According to Kushlick (1980), all severely retarded children and most severely retarded adults who would otherwise need institutional care, can be looked after in 25-bedded residential units by people who have not received special nursing training. Evaluation of children's units of this kind suggests that they are as good or better than the traditional large hospital; however, advocates of 'normalization' criticize these units as still being institutional. Other alternatives to hospital include group homes, adoption, and fostering (see Udall and Corbett 1979). [See Raynes and Sumpton (1987) for a discussion of recent evidence.]

In recent years the reduction of hospital beds has been greater than originally envisaged by the DHSS (1972). In the National Health Service there are now only a thousand beds in England and Wales for children aged under 16. These beds are increasingly used for short stay specialist treatment rather than for long-term placement.

6. Specialist medical services

Retarded children and adults often have physical handicaps or epilepsy for which continuing medical care is needed. In Britain, such medical care is obtained from the ordinary medical services, thus placing a sizeable extra burden on general practitioners and paediatricians. Sometimes this arrangement works well, but there may be difficulties for the patient and his family if doctors and nurses are unaware how to deal with an uncomprehending patient. In some countries, such as Denmark, a special medical service is available for the retarded.

Treatment of psychiatric problems in the mentally retarded

As explained above, psychiatric disorder in the mentally retarded usually comes to notice through changes in behaviour. It should be remembered that behavioural change can also result from physical illness or from stressful events, both of which should be carefully excluded. In the most retarded and especially those with sensory deficits, behavioural disturbance may be due to understimulation rather than excessive stress. Once the cause is clear, the treatment follows. Physical illness should be treated promptly, stressful events reduced if possible, or a more stimulating environment provided when appropriate. If the disturbed behaviour results from a psychiatric disorder, the treatment is similar in many ways to that for a patient of normal intelligence with the same disorder (see below). It is important to advise and support the parents or others who are caring for the patient during the period of treatment. In the more serious and persistent cases, admission to hospital may be needed. [For a review see Reid (1982) and Corbett (1985).]

Drugs

Although antipsychotic drugs are used widely to control abnormal behaviour in the mentally retarded, there have been few controlled trials of their effects. The indications for these drugs are similar to those in patients of normal intelligence. Chlorpromazine or haloperidol are suitable preparations. A particularly careful watch should be kept for side-effects because the patient may not be able to draw attention to them himself. Although antipsychotic drugs may be used for the short-term control of behaviour problems, whenever possible social measures or behavioural treatment should be used for long-term management.

Many mentally retarded patients suffer from epilepsy and require anticonvulsant treatment. Special care is needed in arriving at a drug and a dosage that controls seizures without producing unwanted effects (see p. 646 for the side-effects of anticonvulsant drugs).

Counselling

The patients' limited undertstanding of language sets obvious limitations to the use of psychotherapy. However, simple discussion can help. As noted already, counselling for parents is an important part of treatment.

Behaviour modification

This method has become widely used since it was first introduced in the United States in the 1960s. It can be used to encourage basic skills such as washing, toilet-training, and dressing. Often parents and teachers are taught to carry out the training so that it can be maintained in the patient's everyday environment (see Yule and Carr 1980). The behaviour to be modified is first specified. If the problem is an undesired behaviour a search is made for any environmental factors that seem regularly to provoke it or reinforce it. If possible these environmental factors are changed. In this way problem behaviours are eliminated by ensuring that they are not rewarded inadvertently, and by reinforcing alternative responses. Aggressive behaviour is sometimes dealt with by withdrawing all reinforcement; in so-called 'time out' the patient is ignored or secluded until the behaviour subsides. If the problem is the lack of some socially desirable behaviour, attempts are made to reinforce any such behaviour with material or social rewards, if necessary by 'shaping' the final behaviour from simpler components. Reward should be given immediately after the desired behaviour has taken place (for example using the toilet). For training in skills such as dressing, it is often necessary to provide modelling and prompting in the early stages, and to reduce them gradually later.

Compulsory admission

The relevant provisions of the legislation in England and Wales are referred to in the Appendix.

Further reading

Clarke, A. M., Clarke, A. D. B., and Berg, J. H. C. (1985). *Mental deficiency; the changing outlook* (4th edn). Methuen, London.

Syzmonski, L. S. and Crocker, A. C. (1985). Mental retardation. In *Comprehensive textbook of psychiatry* (ed. H. I. Kaplan and B. J. Sadock). Williams and Wilkins, Baltimore.

Reid, A. H. (1982). *The psychiatry of mental handicap*. Blackwell Scientific Publications, Oxford.

22 Forensic psychiatry

The clinical psychiatrist needs a working knowledge of two sets of laws, those relating to patients seen in ordinary clinical practice, and those relating to mentally abnormal offenders.

The first set of laws (concerned with ordinary patients) consists of two main groups. First are the laws regulating clinical practice, particularly the compulsory detention of patients in hospital and the giving of treatment without the patient's consent. Second are civil laws dealing with issues such as the patient's capacity to make a will or care for his own property.

The second set of laws deals with mentally abnormal offenders, that is criminal offenders who suffer from mental disorder, or mental retardation, or severe personality disorder. Such offenders are a small minority of all offenders, but they present many difficult problems in psychiatry and the law. These problems include issues such as criminal responsibility and fitness to plead; and practical questions such as whether an offender needs psychiatric treatment, and whether such treatment should be provided in the community, in a psychiatric hospital or special hospital, or in prison. For the management of such problems the psychiatrist needs knowledge not only of the law, but also of the relationship between particular kinds of crime and particular kinds of psychiatric disorder.

The term forensic psychiatry is used in two different senses, one narrow and one broad. In its narrow sense the term is applied only to the branch of psychiatry that deals with the assessment and treatment of mentally abnormal offenders. In its broad sense the term is applied to all legal aspects of psychiatry, including the civil law and laws regulating psychiatric practice, as well as the sub-specialty concerned with mentally abnormal offenders. In the title of this chapter the term is used in the broad sense.

The chapter begins with a brief discussion of the law in relation to ordinary psychiatric practice, with particular reference to confidentiality, informed consent, and compulsory admission to hospital. Next comes a short section dealing with the civil law in relation to issues such as fitness to drive and the care and disposal of patients' property.

The main part of the chapter is concerned with the mentally abnormal offender. A brief review of the general causes of crime is followed by discussion of the relationship between crime and the various psychiatric diagnostic categories. Next the role of the psychiatrist is described, with particular reference to the offender's fitness to plead, mental state at the time of the offence, diminished responsibility, and the psychiatric treatment of mentally abnormal offenders. An account is then given of the types of offence (violence, sexual offences, and property offences) most likely to be associated with psychological factors. This is followed by some guidelines for the psychiatrist on the work of the courts, and on interviewing defendants and preparing psychiatric court reports. Dangerousness and violence are then discussed, and finally there is an appendix outlining the main provisions of the Mental Health Act.

In reading this chapter, two important points need to be borne in mind. First, there are substantial differences between the laws of different countries. For this reason, the chapter deals largely with general principles rather than the details of the law. Second, there are differences between the legal and the psychiatric concepts of mental abnormality. These differences are made more complicated because the concept of mental abnormality varies between different parts of the law. In this chapter it is not possible to review all these diverse concepts, but a few examples will be given in relation to such issues as fitness to plead, testamentary capacity (fitness to make a will), and the legal defence of insanity. If a psychiatrist is called upon to give a psychiatric opinion on a legal issue, he should acquaint himself with whichever legal concept of abnormal state of mind is relevant.

The law in relation to ordinary psychiatric practice

In psychiatry the principles concerning *confidentiality* and *informed consent to treatment* are the same as in general medicine, but certain points need to be stressed.

Confidentiality

This is particularly important in psychiatry because information is collected about private and highly sensitive matters. In general, the psychiatrist should not collect information from other informants without the patient's consent. If the patient is too mentally disturbed to give an account of himself, the psychiatrist should use his own discretion about seeking information from someone else. Sometimes such information is of vital importance to assessment and management. The guiding principle should be to try to act in the patient's best interests, and to obtain information as far as possible from close relatives rather than employers. The same principles apply when the psychiatrist needs to give information or an opinion to relatives or other people. In most countries there are legal requirements that medical information be disclosed in certain circumstances (see Hawkins 1985).

Consent to treatment

The patient should have a clear and full understanding of the nature of a treatment procedure and its probable side-effects, and should freely agree to receive the treatment. For most treatments, such as established forms of medication, it is sufficient for the psychiatrist to explain the nature of the treatment and probable side-effects. There are, however, national differences in the degree of explanation required. For example, the concept of informed consent involves a more detailed account of side-effects of treatment in the USA than in the United Kingdom. If there is any doubt about a voluntary patient's capacity to give informed consent to any treatment, a close relative should be consulted wherever possible. Sometimes there is the possibility that doubts or arguments will arise at a later stage; for example, if the patient is very ill, or if the patient or his relatives are critical or litigious. In such cases it is good practice to keep a careful written note of what has been said. [For a general review see Hawkins (1985). Current requirements for consent to treatment in England and Wales are given in the Appendix.]

Compulsory admission and treatment

In all developed countries there are laws to protect a mentally disordered person and to protect society from the consequences of his mental disorder. In a particular society the laws vary with the political system, and with public attitudes towards lawyers and doctors. Generally the need for compulsory psychiatric treatment is smaller in societies that provide good psychiatric treatment which is respected by the community.

Special legal provision is needed for people who are a danger to themselves or others because of mental disorder, and who refuse to accept the treatment they require. Such people usually have little or no insight into their own psychiatric condition. They present a difficult ethical dilemma; on the one hand they have a right to be at liberty, on the other hand they need care and treatment, and society has a right to be protected. Countries vary widely in their approach to this dilemma. In some Scandinavian countries, for example, procedures for compulsory care are simple; whilst in some states of the USA, a court hearing may be required.

In England and Wales, provisions for compulsory admission and treatment are embodied in the Mental Health Act (1983). The relevant sections of this Act are explained in the Appendix, and at this stage only a few practical aspects of patient management will be mentioned. An experienced psychiatrist can often avoid the use of compulsory admission by patiently and tactfully persuading the patient to accept care voluntarily. If persuasion fails and compulsory treatment is inevitable, family members are often called upon to support the patient's admission to hospital. The doctor should consult the family closely and do his best to minimize their anxiety and guilt. Once the patient is in hospital, restrictions should be kept to the minimum required for safety and adequate treatment. Frequently the patient and his family soon realize that compulsory hospital care is virtually the same as that of a voluntary patient. If the hospital staff is patient and adaptable, it is usually possible to maintain treatment without causing lasting harm to relationships between staff, patient, and relatives.

Sometimes a patient admitted under a compulsory order refuses to accept restrictions or medication. Such refusal calls for considerable nursing skill, and the exercise of firmness and flexibility, patience and sympathy.

Another problem is that of the voluntary patient who is judged to need ECT for a severe psychiatric disorder (for example, extreme depression with dangerous refusal of food and drink), but who refuses to consent to ECT. As explained in the Appendix, in England and Wales the procedure is to discuss the problem fully with relatives, to seek an independent psychiatric opinion, and to complete a compulsory treatment order with the relatives' collaboration.

In most legal systems, safeguards against unnecessary detention are provided, and patients are entitled to easy access to appeal procedures. The type of safeguard varies from country to country. The system in England and Wales is reviewed in the Appendix (p. 904). [See Hoggett (1984) for a review of principles and practice, and Unsworth (1987) for a review of the development of mental health legislation in Britain.]

Civil law

As explained in the introduction, civil law deals with laws concerning property and inheritance, and also with contracts. In other words, it deals with the rights and obligations of individuals to one another. In this respect it differs from criminal law, which is concerned with offences against the state (not necessarily against an individual). Proceedings are undertaken by an individual or group who believe they have suffered a breach of the civil law, rather than by an agency of the state as with criminal law.

In matters of civil law, psychiatrists have special responsibility in relation to issues such as fitness to drive, testamentary capacity, torts and contracts, receivership, marriage contracts, and guardianship. These matters are outlined below.

The psychiatrist may be asked to submit a written report on a patient's state of mind in relation to these issues, or to proceedings concerning divorce, compensation, or other matters. In preparing such a report, the psychiatrist should follow the same principles as in writing a court report (see below, p. 892). He should prepare the report only after full discussion with the patient, and only with the patient's full consent. As with all psychiatric reports for legal purposes, the report should be concise and factual, and should give the reasons for any opinions. Finally, the law on these issues is complicated, and it is often advisable for the psychiatrist to seek legal guidance on them, particularly in relation to the legal concept of abnormal mental state relevant to the issue in question. [See Perr (1985) for a review of the principles and practice of law in the USA.]

Fitness to drive

Questions of fitness to drive may arise in relation to most psychiatric disorders, particularly the major mental disorders. Reckless driving may result from suicidal inclinations or manic disinhibition; panicky or aggressive driving may result from persecutory delusions; and indecisive or inaccurate driving from dementia. Concentration on driving may be impaired in severe anxiety or depressive disorders.

The question of fitness to drive also arises in relation to psychiatric drugs, particularly those affecting concentration, such as anxiolytic or antipsychotic drugs in high dosage. A doctor giving an opinion on fitness to drive should consider whether any medical condition or its treatment is liable to: cause loss of control; impair perception or comprehension; impair judgement; reduce concentration; or affect motor functions involved in handling the vehicle.

Testamentary capacity

This term refers to the capacity to make a valid will. If someone is suffering from mental disorder at the time of making a will, the validity of the will may be in doubt, and other people may challenge that validity. However, the will may still be legally valid if the testator is of 'sound disposing mind' at the time of making it.

In order to decide whether or not a testator is of sound disposing mind, the doctor should use four legal criteria:

(1) whether the testator understands what a will is, and what its consequences are;
(2) whether he knows the nature and extent of his property (though not in detail);
(3) whether he knows the names of close relatives, and can assess their claims to his property; and

(4) whether he is free from an abnormal state of mind that might distort feelings or judgements relevant to making the will. (A deluded person may legitimately make a will, provided that the delusions are unlikely to influence it.)

In conducting an examination, the doctor should see the testator alone, but should also see relatives and friends to check the accuracy of factual statements.

Torts and contracts

Torts are wrongs for which a person is liable in civil law as opposed to criminal law. They include, for example, negligence, libel, slander, trespass, and nuisance. If such a wrong is committed by a person of unsound mind, then any damages awarded in a court of law are usually only nominal. In this context the legal definition of unsound mind is restrictive, and it is advisable for a psychiatrist to take the advice of a lawyer on it.

If a person makes a contract and later develops a mental disorder, then the contract is binding. If a person makes a contract and is of unsound mind at the time, then a distinction is made between the 'necessaries' and 'non-necessaries' of life. Necessaries are legally defined as goods (or services) 'suitable to the condition of life of such person and to his actual requirements at the time' (Sale of Goods Act 1893). In a particular case, it is for the court to decide whether any goods or services are necessaries within this definition. Any contract made for necessaries is always binding. In the case of a contract for non-necessaries made by a person of unsound mind, the contract is also binding unless it can be shown both (a) that he did not understand what he was doing, and (b) that the other person was aware of the incapacity.

Power of attorney and receivership

If a patient is incapable of managing his possessions by reason of mental disorder, alternative arrangements must be made, particularly if the incapacity is likely to last a long time. Such arrangements may be required for patients living in the community as well as those in hospital. In English law two methods are available—power of attorney and receivership.

Power of attorney is the simpler method, only requiring the patient to give written authorization for someone else to act for him during his illness. In signing such authorization, the patient must be able to understand what he is doing. He may revoke it at any time.

Receivership is the more formal procedure, and likely to be more in the patient's interests. In England and Wales an application is made to the Court of Protection, which may decide to appoint a receiver (see p. 906).

The procedure is most commonly required for the elderly. The question of receivership is one that places special responsibility on the psychiatrist. If a patient is capable of managing his affairs on admission to hospital, but later becomes incapable by reason of intellectual deterioration, then it is the doctor's duty to advise the patient's relatives about the risks to property. If the relatives are unwilling to take action, then it is the doctor's duty to make an application to the Court of Protection. The doctor may feel reluctant to act in this way; but any actions taken subsequently are the Court's responsibility and not the doctor's.

Family law

A marriage contract is not valid if at the time of marriage either party was so mentally disordered as not to understand the nature of the contract. If mental disorder of this degree can be proved, a marriage may be decreed null and void by a divorce court. If a marriage partner becomes of 'incurably unsound mind' later in a marriage, this may be grounds for divorce.

A doctor may be asked for an opinion about the capacity of parents or a guardian to care adequately for a child. This issue is discussed on p. 810 and the law in England and Wales is summarized in the Appendix.

The mentally abnormal offender

It is possible here to give only a brief outline of patterns of crime. In England and Wales, as in other countries, crime is predominantly an activity of young men. A half of all indictable offences are committed by males aged under 21, and a quarter by males aged under 17. In recent decades crime has increased in amount; since the 1939–45 war there has been a steady rise in the rates of crimes against property and of violent crimes. This rise has included a sharp increase in the numbers of offences committed by women. Four-fifths of all crimes are against property. Only a quarter of first offenders are charged with a further offence. [Readers requiring further information on criminology are referred to Walker (1965), Walker (1987), Radzinowicz and King (1977).]

The causes of crime

In the nineteenth century criminologists were interested in the idea that criminals were degenerate. For example, in 1876 Lombroso published his book *L'Uomo delinquente*, in which he described characteristic physical stigmata in criminals.

In the present century, there has been some interest in a possible genetic basis for antisocial behaviour and criminality. Early studies of twins suggested that concordance rates for criminality were substantially greater in monozygotic twins than in dizygotic twins (Lange 1931). Later adoption studies in Denmark have suggested that the genetic influence is more modest but particularly significant for severe and persistent criminality (see *Lancet* 1983). Chromosomal abnormality has also been studied. It was originally reported that the XYY chromosomal abnormality was more frequent in patients in maximum security hospitals than in the general population (for example Jacobs *et al.* 1965), but recent surveys suggest that the XYY constitution is only weakly associated with criminal behaviour and with aggression in particular (for example Witkin *et al.* 1976). [Mednick *et al.* (1987) have reviewed biological factors contributing to the causes of crime.]

Social studies have drawn attention to numerous social and economic correlates of crime, such as local cultural influences, poverty, and unemployment (Hood and Sparks 1980; Radzinowicz and King 1977).

Nowadays it is generally held that social causes of crime are much more important than psychological causes. Nevertheless, there is a small but important group of offenders whose criminal behaviour seems to be partly explicable by psychological factors (see West 1974). It is this group that particularly concerns the psychiatrist. [See Walker (1987) for a review of the causes of crime.]

Crime and psychiatric disorder

It is difficult to obtain a reliable estimate of the numbers of mentally abnormal offenders. As Walker and McCabe (1973) have pointed out, an unknown but considerable number of mentally abnormal offenders 'bypass' the courts. This group includes offenders whose offences are known to their doctors but not to the police, and those whose offences are known to the police but not prosecuted. The police have considerable discretion as to whether to prosecute, and it is not uncommon for offences to be dealt with unofficially.

Nevertheless it is known that the prisons contain considerable numbers of psychiatrically disturbed people (see Coid 1984; Smith 1984). In a survey of prisons in the south-east region of England, Gunn (1977*a*) found that 31 per cent of prisoners were psychiatrically disturbed. In a study of 708 women admitted to prison, a history of self-harm, psychiatric disorder, or drug abuse was found in half (Turner and Tofler 1986). It has been reported that psychiatric disorder is particularly frequent among offenders sentenced to life imprisonment (Taylor 1986*b*).

A brief review will now be given of the associations between crime and the various psychiatric diagnostic categories. It should be borne in mind that such associations are not necessarily causal. Moreover, if an association of this kind is to have any potential significance, the psychiatric diagnoses must be based on independent evidence and must not be deduced solely from the criminal behaviour, however bizarre.

The psychiatric disorders most likely to be associated with crime are personality disorders, alcohol and drug dependence, and mental retardation. In addition to these categories, there is a sizeable group of recidivist offenders who are socially isolated, and often homeless and unemployed. They are often of low intelligence, and some have chronic schizophrenia. In this group, criminality is just one manifestation of all round incompetence. [See Faulk (1988) for a review of the associations between psychiatric disorder and crime.]

Personality disorder

There are close associations between crime and personality disorder, particularly antisocial personality disorder. Gunn (see 1977*b*) diagnosed abnormal personality in 20 per cent of prisoners in prisons in south-east England; Bluglass (see Gunn 1977*b*) found psychopathic personality disorder in 40 per cent of newly convicted prisoners in a Scottish prison; and Guze (1976) described 70 per cent of prisoners discharged from American prisons as 'sociopathic'. The features, aetiology, and treatment of antisocial personality disorders are discussed in Chapter 5. Offenders with such personality problems are often more susceptible to social than to psychiatric care, but there are sometimes indications for psychological treatment (see Gunn 1979), such as therapeutic community techniques, or treatment for sexual problems or anxiety disorders.

In this book the term antisocial personality disorder is used in preference to 'psychopathic disorder'. However, the latter term is in current legal use, and when working with the courts the psychiatrist is required to use it. In the Mental Health Act (1983), psychopathic disorder is defined as a 'persistent disorder or disability of mind (whether or not including significant impairment of intelligence), which results in abnormally aggressive or seriously irresponsible conduct'. If a compulsory order is to be made on the grounds of psychopathy, then the Act requires that there be evidence that treatment is 'likely to alleviate or prevent a deterioration of (the patient's) condition' as well as the requirement 'that it is necessary for the health and safety of the patient, or the protection of other persons'.

It is widely held that the legal concept of psychopathy is unsatisfactory (see Gunn 1979; Walker and McCabe 1973). The legal definition is difficult to apply in practice (see Hamilton 1987*b*). There is a danger that the diagnosis will be based on the nature of the crime rather than on any independent evidence of psychiatric disorder (Wootton 1959), and that it will be used as a label for people whose behaviour is not acceptable to conventional society (see West 1974). A further criticism is that the stipulation concerning psychiatric treatment is unrealistic, since most patients with psychopathic disorder are not susceptible to psychiatric treatment.

Eysenck (1970*a*) has suggested that there is an association between crime and personality which depends on the rapidity of 'conditioning'. The evidence is contradictory and a single explanation of this kind appears unlikely (see Farrington *et al.* 1982).

Alcohol and drug dependence

There are close links between alcohol and crime. Alcohol intoxication may lead to charges related to public drunkenness, or to driving offences. Intoxication reduces inhibitions and is strongly associated with crimes of violence, including murder. The neuro-psychiatric complications of alco-holism (see Chapter 14) may also be linked with crime. For example, offences may be committed during alcoholic amnesias or 'blackouts' (periods of several hours or days which the heavy drinker cannot sub-sequently recall, although at the time he appeared normally conscious to other people and was able to carry out complicated actions).

Drug intoxication may also lead to criminal behaviour. This may happen for example with cocaine or LSD. A more important link with crime is that drug dependent people may be driven to theft or violence in order to obtain drugs. The relationship between drug dependence and crime is discussed further in Chapter 14.

Mental retardation

Contrary to early beliefs, there is no evidence that most criminals are of markedly low intelligence. Recent surveys have shown that most delin-quent youths are within the lower part of the normal range of intelligence, and only about 3 per cent are mentally retarded. There is no reason to suppose that the distribution of intelligence is any different amongst adult criminals.

Mentally retarded people may commit offences because they do not understand the implications of their behaviour, or because they are susceptible to exploitation by other people. Compared with other offenders, the mentally retarded are more likely to be caught. The closest association between mental retardation and crime is a high incidence of sexual offences, particularly indecent exposure by males (Craft 1984). The exposer is often known to the victim, and the rate of detection is therefore high. There is also said to be an association between mental retardation and arson. The motive for fire-setting may be excitement or revenge on someone in authority (see Reid 1982). Apart from sexual offences and arson, no other crimes are closely associated with mental retardation.

The rest of this section is concerned with the major mental illnesses: organic syndromes, affective disorders, and schizophrenia, none of which is closely related to crime.

Organic mental disorders

Acute organic mental disorders may occasionally be associated with criminal behaviour. Diagnostic problems may arise if the mental disturbance improves before the offender is examined by a doctor.

Senile dementia may sometimes be associated with offences, though crime in general is uncommon among the elderly. Violent offences are rare. Occasionally elderly men commit sexual offences, usually in the form of indecency with children. Such men have usually had life-long sexual difficulties, but no previous offences of any kind. Whenever an elderly man is charged with a sexual offence, it is essential to consider the possibility of dementia.

Epilepsy

It is uncertain whether criminality is more common among epileptics than non-epileptics. The uncertainty results from the use of selected populations and different definitions of epilepsy in different surveys.

It is known that there are more epileptics in prison than would be expected in relation to the general population (see Gunn 1977*a*). This finding holds particularly for young persons and those convicted of violent offences. It appears that fits themselves are not a significant cause of crime. However, some epileptics may suffer from brain disorder that induces both seizures and criminal behaviour; or they may resort to anti-social acts because of general social difficulties. It has often been said that violent behaviour, including a syndrome of episodic dyscontrol, is associated with EEG abnormalities in the absence of clinical epilepsy. However, the evidence is not convincing (see Fenton 1986). It is possible that epileptic automatisms are an extremely rare cause of crime.

Affective disorder

Depressive disorder

This disorder is sometimes associated with shop-lifting (see p. 886). Much more seriously, severe depressive disorder may lead to homicide. When this happens, the depressed person usually has delusions, for example that the world is too dreadful a place for him and his family to live in; he then kills his spouse or children to spare them from the horrors of the world. The killer often commits suicide afterwards. A mother suffering from post-natal depression may sometimes kill her new-born child or her older children. Rarely, a person with severe depressive disorder may commit homicide because of a persecutory belief; for example, that the victim is responsible for the patient's misery. Not uncommonly, ideas of guilt and unworthiness may lead depressed patients to confess to crimes that they did not commit.

There is no convincing evidence for a reported association between affective disorder and sociopathic behaviour [see Reich (1985) for a review].

Mania

Manic patients may spend excessively. They may buy jewellery, fur coats, or cars that they cannot pay for. They may hire cars and fail to return them, or steal other people's cars. They may be charged with fraud or false pretences. Manic patients are also prone to irritability and aggression; this may lead to offences of violence, though seldom to severe violence.

Schizophrenia

The relationship between schizophrenia and crime is still uncertain because of the difficulties in selecting samples and comparison populations. Most research has been concerned with homicide and little is known of other forms of violent crime.

Taylor and Gunn (1984*b*) surveyed 1241 men remanded in prison and found a substantially higher prevalence of schizophrenia among those subsequently convicted of homicide and arson than would have been expected in the general population.

However, in a large study in West Germany of mentally abnormal offenders the risk of homicide was found to be only moderately increased in schizophrenia as compared with the general population (Böker and Häfner 1977).

As mentioned earlier, in some schizophrenics crime is one expression of all-round incompetence. These people are usually apathetic and lacking in judgement. In the past they were often permanent residents in mental hospitals; nowadays they live mostly in the community, and they sometimes become destitute. Their crimes are usually petty, but their repeated offences may lead to many short prison sentences (Valdiserri *et al.* 1986).

In a second group of schizophrenics, criminality results from delusions and hallucinations. According to Planansky and Johnston (1977), violence in schizophrenics may be associated with any of the following features: great fear and loss of self-control in association with non-systematized delusions; irresistible urges; instructions from hallucinatory voices; unaccountable frenzy; and systematized paranoid delusions including the

conviction that enemies must be defended against. Taylor (1985) interviewed remanded psychotic men and concluded that psychiatric symptoms
accounted for most of the very violent behaviour. As mentioned in the
section on dangerousness (p. 894), violent threats in schizophrenics should
be taken very seriously; most serious violence occurs in those already
known to psychiatrists. [See Taylor (1986*a*) for a review of the risk of
violence in psychotic illness.]

Mental disorder in women offenders

In Britain nine times as many men as women are convicted, and 33 times
as many men are imprisoned. Although this may in small part be due to
lower identification and reporting of female crime, it reflects a major
difference in behaviour.

The commonest offence by women is stealing. Shoplifting accounts for
a half of all convictions of women for indictable offences. In contrast,
violent and sexual offences are uncommon (O'Connor 1987). It has been
argued that women indulge in forms of antisocial behaviour that are
regarded less severely by the law than those for which men are prosecuted,
such as soliciting and some forms of social security fraud. However, in
general it would appear that women are more law-abiding than men.

It is widely accepted that a substantial proportion of crime by women is
associated with mental disorder. Psychiatric disorder is common amongst
women admitted to prison (Turner and Tofler 1986). Martin *et al.* (1978)
found that the most powerful predictor of reconviction among women was
psychiatric disorder, (mainly drug dependence and antisocial personality);
and a history of homosexuality.

The premenstrual syndrome is increasingly suggested as an aetiological
factor by defence lawyers and has been accepted as such in a number of
recent court decisions. It is possible that premenstrual symptoms may
complicate or exacerbate pre-existing social and psychological difficulties,
but it is very unlikely that they are ever a primary cause of offences.

Criminal responsibility

Although mentally abnormal offenders are only a small minority of all
offenders, both the forensic psychiatrist and the general psychiatrist can
play an important role by helping to identify, assess, and manage them.
The psychiatrist may be asked to give advice in relation to the following
issues: fitness to plead; mental state at the time of the offence; diminished
criminal responsibility; and the psychiatric management of offenders.

Each of these issues will be discussed in turn. The discussion will be
based on the law in England and Wales, but the principles apply to varying
extents in other countries. [For further information on the criminal law of

England and Wales, the reader is referred to the standard legal texts by Smith and Hogan (1983) and Hoggett (1984), and to the textbook by Faulk (1988).]

Fitness to plead

English law requires that the defendant must be in a fit condition to defend himself. The issue may be raised by the defence, the prosecution, or the judge. It cannot be decided in a magistrates' court, but only by a jury. If the accused is found unfit to plead, an order is made committing him to any hospital specified by the Home Secretary, where he may be detained without limit of time and can be discharged only at the discretion of the Home Secretary. If discharged from hospital he is returned to the penal system for trial.

In determining fitness to plead, it is necessary to determine how far the defendant can: (i) understand the nature of the charge; (ii) understand the difference between pleading guilty and not guilty; (iii) instruct Counsel; (iv) challenge jurors; (v) follow the evidence presented in court.

A person may be suffering from severe mental disorder but still fit to stand trial. An interesting problem arises if the accused has amnesia for the time of the offence; such amnesia has been held to have no bearing on fitness to plead, though it might point to an underlying disorder that could affect the issue. An American study of 85 people judged incompetent to stand trial showed that most had been charged with serious offences. Plans for psychiatric care after release were generally inadequate (Lamb 1987).

Mental state at the time of the offence

Mentally abormal offenders usually stand trial in the same way as other offenders, but when sentence is passed consideration is given to their mental state and to the possibility of psychiatric treatment. In some cases, however, the issue of criminal responsibility is raised at the trial. Underlying this issue is the principle that a person should not be regarded as culpable unless he was able to control his own behaviour and to choose whether to commit an unlawful act or not. It follows from this principle that, in determining whether or not a person is guilty, it is necessary to consider his mental state at the time of the act (see Whitlock 1963).

Before anyone can be convicted of a crime, the prosecution must prove: (i) that he carried out an unlawful act (*actus reus*); (ii) that he had a certain guilty state of mind at the time, namely *mens rea*. The latter is a technical term which is often loosely translated as meaning 'a guilty mind'. However, this translation can be misleading since a person may commit a legal offence whilst completely confident that he is morally right.

The various categories of mens rea are not precisely defined. They vary from crime to crime and are interpreted in the light of the precedents of case law. The categories are:

1. *Intent*. Intent has various meanings but the main principle is that the person perceives and intends that his act of omission will produce unlawful consequences.

The three following definitions are from Smith and Hogan (1983):

2. *Recklessness*. 'Recklessness is the deliberate taking of an unjustifiable risk. A man is reckless with respect to the consequence of his act, when he foresees it may occur but does not desire it. Recklessness with respect to circumstances means the realisation that the circumstances may exist, without either knowing or hoping that they do. D points a gun at P and pulls the trigger; if he does not know that it is loaded, but realises that it may be, he is reckless with respect to that circumstance, whether he hopes it is unloaded or just does not care'.

3. *Negligence*. 'A man acts negligently when he brings about a consequence which a reasonable and prudent man would have foreseen and avoided'.

4. *Blameless inadvertence*. 'A man may reasonably fail to foresee a consequence of his act, as when a slight slap causes the death of an apparently healthy person: or reasonably fail to consider the possibility of the existence of a circumstance, as when goods, which are in fact stolen, are bought in the normal course of business from a trader of high repute'.

Children under 10 are excluded because they are deemed incapable of criminal intent (*doli incapax*). Children aged over 10 and under 14 are excluded unless it can be proved that they knew the nature of their act and knew it to be morally and legally wrong (mischievous discretion); in other words; the law assumes that children in this age group do not have *mens rea* unless it can be proved otherwise.

The degree of *mens rea* required for a conviction varies from crime to crime. For murder, it is necessary to establish 'specific intent'; for manslaughter it is sufficient to establish gross negligence; and for some types of offence such as traffic offences, it is not necessary to establish any degree of *mens rea* at all. For most offences it is necessary to establish some degree of intent.

When a person is charged with an offence, the defence can be made that he is not culpable because he did not have a sufficient degree of *mens rea*. This defence can be raised in several ways:

(1) not guilty by reason of insanity (under the McNaughton rules);

(2) diminished responsibility (not guilty of murder, but guilty of manslaughter, which requires a lesser degree of criminal intent);

(3) incapacity to form an intent because of an automatism.

A further example is that if a mother kills her child in the first year of its life she is not usually held legally responsible for murder but only for the less serious crime of infanticide (see p. 881).

The types of defence listed above will now be considered in turn. [For further information the reader is referred to: Walker (1967); Walker and McCabe (1973); the Committee on Mentally Abnormal Offenders (1975); and the Insanity Defence Work Group (1983).]

Not guilty by reason of insanity

This concept is embodied in the McNaughton Rules. In 1843 Daniel McNaughton, a wood turner from Glasgow, shot and killed Edward Drummond, private secretary to the Prime Minister, Sir Robert Peel. In the trial at the Old Bailey, a defence of insanity was presented on the grounds that McNaughton had suffered from delusions for many years. He believed he was persecuted by spies, and had gone to the police and other public figures seeking help. His delusional system gradually focused on the Tory Party, and he decided to kill their leader, Sir Robert Peel. He killed Peel's secretary but was prevented from firing a second shot at the Prime Minister (see West 1974). In accordance with suggestions made by the judge in summing up, McNaughton was found not guilty on the grounds of insanity, and was admitted to Bethlem Hospital. This verdict outraged public opinion and was debated urgently in the House of Lords. At the request of the Lords, the judges drew up rules which were not enacted in the law but provided guidance as follows:

To establish a defence on the ground of insanity, it must be clearly proved that, at the time of committing the act, the party accused was labouring under such a defect of reason, from disease of the mind, as not to know the nature and quality of the act he was doing, or, if he did know it, that he did not know what he was doing was wrong.

The McNaughton Rules have no statutory basis, but they are accepted by the courts as having the same status as statutory law. If an offender is found 'not guilty by reason of insanity', the court must order his admission to a hospital specified by the Home Secretary (Criminal Procedure (Insanity) Act 1964).

The rules are more restrictive than the summing up in the McNaughton trial. They have been strongly criticized as providing a concept of insanity that is much too narrow. Critics have argued that insanity affects not only cognitive faculties, but also emotions and will power. Both for this reason and because of the increasing concern about capital punishment, the defence of diminished responsibility for murder was introduced in 1957. Since then a defence of insanity in terms of the McNaughton Rules is seldom raised.

The McNaughton Rules are used in several other jurisdictions, and have led to other formulations of the insanity defence. In the USA, the American Psychiatric Association reviewed procedures after public outrage about the finding that, by reason of insanity, Hinkley was not guilty of the attempted murder of the President of the USA. It concluded that further legislation was needed to cover the confinement, treatment, review, and release of such persons (Insanity Defence Work Group 1983).

Diminished responsibility

Diminished responsibility may be pleaded as a defence to the charge of murder. If the defence is upheld, the accused is found guilty only of manslaughter. The concept of diminished responsibility is based on a definition of mental abnormality that is much wider than that embodied in the McNaughton Rules. This point is illustrated by the following extract from the Homicide Act 1957 (section 2):

> where a person kills or is party to a killing of another, he shall not be convicted of murder if he was suffering from such abnormality of mind (whether arising from a condition of arrested or retarded development of mind or any inherent causes or induced by disease or injury) as substantially impaired his mental responsibility for his acts and omissions in doing or being party to the killing.

In practice, if a person is charged with murder, he may plead that he is not guilty of murder but guilty of manslaughter on the grounds of diminished responsibility. If this plea is acceptable to the prosecution and to the judge, there is no trial and a sentence for manslaughter is passed. If on the other hand the plea is not acceptable to the prosecution or the judge, a trial is held. The jury must then consider the evidence, both medical and non-medical, to decide whether at the material time the accused was suffering from abnormality of mind, and if so, whether the abnormality was such as substantially to impair his responsibility. If the accused is convicted of manslaughter, the judge may pass whatever sentence he deems appropriate (which may include life imprisonment) on the grounds of dangerousness. In contrast to this discretion in the sentence for manslaughter, there is a statutory sentence of life imprisonment for a conviction of murder.

Diminished responsibility has been widely interpreted, and has made the insanity defence virtually obsolete. Successful pleas have been based on conditions such as 'emotional immaturity', 'mental instability', 'psychopathic personality', 'reactive depressed state', 'mixed emotions of depression, disappointment and exasperation', and recently, 'premenstrual tension'.

Automatism

If a person has no control over an act, he cannot be held responsible for it. For this reason verdicts of not guilty have been returned when acts of violence were judged to be committed as 'sane automatisms'. Such circumstances are rare, but have occurred in association with hypoglycaemia, concussion, and sleep-walking. If automatism is thought to arise from a 'disease of the mind', it is referred to as 'insane automatism'; the appropriate defence is then insanity, and the McNaughton Rules apply. In legal practice there have been varying interpretations of 'disease of the mind' in this context. A recent House of Lords ruling has defined the significance of epileptic automatism in English law. It rejected the plea of 'sane automatism', and ruled that automatism is a disease of the mind, and as such must be interpreted using the McNaughton Rules.

The law relating to alcohol and drug addiction is complicated. It can be summarized as follows:

1. Involuntary intoxication (as when someone unwittingly takes a drink to which a drug has been added), or automatism occurring as a side-effect of medical treatment, constitutes a valid defence.

2. Self-induced intoxication is not a defence unless (a) it is itself evidence of 'disease of the mind' under the McNaughton Rules: or (b) it is evidence of lack of intent in relation to those crimes for which 'specific intent' must be proved (for example murder, theft, burglary). Self-induced intoxication is not a defence to those crimes for which evidence of 'specific intent' is not required (for example manslaughter, rape, indecent assault, and common assault).

Treatment of the mentally abnormal offender

When sentence is passed in court, the need for psychiatric treatment may be taken into account. After conviction an offender may be treated on a compulsory or voluntary basis (see Hoggett 1984). [Facilities for mentally abnormal offenders are reviewed in the books by Gostin (1985) and Walker (1987). The role of forensic psychiatric services is described by Faulk (1988).]

In Britain special treatment for mentally abnormal offenders is in principle provided by the Home Office (prison medical service and the probation service) as well as by the DHSS (special hospitals and forensic and general psychiatry services). However, many mentally abnormal offenders never receive the psychiatric treatment they require (Taylor and Gunn 1984*b*).

General psychiatrists provide an assessment service and prepare reports for courts. They also offer a range of psychiatric services to offenders given non-custodial sentences. Forensic psychiatrists staff the special hospitals and undertake specialized assessment and court work. They are increasingly helping to provide community forensic services, which include assessment and treatment clinics, and are taking responsibility for secure provision within ordinary psychiatric hospitals.

The mentally abnormal in prison

Surveys have shown a high prevalence of psychiatric morbidity amongst prisoners (see also p. 865). Major psychiatric disorder is no more common than in the general population, but many prisoners suffer from personality, neurotic, and behavioural problems. Alcoholism, drug dependence, and epilepsy are also common. Some of these disorders may be secondary to imprisonment. There is concern that the discharge of chronic patients from mental hospitals has resulted in many chronically handicapped people being sent to prison for petty offences (Coid 1984; Gunn 1985*b*; Valdiserri *et al.* 1986).

The prison medical service has to provide psychiatric care under extremely difficult conditions, and it has been argued that there is a case for a substantial increase in the contribution of psychiatrists to the provision of specialist care within prisons. A few prisons offer psychiatric treatment as a main part of their work; for example, Grendon Underwood in England (Gunn and Robertson 1982). Although there is an undoubted case for good psychiatric care within prisons, there would be considerable disadvantages in a system which actually encouraged the courts to send the mentally abnormal to prison rather than to hospital services (see Gunn 1985*b*; Gunn and Farrington 1982).

Offenders in hospital

In England and Wales a convicted offender may be committed to hospital for compulsory psychiatric treatment under a Mental Health Act hospital order (see Appendix).

There is also provision in law for a prisoner to be transferred from prison to a psychiatric hospital. An important point is that hospital orders have no time limit, while most prison sentences are of fixed length. The length of stay in a psychiatric hospital may therefore be shorter or longer than a prison sentence.

Committal is usually to a local psychiatric hospital, but may be to a special hospital. The first special provision for the criminally insane was made in 1800. Following the trial at which Hadfield was found not guilty by reason of insanity for shooting at King George III, a special criminal wing was established at the Bethlem Hospital. In 1863 Broadmoor, the oldest of the special hospitals, opened under the management of the Home Office. There are now four high security special hospitals in England

and Wales (Broadmoor, Moss Side, Park Lane, and Rampton) which are the responsibility of the DHSS.

The detention of patients in special hospitals is for an indeterminate length of stay. Dell *et al.* (1987) have shown that for those with mental illness (mostly schizophrenia) length of detention at Broadmoor Hospital was associated with the severity or chronicity of the psychiatric disorder rather than the nature of the offence. In contrast, for the quarter of patients suffering from psychopathic disorder, the main determinant of length of stay was the nature of the offence.

The reform of the mental hospitals in the 1950s and following years has had unforeseen consequences for the care of mentally abnormal offenders. There has been a growing emphasis on acute treatment; at the same time there has been less physical security in psychiatric hospitals, and less willingness by hospital staff to tolerate severely disturbed behaviour. As a result it has become increasingly difficult to arrange admission to hospital for offenders, particularly those who are severely disturbed or have chronic handicaps. For severely disturbed offenders, there are alternatives. One is to provide well-staffed secure areas in ordinary psychiatric hospitals; such an arrangement carries the risk of adverse public attitudes towards the hospital. Nevertheless, concern about the need for secure provisions in psychiatric hospitals led the Butler committee (Committee on mentally abnormal offenders 1975) to recommend the setting up of regional secure units within psychiatric hospitals to fill the gap between ordinary hospital care and the special hospitals. This soon became Government policy but progress in setting up such units has been slow. There has been uncertainty about the criteria for selecting patients for these units, and about the role of the units. It has not been established that they will solve the problems they were set up to deal with (see Snowden 1985; Gostin 1985).

Treatment in the community

When a non-custodial sentence is passed, the court may require social and psychological care by the probation service. In addition, psychiatric treatment as an in-patient or out-patient may be made a condition of probation under the Powers of the Criminal Courts Act (1973), which superseded the Criminal Justice Act (1948). When treatment is made a condition of probation, the offender must state that he is willing to comply. Psychiatric treatment for mentally abnormal offenders is similar to that for other patients with the same psychiatric disorder who have not broken the law.

Among offenders with chronic psychiatric handicaps, those who commit repeated petty offences often lack adequate care. In the past they would have been long-stay hospital in-patients, but now they revolve between hospital, prison, and destitution (Rollin 1969). If such people are to lead a better life outside hospital, then the quality of community care must be improved.

The following sections are concerned with offences of the types that are most likely to be associated with psychological factors. These offences can be divided into crimes of violence, sexual offences, and offences against property.

Crimes of violence

Amongst mentally abnormal offenders, violence is associated much more with personality disorder than with psychiatric disorder (see p. 866). Violence is particularly common in people of antisocial personality who abuse alcohol or drugs, or who have marked paranoid or sadistic traits (see Fottrell 1980). Generally violence is part of a persistent pattern of impulsive and aggressive behaviour, but it may be a sporadic response to stressful events in 'overcontrolled' personalities (Megargee 1966). The assessment of dangerousness and the management of violence are discussed in a later section. [See Tardiff (1987) for a review.]

Homicide

Homicide can be divided into several legal categories. The main ones are murder, manslaughter, and infanticide, and these are the subject of this section of the chapter. Murder and manslaughter are defined by historical precedent (common law offences) and not by statute (see Smith and Hogan 1983).

According to a widely quoted definition put forward by Lord Coke in 1797, **murder** occurs:

when a man of sound memory and of the age of discretion unlawfully killeth within any country of the realm any reasonable creature in rerum natura under the King's peace with malice aforethought, either expressed by the party or implied by law, so as the party wounded or hit, etc. die of the wound or hit within a year and a day after the same.

The phrase 'malice aforethought' is important, although it has no statutory definition and can be interpreted only from case law.

According to Smith and Hogan (1983), **manslaughter**:

is a diverse crime covering all unlawful homicides which are not murder. A wide variety of types of homicide fall within this category, but it is customary and useful to divide manslaughter into two main groups which are designated 'voluntary' and 'involuntary' manslaughter respectively. The distinction is that in voluntary manslaughter the defendant may have malice aforethought of murder but the presence of some defined mitigating circumstances reduces his crime to a less serious grade of criminal homicide.

In involuntary manslaughter, there is no malice aforethought; it includes for example causing death by gross negligence.

As mentioned earlier in this chapter the category of manslaughter resulting from diminished responsibility is defined not by common law but by statute, viz. the Homicide Act (1957). This act also provides that the survivor of a genuine suicide pact should be guilty only of manslaughter.

It is common practice to divide homicide into 'normal' and 'abnormal', according to the legal outcome. Homicide is 'normal' if there is a conviction of murder or common law manslaughter; it is 'abnormal' if there is a finding of insane murder, suicide murder, diminished responsibility, or infanticide. This distinction is useful for the interpretation of statistics (see Gibson 1975).

'*Normal*' *homicide* accounts for half to two-thirds of all homicides occurring in Britain. In countries such as the USA where the overall homicide rate is much higher than in Britain, the excess is largely made up of 'normal' homicide. 'Normal' homicide is most likely to be committed by young men of low social class. In Britain the victims are mainly family members or close acquaintances, and they are seldom killed in the course of a robbery or sexual offence. In countries with high homicide rates, there is a greater proportion of killings associated with robbery or sexual offences. When sexual homicide does occur it may result from panic during a sexual offence. Alternatively it may be a sadistic killing, often committed by a shy man with bizarre sadistic and other violent fantasies (Brittain 1970).

'*Abnormal*' *homicide* accounts for a third to half of all homicides in Britain. It is usually committed by older people. Homicide by women is much rarer than by men; when it does occur, it is nearly always 'abnormal', and the commonest category is infanticide. The victims of homicide are usually family members. In those who commit 'abnormal' homicide, the commonest psychiatric diagnosis is depressive disorder, especially in those who afterwards kill themselves. Other associated diagnoses are schizophrenia (see Taylor 1986*a*), personality disorder, and alcoholism. The syndrome of pathological jealousy may be associated with any of the above diagnoses; it has been identified in 12 per cent of insane male murderers and 3 per cent of insane women murderers. It is particularly dangerous because of the risk of the offence being repeated (see the section on pathological jealousy, p. 334).

A large proportion of all murderers are under the influence of alcohol at the time of the crime (Virkunnen 1974). In a survey of 400 people charged with murder in Scotland, 58 per cent of the men and 30 per cent of the women were found to have been intoxicated at the time of the offence (Gillies 1976).

The statistics about the victims of homicide are also of interest. A quarter of all homicide victims are aged under 16; their deaths usually result from 'abnormal' homicide or repeated child abuse by the parents. Amongst adult victims, women outnumber men by three to two. Nearly half of the women victims are killed by their husbands, and the rest mainly by relatives or intimate friends. By contrast, nearly half of the male victims are killed by strangers or chance associates. Bluglass (1979*b*) studied 70 murders, and in over half found that the victim had played a part in the events leading up to death. It has also been shown that about a third of homicide victims were probably intoxicated with alcohol at the time of the crime (Gillies 1976; Bluglass 1979*a*).

Homicide is followed by suicide in about 10 per cent of homicides in England and Wales. West (1965) studied 78 cases occurring in the London area over the years 1954–61. The offenders were strikingly different from homicide offenders in general. They were much more likely to be women, were of higher social class, and had fewer previous convictions than other convicted homicide offenders. The victims were usually children. Half the homicides were 'abnormal' in the sense defined above; in most cases the offender was severly depressed at the time of the offence. In most of the 'normal' offences, the killer appeared to have felt 'driven to suicide by illness or distressing circumstances, the victim being an innocent party involved by virtue of a close relationship'.

Psychiatric assessment in cases of homicide

In England and Wales everyone charged with murder is assessed psychiatrically by a prison doctor. The latter often asks for a second psychiatric opinion, and the defence lawyers often seek independent psychiatric advice. It is good practice for all the doctors involved, whether engaged by the prosecution or defence lawyers, to discuss the case together. If this is done, disagreement is unusual. Copies of the reports are distributed to the judge, and to the prosecution and defence lawyers.

The psychiatric report should be based on full psychiatric and physical examination. It is essential that the psychiatrist read all the depositions by witnesses, statements by the accused, and any previous medical notes and social reports. Family members should be interviewed. The writing of the court report follows the usual format (see p. 892) and should include discussions of mental state at the time of the alleged offence and of fitness to plead.

Parents who kill their children

In Britain a quarter of all victims of murder or manslaughter are under the age of 16. Most of them are killed by a parent who is mentally ill, especially the mother (d'Orban 1979). Classification of child murder is difficult; useful categories suggested by Scott (1973) are mercy killing, psychotic murder, and killing as the end result of battering or neglect. This last category is discussed further on p. 809.

Infanticide

A woman who kills her child may be charged with murder or manslaughter, but under special circumstances the charge may be infanticide. The Infanticide Act (1922), afterwards amended by the Infanticide Act (1938), defined a category of offence which can now be seen as a special case of the later and wider concept of diminished responsibility. Section 1 of the Act provides that:

where a woman causes the death of her child under the age of 12 months, but at the time the balance of her mind was disturbed by reason of her not having fully recovered from the effects of childbirth or lactation consequent upon the birth of the child, she shall be guilty not of murder but infanticide.

The judge has the same freedom of sentencing for a conviction of infanticide as for a conviction of manslaughter. The legal concept of infanticide is unusual in that the accused is required to show only that her mind was disturbed as a result of birth or lactation, but not that the killing was a consequence of her mental disturbance.

Resnick (1969) found that two types of infanticide could be discerned. When the killing occurred within the first 24 hours after birth, in most cases the child was unwanted, and the mother was young and unequipped to care for the child, but not psychiatrically ill. When the killing occurred more than 24 hours after childbirth, in most cases the mother had a depressive disorder and killed the child to save it from the suffering she anticipated for it; about a third of the mothers also tried to take their own lives.

In an analysis of court disposals for infanticide, Walker and McCabe (1973) found that the great majority of the women were either committed to hospital or put on probation; about 1 per cent were sent to prison.

Violence within the family

This subject has received increasing attention in recent years. Several features require emphasis. First, some people are violent only within their family, whilst others are violent outside the family as well. Second, and of particular importance, family violence is strongly associated with excessive drinking. Third, violence in the family can have long-term deleterious effects on the psychological and social development of the children (see Rutter and Madge 1976).

Of the various forms of violence in the family, homicide has been described earlier in this chapter, whilst child abuse is reviewed in Chapter 20, and violence to the elderly is referred to in Chapter 16. Attention has recently been drawn to another aspect of family violence, 'wife battering'. It is difficult to obtain information on this subject, since the husband is usually difficult to interview unless he is in custody. It appears that the perpetrators of wife-battering are mainly men with aggressive personalities, whilst a few are violent only when suffering from psychiatric illness, usually a depressive disorder (see Gayford 1979; Goodstein and Page 1981; Jaffe *et al.* 1986) Other common features in the men are morbid jealousy and heavy drinking. In the management of wife-battering, marital therapy and family therapy are sometimes helpful. In some cases a frightened wife may need practical help to leave the home.

It is important to keep in mind that family violence sometimes leads to homicide in the family.

Child stealing

There has been no psychiatric study of men who steal children, although, according to Trick and Tennent (1981, p. 28) the majority of people charged with the offence are males. In a study of 24 women charged with child stealing, d'Orban (1976) recognized three types of stealing: comforting; manipulative with the intention of influencing someone else; and impulsive stealing in psychiatrically disturbed women.

Sexual offences

In Britain sexual offences account for less than 1 per cent of all indictable offences recorded by the police. Among the various kinds of offenders referred to psychiatrists, sexual offenders make up a relatively large proportion. Even so, only a small proportion of people charged with sexual offences are assessed by psychiatrists. Apart from soliciting for purposes of prostitution, women seldom commit sexual offences. Men commit sexual offences much more frequently, and this section therefore applies almost entirely to men. As a group, sexual offenders are older than other offenders, although they usually have previous non-sexual offences. Reconviction rates are generally lower in sexual offenders than in other offenders, but there is a minority of recidivist sexual offenders who are extremely difficult to manage (see Gunn 1985b).

The commonest sexual offences are indecent assault against women, indecent exposure, and unlawful intercourse with girls aged under 16.

Some sexual offences do not involve violence (for example: indecent exposure; voyeurism; most sexual offences involving children); whilst others may involve considerable violence (for example rape). The nature and treatment of non-violent sexual offences are discussed in Chapter 15, but their forensic aspects are considered here. [See the Howard League Working Party (1985) for a review of social and legal aspects of sexual offences.]

Sexual offences against children

It is illegal to have any heterosexual activity with a person aged under 16, or homosexual activity with people aged under 21. Known sexual offences involving children are common, amounting to over half of all reported sexual offences in Britain. It is probable that many more offences are not reported, particularly those occurring within families. The offences vary in severity from mild indecency to seriously aggressive behaviour, but most do not involve violence.

Adults who commit sexual offences against children are known as paedophiles. They are almost always male. As with other kinds of offender, they are difficult to classify. Some of them are timid and sexually inexperienced; some are mentally retarded and untrained; others have experienced normal sexual relationships but still prefer sexual activity with children. Paedophile murder is rare.

The victims are known to the offender in four-fifths of cases, and belong to the offender's family in a third (see Mohr *et al.* 1964). Girl victims outnumber boys by about two to one. It has been reported that many child victims suffer emotional difficulties later, but according to the Howard League Working Party (1985) serious long-term emotional consequences may be uncommon. More work is needed to decide this issue. Court proceedings, however, are likely to be particularly disturbing to child victims (Weiss and Berg 1982).

The prognosis for sexual offenders against children is generally good. The reconviction rate is low. Most offenders do not progress from less serious to more serious activities; but a few may start with indecent exposure and progress to violent sexual offences later. It is for this reason that psychiatrists are often asked to give an opinion on an offender's dangerousness.

In trying to decide whether the offence is likely to be repeated, and whether there is likely to be a progression to more serious offences, the psychiatrist should consider the duration and frequency of the particular sexual activity in the past; and the offender's predominant sexual orientation (exclusively paedophile inclinations and behaviour indicate greater risk of repetition). Older paedophiles are less likely to be aggressive. It is important to determine whether alcohol or drugs played any part in the offence, and whether the offender feels any regret or guilt. Relevant environmental factors include any stressful circumstances, and the degree of access to children. Finally evidence should be sought of any psychiatric disorder, or personality defects such as lack of self-control.

Psychological treatment is usually directed towards any underlying psychiatric disorder rather than to the undesirable sexual behaviour. Beneficial effects have been reported from psychotherapy and various types of behavioural treatment directed towards encouraging desirable sexual behaviour, but the evidence is uncertain. The use of sex hormones or drugs to reduce sex drive has been advocated, but raises ethical issues.

Sexual abuse of children is also discussed in Chapter 20.

Indecent exposure

In England and Wales, indecent exposure is one of the commonest sexual offences. It is most common in men aged between 25 and 35. The term indecent exposure is the legal name for the offence of indecently exposing the genitals to other people. It is applied to all forms of exposure; exhibitionism is by far the most frequent form, but exposure may also occur as an invitation to intercourse, as a prelude to sexual assault, or as an insulting gesture. Exhibitionism, as explained on p. 582, is the medical name for the behaviour of men who gain sexual satisfaction from repeatedly exposing to women.

Indecent exposers rarely have a history of psychiatric disorder or of other criminal behaviour. The reconviction rate is low, and few offenders proceed to more serious offences.

Indecent assault

Indecent assault embraces a wide range of behaviour from attempting to touch a stranger's buttocks, to sexual assault without attempted penetration. The psychiatrist is most commonly asked to give a psychiatric opinion on adolescent boys, and on men who have assaulted children. Many adolescent boys behave in ways that could be construed as 'indecent'. More serious indecent behaviour is associated with aggressive personality, ignorance and lack of social skill, personal unattractiveness, and occasionally subnormal intelligence. Treatment may include advice and social skills training.

Rape

The Sexual Offences Act 1956 states 'a man commits rape if (a) he has unlawful sexual intercourse with a woman who at the time of the intercourse does not consent to it and (b) at the time he knows that she does not consent to the intercourse or he is reckless as to whether she consents to it.' Forced sexual intercourse within marriage is excluded. Rape does not necessarily include the use of violence. It ranges from the use of deception without violence, to extreme brutality (see also p. 886) Rape and other forms of sexual aggression appear to be much more common in the general population than the number reported to the police would suggest.

Rapists have been classified in various ways (see Gibbens *et al.* 1977; Gunn 1985*b*). Most rapists are young and sexually frustrated, with little experience of sexual intercourse, and most have a record of previous criminal offences. Psychiatric disorder is rare among rapists. Some of the main behavioural types are: (i) aggressive antisocial men who have a history of general criminal behaviour but do not have a formal psychiatric disorder; these are probably the most common; (ii) aggressive sadistic men who wish to humiliate and hurt women; (iii) so-called explosive rapists who are often timid and inhibited, and who carry out the act as a deliberate plan to relieve their frustration; (iv) mentally ill rapists, who most often suffer from mania; this is the least common group. In a study by Amir (1971), a quarter of rapes were found to be committed by three or more men in a group.

The reconviction rate is fairly low. Gibbens *et al.* (1977) found that, among men charged with rape, 12 per cent of those convicted and 14 per cent of those acquitted were convicted of a further sexual offence during a 12-year follow-up. In interpreting these findings it should be remembered that most of the convicted men were in prison and therefore not at risk during part of the follow-up period. In about a third of cases the victim is an acquaintance of the rapist, and in a fifth she appears to have participated initially in the events leading up to the offence. It is sometimes said that women who are raped have frequently encouraged the man initially, or else submitted without much resistance. There is little justification for this view. Amir (1971) found that a half of rape victims were threatened with injury either verbally or with weapons; and about a third were handled roughly or violently. In such a dangerous situation submission without much physical resistance is understandable.

There is evidence that rape victims may suffer long-term psychological effects. Nadelson *et al.* (1982) interviewed 41 women who attended a clinic in a general hospital shortly after being raped. At follow-up one to two and a half years later it was found that half the women were afraid of being alone, and three-quarters were still suspicious of other people. Many women reported depression and sexual difficulties which they attributed to the rape. Those who delay seeking treatment seem particularly liable to report severe distress (Stewart *et al.* 1987). Serious distress may also be experienced by the partners and families of rape victims. In many American general hospitals, crisis intervention centres staffed by multidisciplinary teams have been set up for rape victims. [For reviews of psychological reactions and treatment of rape victims, see Notman and Nadelson (1984); Mezey (1985).]

Sexual violence

Some men who commit rape, homicide or other violent offences have considerable sexual problems or suffer sexual jealousy and these may have contributed to their dangerousness (Gunn 1985*a*). A small group of men obtain sexual pleasure from sadistic assaults on unwilling partners (Mac-Culloch *et al*. 1985). Frequently, the only evidence of psychiatric abnormality is the deviant sexual desire itself.

Incest

In their interviews about sexual behaviour, Kinsey *et al*. (1948) received few reports of incest. This finding is hardly surprising, because incestuous behaviour is particularly unlikely to be revealed to an interviewer. Clinical experience suggests that such statistics underestimate the frequency of incest. Most reported cases involve a father and daughter, but brother–sister relationships are probably more common. Incest between father and daughter often starts as the girl reaches puberty. Several social factors may contribute. There is often a history of marital breakdown and the daughter replaces the mother (see Herman and Hirschman 1981). The family is often socially isolated and sharing bedrooms in crowded accommodation. About a third of the fathers have antisocial personalities, and many of them drink excessively (see Bluglass 1979*b*).

It is likely that many cases are known to the medical or social services but not to the police. Even when cases are known to the police, only half of them are prosecuted. When the girl is a relatively young child, most prosecutions result in imprisonment of the father. Generally the family needs considerable psychological and social support, particularly if the father is imprisoned.

The long-term consequences of incest on the family are uncertain (see Herman *et al*. 1986). If there is a prosecution, any resulting publicity or punishment of the father is likely to have serious repercussions in the family [For reviews of incest see Hendersen 1972; Bluglass 1979*b*; Howard League Working Party 1985; for an account of sexual abuse of children see Chapter 20.]

Offences against property

Shop-lifting

Many adolescents admit occasional shop-lifting, but few admit persistent shop-lifting. Both observational studies (Buckle and Farrington 1984) and the reports of massive losses from shops suggest that among adults shoplifting is very common. Among adults in England and Wales, the number of recorded offences of shop-lifting increased substantially in the 1970s, reaching a figure well over 200 000 per annum. The reasons for this increase are uncertain, but it is generally accepted that most shop-lifters are simply covetous rather than psychiatrically disturbed. In a study of shop-lifters, Gibbens *et al.* (1971) found that nearly two-thirds of those appearing in courts in central London were young foreign girls who appeared to be usually honest but shop-lifted because they were short of money. By contrast, male shop-lifters were likely to have had previous convictions for offences of all kinds, and a third of them had previously been in prison.

In a follow-up study of over 500 women who had been convicted of shop-lifting ten years previously, Gibbens *et al.* (1971) found that the reconviction rate was 11 per cent for first offenders, and 20 per cent for the whole group. Most reconvictions were for further shop-lifting. During the follow-up period the admission rate to mental hospital was three times the expected figure of 2.5 per cent for middle-aged women. The authors distinguished two sub-groups of women. One consisted of 51 women who were persistently and widely deviant; they had committed numerous previous and subsequent offences, and two-fifths of them had committed other offences such as theft, violence, and drunkenness. The other sub-group, comprising 10 to 20 per cent of the total, had suffered from a depressive disorder at the time of the original offence, which was often associated with medical symptoms, or chronic background difficulties, or recent severe life events. These women had generally been of good previous character. Most of these women had no further conviction, but a small minority persisted in shop-lifting. A more recent study in Canada has identified a similar group of shop-lifting women suffering from depressive disorder (Bradford and Balmaceda 1983).

Apart from depressive disorders, various other psychiatric diagnoses may be associated with shop-lifting. Patients with chronic schizophrenia or alcoholism may steal because of economic necessity. In those with acute schizophrenia, mania or anorexia nervosa, shop-lifting may be a manifestation of the psychiatric disorder. In other conditions, shop-lifting may result from distractability; examples are organic mental states, phobic anxiety (especially when occurring in supermarkets), and the effects of psychotropic drugs. The rare condition kleptomania is included in DSMIIIR as a disorder of impulse control, characterized by increasing tension before the theft and pleasure and relief after it.

If a psychiatrist is called upon to assess a person charged with shop-lifting, the procedure is the same as for any other forensic problem. If the accused has a depressive disorder at the time of the examination, the psychiatrist should try to establish whether the disorder was present at the time of the offence, or whether it developed after the charge was brought. The timing is important because, under the Theft Act 1968, a successful prosecution requires that there should have been intention to steal (*mens rea*). The psychiatrist's report should include opinions on the prognosis and the need for treatment. [See Fisher (1984) for a review of psychiatric aspects of shop-lifting.]

Arson

This offence is generally regarded extremely seriously, not only because it threatens life but also because it can result in great damage to property. Most arsonists are males. Although the courts refer many arsonists for psychiatric assessment, the psychiatric literature on arson is small [see Blumberg (1981) for a review]. As often in forensic psychiatry, it is difficult to make a behavioural classification, but certain groups can be recognized. First, there are arsonists who are free from psychiatric disorder, and who start fires for financial or political reasons; they are sometimes referred to as **motivated** arsonists, though the term is unsatisfactory because non-specific. Second, there are so-called **pathological** arsonists, who suffer from mental retardation, mental illness, or alcoholism. In a consecutive series of men remanded in custody, Taylor and Gunn (1984*a*) found an association between psychotic disorder and arson. However, psychotic fire-setters are reported to account for only 10–15 per cent of arsons (see Blumberg 1981). A third group is sometimes said to have pyromania, but this is another unsatisfactory term that should be avoided. This group includes people who are psychiatrically ill, but who raise fires from motives that appear unreasonable; for example, the desire to help the fire brigade in a heroic way, or to obtain sexual arousal by watching a fire (this last practice may be associated with particularly dangerous fires). DSMIIIR includes the term pyromania as a form of impulse control characterized by increasing tension before fire-setting, and the experience of pleasure, gratification, or release at the time of the fire.

It is clearly important to obtain information about the risks of further offences. In a 20-year follow-up, Soothill and Pope (1973) found that only 4 per cent of arsonists were reconvicted for arson, but about half of them were charged with offences of other kinds. An important guideline is that a person convicted of arson a second time is at a much greater risk of further offences.

Apart from this guideline, certain other factors point to an increased risk of a further offence: antisocial personality disorder; mental retardation; persistent social isolation; and evidence that fire-raising was done for sexual gratification or relief of tension.

Children also present with problems of fire-raising (see Showers and Pickrell 1987). Sometimes the behaviour represents extreme mischievousness in psychologically normal children, and sometimes it springs from psychiatric disturbance. The fire-setting sometimes occurs as a group activity. Amongst 104 child fire-setters referred to a child psychiatric clinic in London, two age-peaks were found: at eight and thirteen years. Most of the children had shown marked anti-social and aggressive behaviour. The most frequent diagnosis was conduct disorder (Jacobson 1985). Among children charged with fire-setting, the recurrence rate in the following two years is reported to be under 10 per cent (Strachan 1981).

Victims of crime

It is only recently that criminology has paid attention to the role and needs of victims. Some victims may contribute to an offence by carelessness, provocation or sometimes, as with some child victims of sexual offences, by willing participation (Gibbens and Prince 1965). After an offence the response of the victim is important in determining reporting to the police and enforcement of the law (Walker 1987).

For the victim, the psychological consequences of crime include the immediate distress following the crime and the subsequent distress associated with investigation and court hearings. Long-term adverse consequences can occur, but their frequency is unknown (see Rich and Burgess 1986; Howard League Working Party 1985). Recently there has been growing concern for the victims of rape, and in the USA there are advisory centres to help such victims (see Notman and Nadelson 1984). Psychiatrists may be asked to treat victims suffering from consequential phobic, anxiety, or depressive disorders; they may also be asked for assessments of psychiatric consequences in relation to compensation proceedings. [For reviews of the effects of crime on victims see Walker (1987); and Hamilton 1987*a*.]

Pathological gambling

Pathological ('compulsive') gambling is not itself illegal but it may lead to behaviours that bring the gambler to the attention of the courts; for example fraud or stealing to obtain money to pay for the habit.

Although pathological gambling has been regarded by some psychologists as a form of addictive behaviour (for example, Orford 1985) it is not classified in this way in either DSMIIIR or ICD10 (draft). In DSMIIIR pathological gambling is classified under the rubric 'Impulse control disorders not elsewhere classified', together with kleptomania and pyromania. In the draft of ICD10, pathological gambling is classified under the category 'Abormalities of adult personality and behaviour' in the sub-category 'Habit and impulse disorders'. This sub-category also includes pathological fire-setting and pathological stealing. Since these latter conditions are discussed in this chapter, pathological gambling is also considered here, rather than in Chapter 14, which deals with dependency on drugs and alcohol.

Gambling is pathological when it is repeated frequently and dominates the person's life. The gambling persists when the person can no longer afford to pay his debts; and he may lie, steal, or defraud in order to obtain money or avoid repayment, and to continue the habit. Family life may be demaged, other social relationships impaired, and employment put at risk. The pathological gambler has an intense urge to gamble, which is difficult to control. He is preoccupied with thoughts of gambling, much as a person dependent on alcohol is preoccupied with drink. Often, increasing sums of money are gambled, either to increase the excitement or in an attempt to recover previous losses. Gambling continues despite inability to repay debts, and despite awareness of the resulting social and legal problems. If gambling is prevented, the person becomes irritable and even more preoccupied with the behaviour.

The *prevalence* of pathological gambling is not known. It is probably more frequent among males. Most gamblers seen by psychiatrists are adults, but there is concern that young people are increasingly being involved, usually with gambling machines in amusement arcades and other places. The *causes* of pathological gambling are not known.

In the absence of reliable information about the course of the condition, it is impossible to assess the value of psychiatric *treatment*. The usual management is similar to that for dependence on alcohol. First the gambler takes part in a thorough review of the effects of the habit on himself and his family; then he is given strong encouragement to abstain from gambling. There are self-help groups (Gamblers Anonymous) which resemble Alcoholics Anonymous in providing a combination of individual confession and catharsis, and group support. Help is given to the family, and advice provided about any legal consequences of excessive gambling. [For a review of pathological gambling, see Orford (1985).]

The psychiatrist and the court

The psychiatrist needs some knowledge about the workings of Magistrates' Courts and Crown Courts. He must also be familiar with the role of the psychiatrist in relation to the courts; the psychiatric examination of a defendant; and the preparation of the court report (see Faulk 1988). The psychiatrist is often working outside the familiar conventions of the doctor–patient relationship. It is essential that he has a clear understanding of his role and of ethical issues concerning his relationship to the alleged offender (see Chiswick 1985).

The workings of the courts

In England and Wales, **Magistrates' Courts** deal with 98 per cent of all criminal prosecutions. They also deal with civil cases. Most magistrates are non-stipendiary laymen, who receive some basic legal training, and are advised on legal points by the Clerk to the Justices.

Indictable offences are those that may be tried by a judge and jury in a Crown Court. The Magistrates' Court tries non-indictable offences. Some indictable offences can be tried in a Magistrates' Court; others must go to a Crown Court. Magistrates may impose a sentence, or else (if the offence seems to merit a more severe penalty than can be imposed by a magistrate) refer the case to the Crown Court for sentencing. If a defendant is charged with a serious indictable offence, and even if he chooses to be tried in a Crown Court, the magistrates must first decide whether the prosecution has established a prima facie case.

In the **Crown Courts**, indictable offences are tried by jury and the sentence is passed by a judge.

Appeals against conviction in a Magistrates' Court are heard either in the Crown Court or the Appeal Court; and appeals against convictions in Crown Court are heard in the Appeal Court.

The role of the psychiatrist in relation to the court

The psychiatrist's role is to draw on his special knowledge to help the court. He should not attempt to tell the court what to do. In Britain, an expert medical witness is expected to remain neutral, and not to favour either the accused or the defendant.

The psychiatrist's interview with the defendant

The psychiatrist should prepare himself as thoroughly as possible before the interview. He should have a clear idea as to the purpose of the examination, and particularly as to any question of fitness to plead. He should have details of the present charge and past convictions, together with copies of any statements made by the defendant and witnesses. The psychiatrist should also study any available report of the defendant's social history but during the subsequent interview it is essential to work through the report with the defendant and check its accuracy.

The psychiatrist should begin by explaining to the client the source of the referral, and why the referral was made. He should explain that the psychiatrist's opinion may be given in court and that the defendant is under no obligation to answer any questions if he chooses not to. The interview should be carried out in strict confidence. Detailed notes should be made, recording any significant comments in the defendant's own words.

At some stage in the interview (not necessarily at the start) the alleged crime should be discussed. The defendant may or may not admit guilt. A detailed history of physical illnesses should be taken; particular attention should be paid to neurological disorders including head injury and epilepsy. A careful history of previous psychiatric disorder and treatment should be obtained. If there has been a previous psychiatric opinion or treatment, further information should be sought. Full examination of the present mental state is made in the usual way. Special investigations should be requested if suitable. If the defendant's intelligence level is under question, an assessment should be made by a clinical psychologist who normally submits a separate report.

It is important to obtain further information from relatives and other informants. If the defendant is remanded in custody, the staff may have long periods of contact with the prisoner and may be able to give particularly useful information.

Preparing a psychiatric court report

This section follows guidelines by Scott (1953) and Faulk (1988).

In preparing a court report, the psychiatrist should remember that it will be read by non-medical people. The report should therefore be written in simple English and should avoid jargon. If technical terms are used, they should be defined as accurately as possible. The report should be concise and set out as follows:

1. *A statement* of the psychiatrist's full name, qualifications, present appointment, and whether approved under Section 12 of the Mental Health Act.

2. *Where and when the interview was conducted*, and whether any third person was present.

3. *Sources of information.* Including documents that have been examined.

4. *Family and personal history of the defendant.* Usually this need not be given in great detail, particularly if a social report is available to the court. The focus should be on information relevant to the diagnosis and disposal.

5. *The account of the crime given by the accused.* This will depend on whether the defendant is pleading guilty or not guilty. If the accused admits to the crime, comment may be made on his attitude to it, such as degree of remorse. If he is pleading not guilty any reference to the alleged crime is inadmissible.

6. *Other behaviour.* It may be relevant to mention other items of behaviour, even if not directly involved in the crime, such as: alcohol or

drug abuse; quality of relationships with other people; tolerance of frustration; general social competence.

7. *Present mental state*. Only the salient positive findings should be stated and negative findings should be omitted. A general diagnosis should be given in the terms of the Mental Health Act (mental illness; mental impairment; or psychopathic disorder). A more specific diagnosis can then be given, but the court will be interested in a categorical statement rather than the finer nuances of diagnosis.

8. *Mental state at the time of the crime*. This is often a highly important issue, and yet it can be based only on retrospective speculation. The assessment can be helped by accounts given by eye-witnesses who saw the offender at the time of the crime or soon after. A current psychiatric diagnosis may suggest the likely mental state at the time of the crime. For example, if the accused suffers from chronic schizophrenia or a chronic organic mental syndrome, the mental state may well have been the same at the time of the crime as at the examination. On the other hand, if the accused suffers from a depressive disorder (now or recently) or from an episodic disorder such as epilepsy, it is more difficult to infer what the mental state is likely to have been at the material time. To add to the difficulty, even if it is judged that the defendant was suffering from a mental disorder, a further judgement is needed as to his mens rea at the time of the crime.

9. *Fitness to plead*. It is often helpful for the psychiatrist to include a statement of fitness to plead. (The criteria for deciding this are given on p. 871.)

Advice on medical treatment

One of the psychiatrist's main functions is to give an opinion as to whether or not psychiatric treatment is indicated. The psychiatrist should make sure that his recommendations on treatment are feasible, if necessary by consulting colleagues, social workers, or others. If he recommends hospital treatment, he should let the court know whether or not a suitable placement is available. The assessment of dangerousness is important here (see next section).

The psychiatrist should not recommend any form of disposal other than medical treatment. However, the court often welcomes tactfully worded comments on the suitability of possible sentences, particularly in the case of young offenders.

The psychiatrist appearing in court

The psychiatrist appearing in court should be fully prepared and should have well organized copies of all reports and necessary documents. It is helpful to speak beforehand to the lawyer involved, in order to clarify any points that may be raised in court. When replying to any questions in court, it is important to be brief and clear, to restrict the answers to the psychiatric evidence, and to avoid speculation.

Dangerousness

The psychiatrist may need to assess dangerousness in everyday psychiatric practice, and also in forensic work. In everyday practice, both out-patients and in-patients may appear to be dangerous, and careful assessment may be required so that the most appropriate steps can be taken in the interests of the patient and of other people. Dangerousness is an important criterion for recommending compulsory detention in hospital. In forensic work, the court may ask for the psychiatrist's advice on the defendant's dangerousness so that a suitable sentence can be passed. The psychiatrist may also be asked to comment on offenders who are detained in institutions and who are being considered for release. In both kinds of circumstance there is an ethical dilemma between the need to protect the community from someone who might show violent behaviour and the obligation to respect the human rights of the offender (see Floud and Young 1981; Roth and Bluglass 1985).

There are no fixed rules for assessing dangerousness. Psychiatrists have tried to identify factors associated with dangerousness, but no reliable predictors of violence have been established. Actuarial prediction has been attemped on the basis of mixed groups of offenders and of the limited information available. It has proved to be inaccurate. The assessment of dangerousness remains difficult. There are a few guidelines, as shown in Table 22.1; these guidelines apply to offenders, but the same principles hold for non-offenders. A thorough review should be made of the history of previous violence, characteristics of the current offence, and the circumstances in which it occurred, and of the mental state. In making the review, it is helpful to consider certain key questions; whether any consistent pattern of behaviour can be discerned; whether any circumstances have provoked violence in the past and are likely to occur again in the future; whether there is any good evidence that the defendant is willing to change his behaviour; and whether there is likely to be any response to treatment.

Difficulties may arise in the assessment of dangerousness in people of antisocial personality or in the mentally retarded, both of whom may be poorly motivated to comply with care. Another difficult problem is presented by the person who threatens to commit a violent act such as homicide. Here the assessment is much the same as for suicide threats

Table 22.1. Factors associated with dangerousness

History
    One or more previous episodes of violence
    Repeated impulsive behaviour
    Evidence of difficulty in coping with stress
    Previous unwillingness to delay gratification
    Sadistic or paranoid traits

Offence
    Bizarre violence
    Lack of provocation
    Lack of regret
    Continuing major denial

Mental state
    Morbid jealousy
    Paranoid beliefs plus a wish to harm others
    Deceptiveness
    Lack of self-control
    Threats to repeat violence
    Attitude to treatment

Circumstances
    Provocation or precipitant likely to recur
    Alcohol or drug abuse
    Social difficulties and lack of support

(Gunn 1979). The psychiatrist should ask the threatener about his intent, motivation, and potential victim, and should make a full assessment of mental state. Patients who make threats can often be helped by out-patient support and treatment, but sometimes hospital admission is required. It may be necessary to warn potential victims.

It is a valuable principle for the psychiatrist not to rely entirely on his own evaluation of dangerousness, but to discuss the problem with other colleagues, including psychiatrists, general practitioners, social workers, and relatives.

In the difficult task of trying to gauge whether a person is likely to show violence, probably the best criterion is whether or not he has been violent in the past. [For a review see Scott (1977).]

Violent incidents

Violent incidents are not common in hospitals (Fottrell 1980), but are increasing (Haller and Deluty 1988). It is important that the staff have a clear policy for managing any incidents that do occur. Such a policy calls for attention to the design of wards, arrangements for summoning assistance, and suitable training for the staff.

When violence occurs or is threatened, staff should be available in adequate numbers, and emergency medication such as intramuscular chlorpromazine should be unobtrusively available. Dangerous people can often be calmed by sympathetic discussion and reassurance, preferably given by someone whom the patient knows and trusts. It is important not to challenge the patient. It is inappropriate to reward violent or threatening behaviour by making concessions in treatment or ward rules, but every effort should be made to allow the patient to withdraw from confrontation without loss of face.

After an incident has occurred, the clinical team should meet to consider the future care of the patient, and also any possible changes in the general policy of the ward (see Gunn 1979). For mentally ill patients, there should be a review of the drugs prescribed and their dosage. When violence occurs in a person with a primary personality disorder, medication may be required in an emergency, but it is usually best to avoid maintenance medication. Other measures include trying to reduce factors that provoke violence, or to provide the patient with more constructive ways of managing tension, such as taking physical exercise or asking a member of staff for help.

Further reading

Faulk, M. (1988). *Basic forensic psychiatry*. Blackwell, Oxford.

Hoggett, B. M. (1984). *Mental health law* (2nd edn). Sweet and Maxwell, London.

Kaplan, H. I. and Sadock, B. J.(1985) Chap. 54, 'Forensic psychiatry'. Slovenko, R. 'Law and psychiatry', Adler, G. 'Correctional (Prison) psychiatry' In *Comprehensive textbook of psychiatry* (4th edn). Williams and Wilkins, Baltimore.

Prins, H. (1986). *Dangerous behaviour, the law, and mental disorder*. Tavistock, London.

Smith, J. C. and Hogan, B. (1983). *Criminal law* (5th edn). Butterworths, London.

Walker, N. (1987) *Crime and criminology*. Oxford University Press, Oxford.

Walker, N. and McCabe, S. (1968). *Crime and insanity in England*, Vol. I. Edinburgh University Press, Edinburgh.

Walker, N. and McCabe, S. (1973). *Crime and insanity in England*, Vol. II. Edinburgh University Press, Edinburgh.

Appendix: The law in England and Wales

This appendix is an introduction to the principal sections of the law of England and Wales relating to psychiatric practice. It begins with a review of the Mental Health Act and then outlines the law in relation to child and adolescent psychiatry. More detailed information can be obtained from the works listed under further reading (p. 909) and, of course, from the Act itself. Psychiatrists practising elsewhere than in England and Wales will need to consult guides to their local legislation and its application in clinical practice.

The Mental Health Act

The Mental Health Act 1983 regulates the care of mentally abnormal persons. It consolidates the Mental Health Act 1959 and the Mental Health (Amendment) Act 1982, which made provisions for compulsory treatment and about consent to treatment. It also set up the Mental Health Act Commission, which is an independent multidisciplinary body appointed by the Secretary of State. The Commission has powers to safeguard the interests of detained patients. Its duties are to visit such patients, investigate complaints, receive reports on patients' treatment, and appoint doctors and others to give opinions on consent to treatment.

Parts IV and V of the Mental Health Act provide the legal basis for compulsory admission and detention of psychiatric patients. Provision for compulsory detention is also made by the Criminal Procedure (Insanity) Act 1964, which relates to people found 'not guilty by reason of insanity' or 'unfit to plead' (see pp. 871 and 873).

Under the Mental Health Act there are three main groups of compulsory order for assessment and treatment:
  (a) admission for assessment (Sections 2, 4, 5, 135, 136);
  (b) treatment orders (Section 3 and 7);
  (c) admission and transfer of patients concerned with criminal proceedings (Sections 37, 41, 47, 49).

The short-term orders listed in (a) above apply to any mental disorder, which need not be specified. For the long-term orders listed under (b) and (c), it must be stated that the patient suffers from one of four types of mental disorder: mental illness, psychopathic disorder, mental impairment, and severe mental impairment.

The Act does not define 'mental illness', but it states that no one should be 'treated as suffering from mental disorder by reason only of promiscuity, or other immoral conduct, sexual deviancy or dependence on alcohol or drugs'.

The Act gives the following definitions of the three other types of mental disorder:

(a) **severe mental impairment** means a state of arrested or incomplete development of mind which includes severe impairment of intelligence and social functioning and is associated with abnormally aggressive or seriously irresponsible conduct on the part of the person concerned.

(b) **mental impairment** means a state of arrested or incomplete development of mind (not amounting to severe mental impairment) which includes significant impairment of intelligence and social functioning and is associated with abnormally aggressive or seriously irresponsible conduct on the part of the person concerned.

(c) **psychopathic disorder** means a persistent disorder or disability of mind (whether or not including significant impairment of intelligence) which results in abnormally aggressive or seriously irresponsible conduct on the part of the person concerned.

The Act also specified the various people who may be involved in procedures for admission and treatment:

Responsible medical officer. The doctor in charge of treatment.

Nearest relative. Nearest adult relative (in the order of spouse, son or daughter, father or mother, sibling, grandparent, grandchild, uncle or aunt, nephew or niece). The elder or eldest of relatives of the same kind (for example, siblings) is preferred, and full siblings have precedence over half-siblings. Also preference is given to a relative with whom the patient lives or who cares for him. The definition includes cohabitees (who may be of the same sex as the patient) who have lived with the patient for a specified time. However, they come last on the list of relatives and cannot claim precedence over a husband or wife other than through agreement or under an Order of Court or by desertion.

Approved social worker (formerly mental welfare officer). Social workers approved by the local authority as having appropriate competence in dealing with mentally disordered person.

Approved doctor. A doctor approved under Section 12 of the Act by the Secretary of State as having special experience in the diagnosis or treatment of mental disorder.

The three main groups of compulsory order will now be reviewed in turn.

Admission for assessment

Whilst a full understanding of the proper use of compulsory admission can be gained only from clinical experience, the clinician needs to be aware of the following general conditions governing compulsory detention:

Section 2: Application for admission for assessment (28 days)

The usual procedure for compulsory admission when informal admission is not appropriate in the circumstances. Detention is for assessment, or for assessment followed by medical treatment. The following grounds must be satisfied:

1. The patient suffers from a mental disorder which warrants the patient's detention in hospital for assessment (assessment followed by treatment).

2. Admission is necessary in the interests of the patient's own health or safety or for the protection of others.

The procedure requires:

(a) *Application* by the patient's nearest relative, or an approved social worker who must have seen the patient within the last 14 days. The approved social worker should, so far as it is practicable, consult the nearest relative.

(b) *Medical recommendations* by two doctors, one of whom must be approved under Section 12 of the Act. The two doctors should not be on the staff of the same hospital unless it would cause undesirable delay to find a doctor from elsewhere. There should not be more than five days between the examinations.

Section 4: Emergency order for assessment (72 hours)

This section allows a simpler procedure than Section 2 and provides power to detain patients in emergencies. It is usually completed in the patient's home by the family doctor but is also occasionally used in general hospital casualty departments. Section 4 should be used only when there is insufficient time to obtain the opinion of an approved doctor who could complete Section 2. The grounds are as for Section 2. It is expected that a

Section 4 order will be converted into a Section 2 order as soon as possible after the patient has arrived in hospital. The procedure for a Section 4 order requires:

(a) Application by an approved social worker who must have seen the patient within the previous 24 hours, or the nearest relative.

(b) Medical recommendation by one doctor, who need not be approved under Section 12 of the Act. The patient must be admitted within 24 hours of the examination (or of the application if made earlier).

Section 5: Change to compulsory detention (72 hours)

Section 5 (2) is an order for the emergency detention of a patient who is already in hospital as a voluntary patient but wishes to leave, and the doctor believes an application should be made for compulsory admission under the Act. It requires a single medical recommendation by the doctor in charge of the patient's care or by another doctor who is on the staff of the hospital and nominated by the doctor in charge. (This power applies to a patient in any hospital.) It is usual to consider a change to a Section 2 or 3 order as soon as possible.

If a Section 5 (2) order cannot be obtained immediately, a registered mental nurse or registered nurse for the mentally subnormal may invoke a six-hour Section 5 (4) **holding order**. The nurse must record that the patient is suffering from mental disorder such that, in the interests of the patient's health or safety or for the protection of others, the patient should be restrained from leaving the hospital. The holding order applies only when the patient is already under treatment for a mental disorder. It lapses as soon as the doctor signs Section 5 (2). The latter lasts for a period which commences at the time the original nurses holding order was signed. (This power only applies to patients being treated for mental disorder.)

Section 115: Powers of entry and inspection

An approved social worker can enter and inspect any premises (within the area of the local authority in which the patient lives) if he has reason to believe that a mentally disordered patient is not under proper care. The social worker must be able to provide authenticated documentation of his status.

Section 135: Warrant to search for and remove patients

Any approved social worker who believes that someone is suffering from a mental disorder and is unable to care for himself or is being ill-treated or neglected may apply to a magistrate for a warrant for that person's removal to a place of safety.

Section 136: Mentally disordered person found in a public place

Any police constable who finds in a public place someone who appears to be suffering from a mental disorder may take that person to a place of safety (which usually means a police station or a hospital), if the person appears to be in immediate need of care or control, or if the police constable thinks that it is necessary to do so in the person's interest, or for the further protection of other persons. The person is detained so that he can be examined by a doctor and any necessary arrangements can be made for his treatment or care. The authority under Section 136 expires when these arrangements have been completed or within 72 hours, whichever is the shorter.

Treatment orders

Section 3: Admission for treatment (6 months)

The grounds for this longer-term order are that the patient:

(a) is suffering from mental illness, severe mental impairment, psychopathic disorder or mental impairment, being a mental disorder of a nature or degree which makes it appropriate for him to receive medical treatment in a hospital; and

(b) in the case of psychopathic disorder or mental impairment, that such treatment is likely to alleviate or prevent a deterioration of his condition; and

(c) that it is necessary for the health or safety of the patient or for the protection of other persons that he should receive such treatment and that it cannot be provided unless he is detained under this section.

The procedure requires:
1. *Application*. This is made by the patient's nearest relative or an approved social worker. The latter must, if practicable, consult the nearest relative before making an application and cannot proceed if the nearest relative objects.
2. *Medical recommendation*. As for Section 2. In addition the recommendations must state the particular grounds for the doctor's opinion, specifying whether any other methods of dealing with the patient are available and, if so, why they are not appropriate. The doctor must specify one of the four forms of mental disorder.

3. *Renewal.* The order may be renewed on the first occasion for a further six months and subsequently for a year at a time.

Section 7: Reception into guardianship

Guardianship is more appropriate than the provisions of Section 3 for the long-term treatment of patients living in the community. The application, medical recommendation, duration, and renewal procedure are similar to those for Section 3. The guardian, who is usually but not always the local Social Services Department, is given authority (Section 8) for supervision in the community, including power to:

(a) require the patient to live at a place specified by the guardian;

(b) require the patient to attend places specified by the guardian for medical treatment, occupation, training, or education.

(c) ensure that a doctor, social worker, or other person specified by the guardian can see the patient at his home.

Admission to hospital of those appearing before the courts

These sections of the Mental Health Act allow the Courts to order psychiatric care for those charged with or convicted of an offence punishable by imprisonment. Medical recommendations are required together with an assurance that a hospital place is available.

Remands to hospital and interim hospital orders

Persons on remand (but not in custody) may be treated as voluntary patients. Sometimes psychiatric care may be made a condition of the granting of bail. In addition, the Mental Health Act 1983 gave the courts powers to:

(a) remand an accused person to a hospital for medical reports (Section 35);

(b) remand an accused person to hospital for treatment (except for murder cases) (Section 36);

(c) make an interim hospital order on a convicted person to assess suitability for a hospital order (Section 38).

Procedure (a) requires a medical recommendation by an approved doctor that there is reason to suspect mental disorder. Procedures (b) and

(c) require medical recommendations by two doctors (one of whom must be approved), that the person is suffering from mental disorder.

Section 37: Hospital order

A court may impose a hospital order, which commits an offender to hospital on a similar basis to that of a patient admitted for treatment under the civil provisions of Section 3 of the Act (see above). The duration of the order is six months.

Medical recommendation: two doctors one of whom must be approved.

Section 41: Restriction order

When a Section 37 hospital order is made by a Crown Court, the Court may also make an order under Section 41 of the Act restricting the person's discharge from hospital. The restriction order may be either without limit of time or for a specified period. If it is for a fixed term, once that term expires or otherwise ceases to have effect, the patient will still be detained under a hospital order but without restriction, i.e. Section 37.

Section 47: Transfer to hospital from prison

This section authorizes the Home Secretary to transfer a person serving a sentence of imprisonment to a local NHS hospital or special hospital (Section 48 covers other prisoners not serving sentences for criminal offences). A direction for transfer has the same effect as a hospital order. The patient's status changes to that of a notional Section 37 at the time of the 'earliest date of release'.

The Home Secretary can make the direction with or without special restriction on discharge (Section 49).

Medical recommendation: two doctors one of whom must be approved.

Discharge of patients

Patients on emergency orders (Sections 4,5,135,136) can be discharged by the responsible medical officer. Patients on a Section 2 order can be discharged by the responsible medical officer, the hospital managers, the nearest relative, or a Mental Health Review Tribunal. The same applies to patients on Section 3, except that the responsible medical officer may register an objection to discharge by relatives if he considers that the patient is a danger to himself or others. Patients under guardianship are in the same position as patients on Section 3 except that the local health authority replaces the hospital managers.

The nearest relative has no rights to discharge patients on Section 37 or Section 47 orders. Patients on Section 41 and Section 49 restriction orders can be discharged only by the responsible medical officer with the consent of the Secretary of State for Home Affairs, or by a Mental Health Review Tribunal.

Mental Health Review Tribunals

These are regional tribunals that provide an appeal procedure for patients subject to longer-term orders. They hear appeals against compulsory orders and automatically review certain patients under Sections 3 and 37 (see list below). Review tribunals may order immediate or delayed discharge. The members of a panel are appointed by the Lord Chancellor and include a lay-member, a doctor, and a lawyer who is the chairman. When the patient is subject to a restriction order, the chairman of the panel is a judge. Patients are entitled to be provided with legal representation.

For the various sections of the Act, the timing of application for appeal is specified:

Section 4 and 5:	No appeal
Section 2:	Application must be made within 14 days.
Section 3:	Application can be made in the first six months, second six months, and then annually. Review is automatic if there has been no appeal either in the first six months or in any three-year period.
Section 37 (with or without Section 41)	Application can be made in the second six months, then annually. Review is automatic if there has been no appeal in any three-year period.
Guardianship	An application can be made in each period of detention. No automatic review.

Consent to treatment

Under Common Law, no treatment can be given to a voluntary patient without his valid consent. This requires that the patient voluntarily (that is without being subjected to coercion or unreasonable influence) agrees to the treatment, and is capable of making that decision. Doctors should not give treatment without such consent unless the treatment is essential to safeguard the health or preserve the life of the patient.

The Mental Health Act 1983 introduced provisions to serve two purposes: to give authority for certain treatments to be given without consent, and to safeguard psychiatric patients' interests in relation to treatment procedures.

The Act specifies certain emergency conditions under which treatment can be given without consent to a detained patient. Any treatment (provided it is not irreversible or hazardous) can be given to such a patient without his consent, if it is immediately necessary to save the patient's life, to prevent a serious deterioration in his condition, to alleviate serious suffering, or to prevent violence or danger to the patient himself or to others.

The Act also defines various groups of treatments according to the type of consent required for them. The allocations of particular treatments to these groups are specified in the Act, in Regulations (which are compulsory) and in a Code of Practice (which is advisory). Certain patients are excluded from the stipulations concerning consent to treatment, namely those detained under Sections 4, 5, 135, and 136; those remanded to hospital for reports; and those subject to Section 41 orders but conditionally discharged by the Home Secretary. For these patients the doctor has only 'common-law' rights and duties when giving treatment.

For other patients, three groups of treatments are stipulated, of which all three apply to detained patients, and only the first to voluntary patients.

(1) Treatments which give rise to special concern

This group applies to both voluntary and detained patients. It includes psycho-surgery and other treatments which are yet to be specified, but do not include ordinary medication or ECT. For treatments included in this group the patient must consent, and there must be a second opinion. The second opinion must be provided by an independent doctor who will be required to consult two people (one a nurse, one neither a doctor nor a nurse) who have been professionally concerned with the patient's treatment. He considers both the treatment proposed and the patient's ability to give consent. In addition two independent people must certify as to the patient's ability to give consent.

Approval of treatment by the second opinion procedure may cover a plan of care including more than one form of treatment.

(2) Other treatments listed in Regulations

This group applies to detained patients. It consists of other treatments specified in the Act or in Regulations. It includes some forms of medication and ECT. For these treatments, a second opinion must be obtained as in 1 (a) above if the patient does not consent, cannot give consent, or withdraws consent. Again the second opinion may cover a plan of treatment. However, for most forms of medication these procedures do not apply during the first three months of treatment.

(3) Other forms of treatment

Treatments not referred to in 1 or 2 above can be given to detained patients without their consent. It should be noted that, according to the act, medical treatment 'includes nursing and also includes care, habilitation and rehabilitation under medical supervision'.

The Court of Protection

This Court has a very long history and is responsible for the mentally ill or impaired. Most of its functions are carried out by the Master and other officers appointed by the Lord Chancellor. They are assisted by medical, legal, and general panels of Lord Chancellor's Visitors, who visit patients to review their capacities and the implementation of procedures approved by the Court. Applications to the Court may be made by the nearest relative or any interested party. They should include a medical certificate from a doctor concerned in the patient's care and an affidavit of the patient's family and property. After considering the evidence the judge may appoint a receiver to administer the patients' affairs and also to 'do or secure the doing of all such things as appear necessary or expedient'. During the management of a patient's affairs by the Court, medical opinion may be sought about the patient's ability to make a will and about any application to end the Court management. [See Gostin (1983), for a general review, and MacFarlane (1985) for guidance on providing medical evidence.]

Children and the law

Parental consent is normally required for the medical care of children under the age of sixteen. There are some uncertainties about the occasions on which parents need not be notified when children aged 15 or 16 consult doctors. When in doubt it is sensible to seek further advice from an experienced child psychiatrist, a medical defence society, or another authority.

Compulsory admission under the Mental Health Act is hardly ever used for children under the age of 16 for two reasons. First, there are alternatives such as Care proceedings (see below) or an application for the child to be made a Ward of Court. Secondly, parents have powers up to the age of 16, or up to the age of 18 if the child is not capable of consent. 'The practical answer, therefore, is that where a child is capable but strongly protesting it will usually be unwise to proceed without invoking compulsory powers; where he is capable and consenting it will usually be safe to proceed; and where he is incapable the parents' wishes will prevail unless the compulsory powers are used' (Hoggett 1984, pp 92–93).

Apart from the legal provisions discussed below, a psychiatric opinion may be sought in various types of Civil proceedings, for instance adoption, wardship, divorce, and custody. According to the circumstances it is wise to obtain advice from those with knowledge and experience, such as child psychiatrists, social workers, and lawyers. [See also Hoggett (1984).]

Children convicted of a criminal offence

Children below the age of 10 are not regarded as capable of criminal responsibility (see p. 872). Between the ages of 10 and 14 responsibility must be proved in court. The range of penalties can be summarized thus:

(1) *Absolute or conditional discharge.*

(2) *Fine and compensation.* There are maximum limits to the fines that can be imposed on a child or a young person.

(3) *Binding over parents or guardian.* If the child is found guilty of an offence the Court may order the parent or guardian (with their consent) to enter into recognisance to take proper care of him and exercise proper control.

(4) *Supervision order.* This is the equivalent of a probation order for those aged under 17. It provides for supervision by a probation officer or social worker for a specified period of up to 3 years. Where appropriate, psychiatric treatment may be made a condition of the order under Section 12, Children and Young Persons Act 1969. The offender must consent to this condition.

(5) *Care order* (see below).

(6) *Attendance centre order.* Regular attendance is required for a specified number of hours at a daytime centre for training and constructive occupation.

(7) *Hospital order* (Mental Health Act, 1983) (see above p. 903).

(8) *Detention centre order.* This provides disciplined custodial training lasting three months for offenders aged 14–16 and three to six months for those aged 17–20. Remission of one month is usual for both age groups.

(9) *Borstal training* provides remedial training for young offenders (aged 15–20) who are unsuitable or too old for residential care. The emphasis is intended to be educational rather than punitive. The duration is from 6–24 months.

(10) *Imprisonment.* As specified in section 53 of the Children and Young Persons Act (1933) the court may sentence a child or young person to be detained during Her Majesty's Pleasure when found guilty of an offence which in the case of an adult would carry a long sentence or life imprisonment. Her Majesty's Pleasure may be a determinate or

indeterminate length of time. The latter is not the same as a life sentence. For example, the person is not subject to licence for the rest of life, as is the case with life imprisonment.

Child and Young Persons Act (1969)

This is the most significant legislation affecting the care of children (aged 0–14) and young persons (15–17). It reduces earlier distinctions between those who commit criminal offences and those who are in need of help for other reasons.

Care order

A care order commits a child or young person (up to the age of 17) to the care of the local authority social services department. The order can be made if any of the following conditions are met:

(a) his proper development is being avoidably prevented or neglected or his health is being avoidably impaired or neglected or he is being ill-treated; or

(b) it is probable that the condition set out in the preceding paragraph will be satisfied in his case, having regard to the fact that the court or another court has found that condition is or was satisfied in the case of another child or young person who is or was a member of the household in which he belongs; or

(c) he is exposed to moral danger; or

(d) he is beyond the control of his parent or guardian; or

(e) he is of compulsory school age within the meaning of the Education Act 1944 and is not receiving efficient full time education suitable to his age, ability, and aptitude; or

(f) he is guilty of an offence, excluding homicide.

Child Care Act (1980)

This act covers 'voluntary care and specifies the duties of local authorities to care for children under the age of 17 who have no one to care for them because of death, desertion, illness, or any other reason.'

Hospitals and the police

The police are entitled to question any person, whether suspected or not, who they think may be able to provide useful information. The person need not say anything and cannot be compelled to go to a police station except by arrest. If the police wish to interview a psychiatric patient, it may sometimes be necessary for the doctor to give a medical opinion that the patient's mental condition is such that it would be inappropriate for him to be interviewed.

The Judges' Rules state that, as far as practicable, children and young persons under the age of 17 (whether suspected of a crime or not) should be interviewed only in the presence of a parent or guardian or, in their absence, some person who is not a police officer and who is of the same sex as the child. This recommendation applies to juveniles who are hospital patients. If the parents or guardians cannot be present, the hospital should act *in loco parentis* and an appropriate member of hospital staff of the same sex as the child should be present.

Further reading

Bluglass, R. S. (1983). *A guide to the Mental Health Act 1983*. Churchill Livingstone, Edinburgh.

Hoggett, B. M. (1984). *Mental health law* (2nd edn). Sweet and Maxwell, London.

References

Abel, E. L. (1984). *Fetal alcohol syndrome and fetal alcohol effects*. Plenum Press, New York.

Abraham, K. (1911). Notes on the psychoanalytic investigation and treatment of manic-depressive insanity and allied conditions. In *Selected papers on psychoanalysis*, pp. 137–56. Hogarth Press and Institute of Psychoanalysis, London (1927).

Abrahamson, L. Y., Seligman, M. E. P., and Teasdale, J. (1978). Learned helplessness in humans: critique and reformulation. *Journal of Abnormal Psychology* **87**, 49–74.

Abramowitz, S. I. (1986). Psychosocial outcomes of sex reassignment surgery. *Journal of Consulting and Clinical Psychology* **54**, 183–9.

Abrams, R., Taylor, M. A., Faber, R., Ts'o, T. O. T., Williams, R. A., and Almy, G. (1983). Bilateral versus unilateral electroconvulsive therapy: efficacy in melancholia. *American Journal of Psychiatry* **140**, 463–50.

Acheson, E. D. (1959). The clinical syndrome variously called benign myalgic encephalomyelitis, Iceland disease and epidemic neuromyasthenia. *American Journal of Medicine* **26**, 569–95.

Achté, K. A., Hillbom, E., and Aalberg, V. (1969). Psychoses following war brain injuries. *Acta Psychiatrica Scandinavica* **45**, 1–18.

Acker, W. Aps, E. J., Majumdar, S. K., Shaw, D. K. and Thomson, A. D. (1982). The relationship between brain and liver damage in chronic alcohol patients. *Journal of Neurology, Neurosurgery and Psychiatry* **45**, 984–7.

Acker, W., Ron, M. A., Lishman, W. A., and Shaw, G. K., (1984). A multivariate analysis of psychological clinical and CT scanning measures in detoxified chronic alcoholics. *British Journal of Addiction* **79**, 293–301.

Ackerknecht, E. H. (1968). *A short history of psychiatry*. Hefner, New York.

Ackerman, N. W. (1958). *The psychodynamics of family life*. Basic Books, New York.

Ackner, B. (1954*a*). Depersonalization: I Aetiology and phenomenology. *Journal of Mental Science* **100**, 939–53.

Ackner, B. (1954*b*). Depersonalization II. The clinical syndromes. *Journal of Mental Science* **100**, 954–72.

Ackner, B., and Oldham, A. J. (1962). Insulin treatment of schizophrenia. A three year follow up of a controlled study. *Lancet* **i**, 504–6.

Ackner, B., Cooper, J. E., Gray, C. H., and Kelly, M. (1962). Acute porphyria, a neuro-psychiatric and biochemical study. *Journal of Psychosomatic Research* **6**, 1–24.

Adam, K., Adamson, L., Brezinová, V., Hunter, W. M., and Oswald, I. (1976). Nitrazepam: lastingly effective but trouble on withdrawal. *British Medical Journal* **i**, 1558–60.

Adelstein, A. and Mardon, C. (1975). Suicide 1961–1974: an analysis of trends following the Suicide Act of 1961. *Population Trends* **2**, 13–19.

Adelstein, A. and White, G. (1976). Alcoholism and mortality. *Population Trends* **6**, 7–13.

Ader, R. (1976). Psychosomatic research in animals. In *Modern trends in psychosomatic medicine* (ed. O. W. Hill). Butterworths, London.

Adler, A. (1943). Neuropsychiatric complications in victims of Boston's Coconut Grove disaster. *Journal of the American Medical Association* **123**, 1098–11.

Aduan, R. P., Fauci, A. S., Dale, D. C., Herzberg, J. H. and Wolff, S. M. (1979). Factitious fever and self-induced infection: a report of 32 cases and review of the literature. *Annals of Internal Medicine* **90**, 230–42.

Advisory Committee on Drug Dependence (1968). *Cannabis.* HMSO, London.

Agras, S., Sylvester, D., and Oliveau, D. (1969). The epidemiology of common fears and phobias. *Comprehensive Psychiatry* **10**, 151–6.

Alanen, Y. O. (1958). The mothers of schizophrenic patients. *Acta Psychiatrica Neurologica Scandinavia* **33**, Suppl., 124.

Alanen, Y. O. (1970). The families of schizophrenic patients. *Proceedings of the Royal Society of Medicine* **63**, 227–30.

Albert, M. L., Feldman, R. G., and Willis, A. L. (1974). The 'sub-cortical dementia' of progressive supranuclear palsy. *Journal of Neurology, Neurosurgery and Psychiatry* **37**, 121–30.

Alderson, M. R. (1985). National trends in self poisoning in women. *Lancet* i 974–75.

Alexander, D. A. (1972). 'Senile Dementia' A changing perspective. *British Journal of Psychiatry* **121**, 207–14.

Alexander, F. (1950). *Psychosomatic medicine.* W. W. Norton, New York.

Allderidge, P. (1979). Hospitals, madhouses and asylums: cycles in the care of the insane. *British Journal of Psychiatry* **134**, 321–4.

Allebeck, P. and Wisledt, B. (1986). Mortality in schizophrenia. *Archives of General Psychiatry* **43**, 650–3.

Allen, C. (1969). *A textbook of psychosexual disorders* (2nd edn). Oxford University Press, London.

Alter-Reid, K. A., Gibbs, M. S., Lachenmeyer, J. R., Sigal, J., and Massoll, N. A. (1986). Sexual abuse of children: a review of the empirical findings. *Clinical Psychology Review* **6**, 249–66.

Alzheimer, A. (1897). Beitrage zur pathologischen Anatomie der Hirnrinde und zur anatomischen Grundlage einiger Psychosen. *Monatsschrift für Psychiatrie und Neurologie* **2**, 82–120.

Ambrosini, P. J. and Puig-Antich, J. (1985). Major depression in children and adolescents. In. *The clinical guide to child psychiatry* (ed. D. Shaffer, A. A. Ehrhardt, and L. L. Greenhill). Free Press, New York.

American Psychiatric Association (1980). *Diagnostic and statistical manual of mental disorders* (3rd edn, revised). American Psychiatric Association, Washington, DC.

American Psychiatric Association (1987). *Diagnostic and statistical manual of mental disorders* (3rd edn). American Psychiatric Association, Washington, DC

Amies, P. L., Gelder, M. G., and Shaw, P. M. (1983). Social phobia: a comparative clinical study. *British Journal of Psychiatry* **142**, 174–9.

Amir, M. (1971). *Patterns in forcible rape.* Chicago University Press, Chicago.

Ammerman, R. T., Van Hasselt, V. B., and Herson, M. (1986). Psychological adjustment of visually handicapped children and youth. *Clinical Psychological Review* **6**, 67–85.

Amsterdam, J. D., Winokur, A., Lucki, I., Caroff, S., Snyder, P., and Rickels, K. (1983). A neuroendocrine test battery in bipolar patients and healthy subjects. *Archives of General Psychiatry* **40**, 515–21.

Ananth and Luchins, D. (1977). A review of combined tricyclic and MAOI therapy. *Comprehensive Psychiatry* **18**, 221–30.

Anderson, E. W. (1933). A study of the sexual life in psychoses associated with childbearing. *Journal of Mental Science* **79**, 137–49.

Anderson, H. R., Dick, B., MacNair, R. S., Palmer, J. C., and Ramsey, J. D. (1982). An investigation of 140 deaths associated with volatile substance abuse in the United Kingdom (1971–1981). *Human Toxicology* **1**, 207–21.

Anderson, K. O., Bradley, L. A., Young, L. D., McDaniel, L. K., and Wise, C. M. (1985). Rheumatoid arthritis: review of psychological factors related to etiology, effects and treatment. *Psychological Bulletin* **98**, 358–87.

Anderton, B. H. (1987). Tangled genes and proteins. *Nature* **329**, 106–7.

Andreasen, N. J. C. (1977) Reliability and validity of proverb interpretation to assess mental status. *Comprehensive Psychiatry* **18**, 465–72.

Andreasen, N. J. C. (1982). Negative versus positive schizophrenia: definition and validation. *Archives of General Psychiatry* **36**, 1325–30.

Andreasen, N. J. C. (1985). Post-traumatic stress disorder. In *Comprehensive textbook of psychiatry* (4th edn), Vol. 3 (H. I. Kaplan and B. J. Sadock) Williams and Wilkins, Baltimore.

Andreasen, N. J. C. (ed.) (1986). *Can schizophrenia be localized in the brain?* American Psychiatric Press, Washington DC.

Andreasen, N. J. C. (1987). The diagnosis of schizophrenia. *Schizophrenia Bulletin* **13**, 9–22.

Andreasen, N. J. C. and Norris, A. S. (1972). Management of emotional reactions in severely burned adults. *Journal of Nervous and Mental Disease* **154**, 352–62.

Andreasen, N. J. C., Olsen, S. A., Dennant, J. W., and Smith, M. R. (1982). Ventricular enlargement in schizophrenia: relationship to positive and negative symptoms. *American Journal of Psychiatry* **139**, 297–302.

Angold, A. (1988). Childhood and adolescent depression: 1. Epidemiological aspects. *British Journal of Psychiatry* **152**, 601–17.

Angst, J. (1966). *Zur Aetiologie und Nosologie endogener depressiver Psychosen*. Monographien aus dem Gesamtgebiete der Neurologie und Psychiatrie 112. Springer, Berlin.

Angst, J., Baastrup, P., Grof, P., Hippius, H., Pöldinger, W., and Weiss, P. (1973). The course of monopolar depression and bipolar psychosis. *Psychiatrica, Neurologica, Neurochirurgia* **76**, 486–500.

Annals of Internal Medicine (1985). Health implications of obesity. NIH Health consensus development conference. *Annals of Internal Medicine* **103**, 981–1077.

Anonymous (1984). Lithium and the kidney revisited. *Biological Therapies in Psychiatry* **7**, 9–12.

Anthony, E. J. (1957). An experimental approach to the psychopathology of childhood encopresis. *British Journal of Medical Psychology* **30**, 146–75.

Anthony, W. A. and Liberman R. P. (1986). The practice of psychiatric rehabilitation: historical, conceptual, and research base. *Schizophrenia Bulletin* **13**, 542–9.

Apley, J. and Hale, B. (1973). Children with recurrent abdominal pain: how do they grow up? *British Medical Journal* **ii**, 7–9.

Arie, T. (ed.) (1985). *Recent advances in psychogeriatrics*. Churchill Livingstone, Edinburgh.

Arieti, S. (1974). Individual psychotherapy for schizophrenia. In *American handbook of psychiatry* (ed. S. Arieti). Vol. III, Chapter 27. Basic Books, New York.

Arieti, S. (1977). Psychotherapy of severe depression. *American Journal of Psychiatry* **134**, 864–8.

Armor, D. J., Polich, J. M., and Stambul, H. B. (1976). *Alcoholism and treatment*. Rand Corporation and Wiley Interscience, Santa Monica.

Armstrong, C. N. (1966). Treatment of wrongly assigned sex. *British Medical Journal* ii, 1225–6.

Arnetz, B. B., Horte, L. G., Hedberg, A., Theorell, T., Allender, E., and Malker, H. (1987). Suicide patterns among physicians related to other academics as well as to the general population. *Acta Psychiatrica Scandinavica* 75, 139–43.

Arrindell W. A. and Emelkamp, P. M. G. (1985). Psychological profile of the spouse of the female agoraphobic patient: personality and symptoms. *British Journal of Psychiatry* 146, 405–14.

Arroyave, F., Cooper, S. E., and Harris, A. D. (1980). The role of detoxification in alcoholism: three years' results from the Oxford unit. *Health Trends* 12, 36–8.

Arthur, A. Z. (1964). Theories and explanations of delusions: a review. *American Journal of Psychiatry* 121, 105–15.

Asberg, M., Crönholm, B., Sjöqvist, F., and Tuck, D. (1971). Relationship between plasma level and therapeutic effect of nortriptyline. *British Medical Journal* iii, 331–4.

Asher, R. (1949). Myxoedematous madness. *British Medical Journal* ii, 555–62.

Asher, R. (1951). Munchausen's syndrome. *Lancet* i, 339–41.

Ashton, J. R. and Donnan, S. (1981). Suicide by burning as an epidemic phenomenon: an analysis of 82 deaths and inquests in England and Wales 1978–1979. *Psychological Medicine* 11, 735–9.

Asperger, H. (1944). Die 'Autistischen Psychopathien' Kindesalter. *Archives für Psychiatrie und Nervenkrankheiten* 117, 76–136.

Assal, J. P., Muhlhausar, I., Dernet, A., Gfeller, R., Jorgens, V., and Berger, M. (1985). Patient education as the basis for diabetes care in clinical practice and research. *Diabetologia* 28, 602–13.

Astrup, C. and Ødegaard, Ø. (1960). Internal migration and mental disease in Norway. *Psychiatric Quarterly* 34, supp. 116.

Avni, J. (1980) The severe burns. In *Advances in psychosomatic medicine* (ed. H. Freyburger), Vol. 10. Karger, Basel.

Aylon, T. and Azrin, N. H. (1968). *The token economy: a motivational system for therapy and rehabilitation.* Appleton-Century-Crofts, New York.

Babcock, H. (1930). An experiment in the measurement of mental deterioration. *Archives of Psychology* 117, 5–105.

Bachrach, L. L. (1986). De-institutionalization: What do the numbers mean? *Hospital and Community Psychiatry* 37, 118–21.

Bach-y-Rita, G., Lion, J. R., Climent, C. E., and Ervin, F. R. (1971). Episodic dyscontrol: a study of 130 violent patients. *American Journal of Psychiatry* 127, 1473–8.

Baddeley, A. D. (1976). *The psychology of memory.* Harper and Row, New York.

Bagley, C. (1968). The evaluation of a suicide prevention scheme by an ecological method. *Social Science and Medicine* 2, 1–14.

Bailey, V., Graham, P., and Boniface, D. (1978). How much child psychiatry does a general practitioner do? *Journal of the Royal College of General Practitioners* 28, 621–6.

Baker, R., Hall, J. N., and Hutchinson, K. (1974). A token economy project with chronic schizophrenic patients. *British Journal of Psychiatry* 124, 367–84.

Baker, T. and Duncan, S. (1986). Child sexual abuse. In: *Recent Advances in Paediatrics VIII* (ed. R. Meadow). Churchill Livingstone, London.

Bakwin, H. (1961). Enuresis in children. *Journal of Paediatrics* 58, 806–19.

Baldessarini, R. J. (1984). Treatment of depression by altering monoamine metabolism: precursors and metabolic inhibitors. *Psychopharmacology Bulletin* 20, 224–39.

Baldwin, J. A. and Oliver, J. E. (1975). Epidemiology and family characteristics of severely abused children. *British Journal of Preventive and Social Medicine* **29**, 205–21.

Bale, R. N. (1973). Brain damage in diabetes mellitus. *British Journal of Psychiatry* **122**, 337–41.

Balint, M. (1957). *The doctor, his patient and the illness*. Pitman Medical, London.

Balint, M., Hunt, J., Joyce., D., Marinker, M., and Woodcock, J. (1970). *Treatment or diagnosis: a study of repeat prescriptions in general practice*. Tavistock, London.

Ball, J. R. B. and Kiloh, L. G. (1959). A controlled trial of imipramine in the treatment of depressive states. *British Medical Journal* **ii**, 1052–5.

Ballinger, C. B. (1977). Psychiatric morbidity and the menopause: survey of a gynaecological out-patient clinic. *British Journal of Psychiatry* **131**, 83–9.

Ban, T. A. (1982). Chronic schizophrenias: a guide to Leonhard's classification. *Comprehensive Psychiatry* **23**, 155–69.

Bancroft, J. H. J. (1974). *Deviant sexual behaviour: modification and assessment*. Oxford University Press.

Bancroft, J. H. J. (1975). Homosexuality in the male. In *Contemporary psychiatry* (ed. T. Silverstone and B. Barraclough). *British Journal of Psychiatry*, Special Publication No. 9. London.

Bancroft, J. H. J. (1983). *Human sexuality and its problems*. Churchill Livingstone, Edinburgh.

Bancroft, J. H. J. (1986). Crisis intervention. In: *An introduction to the psychotherapies* (ed. S. Bloch) (2nd edn). Oxford University Press, Oxford.

Bancroft, J. H. J. and Coles, L. (1976). Three years experience in sexual problems clinic. *British Medical Journal* **i**, 1575–7.

Bancroft, J. H. J. and Marks, I. M. (1968). Electric aversion therapy for sexual deviations. *Proceedings of the Royal Society of Medicine* **61**, 796–9.

Bancroft, J. H. J., Reynolds, F., Simkin, S., and Smith, J. (1975). Self-poisoning and self-injury in the Oxford area. *British Journal of Preventive and Social Medicine* **29**, 170–7.

Bancroft, J. H. J., Skrimshire, A. M., Casson, J., Harvard-Watts, O., and Reynolds, F. (1977). People who deliberately poison or injure themselves: their problems and their contacts with helping agencies. *Psychological Medicine* **7**, 289–303.

Bancroft, J. H. J., Simkins, S., Kingston, B., et al. (1979). The reasons people give for taking overdoses: a further inquiry. *British Journal of Medical Psychology* **52**, 353–65.

Bancroft, J. H. J., Tyrer, G., and Warner, P. (1982). The classification of sexual problems in women. *British Journal of Sexual Medicine* **9**, 30–7.

Bancroft, J. H. H., Dickerson, M., Fairburn, C. G., et al. (1986). Sex therapy outcome research: a reappraisal of methodology. *Psychological Medicine* **16**, 851–63.

Bandura, A. (1962). Social learning through imitation. In *Nebraska symposium on motivation* (ed. M. R. Jones). University of Nebraska Press, Lincoln.

Bandura, A. (1969). *Principles of behaviour modification*. Holt, Rinehart and Winston, New York.

Bandura, A. (1971). Psychotherapy based on modelling principles. In *Handbook of psychotherapy and behaviour change* (ed. A. E. Bergin and S. Garfield). Wiley, New York.

Bankowski, Z. and Carballo, M. (1986). *Battered children—child abuse*. World Health Organization and Council for International Organizations of Medical Sciences, Berne.

Banks, M. H. and Jackson, P. R. (1982). Unemployment and risk of minor psychiatric disorder in young people: cross-sectional and longitudinal evidence. *Psychological Medicine* **12**, 789–98.

Bannister, D. (1960). Conceptual structure in thought disordered schizophrenics. *Journal of Mental Science* **106**, 1236–49.

Bannister, D. (1962). The nature and measurement of schizophrenic thought disorder. *Journal of Mental Science* **108**, 825–42.

Bannister, D. and Fransella, F. (1966). A grid test of schizophrenic thought disorder. *British Journal of Social and Clinical Psychology* **5**, 95–102.

Baraitser, M. (1986). Chromosomes and mental retardation. *Psychological Medicine* **16**, 487–95.

Barber, T. X. (1962). Towards a theory of hypnosis: posthypnotic behaviour. *Archives of General Psychiatry* **1**, 321–42.

Barbor, T. F., Ritson, E. B., and Hodgson, R. J. (1986). Alcohol-related problems in the primary health care setting: a review of early intervention strategies. *British Journal of Addiction* **81**, 23–46.

Barcha, R., Stewart, M. A., and Guze, S. B. (1968). The prevalence of alcoholism among general hospital ward patients. *American Journal of Psychiatry* **125**, 681–4.

Barette, J. and Marsden, C. D. (1979). Attitudes of families to some aspects of Huntington's chorea. *Psychological Medicine* **9**, 327–36.

Barker, J. C. (1962). The hospital addiction syndrome (Munchausen syndrome). *Journal of Mental Science* **108**, 167–82.

Barker, J. C. and Barker, A. A. (1959). Deaths associated with electroplexy. *Journal of Mental Science* **105**, 339–48.

Barker, M. G. (1968). Psychiatric illness after hysterectomy. *British Medical Journal* **ii**, 91–5.

Barker, P. (1971). *Basic child psychiatry*. Staples Press, London.

Barnes, J. (1967). Rape and other sexual offences. *British Medical Journal* **i**, 293–4.

Barnes, T. R. E. and Braude, W. M. (1985). Akathisia variants and tardive dyskinesia. *Archives of General Psychiatry* **42**, 874–8.

Barraclough, B. M. (1973). Differences between national suicide rates. *British Journal of Psychiatry* **122**, 95–6.

Barraclough, B. M. (1981). Suicide and epilepsy. In *Epilepsy and psychiatry* (ed. E. H. Reynolds and M. R. Trimble). Churchill Livingstone, Edinburgh.

Barraclough, B. M. (1987). The suicide rate of epilepsy. *Acta Psychiatrica Scandinavica* **76**, 339–45.

Barraclough, B. M. and Mitchell-Heggs, N. A. (1978). Use of neurosurgery for psychological disorder in the British Isles during 1974–6. *British Medical Journal* **ii**, 1591–3.

Barraclough, B. M. and Shea, M. (1970). Suicide and Samaritan clients. *Lancet* **ii**, 868–70.

Barraclough, B. M., and Shepherd, D. M. (1976). Public interest: private grief. *British Journal of Psychiatry* **129**, 109–13.

Barraclough, B. M. Bunch, J., Nelson, B., and Sainsbury, P. (1974). A hundred cases of suicide: clinical aspects. *British Journal of Psychiatry* **125**, 355–73.

Barrash, J., Kroll, J., Carey, K., and Sines, L. (1983). Discriminating borderline personality disorder from other personality disorders: cluster analysis of the diagnostic interview for borderlines. *Archives of General Psychiatry* **40**, 1297–302.

Barsky, A. J. and Klerman, G. L. (1983). Overview: hypochondriasis, bodily complaints and somatic styles. *American Journal of Psychiatry* **140**, 273–83.

Barsky, A. J., Wyshak, G., and Klerman, G. L. (1986). Hypochondriasis: an evaluation of the DSMIII criteria medical out-patients. *Archives of General Psychiatry* **43**, 493–500.

Bartlett, J., Bridges, P., and Kelly, D. (1981). Contemporary indications for psychosurgery. *British Journal of Psychiatry* **138**, 507–11.

Barton, R. (1959). *Institutional neurosis*, John Wright, Bristol.

Baruk, H. (1959). Delusions of passion. Reprinted (1974) in *Themes and variations in European psychiatry* (ed. S. R. Hirsch and M. Shepherd), pp. 375–84. Wright, Bristol.

Basmajian, J. V. (ed.) (1983). *Biofeedback: principles and practice for clinicians*. Williams and Wilkins, Baltimore.

Bass, C. and Wade, C. (1984). Chest pain with normal coronary arteries: a comparative study of psychiatric and social morbidity. *Psychological Medicine* **14**, 51–61.

Bateson, G., Jackson, D., Haley, J., and Weakland, J. (1956). Towards a theory of schizophrenia. *Behavioral Science* **1**, 251–64.

Bayer, R. and Spitzer, R. L. (1985). Neurosis, psychodynamics and DSMIII. *Archives of General Psychiatry* **42**, 187–96.

Beaubrun, M. H. and Knight, F. (1973). Psychiatric assessment of 30 chronic users of cannabis and 30 matched controls. *American Journal of Psychiatry* **130**, 309–11.

Beal, M. F., Benoit, R., Majurek, M., Bird, E. D., and Martin, J. B. (1986). Somatostatin 28 1–12 like immunoreaction is reduced in Alzheimer's disease cerebral cortex. *Brain Research* **368**, 380–3.

Bebbington, P. E., Sturt, E., Tennant, C., and Hurry, J. (1984). Misfortune and resilience: a community study of women. *Psychological Medicine* **14**, 347–63.

Beck, A. T. (1967). *Depression: clinical experimental and theoretical aspects*. Harper and Row, New York.

Beck, A. T. (1976). *Cognitive therapy and the emotional disorders*. International Universities Press, New York.

Beck, A. T., Laude, R., and Bohnert, M. (1974a). Ideational components of anxiety neuroses. *Archives of General Psychiatry* **31**, 319–25.

Beck, A. T., Schuyler, D., and Herman, I. (1974b). Development of suicide intent scales. In *The prediction of suicide* (ed. A. T. Beck, H. L. P. Resaik, and D. J. Lettie). Charles Press, Maryland.

Beck, A. T., Rush, A. J., Shaw, B. F., and Emery, G. (1979). *Cognitive therapy of depression*. Guilford Press, New York.

Beck, A. T., Hollon, S. D., Young, J. E., Bedrosian, R. C., and Budenz, D. (1985a). Treatment of depression with cognitive therapy and amitriptyline. *Archives of General Psychiatry* **42**, 142–8.

Beck, A. T., Steer, R. A., Kovacs, M., and Garrison, B. (1985b). Hopelessness and eventual suicide: a 10-year prospective study of patients hospitalised with suicidal ideation. *American Journal of Psychiatry* **145**, 559–63.

Beech, H. R., Watts, F., and Poole, A. D. (1971). Classical conditioning of a sexual deviation: a preliminary note: *Behaviour Therapy* **2**, 400–2.

Beecher, H. K. (1956). Relationship of significance of wound to the pain experienced. *Journal of the American Medical Association* **161**, 1609–13.

Beidel, D. C. (1987). Psychological factors in organ transplantation. *Clinical Psychology Review* **7**, 677–94.

Benaim, S., Horder, J., and Anderson, J. (1973). Hysterical episode in a classroom. *Psychological Medicine* **3**, 366–73.

Bender, L. and Grugett, A. A. (1952). A follow up report on children who had atypical sexual experiences. *American Journal of Orthopsychiatry* **22**, 825–37.

Bendz, H. (1983). Kidney function in lithium treated patients: a literature survey. *Acta Psychiatrica Scandinavica* **68**, 303–24.

Benedetti, G. (1952). *Die Alkoholhalluzinosen*. Thieme, Stuttgart.

Benjamin, H. (1966). *The transsexual phenomenon*. Julian Press, New York.

Bennett, D. H. (1983). The historical development of rehabilitation services. In *The theory and practice of rehabilitation* (ed. F. N. Watts and D. H. Bennett). Wiley, Chichester.

Bennie, E. H. (1975). Lithium in depression. *Lancet* **i**, 216.

Berg, I. (1981). Child psychiatry and enuresis. *British Journal of Psychiatry* **139**, 247–8.

Berg, I. (1982). When truants and school refusers grow up. *British Journal of Psychiatry* **141**, 208–10.

Berg I. (1984). School refusal. *British Journal of Hospital Medicine* **31**, 59–62.

Berg, I. and Jackson, A. (1985). Teenage school refusers grow up: a follow-up study of 168 subjects, ten years on average after in-patient treatment. *British Journal of Psychiatry* **147**, 366–70.

Berg, J. M. (1965). Aetiological aspects of mental subnormality: pathological factors. In *Mental deficiency: the changing outlook* (ed. A. D. B. Clarke and A. M. Clarke) (2nd edn). Methuen, London.

Berger, M. (1985). Temperament and individual differences. In *Child and adolescent psychiatry: modern approaches* (ed. M. Rutter and L. Hersov) (2nd edn). Blackwell Scientific, Oxford.

Bergin, A. E. and Lambert, M. J. (1978). The evaluation of therapeutic outcomes. In *Handbook of psychotherapy and behaviour change* (ed. S. L. Garfield and A. E. Bergin) (2nd edn). John Wiley, New York.

Bergman, H., Borg, S., Hindmarsh, T., Idestrom, C. -M., and Mutzell, S. (1980). Computed tomography of the brain and neuropsychological assessement of male alcoholic patients. In *Addiction and brain damage* (ed. D. Richter), pp. 201–14. Croom Helm, London.

Bergmann, K., Foster, E. M., Justice, A. W., and Matthews, V. (1978). Management of the demented patient in the community. *British Journal of Psychiatry* **132**, 441–9.

Berne, E. (1966). *Games people play*. André Deutsch, London.

Bernstein, D. A. and Borkovec, T. D. (1973). *Progressive relaxation training: a manual for the helping professions*. Research Press, Champaign, Illinois.

Berridge, V. and Edwards, G. (1981). *Opium and the people*. Allen Lane, London.

Berrios, G. E. (1981*a*). Stupor: a conceptual history. *Psychological Medicine* **11**, 677–88.

Berrios, G. E. (1981*b*). Delirium and confusion in the 19th century. *British Journal of Psychiatry* **139**, 439–49.

Berrios, G. E. (1985). Delusional parasitosis and physical disease. *Comprehensive Psychiatry* **26**, 395–403.

Berrios, G. E. (1987). Dementia during the seventeenth and eighteenth centuries: a conceptual history. *Psychological Medicine* **17**, 829–37.

Berson, R. J. (1983). Capgras' syndrome. *American Journal of Psychiatry* **140**, 969–78.

Bertelsen, A., Harvald, B., and Hauge, M., (1977). A Danish twin study of manic depressive disorders. *British Journal of Psychiatry* **130**, 330–51.

Beskow, J., Gottfries, C. G., Roos, B. -E., and Winblad, B. (1976). Determination of monoamines and monoamine metabolites in human brain: post mortem studies in a group of suicides and a control group. *Acta Psychiatrica Scandinavica* **53**, 7–20.

Betts, T. A., Clayton, A. B., and Mackay, G. M. (1972). Effects of four commonly-used tranquillizers on low-speed driving performance tests. *British Medical Journal* **iv**, 580–4.

Beumont, P. J. V., George G. C. W., and Smart, D. E. (1976). 'Dieters' and 'vomiters and purgers' in anorexia nervosa. *Psychological Medicine* **6**, 617–22.

Beumont, P. J. V., Abram, S. F., and Simson, J. G. (1981). The psychosexual histories of adolescent girls and young women with anorexia nervosa. *Psychological Medicine* **11**, 131–40.

Bewley, B. (1986). The epidemiology of adolescent behaviour problems. *British Medical Bulletin* **42**, 200–3.

Bianchi, G. N. (1971). Patterns of hypochondriasis: a principal components analysis. *British Journal of Psychiatry* **122**, 541–8.

Bibring, E. (1953). The mechanism of depression. In *Affective disorders* (ed. P. Greenacre), pp. 14–47. International Universities Press, New York.

Bicknell, J. (1975). *Pica: a childhood symptom*. Institute for Research into Mental and Multiple Handicap, Monograph 3, Butterworths, London.

Bicknell, J. (1982). Living with a mentally handicapped member of the family. *Postgraduate Medical Journal* **58**, 597–605.

Bieber, I. (1962). *Homosexuality: a psychoanalytic study of male homosexuals*. Basic Books, New York.

Bille, M. and Juel-Nielsen, N. (1968). Incidence of neurosis in psychiatric and other medical services in a Danish county. *Danish Medical Bulletin* **10**, 172–6.

Billings, E. G. (1936). Teaching psychiatry in the medical school general hospital. *Journal of the American Medical Association* **107**, 635–9.

Bilodeau, C. B. and O'Connor, S. O. (1978). Role of nurse clinicians in liaison psychiatry. In *Handbook of general hospital psychiatry* (ed. T. P. Hackett and N. H. Cassem). Mosby, St. Louis.

Binet, A. (1877). Le fétishisme dans l'amour. *Revue Philosophique* **24**, 143.

Binet, A. and Simon, T. (1905). Méthodes nouvelles pour le diagnostic du niveau intellectuel des normaux. *L'Année Psychologique* **11**, 193–244.

Binswanger, O. (1894). *Münchener Medizinische Wochenschrift* **52**, 252.

Bion, W. R. (1961). *Experiences in groups*. Tavistock Publications, London.

Birnbaum, K. (1908). *Psychosen mit Wahnbildung und wahnhafte Einbildungen bei Degenerativen*. Marhold, Halle.

Birren, J. E. and Sloane, R. B. (1980). *Handbook of mental health and ageing*. Prentice Hall, Englewood Cliffs.

Bishop, D. V. M. (1987). The causes of specific developmental language disorder ('Developmental dysphasia'). *Journal of Child Psychology and Psychiatry* **28**, 1–8.

Black, D. (1986). Schoolgirl mothers. *British Medical Journal* **293**, 1047.

Blackburn, I. M., Bishop, S., Glen, A. I. M., Whalley, L. J., and Christie, J. E. (1981). The efficacy of cognitive therapy on depression: a treatment trial using cognitive therapy and pharmacotherapy, each alone and in combination. *British Journal of Psychiatry* **139**, 181–9.

Blacker, K. H., Jones, R. T., Stone, G. C., and Pfefferbaum, D. (1968). Chronic users of LSD: the 'acid heads'. *American Journal of Psychiatry* **125**, 341–8.

Blackwell, B., Galbraith, J. R., and Dahl, D. S. (1984). Chronic pain management. *Hospital and Community Psychiatry* **10**, 999–1008.

Blanchard, E. B. (1986). *Management of chronic headaches*. Pergamon Press, Oxford.

Blanchard, E. B. and Miller, S. T. (1977). Psychological treatment of cardiovascular disease. *Archives of General Psychiatry* **34**, 1402–13.

Blanchard, E. B., Ahles, T. A., and Shaw, E. R. (1979). Behavioural treatment of headaches. *Progress in Behaviour Modification* **8**, 207–48.

Blazer, D. G. (1986). Suicide in late life: Review and commentary. *Journal of the American Geriatric Society* **34**, 519–25.

Bleuler, E. (1906). *Affektivität, Suggestibilität, und Paranoia*. Marhold, Halle.

Bleuler, E. (1911). (English edition 1950). *Dementia praecox or the group of schizophrenias*. International University Press, New York.

Bleuler, E. (1924). *Textbook of psychiatry* (translated by A. A. Brill). Macmillan, New York.

Bleuler, M. (1951). Psychiatry of cerebral disease. *British Medical Journal* **ii**, 1233–8.

Bleuler, M. (1972). (English edition 1978). *The schizophrenic disorders: long term patient and family studies*. Yale Universities Press, New Haven.

Bleuler, M. (1974). The long term course of the schizophrenic psychoses. *Psychological medicine* **4**, 244–54.

Bliss, E. L., Clark, L. D., and West, C. D. (1959). Studies of sleep deprivation: relationship to schizophrenia. *Archives of Neurology and Psychiatry* **81**, 348–59.

Bloch, S. (1979). Assessment of patients for psychotherapy. *British Journal of Psychiatry* **135**, 193–208.

Bloch, S. (1986). Supportive psychotherapy. In *An introduction to the psychotherapies* (ed. S. Bloch) (2nd edn). Oxford University Press, Oxford.

Bloch, S. and Chodoff, P. (1981). *Psychiatric ethics*. Oxford University Press, Oxford.

Bloch, S. and Crouch, E. (1985). *Therapeutic factors in group psychotherapy*. Oxford University Press, Oxford.

Bloch, S., Crouch, E., and Rebstein, J. (1981). Therapeutic factors in group psychotherapy: a review. *Archives of General Psychiatry* **38**, 519–26.

Bluglass, R. (1978). Regional secure units and interim security for psychiatric patients. *British Medical Journal* **i**, 489–93.

Bluglass, R. (1979*a*). The psychiatric assessment of homicide. *British Journal of Hospital Medicine* **22**, 366–77.

Bluglass R. (1979*b*). Incest. *British Journal of Hospital Medicine* **22**, 152–6.

Blumberg, N. H. (1981). Arson update: a review of the literature on firesetting. *Bulletin of the American Academy of Psychiatry and Law* **9**, 255–65.

Blumenthal, E. J. (1955). Spontaneous seizures and related electroencephalographic findings following shock therapy. *Journal of Nervous Mental Disease* **122**, 581–8.

Blumer, D. and Benson, D. F. (1975). Personality changes with frontal and temporal lobe lesions. In *Psychiatric aspects of neurological disease* (ed. D. Benson and D. Blumer). Grune and Stratton, New York.

Blumer, D. and Heilbronn, M. (1982). Chronic pain as a variant of depressive disease. The pain prone disorder. *Journal of Nervous and Mental Disease* **170**, 381–406.

Blurton-Jones, N. G. (1972). Non-verbal communication in children. In *Non-verbal communication* (ed. R. A. Hinde). Cambridge University Press, Cambridge.

Boakes, A. J., Laurence, D. R., Teoh, P. C., Barar, F. S. K., Benedikter, L. T., and Prichard, B. N. C. (1973). Interactions between sympathomimetic amines and antidepressant agents in man. *British Medical Journal* **i**, 311–15.

Bogerts, B., Meertz, E., and Schonfield-Bausch, R. (1985). Basal ganglia and limbic system pathology in schizophrenia: a morphometric study. *Archives of General Psychiatry* **42**, 784–91.

Bogren, L. Y. (1983). Couvade. *Acta Psychiatrica Scandinavica* **68**, 55–63.

Bohman, M. (1978). Some genetic aspects of alcoholism and criminality. *Archives of General Psychiatry* **35**, 269–76.

Bohman, M., Sigvardsson, S., and Cloninger, C. R. (1981). Maternal inheritance of alcohol abuse: cross fostering analysis of adopted women. *Archives of General Psychiatry* **38**, 965–9.

Böker, W. and Häfner, H. (1977). Crimes of violence by mentally disordered offenders in Germany. *Psychological Medicine* **7**, 733–6.

Boll, T. J. and Barth, J. (1983). Mild head injury. *Psychiatric Developments* **3**, 263–75.

Bond, A. J. and Lader, M. H. (1973). Residual effects of flurazepam. *Psychopharmacologia* **32**, 223–35.

Bond, M. R. (1975). Assessment of the psychological outcome after severe head injury. In *Outcome of severe damage to the C.N.S.* Symposium 34. Ciba Foundation, London.

Bondareff, W. (1980). Neurobiology of ageing. In *Handbook of mental health and ageing* (ed. J. E. Birren and R. B. Sloane). Prentice Hall, Englewood Cliffs.

Bondareff, F. W. (1983). Age and Alzheimer disease. *Lancet* i, 1447.

Bonhoeffer, K. (1909). Exogenous psychoses. *Zentralblatt für Nervenheilkunde* **32**, 499–505. Translated by H. Marshall in *Themes and variations in European psychiatry* (ed. S. R. Hirsch and M. Shepherd). Wright, Bristol (1974).

Bonn, J., Turner, P., and Hicks, D. C. (1972). Beta-adrenergic receptor blockade with practolol in the treatment of anxiety. *Lancet* i, 814–15.

Bonn, J. A., Harrison, J., and Rees, W. L. (1971). Lactate-induced anxiety: therapeutic implications. *British Journal of Psychiatry* **119**, 468–71.

Böök, J. A. (1953). A genetic and neuropsychiatric investigation of a North-Swedish population with special regard to schizophrenia and mental deficiencies. *Acta Genetica et Statistica Medica* **4**, 1–100.

Boor, J. W. and Hurtig, W. I. (1977). Persistent cerebellar ataxia after exposure to toluene. *Annals of Neurology* **2**, 440–2.

Boston Collaborative Drug Surveillance Program (1972). Adverse reactions to tricyclic antidepressant drugs. *Lancet* **1**, 529–31.

Boulagouris, J. C. (1977). Variables affecting the behaviour of obsessive-compulsive patients treated by flooding. In *Studies in phobic and obsessive compulsive disorders* (ed. J. C. Boulagouris and A. Rabavilas). Pergamon Press, Oxford.

Bowden, P. (1978). Rape. *British Journal of Hospital Medicine* **20**, 286–90.

Bowen, D. M., Smith, C. B., White, P., and Davison, P. N. (1976). Neurotransmitter-related enzymes and indices of hypoxia in senile dementia and other abiotrophies. *Brain* **99**, 459–96.

Bower, W. H. and Altschule, M. D. (1956). Use of progesterone in the treatment of postpartum psychosis. *New England Journal of Medicine* **254**, 157–60.

Bowlby, J. (1944). Forty-four juvenile thieves. Their characters and home life. *International Journal of Psychoanalysis* **25**, 19–53.

Bowlby, J. (1946). *Forty-four juvenile thieves: their characters and home-life*. Ballière, Tindall and Cox, London.

Bowlby, J. (1951). *Maternal care and maternal health*. World Health Organization, Geneva.

Bowlby, J. (1969). Psychopathology of anxiety: the role of affectional bonds. In *Studies in anxiety* (ed. M. H. Lader). *British Journal of Psychiatry* Special Publication No. 3, London.

Bowlby, J. (1973). *Attachment and loss*, Vol. 2. *Separation, anxiety and anger*. Hogarth Press, London.

Bowlby, J. (1980). *Attachment and loss*, Vol. 3. *Loss, sadness and depression*. Basic Books, New York.

Boyd, J. H. (1983). The increasing rate of suicide by firearms. *New England Journal of Medicine* **308**, 872–4.

Boyd, J. H. and Weissman, M. M. (1982). Epidemiology. In *Handbook of affective disorders* (ed. E. S. Paykel). Churchill Livingstone, Edinburgh.

Brackett, T. O., Condon, N., Kindelan, K. M., and Bassett, L. (1984). The emotional care of a person with a spinal cord injury. *Journal of the American Medical Association* **252**, 793–5.

Braddock, L. (1986). The dexamethasone suppression test: fact and artefact. *British Journal of Psychiatry* **148**, 363–74.

Bradford, J. and Balmaceda, R. (1983). Shoplifting: Is there a specific psychiatric syndrome? *Canadian Journal of Psychiatry* **28**, 248–54.

Bradley, C. (1985). Psychological aspects of diabetes. In: *The Diabetes Annual* (ed. K. G. M. M. Alberti and L. P. Krall). Elsevier, Amsterdam.

Braid, J. (1843). *Neurhypnology: or the rationale of nervous sleep, considered in relation with animal magnetism.* Churchill, London.

Brain, W. R. (1985). *Diseases of the nervous system* (9th edn) (revised by J. N. Walton). Oxford University Press, Oxford.

Brandon, S., Cowley, P., McDonald, C., Neville, P., Palmer, R., and Wellstood-Easen, S. (1984). Electroconvulsive therapy: results in depressive illness from the Leicestershire Trial. *British Medical Journal* **288**, 22–5.

Brauer, A., Horlick, L. F., Nelson, E., Farquar, J. W., and Agras W. S. (1979). Relaxation therapy for essential hypertension: a Veterans Administration out-patient study. *Journal of Behavioural Medicine* **2**, 21–9.

Braun, P., Kuchansky, G., Shapiro, R., Greenberg, S., Gudeman, J. E., Johnson, S., and Shore, M. F. (1981). Overview; reinstitutionalization of psychiatric patients, a critical review of outcome studies. *American Journal of Psychiatry* **138**, 736–49.

Breitner, J. C. S. and Folstein, M. F. (1984). Familial Alzheimer dementia: a prevalent disorder with specific clinical features. *Psychological Medicine* **14**, 63–80.

Brenner, B. (1959). Estimating the prevalence of alcoholism: towards a modification of the Jellinek formula. *Quarterly Journal on Studies of Alcoholism* **20**, 255–69.

Breuer, J. and Freud, S. (1893–5). *Studies on hysteria.* The Standard Edition of the complete psychological works, Vol. 2 (1955). Hogarth Press, London.

Brewer, C. and Perrett, L. (1971). Brain damage due to alcohol consumption: an air-encephalographic, psychometric and electro-encephalographic study. *British Journal of Addiction* **66**, 170–82.

Breslau, N. and Prabucki, M. A. (1987). Siblings of disabled children: effects of chronic stress in the family. *Archives of General Psychiatry* **44**, 1040–46.

Breslau, N., Weitzman, M., and Messenger, K. (1981). Psychologic functioning of the siblings of disabled children. *Pediatrics* **67**, 344–57.

Breslau, W., Starich, K. S., and Mortimer, E. A. (1982). Psychiatric disorders in the mothers of disabled children. *American Journal of Diseases of Childhood* **136**, 682–6.

Bridges, K. W. and Goldberg, D. P. (1985). Somatic presentation of DSMIII psychiatric disorders in primary care. *Journal of Psychosomatic Research* **29**, 563–9.

Brimblecombe, F. S. W. (1979). A new approach to the care of handicapped children. *Journal of the Royal College of Physicians of London* **13**, 231–6.

Brimblecombe, F. S. W. (1985). The needs of young intellectually retarded adults. *British Journal of Psychiatry* **146**, 5–10.

Brill, N. Q., Crumpton, E., Edisuon, S., Grayson, H. M., Hellman, L. I., and Richards, R. A. (1959). Relative effectiveness of varying components of electroconvulsive therapy. *Archives of Neurology and Psychiatry* **81**, 627–35.

Briquet, P. (1859). *Traité clinique et thérapeutique de l'hysterie*. Baillière, Paris.

British Medical Journal (1976). Glutethamide—an unsafe alternative to barbiturate hypnotics. (Editorial.) *British Medical Journal* ii, 1426–7.

British Medical Journal (1980). Phencyclidine: the new American street drug (Editorial). *British Medical Journal* **281**, 1511–12.

British National Formulary (1981). British Medical Association and the Pharmaceutical Society of Great Britain, London.

Brittain, R. P. (1970). The sadistic murderer. *Medicine, Science and the Law* **10**, 198–207.

Broadbent, D.E. (1981). Chronic effects from the physical nature of work. In *Working life: a social science contribution to work reform* (ed. B. Gardell and G. Johansson). Wiley, London.

Broadbent, D. E. and Gath, D. H. (1979). Chronic effects of repetitive and non-repetitive work. In *Response to stress: occupational aspects* (ed. C. G. McKay and T. R. Cox). Independent Publishing Company, London.

Broadwin, I. T. (1932). A contribution to the study of truancy. *American Journal of Orthopsychiatry* **2**, 253–9.

Brockington, I. (1986). Diagnosis of schizophrenia and schizoaffective psychoses. In *The psychopharmacology and treatment of schizophrenia* (ed. P. B. Bradley and S. R. Hirsch). Oxford University Press, Oxford.

Brockington, I. F., Kendell, R. E., Kellett, J. M., Curry, S. H., and Wainwright, S. (1978). Trials of lithium, chlorpromazine and amitriptyline on schizoaffective patients. *British Journal of Psychiatry* **133**, 162–8.

Brockington, I. F. and Leff, J. P. (1979). Schizo-affective psychosis: definitions and incidence. *Psychological Medicine* **9**, 91–9.

Brooks, N. (1984). *Closed head injury*. Oxford University Press, Oxford.

Brown, D. and Pedder, J. (1979). *Introduction to psychotherapy: an outline of psychodynamic principles and practice*. Tavistock, London.

Brown, F. W. (1942). Heredity in the psychoneuroses. *Proceedings of the Royal Society of Medicine* **35**, 785–90.

Brown, G. M. (1976). Endocrine aspects of psychosocial deviation. In *Hormones, behaviour and psychopathology* (ed. E. J. Sachar). Raven, New York.

Brown, G. W. and Birley, J. L. T. (1968). Crisis and life change at the onset of schizophrenia. *Journal of Health and Social Behaviour* **9**, 203–24.

Brown, G. W. and Harris, T. O. (1978). *Social origins of depression*. Tavistock, London.

Brown, G. W. and Harris, T. O. (1986). Stressor, vulnerability, and depression: a question of replication. *Psychological Medicine* **16**, 739–44.

Brown, G. W. and Prudo, R. (1981). Psychiatric disorder in a rural and urban population. 1. Aetiology of depression. *Psychological Medicine* **11**, 581–99.

Brown, G. W. Carstairs, G. M., and Topping, G. G. (1958). *Lancet* ii, 685–9.

Brown, G. W., Monck, E. M., Carstairs, G. M., and Wing, J. K. (1962). Influence of family life on the cause of schizophrenic illness. *British Journal of Preventive and Social Medicine* **16**, 55–68.

Brown, G. W., Bone, M., Dalison, B., and Wing, J. K. (1966). *Schizophrenia and social care*. Maudsley Monograph 17. Oxford University Press, London.

Brown, G. W., Harris, T. O., and Peto, J. (1973*a*). Life events and psychiatric disorders: the nature of the causal link. *Psychological Medicine* **3**, 159–76.

Brown, G. W., Sklair, F., Harris, T. O., and Birley, J. L. T. (1973*b*). Life events and psychiatric disorder: some methodological issues. *Psychological Medicine* **3**, 74–87.

Brown, J. A. C. (1961). *Freud and the post Freudians*. Penguin, Harmondsworth.

Brown, R. *et al.* (1986). Postmortem evidence of structural brain changes in schizophrenia: differences in brain weight, temporal horn area, and parahippocampal gyrus compared with affective disorder. *Archives of General Psychiatry* **43**, 36–42.

Brown, S. W. and Reynolds, E. M. (1981). Cognitive impairment in epileptic patients. In *Epilepsy and psychiatry* (ed. E. H. Reynolds and R. Trimble). Churchill Livingstone, Edinburgh.

Browne, A. and Finkelhor, D. (1986). Impact of child sexual abuse: a review of research. *Psychological Bulletin* **99**, 66–77.

Bruch, H. (1974). *Eating disorders: anorexia nervosa and the person within.* Routledge and Kegan Paul, London.

Brudny, J., Korein, J., Levidow, A., and Friedman, L. W. (1974). Sensory feedback therapy as a modality of treatment in central nervous system disorders of voluntary movement. *Neurology* **24**, 925–32.

Brunt, P. W., Kew, M. C., Scheuer, P. J., and Sherlock, S. (1974). Studies in alcoholic liver disease in Britain. *Gut* **15**, 52–8.

Bryant, B., Trower, P., Yardley, K., Urbieta, H., and Letemendia, F. J. J. (1976). A survey of social inadequacy among psychiatric outpatients. *Psychological Medicine* **6**, 101–12.

Buckle, A. and Farrington, D. P. (1984). An observational study of shop-lifting. *British Journal of Criminology* **24**, 63–73.

Buglass, D. and Duffy, J. C. (1978). The ecological pattern of suicide and parasuicide in Edinburgh. *Social Science and Medicine* **12**, 241–53.

Buglass, D. and Horton, J. (1974). The repetition of parasuicide: a comparison of three cohorts. *British Journal of Psychiatry* **125**, 168–74.

Buglass, D., Clarke, J., Henderson, A. S., Kreitman, N., and Presley, A. S. (1977). A study of agoraphobic housewives. *Psychological Medicine* **7**, 73–86.

Bulbena, A. and Burrows, G. E. (1986). Pseudodementia: Facts and Figures. *British Journal of Psychiatry* **148**, 87–94.

Bulusu, L. and Alderson, M. (1984). Suicide 1950–82. *Population Trends* **35**, 11–17.

Burish, T. G. and Carey, M. P. (1986). Conditioned aversive responses in cancer chemotherapy patients: Theoretical and developmental analysis. *Journal of Consulting and Clinical Psychology* **54**, 593–600.

Burks, J. S., Alfrey, A. C., Huddlestone, J., Norenburg, M. D., and Lewin, E. (1976). A fatal encephalopathy in chronic haemodialysis patients. *Lancet* **i**, 764–8.

Burns, B. H. and Howell, J. B. (1969). Disproportionately severe breathlessness in chronic bronchitis. *Quarterly Journal of Medicine* **38**, 277–94.

Burrow, T. (1927). The group method of analysis. *Psychoanalytic Review* **14**, 268–80.

Butler, G., Cullington, A., Munby, M., Amies, P. L., and Gelder, M. G. (1984). Exposure and anxiety management in the treatment of social phobia. *Journal of Consulting and Clinical Psychology* **52**, 642–50.

Butler, G., Cullington, A., Hibbert, G., Klimes, I., and Gelder, M. G. (1987) Anxiety management for persistent generalized anxiety. *British Journal of Psychiatry* **151**, 535–42.

Bynum, W. F. (1983). Psychiatry in its historical context. In *Handbook of psychiatry* Vol. I (ed. M. Shepherd and O. L. Zangwill). Cambridge University Press, Cambridge.

Byrne, E. A. and Cunningham, C. C. (1985). The effects of mentally handicapped children on families—a conceptual review. *Journal of Child Psychology and Psychiatry* **26**, 847–64.

Cadoret, R. J. (1978*a*). Evidence of genetic inheritance of primary affective disorder in adoptees. *American Journal of Psychiatry* **135**, 463–6.

Cadoret, R. J. (1978*b*). Psychopathology in adopted-away offspring of biologic parents with antisocial behaviour. *Archives of General Psychiatry* **35**, 176–84.

Cadoret, R. J. and Gath, A. (1978). Inheritance of alcoholism in adoptees. *British Journal of Psychiatry* **132**, 252–8.

Cadoret, R. J., Cunningham, L., Loftus, R., and Edwards, J. (1975). Studies of adoptees from psychiatrically disturbed biologic parents—II temperament, hyperactive, antisocial and developmental variables. *Journal of Pediatrics* **87**, 301–6.

Caffey, J. (1946). Multiple fractures in long bones of children suffering from chronic subdural haematomata. *American Journal of Radiology* **56**, 163–73.

Caine, E. D. (1981). Pseudodementia. *Archives of General Psychiatry* **38**, 1359–64.

Cala, L. A., Jones, B., Masatglia, F. L., and Wiley, B. (1978). Brain atrophy and intellectual impairment in heavy drinkers—a clinical, psychosomatic and computerised tomography study. *Australian and New Zealand Medical Journal* **8**, 147–53.

Caldwell, T. and Weiner, M. F. (1981). Stresses and coping in ICU nursing: a review. *General Hospital Psychiatry* **3**, 119–27.

Calne, D. B., Karoum, F., Ruthven, C. J.R., and Sandler, M. (1969). The metabolism of orally administered L-dopa in Parkinsonism. *British Journal of Pharmacology* **37**, 57–68.

Cameron, N. (1938). Reasoning, regression and communication in schizophrenia. *Psychological Monographs* **50**, 1–34.

Campbell, A. M. G., Thomson, J. L. G., Evans, M., and Williams, M. J. (1971). Cerebral atrophy in young cannabis smokers. *Lancet* ii, 1219–24.

Campbell, E., Cope, S., and Teasdale, J. (1983). Social factors and affective disorder: an investigation of Brown and Harris's model. *British Journal of Psychiatry* **143**, 548–53.

Campbell, T. L. (1986). *Family's impact on health: a world review and annotated bibliography*. NIMH series DN6. US Government Policy Office, Washington.

Candy, J. M., Klinowski, J. and Perry, R. H. (1986). Aluminosilicates and senile plaque formation in Alzheimer's Disease. *Lancet* i, 354–6.

Cantwell, D. (1975). Genetics of hyperactivity. *Journal of Child Psychology and Psychiatry* **16**, 261–4.

Cantwell, D. P. (1983). Diagnostic validity of the hyperactive child. (Attention deficit disorder with hyperactivity syndrome). *Psychiatric Developments* **3**, 277–300.

Cantwell, D. P. (1985). Organisation and use of DSMIII. In *The clinical guide to child psychiatry* (ed. D. Shaffer, A. A. Ehrhardt, and L. L. Greenhill). Free Press, New York.

Cantwell, D. P. and Baker, L. (1985*a*). Coordination disorder. In *Comprehensive textbook of psychiatry* (ed. H. I. Kaplan and B. J. Sadock) (4th edn). Williams and Wilkins, Baltimore.

Cantwell, D. P. and Baker, L. (1985*b*). Speech and language: development and disorders. In *Child and adolescent psychiatry: modern approaches* (ed. M. Rutter and L. Hersov) (2nd edn). Blackwell, Oxford.

Capgras, J. and Reboul-Lachaux, J. (1923). L'Illusion des sosies dans un délire systématisé chronique. *Bulletin de la Société Clinique de Médicine Mentale* **11**, 6–16.

Caplan, G. (1961). *An approach to community mental health*. Tavistock, London.

Caplan, H. L. (1970). Hysterical conversion symptoms in childhood. M. Phil. Dissertation, University of London. [See the account in *Child psychiatry:*

modern approaches (ed. M. L. Rutter and L. Hersov) (2nd edn). Blackwell, Oxford (1985).]

Capstick, N. (1975). Clomipramine in the treatment of the true obsessional state: a report on four patients. *Psychosomatics* **16**, 21–5.

Carbotte, R. M., Denbury, S. D., and Denbury, J. A. (1986). Prevalence of cognitive impairment in systemic lupus erythematosus. *Journal of Nervous and Mental Disease* **174**, 357–64.

Carey, G., Gottesman, I. I., and Robins, E., (1980). Prevalence rates among neuroses, pitfalls in the evaluation of familiarity. *Psychological Medicine* **10**, 437–43.

Carlen, P. L., Wortzman, G., Holgate, R. C., Wilkinson, D. A., and Rankin, J. G. (1978). Reversible cerebral atrophy in recent abstinent chronic alcoholics measured by computed tomographic scans. *Science* **100**, 1076–8.

Carlson, G. A. and Goodwin, F. K. (1973). The stages of mania: a longitudinal analysis of the manic episode. *Archives of General Psychiatry* **28**, 221–8.

Carlsson, A. and Lindquist, M. (1963). Effect of chlorpromazine and haloperidol on formation of methoxytyramine and normetanephrine in mouse brain. *Acta Pharmacologia et Toxicologia* **20**, 140–4.

Carney, M. W. P., Roth, M. and Garside, R. F. (1965). The diagnosis of depressive syndromes and the prediction of ECT response. *British Journal of Psychiatry* **111**, 659–74.

Carnwath, T. C. M. and Johnson, D. A. W. (1987). Psychiatric morbidity among spouses of patients with stroke. *British Medical Journal* **294**, 409–11.

Caroff, S. N. (1980). The neuroleptic malignant syndrome. *Journal of Clinical Psychiatry* **41**, 79–83.

Carothers, J. C. (1947). A study of mental derangement in Africans, and an attempt to explain its peculiarities, more especially in relation to the African attitude to life. *Journal of Mental Science* **93**, 548–97.

Carpenter, W. T., Strauss, J. S., and Muleh, S. (1973). Are there pathognomonic symptoms of schizophrenia? An empiric investigation of Schneider's first rank symptoms. *Archives of General Psychiatry* **28**, 847–52.

Carr, S. A. (1980). Interhemispheric transfer of stereognostic information in chronic schizophrenia. *British Journal of Psychiatry* **136**, 53–8.

Carr-Gregg, M. and White, L. (1987). The adolescent with cancer: a psychological overview. *The Medical Journal of Australia* **147**, 496–502.

Carstairs, G. M., O'Connor, N., and Rawnsley, K. (1956). Organisation of a hospital workshop for chronic psychiatric patients. *British Journal of Preventive and Social Medicine* **10**, 136–40.

Carter, C. O., Evans, K. A., and Baraitser, M. (1983). Effect of genetic counselling on the prevalence of Huntington's chorea. *British Medical Journal* **286**, 281–3.

Cartwright, A. (1964). *Human relations and hospital care.* Routledge and Kegan Paul, London.

Catalan, J. (1988). Psychosocial and neuropsychiatric aspects of HIV infection: review of their extent and implications for psychiatry. *Journal of Psychosomatic Research* **32**, 237–48.

Catalan, J., Bradley, M., Gallway, J., and Hawton, K. (1981). Sexual dysfunction and psychiatric morbidity in patients attending a clinic for sexually transmitted diseases. *British Journal of Psychiatry* **138**, 292–6.

Catalan, J., Gath, D., Edmonds, G., and Ennis, J. (1984). The effects of non-prescribing of anxiolytics in general practice: I. Controlled evalation of psychiatric and social outcome. *British Journal of Psychiatry* **144**, 593–602.

Cautela, J. R. (1967). Covert sensitization. *Psychological Reports* **74**, 459–68.

Caviston, P. (1987). Pregnancy and opiate addiction. *British Medical Journal* **295**, 285–6.

Cay, E. L. (1984). Psychological problems in relation to coronary care. In *Recent advances in cardiology* (ed. D. J. Rowlands). Churchill Livingstone, Edinburgh.

Central Health Services Council (1968). *Hospital treatment of acute poisoning.* HMSO, London.

Cerletti, U. and Bini, L. (1938). Un nuovo metodo di shokterapia; 'l'ettroshock'. *Bulletin Accademia Medica di Roma* **64**, 136–8.

Chalkley, A. J. and Powell, G. (1983). The clinical description of forty-eight cases of sexual fetishism. *British Journal of Psychiatry* **142**, 292–5.

Chamberlain, A. S. (1966). Early mental hospitals in Spain. *American Journal of Psychiatry* **123** 143–9.

Chapple, P. A. L., Somekh, D. E., and Taylor, M. E. (1972). Follow-up cases of opiate addiction from the time of notification to the Home Office. *British Medical Journal* **ii**, 680–3.

Charney, D. S., Menkes, D., and Heninger, G. R. (1981). Receptor sensitivity and the mechanism of action of anti-depressant treatment. *Archives of General Psychiatry* **38**, 1160–80.

Charney, D. S., Heninger, G. R., and Breier, A. (1984). Nor-adrenergic function in panic patients. *Archives of General Psychiatry* **41**, 751–62.

Checkley, S. A. (1980). Neuroendocrine tests of monoamine function in man: a review of basic theory and its application to the study of depressive illness. *Psychological Medicine* **10**, 35–53.

Checkley, S. A., Corn, T. H., Glass, I. B., Burton, S. W., and Burke, C. A. (1986). The responsiveness of central alpha-2 adrenoceptors in depression. In *The biology of depression* (ed. J. F. W. Deakin), pp. 100–120. Gaskell, London.

Chick, J., Lloyd, G., and Crombie, E. (1985). Counselling problem drinkers in medical wards: a controlled study. *British Medical Journal* **290**, 965–7.

Chiswick, D. (1985). The use and abuse of psychiatric testimony. *British Medical Journal* **290**, 975–7.

Chopra, G. S. and Smith, J. W. (1974). Psychotic reactions following cannabis use in east Indians. *Archives of General Psychiatry* **30**, 24–7.

Chowdhury, N., Hicks, R. C., and Kreitman, N. (1973). Evaluation of an after-care service for parasuicide ('attempted suicide') patients. *Social Psychiatry* **8**, 67–81.

Christie, A. B. (1985). Survival in dementia: a review. In *Recent advances in psychogeriatrics* (ed. T. Arie). Churchill Livingstone, Edinburgh.

Christie, J. E., Whalley, L. J., Dick, H., Blackwood, D. H. R., Blackburn, I. M., and Fink, G. (1986). Raised plasma cortisol concentrations a feature of drug-free psychotics and not specific for depression. *British Journal of Psychiatry* **148**, 58–65.

Christodoulou, G. N. (1976). Delusional hyper-identifications of the Frégoli type. *Acta Psychiatrica Scandinavica* **54**, 305–14.

Christodoulou, G. N. (1977). The syndrome of Capgras. *British Journal of Psychiatry* **130**, 556–64.

Ciompi, L. (1980). The natural history of schizophrenia in the long term. *British Journal of Psychiatry* **136**, 413–20.

Clancy, J., Noyes, R., Noenk, P. R., and Slymen, D. J. (1978). Secondary depression in anxiety neurosis. *Journal of Nervous and Mental Disease* **166**, 846–50.

Clare, A. (1980). Controversial issues in thought and practice. In *Psychiatry in dissent* (2nd edn). Tavistock, London.

Clare, A. W. (1978). The treatment of premenstrual symptoms. *British Journal of Psychiatry* **135**, 576–9.

Clare, A. W. (1982). Psychiatric aspects of premenstrual complaint. *Journal of Psychosomatic Obstetrics and Gynaecology* **1**, 22–31.

Clare, A. W. (1985). Hormones, behaviour and the menstrual cycle. *Journal of Psychosomatic Research* **29**, 225–33.

Clark, D. M. (1986). A cognitive approach to panic. *Behaviour Research and Therapy* **24**, 461–70.

Clark, D. M. and Teasdale, J. D. (1982). Diurnal variation in clinical depression and accessibility of memories of positive and negative experiences. *Journal of Abnormal Psychology* **91**, 87–95.

Clark, D. M., Salkovskis, P. M., and Chalkley, A. J. (1985). Respiratory control as a treatment for panic attacks. *Journal of Behaviour Therapy and Experimental Psychiatry* **16**, 23–30.

Clark, W. B. (1976). Loss of control, heavy drinking, and drinking problems in a longitudinal study. *Journal of Studies on Alcoholism* **37**, 1256–90.

Clarke, A. M. and Clarke, A. D. B. (1983a). Lifespan development and psychosocial intervention. In *Mental deficiency: the changing outlook* (ed. A. M. Clarke, A. D. B. Clarke, and J. M. Berg) (4th edn). Methuen, London.

Clarke, A. M. and Clarke, A. D. B. (1983b). Classification. In *Mental deficiency: the changing outlook* (ed. A. M. Clarke, A. D. B. Clarke, and J. M. Berg) (4th edn). Methuen, London.

Clarke, A. M., Clarke, A. D. B., and Berg, J. M. (eds.) (1985). *Mental deficiency: the changing outlook* (4th edn). Methuen London.

Clausen, J. A. and Kohn, M. L. (1959). Relation of schizophrenia to the social structure of a small town. In *Epidemiology of mental disorder* (ed. B. Pasamanick). American Association for the Advancement of Science, Washington, D C.

Clayton, P. J. (1979). The sequelae and non-sequelae of conjugal bereavement. *American Journal of Psychiatry* **136**, 1530–4.

Clayton, P. J. (1981). Bereavement. In *Handbook of affective disorders* (ed. E. S. Paykel). Churchill Livingstone, Edinburgh.

Clayton, P. J, Herjanic, M., Murphy, G. E., and Woodruff, R. (1974). Mourning and depression: their similarities and differences. *Canadian Psychiatric Association Journal* **19**, 309–12.

Cleckley, H. M. (1964). *The mask of sanity: an attempt to clarify issues about the so-called psychopathic personality* (4th edn). Mosby, St. Louis.

Clinical Psychiatry Committee (1965). Clinical trials of the treatment of depressive illness: report to the Medical Research Council. *British Medical Journal* i, 881–6.

Clinical Research Centre (Division of Psychiatry) (1984). The Northwick Park ECT trial: predictors of response to real and simulated ECT. *British Journal of Psychiatry* **144**, 227–37.

Cloninger, C. R. (1986). Somatoform and dissociative disorders. In *Medical basis of psychiatry* (ed. G. Winokur and P. Clayton). Saunders, Philadelphia.

Cloninger, C. R. (1987). Diagnosis of somatoform disorders. In *Diagnosis and classification in psychiatry: a critical appraisal of DSM III* (ed. G. L. Tischler) Cambridge University Press, New York.

Cloninger, C. R., Bohman, M., and Sigvardsson, S. (1981). Inheritance of alcohol abuse: cross fostering analysis of adopted men. *Archives of General Psychiatry* **38**, 861–8.

Cloninger, C. R., Reich, T., Suarez, B. K., Price, J. P., and Gottesman, I. I. (1985). The principles of genetics in relation to psychiatry. In *Handbook of Psychiatry* (ed. M. Shepherd), Vol. 5. Cambridge University Press, Cambridge.

Co, B. T., Goodwin, D. W., Gado, M., Mikhael, M., and Hill, S. Y. (1977). Absence of cerebral atrophy in chronic cannabis users: evaluation by computerised transaxial tomography. *Journal of the American Medical Association* **237**, 1229–30.

Cobb, J. P. and Marks, I. M. (1979). Morbid jealousy featuring as obsessive compulsive neurosis. Treatment by behavioural psychotherapy. *British Journal of Psychiatry* **134**, 301–5.

Cobb, S. and Rose, R. M. (1973). Hypertension, peptic ulcer and diabetes in air traffic controllers. *Journal of the American Medical Association* **224**, 489–92.

Cochran, E., Robins, E., and Grote, S. (1976). Regional serotonin levels in the brain: comparison of depressive suicides and alcoholic suicides with controls. *Biological Psychiatry* **11**, 283–94.

Coghill, S. R., Caplan, H. L., Alexandra, H., and Robson, K. M. (1986). Impact of maternal postnatal depression on cognitive development of young children. *British Medical Journal* **292**, 1165–7.

Cohen, F. and Lazarus, R. (1973). Active coping processes, coping dispositions and recovery from surgery. *Psychosomatic Medicine* **35**, 375–89.

Cohen, F. and Lazarus, R. (1979). Coping with stresses of illness. In *Health psychology* (ed. G. C. Stone, F. Cohen, and N. Adler). Jossey Bass, San Francisco.

Cohen, J. (1961). A study of suicide pacts. *Medicolegal Journal* **29**, 144–51.

Cohen, S. (1980). Cushing's syndrome: a psychiatric study of 29 patients. *British Journal of Psychiatry* **136**, 120–4.

Cohen, S. D., Monteiro, W., and Marks, I. M. (1984). Two-year follow-up of agoraphobics after exposure and imipramine. *British Journal of Psychiatry* **144**, 276–81.

Cohen, W. J. and Cohen, N. H. (1974). Lithium carbonate, haloperidol and irreversible brain damage. *Journal of the American Medical Association* **230**, 1283–7.

Cohen-Cole, S. (1980). Training outcome in liaison psychiatry. *General Hospital Psychiatry* **2**, 282–8.

Coid, J. (1979). Mania à potu: a critical review of pathological intoxication. *Psychological Medicine* **9**, 709–19.

Coid, J. (1983). Epidemiology of abnormal homicide and murder followed by suicide. *Psychological Medicine* **13**, 855–86.

Coid, J. (1984). How many psychiatric patients in prison. *British Journal of Psychiatry* **145**, 78–86.

Colbourn, C. J., and Lishman, W. A. (1979). Lateralization of function and psychotic illness: a left hemisphere deficit? In *Hemisphere asymmetries of function in psychopathology* (ed. J. Gruzelier and P. Flor-Henry). Elsevier, Amsterdam.

Cole, J. D., Goldberg, S. C., and Klerman, G. L. (1964). Phenothiazine treatment in acute schizophrenia. *Archives of General Psychiatry* **10**, 246–61.

Committee on the Child Health Services (1976). (Court Committee.) *Fit for the future*. HMSO, London.

Committee into the Education of Handicapped Children and Young People (1978). (Warnock Committee.) *Special educational needs*. HMSO, London.

Committee of Enquiry into Mental Handicap Nursing and Care (1979). (Jay Committee.) HMSO, London.

Committee on Mentally Abnormal Offenders (1975). (Butler Committee.) HMSO, London.

Committee on the Review of Medicines (1980). Systematic review of the benzodiazepines: guidelines for data sheets on diazepam, chlordiazepoxide, medazepam, temazepam, triazolam, nitrazepam and flurazepam. *British Medical Journal* i, 910–12.

Committee on the Safety of Medicines (1981). Mianserin and blood dyscrasia. *Current Problems* No. 7.

Connell, P. H. (1958). *Amphetamine psychosis*. Maudsley Monograph No. 5. Oxford University Press, London.

Connolly, F. H. and Gipson, M. (1978). Dysmorphophobia: a long term study. *British Journal of Psychiatry* **132**, 568–70.

Connolly, J. F., Gruzelier, J. H., Marchanda, R., and Hirsch, S. R. (1983). Visual evoked potentials in schizophrenia. *British Journal of Psychiatry* **142**, 152–5.

Conolly, J. (1856). *Treatment of the insane without mechanical restraints* (reprinted 1973). Dawson, London.

Conrad, K. (1958). *Die beginnende Schizophrenie: versuch einer gestaltanalyse des Wahns*. Thieme, Stuttgart.

Conte, H. R. and Karasu, T. B. (1981). Psychotherapy for medically ill patients: review and critique of controlled studies. *Psychosomatics* **22**, 285–315.

Conte, J. R. (1985). The effects of sexual abuse on children: a critique and suggestions for future research. *Victimology* **10**, 110–30.

Cooper, A. F. (1984). Psychiatric aspects of sensory deficits. In *Handbook of studies on psychiatry and old age* (ed. D. W. K. Kay and G. D. Burrows). Elsevier, Amsterdam.

Cooper, A. J., Ismail, A. A. A., Smith, C. G., and Loraine, J. A. (1970). Androgen function in 'psychogenic' and 'constitutional' types of impotence. *British Medical Journal* iii, 17–20.

Cooper, B. (1978). Epidemiology. In *Schizophrenia. Towards a new synthesis* (ed. J. K. Wing). Academic Press, London.

Cooper, B. (1986). Mental disorder as reaction: the history of a psychiatric concept. In *Life events and psychiatric disorder* (ed. H. Katchnig). Cambridge University Press, Cambridge.

Cooper, B. and Bickel, H. (1984). Population screening and the early detection of dementing disorders in old age: a review. *Psychological Medicine* **14**, 81–95.

Cooper, B. and Sylph, J. (1973). Life events and the onset of neurotic illness: an investigation in general practice. *Psychological Medicine* **3**, 421–35.

Cooper, B., Fry, J., and Kalt, G. W. (1969). A longitudinal study of psychiatric morbidity in a general practice population. *British Journal of Preventive and Social Medicine* **23**, 210–17.

Cooper, J. E., Kendell, R. E., Gurland, B. J., Sharpe, L., Copeland, J. R. M., and Simon, R. (1972). *Psychiatric diagnosis in New York and London*. Maudsley Monograph No. 20. Oxford University Press, London.

Cooper, J. E., Andrews, H., and Barber, C. (1985). Stable abnormalities in the lateralization of early cortical somatosensory evoked potentials in schizophrenic patients. *British Journal of Psychiatry* **146**, 585–93.

Cooper, P. J. and Fairburn, C. G. (1983). Binge eating and self-induced vomiting in the community: a preliminary study. *British Journal of Psychiatry* **142**, 139–44.

Cooper, P. J., Gath, D., Rose, N., and Fieldsend, R. (1982). Psychological sequelae to elective sterilisation: a prospective study. *British Medical Journal* **284**, 461–3.

Cooper, P. J., Campbell, G. A., Day, A., Kennerley, H., and Bond, A. (1988). Non-psychotic psychiatric disorder after childbirth: a prospective study of prevalence, incidence, course and nature. *British Journal of Psychiatry* **152**, 799–806.

Cooper, S. J., Owen, F., Chambers, D. R., Crow, T. J., Johnson, J., and Poulter, M, (1986). Post-mortem neurochemical findings in suicide and depression: a study of the serotonergic system and imipramine. In *The biology of depression* (ed. J. F. W. Deakin). Gaskell, London.

Copeland, J. R. M. (1984). Organisation of services for the elderly mentally ill. In: *Handbook of studies of psychiatry* (ed. D. W. K. Kay and G. D. Burrows). Elsevier, Amsterdam.

Copeland, J. R. M. and Gurland, B. J. (1985). International comparative studies. In *Recent advances in psychogeriatrics* (ed. T. Arie). Churchill Livingstone, Edinburgh.

Copeland, J. R. M., Kelleher, M. J., Kellett, J. M. Barron, G., Cowan, D., and Gourlay, A. J. (1975). Evaluation of a psychogeriatric service: the distinction between psychogeriatric and geriatric patients. *British Journal of Psychiatry* **126**, 21–9.

Coppen, A. J. (1959). Body-build of male homosexuals. *British Medical Journal* **ii**, 1443–5.

Coppen, A. J., (1972). Indoleamines and the affective disorders. *Journal of Psychiatric Research* **9**, 163–71.

Coppen, A. J. and Shaw, D. M. (1963). Mineral metabolism in melancholia. *British Medical Journal* **ii**, 1439–44.

Coppen, A. J. and Wood, K. (1978). Tryptophan and depressive illness. *Psychological Medicine* **8**, 49–57.

Coppen, A. J., Prange, A. J., Whybrow, P. C., Noguera, R., and Praez, J. M. (1969). Methysergide in mania. *Lancet* **ii**, 338–40.

Coppen, A. J. *et al.* (1971). Prophylactic lithium in affective disorders: controlled trial. *Lancet* **i** 275–9.

Coppen, A. J., Whybrow, P. C., Noguera, R., Maggs, R., and Prange, A. J. (1972). The comparative antidepressant value of L-tryptophan and imipramine with and without attempted potentiation by liothyronine. *Archives of General Psychiatry* **26**, 234–41.

Coppen, A. J., Montgomery, S. A., Gupta, R. K., and Bailey, J. (1976). A double blind comparison of lithium carbonate or maprotiline in the prophylaxis of affective disorder. *British Journal of Psychiatry* **128**, 479–85.

Coppen, A. J. *et al.* (1978). Amitryptyline plasma concentration and clinical effect: a World Health Organization Collaborative Study. *Lancet* **i**, 63–6.

Coppen, A. J. *et al.* (1981). Lithium continuation therapy following electroconvulsive therapy. *British Journal of Psychiatry* **139**, 284–7.

Corbett, J. A. (1978). The development of services for the mentally handicapped: a historical and national review. In *The care of the handicapped child* (ed. J. Apley). Heinemann, London.

Corbett, J. A. (1985). Mental retardation—psychiatric aspects. In *Child psychiatry: modern approaches* (ed. M. Rutter and L. Hersov) (2nd edn). Blackwell, Oxford.

Corbett, J. A. and Pond, D. A. (1979). Epilepsy and behaviour disorder in the mentally handicapped. In *Psychiatric illness and mental handicap* (ed. F. F. James and R. P. Snaith). Gaskell, Ashford, Kent.

Corbett, J. A. and Turpin, G. (1985). Tics and Tourette's syndrome. In *Child and adolescent psychiatry: modern approaches* (ed. M. Rutter and L. Hersov) (2nd edn). Blackwell, Oxford.

Corbett, J. A., Matthews, A. M., Connell, P. M., and Shapiro, D. A. (1969). Tics and Gilles de la Tourette syndrome: a follow-up study and a critical review. *British Journal of Psychiatry* **115**, 1229–41.

Corbett, J. A., Harris, R., and Robinson, R. G. (1975). Epilepsy. In *Mental retardation and developmental disabilities: an annual review*, Vol. VII (ed. J. Wortis). Brunner-Mazel, New York.

Corbett, J. A., Trimble, M. R., and Nicol, T. C. (1985). Behavioural and cognitive impairments in children with epilepsy: The long-term effects of anticonvulsant therapy. *Journal of the American Academy of Child Psychiatry* **24**, 17–23.

Corbin, S. L. and Eastwood, M. R. (1986). Sensory deficits and mental disorders of old age: causal or coincidental associations? *Psychological Medicine* **16**, 251–6.

Corr, A. and Corr, D. M. (1983). *Hospice care, principles and practice*. New York, Springer.

Corsellis, J. A. N. (1962). *Mental illness and the ageing brain*. Maudsley Monographs No. 9. Oxford University Press, London.

Corsellis, J. A. N., Bruton, C. J. and Freeman-Browne, D. (1973). The aftermath of boxing. *Psychological Medicine* **3**, 270–303.

Coryell, W., Noyes, R., and Clancy, J. (1982). Excess mortality in panic disorder: comparison with primary unipolar depression. *Archives of General Psychiatry* **39**, 701–3.

Costello, G. G. (1982). Social factors associated with depression: a retrospective community study. *Psychological Medicine* **12**, 329–39.

Costello, R. M. (1975). Alcoholism treatment and evaluation. *International Journal of the Addictions* **10**, 251–75.

Cotard, M. (1882). Du délire de négations. *Archives de Neurologie, Paris* **4**, 152–70 and 282–96. [Translated into English by M. Rohde in S. R. Hirsch and M. Shepherd (eds.) *Themes and variations in European psychiatry*, pp. 353–73. Wright, Bristol.]

Cotterill, J. A. (1981). Dermatological non-disease: a common and potentially fatal disturbance of cutaneous body image. *British Journal of Dermatology* **104**, 611–19.

Coull, D. C., Crooks, J. Dingwell-Fordyce, I., Scott, A. M., and Weir, R. D. (1970). Amitriptyline and cardiac disease: risk of sudden death identified by monitoring system. *Lancet* **ii**, 590–1.

Council on Scientific Affairs. (1986). Dementia. *Journal of the American Medical Association* **256**, 2234–8.

Courbon, P. and Fail, G. (1927). Syndrome 'd'Illusion de Frégoli' et schizophrénie *Bulletin de la Société Clinique de Médecine Mentale* **15**, 121–4.

Covi, L., Lipman, R., and Derogatis, L. (1974). Drugs and group psychotherapy in neurotic depression. *American Journal of Psychiatry* **131**, 191–8.

Cowen, P. J. and Anderson, I. M. (1986). 5HT neuroendocrinology: changes with depressive illness and antidepressant drug treatment. In *The biology of depression* (ed. J. F. W. Deakin), pp. 71–89. Gaskell, London.

Cowie, V. (1961). The incidence of neurosis in the children of psychotics. *Acta Psychiatrica Scandinavica* **37**, 37–71.

Cowie, V. (1980). Injury and insult—considerations of the neuropathological aetiology of mental subnormality. *British Journal of Psychiatry* **137**, 305–12.

Cox, S. M. and Ludwig, A. (1979). Neurological soft signs and psychopathology: 1. Findings in schizophrenia. *Journal of Nervous and Mental Disease* **167**, 161–5.

Craft, A. and Craft, M. (1981) Sexuality and mental handicap: a review. *British Journal of Psychiatry* **139**, 494–505.

Craft, M. (1965). *Ten studies in psychopathic personality*. Wright, Bristol.

Craft, M. (1984). Low intelligence, mental handicap and crime. In *Mentally abnormal offenders* (ed. M. Craft and A. Craft). Baillière Tindall, London.

Craig, T. J. (1982). An epidemiologic study of problems associated with violence among psychiatric inpatients. *American Journal of Psychiatry* **139**, 1262–6.

Craig, T. K. J. and Brown, G. W. (1984). Life events, meaning and physical illness. A review. In *Health care and human behaviour* (eds. A. Steptoe, and A. Mathews). Academic Press, London.

Crammer, J., Barraclough, B., and Heine, B. (1982). *The use of drugs in psychiatry*. Gaskell, London.

Cranshaw, J. A. and Mullen, P. E. (1984). A study of benzhexol abuse. *British Journal of Psychiatry* **145**, 300–3.

Crapper, D., Kirschnan, S. S., and Dalton, A. J. (1973). Brain aluminium distribution in Alzheimer's disease and experimental neurofibrillary degeneration. *Science* **180**, 511–13.

Crauford, D. I. O. and Harris, R. (1986). Ethics of predictive testing for Huntington's chorea: the need for more information. *British Medical Journal* **293**, 249–51.

Crawfurd, M. d'A. (1982). Severe mental handicap: pathogenesis, treatment and prevention. *British Medical Journal* **285**, 762–6.

Creed, F. (1981). Life events and appendectomy. *Lancet* **i**, 1381–5.

Creed, F. (1984). Life events and physical illness. *Journal of Psychosomatic Research* **29**, 113–23.

Creed, F. and Guthrie, E. (1987). Psychological factors in the irritable bowel syndrome. *Gut* **28**, 1307–18.

Creer, C. (1978). Social work with patients and their families. In *Schizophrenia: towards a new synthesis* (ed. J. K. Wing). Academic Press, London.

Creer, C. and Wing, J. K. (1975). Living with a schizophrenic patient. *British Journal of Hospital Medicine* **14**, 73–82.

Cremona, A. (1986). Mad drivers: psychiatric illness and driving performance. *British Journal of Hospital Medicine* **28**, 193–5.

Creutzfeldt, H. E. (1920). Über eine eigenartige herdformige. Erkrankung des zentral Nevensystems. *Zeitschrift für die Gesamte Neurologie und Psychiatrie* **57**, 1–18.

Crisp, A. H. (1977). Diagnosis and outcome of anorexia nervosa: the St. Georges view. *Proceedings of the Royal Society of Medicine* **70**, 464–70.

Crisp, A. H., Palmer, R. L., and Kalucy, R. S. (1976). How common is anorexia nervosa? A prevalence study. *British Journal of Psychiatry* **128**, 549–54.

Critchley, M. (1953). *The parietal lobes*. Edward Arnold, London.

Crome, L. and Stern, J. (1972). *Pathology of mental retardation* (2nd edn). Churchill Livingstone, London.

Cronholm, B. and Molander, L. (1964). Memory disturbance after electroconvulsive therapy. *Acta Psychiatrica Scandinavica* **40**, 211–16.

Cronholm, B. and Ottosson, J. -O. (1960). Experimental studies of the therapeutic action of electroconvulsive therapy in endogenous depression. *Acta Psychiatrica Scandinavica* Suppl. **145**, 69–101.

Crow, T. J. (1980). Molecular pathology of schizophrenia; more than one disease process? *British Medical Journal* **280**, 66–8.

Crow, T. J. (1983). Is schizophrenia an infectious disease? *Lancet* **i**, 173–5.

Crow, T. J. (1984). A re-evaluation of the viral hypothesis: is psychosis the result of retroviral integration at a site close to the cerebral dominance gene? *British Journal of Psychiatry* **145**, 243–53.

Crow, T. J. (1985). The two-syndrome concept: origins and current status. *Schizophrenia Bulletin* **11**, 471–85.

Crow, T. J., Johnstone, E. C., and Owen, F. (1979*a*). Research on schizophrenia. In *Recent advances in clinical psychiatry* (ed. K. Granville-Grossman), Vol. 3, pp. 1–36. Churchill Livingstone, Edinburgh.

Crow, T. J., Baker, H. F. Cross, A. J., Joseph, M. H., Lofthouse, R., Longdon, A., Owen, F., Riley, G. J., Glover, V. and Killpack, W. S. (1979*b*). Monoamine mechanisms in chronic schizophrenia: post mortem neurochemical findings. *British Journal of Psychiatry* **134**, 249–56.

Crow, T. J., Ferrier, I. N., Johnstone, E. C., MacMillan, J. F., Owens, D. G. C., Parry, R. P. and Tyrell, D. A. J. (1979c). Characteristics of patients with schizophrenia or neurological disorder and a virus-like agent in the cerebrospinal fluid. *Lancet* **i**, 842–4.

Crowe, M. J. (1973). Conjoint marital therapy: advice or interpretation. *Journal of Psychosomatic Research* **17**, 309–15.

Crowe, R. R. (1974). An adoption study of antisocial personality. *Archives of General Psychiatry* **31**, 785–91.

Crowe, R. R., Noyes, R., Pauls, D. L., and Slymen, D. (1983). A family study of panic disorder. *Archives of General Psychiatry* **40**, 1065–9.

Crown, S. (1978). *Psychosexual counselling*. Academic Press, London.

Crown, S. (1980). Psychosocial factors in low back pain. *Clinics in Rheumatic Diseases* **6**, 77–92.

Cullen, W. (1772). Nosology. See extracts in I. McAlpine and R. Hunter. *Three hundred years of psychiatry*, pp. 473–9. Oxford University Press, London.

Cummings, J. L. (1986). Subcortical dementia: neuropsychology, neuropsychiatry, and pathophysiology. *British Journal of Psychiatry* **149**, 682–97.

Cunningham, J., Strassberg, D., and Roback, H. (1978). Group psychotherapy for medical patients. *Comprehensive Psychiatry* **19**, 135–40.

Curran, D. (1937). The differentiation of neuroses and manic-depressive psychosis. *Journal of Mental Science* **83**, 156–74.

Cutting, J. (1978). The relationship between Korsakov's syndrome and 'alcoholic dementia'. *British Journal of Psychiatry* **132**, 240–51.

Cutting, J. (1979). Alcohol dependence and alcohol related disabilities. In *Recent advances in clinical psychiatry* (ed. K. Granville-Grossman), Vol. 3 pp. 225–50. Churchill Livingstone, Edinburgh.

Cutting, J. (1980). Physical illness and psychosis. *British Journal of Psychiatry* **136**, 109–19.

Cutting, J. (1985). *The psychology of schizophrenia*. Churchill Livingstone, Edinburgh.

Cutting, J. (1987). The phenomenology of acute psychosis. *British Journal of Psychiatry* **151**, 324–32.

Cybulska, E. and Rucinski, J. (1986). Gross self-neglect in old age. *British Journal of Hospital Medicine* **31**, 21–6.

Da Costa, J. M. (1871). An irritable heart: a clinical study of functional cardiac disorder and its consequences. *American Journal of Medical Science* **61**, 17–52. (See extracts in Jarcho, S. (1959). On irritable heart. *American Journal of Cardiology* **4**, 809–17.)

Dahl, A. A. (1985). A critical examination of empirical studies of the diagnosis of borderline disorders in adults. *Psychiatric Developments* **3**, 1–29.

Dalbiez, R. (1941). *Psychoanalytic method and the doctrine of Freud* (2 vols.). Longmans Green, London.

Dalton, K. (1964). *The premenstrual syndrome*. Heinemann, London.

Dalton, K. (1977). *The premenstrual syndrome and progesterone therapy*. Heinemann, London.

Daly, D. D. (1975). Ictal clinical manifestations of complex partial seizures. In *Advances in neurology* (ed. J. K. Penry and D. Daly), Vol. 11. Raven Press, New York.

Danford, D. E. and Huber, A. M. (1982). Pica among mentally retarded adults. *American Journal of Mental Deficiency* **87**, 141–6.

Davenloo, H. (ed.) (1980). *Short term dynamic psychotherapy.* Aronson, New York.

David, S. A., Wessely, S., and Pelosi, A. J. (1988). Postviral fatigue syndrome: time for a new approach. *British Medical Journal* **296**, 696–700.

Davidson, D. G. D. and Eastham, W. N. (1966). Acute hepatic necrosis following overdose of paracetamol. *British Medical Journal* ii, 497–9.

Davidson, J. R. T. (1972). Postpartum mood change in Jamaican women: a description and a discussion of its significance. *British Journal of Psychiatry* **121**, 659–64.

Davies, A. M. (1986). *Epidemiological data on the health of the elderly: a review of the present state of research* (ed. H. Häfner, G. Moschel, and N. Sartorius). Springer-Verlag, Berlin.

Davies, A. M. and Fleischman, R. (1981). Health status and the use of health services as reported by older residents of the Baka neighbourhood, Jerusalem. *Israeli Medical Sciences* **17**, 138–44.

Davies, B. M. and Morgenstern, F. S. (1960). A case of cysticercosis, temporal lobe epilepsy and transvestism. *Journal of Neurology, Neurosurgery and Psychiatry* **23**, 247–9.

Davies, D. L. (1962). Normal drinking in recovered alcohol addicts. *Quarterly Journal of Studies on Alcohol* **23**, 94–104.

Davies, D. M. (1987). *Textbook of adverse drug reactions* (3rd edn). Oxford University Press, Oxford.

Davis, J. M. (1976). Comparative doses and costs of antipsychotic medication. *Archives of General Psychiatry* **33**, 858–61.

Davis, J. M., Schaffer, C. B., Killian, G. A., Kinard, C., and Chan, C. (1980). Important issues in the drug treatment of schizophrenia. *Schizophrenia Bulletin* **6**, 70–87.

Davis, K. L. and Mohs, R. C. (1986). Cholinergic drugs in Alzheimer's disease. *New England Journal of Medicine* **315**, 1286–7.

Davison, A. N. (1984). Neurobiology and neurochemistry of the developing brain. In *Scientific Studies in Mental Retardation.* (ed J. Dobbing, A. D. B. Clarke, J. A. Corbett, and R. O. Robinson). Royal Society of Medicine and Macmillan, London.

Davison, G. (1968). Elimination of a sadistic fantasy by a client-controlled counter-conditioning technique: a case study. *Journal of Abnormal Psychology* **73**, 84–90.

Davison, K. (1983). Schizophrenia like psychoses associated with cerebral disorders: a review. *Psychiatric Developments* **1**, 1–34.

Davison, K. and Bagley, C. R. (1969). Schizophrenia-like psychoses associated with organic disorders of the central nervous system: a review of the literature. In *Current problems in neuropsychiatry. British Journal of Psychiatry* Special Publication No. 4 (ed. R. N. Herrington). Headley Brothers, Ashford, Kent.

Dawkins, S. (1961). Non-consummation of marriage. *Lancet* ii, 1029–33.

Dawson, J. (1987). Royal Free disease: perplexity continues. *British Medical Journal* **294**, 327–8.

de Alarcón, R. (1969). The spread of heroin abuse in a community. *WHO Bulletin on Narcotics* **21**, 17–22.

de Alarcón, R. D. and Franchesini, J. A. (1984). Hyperparathyroidism and paranoid psychosis; case report and review of the literature. *British Journal of Psychiatry* **145**, 477–86.

Dean, C. (1987). Psychiatric morbidity following mastectomy: preoperative predictors and types of illness. *Journal of Psychosomatic Research* **31**, 385–92.

Dean, C. and Kendell, R. E. (1981). The symptomatology of puerperal illnesses. *British Journal of Psychiatry* **139**, 128–33.

Deary, I. J. and Whalley, L. J. (1988). Recent research on the causes of Alzheimer's disease. *British Medical Journal* **297**, 807–8.

De Clérambault, G. (1921). Les délires passionels. Erotomanie, revendication, jalousie. *Bulletin de la société clinique de Médicine Mentale* 61–71.

De Clérambault, G. G. (1987). Psychoses of passion (English translation). In *The clinical roots of the schizophrenia concept* (ed. J. Cutting and M. Shepherd). Cambridge University Press, Cambridge.

Déjerine, J. and Gauckler, E. (1913). *Psychoneurosis and psychotherapy* (translated by S. E. Jelliffe and J. B. Lippincott. Reissued by Arno Press, New York.)

Delahunty, J. E. and Ardran, G. M. (1970). Globus hystericus: a manifestation of reflux oesophagitis. *Journal of Laryngology and Otology* **84**, 1049–54.

D'Elia, G. and Raotma, H. (1975). Is unilateral ECT less effective than bilateral ECT? *British Journal of Psychiatry* **126**, 83–9.

Dell, S. (1984). *Murder into manslaughter.* Maudsley Monograph No. 27, Oxford University Press, Oxford.

Dell, S. (1987). Detention in Broadmoor. *British Journal of Psychiatry* **150**, 824–7.

Dell, S., Robertson, G., and Parker, E. (1987). Detention in Broadmoor: factors in length of stay. *British Journal of Psychiatry* **150**, 824–7.

de Maré, P. B. and Kreeger, L. C. (1974). *Introduction to group treatments in psychiatry.* Butterworths, London.

Denker, S. J. (1958). A follow-up study of 128 closed head injuries in twins using co-twins as controls. *Acta Psychiatrica Scandinavica* Suppl. **123**, 1–125.

Denko, J. D. and Kaelbling, R. (1962). The psychiatric aspects of hypoparathyroidism. *Acta Psychiatrica Scandinavica* Suppl. **164**, 1–70.

Denmark, J. C. (1985). A study of 250 patients referred to a department of psychiatry for the deaf. *British Journal of Psychiatry* **146**, 282–6.

Department of the Environment (1976). *Drinking and driving. Report of the Departmental Committee.* (Blennerhassett Report.) HMSO, London.

Department of Health and Social Security (1971). *Better services for the mentally handicapped.* HMSO, London.

Department of Health and Social Security (1972). *Services for mental illness related to old age.* HMSO, London.

Department of Health and Social Security (1975). *Better services for the mentally ill.* HMSO, London.

Department of Health and Social Security (1978*a*). *Advisory committee on alcoholism: report on prevention.* HMSO, London.

Department of Health and Social Security (1978*b*). *A happier old age.* HMSO, London.

Department of Health and Social Security (1984). *The management of deliberate self harm.* HM (84) 25. DHSS, London.

Department of Health and Social Security. (1985). *Government response to the second report from the Social Services Committee, 1984–85 Session. Community Care.* HMSO, London.

Derogatis, L. R. *et al.* (1985). Prevalence of psychiatric disorders among cancer patients. *Journal of the American Medical Association* **249**, 751–7.

Detera-Wadleigh, S. D., Berrettini, W. H., Goldini, R., Boorman, D., Anderson, S., and Gershon, E. S. (1987). Close linkage of the C-Harvey-ras-1 and the insulin gene to affective disorder is ruled out in three North American pedigrees. *Nature* **325**, 306–7.

Devlen, J., Maguire, P., Phillips, P., Crowther, D., and Chambers, H., (1987). Psychological problems associated with diagnosis and treatment of lymphomas. *British Medical Journal* **295**, 953–7.

Dew, M. A., Bromet, E. J., Brent, D., and Greenhouse, J. B. (1987). A quantitive literature review of the effectiveness of suicide prevention centers. *Journal of Consulting and Clinical Psychology* **55**, 239–44.

Dewhurst, D. (1969). The neurosyphilitic psychoses today: a survey of 91 cases. *British Journal of Psychiatry* **115**, 31–8.

Dewhurst, K. (1980). *Thomas Willis's Oxford lectures*. Sandford Publications, Oxford.

Dewhurst, K., Oliver, J. E., and McKnight, A. L. (1970). Sociopsychiatric consequences of Huntington's disease. *British Journal of Psychiatry* **116**, 255–8.

Dewhurst, W. G. (1968). Methysergide in mania. *Nature* **219**, 506–7.

Dicks, H. (1967). *Marital tensions: clinical studies towards a psychological theory of interaction*. Routledge and Kegan Paul, London.

Dight, S. E. (1976). *Scottish drinking habits: a survey of Scottish drinking habits and attitudes towards alcohol*. Office of Population Censuses and Surveys. HMSO, London.

DiMascio, A. (1973). The effects of benzodiazepines on aggression: reduced or increased? In *The benzodiazepines* (ed. S. Garattini, E. Mussini and L. O. Randall). Raven Press, London.

DiMascio, A. Weissman, M. M., Prusoff, B. A., Neu, C., Zwiling, M., and Klerman, G. L. (1979). Differential symptom reduction by drugs and psychotherapy in acute depression. *Archives of General Psychiatry* **36**, 1450–6.

Dimsdale, J. E. (1988). A perspective on type A behaviour and coronary disease. *New England Journal of Medicine* **318**, 110–12.

Dodrill, C. B. (1975). Effects of sulthiame upon intellectual, neuro-psychological and social function abilities of adult epileptics: comparison with diphenylhydantoin. *Epilepsia* **16**, 627–5.

Doehrman, S. R. (1977). Psychosocial aspects of recovery from coronary heart disease: a review. *Social Science and Medicine* **11**, 199–218.

Dollard, J. and Miller, N. E. (1950). *Personality and psychotherapy*. McGraw-Hill, New York.

Donnely, J. (1978). The incidence of psychosurgery in the United States 1971–73. *American Journal of Psychiatry* **135**, 1476–80.

d'Orban, P. T. (1976). Child stealing: a typology of female offenders. *British Journal of Criminology* **16**, 275–9.

d'Orban, P. T. (1979). Women who kill their children. *British Journal of Psychiatry* **134**, 560–71.

d'Orban, P. T. (1983). Medicolegal aspects of the premenstrual syndrome. *British Journal of Hospital Medicine* **26**, 404–9.

Dorian, B., and Garfinkel, P. E. (1987). Stress, immunity and illness—a review. *Psychological Medicine,* **17**, 393–407.

Dorner, S. (1976). Adolescents with spina bifida: how they see the situation. *Archives of Disease in Childhood* **51**, 439–44.

Douglas, J. and Richman, N. (1984). *My child won't sleep: a handbook for management for parents*. Penguin, London.

Douglas, J. W. B. and Blomfield, J. M. (1958). *Children under five*. George Allen, London.

Dreifuss, F. E., Bancaud, J., Henricksen, O. *et al.* (1981). Proposal for a revised clinical and electroencephalographic classification of epileptic seizures. *Epilepsia* **22**, 489–503.

Drife, J. O. (1987). Pseudocyesis. *Integrative Psychiatry* **5**, 194–200.

Drossman, D. A. (1982). Patients with psychogenic pain: six years' observation in the medical setting. *American Journal of Psychiatry* **139**, 1549–1557.

Drossman, D. A. (1986). The psychosocial aspects of inflammatory bowel disease. *Stress Medicine* **2**, 119–28.

Drugs and Therapeutics Bulletin (1981*a*). Lithium updated. *Drugs and Therapeutics Bulletin* **19**, 21–4.

Drugs and Therapeutics Bulletin (1981*b*). Sodium valproate reassessed. *Drugs and Therapeutics Bulletin* **19**, 93–5.

Drugs and Therapeutics Bulletin (1983). Drugs which can be given to nursing mothers. *Drugs and Therapeutics Bulletin* **21**, 5–8.

Dubowitz, V. and Hersov, L. (1976). Management of children with non-organic (hysterical) disorders of motor function. *Developmental Medicine and Child Neurology* **18**, 358–68.

Duffy, J. (1977). Estimating the proportion of heavy drinkers. In *The Ledermann curve* (ed. D. L. Davies). Alcohol Education Centre, London.

Dunbar, G. C. and Morgan D. D. V. (1987). The changing pattern of alcohol consumption in England and Wales 1978–85. *British Medical Journal* **295**, 807–10.

Dunbar, H. F. (1954). *Emotions and bodily changes*. Columbia University Press, New York.

Dunbar, J. A., Ogston, S. A., Ritchie, A., Devgun, M. S., Hagart, J., and Martin, B. T. (1985). Are problem drinkers dangerous drivers? An investigation of arrest for drinking and driving, serum gamma glutyl-transpeptidase activities, blood alcohol concentrations and road accidents: the Tayside safe-driving project. *British Medical Journal* **290**, 827–30.

Dunham, H. W. (1965). *Community and schizophrenia: an epidemiological analysis*. Wayne State University Press, Detroit.

Dunlap, K. (1932). *Habits: their making and unmaking*. Liverheight Publishing Corporation, New York.

Dunner, D. L., Ishiki, D., Avery, D. H., Wilson, L. G. and Hyde, T. S. (1986). Effect of alprazolam and diazepam on anxiety and panic attacks in panic disorder: a controlled trial. *Journal of Clinical Psychiatry* **47**, 458–60.

Durkheim, E. (1951). *Suicide: a study in sociology* (translated by J. A. Spaulding and G. Simpson). Free Press, Glencoe, Ill.

Eagles, J. M. and Besson, J. O. (1985). Changes in the incidence of alcohol-related problems in north-east Scotland, 1971–1982. *British Journal of Psychiatry* **147**, 39–43.

Eastwood, R. and Corbin, S. (1985). Epidemiology of mental disorders in old age. In *Recent advances of psychogeriatics* (ed. T. Arie). Churchill Livingstone, Edinburgh.

Eastwood, R. and Trevelyan, M. H. (1972). Relationship between physical and psychiatric disorder. *Psychological Medicine* **2**, 363–72.

Eaton, J. W. and Weil, R. J. (1955). *Culture and mental disorders: a comparative study of the Hutterites and other populations*. Free Press, Glencoe, Ill.

Eaton, L. F. and Menolascino, F. J. (1982). Psychiatric disorders in the mentally retarded: types, problems and challenges. *American Journal of Psychiatry* **139**, 1297–303.

Eddleston, A. l. W. and Davis, M. (1982). Histocompatibility antigens in alcoholic liver disease. *British Medical Bulletin* **38**, 13–16.

Edeh, J. and Toone, B. (1987). Relationship between interictal psychopathology and type of epilepsy. *British Journal of Psychiatry* **151**, 95–101.

Edlund, M. J. and Craig, T. J. (1984). Antipsychotic drug use and birth defects: an epidemiologic assessment *Comprehensive Psychiatry* **25**, 32–7.

Edwards, G. (1976). Cannabis and the psychiatric position. In *Cannabis and health* (ed. J. D. P. Graham). Academic Press, London.

Edwards, G. (1979). British policies on opiate addiction. *British Journal of Psychiatry* **134**, 1–13.

Edwards, G. (1983). Alcohol and advice to the pregnant women. *British Medical Journal* **286**, 247–8.

Edwards, G. (1985). A later follow-up of a classic case series: D. L. Davies' 1962 report and its significance for the present. *Journal of Studies on Alcohol* **46**, 181–90.

Edwards, G., Hensman, C., and Peto, J. (1971). Drinking problems among recidivist prisoners. *Psychological Medicine* **1**, 388–99.

Edwards. G., Chandler, J., and Hensman, C. (1972). Drinking in a London suburb. *Quarterly Journal of Studies on Alcoholism* Suppl. No. 6, 69–128.

Edwards, G., Hawker, A., Hensman, C., Peto, J., and Williamson, V. (1973). Alcoholics known or unknown to agencies: epidemiological studies in a London suburb. *British Journal of Psychiatry* **123**, 169–83.

Edwards, G., Grossman, M. M., Keller, M., Moser, J., and Room, R. (1977*a*). *Alcohol related disabilities*. World Health Organization, Geneva.

Edwards, G. *et al.* (1977*b*). Alcoholism: a controlled trial of 'treatment' and 'advice', *Journal of Studies on Alcohol* **38**, 1004–31.

Egeland, J. A. *et al.* (1987). Bipolar affective disorders linked to DNA markers on chromosome 11. *Nature* **325**, 783–7.

Ehrhardt, A. A., Epstein, R., and Money, J. (1968). Fetal androgens and female gender identity in the early-treated adrenogenital syndrome. *Johns Hopkins Medical Journal* **122**, 160–7.

Eisenberg, L. (1958). School phobia—a study in the communication of anxiety. *American Journal of Psychiatry* **114**, 712–18.

Eisenberg, L. (1980). Adolescent suicide: on taking arms against a sea of troubles. *Paediatrics* **66**, 315–20.

Eisenberg, L. (1986). Does bad news about suicide beget bad news? *New England Journal of Medicine* **315**, 705–7.

Eisenberg, L., Connors, C. K., and Sharpe, L. (1965). A controlled study of the differential application of outpatient psychiatric treatment for children. *Japanese Journal of Psychiatry* **6**, 125–32.

Eisendrath, S. J., Way, L. W., Ostroff, J. W., and Johanson, C. A. (1986). Identification of psychogenic abdominal pain. *Psychosomatics* **27**, 705–12.

Eiser, C. (1986). Effects of chronic illness on the child's intellectual development. *Journal of the Royal Society of Medicine* **79**, 2–3.

Eisinger, A. J., *et al* (1972). Female homosexuality. *Nature* **238**, 157.

Eitinger, L. (1960). The symptomatology of mental disease among refugees in Norway. *Journal of Mental Science* **106**, 947–66.

El-Guebaly, N. and Offord, D. R. (1977). The offspring of alcoholics: a critical review. *American Journal of Psychiatry* **134**, 357–65.

Ellenberg, J. H., Hirtz, D. G. and Nelson, K. B. (1986). Do seizures in children cause intellectual deterioration? *New England Journal of Medicine* **314**, 1085–8.

Ellenberger, H. F. (1970). *The discovery of the unconscious*. Basic Books, New York.

Ellis, A. (1956). The effectiveness of psychotherapy in individuals who have severe homosexual problems. *Journal of Consulting Psychology* **20**, 191–5.

Ellis, A. (1979). *Reasons and emotion in psychotherapy*. Citadel Press, Syracuse, NJ.

Ellis, A. and Brancale, R. (1956). *The physiology of sex offenders*. Thomas, Springfield, Ill.

Ellis, H. (1901). *Studies in the psychology of sex*, Vol. 2. *Sexual inversion*. Davis, Philadelphia.

Ellis, H. (1928). *Studies in the psychology of sex*, Vol. 7. *Eonism and other supplementary studies*. Davis, Philadelphia.

Emery, A. E. H. and Pullen, I. (1984). *Psychological aspects of genetic counselling*. Academic Press, London.

Endicott, J. and Spitzer, R. L. (1978). A diagnostic interview: the schedule for affective disorders and schizophrenia. *Archives of General Psychiatry* **35**, 837–44.

Endicott, J. and Spitzer, R. L. (1979). Use of the research diagnostic criteria and the schedule for affective disorders and schizophrenia to study affective disorders. *American Journal of Psychiatry* **136**, 52–6.

Engel, G. (1958). Psychogenic pain and the pain prone person. *American Journal of Medicine* **26** 899–918.

Engel, G. (1962). *Psychological development in health and disease*. Saunders, Philadelphia.

Engel, G. (1967). Medical education and the psychosomatic approach: a report on the Rochester experience. *Journal of Psychosomatic Research* **11**, 77–83.

Engel, G. (1980). The clinical application of the biopsychosocial model. *American Journal of Psychiatry* **137**, 535–44.

Engel, G. and Romano, J. (1959). Delirium, a syndrome of cerebral insufficiency. *Journal of Chronic Diseases* **9**, 260–77.

Engel, G., Logan, M., and Ferris, E. B. (1947). Hyperventilation: analysis of clinical symptomatology. *Annals of Internal Medicine* **27**, 683–704.

Enoch, M. D. and Trethowan, W. H. (1979). *Uncommon psychiatric syndromes*. Wright, Bristol.

Epstein, A. W. (1960). Fetishism: a study of its psychopathology with particular reference to a proposed disorder in brain mechanisms as an aetiological factor. *Journal of Nervous and Mental Disease* **130**, 107–19.

Epstein, A. W. (1961). Relationship of fetishism and transvestism to brain and particularly to temporal lobe dysfunction. *Journal of Nervous and Mental Disease* **133**, 247–53.

Erkinjuntti, T., Wikstrom, J., Palo, J., and Autio, L. (1986). Dementia among medical in-patients. *Archives of Internal Medicine* **146**, 1923–6.

Errera, P. (1962). Some historical aspects of the concept, Phobia. *Psychiatric Quarterly* **36**, 325–36.

Esquirol, E. (1838). *Des maladies mentales*. Baillière, Paris. (Reprinted in 1976 by Arno Press, New York.)

Esquirol, E. (1845). *Mental maladies: a treatise on insanity*. Lea and Blanchard, Philadelphia.

Essen-Möller, E. (1971). Suggestions for further improvement of the international classification of mental disorders. *Psychological Medicine* **1**, 308–11.

Evans, D. R. (1970). Exhibitionism. In *Symptoms of psychopathology* (ed. C. G. Costello), pp. 7–59. Wiley, New York.

Evans, N. J. R., Baldwin, J. A., and Gath, D. H. (1974). The incidence of cancer among patients with affective disorder. *British Journal of Psychiatry* **124**, 518–5.

Evans, R. W., Hanninen, D. L., Garrison, L.P., *et al.* (1985). Quality of life of patients with end stage renal disease. *New England Journal of Medicine* **312**, 553–9.

Ewing, J. A. and Rouse, B. A. (1976). Failure of an experimental treatment program to inculcate controlled drinking in alcoholics. *British Journal of Addiction* **71**, 123–34.

Ey, H., Bernard, P., and Brisset, C. (1960). Acute delusional psychoses. In *Themes and variations in European psychiatry* (1974) (ed. S. R. Hirsch and M. Shepherd). Wright, Bristol.

Eysenck, H. J. (1952). The effects of psychotherapy: an evaluation. *Journal of Consulting Psychology* **16**, 319–24.

Eysenck, H. J. (1957). *The dynamics of anxiety and hysteria.* Routledge and Kegan Paul, London.

Eysenck, H. J. (1960). *Behaviour therapy and the neuroses.* Pergamon Press, Oxford.

Eysenck, H. J. (1970*a*). *Crime and personality.* Paladin Press, London.

Eysenck, H. J. (1970*b*). A dimensional system of psycho-diagnosis. In *New approaches to personality classification* (ed. A. R. Mahrer), pp. 169–207. Columbia University Press, New York.

Eysenck, H. J. (1976). The learning theory model of neurosis: a new approach. *Behaviour Research and Therapy* **14**, 251–67.

Fabrega, H. (1987). Psychiatric diagnosis. a cultural perspective. *Journal of Nervous and Mental Disease* **175**, 383–94.

Faergeman, P. M. (1963). *Psychogenic psychoses.* Butterworths, London.

Fagan, J. and Shepherd, I. L. (eds.) (1971). *Gestalt therapy now.* Harper Colophon, New York.

Fairburn, C. (1981). A cognitive behavioural approach to the treatment of bulimia. *Psychological Medicine* **11**, 707–11.

Fairburn, C. and Hope, A. (1988). Eating disorder. In *Companion to Psychiatric Studies* (ed. Kendell, R. E. and Zealley, A. K.). Churchill Livingstone, Edinburgh.

Fairburn, C. G. (1985). Cognitive behavioural treatment for bulimia. In *Handbook of psychotherapy for anorexia nervosa and bulimia* (eds. D. M. and P. E. Garfinkel). Guilford Press, New York.

Fairburn, C. G., (1987). The uncertain status of the cognitive approach to bulimia nervosa. In *The psychobiology of bulimia nervosa* (eds. K. M. Pirke, D. Ploog, and W. Vandereycken). Springer, Berlin.

Fairburn, C. G., Wu, F. C., and McCullock, D. K. (1982). The clinical features of diabetic impotence: a preliminary study. *British Journal of Psychiatry* **140**, 447–52.

Faizallah, R., Woodrow, J. C., Krasner, N. K., Walker, R. J., and Morris, A. I. (1982). Are HLA antigens important in the development of alcohol-induced liver disease? *British Medical Journal* **285**, 533–4.

Falloon, I. R. H., McGill, C. W., Boyd, J. L. and Pederson, J. (1987). Family management in the prevention of morbidity of schizophrenia: social outcome of a two-year longitudinal study. *Psychological Medicine* **17**, 59–66.

Fallowfield, L. J., Baum, M., and Maguire, G. P. (1986). Effects of breast conservation on psychological morbidity associated with diagnosis and treatment of early breast cancer. *British Medical Journal* **293**, 1331–4.

Fallowfield, L. J., Baum, M., and Maguire, G. P. (1987). Addressing the psychological needs of the conservative treated breast cancer patient: discussion paper. *Journal of the Royal Society of Medicine* **80**, 696–700.

Falret, J. P. (1854). Mémoire sur la folie circulaire. *Bulletin de l'Academie de Médicine* **19**, 382–415. [Translated into English in Sedler, M. J., and Dessain,

E. C. (1983). Falret's discovery: the origin of the concept of bipolar affective illness. *American Journal of Psychiatry* **140** 1227–33.]

Fanshel, D. (1981). Decision-making under uncertainty: foster care for abused or neglected children? *American Journal of Public Health* **71**, 685–6.

Farde, L., Wiesel, F-A., Hall, H., Halldin, C., Stone-Elander, S., and Sedvall, G. (1987). No D₂ receptor increase in PET study of schizophrenia. *Archives of General Psychiatry* **44**, 671–2.

Farina, A., Barry, H., and Garmezy, N. (1963). Birth order of recovered and non-recovered schizophrenics. *Archives of General Psychiatry* **9**, 224–8.

Faris, R. E. L. and Dunham, H. W. (1939). *Mental disorders in urban areas*. Chicago University Press, Chicago.

Farmer, A., Jackson, R., McGuffin, P., and Storey, P. (1987). Cerebral ventricular enlargement in chronic schizophrenia: consistencies and contradictions. *British Journal of Psychiatry* **150**, 324–30.

Farrell, B. A. (1979). Mental illness: a conceptual analysis. *Psychological Medicine* **9**, 21–35.

Farrell, B. A. (1981). *The standing of psychoanalysis*. Oxford University Press.

Farrington, D. P., Biron, L., and Lerblue, M. (1982). Personality and delinquency. In *Abnormal offenders, delinquency and the criminal justice system* (ed. J. Gunn and D. P. Farrington). Wiley, Chichester.

Faulk, M. (1988). *Basic forensic psychiatry*. Blackwell, Oxford.

Faulstich, M. E. and Williamson, D. A. (1985). An overview of atopic dermatitis: toward a bio-behavioural integration. *Journal of Psychosomatic Research* **29**, 647–54.

Fawcett, J., Scheftner, W., Clark, D., Gibbens, R., and Coryell, W. (1987). Clinical predictors of suicide in patients with major affective disorders: a controlled prospective study. *American Journal of Psychiatry* **144**, 35–40.

Feighner, J. P., Robins, E., Guze, S. B., Woodruff, R. A., Winokur, G., and Munoz, R. (1972). Diagnostic criteria for use in psychiatric research. *Archives of General Psychiatry* **26**, 57–63.

Feingold, B. F. (1975). Hyperkinesis and learning difficulties linked to artificial food and colors. *American Journal of Nursing* **75**, 797–803.

Feinmann, C. and Harris M., (1984). Psychogenic facial pain. Part 1: The clinical presentation. *British Dental Journal* **156**, 165.

Feinmann, C., Harris, M., and Cawley, R. (1984). Psychogenic facial pain: presentation and treatment. *British Medical Journal* **288**, 436–8.

Feldman, F., Cantor, D., Soll, S., and Bachrach, W. (1967). Psychiatric study of a consecutive series of 34 patients with ulcerative colitis. *British Medical Journal* **iii**, 711–14.

Feldman, M. P. and McCulloch, M. J. (1979). *Homosexual behaviour, therapy and assessment*. Pergamon Press, Oxford.

Fenichel, O. (1945). *The psychoanalytic theory of neurosis*. Kegan Paul, Trench and Trubner, London.

Fenton, G. W. (1983). Epilepsy, personality and behaviour. In *Research progress in epilepsy* (ed. F. C. Rose). Pitman, Bath.

Fenton, G. W. (1986). Epilepsy and hysteria. *British Journal of Psychiatry* **149**, 28–37.

Fenton, W. S., Mosher, L. R., and Matthews, S. M. (1981). Diagnosis of schizophrenia: a critical review of current diagnostic systems. *Schizophrenia Bulletin* **7**, 452–76.

Ferdijae, W. E. (1978). Learning process in pain. In *The psychology of pain* (ed. R. A. Steinback). Raven Press, New York.

Fernando, S., and Storm, V. (1984). Suicide among psychiatric patients of a district general hospital. *Psychological Medicine* **14**, 661–72.

Ferrari, M. (1984). Chronic illness: psychosocial effects on siblings. *Journal of Child Psychology and Psychiatry* **25**, 459–76.

Ferreira, A. J. and Winter, W. D. (1965). Family interaction and decision making. *Archives of General Psychiatry* **13**, 214–23.

Ferrier, I. N., Roberts, G. W., Crow, T. J., *et al.* (1983). Reduced cholecystokinin-like and somatostatin-like immunoreactivity in limbic lobe is associated with negative symptoms of schizophrenia. *Life Sciences* **3**, 475–82.

Field, E. (1967). *A validation of Hewitt and Jenkins' hypothesis.* Home Office Research Unit Publication No. 10. HMSO, London.

Fielding, D., Moore, B., Dewey, M., Ashley, P., McKendrick, T., and Pinkerton, P. (1985). Children with end-stage renal failure: psychological effects on patients, siblings and parents. *Journal of Psychosomatic Research* **29**, 457–65.

Fieve, R. R., Platman, S. R., and Plutchik, R. R. (1968). The use of lithium in affective disorders: I. Acute endogenous depression. *American Journal of Psychiatry* **125**, 487–91.

Finkelhor, D. (1984). *Child sexual abuse: new theory and research*, Chapter 5, pp. 53–68. Free Press, London.

Firth, M. A. (1983). Diagnosis of Duchenne muscular dystrophy: experience of parents of sufferers. *British Medical Journal* **286**, 700–1.

Fischer, M. (1973). Genetic and environmental factors in schizophrenia: a study of twins and their families. *Acta Psychiatrica Scandinavica* Suppl. **238**.

Fish, F. J. (1974). *Clinical psychopathology* (revised by M. Hamilton). Wright, Bristol.

Fishbain, D. A., and Aldrich, T. E. (1985). Suicide pacts: international comparisons. *Journal of Clinical Psychiatry,* **46**, 11–15.

Fisher, C. (1984). Psychiatric aspects of shoplifting. *British Journal of Hospital Medicine* **27**, 209–12.

Fisher, C. M. and Adams, R. D. (1958). Transient global amnesia. *Transactions of the American Neurological Association* 143–6.

Fisher, C. M. and Adams, R. D. (1964). Transient global amnesia. *Acta Neurologica Scandinavica* Suppl. 9, 7–83.

Fisher, S. and Greenberg, R. P. (1977). *The scientific credibility of Freud's theories and therapy.* Basic Books, New York.

Fitzgerald, R. G. (1970). Reactions to blindness. *Archives of General Psychiatry* **22**, 370–9.

Fitzpatrick, R. and Hopkins, A. (1981). Referrals to neurologists for headaches not due to structural disease. *Journal of Neurology, Neurosurgery and Psychiatry* **44**, 1061–7.

Floud, J. and Young, W. (1981). *Dangerousness and criminal justice.* Heinemann, London.

Folks, D. G. and Freeman, A. M. (1985). Munchausen's syndrome and other factitious illness. *Psychiatric Clinics of North America* **8**, 263–78.

Follick, M. J., Smithy, T. W., and Turk, D. C. (1984). Psychosocial adjustment following ostomy. *Health Psychology* **3**, 505–17.

Folsom, J. C. (1967). Intensive hospital therapy for psychogeriatric patients. *Current Psychiatric Therapy* **7**, 209–15.

Folstein, M. F., Folstein, S. E., and McHugh, P. R. (1975). 'Mini-mental state'. A practical method for grading the cognitive state of patients for the clinician. *Journal of Psychiatric Research* **12**, 189–98.

Folstein, S. and Rutter, M. (1971). Infantile autism: a genetic study of 21 twin pairs. *Journal of Child Psychology and Psychiatry* **18**, 297–321.

Folstein, S. E., Abbott, M. H., Chase, G. A., Jensen, B. A., and Folstein, M. F. (1983). The association of affective disorder with Huntington's disease in a case series and in families. *Psychological Medicine* **13**, 537–42.

Foncin, J. F. and El Hachini, K. H. (1986). Neurofibrillary degeneration in Alzheimer's disease: a discussion with a contribution to aluminum pathology in man. In *Senile dementias: early detection* (ed. J. Bes, J. Cahn, R. Cahn, S. Hoyer, J. P. Marc-Vergnes, and H. M. Wisniewski), pp. 191–201. Eurotext, London.

Ford, C. S. and Beach, F. A. (1952). *Patterns of sexual behaviour.* Eyre and Spottiswoode, London.

Ford, M. J. (1986). The irritable bowel syndrome. *Journal of Psychosomatic Research* **30**, 399–401.

Ford, M. J., Eastwood, J., and Eastwood, M. A. (1982). The irritable bowel syndrome: soma and psyche. *Psychological Medicine* **12**, 705–8.

Fordyce, W. E. (1982). A behavioural perspective on chronic pain. *British Journal of Clinical Psychology* **21**, 313–20.

Forester, B., Kornfeld, D. S., and Fleiss, J. L. (1985). Psychotherapy during radiotherapy: effects on emotional and physical distress. *American Journal of Psychology* **142**, 22–7.

Forreyt, J. P., Goodrick, G. K., and Gotto, A. M. (1981). Limitations of behavioural treatment of obesity: review and analysis. *Journal of Behavioral Medicine* **4**, 159–74.

Foster, E. M., Kay, D. W. K., and Bergmann, K. (1976). The characteristics of old people receiving and needing domiciliary services. *Age and Ageing* **5**, 345–55.

Fottrell, E. (1980). A study of violent behaviour among patients in psychiatric hospitals. *British Journal of Psychiatry* **136**, 216–21.

Foulds, G. A. (1965). *Personality and personal illness.* Tavistock, London.

Foulds, G. A. (1976). *The hierarchical nature of personal illness.* Academic Press, London.

Foulkes, S. H. (1948). *Introduction to group-analytic psychotherapy.* Heinemann, London.

Foulkes, S. H. and Anthony, E. J. (1957). *Group psychotherapy: the psychoanalytic approach.* Penguin, Harmondsworth.

Foulkes, S. H. and Lewis, E. (1944). Group analysis: a study in the treatment of groups on psychoanalytic lines. *British Journal of Medical Psychology* **20**, 175–82.

Foundeur, M., Fixsen, C., Triebel, W. A., and White, M. A. (1957). Post-partum mental illness. *Archives of Neurology and Psychiatry* **77**, 503–12.

Fowler, R. C., Rich, C. L., and Young, D. (1986). San Diego suicide study. II. substance abuse in young cases. *Archives of General Psychiatry* **43**, 962–5.

Fox, B. H. (1978). Premorbid psychological factors as related to cancer incidence. *Journal of Behavioural Medicine* **1**, 45–133.

Fox, J. H., Ramsey, R. G., Huckman, M. S., and Proske, A. E. (1976). Cerebral ventricular enlargement. Chronic alcoholics examined by computerised tomography. *Journal of the American Medical Association* **236**, 365–8.

Frank, J. D., Bliedman, L. H., Imber, S. D., Nash, E. H., and Stone, A. R. (1957). Why patients leave psychotherapy. *Archives of Neurology and Psychiatry* **77**, 283–99.

Frank, J. D., Hoehn-Sarik, R., Imber, S. D., Liberman, B. L., and Stone, A. R. (1978). *Effective ingredients of successful psychotherapy.* Brunner-Mazel, New York.

Frank, R. G., Kashani, J. H., Kashani, S. R., Wanderlich, S. A., Umlauf, R. L., and Ashkazai, G. S. (1984). Psychological response to amputation as a function of age and time since amputation. *British Journal of Psychiatry* **144**, 493–7.

Frank, R. G., Elliott, T. R., Corcoran, J. R., and Wonderlich, S. A. (1987). Depression after spinal cord injury: is it necessary? *Clinical Psychology Review* **7**, 611–30.

Frank, O. S. (1985) Dysmorphophobia. In *Current themes in psychiatry* (ed. R. N. Gaind, F. I. Fawzy, B. L. Hudson, and R. O. Pasnau), Vol. 4. Medical and Scientific Books, New York.

Fras, I., Litin, E. M., and Pearson, J. S. (1967). Comparison of psychiatric symptoms in carcinoma of the pancreas with those in some other intra-abdominal neoplasms. *American Journal of Psychiatry* **123**, 1553–62.

Fraser, R. (1947). The incidence of neurosis among factory workers. *Industrial Health Research Board Report* Number 90. HMSO, London.

Frederiks, J. A. M. (1969). Disorders of the body schema. In *Handbook of clinical neurology* (ed. P. J. Vinken and G. W. Bruyn), Vol. 4, Chapter 11, pp. 207–40. North Holland, Amsterdam.

Freeman, C. P. L., and Kendell, R. E. (1980). ECT: patients' experiences and attitudes. *British Journal of Psychiatry* **137**, 8–16.

Freeman, C. P. L., Basson, J. V., and Crighton, A. (1978). Double blind controlled trial of electroconvulsive therapy (ECT) and simulated ECT in depressive illness. *Lancet* **i**, 738–40.

Freeman, C. P. L. Weeks, D., and Kendell, R. E. (1980). ECT: II patients who complain. *British Journal of Psychiatry* **137**, 17–25.

Freeman, H. (ed.) (1984). *Mental health and the environment*. Churchill Livingstone, Edinburgh.

Freeman, M. D. A. (1979). The law and sexual deviation. In *Sexual deviation* (ed. I. Rosen) (2nd edn). Oxford University Press, Oxford.

Freeman, W. and Watts, J. W. (1942). *Psychosurgery*. Thomas, Springfield, Ill.

Fremming, K. H. (1951). The expectation of mental infirmity in a sample of the Danish population. *Occasional Papers on Eugenics*, No. 7. Cassell, London.

Freud, A. (1936). *The ego and the mechanisms of defence*. Hogarth Press, London.

Freud, A. (1958). Adolescence. I. Adolescence in the psychoanalytic theory. In *The psychoanalytic study of the child* (ed. A. Freud) Vol. XIII. International University Press, New York.

Freud, A. (1966). *Normality and pathology in childhood: assessments of development*. Hogarth Press and Institute of Psychoanalysis, London.

Freud, S. (1893). On the psychical mechanisms of hysterical phenomena. *The standard edition of the complete psychological works* (ed. J. Strachey), Vol. 3, pp. 25–42. Hogarth Press, London.

Freud, S. (1895*a*). Obsessions and phobias, their psychical mechanisms and their aetiology. In *The standard edition of the complete psychological works* (ed. J. Strachey) Vol. 3. Hogarth Press, London.

Freud, S. (1895*b*). The justification for detaching from neurasthemia a particular syndrome: the anxiety neurosis. *Neurologisches Zentralblatt* **14**, 50–66. [Reprinted (translated J. Riviere) 1940 in Collected Papers **1**, 76–106.]

Freud, S. (1911). Psychoanalytic notes upon an autobiographic account of cases of paranoia. (Schreber.) In *The standard edition of the complete psychological works* (1958) Vol. 12, pp. 1–82. Hogarth Press, London.

Freud, S. (1914). *Psychopathology of everyday life*. Fisher Unwin, London.

Freud, S. (1917). Mourning and melancholia. *The standard edition of the complete psychological works*, Vol. 14, pp. 243–58. Hogarth Press, London.

Freud, S. (1923). Psychoanalysis. In *The standard edition of the complete psychological works*, Vol. 18, pp. 235–54. Hogarth Press, London.

Freud, S. (1927). Fetishism. *International Journal of Psychoanalysis* **9**, 161–6. Also in *The standard edition of the complete psychological works*, Vol. 21, pp. 147–57. Hogarth Press, London.

Freud, S. (1933). Anxiety and instinctual life. In *The standard edition of the complete psychological works* (ed. J. Strachey), Vol. 22. Hogarth Press, London.

Freud, S. (1935). *An autobiographic study*. Hogarth Press, London.

Friedhoff, A. and van Winkle, E. (1962). The characteristics of an amine found in the urine of schizophrenic patients. *Journal of Nervous and Mental Disease* **135**, 550–5.

Friedman, A. S. (1975). Interaction of drug therapy with marital therapy for depressed patients. *Archives of General Psychiatry* **32**, 619–37.

Friedman, D. E. L. (1966). A new technique for the systematic desensitization of phobic symptoms. *Behaviour Research and Therapy* **4**, 139–40.

Freidman, L. J. (1962). *Virgin wives: a study of unconsummated marriage*. Tavistock, London.

Friedman, M. and Rosenman, R. H. (1959). Association of specific behaviour pattern with blood and cardiovascular findings. *Journal of the American Medical Association* **169**, 1286–96.

Friedman, M., Thorensen, C. E., Gill, J. J., *et al.* (1982). Feasibility of altering type A behaviour pattern after myocardial infarction. Recurrent coronary prevention project study: methods, base line results and preliminary findings. *Circulation* **66**, 83–92.

Friedman, M., Thorensen, C. E., Gill, J. J. (1986). Alteration of Type A behaviour and its effect on cardiac recurrences in post myocardial infarction patients: summary results of the recurrent coronary prevention project. *American Heart Journal* **112**, 653–65.

Friedman, S. B., Chodoff, P., Mason, J. W., and Hamburg, D. A. (1963). Behavioural observations on patients anticipating the death of a child. *Pediatrics* **32**, 610–25.

Friedman, T. and Gath, D. (1988). The psychiatric consequences of spontaneous abortion. (In press.)

Fromm, E. (1942). *The fear of freedom*. Kegan Paul, London.

Fromm-Reichman, F. (1948). Notes on the development of treatment of schizophrenia by psychoanalytic psychotherapy. *Psychiatry* **11**, 263–73.

Furniss, T., Bingley-Miller, L., and Bentovim, A. (1984). Therapeutic approach to sexual abuse. *Archives of Disease in Childhood* **59**, 865–70.

Gale, E. and Ayer, W. A. (1969). Treatment of dental phobias. *Journal of the American Dental Association* **78**, 1304–7.

Ganser, S. J. (1898). Über einen eigenartigen hysterischen Dämmerzustand. *Archiv für Psychiatrie und Nervenkrankheiten* **30**, 633–40. [Translated by Schorer, C. E. in *British Journal of Criminology* **5**, 120–6 (1965).]

Garbarino, J., Guttman, E., and Seeley, J. W. (1986). *The psychologically battered child*. Jossey Bass, London.

Gardner, R. (1970). Deaths in United Kingdom opioid users 1965–69. *Lancet* **ii**, 650–3.

Gardner, R., Hanka, R., O'Brien, V. C., Page, A. J. F., and Rees, R. (1977). Psychological and social evaluation in cases of deliberate self-poisoning admitted to a general hospital. *British Medical Journal* **ii**, 1567–70.

Garfield, S. L. (1980). *Psychotherapy: an eclectic approach*. Wiley, New York.

Garfield, S. L. and Bergin, A. E. (eds.) (1986). *Handbook of psychotherapy and behaviour change* (3rd edn). Wiley, New York.

Garfinkel, B. D., Froese, A., and Hood, J. (1982). Suicide attempts in children and adolescents. *American Journal of Psychiatry* **139**, 1257–61.

Garfinkel, P. E. and Garner, D. N. (1982). *Anorexia nervosa: a multidimensional perspective*. Brunner-Mazel, New York.

Garfinkel, P. E., Modofsky, H., and Garner, D. N. (1980*a*). The heterogeneity of anorexia nervosa. *Archives of General Psychiatry* **37**, 1036–40.

Garfinkel, P. E., Stancer, H. C., and Persad, E. (1980*b*). A comparison of haloperidol, lithium carbonate and their combination in the treatment of mania. *Journal of Affective Disorders* **2**, 279–88.

Garner, D. M. (1981). Body image in anorexia nervosa. *Canadian Journal of Psychiatry* **26**, 224–7.

Garner, D. M. and Garfinkel, P. E. (1980). Socio-cultural factors in the development of anorexia nervosa. *Psychological Medicine* **10**, 647–56.

Garraway, M. (1985). Stroke rehabilitation units: concepts, evaluation and unresolved issues. *Stroke* **16**, 178–81.

Garrick, T. R. and Stottard, N. L. (1982). How to write a psychiatric consultation. *American Journal of Psychiatry* **139**, 849–55.

Garver, D. E. and Davis, L. M. (1979). Biogenic amine hypothesis of affective disorders. *Life Science* **24**, 383–94.

Gastaut, M. (1969). Clinical and electroencephalographic classification of epileptic seizures. *Epilepsia* Suppl. **10**, 2–21.

Gath, A. (1978). *Down's syndrome and the family*. Academic Press, London.

Gath, A. (1984). Emotional abuse. *Journal of Maternal and Child Health* **9**, 229–32.

Gath, A. and Gumley, D. (1986). Behaviour problems in retarded children with special reference to Down's syndrome. *British Journal of Psychiatry* **149**, 156–61.

Gath, D. (1980). Psychiatric aspects of hysterectomy. In *The social consequences of psychiatric illness* (ed. L. Bosin *et al.*). Brunner-Mazel, New York.

Gath, D. and Cooper, P. (1982). Psychiatric aspects of hysterectomy and female sterilisation. In *Recent advances in psychiatry* (ed. K. Granville-Grossman),Vol. 4. Churchill Livingstone, Edinburgh.

Gath, D. and Iles, S. (1988). Treating the premenstrual syndrome. *British Medical Journal* **297**, 237–8.

Gath, D., Hensman, C., Hawker, A., Kelly, M., and Edwards, G. (1968). The drunk in court: survey of drunkenness offenders from two London courts. *British Medical Journal* **iv**, 808–11.

Gath, D., Cooper. P., Gattoni, F., and Rockett, D. (1977). *Child guidance and delinquency in a London Borough*. Maudsley Monograph No. 24. Oxford University Press, London.

Gath, D., Cooper, P., and Day, A. (1982*a*). Hysterectomy and psychiatric disorder: I. Levels of psychiatric morbidity before and after hysterectomy. *British Journal of Psychiatry* **140**, 335–42.

Gath, D., Cooper, P., Bond, A., and Edmonds, G. (1982*b*). Hysterectomy and psychiatric disorder: II. Demographic psychiatric and physical factors in relation to psychiatric outcome. *British Journal of Psychiatry* **140**, 343–50.

Gath, D., Osborn, M., Bungay, G., Iles, S., Day, A., Bond, A., and Passingham, C. (1987). Psychiatric disorder and gynaecological symptoms in middle-aged women: a community survey. *British Medical Journal* **24**, 213–18.

Gath, D. H., Hassall, C., and Cross, K. W. (1973). Whither psychiatric day care? *British Medical Journal* **1**, 94–8.

Gaupp, R. (1914). The scientific significance of the case of Ernst Wagner. In

Themes and variations in European psychiatry (ed. S. R. Hirsch and M. Shepherd) pp. 121–33 (1974).

Gayford, J. J. (1979). Battered wives. *British Journal of Hospital Medicine* **22**, 496–503.

Gayford, J. J. (1981). Indecent exposure: a review of the literature. *Medicine, Science and the Law* **21**, 233–42.

Gazzard, R. G., Davis, M., Spooner, J., and Williams, R. (1976). Why do people use paracetamol for suicide? *British Medical Journal* i, 212–13.

Gebhard, P. H., Raboch, J., and Giese, H. (1970). *The sexuality of women* (translated by C. Bearne). André Deutsch, London.

Gelder, M. G. (1978). Hormones and post partum depression. In *Mental illness in pregnancy and the puerperium* (ed. M. Sandler). Oxford University Press, Oxford.

Gelder, M. G. (1986*a*). Neurosis: another tough old word. *British Medical Journal* **292**, 972–3.

Gelder, M. G. (1986*b*). Panic disorder: new approaches to an old problem. *British Journal of Psychiatry* **149**, 346–52.

Gelder, M. G., Marks, I. M., and Wolff, H. (1967). Desensitization and psychotherapy in phobic states: a controlled enquiry. *British Journal of Psychiatry* **113**, 53–73.

Gelder, M. G., Bancroft, J. H. J., Gath, D. H., Johnston, D. H., Matthews, A. M., and Shaw, P. M. (1973). Specific and non-specific factors in behaviour therapy. *British Journal of Psychiatry* **123**, 445–62. .

Gelter, J. L. and Bertsch, G. (1985). Fire-setting behaviour in the histories of a state hospital population. *American Journal of Psychiatry* **12**, 283–99.

General Register Office (1968). A glossary of mental disorders. *Studies on Medical and Population Subjects 22*. HMSO, London.

Gerbert, B. (1980). Psychological aspects of Crohn's disease. *Journal of Behavioral Medicine* **3**, 41–58.

German, G. A. (1972). Aspects of clinical psychiatry in Sub-Saharan Africa. *British Journal of Psychiatry* **121**, 461–79.

German. G. A. and Arya, O. P. (1969). Psychiatric morbidity amongst a Uganda student population. *British Journal of Psychiatry* **115**, 1323–9.

Gershon, E. S. and Bunney, W. E. (1976). The question of linkage in manic depressive illness. *Journal of Psychiatric Research* **13**, 99–117.

Gershon, E. S., Mark, A., Cohen, N., Belizon, N., Barron, M., and Knobe, K. E. (1975). Transmitted factors in the morbidity of affective disorders: a controlled study. *Journal of Psychiatric Research* **12**, 283–99.

Gibb, W. R. G. and Lees, A. J. (1985). The neuroleptic malignant syndrome—a review. *Quarterly Journal of Medicine* **56**, 421–9.

Gibbens, T. C. N. and Prince, J. (1965). *Child victims of sex offences*. Institute for the Study and Treatment of Delinquency, London.

Gibbens, T. C. N. and Robertson, G. (1985). Survey of criminal careers of hospital order patients. *British Journal Psychiatry* **143**, 362–9.

Gibbens, T. C. N., Pond, D. A., and Stafford Clark, D. A. (1959). A follow-up study of criminal psychopaths. *Journal of Mental Science* **105**, 108–15.

Gibbens, T. C. N., Palmer, C., and Prince, J. (1971). Mental health aspects of shoplifting. *British Medical Journal* iii, 612–15.

Gibbens, T. C. N., Way, C., and Soothill, K. L. (1977). Behavioural types of rape. *British Journal of Psychiatry* **130**, 32–42.

Gibbons, J. S., Butler, J., Urwin, P., and Gibbons, J. L. (1978). Evaluation of a social work service for self-poisoning patients. *British Journal of Psychiatry* **133**, 111–18.

Gibbs, C. J., Gajdusek, D. C., Asher, D. M., Alpers, M. P., Beck, E., Daniel, P.M., and Mathews, W. B. (1968). Creutzfeldt-Jacob disease (spongiform encephalopathy): transmission to the chimpanzee. *Science* **161**, 388–9.

Gibson, A. J., Moyes, I. C. A., and Kendrick, D. (1980). Cognitive assessment of the elderly long stay patient. *British Journal of Psychiatry* **137**, 551–7.

Gibson, E. (1975). Homicide in England and Wales. 1967–71. *Home Office Research Study* No. 31. HMSO, London.

Gibson, S. and Becker, J. (1973). Changes in alcoholics' self-reported depression. *Quarterly Journal of Studies on Alcohol* **34**, 829–36.

Gillespie, R. D. (1928). Hypochondria: definition, nosology and psychopathology. *Guy's Hospital Reports* **78**, 408–60.

Gillespie, R. D. (1929). Clinical differentiation of types of depression. *Guy's Hospital Reports* **79**, 306–44.

Gillies, N. (1976). Homicide in the west of Scotland. *British Journal of Psychiatry* **128**, 105–27.

Gittelman, R. (1985). Controlled trials of remedial approaches to reading disability. *Journal of Child Psychology and Psychiatry* **6**, 843–6.

Gittelson, N. L., Eacott, S. E., and Mehta, B. M. (1978). Victims of indecent exposure. *British Journal of Psychiatry* **132**, 61–6.

Gjessing, R. (1947). Biological investigations in endogenous psychoses. *Acta Psychiatrica* (Kbh) Suppl. 47.

Glaister, B. (1982) Muscle relaxation training for fear reduction of patients with psychological problems: a review on controlled studies. *Behaviour Research and Therapy* **20**, 493–504.

Glaser, G. H. (1972). Diphenylhydantoin toxicity. In *Antiepileptic drugs* (ed. M. Dixon, J. Woodbury, J. Kiffin Penry, and R. P. Schmidt), Chapter 20. Raven Press, London.

Glatt, M. M. (1976). Alcoholism: disease concept and lack of control revisited. *British Journal of Addiction* **71**, 135–44.

Glen, A. I. M., Doig, M., Hulme, E. B., and Kreitman, N. (1979). Mortality on lithium. *Neuropsychobiology* **5**, 167–73.

Glen, A. I. M., Johnson, A. L., and Shepherd, M. (1984). Continuation therapy with lithium and amitriptyline in unipolar depressive illness: a randomized, double-blind controlled trial. *Psychological Medicine* **14**, 37–50.

Glickman, L. S. (1980). *Psychiatric consultation in the general hospital.* Marcel Dekker, New York.

Glue, P. W., Nutt, D. J., Cowen, P. J., and Broadbent, D. (1987). Selective effects of lithium on cognitive performance in man. *Psychopharmacology* **91**, 109–11.

Godfrey, H. P. D. and Knight, R. G. (1987). Interventions for amnesics: a review. *British Journal of Clinical Psychology* **26**, 83–91.

Goffman, E. (1961). *Asylums: essays on the social situation of mental patients and other inmates.* Doubleday, New York.

Göktepe, E. O., Young, L. B., and Bridges, P. K. (1975). A further review of the results of stereotactic tractotomy. *British Journal of Psychiatry* **126**, 270–81.

Goldberg, D. (1972). *The detection of psychiatric illness by questionnaire.* Maudsley Monograph No. 21. Oxford University Press, London.

Goldberg, D. (1986). Implementation of mental health policies in the North West of England. In *The provision of mental health services in Britain* (ed. G. Wilkinson and H. Freeman). Gaskell, London.

Goldberg, D. and Blackwell, B. (1970). Psychiatric illness in general practice. A detailed study using a new method of case identification. *British Medical Journal* **ii**, 439–43.

Goldberg, D. and Huxley, P. (1980). *Mental illness in the community*. Tavistock, London.

Goldberg, D., Richels, J., Downing, R., and Hesbacher, P. (1976). A comparison of two psychiatric screening tests. *British Journal of Psychiatry* **129**, 61–7.

Goldberg, E. M. and Morrison, S. L. (1963). Schizophrenia and social class. *British Journal of Psychiatry* **109**, 785–802.

Goldberg, I., Reglier, D., and McInery, T. K. (1929). The role of the pediatrician in the delivery of the mental health services to children. *Pediatrics* **63**, 898–909.

Goldfried, M. R. and Goldfried, A. P. (1975). Cognitive change methods. In *Helping people change* (ed. F. H. Kafner and A. P. Goldstein). Pergamon Press, London.

Goldiamond, I. (1965). Self-control procedures in personal behaviour problems. *Psychological Reports* **17**, 851–68.

Goldstein, A., Aronow, L., and Kalman, S. M. (1974). *Principles of drug action: the basis of pharmacology* (2nd edn). Wiley, New York.

Goldstein, K. (1944). Methodological approach to the study of schizophrenic thought disorder. In *Language and thought in schizophrenia* (ed. J. S. Kasanin). University of California Press, Berkeley.

Goldstein, K. (1975). Functional disturbance in brain damage. In *American handbook of psychiatry*, (ed. S. Arieti and M. F. Reisser) (2nd edn), Vol. 4 Basic Books, New York.

Goldstein, K. and Scheerer, M. (1941). Abstract and concrete behaviour: an experimental study with special tests. *Psychological Monographs* **53** No. 239.

Gomez, J. (1975). Subjective side-effects of E. C. T. *British Journal of Psychiatry* **127**, 609–11.

Gomez, J. and Dally, P. (1977). Psychologically mediated abdominal pain in surgical and medical out-patient clinics. *British Medical Journal* i, 1451–3.

Goodstein, R. K. and Page, A. W. (1981). Battered wife syndrome: overview of dynamics and treatment. *American Journal of Psychiatry* **1387**, 1036–44.

Goodwin, D. W. (1971). Is alcoholism hereditary? *Archives of General Psychiatry* **25**, 545–9.

Goodwin, D. W. (1985). Alcoholism and genetics. *Archives of General Psychiatry* **42**, 171–4.

Goodwin, F. K. and Zis, A. O. (1979). Lithium in the treatment of mania: comparisons with neuroleptics. *Archives of General Psychiatry* **36**, 840–4.

Goodwin, F. K., Murphy, D. L., and Bunney, W. E. (1969). Lithium carbonate treatment in depression and mania: a longitudinal double blind study. *Archives of General Psychiatry* **21**, 486–96.

Goodwin, F. K., Schulsinger, F., Hermansen, L., Guze, S. B., and Winokur, G. (1973). Alcohol problems in adoptees raised apart from alcoholic biological parents. *Archives of General Psychiatry* **28**, 238–43.

Goodwin, F. K., Prange, A. J., Post, R. M., Muscettola, G., and Lipton, M. A. (1982). Potentiation of antidepressant effects by 1-triiodothyronine in tricyclic non-responders. *American Journal of Psychiatry* **139**, 34–8.

Goodyer, I. and Taylor, D. C. (1985). Hysteria. *Archives of Diseases in Childhood* **60**, 680–1.

Gossop, M. (1978). A review of the evidence for methadone maintenance as a treatment for narcotic addiction. *Lancet* i, 812–15.

Gossop, M. (1981). *Theories of neurosis*. Springer, Berlin.

Gossop, M., Green, L., Phillips, G., and Bradley, B. (1987). What happens to opiate addicts immediately after treatment: a prospective follow-up study. *British Medical Journal* **294**, 1377–80.

Gostin, L. (1983). *The court of protection*. Mind, London.

Gostin, L. (1985). *Secure provision* (ed. L. Gostin). Tavistock, London.

Gottesman, I. and Shields, J. A. (1967). A polygenic theory of schizophrenia. *Proceedings of the National Academy of Science* **58**, 199–205.

Gottesman, I. and Shields, J. A. (1972). *Schizophrenia and genetics; a twin study vantage point*. Academic Press, New York.

Gottesman, I. I., McGuffin, P., and Farmer, A. E. (1987). Clinical genetics as clues to the 'real' genetics of schizophrenia. *Schizophrenia Bulletin* **13**, 22–47.

Grad, J. and Sainsbury, P. (1966). Evaluating the community psychiatric service in Chichester: results. *Millbank Research Fund Quarterly* **44**, 246–77.

Graham, J. D. P. (ed.) (1976). *Cannabis and health*. Academic Press, London.

Graham, P. (1974). Depression in prepubertal children. *Developmental Medicine and Child Neurology* **16**, 340–9.

Graham, P. (1986). *Child psychiatry: a developmental approach*. Oxford University Press, Oxford.

Graham, P. and Rutter, M. (1968). Organic brain dysfunction and child psychiatric disorder. *British Medical Journal* **iii**, 695–700.

Graham, P. and Rutter, M. (1970). Psychiatric aspects of physical disorder. In *Education, health and behaviour* (ed. M. Rutter, J. Tizard, and K. Whitmore). Longman, London.

Graham, P. and Rutter, M. (1973). Psychiatric disorder in the young adolescent: a follow-up study. *Proceedings of the Royal Society of Medicine* **66**, 1226–9.

Graham, P. and Stevenson, J. (1987). Temperament and psychiatric disorder: the genetic contribution to behaviour in childhood. *Australian and New Zealand Journal of Psychiatry* **21**, 267–74.

Graham, P. S. (1982). Late paraphrenia. *British Journal of Hospital Medicine* **27**, 522–8.

Grahame-Smith, D. G., Green, A. R., and Costain, D. W. (1978). Mechanisms of the antidepressant action of electroconvulsive therapy. *Lancet* **i**, 254–6.

Gralnick, A. (1942). Folie à deux. The psychosis of association. *Psychiatric Quarterly* **16**, 230–63.

Grant, I., Heaton, R. K., McSweeny, J., Adams, K. M., and Timms, R. M. (1982). Neuropsychological findings in hypoxemic chronic obstructive pulmonary disease. *Archives of Internal Medicine* **142**, 1470–6.

Gray, J. A. (1971). *The psychology of fear and stress*. Weidenfeld and Nicholson, London.

Green, A. R. and Costain, D. W. (1979). The biochemistry of depression. In *Psychopharmacology of affective disorders* (ed. E. S. Paykel and A. Coppen). Oxford University Press, Oxford.

Green, A. R. and Costain, D. W. (1981). *Pharmacology and biochemistry of psychiatric disorders*. Wiley, Chichester.

Green, A. R., and Goodwin, G. M. (1986). Antidepressants and mono-amines: actions and interactions. In *The biology of depression* (ed. J. F. W. Deakin), pp. 174–89. Gaskell, London.

Green, J. R., Troupin, A. S., Halpern, L. M., Friel, P., and Kanarek, P. (1974). Sulthiame: evaluation as an anticonvulsant. *Epilepsia* **15**, 329–49.

Green, R. (1974). *Sexual identity conflict in children and adults*. Duckworth, London.

Green, R. (1985). Atypical psychosexual development. In *Child and adolescent psychiatry* (ed. M. Rutter and L. Hersov) (2nd edn). Blackwell, Oxford.

Green, R. and Money, J. (1961). Effeminacy in prepubertal boys: summary of eleven cases and recommendations for case management. *Pediatrics* **27**, 286–91.

Green, R. and Money, J. (1969). *Transsexualism and sex reassignment*. Johns Hopkins Press, Baltimore.

Green, W. H., Campbell, M., and David, R. (1984). A comparison of schizophrenic and autistic children. *Journal of the American Academy of Child Psychiatry* **23**, 399–409.

Greenblatt, M., Grosser, G. H., and Wechsler, H. (1964). Differential response of hospitalized patients to somatic therapy. *American Journal of Psychiatry* **120**, 935–43.

Greenson, R. R. (1967). *The techniques and practice of psychoanalysis.* Hogarth Press, London.

Greer, H. S., Lal, S., Lewis, S. C., Belsey, E. M., and Beard, R. W. (1976). Psychosocial consequences of therapeutic abortion. *British Journal of Psychiatry* **128**, 74–9.

Greer, S. (1969). The prognosis of anxiety states. In *Studies in Anxiety* (ed. M. H. Lader), pp. 151–7. Royal Medicopsychological Association, London.

Greer, S. (1985). Cancer: psychiatric aspects. In *Recent advances in psychiatry* (ed. K. Granville-Grossman), Vol. 5. Churchill Livingstone, Edinburgh.

Greer, S. and Bagley, C. (1971). Effects of psychiatric intervention in attempted suicide: a controlled study. *British Medical Journal* **i**, 310–12.

Greer, S. and Cawley, R. H. (1966). *Some observations on the natural history of neurotic illness.* Australian Medical Medical Association. Mervyn Archdall Medical Monograph No. 3. Australasian Medical Publishing Company.

Greer, S. Marcus, T., and Pettingale, K. W. (1979). Psychological response to breast cancer: effect on outcome. *Lancet* **ii**, 785–7.

Gregory, S., Shawcross, C. R., and Gill, D. (1985) The Nottingham ECT study: a double blind comparison of bilateral, unilateral and simulated ECT in depressive illness. *British Journal of Psychiatry* **146**, 520–4.

Griesinger, W. (1867). *Mental pathology and therapeutics* (translated from the German 2nd edn by C. Lockhart Robertson and J. Rutherford). New Sydenham Society, London.

Griffin, J. C., Ricketts, M. S., Williams, D. E., Locke, B. J., Altmeyer, B. K., and Stark, M. T. (1987). A community survey of self-injurious behavior among developmentally disabled children and adolescents. *Hospital and Community Psychiatry* **38**, 959–63.

Griffin, N., Draper, R. J., and Webb, M. G. T. (1981). Addiction to tranylcypromine. *British Medical Journal* **283**, 346.

Gross, M. M., Rosenblatt, S. M., Lewis, E., Malenowski, B., and Broman, M. (1971). Hallucinations and clouding of sensorium during alcohol withdrawal. *Quarterly Journal of Studies on Alcohol* **32**, 1061–9.

Grundy, E. (1987). Community care for the elderly 1976–84. *British Medical Journal* **294**, 626–9.

Guerrant, J., Anderson, W. W., Fischer, A., Weinstein, M. R., Jaros, R. M., and Deskins, A. (1962). *Personality in epilepsy.* Thomas, Springfield, Ill.

Guggenheim, F. G. (1986). Psychological aspects of surgery. *Advances in psychosomatic medicine*, Vol. 15. Karger, Basel.

Gulleminault, C. and Mandini, S. (1984). Sleep disorders. In *Recent advances in clinical neurology* (ed. W. B. Mathews and G. H. Glaser). Churchill Livingstone, Edinburgh.

Gunn, J. (1977*a*). *Epileptics in prison.* Academic Press, London.

Gunn, J. (1977*b*). Criminal behaviour and mental disorder. *British Journal of Psychiatry* **130**, 317–29.

Gunn, J. (1979). Forensic psychiatry. In *Recent advances in clinical psychiatry* (ed. K. Granville-Grossman), Vol. 3. Churchill Livingstone, Edinburgh.

Gunn, J. (1985*a*). Sexual offenders. In *Current themes in psychiatry* (ed. R. N.

Gaind, A. Fawzy, B. L. Hudson, and R. O. Pasnau), Vol. 4. Spectrum, New York.

Gunn, J. (1985*b*). The role of psychiatry in prisons and the right to punishment. In *Psychiatry, human rights and the law* (ed. M. Roth and R. Bluglass). Cambridge University Press, Cambridge.

Gunn, J. and Farrington, D. P. (1982) *Abnormal offenders: delinquency and the criminal justice system.* Wiley, Chichester.

Gunn, J. and Fenton, G. W. (1971). Epilepsy, automatism and crime. *Lancet* **i**, 1173–6.

Gunn, J. and Robertson, G. (1982). An evaluation of Grendon Prison. In *Abnormal offenders, delinquency and the criminal justice system* (ed. J. Gunn and D. P. Farrington). Wiley, Chichester.

Gupta, M. A., Gupta, A. K., and Haberman, H. F. (1987*a*). The self-inflicted dermatoses: a critical review. *General Hospital Psychiatry* **9**, 45–52.

Gupta, M. A., Gupta, A. K., and Haberman, H. F. (1987*b*). Psoriasis and psychiatry: an update. *General Hospital Psychiatry* **9**, 157–66.

Gur, R. E. (1986). Cognitive aspects of schizophrenia. *Psychiatry update: the American Psychiatric Association annual review.* (ed. A. J. Frances and R. E. Hales), Vol. 5. American Psychiatric press, Washington, DC.

Gurland, B., *et al.* (1979). A cross-national comparison of the institutionalised elderly in the cities of New York and London. *Psychological Medicine* **9**, 781–8.

Gurman, A. S. (1979). Research on marital and family therapy: progress, perspective and prospect. In *Handbook of psychotherapy and behaviour change* (ed. S. L. Garfield and A. E. Bergin) (2nd edn). Wiley, New York.

Gurman, A. S., Kniskern, D. P., and Pinsof, W. M. (1986). Research on the process and outcome of marital and family therapy. In *Handbook of psychotherapy and behaviour change* (ed. S. Garfield and A. E. Bergin) (3rd edn). Wiley, New York.

Gusella, J. F., Wexler, N. S., Conneally, P. M., *et al.* (1983). Polymorphic DNA marker genetically linked to Huntington's disease. *Nature* **306**, 234–8.

Gussow, Z. (1963). A preliminary report of kayak-angst among the eskimo of west Greenland: a study in sensory deprivation. *International Journal of Social Psychiatry* **9**, 18–26.

Guttman, E. and Maclay, W. S. (1936). Mescalin and depersonalization; therapeutic experiments. *Journal of Neurology and Psychopathology* **16**, 193–212.

Guze, S. B. (1976). *Criminality and psychiatric disorders.* Oxford University Press, New York.

Guze, S. B. Woodruff, R. A., and Clayton, P. J. (1971). 'Secondary' affective disorder: a study of 95 cases. *Psychological Medicine* **1**, 426–8.

Guze, S. B., Cloninger, C. R., Martin, R. L., and Clayton, P. J. (1986). A follow-up and family study of Briquets' syndrome. *British Journal of Psychiatry* **149**, 17–23.

Hachinski, V., Lassen, N. A., and Marshall, J. (1974). Multi-infarct dementia. *Lancet* **ii**, 207–9.

Hachinski, V. C., Iliff, L. D., and Zilkha, E. (1975). Cerebral blood flow in dementia. *Archives of Neurology* **32**, 632–7.

Hackett, T. P. and Cassem, N. H. (1978). *Handbook of general hospital psychiatry.* Mosby, St. Louis.

Hackett, T. P. and Weissman, A. (1962). The treatment of the dying. *Current Psychiatric Therapy* **2**, 121–6.

Häfner, H. (1987*a*). Do we still need beds for psychiatric patients? *Acta Psychiatrica Scandinavica* **75**, 113–26.

Häfner, H. (1987b). The concept of disease in psychiatry. *Psychological Medicine* **17**, 11–14.

Häfner, H. and Reimann, H. (1970). Spatial distribution of mental disorders in Mannheim. In *Psychiatric epidemiology* (ed. E. H. Hare and J. K. Wing). Oxford University Press, London.

Hagnell, O. (1966). *A prospective study of the incidence of mental disorder*. Scandinavian University Books, Denmark.

Hagnell, O. (1970). Incidence and duration of episodes of mental illness in a total population. In *Psychiatric epidemiology* (ed. E. H. Hare and J. K. Wing). Oxford University Press, London.

Hagnell, O., Lanke, J., Rorsman, B., Ohhmon, R., and Ojesjo (1983). Current trends in the incidence of senile and multiinfarct dementia. *Archiv für Psychiatrie und Nervenkrankheiten* **233**, 423–38.

Hakim, S. and Adams, R. D. (1965). The special problem of symptomatic hydrocephalus with normal cerebrospinal fluid pressures: observations on cerebrospinal fluid hydrodynamics. *Journal of Neurological Sciences* **2**, 307–27.

Haley, J. (1963). *Strategies of psychotherapy*. Grune and Stratton, New York.

Hall, G. S. and Lindzey, G. (1980). *Theories of personality* (3rd edn). Wiley, Chichester.

Hall, J. (1983). Ward based rehabilitation programmes. In *Theory and practice of psychiatric rehabilitation* (ed. F. N. Watts and D. H. Bennett). Wiley, Chichester.

Hall, R. C. W. (1980). *Psychiatric presentation of medical illness: somatopsychic disorders*. MTP, Lancaster.

Hall, R. C. W., Gardner, E. R., Stickney, S. K., Lecann, A. F., and Popkin, M. K. (1980). Physical illness manifesting as psychiatric disease II: analysis of a state hospital in-patient population. *Archives of General Psychiatry* **37**, 989–95.

Hallam, R., Rachman, S., and Hinchcliffe, R. (1984). Psychological aspects of tinnitis. In *Contributions to medical psychology* (ed. S. Rachman), Vol. 3. Pergamon, Oxford.

Haller, R. M. and Deluty, R. H. (1988). Assaults on staff by psychiatric in-patients: a critical review. *British Journal of Psychiatry* **152**, 174–9.

Hallett, E. C. and Pilowsky, I. (1982). The response to treatment in a multidisciplinary pain clinic. *Pain* **12**, 365–4.

Hallgren, B. (1960). Nocturnal enuresis in twins. *Acta Psychiatrica Scandinavica* **35**, 73–90.

Halliday, J. L. (1937). Epidemiology and the psychosomatic affections: a study in social medicine. *Lancet* **ii** 185–91.

Hallstrom, C. (1985). Benzodiazepines: clinical practice and central mechanisms. In *Recent advances in psychiatry* (ed. K. Granville-Grossman), Vol. 5. Churchill Livingstone, Edinburgh.

Hamburg, D. A. and Adams, J. E. (1967). A perspective on coping behaviour. *Archives of General Psychiatry* **17**, 277–84.

Hamburg, D. A., Artz, P., Reiss, E., Amspacker, W., and Chambers, R. E. (1953). Clinical importance of emotional problems in the care of patients with burns. *New England Journal of Medicine* **248**, 355–9.

Hamilton, J. A. (1962). *Post partum psychiatric problems*. Mosby, St. Louis.

Hamilton, J. R. (1987a). Violence and victims: the contribution of victimiology to forensic psychiatry. *Lancet* **i**, 147–50.

Hamilton, J. R. (1987b). The management of psychopathic offenders. *British Journal of Hospital Medicine* **38**, 245–50.

Hamilton, J. R. and Freeman, H (1982). *Dangerousness: psychiatric assessment and management*. Gaskell, London.

Hamilton, J. R., Griffith, A., Ritson, E. B., and Aitken, R. C. B. (1977). A detoxification unit for habitual drunken offenders. *Health Bulletin* **35**, 146–54.

Hamilton, M. (ed.) (1984). *Fish's schizophrenia* (3rd edn). Wright, Bristol.

Hamilton, M. (ed.) (1985). *Fish's clinical psychopathology* (2nd edn). Wright, Bristol.

Hampson, J. L. and Hampson, J. G. (1961). The ontogenesis of sexual behaviour in man. In *Sex and internal secretions* (ed. W. C. Young) (3rd edn). Johns Hopkins Press, Baltimore.

Hans, M. and Koeppen, A. H. (1980). Huntington's chorea: its impact on the spouse. *Journal of Nervous and Mental Disease* **168**, 209–14.

Hanson, D. R., Gottesman, I. I., and Heston, L. L. (1976). Some possible childhood indications of adult schizophrenia inferred from children of schizophrenics. *British Journal of Psychiatry* **129**, 142–54.

Hanson, J. W., Jones, K. L., and Smith, D. W. (1976). Fetal alcohol syndrome: an experiment with 41 patients. *Journal of the American Medical Association* **235**, 1458–60.

Harding, C. M., Zubin, J., and Strauss, J. S. (1987). Chronicity in schizophrenia: fact, partial fact, or artifact? *Hospital and Community Psychiatry* **38**, 477–86.

Hardy, J., Adolfsson, R., and Alafuzuff, I. (1985). Transmitter deficits in Alzheimer's disease. *Neurochemistry International* **7**, 545–63.

Hare, E. H. (1956*a*). Mental illness and social conditions in Bristol. *Journal of Mental Science* **102**, 349–57.

Hare, E. H. (1956*b*). Family setting and the urban distribution of schizophrenia. *Journal of Mental Science* **102**, 753–60.

Hare, E. H. (1959). The origin and spread of dementia paralytica. *Journal of Mental Science* **105**, 594–626.

Hare, E. H. (1973). A short note on pseudo-hallucinations. *British Journal of Psychiatry* **122**, 469–76.

Hare, E. H. (1975). Season of birth in schizophrenia and neurosis. *American Journal of Psychiatry* **132**, 1168–71.

Hare, E. H. and Shaw, G. K. (1965). *Mental health on a new housing estate: a comparative study of two districts of Croydon*. Maudsley Monographs No. 12, Oxford University Press, London.

Harper, C. and Kril, J. (1985). Brain atrophy in chronic alcoholic patients: a quantitative pathological study. *Journal of Neurology, Neurosurgery and Psychiatry* **48**, 211–17.

Harris, A. I., Cox, E., and Smith, C. R. W. (1971). Handicapped and impaired in Great Britain, Part 1. *Office of Population Censuses and Surveys* . HMSO, London.

Harris, E. L. and Fitzgerald, J. D. (1970). *The principles and practice of clinical trials*. Livingstone, Edinburgh.

Harris, P. (1982). The symptomatology of abnormal appearance: an anecdotal survey. *British Journal of Plastic Surgery* **35**, 312–13.

Harrison, G. (1980). The abuse of anti-cholinergic drugs in adolescents. *British Journal of Psychiatry* **137**, 494–6.

Hartmann, H. (1964). *Essays on ego psychology*. Hogarth Press, London.

Hartman, V. (1965). Notes on group therapy with pedophiles. *Canadian Psychiatric Association Journal* **10**, 283–8.

Harvey, R. F., Mauad, E. C., and Brown, A. M. (1987). Prognosis in the irritable bowel syndrome: a five-year prospective study. *Lancet* **ii**, 963–5.

Harvey Smith, E. A. and Cooper, B. (1970). Patterns of neurotic illness in the community. *Journal of the Royal College of General Practitioners* **19**, 132–9.

Haug, J. O. (1962). Pneumoencephalographic studies in mental disease. *Acta Psychiatrica Scandinavica* Suppl. **165**, 1–114.

Havard, J. D. J. (1977). Alcohol and road accidents. In *Alcoholism: new knowledge and new responses* (ed. G. Edwards and M. Grant). Croom Helm, London.

Havdala, H. S., Borison, R. L., and Diamond, B. T. (1979). Potential hazards and applications of lithium in anesthesiology. *Anesthesiology* **50**, 534–7.

Hawker, A. (1978). *Adolescents and alcohol*. Edsall, London.

Hawkins, C. (1985). *Mishap or malpractice?* Blackwell, Oxford.

Hawthorne, M. and O'Connor, S. (1987). The psychological side of tinnitus. *British Medical Journal* **294**, 1441–2.

Hawton, K. (1980). Current trends in sex therapy. In *Current trends in treatment in psychiatry* (ed. T. G. Tennant). Pitman Medical, Tunbridge Wells.

Hawton, K. E. (1978). Deliberate self-poisoning and self-injury in the psychiatric hospital. *British Journal of Medical Psychology* **51**, 253–9.

Hawton, K. E. (1982). Attempted suicide in children and adolescents. *Journal of Child Psychology and Psychiatry* **23**, 497–503.

Hawton, K. E. (1985). *Sex therapy: a practical guide.* Oxford University Press, Oxford.

Hawton, K. E. (1986). *Suicide and attempted suicide among children and adolescents.* Sage, Beverley Hills.

Hawton, K. E. (1987). Assessment of suicide risk. *British Journal of Psychiatry* **150**, 145–53.

Hawton, K. E. and Catalan, J. (1987). *Attempted suicide: a practical guide to its nature and management* (2nd edn). Oxford University Press, Oxford.

Hawton, K. E. and Fagg, J. (1983). Suicide, and other causes of death, following attempted suicide. *British Journal of Psychiatry* **152**, 359–66.

Hawton, K. E. and Oppenheimer, C. (1983). Women's sexual problems. In *Women's problems in general practice* (ed. A. Anderson and A. McPherson). Oxford University Press, Oxford.

Hawton, K. E., Crowle, J., Simkin, S., and Bancroft, J. H. J. (1978). Attempted suicide and suicide among Oxford University students. *British Journal of Psychiatry* **132**, 506–9.

Hawton, K. E., Gath, D., and Smith, E. (1979). Management of attempted suicide in Oxford. *British Medical Journal* **ii**, 1040–2.

Hawton, K. E., Fagg, J., and Marsack, P. (1980). Association between epilepsy and attempted suicide. *Journal of Neurology, Neurosurgery and Psychiatry* **43**, 168–70.

Hawton, K. E., Bancroft, J., Catalan, J., Kingston, B., Stedeford, A., and Welch, N. (1981). Domiciliary and out-patient treatment of self-poisoning patients by medical and non-medical staff. *Psychological Medicine* **116**, 169–77.

Hawton, K. E., O'Grady, J. Osborn, M., and Cole, D. (1982). Adolescents who take overdoses: their characteristics, problems and contacts with helping agencies. *British Journal of Psychiatry* **140**, 118–23.

Hawton, K. E., Roberts, J., and Goodwin, G. (1985). The risk of child abuse among attempted suicide mothers with young children. *British Journal of Psychiatry* **146**, 486–9.

Hawton, K. E., Catalan, J., Martin, P., and Fagg, J. (1986). Long-term outcome of sex therapy. *Behaviour Research and Therapy* **24**, 665–75.

Hawton, K. E., McKeown, S., Day, A., Martin, P., O'Connor, M. and Yule, J. (1987). Evaluation of out-patient counselling compared with general practitioner care following overdoses. *Psychological Medicine* **17**, 751–62.

Hay, G. G. (1970a). Psychiatric aspects of cosmetic nasal operations. *British Journal of Psychiatry* **116**, 85–97.

Hay, G. G. (1970b). Dysmorphophobia. *British Journal of Psychiatry* **116**, 399–406.

Hay, G. G. (1983). Feigned psychosis: a review of the simulation of mental illness. *British Journal of Psychiatry* **43**, 8–10.

Hay, G. G., and Heather, B. B. (1973). Changes in psychometric test results following cosmetic nasal operations. *British Journal of Psychiatry* **122**, 81–90.

Haynes, R. B., Taylor, D. W., and Sackett, D. L. (eds.) (1979). *Compliance in health care*. Johns Hopkins University Press, Baltimore.

Haynes, S. G., Feinleib, M., and Kannel, W. B. (1980). The relationship of psychosocial factors to coronary heart disease in the Framingham study. III: Eight year incidence of coronary heart disease. *American Journal of Epidemiology* **111**, 37–58.

Head, H. (1920). *Studies in neurology*, Vol. 2. Oxford University Press, Oxford.

Health Advisory Service (1983). *The rising tide*. Department of Health and Social Security, London.

Heath, R. G., Franklin, D. E., and Shraberg, D. (1979). Gross pathology of the cerebellum in patients diagnosed and treated as functional psychiatric disorder. *Journal of Nervous and Mental Disorder* **167**, 585–92.

Heber, R. (1981). A manual on terminology and classification in mental retardation. *American Journal of Mental Deficiency*. Suppl. 64.

Heber, R. and Garber, H. (1975). The Milwaukee project: a study of the use of family intervention to prevent cultural familial retardation. In *The exceptional infant* (ed. B. Z. Friedlander, G. M. Sternt, and C. E. Kirk), Vol. 3. Brunner-Mazel, New York.

Hecker, E. (1871). Die Hebephrenie. *Virchows Archiv für Pathologie und Anatomie* **52**, 394–429. (See *American Journal of Psychiatry* **142**, 1265–71.)

Heimann, P. (1950). On countertransference. *International Journal of Psychoanalysis* **31**. 81–4.

Helgason, T. (1964). Epidemiology of mental disorders in Iceland. A psychiatric and demographic investigation of 5395 Icelanders. *Acta Psychiatrica Scandinavica*. Suppl. 173.

Helweg-Larsen, P., Hoffmeyer, H., Kieler, J., Thaysen, E. H., Thaysen, J. H., Thygesen, P., and Wulff, M. H. (1952). Famine disease in German concentration camps: complications and sequels. *Acta Psychiatrica et Neurologica Scandinavica* Suppl. **83**, 1–460.

Helzer, J. E. and Winokur, G. (1974). A family interview study of male manic depressives. *Archives of General Psychiatry* **31**, 73–7.

Helzer, J. E., Kendell, R. E., and Brockington, I. F. (1983). Contribution of the six-month criteria to the predictive validity of the DSMIII definition of schizophrenia. *Archives of General Psychiatry* **40**, 1277–80.

Helzer, J. E., Chammas, S., Norland, C. C., Stillings, W. A., and Alpers, D. H. (1984). A study of the association between Crohn's disease and psychiatric illness. *Gastroenterology* **86**, 324–30.

Hempel, C. G. (1961). Introduction to problems of taxonomy. In *Field studies in the mental disorders* (ed. J. Zubin). Grune and Stratton, New York.

Hemphill, R. E. (1952). Puerperal psychiatric illness. *British Medical Journal* **ii**, 1232–5.

Henderson, A. S. (1986). Epidemiology of mental illness. In *Mental health in the elderly: a review of the present state of research* (ed. H. Häfner, G. Moschel, and N. Sartorius). Springer, Berlin.

Henderson, A. S., Krapowski, J., and Stoller, A. (1971). Epidemiological aspects of adolescent psychiatry. In *Modern perspectives in adolescent psychiatry* (ed. J. G. Howells). Oliver and Boyd, Edinburgh.

Henderson, D. K. (1939). *Psychopathic states*. Chapman and Hall, London.

Henderson, J. J. (1972). Incest: a synthesis of data. *Canadian Psychiatric Association Journal* **17**, 291–313.

Henderson, S., Duncan-Jones, P., McAuley, H., and Ritchie, K. (1978). The patient's primary group. *British Journal of Psychiatry* **132**, 74–86.

Henderson, S., Byrne, D. G., and Duncan-Jones, P. (1982). *Neurosis and the social environment*. Academic Press, London.

Henderson, S. E. (1987). The assessment of 'clumsy' children: old and new approaches. *Journal of Child Psychology and Psychiatry* **28**, 511–27.

Hendren, R. L. (1986). Adolescent alcoholism and substance abuse. *American Psychiatric Associations Annual Review* 5. (ed. A. J. Frances, and R. E. Hales). American Psychiatric Association, Washington D. C.

Hendriksen, C. and Binder, V. (1980). Social prognosis in patients with ulcerative colitis. *British Medical Journal* ii, 581–3.

Heninger, G. R., Charney, D. S., and Menkes, D. B. (1983*a*). Receptor sensitivity and the mechanism of action of antidepressant treatment. In *Treatment of depression: old approaches and new controversies* (ed. P. J. Clayton and J. E. Barrett). Raven Press, New York.

Heninger, G. R., Charney, D. S., and Sternberg, D. E. (1983*b*). Lithium carbonate augmentation of antidepressant treatment. *Archives of General Psychiatry* **40**, 1335–42.

Heninger, G. R., Charney, D. S., and Sternberg, D. E. (1984). Serotonergic function in depression: prolactin response to intravenous tryptophan in depressed patients and healthy subjects. *Archives of General Psychiatry* **41**, 398–402.

Henry, G. W. (1929). Some modern aspects of psychiatry in general hospital practice. *American Journal of Psychiatry* **86**, 623–30.

Henry, J. P., Meehan, J. P., and Stephens, P. M. (1967). Use of psychosocial stimuli to induce prolonged systolic hypertension in mice. *Psychosomatic Medicine* **29**, 408–32.

Herbert, D., Kleber, M. D., Riordan, C. E. *et al.* (1985). Clonidine in out-patient detoxification from methadone maintenance. *Archives of General Psychiatry* **42**, 391–8.

Herman, J. and Hirschman, L. (1981). Families at risk for father-daughter incest. *American Journal of Psychiatry* **138**, 967–70.

Herman, J., Rossell, D., and Trocki, K. (1986). Long-term effects of incestuous abuse in childhood. *American Journal of Psychiatry* **143**, 1293–6.

Hermann, B. P. and Whitman, S. (1984). Behavioural and personality correlates of epilepsy: a review, methodological critique, and conceptual model. *Psychological Bulletin* **95**, 451–97. –

Hermelin, B. and O'Connor, N. (1983). The idiot savant: flawed genius or clever Hans? *Psychological Medicine* **13**, 479–81.

Herold, S., Leenders, K. L., Turton, D. R., *et al.* (1985). Dopamine receptor binding in schizophrenic patients as measured with C-methylspiperone and P. E. T. *Journal of Cerebral Blood Flow and Metabolism* **5** (Suppl. 1), 191–2.

Hershon, H. I. (1977). Alcohol withdrawal symptoms and drinking behaviour. *Journal of Studies on Alcoholism* **38**, 953–71.

Hersov, L. (1960). Refusal to go to school. *Journal of Child Psychology and Psychiatry* **1**, 137–45.

Hersov, L. (1985). Encopresis. In *Child psychiatry: modern approaches* (ed. L. Hersov and M. Rutter) (2nd edn). Blackwell, Oxford.

Hersov, L. and Berg, I. (eds.) (1980). *Out of school*. Wiley, Chichester.

Herstbech, S., Hansea, H. E., Amdisen, A., and Olsen, S. (1977). Chronic renal lesions following long term treatment with lithium. *Kidney International* **12**, 205–13.

Herzberg, J. L. (1987). No fixed abode. A comparison of men and women admitted to an east London psychiatric hospital. *British Journal of Psychiatry* **150**, 621–7.

Herzog, A. and Detre, T. (1967). Psychotic reaction associated with childbirth. *Diseases of the Nervous System* **37**, 229–35.

Herzog, D. B., Keller, M. B., and Lavori, P. W. (1988). Outcome in anorexia nervosa and bulimia nervosa. *Journal of Nervous and Mental Diseases* **176**, 131–43.

Heshe, J. and Roeder, E. (1976). Electroconvulsive therapy in Denmark. *British Journal of Psychiatry* **128**, 241–5.

Hesse, K. A. F. (1975). Meeting the psychosocial needs of pacemaker patients, *International Journal of Psychiatry in Medicine* **6**, 359–72.

Heston, L. J. (1966). Psychiatric disorders in foster home reared children of schizophrenic mothers. *British Journal of Psychiatry* **112**, 819–25.

Heston, L. J. and Shields, J. (1968). Homosexuality in twins: a family study and a registry study. *Archives of General Psychiatry* **18**, 149–60.

Heston, L. J., Mastri, A. R., Anderson, V. E., and White, J. (1981). Dementia of the Alzheimer type. Clinical genetics, natural history and associated conditions. *Archives of General Psychiatry* **38**, 1085–90.

Heston, L. J., White, J. A., and Mastri, A. R. (1987). Pick's disease. Clinical genetics and natural history. *Archives of General Psychiatry* **44**, 409–11.

Hewett, L. E. and Jenkins, R. L. (1946). *Fundamental patterns of maladjustment: the dynamics of their origin*. Thomas, Springfield, Ill.

Hewett, S. H. and Ryan, P. J. (1975). Alternatives to living in psychiatric hospitals—a pilot study. *British Journal of Hospital Medicine* **14**, 65–70.

Hibbert, G. A. (1984a). Ideational components of anxiety, their origin and content. *British Journal of Psychiatry* **144**, 618–24.

Hibbert, G. A. (1984b). Hyperventilation as a cause of panic attacks. *British Medical Journal* **288**, 263–4.

Hill, D. (1952). EEG in episodic psychotic and psychopathic behaviour: a classification of data. *Electroencephalography and Clinical Neurophysiology* **4**, 419–42.

Hill, D. (1953). Psychiatric disorders of epilepsy. *Medical Press* **229**, 473–5.

Hill, D. (1981). Historical review. In *Epilepsy and psychiatry* (ed. E. M. Reynolds and M. R. Trimble). Churchill Livingstone, Edinburgh.

Hill, O. W. (1972). Functional vomiting. *British Journal of Hospital Medicine* **7**, 755–8.

Hill-Beuff, A. and Porter, J. D. R. (1984). Children coping with impaired appearance: social and psychologic influences. *General Hospital Psychiatry* **6**, 294–301.

Hinde, R. A. (1977). Mother–infant separation and the nature of inter-individual relationships: experiments with rhesus monkeys. *Proceedings of the Royal Society of London* (B) **196**, 29–50.

Hinde, R. A. (1985). Ethiology in relation to psychiatry. In *Handbook of Psychiatry,* (ed. M. Shepherd) Vol 5. Cambridge University Press, Cambridge.

Hinde, R. A. and Spencer Booth, Y. (1970). Individual differences in the responses of rhesus monkeys to a period of separation from their mothers. *Journal of Child Psychology and Psychiatry* **11**, 159–76.

Hinkle, L. E. and Wolff, H. G. (1958). Ecological investigation of the relationship between illness, life experience and the social environment *Annals of Internal Medicine* **49**, 1373.

Hirsch, S. R. (1982). Depression revealed in schizophrenia. *British Journal of Psychiatry* **140**, 421–3.

Hirsch, S. R. (1986*a*). Clinical treatment of schizophrenia. In *The psychopharmacology and treatment of schizophrenia* (ed. P. Bradley and S. R. Hirsch). Oxford University Press, Oxford.

Hirsch, S. R. (1986*b*). Influence of social experience and environment. In *The psychopharmacology and treatment of schizophrenia* (ed. P. Bradley and S. R. Hirsch). Oxford University Press, Oxford.

Hirsch, S. R. (1987). Planning for bed needs and resource requirements in acute psychiatry. *Bulletin of the Royal College of Psychiatrists* **11**, 398–407.

Hirsch, S. R. and Leff, J. (1975). *Abnormalities in parents of schizophrenics.* Maudsley Monograph No. 22. Oxford University Press, London.

Hirsch, S. R., Gaind, R., Rohde, P. D., Stevens, B. C., and Wing, J. K. (1973). Outpatient maintenance of chronic schizophrenic patients with long acting fluphenazine: double blind placebo trial. *British Medical Journal* **i**, 633–7.

Hirschfeld, M. (1936). *Sexual anomalies and perversions.* Aldor, London.

Hirschfeld, M. (1944). *Sexual anomalies and perversions: physical and psychological development and treatment.* Aldor, London.

Hobson, R. F. (1953). Prognostic factors in electric convulsive therapy. *Journal of Neurology, Neurosurgery and Psychiatry* **16**, 275–81.

Hoch, P. H. and Polantin, P. (1949). Pseudoneurotic forms of schizophrenia. *Psychiatric Quarterly* **23**, 249–96.

Hodgkinson, S. *et al.* (1987). Molecular genetic evidence for heterogeneity in manic depression. *Nature* **325**, 805–6.

Hodkinson, H. M. (1973). Mental impairment in the elderly. *Journal of the Royal College of Physicians* **7**, 305–7.

Hoehn-Sarik, R., Frank, J. D., Imber, S. D., Nash, E. H., Stone, A. R., and Battle, C. R. (1964). Systematic preparation of patients for psychotherapy I: Effect on therapy behaviour and outcome. *Journal of Psychiatric Research* **2**, 267–81.

Hoenig, J. and Kenna, J. C. (1974). The prevalence of transsexualism in England and Wales. *British Journal of Psychiatry* **124**, 181–90.

Hoffman, B. F. (1986). How to write a psychiatric report for litigation following a personal injury. *American Journal of Psychiatry* **143**, 164–9.

Hogarty, G. E. and Ulrich, R. (1977). Temporal effects of drug and placebo in delaying relapse in schizophrenic out-patients. *Archives of General Psychiatry* **34**, 297–301.

Hogarty, G. E., Goldberg, S. C., and Schooler, N. (1974). Drugs and sociotherapy in the aftercare of schizophrenic patients II. Two year relapse rates. *Archives of General Psychiatry* **31**, 603–8.

Hogarty, G. E., Anderson, C. M., Reiss, D. J., *et al.* (1986). Family psychoeducation, social skills training and maintenance chemotherapy in the aftercare treatment of schizophrenia. *Archives of General Psychiatry* **43**, 633–42.

Hoggett, B. (1984). *Mental health law* (2nd edn). Sweet and Maxwell, London.

Holding, T. A. and Barraclough, B. M. (1975). Psychiatric morbidity in a sample of a London coroner's open verdicts. *British Journal of Psychiatry* **127**, 133–43.

Holding, T. A. Buglass, D., Duffy, J. C., and Kreitman, N. (1977). Parasuicide in Edinburgh—a seven year review, 1968–1974. *British Journal of Psychiatry* **130**, 534–43.

Holland, A. J., Hall, A., Murray, R., Russell, G. F. M., and Crisp, A. H. (1984).

Anorexia nervosa: a study of 34 twin pairs and a set of triplets. *British Journal of Psychiatry* **145**, 414–19.

Holland, J. C. *et al.* (1986). Comparative psychological disturbance in patients with pancreatic and gastric cancer. *American Journal of Psychiatry* **143**, 982–6.

Hollingshead, A. B. and Redlich, F. C. (1958). *Social class and mental illness: a community study.* Wiley, New York.

Holmes, T. and Rahe, R. H. (1967). The social adjustment rating scale. *Journal of Psychosomatic Research* **11**, 213–18.

Holmes, T. H., Hawkins, N. G., Bowerman, E., Clarke, R., and Joffe, J. R. (1957). Psychosocial and psychophysiologic studies of tuberculosis. *Psychosomatic Medicine* **19**, 134–43.

Holt, S., Stewart, I. C., Dixon, J. M., Elton, R. A., Taylor, T. V., and Little, K. (1980). Alcohol and the emergency service patient. *British Medical Journal* **281**, 638–40.

Hood, R. and Sparks, R. (1980) *Key issues in criminology.* Weidenfeld and Nicholson, London.

Hooley, J. M., Orley, J., and Teasdale, J. D. (1986). Levels of expressed emotion and relapse in depressed patients. *British Journal of Psychiatry,* **148**, 642–7.

Hopkins, J., Marcus, M., and Campbell, S. B. (1984). Postpartum depression: a critical review. *Psychological Bulletin* **95**, 498–513.

Hore, B. D. and Wilkins, R. H. (1976). A general-practice study of the commonest presenting symptoms of alcoholism. *Journal of the Royal College of General Practitioners* **26**, 140–2.

Horgan, J. H. (1987). Cardiac tamponade. *British Medical Journal* **295**, 563.

Horn, G. van (1987). Dementia. *The American Journal of Medicine* **83**, 101–10.

Horne, R. L., Pettinati, H. M., Sugarman, A., and Varga, E. (1985). Comparing bilateral to unilateral electroconvulsive therapy in a randomised study with EEG monitoring. *Archives of General Psychiatry* **42**, 1087–92.

Horney, K. (1939). *New ways in psychoanalysis.* Kegan Paul, London.

Hoult, J. (1986). Community care of the acutely mentally ill. *British Journal of Psychiatry* **149**, 137–44.

House, A. (1987*a*). Psychosocial problems on the renal unit and their relation to treatment outcome. *Journal of Psychosomatic Research* **31**, 441–52.

House, A. (1987*b*). Depression after stroke. *British Medical Journal* **294**, 76–8.

Houston, F. and Royse, A. B. (1954). Relationship between deafness and psychotic illness. *Journal of Mental Science* **100**, 990–3.

Howard League Working Party (1985). *Unlawful sex.* Waterlow, London.

Howlin, P., Marchant, R., Rutter, M., Berger, M., Hersov, L., and Yule, W. (1973). A home-based approach to the treatment of autistic children. *Journal of Autism and Child Schizophrenia* **3**, 308–16.

Hsu, L. K. G. (1986). The treatment of anorexia nervosa. *American Journal of Psychiatry* **143**, 573–81.

Huber, G., Gross, G., and Schuttler, R. (1975). A long-term follow up study of schizophrenia: psychiatric course of illness and prognosis. *Acta Psychiatrica Scandinavica* **52**, 49–57.

Hughson, A. V. M., Cooper, A. F., McArdle, C. S., and Smith, D. C. (1987). Psychosocial effects of radiotherapy after mastectomy. *British Medical Journal* **294**, 1515–18.

Hull, C. L. (1943). *Principles of behaviour.* Appleton, New York.

Hume, D. (1958). *A treatise of human nature* (ed. L. A. Selby-Bigge). Oxford University Press, Oxford.

Hunter, M. (1979). Forensic psychiatry and mental handicap. In *Psychiatric illness and mental handicap* (ed. F. E. James and R. P. Snaith). Gaskell, Ashford, Kent.

Huntington, G. (1872). On chorea. *Medical and Surgical Reporter. Philadelphia* **26**, 317–21.

Hussebye, D. G., Westlie, L., Thomas, J. S., and Kjellstrand, C. M. (1987). Psychological, social, and somatic prognostic indicators in old patients undergoing long-term dialysis. *Archives of Internal Medicine* **147**, 1921–4.

Hutchings, B. and Mednick, S. A. (1974). Registered criminality in the adopted and biological parents of registered male criminal adoptees. In *Genetic researches in psychiatry* (ed. R. R. Fieve *et al.*). Johns Hopkins University Press, Baltimore.

Huxley, P. J., Goldberg, D. P., Maguire, E. P., and Kincey, V. (1979). The prediction of the course of minor psychiatric disorders. *British Journal of Psychiatry* **135**, 535–43.

Hyde, C., Bridges, K., Goldberg, D., Lowson, K., Sterling, C., and Faragher, B. (1987). The evaluation of a hostel ward: a controlled study using modified cost-benefit analysis. *British Journal of Psychiatry* **151**, 805–12.

Illingworth, R. S. (1980). *Development of the infant and young child*. Churchill Livingstone, Edinburgh.

Imboden, J. B. (1972). Psychosocial determinants of recovery. In *Psychosocial aspects of physical illness* (ed. Z. J. Lipowski). Karger, Basel.

Imboden, J. B., Canter, A., and Cluff, L. E. (1959). Brucellosis III. Psychological aspects of delayed convalescence. *Archives of Internal Medicine* **103**, 406–14.

Imboden, J. B., Canter, A., and Cluff, L. E. (1961). Convalescence from influenza: a study of the psychological and clinical determinants. *Archives of Internal Medicine* **108**, 393–9.

Insanity Defense Work Group (1983). American Psychiatric Association statement of the insanity defense. *American Journal of Psychiatry* **140**, 681–8.

Isbell, H., Altschul, S., Kornetsky, C. H., Eisenman, A. J., Flanary, H. G., and Graser, H. F. (1950). Chronic barbiturate intoxication. *Archives of Neurology and Psychiatry* **64**, 416–18.

Isbell, H., Fraser, H. F., Wikler, A., Belleville, R., and Eisenman, A. J. (1955). An experimental study of the etiology of 'rum fits' and 'delirium tremens'. *Quarterly Journal of Studies on Alcoholism* **16**, 1–33.

Jablensky, A. (1986). Epidemiology of schizophrenia: a European perspective. *Schizophrenia Bulletin* **12**, 52–73.

Jablensky, A. (1987). Multicultural studies and the nature of schizophrenia: a review. *Journal of the Royal Society of Medicine* **80**, 162–7.

Jablensky, A., Korten, A., Ernberg, G., Anker, M., Cooper, J. E., and Day, R. (1986). Manifestations and first-contact incidence of schizophrenia in different cultures. *Psychological Medicine* **16**, 909–28.

Jackson, B. M. (1969). A case of voyeurism treated by counterconditioning. *Behaviour Research and Therapy* **7**, 133–4.

Jacobs, P. A., Brunton, M., Melville, M. M., Brittain, R. P., and McClemont, W. F. (1965). Aggressive behaviour and subnormality. *Nature* **208**, 1351–2.

Jacobs, S. and Myers, J. (1976). Recent life events and acute schizophrenic psychosis: a controlled study. *Journal of Nervous and Mental Disease* **162**, 75–87.

Jacobs, S., Prusoff, B. A., and Paykel, E. S. (1974). Recent life events in schizophrenia and depression. *Psychological Medicine* **4**, 444–52.

Jacobson, E. (1938). *Progressive relaxation*. Chicago University Press, Chicago.

Jacobson, E. (1953). Contribution to the metapsychology of cyclothymic depression. In *Affective disorders* (ed. P. Greenacre). International Universities Press, New York.

Jacobson, E., Kales, A., Lehmann, D., and Zweizig, J. R. (1965). Somnambulism: all night electro-encephalographic studies. *Science* **148**, 975–7.

Jacobson, R. R. (1985). Child firesetters: a clinical investigation. *Journal of Child Psychology and Psychiatry* **26**, 759–68.

Jacoby, R. (1981). Dementia, depression and the CT scan. *Psychological Medicine* **11**, 673–6.

Jacoby, R. and Levy, R. (1980). Computed tomography in the elderly II: Senile dementia: diagnosis and functional impairment. *British Journal of Psychiatry* **136**, 256–69.

Jaffe, P., Wolfe, D. A., Wilson, S., and Zak, L. (1986). Emotional and physical health problems of battered women. *Canadian Journal of Psychiatry* **31**, 625–9.

Jahoda, G. and Cramond, J. (1972). *Children and alcohol. A developmental study in Glasgow*, Vol. 1. HMSO, London.

Jakes, S. C., Hallam, R. S., Rachman, J., and Hinchcliffe, R. (1986). The effects of reassurance, relaxation training and distraction on chronic tinnitus sufferers. *Behaviour Research and Therapy* **24**, 497–507.

Jakob, A. (1921). Über eingenarte Erkrankungen des Zentralnervensystems mit bemerkenswerten anatomischen Befunde. *Zeitschrift für die gesamte Neurologie und Psychiatrie* **64**, 147–228.

James, I. P. (1967). Suicide and mortality among heroin addicts in Britain. *British Journal of Addictions* **62**, 391–8.

Janet, P. (1894). *L'état mental des hystériques*. Rueff, Paris.

Janet, P. (1909). *Les névroses*. Flammarion, Paris.

Janet, P. (1925). *Psychological healing*. Allen and Unwin, London.

Janicak, P. G., Davis, J. M., Gibbons, R. D., Ericksen, S., Chang, S., and Gallagher, P. (1985). Efficacy of ECT: a meta-analysis. *American Journal of Psychiatry* **142**, 297–302.

Janis, I. L. (1958). *Psychological stress: psychoanalytic and behavioural studies of surgical patients*. Wiley, New York.

Jannoun, L., Munby, M., Catalan, J., and Gelder, M. G. (1980). A home based treatment program for agoraphobia. *Behaviour Therapy* **11**, 294–305.

Jarman, C. M. B. and Kellet, J. M. (1979). Alcoholism in the general hospital. *British Medical Journal* **ii**, 469–71.

Jaspers, K. (1913). *Allgemeine Psychopathologie*. Springer, Berlin.

Jaspers, K. (1963). *General psychopathology* (*Allgemeine Psychopathologie*, 7th edn, 1959, trans. by J. Hoenig and M. W. Hamilton). Manchester University Press.

Jeavons, P. M. (1970). Choice of drug therapy in epilepsy. *Practitioner* **219**, 542–56.

Jeavons, P. M. (1983). Non-epileptic attacks in childhood. In *Research progress in epilepsy* (ed. F. C. Rose). Pitman, Bath.

Jellinek, E. M. (1959). Estimating the prevalence of alcoholism: modified values in the Jellinek formula and an alternative approach. *Quarterly Journal of Studies on Alcohol* **20**, 261–9.

Jellinek, E. M. (1960). *The disease concept of alcoholism*. Hillhouse Press, New Brunswick.

Jenkins, C. D. (1976). Recent evidence supporting psychologic and social risk factors for coronary disease. *New England Journal of Medicine* **294**, 987–94 and 1033–8.

Jenkins, C. D. (1982). Psychosocial risk factors for coronary heart disease. *Acta Medica Scandinavica* Suppl. 660, 123–36.

Jenkins, L., Tarnopolsky, A., and Hand, D. (1981). Psychiatric admissions and aircraft noise from London Airport: four year, three-hospitals' study. *Psychological Medicine* 11, 765–82.

Jennings, C., Barraclough, B. M., and Moss, J. R. (1978). Have the Samaritans lowered the suicide rate? A controlled study. *Psychological Medicine* 8, 413–22.

Jesness, C. F. (1962). *The Jesness inventory: development and validation.* Research report no. 29. California Youth Authority, Sacramento.

Johnson, A. M., Falstein, E. K., Szorek, S. A., and Svendsen, M. (1941). School phobia. *American Journal of Orthopsychiatry* 11, 702–11.

Johnson, D. A. W. (1986). Depressive symptom in schizophrenia: some observations on frequency, morbidity and possible causes. In *Contemporary issues in schizophrenia* (ed. A. Kerr and P. Snaith). Gaskell, London.

Johnson, J. (1969). Organic psychosyndromes due to boxing. *British Journal of Psychiatry* 115, 45–53.

Johnson, J. (1984). Stupor: a review of 25 cases. *Acta Psychiatrica Scandinavica* 70, 376–7.

Johnson, S. B. (1980). Psychosocial factors in juvenile diabetes: a review. *Journal of Behavioural Medicine* 3, 95–116.

Johnson, S. B. (1985). Situational fears and objects phobias. In: *The clinical guide to child psychiatry* (ed. D. Shaffer, A. A. Ehrhardt, and L. L. Greenhill). Free Press, New York.

Johnston, D. W. (1985). Psychological intervention in cardiovascular disease. *Journal of Psychosomatic Research* 29, 447–56.

Johnston, M. (1986). Preoperative emotional status and post operative recovery. In *Psychological aspects of surgery. Advances in Psychosomatic Medicine,* Vol. 15, 1–22.

Johnstone, E. C., and Marsh, W. (1973). Acetylator status and response to phenelzine in depressed patients. *Lancet* i, 567–70.

Johnstone, E. C., Crow, T. J., Frith, C. D., Husband, J., and Kreel, L. (1976). Cerebral ventricular size and cognitive impairment in chronic schizophrenia. *Lancet* ii, 924–6.

Johnstone, E. C., Crow, T. J., and Masheter, K. (1977). Anterior pituitary hormone secretion in chronic schizophrenia—an approach to neurohormonal mechanisms. *Psychological Medicine* 7, 223–8.

Johnstone, E. C., Crow, T. J., Frith, C. D., Carney, M. W. P., and Price, J. S. (1978). Mechanism of the antipsychotic effect in the treatment of acute schizophrenia. *Lancet* i, 848–51.

Johnstone, E. C., Deakin, J. F. W., Lawler, P., Frith, C. D., Stevens, M., McPherson, K., and Crow, T. J. (1980). The Northwick Park electroconvulsive therapy trial. *Lancet* ii, 1317–20.

Johnstone, E. C., Cunningham-Owens, D. G., Gold, A., Crow, T. J., and MacMillan, J. F. (1981). Institutionalisation and the defects of schizophrenia. *British Journal of Psychiatry* 139, 195–203.

Johnstone, E. C., Owens, D. G. C., Gold, A., Crow, T. J., and MacMillan, J. F. (1984). Schizophrenia patients discharged from hospital—a follow-up study. *British Journal of Psychiatry* 145, 586–90.

Johnstone, E. C., Crow, T. J., Johnstone, A. L., and MacMillan, J. F. (1986). The Northwick Park study of first episodes of schizophrenia. I. Presentation of the illness. Problems relating to admission. *British Journal of Psychiatry* 148, 115–120.

Johnstone, J. M., Hunt, A. C., and Ward, E. M. (1960). Plastic bag asphyxia in adults. *British Medical Journal* ii, 1714–15.

Jolliffe, N. and Jellinek, E. M. (1941). Vitamins and liver cirrhosis in alcoholism: VII cirrhosis of the liver. *Quarterly Journal of Studies on Alcohol* 2, 544–83.

Jones, D. P. H. (1986). Individual psychotherapy for the sexually abused child. *Child Abuse and Neglect* 10, 377–86.

Jones, D. P. H., and Alexander, H. (1978). Treating the abusive family within the family care system. In *The battered child* (ed. R. E. Helfer, and R. S. Kempe) (4th edn). University of Chicago Press, London.

Jones, D. P. H., and MacQuiston, M. (1988). *Interviewing the sexually abused child* (3rd edn). Gaskell Press, London.

Jones, K. (1972). *A history of the mental health services*. Routledge and Kegan Paul, London.

Jones, K. and Smith, D. W. (1973). Recognition of the fetal alcohol syndrome in early infancy. *Lancet* ii, 999–1001.

Jones, M. (1952). *Social psychiatry: a study of therapeutic communities*. Tavistock, London.

Jorm, A. F. (1985). Subtypes of Alzheimer's dementia: a conceptual analysis and critical review. *Psychological Medicine* 15, 543–53.

Jorm, A. F., Korten, A. E., and Henderson, A. F. (1987). The prevalence of dementia: a quantitive integration of the literature. *Acta Psychiatrica Scandinavica* 76, 465–79.

Jowett, S. and Ryan, T. (1985). Skin disease and handicap: an analysis of the impact of skin conditions. *Social Science and Medicine* 20, 421–5.

Kahlbaum, K. (1863). *Die Gruppirung der psychichen Krankheiten*. Kafemann, Danzig.

Kahn, E. (1928). Die psychopäthischen Persönlichkeiten. In *Handbuch der Geisteskrankheiten*, Vol. 5, p. 227. Springer, Berlin.

Kales, A., Soldatos, C. R., and Kales, J. D. (1987). Sleep disorders: insomnia, sleepwalking, night terrors, nightmares, and enuresis. *Annals of Internal Medicine* 106, 582–92.

Kalinowsky, L. B. and Hoch, P. H. (1947). *Shock treatments and other somatic procedures in psychiatry*. Heinemann Medical, London.

Kallen, B. and Tandberg, A. (1983). Lithium and pregnancy—a cohort study of manic depressive women. *Acta Psychiatrica Scandinavica* 62, 134–9.

Kallmann, F. J. (1938). *The genetics of schizophrenia*. Augustin, New York.

Kallmann, F. J. (1946). The genetic theory of schizophrenia: an analysis of 691 schizophrenic twin index families. *American Journal of Psychiatry* 103, 309–22.

Kallmann, F. J. (1952). Study on the genetic affects of male homosexuality. *Journal of Nervous and Mental Disease* 115, 1283–98.

Kalucy, R. S., Crisp, A. H., and Harding, B. (1977). A study of 56 families with anorexia nervosa. *British Journal of Medical Psychology* 50, 381–95.

Kaminski, M., Rumeau-Rouquette, C., and Schwartz, D. (1976). Consommation d'alcool chez les femmes enceintes et issue de la grossesse. *Revue d'Epidemiologie et de Santé Publique* 24, 27–40.

Kane, J. M. (1986). Somatic therapy. In *Psychiatry update. The American Psychiatric Association annual review*, Vol. 5 (ed. A. J. Frances, and R. E. Hales). American Psychiatric Press, Washington, D. C.

Kane, J. M. (1987). Treatment of schizophrenia. *Schizophrenia Bulletin* 13, 133–56.

Kane, J. M. and Smith, J. M. (1982). Tardive dyskinesia: prevalence and risk factors, 1959–1979). *Archives of General Psychiatry* 39, 473–81.

Kane, R. L. (1985). Special needs of the elderly. In *Oxford textbook of public health* (ed. W. W. Holland), Vol. 4. Oxford University Press, Oxford.

Kanner, L. (1943). Autistic disturbance of affective contact. *Nervous Child* **2**, 217–50.

Kantor, J. S., Zitrin, C. M., and Zeldis, S. M. (1980). Mitral valve prolapse in agoraphobic patients. *American Journal of Psychiatry* **137**, 467–9.

Kaplan, H. I., Freedman, A. M., and Sadock, B. J. (eds.) (1980). *Comprehensive textbook of psychiatry* (3rd edn). Williams and Wilkins, Baltimore.

Kaplan, N. (1985). Non-drug treatment of hypertension. *Annals of Internal Medicine* **102**, 359–73.

Karasu, T. B. (1979). Psychotherapy of the medically ill. *American Journal of Psychiatry* **136**, 1–11.

Karush, A., Daniels, G. E., O'Connor, J. F., and Stern, L. O. (1977). *Psychotherapy in chronic ulcerative colitis*. Saunders, Philadelphia.

Kasanin, J. (1933). The acute schizoaffective psychoses. *American Journal of Psychiatry* **13**, 97–126.

Katon, W. J., Ries, R. K., Bokan, J. A., and Kleinman, A. (1980). Hyperemesis gravidarum: a biopsychosocial perspective. *International Journal of Psychiatry in Medicine* **10**, 151–62.

Katon, W., Kleinman, A., and Rosen, G. (1982). Depression and somatization: a review. Part I. *American Journal of Medicine* **72**, 127–35.

Katon, W., Ries, R. K., and Kleinman, A. (1984). A prospective DSMIII study of 100 consecutive somatization patients. *Comprehensive Psychiatry* **25**, 305–14.

Katon, W., Egan, K., and Miller, D. (1985). Chronic pain: lifetime psychiatric diagnosis and family history. *American Journal of Psychiatry* **142**, 1156–60.

Katz, S. E. (1985). Partial hospitalization and comprehensive community services. In *Comprehensive textbook of psychiatry* (ed. H. I. Kaplan and B. J. Sadock) (4th edn). Williams and Wilkins, Baltimore.

Kavka, J. (1949). Pinel's conception of the psychopathic state. *Bulletin of the History of Medicine* **23**, 461–8.

Kay, D. W. K. (1962). Outcome and cause of death in mental disorders of old age. *Acta Psychiatrica Scandinavica* **38**, 249–76.

Kay, D. W. K. (1963). Late paraphrenia and its bearing on the aetiology of schizophrenia. *Acta Psychiatrica Scandinavica* **39**, 159–69.

Kay, D. W. K. and Bergmann, K. (1980). Epidemiology of mental disorder among the aged in the community. In *Handbook of mental health and ageing* (ed. J. E. Birren and R. B. Sloane). Prentice Hall, Englewood Cliffs.

Kay, D. W. K. and Roth, M. (1961). Environmental and hereditary factors in the schizophrenias of old age ('late paraphrenia') and their bearing on the general problem of causation in schizophrenia. *Journal of Mental Science* **107**, 649–86.

Kay, D. W. K., Beamish, P., and Roth, M. (1964). Old age mental disorders in Newcastle-upon-Tyne: 1: a study in prevalence. *British Journal of Psychiatry* **110**, 146–58.

Kay, D. W. K. Bermann, K., Foster, E. M., McKechnie, A. A., and Roth, M. (1970). Mental illness and hospital usage in the elderly: a random sample followed up. *Comprehensive Psychiatry* **11**, 26–35.

Kay, D. W. K., Cooper, A. F., Garside, R. F., and Roth, M. (1976). The differentiation of paranoid and affective psychoses by patients' premorbid characteristics. *British Journal of Psychiatry* **129**, 207–15.

Kedward, H. B. and Cooper, B. (1966). Neurotic disorders in urban practice: a 3 year follow-up. *Journal of the Royal College of General Practitioners* **12**, 148–63.

Keefe, F. J. and Gil, K. M. (1986). Behavioural concepts in the analysis of chronic pain syndromes. *Journal of Consulting and Clinical Psychology* **54**, 776–83.

Keefe, F. J., Gil, K. M., and Rose, S. C. (1986). Behavioural approaches in the multidisciplinary management of chronic pain: programs and issues. *Clinical Psychology Review* 6, 87–113.

Keeley, S. M., Shemberg, K. M., and Carbonell, J. (1976). Operant clinical intervention: behaviour management or beyond? Where are the data? *Behaviour Therapy* 7, 292–305.

Kellam, A. M. P. (1987). The neuroleptic malignant syndrome, so called: a survey of the world literature. *British Journal of Psychiatry* 150, 752–9.

Kellar, K. J. and Stockmeier, C. A. (1986). Effects of electroconvulsive shock and serotonin axon lesions on beta-adrenergic and serotonin-2 receptors in rat brain. In *Basic research issues* (ed. S. Malitz and H. A. Sackheim), *Annals of the New York Academy of Science,* 467, 76–90.

Keller, M. (1976). The disease concept of alcoholism revisited. *Journal of Studies on Alcohol* 37, 1694–717.

Keller, M. B., Klerman, G. L., Lavori, P. W., Coryell, W., Endicott, J., and Taylor, J. (1984). Long-term outcome of episodes of major depression: clinical and public health significance. *Journal of the American Medical Association* 252, 788–92.

Keller, M. B., Beardslee, W. R., Dorer, D. J., Lavori, P. W., Samuelson, H., and Klerman, G. L. (1986). Impact of severity and chronicity of parental affective illness on adaptive functioning and psychopathology in children. *Archives of General Psychiatry* 43, 930–7.

Kellner, R. (1985). Functional somatic symptoms and hypochondriasis. A survey of empirical studies. *Archives of General Psychiatry* 42, 821–33.

Kellner, R. (1987). Hypochondriasis and somatization. *Journal of the American Medical Association* 258, 2718–21.

Kelly, G. A. (1955). *The psychology of personal constructs*, Vols. 1 and 2. Norton, New York.

Kelly, W. F., Checkley, S. A., Bender, D. A., and Mashifer, K. (1985). Cushing's syndrome and depression—a prospective study of 26 patients. *British Journal of Psychiatry* 142, 16–19.

Kemmer, F. W. Bisping, R., Steingruber, H. J., *et al.* (1986). Psychological stress and metabolic control in patients with type 1 diabetes mellitus. *New England Journal of Medicine* 314, 1078–84.

Kemp, N. J. (1981). Social-psychological aspects of blindness: a review. *Current Psychological Reviews* 1, 69–89.

Kempe, C. H., Silverman, F. N., Steele, B. F., Droegemueller, W., and Silver, H. K. (1962). The battered child syndrome. *Journal of the American Medical Association* 181, 17–24.

Kempe, R. S. and Goldbloom, R. B. (1987) Malnutrition and growth retardation (failure to thrive) in the context of child abuse and neglect. In *The battered child* (ed. R. E. Helfer and R. S. Kempe), Chapter 16, pp. 315–35. University of Chicago Press, London.

Kendell, R. E. (1968). *The classification of depressive illness*. Maudsley Monograph No. 18. Oxford University Press, London.

Kendell, R. E. (1975). *The role of diagnosis in psychiatry*. Blackwell, Oxford.

Kendell, R. E. (1981). The present status of electroconvulsive therapy. *British Journal of Psychiatry* 139, 265–83.

Kendell, R. E. (1983). DSMIII: a major advance in psychiatric nosology. In *International perspectives on DSMIII* (ed. R. L. Spitzer, J. R. W. Williams, and A. E. Skodol). American Psychiatric Association Press, Washington, DC.

Kendell, R. E. (1985). Emotional and physical factors in the genesis of puerperal mental disorders. *Journal of Psychosomatic Research* 29, 3–11.

Kendell, R. E., Hall, D. J., Pichot, P., and von Cranach, M. (1974). Diagnostic criteria of English, French and German psychiatrists. *Psychological Medicine* **4**, 187–95.

Kendell, R. E., Hall, D. J., Wainwright, S., Hailey, A., and Shannon, B. (1976). The influence of childbirth on psychiatric morbidity. *Psychological Medicine* **6**, 297–302.

Kendell, R. E., Hall, D. J., Rennie, D., Clarke, J. A., and Dean, C. (1981). The social and obstetric correlates of psychiatric admission in the puerperium. *Psychological Medicine* **11**, 341–50.

Kendell, R. E., de Roumanie, M., and Ritson, E. B. (1983). Influence of an increase in excise duty on alcohol consumption and its adverse effects. *British Medical Journal* **287**, 809–11.

Kendell, R. E., Chalmers, J. C., and Platz, C. (1987). Epidemiology of puerperal psychoses. *British Journal of Psychiatry* **150**, 662–73.

Kendler, K. S. (1982). Demography of paranoid psychosis (delusional disorder). *Archives of General Psychiatry* **39**, 890–902.

Kendler, K. S. (1986). Genetics of schizophrenia. In *American Psychiatric Association annual review* (ed. A. J. Frances and R. E. Hales), Vol. 5. American Psychiatric Press, Washington, D. C.

Kendler, K. S. (1987). Paranoid disorders in DSM-III, a critical review. In: *Diagnosis and classification in psychiatry* (ed. G. L. Tischler). Cambridge University Press, Cambridge.

Kendler, K. S. and Davis, K. L. (1981). The genetics and biochemistry of paranoid schizophrenia and other paranoid psychoses. *Schizophrenia Bulletin* **7**, 689–769.

Kendler, K. S. and Gruenberg, A. M. (1984). An independent analysis of the Danish adoption study of schizophrenia. VI. The relationship between psychiatric disorders as defined by DSMIII in the relatives and adoptees. *Archives of General Psychiatry* **41**, 555–64.

Kendler, K. S. and Tsuang, M. T. (1981). Nosology of paranoid schizophrenia and other paranoid psychoses. *Schizophrenia Bulletin* **7**, 594–610.

Kendler, K. S., Gruenberg, A. M., and Strauss, J. S. (1981). An independent analysis of the Copenhagen sample for the Danish adoption study of schizophrenia. The relationship between schizotypal personality disorder and schizophrenia. *Archives of General Psychiatry* **38**, 982–7.

Kennedy, A. and Neville, J. (1957). Sudden loss of memory. *British Medical Journal* **ii**, 428–33.

Kennedy, P. (1972). Efficacy of a regional poisoning treatment centre in preventing further suicidal behaviour. *British Medical Journal* **iv**, 255–7.

Kennedy, P. and Kreitman, N. (1973). An epidemiological survey of parasuicide ('attempted suicide') in general practice. *British Journal of Psychiatry* **123**, 23–34.

Kennedy, W. A. (1965). School phobia: a rapid treatment of 50 cases. *Journal of Abnormal Psychology* **70**, 285–9.

Kennerley, H., and Gath, D. (1986). Maternity blues reassessed. *Psychiatric Developments* **1**, 1–17.

Kenyon, F. E. (1964). Hypochondriasis: a clinical study. *British Journal of Psychiatry* **110**, 478–88.

Kenyon, F. E. (1965). Hypochondriasis: a survey of some historical, clinical and social aspects. *British Journal of Medical Psychology* **38**, 117–33.

Kenyon, F. E. (1968). Studies in female homosexuality: social and psychiatric aspects: sexual development, attitudes and experience. *British Journal of Psychiatry* **114**, 1337–50.

Kenyon, F. E. (1980). Homosexuality in gynaecological practice. *Clinics in Obstetrics and Gynaecology* 1, 363–86.

Kerr, T. A., Roth, M., Shapira, K., and Gurney, C. (1972). The assessment and prediction of outcome in affective disorders. *British Journal of Psychiatry* 121, 167–74.

Kerr, T. A., Roth, M., and Shapira, K. (1974). Prediction of outcome in anxiety states and depressive illness. *British Journal of Psychiatry* 124, 125–31.

Kessel, N. (1977a). Self-poisoning. *British Medical Journal* ii, 1265–70 and 1336–40.

Kessel, N. (1977b). The foetal alcohol syndrome from the public health standpoint. *Health Trends* 9, 86–9.

Kessel, N. (1978). *Report of the Advisory Committee on Alcoholism*. HMSO, London.

Kessel, N. and Grossman, G. (1965). Suicide in alcoholics. *British Medical Journal* ii, 1671–2.

Kessler, S. (1980). The genetics of schizophrenia: a review. *Schizophrenia Bulletin* 6, 404–16.

Kety, S. (1980). The syndrome of schizophrenia. *British Journal of Psychiatry* 136, 421–36.

Kety, S. (1983). Mental illness in the biological and adoptive relatives of schizophrenic adoptees: findings relevant to genetic and environmental factors in etiology. *American Journal of Psychiatry* 140, 720–7.

Kety, S., Rosenthal, D., Wender, P. H., Schulsinger, F., and Jacobsen, B. (1975). Mental illness in the biological and adoptive families of adopted individuals who have become schizophrenic. In *Genetic research in psychiatry* (ed. R. R. Fieve, D. Rosenthal and H. Bull). Johns Hopkins University Press, Baltimore.

Khoo, C. T. K. (1982). Cosmetic surgery—where does it begin? *British Journal of Plastic Surgery* 35, 277–80.

Kidd, C. B. (1962). Misplacement of the elderly in hospital. *British Medical Journal* ii, 1491–5.

Kidson, M. A. (1973). Personality and hypertension. *Journal of Psychosomatic Research* 17, 35–41.

Kiev, A. (1971). Suicide prevention. In *Identifying suicide potential* (ed. D. B. Anderson and L. J. McClean), pp. 3–13. Behaviour Publications, New York.

Kiev, A. (1972). *Transcultural psychiatry*. Penguin, Harmondsworth.

Kilmann, P. R. (1982). The treatment of sexual paraphilias: a review of outcome research. *Journal of Sex Research* 18, 193–252.

Kiloh, L. G. and Garside, R. F. (1963). The independence of neurotic depression and endogenous depression. *British Journal of Psychiatry* 109, 451–63.

Kiloh, L. G., Child, J. P., and Latner, G. (1960). A controlled trial in the treatment of endogenous depression. *Journal of Mental Science* 106, 1139–44.

Kiloh, L. G., Ball, J. R. B., and Garside, R. F. (1962). Prognostic factors in treatment of depressive states with imipramine. *British Medical Journal* i, 1225–7.

Kiloh, L. G., Andrews, G., Nielson, M., and Bianchi, G. N. (1972). The relationship between the syndromes called endogenous and neurotic depression. *British Journal of Psychiatry* 121, 183–96.

Kind, D. (1958). Die psychiatrie der hypophyseninsuffizienz speziell der Simmondsschen Krankheit. *Forschritte der Neurologie-Psychiatrie* 26, 501–63.

King, B. H. and Ford, C. V. (1988). Pseudologia fantastica. *Acta Psychiatrica Scandinavica* 77, 1–6.

King, J. R. and Hullin, R. P. (1983). Withdrawal symptoms from lithium; four case reports and a questionnaire study. *British Journal of Psychiatry* 143, 30–35.

King, R., Raynes, N., and Tizard, J. A. (1971). *Patterns of residential care.* Routledge and Kegan Paul, London.

Kingman, R. and Jones, D. P. H. (1987). Incest and other forms of sexual abuse. In *The battered child* (eds. R. E. Helfer and R. S. Kempe) (4th edn). University of Chicago Press, London.

Kinnell, H. G. (1987). Fragile X syndrome: an important preventable cause of mental handicap. *British Medical Journal.* **295**, 564.

Kinsey, A. C., Pomeroy, W. B., and Martin, C. E. (1948). *Sexual behavior in the human male.* Saunders, Philadelphia.

Kinsey, A. C., Pomeroy, W. B., Martin, C. E., and Gebhard, P. H. (1953). *Sexual behaviour in the human female.* Saunders, Philadelphia.

Kirman, B. (1987). Self-injury and mental handicap. *British Medical Journal,* **295**, 1085–6.

Kirsner, J. B. (1981). The irritable bowel syndrome: a clinical review and ethical consideration. *Archives of Internal Medicine* **141**, 635–9.

Kitson, T. M. (1977). The disulfiram-ethanol reaction. *Journal of Studies on Alcoholism* **38**, 96–113.

Klaf, F. S. and Hamilton, J. G. (1961). Schizophrenia—a hundred years ago and today. *Journal of Mental Science* **107**, 819–28.

Klein, D. F. (1964). Delineation of two drug-responsive anxiety syndromes. *Psychopharmacologia* **5**, 397–408.

Klein, M. (1934). A contribution to the psychogenesis of manic-depressive states. Reprinted in *Contributions to psychoanalysis 1921–1945: developments in child and adolescent psychology,* pp. 282–310. Hogarth Press, London (1948).

Klein, M. (1963). *The psychoanalysis of children* (translated by A. Strachey). Hogarth Press and Institute of Psychoanalysis, London.

Klein, R. H. and Nimorwicz, P. (1982). Psychosocial aspects of hemophilia in families: assessment strategies and instruments. *Clinical Psychology Review* **2**, 153–69.

Kleinknecht, R. A., Klepac, R. K., and Alexander, L. D. (1973). Origin and characteristics of fear of dentistry. *Journal of the American Dental Association* **86**, 842–8.

Kleinman, A. (1982). Neurasthenia and depression: a study of somatization and culture in China. *Culture Medicine and Psychiatry* **6**, 117–96.

Kleist, K. (1928). Cycloid paranoid and epileptoid psychoses and the problem of the degenerative psychosis. Reprinted in *Themes and variations in European psychiatry* (ed. S. R. Hirsch and M. Shepherd). Wright, Bristol (1974).

Kleist, K. (1930). Alogical thought disorder: an organic manifestation of the schizophrenic psychological deficit. In *The clinical roots of the schizophrenic concept* (ed. J. Cutting and M. Shepherd). Cambridge University Press, Cambridge (1987).

Knight, G. (1972). Neurosurgical aspects of psychosurgery. *Proceedings of the Royal Society of Medicine* **65**, 1099–104.

Knights, A. and Hirsch, S. R. (1981). Revealed depression and drug treatment for schizophrenia. *Archives of General Psychiatry* **38**, 806–11.

Knights, E. B. and Folstein, M. F. (1977). Unsuspected emotional and cognitive disturbance in medical patients. *Annals of Internal Medicine* **87**, 723–4.

Knott, D. G. and Beard, J. D. (1971). In *Treatment of the alcohol withdrawal syndrome* (ed. F. A. Seixas), p. 29. National Council on Alcoholism, New York.

Koch, J. L. A. (1891). *Die Psychopathischen Minderwertigkeiter.* Dorn, Ravensburg.

Koegel, R., Schreibman, L., O'Neil, R. E., and Burke, J. C. (1983). The personality and family interaction characteristics of parents with autistic children. *Journal of Consulting and Clinical Psychology* **51**, 683–92.

Koehler, K. (1979). First rank symptoms of schizophrenia: questions concerning clinical boundaries. *British Journal of Psychiatry* **134**, 236–48.

Koehler, T. (1985). Stresses and rheumatoid arthritis: a survey of empirical evidence in human and animal studies. *Journal of Psychosomatic Research* **29**, 655–63.

Kolle, K. (1931). *Die primare Verrucktheit: psychopathologishe, klinische und genealogische Untersuchungen*. Thieme, Leipzig.

Kolodny, R. C., Master, W. H., and Johnson, V. E. (1979). *Textbook of sexual medicine*. Little Brown, Boston.

Kolvin, I. and Fundudis, T. (1981). Elective mute children: psychological development and background factors. *Journal of Child Psychology and Psychiatry* **22**, 219–32.

Kolvin, I. Garside, R. F., and Nichol, A. R. (1981). *Help starts here: the maladjusted child in the ordinary school*. Tavistock, London.

Kopelman, M. D. (1986). Clinical tests of memory. *British Journal of Psychiatry* **148**, 517–625.

Kopelman, M. D. (1987). Amnesia: organic and psychogenic. *British Journal of Psychiatry* **150**, 428–42.

Kornfeld, D. S. (1980). The intensive care unit in adults: coronary care and general medical/surgical. *Advances in Psychosomatic Medicine* **10**, 1–29.

Korobkin, R., Ashbury, A. K., Sumner, A. J., and Nielsen, M. D. (1975). Glue-sniffing neuropathy. *Archives of Neurology* **32**, 158–62.

Korsakov, S. S. (1889). Translated and reprinted as 'Psychic disorder in conjunction with multiple neuritis.' *Neurology* **5**, 394–406.

Koryani, E. K. (1979). Morbidity and rate of undiagnosed physical illness in a psychiatric clinic population. *Archives of General Psychiatry* **36**, 414–19.

Koss, M. P., Gidycz, C. A., and Wisniewski, N. (1987). The scope of rape: incidence and prevalence of sexual aggression and victimization in a national sample of higher education students. *Journal of Consulting and Clinical Psychology* **55**, 162–70.

Kosviner, A. (1976). Social science and cannabis use. In *Cannabis and health* (ed. J. D. F. Graham). Academic Press, London.

Kotin, J. and Goodwin, F. K. (1972). Depression during mania. Clinical observations and theoretical implications. *American Journal of Psychiatry* **129**, 679–86.

Kovacs, M. and Beck, A. T. (1977). An empirical clinical approach toward a definition of childhood depression. In *Depression and childhood* (ed. J. G. Schulterbrandt and A. Raskin). Raven Press, New York.

Kraepelin, E. (1897). Dementia praecox. In *Clinical roots of the schizophrenia concept*. (ed. J. Cutting and M. Shepherd). Cambridge University Press. Cambridge (1981).

Kraepelin, E. (1904). *Clinical psychiatry: a textbook for students and physicians*. (edited and translated from 7th edition of Kraepelin's Textbook by A. R. Diefendof). Macmillan, New York.

Kraepelin, E. (1912). Uber paranoide Erkrankungen. *Zentralblatt für die gesamte Neurologie und Psychiatrie* **11**, 617–38.

Kraepelin, E. (1915). Der Verfolgungswahn der Schwerhörigen. *Psychiatrie* Auflage 8, Band IV. Barth, Leipzig.

Kraepelin, E. (1919). *Dementia praecox and paraphrenia*. Livingstone, Edinburgh.

Kraepelin, E. (1920). Patterns of mental disorder. Reprinted in *Themes and variations in European psychiatry* (ed. S. R. Hirsch and M. Shepherd). Wright, Bristol (1974).

Kraepelin, E. (1921). Manic depressive insanity and paranoia (translated by R. M. Barclay from the 8th edition of *Lehrbuch der Psychiatrie*, Vols. III and IV). E. and S. Livingstone, Edinburgh.

Krafft-Ebing. R. (1888). *Lehrbuch der Psychiatrie*. Enke, Stuttgart.

Krafft-Ebing, R. (1924). *Psychopathic sexuality with special reference to contrary sexual instinct*. Authorized translation of the 7th German edition by C. G. Chaddock. F. A. Davis, Philadelphia.

Kral, A. A. (1978). Benign senescent forgetfulness. In *Alzheimer's disease: senile dementia and related disorders* (ed. R. Katzman, R. D. Terry, and K. L. Bick). Raven Press, New York.

Krauthammer, C. and Klerman, G. L. (1978). Secondary mania. *Archives of General Psychiatry* **35**, 1333–9.

Krauthammer, C. and Klerman, G. L. (1979). The epidemiology of mania. In *Manic illness* (ed. B. Shopsin) pp. 11–28. Raven Press, New York.

Kreitman, N. (ed.) (1977). *Parasuicide*. Wiley, London.

Kreitman, N. and Dyer, J. A. T. (1980). Suicide in relation to parasuicide. *Medicine* 2nd series, 1826–30.

Kreitman, N., Sainsbury, P., Pearce, K., and Costain, W. R. (1965). Hypochondriasis and depression in out-patients at a general hospital. *British Journal of Psychiatry* **111**, 607–15.

Kreitman, N., Smith, P., and Tan, E. S. (1969). Attempted suicide in social networks. *British Journal of Preventive and Social Medicine* **23**, 116–23.

Kreitman, N., Collins, J., Nelson, B., and Troop, J. (1970). Neurosis and marital interaction. *British Journal of Psychiatry* **117**, 33–46 and 47–58.

Kretschmer, E. (1921). *Physique and character*. Translated from the original German. Harcourt Brace, New York.

Kretschmer, E. (1924). *Physique and character*. Kegan Paul, London.

Kretschmer, E. (1927). Der sensitive Beziehungswahn. Reprinted and translated as Chapter 8 in *Themes and variations in European psychiatry* (ed. S. R. Hirsch and M. Shepherd). Wright, Bristol (1974).

Kretschmer, E. (1936). *Physique and character* (2nd edn) (translated by W. J. H. Sprott and K. Paul Trench). Trubner, New York.

Kretschmer, E. (1961). *Hysteria, reflex and instinct* (translated into English by V. and W. Baskin from the German). Peter Owen, London.

Kringlen, E. (1965). Obsessional neurosis: a long term follow up. *British Journal of Psychiatry* **111**, 709–22.

Kringlen, E. (1967). *Heredity and environment in the functional psychoses*. Heinemann, London.

Kringlen, E. (1980). Schizophrenia: research in Nordic countries. *Schizophrenia Bulletin* **6**, 566–78.

Kripke, D. F., Risch, S. C., and Janowsky, D. S. (1983). Bright light alleviates depression. *Psychiatry Research* **10**, 105–112.

Krishnan, H. R. R., Davidson, J. R. T., and Guajardo, C. (1985). Trichotillomania—a review. *Comprehensive Psychiatry* **26**, 123–8.

Kroll, J. (1979). Philosophical foundation of French and U. S. nosology. *American Journal of Psychiatry* **136**, 1135–8.

Kubler-Ross, E. (1969). *On death and dying*. Macmillan, New York.

Kuhn, R. (1957). Über die Behandlung depressiver Zustände mit einem Iminodibenzylderivat. *Schweizerische medizinische Wochenschrift* **36**, 1135–40.

Kushlick, A. (1980). Evaluation of residential facilities for the severely mentally handicapped. *Advances in Behaviour Research and Therapy* **3**, No. 1.

Kushlick, A. and Blunden, R. (1974). The epidemiology of mental subnormality.

In *Mental deficiency: the changing outlook* (ed. A. M. Clarke and A. D. B. Clarke) (3rd edn). Methuen, London.

Lacey, J. I. and Lacey, B. C. (1958). Verification and extension of autonomic response stereotype. *American Journal of Psychology* **71**, 50–75.

Lader, M. H. (1969). Psychophysiological aspects of anxiety. In *Studies of anxiety* (ed. M. H. Lader). *British Journal of Psychiatry* Special Publication, No 3.

Lader, M. H. (1975). *The psychophysiology of mental illness*. Routledge and Kegan Paul, London.

Lader, M. H. and Sartorius, N. (1968). Anxiety in patients with hysterical conversion symptoms. *Journal of Neurology, Neurosurgery and Psychiatry* **31**, 490–7.

Lader, M. H. and Wing, L. (1966). *Physiological measures, sedative drugs and morbid anxiety*. Maudsley Monograph No. 14. Oxford University Press, London.

Lader, M. H., Ron, M., and Petursson, H. (1984). Computed axial brain tomography in long-term benzodiazepine users. *Psychological Medicine* **14**, 203–6.

Laidlaw, J., Richens, A., and Oxley, J. (1988). *A textbook of epilepsy* (3rd edn). Churchill Livingstone, Edinburgh.

Laing, R. (1965). *The divided self*. Penguin, Harmondsworth.

Lamb, H. R. (1987). Incompetency to stand trial: appropriateness and outcome. *Archives of General Psychiatry* **44**, 754.

Lamb, H. R. and Talbott, J. A. (1986). The homeless mentally ill. *Journal of the American Medical Association* **256**, 498–501.

Lambourn, J. and Gill, D. (1978). A controlled comparison of simulated and real ECT. *British Journal of Psychiatry* **133**, 514–19.

Lancet (1979). Lithium and the kidney. Grounds for cautious optimism (Editorial). *Lancet* **ii**, 1056–7.

Lancet (1981). Epilepsy and violence (Editorial). *Lancet* **ii**, 966–7.

Lancet (1982a). Solvent abuse (Editorial). *Lancet* **ii**, 1139–40.

Lancet (1982b). Trials of coronary heart disease prevention (Editorial). *Lancet* **ii**, 803–4.

Lancet (1983). Crime as destiny (Editorial). *Lancet* **i**, 35–6.

Lancet (1986). Secure accommodation in psychiatric hospitals (Editorial). *Lancet* **2**, 24–5.

Lancet (1987a). Non-convulsive status epilepticus (Editorial). *Lancet* **1**, 958–9.

Lancet (1987b). Psychiatric day hosptials for all? (Editorial). *Lancet* **2**, 1184–5.

Lander, E. S. (1988). Splitting schizophrenia. *Nature* **336**, 105–6.

Landesmann-Dyer, S. (1981). Living in the community. *American Journal of Mental Deficiency* **86**, 223–34.

Lange, J. (1929). *Verbrechen als Schisksal: Studien kriminellen Zwillingen*. Thieme, Leipzig.

Lange, J. (1931). *Crime as destiny* (translated by C. Haldane). George Allen, London.

Langfeldt, G. (1938). The prognosis in schizophrenia and the factors influencing the course of the disease. *Acta Psychiatrica et Neurologica Scandinavica* Suppl. 13.

Langfeldt, G. (1939). *The schizophreniform states*. Munksgaard, Copenhagen.

Langfeldt, G. (1960). Diagnosis and prognosis of schizophrenia. *Proceedings of the Royal Society of Medicine* **53**, 1047–51.

Langfeldt, G. (1961). The erotic jealousy syndrome. A clinical study. *Acta Psychiatrica Scandinavica* Suppl. 151.

Langsley, D. G. (1985). Community psychiatry. In *Comprehensive textbook of psychiatry* (ed. H. I. Kaplan and B. J. Sadcock) (4th edn). Williams and Wilkins, Baltimore.

Larson, E., Reifler, B. V., Featherstone, H. J., and English, D. R. (1984). Dementia in elderly out-patients: a prospective study. *Annals of Internal Medicine* **100**, 417–23.

Larsson, T., Sjögren, T., Jacobson, G. with the assistance of Sjögren, G. (1963). Senile dementia. A clinical, socio-medical and genetic study. *Acta Psychiatrica Scandinavica* Suppl. **167**, 1–259.

Lasègue, C. (1877). Les exhibitionnistes. *Union Medicale* **23**, 709–14.

Latcham, R. W. (1985). Familial alcoholism: evidence from 237 alcoholics. *British Journal of Psychiatry* **147**, 54–7.

Latimer, P. R. (1978). Crohn's disease: a review of the psychological and social outcome. *Psychological Medicine* **8**, 649–56.

Latimer, P. R. (1981). Irritable bowel syndrome: a behavioural model: *Behaviour Research and Therapy* **19**, 475–83.

Laurell, B. (1970). Comparison of electric and flurothyl convulsive therapy. II antidepressive effect. *Acta Psychiatric Scandinavica* Suppl. **145**, 22–35.

Lauter, I. H. and Meyer, J. E. (1968). Clinical and nosological concepts of dementia. In *Senile dementias* (ed. C. Müller and L. Ciompi). Hans Hüber, Bern.

Lazar, I., Darlington, R., Murray, H., Royce, J., and Snipper, A. (1982). Lasting effects of early education. *Monographs of the Society for Research and Child Development* **47**, (1–2, Serial No. 194).

Lazarus, R. S. (1966). *Psychological stress and the coping processes*. McGraw-Hill, New York.

Leach, J. and Wing, J. K. (1980). *Helping destitute men*. Tavistock, London.

Ledermann, S. (1956). *Alcool, alcoolisme, alcoolisation*. Presses Universitaires de Paris, Paris.

Lee, K., Miller, L., Hardt, F., Haubek, A., and Jensen, E. (1979). Alcohol-induced brain and liver damage in young males. *Lancet* **ii**, 759–61.

Leff, J. (1978). Social and psychological causes of the acute attack. In *Schizophrenia: towards a new synthesis* (ed. J. K. Wing). Academic Press, London.

Leff, J. (1981). *Psychiatry around the globe: a transcultural view*. Marcel Dekker, New York.

Leff, J. (1985). Family treatment of schizophrenia. In *Recent advances in clinical psychiatry* (ed. K. Granville-Grossman), Vol. 5. Churchill Livingstone, London.

Leff, J. (1986). Planning a community psychiatric service: from theory to practice. In *The provision of mental health services in Britain* (ed. G. Wilkinson and H. Freeman). Gaskell, London.

Leff, J. and Isaacs, A. D. (1978). *Psychiatric examination in clinical practice*. Blackwell, Oxford.

Leff, J. and Vaughn, C. (1972). Psychiatric patients in contact and out of contact with services; a clinical and social assessment. In *Evaluating a community psychiatric service* (ed. J. K. Wing and A. M. Hailey). Oxford University Press, London.

Leff, J. and Vaughn, C. (1981). The role of maintenance therapy and relative expressed emotion in relapse of schizophrenia: a two year follow up. *British Journal of Psychiatry* **139**, 102–4.

Leff, J. and Wing, J. K. (1971). Trial of maintenance therapy in schizophrenia. *British Medical Journal* **iii**, 599–604.

Leff, J. Kuipers, L., Berkowitz, R., Everlein-Vries, R., and Sturgeon, D. A. (1982). A controlled trial of social intervention in the families of schizophrenic patients. *British Journal of Psychiatry* **141**, 121–34.

Leff, J. P., Kuipers, L., Berkowitz, R., and Sturgeon, D. (1985a). A controlled trial of intervention in the families of schizophrenic patients: two year follow-up. *British Journal of Psychiatry* 146, 594–600.

Leff, J., Kuipers, L., Berkowitz, R., Vaughn, C., and Sturgeon D. (1985b). Life events, relative expressed emotion and maintenance narcoleptics in schizophrenic relapse. *Psychological Medicine* 13, 799–806.

Leff, J., Wig, N. N., Ghosh, A. *et al.* (1987). Influence of relatives' expressed emotion on the course of schizophrenia in Chandigarh. *British Journal of Psychiatry* 151, 166–73.

Lehrke, R. (1972). A theory of X-linkage of major intellectual traits. *American Journal of Mental Deficiency* 76, 611–19.

Lemere, F., Voegtlin, W. L., Broz, W. R., O'Hallaren, P., and Tupper, W. E. (1942). Conditioned reflex treatment of chronic alcoholism. VIII: a review of six years experience with this treatment of 1526 patients. *Journal of the American Medical Association* 120, 269–70.

Lemert, E. (1951). *Social pathology: a systematic approach to the theory of sociopathic behaviour.* McGraw-Hill, New York.

Lemoine, P., Harousseau, H., Borteyru, J.-P., and Menuet, J.-C. (1968). Les enfants de parents alcooliques: anomalies observées à propos de 127 cas. *Ouest Médical* 25, 477–82.

Leonhard, K. (1957). *The classification of endogenous psychoses.* English translation of the 8th German edition of *Aufteilung der Endogenen Psychosen* by R. Berman. Irvington, New York (1979).

Leonhard, K., Korff, I., and Schulz, H. (1962). Die Temperamente und den Familien der monopolaren und bipolaren phasishen Psychosen. *Psychiatrie und Neurologie* 143, 416–34.

Lerer, B., Moore, N., Meyendorff, E., Cho, S. R., and Gershon, S. (1987). Carbamazepine versus lithium in mania: a double blind study. *Journal of Clinical Psychiatry* 48, 89–93.

Lerman, C. E. (1987). Rheumatoid arthritis: psychological factors in the etiology, course, and treatment. *Clinical Psychology Review* 7, 413–25.

Levenson, J. L., Hamer, R. M., Myers, T., Hart, R. P., and Kaplowitz, L. G. (1987). Psychological factors predict symptoms of severe recurrent genital herpes infection. *Journal of Psychosomatic Research* 31, 153–9.

Levy, N. B. (1986). Renal transplantation in the new medical era. *Advances in Psychosomatic Medicine* 15, 167–79.

Levy, R. and Post, F. (1982). *The psychiatry of late life.* Blackwell, Oxford.

Levy, R., Isaacs A., and Hawks, G. (1970). Neurophysiological correlates of senile dementia: I. Motor and sensory nerve conduction velocity. *Psychological Medicine* 1, 40–7.

Levy, R., Janssen, R., Bush, T., and Rosenblum M. (1988). Neuroepidemiology of AIDS. *Journal of Acquired Immune-Deficiency Syndromes* 1, 81–8.

Lewis, A. J. (1934). Melancholia: a clinical survey of depressive states. *Journal of Mental Science* 80, 277–8.

Lewis, A. J. (1936a). Melancholia: prognostic study and case material. *Journal of Mental Science* 82, 488–558.

Lewis, A. J. (1936b). Problems of obsessional neurosis. *Proceedings of the Royal Society of Medicine* 29, 325–36.

Lewis, A. J. (1938). States of depression: their clinical and aetiological differentiation. *British Medical Journal* ii, 875–8.

Lewis, A. J. (1942). Discussion on differential diagnosis and treatment of post confusional states. *Proceedings of the Royal Society of Medicine* 35, 607–14.

Lewis, A. J. (1953*a*). Hysterical dissociation in dementia paralytica. *Monatsschrift für Psychiatrie und Neurologie* **125**, 589–604.

Lewis, A. J. (1953*b*). Health as a social concept. *British Journal of Sociology* **4**, 109–24.

Lewis, A. J. (1956). Psychological medicine. In *Price's textbook of the practice of medicine* (ed. D. Hunter) (9th edn). Oxford University Press, London.

Lewis, A. J. (1957). Obsessional illness. *Acta Neuropsiquiàtrica Argentina* **3**, 323–35. Reprinted as Chapter 7 in *Inquiries in psychiatry: clinical and social investigations*. Routledge and Kegan Paul, London.

Lewis, A. J. (1968). A glossary of mental disorders. Studies on medical and population subjects 22. General Register Office. HMSO, London.

Lewis, A. J. (1970). Paranoia and paranoid: a historical perspective. *Psychological Medicine* **1**, 2–12.

Lewis, A. J. (1976). A note on classification of phobia. *Psychological Medicine* **6**, 21–2.

Lewis, E. (1979). Grieving by the family after a stillbirth or neonatal death. *Archives of the Diseases of Childhood* **54**, 303–6.

Lewis, E. O. (1929). Report on an investigation into the incidence of mental deficiency in six areas. 1925–27. In *Report of the mental deficiency committee*, Part IV. HMSO, London.

Lewis, H. R. and Streitfeld, H. S. (1970). *Growth games.* Harcourt Brace Jovanovich, New York.

Lewis, N. D. S. and Yarnell, P. (1951). *Pathological firesetting.* Nervous and Mental Diseases Monograph No. 82. New York.

Lex, B. W. (1985). Alcohol problems in special populations. In *The diagnosis and treatment of alcoholism* (ed. J. H. Mendelson and N. K. Mello). McGraw-Hill, New York.

Ley, P. (1977). Psychological studies of doctor patient communication. In *Contributions to medical psychology* (ed. S. Rachman), Vol. 1. Pergamon Press, Oxford.

Ley, P. (1982). Satisfaction, compliance and communication. *British Journal of Clinical Psychology* **21**, 241–54.

Lhermitte, J. (1951). Visual hallucinations of the self. *British Medical Journal* i, 431–4.

Liakos, A. (1967). Familial transvestism. *British Journal of Psychiatry* **113**, 49–51.

Liberman, R. P., Mueser, K. T., Wallace, C. J., *et al.* (1986). Training skills in the psychiatrically disabled: learning coping and competence. *Schizophrenia Bulletin* **12**, 631–47.

Lidz, R. W. and Lidz, T. (1949). The family environment of schizophrenic patients. *American Journal of Psychiatry* **106**, 332–45.

Lidz, T., Fleck, S., and Cornelison, A. (1965). *Schizophrenia and the family.* International Universities Press, New York.

Lieberman, M. A., Yalom, I. D., and Miles, M. B. (1973). *Encounter groups: first facts.* Basic Books, New York.

Liebowitz, M. R. (1979). Is borderline a distinct entity? *Schizophrenia Bulletin* **5**, 23–38.

Liebowitz, M. R., Gorman, J. M., Fyer, A. J., and Klein, D. F. (1985). Social phobia: review of a neglected anxiety disorder. *Archives of General Psychiatry*, **42**, 729–36.

Liem, J. H. (1980). Family studies of schizophrenia: an update and commentary. *Schizophrenia Bulletin* **6**, 429–55.

Lim, L., Ron, M. A., Ormerod, I. E. C., David, J., Miller, D. H., Logsdail, S. J., Walport, M. J., and Harding, A. E. (1988). Psychiatric and neurological manifestations in systemic lupus erythematosus. *Quarterly Journal of Medicine* **66**, 27–38

Lind, K. (1982). A synthesis of studies on stroke rehabilitation. *Journal of Chronic Disorders* **35**, 133–49.

Lindemann, E. (1944). Symptomatology and management of acute grief. *American Journal of Psychiatry* **101**, 141–8.

Lindsay, J. (1986). Suicide and attempted suicide in old age. In *Affective disorders in the elderly* (ed. E. Murphy). Churchill Livingstone, Edinburgh.

Lindsay, M. (1985). Emotional management. In *Care of the child with diabetes*. (ed. J. D. Baum and A. L. Kinmonth) Churchill Livingstone, Edinburgh.

Lindstedt, G., Nilsson, L. A., Walinder, J., Skott, A., and Ohman, R. (1977). On the prevalence, diagnosis and management of lithium-induced hypothyroidism in psychiatric patients. *British Journal of Psychiatry* **130**, 452–8.

Lineberger, H. P. (1981). Social characteristics of a haemophiliac clinic population. *General Hospital Psychiatry* **3**, 157–63.

Ling, M. H. M., Perry, P. J., and Tsuang, M. T. (1981). Side effects of corticosteroid therapy. *Archives of General Psychiatry* **38**, 471–7.

Lingjaerde, O., Edlund, A. H., Gormsen, C. A., Gottfries, C. G., Haugstad, A., Hermann, I. L., Hollnagel, P., Mäkimattila, A.,, Rasmussen, K. E., Remvig, J., and Robak, O. H. (1974). The effects of lithium carbonate in combination with tricyclic antidepressants in endogenous depression. *Acta Psychiatrica Scandinavica* **50**, 233–42.

Linn, M. W., Caffey, E. M., Klett, J., Hogarty, G. E., and Lamb, R. (1979). Day treatment and psychotropic drugs in the aftercare of schizophrenic patients. *Archives of General Psychiatry* **36**, 1055–66.

Linton, S. J. (1986). Behavioural remediation of chronic pain, a status report. *Pain* **24**, 125–41.

Lipkin, M., Fisher, L., Rawley, P. T., Loader, S., and Iker, H. P. (1986). Genetic counselling of symptomatic carriers in a primary care setting. *Annals of Internal Medicine* **105**, 115–23.

Lipowski, Z. J. (1980a). *Delirium. Acute brain failure in man.* Thomas, Springfield, Ill.

Lipowski, Z. J. (1980b). Organic mental disorders: introduction and review of syndromes. In *Comprehensive textbook of psychiatry*, (ed. H. I. Kaplan, A. M. Freedman, and B. J. Sadock) (3rd edn). Williams and Wilkins, Baltimore.

Lipowski, Z. J. (1983). Transient cognitive disorders (delirium, acute confusional states) in the elderly. *American Journal of Psychiatry* **140**, 1426–36.

Lipowski, Z. J. (1984). Organic brain syndromes: new classification, concepts and prospects. *Canadian Journal of Psychiatry* **29**, 198–204.

Lipowski, Z. J. (1985). *Psychosomatic medicine and liaison psychiatry*. Plenum, New York.

Lipowski, Z. J. (1986). Consultation-liaison psychiatry: the first half century. *General Hospital Psychiatry* **8**, 305–15.

Lishman, W. A. (1968). Brain damage in relation to psychiatric disability after head injury. *British Journal of Psychiatry* **114**, 373–410.

Lishman, W. A. (1978). Research into the dementias. . *Psychological Medicine* **8**, 353–6.

Lishman, W. A. (1981). Cerebral disorder in alcoholism: syndromes of impairment. *Brain* **104**, 1–20.

Lishman, W. A. (1987). *Organic psychiatry* (2nd edn). Blackwell, Oxford.

Lishman, W. A., Ron, M., and Acker, W. (1980). Computed tomography of the brain and psychometric assessment of alcoholic patients—a British study. In *Addiction and brain damage* (ed. D. Richter). Croom Helm, London.

Liskow, B., Othmer, E., Renick, E. C., De Souza, C., and Gabelli, W. (1986). Is Briquet's syndrome a heterogeneous disorder? *American Journal of Psychiatry* **143**, 626–9.

Liston, E. H. and La Rue, A. (1985). Clinical differentiatioin of primary degenerative and multi-infarct dementia: a critical review of the evidence. Part 1: clinical studies. *Biological Psychiatry* **18**, 1451–65.

Litman, R. E., Curphey, T., Shneidman, E. S., Farberow, N. C., and Tabachnick, N. (1963). The psychological autopsy of equivocal suicides. *Journal of the American Medical Association* **184**, 924–9.

Littlewood, R. and Lipsedge, M. (1988). Psychiatric illness among British Afro-Caribbeans. *British Medical Journal* **296**, 950–1.

Livingston, M. G. (1986). Assessment of need for coordinated approach in families with victims of head injury. *British Medical Journal* **293**, 742–4.

Livingston, M. G., Brooks, D. N., and Bond, M. R. (1985). Patient outcome in the year following severe head injury and relatives psychiatric and social functioning. *Journal of Neurology, Neurosurgery and Psychiatry* **48**, 876–81.

Ljungberg, L. (1957). Hysteria. *Acta Psychiatrica Scandinavica* Suppl. 12.

Lloyd, G. G. (1980). Whence and whither 'liaison' psychiatry? *Psychological Medicine* **10**, 11–14.

Lloyd, G. G. (1985). Emotional aspects of physical illness In *Recent advances in clinical psychiatry* (ed. K. Granville-Grossman) Vol. 5. London.,

Lloyd, G. G., Parke, A. C., Ludlam, C. A., and Macguire, R. I. (1984). Emotional impact of diagnosis and early treatment of lymphomas. *Journal of Psychological Research* **28**, 157–62.

Lloyd, K. G., Farley, I. J., Deck, J. H. N., and Hornykiewicz, O. (1974). Serotonin and 5-hydroxyindolacetic acid in discrete areas of the brain stem of suicide victims and control patients. *Advances in Biochemical Psychopharmacology* **11**, 387–97.

Longsley, D. G. (1985). Community psychiatry. In *Comprehensive textbook of psychiatry* (ed. H. I. Kaplan and B. J. Sadock) (4th edn). Williams and Wilkins, Baltimore.

Loudon, J. B. (1987). Prescribing in pregnancy: psychotropic drugs. *British Medical Journal* **293**. 167–9.

Loudon, J. B. and Waring, H. (1976). Toxic reactions to lithium and haloperidol. *Lancet* **ii**, 1088.

Lovibond, S. H. (1964). *Conditioning and enuresis*. Pergamon Press, Oxford.

Lovibond, S. H. and Coote, M. A. (1970). Enuresis. In *Symptoms of psychopathology* (ed. G. G. Costello). Wiley, New York.

Lowman, R. L. and Richardson, L. M. (1987). Pseudoepileptic seizures of psychogenic origin: a review of the literature. *Clinical Psychology Review* **7**, 363–89.

Lown, B., (1982). Mental stress, arrhythmias and sudden death. *American Journal of Medicine* **72**, 177–80.

Lown, B., de Silva, R. A., Reich, P., and Murawski, B. J. (1980). Psychophysiologic factors in sudden cardiac death. *American Journal of Psychiatry* **137**, 1325–35.

Luborsky, L., Singer, B., and Luborsky, L. (1975). Comparative studies of psychotherapies. *Archives of General Psychiatry* **31**, 995–1008.

Lukianowicz, N. (1958). Autoscopic phenomena. *Archives of Neurology and Psychiatry* **80**, 199–220.

Lukianowicz, N. (1959). Survey of various aspects of transvestism in the light of our present knowledge. *Journal of Nervous and Mental Disease* **128**, 36–64.

Lukianowicz, N. (1967). 'Body image' disturbances in psychiatric disorders. *British Journal of Psychiatry* **113**, 31–47,

Lundberg, S. G. and Guggenheim, F. (1986). Sequelae of limb amputation. In: Psychological aspects of surgery. *Advances in Psychosomatic Medicine* **15**, 199–210.

Lundquist, G. (1945). Prognosis and course in manic depressive psychosis. A follow-up study of 319 first admissions. *Acta Psychiatrica Scandinavica* Suppl. 35.

Luxenberger, H. (1928). Vorläufiger Bericht über psychiatrische Serienuntersuchungen an Zwillingen. *Zeitschrift für die gesamte Neurologie and Psychiatrie* **116** 297–326.

Lynch, M. and Roberts, J. (1982). *Consequences of child abuse*. Academic Press, London.

MacAlpine, I. and Hunter, R. (1966). The 'insanity' of King George III: a classic case of porphyria. *British Medical Journal* i, 65–71.

McCabe, B. J. (1986). Dietary tyramine and other pressor-amines in MAOI regimens: a review. *Journal of the American Dietetic Association* **86**, 1059–64.

MacCarthy, D. (1981). The effects of emotional disturbance and deprivation and somatic growth. In *Scientific foundations of paediatrics* (ed J. A. Davis and J. Dobbing), pp. 54–73. Heinemann, London.

McCarthy, P. D. and Walsh, D. (1975). Suicide in Dublin: 1. The under-reporting of suicide and the consequences for national statistics. *British Journal of Psychiatry* **126**, 301–8.

McClure, G. M. G. (1984a). Recent trends in suicide amongst the young. *British Journal Psychiatry* **144**, 134–8.

McClure, G. M. G. (1984b). Suicide in England and Wales 1975–84. *British Journal of Psychiatry* **150**, 309–14.

McCombie, S. L., Bassuk, E., Savitz, R., and Pell, S. (1976). Development of a medical center rape crisis intervention programme. *American Journal of Psychiatry* **133**, 418–21.

McCreadie, R. G., and Farmer, J. G. (1985). Lithium and hair texture. *Acta Psychiatrica Scandinavica* **72**, 387–8.

McCulloch, D. K., Young, R. J., Prescott, R. J., Campbell, I. W., and Clark, B. F. (1984). Natural history of impotence in diabetic men. *Diabetologia* **26**, 437–40.

MacCulloch, M. J., Snowden, P. R., Wood, P. J. W., and Mills, H. E. (1985). Sadistic fantasy, sadistic behaviour, and offending. *British Journal of Psychiatry* **143**, 20–9.

McDonald, C. (1969). Clinical heterogeneity in senile dementia. *British Journal of Psychiatry* **115**, 267–72.

MacDonald, J. M. (1964). The threat to kill. *American Journal of Psychiatry* **120**, 125–30.

McEvedy, C. P. and Beard, A. W. (1970). Concept of benign myalgic encephalomyelitis. *British Medical Journal* i, 11–15.

MacFarlane, A. B. (1985). Medical evidence in the Court of Protection. *Bulletin of the Royal College of Psychiatrists* **9**, 26–8.

McGuffin, P. (1984). Principles and methods in psychiatric genetics. In *The scientific principles of psychopathology* (ed. P. McGuffin, M. F. Shanks, and R. J. Hodgson). Academic Press, London.

McGuffin, P. (1987). The new genetics and childhood psychiatric disorder. *Journal of Child Psychology and Psychiatry* **28**, 215–22.

McGuffin, P. and Katz, R. (1986). Nature, nuture and affective disorder. In *The biology of depression* (ed. J. F. W. Deakin), pp. 26–52. Gaskell, London.

McGuffin, P., Farmer, A. E., Gottesman, M., Murray, R. M., and Reveley, A. M. (1984). Twin concordance for operationally defined schizophrenia. *Archives of General Psychiatry* **49**, 541–5.

McHugh, P. R. and Slavney, P. R. (1986). *The perspectives of psychiatry*. Johns Hopkins University Press, Baltimore.

MacKay, A. V. P. and Sheppard, G. P. (1979). Pharmacotherapeutic trials in tardive dyskinesia. *British Journal of Psychiatry* **135**, 489–99.

Mackay, R. I. (1982). The causes of severe mental handicap. *Developmental Medicine and Child Neurology* **24**, 386–93.

McKenna, P. J. (1984). Disorders with overvalued ideas. *British Journal of Psychiatry* **145**, 579–85.

McKinney, W. T., Suomi, S. J., and Harlow, H. F. (1972). Repetitive peer separation of juvenile-age rhesus monkeys. *Archives of General Psychiatry* **27**, 200–3.

Macleod, J. and Walton, H. (1969). Liaison between physicians and psychiatrists in a teaching hospital. *Lancet* **ii**, 789–92.

McLoone, P. and Crombie, I. K. (1987). Trends in suicide in Scotland 1974–84: an increasing problem. *British Medical Journal* **295**, 629–31.

McLoughlin, I. J. (1986). Bereavement in the mentally handicapped. *British Journal of Hospital Medicine* **31**, 256–60.

McLoughlin, I. J. (1987). The picas. *British Journal of Hospital Medicine* **37**, 286–90.

MacMillan, J. F., Crow, T. J., Johnson, A. L., and Johnstone, E. C. (1986). The Northwick Park study of first episodes of schizophrenia. IV. Expressed emotion and relapse. *British Journal of Psychiatry* **148**, 133–43.

McSweeney, A. J., Grant, I., Medlen, R. K., Adams, K. M., and Timms, R. M. (1982). Life quality of patients with chronic obstructive pulmonary disease. *Archives of Internal Medicine* **142**, 473–8.

Madanes, C. and Haley, J. (1977). Dimensions of family therapy. *Journal of Nervous and Mental Disease* **165**, 88–98.

Maguire, G. P. (1983). Psychological and social aspects of childhood malignancy. *Annales Nestlé* **41**, 32–43.

Maguire, G. P. (1985). Psychosocial intervention in women with breast cancer. In: *Psychological aspects of cancer* (eds. M. Watson and T. Morris). Pergamon Press, Oxford.

Maguire, G. P. and Granville-Grossman, K. L. (1968). Physical illness in psychiatric patients. *British Journal of Psychiatry* **115**, 1365–9.

Maguire, G. P., Julier, D. L., Hawton, K. E., and Bancroft, J. H. J. (1974). Psychiatric morbidity and referral on two general medical wards. *British Medical Journal* **i**, 268–70.

Maguire, G. P., Lee, E. O., Bevington, D. J., Kucheman, C. S., Crabtree, R. J., and Cornell, C. E. (1978). Psychiatric problems in the first year after mastectomy. *British Medical Journal* **i**, 963–5.

Maguire, G. P., Tait, A., Brooke, M., Thomas, C., and Sellwood, R. (1980). Effect of counselling on the psychiatric morbidity associated with mastectomy. *British Medical Journal* **281**, 1454–6.

Mahendra, B. (1981). Where have all the catatonics gone? *Psychological Medicine* **11**, 669–71.

Mahl, G. F. (1953). Physiological changes during chronic fear. *Annals of the New York Academy of Science* **56**, 240–9.

Make, B. J. (1986). Introduction to pulmonary rehabilitation. *Clinics in Chest Medicine* **7**, 519–48.

Malan, D. H. (1963). *A study of brief psychotherapy.* Tavistock, London.

Malitz, S., Sackheim, H. A., Decina, P., Kanzler, M., and Ker, B. (1986). The efficacy of electroconvulsive therapy: dose–response interactions with modality. In *Electroconvulsive therapy: clinical and basic research issues. Annals of the New York Academy of Science* **467**, 56–64.

Maletzky, B. M. (1973). The episodic dyscontrol syndrome. *Diseases of the Nervous System* **34**, 178–84.

Maletzky, B. M. (1974). 'Assisted' covert sensitization in the treatment of exhibitionism. *Journal of Consulting and Clinical Psychology* **42**, 34–40.

Maletzky, B. M. (1976). The diagnosis of pathological intoxication. *Journal of Studies on Alcoholism* **37**, 1215–20.

Maletzky, B. M. (1977). 'Booster' sessions in aversion therapy: the permanency of treatment. *Behaviour Therapy* **11**, 655–7.

Malin, N., Race, D., and Jones, G. (1980). *Services for the mentally handicapped in Britain.* Croom Helm, London.

Malmo, R. B. (1962). Activation. In *Experimental foundations of clinical psychology* (ed. A. J. Bachrach). Basic Books, New York.

Malzberg, B. and Lee, E. S. (1956). *Migration and mental disease: a study of first admission to hospitals for mental disease in New York 1939–41.* Social Science Research Council, New York.

Mann, A. H. (1977). The psychological effect of a screening programme and clinical trial for hypertension upon the participants. *Psychological Medicine* **7**. 431–8.

Mann, A. H. (1986). Psychological aspects of essential hypertension. *Journal of Psychosomatic Research* **30**, 527–41.

Mann, A. H., Jenkins, R., and Belsey, E. (1981). The twelve-month outcome of patients with neurotic illness in general practice. *Psychological Medicine* **11**, 535–50.

Mann, J. J., Stanley, M., McBride, P. A., and McEwen, B. S. (1986). Increased serotonin, and beta-adrenergic receptor binding in the frontal cortices of suicide victims. *Archives of General Psychiatry* **43**, 954–9.

Mann, S. A. and Cree, W. (1976). New long stay patients: a national survey of 15 mental hospitals in England and Wales 1972–3. *Psychological Medicine* **6**, 603–16.

Manschreck, T. C., Maher, B. A., Rucklos, M. E., and Vereen, D. R. (1982). Disturbed voluntary motor activity in schizophrenic disorder. *Psychological Medicine* **12**, 73–84.

Mapother, E. (1926). Manic depressive psychosis. *British Medical Journal* **ii**, 872–9.

Marcé, L. V. (1858). *Traité de la folie des femmes enceintes, des nouvelles accouchés et des nourrices.* Baillière, Paris.

Marks, I. M. (1969). *Fears and phobias*, Heinemann, London.

Marks, I. M. (1981). Space phobia: a pseudo-agoraphobic syndrome. *Journal of Neurology, Neurosurgery and Psychiatry* **44**, 387–91.

Marks, I. M. and Gelder, M. G. (1966). Different ages of onset of varieties of phobia. *American Journal of Psychiatry* **123**, 218–21.

Marks, I. M. and Gelder, M. G. (1967). Transvestism and fetishism; clinical and psychological changes during faradic aversion. *British Journal of Psychiatry* **113**, 711–29.

Marks, I. M., Rachman, S., and Gelder, M. G. (1965). Method for the assessment of aversion therapy in fetishism with narcissism. *Behaviour Research and Therapy* **3**, 253–8.

Marks, I. M., Stern, R. S., Mawson, D., Cobb, J., and McDonald, R. (1980). Clomipramine and exposure for obsessive compulsive rituals. *British Journal of Psychiatry* **136**, 1–25.

Marks, I. M., Gray, S., Cohen, D., Hill, R., Mawson, D., Ramm, E., and Stern, R. S. (1983). Imipramine and brief therapist-aided exposure in agoraphobics having self-exposure homework. *Archives of General Psychiatry* **40**, 153–62.

Marks, V. and Rose, F. C. (1965). *Hypoglycaemia*. Blackwell, Oxford.

Marsden, C. D. (1983). Pain, as illustrated by the problems of headache and facial pain. In *Handbook of Psychiatry*, Vol. 2. *Mental disorders and somatic illness*. (ed. M. H. Lader). Cambridge University Press, Cambridge.

Marsden, C. D. (1984). Neurological causes of dementia other than Alzheimer's Disease. In *Handbook of studies on psychiatry and old age* (eds. D. W. K. Kay and G. D. Burrows). Elsevier, Amsterdam.

Marsden, C. D. and Jenner, R. (1980). Pathophysiology of extrapyramidal side-effects of neuroleptic drugs. *Psychological Medicine* **10**, 55–72.

Martin, P. R. (1982). Spasmodic torticollis; a behavioral perspective. *Journal of Behavioral Medicine* **5**, 249–74.

Martin, P. R. and Mathews, A. (1978). Tension headaches: a physiological investigation. *Journal of Psychosomatic Research* **22**, 389–99.

Masters, W. H. and Johnson, V. E. (1970). *Human sexual inadequacy*. Churchill, London.

Masters, W. H. and Johnson, V. E. (1979). *Homosexuality in perspective*. Little Brown, Boston.

Mathews, A. and Ridgeway, V. (1981). Personality and surgical recovery: a review. *British Journal of Clinical Psychology* **20**, 243–60.

Mathews, A., Gelder, M. G., and Johnston, D. (1981). *Agoraphobia: nature and treatment*. Tavistock, London.

Maudsley, H. (1879). *The pathology of mind*. Macmillan, London.

Maudsley, H. (1885). *Responsibility in mental disease*. Kegan Paul and Trench, London.

Maughan, B., Gray, G., and Rutter, M. (1985). Reading retardation and antisocial behaviour: a follow-up into employment. *Journal of Child Psychology and Psychiatry* **25**, 741–58.

Mavissakalian, M., Salerni, R., Thompson, M. E., and Mitchelson, L. (1983). Mitral valve prolapse and agoraphobia. *American Journal of Psychiatry* **140**, 1612–40.

May, P. R. A. (1968). *Treatment of schizophrenia*. Science House, New York.

Mayer, W. (1921). Über paraphrene psychosen. *Zentralblatt für die gesamte Neurologie und Psychiatrie* **71**, 187–206.

Mayer-Gross, W. (1932). Die Schizophrenie. In *Bumke's Handbuch der Geistes-krankheiten*, Vol. 9. Springer, Berlin.

Mayer-Gross, W. (1935). On depersonalization. *British Journal of Medical Psychology* **15**, 103–26.

Mayer-Gross, W., Slater, E., and Roth, M. (1969). *Clinical psychiatry*. Ballière Tindall and Cox, London.

Mayfield, D., Millard, G., and Hall, P. (1974). The CAGE questionnaire: validation of a new alcoholism screening instrument. *American Journal of Psychiatry* **131**, 1121–3.

Mayou, R. A. (1975). Psychological morbidity in a clinic for sexually transmitted disease. *British Journal of Venereal Disease* **51**, 57–60.

Mayou, R. A. (1976). The nature of bodily symptoms. *British Journal of Psychiatry* **129**, 55–60.

Mayou, R. A. (1979). The course and determinants of reactions to myocardial infarction. *British Journal of Psychiatry* **134**, 588–94.

Mayou, R. A. (1986). The psychiatric and social consequences of coronary artery surgery. *Journal of Psychosomatic Research* **30**, 255–71.

Mayou, R. A. and Hawton, K. E. (1986). Psychiatric disorder in the general hospital. *British Journal of Psychiatry* **149**, 172–90.

Mayou, R. A., Sleight, P., MacMahon, D., and Florencio, M. J. (1981). Early rehabilitation after myocardial infarction. *Lancet* **ii**, 1399–401.

Meacher, M. (1972). *Taken for a ride*. Longmans, London.

Meadow, R. (1985). Management of Munchausen syndrome by proxy. *Archives of Diseases of Childhood* **60**, 385–93.

Mechanic, D. (1962). The concept of illness behaviour. *Journal of Chronic Diseases* **15**, 189–94.

Mechanic, D. (1978). *Medical sociology* (2nd edn). Free Press, Glencoe.

Mechanic, D. (1979). *Future issues in health care; social policy and the rationing of medical services*, Free Press, New York.

Mechanic, D. and Aiken, L. H. (1987). Improving the care of patients with chronic mental illness. *New England Journal of Medicine* **317**, 1634–8.

Medical Research Council Drug Trials Subcommittee (1981). Continuation therapy with lithium and amitriptyline in unipolar depressive illness: a controlled clinical trial. *Psychological Medicine* **11**, 409–16.

Mednick, S. A. (1958). A learning theory approach to research in schizophrenia. *Psychological Bulletin* **55**, 316–27.

Mednick, S. A. and Schulsinger, F. (1968). In *The transmission of schizophrenia* (ed. D. Rosenthal and S. Kety). Pergamon Press, Oxford.

Mednick, S. A., Moffitt, T. E., and Stack, S. (1987). *The causes of crime. New biological approaches*. Cambridge University Press, Cambridge.

Meduna, L. (1938). General discussion of cardiazol therapy. *American Journal of Psychiatry* **94**, Suppl. 40.

Meecham, W. C. and Smith, N. (1977). Effects of jet aircraft noise on mental hospital admissions. *British Journal of Audiology* **11**, 81–5.

Megargee, E. I. (1966). Uncontrolled and overcontrolled personality type in extreme antisocial aggression. *Psychological Monographs* **80**, No. 3.

Meichenbaum, D. H. (1977). *Cognitive-behaviour modification*. Plenum, New York.

Mellinger, G. D., Balter, M. B., and Uhlenhuth, E. H. (1985). Insomnia and its treatment. *Archives of General Psychiatry* **42**, 225–32.

Mellor, C. S. (1982). The present status of first-rank symptoms. *British Journal of Psychiatry* **140**, 423–4.

Meltzer, E. S. and Kumar, R. (1985). Puerperal mental illness, clinical features and classification: a study of 142 mother-and-baby admissions. *British Journal of Psychiatry* **147**, 647–54.

Melzack, R. and Wall, P. D. (1965). Pain mechanisms: a new theory. *Science* **130**, 971–9.

Mendels, J. (1965). Electroconvulsive therapy and depression I: the prognostic significance of clinical features. *British Journal of Psychiatry* **111**, 675–81.

Mendels, J., Secunda, S. K., and Dyson, W. L. (1972). A controlled study of the antidepressant effects of lithium carbonate. *Archives of General Psychiatry* **26**, 456–72.

Mendelson, M. (1982). Psychodynamics of depression. In *Handbook of affective disorders* (ed. E. S. Paykel). Churchill Livingstone, Edinburgh.

Mendelson, W. B. (1980). *The use and misuse of sleeping pills: a clinical guide.* Plenum, New York.

Mendelwicz, J. and Rainer, J. D. (1977). Adoption study supporting genetic transmission of manic depressive illness. *Nature* **268**, 327–9.

Menninger, K. (1948). *Changing concepts of disease.* Viking Press, New York.

Merikangas, K. R., Leckman, J. F., Prusoff, B. A., Pauls, D. L., and Weissman, M. M. (1985). Familial transmission of depression and alcoholism. *Archives of General Psychiatry* **42**, 367–72.

Merskey, H. (1980). Psychiatry and the treatment of pain. *British Journal of Psychiatry* **136**, 600–2.

Merskey, H. (1984). Too much pain. *British Journal of Hospital Medicine* **30**, 63–66.

Merskey, H. and Spear, F. G. (1967). *Pain, psychological and psychiatric aspects.* Baillière, Tindall and Cassell, London.

Meyer, A. J. and Henderson, J. B. (1974). Multiple risk factor reductions in the prevention of cardiovascular disease. *Preventive Medicine* **3**, 225–36.

Meyer, J. K. and Reter, D. J. (1979). Sex reassignment: follow up. *Archives of General Psychiatry* **36**, 1010–15.

Meyer, V. and Levy, R. (1971). Treatment of obsessive compulsive neurosis. *Proceedings of the Royal Society of Medicine* **64**, 1115–18.

Meyers, S., Walfish, J. S., Sachar, D. B., Greenstein, A. J., Hill, A. G., and Janowitz, H. D. (1980). Quality of life after surgery for Crohn's disease: a psychosocial survey. *Gastroenterology* **78**, 1–6.

Mezey, G. C. (1985). Rape—victimological and psychiatric aspects. *British Journal of Hospital Medicine* **28**, 152–8.

Mezzich, J. E., Fabrega, H., Mezzich, A. C., and Coffman, G. A. (1985). International Experience with DSMIII. *Journal of Nervous and Mental Disorders* **173**, 738–41.

Michael, R. P. and Gibbons, J. L. (1963). Interrelationships between the endocrine system and neuropsychiatry. *International Review of Neurobiology* **5**, 243–302.

Milano, M. R. and Kornfeld, D. S. (1984). Psychiatry and surgery. In: *Psychiatry update. The American Psychiatric Association Annual review*, Vol. 3. (ed. L. Grinspoon) American Psychiatric Press, Washington.

Miles, A. (1979). Some psychosocial consequences of multiple sclerosis: problems of social interaction and group identity. *British Medical Journal* **iii**, 321–31.

Miles, P. (1977). Conditions predisposing to suicide: a review. *Journal of Nervous and Mental Diseases* **164**, 231-46.

Miller, D. H., Clancy, J., and Cumming, E. (1953). A comparison between unidirectional current non-convulsive electrical stimulation given with Reiter's machine, standard alternating current electroshock (Cerletti method) and pentothal in chronic schizophrenia. *American Journal of Psychiatry* **109**, 617–20.

Miller, E. (1980*a*). Cognitive assessment of the older adult. In *Handbook of mental health* (ed. J. E. Birren and R. E. Sloane). Prentice Hall, Englewood Cliffs.

Miller, E. (1980*b*). Psychological intervention in the management and rehabilitation of neuropsychological impairments. *Behaviour Research and Therapy* **18**, 527–35.

Miller, G. H. and Agnew, N. (1974). The Lederman model of alcohol consumption. *Quarterly Journal of Studies on Alcoholism* **35**, 877–98.

Miller, H. (1961). Accident neurosis. *British Medical Journal* **i**, 919–25 and 992–8.

Miller, H. and Stern, G. (1965). The long-term prognosis of severe head injury. *Lancet* **i**, 225–9.

Miller, H. L., Coombs, D. W., Leeper, J. D., and Barlor, S. N. (1984). An analysis of the effects of suicide prevention facilities on suicide rates in the United States. *Journal of Public Health* **74** 340–3.

Miller, R. J., Horn, A. S., and Iversen, L. L. (1974). The action of neuroleptic drugs on dopamine-stimulated adenosine cyclic 3'5' monophosphate production in rat neostriatum and limbic forebrain. *Molecular Pharmacology* **10**, 759–66.

Mindham, R. H. S. (1970). Psychiatric symptoms in Parkinsonism. *Journal of Neurology, Neurosurgery and Psychiatry* **33**, 188–91.

Mindham, R. H. S. (1974). Psychiatric aspects of Parkinson's disease. *British Journal of Hospital Medicine* **11**, 411–14.

Mindham, R. H. S. (1979). Tricyclic antidepressants and amine precursors. In *Psychopharmacology of affective disorders* (ed. E. S. Paykel and A. Coppen). Oxford University Press, Oxford.

Mindham, R. H. S., Bagshaw, A., Howland, C., and Shepherd, M. (1973). An evaluation of continuation therapy with tricyclic antidepressants in depressive illness. *Psychological Medicine* **3**, 5–17.

Mindham, R. H. S., Ahmed, S. W., and Clough, S. G. (1982). A controlled study of dementia in Parkinson's disease. *Journal of Neurology, Neurosurgery and Psychiatry* **45**, 969–74.

Minski, L. and Guttmann, E. (1938). Huntington's chorea: a study of thirty four families. *Journal of Mental Science* **84**, 21–96.

Minuchin, S. (1974). *Families and family therapy*. Tavistock, London.

Minuchin, S. and Fishman, H. C. (1981). *Family therapy techniques*. Harvard University Press, Cambridge, Mass.

Minuchin, S., Rosman, B., and Baker, L. (1978). *Psychosomatic families: anorexia nervosa in context*. Harvard University Press, Cambridge, Mass.

Mitchell, A. R. K. (1985). Psychiatrists in primary health care settings. *British Journal of Psychiatry* **147**, 371–9.

Mitchell, J. E. (1986). Anorexia nervosa: medical and physiological aspects. In: *Handbook of eating disorders: physiology, psychology and treatment of obesity, anorexia and bulimia* (eds. K. D. Brownell, and K. J. P. Forreyt). Basic Books, New York.

Mitchell, W., Falconer, M. A., and Hill, D. (1954). Epilepsy with fetishism relieved by temporal lobectomy. *Lancet* **ii**, 626–30.

Mitchell-Heggs, N., Kelly, D., and Richardson, A. (1976). Stereotactic limbic leucotomy—a follow-up after 16 months. *British Journal of Psychiatry* **128**, 226–41.

Mitcheson, M. C. (1983). Drug addiction. In *The Oxford textbook of medicine* (ed. D. J. Weatherall, J. G. G. Ledingham, and D. A. Warrell). Oxford University Press, Oxford.

Mohr, J. W., Turner, R. E., and Jerry, M. B. (1964). *Pedophilia and exhibitionism*. University Press, Toronto.

Monteiro, W., Marks, I. M., and Ramm, E. (1985). Marital adjustment and treatment outcome in agoraphobia. *British Journal of Psychiatry* **146**, 383–90.

Morel, B. A. (1860). *Traité des malades mentales*. Masson, Paris.

Morgan, H. G. (1979). *Death wishes? The understanding and management of deliberate self-harm*. Wiley, Chichester.

Morgan, H. G. (1985). Functional vomiting. *Journal of Psychosomatic Research* **29**, 341–52.

Morgan, H. G., Burns-Cox, C. J., Pocock, H., and Pottle, S. (1975). Deliberate self-harm: clinical and socio-economic characteristics of 368 patients. *British Journal of Psychiatry* **127**, 564–74.

Morris, P. (1969). *Put away*. Routledge and Kegan Paul, London.

Morrison, J. R. (1975). The family histories of manic-depressive patients with and without alcoholism. *Journal of Nervous and Mental Diseases* **160**, 227–9.

Morselli, E. (1886). Sulla dismorfofobia e sulla tabefobia. *Bolletin Academica Medica* **VI**, 110–19.

Morstyn, R., Duffy, F. H., and McCarley, R. W. (1983). Altered P_{300} topography in schizophrenia. *Archives of General Psychiatry* **40**, 729–34.

Mortimer, P. S. and Dawber, R. P. R. (1984). Hair loss and lithium, commentary. *International Journal of Dermatology* **23**. 603–4.

Mosher, L. R. (1983). Alternatives to psychiatric hospitalisation. *New England Journal of Medicine* **309**, 1579–80.

Mosher, L. and Keith, S. (1980). Psychosocial treatment: individual, group, family and community support approaches. *Schizophrenia Bulletin* **6**, 10–41.

Moss, A. R. (1987). AIDS and intravenous drug use: the real heterosexual epidemic. *British Medical Journal* **294**, 389–90.

Moss, P. D. and McEvedy, C. P. (1966). An epidemic of overbreathing among schoolgirls. *British Medical Journal* **ii**, 1295–300.

Mowat, R. R. (1966). *Morbid jealousy and murder*. Tavistock, London.

Mowrer, O. H. (1950). *Learning theory and personality dynamics*. Ronald Press, New York.

Mrazek, D. and Mrazek, P. (1985) Child maltreatment. In *Child and adolescent psychiatry* (ed. M. Rutter and L. Hersov) (2nd edn). Blackwell, Oxford.

Mrazek, D., Secunda, S. K., and Dyson, W. L. (1972). A controlled study of the antidepressant effects of lithium carbonate. *Archives of General Psychiatry* **26**, 154–7.

Mrazek, D., Stinnett, J. L., Burns, D., and Frazer, A. (1975). Amine precursors and depression. *Archives of General Psychiatry* **32**, 22–30.

Mullen, P. E. and Maack, L. H. (1985). Jealousy, pathological jealousy and aggression. In *Aggression and dangerousness* (ed. D. P. Farington and J. Gunn). Wiley, Chicester.

Munetz, M. R. and Cornes, C. L. (1982). Akathisia, pseudo-akathisia and tardive dyskinesia. *Comprehensive Psychiatry* **23**, 345–52.

Munro, A. (1980). Monosymptomatic hypochondriacal psychosis. *British Journal of Hospital Medicine* **24**, 34–8.

Munro, A. (1987). Paranoid (delusional) disorders: DSMIIIR and beyond. *Comprehensive Psychiatry* **28**, 35–9.

Munroe, R. L. (1955). *Schools of psychoanalytic thought*. Hutchinson Medical, London.

Munthe-Kaas, A. (1980). Rectal administration of diazepam: theoretical basis and clinical experience. In *Antiepileptic therapy: advances in drug monitoring* (ed. S. L. Johannensen *et al.*). Raven Press, New York.

Murphy, E. (1986). *Affective disorders in the elderly*. Churchill Livingstone, Edinburgh.

Murphy, E., Lindesay, J., and Grundy, E. (1986). 60 years of suicide in England and Wales. *Archives of General Psychiatry* **43**, 969–76.

Murphy, E., Smith, R., Lindesay, J., and Slattery, J. (1988). Increased mortality rates in late-life depression. *British Journal of Psychiatry* **152**, 347–53.

Murphy, G. E. (1982). Social origins of depression in old age. *British Journal of Psychiatry* **141**, 135–42.

Murphy, G. E. (1983). The prognosis of depression in old age. *British Journal of Psychiatry* **142**, 111–19.

Murphy, G. E. (1986). Suicide and alcoholism. In *Suicide* (ed. A. Roy). Williams and Wilkins, Baltimore.

Murphy, G. E. and Guze, S. B. (1960). Setting limits: the management of the manipulative patient. *American Journal of Psychotherapy* **14**, 30–47.

Murphy, G. E., Simons, A. D., Wetzel, R. D., and Lustman, P. J. (1984). Cognitive therapy and pharmacotherapy: singly and together in the treatment of depression. *Archives of General Psychiatry* **41**, 33–41.

Murphy, H. B. M. (1968). Cultural factors in the genesis of schizophrenia. In *The transmission of schizophrenia* (ed. D. Rosenthal and S. S. Kety). Pergamon Press, Oxford.

Murphy, H. B. M. (1977). Migration, culture and mental health. *Psychological medicine* **7**, 677–84.

Murphy, H. B. M. and Raman, A. C. (1971). The chronicity of schizophrenia in indigenous tropical people. *British Journal of Psychiatry* **118**, 489–97.

Murphy, S. B. and Donderi, D. C. (1980). Predicting the success of cataract surgery. *Journal of Behavioral Medicine* **3**, 1–14.

Murray, R. M. (1976). Characteristics and prognosis of alcoholic doctors. *British Medical Journal* **2**. 1537–9.

Murray, R. M. and Reveley, A. (1981). The genetic contributioin to the neuroses. *British Journal of Hospital Medicine* **25**, 185–90.

Murray, R. M., Reveley, A. M., and McGuffin, P. (1986). Genetic vulnerability to schizophrenia. In *Psychiatric clinics of North America* (ed. A. Roy), Vol. 9. Saunders, Philadelphia.

Myers, J. B., Morgan, T. O., Carney, S. L., and Ray, C. (1980). Effects of lithium on the kidney. *Kidney International* **18**, 601–8.

Myers, J. K. *et al.* (1984). Six-month prevalence of psychiatric disorder in three communities, 1980–1982. *Archives of General Psychiatry* **41**, 959–67.

Nadelson, C. C., Notman, M. T., Zackson, H., and Garnick, J. (1982). A follow-up study of rape victims. *American Journal of Psychiatry* **139**, 1266–70.

Nagler, S. H. (1957). Fetishism. *Psychiatric Quarterly* **31**. 713–41.

Naguib, M. and Levy, R. (1982). Prediction of outcome in senile dementia—a computed tomography study. *British Journal of Psychiatry* **140**, 263–7.

Navia, B. and Price, R. (1987). AIDS dementia complex and the presenting or sole manifestation of HIV infection. *Archives of Neurology* **44**, 65–9.

Naylor, G. J., Dick, D. A. T., Dick, E. G., Le Poidevin, D., and Whyte, S. F. (1973). Electrolyte membrane cation carrier in depressive illness. *Psychological Medicine* **3**, 502–8.

Naylor, G. T., Worrall, E. P., Peet, M., and Dick, P. (1976). Whole blood adenosine triphosphate in manic depressive illness. *British Journal of Psychiatry* **129**, 233–5.

Naysmith, A., Hinton, J. M., Meredith, R., Marks, M. D., and Berry, R. J. (1983). Surviving malignant disease. Psychological and family aspects. *British Journal of Hospital Medicine* **30**, 22–27.

Ndetei, D. M. and Muhangi, J. (1979). The prevalence and clinical presentation of psychiatric illness in a rural setting in Kenya. *British Journal of Psychiatry* **135**, 269–72.

Neale, J. M. and Oltmans, T. F. (1980). *Schizophrenia*, Chapter 6. Wiley, Chichester.

Neary, D., Snowden, J. S., and Mann, D. M. A. (1986). Alzheimer's disesase: a correlative study. *Journal of Neurology, Neurosurgery and Psychiatry* **49**, 229–37.

Needleman, H., Gunnoe, C., Leviton, A., Reed, R., Peresie, H., Muher, C., and Barrett, P. (1979). Deficits in psychologic and classroom performances of children with elevated dentine lead levels. *New England Journal of Medicine* **300**, 689–95.

Neligan, G. and Prudham, D. (1969). Norms for four standard developmental milestones by sex, social class and place in the family. *Developmental Medicine and Child Neurology* **11**, 413–22.

Nemiah, J. C. and Sifneos, P. E. (1970). Psychosomatic illness: a problem of communication. *Psychotherapy and Psychosomatics* **18**, 154–60.

Newson-Smith, J. G. B. and Hirsch, S. R. (1979*a*). Psychiatric symptoms in self poisoning patients. *Psychological Medicine* **9**, 493–500.

Newson-Smith, J. G. B. and Hirsch, S. R. (1979*b*). A comparison of social workers and psychiatrists in evaluating suicide. *British Journal of Psychiatry* **134**, 335–42.

Nichols, P. J. R. (1975). Some psychosocial aspects of rehabilitation and their implication in research. *Proceedings of the Royal Society of Medicine* **68**, 537–44.

Nicholson, W. A. (1967). Collection of unwanted drugs from private homes. *British Medical Journal* **iii**, 730–1.

Nicol, A. R. (1982). Psychogenic abdominal pain in childhood. *British Journal of Hospital Medicine* **27**, 351–3.

Nielsen, J. and Sorensen, K. (1979). Alcohol policy: alcohol consumption, alcohol prices, delirium tremens and alcoholism as causes of death in Denmark. *Social Psychiatry* **14**, 133–8.

Nilsson, A., Kay, L., and Jacobson, L. (1967). Postpartum mental disorder in an unselected sample: psychiatric history. *Journal of Psychosomatic Research* **11**, 327–40.

NiNuallain, M., O'Hare, A., and Walsh, D. (1987). Incidence of schizophrenia in Ireland. *Psychological Medicine* **17**, 943–8.

Nirje, B. (1970). Normalisation. *Journal of Mental Subnormality* **31**, 62–70.

Notman, M. T. and Nadelson, C. C. (1984). The rape victim. In *Manual of psychiatric consultation and emergency care* (ed. F. G. Guggenheim and M. Weiner). Jason Aronson, New York.

Nott, P. N., Franklin, M., Armitage, C., and Gelder, M. G. (1976). Hormonal changes and mood in the puerperium. *British Journal of Psychiatry* **128**, 379–83.

Noyes, R. and Clancy, J. (1976). Anxiety neurosis: a 5 year follow up. *Journal of Nervous and Mental Disease* **162**, 200–5.

Noyes, R. and Kathol, R. G. (1986). Depression and cancer. *Psychiatric Developments* **2**, 77–100.

Noyes, R., Kathol, R. G., Crowe, R., Hoenk, P. R., and Slymen, D. J. (1978). The familial prevalence of anxiety neurosis. *Archives of General Psychiatry* **35**, 1057–9.

Nurnberger, J. I. and Gershon, E. S. (1982). Genetics. In *Handbook of affective disorders* (ed. E. S. Paykel), pp. 126–45. Churchill Livingstone, Edinburgh.

Oates, R. K., Peacock, A., and Forrest, D. (1985). Long-term effects of non-organic failure to thrive. *Paediatrics* **75**, 36–40.

O'Brien, S. J. (1986). The controversy surrounding epilepsy and driving: a review. *Public Health* **100**, 21–7.

O'Connor, A. A. (1987). Female sex offenders. *British Journal of Psychiatry* **150**, 615–20.

O'Connor, N. (1968). Psychology and intelligence. In *Studies in psychiatry* (ed. M. Shepherd and D. L. Davis). Oxford University Press, London.

Ødegaard, Ø. (1932). Emigration and insanity. *Acta Psychiatrica Scandinavica* Suppl. 4.

Odlum, D. (1955). Fetishism. *British Medical Journal* **i**, 302.

Office of Health Economics. (1986*a*). *Cystic fibrosis*. Office of Health Economics, London.

Office of Health Economics (1986*b*). *Mental handicap. Partnership in the community?* Office of Health Economics, London.

Okuma, T., Inanaga, K., Otsuki, S., Sarai, K., Takayashi, R., Hazama, H., Mori, A., and Watanabe, M. (1981). A preliminary double-blind study of the efficacy of carbamazepine in the prophylaxis of manic-depressive illness. *Psychopharmacology* **73**, 95–6.

Oliver, C. and Holland, A. J. (1986). Down's syndrome and Alzheimer's disease: a review. *Psychological Medicine* **16**, 307–22.

Oliver, J. E. (1970). Huntington's chorea in Northamptonshire. *British Journal of Psychiatry* **116**, 241–53.

Olsen, M. R. (1985). The care of the chronically mentally ill. *Current themes in psychiatry* (ed. R. N. Gaind *et al.*) Vol. 4. Spectrum. New York.

Olsen, R. (1979*a*). Services for the elderly and mentally infirm. In *Community care for the mentally disabled* (ed. J. K. Wing and R. Olsen). Oxford University Press, Oxford.

Olsen, R. (1979*b*). *Alternative patterns of residential care for discharged psychiatric patients*. British Association of Social Workers, London.

O'Malley, T., Everitt, D. E., O'Malley, H. C., and Campion, W. (1983). Identifying and preventing family-mediated abuse and neglect of elderly persons. *Annals of Internal Medicine* **98**, 998–1005.

Orford, J. (1973). A comparison of alcoholics whose drinking is totally uncontrolled and those whose drinking is mainly controlled. *Behaviour Research and Therapy* **11**, 565–76.

Orford, J. (1985). *Excessive appetites: a psychological view of addictions*. Wiley, Chicester.

Orford, J. (1979). Alcohol and the family. In *Alcoholism in perspective* (ed. M. Grant and P. Gwinner). Croom Helm, London.

Orford, J. and Edwards, G. (1977). *Alcoholism*. Maudsley Monographs No. 26. Oxford University Press, London.

Orley, J., and Wing, J. K. (1979). Psychiatric disorder in two African villages. *Archives of General Psychiatry* **36**, 513–20.

Orme, M. L'E. (1984). Antidepressants and health disease. *British Medical Journal* **289**, 1–2,

Osberg, J. W., Meares, G. J., McKee, D. C. M., and Burnett, G. B. (1982). Intellectual functioning in renal failure and chronic dialysis. *Journal of Chronic Diseases* **35**, 445–57.

Osborn, M. (1981). Physical and psychological determinants of premenstrual tension: research issues and a proposed methodology. *Journal of Psychosomatic Research* **25**, 363–7.

Osborn, M. (1984). Depression at the menopause. *British Journal of Hospital Medicine* 126–9.

Osborn, M., Hawton, K., and Gath, D. (1988). Sexual dysfunction among middle-aged women in the community. *British Medical Journal* **296**, 959–62

Osler, W. (1910). Angina pectoris. *Lancet* **i**, 697–702 and 839–44.

Osmond, H., Smythies, J. R., and Harley-Mason, J. (1952). Schizophrenia: a new approach. *Journal of Mental Science* **98**, 309–15.

Osofsky, H. J. and Blumenthal, S. T. (1985). *Premenstrual syndrome: current findings and current directions*. American Psychiatric Association Press, Washington, D. C.

Ovenstone, I. M. K. and Kreitman, N. (1974). Two syndromes of suicide. *British Journal of Psychiatry* **124**, 336–45.

Owen, F., Cross, A. J., Crow, T. J., Longden, A., Pulter, M., and Riley, G. J. (1978). Increased dopamine receptor sensitivity in schizophrenia. *Lancet* **ii**, 223–5.

Owens, D. G. C., Johnstone, E. C., Crow, T. J., Frith, C. D., Jagoe, J. R., and Kreel, L. (1985). Lateral ventricular size in schizophrenia: relationship to the disease process and its clinical manifestations. *Psychological Medicine* **15**, 27–41.

Pachalis, A. P., Kimmel, H. D., and Kimmel, E. (1972). Further study of diurnal instrumental conditioning in the treatment of enuresis nocturna. *Journal of Behaviour Research and Experimental Psychiatry* **3**, 253–6.

Packard, E. H. (1909). An analysis of the psychoses associated with Graves' disease. *American Journal of Insanity* **66**, 189–202.

Paffenberger, R. S. (1964). Epidemiological aspects of post-partum mental illness. *British Journal of Social and Preventive Medicine* **18**, 189–95.

Pare, C. M. B. and Sandler, M. J. (1959). A clinical and biochemical study of a trial of iproniazid in the treatment of depression. *Journal of Neurology, Neursurgery and Psychiatry* **22**, 247–51.

Parker, G. (1979). Parental characteristics in relation to depressive disorders. *British Journal of Psychiatry* **134**, 138–47.

Parkes, C. M. (1978). Psychological reactions to loss of a limb. In *Modern perspectives in the psychological aspects of surgery* (ed. J. G. Howells). Macmillan, London.

Parkes, C. M. (1985). Bereavement. *British Journal of Psychiatry* **146**, 11–17.

Parkes, C. M. and Brown, R. J. (1972). Health after bereavement: a controlled study of young Boston widows and widowers. *Psychosomatic Medicine* **34**, 449–61.

Parkes, C. M. Benjamin, B., and Fitzgerald, R. G. (1969). Broken heart: a statistical study of increased mortality among widowers. *British Medical Journal* **i**, 740–3.

Parkes, J. D. (1985). *Sleep and its disorders*. Saunders, London.

Parkes, K. R. (1982). Occupational stress among student nurses: a natural experiment. *Journal of Applied Psychology* **67**, 784–96.

Parloff, M. B., Waskow, I. E., and Wolfe, B. E. (1978). Research on therapist variables in relation to process and outcome. In *Handbook of psychotherapy and behaviour change* (ed. S. L. Garfield and A. E. Bergin (2nd edn). Wiley, New York.

Parnas, J., Schulsinger, F., Teasdale, T. W., Schulsinger, H., Feldman, P. M., and Mednick, S. A. (1982). Perinatal complications and clinical outcome within the schizophrenia spectrum. *British Journal of Psychiatry* **140**, 416–20.

Parry-Jones, W. Ll. (1972). *The trade in lunacy*. Routledge and Kegan Paul, London.

Parry-Jones, W. Ll. (1973). Criminal law and complicity in suicide and attempted suicide. *Medicine, Science and the Law* **13**, 110–19.

Parry-Jones, W. L., Santer-Westrate, H. C., and Crawley, R. C. (1970). Behaviour therapy in a case of hysterical blindness. *Behaviour Research and Therapy* **8**, 79–85.

Parsons, T. (1951). *The social system*. Free Press, Glencoe.

Pasamanick, B. and Knobloch, H. (1966). Retrospective studies on the epidemiology of reproductive casualty: old and new. *Merril-Palmer Quarterly of Behavioral Development* **12**, 7–26.

Pasamanick, B., Scarpitti, F. R., and Lefton, M. (1964). Home versus hospital care for schizophrenics. *Journal of the American Medical Association* **187**, 177–81.

Patel, C. (1975). 12 month followup of yoga and biofeedback in the management of hypertension. *Lancet* **i**, 62–4.

Paton, W. D. M. (1969). A pharmacological approach to drug dependence and drug tolerance. In *Scientific basis of drug dependence* (ed. H. Steinberg). Churchill, London.

Patterson, E. M. (1977). *The experience of dying*. Prentice-Hall, London.

Patterson, R. L. and Jackson, G. M. (1980). Behaviour modification with the elderly. *Progress in Behaviour Modification* **9**, 205–39.

Pattison, E. M. (1966). A critique of alcoholism treatment concepts. *Quarterly Journal of Studies on Alcoholism* **27**, 49–71.

Pauls, D. L., Cohen, D. J., Heimbuch, R., Detlor, J., and Kidd, K. K. (1981). Familial pattern and transmission of Gilles de la Tourette syndrome and multiple tics. *Archives of General Psychiatry* **38**, 1091–3.

Paykel, E. S. (1974). Recent life events and clinical depression. In *Life stress and illness* (ed. E. G. Gunderson and R. H. Rahe) pp. 134–63. Thomas, Springfield, Ill.

Paykel, E. S. (1978). Contribution of life events to causation of psychiatric illness. *Psychological Medicine* **8**, 245–53.

Paykel, E. S. (1981). Have multivariate statistics contributed to classification? *British Journal of Psychiatry* **139**, 357–62.

Paykel, E. S. (1982). Life events and environment. In *Handbook of affective disorder* (ed. E. S. Paykel), pp. 146–61. Churchill Livingstone, Edinburgh.

Paykel, E. S. (1983). Methodological aspects of life event research. *Journal of Psychosomatic Research* **27**, 341–52.

Paykel, E. S., Myers, J. K., Dienelt, M. N., Klerman, G. L., Lindenthal, J. J., and Pepper, M. P. (1969). Life events and depression: a controlled study. *Archives of General Psychiatry* **21**. 753–60.

Paykel, E. S. Prusoff, B. A., and Myers, J. K. (1975a). Suicide attempts and recent life events: a controlled comparison. *Archives of General Psychiatry* **32**, 327–33.

Paykel, E. S., Di Mascio, A., Haskell, D., and Prusoff, B. A. (1975b). Effects of maintenance amitriptyline and psychotherapy on symptoms of depression. *Psychological Medicine* **5**, 67–77.

Paykel, E. S., Emms, E. M., Fletcher, J., and Rassaby, E. S. (1980). Life events and support in puerperal depression. *British Journal of Psychiatry* **136**, 339–46.

Paykel, E. S., Rao, B. M., and Taylor, C. N. (1984). Life stress and symptom pattern in outpatient depression. *Psychological Medicine* **14**, 559–68.

Paykel, E. S., Griffith, J. H., and Mangen, S. P. (1985). Community psychiatric nursing. In *Current themes in psychiatry* (ed. R. N. Gaind, F. I. Fawzy, B. L. Hodson, and R. O. Pasnau), Vol. 4. Spectrum. New York.

Payne, B. and Norfleet, M. A. (1986). Chronic pain and the family: a review. *Pain* **26**, 1–22.

Payne, R. W. (1962). An object classification test as a measure of over-inclusiveness in schizophrenic patients. *British Journal of Social and Clinical Psychology* **1**, 213–21.

Payne, R. W. (1973). Cognitive abnormalities. In *Handbook of abnormal psychology* (ed. H. J. Eysenck) (2nd edn). Pitman Medical, London.

Payne, R. W. and Friedlander, D. (1962). A short battery of simple tests for measuring over-inclusive thinking. *Journal of Mental Science* **108**, 362–7.

Pedley, T. A. and Meldrum, B. S. (eds.) (1983). *Recent advances in epilepsy*, Vol. 1. Churchill Livingstone, Edinburgh.

Pedley, T. A. and Meldrum B. S. (eds.) (1985). *Recent advances in epilepsy*, Vol. 2. Churchill Livingstone, Edinburgh.

Pedley, T. A. and Meldrum, B. S. (eds.) (1986). *Recent advances in epilepsy*, Vol. 3. Churchill Livingstone, Edinburgh.

Penrose, L. (1938). *A clinical and genetic study of 1280 cases of mental deficiency.* HMSO, London.

Penrose, R. J. J. and Storey, P. (1972). Life events before subarachnoid haemorrhage. *Journal of Psychosomatic Research* **16**, 329–33.

Perley, M. J. and Guze, S. B. (1962). Hysteria—the stability and usefulness of clinical criteria. *New England Journal of Medicine* **266**, 421–6.

Perlmutter, L. C., Hakami, M. K., Hodgson-Harrington, C., Ginsberg, J., Katz, J., Singer, D. E., and Nathan, D. M. (1984). Decreased cognitive function in aging non-insulin-dependent diabetic patients. *American Journal of Medicine* **77**, 1043–48.

Perls, F., Hefferline, R. F., and Goodman, P. (1951). *Gestalt therapy: excitement and growth in human personality.* Penguin, Harmondsworth.

Peroutka, S. J., Lebovitz, R. M., and Snyder, S. H. (1986). Two distinct serotonin receptors with different physiological functions. *Science* **212**, 827–9.

Perr, I. N. (1985). Liability of the mentally ill and their insurers in negligence and other civil actions. *American Journal of Psychiatry* **142**, 1414–18.

Perrin, G. M. (1961). Cardiovascular aspects of electric shock therapy *Acta Psychiatrica Scandinavica* **36**, Suppl. 152, 1–45.

Perris, C. (1966). A study of bipolar (manic depressive) and unipolar recurrent depressive psychoses. *Acta Psychiatrica Scandinavica* **42**, Suppl. 194.

Perris, C. (1974). A study of cycloid psychoses. *Acta Psychiatrica Scandinavica* Suppl. 253.

Perry, E. K., Perry, R. H., Blessed, G., and Tomlinson, B. E. (1977). Necropsy evidence of central cholinergic deficits in senile dementia. *Lancet* **i**, 189.

Perry, E. K. Tomlinson, B. E., and Blessed, G. (1978). Correlation of cholinergic abnormalities with senile plaques and mental test scores in senile dementia. *British Medical Journal* **ii**, 1457–9.

Perry, E. K., Oakley, A. E., and Candy, J. M. (1981). Neurochemical activities in human temporal lobe related to ageing and Alzheimer-type changes. *Neurobiology of Ageing* **2**, 251–6.

Perry, P. S., Morgan, D. E., Smith, R. E., and Tsuang, M. T. (1982). Treatment of unipolar depression accompanied by delusions. *Journal of Affective Disorders* **4**, 195–200.

Perry, R. and Perry, E. K. (1982). The ageing brain and its pathology. In *The psychiatry of late life* (ed. R. Levy and F. Post). Blackwell, Oxford.

Perry, T. L., Hansen, S., and Kloster, M. (1973). Huntington's chorea: deficiency of gamma-aminobutyric acid in brain. *New England Journal of Medicine* **288**, 337–42.

Peters, S. D., Wyatt, G. E., Finkelhor, D. (1986). Prevalence. In *A source book on child sexual abuse* (ed. D. Finkelhor). Sage, London.

Petersen, P. (1968). Psychiatric disorders in primary hyperparathyroidism. *Journal of Clinical Endocrinology and Metabolism* **28**, 1491–5.

Peterson, B., Kristenson, H., Sternby, N. H., Trell, E., Fex, G., and Hood, B. (1980). Alcohol consumption and premature death in middle-aged men. *British Medical Journal* **i**, 1403–6.

Petursson, H. and Lader, M. H. (1984). *Dependence on tranquillizers.* Oxford University Press, Oxford.

Pfohl, B. and Andreasen, N. C. (1986). Schizophrenia: diagnosis and classification. In *American Psychiatric Association annual review* (ed. A. J. Frances and R. E. Hales), Vol. 5. American Psychiatric Press, Washington, DC.

Philippopoulos, G. S., Wittkower, E. D., and Cousineau, A. (1958). The etiologic significance of emotional factors in onset and exacerbations of multiple sclerosis. *Psychosomatic Medicine* **20**, 458–74.

Pichot, P. (1982). The diagnosis and classification of mental disorders in French speaking countries: background, current view and comparison with other nomenclature. *Psychological Medicine* **12**, 475–92.

Pichot, P. (1984). The French approach to classification. *British Journal of Psychiatry* **144**, 113–18.

Pilowsky, I. (1969). A general classification of abnormal illness behaviours. *British Journal of Medical Psychology* **51**, 131–7.

Pilowsky, I. (1978). Psychodynamic aspects of pain experience. In *The psychology of pain* (ed. R. A. Sternbach). Raven Press, New York.

Pilowsky, I. and Spence, N. D. (1975). Patterns of illness behaviour in patients with intractable pain. *Journal of Psychosomatic Research* **19**, 279–87.

Pincus, J. H. and Tucker, G. J. (1985). *Behavioural neurology* (3rd edn). Oxford University Press, New York.

Pinel, P. (1806). *A treatise on insanity* (translated by D. D. Davis). Reprinted 1962. Hafner, New York.

Pippard, J. and Ellam, L. (1981). *Electroconvulsive treatment in Great Britain.* Gaskell, London.

Pitres, A. and Régis, E. (1902). *Les obsessions et les impulsions.* Doin, Paris.

Pitt, B. (1968). 'Atypical' depression following childbirth. *British Journal of Psychiatry* **114**, 1325–35.

Pitts, F. N. and McClure, J. N. (1967). Lacate metabolism in anxiety neurosis. *New England Journal of Medicine* **25**, 1329–36.

Pitts, F. N. and Winokur, G. (1964). Affective disorders III: diagnostic correlates and incidence of suicide. *Journal of Nervous and Mental Disease* **139**, 176–81.

Planansky, K. and Johnston, R. (1977). Homicidal aggression in schizophrenic men. *Acta Psychiatrica Scandinavia* **55**, 65–73.

Plant, M. A. (1975). *Drug takers in an English Town*, Tavistock, London.

Plant, M. A., Peck, D. F., and Stuart, R. (1982). Self-reported drinking habits and alcohol-related consequences among a cohort of Scottish teenagers. *British Journal of Addiction* **77**, 75–90.

Plant, M. A., Peck, D. F., and Samuel, E. (1985). *Alcohol, drugs and school leavers.* Tavistock, London.

Platt, S. (1986). Parasuicide and unemployment. *British Journal of Psychiatry* **149**, 401–3.

Platt, S. (1987). Suicide trends in 24 European countries 1972–1984. In *Current issues in suicidology* (ed. J. Möller, A. Schmidtke, and R. Wetz). Springer, Berlin.

Pokorny, A. (1964). Suicide rates in various psychiatric disorders. *Archives of General Psychiatry* **139**, 499–506.

Pollard, R. (1973). Surgical implications of some types of drug dependence. *British Medical Journal* **i**, 784–7.

Pollin, W. and Stabenau, J. (1968). Biological, psychological, and historical differences in a series of monozygotic twins discordant for schizophrenia. In *Transmission of schizophrenia* (ed. D. Rosenthal and S. Kety). Pergamon Press, London.

Pollin, W., Cardon, P. V. Jr, and Kety, S. S. (1961). Effects of aminoacid feedings in schizophrenic patients treated with iproniazid. *Science* **133**, 104–5.

Pollitt, J. (1957). Natural history of obsessional states. *British Medical Journal* **i** 194–8.

Pollitt, J. (1960). Natural history studies in mental illness: a discussion based upon a pilot study of obsessional states. *Journal of Mental Science* **106**, 93–113.

Pond, D. A. (1957). Psychiatric aspects of epilepsy. *Journal of the Indian Medical Profession* 3, 1441–51.

Pond, D. A. and Bidwell, B. H. (1960). A survey of epilepsy in fourteen general practices. II. Social and psychological aspects. *Epilepsia* 1, 285–99.

Pond, D. A., Bidwell, B. H., and Stein, L. (1980). A survey of epilepsy in fourteen general practices. I: Demographic and medical data. *Psychiatrica, Neurologia, et Neurochirurgia* 63, 217–36.

Pope, H. G., Jonas, J. M., Hudson, J. I., Cohen, B. M., and Gunderson, J. G. (1983). The validity of DSM III borderline personality disorder: a phenomenological, family history, treatment response, and long term follow-up study. *Archives of General Psychiatry* 40, 23–30.

Popham, R. E. (1956). The Jellinek alcoholism estimation formula and its application to Canadian data. *Quarterly Journal of Studies on Alcohol* 17, 559–93.

Popkin, M. K., Callies, A. L., and Mackenzie, J. D. (1985). The outcome of antidepressant use in the medically ill. *Archives of General Psychiatry* 42, 1160–3.

Post, F. (1965). *The clinical psychiatry of late life.* Pergamon Press, New York.

Post, F. (1966). *Persistent persecutory states in the elderly.* Pergamon Press, London.

Post, F. (1971). Schizo-affective symptomatology in late life. *British Journal of Psychiatry* 118, 437–45.

Post, F. (1972). The management and nature of depressive illnesses in late life: a follow-through study. *British Journal of Psychiatry* 121, 393–404.

Post, R. M., Uhde, T. W., Ballenger, J. C., and Squillace, K. M. (1983). Prophylactic efficacy of carbamazepine in manic-depressive illness. *American Journal of Psychiatry* 140, 1602–4.

Post, R. M., Uhde, T. W., Roy-Byrne, P. P., and Joffe, R. T. (1986). Antidepressant effects of carbamazepine. *American Journal of Psychiatry* 143, 29–34.

Powell, G. F., Brasel, J. A., and Blizzard, R. M. (1967). Emotional deprivation and growth retardation simulating idiopathic hypopituitarism. *New England Journal of Medicine* 276, 1271–83.

Power, D. J. (1969). Subnormality and crime. *Medicine, Science and the Law* 9, 82–93 and 162–71.

Power, D. J., Benn, R. T., and Homes, J. N. (1972). Neighbourhood, school and juveniles before courts. *British Journal of Criminology* 12, 111–32.

Pratt, J. H. (1908). Results obtained in treatment of pulmonary tuberculosis by the class method. *British Medical Journal* ii, 1070–1.

Pratt, R. T. C. (1951). An investigation of psychiatric aspects of disseminated sclerosis. *Journal of Neurology, Neurosurgery and Psychiatry* 14, 326–35.

President's Panel on Mental Retardation (1972). *National action to combat mental retardation.* United States Government Printing Office, Washington, DC.

Price, J. (1968). The genetics of depressive behaviour. In *Recent developments affective disorders* (ed. A. Coppen and S. Walk). *British Journal of Psychiatry* Special Publication No. 2.

Price, L. H., Charney, D. S., and Heninger, G. R. (1985). Efficacy of lithium-tranylcypromine treatment in refractory depression. *American Journal of Psychiatry* 142, 619–23.

Prichard, J. C. (1835). *A treatise on insanity.* Sherwood Gilbert and Piper, London.

Prien, R. F. and Kupfer, D. J. (1986). Continuation drug therapy for major depressive episodes: how long should it be maintained? *American Journal of Psychiatry* 143, 18–23.

Prien, R. F., Caffey, E. M., and Glett, C. J. (1972). Comparison of lithium carbonate and chlorpromazine in the treatment of mania. *Archives of General Psychiatry* **26**, 146–53.

Prien, R. F., Caffey, E. M., and Glett, C. J. (1973). Prophylactic efficacy of lithium carbonate in manic depressive illness. *Archives of General Psychiatry* **28**, 337–41.

Prien, R. F., Kupfer, D. J., Mansky, P. A., Small, J. G., Tuason, V. B., Voss, C. B., and Johnson, W. E. (1984). Drug therapy in the prevention of recurrences in unipolar and bipolar affective disorders: report of the NIMH collaborative study group comparing lithium carbonate, imipramine, and lithium carbonate—imipramine combination. *Archives of General Psychiatry* **41**, 1096–104.

Prigatano, G. P., Wright, E. C., and Levin, D. (1984). Quality of life: its predictors in patients with mild hypoxaemia and chronic obstructive pulmonary disease. *Archives of Internal Medicine* **144**. 1613–19.

Prince, Morton (1908). *Dissociation of personality, a biographical study in abnormal psychology*. Longmans Green, New York.

Pritchard, M. (1982). Psychological problems in a renal unit. *British Journal of Hospital Medicine* **27**, 512–15.

Pritchard, M. and Graham, P. (1966). An investigation of a group of patients who have attended both the child and adult departments of the same psychiatric hospital. *British Journal of Psychiatry* **112**, 603–12.

Protheroe, C. (1969). Puerperal psychoses: a long term study, 1927–1961. *British Journal of Psychiatry* **115**, 9–30.

Prusoff, B. A., Weissman, M. M., Klerman, G. L., and Rounsaville, B. J. (1980). Research diagnostic criteria subtypes of depression as predictors of differential response to psychotherapy and drug treatment. *Archives of General Psychiatry* **37**, 796–801.

Prys-Williams, G. and Glatt, M. M. (1966). The incidence of longstanding alcoholism in England and Wales. *British Journal of Addiction* **61**, 257–68.

Pugh, R., Jerath, B. K., Schmidt, W. M., and Reed, R. B. (1963). Rates of mental disease related to child bearing. *New England Journal of Medicine* **22**, 1224–8.

Quay, H. C. (1986). Classification. In *Psychopathological disorders of childhood* (ed. H. C. Quay and J. S. Werry) (3rd edn). John Wiley, New York.

Quay, H. C. and Werry, J. S. (1986). *Psychopathological disorders of Childhood* (3rd edn). John Wiley, New York.

Querido, A. (1959). Forecast and follow-up. An investigation into the clinical, social and mental factors determining the results of hospital treatment. *British Journal of Preventive and Social Medicine* **13**, 334–9.

Quine, L. (1986). Behaviour problems in severely mentally handicapped children. *Psychological Medicine* **16**, 895–907.

Quitkin, F., Rifkin, A., and Klein, D. (1976). Neurologic soft signs in schizophrenia and character disorders. *Archives of General Psychiatry* **33**, 845–53.

Quitkin, F. M., Rabkin, J. G., Ross, D., and McGrath, P. J. (1984). Duration of antidepressant drug treatment: what is an adequate trial? *Archives of General Psychiatry* **41**, 238–45.

Rachman, S. (1966). Sexual fetishism—an experimental analogue. *Psychological Record* **16**, 293–6.

Rachman, S. (1974) Primary obsessional slowness. *Behaviour Research and Therapy* **11**, 463–71.

Rachman, S. and Hodgson, R. J. (1980). *Obsessions and compulsions*. Prentice-Hall, New Jersey.

Rachman, S. and Teasdale, J. (1969). *Aversion therapy and behaviour disorders: an analysis*. Pergamon Press, Oxford.

Radomski, J. K., Fuyat, H. N., Belson, A. A., and Smith, P. K. (1950). The toxic effects, excretion and distribution of lithium chloride. *Journal of Pharmacology and Experimental Therapeutics* **100**, 429–44.

Radzinowicz, L. (1957). *Sexual offences*. Macmillan, London.

Radzinowicz, L. and King, J. (1977). *The growth of crime*. Penguin, Harmondsworth.

Rae, W. A. (1977). Childhood conversion reactions: a review of incidence in pediatric settings. *Journal of Clinical Child Psychology* **6**, 66–72.

Rahe, R. (1973). Subjects recent life changes and the near future illness reports. *Annals of Clinical Research* **4**, 1–16.

Rahe, R., Gunderson, E. K. E., and Arthur, R. J. (1970). Demographic and psychosocial factors in acute illness reporting. *Journal of Chronic Diseases* **23**, 245–55.

Rahe, R. H., McKean, J. D., and Ransom, J. A. (1967). A longitudinal study of life-changes and illness patterns. *Journal of Psychosomatic Research* **10**, 355–66.

Ramsay, A. M. (1973). Benign myalgic encephalomyelitis. *British Journal of Psychiatry* **122**, 618–19.

Rapoport, J. L. (1986). Childhood obsessive compulsive disorders. *Journal of Child Psychology and Psychiatry* **27**, 289–95.

Rapoport, R. N. (1960). *Community as doctor*. Tavistock, London.

Ratcliffe, S. G. (1982). Speech and learning disorders in children with sex chromosome abnormalities. *Developmental Medicine and Child Neurology* **24**, 80–4.

Ratnoff, O. D. (1980). The psychogenic purpuras: a review of autoerythrocyte sensitization to DNA, 'Hysterical' and facticial bleeding, and the religious stigmata. *Seminars in Hematology* **17**, 192–213.

Rawnsley, K. (1984). Alcoholic doctors. *Alcohol and Alcoholism* **19**, 257–60.

Raynes, N. V. and Sumpton, R. C. (1987). Differences in the quality of residential provision for mentally handicapped people. *Psychological Medicine* **17**, 999–1008.

Razani, J., White, J., Simpson, G., Sloane, R. B., Rebal, R., and Palmer, R. (1983). The safety and efficacy of combined amitriptyline and tranylcypromine antidepressant treatment. *Archives of General Psychiatry* **40**, 657–61.

Razin, A. M. (1982). Psychosocial intervention in coronary artery disease: a review. *Psychosomatic Medicine* **44**, 363–87.

Reed, G. F. and Sedman, G. (1964). Personality and depersonalization under sensory deprivation conditions. *Perceptual and Motor Skills* **18**, 659–60.

Reed, T. E. and Chandler, J. H. (1958). Huntington's chorea in Michigan. I Demography and genetics. *American Journal of Human Genetics* **10**, 201–25.

Rees, W. D. and Lutkins, S. G. (1967). Mortality of bereavement. *British Medical Journal* **iv**, 13–16.

Reich, J. (1985). The relationship between antisocial behaviour and affective illness. *Comprehensive Psychiatry* **26**, 296–303.

Reich, P. and Gottfried, L. A. (1983). Factitious disorders in a teaching hospital. *Annals of Internal Medicine* **99**, 240–7.

Reich, P., Regestein, Q. R., Murawski, B. J., De Silva, R. A., and Lown, B. (1983). Unrecognized organic mental disorders in survivors of cardiac arrest. *American Journal of Psychiatry* **140**, 1194–7.

Reid, A. H. (1982). *The psychiatry of mental handicap*. Blackwell, Oxford.

Reid, A. H. and Ballinger, B. R. (1987). Personality disorder in mental handicap. *Psychological Medicine* **17**, 983–7.

Reisberg, B. (1983). *Alzheimer's disease*. Collier Macmillan, London.

Reisberg, B., Ferris, S. H., and Gershon, S. (1981). An overview of pharmacologic treatment of cognitive decline in the aged. *American Journal of Psychiatry* **138**, 593–600.

Resnick, P. J. (1969). Child murder by parents. *American Journal of Psychiatry* **126**, 325–34.

Reuler, J. B., Girard, D. E., and Nardone, D. A. (1980). The chronic pain syndrome: misconceptions and management. *Annals of Internal Medicine* **93**, 588–96.

Reynolds, E. H. (1968). Mental effects of anticonvulsants and folic acid metabolism. *Brain* **91**, 197–214.

Reynolds, E. H., Preece, J., and Chanarin, I. (1969). Folic acid and anticonvulsants. *Lancet* **i**, 1264–5.

Reynolds, E. H. and Trimble, M. R. (eds.) (1981). *Epilepsy and psychiatry*. Churchill Livingstone, Edinburgh.

Reynolds, G. P. (1983). Increased concentration and lateral asymmetry of amygdala dopamine in schizophrenia. *Nature* **305**, 527–9.

Rich, R. F. and Burgess, A. W. (1986). Panel recommends comprehensive program for victims of violent crime. *Hospital Community Psychiatry* **37**, 437–45.

Richards, J. S. (1986). Psychologic adjustment to spinal cord injury during the first post discharge year. *Archives of Physical Medicine and Rehabilitation* **67**, 362–3.

Richardson, A. (1973). Stereotactic limbic leucotomy: surgical technique. *Postgraduate Medical Journal* **49**, 860.

Richings, J. S., Khara, G. S., and McDowell, M. (1986). Suicide in young doctors. *British Journal of Psychiatry* **149**, 475–8.

Richman, N., Stevenson, J., and Graham, P. (1982). *Preschool to school: a behavioural study*. Academic Press, London.

Richman, N., Douglas, J., Hunt, H., Lansdown, R., and Levine, R. (1985). Behavioural methods in the treatment of sleep disorders—a pilot study. *Journal of Child Psychology and Psychiatry* **26**, 581–90.

Rickles, N. K. (1950). *Exhibitionism*. Lippincott, Philadelphia.

Ridges, A. P. (1973). Abnormal metabolites in schizophrenia. In *Biochemistry and mental illness* (ed. L. L. Iversen and S. P. R. Rose) pp. 175–88. Biochemical Society Special Publication No. 1.

Ridgeway, V. and Mathews, A. (1982). Psychological preparation for surgery: a comparison of methods. *British Journal of Clinical Psychology* **21**, 271–80.

Rimm, D. C. and Masters, J. C. (1974). *Behaviour therapy: techniques and empirical findings*. Academic Press, New York.

Rimmer, E. M. and Richens, A. (1982). Clinical pharmacology and medical treatment. In *A textbook of epilepsy* (ed. J. Laidlaw, A. Richens, and J. Oxley) (3rd edn). Churchill Livingstone, Edinburgh.

Ritson, B. (1977). Alcoholism and suicide. In *Alcoholism: new knowledge and new responses* (ed. G. Edwards and M. Grant). Croom Helm, London.

Ritson, B. (1982). Helping the problem drinker. *British Medical Journal* **284**, 327–9.

Rivinus, T. M., Jamison, D. L., and Graham, P. J. (1975). Childhood organic neurological disease presenting as psychiatric disorder. *Developmental Medicine and Child Neurology* **23**, 747–60.

Rix, B., Pearson, D. J., and Bentley, S. J. (1984). A psychiatric study of patients with supposed food allergy. *British Journal of Psychiatry* **145**, 121–6.

Roberts, A. H. (1969). *Brain damage in boxers*. Pitman, London.

Roberts, J. and Hawton, K. (1980). Child abuse and attempted suicide. *British Journal of Psychiatry* **137**, 319–23.

Robin, A. A. and Harris, J. A. (1962). A controlled comparison of imipramine and electroplexy. *Journal of Mental Science* **108**, 217–19.

Robin, A. A. and deTissera, S. A. (1982). A double-blind controlled comparison of the therapeutic effects of low and high energy electroconvulsive therapies. *British Journal of Psychiatry* **141**, 357–66.

Robin, A. A., Binne, C. D., and Copas, J. B. (1985). Electrophysiological and hormonal responses to three types of electroconvulsive therapy. *British Journal of Psychiatry* **147**, 707–12.

Robins, E., Gassner, S., Kayes, J., Wilkinson, R. H., and Murphy, G. E. (1959). The communication of suicidal intent: a study of 134 successful (completed) suicides. *American Journal of Psychiatry* **115**, 724–33.

Robins, L. N. (1966). *Deviant children grown up*. Williams and Wilkins, Baltimore.

Robins, L. (1970). Follow up studies investigating childhood disorders. In *Psychiatric epidemiology* (ed. E. H. Hare and J. K. Wing). Oxford University Press, London.

Robins, L. N. (1978). Sturdy childhood predictors of adult antisocial behaviour: replications from longitudinal studies. *Psychological Medicine* **8**, 611–22.

Robins, L. N. (1979*a*). Follow-up studies. In *Pathological disorders of childhood* (ed. H. C. Quay and J. S. Werry) pp. 483–513. Wiley, New York.

Robins, L. N. (1979*b*). *N. I. M. H. diagnostic interview*. National Institutes of Mental Health, Bethesda.

Robins, L. N., Davis, D. H., and Goodwin, D. W. (1974). Drug use by the US army enlisted men in Vietnam: a follow-up on their return home. *American Journal of Epidemiology* **99**, 235–49.

Robins, L. N., Helzer, J. E., Ratcliff, K. S., and Seyfried, W. (1982). Validity of the Diagnostic Interview Schedule, version II: DSMIII diagnoses. *Psychological Medicine* **12**, 855–70.

Robins, L. N., Helzer, J. E., Weissman, M. M., Orschavel, H., Gruenberg, E., Burke, J. D., and Regier, D. A. (1984). Lifetime prevalence of specific psychiatric disorder in three sites. *Archives of General Psychiatry* **41**, 949–58.

Robinson, D. (1978). Self-help groups. *British Journal of Hospital Medicine* **20**, 306–11.

Robinson, D. (1979). *Talking out of alcoholism: the self-help process of Alcoholics Anonymous*. Croom Helm, London.

Robinson, G. E., Stewart, D. E., and Flak, E. (1986*a*). Rational use of psychotropic drugs in pregnancy and post partum. *Canadian Journal of Psychiatry* **31**, 183–90.

Robinson, R. G., Bolla-Wilson, K., Kaplan, E., Lipsey, J. R., and Price, T. R. (1986*b*). Depression influences intellectual impairment in stroke patients. *British Journal of Psychiatry* **148**, 541–47.

Robinson, R. G., Kubos, K. L., Storr, L. B., Krisha, R., and Price, T. R. (1984). Mood disorders in stroke patients: importance of location of lesion. *Brain* **107**, 87–94.

Rochford, J. M., Detre, T., Tucker, G. J., and Harrow, M. (1970). Neuropsychological impairments in functional psychiatric disease. *Archives of General Psychiatry* **22**, 114–19.

Rodin, G. M., Johnson, L. E., Garfunkel, P. E., Daneman, D., and Kenshole, A. B. (1986). Eating disorders in female adolescents with insulin-dependent diabetes mellitus. *International Journal of Psychiatry in Medicine* **16**, 49–57.

Rodnight, R., Murray, R. M., Oon, M. C. H., Brockington, I. F., Nicholls, P., and Birley, J. L. T. (1977). Urinary dimethyltryptamine and psychiatric symptomatology and classification. *Psychological Medicine* **6**, 649–57.

Rodrigo, E. K. and Williams, P. (1986). Frequency of self-reported 'anxiolytic withdrawal' symptoms in a group of female students experiencing anxiety. *Psychological Medicine* **16**, 467–72.

Rogers, C. R. and Dymond, R. F. (ed.) (1954). *Psychotherapy and personality change*. University of Chicago Press.

Rogers, M. and Reich, P. (1986). Psychological intervention with surgical patients: evaluation of outcome. *Advances in Psychosomatic Medicine* **15**, 25–30.

Rogers, S. C. and May, P. M. (1975). A statistical review of controlled trials of imipramine and placebo in the treatment if depressive illness. *British Journal of Psychiatry* **127**, 599–603.

Rollin, H. R. (1969). *The mentally abnormal offender and the law*. Pergamon, Oxford.

Romans-Clarkson, S. E., Clarkson, J. E., and Dittmer, I. D. (1986). Impact of a handicapped child on mental health of patients. *British Medical Journal* **293**, 1395–417.

Ron, M. A. (1977). Brain damage in chronic alcoholism: a neuropathological, neuro-radiological and psychological review. *Psychological Medicine* **7**, 103–12.

Ron, M. A. (1986*a*). Volatile solvent abuse; a review of possible long-term neurological, intellectual and psychiatric sequellae. *British Journal of Psychiatry* **148**, 235–6.

Ron, M. A. (1986*b*). Multiple sclerosis: a psychiatric and psychometric abnormalities. *Journal of Psychosomatic Research* **30**, 3–11.

Ron, M. A., Acker, W., and Lishman, W. A. (1980). Morphological abnormalities in the brains of chronic alcoholics. A clinical, psychological and computerised axial tomographic study. *Acta Psychiatrica Scandinavica* Suppl. 286, 51–6.

Ron, M. A., Toone, B. K., Garralda, M. E., and Lishman, W. A. (1979). Diagnostic accuracy in presenile dementia. *British Journal of Psychiatry* **134**, 161–8.

Ron, M. A., Acker, W., Shaw, K. K., and Lishman, W. A. (1982). Computerized tomography of the brain in chronic alcoholism. *Brain* **105**, 497–514.

Rook, A. (1959). Student suicides. *British Medical Journal* i, 600–3.

Rooth, F. G. (1971). Indecent exposure and exhibitionism. *British Journal of Hospital Medicine* **5**, 521–33.

Rooth, F. G. (1973). Exhibitionism, sexual violence and paedophilia. *British Journal of Psychiatry* **122**, 705–10.

Rooth, F. G. (1980). Exhibitionism: an eclectic approach to its management. *British Journal of Hospital Medicine* **23**, 366–70.

Rooth, F. G. and Marks, I. M. (1974). Persistent exhibitionism: short-term response to aversion self regulation and relaxation treatment. *Archives of Sexual Behaviour* **3**, 227–43.

Rosalki, S. B., Rau, D., Lehmann, D., and Prentice, M. (1970). Determination of serum gamma-glutamyl transpeptidase activity and its clinical applications. *American Journal of Clinical Biochemistry* **7**, 143–7.

Rosanoff, A. J., Handy, L. M., and Rosanoff, I. A. (1934). Criminality and delinquency in twins. *Journal of Criminal Law and Criminology* **24**, 923–34.

Rosanoff, A. J., Handy, L. M., and Plesset, I. R. (1941). *The ecology of child behaviour difficulties, juvenile delinquency and adult criminality with special reference to the occurrence in twins*. Psychiatric Monograph (California) No. 1. Department of Institutions, Sacramento.

Rosen, B. K. (1981). Suicide pacts: a review. *Psychological Medicine* **11**, 525–33.

Rosen, I. (1979). Exhibitionism, scopophilia and voyeurism. In *Sexual deviations* (ed. I. Rosen) (2nd edn). Oxford University Press, Oxford.

Rosenbaum, M. (1983). Crime and punishment—the suicide pact. *Archives of General Psychiatry* **40**, 979–82.

Rosenham, D. (1973). On being sane in insane places. *Science* **179**, 250–8.

Rosenman, R. H., Brand, R. J., Jenkins, C. D., Friedman, H., Straus, R., and Wurner, H. (1975). Coronary heart disease: a western collaborative group study. Final follow up experience of eight and a half years. *Journal of the American Medical Association* **233**, 872–7.

Rosenthal, A. and Levine, S. V. (1971). Brief psychotherapy with children: process and therapy. *American Journal of Psychiatry* **128**, 141–5.

Rosenthal, D., Wender, P. H., Kety, S. S., and Welner, J. (1971). The adopted-away offspring of schizophrenics. *American Journal of Psychiatry* **128**, 307–11.

Rosenthal, N. E., Sack, D. A., Gillin, J. C., Lewy, A. J., Goodwin, F. K., Davenport, Y., Mueller, P. S., Newsome, D. A., and Weher, T. A. (1984). Seasonal affective disorder. *Archives of General Psychiatry* **41**, 72–80.

Rosenthal, N. E., Sack, D. A., Carpenter, C. J., Parry, B. L., Mendelson, W. B., Wehr, T. A. (1985). Antidepressant effect of light in seasonal affective disorder. *American Journal of Psychiatry* **142**, 163–70.

Rosenthal, P. A. and Rosenthal, S. (1984). Suicide behaviour by pre-school children. *American Journal of Psychiatry* **141**, 520–5.

Rosenthal, R. and Bigelow, L. B. (1972). Quantitative brain measurements in chronic schizophrenia. *British Journal of Psychiatry* **121**, 259–64.

Rosie, J. S. (1987). Partial hospitalization: a review of recent literature. *Hospital and Community Psychiatry* **38**, 1291–99.

Ross, T. A. (1937). *The common neuroses: their treatment by psychotherapy* (2nd edn). Edward Arnold, London.

Rosser, A. M. and Guz, A. (1981). Psychological approach to breathlessness and its treatment. *Journal of Psychosomatic Research* **25**, 439–47.

Roth, B., Neusimalova S., and Rechtschaffen, W. L. (1972). Hypersomnia with sleep drunkenness. *Archives of General Psychiatry* **26**, 456–72.

Roth, M. (1955). The natural history of mental disorder in old age. *Journal of Mental Science* **101**, 281–301.

Roth, M. (1959). The phobic anxiety-depersonalization syndrome. *Proceedings of the Royal Society of Medicine* **52**, 587–95.

Roth, M. (1971). Classification and aetiology in mental disorders of old age: some recent developments. In *Recent developments in psychogeriatrics* (ed. D. W. K. Kay and A. Walk). Headley Brothers, Ashford.

Roth, M. and Ball, J. R. B. (1964). Psychiatric aspects of intersexuality. In *Intersexuality in vertebrates including man* (ed. C. N. Armstrong and A. J. Marshall). Academic Press, London.

Roth, M. and Bluglass, R. (1985). A postscript on the discussions at the Cambridge Conference on society, psychiatry and the law. In *Psychiatry, human rights and the law* (ed. M. Roth and R. Bluglass) pp. 228–41. Cambridge University Press, Cambridge.

Roth, M. and Iverson, L. (eds.) (1986). Alzheimer's disease and related disorders. *British Medical Bulletin* **42**, 1–115.

Roth, M. and Kroll, J. (1987). *The reality of mental illness*. Cambridge University Press, Cambridge.

Rothman, D. (1971). *The discovery of the asylum*. Little Brown, Boston.

Rothschild, D. (1942). Neuropathological changes in arteriosclerotic psychosis and their psychiatric significance. *Archives of Neurology and Psychiatry, Chicago* **48**, 417–36.

Rowan, P. R., Paykel, E. S., and Parker, R. P. (1982). Phenelzine and amitriptyline effects on symptoms of neurotic depression. *British Journal of Psychiatry* **140**, 475–83.

Roy, A. (1976). Psychiatric aspects of narcolepsy. *British Journal of Psychiatry* **128**, 562–5.

Roy, A. (1982). Suicide in chronic schizophrenia. *British Journal of Psychiatry* **141**, 171–7.

Roy, A. (1985). Suicide in doctors. *Psychiatric Clinics of North America* **8**, 377–87.

Roy, A. and Bhanji, S. (1976). Sleep deprivation in depression: a review. *Postgraduate Medical Journal* **52**, 50–2.

Royal College of Physicians (1981). Organic mental impairment in the elderly. Report of the College Committee on geriatrics. *Journal of the Royal College of Physicians* **15**, 141–67.

Royal College of Physicians. (1984). Medication for the elderly. *Journal of the Royal College of Physicians* **18**, 7–17.

Royal College of Physicians (1987). *A great and growing evil: the medical consequences of alcohol abuse*. Tavistock, London.

Royal College of Physicians and the British Nutrition Foundation. (1984). Food intolerance and food aversion. *Journal of the Royal College of Physicians* **18**, 83–123.

Royal College of Psychiatrists (1977). Memorandum on the use of electroconvulsive therapy. *British Journal of Psychiatry* **131**, 261–72.

Royal College of Psychiatrists (1979). *Alcohol and alcoholism. The report of a special committee of the Royal College of Psychiatrists*. Tavistock, London.

Royal College of Psychiatrists (1986). *Alcohol: our favourite drug: new report on alcohol and alcohol related problems*. Tavistock, London.

Rubinow, D. R. and Roy-Byrne, P. (1984). Premenstrual syndromes: overview from a methodologic perspective. *American Journal of Psychiatry* **141**, 163–72.

Rüdin, E. (1916). Studien über Vererbung und Entstehung geistiger Störungen: *I. Zur Vererbung und Neuentstehung der Dementia Praecox*. Springer, Berlin.

Rüdin, E. (1953). Ein Beitrag zur Frage der Zwangskrankeit, unsbesondere ihrer hereditären Beziehungen. *Archiv für Psychiatrie und Nervenkrankheiten* **191**, 14–54.

Rund, D. A. and Huter, J. C. (1983). *Emergency psychiatry*. Mosby, St. Louis.

Rush, A. J., Beck, A. T., Kovacs, M., and Hollon, S. (1977). Comparative efficacy of cognitive therapy and imipramine in the treatment of depressed outpatients. *Cognitive Therapy and Research* **1**, 17–31.

Rush, Benjamin (1830). *Medical inquiries and observations upon the diseases of the mind* (4th edn). Philadelphia.

Russell, G. F. M. (1977). The present status of anorexia nervosa. *Psychological Medicine* **7**, 363–7.

Russell, G. F. M. (1979). Bulimia nervosa: an ominous variant of anorexia nervosa. *Psychological Medicine* **9**, 429–48.

Russell, G. F. M. (1981). The current treatment of anorexia nervosa. *British Journal of Psychiatry* **138**, 164–6.

Russell, O. (1970). Autistic children: infancy to adulthood. *Seminars in Psychiatry* **2**, 435–40.

Russell, O. (1971). Normal psychosexual development. *Journal of Child Psychology and Psychiatry* **11**, 259–83.

Russell, O. (1985). *Mental handicap*. Churchill Livingstone, Edinburgh.

Rutter, M. (1971). Parent–child separation: psychological effects on the children. *Journal of Child Psychology and Psychiatry* **14**, 201–8.

Rutter, M. (1972). Relationships between child and adult psychiatric disorders. *Acta Psychiatrica Scandinavica* **48**, 3–21.

Rutter, M. (ed.) (1980). *Scientific foundations of developmental psychiatry*. Heinemann, London.

Rutter, M. (1981). *Maternal deprivation reassessed*. Penguin, Harmondsworth.

Rutter, M. (1982). Syndromes attributed to 'minimal brain dysfunction' in childhood. *American Journal of Psychiatry* **139**, 21–33.

Rutter, M. (1985a). Infantile autism and other pervasive developmental disorders. In: *Child and adolescent psychiatry: modern approaches* (eds. M. Rutter and L. Hersov) (2nd edn). Blackwell, Oxford.

Rutter, M. (1985b). Resilience in the face of adversity: protective factors and resistance to psychiatric disorder. *British Journal of Psychiatry* **147**, 598–611.

Rutter, M. (1985c). The treatment of autistic children. *Journal of Child Psychology and Psychiatry* **2**, 193–214.

Rutter, M. and Giller, H. (1983). *Juvenile delinquency. trends and perspectives*. Penguin, Harmondsworth.

Rutter, M. and Gould, M. (1985). Classification In *Child and adolescent psychiatry: modern approaches*. (ed. M. Rutter and L. Hersov) (2nd edn). Blackwell, Oxford.

Rutter, M. L. and Hersov, L. (1985). *Child and adolescent psychiatry. Modern approaches*, Blackwell, Oxford.

Rutter, M. and Lockyer, L. (1967). A five to fifteen year follow-up study of infantile psychosis: I. Description of sample. *British Journal of Psychiatry* **113**, 1169–82.

Rutter, M. and Madge, N. (1976). *Cycles of disadvantage: a review of research*. Heinemann, London.

Rutter, M. Graham, P., and Birch, H. G. (1970a). *A neuropsychiatric study of childhood*. Clinics in Developmental Medicine No. 35/36. Heinemann, London.

Rutter, M., Tizard, J., and Whitmore, K. (eds.) (1970b). *Education, health and behaviour*. Longmans, London.

Rutter, M., Yule, W., Berger, M., Yule, B., Morton, J., and Bagley, C. (1974). Children of West Indian immigrants. I. Rates of behavioural deviance and of psychiatric disorder. *Journal of Child Psychology and Psychiatry* **15**, 241–62.

Rutter, M., Shaffer, D., and Shepherd, M. (1975a). *A multiaxial classification of child psychiatric disorders*. World Health Organization, Geneva.

Rutter, M. L., Cox, A., Tupling, C., Berger, M., and Yule, W. (1975b). Attainment and adjustment in two geographical areas: I. Prevalence of psychiatric disorders. *British Journal of Psychiatry* **126**, 493–509.

Rutter, M., Yule, B. Quinton, D., Rowlands, O., Yule, W., and Berger, N. (1975c). Attainment and adjustment in two geographical areas III: Some factors accounting for area differences, *British Journal of Psychiatry* **126**, 520–33.

Rutter, M., Tizard, J., Yule, W., Graham, P., and Whitmore, K. (1976a). Isle of Wight Studies 1964–1974. *Psychological Medicine* **6**, 313–32.

Rutter, M., Graham, P., Chadwick, O., and Yule, W. (1976b). Adolescent turmoil: fact or fiction. *Journal of Child Psychology and Psychiatry* **17**, 35–56.

Rutter, M., Izard, C., and Read, P. (1986). *Depression in young people*. Guilford Press, London.

Ryan, N. D. and Puig-Antich, J. (1986). Affective illness in adolescence. *American Psychiatric Association Annual Review* 5 (eds. A. J. Frances and R. E. Hales).American Psychiatric Association, Washington DC.

Ryan, P. (1979). Residential care for the mentally disabled. In *Community care for the mentally disabled* (ed. J. K. Wing and R. Olsen). Oxford University Press.

Saario, I., Linnoila, M., and Maki, M. (1975). Interaction of drugs with alcohol on human psychomotor skills related to driving: effects of sleep deprivation or two weeks treatment with hypnotics. *Journal of Clinical Pharmacology* **15**, 52–9.

Sachar, E. J. (1982). Endocrine abnormalities in depression. In *Handbook of affective disorders* (ed. E. S. Paykel). Churchill Livingstone, Edinburgh.

Sacks, O. (1973). *Awakenings*. Duckworth, London.

Saghir, M. T. and Robins, E. (1973). *Male and female homosexuality: a comprehensive investigation*. Williams and Wilkins, Baltimore.

Sainsbury, P. (1955). *Suicide in London*. Maudsley Monograph No. 1. Chapman and Hall, London.

Sainsbury, P. (1962). Suicide in later life. *Gerontologia Clinica* 4, 161–70.

Sainsbury, P. (1986). The epidemiology of suicide. In *Suicide*. (ed. A. Roy). Williams and Wilkins, Baltimore.

Sainsbury, P. and Barraclough, B. (1968). Differences between suicide rates. *Nature* 220, 1252–3.

St George-Hyslop, P. H. *et al.* (1987). The genetic defect causing familial Alzheimer's disease maps on chromosome 21. *Science* 20, 885–9.

Sakel, M. (1938). *The pharmacological shock treatment of schizophrenia*. Nervous and Mental Diseases Monograph Series No. 62. Nervous and Mental Diseases Publications Co., New York.

Salkovskis, P. M. and Warwick, H. M. C. (1986). Morbid preoccupations, health anxiety and reassurance: a cognitive-behavioural approach to hypochondriasis. *Behaviour Research and Therapy* 24, 597–602.

Salter, A. (1949). *Conditioned reflex therapy*. Farrar Strauss, New York.

Sammons, M. T. and Karoly, P. (1987). Psychosocial variables in irritable bowel syndrome: a review and proposal. *Clinical Psychology Review* 7, 187–204.

Sander, J. W. A. S. and Shorvon, S. D. (1987). Incidence and prevalence studies in epilepsy and their methodological problems: a review. *Journal of Neurology, Neurosurgery and Psychiatry* 50, 829–39.

Sanders, S. H. (1979). Behavioural assessment and treatment of clinical pain: appraisal of current status. *Progress in Behaviour Modification* 8, 249–92.

Sandifer, M. G., Hordern, A., Timbury, G. C., and Green, L. M. (1968). Psychiatric diagnosis: a comparative study in North Carolina. *British Journal of Psychiatry* 114, 1–9.

Sandler, J., Dare, C., and Holder, A. (1970a). Basic psychoanalytic concepts: II. The treatment alliance. *British Journal of Psychiatry* 116, 555–8.

Sandler, J., Dare, C. and Holder, A. (1970b). Basic psychoanalytic concepts: III. Transference. *British Journal of Psychiatry* 116, 667–72.

Sandler, J., Dare, C. and Holder, A. (1970c). Basic psychoanalytic concepts: IV. Countertransference. *British Journal of Psychiatry* 117, 83–8.

Sandler, J., Dare, C. and Holder, A. (1970d). Basic psychoanalytic concepts: V. Resistance *British Journal of Psychiatry* 117, 215–21.

Sandler, J., Dare, C. and Holder, A. (1970e). Basic psychoanalytic concepts: VI. Acting out. *British Journal of Psychiatry* 117, 329–35.

Sargant, W. and Dally, P. (1962). Treatment of anxiety state by antidepressant drugs. *British Medical Journal* i, 6–9.

Sargant, W. and Slater, E. (1940). Acute war neuroses. *Lancet* ii, 1–2.

Sargant, W. and Slater, E. (1963). *An introduction to physical methods of treatment in psychiatry*. Livingstone, Edinburgh.

Sartorius, N., Jablensky, A., Cooper, J. E., and Burke, J. D. (eds.) (1988). Psychiatric classification in an international perspective. *British Journal of Psychiatry* 152, Suppl. 1.

Satir, V. (1967). *Conjoint family therapy*. Science and Behaviour Books, Palo Alto.

Saunders, C. (1969). The moment of truth: care of the dying person. In *Death and dying* (ed. L. Pearson). Case Western Reserve University Press, Cleveland.

Saunders, J. B., Davis, M., and Williams, R. (1981). Do women develop alcoholic liver disease more readily than men? *British Medical Journal* **282**, 1140–3.

Savage, R. L. (1976). Drugs and breast milk. *Adverse Drug Reactions Bulletin* **61**, 212–14.

Scadding, J. G. (1963). Meaning of diagnostic terms in bronchopulmonary disease. *British Medical Journal* ii, 1425–30.

Schade, D. S., Drumm, D. A., Eaton, R. P., and Sterling, W. A. (1985). Factitious brittle diabetes mellitus. *The American Journal of Medicine* **78**, 777–83.

Schaefer, C. (1979). *Childhood encopresis and enuresis*. Van Nostrand, New York.

Schaefer, C., Coyne, J. C., and Lazarus, R. S. (1981). The health-related functions of social support. *Journal of Behavioral Medicine* **4**, 381–406.

Schapira, K., Davison, K., and Brierley, H. (1979). The assessment and management of transsexual problems. *British Journal of Hospital Medicine* **22**, 63–9.

Schapira, K., Roth, M., Kerr, T. A., and Gurney, C. (1972). The prognosis of affective disorders. The differentiation of anxiety states from depressive illness. *British Journal of Psychiatry* **121**, 175–81.

Scharfetter, C. (1980). *General psychopathology: an introduction* (translated from the German by H. Marshall). Cambridge University Press, Cambridge.

Scheff, T. J. (1963). The role of the mentally ill and the dynamics of mental disorder: a research framework. *Sociometry* **26**, 436–53.

Schilder, P. (1935). *The image and appearance of the human body*. International Universities Press, New York.

Schizophrenia Bulletin (1987). High risk research. *Schizophrenia Bulletin* **13**, 369–496.

Schmideberg, M. (1947). The treatment of psychopaths and borderline patients. *American Journal of Psychotherapy* **1**, 45–70.

Schmidt, W. and de Lint, J. E. E. (1972). The causes of death in alcoholics. *Quarterly Journal of Studies on Alcoholism* **33**, 171–85.

Schneider, K. (1950). *Psychopathic personalities* (translation of 9th edition by M. W. Hamilton). Cassel, London.

Schneider, K. (1959). *Clinical psychopathology*. Grune and Stratton, New York.

Schooler, N. R., Levine, J., Severe, J. B., Bruazer, B., diMascio, A., Klerman, G., and Tuason, V. B. (1980). Prevention of relapse in schizophrenia. *Archives of General Psychiatry* **37**, 16–24.

Schou, M., Amisden, A., Jensen, S. E., and Olsen, T. (1968). Occurrence of goitre during lithium treatment. *British Medical Journal* iii, 710–13.

Schreiner-Engel, P., and Schiavi, R. C. (1986). Lifetime psychopathology in individuals with low sexual desire. *Journal of Nervous and Mental Disease* **174**, 646–51.

Schrenck-Notzing, A. von (1895). *The use of hypnosis in psychopathia sexualis with special reference to contrary sexual instinct*. Trans. by C. G. Chaddock. The Institute of Research in Hypnosis Publication Society and the Julian Press, New York (1956).

Schulberg, H. C. (1984). *The treatment of psychiatric patients in general hospitals: a research agenda and annotated bibliography*. National Institutes of Mental Health, Rockville.

Schulsinger, F. (1982). Psychopathy: heredity and environment. *International Journal of Mental Health* **1**, 190–206.

Schultz, J. H. (1932). *Das autogene training*. Thieme, Liepzig.

Schultz, J. H. and Luthe, W. (1959). *Autogenic training: a psychophysiological approach*. Grune and Stratton, New York.

Schwartz, M. A. (1973). Pathways of metabolism of diazepines. *The benzodiaze-pines* (ed. S. Garrattini, E. Mussini, and L. O. Randall). Raven Press, New York.

Scott, P. D. (1953). Psychiatric reports for magistrates courts. *British Journal of Delinquency* 4, 82–98.

Scott, P. D. (1957). Homosexuality with special reference to classification. *Proceedings of the Royal Society of Medicine* 50, 655–9.

Scott, P. D. (1960). The treatment of psychopaths. *British Medical Journal* i, 1641–6.

Scott, P. D. (1965). The Ganser syndrome. *British Journal of Criminology* 5, 127–34.

Scott, P. D. (1973). Parents who kill their children. *Medicine Science and the Law* 13, 120–6.

Scott, P. D. (1977). Assessing dangerousness in criminals. *British Journal of Psychiatry* 131, 127–42.

Seager, C. P. and Flood, R. A. (1965). Suicide in Bristol. *British Journal of Psychiatry* 111, 919–32.

Sedler, M. J. (1985). The legacy of Ewald Hecker: a new translation of 'Die Hebephrenie.' *American Journal of Psychiatry* 142, 1265–71.

Sedman, G. (1966). A phenomenological study of pseudo-hallucinations and related experiences. *British Journal of Psychiatry* 113, 1115–21.

Sedman, G. (1970). Theories of depersonalization: a reappraisal. *British Journal of Psychiatry* 117, 1–14.

Sedvall, G., Farde, L., Persson, A., and Wiesel, F. A. (1986). Imaging of neurotransmitter receptors in the living human brain. *Archives of General Psychiatry* 43, 995–1005.

Segal, H. (1963). *Introduction to the work of Melanie Klein.* Heinemann Medical Books, London.

Seguin, E. (1864). Origin of the treatment and training of idiots. In *History of mental retardation*, (ed. M. Rosen, G. R. Clark, and M. S. Kivitz), Vol. 1. University Park Press, Baltimore (1976).

Seguin, E. (1866). *Idiocy and its treatment by the physiological method.* Brandown, Albany.

Seidel, U., Chadwick, O. F. D., and Rutter, M. L. (1975). Psychological disorder in crippled children: a comparative study of children with and without brain damage. *Developmental Medicine and Child Neurology* 17, 563–73.

Seligman, M. E. P. (1975). *Helplessness: on depression, development and death.* Freeman, San Francisco.

Selye, H. (1950). *Stress.* Acta, Montreal.

Serieux, P. and Capgras, J. (1987). Misinterpretation delusional states (English translation). In *The clinical roots of the schizophrenia concept* (ed. J. Cutting and M. Shepherd). Cambridge University Press, Cambridge.

Settle, E. C. (1984). Rapid neuroleptization. In *Manual of psychiatric consultation and emergency care* (ed. F. Guggenheim and M. Weiner). Jason Aronson, New York.

Shaffer, D. (1974). Suicide in childhood and early adolescence. *Journal of Child Psychology and Psychiatry* 15, 275–91.

Shaffer, D. (1985a). Enuresis. In *Child psychiatry: modern approaches* (ed. M. Rutter and L. Hersov) (2nd edn). Blackwell, Oxford.

Shaffer, D. (1985b). Brain damage. In *Child and adolescent psychiatry: modern approaches.* (ed. M. Rutter and L. Hersov) (2nd edn). Blackwell, Oxford.

Shaffer, D. Costello, A. J., and Hill, I. D. (1968). Control of enuresis with imipramine. *Archives of Diseases of Childhood* 43, 665–71.

Shalev, A. and Munitz, H. (1986). The neuroleptic malignant syndrome; agent and host interaction. *Acta Psychiatrica Scandinavica* **73**, 337–47.

Shannon, F. T., Fergusson, D. M., and Dimond, M. E. (1984). Early hospital admissions and subsequent behaviour problems in six-year-olds. *Archives of Diseases of Childhood* **59**, 815–19.

Shapiro, A. K., Shapiro, E. S., Bruun, R. D., and Street, R. D. (1978). *Gilles de la Tourette Syndrome*. Raven Press, New York.

Shapiro, D. (1976). The effects of therapeutic conditions: positive results revisited. *British Journal of Medical Psychology* **49**, 315–23.

Shapiro, P. A. and Kornfeld, D. S. (1987). Psychiatric aspects of head and neck cancer surgery. *Psychiatric Clinics of North America* **10**, 87–100.

Sharan, S. N. (1965). Family interaction with schizophrenia and their siblings. *Journal of Abnormal Psychology* **71**, 345–53.

Shaw, P. M. (1979). A comparison of three behaviour therapies in the treatment of social phobias. *British Journal of psychiatry* **134**, 620–3.

Shaw, S. (1980). The causes of increasing drinking problems among women. In *Women and alcohol*. Tavistock, London.

Sheehan, D. V., Ballenger, J., and Jacobson, G. (1980). Treatment of endogenous anxiety with phobic hysterical and hypochondriacal symptoms. *Archives of General Psychiatry* **37**, 51–9.

Sheldon, W. H. Stevens, S. S., and Tucker, W. B. (1940). *The varieties of human physique*. Harper, London.

Sheldon, W. H., Stevens, S. S., and Tucker, W. B. (1942). *The varieties of temperament*. Harper, London.

Shepherd, M. (1961). Morbid jealousy: some clinical and social aspects of a psychiatric symptom. *Journal of Mental Science* **107**, 687–753.

Shepherd, M. (ed.) (1983). *Handbook of psychiatry*. Vols. 1–5. Cambridge University Press.

Shepherd, M. and Gruenberg, E. M. (1957). The age for neuroses. *Millbank Memorial Fund Quarterly* **35**, 258–65.

Shepherd, M. and Watt, D. C. (1977). Long term treatment with neuroleptics in psychiatry. *Current Developments in Psychopharmacology* **4**, 217–47.

Shepherd, M., Cooper, B., Brown, A. C., and Kalton, G. W. (1966). *Psychiatric illness in general practice*. Oxford University Press, London.

Shepherd,M., Lader, M., and Rodnight, R. (1968). *Clinical psychopharmacology*. English Universities Press, London.

Shepherd, M., Harwin, B. G., Depla, C., and Cairns, V. (1979). Social work and primary care of mental disorder. *Psychological Medicine* **9**, 661–70.

Shepherd, M., Wilkinson, G., and Williams, P. (1986). *Mental illness in primary care settings*. Tavistock, London.

Sheppard, G., Gruzella, J., Manchadra, R., *et al.* (1983). 150 positron emmission tomographic scanning in predominantly never-treated patients. *Lancet* **2**, 1448–52.

Sheppard, N. P., O'Loughlin, S., and Malone, J. P. (1986). Psychogenic skin disease. A review of 35 cases. *British Journal of Psychiatry* **149**, 636–43.

Sherman, R. A., Sherman, C. J., and Bruno, G. M. (1987). Psychological factors influencing chronic phantom limb pain: an analysis of the literature. *Pain* **28**, 285–95.

Shields, J. (1962). *Monozygotic twins brought up apart and brought up together*. Oxford University Press, London.

Shields, J. (1976). Heredity and environment. In *Textbook of human psychology* (ed. H. J. Eysenck and G. D. Wilson). MTP, Lancaster.

Shields, J. (1978). Genetics. In *Schizophrenia: towards a new synthesis* (ed J. K. Wing). Academic Press, London.

Shields, J. (1980). Genetics and mental development. In *Scientific foundations of developmental psychiatry* (ed. M. Rutter). Heinemann Medical, London.

Shillito, F. H., Drinker, C. K., and Shaughnessy, T. J. (1936). The problem of nervous and mental sequelae of carbon monoxide poisoning. *Journal American Medical Association* **106**, 669–74.

Shneidman, E. S. (1976). Suicide notes reconsidered. In *Suicidology: contemporary developments* (ed. E. S. Shneidman), pp. 253–78. Grune and Stratton, New York.

Shneidman, E. S., Farberow, N. L., and Litman, R. E. (1961). The suicide prevention centre. In *The cry for help* (ed. N. L. Farberow and E. S. Shneidman), pp. 6–118. McGraw-Hill, New York.

Shorvon, H. J., Hill, J. D. N., Burkitt, E., and Hastead, H. (1946). The depersonalization syndrome. *Proceedings of the Royal Society of Medicine* **39**, 779–92.

Showers, J. and Pickrell, E. (1987). Child firesetters: a study of three populations. *Hospital and Community Psychiatry* **38**, 495–501.

Shulman, K. and Post, F. (1980). Bipolar affective disorder in old age. *British Journal of Psychiatry* **136**, 26–32.

Shulman, K. T. (1986). Mania in old age. In *Affective disorders in the elderly* (ed. E. Murphy). Churchill Livingstone, Edinburgh.

Shulman, R. (1967). Vitamin B_{12} deficiency and psychiatric illness. *British Journal of Psychiatry* **113**, 252–6.

Siegelman, M. (1974). Parental background of male homosexuals and heterosexuals. *Archives of Sexual Behaviour* **3**, 3–18.

Sifneos, P. E. (1972). *Short-term psychotherapy and emotional crisis*. Harvard University Press, Cambridge, Massachusetts.

Sigurdsson, B. and Gudmundsson, K. B. (1956). Clinical findings six years after an outbreak of Alkureyri disease. *Lancet* i, 766–8.

Silberfarb, P., Philibert, D., and Levine, P. M. (1980). Psychological aspects of neoplastic disease: II. Affective and cognitive effects of chemotherapy in cancer patients. *American Journal of Psychiatry* **137**, 597–601.

Simmons, R. G., Anderson, C., and Kamstra, L. (1986). Comparison of quality of life on continuous ambulatory peritoneal dialysis, hamodialysis, and after transplantation. *American Journal of Kidney Disease* **4**, 253–5.

Simon, N. M., Garber, E., and Arieff, A. J. (1977). Persistent nephrogenic diabetes insipidus after lithium carbonate. *Annals of Internal Medicine* **86**, 446–7.

Simons, R. C. and Hughes, C. C. (1985). *Culture bound syndromes: folk illnesses of psychiatric and anthropological interest*. Reidel, Dordrecht.

Simpson, M. A. (1976). Self mutilation. *British Journal of Hospital Medicine* **16**, 430–8.

Sims, A. (1973). Mortality and neurosis. *Lancet* ii, 1072–5.

Sims, A. C. P. (1978). Hypothesis linking neuroses with premature mortality. *Psychological Medicine* **8**, 255–63.

Singer, H. S. (1982). Tics and Tourette syndrome. *Johns Hopkins Medical Journal* **151**, 30–5.

Singer, M. T. and Wynne, L. C. (1965). Thought disorder and family relations of schizophrenics: IV. Results and implications. *Archives of General Psychiatry* **12**, 201–12.

Sjöbring, H. (1973). Personality structure and development: a model and its applications. *Acta Psychiatrica Scandinavica* Suppl. 244.

Sjögren, T., Sjögren, H., and Lindgren, A. G. H. (1952). Morbus Alzheimer and morbus Pick. A genetic, clinical and patho-anatomical study. *Acta Psychiatrica Neurologica Scandinavica* Suppl. 82.

Skeels, H. (1966). Adult status of children with contrasting life experiences: a follow-up study. *Monograph of the Society for Research into Child Development* **31**, No. 3.

Skegg, D. C. G., Doll, R., and Perry, J. (1977). Use of medicines in general practice. *British Medical Journal* i, 1561–3.

Skevington, S. M. (1986). Psychological aspects of pain in rheumatoid arthritis: a review. *Social Science and Medicine* **23**, 567–75.

Skinner, B. F. (1953). *Science and human behaviour*. Macmillan, New York.

Sklar, L. S. and Anisman, H. (1981). Stress and cancer. *Psychological Bulletin* **89**, 369–406.

Skuse, D. (1985). Non-organic failure to thrive. *Archives of Disease in Childhood* **60**, 173–8.

Skuse, D. and Burrell, S. (1982). A review of solvent abusers and their management by a child psychiatric outpatient service. *Human Toxicology* **1**, 321–9.

Skynner, A. C. R. (1969). Indications for and against conjoint family therapy. *International Journal of Social Psychiatry* **15**, 245–9.

Skynner, A. C. R. (1976). *One flesh, separate persons: principles of family and marital psychotherapy*. Constable, London.

Skynner, A. C. R. and Brown, D. G. (1981). Referral of patients for psychotherapy. *British Medical Journal* **282**, 1952–5.

Slater, E. (1943). The neurotic constitution: a statistical study of 2000 soldiers. *Journal of Neurology and Psychiatry* **6**, 1–16.

Slater, E. (1951). Evaluation of electric convulsion therapy as compared with conservative methods in depressive states. *Journal of Mental Science* **97**, 567–9.

Slater, E. (1953). *Psychotic and neurotic illness in twins*. HMSO, London.

Slater, E. (1958). The monogenic theory of schizophrenia. *Acta Genetica Statistica Medica* **8**, 50–6.

Slater, E. (1961). Hysteria 311. *Journal of Mental Science* **107**, 359–81.

Slater, E. (1965). The diagnosis of hysteria. *British Medical Journal* i, 1395–9.

Slater, E. and Cowie, V. (1971). *The genetics of mental disorders*. Oxford University Press, London.

Slater, E. and Glithero, E. (1965). A follow-up of patients diagnosed as suffering from hysteria. *Journal of Psychosomatic Research* **9**, 9–13.

Slater, E. and Shields, J. (1969). Genetical aspects of anxiety. In *Studies of anxiety* (ed. M. H. Lader). *British Journal of Psychiatry* Special Publication No. 3.

Slater, E., Beard, A. W., and Glithero, E. (1963). The schizophrenia-like psychoses of epilepsy. *British Journal of Psychiatry* **109**, 95–150.

Sloan, F. A., Khakoo, R., Cluff, L. E., and Waldman, R. M. (1979). Impact of infection and allergic disease on the quality of life. *Social Science and Medicine* **13**, 473–82.

Slovenko, R. (1985). Forensic psychiatry. In *Comprehensive textbook of psychiatry* (ed. H. I. Kaplan and B. J. Sadock) (4th edn). Williams and Wilkins, Baltimore.

Small, G. W. (1986). Pseudocyesis: an overview. *Canadian Journal of Psychiatry* **31**, 452–7.

Small, I. F., Heimburger, R. F., Small, J. G., Milstein, V., and Moore, D. F. (1977). Follow up of stereotaxic amygdalotomy for seizure and behaviour disorders. *Biological Psychiatry* **12**, 401–11.

Small, J. G., Milstein, V., Klapper, M. H., Kellams, J. J., Miller, M. J., and Small, I. F. (1986). Electroconvulsive therapy in the treatment of manic episodes. In *Electroconvulsive therapy: clinical and basic research issues* (eds. S.

Malitz and H. A. Sackheim). *Annals of the New York Academy of Science* **462**, pp. 37–49.

Smart, R. G. and Cutler, R. E. (1976). The alcohol advertising ban in British Columbia: problems and effects on beverage consumption. *British Journal of Addiction* **71**, 13–21.

Smigman, L. and Perris, C. (1983). Memory functions and prophylactic treatment with lithium. *Psychological Medicine* **13**, 529–36.

Smith, G. R., Hanson, R. A., and Ray, D. C. (1986). Patients with multiple unexplained symptoms. *Archives of Internal Medicine* **146**, 69–72.

Smith, J. C. and Hogan, B. (1983). *Criminal law* (5th edn). Butterworths, London.

Smith, J. S. and Brandon, S. (1973). Morbidity from acute carbon monoxide poisoning at 3 year follow up. *British Medical Journal* i, 318–21.

Smith, M. (1986). Recent work on low level lead exposure and its impact on behaviour, intelligence and learning: a review. *Journal of the American Academy of Child Psychiatry* **24**. 24–32.

Smith, M. L. and Glass, G. V. (1977). Meta-analysis of psychotherapy outcome studies. *American Psychologist* **32**, 752–60.

Smith, R. (1981). Alcohol, women, and the young: the same old problem? *British Medical Journal* **283**, 1170–2.

Smith, R. (1984). The mental health of prisoners. I—How many mentally abnormal offenders? *British Medical Journal* **288**, 308–10.

Smith, R. (1985). Occupationless health. *British Medical Journal* **291**, 1024–7; 1191–5; 1338–41; 1409–12.

Smith, S. L. (1970). School refusal with anxiety: a review of sixty-three cases. *Canadian Psychiatric Association Journal* **15**, 257–64.

Smith, T. (1983). Denmark: the elderly living in style. *British Medical Journal* **287**, 1053–5.

Smith, W. J. (1982). Long term outcome of early onset anorexia nervosa. *Journal of American Academy of Child Psychiatry* **21**, 38–46.

Smoller, J. W., Wadden, T. A., and Stunkard, A. J. (1987). Dieting and depression: a critical review. *Journal of Psychosomatic Research* **31**, 429–40.

Snaith, P. (1981). *Clinical neurosis*. Oxford University Press, Oxford.

Snaith, R. P. and Taylor, C. M. (1985). Irritability: definition, assessment and associated factors. *British Journal of Psychiatry* **147**, 127–36.

Sneddon, I. B. (1983). Simulated disease: problems in diagnosis and management. *Journal of the Royal College of Physicians,* **17**, 199–205.

Sneddon, I. B. and Sneddon, J. (1975). Self-inflicted injury: a follow-up study of 43 patients. *British Medical Journal* iii, 527–30.

Snowden, P. (1985). A survey of the regional secure unit programme. *British Journal of Psychiatry* **147**, 499–507.

Sobell, L. C. and Sobell, M. B. (1973a). A self-feedback technique to monitor drinking behaviour in alcoholics. *Behaviour Research and Therapy* **11**, 237–8.

Sobell, M. B. and Sobell, L. C. (1973b). Alcoholics treated by individualized behaviour therapy: one year treatment outcome. *Behaviour Research Therapy* **11**, 599–618.

Solomon, Z. and Bromet, E. (1982). The role of social factors in affective disorder: an assessment of the vulnerability model of Brown and his colleagues. *Psychological Medicine* **12**. 123–30.

Solyom, L., Beck, P., Solyom, C., and Hugel, R. (1974). Some etiological factors in phobic neurosis. *Canadian Psychiatric Association Journal* **19**, 69–78.

Soothill, K. L. and Pope, P. J. (1973). Arson: a twenty-year cohort study. *Medicine, Science and the Law* **13**, 127–38.

Sourindrin, I. (1985). Solvent abuse. *British Medical Journal* **290**, 94–5.

Sourindrin, I. and Baird, J. A. (1984). Management of solvent abuse: a Glasgow community approach. *British Journal of Addiction* **79**, 227–32.

Southard, E. E. (1910). A study of the dementia praecox group in the light of certain cases showing anomalies or sclerosis in particular brain regions. *American Journal of Insanity* **67**, 119–76.

Sowerby, P. (1977). Balint reassessed. *Journal of the Royal College of Practitioners* **27**, 583–9.

Sox, G. C. (1979). Quality of care by nurse, practitioner and physician and assistants: a ten year perspective. *Annals of Internal Medicine* **91**, 459–68.

Spicer, R. F. (1985). Adolescents. In *Oxford textbook of public health* (ed. W. Holland, R. Detels, and G. Knox), Vol. 4. Oxford University Press, Oxford.

Spitzer, R. L. and Endicott, J. (1968). DIAGNO: a computer programme for psychiatric diagnosis utilizing the differential diagnostic procedures. *Archives of General Psychiatry* **18**, 746–56.

Spitzer, R. L. and Williams, J. B. W. (1985). Classification in psychiatry. In *Comprehensive textbook of psychiatry* (ed. H. I. Kaplan and B. J. Sadock) (4th edn). Williams and Wilkins, Baltimore.

Spitzer, R. L., Endicott, J. and Robins, E. (1975). Clinical criteria for psychiatric diagnosis and DSM III. *American Journal of Psychiatry* **132**, 1187–92.

Spitzer, R. L., Endicott, J., and Robins, E. (1978). Research diagnostic criteria: rationale and reliability. *Archives of General Psychiatry* **35**, 773–82.

Spitzer, R. L., Endicott, J., and Gibson, M. (1979) Research diagnostic criteria: rationale and reliability. *Archives of General Psychiatry* **36**, 17–24.

Squire, L. R., and Zouzounis, J. A. (1986) ECT and memory: brief pulse versus sine wave. *American Journal of Psychiatry* **143**, 596–601.

Srinivasan, D. P. and Hullin, R. P. (1980). Current concepts of lithium. *British Journal of Hospital Medicine* **24**, 466–75.

Srole, T., Langner, T., Michael, S., Opler, M., and Rennie, T. (1962). *Mental health in the metropolis*. McGraw-Hill, New York.

Stahl, S. (1986). Tardive dyskinesia: natural history studies assist the pursuit of preventive therapies. *Psychological Medicine* **16**, 491–4.

Stam, H. J., Bultz, B. D., and Pittman, C. A. (1986). Psychosocial problems and interventions in a referred sample of cancer patients. *Psychosomatic Medicine* **48**, 539–47.

Stark, O., Atkins, E., Wolff, O. H., and Douglas, J. W. B. (1981). Longitudinal study of obesity in the national survey of health and development. *British Medical Journal* **283**, 13–17.

Stedeford, A. (1984). *Facing death: patients, families and professionals*. William Heinemann, London.

Stedeford, A. and Bloch, S. (1979). The psychiatrist in the terminal care unit. *British Journal of Psychiatry* **135**, 7–14.

Stein, L. I. and Test, M. A. (1980). An alternative to mental hospital treatment. *Archives of General Psychiatry* **37**, 392–7.

Steinberg, D. (1982). Treatment, training, care or control. *British Journal of Psychiatry* **141**, 306–9.

Stekel, W. (1952). *Sexual aberrations; the phenomena of fetishism in relation to sex*, 2 Vols (English translation by S. Parker). Vision Press, London.

Stekel, W. (1953). *Sadism and machosism*, 2 Vols. Liveright, London.

Stengel, E. (1941). On the aetiology of fugue states. *Journal of Mental Science* **87**, 572–99.

Stengel, E. (1945). A study of some clinical aspects of the relationship between obsessional neurosis and psychotic reaction types. *Journal of Mental Science* **91**, 166–87.

Stengel, E. (1952). Enquiries into attempted suicide. *Proceedings of the Royal Society of Medicine* **45**, 613–20.

Stengel, E. (1959). Classification of mental disorders. *Bulletin of the World Health Organization* **21**, 601–63.

Stengel, E. and Cook, N. G. (1958). *Attempted suicide: its social significance and effects*. Maudsley Monograph No. 4. Chapman and Hall, London.

Stengel, E., Zeitlyn, B. B., and Rayner, E. H. (1958). Post operative psychosis. *Journal of Mental Science* **104**, 389–402.

Stenstedt, A. (1952). A study of manic depressive psychosis: clinical, social and genetic investigations. *Acta Psychiatrica et Neurologica Scandinavica* Suppl. **79**, 3–85.

Stenstedt, A. (1981). Involutional melancholia: an aetiological, clinical and social study of endogenous depression in later life with special reference to genetic factors. *Acta Psychiatrica Scandinavica* Suppl. 127.

Stephens, J. H. (1978). Long term prognosis and follow up in schizophrenia. *Schizophrenia Bulletin* **4**, 25–47.

Steptoe, A. (1981). *Psychological factors in cardiovascular disease*. Academic Press, London.

Steptoe, A. (1984). Psychological aspects of bronchial asthma. In *Contributions to medical psychology* 3 (ed. S. Rachman). Pergamon Press, Oxford.

Steptoe, A. (1985). Type-A coronary prone behaviour. *British Journal of Hospital Medicine* **27**, 257–60.

Stern, N. J. and Cleary, P. (1982). The national exercise and heart disease project: long term psychosocial outcome. *Archives of Internal Medicine* **142**, 1093–7.

Stern, R. S., Lipsedge, M. A., and Marks, I. M. (1973). Thought-stopping of neutral and obsessional thoughts: a controlled trial. *Behaviour Research and Therapy* **11**, 659–62.

Stern, Z. A. and Susser, M. (1977). Recent trends in Down's syndrome. In *Research to practice in mental retardation: biomedical aspects*, (ed. P. Mittler), Vol. III. University Park Press, Baltimore.

Sternbach, R. A. (1986). *The psychology of pain* (2nd edn). Raven Press, New York.

Stevens, J. (1987). Brief psychoses: do they contribute to the good prognosis and equal prevalence of schizophrenia in developing countries? *British Journal of Psychiatry* **151**, 393–6.

Stevens, J. R. (1966). Psychiatric implications of psychomotor epilepsy. *Archives of General Psychiatry* **14**, 461–71.

Stevenson, J. and Richman, N. (1976). The prevalence of language delay in a population of 3-year-old children and its association with general retardation. *Developmental Medicine and Child Neurology* **18**, 431–41.

Stewart, B. D., Hughes, C., Frank, E., Anderson, B., Kendall, and West D. (1987). The aftermath of rape. Profiles of immediate and delayed treatment seekers. *Journal of Nervous and Mental Disease* **175**, 90–4.

Stewart, W. F. R. (1978). Sexual fulfillment for the handicapped. *British Journal of Hospital Medicine* **22**, 676–80.

Stimson, G. V., Oppenheimer, E., and Thorley, A. (1978). Seven-year follow-up of heroin addicts. *British Medical Journal* i, 1190–2.

Stokes, P. E., Stoll, P. M., Shamoian, C. A., and Patton, M. J. (1971). Efficacy of lithium as acute treatment of manic depressive illness. *Lancet* i, 1319–25.

Stone, A. R., Frank, J. D., Nash, E. H., and Imber, S. D. (1961). An intensive five year follow up study of treated psychiatric outpatients. *Journal of Nervous and Mental Disease* **133**, 410–22.

Stone, W. N. and Tieger, M. E. (1971). Screening for T-groups: the myth of healthy candidates. *American Journal of Psychiatry* **127**, 1485–90.

Stores, G. (1978). Antiepileptics (anticonvulsants). In *Paediatric psychopharmacology* (ed. J. S. Werry). Brunner-Mazel, New York.

Stores, G. (1981). Problems of learning and behaviour in children with epilepsy. In *Epilepsy and psychiatry* (ed. E. H. Reynolds and M. R. Trimble). Churchill Livingstone, Edinburgh.

Stores, G. (1986). Psychological aspects of nonconvulsive status epilepticus and children. *Journal of Child Psychology and Psychiatry* **27**, 575–82.

Storey, P. B. (1967). Psychiatric sequelae of subarachnoid haemorrhage. *Journal of Psychosomatic Research* **13**, 175–82.

Storey, P. B. (1970). Brain damage and personality change after subarachnoid haemorrhage. *British Journal of Psychiatry* **117**, 129–42.

Stoudemire, A., Cotanch, P., and Laszlo, J. (1984). Recent advances in the pharmacologic and behavioural management of chemotherapy-induced emesis. *Archives of Internal Medicine* **144**, 1029–33.

Strachan, J. G. (1981). Conspicuous firesetting in children. *British Journal of Psychiatry* **138**, 26–9.

Strain, J. J. and Grossman, S. (1975). *Psychological care of the medically ill.* Appleton-Century-Crofts, New York.

Strassman, R. J. (1984). Adverse reactions to psychedelic drugs. *Journal of Nervous and Mental Disease* **172**, 577–95.

Strathdee, G. (1987). Primary care—psychiatry interaction: a British perspective. *General Hospital Psychiatry* **9**, 102–10.

Straus, S. K., (1987). EB or not EB—that is the question. *Journal of the American Medical Association* **257**, 2335–6.

Strauss, A. and Lehtinen, V. (1947). *Psychopathology and education of the brain-injured child*, Vol. 1. Grune and Stratton, New York.

Strauss, J. S. and Carpenter, W. T. (1974). The prediction of outcome of schizophrenia. *Archives of General Psychiatry* **31**, 37–42.

Strauss, J. S. and Carpenter, W. T. (1977). Prediction of outcome in schizophrenia III. Five-year outcome and its predictors. *Archives of General Psychiatry* **34**, 159–63.

Streissguth, A. P., Clarren, S. K., and Jones, K. L. (1985). Natural history of the fetal alcohol syndrome: a 10-year follow-up of eleven patients. *Lancet* ii, 85–91.

Stroebel, C. F. (1985). Biofeedback and behavioural medicine. In *Comprehensive textbook of psychiatry* (ed. H. I. Kaplan and B. J. Sadock) (4th edn), pp. 1467–73. Williams and Wilkins, Baltimore.

Strömgren, E. (1968). Psychogenic psychoses. In *Themes and variations in European psychiatry* (ed. S. R. Hirsch and M. Shepherd) pp. 97–120. Wright, Bristol (1974).

Strömgren, E. (1985). World-wide issues in psychiatric diagnosis and classification and the Scandanavian point of view. In *Mental disorders, alcohol and drug related problems*. Excerpta Medica, Amsterdam.

Strömgren, E. (1986). The development of the concept of reactive psychoses. *Psychopathology* **20**, 62–67.

Ström-Olsen, R. and Carlisle, S. (1971). Bifrontal stereotactic tractotomy. *British Journal of Psychiatry* **118**, 141–54.

Strunk, R. C., Mrazek, D. A., Fuhimann, G. S. W., and La Breque, J. F. (1985). Physiologic and psychological characteristics associated with death due to asthma in childhood. *Journal of the American Medical Association* **254**, 1193–8.

Strupp, H. H., Hadley, S. W., and Gomes-Schwartz, B. (1977). *Psychotherapy for better or worse*. Aronson, New York.

Stuart, R. B. (1969). Operant interpersonal treatment for mental disorder. *Journal of Consulting and Clinical Psychology* 33, 675–82.

Stunkard, A. (1980). Obesity. In *Comprehensive textbook of psychiatry* (ed. H. I. Kaplan, A. M. Freedman, and B. J. Sadock) (3rd edn), Vol. 2. Williams and Wilkins, Baltimore.

Stunkard, A. and McLaren-Hume, M. (1959). The results of treatment for obesity. *Archives of Internal Medicine* 103, 79–85.

Stunkard, A. J., Foster, G. D., and Grossman, R. T. (1986). Surgical treatment of obesity. *Advances in Psychosomatic Medicine* 12, 140–66.

Sturgeon, D., Turpin, G., Kuipers, L., Berkowitz, R., and Leff, J. (1984). Psychophysiological responses of schizophrenia patients to high and low expressed emotion relatives: a follow-up study. *British Journal of Psychiatry* 145, 62–9.

Stürup, G. K. (1968). *Treating the 'untreatable': chronic criminals at Herstedvester.* Johns Hopkins University Press, Baltimore.

Suinn, R. and Richardson, F. (1971). Anxiety management training: a non-specific behaviour therapy programme for anxiety control. *Behaviour Therapy* 2, 498–510.

Sullivan, C., Grant, M. Q., and Grant, J. D. (1959). The development of interpersonal maturity: applications to delinquency. *Psychiatry* 20, 373–85.

Sulloway, F. J. (1979). *Freud: biologist of the mind.* Fontana, London.

Summerskill, W. H. J., Davidson, E. A., Sherlock, S., and Steiner, R. E. (1956). The neuropsychiatric syndrome associated with hepatic cirrhosis and an extensive portal collateral circulation. *Quarterly Journal of Medicine* 25, 245–66.

Suomi, S. J., Eisele, C. D., Gardy, S. A., and Harlow, H. F. (1975). Depressive behaviour in adult monkeys following separation from family environment. *Journal of Abnormal Psychology* 84, 576–8.

Surgeon General [US] (1981). Surgeon General's advice on alcohol and pregnancy. *FDA Drug Bulletin* 11, 9–10.

Surman, O. S (1978). The surgical patient. In *Massachusetts General Hospital handbook of general hospital psychiatry* (ed. T. P. Hackett and N. H. Cassem). Mosby, St. Louis.

Surridge, D. (1969). An investigation into some psychiatric aspects of multiple sclerosis. *British Journal of Psychiatry* 115, 749–64.

Surridge, D. H. C., Erdahl, D. L. W., Lawson, J. S., Donald, M. W., Monga, T. N., Bird, C. E., and Letemendia, F. J. J. (1984). Psychiatric aspects of diabetes mellitus. *British Journal of Psychiatry* 145, 269–76.

Swan, W. and Wilson, L. J. (1979). Sexual and marital problems in a psychiatric outpatient population. *British Journal of Psychiatry* 135, 310–15.

Swan-Parente, A. (1982). Psychological problems in a neonatal ITU. *British Journal of Hospital Medicine* 27, 266–8.

Swartz, M. S. and Blazer, D. G. (1986). The distribution of affective disorders in old age. In *Affective disorders in the elderly* (ed. E. Murphy). Churchill Livingstone, Edinburgh.

Swyer, G. I. M. (1985). Post partum mental disturbance and hormone changes. *British Medical Journal* 290, 1232–3.

Symmers, W. St. C. (1968). Carcinoma of breast in transsexual individuals after surgical and hormonal interference with primary and secondary sex characteristics. *British Medical Journal* ii, 83–5.

Symonds, R. L. (1985). Psychiatric aspects of railway fatalities. *Psychological Medicine* 15, 609–21.

Symonds, A. and Symonds, M. (1985). Karen Horney. In *Comprehensive textbook of psychiatry* (ed. H. I. Kaplan and B. J. Sadock), Vol. 1, pp. 419–25. Williams and Wilkins, Baltimore.

Szasz, T. S. (1957). *Pain and pleasure. A study in bodily feelings*. Basic Books, New York.

Szasz, T. S. (1960). The myth of mental illness. *American Psychologist* **15**, 113–18.

Szasz, T. S. (1976). *Schizophrenia: the sacred symbol of psychiatry*. Oxford University Press, Oxford.

Szmukler, G. I. (1985). The epidemiology of anorexia nervosa and bulimia. *Journal of Psychiatric Research* **19**, 143–53.

Szmukler, G. I. and Russell, G. F. M. (1986). Outcome and prognosis of anorexia nervosa. In *Handbook of eating disorders: physiology, psychology and treatment of obesity, anorexia and bulimia*. (ed. K. D. Brownell, and J. P. Goreyt) Basic Books, New York.

Talbott, J. A. (1985). Community care for the chronically mentally ill. *Psychiatric Clinics of North America* **8**, 437–48.

Talbott, J. A. and Glick, I. D. (1986). The inpatient care of the chronically mentally ill. *Schizophrenia Bulletin* **12**, 129–40.

Tan, E., Marks, I. M., and Marset, P. (1971). Bimedial leucotomy in obsessive compulsive neurosis: a controlled serial enquiry. *British Journal of Psychiatry* **118**, 155–64.

Tanguay, P. E. and Cantor, S. L. (1986). Schizophrenia in children. *Journal of the American Academy of Child Psychiatry* **25**, 591–4.

Tansella, M. and Williams, P. (1987). The Italian experience and its implications. *Psychological Medicine* **17**, 283–9.

Tantam, D. (1985). Alternatives to psychiatric hospitalisation. *British Journal of Psychiatry* **146**, 1–4.

Tanzi, R. E. *et al.* (1987). The genetic defect in familial Alzheimer's disease is not tightly linked to the amyloid B-protein gene. *Nature* **329**, 156–7.

Tardiff, K. (1987). Violence and the violent patient. In *Annual Review*, Vol. 6. American Psychiatric Association, Washington DC.

Tarnopolsky, A., and Berelowitz, M. (1987). Borderline personality: a review of recent research. *British Journal of Psychiatry* **151**, 724–34.

Tarnopolsky, A., Watkins, G. V., and Hand, D. J. (1980). Aircraft noise and mental health: I. Prevalence of individual symptoms. *Psychological Medicine* **10**, 683–98.

Tarsh, M. J. and Royston, C. (1985). A follow-up study of accident neurosis. *British Journal of Psychiatry* **146**, 18–25.

Task Force of the American Psychiatric Association (1980). Tardive dyskinesia. *American Journal of Psychiatry* **137**, 163–72.

Tattersall, R. B. (1981). Psychiatric aspects of diabetes—a physician's view. *British Journal of Psychiatry* **139**, 485–93.

Tattersall, R. B. (1985). Brittle diabetes. *British Medical Journal* **291**, 555–6.

Taylor, C. B., Housten-Miller, N., Ahn, D. K., Haskell, W., and De Busk, R. F. (1986). Effects of an exercise training programme on psychosocial improvement in uncomplicated postmyocardial infarction patients. *Journal of Psychosomatic Research* **30**, 581–7.

Taylor, E. A. (1984). Diet and behaviour. *Archives of Disease of Childhood* **59**, 97–8.

Taylor, E. A. (1986). Childhood hyperactivity. *British Journal of Psychiatry* **149**, 562–73.

Taylor, F. H. (1966). The Henderson therapeutic community. In *Psychopathic disorders* (ed. M. Craft). Pergamon Press, Oxford.

Taylor, F. K. (1958). A history of group and administrative therapy in Great Britain. *British Journal of Medical Psychology* **3**, 153–73.

Taylor, F. K. (1979). *Psychopathology: its causes and symptoms.* Quartermaine House, Sunbury on Thames.

Taylor, F. K. (1981). On pseudo-hallucinations. *Psychological Medicine* **11**, 265–72.

Taylor, G. J. (1984). Alexithymia: concept, measurement and implications for treatment. *American Journal of Psychiatry* **141**, 725–32.

Taylor, P. J. (1985). Motives for offending among violent and psychotic men. *British Journal of Psychiatry* **147**, 491–8.

Taylor, P. J. (1986*a*). The risk of violence in psychotics. *Integrative Psychiatry* **4**, 12–24.

Taylor, P. J. (1986*b*). Psychiatric disorder in London's life-sentenced offenders. *British Journal of Criminology* **26**, 63–78.

Taylor, P. J. and Fleminger, J. J. (1980). ECT for schizophrenia. *Lancet* **i**, 1380–2.

Taylor, P. J. and Gunn, J. (1984*a*). Violence and psychosis. I—Risk of violence among psychotic men. *British Medical Journal* **288**, 1945–9.

Taylor, P. J. and Gunn, J. (1984*b*). Violence and psychosis. II—Effect of psychiatric diagnosis on conviction and sentencing of offenders. *British Medical Journal* **289**, 9–12.

Taylor, P. J. and Kopelman, M. D. (1984). Amnesia for a criminal offence. *Psychological Medicine* **14**, 581–8.

Taylor, P. J. and Parrott, J. M. (1988). Elderly offenders: a study of age-related factors among custodially remanded prisoners. *British Journal of Psychiatry* **152**, 340–6.

Taylor, P. J., Mahandra, B., and Gunn, J. (1983). Erotomania in males. *Psychological Medicine* **13**, 645–50.

Taylor, S. E., Falke, R. L., Shoptow, S. J., and Lichtman, R. R. (1986). Social support, support groups and the cancer patient. *Journal of Consulting and Clinical Psychology* **54**, 608–15.

Taylor, S. J. L. and Chave, S. (1964). *Mental health and environment.* Longman, London.

Teasdale, J. D. (1983). Changes in cognition during depression: psychopathological implications. *Journal of the Royal Society of Medicine* **76**, 1038–44.

Teasdale, J. D. and Bancroft, J. (1977). Manipulation of thought content as a determinant of mood and corrugator electromyographic activity in depressed patients. *Journal of Abnormal Psychology* **86**, 235–41.

Teasdale, J. D. and Fogarty, S. (1979). Differential aspects of induced mood on the retrieval of pleasant events from episodic memory. *Journal of Abnormal Psychology* **88**, 248–57.

Teasdale, J. D., Taylor, R., and Fogarty, S. J. (1980). Effects of induced elation-depression on accessibility of memories of happy and unhappy experiences. *Behaviour Research and Therapy* **18**, 339–46.

Teasdale, J. D., Fennell, M. J. V., Hibbert, G. A., and Amies, P. L. (1984). Cognitive therapy for major depressive disorder in primary care. *British Journal of Psyhchiatry* **144**, 400–6.

Tellenbach, R. (1975). Typologische untersuchungen zur prämorbiden Persönlichkeit von Psychotikern unter besonderer Berucksichtigung manisch-depressiver. *Confinia Psychiatrica* **18**, 1–15.

Temkin, O. (1971). *The falling sickness.* Johns Hopkins Press, Baltimore.

Tennant, C. (1985). Female vulnerability to depression. *Psychological Medicine* **15**, 733–7.

Tennant, C. (1988). Psychosocial causes of duodenal ulcer. *Australian and New Zealand Journal of Psychiatry* **22**, 195–201.

Tennant, C. and Bebbington, P. (1978). The social causation of depression: a critique of the work of Brown and his colleagues. *Psychological Medicine* **8**, 565–75.

Tennant, C., Bebbington, P., and Hurry, J. (1981a). The short-term outcome of neurotic disorders in the community: the relation of remission to clinical factors and to 'neutralizing' life events. *British Journal of Psychiatry* **139**, 213–20.

Tennant, F. S., Rawson, R. A., and McCann, M. (1981b). Withdrawal from chronic phencyclidine (PCP) dependence with desimipramine. *American Journal of Psychiatry* **138**, 845–6.

Teta, M. J., Del Po, M. C., Kasl, S. V., Meigs, J. W., Myers, M. H., and Muluihill, J. J. (1986). Psychosocial consequences of childhood and adolescent cancer survival. *Journal of Chronic Diseases* **39**, 751–9.

Theander, S. (1970). Anorexia nervosa: a psychiatric investigation of female patients. *Acta Psychiatric Scandinavica* Suppl. 214.

Theander, S. (1985). Outcome and prognosis in anorexia nervosa and bulimia: some results of previous investigations, compared with those of a Swedish long-term study. *Journal of Psychiatric Research* **19**, 493–508.

Theorell, T. and Lind, E. (1973). Systolic blood pressure, serum cholesterol, and smoking in relation to sociological factors and myocardial infarctions. *Journal of Psychosomatic Research* **17**, 327–32.

Thigpen, C. H., Thigpen, H., and Cleckley, H. M. (1957). *The three faces of Eve.* McGraw-Hill, New York.

Thomas, A., Chess, S., and Birch, H. G. (1968). *Temperament and behaviour disorders in children.* University Press, New York.

Thomas, A. J. (1981). Acquired deafness and mental health. *British Journal of Medical Psychology* **54**, 219–29.

Thomas, C., Madden, F., and Jehu, D. (1984). Psychosocial morbidity in the first three months following stoma surgery. *Journal of Psychosomatic Research* **28**, 251–7.

Thomas, C., Madden, F., and Jehu, D. (1987). Psychological effects of stomas—I. Psychosocial morbidity one year after surgery. *Journal of Psychosomatic Research* **31**, 311–16.

Thomas, P. K. (1986). Brain atrophy and alcoholism. *British Medical Journal* **292**, 787.

Thompson, W. G. and Heaton, K. W. (1980). Functional bowel disorder in apparently healthy people. *Gastroenterology* **79**, 283–8.

Thorndike, E. L. (1913). *Educational psychology*, Vol. II. *the psychology of learning.* Teachers College, Columbia University, New York. [Also Kegan Paul, Trench, and Trubner, London (1923).]

Tienari, P. (1968). Schizophrenia in monozygotic male twins. In *The transmission of schizophrenia* (ed. D. Rosenthal and S. S. Kety). Pergamon Press, New York.

Tizard, B. (1962). The personality of epileptics: discussion of the evidence. *Psychological Bulletin* **59**, 196–210.

Tizard, J. (1964). *Community services for the mentally handicapped.* Oxford University Press, London.

Tizard, J. (1968). Social psychiatry and mental subnormality. In *Studies in psychiatry* (ed. M. Shepherd and D. L. Davies). Oxford University Press, London.

Tizard, J. (1974). Services and evaluation of services. In *Mental deficiency: the changing outlook* (ed. A. M. Clarke, and A. D. M. Clarke). Methuen, London.

Tizard, J. and Grad, J. C. (1961). *Mentally handicapped children and their families.* Oxford University Press, London.

Tollison, C. D. and Adams, H. E. (1979). *Sexual disorders: treatment, theory and research.* Gardner Press, New York.

Tomlinson, B. E., Blessed, G., and Roth, M. (1970). Observations on the brains of demented old people. *Journal of the Neurological Sciences* **11**, 205–42.

Tonks, C. M. (1964). Mental illness in hypothyroid patients. *British Journal of Psychiatry* **110**, 706–10.

Toone, B. (1985). Sexual disorders in epilepsy. In *Recent advances in epilepsy* 2 (ed. T. A. Pedley and B. S. Meldrum). Churchill Livingstone, Edinburgh.

Torgersen, S. (1979). The nature and origin of common phobic fears. *British Journal of Psychiatry* **134**, 343–51.

Torgersen, S. (1984). Genetic and nosological aspects of schizotypal and borderline personality disorders: a twin study. *Archives of General Psychiatry* **41**, 546–54.

Touwen, B. C. L. and Prechtl, H. F. R. (1970). The neurological examination of the child with minor nervous dysfunction. *Clinics in Developmental Medicine* No. 38. Spastics International Medical Publications and William Heinemann Medical, London.

Townsend, P. (1962). *The last refuge.* Routledge and Kegan Paul, London.

Treiman, D. M. and Delgado-Escueta, A. V. (1983). Violence and epilepsy: a critical review. In *Recent advances in epilepsy* 1 (ed. T. A. Pedley and B. S. Meldrum), Vol. 1. Churchill, Livingstone, Edinburgh.

Trethowan, W. (1979). Some rare psychiatric disorders. In *Current themes in psychiatry*, Vol. 2 (ed. R. Gaind and B. Hudson). Macmillan, London.

Trick, K. L. K. and Tennent, T. G. (1981). *Forensic psychiatry: an introductory text.* Pitman, London.

Trimble, M. R. (1981). *Post-traumatic neurosis: from railway spine to the whiplash.* Wiley, Chichester.

Trimble, M. R. (1985). Psychiatric and psychological aspects of epilepsy. In *The epilepsies* (ed. R. J. Porter, and P. L. Marselli). Butterworths, London.

Trimble, M. R. (ed.) (1986). *New brain imaging techniques and psychopharmacology.* British Association for Psychopharmacology Monograph No. 9. Oxford University Press, Oxford.

Trimble, M. and Reynolds, E. H. (1984). Neuropsychiatric toxicity of anticonvulsant drugs. In: *Recent advances in clinical neurology* (ed. W. B. Mathews and G. H. Glaser) Churchill Livingstone, Edinburgh.

Trower, P. E., Bryant, B., and Argyle, M. (1978). *Social skills and mental health.* Methuen, London.

Truax, C. B. and Carkhuff, R. R. (1967). *Towards effective counselling and psychotherapy.* Aldine, Chicago.

Tsuang, M. T. (1978). Suicide in schizophrenics, manics, depressives·and surgical controls. *Archives of General Psychiatry* **35**, 153–5.

Tsuang, M. T. (1980). *Genetic issues in epidemiology.* Washington University Press, Washington DC.

Tsuang, M. T. and Simpson, J. C. (1984). Schizoaffective disorder: concept and reality. *Schizophrenia Bulletin* **10**, 14–25.

Tsuang, M. T., Woolson, R. F., and Fleming, J. A. (1979). Long-term outcome of major psychosis: I Schizophrenia and affective disorder compared with psychiatrically symptom free surgical controls. *Archives of General Psychiatry* **36**, 1295–301.

Tucker, P. (1986). The burn victim—a review of psychosocial issues. *Australian and New Zealand Journal of Psychiatry* **20**, 413–20.

Tuckman, J. and Youngman, W. F. (1968). A scale for assessing suicide risk of attempted suicide. *Journal of Clinical Psychology* **24**, 17–19.

Tuke, D. H. (1872). *Illustrations of the influence of the mind upon the body in health and disease.* J. and A. Churchill, London.

Tuke, D. H. (1892). *A dictionary of psychological medicine.* J. and A. Churchill, London. Reprinted by Arno Press (1976).

Tuke, S. (1813). *A description of the retreat* (reprinted 1964). Dawson, London.

Tune, L. and Folstein, M. 1986). Post-operative delirium. In *Advances in psychosomatic medicine,* Vol. 15. *Psychological aspects of surgery.* Karger, Basel.

Tune, L. E., Folstein, M., Rabins, P., Jayaram, G., and McHugh, P. (1982). Familial manic-depressive illness and familial Parkinson's disease: a case report. *Johns Hopkins Medical Journal* **151**, 65–70.

Tunving, K. (1985). Psychiatric effects of cannabis use. *Acta Psychiatrica Scandinavica* **72**, 209–17.

Turk, D. C. and Rudy, T. E. (1987). Towards a comprehensive assessment of chronic pain patients. *Behaviour Research and Therapy* **25**, 237–49.

Turner, G. (1982). X-linked mental retardation. *Psychological Medicine* **12**, 471–3.

Turner, R. K. (1973). Conditioning treatment of nocturnal enuresis: present status. In Bladder control and enuresis. *Clinics in Developmental Medicine,* Nos. 48–49 (ed. I. Kolvin, R. McKeith, and S. R. Meadows). Spastics International Medical Publications and Heinemann, London.

Turner, T. J. and Tofler, D. S. (1986). Indications of psychiatric disorder among women admitted to prison. *British Medical Journal* **292**, 651–3.

Twaddle, A. (1972). The concepts of the sick role and illness behaviour. In *Advances in psychosomatic medicine,* Vol. 8. *Psychological aspects of physical illness* (ed. Z. J. Lipowski). Karger, Basel.

Tyrer, P. (1976). Towards rational therapy with mono-amine oxidase inhibitors. *British Journal of Psychiatry* **128**, 354–60.

Tyrer, P. and Steinberg, D. (1975). Symptomatic treatment of agoraphobia and social phobias: a follow-up study. *British Journal of Psychiatry* **127**, 163–8.

Tyrer, P., Rutherford, D., and Huggett, T. (1981). Benzodiazepine withdrawal symptoms and propanolol. *Lancet* i, 520–2.

Tyrer, S. P. (1986). Learned pain behaviour. *British Medical Journal* **292**, 1–2.

Udall, E. T. and Corbett, J. A. (1979). New hospital residential care of adults with mental retardation. In *Community care for the mentally disabled* (ed. J. K. Wing and R. Olsen). Oxford University Press, Oxford.

Unsworth, C. (1987). *The politics of mental health legislation.* Oxford University Press, Oxford.

Urwin, P. and Gibbons, J. L. (1979). Psychiatric diagnosis in self-poisoning patients. *Psychological Medicine* **9**, 501–8.

Vaillant, G. and Perry, J. C. (1985). Personality disorders. In *Comprehensive textbook of psychiatry* (ed. H. I. Kaplan and B. J. Sadock), Vol. 1 (4th edn). pp. 958–86. Williams and Wilkins, Baltimore.

Valdiserri, E. V., Carroll, K. R., and Hartl, A. J. (1986). A study of offenses committed by psychotic inmates in a county jail. *Hospital and Community Psychiatry* **37**, 163–6.

Valentine, M., Keddie, K., and Dunne, D. (1968). A comparison of techniques of electroconvulsive therapy. *British Journal of Psychiatry* **114**, 989–96.

Van Broeckhoven, C., Genthe, A. M., Vandenberghe, A., *et al.* (1987). Failure of familial Alzheimer's disease to segregate with the A4-amyloid gene in several European families. *Nature* **329**, 153–5.

Van der Plate, C. and Aral, S. O. (1987). Psychosocial aspects of genital herpes virus infection. *Health Psychology* **6**, 57–72.

Van Dongen-Melman, J. E. W. M. and Sanders-Woudstra, J. A. R. (1986). Psychosocial aspects of childhood cancer: a review of the literature. *Journal of Child Psychology and Psychiatry* **27**, 145–80.

Van Krevelin, D. A. (1971). Early infantile autism and autistic psychopathy. *Journal of Autism and Child Schizophrenia* **1**, 82–6.

Van Loon, F. H. G. (1927). Amok and latah. *Journal of Abnormal and Social Psychology* **21**, 434–44.

Van Praag, H. M. (1982). Neurotransmitters and depression. Part B. catecholamines and depression. In *Handbook of psychiatry and endocrinology* (ed. P. J. V. Beumont and G. D. Burrows). Elsevier Biomedical, Amsterdam.

Van Praag, H. M. and Korf, J. (1971). Retarded depression and dopamine metabolism. *Psychopharmacologia* **19**, 199–203.

Van Putten, T. and May, P. R. A. (1978). 'Akinetic depression' in schizophrenia. *Archives of General Psychiatry* **35**, 1101–7.

Vaughn, C. E. and Leff, J. P. (1976). The influence of family and social factors as the course of psychiatric illness. *British Journal of Psychiatry* **129**, 125–37.

Vaukhonen, K. (1968). On the pathogenesis of morbid jealousy. *Acta Psychiatrica Scandinavica* Suppl. 202.

Veith, I. (1965). *Hysteria: the case history of a disease*. University of Chicago Press, Chicago.

Veith, R. C., Raskind, M. A., Caldwell, J. H., Barnes, R. F. Gumbrecht, G., and Ritchie, J. L. (1982). Cardovascular effects of tricyclic antidepressants in depressed patients with chronic heart disease. *New England Journal of Medicine* **306**, 954–9.

Venables, P. M. (1977). The electrodermal physiology of schizophrenics and children at risk for schizophrenia. *Schizophrenia Bulletin* **3**, 28–48.

Venables, P. M. and Wing, J. K. (1962). Level of arousal and the subclassification of schizophrenia. *Archives of General Psychiatry* **7**, 114–19.

Victor, M. (1964). Observations on the amnesic syndrome in man and its anatomical basis. In *Brain function: RNA and brain function, memory and learning*, Vol. ii (ed. M. A. B. Brazier). University of California Press, Berkeley.

Victor, M. and Adams, R. D. (1953). The effect of alcohol on the nervous system. *Proceedings of the Association for Research in Nervous and Mental Diseases* **32**, 526–73.

Victor, M., Adams, R. D., and Collins, G. H. (1971). *The Wernicke–Korsakoff syndrome*. Blackwell, Oxford.

Vieweg, W. W. R., David, J. J., Rowe, W. T., Wampler, G. J., Burns, W. J., and Virkunnen, M. (1974). Alcohol as a factor precipitating aggression and conflict behaviour leading to homicide. *British Journal of Addiction* **69**, 149–54.

Vislie, H. (1956). Puerperal mental disorders. *Acta Psychiatrica et Neurologica Scandinavica* Suppl. 111.

Visotsky, H. M., Hamburg, D. A., Gross, M. E., and Lebovitz B. Z. (1967). Coping behaviour under extreme stress. *Archives of General Psychiatry* **56**, 423–48.

Von Economo, C. (1929). *Encephalitis lethargica: Its sequelae and treatment*. Translated by Newman, K. O. (1931). Oxford University Press, Oxford.

Von Hartitzsch, B., Hoenich, N. A., Leigh, R. J., Wilkinson, R., Frost, T. H., Weddel, A., and Posen, G. A. (1972). Permanent neurological sequelae despite haemodialysis for lithium intoxication. *British Medical Journal* **iv**, 757–9.

Von Korff, R., Eaton, W. W., and Keyl, P. M. (1985). The epidemiology of panic attacks and panic disorder: results in three community surveys. *American Journal of Epidemiology* **122**, 970–81.

Wadden, T. A. and Stunkard, A. J. (1985). Social and psychological consequences of obesity. *Annals of Internal Medicine* **103**, 1062–7.

Wadden, T. A., Luborsky, L., Green, S., and Crits-Christoph, P. (1984). The behavioural treatment of essential hypertension: An update and comparison with pharmacological treatment. *Clinical Psychology Review* **4**, 403–29.

Wade, S. T., Legh-Smith, J. and Hewer, R. L. (1986). Effects of living with and looking after survivors of a stroke. *British Medical Journal* **293**, 418–20.

Wadsworth, M. E. J., Butterfield, W. J. H., and Blaney, R. (1972). *Health and sickness, the choice of treatment*. Tavistock, London.

Wakeling, A. (1979). A general psychiatric approach to sexual deviation. In *Sexual deviation* (ed. I. Rosen) (2nd edn). Oxford University Press.

Wålinder, J. (1967). *Transsexualism: a study of 43 cases*. Akademi-förlaget Göteborg.

Wålinder, J. (1968). Transsexualism—definition, prevalence and sex distribution. *Acta Psychiatrica et Neurologica Scandinavica* Suppl. **203**, 255–8.

Wålinder, J. and Thuwe, I. (1977). A study of consanguinity between the parents of transsexuals. *British Journal of Psychiatry* **131**, 73–4.

Walker, N. (1965). *Crime and punishment in Britain*. Edinburgh University Press.

Walker, N. (1967). *Crime and insanity in England*, Vol. 1. *The historical perspective*. Edinburgh University Press.

Walker, N. (1987). *Crime and criminology*. Oxford University Press, Oxford.

Walker, N. and McCabe, S. (1973). *Crime and insanity in England*, Vol. 2. Edinburgh University Press.

Walker, S., Yesavage, J. A., and Tinklenberg, J. R. (1981). Acute phencylidine (PCP) intoxication: quantitative urine levels and clinical management. *American Journal of Psychiatry* **138**, 674–5.

Walker, V. and Beech, H. R. (1969). Mood state and the ritualistic behaviour of obsessional patients. *British Journal of Psychiatry* **115**, 1261–3.

Wallace, C., Nelson, C., and Liberman, R. (1980). A review and critique of social skills and training with schizophrenic patients. *Social Bulletin* **6**, 42–63.

Walsh, B. W. and Rosen, P. R. (1985). Self mutilation and contagion: an empirical test. *American Journal of Psychiatry* **142**, 119–20.

Walsh, D. (1982). *Alcohol related medicosocial problems and their prevention*. (Public Health in Europe, No. 17). World Health Organization, Copenhagen.

Walters, A. (1961). Psychogenic regional pain alias hysterical pain. *Brain* **84**, 1–18.

Walton, D. (1961). Experimental psychology and the treatment of the ticquer. *Journal of Child Psychology* **2**, 148–55.

Walton, J. N. (ed.) (1985). *Brain's diseases of the nervous system* (9th edn). Oxford University Press, Oxford.

Ward, C. H., Beck, A. T., Mendelson, M., Mock, J. E., and Erbaugh, J. K. (1962). The psychiatric nomenclature. *Archives of General Psychiatry* **7**, 198–205.

Warr, P. and Jackson, P. (1985). Factors influencing the psychological impact of prolonged unemployment and of re-employment. *Psychological Medicine* **15**, 795–808.

Warren, E. W. and Groome, D. H. (1984). Memory test performance under three different waveforms of ECT for depression. *British Journal of Psychiatry* **144**, 370–5.

Warren, M. Q. (1969). The case for differential treatment of delinquents. *Annals of the American Academy of Political and Social Science* **381**, 47–59.

Warren, M. Q. (1973). Correctional treatment in community settings. *Proceedings of the International Congress of Criminology*, Madrid.

Warrington, E. K. and Weiskrantz, L. (1970). Amnesic syndrome—consolidation or retrieval? *Nature* **228**, 628–30.

Watanabe, S., Ishino, M., and Otsuki, S. (1975). Double blind comparison of lithium carbonate and imipramine in the treatment of depression. *Archives of General Psychiatry* **32**, 659–68.

Watson, J. B. and Rayner, R. (1920). Conditioned emotional reactions. *Journal of Experimental Psychology* **3**, 1–14.

Watson, J. M. (1982). Solvent abuse: presentation and clinical diagnosis *Human Toxicology* **1**, 249–56.

Watson, M. (1983). Psychosocial intervention with cancer patients: a review. *Psychological Medicine* **13**, 839–46.

Watt, N. F., Anthony, E. J., Wynne, L. C., and Rolf, J. E. (1984). *Children at risk for schizophrenia*. Cambridge University Press, Cambridge.

Watts, F. N. and Bennett, D. H (1983). *Theory and practice of psychiatric rehabilitation*. Wiley, Chichester.

Watzlawick, P., Bearn, J. H., and Jackson, D. D. (1968). *Pragmatics of human communication*. Faber, London.

Weatherall, D. J. (1986). *The new genetics and clinical practice* (2nd edn). Oxford University Press, Oxford.

Weatherall, D., Ledingham, J. G. G., and Warrell, D. (1987) *Oxford textbook of medicine*, 2nd edn. Oxford University Press, Oxford.

Wechsler, D. (1945). A standardized memory scale for clinical use. *Journal of Psychology* **19**, 87–95.

Wechsler, H., Grosser, G. H., and Greenblatt, M. (1965). Research evaluating antidepressant medications on hospitalized mental patients: a survey of published reports during a five year period. *Journal of Nervous and Mental Disease* **141**, 231–9.

Weeks, D., Freeman, C. P. L., and Kendell, R. E. (1980). E.C.T.:III Enduring cognitive deficits. *British Journal of Psychiatry* **137**, 26–37.

Weeks, H. A. (1958). The Highfields project and its success. In *The sociology of punishment and correction* (ed. N. Johnston, L. Savitz, and M. W. Wolfgang). Wiley, New York.

Wehr, T. A., Jacobsen, F. M., Arendt, J., Tamarkin, L., and Rosenthal, N. E. (1986). Phototherapy of seasonal affective disorder. *Archives of General Psychiatry* **43**. 870–7.

Weighill, V. E. (1983). Compensation neurosis: A review of the literature. *Journal of Psychosomatic Research* **27**, 97–104.

Weinberger, D. R. and Kleinman, J. E. (1986). Observations on the brain in schizophrenia. *Psychiatry update: the American Psychiatric Association Annual Review*, Vol. 5 (ed. A. J. Frances and R. E. Hales). American Psychiatric Press, Washington DC.

Weinberger, D. R., Bigelow, L. B., Kleinman, J. E., Klein, S. T., Rosenblatt, J. E., and Wyatt, R. J. (1980*a*). Cerebral ventricular enlargement in chronic schizophrenia. *Archives of General Psychiatry* **37**, 11–13.

Weinberger, D. R., Cannon-Spoor, E., Potkin, S. G., and Wyatt, R. J. (1980*b*). Poor premorbid adjustment and CT scan abnormalities in chronic schizophrenia. *American Journal of Psychiatry* **137**, 1410–13.

Weinberger, D. R., Cannon-Spoor, E., and Potkin, S. G. (1981). Familial aspects of CT scan abnormalities in chronic schizophrenic patients. *Psychological Research* **4**, 65–71.

Weiner, H. (1977). *Psychobiology and human disease.* Elsevier, New York.

Weinstein, E. A. and Kahn, R. L. (1955). *Denial of illness: symbolic and physiological aspects.* Thomas, Springfield, Ill.

Weinstein, M. R. (1980). Lithium treatment of women during pregnancy and in the post delivery period. In *Handbook of lithium therapy* (ed. F. N. Johnson) (2nd edn), pp. 421–9. MTP, Lancaster.

Weiss, E. M. and Berg, R. F. (1982). Child victims of sexual assault: impact of court procedures. *Journal of the American Academy of Child Psychiatry* **21**, 513–18.

Weiss, S. M., Krantz, D. S., and Mathews, K. A. (1984). Coronary prone behaviour. In *Recent advances in cardiology*, Vol. 9. Churchill Livingstone, Edinburgh.

Weissman, A. D. (1974). The epidemiology of suicide attempts. 1960–1971. *Archives of General Psychiatry* **30**, 737–46.

Weissman, M. M. and Boyd, J. H. (1985). Affective disorders: epidemiology. In *Comprehensive textbook of psychiatry* (ed. H. I. Kaplan and B. J. Sadock) (4th edn), Vol. I, pp. 764–9. Williams and Wilkins, Baltimore.

Weissman, M. M. and Klerman, G. L. (1978). Epidemiology of mental disorder: emerging trends in the U. S. *Archives of General Psychiatry* **35**, 705–12.

Weissman, M. M. and Merikangas, K. R. (1986). The epidemiology of anxiety and panic disorders. *Journal of Clinical Psychiatry* **47** (suppl.), 11–17.

Weissman, M. and Slaby, A. (1973). Oral contraceptives and psychiatric disturbance: evidence from research. *British Journal of Psychiatry* **123**, 513–18.

Weissman, M., Pottenger, M., Kleber, H., Ruben, H. L., Williams, D., and Thompson, W. D. (1977). Symptom patterns in primary and secondary depression: a comparison of primary depressives, with depressed opiate addicts, alcoholics and schizophrenics. *Archives of General Psychiatry* **34**, 854–62.

Weissman, M., Prusoff, B. A., DiMascio, A., Neu, C., Goklaney, M., and Klerman, G. L. (1979). The efficacy of drugs and psychotherapy in the treatment of acute depressive episodes. *American Journal of Psychiatry* **136**, 555–8.

Weissman, M. M., Merikangas, K. R., John, K., Wickramaratne, P., Prusoff, B. A. and Kidd, K. K. (1986). Family-genetic studies of psychiatric disorders. *Archives of General Psychiatry* **43**, 1104–16.

Welch, C. A. (1981). Psychiatric medicine and the burn patient. In *Psychiatric medicine update: Massachusetts General Hospital reviews for physicians* (ed. T. C. Manschrek). Churchill Livingstone, Edinburgh.

Wells, C. E. (1978). Chronic brain disease: an overview. *American Journal of Psychiatry* **135**, 1–12.

Welner, J. and Strömgren, E. (1958). Clinical and genetic studies on benign schizophreniform psychoses based on a follow up. *Acta Psychiatrica Neurologica Scandinavica* **33**, 377–99.

Wender, P., Rosenthal, D., Kety, S. S., Schulsinger, F., and Welner, J. (1974). Cross-fostering: a research strategy for clarifying the role of genetic and experimental factors in the aetiology of schizophrenia. *Archives of General Psychiatry* **30**, 121–8.

Wender, P. H., Kety, S. S., Rosenthal, D., Schulsinger, F., Ortmann, J., and Lunde, I. (1986). Psychiatric disorder in the biological and adoptive families of adopted individuals with affective disorders. *Archives of General Psychiatry* **43**, 923–9.

Wernicke, C. (1881). *Lehrbuch der Gehirnkrankheiten*, part 2, p. 229. Kassel, Berlin.

Wernicke, C. (1900). *Grundriss der Psychiatrie*. George Thieme, Leipzig.

West, D. (1965). *Murder followed by suicide*. Heinemann, London.

West, D. (1974). Criminology, deviant behaviour and mental disorder. *Psychological Medicine* **4**, 1–3.

West, D. (1977). Delinquency. In *Child psychiatry. Modern approaches* (ed. M. Rutter and L. Hersov). Blackwell, Oxford.

West, D. and Farrington, D. P. (1973). *Who becomes delinquent?* Heinemann Educational, London.

West D. and Farrington, D. P. (1977) *The delinquent way of life*. Heinemann. London

West, D. and Walk, A. (eds.) (1977). *Daniel McNaughton: his trial and aftermath*. Gaskell Books, Ashford, Kent.

West, E. D. (1981). Electric convulsion therapy in depression: a double blind controlled trial. *British Medical Journal* **282**, 355–7.

Wexler, L., Weissman, N. M., and Kasl, S. V. (1978). Suicide attempts 1970–75. Updating a United States study and comparisons with international trends. *British Journal of Psychiatry* **132**, 180–5.

Whalley, L. J., Borthwick, N., Copolov, D., Dick, H., Christie, J. E., and Fink, G. (1986). Corticosteroid receptors and depression. *British Medical Journal* **292**, 859–61.

Whalley, L. J., Carothers, A. D., Collyer, S., DeMey, R., and Frackiewicz, A. (1982*a*). A study of familial factors in Alzheimer's disease. *British Journal of Psychiatry* **140**, 249–56.

Whalley, L. J., Rosie, R., Dick, H., Levy, G., Watts, A. G., Sheward, W. J., Christie, J. E., and Fink, G. (1982*b*). Immediate increases in plasma prolactin and neurophysin but not other hormones after electroconvulsive therapy. *Lancet* **ii**, 1064–8.

Wheeler, E. O., White, P. D., Reed, E. W., and Cohen, M. E. (1950). Neurocirculatory asthenia (anxiety neurosis, effort syndrome, neurasthenia). A twenty year follow up of one hundred and seventy three patients. *Journal of the American Medical Association* **142**, 878–89.

Wheeler, K., Leiper, A. D., Jannoun, L., and Chessells, J. M. (1988). Medical cost of curing childhood acute lymphoblastic leukaemia. *British Medical Journal* **296**, 162–6.

White, K. and Simpson, G. (1981). Combined MAOI-tricyclic antidepressant treatment: a re-evaluation. *Journal of Clinical Psychopharmacology* **1**, 264–82.

Whitehead, A. (1984). Psychological intervention in dementia. In *Handbook of studies on psychiatry and old age* (ed. D. W. K. Kay and G. B. Burrows). Elsevier, Amsterdam.

Whitehorn, J. C. and Betz, B. J. (1954). A study of psychotherapeutic relationship between physicians and schizophrenic patients. *American Journal of Psychiatry* **111**, 321–31.

Whitehouse, P. J. (1986). The concept of subcortical and cortical dementia: another look. *Annals of Neurology* **19**, 1–6.

Whiteley, J., Stuart, J., and Gordon, J. (1979). *Group approaches in psychiatry*. Routledge and Kegan Paul, London.

Whiteley, S. (1975). The psychopath and his treatment. In *Contemporary psychiatry* (ed. T. Silverstone and R. B., Barraclough). *British Journal of Psychiatry* Special Publication No. 9.

Whitlock, F. (1961). The Ganser syndrome. *British Journal of Psychiatry* **113**, 19–29.

Whitlock, F. (1963). *Criminal responsibility*. Butterworths, London.

Whitlock, F. (1973*a*). Suicide in England and Wales 1959–1963. Part 1. The county boroughs. *Psychological Medicine* **3**, 350–65.

Whitlock, F. (1973*b*). Suicide in England and Wales 1959–1963. Part 2, London. *Psychological Medicine* **3**, 411–20.

Whitlock, F. (1976). *Psychological aspects of skin disease.* Saunders, London.

Whitlock, F. A. (1982). *Symptomatic affective disorders.* Academic Press, London.

Whitlock, F. A. (1986*a*). Suicide and physical illness. In *Suicide* (ed. A. Roy). Williams and Wilkins, Baltimore.

Whitlock, F. A. (1986*b*). The psychiatric complication of Parkinson's disease. *Australian and New Zealand Journal of Psychiatry* **20**, 114-21.

Whybrow, P. C. and Hurwitz, T. (1976). Psychological disturbances associated with endocrine disease and hormone therapy. In *Hormones, behaviour and psychopathology* (ed. E. J. Sachar). Raven Press, New York.

Wilkin, D. (1979). *Caring for the mentally handicapped child.* Croom Helm, London.

Wilkin, D., Evans, G., Hughes, B., and Jolley, D. (1982). The implications of managing confused and disabled people in non-specialist residential homes for the elderly. *Health Trends* **14**, 98–100.

Wilkin, D., Hughes, B. and Jolley, D. J. (1985). Quality of care in institutions. In *Recent advances in psychogeriatrics.* Churchill Livingstone, Edinburgh.

Wilkins, R. H. (1974). *The hidden alcoholic in general practice. A method of detection using a questionnaire.* Elek Science, London.

Wilkinson, G. (1987). The influence of psychiatric, psychological and social factors on the control of insulin dependent diabetes mellitus. *Journal of Psychosomatic Research* **31**, 277–86.

Wilkinson, G. and Pelosi, A. J. (1987). The economics of mental health services. *British Medical Journal* **294**, 139–40.

Williams, D. (1969). Neural factors related to habitual aggression: consideration of the differences between those habitual aggressive and others who have committed crimes of violence. *Brain* **92**, 503–20.

Williams, J. B. W. (1985). The multixial system of DSMIII: where did it come from and where should it go? *Archives of General Psychiatry* **42**, 175–86.

Williams, J. B. W. and Spitzer, R. L. (1982). Idiopathic pain disorder: a critique of pain-prone disorder and a proposal for a revision of the DSMIII category psychogenic pain disorder. *Journal of Nervous and Mental Disorders* **170**, 415–19.

Williams, R. and Davis, M. (1977). Alcohol liver injury. *Proceedings of the Royal Society of Medicine* **70**, 33–6.

Williamson, J., Stokoe, I. H., Gray, S., Fisher, M., Smith, A., McGhee, A., and Stephenson, E. (1964). Old people at home: their unreported needs. *Lancet* **i**, 1117–20.

Williamson, P. D. and Spencer, S. S. (1986). Clinical and EEG features of complex partial seizures of extra temporal origin. *Epilepsia.* Suppl. **2**, 546–63.

Willner, A. E. and Rabiner, C. J. (1979). Psychopathology and cognitive dysfunction five years after open heart surgery. *Comprehensive Psychiatry* **20**, 409–18.

Wimmer, A. (1916). Psykogene sindssygdomsformer. [Psychogenic varieties of mental diseases.] In *St. Hans Hospital 1816–1916. Jubilee Publication*, pp. 85–216. Gad, Copenhagen.

Wilson, G. D. (1981). *Love and instinct.* Temple Smith, London.

Wilson, P. (1980). *Survey of drinking in England and Wales.* Office of population censuses and surveys. HMSO, London.

Wilson, S. (1978). The effect of treatment in a therapeutic community on intravenous drug abuse. *British Journal of Addiction* **73**, 407–11.

Wilson, S. and Mandelbrote, B. (1978). The relationship between duration of treatment in a therapeutic community for drug abusers and subsequent criminality. *British Journal of Psychiatry* **132**, 487–91.

Wing, J. K. (1978). *Schizophrenia. Towards a new synthesis*. Academic Press, London.

Wing, J. K. (ed.) (1982). Long term community care: experience in a London Borough. *Psychological Medicine Monograph* Suppl. No. 2.

Wing, J. K. (1986). The cycle of planning and evaluation. In *The provision of mental health services in Britain: the way ahead* (ed. G. Wilkinson and H. Freeman). Gaskell, London.

Wing, J. K. and Brown, G. W. (1970). *Institutionalism and schizophrenia*. Cambridge University Press, London.

Wing, J. K. and Fryers, T. (1976). *Psychiatric services in Camberwell and Salford*. MRC Social Psychiatry Unit, London.

Wing, J. K. and Furlong, R. (1986). A haven for the severely disabled within the context of a comprehensive psychiatric community service. *British Journal of Psychiatry* **149**, 449–57.

Wing, J. K. and Hailey, A. M. (ed). (1972). *Evaluating a community psychiatric service*. Oxford University Press, London.

Wing, J. K. and Morris, B. (1981). *Handbook of rehabilitation practice*. Oxford University Press, Oxford.

Wing, J. K. and Olsen, R. (1979). *Community care for the mentally disabled*. Oxford University Press, London.

Wing, J. K., Bennett, D. H., and Denham, J. (1964). *The industrial rehabilitation of long stay psychiatric patients*. Medical Research Council Memorandum. No. 42. HMSO, London.

Wing, J. K. Cooper, J. E., and Sartorius, N. (1974). *Measurement and classification of psychiatric symptoms*. Cambridge University Press, Cambridge.

Wing, R. R., Epstein, L. H., Nowalk, M. P., and Lampaski, D. M. (1986). Behavioural self-regulation in the treatment of patients with diabetes mellitus. *Psychological Bulletin* **99**, 78–89.

Winickoff, R. N. and Murphy, P. K. (1987). The persistent problem of poor blood pressure control. *Archives of Internal Medicine* **147**, 1393–6.

Winokur, G., Cardoret, R., Dorzab, J., and Baker, M. (1971). Depressive disease: a genetic study. *Archives of General Psychiatry* **24**, 135–44.

Winterborn, M. H. (1987). Growing up with chronic renal failure. *British Medical Journal,* **295**, 870.

Witkin, H. A., Mednick, S. A., and Schulsinger, F. (1976). Criminality and XYY and XXY man. *Science* **193**, 547–8.

Witte, R. A. (1985). The psychosocial impact of a progressive physical handicap and terminal illness. (Duchenne muscular dystrophy) on adolescents and the families. *British Journal Medical Psychology* **58**, 179–87.

Witzig, J. S. (1968). The group treatment of male exhibitionists. *American Journal of Psychiatry* **125**, 179–85.

Woerner, M. G., Pollack, M., and Klein, D. F. (1973). Pregnancy and birth complications in psychiatric patients: a comparison of schizophrenic and personality disorder patients with their siblings. *Acta Psychiatrica Scandinavica* **49**, 712–21.

Wolberg, L. R. (1948). *Medical hypnosis*. Grune and Stratton, New York.

Wolberg, L. R. (1977). *The techniques of psychotherapy*. Grune and Stratton, New York.

Wolf, S. and Wolff, H. G. (1947). *Human gastric function*. Oxford University Press, New York.

Wolfe, D. A. (1985). Child abusive parents: an empirical review and analysis. *Psychological Bulletin* **97**, 462–82.

Wolfe, F. (1986). The clinical syndrome of fibrositis. *American Journal of Medicine* **81**, (Suppl. 3A), 7.

Wolfensberger, W. (1980). The definition of normalisation—update, problems, disagreements, and misunderstandings. In *Normalisation, social integration and community services* (ed. R. J. Flynn and K. E. Nitsch). University Park Press, Baltimore.

Wolff, C. (1971). *Love between women*. Duckworth, London.

Wolff, H. G. (1962). A concept of disease in man. *Psychosomatic Medicine* **24**, 25–30.

Wolff, H. G. and Curran, D. (1935). Nature of delirium and allied states. *Archives of Neurology and Psychiatry* **35**, 1175–215.

Wolff, S. (1961). Symptomatology and outcome of preschool children with behaviour disorders attending a child guidance clinic. *Journal of Child Psychology and Psychiatry* **2**, 269–76.

Wolkind, S. and Zajicek, E. (1981). *Pregnancy—a psychological and social study*. Academic Press, London.

Wolpe, J. (1958). *Psychotherapy by reciprocal inhibition*. Stanford University Press, Stanford.

Wong, D. F., Wagner, H. N., Tune, L. E., *et al.* (1986). Positron emission tomography reveals elevated D_2 dopamine receptors in drug-naive schizophrenics. *Science* **234**, 1558–63.

Wood, P. (1941). Da Costa's syndrome (or effort syndrome). *British Medical Journal* **1**, 767–74; 805–11; 846–51.

Woodruff, R. A., Guze, S. B., Clayton, P. J., and Carr, D. (1973). Alcoholism and depression. *Archives of General Psychiatry* **28**, 97–100.

Woods, R. (1982). The psychology of ageing. In *The psychiatry of late life.* (ed. R. Levy and F. Post). Blackwell, Oxford.

Wooff, K., Goldberg, D. P., and Fryers, T. (1986). Patients in receipt of community psychiatric nursing care in Salford 1976–82. *Psychological Medicine* **16**, 407–14.

Woolley, D. W. and Shaw, E. (1954). A biochemical and pharmacological suggestion about certain mental disorders. *Proceedings of the National Academy of Sciences* **40**, 228–31.

Woolston, J. L. (1987). Obesity in infancy and early childhood. *American Academy of Child and Adolescent Psychiatry* **20**, 123–60.

Wootton, B. (1959). *Social science and social pathology*, Chapter 7, pp. 203–26. George Allen and Unwin, London.

Worden, J. W. and Weissman, A. D. (1984). Prevententive psychosocial intervention with newly diagnosed cancer patients. *General Hospital Psychiatry* **6**, 243–9.

World Health Organization (1973). *Report of the International Pilot Study of Schizophrenia*, Vol. 1. World Health Organization, Geneva.

World Health Organization (1978). *Mental disorders: glossary and guide to their classification in accordance with the ninth revision of the International Classification of Diseases*. World Health Organization, Geneva.

World Health Organization (1979). *Schizophrenia: an initial follow up*. Wiley, Chichester.

World Health Organization (1980). Changing patterns in mental health care. *Euro Reports and Studies 25*. World Health Organization, Copenhagen.

World Health Organization (1981). *Current state of diagnosis and classification in the mental health field*. World Health Organization, Geneva.

World Health Organization (1984). *Mental health care in developing countries: a critical appraisal of research findings*. Technical Report Series 698. World Health Organization, Geneva.

World Health Organization. (1987). *ICD–10, 1986 Draft of Chapter V. Mental behavioural and developmental disorders*. World Health Organization, Geneva.

Worrall, E. P., Moody, P. J., Peet, M., Dick, P., Smith, A., Chambers, C., Adams, M., and Naylor, G. J. (1979). Controlled studies of the antidepressant effects of lithium. *British Journal of Psychiatry* **135**, 255–62.

Wright, J., Perreault, R., and Mathieu, M. (1977). The treatment of sexual dysfunction: a review. *Archives of General Psychiatry* **34**, 881–90.

Wyant, G. M. and MacDonald, W. B. (1980). The role of atropine in electroconvulsive therapy. *Anaesthesia and Intensive Care* **8**, 445–50.

Wyke, T. (1980). Language and schizophrenia. *Psychological Medicine* **10**, 403–6.

Wyke, T. (1982). A hostel ward for 'new' long stay patients: an evaluative study of 'a ward in a house'. *Psychological Medicine* **2**, 15–27.

Wynne, L. C. (1981). Current concepts about schizophrenics and family relationships. *The Journal of Nervous and Mental Disease* **169**, 82–9.

Wynne, L. C. and Singer, M. T. (1963). Thought disorder and family relationships of schizophrenics: II. A classification of forms of thinking. *Archives of General Psychiatry* **9**, 199–206.

Wynne, L. C. Ryckoff, I., Day, J., and Hirsch, S. (1958). Pseudomutuality in the family relations of schizophrenics. *Psychiatry* **21**, 205–20.

Yalom, I. (1980). *Existential psychotherapy*. Basic Books, New York.

Yalom, I. D. (1985). *The theory and practice of group psychotherapy* (3rd edn). Basic Books, New York.

Yalom, I. Hovts, P. S., Newell, G., and Rand, K. H. (1967). Preparation of patients for group therapy. *Archives of General Psychiatry* **17**, 416–27.

Yalom, I. Linde, D., Moos, R. M., and Hamburg, D. A. (1968). 'Post partum blues' syndrome. A description and related variables. *Archives of General Psychiatry* **18**, 16–27.

Yap, P. M. (1951). Mental diseases peculiar to certain cultures: a survey of comparative psychiatry. *Journal of Mental Science* **97**, 313–27.

Yap, P. M. (1965). Koro—a culture-bond depersonalization syndrome. *British Journal of Psychiatry* **111**, 43–50.

Yap, P. M. Green, R., and Fisk, N. (1973). Prenatal exposure to female hormones: effects on the psychosexual development of boys. *Archives of General Psychiatry* **28**, 554–61.

Yardley, K. M. (1976). Training in feminine skills in a male transsexual: preoperative procedure. *British Journal of Medical Psychology* **49**, 329–39.

Yates, W. R., Jacoby, C. G., and Andreasen, N. C. (1987). Cerebellar atrophy in schizophrenia and affective disorder. *The American Journal of Psychiatry* **144**, 465–7.

Young, J. P. R., Lader, M. H., and Hughes, W. C. (1979). Controlled trial of trimipramine, monamine oxidase inhibitors and combined treatment in depressed outpatients. *British Medical Journal* **2**, 1315–17.

Young, R. J. and Clarke, B. F. (1985). Pain relief and diabetic neuropathy: the effectiveness of imipramine and related drugs. *Diabetic Medicine* **2**, 363–6.

Young, W., Goy, R., and Phoenix, C. (1964). Hormones and sexual behaviour. *Science* **143**, 212–18.

Yule, W. (1967). Predicting reading ages on Neale's analysis of reading ability. *British Journal of Educational Psychology* **37**, 252–5.

Yule, W. and Carr, J. (1980). *Behaviour modification for the mentally handicapped*. Croom Helm, London.

Yule, W. and Rutter, M. (1985). Reading and other learning difficulties. In *Child and adolescent and psychiatry. Modern approaches* (2nd edn). (ed. M. Rutter and L. Hersov). Blackwell, Oxford.

Zall, H., Therman, P.-O. G., and Myers, J. M. (1968). Lithium carbonate: a clinical study. *American Journal of Psychiatry* **125**, 549–55.

Zeitlin, H. (1986). *The natural history of psychiatric disorder in children*. Maudsley Monograph No. 29. Oxford University Press, Oxford.

Zerssen, D. von (1976). Physique and personality. In *Human behaviour genetics* (ed. A. R. Kaplan) pp. 230–78. Thomas, Springfield, Ill.

Zimberg, S. (1983). Alcohol problems in the elderly. *Journal of Psychiatric Treatment and Evaluation* **5**, 515–20.

Zitrin, C. M., Klein, D. F., and Woerner, M. G. (1978). Behaviour therapy, supportive psychotherapy, imipramine and phobias. *Archives of General Psychiatry* **35**, 307–16.

Zitrin, C. M., Klein, D. F., Woerner, M. G., and Ross, D. C. (1983). Treatment of phobias: I. Comparison of imipramine hydrochloride and placebo. *Archives of General Psychiatry* **40**, 125–38.

Zola, I. (1966). Culture and symptoms—an analysis of patients' persistent complaints. *American Sociological Review* **31**, 615–30.

Zuger, B. (1984). Early effeminate behaviour in boys: outcome and significance for homosexuality. *Journal of Nervous and Mental Diseases* **172**, 90–7.

Author Index

Subject Index